Portugal

The Minho
(p419)

Porto,
the Douro &
Trás-os-Montes
(p352)

The Beiras
(p295)

Estremadura
& Ribatejo
(p258)

Lisbon &
Around
(p58)

The Alentejo
(p206)

The Algarve
(p148)

Kate Armstr

Contents

LISBON P62

TAVIRA P163

Contents

Welcome to Portugal

Medieval castles, cobblestone villages, captivating cities and golden beaches: the Portugal experience can be many things. History, great food and idyllic scenery are just the beginning...

Ghosts of the Past

Celts, Romans, Visigoths, Moors and Christians all left their mark on the Iberian nation. Here, you can gaze upon 20,000-year-old stone carvings in the Vila Nova de Foz Côa, watch the sunset over mysterious megaliths outside Évora or lose yourself in the elaborate corridors of Unesco World Heritage sites in Tomar, Belém, Alcobaça or Batalha. You can pack an itinerary visiting palaces set above mist-covered woodlands, craggy clifftop castles and stunningly preserved medieval town centres.

The Portuguese Table

Freshly baked bread, olives, cheese, red wine or crisp *vinho verde* (sparkling wine), *cataplana* (seafood stew), smoked meats – the Portuguese have perfected the art of cooking simple, delicious meals. Sitting down to table means experiencing the richness of Portugal's bountiful coastline and fertile countryside. Of course, you don't have to sit, you can take your piping-hot *pastel de nata* (custard tart) standing up at an 1837 patisserie in Belém, or wander through scenic vineyards sipping the velvety ports of the Douro valley. You can shop the produce-filled markets, or book a table in one of the country's top dining rooms.

Cinematic Scenery

Outside the cities, Portugal's beauty unfolds in all its startling variety. You can go hiking amid the granite peaks of Parque Nacional da Peneda-Gerês or take in the pristine scenery and historic villages of the little-explored Beiras. More than 800km of coast offers a multitude of places to soak up the splendour. Gaze out over dramatic end-of-the-world cliffs, surf stellar breaks off dune-covered beaches or laze peacefully on sandy islands fronting calm blue seas. You'll find dolphin-watching in the lush Sado estuary, boating and kayaking along the meandering Rio Guadiana and memorable walks and bike rides all across the country.

Rhythms of Portugal

Festivals pack Portugal's calendar. Drink, dance and feast your way through such all-night revelries as Lisbon's Festa de Santo António or Porto's Festa de São João. There are kick-up-your-heels country fairs in the hinterlands, and rock- and world-music fests all along the coast. Any time of year is right to hear the mournful music of fado in the Alfama, join the dance party in Bairro Alto or hit the bars in Porto, Coimbra and Lagos.

Why I Love Portugal

By Regis St Louis, Coordinating Author

I'm enamoured by the scenery, the traditions of village life and Portugal's outstanding, afford-able seafood – especially *percebes* (goose barnacles) or whatever is the fresh catch of the day, grilled to perfection. I love taking in the stunning views along the coast (from the hidden beach-es in Parque Natural da Arrábida to the windswept cliffs dotting the southwest shores), going for mountain treks in the Serra da Estrela (where I often bump into a shepherd or two along the way), and wandering through the pretty towns of the Minho (especially on a market day). Portu-gal is full of surprises, and I never tire of exploring this small but endlessly fascinating country.

For more about our authors, see page 544

Above: Praia da Dona Ana (p187), Lagos

Portugal

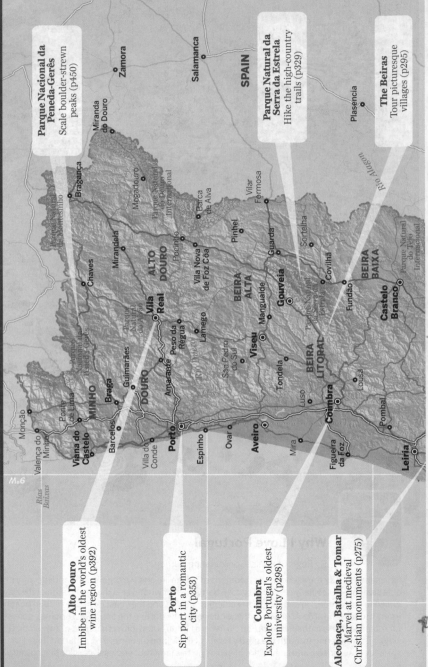

Parque Nacional da Peneda-Gerês
Scale boulder-strewn peaks (p450)

Parque Natural da Serra da Estrela
Hike the high-country trails (p329)

The Beiras
Tour picturesque villages (p295)

Alto Douro
Imbibe in the world's oldest wine region (p392)

Porto
Sip port in a romantic city (p353)

Coimbra
Explore Portugal's oldest university (p298)

Alcobaça, Batalha & Tomar
Marvel at medieval Christian monuments (p275)

SPAIN

80 km
40 miles

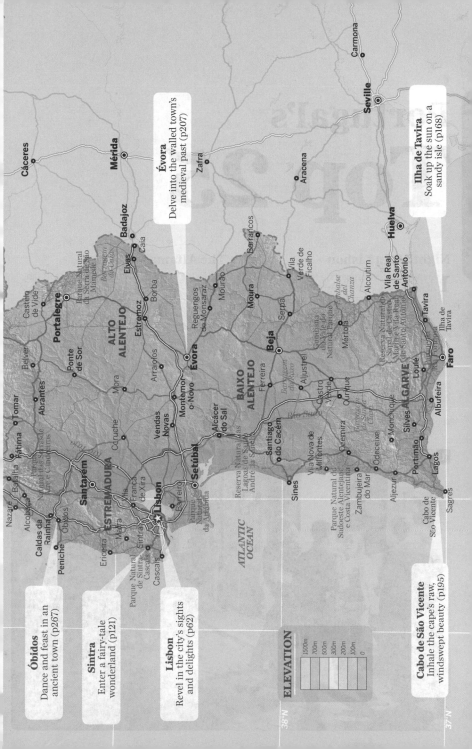

Évora
Delve into the walled town's medieval past (p207)

Ilha de Tavira
Soak up the sun on a sandy isle (p168)

Óbidos
Dance and feast in an ancient town (p267)

Sintra
Enter a fairy-tale wonderland (p121)

Lisbon
Revel in the city's sights and delights (p62)

Cabo de São Vicente
Inhale the cape's raw, windswept beauty (p195)

ELEVATION

1500m
700m
500m
300m
200m
100m
0

ATLANTIC OCEAN

38°N

37°N

Portugal's
Top 25

Nightlife in Lisbon

1 Lisbon's dizzying nightlife (p106) is a mix of old-school drinking dens, brassy jazz clubs and stylish lounges. The challenge is where to begin. You can start the evening with sunset drinks on a panoramic terrace overlooking the city, then head to Bairro Alto for tapas and early-evening cocktails on people-packed, bar-lined streets. Then head downhill to Cais do Sodré, a former red-light district turned hipster playground, or to Bica for a lively local bar scene. At the end of the night there's always riverside Lux, still one of Portugal's best night-spots. Below: Bairro Alto district (p67)

The Alfama

2 Lisbon's Alfama district (p70), with its laby-rinthine alleyways, hidden courtyards and curving shadow-filled lanes, is a magical place in which to lose all sense of direction and delve into the soul of the city. You'll pass breadbox-sized grocers, brilliantly tiled buildings and cosy taverns filled with easygoing chatter, accompa-nied by the scent of chargrilled sardines and the mournful rhythms of fado drifting in the breeze. Round a bend and catch sight of steeply pitched rooftops leading down to the glittering Tejo, and you know you're hooked...

ADINA TOVY / GETTY IMAGES ©

HEINRICH VAN DEN BERG / GETTY IMAGES ©

STEFAN CIOATA / GETTY IMAGES ©

Sintra

3 Less than an hour by train from the capital, Sintra (p121) feels like another world. Like a page torn from a fairy tale, Sintra is a quaint village sprinkled with stone-walled taverns and with a whitewashed palace looming over town. Forested hillsides form the backdrop to the storybook setting, with imposing castles, mystical gardens, strange mansions and centuries-old monasteries hidden among the woodlands. The fog that sweeps in by night adds another layer of mystery, and cool evenings are best spent fireside in one of Sintra's many charming B&Bs. Above: Palácio Nacional de Sintra (p122)

Parque Natural da Ria Formosa

4 This special spot (p161) feels like it's in the middle of wilderness, yet it's right off the Algarvian coast. Enclosing a vast area of *sapais* (marshes), *salinas* (salt pans), creeks and dune islands, the protected lagoon system stretches for an incredible 60km and encompasses 18,000 hectares. And it's all accessible from various towns – have a boat drop you at a deserted beach, or amble along the nature trail among the precious wetland birdlife. Top right: purple gallinule (p199)

Historic Évora

5 The Queen of the Alentejo and one of Portugal's most beautifully preserved medieval towns, Évora (p207) is an enchanting place to spend several days delving into the past. Inside the 14th-century walls, Évora's narrow, winding lanes lead to striking architectural works: an elaborate medieval cathedral and cloisters, Roman ruins and a picturesque town square. Historic and aesthetic virtues aside, Évora is also a lively university town, and its many attractive restaurants serve up excellent, hearty Alentejan cuisine. Above: Sé (p211)

Fado

6 Born in a working-class neighbourhood of Lisbon, the melancholic music of fado (p494) has been around for centuries. Despite its years, fado remains a living art, heard in tiny restaurants and elegant music halls alike. A lone, powerful voice coupled with the 12-string Portuguese *guitarra* are all the tools needed to bring some listeners to tears, as songs recall broken hearts, unfulfilled dreams and lost days of youth. In fado, raw emotion often conveys more than mere lyrics can; even non-Portuguese speakers find themselves moved by great fadistas.

Below: Clube de Fado (p112)

Sipping the Douro

7 The exquisite Alto Douro wine country (p392) is the oldest demarcated wine region on earth. Its steeply terraced hills, stitched together with craggy vines that have produced luscious wines for centuries, loom on both sides of the sinuous Rio Douro. Whether you get here by driving the impossibly scenic back roads, or catch a train or boat from Porto, take the time to hike, cruise and taste. Countless vintners receive guests for tours, tastings and overnight stays, and if you find one that's still family-owned, don't be surprised if you sample something very old and very special.

GREG ELMS / GETTY IMAGES ©

OLIVER STREWE / GETTY IMAGES ©

The Cliffs of Cabo de São Vicente

8 There's something thrilling about standing at Europe's most southwestern edge (p195), a headland of barren cliffs to which Portuguese sailors bid a nervous farewell as they sailed past, venturing into the unknown during Portugal's golden years of exploration. The windswept cape is redolent of history – if you squint hard (really hard), you'll see the ghost of Vasco da Gama sailing past. These days, a fortress and lighthouse perch on the cape. A new museum beautifully highlights Portugal's maritime navigation history.

Megaliths Around Évora

9 Spiritual, magical, historical, incredible – a visit to the many ancient megaliths around Évora (p219) will make your hairs stand on end. As a traveller, you will more often than not have these sites to yourself. And what better way to ponder the mysteries of places so ancient they cannot fully be explained? How did such massive rocks get hauled into place? Were they fertility symbols or proprietal land boundaries? They beg questions, yet – refreshingly in a world of reasoning – provide few answers. Somehow, part of their appeal lies in not knowing.

Porto

10 It would be hard to dream up a more romantic city than Portugal's second largest (p353). Laced with narrow pedestrian laneways, it is blessed with countless baroque churches, epic theatres and sprawling plazas. Its Ribeira district – a Unesco World Heritage site – is just a short walk across a landmark bridge from centuries-old port wineries in Vila Nova de Gaia, where you can sip the world's best port. And though some walls are crumbling, renewal – in the form of spectacular modern architecture, cosmopolitan restaurants, burgeoning nightlife and a vibrant arts scene – is palpable.

Parque Nacional da Peneda-Gerês

11 The vast rugged wilderness of Portugal's northernmost park (p450) is home to dramatic peaks, meandering streams and rolling hillsides covered with wildflowers. Its age-old stone villages seem lost in time and, in remote areas, wolves still roam. As always, the best way to feel nature's power is on foot along one of more than a dozen hiking trails. Some scale peaks, a few link to old Roman roads, others lead to castle ruins or waterfalls.

Above: Castro Laboreiro (p453) ruins

Staying in a Pousada

12 Portugal has its share of lavish accommodation, but some of its most memorable lodgings are found in government-run *pousadas*. The settings are historic and jaw-dropping: 300-year-old castles, atmospheric monasteries and clifftop mansions are among the 40 different *pousadas* available. Where else can you lodge in rooms where dukes once slept, contemplating the age-old beauty of the landscape? Pulling aside curtains, you'll gaze upon rolling vineyards, boulder-strewn mountains or the glimmering coastline.

Below: Pousada do Palácio de Estoi (p159)

Ilha de Tavira

13 This place (p168) has the lot for sun-seekers, beach bums, nature lovers (and naturists): mile after mile of golden beach (think sand, sand, sand, as far as the eye can see), a designated nudist area, transport via miniature train, busy restaurants and a campground. To top it off, it's part of the protected Parque Natural da Ria Formosa. Outside the high season, the island feels wonderfully remote and empty, but be warned: during high season (July and August) the hordes descend.

TRAVEL INK / GETTY IMAGES ©

JOE DANIEL PRICE / GETTY IMAGES ©

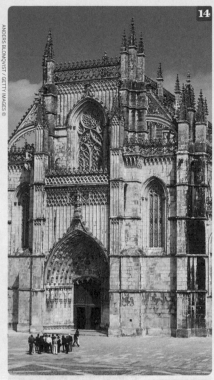

Batalha, Alcobaça & Tomar

14 These medieval Christian monuments constitute one of Portugal's greatest national treasures. Each has its own magic: the whimsy of Manueline adornments and haunting roofless shell of the unfinished Capelas Imperfeitas at Batalha's monastery (p277); the great kitchen at Alcobaça's monastery (p275), where a fish-stocked river once stoked the appetites of countless monks; or the labyrinthine courtyards and mysterious 16-sided chapel of the Knights Templar at Tomar's Convento de Cristo (p290). Above: Mosteiro de Santa Maria da Vitoria (p277)

Festivals

15 There's always something to celebrate in Portugal. For Easter processions, head to Braga. Romantics will love Lisbon's mid-June Festa de Santo António, with ubiquitous parties and locals plying sweethearts with poems and pots of aromatic basil. In August, catch Viana do Castelo's Romaria de Nossa Senhora d'Agonia, where *gigantones* (giants) parade down sawdust-painted streets alongside gold-and scarlet-clad women. And in winter, young lads wear masks and colourful garb in Trás-os-Montes' villages during the Festa dos Rapazes. Top right: Romaria de Nossa Senhora D'Agonia (p438)

Barcelos Market

16 The Minho is famous for its sprawling outdoor markets, but the largest, oldest and most celebrated is the Feira de Barcelos (p427), held every Thursday in this ancient town on the banks of the Rio Cávado. Most outsiders come for the yellow-dotted louça de Barcelos ceramics and the gaudy figurines à la local potter Rosa Ramalho, while rural villagers are more interested in the scrawny chickens, hand-embroidered linen, hand-woven baskets and hand-carved ox yokes.

DAVID LOPES / GETTY IMAGES ©

ANDERS BLOMQVIST / GETTY IMAGES ©

Óbidos

17 Wandering through the tangle of ancient streets and whitewashed houses of Óbidos (p267) is enchanting any time of year, but come during one of its festivals and you're in for a special treat. Whether attending a jousting match or climbing the castle walls at the medieval fair, searching for the next Pavarotti at the Festival de Ópera, or sampling chocolate at the Festival Internacional do Chocolate, you couldn't ask for a better backdrop.

Coimbra

18 Portugal's atmospheric college town, Coimbra (p298) rises steeply from the Rio Mondego to a medieval quarter housing one of Europe's oldest universities. Students roam the narrow streets clad in black capes, while strolling fado musicians give free concerts beneath the Moorish town gate. Kids can keep busy at Portugal dos Pequenitos, a theme park with miniature versions of Portuguese monuments; adults will appreciate the upper town's student-driven nightlife and the new cluster of bars and restaurants in the riverside park below. Top right: Velha Universidade (p299)

Azulejos

19 Some of Portugal's most captivating works of art are out on the streets – free viewing for anyone who happens to stroll past. A great legacy of the Moors, the *azulejo* (hand-painted tile) was adopted by the Portuguese, and put to stunning use over the centuries. Exquisite displays cover Porto's train station and iconic churches, with larger-than-life stories painted on the ceramic tiles. Lisbon has even more eye candy, with *azulejo*-adorned buildings all over town. The best place to start the hunt: Museu Nacional do Azulejo (p63). Far right: Igreja de São Lourenço de Matos (p170)

JOSE FUSTE RAGA / CORBIS ©

Seafood

20 Always a seafaring culture, the Portuguese know a thing or two about cooking fish. Taste the culinary riches of Portugal's coast in dishes like *caldeirada de peixe* (fish stew layered with tomatoes, potatoes and rice), *açorda de camarãoes* (a tasty stew of shrimp, garlic and cilantro thickened with bread crumbs), *cataplana* (shellfish stewed with wine, garlic and tomatoes in a traditional domed copper pan) or *ensopada de enguias* (eel stew). Or content yourself with the simplest of all Portuguese treats – fresh-grilled sardines, straight out of the ocean and onto the fire!

SHYMAN / GETTY IMAGES ©

Parque Natural da Serra da Estrela

21 Portugal's highest mountains (p329) blend rugged scenery, outdoor adventure and vanishing traditional ways. At Torre, the country's highest point (artificially pushed up to 2000m by the addition of a not-so-subtle stone monument!), you can slalom down the country's only ski slope. Hikers can choose from a network of high country trails with stupendous vistas. Oh, and did we mention the furry sheepdog puppies that frolic by the roadside? You'll long to take one home.

Beaches of the Algarve

22 Sunseekers have much to celebrate when it comes to beaches. On Portugal's south coast, the Algarve (p148) has a varied coastline. There are sandy islands reachable only by boat, dramatic cliff-backed shores, rarely visited beaches and people-packed sands near buzzing nightlife. Days are spent playing in the waves, taking long oceanfront strolls and surfing memorable breaks. For endless days of sun and refreshing ocean temperatures, come in the summer; but to escape the crowds, plan an off-season visit, when prices dive and crowds disperse. Bottom: Praia da Marinha

JOEL SANTOS / GETTY IMAGES ©

FRANCISLM PHOTOGRAPHY / GETTY IMAGES ©

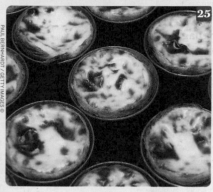

Braga

23 The country's third-largest city (p421) is blessed with terrific restaurants, a vibrant university and raucous festivals, but when it comes to historic sites it is unparalleled in Portugal. Here's the remarkable 12th-century cathedral, there's a 14th-century church. Braga has not one, but two sets of Roman ruins, countless 17th-century plazas and an 18th-century palace turned museum. Then there's that splendid baroque staircase: Escadaria do Bom Jesus (p428), the target of penitent pilgrims who come to make offerings at altars on the way to the mountaintop throughout the year. Above: Bom Jesus do Monte (p428)

Villages of the Beiras

24 From schist-walled communities spilling down terraced hillsides to spiky-edged sentinels that once guarded the eastern border against Spanish incursions, the inland Beiras (p295) are filled with picturesque and historical villages: Piódão, Trancoso, Sortelha, Monsanto... Today mostly devoid of residents but not yet overwhelmed by mass tourism, they are some of the country's most peaceful and appealing destinations. String a few together into the perfect road trip – or better yet, don your walking shoes and experience these ancient places at a medieval pace. Top right: Piódão (p323)

Pastries

25 One of the great culinary wonders of Portugal, the cinnamon-dusted *pastel de nata* (custard tart), with its flaky crust and creamy centre, lurks irresistibly behind pastry counters across the country; the best are served piping hot in Belém. Of course, when it comes to dessert, Portugal is more than a one-hit wonder, with a dazzling array of regional sweets – from the jewel-like Algarve marzipan to Sintra's heavenly almond-and-egg *travesseiros* to Serpa's cheesecake-like *queijadas*. Above: *pastéis de nata*

MG THERIN WEISE / GETTY IMAGES ©

AHMAD KAVOUSIAN / GETTY IMAGES ©

PAUL BERNHARDT / GETTY IMAGES ©

Need to Know

For more information, see Survival Guide (p497)

Currency
The euro (€)

Language
Portuguese

Visas
Generally not required for stays of up to 90 days; some nationalities will need a Schengen visa.

Money
ATMs widely available. Credit cards accepted at most midrange and top-end hotels and restaurants.

Mobile Phones
Local SIM cards can be used in unlocked European, Australian and quad-band US mobiles.

Time
GMT/UTC in winter, GMT/UTC plus one hour in summer.

When to Go

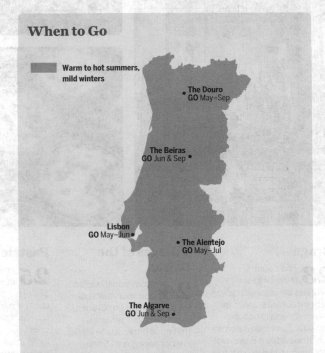

Warm to hot summers, mild winters

The Douro
GO May–Sep

The Beiras
GO Jun & Sep

Lisbon
GO May–Jun

The Alentejo
GO May–Jul

The Algarve
GO Jun & Sep

High Season (Jul–Aug)
➡ Accommodation prices increase by 30%.

➡ Expect big crowds in the Algarve and coastal resort areas.

➡ Sweltering temperatures are commonplace.

➡ Warmer ocean temperatures.

Shoulder (May, Jun & Sep)
➡ Wildflowers and mild days are ideal for hikes and outdoor activities.

➡ Lively festivals take place in June.

➡ Crowds and prices are average.

➡ Colder ocean temperatures.

Low Season (Dec–Mar)
➡ Shorter, rainier days with freezing temperatures in the interior.

➡ Lower prices, fewer crowds.

➡ Attractions keep shorter hours.

➡ Frigid ocean temperatures.

Websites

Lonely Planet (www.lonely planet.com/portugal) Destination information, hotel bookings, traveller forum and more.

Portugal Tourism (www.visit portugal.com) Portugal's official tourism site.

Inside Portugal Travel (www.insideportugaltravel.com) The Portuguese National Tourist Office site in North America.

ViniPortugal (www.viniportugal.pt) Fine overview of Portugal's favourite beverage, covering wine regions, grape varieties and wine routes.

Important Numbers

Country Code	☏351
International Access Code	☏00
Ambulance	☏112
Fire	☏112
Police	☏112

Exchange Rates

Australia	A$1	€0.70
Canada	C$1	€0.72
Japan	¥100	€0.74
New Zealand	NZ$1	€0.62
UK	£1	€1.18
USA	US$1	€0.74

For current exchange rates see www.xe.com.

Daily Costs

Budget: less than €50

➡ Dorm bed: €15–22

➡ Self-catering

➡ Plan sightseeing around free admission days (often Sunday mornings)

➡ Youth cards save on sights and transport

Midrange: €50–120

➡ Double room in a midrange hotel: €50–100

➡ Lunch and dinner in a midrange restaurant: €20–30

➡ Book online to save money on accommodation

Top End: more than €120

➡ Boutique hotel room: from €120

➡ Three-course meal in a top restaurant: from €40

Opening Hours

Opening hours vary throughout the year. We provide high-season opening hours; hours will generally decrease in the shoulder and low seasons.

Restaurants noon–3pm & 7–10pm

Cafés 9am–7pm

Shops 9.30am–noon & 2–7pm Mon–Fri, 10am–1pm Sat

Bars 7pm–2am

Nightclubs 11pm–4am Thu–Sat

Malls 10am–10pm

Banks 8.30am–3pm Mon–Fri

Arriving in Portugal

Aeroporto de Lisboa (Lisbon; p118)

Metro: €1.90 (including €0.50 Viva Viagem card); red line from Aeroporto station; transfer at Alameda for blue line to Rossio and Baixa-Chiado. Twenty minutes to the centre; frequent departures from 6.30am to 1am.

AeroBus: €3.50; every 20 minutes from 7.45am to 8.15pm.

Taxi: €12–16; around 20 minutes to the centre.

Aeroporto Francisco Sá Carneiro (Porto; p379)

Metro: €2.30 (including €0.50 Andante card); 45 minutes to the centre; frequent departures.

Taxi: €22–28; around 30 to 60 minutes to the centre.

Aeroporto de Faro (Faro)

Bus: €1.60; every 30 minutes weekdays, every two hours weekends.

Taxi: €10–14; around 20 minutes to the centre.

Getting Around

Transport in Portugal is reasonably priced, quick and efficient.

Train Extremely affordable, with a decent network between major towns from north to south. Visit Comboio Portugal (www.cp.pt) for schedules and prices.

Car Useful for visiting small villages, national parks and other regions with minimal public transport. Cars can be hired in major towns and cities. Drive on the right.

Bus Cheaper and slower than trains. Useful for more remote villages that aren't serviced by trains. Infrequent service on weekends.

For much more on **getting around**, see p508

First Time Portugal

For more information, see Survival Guide (p497)

Checklist

➡ Check whether you can use your phone in Portugal and ask about roaming charges

➡ Book your first night's accommodation

➡ Check the calendar (p27) to see which festivals to visit (or avoid!)

➡ Organise travel insurance (p502)

➡ Check airline baggage restrictions

➡ Inform your debit- and credit-card company of your travel plans

What to Pack

➡ Phrasebook

➡ Travel plug

➡ Good walking shoes

➡ Earplugs for thin-walled guest houses and noisy weekend nights

➡ Sunscreen

➡ Swimming towel

➡ Rain jacket (especially in the winter)

➡ English-language reading material

Top Tips for Your Trip

➡ Portugal's *mercados* (markets) are a great way to sample the country's culinary bounty. You'll find breads, cheeses, olives, smoked meats, fruits and vegetables – all ideal for picnics.

➡ Get off the main highways and take to the backroads. Sleepy villages, roadside fruit stands and tiny roads leading to remote beaches are a few reasons to get off the beaten path.

What to Wear

Portugal is a fairly casual destination, though most Portuguese tend to wear trousers (rather than shorts) outside of resort areas. For upscale dining, smart casual is all that's required – no restaurant will insist on jackets or ties, and nor will any theatre or concert hall.

Nights can get windy or chilly, so bring a lightweight jacket in the summer, and be prepared for rain and cooler temperatures in the winter.

Sleeping

Although you can usually show up in any town and find a room on the spot, it's worthwhile booking ahead. You'll find more charming options, and better rooms in guesthouses by reserving in advance. For summer months, especially July and August, plan well ahead.

➡ **Guesthouses** For a local experience, stay in a *pensão* or *residencial*. These are small, often family-run places, and some are set in historic buildings. Amenities range from simple to luxury.

➡ **Hostels** Portugal has a growing network of hostels, with stylish, award-winning options in both Lisbon and Porto.

➡ **Turihab Properties** Unique options to stay in manor houses, restored farmhouses or in self-contained stone cottages.

➡ **Pousadas** Accommodation set inside former castles, monasteries and estates. Nearly three dozen *pousadas* are spread across the country, and are well worth planning a trip around.

➡ **Private rooms and apartments** Airbnb (www.airbnb.com) has loads of listings throughout Portugal.

Money

ATMs are the easiest way to get cash in Portugal, and they're easy to find in most cities and towns. Tiny rural villages probably won't have ATMs, so it's wise to get cash in advance. The ATM withdrawal limit is €200 per day, and many banks charge a foreign transaction fee (typically around 2% or 3%).

Most hotels accept credit cards; smaller guesthouses and budget hotels might not, so be sure to inquire before booking. Likewise, smaller restaurants don't often take credit, so it's wise to have cash with you. Armed robbery is virtually unheard of in Portugal. Petty thievery (such as pickpocketing) is a concern in popular tourist areas.

For more information, see p503.

Bargaining

Gentle haggling is common in markets (less so in produce markets); in all other instances you're expected to pay the stated price.

Tipping

➡ **Restaurants** 10% on average, up to 15% in pricier places.

➡ **Bars** Not expected unless table service is provided, then around 10%.

➡ **Snack bars** It's courteous to leave a bit of spare change.

➡ **Taxis** Not expected, but it's polite to round up to the nearest euro.

➡ **Hotels** €1 per bag is standard; gratuity for cleaning staff is at your discretion.

Language

English is spoken in larger cities and in popular tourist areas (especially the Algarve), but is less common in rural areas and among older Portuguese. Many restaurants have English-language menus, though smaller family-run places typically do not (but may have English-speaking staff on hand to help out). Smaller museums are likely to have signs in Portuguese only. The Portuguese always appreciate the effort: a few key words, such as 'bom dia', 'boa tarde', 'obrigado/obrigada' and 'por favor', can go a long way.

See Language (p514), for more information.

Etiquette

➡ **Greetings** When greeting females or mixed company, an air kiss on both cheeks is common courtesy. Men give each other a handshake.

➡ **Visiting Churches** It is considered disrespectful to visit churches as a tourist during Mass. Taking photos at such a time is definitely inappropriate.

➡ **'Free' Appetisers** Whatever you eat, you must pay for, whether or not you ordered it. It's common practice for restaurants to bring bread, butter, cheese and other goodies to the table, but these are never free and will be added to your bill at the end. If you don't want them, a polite 'no thank you' will see them returned to the kitchen.

If You Like...

Food

Renowned for its seafood, hearty country cooking and the many regional specialities, Portugal offers many temptations to the food-minded traveller. Celebrated new chefs have brought much attention to many dining rooms; while those who enjoy the simple things – freshly baked bread, olives, cheeses, roast meats, fish sizzling on the grill – will enjoy memorable meals in traditional restaurants all across the country.

Chiado district This Lisbon neighbourhood is home to some of Portugal's most elegant dining rooms. (p97)

Food festivals The Algarve elevates its seafood and regional delicacies to high art in these food-minded celebrations. (p148)

Vila Joya Overlooking the beach, this two-Michelin-starred restaurant is one of Portugal's finest. (p175)

Cataplana This decadent seafood stew is a south-coast speciality; Olhão serves an excellent version. (p161)

DOC Serves delectable haute cuisine in a beautiful setting on the Douro. (p395)

Wine & Port

Home to some of the oldest vineyards on earth, Portugal has some fantastic (and deliciously affordable) wines. Each region has its enticements, from full-bodied Alentejan reds to Minho's refreshing *vinho verde* (slightly sparkling wine), along with the famous ports from the Douro. Stylish wine bars and bucolic vineyards provide memorable settings to taste Portugal's great fruits of the vine.

Wine Bar do Castelo Sample the country's finest – over 150 Portuguese wines – at Lisbon's best wine bar. (p109)

Herdade do Esporão An acclaimed winery outside Reguengos de Monsaraz, with vineyards dating back hundreds of years. (p220)

Palácio de Mateus Inside a palace, drink in the grandeur while sipping distinctive and rare Alvarelhão. (p397)

Solar do Vinho do Porto With views over the Douro, this elegant garden bar serves an astounding variety of ports. (p108)

Douro Vineyards Breathtaking views from 18th-century manors and velvety rich wines make the Douro a requisite stop for wine lovers. (p393)

Beaches

With 830km of coastline, you'll find sun-kissed shores of every type from festive, people-packed coves to remote windswept shores that invite endless wandering.

Ilha de Tavira This sandy island off the southern coast is a remarkable getaway. (p168)

São Jacinto To escape the crowds, head to this wild beach backed by dunes west of Aveiro. (p318)

Vila Nova de Milfontes Star of the Alentejo coastline is this lovely and vibrant village overlooking several pretty beaches. (p254)

Costa da Caparica Just across the Tejo from Lisbon, you'll find 8km of pretty coastline, with stylish beach bars sprinkled along it. (p138)

IF YOU LIKE... SEEING DOLPHINS

Setúbal has memorable dolphin-watching cruises in the Sado estuary (p142).

Lagos This popular Algarve resort town offers a mix of lively surfing beaches and secluded sandstone-backed shorelines further out of town. (p186)

Architecture

Taking in Portugal's wildly varied architecture involves delving into the past as you gaze upon medieval monasteries, imposing hilltop castles and ancient ruins.

Fortaleza de Sagres Contemplate Portugal's seafaring past from this clifftop perch over the Atlantic. (p195)

Casa da Música Rem Koolhaas' stunning music hall, completed in 2005, is an architectural gem. (p377)

Mosteiro dos Jerónimos Dom Manuel I's fantastical tribute to the great explorers of the 15th century. (p79)

Convento de Cristo Former headquarters of the Knights Templar, this Unesco World Heritage site is stunning to behold. (p290)

Conímbriga The best-preserved Roman ruins on the Iberian Peninsula provide a window into the rise and fall of the once great empire. (p309)

Palácio Nacional de Mafra The construction of this exuberant palace with its 1200 rooms nearly bankrupted the nation. (p136)

Music

The national music of Portugal is undoubtedly fado, that stirring, melancholic sound that's so prevalent in Lisbon (its birthplace) and Coimbra. Other genres also have their followers, and you can catch live rock, jazz and a wide range of world sounds.

(Above) Palácio de Mateus (p397), Vilareal
(Below) Near Cais do Sodre, Lisbon (p59)

The Alfama The birthplace of fado has many authentic places in which to hear it live – as well as tourist traps to avoid. (p110)

A Capella Coimbra also has a fado-loving heart; this converted 14th-century chapel is the best place to hear it live. (p308)

Festival do Sudoeste One of Portugal's biggest music fests erupts each August in the seaside town of Zambujeira do Mar. (p29)

Casa da Música Rem Koolhaas' concert hall is both an architectural masterpiece and a vibrant set piece for year-round music events. (p377)

Music Box Long-lived Lisbon space hosting an eclectic line-up of rock, folk, funk and more. (p110)

Art

In the Portuguese art world, quality trumps quantity. You may not find massive art institutions here, but you will find galleries showcasing unique works from the past and present – including Portugal's own home-grown legends.

Museu Calouste Gulbenkian One of Lisbon's finest museums houses an epic collection of magnificent artwork from East and West. (p77)

Museu Colecção Berardo In Belém, this free museum hosts some of Portugal's most daring exhibits. (p81)

Casa das Histórias Paula Rego Cascais' best exhibition space celebrates the artwork of Paula Rego, one of Portugal's finest living painters. (p130)

Casa de Serralves Porto's art lovers don't miss the cutting-edge exhibits inside this art-deco mansion in the park. (p359)

Museu da Tapeçaria de Portalegre Guy Fino Be dazzled by colour at this fine tapestry museum in the Alentejo. (p234)

Museu de Lamego Superb collection of works from 16th-century luminary Grão Vasco. (p388)

Nightlife

When the sun goes down, things start to get interesting. Whether you want to party like a rock star or sip cocktails with a more laid-back, bohemian crowd, you'll find these and dozens of other scenes in Portugal.

Lagos Packed with music-filled bars and lounges, Lagos is the nightlife centre of the Algarve. (p186)

Forte São João Baptista In a striking 17th-century fort, this

hotel, restaurant and nightclub throws some of the best summer parties in the north. (p385)

Cais do Sodré Lisbon's new nightlife epicentre has colourful bars, tapas joints and DJ-spinning clubs that stay open till the early morning. (p110)

Porto Nightlife has exploded in recent years, with revellers packing the bar- and gallery-lined streets near Rua das Carmelitas. (p373)

Historic Villages

Portugal is home to many enchanting villages, where a stroll along peaceful cobblestone lanes is like strolling back in time.

Óbidos Medieval architecture, lively festivals and charming guesthouses await in this fortified town an hour north of Lisbon. (p267)

Mértola Set high above the Rio Guadiana, this remarkably well-preserved Alentejo town is considered an open-air museum. (p241)

Monsanto A forlorn village surrounding an age-old, boulder-strewn castle, with great walking trails nearby through rolling countryside. (p326)

Miranda do Douro A remote fortress town on the edge of Spain, with an imposing 16th-century castle and street signs in the ancient language of Mirandês. (p414)

Castelo de Vide Wander the medieval Jewish quarter and take in sweeping views over the surrounding cork and olive groves. (p236)

IF YOU LIKE... SCENIC TRAIN RIDES

The Douro line heading east to Pocinho (p392) has stunning views of the river and vineyard-covered hillsides.

Month by Month

February

Winter sees fewer crowds and lower prices along with abundant rainfall, particularly in the north. Coastal temperatures are cool but mild, while inland sees frigid days. Many resorts remain shuttered until spring.

Carnaval

Portugal's Carnaval features much merry-making in the pre-Lenten celebrations. Loulé boasts the best parades, while Lisbon, Nazaré and Viana do Castelo all throw a respectable bash.

Fantasporto

Porto's world-renowned two-week international festival (www.fantasporto. com) of fantasy, horror and just plain weird films.

March

March days are rainy and chilly in much of Portugal, though the south sees more sunshine. Prices remain low, and travellers few and far between.

Festival Internacional do Chocolate

For several days in early March Óbidos celebrates the sweet temptation of the cacao bean.

April

Spring arrives, bringing warmer temperatures and abundant sunshine in both the north and the south. Late April sees a profusion of wildflowers in the south.

Semana Santa

The build-up to Easter is magnificent in the Minho's saintly Braga. During Holy Week, barefoot penitents process through the streets, past rows of makeshift altars, with an explosion of jubilation at the cathedral on the eve of Easter.

Ovibeja

This huge nine-day agricultural fair in Beja features concerts every night, with handicrafts booths and abundant food stalls.

May

Lovely, sunny weather and the lack of peak-season crowds makes May an ideal time to visit. The beaches of the Algarve awake from their slumber and see a smattering of travellers passing through.

Feira das Cantarinhas

A huge three-day street fair of traditional handicrafts in Bragança.

Queima das Fitas

Join the mayhem of Burning of the Ribbons at the University of Coimbra (Portugal's Oxford), as students celebrate the end of the academic year with concerts, a parade and copious amounts of drinking. (p303)

Festa das Cruzes

Barcelos turns into a fairground of flags, flowers, lights and open-air concerts at the Festival of the Crosses. The biggest days are 1 to 3 May. Monsanto, in the Beiras, also celebrates, with singing and dancing beside a medieval castle.

✺ Festa do Mar

Celebrating the age-old love of the sea (and the patron saints of fishermen), this lively fest brings a flotilla of fishing boats to Nazaré's harbour, as well as a colourful parade of elaborately decorated floats. There's plenty of eating and drinking.

◉ Fátima Romaris

Hundreds of thousands make the pilgrimage to Fátima each year to commemorate the apparitions of the Virgin that occurred on 13 May 1917. The pilgrimage also happens in October (12 and 13).

June

Early summer is one of the liveliest times to visit, with a packed festival calendar. Warm sunny days are the norm, and while tourism picks up, the hordes have yet to arrive.

☆ Festa do Fado

Lisbon's love affair with fado reaches a high point at this annual songfest held at the cinematic Castelo de São Jorge. You can also hear free fado on trams every Thursday and Sunday in June. (p70)

☆ Festival Ollin Kan Portugal

Erupting in Vila do Conde, just north of Porto, is this world-music fest (www.ollinkanportugal.com). Hear top acts for free during the three-night event on the banks of the Rio Ave.

✺ Festa do Corpo de Deus

This religious fest happens all across Northern Portugal on Corpus Christi, but is liveliest in Monção, with an old-fashioned medieval fair, theatrical shows and over-the-top processions.

☆ FestivalMed

Loulé's world-music festival (www.festivalmed.com.pt), held over three days, brings more than 50 bands playing an incredible variety of music. World cuisine accompanies the global beats.

✺ Vaca das Cordas & Corpus Christi

Ponte de Lima gets rowdy during this unusual event, which features a bull on a rope let loose on the streets. A more solemn event follows suit with religious processions along flower-strewn streets.

✺ Festas de Junho

Amarante goes wild for its favourite saint and patron of lovers, São Gonçalo. All-night music, fireworks, markets and processions mark the occasion.

✺ Festa de Santo António

The lively Festival of St Anthony is celebrated with fervour in Lisbon's Alfama and Madragoa districts, with feasting, drinking and dancing in some 50 *arraiais* (street parties).

✺ Festa de São João

St John is the favourite up north, where Porto, Braga and Vila do Conde celebrate with elaborate processions, music and feasting, while folks go around whacking

each other with plastic hammers. (p366)

✺ Feira Nacional da Agricultura

One of Portugal's biggest country fairs, this family-fun event turns Santarém into an oversized playground for horse-racing, bullfights, live music, feasting and dancing; there's loads of entertainment for kids.

✺ Festas Populares

Celebrating the feast days of São João and São Pedro, Évora hosts a lively 12-day event that kicks off in late June. There's a traditional fairground, art exhibitions, gourmet food and drink, cultural events and sporting competitions.

July

The summer heat arrives, bringing sun-seekers who pack the resorts of the Algarve. Lisbon and Porto also swell with crowds and prices peak in July and August.

☆ Festival Internacional de Folclore

The week-long International Folk Festival in late July brings costumed dancers and traditional groups to Porto.

✺ Mercado Medieval

Don your armour and head to the castle grounds for this lively two-week medieval fair in Óbidos. Attractions include wandering minstrels, jousting matches and plenty of grog. Other medieval fairs are held in Silves and other castle towns.

August

The mercury rises higher in August, with sweltering days best spent at the beach. This is Portugal's busiest tourist month, and reserving ahead is essential.

✲ Festas de Cidade e Gualterianas

The old city of Guimarães brings revellers from across the region to its colourful processions with allegorical floats, plus folk dancing, fireworks and bands (www.aoficina.pt).

☆ Festival do Sudoeste

The Alentejan Glastonbury, in Zambujeira do Mar, attracts a young, surfy crowd with huge parties and big-name bands headlining.

✕ Festival do Marisco

Seafood lovers should not miss this grand culinary fest in Olhão. Highlights include regional specialities such as chargrilled fish, *caldeirada* (fish stew) and *cataplana* (a kind of Portuguese paella); there's also live music.

✲ Romaria de Nossa Senhora d'Agonia

The Minho's most spectacular festival, in Viana do Castelo, has elaborate street paintings, folk cos-

tume parades, drumming, giant puppets and much merry-making. (p438)

✲ Feira de São Mateus

Folk music, traditional food and fireworks rule the day at St Matthew's Fair in Viseu.

☆ Folkfaro

A musician's treat, the Folkfaro brings local and international folk performers to the city of Faro for staged and impromptu performances across town. Street fairs accompany the event.

☆ Noites Ritual Rock

Towards the end of summer, Porto hosts a free weekend-long rock bash (www.noitesritual.com) that sees up-and-coming bands from around Portugal work big crowds at the Jardins do Palácio de Cristal.

✲ Festa de Nossa Senhora dos Remédios

Head to Lamego, in the Douro, for a mix of religious devotion and secular revelry. In early September, rock concerts and all-night celebrations coincide with pious processions winding through the streets.

September

Peak tourist season officially runs until mid-September, when ongoing warm weather ensures beaches remain packed.

Things cool down a bit, and prices dip, as the crowds dissipate by late September.

✲ Nossa Senhora da Nazaré

The festival of Our Lady of Nazaré brings much life to this eponymous town in Estremadura, with rich processions, folk music and dancing, bullfights and other competitions.

✲ Feiras Novas

One of Portugal's oldest ongoing events, the New Fairs festival has a massive market and fair, with folk dances, fireworks and brass bands at Ponte de Lima.

December

December means rain and colder temperatures. Few travellers venture south, where many resorts close for the winter. Christmas and New Year's Eve bring merriment to the somewhat dreary season.

✲ Festa dos Rapazes

Just after Christmas, the so-called Festival of the Lads is a rollicking time of merry-making by young unmarried men who light bonfires and rampage around in rags and wooden masks. Catch it in Miranda do Douro.

☆ New Year's Eve

Ring in the Ano Novo in Lisbon with fireworks, free concerts and DJs down by the Tejo.

Plan Your Trip
Itineraries

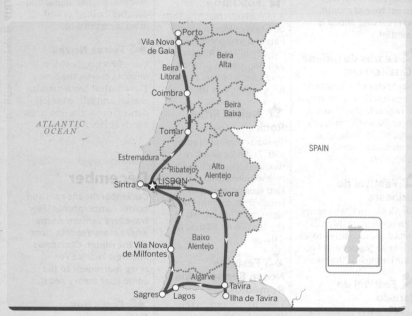

ATLANTIC OCEAN

Porto
Vila Nova de Gaia
Beira Alta
Beira Litoral
Coimbra
Beira Baixa
Tomar
Estremadura
SPAIN
Ribatejo
Alto Alentejo
Sintra
LISBON
Évora
Baixo Alentejo
Vila Nova de Milfontes
Algarve
Sagres
Lagos
Tavira
Ilha de Tavira

2 WEEKS **Highlights of Portugal**

This grand journey takes you from the vibrant Portuguese capital to the sunny beaches of the Algarve and up north to the striking riverside city of Porto. Along the way, you'll visit Unesco World Heritage sites, stroll medieval town centres and sample the varied cuisines from the north, south and centre.

Start in **Lisbon**, spending two days exploring the city's enchanting neighbourhoods, fado-filled taverns, atmospheric cafes and restaurants, and late-night street parties. Take in vertiginous tram rides, the hilltop

castle and viewing points, museums and historic sites. On day three, head to nearby **Sintra**, for quaint village life amid woodlands and palaces. Next enjoy two days exploring fascinating **Évora** and its nearby megaliths. From there, go south and spend a day in peaceful **Tavira**, one of the Algarve's prettiest towns. Take the ferry out to car-free **Ilha de Tavira**. Continue west to beach- and nightlife-loving **Lagos**. Don't miss the pretty beaches (Batata, Dona Ana and Camilo) south of town. Keep going west until you hit laid-back **Sagres**, where you can visit its dramatically sited fort, surf good waves

Rua Augusta, Baixa (p63), Lisbon

and contemplate the endless horizon at the cliffs near town. Go north back to Lisbon, stopping en route in the coastal town of **Vila Nova de Milfontes**, a great spot for uber-fresh seafood grilled up to perfection. You can eat it right on the waterfront. Spend one day in **Tomar**, a sleepy river town that's home to the staggering Convento de Cristo. Then book two nights in the venerable university town of **Coimbra**, wandering the old quarters, visiting medieval convents and churches, and enjoying good meals, lively bars (during the academic year) and live music. Spend your last two days in **Porto**, Lisbon's rival in beauty.

Enjoy a day exploring the Ribeira, visiting avant-garde galleries and museums, and taking in the nightlife in the city centre. Then head across the river to **Vila Nova de Gaia**, for an introduction to the country's great ports. If time allows, take a boat trip along the Rio Douro, taking in some dramatic gorge scenery and centuries-old vineyards.

Vila do Conde
Foz do Douro
Porto
Douro
Alto Daro

Reserva Natural das
Dunas de São Jacinto
Aveiro
Beira
Alta

ATLANTIC
OCEAN
Beira
Litoral

Figueira da Foz
Montemor-
o-Velho
Beira
Baixa
SPAIN

Nazaré
Batalha
Alcobaça

Berlenga
Grande
Baleal
Peniche
Óbidos
Ribatejo

Ericeira
Estremadura

Cabo da Roca
Sintra
Alto
Alentejo
Praia do Guincho
LISBON
Cascais

Exploring the Atlantic Coast

3 WEEKS

Scenic shorelines, captivating towns and staggering architectural monuments set the stage for this memorable journey down the Atlantic coast.

Begin in **Porto**, the port-wine capital at the mouth of the Douro. Spend two days exploring its historic centre, museums, parks and gardens, plus the beach neighbourhood of **Foz do Douro**. On the third day go north to the seaside town of **Vila do Conde**, a quick and popular beach getaway. Next, head south to **Aveiro**, for rides along its scenic canals on high-prowed *moliceiros* (traditional boats). For a fine day trip from here take a bus and ferry out to the **Reserva Natural das Dunas de São Jacinto**, a scenic nature reserve and birdwatching site. The popular resort town of **Figueira da Foz** is the next stop; you'll find prime surfing, a touch of nightlife and wide people-packed beaches, with more isolated sands out of town. After a day of sunbaking, make an inland day trip to the striking mountain-top castle of **Montemor-o-Velho**. The picturesque and fun-loving beach town of **Nazaré** is next and here you can frolic in the waves, enjoy traditional seafood restaurants and take the funicular to a clifftop promontory for superb views. Nazaré is also a good base for exploring the architecturally stunning monasteries (and Unesco World Heritage sites) in **Alcobaça** and **Batalha**. From there, head south to **Óbidos**, with its cobblestone lanes and upmarket inns. Go west back to the coast to reach **Peniche**, where you'll find excellent beaches, particularly in nearby **Baleal**. From Peniche, be sure to take a boat out to the remote island of **Berlenga Grande**. You can even stay overnight (reserve well ahead). Continue south to **Ericeira**, a whitewashed village perched atop sandstone cliffs. Explore the beaches, feast on seafood, then continue on to the fairy-tale setting of **Sintra**, where picturesque guesthouses make a fine overnight stay. Take the road to the coast, and follow it out to the dramatically set **Cabo da Roca** and down to the windswept beach of **Praia do Guincho**. The next stop is the pretty village of **Cascais**, home to narrow pedestrian lanes, lively outdoor restaurants and leafy gardens. End your journey in **Lisbon**, spending a few days exploring Portugal's vibrant capital.

PLAN YOUR TRIP ITINERARIES

Top: Ericeira (p260)
Bottom: Traditional boat, Aveiro (p318)

10 DAYS

Circling the Centre

Dramatic scenery, frozen-in-time villages and clifftop castles make for a charming journey on this loop around Portugal's often overlooked interior.

From Lisbon head 200km southeast to the historic village of **Castro Verde**. Visit the royal basilica in town then the LPN Interpretative and Environmental Centre, a great spot for bird-watching some 5km north of town. Drive east to **Mértola**, a picturesque medieval settlement set high above the placid Rio Guadiana. Wander the old streets, go kayaking on the river, sample wild boar (a local speciality) and overnight in one of the area's charming inns. From Mértola, drive north to **Beja**, a lively town with a walled centre, intriguing museums and a 13th-century castle with sweeping views over golden wheat fields beyond town. Keep north to reach **Évora**, the most vibrant town in the Alentejo. Its large cobblestone centre is a great place to wander, and is packed with history (don't miss the Bone Chapel and Roman temple). Évora has great traditional restaurants and makes a good base for visiting neolithic sites in the countryside. Head northeast to the marble town of **Vila Viçosa**, home to a staggering palace and a peaceful town centre. Next up is **Castelo de Vide**, a wildly remote-feeling town perched on a clifftop. Have a wander through the sleepy streets, have lunch, and then continue to **Monsanto**, another photogenic castle-in-the-sky town. Leave early for the two-hour drive to **Vila Nova de Foz Côa**, gateway to some of Iberia's most extensive petroglyphs. From here, it's an easy detour to the vineyards along the Douro. Otherwise, head southwest into the **Parque Natural da Serra da Estrela**, a scenic, mountainous area with great hiking, and peaceful guesthouses where you can soak up the scenery. **Manteigas** makes a great base. After a day or two in the mountains, head west to the lively university town of **Coimbra**. Visit the historic campus, stroll the riverbank, feast on hearty Portuguese cooking and catch live Coimbra-style fado. Visit **Conímbriga** southwest of Coimbra for a look at Roman ruins, then continue to **Santarém**, with Gothic architecture, atmospheric restaurants and panoramic views, before finishing the tour in **Lisbon**.

Top: Monsanto (p326)

Bottom: Monsanto resident

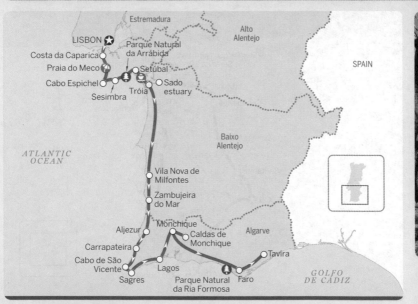

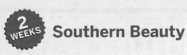

Southern Beauty

This trip will give you a chance to see spectacular contrasts in scenery by following Portugal's southern rivers, beaches and ridges.

From **Lisbon** head to the **Costa da Caparica**, taking in the festive beaches near the town, and then escaping the crowds on wilder beaches to the south. Next head down to **Praia do Meco** for more sandy action and some great seafood. Keep going south to reach the desolate cliffs of **Cabo Espichel**. A good place to stay for the night is at a rural guesthouse outside of **Sesimbra**, a former fishing village turned resort with open-air restaurants and family-friendly beaches. On the next day, continue east, stopping for a picnic on the forest-lined shores of **Parque Natural da Arrábida**. At night, stay in **Setúbal** for more seafood feasting and a wander through the sleepy old-town quarters. The next day, book a dolphin-watching boat trip along the **Sado estuary**. From Setúbal, take the ferry across to handsomely sited **Tróia**. Continue south to overnight in **Vila Nova de Milfontes**, a lovely seaside town with fine beaches and charming guesthouses. Next is **Zambujeira do Mar**, a tiny village perched above a pretty beach. Follow the coast to **Aljezur**, with its unspoilt, cliff-backed sands, and into the rustic town of **Carrapateira**, with more wild, untouched beaches, plus cafes and guesthouses catering to the surf-loving crowd. Head south, and you'll reach the southern coast at pretty, laid-back **Sagres**, another surf-loving town. Visit Sagres' sea-cliff fortress, then the surreal cliffs of **Cabo de São Vicente**. Go east to **Lagos**, one of the Algarve's liveliest towns with loads of good sleeping, eating and drinking options. Afterwards, go inland to **Monchique**, with its densely wooded hillsides that offer picturesque walking, cycling and pony-trekking opportunities, followed by a spa visit in **Caldas de Monchique**. Back on the coast, stay overnight in the lively **Faro**, before journeying out to the **Parque Natural da Ria Formosa**, a lagoon system full of marsh, creeks and dune islands. From there, head to **Tavira**, set with genteel 18th-century buildings straddling the Rio Gilão.

Top: Lagos (p186)
Bottom: Vila Nogueira de Azeitao, Setubal (p139)

Off the Beaten Track: Portugal

PONTE DE LIMA

A picturesque Minho town with long riverside walks and river kayaking. Visit on alternate Mondays, when a massive market spreads along the banks. (p444)

CITÂNIA DE BRITEIROS

A mysterious fortified village that was the last stronghold of Celtiberians against invading Romans some 2000 years ago. (p434)

MATA NACIONAL DO BUÇACO

Surrounding a palace-turned-upscale-hotel, this rambling forest is dotted with ponds, fountains and crumbling ruins. The spa town of Luso is just downhill. (p311)

SERRA DA PENEDA

Superb hiking amid wild, boulder-strewn countryside in the northern, least-visited section of the Parque Nacional da Peneda-Gerês. (p452)

MIRANDA DO DOURO

Some folks still speak the ancient tongue of Mirandês in this rugged fortress town, and it's a great base for exploring the canyons and cliffs of remote Parque Natural de Montesinho. (p414)

PIODÃO

Perched along the edge of a valley, this picturesque stone village offers a window into old-world Portugal – until 1970, the only way here was on foot. (p323)

SERPA

Famed for its sheep's milk cheese, Serpa has several curious museums (including one dedicated to timepieces), but it's the traditional Alentejo cooking that is the real draw. (p249)

SÃO DOMINGOS

A former mining settlement that became a ghost town when the mine closed in the 1960s. (p244)

ALCOUTIM

Home to a castle, a pretty riverside beach and few tourists, this Algarve town is a great place to escape the crowds. (p171)

CARRAPATEIRA

Laid-back village near pristine, undeveloped beaches backed by cliffs. It's a great place to surf or learn the ropes. (p199)

Cáceres

Badajoz

Portalegre

Parque Natural da Serra de São Mamede

Barragem do Caia

RIBATEJO

Rio Guadiana

SERPA

Évora

Beja

SÃO DOMINGOS

Rio Guadalquivir

Seville

Huelva

ALCOUTIM

BAIXO ALENTEJO

Parque Natural do Vale do Guadiana

Gundiana du Vale do Natural Parque

Reserva Natural do Sapal de Castro, Marín e Vila Real de Santo António

Ilha de Tavira

Faro

ALGARVE

Monchique

Parque Natural das Serrasde Aire e Candeeiros

ESTREMADURA

Santarem

Rio Tejo

LISBON

Parque Natural da Arrábida

Setúbal

Rio Sado

Reserva Natural das Lagoas de Santo André da Sancha

Parque Natural de Sintra-Cascais

Parque Natural do Sudoeste Alentejano e Costa Vicentina

CARRAPATEIRA

ATLANTIC OCEAN

Plan Your Trip
Portugal Outdoors

Outdoors enthusiasts will find plenty to appreciate in Portugal. With 830km of coastline, there's first-rate surfing all along the coast. Inland, rolling cork fields, granite peaks and precipitous river gorges form the backdrop for a host of other activities – from walking to birdwatching, horse riding to paragliding.

Best Outdoors

Best Surf Spots
Peniche (p263)

Ribeira d'Ilhas (p260)

Carrapateira (p200)

Cabedelo, Viana do Castelo (p437)

Meia Praia, Lagos (p187)

Best Places to Walk
Parque Nacional da Peneda-Gerês (p450)

Parque Natural da Serra da Estrela (p329)

Via Algarviana (p158)

Parque Natural de Montesinho (p411)

Rota Vicentina (p256)

Best Places to Watch Wildlife
Parque Natural da Ria Formosa (p161)

Sado estuary (p141)

Parque Natural do Douro Internacional (p417)

Surfing

Portugal has some of Europe's most curvaceous surf, with 30 to 40 major reefs and beaches. It picks up swells from the north, south and west, giving it remarkable consistency. It also has a wide variety of waves and swell sizes, making it ideal for surfers of all levels. Numerous surf schools in the Algarve and along Portugal's western Atlantic coast offer classes and all-inclusive packages for all skill levels, from beginners to advanced.

When to Surf

The best waves in southern Portugal generally occur in the winter from November to March. Further north, spring and autumn tend to be the best seasons for surfing action. Waves at these times range from 2m to 4.5m high. This is also the low season, meaning you'll pay less for accommodation, and the beaches will be far less crowded. Even during the summer, however, the coast gets good waves (1m to 1.5m on average) and, despite the crowds, it's fairly easy to head off and find your own spots (with your own wheels, you can often be on your own stretch of beach just by driving a few minutes up the road).

What to Take

The water temperature here is colder than it is in most other southern European countries, and even in the summer you'll probably want a wetsuit. Board and wet-suit hire are widely available at surf shops and surf camps; you can usually score a discount if you rent long-term – otherwise, you'll be paying around €20 to €30 per day for a board and wetsuit, or €15 to €25 per day for the board only.

Prime Spots

One of Portugal's best breaks is around Peniche (p264), where you can count on good waves with just about any wind. An excellent hostel and several residential surf camps make this an affordable base. Supertubos and Baleal are the most popular local beaches.

Other fabled surf spots include Ribeira d'Ilhas in Ericeira (p260) and Praia do Guincho (p131) near Cascais, which often host international championships. Another break that's famous among the global surf-ing community is Carrapateira (p200) in the western Algarve. Schools and clubs head over this way from Lagos and further afield to take advantage of the crashing waves. Nearby, the area around Praia do Penedo is a good choice for beginners.

There are countless other good surf spots up and down the coast including, but by no means limited to, the following, from north to south: Viana do Castelo (p435), Praia da Barra (p319), Costa Nova (p319), Figueira da Foz (p313), Nazaré (p272), Costa da Caparica (p138), Sesimbra (p145), Vila Nova de Milfontes (p254) and Zambujeira (p256).

Information

There are dozens of schools that can help you improve your surfing. Most offer weekly packages including simple accom-modation (dorms, bungalows or camping), meals and transport to the beach.

Recommended surf camps north of Lis-bon include Ericeira's Ribeira Surf Camp (p260) and the camps at Baleal (p263).

In the Algarve you'll have your pick of countless operators, many of them concen-trated around Lagos (p187), Sagres (p195) and Carrapateira (p199).

Surfer Sites

For information on wave conditions, com-petitions and more, surf on over to one of these helpful sites.

www.magicseaweed.com International site with English-language surf reports for many Portu-guese beaches.

www.surfingportugal.com Official site of the Portuguese Surfing Federation.

www.surftotal.com/pt Portuguese-language site with news about the national surf scene and webcams showing conditions at a dozen popular beaches around Portugal.

Walking

Portugal's wonderful walking potential is all the better because so few people know about it. Most organised walking clubs are found in the Algarve, there is a cluster of organisations around Monchique but other good bases are Sagres and Vila Real de Santo António. Northern Portugal has more mountainous terrain and several lovely, little-visited natural parks.

WORLD CHAMPIONSHIP WAVES

In 2009 Portugal's surf scene got a real shot in the arm when **Supertubos** beach near Peniche was chosen as one of 10 stops on the ASP World Tour, the most prestig-ious international competitive surfing event. For 12 days in October, the beach was packed with surfers from around the world showing off their best moves. The event's organisers apparently liked what they saw – Supertubos has hosted the interna-tional contest every year since then.

Supertubos isn't the only spot in Portugal with great breaks. Some 60km north of Peniche, you'll find some of the world's tallest waves, thanks to a deep-water canyon connected to the shoreline. In 2011 Hawaiian surfer Garret McNamara set the world record for the biggest wave ever ridden by riding a wave reportedly 30.5m (100ft) high.

Portugal Outdoors

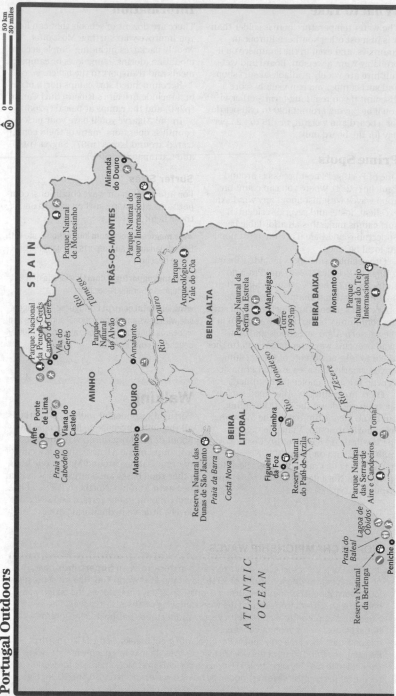

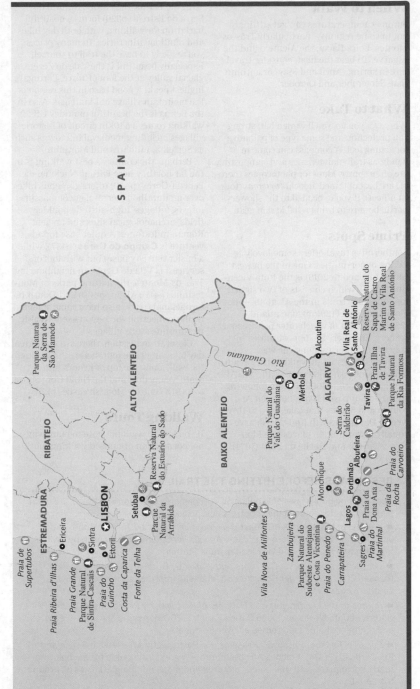

When to Walk

Summer temperatures can get stiflingly hot in some regions – particularly Trás-os-Montes, Beira Baixa, the Alentejo and the Algarve. To beat the heat, consider travelling in spring (April and May) or autumn (late September and October).

What to Take

Wherever you go, you'll want a hat, strong sun protection and some type of palliative for aching feet. A compass can come in handy, as trail maintenance and signposting are often spotty. Maps (or photocopies thereof) are best obtained at local *turismos* (tourist offices). If you're headed to the showery north, be sure to bring reliable rain gear.

Prime Spots

Southern Portugal offers some lovely hiking opportunities. One of the newest routes (opened in 2013) is the Rota Vicentina (p256), which consists of two signed long-distance trails in the Alentejo – one along the coast (120km), one inland (230km) – both of which offer picturesque scenery, and there are opportunities to stay in guesthouses along the way.

Those interested in walking the breadth of the country should consider the Via Algarviana (p158), a 300km route following paved and unpaved roads between Alcoutim and Sagres that takes two to three weeks. Day hikers will find the Algarve equally rewarding, in places like Monchique (p203) and Rocha da Pena (p174).

In the Beiras, the Parque Natural da Serra da Estrela (p329) forms a beautiful backdrop for walking, with both day hikes and multiday itineraries. In many places you're likely to have the trail to yourself. Especially beautiful is the Vale do Zêzere, a glacial valley at the foot of Torre, Portugal's highest peak. A good base in this region is the mountain village of Manteigas. Also in the Beiras is the beautiful multiday GR-22 walking route, a 540km circuit of historic villages including medieval hill towns such as Sortelha, Linhares and Monsanto.

Perhaps the country's best walking is in the far north, where Parque Nacional da Peneda-Gerês (p450) offers gorgeous hikes over mountainous terrain, encompassing forests, villages, high-altitude boulder fields, archaeological sites and ancient Roman milestones. A quiet base for adventure is **Campo do Gerês** (p457), while a busier touristy base (but with lots of services) is Vila do Gerês. In neighbouring Trás-os-Montes, the natural parks of Montesinho (p411), Alvão (p400) and Douro Internacional (p417) also have some splendid trails connecting the region's remarkably picturesque stone villages.

Closer to civilisation, there are some great day hikes in prime tourist areas, including the walk along the top of Évora's 16th-century aqueduct and the climb from Sintra to its 9th-century Moorish castle (p121).

Walking Tours

If you love to walk but hate to plan, why not consider an organised walking tour?

BEST READS BEFORE HITTING THE TRAIL

The following books, available online or at bookstores in Lisbon and Porto, are great planning aids for some of the country's best hikes.

➡ *Walking in the Algarve: 40 Coastal & Mountain Walks*, by Julie Statham and June Parker (2006), Cicerone Press – An excellent guide co-authored by British-born Algarve resident and tour leader, Julie Statham.

➡ *Landscapes of Algarve: Car Tours and Walks*, by Brian and Eileen Anderson (revised 2012), Sunflower Books – Lots of useful information for exploring the southern coast.

➡ *Routes to the Landscapes and Habitats of Portugal*, by Pedro Castro Henriques, Renato Neves and João Carlos Farinha (2005), Assirio & Alvim – Features environmentally-focused routes all over Portugal.

➡ *Portugal Passo-a-Passo: 20 Passeios por Portugal*, by Abel Melo e Sousa and Rui Cardoso (2004), Edições Afrontamento – A great little guide for anyone who reads Portuguese, with full-colour pictures and maps outlining 20 hikes all around the country.

The companies listed here offer both group walking tours – complete with tour leader – and self-guided tours where you walk independently, following an itinerary provided by the tour company, with pre-arranged meals and lodging included in the price.

Based about 10km north of Sagres, **Portugal Walks** (www.portugalwalks.com) offers week-long packages (self-guided/group walks from €490/610) in mainland Portugal as well as Madeira and the Azores.

Another dependable Portuguese outfitter offering guided walks is **A2Z Adventures** (www.a2zadventures.com).

Ecotourism company Sistemas de Ar Livre (p142), in Setúbal, arranges activities including three-hour guided walks. Also try the following UK-based companies:

ATG Oxford (www.atg-oxford.co.uk) Offers weeklong guided walking holidays between Sintra and Cascais, and also in the Azores.

Headwater (www.headwater.com) Weeklong jaunts in the Serra da Estrela, Alentejo and Algarve regions.

Ramblers Holidays (www.ramblersholidays.co.uk) Guided seven- to 10-day walking holidays in the Minho, the Douro and the Algarve.

VBT Bicycling & Walking Vacations (www.vbt.com) Guided weeklong walking tours in the Douro region.

Information

Many *turismos* and natural-park offices offer free brochures about local walks, although materials frequently go out of print due to insufficient funding. Other organisations that produce free maps of their own trails include Odiana in the Algarve and the Centro de Interpretaçaõ da Serra da Estrela (CISE) in the Serra da Estrela.

Portugal uses a system of coloured blazes to mark its trails. White and red are the colours of choice for the major multiday trails known as Grandes Rotas, while red and yellow blazes indicate Pequenas Rotas (shorter day hikes). Common blaze patterns and their meanings are outlined here.

Other Outdoor Activities

While walking and cycling can be done at the drop of a hat, many other outdoor activities need a bit more organisation –

PLAN YOUR TRIP PORTUGAL OUTDOORS

SANTIAGO DE COMPOSTELA

Every year thousands of walkers from around the world hike the **Camino de Santiago**, the classic pilgrimage route from France to Santiago de Compostela, Spain. But what if you're already in Portugal? Portuguese pilgrims have their own route to Santiago, less crowded but just as interesting. Like its sister trail to the north, the **Caminho Português** has multiple starting points, but the best-known section originates in Porto. Information is available through the **Associação dos Amigos do Caminho Português de Santiago** (www.caminhoportuguesdesantiago.com).

and often specialist gear, as well as guides or instructors. Below are a few ideas to inform and inspire. If you need more details while you're travelling in Portugal, *turismos* can advise about specialist local operators and adventure centres.

Rock Climbing, Paragliding & Adrenalin Sports

In the far north, the granite peaks of Parque Nacional da Peneda-Gerês (p450) are a climber's paradise. Other popular places are the schist cliffs at Nossa Senhora do Salto, east of Porto; the 500m-tall granite Cántaro Magro in the Serra da Estrela (p330); the limestone crags of Rceguengo do Fetal near Fátima; the sheer rock walls of Penedo da Amizade, just below Sintra's Moorish castle; the dramatic quartzite ridge of Penha Garcia (p326), near Monsanto in Beira Baixa; and Rocha da Pena (p174) in the Algarve.

Useful climbing organisations include **Clube Nacional de Montanhismo** (www.cnm.org.pt) and **Grupo de Montanha e Escalada de Sintra** (www.gmesintra.com). The latter publishes free downloadable guides to crags as well as the online climbing magazine, **Vertigem** (www.vertigem-mag.com).

Paragliding is also popular in the north. Two prime launch sites are Linhares (p334) in the Serra da Estrela and Alvados (p284) in the Parque das Serras de Aire e Candeeiros.

Several local adrenalin-sports outfitters have English-language websites.

Eco-aware, Sesimbra-based Vertente Natural (p145) offers trekking, canyoning, canoeing, diving and rappelling.

Capitão Dureza (☎239 918 148; www.capitaodureza.com) This outfit located outside of Coimbra organises high-adrenalin activities including rafting, canyoning, abseiling (rappelling), mountain biking and trekking.

Freetour (www.freetour.pt) This Leiria-based agency organises rafting, canyoning, abseiling,

mountain biking and trekking, plus paragliding and skydiving throughout Portugal.

Trilhos (www.trilhos.pt) A Porto-based company promoting environmental tourism, offering climbing, caving, canyoning, trekking and other adventure sports.

Boating

Along the coast, especially in the Algarve, pleasure boats predominate, offering

NATURAL PARKS & RESERVES

Portugal's mixed bag of natural parks and reserves is worth the effort. The Parque Nacional da Peneda-Gerês is the country's only bona fide *parque nacional* (national park), but there are 24 other parks of varying designations. These areas total some 6500 sq km – just over 7% of Portugal's land area.

The **Instituto da Conservação da Natureza e da Biodiversidade** (ICNB; http://portal.icn.pt) is the government agency responsible for the parks. It has general information, but detailed maps and English-language materials are sometimes hard to come by. Standards of maintenance and facilities vary wildly. For a picture of all the rich wildlife and diverse landscapes on offer, browse the table below.

PARK/RESERVE	FEATURES
Parque Nacional da Peneda-Gerês (p450)	lushly forested mountains, rock-strewn plateaus, deer, birds of prey, hot springs, wolves, long-horned cattle
Parque Natural da Arrábida (p144)	coastal mountain range, birds of prey, diverse flora, damaged by wildfire
Parque Natural da Ria Formosa (p161)	salty coastal lagoons, lakes, marshes, dunes, rich bird life, beaches, Mediterranean chameleons
Parque Natural da Serra da Estrela (p329)	pristine mountains – Portugal's highest, rich bird life, rare herbs
Parque Natural das Serras de Aire e Candeeiros (p284)	limestone mountains, cave systems, covered in gorse & olive trees
Parque Natural de Montesinho (p411)	remote oasis of peaceful grassland & forest, last wild refuge for Iberian wolf
Parque Natural de Sintra-Cascais	rugged coastline & mountains, diverse flora
Parque Natural do Alvão (p400)	granite basin, pine forest, waterfalls, rich bird life, deer, boar
Parque Natural do Douro Internacional (p417)	canyon country with high cliffs & lakes, home to many endangered birds of prey
Parque Natural do Vale do Guadiana (p242)	gentle hills & plains, rivers, rare birds of prey, snakes, toads, prehistoric sites
Parque Natural do Sudoeste Alentejano e Costa Vicentina (p254)	coastal cliffs & remote beaches, unique plants, otters, foxes, 200 bird types
Reserva Natural da Berlenga (p266)	remote islands in clear seas, rock formations, caves, seabirds
Reserva Natural das Dunas de São Jacinto (p318)	thickly wooded coastal park, rich in bird life
Reserva Natural do Estuário do Sado (Sado estuary; p141)	estuary of mud, marshes, lagoons & dunes, bird life including flamingos, molluscs, bottlenose dolphins
Reserva Natural do Sapal de Castro Marim e Vila Real de Santo António (p170)	marshland & salt pans, flamingos, spoonbills, avocet, Caspian terns, white storks

everything from barbecue cruises and grotto tours to dolphin-spotting excursions. Inland, Portugal's rivers, lagoons and reservoirs offer a wide variety of boating opportunities, including kayaking, sailing, rafting and canoeing. Rivers popular for boating include the Guadiana, Mondego, Zêzere, Paiva, Minho and Tâmega.

Companies that rent boats and/or operate boat trips can be found in Lagos, Mértola, Barragem do Alqueva, Tomar, Coimbra, Ponte de Lima, Rio Caldo and Amarante, just to name a few.

Cycling

Portugal has many exhilarating opportunities for **mountain biking** (*bicicleta todo terreno;* BTT). Monchique (p203) and Tavira in the Algarve, Sintra (p124) and Setúbal (p141) in central Portugal and Parque Nacional da Peneda-Gerês (p450) in the north are all popular starting points.

Bicycle trails are also growing in popularity. Rio Lima in the north has a handful of short greenways (ranging from 8km to 13.3km) that are popular with cyclists, walkers and runners. Another rail-to-trails initiative, the 49km **Ecopista do Dão** between Viseu and Santa Comba Dão in the Beiras, opened in 2011. There are even places to rent bikes near the start in Santa Comba Dão. Down south, the ambitious **Ecovia do Litoral** is a 214km cycling route across the Algarve that will eventually connect Cabo de Sao Vicente at Portugal's southwestern tip to Vila Real de Santo António on the Spanish border. Meanwhile, bike paths have become fixtures of the urban landscape around Lisbon and in northern cities like Porto, Coimbra and Guarda; popular bike trails have also cropped up in coastal venues such as the Estremadura's Pinhal de Leiria and the Lisbon coast between Cascais and Praia do Guincho.

Cycling Tours

If you're looking for a good day trip or a longer cycling holiday, the following excellent local companies can point you in the right direction.

Portugal Bike (www.portugalbike.com) Lisbon-based operator that offers an excellent selection of bike tours – on road bikes, mountain bikes or hybrids – available year-round. Trips go through the Algarve, Minho or Alentejo. There's also a route that follows the Camino de Santiago through northern Portugal and into Spain. Tours run five to 10 days and are available guided or self-guided.

> ### PENNILESS PEDALLING
>
> Fancy a ride without spending a euro-cent? An increasing number of Portuguese towns have adopted **free bike programs**. In places like Aveiro and Cascais you can show up at the local free bike agency, provide a photo ID, fill out a short form and presto! – off you go on your very own bicycle.

Blue Coast Bikes (Map p140; ☎265 092 172; www.bluecoastbikes.travel; Rua das Fontaínhas 82; bike hire per day from €15, guided tours from €70) An American-Portuguese partnership based in Setúbal, offers six- and eight-day guided tours through the Douro Valley, around the Alentejo and along the Costa Azul. Their mechanic is a former Portuguese downhill and cross-country champion.

Pedal in Portugal (www.pedalinportugal.com) A well-established, Portugal-based company offering both guided and self-guided road- and mountain-bike tours in both the Alentejo and the Algarve. It also runs day tours in the Algarve.

You can also try the following UK- and US-based companies.

Easy Rider Tours (www.easyridertours.com) Features several guided cycling itineraries in the Minho, Alentejo and Algarve and along the Lisbon coast near Sintra.

Saddle Skedaddle (www.skedaddle.co.uk) Offers both guided and self-guided tours lasting eight to nine days. Trips go through the eastern Beiras and the Alentejo (with a coastal and an inland route). The ambitious can sign on for a 16-day trip.

Saranjan Tours (www.saranjan.com) High-end cycling tours in the Algarve, Alentejo, Minho and Douro regions.

Diving

Portugal's best dive sites are concentrated in the Algarve. The water temperature is a bit crisp (around 14°C to 16°C, though it doesn't vary much between summer and winter); most divers prefer a 5mm suit. Visibility is usually between 4m and 6m; on the best days, it can range from 15m to 20m.

One of the best places for beginners to learn to dive is off Praia do Carvoeiro (p177), with several operators offering PADI-accredited courses in English. PADI-accredited courses are also offered in Lagos (p187) and Sagres (p196).

Closer to Lisbon, there are diving outfits at Costa da Caparica (p138), Sesimbra (p145) and Reserva Natural da Berlenga (p266).

Golf

Portugal is a golf mecca, and its championship courses are famous for their rolling greens and ocean vistas. Although many courses are frequented mainly by club members, anyone with a handicap certificate can play here. Greens fees run from €35 to more than €120 per round.

Estoril has nearly a dozen spectacular courses. Golf do Estoril, one of Portugal's best-known, has hosted the Portuguese Open Championship 20 times. It's 5262m long and set among eucalyptus, pine and mimosa trees. Two other Portuguese Open venues lie nearby: Oitavos Dunes, which rolls over windblown dunes and rocky outcrops; and Penha Longa, ranked one of Europe's best courses, with superb views of the Serra de Sintra. See www.estorilsin tragolf.net or the Estoril and Cascais *turismos* for full details of all courses.

Two well-regarded courses around Lisbon are Troia Golf near Setúbal and Praia d'El Rey Golf & Beach Resort near Óbidos.

The Algarve has three-dozen courses at last count – including the renowned Vilamoura Oceânico Victoria, San Lorenzo, Monte Rei and Vale do Lobo courses. For a general overview, see the complete course guide at www.algarve-golf.com.

For golfing packages around Lisbon and in the Algarve, try UK-based **3D Golf** (www.3dgolf.com).

Bear in mind that golf courses' toll on the environment can be significant, especially in fragile coastal settings like the Algarve.

Horse Riding

Horse riding is a fantastic way to experience Portugal's countryside. Lusitano thoroughbreds hail from Portugal, and experienced riders can take dressage lessons in Estremadura. Otherwise, there are dozens of horse-riding centres – especially in the Alentejo, and in the Algarve at places like Silves, Lagos, Portimão and Albufeira. Northern Portugal also offers some pleasant settings for rides, including **Campo do Gerês** (p457) at the edge of Parque Nacional da Peneda-Gerês. Rates are usually around €20 to €30 per hour.

Switzerland-based **Equitour** (www.equitour.com) offers eight-day riding holidays around Portugal costing €998 to €1710 per person, including accommodation and some meals. Its signature tour follows the Alentejo Royal Horse Stud Trail, with stays at grand country estates.

GREAT OUTDOOR ADVENTURES FOR FAMILIES

➡ Mountain bike through the outback to see the Palaeolithic petroglyphs at **Parque Arqueológico do Vale do Côa** (p395).

➡ Kayak with your kids down the **Rio Mondego** (p303) from Penacova to Coimbra.

➡ Learn to surf with the whole family at **Hooked Surf School** (p138) in Costa da Caparica.

➡ Take the invigoratingly bouncy **boat ride** (p265) from Peniche to Berlenga Grande, then stay overnight in a 17th-century fort converted into a **hostel** (p267).

➡ Look for **dolphins** (p176) – and learn about them from an onboard marine biologist – as you ply the Atlantic waters off the Algarve coast.

➡ Walk through a landscape of dramatic mountains and stone shepherds' huts as you climb the glacial Zêzere Valley, then cool off with icy water from a natural spring in **Parque Natural Serra da Estrela** (329).

➡ Scan the horizon for pirates from the 17th-century **fort** (p145), play king of the castle at the Moorish *castelo*, or build sandcastles of your own on the beach at Sesimbra.

➡ Take the narrow-gauge train to the lovely, wild beaches along **Costa da Caparica** (p138).

➡ See dinosaur footprints – yes, *real* dinosaur footprints! – at **Cabo Espichel** (p146) or **Monumento Natural das Pegadas dos Dinossáurios** (p284).

The Wyoming-based outfit **Equitours** (www.ridingtours.com), offers a year-round classical dressage program on Lusitano horses at the Escola de Equitação de Alcainça, near Mafra, including accommodation plus 90 minutes/three hours of riding per day for US$195/240 in the low season, to US$220/265 in the high season.

Wildlife Watching

Portugal has excellent **birdwatching**, especially in Atlantic coastal lagoons and the deep river canyons along the Spanish border. In the south, prime spots include the Serra do Caldeirão (p174), Parque Natural da Ria Formosa (p161), Parque Natural do Vale do Guadiana (p242) and the Reserva Natural do Sapal de Castro Marim e Vila Real de Santo Antonio (p170). In the Alentejo, Castro Verde is near good birdwatching (in particular the LPN Interpretative and Environmental Centre; p245), while the nature reserve of the Sado estuary (Reserva Natural do Estuário do Sado; p141) near Setúbal is also a big draw.

North of Lisbon, the Ilhas Berlengas are a perfect place to observe seabirds. Other good places for birdwatching include Reserva Natural do Paúl de Arzila near Coimbra; Dunas de São Jacinto (p318) near Aveiro; and the Tejo and Douro gorges, where vultures and eagles nest in the Parque Natural do Tejo Internacional (p325) and Parque Natural do Douro Internacional (p417).

Portugal's leading ornithological society is the **Sociedade Portuguêsa para o Estudo de Aves**, which runs government-funded projects to map the distribution of Portugal's breeding birds.

For birdwatching and other nature-oriented **guided excursions** in the Algarve, there are several excellent options:

Wildaway (www.wildaway.com), based in Portugal, offers day tours of the Algarve's lagoons, wetlands, salt marshes and tidal flats. Prices for a guided seven-hour day trip start at €120 for one to three people without transport, or €180 with transport. Multiday group and private tours can also be arranged.

UK-based **Naturetrek** (p513) runs an eight-day birdwatching excursion around southern Portugal starting at £1295.

SKI PORTUGAL?

Switzerland it isn't – or not even Spain! – but believe it or not, Portugal has a downhill ski run. The country's highest peak, 1993m-high Torre in **Parque Natural da Serra da Estrela** (p330), offers basic facilities including three lifts and equipment rental. Truth be told, Torre offers more curiosity value than actual skiing excitement, and the mountain landscape is so fragile that it's hard to recommend this as sustainable tourism. If you're really hard-up, and want a (slightly) less environmentally damaging alternative, you can always hit the rather surreal 'dry ski' run at **SkiParque** (p335) east of Manteigas.

Various companies in the Algarve and around the Sado estuary offer **dolphin-spotting** trips, including Mar Ilimitado (p197), Dolphins Driven (p176), and Algarve Dolphins (p189).

Formosamar (www.formosamar.com) The local environmental organisation offers three-hour tours for €140 per tour (one to four people) in Parque Natural da Ria Formosa, employing marine biologists and raptor specialists as guides.

Windsurfing & Kitesurfing

Praia do Guincho, west of Sintra, and Portimão in the Algarve are both world-championship windsurfing sites. Other prime spots include (from north to south) Viana do Castelo's Praia do Cabedelo (p435); Lagoa de Óbidos, a pretty lagoon that draws both sailors and windsurfers; and (closer to Lisbon) the Costa da Caparica's Fonte da Telha. In the Algarve, Sagres (p195) attracts pros (its strong winds and fairly flat seas are ideal for free-riding), while Lagos (p187), Albufeira (p176) and Praia da Rocha (p185) cater to all.

Popular venues for windsurfing and kitesurfing lessons include the beaches around Viana do Castelo (p435), Foz do Arelho (p270), Peniche (p264), Praia do Guincho (p131), Lagos (p187) and Tavira (p163).

Classic Portuguese fare: bread and port (p374)

Plan Your Trip
Eat & Drink Like a Local

Settling down to a meal with friends is one of life's great pleasures for the Portuguese, who take pride in simple but flavourful dishes honed to perfection over the centuries. Seafood, roast meats, freshly baked bread and velvety wines are key staples in the everyday feast that is eating in Portugal.

The Year in Food

Spring

In late spring and early summer, you'll see signs advertising *caracois* (snails). These little delicacies are cooked in olive oil, garlic and herbs and are quite tasty. They go nicely with a cold beer.

Summer

Head to the market for bountiful fruits and vegetables: plump tomatoes, juicy peaches, *nísperos* (loquats), strawberries and other delights. Sardines, much loved along the coast (especially in Lisbon), are available from May through October, and generally bigger and juicier in July and August.

Autumn

In September the Douro valley begins its annual grape harvest; it's a festive time to visit, and some wineries allow visitors to take part.

Winter

During cold days Portuguese hunker down over hearty dishes such as *cozido à portuguesa*, a dish of mixed roast meats, potatoes, cabbage and carrots. Rich soups such as *canja* (chicken soup) and *sopa de peixe* (fish soup) are also popular. In the Minho, January to March is the season for tender grilled eels.

Food Experiences

Meals of a Lifetime

➡ **Vila Joya** Delightful two-Michelin-star restaurant by the sea. (p175)

➡ **100 Maneiras** Brilliantly creative, multi-course extravaganza in Lisbon. (p100)

➡ **Botequim da Mouraria** Fantastic traditional Alentejan cooking in a tiny, unpretentious tavern in Évora. (p217)

➡ **Tasca do Celso** Wonderful cuisine and charming rustic ambience on the Alentejo coast in Vila Nova de Milfontes. (p255)

➡ **Sítio do Rio** Excellent grilled fish in the laid-back coastal enclave of Carrapateira. (p200)

➡ **DOC** Delectable fare and an unmatched wine list at an indoor-outdoor restaurant right on the Douro. (p394)

➡ **Esplanada Furnas** Seafood feasts served on a cliff overlooking the waves in Ericeira. (p262)

➡ **Pedra de Sal** A cosy dining room that serves phenomenal Iberian pork dishes. (p312)

➡ **O Albertino** The superb traditional fare is well worth the drive to this spot tucked away in the mountainous northern reaches of Portugal. (p334)

➡ **Belcanto** Prepare for a dazzling meal at this celebrated restaurant of José Avillez in Lisbon. (p98)

➡ **Adraga** Excellent fresh fish served just steps from the ocean in a famous, but unfussy spot west of Sintra. (p129)

Cheap Treats

➡ **Pastel de nata** Custard tart, ideally served warm and dusted with cinnamon.

➡ **Travesseira** A rolled puff pastry filled with almond-and-egg-yolk custard. Find them in Sintra.

➡ **Tinned fish** Sardines, mackerel and tuna served with bread, olives and other accompaniments are the latest snack craze in Lisbon. Try Sol e Pesca (p102).

➡ **Francesinha** Porto's favourite hangover snack is a thick open-faced sandwich covered in melted cheese.

➡ **Marzipan** In the Algarve, this very sweet almond-infused confection is a local favourite.

➡ **Grilled chicken** Rotisserie chicken is an art form in Portugal. Spice it up with piri-piri (hot sauce).

➡ **Bifana** A bread roll served with a slice of fried pork inside. They're best in the Alentejo.

Dare to Try

➡ **Tripe** People from Porto aren't called *tripeiros* (tripe-eaters) for nothing. Try the surprisingly tasty *tripas à modo do Porto,* made of tripe, beans and sausage.

➡ **Arroz de cabidelo** Rice soaked in chicken's blood may sound foul, but it's a bloody good delicacy. The pork variant is called *arroz de sarrabulho.*

➡ **Morcela** Blood sausage made with pig's blood and perhaps rice and pork.

TOP MARKETS

Every sizable town has a local produce market where you can assemble a feast of a picnic (breads, cheeses, olives, fruits, vegetables, smoked meats and more) for very little cash. Here are a few of our favourites:

➡ **Mercado da Ribeira** (p117), Lisbon

➡ **Mercado do Livramento** (p143), Setúbal

➡ **Mercado** (p161), Olhã

➡ **Mercado Municipal** (p217), Évora

➡ **Mercado Municipal Dom Pedro V** (p306), Coimbra

➡ **Mercado Municipal** (p425), Braga

➡ **Mercado do Bolhão**, Porto

➡ **Caracois** Smaller and less fancy than escargots, these are snails, plain and simple.

➡ **Torresmos** Slices of pig skin and fat served up deep-fried. Makes a great bar snack.

Food & Wine Festivals

➡ **Rota de Sabores Tradicionais** Running from January to May, this culinary fair in Évora features traditional specialities served at select restaurants throughout the town. (p215)

➡ **Festival Internacional do Chocolate** Chocolate lovers descend on the pretty medieval town of Óbidos in March. (p268)

➡ **Festa de Santo António** Lisbon's lively street party is a great opportunity to feast on chargrilled sardines and roast suckling pig. (p87)

➡ **Feira do Alvarinho** In July, Monção in the Minho pays its respects to its most famous produce, the refreshing Alvarinho white wine. (p443)

➡ **Festival do Marisco** A sinful seafood festival held in August in the Algarve. (p87)

➡ **Cozinha dos Ganhões** The lively culinary festival held in Estremoz runs from late November to early December. (p225)

Local Specialities

Bread remains integral to every meal, and it even turns up in some main courses. Be

Market fruit

on the lookout for *açorda* (bread stew, often served with shellfish), *migas* (bread pieces prepared as a side dish) and *ensopados* (stews with toasted or deep-fried bread).

Seafood stews are superb here, particularly *caldeirada*, which is a mix of fish and shellfish in a rich broth, not unlike a bouillabaisse. *Bacalhau* (salted cod) is bound up in myth, history and tradition, and is excellent in baked dishes.

Lisbon

Simplicity, pristine ingredients and creativity mark Lisbon's gourmet scene. Chefs such as Henrique Sá Pessoa (Alma; p103), José Cordeiro (Feitoria; p106), José Avillez (Belcanto; p98) and Ljubomir Stanisic (100 Maneiras; p100), among others, have put the Portuguese capital on the gastro map with ingredient-focused tasting menus that often put a spin on comfort foods such as slow-cooked suckling pig and *bacalhau*.

The Algarve

This is a bivalve zone, with hordes of fresh clams, oysters, mussels, cockles and

Chouriço (spicy sausage) for sale at a market stall, Sintra (p121)

whelks. Don't go past the seafood *cataplana* (a Portuguese version of the Spanish paella) and *xerém* (corn mash made with cockles).

Alentejo

Warning to vegetarians: pork will confront you at every repast. Bread also figures heavily; you'll find it in gazpacho or *açorda*. During hunting season, *perdiz* (partridge), *lebre* (hare) and *javali* (wild boar) are the go. The Alentejo also has surf-and-turf blends such as *carne de porco à alentejana* (braised pork with baby clams).

Estremadura & Ribatejo

Seafood dominates the culinary palate in Estremadura; *caldeiradas de peixe* (fish stews) rule the menus, closely followed by *escabeche* (marinated vinegar fish stew) and *sopas de mariscos* (shellfish soups). Carnivores should head to Ribatejo – this is meat and tripe country.

The Beiras

There's plenty of *bacalhau* and *ovos moles* (thickened sweet egg yolks), egg cakes and *chanfana* (goat or lamb stews), plus Atlantic seafood. Sausages are popular, as are cheeses, especially Rabaçal cheese and *Queijo Serra da Estrela* (Serra cheese).

The Minho

The Minho produces the famous *vinho verde* (green wine – 'green' because it's made from immature grapes, either red or white), *Caldo verde* (Galician kale and

---

NOTHING IS FREE

Throughout the country, waiters bring bread, olives and other goodies to your table when you sit down. This unordered appetizer is called *'couvert'* and it is never free (*couvert* can cost from €1 to upwards of €8 per person at flashier places). If you don't want it, send it away, no offence taken.

Seaside dining, Albufeira (p175)

potato soup), *broa de Milho* (golden corn loaf), thrifty *sopa seca* (dry soup) and seasonal eel-like lamprey, trout and salmon dishes.

Douro & Trás-os-Montes

The north is known for its pork dishes, *cabrito assado* (roast kid) and *posta de barrosã* (beef from a rare breed of cattle). The pork-free *alheira* (a bread and meat sausage) was invented by the Jewish people during the Inquisition. Crops of figs, cherries, almonds, chestnuts and oranges abound.

How to Eat & Drink

For an explanation of the dishes you'll find on Portuguese menus, see p521.

When to Eat

Common meal times are as follows:

➡ **Breakfast** 8am to 10am

➡ **Lunch** noon to 3pm

➡ **Dinner** 7pm to 10pm

Where to Eat

➡ **Tasca** Old-fashioned place with daily specials, fair prices and a local crowd.

➡ **Churrasqueira** Restaurant that specializes in chargrilled meats.

➡ **Marisqueira** Seafood house that serves up fish and crustaceans, often priced by the kilo.

➡ **Cervejaria** Beer hall; good for snacking and socializing.

➡ **Adega** Literally 'wine cellar', usually decorated with wine casks and a rustic, cosy ambience. Expect hearty inexpensive meals.

Regions at a Glance

Lisbon & Around

History
Food & Wine
Nightlife

History
History lurks around every corner, from roofless cathedrals that bore witness to Europe's most devastating earthquake, to the 1000-year-old castle on the hill – the scene of bloody Crusades battles. There are Roman ruins, medieval churches, 16th-century convents and more.

Food & Wine
Ever-inventive chefs showcase the bounty from field and ocean, alongside traditional restaurants serving Spanish, Italian, Indian, French and other cuisines. Cinematic views, alfresco meals and buzzing dining rooms complete the experience.

Nightlife
Nights out range from curbside drinking in Bairro Alto to live fado shows in Alfama. Put your hands in the air at club Lux, listen to up-and-coming bands at Music Box: the options are limitless.

p58

The Algarve

Beaches
Seafood
Activities

Beaches
Sun-kissed beaches come in many forms in the Algarve: scenic coves, family-friendly bays, pounding surf. Beaches along the west coast are more remote and natural. Those further east have bigger tourist infrastructures, and swell with holiday-makers in summer.

Seafood
Seafood plays a starring role in the Algarve – with superb *cataplanas* (stews) and a vast range of grilled fish. You'll find all levels of restaurants, from Michelin-starred to beachside shacks.

Activities
The Algarve offers a plethora of organised activities, especially for children, with water parks, horse riding and pirate-ship cruises. There's also bird-watching, walking, thermal baths, surfing and boat trips.

p148

The Alentejo

Medieval Villages
Food & Wine
Scenery

Medieval Villages
Medieval villages proliferate in the Alentejo. Marvão, Monsaraz, Mértola, Estremoz and Elvas all have striking castles that played a role in shaping Portugal's history.

Food & Wine
The Alentejo is known for its produce, especially *porco preto* (black pork), and its *doces conventuais* (sweets). Vineyards cover the region, with a well-established network of wineries.

Scenery
This region boasts great walks and scenic drives. Highlights include craggy mountains, rivers, gorges, and hillsides dotted with cork trees, olive groves and wildflowers. Parque Natural do Vale do Guadiana is particularly striking.

p206

Estremadura & Ribatejo

Monasteries
Seafood
Surfing

Monasteries

A cluster of Unesco World Heritage sites, Tomar, Batalha and Alcobaça are splendid religious monuments easily reached from Lisbon. With soaring arches, Manueline ornamentation and pretty courtyards, these medieval-Renaissance masterpieces are *the* reason to visit central Portugal.

Seafood

Ask a Lisboeta where to go for seafood, and they'll point you to Ericeira. This coastal village is full of restaurants where you choose the catch of the day and it is grilled on the spot.

Surfing

The waves of Baleal, Supertubos and Ribeira d'Ilhas draw throngs from around the globe, and national championships are often held here.

p258

The Beiras

Frontier Towns
Scenery
University Life

Frontier Towns

The inland Beiras are filled with castles and fortresses that once guarded the country's eastern frontier with Spain. From Folgosinho's fairytale minicastle to the elaborate star-shaped ramparts of Almeida, they tell tales of a rambunctious time in Portugal's history.

Scenery

The rocky heights of Serra da Estrela are a revelation of cool air, magnificent vistas and great walks. Portugal's highest mountains, once the domain of shepherds, now sees a stream of outdoor enthusiasts.

University Life

Portugal's oldest university town, Coimbra, wears its tradition proudly, as evidenced by its medieval architecture and the black capes still worn by students.

p295

Porto, the Douro & Trás-os-Montes

Scenery
Wine & Port
Nightlife

Scenery

Porto captivates with its pretty squares and riverside setting. Other stars include stone villages, natural parks, and 30,000-year-old rock carvings at Vila Nova de Foz Côa.

Wine & Port

Taste the world's best ports in Vila Nova de Gaia followed by a wine-tasting ramble through vineyard country in the Douro and southern Trás-os-Montes.

Nightlife

Porto's nightlife encompasses wine bars, bohemian art-music spaces and ocean-front bars (in nearby Foz do Douro). There's a lively drinking scene in Vila Nova de Gaia and great nightlife in Vila do Conde.

p352

The Minho

History
Food & Wine
Activities

History

Head to medieval Guimarães to discover Portugal's birthplace. Even more stunning is Braga, with its 1000-year-old cathedral and colourful festivals. Then there's the Celtic settlement of Citânia de Briteiros, atmospheric Viana do Castelo and cinematic citadel Valença do Minho.

Food & Wine

Braga has first-rate restaurants, while Viana do Castelo and Guimarães also have gems. Home to *vinho verde* (green wine), the Minho produces some great wines, including the refreshing Alvarinho.

Activities

There's top surfing in Minho, particularly off Praia do Cabedelo. Parque Nacional da Peneda-Gerês has great hiking.

p419

On the Road

The Minho
(p419)

**Porto,
the Douro &
Trás-os-Montes**
(p352)

The Beiras
(p295)

**Estremadura
& Ribatejo**
(p258)

**Lisbon &
Around**
(p58)

The Alentejo
(p206)

The Algarve
(p148)

Lisbon & Around

Includes ➡

Best Places to Eat

➡ 100 Maneiras (p100)
➡ Belcanto (p98)
➡ Taberna Ideal (p103)

Best Places to Stay

➡ Casa Balthazar (p92)
➡ Chiado 16 (p92)
➡ Casa Amora (p94)

Why Go?

Spread across steep hillsides that overlook the Rio Tejo, Lisbon has captivated visitors for centuries. Windswept vistas reveal the city in all its beauty: Roman and Moorish ruins, white-domed cathedrals, grand plazas lined with sun-drenched cafes. The real delight of discovery, though, is delving into the narrow cobblestone lanes.

As yellow trams clatter through tree-lined streets, *lisboêtas* stroll through lamplit old quarters, much as they've done for centuries. Gossip is exchanged over fresh bread and wine at tiny patio restaurants as fado singers perform in the background. In other parts of town, Lisbon reveals its youthful alter ego at bohemian bars and riverside clubs, late-night street parties and eye-catching boutiques selling all things classic and cutting-edge.

Just outside Lisbon, there's more – enchanting woodlands, gorgeous beaches and seaside villages, all ripe for discovery.

When to Go
Lisbon

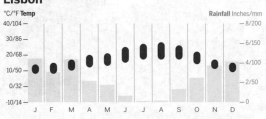

May After the winter rains, late spring is lovely, with sunny days and flowers in bloom.

Jun Early summer brings festivals, warm weather and perfect beach days.

Sep Lisbon is pure magic, with cooler days and nights and a lack of summer crowds.

Lisbon's Neighbourhoods in a Nutshell

Baixa, near the riverfront, and Rossio, just north of there, are the heart of old Lisbon, with pedestrian streets and picturesque plazas. Follow the rattling trams to the east and you'll reach Alfama, with its medina-like lanes, and tiny, fado-filled restaurants. Above the Alfama looms the ramparts of an ancient castle, with great viewpoints here and in other parts of the aptly named Castelo neighbourhood.

A steep climb west of Baixa leads into the swanky shopping and dining district of Chiado; further uphill lie the narrow streets of nightlife-haven Bairro Alto. Nearby Santa Catarina, with its tiny bars and old-fashioned funicular, has a more laid-back vibe. Further downhill towards the river is Cais do Sodré, a red-light district turned hipster centre, with late-night bars and eateries.

The World Heritage sites of Belém lie further west along the river – an easy tram ride from Baixa or Cais do Sodré.

FREE LISBOA

It's easy to enjoy Lisbon without breaking the bank as its biggest draws are outdoors: from astounding views at hilltop *miradouros* (lookouts) to tranquil squares and magical strolls in the Alfama.

Many museums have free admission on Sunday mornings. For a free cultural fix on other days, visit the design showcase of MUDE (the Museu de Design e da Moda; p63), tour underground Roman ruins at Núcleo Arqueológico (p66), and sample free wine at ViniPortugal (p83). Gawk at gorgeous churches like the Sé (p71), Igreja de São Roque (p67) and the surreal Igreja de São Domingos (p66). Also, don't miss Belém's avant-garde (and always-free) Museu Colecção Berardo (p81). Most hostels also offer free walking tours.

Panoramic Views

➡ **Largo das Portas do Sol** Stunning angles over Alfama's jumble rooftops, with the Tejo beyond.

➡ **Miradouro de Santa Luzia** (p86) A fountain, bougainvillea and blue-and-white *azulejos* (tiles) depicting the Siege of Lisbon in 1147.

➡ **Miradouro da Graça** (p109) Pine-fringed square, with cafe, that makes a great spot for sundowners.

➡ **Miradouro da Senhora do Monte** Relaxed vibe and the best views of the castle on the hill opposite.

➡ **Jardim do Torel** Little visited with a concealed indoor-outdoor cafe (go down the steps on the right) with a DJ or live music most summer weekend nights.

➡ **Miradouro de São Pedro de Alcântara** Great views, drinks and people-watching just below Bairro Alto.

DON'T MISS

Eating a *pastel de nata* (custard tart), having an afternoon swizzle of *ginjinha* (cherry brandy; p106) or sampling market fare at Mercado da Ribeira (p117).

LISBON & AROUND

Best Day Trips

➡ **Cascais** (p130) Charming seaside village.

➡ **Costa da Caparica** (p138) – Beautiful beaches, great surf.

➡ **Sintra** (p121) Enchanted woodlands dotted with palaces, mansions and gardens.

➡ **Cacilhas** (p104) Waterfront restaurants a ferry ride away.

➡ **Queluz** (p135)Portugal's answer to Versailles.

Off the Beaten Track

The neighbourhood of Madragoa with its narrow lanes and charming restaurants, is reminiscent of Alfama, but with a fraction of the tourists. It's west of Baixa; take tram 25 from Praça do Comércio to get there.

Resources

➡ www.visitlisboa.com Official tourism website.

➡ www.lisbonlux.com City guide.

➡ www.spottedbylocals.com/lisbon Insider tips.

➡ www.golisbon.com Dining, drinking and nightlife insights.

Lisbon & Around Highlights

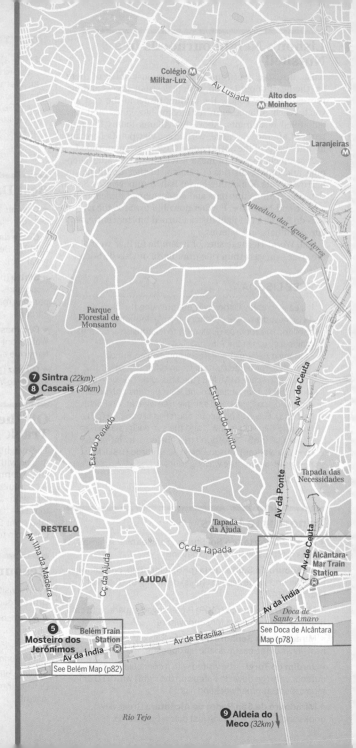

1 Get lost in the narrow village-like lanes of the **Alfama** (p92), searching for the soul of fado.

2 Bar-hop your way through the cobblestone streets of nightlife-loving **Bairro Alto** (p107).

3 Take in the pleasant outdoor cafes and restaurants of elegant **Chiado** (p97).

4 Take a rattling roller-coaster ride through the city aboard **tram 28** (p86).

5 Gaze upon the Manueline fantasy of **Mosteiro dos Jerónimos** (p79).

6 Check out the burgeoning new bar scene in **Cais do Sodré** (p110).

7 Stride through enchanted forests to above-the-clouds palaces and castles in **Sintra** (p121).

8 Spend the day taking in the village lanes and outdoor eateries of laid-back **Cascais** (p130).

9 Frolic in the waves off the beautiful beaches around **Aldeia do Meco** (p146).

LISBON

POP 580,000

History

Imperial riches, fires, plague, Europe's worst recorded earthquake, revolutions, coups and a dictatorship – Lisbon has certainly had its ups and downs.

It's said that Ulysses was here first, but the Phoenicians definitely settled here 3000 years ago, calling the city Alis Ubbo (Delightful Shore). Others soon recognised its qualities: the Greeks, the Carthaginians and then, in 205 BC, the Romans, who stayed until the 5th century AD. After some tribal chaos, the city was taken over by North African Moors in 714. They fortified the city they called Lissabona and fended off the Christians for 400 years.

But in 1147, after a four-month siege, Christian fighters (mainly British crusaders) under Dom Afonso Henriques captured the city. In 1255, Afonso III moved his capital here from Coimbra, which proved far more strategic given the city's excellent port and central position.

In the 15th and 16th centuries Lisbon boomed as the opulent centre of a vast empire after Vasco da Gama found a sea route to India. The party raged on into the 1800s, when gold was discovered in Brazil. Merchants flocked to the city, trading in gold, spices, silks and jewels. Frenzied, extravagant architecture held up a mirror to the era, as seen in Manueline works such as Belém's Mosteiro dos Jerónimos.

But at 9.40am on All Saints' Day, 1 November 1755, everything changed. Three major earthquakes hit, as residents celebrated Mass. The tremors brought an even more devastating fire and tsunami. Some estimate that as many as 90,000 of Lisbon's 270,000 inhabitants died. Much of the city was ruined, never to regain its former status. Dom João I's chief minister, the formidable Marquês de Pombal, immediately began rebuilding in a simple, cheap, earthquake-proof style that created today's formal grid.

Two bloodless coups (in 1926 and 1974) rocked the city. In 1974 and 1975 there was a massive influx of refugees from the former African colonies, changing the demographic of the city and culturally, if not financially, adding to its richness.

After Portugal joined the European Community (EC) in 1986, massive funding fuelled redevelopment, which was a welcome boost after a 1988 fire in Chiado. Streets became cleaner and investment improved facilities. Lisbon then spent years dashing in and out of the limelight as the 1994 European City of Culture, and host of Expo '98 and the 2004 European Football Championships. Major development projects throughout the city

---

LISBON IN...

Two Days

Take a ride on tram 28 (p86), hopping off to scale the ramparts of Castelo de São Jorge (p70). Sample Portugal's finest at Wine Bar do Castelo (p109), then stroll the picturesque lanes of Alfama, having a classic meal of sizzling grilled sardines at open-air Páteo 13 (p101). Glimpse the fortress-like sé (cathedral; p71) en route to shopping in pedestrianised Baixa (p114). By night, return to lantern-lit Alfama for fado at Bela (p112).

On day two breakfast on pastries in Belém, then explore the fantastical Mosteiro dos Jerónimos (p79), the riverfront Torre de Belém (p81) and the avant-garde Museu Colecção Berardo (p81). Head back for sundowners and magical views at Noobai (p107), dinner at 100 Maneiras (p100) and bar-crawling in Bairro Alto (p107). End the night at **Pensão Amor** (Map p68; Rua Nova do Carvalho 36; ⊙noon-2am Mon-Wed, to 4am Thu & Fri, 6pm-4am Sat), down in Cais do Sodré.

Four Days

Go window-shopping and cafe-hopping in well-heeled Chiado (p97), then head to futuristic Parque das Nações for riverfront gardens and the head-spinning Oceanário (p83). Dine at Belcanto (p98) or Taberna Ideal (p103), then go dancing in clubbing temple Lux (p109).

On day four catch the train to Sintra (p121) for walks through boulder-speckled woodlands to fairy-tale palaces. Back in Rossio, toast your trip with cherry liqueur at A Ginjinha (p106) and a seafood feast at Ramiro (p105).

have continued recently, from the continued expansion of the metro (which now reaches the airport) to much-needed building rehab in the Alfama.

 Sights

Baixa & Rossio

After the devastating earthquake of 1755, the Baixa was reborn as a grid – the world's first ever – as envisioned by the Marquês de Pombal. Wide commercial streets were laid, with grand plazas, fountains and a triumphal arch evoking the glory of Portuguese royalty. Today the main drag, pedestrianised Rua Augusta, buzzes with bag-toting shoppers, camera-wielding tourists and shrill-voiced buskers. For a taste of the trades that once flourished here, stroll down streets named after *sapateiros* (shoemakers), *correeiros* (saddlers), *douradores* (gilders), *fanqueiros* (cutlers) and even *bacalhoeiros* (cod-fishing vessels).

Praça do Comércio   PLAZA
(Terreiro do Paço; Map p64) With its grand 18th-century arcades, lemon-meringue facades and mosaic cobbles, the riverfront Praça do Comércio is a square to out-pomp them all. Everyone arriving by boat used to disembark here, and it still feels like the gateway to Lisbon, thronging with activity and rattling trams. At its centre rises the dashing equestrian **statue of Dom José I** (Map p64), hinting at the square's royal roots as the pre-earthquake site of Palácio da Ribeira.

In 1908 the square witnessed the fall of the monarchy, when anarchists assassinated Dom Carlos I and his son. The biggest crowd-puller is Verissimo da Costa's triumphal **Arco da Victória** (Map p64), crowned with bigwigs such as 15th-century explorer Vasco da Gama; come at dusk to see the arch glow gold. Ongoing renovations have opened pedestrian access to the Tejo once again (though watch the traffic crossing the street).

Lisbon Story Centre   MUSEUM
(Map p64; www.lisboacentre.pt; Praça do Comércio 78; adult/child €7/3; ⊙10am-7pm) This newly opened museum takes visitors on a 60-minute journey through Lisbon's history, from its early foundation (pre-Ancient Roman days) to modern times. An audioguide and multimedia exhibits describe key episodes, including New World discoveries, the

MUSEU NACIONAL DO AZULEJO

You haven't been to Lisbon until you've been on the tiles at the **Museu Nacional do Azulejo** (www.museudo azulejo.pt; Rua Madre de Deus 4; admission €5, free 10am-2pm Sun; ⊙10am-6pm Tue-Sun). Housed in a sublime 16th-century convent, the museum covers the entire *azulejo* spectrum, from early Ottoman geometry to zinging altars, scenes of lords a-hunting to Goan intricacies. Star exhibits are a 36m-long panel depicting pre-earthquake Lisbon, a Manueline cloister with weblike vaulting and exquisite blue-and-white *azulejos*, and a gold-smothered baroque chapel. Food-inspired *azulejos* – ducks, pigs and the like – adorn the restaurant opening onto a vine-clad courtyard.

terrifying 1755 earthquake (with a vivid film re-enacting the horrors) and the ambitious reconstruction that followed.

The final room shows the events that have taken place in the Praça do Comércio over the years, from early arrivals at the waterfront gates to the city, to the 1974 revolution and its less illustrious days as a parking lot in the 1980s.

Museu de Design e da Moda   MUSEUM
(Map p64; www.mude.pt; Rua Augusta 24; ⊙10am-6pm Tue-Sun) **FREE** Baixa's newest star is the Museum of Design and Fashion, a cavernous concrete-walled space – set in a former bank – that contains furniture, industrial design and couture dating from the 1930s to the present. Exhibits are arranged by decade, with signs in both English and Portuguese.

Highlights include iconic furniture by Arne Jacobsen, Charles Eames and Frank Gehry, plus haute couture by the likes of Givenchy, Christian Dior and Balenciaga. Don't miss temporary exhibitions staged downstairs in the former vaults.

Elevador de Santa Justa   ELEVATOR
(Map p68; cnr Rua de Santa Justa & Largo do Carmo; admission €5; ⊙7am-10pm) If the lanky, wrought-iron Elevador de Santa Justa seems uncannily familiar, it's probably because the neo-Gothic marvel is the handiwork of Raul Mésnier, Gustave Eiffel's apprentice. It's Lisbon's only vertical street lift. Get there early

Baixa & Rossio

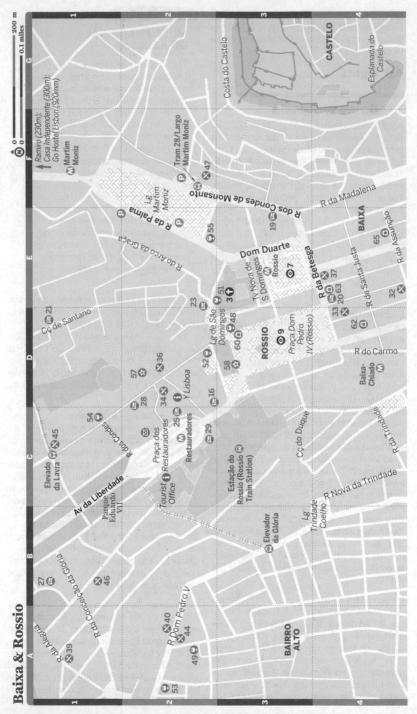

200 m
0.1 miles

Ramiro (230m);
Casa Independente (300m);
Go Hostel Lisbon (920mm)

Martim
Moniz

R da Palma

R do Arco da Graça

Cç de Santano

Cç de Santano

Elevado
da Lavra

Av da Liberdade

Parque
Eduardo
VII

R da Alegria

R da Conceição da Glória

R dos Condes

Praça dos
Restauradores

Tourist
Office

Restauradores

Estação do
Rossio (Rossio
Train Station)

Elevador
da Glória

R Dom Pedro V

BAIRRO
ALTO

Lg
Trindade
Coelho

Cç do Duque

R Nova da Trindade

R da Trindade

Baixa-
Chiado

R do Carmo

ROSSIO

Praça Dom
Pedro
IV (Rossio)

Lg de São
Domingos

Tv Nova de
S Domingos

Rossio

Dom Duarte

R da Betesga

BAIXA

R da Madalena

R da Assunção

R de Santa Justa

Tram 28/Largo
Martim Moniz

Lg
Martim
Moniz

R dos Condes de Monsanto

Costa do Castelo

CASTELO

Esplanada do
Castelo

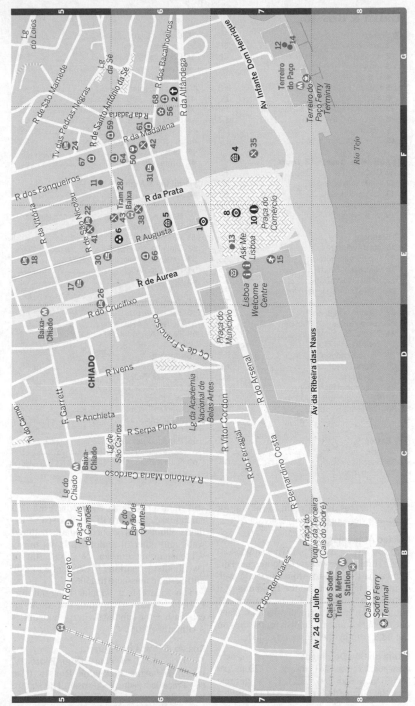

Baixa & Rossio

to beat the crowds and zoom to the top for sweeping views over the city's skyline.

Núcleo Arqueológico
RUINS
(Map p64; Rua Augusta 96; ⊙10am-5pm Mon-Sat) **FREE** Hidden under Banco Comercial Portuguesa is the Núcleo Arqueológico, a web of tunnels believed to be the remnants of a Roman spa dating from the 1st century AD. You can descend into the depths on a fascinating guided tour in English (departing on the hour) run by the Museu da Cidade.

Igreja de São Domingos
CHURCH
(Map p64; Largo de São Domingos; ⊙7.30am-7pm Mon-Fri, noon-6pm Sat) **FREE** It's a miracle that the enigmatic Igreja de São Domingos

still stands, having barely survived the 1755 earthquake, then fire in 1959. A sea of tea lights illuminates gashed pillars, battered walls and ethereal sculptures in its musty yet enchanting interior. Note the Star of David outside marking the spot of a bloody anti-Semitic massacre in 1506.

The square is a popular hang-out for Lisbon's African community. At dusk locals gather for sundown cherry liqueurs at A Ginjinha (p106).

Rossio & Praça da Figueira
PLAZAS
All roads lead to Praça Dom Pedro IV, which *lisboêtas* nickname **Rossio** (Map p64; Praça Dom Pedro IV; 🚇Rossio). The square has a 24-hour buzz: office workers, hash-

peddlers and sightseers drift across its wave-like cobbles, bask in the spray of fountains and gaze up to **Dom Pedro IV** (Brazil's first emperor), perched high on a marble pedestal.

Standouts feature the filigree horseshoe-shaped arches of neo-Manueline **Rossio train station**, where trains depart for Sintra; and neoclassical **Teatro Nacional de Dona Maria II**, hiding a dark past as the seat of the Portuguese Inquisition.

Rossio's sidekick is bustling Figueira (Map p64; Rossio), flanked by baline town houses and aimed at tourists for sipping a *bica* (espresso) and admiring the castle on the hillside.

◉ Chiado & Bairro Alto

Framed by the ethereal arches of Convento do Carmo, well-heeled Chiado harbours old-world cafes with literary credentials, swish boutiques, grand theatres and elegant 18th-century town houses. Designer divas seeking Portuguese couture, art buffs hunting Rodin originals and those content to people-watch from a cafe terrace flock here.

Sidling up to Chiado is the party-loving Bairro Alto, whose web of graffiti-slashed streets is sleepy by day. The district comes alive at twilight when hippy chicks hunt for vintage glitz in its retro boutiques and revellers hit its wall-to-wall bars and bistros. Beyond Bairro Alto you'll find the leafy squares, shops and cafes around Príncipe Real.

Convento do Carmo
& Museu Arqueológico   MUSEUM
(Map p68; Largo do Carmo; adult/child €3.50/free; ◉10am-7pm Mon-Sat) Soaring high above Lisbon, the skeletal Convento do Carmo was all but devoured by the 1755 earthquake and it's precisely that which makes it so captivating. Its shattered pillars and wishbone-like arches are completely exposed to the elements. The Museu Arqueológico shelters archaeological treasures from Lisbon and beyond, such as 4th-century sarcophagi, griffin-covered column fragments from the 10th-century, 18th-century *azulejo* (hand-painted tile) panels, a curious belt buckle from Visigothic times and two gruesome 16th-century Peruvian mummies.

Museu do Chiado   MUSEUM
(Map p68; ☏ 213 432 148; www.museuartecontemporanea.pt; Rua Serpa Pinto 4; adult/child €4/free,

admission free 10am-2pm Sun; ◉10am-6pm Tue-Sun) Contemporary art fans flock to Museu do Chiado, housed in the strikingly converted Convento de São Francisco. Temporary exhibitions lean towards interactive multimedia installations, while the gallery's permanent collection of 19th- and 20th-century works features pieces by Rodin, Jorge Vieira and José de Almada Negreiros. Revive over calm in the sculpture garden.

Miradouro de Santa Catarina   VIEWPOINT
(Rua de Santa Catarina; ◉24hr; El-da Bica) FREE Students bashing out drums, pot-smoking hippies, shrieking parents and loved-up couples meet at this precipitous spot. Santa Catarina stretching down to Avenida 24 de Abril and Cais do Sodré.

If you're coming from Cais do Sodré, it's fun to take the arthritic, 19th-century **Elevador da Bica** (Rua de São Paulo; €1.35; ◉7am-9pm Mon-Sat, 9am-9pm Sun; Cais do Sodré) funicular up chasm-like Rua da Bica de Duarte Belo to reach the lookout. At research time, the viewpoint was closed and under renovation. Next door, however, you can enjoy the same vista over drinks at laid-back Noobai Café (p107).

Igreja & Museu São Roque   CHURCH, MUSEUM
(Map p68; Largo Trindade Coelho; church free, museum €2.50, free 10am-2pm Sun ; ◉10am-6pm Tue, Wed & Fri-Sun, 2-9pm Thu) The plain facade of 16th-century Jesuit Igreja de São Roque belies its dazzling interior of gold, marble and Florentine *azulejos* – bankrolled by Brazilian riches. Its star attraction is **Capela de São João Baptista**, to the left of the altar, a lavish confection of amethyst, alabaster, lapis lazuli and Carrara marble. The museum adjoining the church is packed with elaborate sacred art and holy relics; the bamboo-lined courtyard restaurant is a treat.

Miradouro de São
Pedro de Alcântara   VIEWPOINT
(Map p68; Rua São Pedro de Alcântara; ◉viewpoint 24hr, cafe 10am-midnight Mon-Wed, to 2am Thu-Sun; Restauradores) Hitch a ride on vintage **Elevador da Glória** from Praça dos Restauradores, or huff your way up steep Calçada da Glória to this terrific hilltop viewpoint. Fountains and Greek busts add a regal air to the surroundings, and the open-air cafe doles out wine, beer and snacks, which you can enjoy while taking in the castle views.

Chiado & Bairro Alto

200 m
0.1 miles

BAIRRO ALTO

SANTA CATARINA

CHIADO

Estação do Rossio (Rossio Train Station)

Praça da Figueira

Praça Dom Pedro IV (Rossio)

R 1 de Dezembro

Cç do Duque

R do Duque

R da Condessa

R da Oliveira

Lg do Trindade Coelho

Largo da Trindade

R Nova da Trindade

R da Misericórdia

R das Gáveas

R do Norte

Tv da Espera

R das Salgadeiras

Praça Luís de Camões

R do Loreto

R Luz Soriano

Tv das Mercês

Tv dos Fiéis de Deus

Tv da Boa Hora

Tv da Água da Flor

Tv da Cara

Tv de S Pedro

R do Teixeira

R dos Mouros

R da Atalaia

R da Rosa

R S Boaventura

Cç do Tijolo

R dos Inglesinhos

R do Século

Cç do Combro

R S Pedro de Alcântara

R das Taipas

R de Santa Justa

R de Áurea

R do Carmo

Baixa-Chiado

Baixa-Chiado

Lg do Carmo

R Garrett

Livraria Bertrand

R Serpa Pinto

Lg Rafael Bordalo Pinheiro

Tv do Carmo

Baixa-Chiado

Lg do Chiado

Lg da Trindade

R da 23

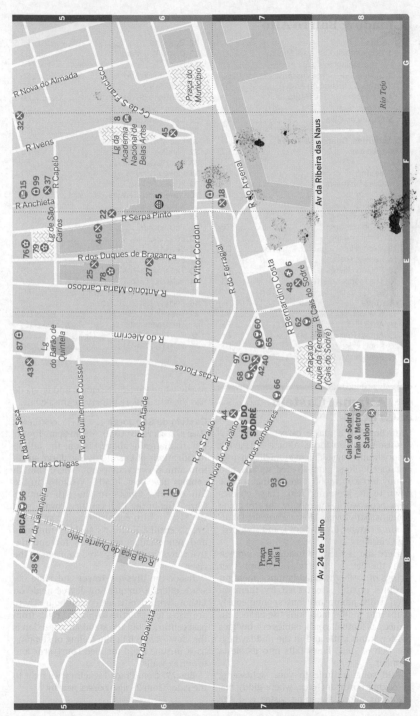

⊙ Alfama, Castelo & Graça

Unfurling like a magic carpet at the foot of Castelo de São Jorge, Alfama is Lisbon's Moorish time capsule: a medina-like district of tangled alleys, palm-shaded squares and skinny, terracotta-roofed houses that tumble down to the glittering Tejo. These cobbles have been worn smooth by theatre-going Romans, bath-loving Moors who called it *al-hamma* (Arabic for 'springs'), and stamped-ing Crusaders.

Here life is literally inside out: women dish the latest *mexericos* (gossip) over strings of freshly washed laundry, men gut sardines on the street then fry them on open grills, plump matrons spontaneously erupt into wailful fado, kids use chapel entrances as football goals, babies cry, budgies twitter, trams rattle and in the midday heat the web of steep lanes falls into its siesta slumber.

Add some altitude to your sightseeing by edging north to Graça, where giddy *miradouros* afford sweeping vistas and the pearly-white Panteão Nacional and Igreja de São Vicente de Fora punctuate the skyline.

Castelo de São Jorge   CASTLE RUINS
(Map p72; admission €7.50; ⊙9am-9pm) Towering dramatically above Lisbon, the hilltop fortifications of Castelo de São Jorge sneak into almost every snapshot. These smooth cobbles have seen it all – Visigoths in the 5th century, Moors in the 9th century, Christians in the 12th century, royals from the 14th to 16th centuries, and convicts in every century. Roam its snaking ramparts and pine-shaded courtyards for superlative views over the city's red rooftops to the river.

Inside the **Ulysses Tower**, a camera obscura offers a unique 360-degree angle on Lisbon, with demos every half-hour. There are also a few galleries displaying relics from past centuries, but the standout attraction is the view – as well as the feeling of stepping back in time amid fortified courtyards and towering walls.

Bus 737 from Praça Figueira goes right to the gate. Tram 28 also passes nearby.

Sé   CATHEDRAL
(Map p72; 📞218 866 752; ⏱9am-7pm Tue-Sat, 9am-5pm Mon & Sun) FREE One of Lisbon's icons is the fortress-like *sé*, built in 1150 on the site of a mosque soon after Christians recaptured the city from the Moors. It was sensitively restored in the 1930s. Despite the masses outside, the rib-vaulted interior, lit by a rose window, is calm. Stroll around the cathedral to spy leering gargoyles peeking above the orange trees.

History buffs shouldn't miss the less-visited **Gothic cloister** (Map p72; admission €2.50; ⏱10am-5pm Mon, 10am-6.30pm Tue-Sat), which opens onto a deep pit full of archaeological excavations going back more than 2000 years. You have to squint hard to imagine it, but you'll see remnants of a Roman street and shopfronts, an Islamic-era house and dump, as well as a medieval cistern. The **treasury** (Map p72; admission €2.50; ⏱10am-5pm Mon-Sat) showcases religious artwork.

Igreja de São Vicente de Fora   CHURCH
(Map p72; 📞218 824 400; Largo de São Vicente; admission €5; ⏱10am-6pm Tue-Sun) Graça's serene, gorgeous Igreja de São Vicente de Fora was founded as a monastery in 1147, revamped by the Italian architect Felipe Terzi in the late 16th century, and devastated in the 1755 earthquake when its dome collapsed on worshippers. Elaborate

---

GET LOST IN ALFAMA

There's no place like the labyrinthine Alfama for ditching the map to get lost in sun-dappled alleys and squares full of beauty and banter. Its narrow *becos* (cul de sacs) and *travessas* (alleys) lead you on a spectacular wild goose chase past chalk-white chapels and tiny grocery stores, patios shaded by orange trees, and João's freshly washed underpants. The earthy, working-class residents, *alfacinhas*, fill the lanes with neighbourly chatter, wafts of fried fish and the mournful ballads of fado. Experiencing Alfama is more about luxuriating in the everyday than ticking off the big sights. Take a serendipitous wander through lanes fanning out from Rua de São Miguel, Rua de São João da Praça and Rua dos Remédios.

Alfama, Castelo & Graça

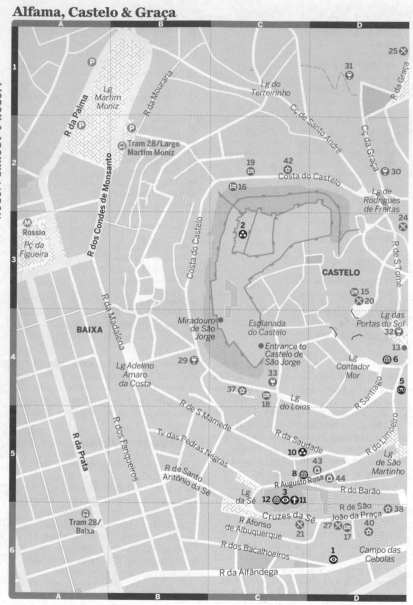

blue-and-white *azulejos* dance across almost every wall, echoing the curves of the architecture, across the white cloisters and up to the 1st floor. Here you'll find a one-off collection of panels depicting La Fontaine's moral tales of sly foxes and greedy wolves. Under the marble sacristy lie the crusaders' tombs. Seek out the weeping, cloaked woman holding stony vigil in the eerie mausoleum. Have your camera handy to snap some of the superb views from the tower.

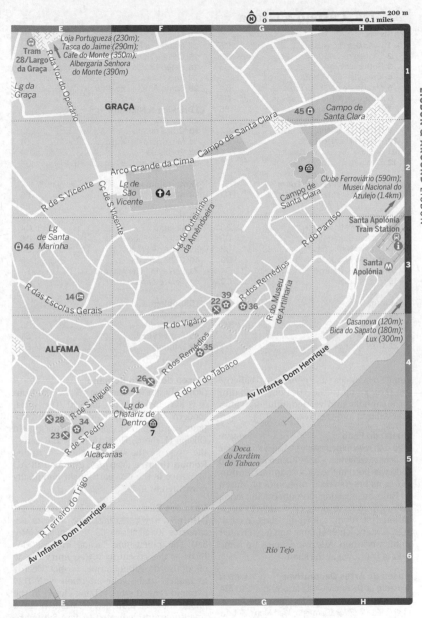

Panteão Nacional MUSEUM
(Map p72; ☎ 218 854 820; Campo de Santa Clara; adult/child €3/free, free 10am-2pm Sun; ☉ 10am-5pm Tue-Sun) Perched high and mighty above Graça's Campo de Santa Clara, the porcelain-white Panteão Nacional is a baroque beauty. Originally intended as a church, it now pays homage to Portugal's heroes and heroines, including 15th-century explorer Vasco da Gama and *fadista* Amália Rodrigues. Lavishly adorned with pink marble and gold swirls, its echoing

Alfama, Castelo & Graça

dome resembles an enormous Fabergé egg. Trudge up to the 4th-floor viewpoint for a sunbake and vertigo-inducing views over Alfama and the river.

Museu do Fado   MUSEUM
(Map p72; www.museudofado.pt; Largo do Chafariz de Dentro; admission €5; ⊙10am-6pm Tue-Sun) Fado was born in the Alfama. Immerse yourself in its bittersweet symphonies at Museu do Fado, an engaging museum tracing fado's history from its working-class roots to international stardom, taking in discs, recordings, posters, a hall of fame and a re-created guitar workshop. Afterwards, pick up some fado of your own at the shop.

Museu de Artes Decorativas   MUSEUM
(Museum of Decorative Arts; Map p72; ☑218 814 600; www.fress.pt; Largo das Portas do Sol 2; adult/child €4/2; ⊙10am-5pm Wed-Mon) Set in a petite 17th-century palace, the Museu de Artes Decorativas creaks under the weight of treasures including blingy French silverware, priceless Qing vases and Indo-Chinese furniture. It's worth a visit alone to admire the lavish apartments, embellished with baroque *azulejos,* frescos and chandeliers.

Museu do Teatro Romano   MUSEUM
(Roman Theatre Museum; Map p72; Pátio do Aljube 5; ⊙10am-1pm & 2-6pm Tue-Sun) The ultramodern Museu do Teatro Romano catapults you back to Emperor Augustus' rule in Olisipo (Lisbon). Head upstairs and across the street for the star attraction – a ruined **Roman theatre** (Map p72), extended in AD 57, buried in the 1755 earthquake and finally unearthed in 1964.

Casa dos Bicos   HISTORIC SITE
(Map p72; www.josesaramago.org; Rua dos Bacalhoeiros 10; admission €3; ⊙10am-6pm Mon-Sat) The pincushion facade of Casa dos Bicos – the eccentric 16th-century abode of Afonso de Albuquerque, former viceroy to India – grabs your attention with 1125 pyramid-shaped stones. Long closed to the public, the Casa reopened in 2012 to house a small museum dedicated to José Saramago (1922–2010), Portugal's most famous writer.

Known for his discursive, cynical and darkly humorous novels, Saramago gained worldwide attention after winning the Nobel Prize in 1998. His best works mine the depth of the human experience and are often set in a uniquely Portuguese landscape. Stop in the bookstore to pick up one of his works, and don't miss the olive tree planted out front, taken from his birthplace of Azinhaga. Below the tree are the ashes of the great writer.

◉ Príncipe Real, Santos & Estrela

West of Bairro Alto, these serene and affluent tree-fringed neighbourhoods slope down to the Rio Tejo, and are dotted with boutique hotels, art galleries, vine-clad courtyards and antique shops. This offbeat corner of Lisbon harbours a handful of must-sees including a neoclassical basilica, exotic gardens, a cavernous ancient art museum, plus the neoclassical Palácio da Assembleia da República, home to Portugal's parliament.

Casa Museu de
Amália Rodrigues   MUSEUM
(Map p76; ☑ 213 971 896; www.amaliarodrigues.pt; Rua de São Bento 193; admission €5; ☺ 10am-1pm & 2-6pm Tue-Sun) A pilgrimage site for fado fans, Casa Museu de Amália Rodrigues is where the Rainha do Fado (Queen of Fado) Amália Rodrigues lived; note graffiti along the street announcing it as Rua Amália. Born in Lisbon in 1920, the diva popularised the genre with her heartbreaking trills and poetic soul. Short tours take in portraits, glittering costumes and crackly recordings of her performances.

Museu da Marioneta   MUSEUM
(Puppet Museum; Map p76; ☑ 213 942 810; www.museudamarioneta.pt; Rua da Esperança 146; adult/child €5/3; ☺ 10am-1pm & 2-6pm Tue-Sun) Discover your inner child at the enchanting Museu da Marioneta, a veritable Geppetto's workshop housed in the 17th-century Convento das Bernardas. Superstars such as impish Punch and his Russian equivalent Petruschka are displayed alongside rarities: Vietnamese water puppets, Sicilian opera marionettes and intricate Burmese shadow puppets. Tots can try their hand at puppetry. The museum also hosts periodic performances and puppet-making workshops. There's also a superb restaurant, **A Travessa** (Map p76; ☑ 213 902 034; Travessa do Convento das Bernardas 12; ☺ 12.30-3.30pm & 8pm-midnight Mon-Fri, dinner only Sat; ☐ 706, ☐ 25), in the convent.

Basílica da Estrela   CHURCH
(Map p76; ☑ 213 960 915; Praça da Estrela; basilica free, nativity scene €1.50, roof €4; ☺ 9.30am-noon & 2-7pm) The curvaceous, sugar-white dome and twin belfries of Basílica da Estrela are visible from afar. The echoing interior is awash with pink-and-black marble, which creates a kaleidoscopic effect when you gaze up into the cupola. The neoclassical beauty was completed in 1790 by order of Dona Maria I (whose tomb is here) in gratitude for a male heir.

Do not miss the incredibly elaborate 500-piece Nativity Scene made of cork and terra cotta by celebrated 18th-century sculptor Joaquim Machado de Castro; it's in a room just beyond the tomb. Climb the dome for far-reaching views over Lisbon.

Jardim da Estrela   GARDENS
(Map p76; Largo da Estrela; ☺ gardens 7am-midnight, cafe 10am-11pm) **FREE** Seeking green respite? Opposite the Basílica da Estrela, this garden is perfect for a stroll, with paths weaving past pine, monkey puzzle and palm trees, rose and cacti beds and the centrepiece – a giant banyan tree. Kids love the duck ponds and animal-themed playground. There are several open-air cafes where you can recharge.

Jardim Botânico   GARDENS
(Botanical Garden; Map p76; ☑ 213 921 800; Rua da Escola Politécnica 58; admission €2; ☺ gardens 9am-8pm, butterfly house 11am-5pm Tue-Sun) Nurtured by green-fingered students, the Jardim Botânico is a quiet pocket of lushness just north of Bairro Alto. Look out for Madeiran geraniums, sequoias, purple jacarandas and, by the entrance (upper level gardens), a gigantic Moreton Bay fig tree. It's also worth a peek inside the butterfly house.

Palácio da Assembleia da
República   NOTABLE BUILDING
(Assembly of the Republic; Map p76; Rua de São Bento; ☺ closed to the public) The columned, temple-like Palácio da Assembleia da República is where Portugal's parliament, the Assembleia da República, makes its home. It was once the enormous Benedictine Mosteiro de São Bento, and is decorated with lofty Doric columns and graceful statues of temperance, prudence, fortitude and justice.

British Cemetery   CEMETERY
(Map p76; Rua de São Jorge; ☺ 9am-1pm) **FREE** Overgrown with cypress trees, the Cemitério dos Ingleses was founded in 1717. Expats at

Príncipe Real, Santos & Estrela

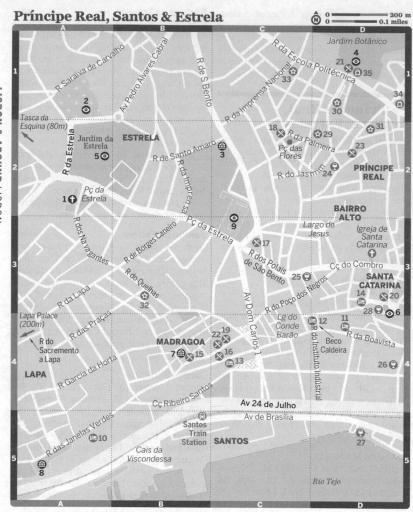

rest here include Henry Fielding (author of *Tom Jones*), who died during a fruitless visit to Lisbon in 1754 to improve his health. At the far corner are the remains of Lisbon's old Jewish cemetery.

◉ Doca de Alcântara

Near the scenic but gratingly noisy suspension bridge (and Golden Gate lookalike) Ponte 25 de Abril, the reborn Alcântara dock is sprinkled with outdoor restaurants and drinking spots. For sightseers, the number one attraction is the impressive Museu do Oriente; this spectacularly converted warehouse turns the spotlight on Portugal's links with Asia.

Getting here on westbound tram 28 or 25 is fun. You can also get here by taking the riverside bike path from Cais do Sodré.

Museu do Oriente   MUSEUM
(Map p78; ☎ 213 585 200; www.museudooriente.pt; Doca de Alcântara; adult/child €5/2, admission free 6-10pm Fri; ⊙10am-6pm Tue-Sun, 10am-10pm Fri) The beautifully designed Museu do Oriente highlights Portugal's ties with Asia, from colonial baby steps in Macau to ancestor

Príncipe Real, Santos & Estrela

worship. The cavernous museum occupies a revamped 1940s *bacalhau* (dried salt-cod) warehouse – a €30 million conversion. Strikingly displayed in pitch-black rooms, the permanent collection focuses on the Portuguese presence in Asia, and Asian gods.

Standouts on the 1st floor include rare Chinese screens and Ming porcelain, plus East Timor curiosities such as the divining conch and delicately carved umbilical-cord knives. Upstairs, cult classics include peacock-feathered effigies of Yellamma (goddess of the fallen), Vietnamese medium costumes and an eerie, faceless Nepalese exorcism doll.

◎ Rato, Marquês de Pombal & Saldanha

Up north Lisbon races headlong into the 21st century with gleaming high-rises, dizzying roundabouts, shopping malls and the Parisian-style boulevard Avenida da Liberdade, which poet Fernando Pessoa dubbed 'the finest artery in Lisbon'. The contrast to the old-world riverfront districts is startling.

Though often overlooked, these neighbourhoods reveal some gems: from René Lalique glitterbugs at Museu Calouste Gulbenkian to Hockney masterpieces at Centro de Arte Moderna, hothouses in Parque Edu-

ardo VII to the lofty arches of Aqueduto das Águas Livres.

Museu Calouste Gulbenkian MUSEUM
(Map p80; Avenida de Berna 45; admission €4; ◉10am-6pm Tue-Sun) Famous for its outstanding quality and breadth, Museu Calouste Gulbenkian showcases an epic collection of Western and Eastern art. The chronological romp kicks off with highlights such as gilded Egyptian mummy masks, Mesopotamian urns, elaborate Persian carpets and Qing porcelain (note the grinning Dogs of Fo). Going west, art buffs bewonder masterpieces by Rembrandt (*Portrait of an Old Man*), Van Dyck and Rubens (including the frantic *Loves of the Centaurs*).

Be sure to glimpse Rodin's passionate *Spring Kiss*. The grand finale is the collection of exquisite René Lalique jewellery, including the otherworldly *Dragonfly*.

Casa Museu Dr Anastácio Gonçalves MUSEUM
(Map p80; Av 5 de Outubro 6; admission €3, free 10am-2pm Sun; ◉2-6pm Tue, 10am-6pm Wed-Sun) This architecturally intriguing house museum (built in 1905) contains a small but fascinating collection of 19th-century paintings by Portuguese artists, as well as rare Chinese porcelain and furnishings dating as far back as the 1600s.

Doca de Alcântara

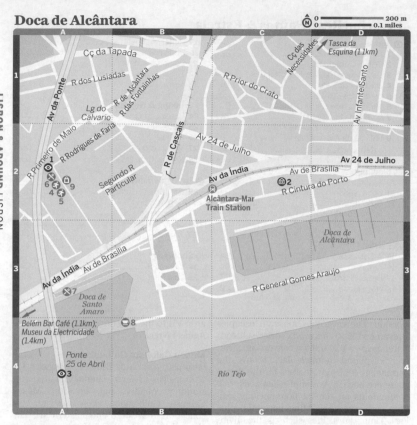

LISBON & AROUND LISBON

Doca de Alcântara

Centro de Arte Moderna MUSEUM
(Modern Art Centre; Map p80; Rua Dr Nicaulau de Bettencourt; admission €5; ⊙10am-6pm Tue-Sun) Situated in a sculpture-dotted garden alongside Museu Calouste Gulbenkian, the Centro de Arte Moderna reveals a stellar collection of 20th-century Portuguese and international art, including works by David Hockney, Anthony Gormley and José de Almada Negreiros. Feast your eyes on gems like Paula Rego's warped fairy-tale series *Contos Populares* and Sonia Delaunay's geometrically bold *Chanteur Flamenco*. There's also a well-stocked bookshop and garden cafe.

Casa-Museu Medeiros e Almeida MUSEUM
(Map p80; www.casa-museumedeirosealmeida. pt; Rua Rosa Araújo 41; adult/youth/child €5/3/ free; ⊙1-5.30pm Mon-Sat) Housed in a stunning art-nouveau mansion, this little known museum presents António Medeiros e Almeida's exquisite fine- and decorative-arts collection. Highlights include 18th-century

Flemish tapestries, Qing porcelain, Thomas Gainsborough paintings, wondrous mechanised clocks and pendulums, and a dinner service that once belonged to Napoleon Bonaparte.

Parque Eduardo VII
PARK

(Map p80; Alameda Edgar Cardoso; ⊘daylight hours) FREE An urban oasis with British roots, Parque Eduardo VII is named after his highness Edward VII, who visited Lisbon in 1903. The sloping parterre affords sweeping views over the whizzing traffic of Praça Marquês de Pombal to the river. The **estufas** (Greenhouses; Map p80; adult/child €3.10/2.30, free 9am-2pm Sun; ⊘9am-6pm) are a highlight, with lush foliage and tinkling fountains.

Look out for tree ferns and camellias in the *estufa fría* (cool greenhouse) and coffee and mango trees in the *estufa quente* (hot greenhouse).

Mãe d'Água
HISTORIC BUILDING

(Mother of Water; Map p80; 🖫218 100 215; Praça das Amoreiras; admission €2; ⊘10am-5.30pm Tue-Sat) The king laid the aqueduct's final stone at Mãe d'Água, the city's massive 5500-cu-metre main reservoir. Completed in 1834, the reservoir's cool, echoing chamber is a fine place to admire the 19th-century technology. Climb the stairs for an excellent view of the aqueduct and the surrounding neighbourhood.

Campo Pequeno Bullring
STADIUM

(Avenida da República) This red-brick, neo-Moorish building hosts big concerts and other events, including bullfighting. Below the stadium is a shopping centre, cinema and food court – and it's a popular destination all year long.

In the Portuguese version of bullfighting the animal is not killed publicly, though throughout the event theatrically dressed horsemen plant spears in the bull's neck. During the final phase (or *pega*) eight *forcados,* dressed in breeches and short jackets, face the weakened bull barehanded. The leader swaggers towards the bull, provoking it to charge. Bearing the brunt of the attack, he throws himself onto the animal's head and grabs the horns while his mates rush in to grab the beast, often being tossed in all directions. Their success wraps up the contest and the cows are sent in to the arena to lure the bull out.

Though Portuguese bullfighting rules prohibit a public kill, the animals are killed after the show by a professional butcher – you just don't witness the final blow.

◉ Belém

As well as Unesco World Heritage–listed Manueline stunners such as Mosteiro dos Jerónimos and the whimsical Torre de Belém, this district 6km west of the centre offers a tranquil botanical garden, fairy-tale golden coaches, Lisbon's tastiest *pastéis de nata* (custard tarts) and a whole booty of other treasures.

The best way to reach Belém is on the zippy tram 15 from Praça da Figueira or Praça do Comércio.

★ Mosteiro dos Jerónimos
MONASTERY

(Map p82; www.mosteirojeronimos.pt; Praça do Império; admission €7; ⊘10am-6.30pm Tue-Sun) Belém's undisputed heart-stealer is this Unesco-listed monastery. The *mosteiro* is the stuff of pure fantasy; a fusion of Diogo de Boitaca's creative vision and the spice and pepper dosh of Manuel I, who commissioned it to trumpet Vasco da Gama's discovery of a sea route to India in 1498.

Wrought for the glory of God, Jerónimos was once populated by monks of the Order of St Jerome, whose spiritual job for four centuries was to comfort sailors and pray for the king's soul. When the order was dissolved in 1833, the monastery was used as a school and orphanage until about 1940.

Entering the church through the western portal, you'll notice tree-trunk-like columns that seem to grow into the ceiling, which is itself a spiderweb of stone. Windows cast a soft golden light over the church. Superstar Vasco da Gama is interred in the lower chancel, just left of the entrance, opposite venerated 16th-century poet Luís Vaz de Camões. From the upper choir, there's a superb view of the church; the rows of seats are Portugal's first Renaissance woodcarvings.

There's nothing like the moment you walk into the honey-stone Manueline cloisters, dripping with organic detail in their delicately scalloped arches, twisting auger-shell turrets and columns intertwined with leaves, vines and knots. It's just wow. Keep an eye out for symbols of the age like the armillary sphere and the cross of the Military Order, plus gargoyles and fantastical beasties on the upper balustrade.

If you plan to visit both the monastery and Torre de Belém, you can save a little by

Rato, Marquês de Pombal & Saldanha

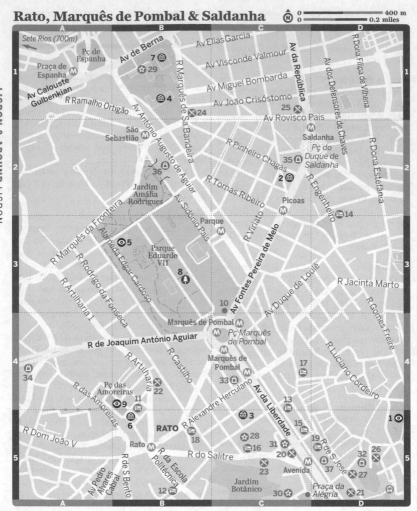

purchasing a €10 admission pass valid for both, or a €13 pass including the Palácio Nacional de Ajuda.

Palácio Nacional de Ajuda
PALACE
(☏213 637 095; www.palacioajuda.pt; Largo da Ajuda; admission varies; ☺10am-5pm Thu-Tue) Built in the early 19th century, this staggering neoclassical palace served as the royal residence from the 1860s until the end of the monarchy in 1910. You can tour through private apartments and state rooms, getting an eyeful of the crystal chandeliers, Flemish tapestries, fresco-covered ceilings, gilded furnishings and exquisite artworks dating back five centuries.

It's a long uphill walk from Belém, or you can take tram 18 or several buses from downtown, including 760 from Praça do Comércio.

Museu de Marinha
MUSEUM
(Naval Museum; Map p82; ☏213 620 019; Praça do Império; adult/child €5/2.50, free 10am-2pm Sun; ☺10am-6pm Tue-Sun) The Museu de Marinha is a nautical flashback to the Age of Discovery, with its armadas of model ships, cannonballs and shipwreck booty. Dig for

Rato, Marquês de Pombal & Saldanha

buried treasure such as Vasco da Gama's portable wooden altar, 17th-century globes (note Australia's absence) and the polished private quarters of UK-built royal yacht *Amélia*. A separate building houses ornate royal barges, 19th-century fire-fighting machines and several seaplanes.

Padrão dos Descobrimentos MUSEUM
(Discoveries Monument; Map p82; ☑ 213 031 950; Av de Brasília; adult/child €3/2; ⊙ 10am-7pm, closed Mon in low season) Like a caravel frozen in mid-swell, the monolithic Padrão dos Descobrimentos was inaugurated in 1960 on the 500th anniversary of Henry the Navigator's death. The 52m-high limestone giant is chock-full of Portuguese bigwigs. At the prow is Henry, while behind him are explorers Vasco da Gama, Diogo Cão, Fernão de Magalhães and 29 other greats. Do take the lift (or puff up 267 steps) to the windswept *miradouro* for 360-degree views over the river. The mosaic in front of the monument charts the routes of Portuguese mariners.

Torre de Belém TOWER
(www.torrebelem.pt; admission €5, free 10am-2pm Sun; ⊙ 10am-6.30pm Tue-Sun) Jutting out onto the Rio Tejo, the World Heritage–listed fortress of Torre de Belém epitomises the Age of Discoveries. Francisco de Arruda designed the pearly-grey chess piece in 1515 to defend Lisbon's harbour and nowhere else is the lure of the Atlantic more powerful. The Manueline show-off flaunts filigree stonework, meringue-like cupolas and – just below the western tower – a stone rhinoceros.

The ungulate depicts the one Manuel I sent Pope Leo X in 1515, which inspired Dürer's famous woodcut. Breathe in to climb a narrow spiral staircase to the tower, affording sublime views over Belém and the river. Crowds can be intense on weekends (especially Sunday) – a warning to claustrophobes.

Museu Colecção Berardo MUSEUM
(Map p82; www.museuberardo.pt; Praça do Império; ⊙ 10am-7pm Tue-Sun) FREE Culture fiends get their contemporary art fix for free at Museu Colecção Berardo, the star of the Centro Cultural de Belém. The ultrawhite, minimalist gallery displays billionaire José Berardo's eye-popping collection of abstract, surrealist and pop art. Temporary exhibitions are among the best in Portugal. Also in the complex is a cafe, a restaurant that faces a grassy lawn, a bookshop and a crafty museum store.

Belém

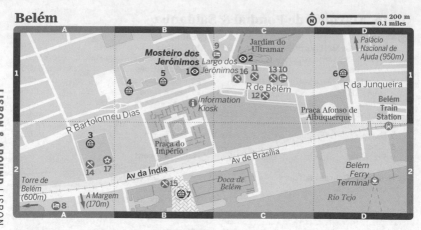

Museu Nacional de Arqueologia MUSEUM
(National Archaeology Museum; Map p82; ☎213 620 000; www.museuarqueologia.pt; Praça do Império; adult/child €5/free, free 10am-2pm Sun; ⊙10am-6pm Tue-Sun) Housed in Mosteiro dos Jerónimos' western wing, this intriguing stash contains Mesolithic flintstones, Egyptian mummies inside elaborately painted sarcophagi and beautifully wrought Bronze Age jewellery. Even more curious is

the collection of statues dedicated to Roman deities.

Museu Nacional dos Coches MUSEUM
(National Coach Museum; Map p82; ☎213 610 850; http://en.museudoscoches.pt; Praça Afonso de Albuquerque; adult/child €5/2.50, free 10am-2pm Sun; ⊙10am-6pm Tue-Sun) Cinderella wannabes feel right at home at the palatial Museu Nacional dos Coches, which dazzles with its world-class collection of 17th- to 19th-century coaches. The stuccoed, frescoed halls of the former royal riding stables display gold coaches so heavy and ornate, it's a wonder they could move at all. Stunners include Pope Clement XI's scarlet-and-gold *Coach of the Oceans*.

Jardim Botânico Tropical GARDENS
(Map p82; Calçada do Galvão; adult/child €2/free; ⊙9am-5pm Mon-Fri, 11am-5pm Sat & Sun) Far from the madding crowd, these botanical gardens bristle with hundreds of tropical species from date palms to monkey puzzle trees. Spread across 7 hectares, it's a peaceful, shady retreat on a sweltering summer's day. A highlight is the Macau garden complete with mini pagoda, where bamboo rustles and a cool stream trickles. Tots love to clamber over the gnarled roots of a banyan tree and spot the waddling ducks and geese.

Museu da Electricidade MUSEUM
(Av de Brasília; ⊙10am-6pm Tue-Sun) FREE On the riverfront, this red-brick building and former power station dates from 1900, with original machinery and interactive exhibits providing a window into its coal-burning

past. More appealing for non-science nerds are first-rate temporary exhibitions (like the World Press photo shows held here each year). There's an on-site sushi restaurant, cafe and waterfront esplanade bar.

◉ Parque das Nações

A shining model of urban regeneration, Parque das Nações has almost single-handedly propelled the city into the 21st century since Expo '98. Here you'll find an impressive aquarium, riverside gardens, public art installations, and outdoor dining options galore.

To reach the Parque das Nações, take the train or metro to Gare do Oriente and follow the signs to the waterfront. The riverside promenade is great for two-wheel adventures. To rent your own set of wheels, check out Tejo Bike (p119), located just east of the Centro Vasco da Gama. For a bird's-eye view of the park, take a ride on the **Teleférico** (Aerial Tram; www.telecabinelisboa.pt; Passeio do Tejo; adult/child one-way €4/2; ◉ 11am-1.30pm & 2.45-7pm), which glides above the river's edge.

Oceanário   AQUARIUM
(www.oceanario.pt; Doca dos Olivais; adult/child €13/9; ◉ 10am-8pm) The closest you'll get to scuba-diving without a wetsuit, Lisbon's Oceanário is mind-blowing. No amount of hyperbole does it justice, with 8000 species splashing around in 7 million litres of seawater. Huge wraparound tanks make you feel as if you are underwater, as you eyeball zebra sharks, honeycombed rays, gliding mantas and schools of neon fish.

Keep an eye out for oddities such as filigree seadragons, big ocean sunfish, otherworldly jellyfish and frolicsome sea otters. You'll also want to see the recreated rainforest, Indo-Pacific coral reef and Magellan penguins on ice. The conservation-oriented oceanarium arranges family activities from behind-the-scenes marine tours to sleeping with the sharks.

Pavilhão do Conhecimento   MUSEUM
(www.pavconhecimento.pt; Living Science Centre; adult/child €7/4; ◉ 10am-6pm Tue-Fri, 11am-7pm Sat & Sun) Kids won't grumble about science at the interactive Pavilhão do Conhecimento, where they can launch hydrogen rockets, lie unhurt on a bed of nails, experience the gravity on the moon and get dizzy on a highwire bicycle. Budding physicists have fun

whipping up tornadoes and blowing massive soap bubbles, while tots run riot in the adult-free unfinished house.

Gare do Oriente   NOTABLE BUILDING
(Oriente Station) Designed by acclaimed Spanish architect Santiago Calatrava, the space-age Gare do Oriente is an extraordinary vaulted structure, with slender columns fanning out into a concertina roof to create a kind of geometric, crystalline forest.

Jardim Garcia de Orta   GARDENS
(Garcia de Orta Garden; Rossio dos Olivais) Bristling with exotic foliage from Portugal's former colonies, the Jardim Garcia de Orta is named after a 16th-century Portuguese naturalist and pioneer in tropical medicine. Botanical rarities include Madeira's bird of paradise and serpentine dragon tree. Stroll the Brazilian garden, shaded by bougainvillea, silk-cotton, frangipani and Tabasco pepper trees. There's also a music garden where kids can bash out melodies on giant triangles and gongs.

🏃 Activities

ViniPortugal   WINE TASTING
(Map p64; www.viniportugal.pt; Praça do Comércio; ◉ 11am-7pm Tue-Sat) **FREE** A few doors down from the tourist office, this viticultural organisation offers free wine tastings four or five times a day (stop in or check the schedule posted out front). Each tasting features three different wines, which range from good to rather undrinkable – depending on what's being opened for the day.

WATER FEATURE

The 109 arches of the **Aqueduto das Águas Livres** (Aqueduct of the Free Waters) lope across the hills into Lisbon from Caneças, more than 18km away; they are most spectacular at Campolide, where the tallest arch is an incredible 65m high. Built between 1728 and 1835, by order of Dom João V, the aqueduct is a spectacular feat of engineering and brought Lisbon its first clean drinking water. Its more sinister claim to fame is as the site where 19th-century mass murderer Diogo Alves pushed his victims over the edge. One of the best places to see the aqueduct is in the leafy **Praça das Amoreiras** (Map p80), next to the Mãe d'Água.

A WONDROUS ART COLLECTION

Set in a lemon-fronted, 17th-century palace, the **Museu Nacional de Arte Antiga** (Ancient Art Museum; Map p76; www.museudearteantiga.pt; Rua das Janelas Verdes; admission €5, free 10am-2pm Sun; ⊙ 2-6pm Tue, 10am-6pm Wed-Sun) is Lapa's biggest draw. It presents a star-studded collection of European and Asian paintings and decorative arts. Keep an eye out for highlights such as Nuno Gonçalves' naturalistic *Panels of São Vicente*, Albrecht Dürer's *St Jerome*, Lucas Cranach's haunting *Salomé*, and Gustave Courbet's bleak *Snow*. Other gems include golden wonder the *Monstrance of Belém*, a souvenir from Vasco da Gama's second voyage; and 16th-century Japanese screens depicting the arrival of the *namban* (southern barbarians), namely big-nosed Portuguese explorers.

Tours

Jeep, Bus, Tram & Tuk Tuk Tours

We Hate Tourism Tours TOUR
(☑ 913 776 598; www.wehatetourismtours.com; per person from €25) One memorable way to explore the city is aboard an open-topped UMM (a Portuguese 4WD once made for the army). In addition to the King of the Hills tour, this alternative outfit organises evening meals followed by a night tour around Lisbon, plus beach trips, longer city tours and excursions to Sintra. Most trips depart from Praça Luís de Camões, near the Chiado.

Carristur TOUR
(☑ 213 582 334; www.yellowbustours.com; tram tour adult/child €18/9; ⊙ 10am-7pm Jun, 9.20am-7pm Jul-Sep, 10.20am-5.40pm Oct-May) Tram 28 covers the major sights, but if you'd prefer to join a group, Carristur runs 1½-hour tram tours of city highlights in Alfama and Baixa departing from Praça do Comércio. Other Carristur tours take in the highlights of Belém by bus (adult/child €5/2.50), while another goes from Praça da Figueira out to Parque das Nações (adult/child €15/7.50), with stops along the way. All are hop-on hop-off tours. Tours depart every 20 minutes from June to September, and every 40 minutes from October to May.

Cityrama BUS TOUR
(Map p80; ☑ 213 191 090; www.cityrama.pt; hop-on hop-off tour €12-25) This outfit runs open-topped double-decker bus tours that travel several routes in Lisbon, heading towards Castelo, Oriente, Belém or Cascais. All depart from Marquês de Pombal.

Tuk Tuk TOUR
(Map p72; ☑ 213 478 103; www.tuk-tuk-lisboa. pt; Largo das Portas do Sol ; 30-/60-minute tour €35/45; ⊙ 10am-6pm) Toodle around Lisbon in a small, open-topped, four-person tuk tuk – those quaint, three-wheel vehicles popular in South Asia. You can select from a range of circuits, the best of which head up to various lookouts, giving you dazzling views over the city without the serious legwork. Reserve ahead or show up at Largo das Portas do Sol, where they park.

River Cruises & Dinner Cruises

Transtejo CRUISE
(Map p64; ☑ 210 422 417; www.transtejo.pt; Terreiro do Paço ferry terminal; adult/child €20/10; ⊙ May-Oct) These 2½-hour river cruises are a laid-back way to enjoy Lisbon's sights with multilingual commentary.

Lisboa Vista do Tejo FERRY, CRUISE
(Map p64; ☑ 213 913 030; www.lvt.pt; Terreiro do Paço terminal; ferry ticket one-way/return €12/16; ☎) This outfit sails twice daily between Caís do Sodré and Belém, where it docks near the Torre de Belém. LVT also offers several three-hour dinner cruises (per person €80) per week; these depart from Docas de Alcântara.

Speciality Tours

GoCar Touring DRIVING TOUR
(Map p64; ☑ 210 965 030; www.gocartours.pt; Rua dos Douradores 16; per hr/day €29/99; ⊙ 9.30am-6.30pm) These self-guided tours put you behind the wheel of an open-topped, two-seater mini-car with a talking GPS that guides you along one of several pre-determined routes. Helmets included.

Walking Tours

Lisbon Walker WALKING TOUR
(Map p64; ☑ 218 861 840; www.lisbonwalker.com; Rua dos Remédios 84; 3hr walk adult/child €15/ free; ⊙ 10am & 2.30pm) This excellent company, with well-informed, English-speaking guides, offers themed walking tours through Lisbon such as 'Old Town' (the history and lore of the Alfama) and 'Legends and Mysteries'. Walking tours depart from the northwest corner of Praça do Comércio.

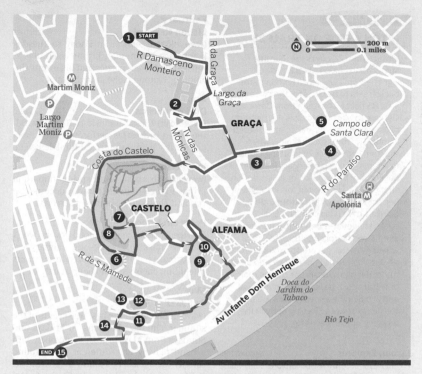

Walking Tour
Exploring the Alfama

START MIRADOURO DA SENHORA DO MONTE
FINISH PRAÇA DO COMÉRCIO
DISTANCE 3KM
DURATION TWO TO THREE HOURS

This scenic route starts on tram 28 from Largo Martim Moniz or the Baixa, taking in the city's best tram route *and* avoiding uphill slogs. Take the tram up to Largo da Graça. From here, stroll north and turn left behind the barracks for breathtaking views from Lisbon's highest lookout, **①Miradouro da Senhora do Monte**. Next, walk south and turn right to pine-shaded **②Miradouro da Graça** (p109), where central Lisbon spreads out before you. Retrace your steps and head east to admire the exquisitely tiled cloisters of **③Igreja de São Vicente de Fora** (p71), and the cool, echoing **④Panteão Nacional** (p73). If it's Tuesday or Saturday, make a detour to the buzzy **⑤Feira da Ladra** (Thieves Market; p117) to hunt for buried treasure. Otherwise, go west along Arco Grande da Cima until you

reach Largo de Rodrigues de Freitas. Take the Costa do Castelo fork, continuing west to skirt the castle battlements along narrow cobbled streets affording stunning views. Pass in front of **⑥Solar dos Mouros** (p93), then turn left up to the **⑦Castelo de São Jorge** (p70) and its **⑧viewpoint**. Next, head down the steep lanes to Largo das Portas do Sol, and another fine vista from bougainvillea-clad **⑨Miradouro de Santa Luzia**. From here wander northward, past whitewashed **⑩Igreja de Santa Luzia** and turn right into the atmospheric lane of Beco de Santa Helena, threading through labyrinthine Alfama to Largo das Alcaçarias. Take Rua de São João da Praça westwards, pausing for a bite or a drink at **⑪Cruzes Credo Cafe** (p101), before continuing on to the fortresslike **⑫sé** (p71) and **⑬Igreja de Santo António**. Continue downhill, stopping for a look at the intricate Manueline facade of **⑭Igreja da Conceição Velha**, before ending at **⑮Praça do Comércio**, Europe's largest square.

HITCH A RIDE ON TRAM 28

Vintage tram 28 offers the ultimate spin around Lisbon's blockbuster sights – from Basílica da Estrela to the backstreets of **Baixa** – for the price of a €2.85 ticket. The route from Campo Ourique to Martim Moniz is 45 minutes of astonishing views and absurdly steep climbs. The most exciting bit is when the tram commences its rattling climb to Alfama, where passengers lean perilously out of the window for an in-motion shot of the *sé* or hop out for postcard-perfect views from **Miradouro de Santa Luzia** (Map p72). The final stretch negotiates impossibly narrow streets and hairpin bends up to Graça, where most folk get out to explore Igreja de São Vicente de Fora (p71). Keep in mind that many locals use this as their only transport; be kind and offer a seat, and avoid riding at peak hours. Beat the heavy crowds by going early in the morning or in the evening.

Lisbon Explorer　　　WALKING TOUR
(☑969 219 059; www.lisbonexplorer.com; adult/child from €35/free) Top-notch English-speaking guides peel back the many layers of Lisbon's history during the three-hour walking tours offered by this highly rated outfit. Top picks include 'Around Alfama', taking in the castle, *sé* and the narrow back lanes of the neighbourhood; and 'Hidden Lisbon', delving into the Baixa, Chiado and Bairro Alto. There are also tours to Sintra and Belém, and a food- and wine-tasting tour. The fee includes admissions and public transport costs during the tour. Tours typically depart from Praça do Comércio or other central locations. You'll receive the meeting point upon booking.

✥ Festivals & Events

Lisboêtas celebrate their seasons with fervour. Rio-style carnivals and indie flicks heat up the cooler months, while summer spells high-octane concerts, sparkly pride parading and saintly celebrations of feasting and indecent proposals. *Fazer a festa* (partying) is considered a birthright in Portugal's live-wire capital. For up-to-date listings, pick up the tourist board's free magazine *Follow Me Lisboa*.

February

Lisbon Carnival　　　CULTURE
(www.visitlisboa.com) From Friday to Tuesday before Ash Wednesday, Lisbon celebrates at music-filled street parties and big events (including costume balls) at nightclubs.

April

Dias da Música　　　MUSIC
(www.ccb.pt) Classical-music buffs see world-renowned orchestras perform at this three-day festival held at Centro Cultural de Belém.

Indie Lisboa　　　FILM
(www.indielisboa.com) This spring filmathon brings 10 days of indie features, documentaries and shorts to Lisbon's big screens.

Peixe em Lisboa　　　FOOD
(www.peixemlisboa.com) Seafood lovers won't want to miss this week-long culinary extravaganza, put on by a dozen restaurants (including chefs with Michelin stars).

May

Out Jazz　　　MUSIC
(www.ncs.pt) One of the best free events of the summer, Out Jazz happens on Fridays and Sundays from May through September, with a band playing at a different park around the city each week. DJs follow the live music. Bring a picnic blanket and join the festive summer crowds.

June

Festival ao Largo　　　MUSIC
(Map p68; www.festivalaolargo.pt; Largo de São Carlos) Free outdoor performances – classical concerts, ballet and opera – from late June to late July in front of the Teatro Nacional de São Carlos.

July

BaixAnima　　　CULTURE
Baixa's summertime shindig entertains the crowds for free on weekends from July to September with circus acts and live music, improvised theatre and mime.

Delta Tejo　　　MUSIC
(www.deltatejo.com) Alto Ajuda's environmentally sustainable festival stages three days of live music under a starry sky – from reggae and fado to mellow Brazilian grooves.

August

Jazz em Agosto　　　MUSIC
(www.musica.gulbenkian.pt) Fundação Calouste Gulbenkian welcomes established and fresh talent to the stage at this soulful jazz fest.

November

Arte Lisboa ART
(www.artelisboa.fil.pt) In the spotlight: the contemporary art of 40 Portuguese and international galleries at this massive fair in Parque das Nações.

December

New Year's Eve CULTURE
Ring in the *ano novo* (new year) with fireworks, free concerts and DJs down by the river.

🛏 Sleeping

Lisbon has an array of boutique hotels, upmarket hostels and both modern and old-fashioned guesthouses. Be sure to book ahead during the high season (July to September). If you arrive without a reservation, head to a tourist office, where staff can call around for you.

A word to those with weak knees and/ or heavy bags: many guesthouses lack lifts, meaning you'll have to haul your luggage up three flights or more. If this disconcerts, be sure to book a place with an elevator.

🛏 Baixa & Rossio

Sandwiched between the Alfama and Bairro Alto, this central area is packed with options, including high-end hotels, modest and upper-end guesthouses and first-rate hostels. You can walk everywhere and there's great public transit.

Travellers House HOSTEL €
(Map p64; ☑ 210 115 922; www.travellershouse.com; Rua Augusta 89; dm/s/d €22/35/65; @ 🛜) Travellers enthuse about this super-friendly hostel set in a converted 250-year-old house on Rua Augusta. As well as cosy dorms, there's

a retro lounge with beanbags, an internet corner and a communal kitchen. Tiago and Gonçalo know what travellers like, from scrambled eggs for breakfast to evening Alfama tours and periodic happy hours.

Goodnight Hostel HOSTEL €
(Map p64; ☑ 213 430 139; www.goodnighthostel. com; Rua dos Correiros 113; dm/d €21/55; @ 🛜) Set in a converted 18th-century town house, this glam hostel rocks with its fab location, retro design and friendly staff. The high-ceilinged dorms offer vertigo-inducing views over Baixa.

Lisbon Lounge Hostel HOSTEL €
(Map p64; ☑ 213 462 061; www.lisbonlounge hostel.com; Rua de São Nicolau 41; dm/d €22/64; @ 🛜) These stylish Baixa digs have immaculate dorms and an artfully designed lounge complete with turntable and faux moose head. The fun team hosts nightly dinners, bar crawls and other events. It's a great spot to meet other travellers.

Pensão Brasil-África GUESTHOUSE €
(Map p64; ☑ 218 869 266; www.pensaobrasilafrica. com; Travessa das Pedras Negras 8; s/d €25/35; 🛜) Tucked down a quiet street, this old-school guesthouse near the *sé* offers sunny, wood-floored rooms with floral prints. Shared bathrooms are fairly clean. There's everything you need to rustle up a light breakfast in the lounge.

Pensão Imperial GUESTHOUSE €
(Map p64; ☑ 213 420 166; Praça dos Restauradores 78, Rossio; s/d from €20/30) Cheery Imperial has a terrific location, but you'll need to grin and lug it, as there's no lift. The rooms with high ceilings and wooden furniture are nothing flash, but some have flower-draped balconies overlooking the *praça*. Bathrooms

---

SAINTLY CELEBRATIONS

Come all ye faithful lovers of *vinho*-swigging, sardine-feasting, dancing and merrymaking to June's **Festas dos Santos Populares** (Festivals of the Popular Saints), three weeks of midsummer madness. There are a couple of key saintly festivities:

Festa de Santo António (Festival of St Anthony) This lively fest is celebrated with particular fervour in Alfama and Madragoa from June 12 to 13, with feasting, drinking, *bailes* (balls) and some 50 *arraiais* (street parties). St Anthony has a bit of a reputation as a matchmaker. *Lisboêtas* declare their undying love by giving *manjericos* (basil plants) with soppy poems. Around 300 hard-up couples get hitched for free!

Festa de São Pedro (Festival of St Peter) Lisbon pulls out all the stops for St Peter, the patron saint of fishermen, from June 28 to 29. There are slap-up seafood dinners and river processions in his barnacled honour.

are shared, though some rooms have a shower or sink.

Pensão Galicia GUESTHOUSE €

(Map p64; ☎213 428 430; 4th fl, Rua do Crucifixo 50; s/d with shared bathroom €25/40) Central for Baixa, this homey, no-frills guesthouse exudes tattered charm. Its 11 small rooms are decked out in chintzy pastels, rag rugs and old-style furnishings; the best have little balconies.

Residencial Restauradores GUESTHOUSE €

(Map p64; ☎213 475 660; http://residencialrestauradores.pai.pt; 4th fl, Praça dos Restauradores 13; d €35; ❄) Run by a kindhearted old soul, this guesthouse has clean, old-fashioned rooms with homey furnishings. Most rooms have showers, but the toilets are shared. The best have fine views over the plaza. French, English and Spanish spoken.

Lavra Guest House GUESTHOUSE €€

(Map p64; ☎218 820 000; www.lavra.pt; Calçada de Santano 198; d not incl breakfast €59-69; 📶) Set in a former convent that dates back two centuries, this place has stylishly set rooms with wood floors and tiny balconies. Some bathrooms are cramped. It's a short stroll from the Elevador da Lavra, or a steep climb from Largo de São Domingos.

Brown's Downtown BOUTIQUE HOTEL €€

(Map p64; ☎213 431 391; www.brownsdowntown.com; Rua dos Sapateiros 69; d €90-120) Brown's Downtown offers attractive, high-tech rooms complete with iMacs and well-anchored iPads, and an excellent location in the Baixa. On the downside, rooms can be on the smallish side, the walls are thin, and the heating/cooling and showers (which sometimes flood) could use some tweaking.

Lisbon Story Guesthouse GUESTHOUSE €€

(Map p64; ☎218 879 392; www.lisbonstoryguesthouse.com; Largo de São Domingos 18; d €100-120, shared bathrooms €60-80; @📶) Overlooking Praça São Domingos, Lisbon Story is a small, welcoming guesthouse with nicely maintained rooms, some of which sport Portuguese themes (the river-blue Tejo room, a handicraft-lined 'Culturas' room). Rooms range from cramped to spacious, and the best room has fine views and pays homage to Portugal's greatest writers. Three rooms have private bathrooms; the other eight share three bathrooms. The shoe-free lounge, with throw pillows and low tables, is a nice touch.

Residencial Alegria GUESTHOUSE €€

(Map p64; ☎213 220 670; www.alegrianet.com; Praça da Alegria 12; d €60-83; ❄) Overlooking a palm-dotted plaza, this lemon-fronted belle-époque gem is ablaze with pink geraniums in summer. Rooms are peaceful and airy with plaids and chunky wood, while corridors reveal stucco and antiques.

Hotel Lisboa Tejo HOTEL €€

(Map p64; ☎218 866 182; http://lisboatejohotel.com; Rua dos Condes de Monsanto 2; s/d from €70/80; ❄@📶) Once a broom-maker's, this 58-room hotel has wood-floored chambers with cornflower-blue hues, theatrical chairs and satellite TV. Don't miss the Roman *poço* (well) near the entrance.

Residencial Florescente GUESTHOUSE €€

(Map p64; ☎213 426 609; www.residencialflorescente.com; Rua das Portas de Santo Antão 99; s/d from €50/75; ❄@📶) The best feature of Florescente is the excellent location, just a short stroll from Rossio. Rooms are clean and simple, though the ones in the back lack natural light. It's on a pedestrian street lined with alfresco restaurants.

Pensão Royal GUESTHOUSE €€

(Map p64; ☎213 479 006; www.royal-guesthouse.com; 3rd fl, Rua do Crucifixo 50; d €55-70; ❄📶) This petite seven-room guesthouse has pleasant, colourful rooms, some of which are decorated with *azulejos*. Friendly service, big breakfasts and excellent local advice add to the value. French, Italian and English spoken.

Internacional Design Hotel BOUTIQUE HOTEL €€€

(Map p64; ☎213 240 990; http://idesignhotel.com; Rua da Betesga 3; d €130-250; ❄📶) This high-concept hotel has four types of rooms, each conjuring a radically different aesthetic. Urban rooms have brightly coloured artwork and duvets; Tribu rooms have wood details and tree silhouettes; Zen aims for simple elegance; while Pop features eye-catching art and bubblegum-coloured floors and walls. The enticing cafe-restaurant on the 1st floor has views over Rossio.

Vincci BOUTIQUE HOTEL €€€

(Map p64; ☎218 803 190; www.vinccihoteles.com; Rua do Comércio 32; r from €167; ❄📶) In a great location near the Praça do Comércio, Vincci has attractive rooms with a modern design and good lighting. Some rooms are a bit on the small side, and the narrow closets don't allow much storage. Good soundproofing ensures a quiet night's rest.

Altis Avenida
BOUTIQUE HOTEL €€€

(Map p64; ☑808 200 504; www.altishotels.com; Rua 1 Dezembro 120; d €185-215; P❋🐾) It's hard to fault the Altis Avenida. Rooms are spotless and handsomely appointed, the service is friendly, and the central location (facing Rossio train station) is excellent. Minuses: rooms aren't huge and the breakfast is fairly average. It's worth stopping in for an evening drink at the rooftop bar even if you don't stay here.

🛌 Chiado, Bairro Alto & Around

Well-heeled Chiado has high-quality top-end and budget options, but little in between. Bairro Alto is nightlife central, meaning you won't get much rest amid the late-night revelry. The hip Santa Catarina district has a few options.

Living Lounge
HOSTEL €

(Map p68; ☑213 461 078; www.livinglounge hostel.com; 2nd fl, Rua do Crucifixo 116; dm/s/d €22/37/64; @🐾) The Living Lounge has a stylish design, attractive rooms, friendly staff and excellent amenities (full kitchen, wi-fi, bicycle hire). The nightly dinners and wide range of tours provide a fine opportunity to meet other travellers.

The Independente
HOSTEL €

(Map p68; ☑213 461 381; www.theindependente.pt; Rua de São Pedro de Alcântara 81; dm €18-20, ste without/with view €110/120; 🐾) Located on the edge of the Bairro Alto, this stylish new place has 11 dorm rooms (with six to 12 beds in each) and a handful of roomier suites with balconies overlooking the Tejo. Common areas feature vintage furnishings and art-deco details, and the restaurant (p100) and bar are great places to start off the night. Light sleepers beware: noise is a major issue.

Shiado Hostel
HOSTEL €

(Map p68; ☑213 429 227; www.shiadohostel.com; 3rd fl, Rua Anchieta 5; dm/d with shared bathroom from €20/60; ❋@🐾) Beautifully located on an elegant street in the Chiado, this handsomely maintained upper-floor hostel (with lift) has bright, Zen-like rooms with polished floors and a simple but inviting colour scheme, and artwork around the common areas. It's a welcoming, peaceful place;

SELF-CATERING IN STYLE

Lisbon has great deals on modern, fully furnished apartments, particularly if you're staying for more than a few nights. Rates in central districts such as Alfama, Baixa and Chiado start at around €50 per night, with many places offering substantial discounts for stays of more than a week. There's also Airbnb, where you can rent both apartments and spare rooms from locals. Good websites to try include the following:

➡ www.travelingtolisbon.com

➡ www.lisbon-holiday-apartments.com

➡ www.airbnb.com

---

there's a yoga studio and a macrobiotic institute in the same building.

Lisbon Calling
HOSTEL €

(Map p68; ☑213 432 381; www.lisboncalling.net; 3rd fl, Rua de São Paulo 126; dm/d €20/60; @🐾) This stylish, unsigned backpacker favourite near Santa Catarina features original frescos, *azulejos* and hardwood floors – all lovingly restored by the friendly English-Portuguese owners. It's a charming pad with bright, spacious dorms, a groovy lounge with internet, and a brick-vaulted kitchen where breakfast is served.

Oasis Lisboa
HOSTEL €

(Map p76; ☑213 478 044; www.oasislisboa.com; Rua de Santa Catarina 24; dm/d €20/60; @🐾) Behind bright yellow walls, this self-described backpacker mansion offers wood-floored dorms, a sleek lounge and kitchen, and a rooftop terrace with stunning views to the river. The young team arranges activities from cocktail hours to barbecues.

Pensão Globo
GUESTHOUSE €€

(Map p68; ☑213 462 279; www.blueangelhotel. com/pensaoglobo; Rua do Teixeira 37; r from €50) Tucked down a quietish street, this guesthouse offers 16 tidy, individually decorated rooms – from scarlet ones with postage-stamp-sized courtyards to lime-green and leafy jobs; all have ultramodern bathrooms. Payment is cash only.

★Lisboa Carmo Hotel
HOTEL €€€

(Map p68; ☑213 264 710; www.lisboacarmohotel. com; Rua da Oliveira ao Carmo 1; r €120-200;

Lisbon's Architectural Highs

Lisbon is packed with stunning architectural works that span more than five centuries. You'll find wildly intricate Unesco World Heritage sites commemorating Portugal's Golden Age of Discoveries, whimsical works of wrought-iron elegance (with grand views over the old city) and cutting-edge designs of the late 20th century.

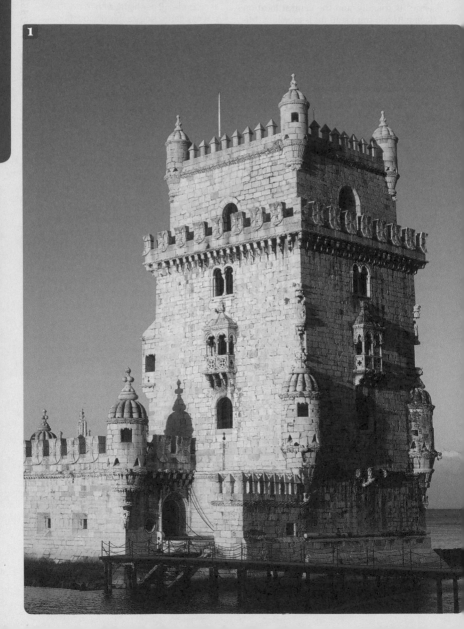

1. Torre de Belém (p81), Belém
Built in 1515, the Manueline-period architecture of Torre de Belém epitomises the Age of Discoveries era.

2. Gare do Oriente (p83), Parque das Nações
The futuristic Gare do Oriente was built by Spanish architect Santiago Calatrava for Expo '98.

3. Elevador de Santa Justa (p63), Baixa
Ride this neo-Gothic street lift for views of the city.

4. Sé (p71), Alfama
This iconic Lisbon cathedral was built on the site of a mosque in 1150.

❄️🛜) On the edge of one of Lisbon's prettiest plazas, this 48-room hotel has classically designed rooms, the best of which have sweeping Lisbon views. It earns high marks for its use of Portuguese products both in the rooms (bed linens, towels, bath products) and in the pleasant ground-floor restaurant.

★ Casa Balthazar
GUESTHOUSE €€€

(Map p68; ☎ 917 085 568; www.casabalthazar lisbon.com; Rua do Duque 26; r €160-220; P ❄️🛜🏊) Tucked down a quiet lane, Casa Balthazar has undeniable appeal with beautifully furnished rooms, friendly service and a grassy courtyard with a pool. Each of the nine rooms has been appointed with high-end fittings (iPod docks, big flat-screen TVs, luxury bedding), and pricier rooms have magnificent views (some even have private terraces).

★ Chiado 16
BOUTIQUE HOTEL €€€

(Map p68; ☎ 213 941 616; www.chiado16. com; Academia Nacional das Belas Artes 16; d/ste from €156/285; P ❄️🛜) On an elegant street in the lower Chiado, this boutique charmer has just seven rooms: three large guestrooms with river views and four suites (with full kitchens, making them ideal for families) – two of which have panoramic views. All feature unique designs with rich colour schemes and high-end furnishings. The first-rate cooked breakfast costs extra (€12.30 per person).

Hotel do Chiado
HOTEL €€€

(Map p68; ☎ 213 256 100; www.hoteldochiado.com; Rua Nova do Almada 114; s/d from €142/162; ❄️🛜) Fusing 19th-century charm with 21st-century cool, the well-located Hotel do Chiado offers carpeted, well-appointed rooms that come in three styles: classics (small and boxy, with no view), superiors (brighter and roomier with French balconies) and premiums (top-floor rooms that open onto grassy, bougainvillea-clad terraces with views to the river and castle). Open from 11am to midnight, the 7th-floor bar offers superb vistas for all.

Mercy Hotel
BOUTIQUE HOTEL €€€

(Map p68; ☎ 212 481 480; www.mercyhotel.com; Rua da Misericórdia 76; r €135-205; ❄️🛜) This luxury hotel has sleek ultra-modern rooms, though the black colour scheme (for both the rooms and bathrooms) may seem overly dramatic. The cheapest quarters (the 'cosy' rooms) are quite small. Top-floor rooms

have magnificent views. It also has friendly efficient service, a first-rate Japanese restaurant onsite and a great location a short stroll from both the Chiado and Bairro Alto.

🛏️ Alfama, Castelo & Graça

Alfama's cobbled lanes generally offer peaceful slumber, though choose wisely or else you might find yourself being serenaded to sleep by a warbling *fadista*. On its hilltop perch above Lisbon, leafy Graça has dramatic views.

This is Lisbon
HOSTEL €

(Map p72; ☎ 218 014 549; www.thisislisbonhostel. com; Rua da Costa do Castelo 63; dm/d/apt from €17/60/96; @🛜) Great views and an easy-going vibe draw a good mix of travellers to this Brazilian-run hilltop perch in Castelo. In addition to dorms, there's a private apartment with kitchen for rent next door. It's a good place to meet other travellers, with yoga on the terrace, surf classes, pub crawls, nightly dinners and occasional barbecues.

Alfama Patio Hostel
HOSTEL €

(Map p72; ☎ 218 883 127; http://alfama.destina tionhostels.com; Rua das Escolas Gerais 3; dm/d €23/60; @🛜) In the heart of the Alfama, this beautifully run hostel is a great place to meet other travellers, with loads of activities (from pub crawls through the Bairro Alto to day trips to the beach), plus regular barbecues on the hostel's laid-back garden-like patio. There's a stylish lounge and fantastic staff.

Pensão Ninho das Águias
GUESTHOUSE €

(Map p72; ☎ 218 854 070; http://ninhodasaguias. pai.pt/; Costa do Castelo 74; s/d/tr with shared bathroom €30/40/60) It isn't called 'eagle's nest' for nothing: this guesthouse has a Rapunzel-esque turret affording magical 360-degree views over Lisbon. Let your hair down in the light and breezy rooms, or on the flowery terrace. Service is grumpy.

Pensão São João da Praça
GUESTHOUSE €

(Map p72; ☎ 218 862 591; 218862591@sapo.pt; 2nd fl, Rua de São João da Praça 97; s/d with shared bathroom €30/40, d with private bathroom €45-55; 🛜) So close to the *sé* you can almost touch the gargoyles, this 19th-century guesthouse has a pick-and-mix of sunny rooms with fridges and TVs; the best have river-facing verandahs.

GREE T ESCAPES

Some of Lisbon's greenest and most peaceful *praças* (town squares) are perfect for a crowd-free stroll or picnic. A few of our favourites:

Praça da Alegria Swooping palms and banyan trees shade tranquil Praça da Alegria, which is actually more round than square. Look out for the bronze bust of 19th-century Portuguese painter and composer Alfredo Keil.

Praça do Príncipe Real A century-old cedar tree forms a giant natural parasol at the centre of this palm-dotted square, popular among grizzled card players by day and gay cruisers by night. There's a kids' playground and a relaxed cafe with alfresco seating.

Praça das Flores Centred on a fountain, this romantic, leafy square has cobbles, pastel-washed houses and enough doggie-do to make a Parisian proud.

Campo dos Mártires da Pátria (Map p80) Framed by elegant buildings, this grassy square is dotted with pine, weeping willow and jacaranda trees, with a pond for ducks and a pleasant indoor-outdoor cafe. *Lisboêtas* in search of cures light candles before the statue of Dr Sousa Martins, who was renowned for his healing work among the poor.

Albergaria Senhora do Monte HOTEL €€
(📋218 866 002; www.albergariasenhoradomonte.com; Calçada do Monte 39; s/d from €80/98; ❄️) Well off the beaten path, this friendly hotel has clean but slightly dated rooms with stunning views. It's worth shelling out extra for a verandah. There's also a restaurant and sunny terrace – both with panoramic views. Tram 28 passes nearby.

Palácio Belmonte LUXURY HOTEL €€€
(Map p72; 📋218 816 600; www.palaciobelmonte.com; Páteo Dom Fradique 14; ste from €300; ❄️🏊) Nestled beside Castelo de São Jorge, this 15th-century palace turns on the VIP treatment with its 11 suites, named after Portuguese luminaries and lavishly adorned with 18th-century *azulejos,* silks, marble and antiques. There's a pool framed by herb gardens, a wood-panelled library where classical music plays, and numerous other luxuries to justify the price tag.

Solar dos Mouros BOUTIQUE HOTEL €€€
(Map p72; 📋218 854 940; www.solardosmouros.pt; Rua do Milagre de Santo António 4; d €70-170; ❄️) Blink and you'll miss this boutique pad near the castle. Its art-slung interior reveals a passion for Africa and primary colours. Affording castle views or more panoramic vistas over the river, the 12 rooms bear the imprint of artist Luís Lemos and offer trappings such as flat-screen TVs and minibars. There's a water garden for catnapping between sights.

🛏 Príncipe Real, Santos & Estrela

Leafy neighbourhoods and plenty of style set the scene for an overnight stay in the top-notch boutique hotels here. It's ideal for escapists who prefer pin-drop peace to central bustle.

Maná Guesthouse GUESTHOUSE €
(Map p76; 📋213 931 060; pensaomana@sapo.pt; Calçada do Marquês de Abrantes 97; d €50; 📶) Small and welcoming, Maná has ultraclean rooms with polished wood floors, high ceilings and decorative balconies. Breakfast is served under the fruit trees in the garden.

Casa de Santos GUESTHOUSE €
(Map p76; 📋915 696 177; www.casadesantos.net; Rua da Boavista 102; d/ste €50/90; ❄️📶) Casa de Santos has appealing wood-floored rooms decorated with artwork and eclectic furnishings – including pieces from the Far East. The location is good for those interested in exploring the less touristy neighbourhoods of Santa Catarina and Santos. If you don't mind the shared bathrooms (six rooms share two bathrooms), it's excellent value.

Casa do Bairro B&B €€
(Map p76; 📋218 054 784; http://shiadu.com; Beco Caldeira 1 ; d €99-139 ; ❄️📶) This small welcoming guesthouse has bright rooms furnished in an attractive contemporary style, and staff have great tips on the city. Some rooms are small, and bathrooms can be rather cramped. It's hard to find (it's located on a staircase lane), so get good directions

before arriving. The owners also operate four other B&Bs in Lisbon, and one in Porto.

Lapa Palace　　　LUXURY HOTEL €€€
(☑ 213 949 494; www.lapapalace.com; Rua do Pau de Bandeira 4; d from €350; ❋ @ ? ☎) Set in landscaped gardens, this belle-époque mansion offers the red-carpet treatment in swanky quarters with five-star trimmings.

As Janelas Verdes　　　BOUTIQUE HOTEL €€€
(Map p76; ☑ 213 968 143; www.heritage.pt; Rua das Janelas Verdes 47; d €250; ❋ @) This romantic 18th-century mansion inspired Eça de Queirós' novel *Os Maias*. Retreat to the wood-panelled library for sweeping views to the river and a stargazing telescope. When the sun's out, have your breakfast in the bougainvillea-draped courtyard.

🛏 Rato, Marquês de Pombal & Saldanha

Go Hostel Lisbon　　　HOSTEL €
(☑ 218 229 816; Rua Maria da Fonte 55; dm €16-20, d €55-70; ❋ @ ?) Set inside a sprawling 150-year-old mansion (the Palacio Andrade), this hostel has loads of character, including frescos in some rooms, skylights, mural-covered stairwells, an elegant lounge and a grassy courtyard that sometimes hosts concerts and DJ nights. It's located in a tourist-free residential area, a short walk from Intendente metro station; tram 28 also rattles past.

Dom Sancho I　　　GUESTHOUSE €
(Map p80; ☑ 213 513 160; www.domsancho.com; 2nd fl, Av da Liberdade 202; s/d from €55/60; ❋ @ ?) In a grand 18th-century edifice overlooking the leafy but busy Avenida da Liberdade, Dom Sancho I offers small but comfortably furnished rooms – the best with polished wood floors, marble bathrooms and decorative balconies. Breakfast and wi-fi are available, but may cost extra (depending on where you booked).

★Casa Amora　　　GUESTHOUSE €€
(Map p80; ☑ 919 300 317; http://solisbon.com; Rua João Penha 13; d €100-140; ❋ ?) Opened in 2012, the Casa Amora has five beautifully designed guestrooms and one private studio with a small kitchen. Rooms are bright, elegantly furnished and uniquely designed, and each pays homage to a different Portuguese artist (poet Fernando Pessoa, fadista Amália Rodrigues, painter Amadeo Souza Cardoso).

There's a lovely garden patio where the first-rate breakfast is served. It's located in the peaceful neighbourhood of Amoreiras, a few steps from one of Lisbon's prettiest squares.

Lisbon Dreams　　　GUESTHOUSE €€
(Map p80; ☑ 213 872 393; www.lisbondreams guesthouse.com; Rua Rodrigo da Fonseca 29; s/d with shared bathroom €50/60; @ ?) On a quiet street lined with jacaranda trees, Lisbon Dreams offers excellent value for its bright modern rooms with high ceilings and excellent mattresses. The green apples are a nice touch, and there are attractive common areas to unwind in. All bathrooms are shared, but are spotlessly clean.

Fontana Park Hotel　　　HOTEL €€
(Map p80; ☑ 210 410 600; www.fontanaparkhotel. com; Rua Engenheiro Vieira da Silva 2; d from €88; ❋ @ ?) In Saldanha, this 1908 iron-factory-turned-cutting-edge hotel, flaunts smooth contours, space-age lighting and sylvan flourishes. The 140 monochrome rooms are temples to minimalism, with granite bathrooms with transparent walls. There's also a Japanese restaurant and bamboo-fringed garden with cascading fountain.

Inspira Santa Marta　　　HOTEL €€
(Map p80; ☑ 210 440 900; www.inspirasanta martahotel.com; Rua de Santa Marta 48; d from €100; ❋ @ ?) 🌿 The 89-room Inspira Santa Marta is an ecofriendly designer hotel set in a converted 19th-century building. Rooms are stylish but functional and incorporate five different feng-shui themes, including earth-toned Terra rooms and cork-floored Arvore (tree) rooms with sky-blue details. There's an inviting brasserie that showcases locally grown ingredients, a bar with fireplace, a games room with billiards table, and a spa.

Hotel Eurostars das Letras　　　HOTEL €€
(Map p80; ☑ 213 573 094; www.eurostarsdaslet ras.com; Rua Castilho 6; d/ste €98/147; P ❋ @ ?) The Hotel Eurostars has high-tech rooms painted in earthy tones, with wood floors, walnut headboards, black armchairs and brown comforters. Rooms have a literary bent, with quotes by famous writers (Shakespeare, Borges, Pessoa) over the beds. Top-floor rooms have balconies. Breakfast costs an extra €7 per person.

Casa de São Mamede　　　GUESTHOUSE €€
(Map p80; ☑ 213 963 166; www.casadesao mamede.com; Rua da Escola Politécnica 159; s/d from €70/80; ❋ ?) This 18th-century,

family-run villa has class: from the red carpet gracing the staircase to the tinkling chandeliers in the exquisitely tiled breakfast room. Large and serene, rooms sport period furnishings. It's a short stroll from Bairro Alto and the botanical gardens.

Hotel Britania HOTEL €€€
(Map p80; ☑ 213 155 016; www.heritage.pt; Rua Rodrigues Sampaio 17; d from €205; ✸ @ ☎) Art deco rules the waves at Britania, a boutique gem near Avenida da Liberdade. Cassiano Branco put his modernist stamp on the rooms with chrome lamps, plaid fabrics and shiny marble bathrooms. Hobnob over a G&T at the bar, chat with the affable staff and let this 1940s time capsule work its charm.

Mercador APARTMENT €€€
(Map p80; ☑ 919 300 317; http://solisbon.com; Rua São José 164; ste €125-145; ☎) Mercador consists of three lavish apartments suitable for royalty. It's on a peaceful street one block back from grand Avenida da Liberdade. It's best for self-caterers, as there's no reception area and minimal amenities (although the suites are cleaned daily and the refrigerator is stocked for breakfast).

🛏 Belém

Pensão Residencial Setúbalense GUESTHOUSE €
(Map p82; ☑ 213 636 639; www.setubalense.pt; Rua de Belém 28; s/d from €45/50; ✸) A short toddle east of the Mosteiro dos Jerónimos (p79), this 17th-century guesthouse has twee but comfy rooms with tiled floors, floral fabrics and modern bathrooms. Corridors are a tad dark, but *azulejos* and potted plants add a homely touch.

Jerónimos 8 BOUTIQUE HOTEL €€
(Map p82; ☑ 213 600 900; www.jeronimos8.com; Rua dos Jerónimos 8; d from €102; ✸ @ ☎) Belém's first boutique hotel, Jerónimos 8 ups the style ante with clean lines, floor-to-ceiling windows and designer flourishes aplenty. The slick rooms, dressed in cream and caramel hues with natural fabrics, feature cable TV, minibar and wi-fi. Chill in the pepper-red bar or on the deck. The monastery views are superb.

Altis Belém HOTEL €€€
(Map p82; ☑ 210 400 200; www.altishotels.com; Doca do Bom Sucesso; d from €230; ℗ ✸ @ ☎) Near the waterfront, this hypermodern

boutique hotel and spa offers stylish rooms that range from small to large with all the high-end fittings – Egyptian-cotton bed linen, glass-walled marble bathrooms, and outdoor jacuzzis in some suites. All have balconies, and the best have enviable views over the Tejo. There's also a full-service spa and several enticing restaurants (one with an outdoor deck facing the marina).

🛏 Parque das Nações

Myriad LUXURY HOTEL €€€
(Vasco da Gama Tower; ☑ 211 107 600; http://myriad.pt; Rua Cais das Naus; s/d from €210/240; @ ☎ ⚊) Formerly part of the Expo, the 145m-high, concrete-and-steel Torre Vasco da Gama today houses this luxury hotel. All rooms are lavishly appointed, if a touch on the garish side, with ruby red carpets and red pillows accenting an otherwise subdued colour scheme. Big windows provide stunning river views. There's a spa, indoor pool and restaurant, and the open-air riverside lounge juts out over the water.

✕ Eating

Creative new-generation chefs at the stove, first-rate raw ingredients and a generous pinch of world spice has transformed Lisbon into a buzzing culinary capital.

✕ Baixa & Rossio

Many of Baixa's old-school bistros and outdoor cafes heave with tourists, but tiptoe away from the main drag, Rua Augusta, and you'll find some gems in streets such as Rua dos Correiros and Rua dos Sapateiros.

Amorino ICE CREAM €
(Map p64; Rua Augusta 209; small/large ice cream €3.50/5.50; ☺11am-9pm) For lovers of sweet treats, Amorino serves the city's best gelato – creamy, rich decadence made from organic, high-quality ingredients.

Oishi Sushi JAPANESE €
(Map p64; Rua dos Correios 42; 8 rolls €6-8; ☺lunch & dinner Mon-Sat) Oishi (which means 'yummy' in Japanese) delivers the goods with plump, mouthwatering sushi and *temaki* (hand rolls). There's limited seating fronting the fast food–like counter, so you want to get it to go, and have an impromptu picnic on nearby Praça do Comércio.

Bacalhoeiro
PORTUGUESE €

(Map p64; Rua dos Sapateiros 218; mains €7-10; ⊘lunch & dinner Mon-Sat) A standout among the tourist traps of Baixa, Bacalhoeiro serves good-value Portuguese fish and meat dishes. True to name, the *bacalhau* (cod) is excellent, the wines refreshing and affordable, and the atmosphere is buzzing and casual.

Moma
FUSION €

(Map p64; Rua de São Nicolau 47; mains €7.50-9; ⊘12.30pm-6pm Mon-Fri) A nice break from grilled sardines and menu-touting hawks in Baixa, this local haunt boasts black-and-white tile floors and a small but creative menu (spicy crispy prawns, pasta with wild mushrooms, and arugula salad with goat cheese and grilled eggplant are three recent favourites).

Nova Pombalina
PORTUGUESE €

(Map p64; Rua do Comércio 2; sandwiches €3.50; ⊘7am-8pm) The reason this bustling tradi-tional restaurant is always packed around midday is its delicious *leitão* (suckling pig) sandwich, served on freshly baked bread in 60 seconds or less by the lightning-fast crew behind the counter. Other sandwich favourites include prosciutto and roast chicken.

Fragoleto
ICE CREAM €

(Map p64; Rua da Prata 61; small/medium/large €2.20/3.50/5; ⊘9am-8pm Mon-Sat; 🖉) Frago-leto serves creamy, rich, Italian-style gelato made from seasonal fruit – and there are even vegan options.

Confeitaria Nacional
PATISSERIE €€

(Map p64; 🖉213 461 720; Praça da Figueira 18; lunches €9-11; ⊘8am-8pm Mon-Sat) Expanding waistlines since 1829, this stuccoed patis-serie entices with strong *bica*, macaroons and *pastéis de nata*. Upstairs, the restaurant dishes up hearty quiches, soups and daily lunch specials.

LOCAL KNOWLEDGE

LISBON'S CULINARY REVOLUTION

Sarajevo-born Ljubomir Stanišić is one of Lisbon's most celebrated chefs, the master-mind behind the award-winning restaurant **100 Maneiras** (p100) and a **bistro** (p98) of the same name. Here he gives the dish on Portugal's dynamic culinary scene.

What influences your cooking?

My cooking is based on French knowledge and techniques, but I'm also interested in ex-ploring everyday types of cuisine on the travels I make (come with us on www.papakms.com). Asia is also a huge inspiration, as is Africa. So, the world is, in fact, a daily inspira-tion. I love to taste and to see what others do and then take bits of this and bits of that...

How would you describe the current dining scene in Lisbon?

Portuguese traditional gastronomy is very rich but has grown even richer in the past five years. With the economic crisis, haute cuisine has fallen out of fashion, and the emerg-ing trend (even among high-level chefs) is to focus on bistro-style *tascas* or *tavernas* – more relaxed, less expensive and informal.

What's the one thing that distinguishes Portuguese cooking from other cuisines?

The perfect mixture between olive oil, garlic, coriander and wine. And definitely the best fish in the world.

Aside from your own restaurants, what are your favourite restaurants in Lisbon?

Tasca da Esquina (p103), Ramiro (p105), O Pitéu (p101), Jesus é Goês (p105) and Solar dos Presuntos (p97), among others.

Do you have any insider tips for visitors seeking an authentic Lisbon dining experience?

The fresh grilled fish and the seafood like *bruxas* and *percebes* at Mar do Inferno (p133), in Cascais; the fried *carabineiros* at Ramiro (p105), in Lisbon – they're not on the menu, so ask; a fresh-squeezed juice with the best terrace-view in town at Noobai (p107); and several glasses of excellent Portuguese wine at Wine Bar do Castelo (p109).

Casa do Alentejo
PORTUGUESE €€

(Map p64; Rua Portas de Santo Antão 58; mains €11-14; ⊙lunch & dinner Mon-Sat) Hidden behind a plain facade, the Casa do Alentejo has a magnificent Moorish-style interior; head upstairs to a series of tile-filled dining rooms where you can feast on pork with clams, lamb stew and other Alentejan favourites. The changing €8 lunch specials are good value.

Jardim dos Sentidos
VEGETARIAN €€

(Map p64; ☑213 423 670; Rua Mãe d'Água 3; lunch buffet €9-11; ⊙lunch Mon-Fri, dinner Mon-Sat; ☑) Vegetarian-minded diners flock to this attractive restaurant with a back garden and an extensive lunch buffet. Among the offerings: four-cheese lasagna, vegetarian chilli, warm goat's-cheese salad and stuffed eggplant, plus a substantial tea menu.

Tamarind
INDIAN €€

(Map p64; ☑213 466 080; Rua da Glória 43; mains €9-14; ⊙lunch Sun-Fri, dinner daily; ☑) Dave Walia cooks up an Indian storm at this calm restaurant in Ayurveda-inspired pink and blue tones. His rich prawn kormas and lamb curries are inflected with chilli, ginger and fresh herbs.

Bonjardim
PORTUGUESE €€

(Map p64; ☑213 424 389; Travessa de Santo Antão 11; roast chicken for 2 €13; ⊙lunch & dinner) Juicy, spit-roast *frango* (chicken) is served with a mountain of fries at this local favourite. Add piri-piri for extra spice. The pavement terrace is elbow-to-elbow in summer.

Can the Can
MEDITERRANEAN €€

(Map p64; Praça do Comércio 82; mains €12-19; ⊙9am-midnight) One of numerous indoor-outdoor restaurants facing Lisbon's biggest plaza, Can the Can pays homage to the humble tinned fish in appetisers and sharing plates (not to mention the giant chandelier). Not everything comes out of a can: savoury salads, roast meats and grilled fish and veggies are all fresh and nicely prepared. There's live fado on Friday nights from 9.30pm.

Solar dos Presuntos
PORTUGUESE €€€

(Map p64; ☑213 424 253; Rua das Portas de Santo Antão 150; mains €15-28; ⊙lunch & dinner Mon-Sat) Don't be fooled by the smoked *presunto* (ham) hanging in the window; this iconic restaurant is renowned for its excellent seafood – as well as its smoked and grilled meats. There's a pleasant buzz to the folksy and welcoming space, with photos of admirers lining the restaurant's walls. Prawn and lobster curry, salt-baked sea bass and delectable seafood paella are among the top choices.

✗ Chiado

The elegant back streets of Chiado have some memorable dining options, some of which have vistas overlooking peaceful tree-fringed plazas. Good places to browse restaurant options include Rua dos Duques de Bragança, Rua Nova de Trindade and around pretty Largo do Carmo. You'll also find a handful of restaurants on a well-concealed plaza off Rua Garrett, just east of Livraria Bertrand.

If you're self-catering or simply after a picnic, **Brio** (Map p68; Travessa do Carmo 1; ⊙9am-8pm Mon-Fri, 10am-8pm Sat, noon-7pm Sun) – an organic, reasonably priced grocer – stocks the essentials: wines, yoghurts, granolas, cold drinks, chocolates, cheeses, breads and more. There's also a small cafe, with outdoor tables in front.

Eric Kayser
CAFE, PATISSERIE €

(Map p68; Rua do Carmo 70; pastries €1.50-2.50; ⊙8am-10pm) This Parisian boulangerie opened in the Chiado in 2012, and has earned much acclaim for its delectable pastries, tarts and baguettes. Lunch and dinner specials include a light main (sandwich, salad, quiche), a drink and dessert for €7 to €9.

ACISJF
PORTUGUESE €

(Map p68; top fl, Travessa do Ferragial 1; mains €7; ⊙lunch Mon-Fri) Sweet nuns dressed as lunch ladies run this small, sunny cafeteria, dishing up a daily soup (the gazpacho is great!), several mains – of the beef, sardines or codfish variety – and fresh fruit for dessert. The river views from the sun-drenched terrace are astounding.

Faca & Garfo
PORTUGUESE €

(Map p68; Rua da Condessa 2; mains €7-10; ⊙lunch & dinner Mon-Sat) The sweet *azulejo*-filled Faca & Garfo (which means 'knife and fork') has earned a loyal local following for its tasty, carefully prepared Portuguese recipes, reasonable prices and friendly service. Try the authentic *alheira de Mirandela* (chicken sausage) or the *bife à casa* (steak with cream and port-wine sauce).

Jardim das Cerejas
VEGETARIAN €

(Map p68; Calçada do Sacramento 36; buffet lunch/dinner €7.50/9.50; ⊙lunch & dinner; ☑)

On a restaurant-lined stretch of Chiado, Jardim das Cerejasoffers a small but tasty buffet, with many vegan items.

Tartine
CAFE €€

(Map p68; Rua Serpa Pinto 15; mains €8-10; ☺10pm Mon-Fri, 10am-8pm Sat; 🛜) This stylish modern cafe and bakery has a tempting display case of almond croissants, eclairs and other baked goodies. Head upstairs to the wooden tables to peruse newspapers or join locals over big bowls of coffee and tasty lunch specials (quiche, risotto, pasta). There's also a small terrace.

Kaffeehaus
CAFE €€

(Map p68; Rua Anchieta 3; mains €9-13; ☺noon-midnight Tue-Sat, to 8pm Sun) Kaffee Haus has a bright interior with classic lines and big windows overlooking a peaceful corner of the Chiado, and it's a favourite eating and drinking spot among a cool but unpretentious crowd. Check the chalkboard for daily specials, including big salads, tasty schnitzels, strudels, cakes and more. Expect big crowds (and great food) at weekend brunches.

Fábulas
CAFE €€

(Map p68; Calçada Nova de São Francisco 14; mains €10-15, lunch specials €6-7; ☺10am-midnight; 🛜🖉) Exposed stone walls, low lighting and twisting corridors that open onto cosy nooks do indeed conjure a *fábula* (storybook fable). Couches and wooden tables are fine spots to while away a few hours over coffee, drinks or globally inspired dishes – curry shrimp with basmati rice, quinoa with vegetables, and duck magret with chestnut risotto. There's also alfresco dining on the back courtyard, adjoining a handful of other restaurants.

Café no Chiado
PORTUGUESE €€

(Map p68; 213 460 501; R dos Duques de Bragança; mains €15-18; prix-fixe lunch/dinner €13/16; ☺10am-2am) Near the Teatro São Luís, this atmospheric cafe serves Portuguese classics such as *bacalhau à brás* (shredded cod with scrambled eggs), *arroz de pato* (oven-cooked duck with rice) and creamy desserts. Tram 28 rattles right by the shaded sidewalk terrace, which is great for people-watching. Multi-course lunch or dinner specials including wine are available on weekdays.

Taberna da Rua das Flores
PORTUGUESE €€

(Map p68; 213 479 418; Rua das Flores 103; small plates €6-8; ☺11am-midnight Mon-Sat) This vintage-looking space channels the nostalgia of the old-fashioned tavern with marble-topped tables and classic Portuguese products on display. Excellent cocktails and local wines from the surrounding region go nicely with tapas plates like the mussels in garlic and coriander sauce, seared razor clams and pork shoulder sandwiches.

Cervejaria da Trindade
PORTUGUESE €€

(Map p68; 213 423 506; Rua Nova da Trindade 20c; mains €8-20; ☺noon-midnight daily) This 13th-century monastery turned clattering beer hall oozes atmosphere with its vaults and *azulejos* of quaffing clerics and seasonal goddesses. Feast away on huge steaks or lobster stew, washed down with foaming beer.

Tagide Wine & Tapas Bar
FUSION €€

(Map p68; 213 404 010; Largo da Academia Nacional de Belas Artes 20; tapas €4-9; ☺noon-3pm & 7pm-midnight Mon-Fri, 1pm-midnight Sat) Not to be confused with the pricier Tagide next door, this less-formal place has an airy modern setting with dark wood floors and narrow windows with pretty views to the river (the TV, though thankfully silent, seems out of place). Small sharing plates feature imaginative combinations that are packed with flavour. Two-course lunch specials cost €8.50.

★Belcanto
PORTUGUESE €€€

(Map p68; 213 420 607; Largo de São Carlos 10; mains €35-38, tasting menu €65-85; ☺lunch & dinner Tue-Sat) One of Lisbon's best restaurants, Michelin-starred Belcanto has wowed many diners with its small but creative menu, delicious cuisine and first-rate service (the rather stuffy ambience, however, is another story). Suckling pig, sea bass with seaweed and bivalves, and lamb with marinated vegetables are superb. For true decadence, try the tasting menu, and do trust the top-notch sommelier. As with any of José Avillez' restaurants, you'll need to reserve ahead.

Bistro 100 Maneiras
FUSION €€€

(Map p68; 910 307 575; Largo da Trindade 9; mains €18-24; ☺6pm-2am Mon-Sat) The mastermind behind 100 Maneiras (p100) in Bairro Alto opened this creatively charged bistro to much fanfare in 2010. It has earned rave reviews for its beautifully prepared dishes, which showcase high-end Portuguese ingredients. It stays open late (though the kitchen closes around 12.30am), making it a good option for late-night dining. Reserve ahead.

LISBON FOR CHILDREN

Amusing kids is child's play in Lisbon, where even little things spark the imagination – from bumpy rides on bee-yellow trams to gooey *pastéis de nata*, acting out fairy tales at Castelo de São Jorge (p70) to munching colourful *pipocas* (popcorn).

Lisboêtas are well prepared for families, with free or half-price tickets for little 'uns at major sights, half portions (ask for *uma meia dose*) at many restaurants, and free transport for under-fives. Hotels will often squeeze in cots or beds for tots at no extra charge.

Prime kiddie territory is Parque das Nações, where little nippers love to spot toothy sharks and sea otters at the eye-popping Oceanário (p83), launch rockets and ride the high-wire bicycle at the hands-on Pavilhão do Conhecimento (p83), then get utterly soaked at the splashy **Jardins d'Água** (Water Gardens; Passeio de Neptuno; ⊙24hr; underground rail Oriente) `FREE`.

Most of Lisbon's squares and parks have playgrounds for tykes to let off excess energy, including Parque Eduardo VII (p79) and an animal-themed one at Jardim da Estrela (p75).

Go west to relive the nautical adventures of the Age of Discovery in Belém's barge-stuffed Museu de Marinha (p80), or marvel at the puppets in Lapa's enchanting Museu da Marioneta (p75). Hard-to-please teens in tow? Take them shopping in Bairro Alto's groovy boutiques such as Sneakers Delight (p116).

When the weather warms up, take the train to Cascais for some ice-cream-licking, bucket-and-spade fun. Kids can make finny friends on a dolphin-watching tour in Setúbal, or play king of the castle in the fantastical turrets and woodlands of Sintra.

Aqui Há Peixe
SEAFOOD €€€

(Map p68; ✆213 432 154; Rua da Trindade 18; mains €15-20; ⊙lunch Tue-Fri, dinner Tue-Sun) Stone walls, sea-green banquettes and nautical knick-knacks remind diners that indeed '*aqui ha peixe*' (here there is fish). Prices are high, but so is the quality with favourites such as oysters, octopus salad, grilled sea bass and lobster.

Cantinho do Avillez
PORTUGUESE €€€

(Map p68; ✆211 992 369; Rua dos Duques de Bragança 7; small plate €5-10, mains €18-20; ⊙lunch & dinner Mon-Sat) Celebrated chef José Avillez has several restaurants in the neighbourhood, including this buzzing, warmly lit bistro. Small plates are a great way to sample a variety of inventive dishes, including partridge pie, Alentejo-style black pork and marinated scallops with avocado. Steak sandwiches and hearty mains (cod with eggs, grilled tuna) are nicely prepared, if a little unimaginative.

✖ Bairro Alto & Around

For a preclubbing vibe, caipirinhas and a side order of cool, it has to be loud and lively Bairro Alto. The rhythmic sizzle of grills, wafts of garlic and pumping music fill the narrow lanes come twilight.

Flower Power
CAFE €

(Map p68; Calçada do Combro 2; snacks €4-6; ⊙11am-8pm) True to name, this stylish little cafe is packed with artfully arranged floral displays (owner Carlos Filipe runs a flower shop in the same space). The menu features soups, salads, sandwiches, quiches and desserts. Sidewalk tables are a fine vantage point for taking in the passing people parade.

Casa da India
PORTUGUESE €

(Map p68; Rua do Loreto 49; mains €7-9; ⊙noon-2am Mon-Sat) Despite the name, this is a traditional joint with a Portuguese menu. It's a local haunt with a buzzing, if downmarket, atmosphere (the green and beige tiles aren't winning any design awards) and a grillmaster in front who whips up tasty grilled meats and seafood; the *chocos* (cuttlefish) are excellent.

Cultura do Chá
CAFE €

(Map p68; Rua das Salgadeiras 38; snacks €3-4; ⊙noon-10pm Mon-Sat) One of Bairro Alto's rare quiet nooks, this tearoom has comfy chairs, stone walls and arches, and a relaxing vibe that goes well with the little pots of lapsang, sencha and 15 other teas on offer. Simple sandwiches and salads along with pastries and cakes round out the menu.

Toma Lá-Dá-Cá PORTUGUESE €
(Map p68; ☑ 213 479 243; Travessa do Sequeiro 38; mains €7-12; ☺ lunch & dinner) There's always a buzzing crowd filling this Santa Catarina gem, which is famed for its simple classics such as grilled fish and roasted meat dishes.

Tease CAFE €
(Map p68; Rua do Norte 31; cupcakes €2.50; ☺ 11am-midnight Mon-Sat) This rock 'n' roll bakery specialises in decadent cupcakes piled high with frosting, as well as scones and freshly brewed teas. The gold disco ball, delicate armchairs and black skull wallpaper add to the fun.

Pastelaria São Roque PATISSERIE €
(Map p64; Rua Dom Pedro V; pastries €1-3; ☺ 7am-7pm) This wedding cake of a patisserie drips with exquisite *azulejos,* gold-topped columns and mirrors. Bag a seat in one of the alcoves to indulge in buttery cakes, freshly made bread and people-watching.

Lost in Esplanada INTERNATIONAL €€
(Map p64; Rua Dom Pedro V 56; mains €11-17; ☺ 4pm-midnight Mon, 12.30pm-midnight Tue-Sat) Hidden behind an Indian textile shop, this well-concealed terrace is set up with painted wicker chairs, a gurgling fountain and a Krishna mural, though the view over the city is the real attraction. Veggie burgers, prawn curry and Portuguese sharing plates comprise the menu. There's live jazz on Thursdays from 9pm to 11pm.

Flor da Laranja MOROCCAN €€
(Map p68; ☑ 213 422 996; Rua da Rosa 206; mains €14-16; ☺ dinner Mon-Sat) A great place to linger over a meal, Flor da Laranja earns rave reviews for its warm welcome, cosy ambience and delicious Moroccan cuisine (the owner hails from Casablanca). Top picks include dolmas, mouth-watering couscous dishes, lamb tagine, and fresh berry crepes for dessert.

Le Petit Bistro FUSION €€
(Map p68; Rua do Almada 31; mains €9-14; ☺ dinner Tue-Fri, lunch & dinner Sat & Sun) On a lively stretch of Bica, the bohemian Petit Bistro serves both tapas-size plates and heartier mains from France and beyond (duck confit, gazpacho, wraps, lasagna, couscous dishes, hummus with bruschetta). Good late brunches (from 1pm) on weekends.

Beef Burger Bar BURGERS €€
(Map p68; ☑ 213 424 266; Rua de Sao Boaventura 16; mains €9-14; ☺ 5pm-2am Wed-Mon) Vintage toys hanging from the ceilings, walls plastered with black-and-white photos, and paintings of bullfighters set the scene at this wildly decorated – if unimaginatively named – restaurant. In addition to thick burgers (which can be a little undercooked) and refreshing Estrella draughts, you'll find a selection of classic Spanish tapas.

Antigo Primeiro de Maio PORTUGUESE €€
(Map p68; Rua da Atalaia 8; mains €10-12; ☺ dinner Mon-Sat, lunch Mon-Fri) Always packed with regulars, this small but festive *tasca* (tavern) serves excellent traditional Portuguese dishes amid tiled walls, a garrulous crowd and a harried but friendly waiters.

Decadente PORTUGUESE €€
(Map p68; ☑ 213 461 381; Rua de São Pedro de Alcântara 81; mains €9-14; ☺ lunch Sun-Fri, dinner daily) This beautifully designed restaurant, with touches of industrial chic, geometric artwork and an enticing back patio, attracts a mix of hip *lisboetas* and foreign guests staying at the Independente. All come for inventive dishes showcasing high-end Portuguese ingredients at excellent prices. The changing three-course lunch menu (€10) is first-rate. Start off with creative cocktails in the front bar. There's also bistro fare in the bar from 4pm to 7pm.

Pharmacia MEDITERRANEAN €€
(Map p76; ☑ 213 462 146; Rua Marechal Saldanha 1; tapas €7-11; ☺ 1pm-1am Tue-Sun) Within Lisbon's apothecary museum, this wonderfully quirky restaurant dispenses tasting menus and tapas that sing with flavours that are market fresh and Mediterranean influenced. Waiters in white lab coats, appetisers served in test tubes, and cabinets brimming with pill bottles and flacons – it's all part of the pharmaceutical fun. The terrace is a great afternoon spot for cocktails.

★100 Maneiras FUSION €€€
(Map p68; ☑ 910 307 575; Rua do Teixeira 35; tasting menus €45; ☺ dinner) One of Lisbon's best-rated restaurants, 100 Maneiras has no menu, just a 10-course tasting menu that changes daily and features creative, delicately prepared dishes. The courses are all a surprise – part of the charm – though the chef will take special diets and food allergies into consideration. There's a lively buzz to the elegant and small space. Reservations essential.

Pap'Açorda PORTUGUESE €€€
(Map p68; ☑ 213 464 811; Rua da Atalaia 57; mains €17-29; ☺ lunch & dinner) Pap'Açorda lures the

beauty set with its cascading chandeliers, pink-champagne walls and Right Said Fred lookalike waiters. Dishes are traditional and include the likes of *açorda* (bread and shellfish stew), lamb chops, grilled stone-bass and rich chocolate mousse for dessert.

Sea Me
SEAFOOD €€€

(Map p68; ☑ 213 461 564; Rua do Lareto 21; mains €18-30; ⊘ lunch & dinner) One of Lisbon's best seafood restaurants serves up magnificent grilled fish by the kilo (check out the tempting fresh selection in the back) as well as flavourful plates with international accents – risotto with shrimp, Thai green curry with grilled salmon, seared scallops with mango relish, and fish ceviche among other standouts.

✖ Alfama, Castelo & Graça

Peppered with small family bistros whose owners might spontaneously break out in song, Alfama's twisting, lantern-lit lanes are made for romantic *tête-à-têtes*. Come for alfresco dining on the cobblestones and impromptu *fado vadio* (street fado).

Cafe Belmonte
CAFE €

(Map p72; Páteo Dom Fradique 14; mains €4-6; ⊘ 11am-7pm; ☏) A peaceful and beautifully located cafe with old stone walls and an outdoor terrace a few steps from the castle.

Marcelino Pão e Vinho
PORTUGUESE €

(Map p72; Rua do Salvador 62; snacks €2-4; ⊘ 10.30am-midnight Thu-Tue; ☏) This narrow cafe has just three tables inside and two on the quiet lane outside. What it lacks in space, however, it makes up for in atmosphere, with changing artwork (featuring local artists) on the walls, occasional live music, refreshing sangria, and salads, sandwiches, quiches, desserts and other light bites.

Cafe do Monte
CAFE €

(Rua Senhora do Monte; mains €5-8; ⊘ noon-3pm & 7-11pm Mon-Fri, 10am-10.30pm Sat & Sun) Near the panoramic overlook of Miradouro da Senhora do Monte, this sweet little cafe with its burgundy walls, old film posters and ambient electrogrooves attracts an easy-going, mostly local crowd who come for warm goat-cheese salads, toasted sandwiches and *tabuas* (sharing platters) of cheese and smoked meats. Drinks by night and week-

end breakfasts (yoghurt, fruit and muesli, and the like).

Pois Café
CAFE €

(Map p72; Rua de São João da Praça 93; mains €7-10; ⊘ 11am-10pm Tue-Sun) Boasting a laid-back vibe, Pois Café has creative salads, sandwiches and fresh juices, plus a delicious daily special (soup and main for €9.50). Its sofas invite lazy afternoons spent reading novels and sipping coffee.

Páteo 13
PORTUGUESE €€

(Map p72; Calçadinha de Santo Estêvão 13; mains €8-12; ⊘ lunch & dinner) Follow the scent of chargrilled fish to this local favourite, tucked away on a small, festively decorated plaza in the Alfama. Join buzzing crowds hunkered over picnic tables as they feast on barbecued seafood and meats, washed down with ever-flowing Alentejan reds.

O Piteu
PORTUGUESE €€

(Map p72; ☑ 218 871 067; Largo da Graça 95; mains €9-14; ⊘ lunch Mon-Sat, dinner Mon-Fri) Off the beaten path, this unassuming place draws a local crowd who come for beautifully prepared, good-value dishes. Join them in savouring flavourful Alentejan pork, *figado* (liver) and excellent fish dishes – especially the grilled *dourada* (golden bream) and fried *carapauzinhos* (small mackerel). The portions are huge, the wine reasonably priced, and the staff friendly (if almost exclusively Portuguese-speaking).

Cruzes Credo Café
CAFE €€

(Map p72; Rua Cruzes da Sé 29; mains €7-12; ⊘ 10am-2am) In the shadow of the grand cathedral, this youthful, jazz-loving cafe has earned a local following for its cozy ambience and eclectic menu. Stop in for coffees, drinks, salads, sandwiches, crepes, burgers, and decadent chocolate cake.

Santo António de Alfama
PORTUGUESE €€

(Map p72; ☑ 218 881 328; Beco de Saõ Miguel 7; mains €15-21; ⊘ lunch & dinner) This bistro wins the award for Lisbon's loveliest courtyard: all vines, twittering budgies and fluttering laundry. The interior is a silverscreen shrine, while the menu stars tasty *petiscos* (appetisers): gorgonzola-stuffed mushrooms, roasted aubergines with yoghurt, as well as more filling traditional Portuguese dishes.

Malmequer Bemmequer
PORTUGUESE €€

(Map p72; ☑ 218 876 535; Rua de São Miguel 23; dishes €8-15; ⊘ lunch & dinner Wed-Sun) Look for the sign with a daisy for this bright check-tablecloth-and-tile number overlooking a pretty square. It rolls out charcoal-grilled dishes such as lamb chops, shrimp and fish kebabs, and classic sardines.

Casanova
PIZZA €€
(☑ 218 877 532; Cais da Pedra á Bica do Sapato; mains €8-16; ☺ lunch & dinner) Casanova seduces with wood-fired pizza that's thin, crisp and authentically Italian. Bag a table on the riverside terrace (heated in winter).

Grelhador de Alfama
PORTUGUESE €€
(Map p72; ☑ 218 886 298; Rua dos Remédios 135; mains €10-12; ☺ lunch & dinner Mon-Sat) Exposed stone and fado paraphernalia create a cosy-meets-kitsch setting for barbecued fish or steak at this no-fuss grill house. The pocket-sized terrace fills up fast in summer.

Tentações de Goa
INDIAN €€
(Map p64; ☑ 218 875 824; Rua São Pedro Mártir 23; mains €7-14; ☺ lunch Tue-Sat, dinner Mon-Sat) Friendly and usually full, this family affair is tucked down a backstreet near Martim Moniz. Reserve a table to munch on spicy Goan nosh such as crab curry with perfectly fluffy basmati.

Chapitô
CONTEMPORARY, PORTUGUESE €€€
(Map p72; ☑ 218 867 334; Costa do Castelo 7; mains €17-20; ☺ lunch & dinner) Part of the Chapitô arts cooperative, this tree-filled courtyard hums with arty types tucking into tapas or barbecued steaks. Zebra and giraffe prints glam up the top-floor restaurant, which affords mesmerising views over Lisbon.

Bica do Sapato
FUSION €€€
(☑ 218 810 320; Cais da Pedra á Bica do Sapato; mains €19-32; ☺ lunch Tue-Sat, dinner Mon-Sat) Part-owned by John Malkovich, this uberhip dockside venue is all glass walls, artful lighting and airy river views. Upstairs, scenesters nibble on sashimi in the minimalist sushi bar, while downstairs the design-conscious restaurant serves highlights such as roasted meats, mushroom risotto and oven-baked fish. There's also an open-air patio cafe facing the river with several other restaurant-cafes next door.

✖ Cais do Sodré

Near the waterfront a handful of restaurants and cafes have opened their doors in recent years, meaning you can grab a bite before hitting the bars nearby.

Sol e Pesca
PORTUGUESE €
(Map p68; Rua Nova do Carvalho 44; tinned fish around €3; ☺ noon-2am Tue-Thu, to 4am Fri & Sat) Rods, nets, hooks and fish charts give away this tiny bar's former life as a fishing-tackle shop. Cabinets are stacked with vintage-looking tins of sardines, tuna, mackerel and other preserved delicacies. Grab a chair, order a tin or two, and accompany it with bread, olives and wine, and you have the makings of a fine and quite affordable meal.

Cafe Tati
CAFE €
(Map p68; ☑ 213 461 279; http://cafetati.blogspot.com; Rua da Ribeira Nova 36; mains €7-8; ☺ 11am-1am Tue-Sun) Opposite the Mercado da Ribeira, Cafe Tati has undeniable charm amid its smattering of well-lit stone-arched rooms with stencilled walls. Along with inventive tostas (Parma ham and raclette) and salads (goat cheese and green apple), four changing daily specials round out the menu and feature the likes of fluffy quiche and chicken with ratatouille. Live jazz and jam sessions, held several nights a week, bring in a festive, alternative crowd.

Povo
PORTUGUESE €
(Map p68; Rua Nova do Carvalho 32; small plates €4-8; ☺ noon-2am Tue-Sat, 6pm-1am Sun & Mon) On bar-lined Rua Nova do Carvalho, Povo serves up tasty Portuguese comfort food in the form of petiscos (small plates). Try the favinhas e chouriço (fava beans with chorizo), salada de polvo (octopus salad) or camarão ao alhinho (garlic prawns). There's also outdoor seating and live fado nights (Thursdays are best).

Green Room
INTERNATIONAL €
(Map p68; Rua Cais do Sodré 16; mains €7.50; ☺ 11am-midnight Mon-Sat, to 8pm Sun; 🔊🖉) This American-run cafe and restaurant serves an eclectic, reasonably priced menu that changes weekly. Jambalaya, Cajun chicken salad, Moroccan couscous and vegan pizza with roasted pumpkin are recent hits, and there are always vegetarian options. You can eat at sidewalk tables outside, though to beat the traffic noise, head inside to the cosy, brick vaulted interior, which also makes a fine setting for an afternoon pick-me-up. Big breakfasts available.

Taberna Tosca
TAPAS €€
(Map p68; ☑ 218 034 563; Praça São Paulo 21; tapas €7-8; ☺ noon-midnight Mon-Thu, to 2am Fri, from 3pm Sat) A peaceful retreat from the nearby mayhem on Rua Nova do Carvalho,

Taberna Tosca is an enticing spot for Portuguese tapas and bold reds from the Douro. Open-air seating is on the leafy plaza (Praça São Paulo) in front, opposite an 18th-century church, all of which makes it feel like a hidden corner of Lisbon.

✗ Príncipe Real, Santos & Estrela

Elegant Príncipe Real, with its peaceful streets and leafy plazas, has a mix of charming outdoor cafes and locally loved restaurants. Santos, closer to the waterfront, has some innovative, beautifully designed dining rooms currently in vogue with Lisbon's style set.

Poison d'Amour   CAFE €
(Map p76; Rua da Escola Politécnica 32; pastries €2-3; ☉10am-8pm Tue-Fri, 9am-8pm Sat & Sun) Poison d'Amour is an elegant cafe and patisserie with a glittering display counter of tarts, macaroons, almond croissants and other temptations. You'll also find a good tea selection, wines and champagne cocktails, light lunches (sandwiches, quiches) and a pleasant terrace-garden in the back.

★Taberna Ideal   FUSION €€
(Map p76; ☑ 213 962 744; Rua da Esperança 112; small plates €8-12; ☉ dinner Wed-Sat, lunch & dinner Sun) In a cosy, atmospheric dining room, Taberna Ideal wows diners with flavourful dishes that blend Alentejan recipes with a modern edge. The inventive menu changes daily and features plates designed for sharing. Recent favourites include goat cheese, honey and rosemary bruschetta; braised pork; scrambled eggs with game sausage; and chestnut pastries filled with mushrooms. Reserve ahead. Cash only.

Petiscaria Ideal   FUSION €€
(Map p76; ☑ 213 971 504; Rua da Esperança 100; small plates €9-11; ☉ dinner Tue-Sat) This small buzzing spot serves up delicious fare – octopus with tomato sauce and sweet potatoes, black sausage with apple puree, and soft polenta with clams followed by chocolate cake with fresh cream and wild berries. Dining is at long communal tables, and there's a spirited rock-and-roll vibe to the place.

Tasca da Esquina   FUSION €€
(☑ 210 993 939; Rua Domingos Sequeira 41; mains €15-20, lunch specials €9, tapas €6-9; ☉lunch Tue-Sat, dinner Mon-Sat) Headed by celebrated chef Vitor Sobral, the 'tavern on the corner' serves rich and inventive dishes featuring classic Portuguese ingredients. It's a small place, with a sizzling grill in front and a cheery sunroom where well-dressed diners fill the tables most days. *Petiscos* (tapas) and multi-course tasting menus are a good way to sample a variety of dishes.

Bebel Bistro   FUSION €€
(Map p76; ☑ 213 952 639; Rua de São Bento 107; mains €7-16; ☉ 8.30am-8pm Mon-Wed, to 11pm Thu & Fri, 11.30am-3pm Sat & Sun) Facing the Portuguese parliament building, Belgian-owned Bebel Bistro serves up a mix of European dishes in a relaxed atmosphere with vintage furnishings. Mussels and fries, rice with razor clams, turkey cutlets, and dessert crepes are among the varied offerings.

Nova Mesa   FUSION €€
(Map p76; ☑ 213 966 287; Rua Marcos Portugal 1; 3-course lunch/dinner €14/24; ☉ lunch & dinner Tue-Sat, lunch Sun) Overlooking the peaceful Praça das Flores, Nova Mesa serves innovative world cuisine, including curry with scallops and prawns, duck with sweet potato, and chicken samosas. Nearby are several other cafe terraces facing the plaza.

Terra   VEGETARIAN €€
(Map p76; ☑ 213 421 407; Rua da Palmeira 15; buffet €13-16; ☉ lunch & dinner Tue-Sun; ☑) ✦ Vegetarians sing the praises of Terra for its superb buffet (including vegan options) of salads, kebabs and curries, plus organic wines and juices. A fountain gurgles in the tree-shaded courtyard, lit by twinkling lights after dark.

Alma   CONTEMPORARY, PORTUGUESE €€€
(Map p76; ☑ 213 963 527; Calçada Marquês de Abrantes 92; 3-course menu €38; ☉ dinner Tue-Sat) Henrique Sá Pessoa, one of Portugal's most talented chefs, consistently receives stellar reviews for the nouveau Portuguese cuisine he so masterfully prepares at this stylish, all-white restaurant in Santos. The multicourse tasting menus provide excellent value for money and the service is first-rate.

✗ Doca de Alcântara

There's a string of waterfront restaurants around the Doca area, near the grating noise of traffic on **Ponte 25 de Abril** (Map p78; Doca de Santo Amaro). Take a stroll to see what takes your fancy. After dark, the riverfront switches into party mode.

WORTH A TRIP

CACILHAS

This sleepy seaside suburb lies just across the Rio Tejo from the capital. Its star attraction – visible from almost everywhere in Lisbon – is 110m-high **Cristo Rei**. Perched on a pedestal, the statue of Christ with outstretched arms is a slightly more baroque version of Rio de Janeiro's *Christ the Redeemer*. It was erected in 1959 to thank God for sparing Portugal from the horrors of WWII. A **lift** (summer/winter €5/4; ⊙ 9.30am-6.30pm) zooms you up to a platform, from where Lisbon spreads magnificently before you. It's a fantastic place for photos. To reach the statue from Cacilhas, take bus 101 (€1.35).

Lisboêtas also flock to Cacilhas for the *cervejarias* (beer halls) serving fresh seafood, refreshing brews and fine views of the sun setting over the river.

Near the ferry terminal, **Cervejaria O Farol** (☑ 212 765 248; Largo Alfredo Dinis 1; mains around €14, seafood platter for two €45; ⊙ 10am-midnight) is a buzzy haunt that cooks crustaceans, including garlicky clams and shrimps, to finger-licking perfection.

A 15-minute stroll along the waterfront brings you to **Ponto Final** (☑ 212 760 743; Cais do Ginjal 72; mains €12-18; ⊙ noon-11pm Wed-Mon). The grilled fish, codfish cakes and monkfish rice are quite good, though the view from the outdoor tables along the river's edge is the real star. It's also a great spot for sunset drinks.

Ferries to Cacilhas (€1.20, 10 minutes, 5.40am to 1.20am) run frequently from Lisbon's Cais do Sodré.

Doca Peixe   SEAFOOD €€€
(Map p78; ☑ 213 973 565; Doca de Santo Amaro; mains €15-30; ⊙ lunch & dinner Tue-Sun) Famous for market-fresh seafood, Doca Peixe is practically under Ponte 25 de Abril. Savour lemony oysters or cod with clams on the terrace.

✕ Rato, Marquês de Pombal & Saldanha

Head north of the centre to splurge at some of Lisbon's top restaurants.

Velocité   CAFE €
(Map p80; Av Duque de Ávila 120; mains €4.20-6.50; ⊙ 10am-8pm; ☑) One for the bike lovers, Velocité is perfectly sited off a bike path. Stop in for healthy salads (pear and gorgonzola; feta and quinoa), soups, *tostas*, burgers and veggie burgers. There's outdoor seating and a bright, open interior. Bike hire is available (per hour/day €5/15).

Cinemateca Portuguesa   CAFE €
(Map p80; Rua Barata Salgueiro 39; mains €6-8; ⊙ 1-11.30pm Mon-Fri, from 2.30pm Sat) Hidden on the 2nd floor of the indie-loving cinema, this bright, wood-filled cafe with its sunny terrace makes a fine retreat for an afternoon or evening pick-me-up. The menu features light snacks, drinks and daily specials.

Versailles   PATISSERIE €
(Map p80; ☑ 213 546 340; Av da República 15A; pastries €2-4; ⊙ 7.30am-10pm) With a marble chandelier and icing-sugar stucco confection, this sublime patisserie is where well-coiffed ladies come to devour cream cakes (or scones with jam) and gossip.

Xuventude de Galicia   PORTUGUESE, SPANISH €
(Map p80; ☑ 218 821 392; Rua Julio Andrade 3; mains €6-10; ⊙ noon-10pm Tue-Sat, to 4pm Sun) Near the leafy Campo Mártires park above Av da Liberdade, this Galician cultural centre has a little-known restaurant that serves up tender *polvo à lagareiro* (octopus with potatoes), *peixe espada grelhado* (grilled swordfish), paella and tapas plates to fine views. The peaceful courtyard is a relaxing spot for a coffee.

Os Tibetanos   VEGETARIAN €
(Map p80; ☑ 213 142 038; Rua do Salitre 117; daily special €8; ⊙ lunch & dinner Mon-Sat; ☑) Part of a Tibetan Buddhism school the mantra here is fresh vegetarian food, with daily specials such as quiche and curry. Sit in the serene courtyard if the sun's out and save room for rose-petal ice cream.

Mezzaluna   ITALIAN €€
(Map p80; ☑ 213 879 944; Rua Artilharia Um 16; mains €16-20; ⊙ lunch Mon-Fri, dinner Mon-Sat) Run by a Neopolitan chef who grew up in New York, Mezzaluna prepares beautifully turned-out dishes that blend classic Italian recipes with mouthwatering fresh Portuguese ingredients. Start off with tender carpaccio or endive leaves wrapped in

prosciutto, parmesan and *ginja* (cherry brandy) reduction, before moving on to linguine with octopus or pan-seared duck breast with prune sauce.

Jesus é Goês
INDIAN €€

(Map p80; ☑ 211 548 812; Rua de São José 23; mains €10-15; ◔ noon-3pm & 7-11pm Mon-Sat) Inside one of Lisbon's best Indian restaurants, jovial chef Jesus Lee whips up South Indian delicacies with a contemporary twist. Rice sack tablecloths and colourful murals by Mario Belém (note the playful blend of Christian-Hindu imagery: ie Ganesh with crown of thorns) set the scene for feasting on shrimp samosas, crab with coconut, and goat with 11 spices – followed by date samosas with ginger and cardamom ice cream for dessert.

Don't miss creative cocktails like the *gin à Jesus*, a beautifully reimagined gin and tonic with basil, rosemary, fennel seeds and pink tonic water made from Indian peppers. Reserve ahead.

Cervejaria Ribadouro
SEAFOOD €€

(Map p80; ☑ 213 549 411; Rua do Salitre 2; mains €11-20, prawns/lobster per kg from €41/76; ◔ lunch & dinner) Bright, noisy and full to the gills, this bustling beer hall is popular with the local seafood fans. The shellfish are plucked fresh from the tank, weighed and cooked to lip-smacking perfection.

Zé Varunca
PORTUGUESE €€

(Map p80; Rua de São José 54; mains €10-14; ◔ lunch & dinner Mon-Sat) Zé is a small, rustically decorated, charming restaurant specialising in Alentejan cuisine, with regional favourites such as roast pork with clam sauce, gazpacho with fried fish, and *migas de bacalhau* (a bread-based dish cooked with cod).

★ Ramiro
SEAFOOD €€€

(Av Almirante Reis 1; seafood per kg around €40-80; ◔ noon-3pm & 7.30pm-midnight Tue-Sun) Opened in 1956, Ramiro has a legendary status among Lisbon's seafood lovers. Here you can feast on rich plates of giant tiger prawns, *percebes* (goose barnacles), lobster, crab and clams – and a juicy steak sandwich for non-pescatarians. Despite the high prices, the atmosphere is bustling and informal, with garrulous crowds quaffing more beer than wine. Ramiro doesn't take reservations, so arrive early and prepare to queue.

✗ Belém

Antiga Confeitaria de Belém
PATISSERIE €

(Map p82; ☑ 213 637 423; Rua de Belém 86-88; pastries €1.05; ◔ 8am-11pm) Since 1837 this patisserie has been transporting locals to sugar-coated nirvana with heavenly *pastéis de belém*: crisp pastry nests filled with custard cream, baked at 200°C for that perfect golden crust, then lightly dusted with cinnamon. Admire *azulejos* in the vaulted rooms or devour a still-warm tart at the counter and try to guess the secret ingredient. Go early midweek to beat the crowds.

Pão Pão Queljo Queijo
CAFE €

(Map p82; ☑ 213 626 369; Rua de Belém 124; sandwiches around €4; ◔ 8am-midnight Mon-Sat, 8am-8pm Sun; ☑) Join the snaking queue for Belém's tastiest falafel (both hands required), sardine baguettes and Mexican salads.

Bem Belém
PORTUGUESE €

(Map p82; Rua Vieira Portuense 72; mains €8-12; ◔ lunch Wed-Mon, dinner Wed-Sun) Bem Belém's sunny patio facing the park is a magnet for lunchtime crowds, who refuel over generous portions of chargrilled sardines and other Portuguese classics.

Este Oeste
INTERNATIONAL €

(Map p82; Centro Cultural de Belém, Praça do Império; mains €9-11; ◔ 10am-11pm Tue-Sun; ☑) This strange hybrid manages to bridge east (este) and west (oeste) surprisingly well, with tasty thin-crust pizzas fired up in the geometric oven and an inviting sushi display at the other end of the front counter. There's an airy interior, patio seating and a grassy lawn where kids frolic and adults lounge about. Behind the restaurant is a cafe.

Nosolo Italia
ITALIAN €€

(Map p82; Av de Brasília 202; mains €10-14; ◔ noon-10pm) This bustling eatery, with outdoor tables perched over the water, has a big menu of pizzas, pastas, salads and crepes; there's also a popular ice-cream counter.

Enoteca de Belém
PORTUGUESE, WINE BAR €€

(Map p82; ☑ 213 631 511; Travessa do Marta Pinto 10; mains €12-17; ◔ 1-11pm Tue-Sun) Tucked down a quiet lane just off Belém's main thoroughfare, this wine bar serves tasty Portuguese classics (try the octopus or the grilled Iberian pork), matched by an excellent selection of full-bodied Douro reds and refreshing Alentejan whites. The atmosphere is a mix of elegance (artwork, bottle-lined walls) and casual (soundless football playing on the TV).

A Margem
FUSION €€

(☑ 918 225 548; Doca do Bom Sucesso; salads €10-14; ☺ 10am-1am) Well-sited near the river's edge, this small sun-drenched cube of glass and white stone boasts an open patio and large windows facing the Tejo. Locals come for fresh salads, cheese plates, bruschetta and other light bites that go niccly with wine and other drinks. Sunglasses are essential. To get here, follow the river's edge 200m west from the Padrão dos Descobrimentos.

Feitoria
CONTEMPORARY, PORTUGUESE €€€

(Map p82; ☑ 210 400 200; Altis Belém Hotel, Doca do Bom Sucesso; mains €34-42; ☺ lunch Tue-Fri, dinner Tue-Sat) José Cordeiro serves decadent, seasonally inspired masterpieces at this Michelin-starred restaurant overlooking the riverfront. Rich textures and mouthwatering flavours feature in dishes like roasted *cantaril* (redfish) and crispy squid stuffed with crab and green-pea texture, and oven-roasted partridge with chestnut purée and wild mushrooms. Excellent wines.

✕ Parque das Nações

Many of the waterfront cafes and restaurants have outdoor seating and do double duty as pulsating bars after dark.

GINJINHA BARS
....

Come dusk, the area around Largo de São Domingos and the adjacent Rua das Portas de Santo Antão buzzes with locals getting their cherry fix in a cluster of *ginjinha* bars. A Ginjinha (p106) is famous as the birthplace of the sugary sweet tipple thanks to a quaffing friar from Igreja Santo Antonio who revealed the secret to an entrepreneurial Galician by the name of Espinheira. Order your €1 *ginjinha sem* (without) or – our favourite – *com* (with) the alcohol-soaked cherries. Other postage-stamp-sized bars nearby include **Ginjinha Sem Rival** (Map p64; Rua Portas de Santo Antão 61; ☺ 7am-midnight) and **Ginjinha Rubi** (Map p64; Rua Barros Queirós 27; ☺ 7am-midnight; underground rail Rossio).

Art Cafe
CAFE €

(Alameda dos Oceanos; light meals €4-7; ☺ 10am-8pm Mon-Sat; 🛜 ☑) Scarlet walls and vibrant paintings give this high-ceilinged cafe an arty feel. It's a relaxed spot for a *bica* or light bites such as quiches, salads and sandwiches. The terrace in the back has fine Tejo views. It's near the Oceanário.

Arrigato
JAPANESE €€€

(☑ 218 967 132; Alarneda dos Oceanos; lunch/dinner buffet €16/21; ☺ lunch & dinner Mon-Sat) Blonde wood and clean lines define this gallery-style restaurant. The buffet has an excellent variety of flavourful sushi and sashimi, and there's outdoor dining when the weather is nice.

Drinking & Nightlife

Late-night street parties in Cais do Sodré and Bairro Alto, sunset *ginjinhas* on Rossio's sticky cobbles, drinks with indie kids in Santa Catarina – Lisbon has one of Europe's most eclectic nightlife scenes.

Baixa & Rossio

Bar Trobadores
BAR

(Map p64; Rua de São Julião 27; ☺ 5pm-2am Mon-Sat) In nightlife-starved Baixa, Bar Trobadores harks back to the Middle Ages with a candle-lit interior, solid wood tables and low-hanging iron chandeliers. There's live music most weekends (minstral-inspired groups, Celtic, fado) and a good beer selection (including Duvel, Chimay and other Belgian brews).

Rooftop Bar
BAR

(Map p64; Hotel Mundial, Praça Martim Moniz 2; ☺ 5.30-11.30pm) Grab a table at sundown on the Hotel Mundial's roof terrace for a sweeping view of Lisbon and its hilltop castle. Its backlit bar, white sofas and ambiant sounds (plus live jazz on Thursday nights in summer) set the stage for evening drinks and sharing plates.

Bar Rossio
BAR

(Map p64; Altis Avenida Hotel, Rua 1 Dezembro 120; ☺ 7am-1am) A terrific rooftop spot for an afternoon coffee or drinks as the city lights begin to glow.

A Ginjinha
BAR

(Map p64; Largo de Saõ Domingos 8; ☺ 9am-10pm) Hipsters, old men in flat caps, office workers and tourists all meet at this microscopic *ginjinha* bar for that moment of cherry-licking, pip-spitting pleasure their euro buys. Watch the owner line 'em up at the bar under the beady watch of the drink's 19th-century inventor, Espinheira. It's less about the grog, more about the event.

Primeiro Andar
BAR

(Map p64; Rua das Portas de Santo Antão 110, Ateneu Comerical de Lisboa; ⊙3pm-1am Mon-Fri, 7pm-2am Sat) Although it's right above a touristy pedestrian street, this delightful cafe and bar remains well-concealed from the masses. To get there, take the small alley about 30m south of the Ateneu Comerical de Lisboa building, go to the end and head inside the dark entrance. Don't be shy, it's a welcoming, laid-back place, good for a pick-me-up in the afternoon (or an inexpensive meal) and drinks with friends by night.

🍸 Chiado & Bairro Alto

Bairro Alto is like a student at a house party: wasted on cheap booze, flirty and everybody's friend. At dusk, the nocturnal hedonist rears its head with bars trying to out-decibel each other, hash-peddlers lurking in the shadows and kamikaze taxi drivers forcing kerbside sippers to leap aside. For a more sophisticated and more artistically minded crowd, head a few blocks south to Bica.

Noobai Café
BAR

(Map p76; Miradouro de Santa Catarina; ⊙noon-10pm Tue-Thu, to midnight Fri & Sat, to 8pm Sun) Great views, winning cocktails and a festive crowd make Noobai a popular draw for a sundowner. Though it's next to Miradouro de Santa Catarina, most people don't realise this bar is here until they descend the steps and a terrace unfurls before them. The vibe is laid-back, the music is funky jazz and the views over the Tejo are magical.

Alfaia Garrafeira
WINE BAR

(Rua Diário de Noticias 125; ⊙2pm-1am Mon-Fri, from 4pm Sat & Sun) This cosy spot with outdoor tables serves a decent selection of wine and tapas plates (€4 to €7), making it a good pre-dinner spot. Skip the lacklustre restaurant of the same name across the street.

Bairro Alto Hotel
BAR

(Map p68; ☑213 408 288; Praça Luís de Camões 2; ⊙12.30pm-midnight) Rise in the gold-mesh lift to the 6th floor of Bairro Alto Hotel for sundowners and dazzling views over the rooftops to the river. It's a smart, grown-up lounge for cocktails and conversation as Lisbon starts to sparkle.

Bicaense
BAR

(Map p68; Rua da Bica de Duarte Belo 42a; ⊙8pm-2am Tue-Sat) Indie kids have a soft spot for this chilled Santa Catarina haunt, kitted out with retro radios, projectors and comfy armchairs. DJs spin house to the preclubbing crowd and the back room stages occasional gigs. There are lots of other great drinking spots nearby – and it's less of a teenage drinking scene than Bairro Alto.

Maria Caxuxa
BAR

(Map p68; Rua da Barroca 6; ⊙5pm-2am) Set in a former bakery, Maria Caxuxa has effortless style – its several rooms are decked out with giant mixers, 1950s armchairs and sofas, marble and *azulejo*-lined walls and incongruous photos. Funk-laden jazz plays overhead, with DJs adding to the eclectic setting.

A Brasileira
CAFE

(Map p68; Rua Garrett 120-122; ⊙8am-2am) All gold swirls and cherubs, this art-deco cafe has been a Lisbon institution since 1905. Sure, it's touristy, but the terrace is brilliant for watching street entertainers beside the bronze statue of poet Fernando Pessoa. Order a *bica,* which takes its name from A Brasileira's 1905 catchphrase: *beba isto com açúcar* (drink this with sugar).

Wine Lover
WINE BAR

(Map p68; Rua das Gaveas 38; ⊙3pm-midnight Tue-Sun) This festive spot with outdoor seating has a good selection of wines by the glass and tapas plates. Skip the underwhelming restaurant that adjoins the space.

Frágil
CLUB

(Map p68; ☑213 469 578; Rua da Atalaia 126; ⊙11pm-4am Thu-Sat) In the beginning there was Frágil, Manuel Reis' first love. This small, loud and sweaty club has been rocking Bairro Alto since the 1980s. DJs spin progressive house and electronica to a mixed gay-straight crowd.

Capela
BAR

(Map p68; Rua da Atalaia 45; ⊙8pm-2am Mon-Sat) Once a Gothic chapel, today Capela's gospel is an experimental line-up of electronica and funky house. Get there early (before midnight) to appreciate the DJs before the crowds descend. Frescos, Renaissance-style nude murals and dusty chandeliers add a boho-chic touch.

CLUBBING TIPS

Superstar DJs heating up dance floors at clubbing temples such as Lux (p109) have put Lisbon firmly on Europe's must-party map. Sleep is overrated in a city where locals don't even think about showing up at a club before 2am.

Though getting in is not as much of a beauty contest as in other capitals, you'll stand a better chance of slipping past the fashion police if you dress smartish and don't rock up on your lonesome. Most clubs charge entry (around €5 to €20, which usually includes a drink or two), and some operate a card-stamping system to ensure you spend a minimum amount. Many close Sunday and Monday.

Majong BAR
(Map p68; Rua da Atalaia 3) Long-time favourite Majong oozes shabby chic with cabbage-shape lights, deep-red walls and school chairs. Mojitos flow as DJs spin minimalist techno, rock and reggae.

Portas Largas BAR
(Map p68; ☑ 218 466 379; Rua da Atalaia 105) Once a *tasca*, this Bairro Alto linchpin retains original fittings including black-and-white tiles, columns and porticos. It throws open *portas largas* (wide doors) to a mishmash of gays, straights and not-sures, who spill onto the cobbles with zingy *caipirinhas*. Live bands most weekends.

Old Pharmacy WINE BAR
(Map p68; Rua Diario de Noticias 83; ⊘ 5.30pm-midnight) True to name, this dimly lit space was once a pharmacy, its backlit built-in cabinets lined with the diverse wines of Portugal. There are dozens of wines to choose from (and good staff recommendations), plus appetisers, outdoor seating, and a more grown-up vibe than most other Bairro Alto spots. A glass starts at €2.20.

Solar do Vinho do Porto WINE BAR
(Map p68; ☑ 213 475 707; Rua São Pedro de Alcântara 45; ⊘ 11am-midnight Mon-Fri, from 2pm Sat) The glug, glug of a 40-year-old tawny being poured is music to port-lovers' ears. Part of an 18th-century mansion, the low-lit, beamed cavern is ideal for nursing a glass of Portugal's finest.

Club Carib BAR
(Map p68; Rua da Atalaia 78; ⊘ 6pm-2am daily) A dance-loving crowd flocks to Carib, drawn by DJs spinning a dizzying variety of world beats – Afro-Cuban jazz, Brazilian MPB and samba, African funk, salsa, tango and more.

Associação Loucos & Sonhadores BAR
(Map p64; Travessa do Conde de Soure 2; ⊘ 10pm-2am Mon-Sat) Though it's in Bairro Alto, this bohemian drinking den feels secreted away from the heaving masses on nearby streets. Kitschy decor, free (salty) popcorn and eclectic tunes – it's a great place for conversation rather than pounding shots.

Bedroom BAR
(Map p68; Rua do Norte 86) It might be a bedroom, but these beauties aren't sleeping. Join them on the dance floor for electro and hip hop, or recline on the beds in the lounge shimmering with gold wallpaper and chandeliers.

Alfaia Garrafeira WINE BAR
(Map p68; Rua do Diário de Notícias 125; ⊘ 2pm-1am Mon-Fri, from 4pm Sat & Sun) On a quiet stretch of Bairro Alto, this tiny wine shop and charcuterie serves wines by the glass as well as cheeses and smoked meats. Arrive early to score one of the few wine-cask tables in front.

Café Suave BAR
(Map p68; Rua do Diário de Notícias 6) A laid-back spot that attracts a mix of foreigners and locals, with decent grooves. It's a good place to start off the night.

Artis WINE BAR
(Map p68; Rua Diário de Notícias 95; ⊘ 4.30pm-2am Tue-Sun) Down a few steps from street level, Artis is a warmly lit place with old wood details, a jazzy soundtrack and an excellent selection of wines by the glass or bottle. Nicely turned out *petiscos* (appetisers) add to the appeal, with Galician-style octopus, flambéed Portuguese sausage and mixed cheese platters.

Alface Hall LIVE MUSIC
(Map p68; Rua do Norte 96; ⊘ noon-midnight) With one wall covered in LPs, a pair of barbershop chairs (?) and a tiny stage, there's an old-time feel to this jazz and blues bar in Bairro Alto. Free concerts happen nightly at 9pm: blues from Monday to Wednesday, jazz on Thursday to Sunday.

Príncipe Real, Santos & Estrela

Just north of Bairro Alto, Príncipe Real is the epicentre of Lisbon's gay scene (see boxed text, p111) and home to some quirky drinking dens.

Pavilhão Chinês   LOUNGE

(Map p64; Rua Dom Pedro V 89-91; ☺ 6pm-2am daily) Pavilhão Chinês is an old curiosity shop of a bar with oil paintings and model spitfires dangling from the ceiling, and cabinets brimming with glittering Venetian masks and Action Men. Play pool or bag a comfy armchair to nurse a port or beer. Prices are higher than elsewhere, but such classy kitsch doesn't come cheap.

Cinco Lounge   LOUNGE

(Map p76; Rua Ruben António Leitão 17; ☺ 9pm-2am) Take an award-winning London-born mixologist, add a candlelit, gold-kissed setting and give it a funky twist – et voilà – you have Cinco Lounge. Come here to converse and sip legendary cocktails.

Incógnito   CLUB

(Map p76; Rua dos Polais de São Bento 37; ☺ 11pm-4am Thu-Sat) No-sign, pint-sized Incógnito offers an alternative vibe and DJs thrashing out indie rock and electropop. Sweat it out with a fun crowd on the tiny basement dance floor, or breathe more easily in the loft bar upstairs.

Intendente

Casa Independente   BAR

(Largo do Intendente 45; ☺ 11am-midnight Tue-Thu, to 2am Fri & Sat) There's always something going on at this creative space overlooking a sleepy plaza just north of Largo Martim Moniz. You can wander through rooms looking at strange and curious artwork, join the smokers on the plant-filled back patio, or nurse drinks in quiet corners of this rambling old space. Bands play on weekends (you can't miss the photogenic tiger that dominates the stage), and you can also pop by in the day for snacks and coffee.

Alfama, Castelo, Graça & Santa Apolónia

Alfama and Graça are perfect for a relaxed drink with a view.

Lux   CLUB

(www.luxfragil.com; Avenida Infante Dom Henrique, Santo Apolónia; ☺ 10pm-6am Tue-Sat) Lisbon's ice-cool, must-see club, Lux is run by ex-Frágil maestro Marcel Reis and part-owned by John Malkovich. Special but not snooty, Lux hosts big-name DJs spinning electro and house. Grab a spot on the roof terrace to see the sun rise over the Tejo. Style policing is heartwarmingly lax but get here after 4am on a Friday or Saturday and you might have trouble getting in because of the crowds.

Clube Ferroviário   CLUB

(Rua de Santa Apolónia 59; ☺ 4pm-2am Mon-Sat) Above Santa Apolónia train station, this former social club of Lisbon's railworkers has been transformed into an intriguing nightspot with DJs and occasional concerts; the best feature is the roof terrace with Tejo views.

Bar das Imagens   BAR

(Map p72; Calçada Marquês de Tancos 1; ☺ noon-midnight Tue-Sun) With a terrace affording vertigo-inducing views over the city, this tiny bar serves potent Cuba libres and other well-prepared cocktails.

Wine Bar do Castelo   WINE BAR

(Map p72; ☎ 218 879 093; Rua Bartolomeu de Gusmão 13; ☺ noon-10pm) Located near the entrance to the Castelo São Jorge, this laid-back wine bar serves more than 150 Portuguese wines by the glass, along with gourmet smoked meats, cheeses, olives and other tasty accompaniments. Nuno, the multilingual owner, is a welcoming host and a fount of knowledge about all things wine-related.

Graça do Vinho   WINE BAR

(Map p72; Calçada da Graça 10; ☺ 11am-10pm Wed-Mon, til midnight Fri & Sat) A welcome new addition to Graça, this former pharmacy serves up a refreshing variety of wines by the glass (from €3) or bottle (from €7), which go nicely with cheeses, sardines, smoked meats and other appetisers. It's a short stroll downhill from the Miradouro da Graça.

Miradouro da Graça   KIOSK

(Map p72; ☺ 10am-8pm) There are far reaching vistas from this terrace, with shaded cafe tables, and coffee, beer, wine and snacks.

Portas do Sol   BAR

(Map p72; Largo das Portas do Sol; ☺ 11am-midnight) Near one of Lisbon's iconic viewpoints, this spacious sun-drenched terrace has a mix of sofas and white patio furniture on which to sip cocktails while taking in magnificent river views. DJs bring animation to the darkly lit industrial interior on weekends.

Cais do Sodré & Santos

For years Cais do Sodré was the haunt of whisky-slugging sailors craving after-dark sleaze. Then, in late 2011, the district went from seedy to stylish. Rua Nova do Carvalho was painted pink and the call girls were sent packing, but the edginess and decadence on which Lisbon thrives remains. Now party central, its boho bars, live-music venues and burlesque clubs are perfect for a late-night bar crawl.

Music Box CLUB
(Map p68; www.musicboxlisboa.com; Rua Nova do Carvalho 24; ⊙11pm-6am Mon-Sat) Under the brick arches on Rua Nova do Carvalho lies one of Lisbon's hottest clubs. The pulsating Music Box hosts loud and sweaty club nights with music shifting from electro to rock, plus gigs by up-and-coming bands.

Meninos do Rio OUTDOOR BAR
(Map p76; Rua da Cintura do Porto de Lisboa, Armação 255, Santos; ⊙noon-2am) Perched on the river's edge, Meninos do Rio has palm trees, wooden decks, reggae-playing DJs and tropical cocktails, giving it a vibe that's more Caribbean than Iberian. It's a great spot at sunset.

Discoteca Jamaica CLUB
(Map p68; Rua Nova do Carvalho; ⊙11pm-4am) Gay and straight, black and white, young and old – everyone has a soft spot for this offbeat club. It gets going around 2am at weekends with DJs pumping out reggae, hip hop and retro.

O'Gílíns PUB
(Map p68; Rua dos Remolares 10; ⊙noon-2am daily) To be sure the best craic in Lisbon, O'Gílíns serves Guinness, big-screen sports and live music some nights.

Hennessy's PUB
(Map p68; Rua Cais do Sodré 32-38; ⊙noon-2am daily) A relaxed Irish pub with banter, occasional live music and Kilkenny on tap.

Lounge LIVE MUSIC
(Map p76; www.loungelisboa.com.pt; Rua da Moeda 1; ⊙10pm-4am Tue-Sun) Little miss popular on the Cais do Sodré circuit, this laid-back indie club is jam-packed and pumping most

nights. DJs, live acts and rock gigs are first-rate.

Doca de Alcântara & Doca de Santo Amaro

The dockside duo of Doca de Alcântara and Doca de Santo Amaro harbour wall-to-wall bars with a preclubbing vibe. Many occupy revamped warehouses, with terraces facing the river and the lit-up Ponte 25 de Abril. Most people taxi here, but you can take the train from Cais do Sodré to Alcântara Mar or catch tram 15 from Praça da Figueira.

Op Art Café CAFE, BAR
(Map p78; Doca de Santo Amaro; ⊙1pm-2am Sun-Thu, to 6am Fri & Sat) Located on the water's edge this slightly hidden glass-and-wood cafe attracts a more laid-back bunch than other Docas bars. On Saturday nights the DJs spin house and lounge until dawn.

Belém Bar Café LOUNGE
(Av Brasília, Pavilhão Poente; ⊙midnight-6am Fri & Sat) The self-consciously cool BBC attracts a well-moneyed crowd to its glass-walled lounge bar and terrace with views of Ponte 25 de Abril. DJs fill the dance floor with hip hop and electronica on weekend nights. There's a pricey restaurant attached.

☆ Entertainment

Lisbon entertains with high culture, experimental art and everything in between. One minute it's sumptuous strings and street theatre in Chiado, the next it's the melancholic soul of fado in Alfama's atmospheric lanes.

For event listings during your stay, grab a copy of the free monthly *Follow Me Lisboa* from tourist offices. If you speak Portuguese, click onto **Time Out Lisboa** (http://timeout. sapo.pt), **Guia da Noite** (www.guiadanoite.com) and **Agenda Cultural Lisboa** (www.lisboacul tural.pt) for info on performances and screenings; cinema listings can also be found in the daily *Diário de Notícias*. Tickets are available in a number of outlets: **ABEP** (Praça dos Restauradores), Fnac (p115) and **Ticket Line** (✆210 036 300; www.ticketline.sapo.pt).

Fado

Infused by Moorish song and the ditties of homesick sailors, bluesy, bittersweet fado encapsulates the Lisbon psyche like nothing else. Ask 10 *lisboêtas* to explain it and each will give a different version. This is because

GAY & LESBIAN LISBON

The gay and lesbian community had much to celebrate in 2010, with the passing of a bill that legalised gay marriage. The big events worth looking out for are **Lisbon Pride** (www.portugalpride.org) in June, and the **Festival de Cinema Gay e Lésbico** (www.queerlisboa.pt) in late September.

The Scene

From camp to cruisy, Praça do Príncipe Real, just north of Bairro Alto, is king of Lisbon's gay and lesbian scene. Most nightclubs, especially Lux (p109), draw a mixed gay-straight crowd. It's worth planning a trip around big events like the **Conga Club Party** (www.facebook.com/congaclubparty), held one Saturday a month at different locations. For more listings, check out *Time Out* (http://timeout.sapo.pt), with a Gay section updated weekly.

Bar 106 (Map p76; ☑ 213 427 373; www.bar106.com; Rua de São Marçal 106; ⊗ 9pm-2am) Young and fun with an upbeat, preclubbing vibe and crazy events such as Sunday's message party.

Clube da Esquina (Map p68; ☑ 213 427 149; Rua da Barroca 30; ⊗ 9.30pm-2am Mon-Sat; underground rail Baixa-Chiado) DJs playing hip hop and house to a beautiful and fashionable crowd.

Construction (Map p76; www.constructionlisbon.com; Rua Cecílio de Sousa 84; admission €6; ⊗ midnight-6am Fri & Sat) The top club of the moment has a somewhat industrial design, pumping house music and a dark room.

Finalmente (Map p76; ☑ 213 479 923; www.finalmenteclub.com; Rua da Palmeira 38; admission €6; ⊗ midnight-5am) This popular club has a tiny dance floor, nightly drag shows and wall-to-wall crowds.

Purex (Map p68; Rua das Salgadeiras 28; ⊗ 10pm-2am Fri & Sat) One for the girls, this unsigned Bairro Alto spot draws a lesbian and mixed crowd, with DJ nights and a small dance floor.

Sétimo Céu (Map p68; Travessa da Espera 54; ⊗ 10pm-2am Mon-Sat) A mainstay of the Bairro Alto scene, this old-school bar attracts a young and vibrant crowd. Excellent *caipirinhas*.

Trumps (Map p76; www.trumps.pt; Rua da Imprensa Nacional 104b; admission €10; ⊗ midnight-6am Fri & Sat) Lisbon's hottest gay club with cruisy corners, a sizeable dance floor and events from live music to drag.

fado is deeply personal and explanations hinge on the mood of the moment. Recurring themes are love, destiny, death and the omnipresent *saudade* or 'nostalgic longing'; a kind of musical soap opera.

Though a *fadista* is traditionally accompanied by a classical and 12-string Portuguese guitar, many new-generation stars such as Mariza, Ana Moura and Joana Amendoeira are putting their own spin on the genre, giving it a twist of Cuban *son* or a dash of Argentine tango.

At Bairro Alto's touristy, folksy performances, you'll only be skating the surface. For authentic fado, go to where it was born – Alfama. While wandering the narrow lanes by night you'll be serenaded by mournful ballads.

There's usually a minimum cover of €15 to €25 and, as food is often mediocre, it's worth asking if you can just order a bottle of wine. Book ahead at weekends. If you prefer a spontaneous approach, seek out *fado vadio* where anyone can – and does – have a warble.

A Baîuca

FADO

(Map p72; ☑ 218 867 284; abaiuca@sapo.pt; Rua de São Miguel 20; ⊗ dinner Thu-Mon) On a good night, walking into A Baîuca is like gate-crashing a family party. It's a special place with *fado vadio*, where locals take a turn and spectators hiss if anyone dares to chat during the singing. The food stops around 10pm but the fado goes on until midnight. Reserve ahead.

FACTORY OF THE ARTS

Set in a converted 19th-century industrial complex, **LX Factory** (Map p78; www.lxfactory.com; Rua Rodrigues de Faria 103, Alcântara) is Lisbon's new hub of creativity. In 2007 some 23,000 sq m of abandoned warehouses were transformed into art studios, galleries, and printing and design companies. Creative restaurants, bars and shops have added to the energy, and today LX Factory is a great spot to check out an alternative side of Lisbon. It's liveliest on weekend nights, though it's also worth stopping by the open-air market (vintage clothes, crafts) held on Sundays from 11am to 7pm. Get there on tram 15 or 18.

Other highlights include the following:

Kiss the Cook (Map p78; www.kissthecook.pt) Offers cooking classes (the chef speaks English).

LX Massagens (Map p78; www.lxmassagens.com A very peaceful setting for a relaxing massage.

Kare Design (Map p78; www.kare-design.com) An imaginative home-design store.

Ler Devagar (Map p78; www.lerdevagar.com) Great bookshop and cosy cafe. Don't miss the wild exhibits on upper floors.

1300 Taberna (Map p78; ☑ 213 649 170; www.1300taberna.com; five-course menu €30; ⊘lunch & dinner Tue-Sat) Excellent restaurant featuring creative takes on Portuguese fare.

Funky (Map p78; ⊘ 4pm-4am Tue-Sat) Atmospheric bar with DJs spinning vintage grooves, and occasional live concerts.

Faktory (Map p78; ⊘11pm-5am Fri & Sat) Two-floor club with lounge space (couches beneath chandeliers and tall ceilings) and a dance floor.

Clube de Fado   FADO
(Map p72; ☑ 218 852 704; www.clube-de-fado.com; Rua de São João da Praça; admission €15; ⊘9pm-2.30am Mon-Sat) Clube de Fado hosts the cream of the fado crop in vaulted, dimly lit surrounds. Big-name *fadistas* performing here include Joana Amendoeira and Miguel Capucho, alongside celebrated guitarists such as José Fontes Rocha. The food is less outstanding, so come for drinks and perhaps appetisers.

Mesa de Frades   FADO
(Map p72; ☑ 917 029 436; www.mesadefrades.com; Rua dos Remédios 139a; admission from €15; ⊘dinner Wed-Mon) A magical place to hear fado, tiny Mesa de Frades used to be a chapel. It's tiled with exquisite *azulejos* and has just a handful of tables. The show begins around 11pm. Skip the food (which is hit-or-miss) and stick to drinks.

Parreirinha de Alfama   FADO
(Map p72; ☑ 218 868 209; Beco do Espírito Santo 1; minimum €15; ⊘8pm-2am) Owned by fado legend Argentina Santos, this place offers good food and ambience; it attracts an audience that often falls hard for the top-quality *fadistas*. Book by 4pm.

Senhor Vinho   FADO
(Map p76; ☑ 213 972 681; Rua do Meio á Lapa; minimum €15; ⊘8pm-2am) Fado star Maria da Fé owns this small place, welcoming first-rate *fadistas*. Even the legendary Mariza has performed here.

Bela   FADO
(Map p72; Rua dos Remédios 190; ⊘8pm-2am) This spot features live fado on Wednesdays and Sundays, and eclectic cultural fare (poetry readings, jazz nights) on other nights. Unlike most fado houses, you won't have to buy a pricey meal as it's an appetisers-and-drinks kind of place.

Tasca do Jaime   FADO
(Rua da Graça 91; ⊘noon-midnight) This low-key restaurant in Graça hosts authentic, sing-for-your-dinner fado on weekends from about 4pm to 8pm. Decorated with *azulejos* and photos of prominent *fadistas*, it's a tiny space, so arrive early if you want to score a table.

Adega dos Fadistas   FADO RESTAURANT
(Map p72; ☑211 510 368; Rua dos Remedios; ☺8pm-2am Thu-Tue) One of the top new fado houses in the Alfama, the Adega dos Fadistas serves up first-rate fado in a medieval-like stone-walled dining room. Mains cost around €17, and the added music charge is €10. Shows start at 9pm most nights.

Fado in Chiado   CONCERTS
(Map p68; ☑213 430 184; Espaço Chiado, Rua da Miséricordia 14; admission €16; ☺7pm Mon-Sat) Inside a small theatre, the 50-minute nightly shows feature high-quality fado – a male and a female singer and two guitarists – and it is held early so you can grab dinner afterwards.

Alternative Culture
Lisbon may flirt with high culture and embrace fado, but it also has an ongoing relationship with the underdog. Individuality trumps conformity and alternative culture rules in these offbeat cultural centres.

Bacalhoeiro   BAR
(Map p64; ☑218 864 891; http://bacalhoeiro.blog spot.com; 2nd fl, Rua dos Bacalhoeiros 125, Baixa; ☏) Nonconformist, laid-back Bacalhoeiro shelters a cosy bar and hosts everything from jazz jams (on Sundays) to rock, blues and funk, plus DJ nights featuring an even wider range of sounds.

Chapitô   THEATRE
(Map p72; ☑218 855 550; www.chapito.org; Costa do Castelo 1-7; ☺noon-2am) Chapitô offers physical theatre performances, with a circus school attached. There's a jazz cafe downstairs with dentist chair decor and live music Thursday to Saturday. Come for the spectacular views and excellent restaurant.

Culturgest   ECLECTIC
(☑217 905 155; www.culturgest.pt; Rua do Arco do Cego; admission €5-12) Culturgest's experimental and occasionally provocative line-up encompasses exhibitions, dance, poetry, music and theatre.

Cinemas
For blockbusters try the multiplexes in the Complexo das Amoreiras (p116), Centro Comercial Colombo (p116) and **Centro Vasco da Gama** (www.centrovascodagama.pt) malls. The **São Jorge** (Map p80; Avenida da Liberdade 175) and, just around the corner, **Cinemateca Portuguesa** (Map p80; www. cinemateca.pt; Rua Barata Salgueiro 39) screen offbeat, art-house, world and old films.

For details of screen times and venues, visit www.7arte.net.

Music, Theatre & Dance
Teatro Nacional de Dona Maria II   THEATRE
(Map p64; ☑213 250 800; www.teatro-dmaria.pt; Praça Dom Pedro IV) Rossio's graceful neoclassical theatre has a somewhat hit-and-miss schedule due to underfunding. Guided tours on Mondays at 11.30am (€6).

Teatro Nacional de São Carlos   OPERA, BALLET
(Map p68; ☑213 253 045; www.saocarlos.pt; Rua Serpa Pinto 9) Worth visiting just to see the sublime gold-and-red interior, this theatre has opera, ballet and theatre seasons. The summertime Festival ao Largo (p86) features free outdoor concerts on the plaza facing the theatre.

Teatro Municipal de São Luiz   OPERA, BALLET
(Map p68; ☑213 257 640; www.teatrosaoluiz.pt; Rua António Maria Cardosa 38) This venue stages opera, ballet and theatre.

Teatro Taborda   THEATRE
(Map p72; ☑218 854 190; www.teatrodagaragem. com; Costa do Castelo 75; @) This cultural centre shows contemporary dance, theatre and world music. It also has spectacular views from its cafe-restaurant.

Teatro da Trindade   THEATRE
(Map p68; ☑213 420 000; http://teatrotrindade. inatel.pt; Largo da Trindade 7) This early-20th-century gem stages an assortment of national and foreign productions.

Centro Cultural de Belém   THEATRE
(CCB; Map p82; ☑213 612 627; www.ccb.pt; Praça do Império) CCB presents a diverse program spanning experimental jazz, contemporary ballet, boundary-crossing plays and performances by the Portuguese Chamber Orchestra.

Coliseu dos Recreios   CONCERT HALL
(Map p64; ☑213 240 580; www.coliseulisboa.com; Rua das Portas de Santo Antão 96) This concert hall stages big-name concerts, theatre, dance and opera. The recent roll-call has included David Byrne, Gilberto Gil and the Foals.

Fundação Calouste Gulbenkian   CLASSICAL MUSIC
(Map p80; ☑217 823 700; www.musica.gulben kian.pt; Av de Berna) Home to the Gulbenkian Orchestra, this classical-music heavyweight stages first-rate concerts and ballets.

Hot Clube de Portugal · JAZZ
(Map p80; ☑213 619 740; www.hcp.pt; Praça da Alegria 48) As hot as its name suggests, this small, poster-plastered cellar has staged top-drawer jazz acts since the 1940s.

Onda Jazz Bar · JAZZ
(Map p72; www.ondajazz.com; Arco de Jesus 7, Alfama; ☉8pm-2am Tue-Sat) This vaulted cellar features a menu of mainstream jazz, plus more-eclectic beats of bands hailing from Brazil and Africa. Don't miss Wednesday's free jam session (10.30pm).

Zé dos Bois · LIVE MUSIC
(Map p68; ☑213 430 205; www.zedosbois.org; Rua da Barroca 59, Bairro Alto; ☉7pm-2am) Focusing on tomorrow's performing arts and music trends, Zé dos Bois is an experimental venue with a graffitied courtyard, and an eclectic line-up of theatre, film, visual arts and live music. The boho haunt has welcomed bands such as Black Dice and Animal Collective to its stage.

Football
Lisboêtas are mad about football. It's hardly surprising given that the capital is home to two of Portugal's 'big three' clubs – SL Benfica and Sporting Clube de Portugal.

The season runs from September to mid-June, with most league matches on Sunday; check details in the papers (especially *Bola,* the daily football paper) or ask at the tourist office. Tickets cost about €23 to €55 at the stadium on match day or, for higher prices, at the ABEP ticket agency (p110).

Estádio da Luz · STADIUM
(☑217 219 555; www.slbenfica.pt) SL Benfica plays at this 65,000-seat stadium in the northwestern Benfica district. The nearest metro station is Colégio Militar-Luz. The 2014 Champions League Final is scheduled to take place here.

Estádio José de Alvalade · STADIUM
(Rua Prof Fernando da Fonseca) Just north of the university, this state-of-the-art 54,000-seat stadium hosts Sporting Clube's matches. Take the metro to Campo Grande.

🛍 Shopping

Le freak, c'est retro *chic* in grid-like Bairro Alto, attracting vinyl lovers and vintage devotees to its cluster of late-opening boutiques. Alfama, Baixa and Rossio have frozen-in-time stores dealing exclusively in buttons and kid gloves, tawny port and tinned fish. Elegant Chiado is the go-to place for high-street and couture shopping to the backbeat of buskers.

🛍 Baixa & Rossio

Conserveira de Lisboa · FOOD
(Map p64; ☑218 864 009; Rua dos Bacalhoeiros 34; ☉9am-7pm Mon-Sat) In Rua dos Bacalhoeiros (cod-vessel street) lies a store dedicated wholly to tinned fish, and whose walls are clad in a mosaic of retro wrappings. An elderly lady and her son tot up on a monstrous old till and wrap purchases in brown paper.

Discoteca Amália · MUSIC
(Map p64; ☑213 421 485; Rua de Áurea 272; ☉10am-7pm Mon-Sat) This shrine to *fadista* Amália Rodrigues stocks an excellent range of fado and classical CDs.

Papabubble · FOOD
(Map p64; Rua da Conçeicão 117; ☉10am-7pm Mon-Sat) Papabubble makes and sells old-fashioned hard candy in a variety of classic and creative flavours (including passion-fruit, kiwi and aniseed). Kids might enjoy seeing the candymakers in action behind the counter.

CATWALK QUEENS

Make way for Lisbon's trio of catwalk queens, revamping wardrobes with their majestic collections:

Ana Salazar (Map p68; ☑213 472 289; Rua do Carmo 87; ☉10am-7pm Mon-Sat) Ana's sassy, feminine styles reveal a passion for stretchy fabrics, bold prints and earthy hues. Her flagship boutique, with a striking arched glass ceiling, is in the heart of Chiado.

Fátima Lopes (Map p68; ☑213 240 546; www.fatima-lopes.com; Rua da Atalaia 36) Divas love Fátima's immaculate collection of figure-hugging, Latin-inspired threads – from slinky suits to itsy-glitzy prom dresses and hot-pink ball gowns.

Lena Aires (Map p68; ☑213 461 815; www.lena-aires.com; Rua da Atalaia 96) Lena's funky Bairro Alto boutique brims with citrus-bright knits and fresh-faced fashion.

Silva & Feijó FOOD
(Map p64; Rua dos Bacalhoeiros 117; ☺10am-1pm & 2.30-7pm Mon-Sat) Planning a picnic? Stop by this beamed store for sheep's cheese from the Seia mountains, sardine pâté, rye bread, *salsichas* (sausages) and other Portuguese goodies.

Amatudo CRAFT
(Map p64; Rua da Madalena 76; ☺10.30am-7.30pm Mon-Sat) This is a one-stop shop for nonkitschy Portuguese gifts like Tricana sardines, beautifully packaged Confiança soaps, 3D Belém or tram puzzles, and humorous takes on the Barcelos cockerel.

Santos Oficios HANDICRAFTS
(Map p64; Rua da Madalena 87; ☺10am-8pm Mon-Sat) If you have always fancied a hand-embroidered fado shawl, check out this brick-vaulted store. Santos is a must-shop for Portuguese folk art including Madeira lace, blingy Christmas decorations and glazed earthenware.

Outra Face da Lua VINTAGE
(Map p64; Rua da Assunção 22; ☺10am-7.30pm Mon-Sat; 🐾) Vintage divas make for this retro boutique in Baixa, crammed with puff ball dresses, lurex skirts and wildly patterned '70s shirts. Jazz and electronica play overhead. Revive over salads, sandwiches, cocktails and cosmic iced tea at the in-store cafe.

Napoleão WINE, PORT
(Map p64; ☑218 861 108; Rua dos Fanqueiros 70; ☺9.30am-8pm Mon-Fri, noon-7pm Sat) This friendly, English-speaking cellar is the go-to place for Portuguese wines and ports, with hundreds of bottles to choose from. Ships worldwide.

Azevedo Rua CLOTHING
(Map p64; ☑213 427 511; Praça Dom Pedro IV 73; ☺10am-7pm Mon-Fri, 10am-noon Sat) Lisbon's maddest hatters have been covering bald spots since 1886. Expect old-school service and wood-panelled cabinets full of flat caps and Ascot-worthy headwear.

Manuel Tavares FOOD, WINE
(Map p64; ☑213 424 209; Rua da Betesga 1A; ☺10am-7pm Mon-Sat) For a lingering taste of Lisbon, nip into this wood-fronted store, which has been tempting locals since 1860 with *pata negra* (cured ham), pungent cheeses, *ginjinha,* port and other Portuguese treats.

🅰 Chiado

Vida Portuguesa GIFTS
(Map p68; Rua Anchieta 11; ☺10am-8pm Mon-Sat, from 11am Sun) A flashback to the late 19th century with its high ceilings and polished cabinets, this store lures nostalgics with all-Portuguese products from retro-wrapped Tricona sardines to lime-oil soap and Bordallo Pinheiro porcelain swallows.

Fábrica Sant'Ana HANDICRAFTS
(Map p68; Rua do Alecrim 95; ☺9.30am-7pm Mon-Fri, 10am-2pm Sat) Hand-making and painting *azulejos* since 1741, this is the place to get some eye-catching porcelain tiles for your home.

Story Tailors CLOTHING
(Map p68; ☑213 432 306; Calçada do Ferragial 8; ☺noon-8pm Tue-Sat) Luís Sanchez and João Branco bewitch with floaty, feminine polka-dot, gingham and ruffle designs at their enchanted forest of fashion, bedecked with a hanging swing, chandeliers and gnarled wood.

Livraria Bertrand BOOKS
(Map p68; ☑213 421 941; Rua Garrett 73; ☺9am-10pm Mon-Sat, 11am-8pm Sun) Amid 18th-century charm, Bertrand has excellent selections, including titles in English, French and Spanish.

Fnac BOOKS, MUSIC
(Map p68; ☑213 221 800; www.fnac.pt; Armazéns do Chiado, Rua do Carmo 3; ☺10am-10pm) One of the city's biggest book and music stores.

Armazéns do Chiado MALL
(Map p68; Rua do Carmo 2; ☺10am-11pm) Fashion, books, music and cosmetics in the heart of Chiado. Inexpensive eating (with views) on the upper level.

Trem Azul MUSIC
(Map p68; www.tremazul.com; Rua do Alecrim 21A; ☺10am-7.30pm Mon-Fri, from 2pm Sat) Trem Azul stocks an excellent selection of jazz and world beats on both vinyl and CD. There's a small stage in the back, where small concerts and release parties are sometimes held.

Luvaria Ulisses CLOTHING
(Map p68; ☑213 420 295; Rua do Carmo 87A; ☺10am-7pm Mon-Sat) So tiny it's almost an optical illusion, this magical art-deco store is chock-full of soft handmade leather gloves in kaleidoscope shades.

Louie Louie
MUSIC

(Map p68; ☑ 213 472 232; Rua Nova da Trindade 8; ⊗ 11am-7.30pm Mon-Sat) Clued-up DJs head for this funky music store stocking second-hand vinyl and the latest house, dance and electronica grooves.

🏠 Bairro Alto & Príncipe Real

Vellas Loreto
HOMEWARES

(Map p68; ☑ 213 425 387; Rua do Loreto 53; ⊗ 9am-7pm Mon-Fri, to 1pm Sat) *Lisboêtas* have been waxing lyrical about this specialist candle-maker since 1789. The wood-panelled, talc-scented store sells myriad candles, from cherubs and peppers to Christmas trees and water lilies.

Loja Real
DESIGN

(Map p76; Praça do Príncipe Real 20; ⊗ 10.30am-8pm Mon-Sat) A showcase for largely Portuguese designers, Loja Real features a wide assortment of unique, high-quality products that run the gamut from home decor (cushions, teapots, vases), fashion (clothing, jewellery) and artwork to items for children (clothing, books and toys). The emphasis is 'slow retail': nothing mass-produced or made with plastics or cheap materials.

There's also a food component on Thursday and Friday nights (from 6.30pm to 10.30pm), and you can stop in for an aperitif and *stuzzichini* (tapas-like finger food) prepared by the Italian chef.

SHOPPING MALLS
....

When you need a break from the heat, step into air-conditioned splendour. All of the following malls have cinemas, good food courts and, of course, shops.

Centro Comercial Colombo (www. colombo.pt; Av Lusíada; ⊗ 9am-midnight)

Complexo das Amoreiras (Map p80; ☑ 213 810 200; www.amoreiras.com; Av Duarte Pacheco; ⊗ 10am-11pm)

El Corte Inglês (Map p80; www. elcorteingles.pt; Av António Augusto de Aguiar 31; ⊗ 10am-10pm Mon-Sat, to 8pm Sun)

Dolce Vita (Map p80; www.dolcevita.pt; Ave Cruzeiro Seixas & Radial da Pontinha, Amadora; ⊗ 10am-10pm Mon-Sat, to 8pm Sun)

Poise & Matéria Prima
ACCESSORIES, MUSIC

(Map p68; Rua da Rosa 197; ⊗ 2-8pm Mon-Sat) This store has two sides. The first is Poise, a boutique that sells beautifully crafted handbags made from 100% Portuguese materials, and made in the atelier onsite. The adjoining space (Matéria Prima) is devoted to music – cutting-edge electronica, indie rock and esoteric sounds.

Cork & Company
GIFTS

(Map p68; Rua das Salgadeiras 10; ⊗ noon-9pm Mon-Thu, 11am-midnight Fri & Sat) At this elegantly designed shop in the lower Bairro Alto, you'll find cork put to surprisingly imaginative uses, with well-made cork hand-bags, pens, wallets, journals, candle holders, hats, scarves, place mats, umbrellas and even iPhone covers.

A Carioca
COFFEE, TEA

(Map p68; ☑ 213 420 377; Rua da Misericórdia 9; ⊗ 9am-7pm Mon-Fri, to 1pm Sat) Little has changed since this old-world store opened in 1924: brass fittings still gleam, the coffee roaster is still in action and home blends, sugared almonds and toffees are still lovingly wrapped in green paper.

Arte Assinada
DESIGN

(Map p68; Largo Trindade Coelho 13; ⊗ 10am-8pm Mon-Sat) In an industrial-chic space across from the São Roque church, this high-concept store has geometric jewellery, elegant vases and artful objects for the home. You might not walk out with anything, but it's a fun place to browse.

Espaço B
FASHION

(Map p76; Rua Dom Pedro V 120; ⊗ 11am-8pm Mon-Sat) This high-end fashion boutique offers well-tailored men's and women's fashions by the likes of Racines du Ciel, Fred Perry and Comme des Garçons. Clothing aside, Espaço B stocks scarves (for men and women), artfully designed jewellery, designer sneakers and other collectibles.

El Dorado
VINTAGE

(Map p68; ☑ 213 423 935; Rua do Norte 23) A gramophone plays vinyl classics as divas bag vintage styles from psychedelic prints to 6in platforms and pencil skirts at this Bairro Alto hipster. There's also a great range of clubwear.

Sneakers Delight
SHOES

(Map p68; ☑ 213 479 976; Rua do Norte 30; ⊗ 1-10pm Mon-Sat) You'll find limited edition

Adidas trainers at this groovy store, with DJs spinning on weekends.

Alfama, Castelo & Graça

Feira da Ladra
MARKET
(Map p72; Campo de Santa Clara; ⊙7am-5pm Tue & Sat) Browse for back-of-the-lorry treasures at this massive flea market. You'll find old records, coins, baggy pants, dog-eared poetry books and other attic junk. Haggle hard and watch your wallet – it isn't called 'thieves market' for nothing.

Arte da Terra
GIFTS
(Map p72; Rua Augusto Rosa 40; ⊙11am-8pm) In the stables of a centuries-old bishop's palace, Arte da Terra brims with authentic Portuguese crafts including Castello Branco embroideries, nativity figurines, handpainted *azulejos*, fado CDs and quality goods (umbrellas, aprons, writing journals) made from cork.

Loja Portugueza
GIFTS
(Rua do Graça 107; ⊙9am-7pm) This tiny store stocks tins of olive oil with vintage designs, retro coffee packs, grocery bags with colourful designs and other objects that make fine gifts.

Fabula Urbis
BOOKS
(Map p72; Rua Augusto Rosa 27; ⊙10am-2pm & 3-8pm) A great little bookshop that celebrates works about Portugal, both by home-grown and expat authors. All the best works by Lobo Antunes, Saramago, Pessoa, Richard Zimler and Robert C Wilson are here and available in English, French, Spanish and, of course, Portuguese.

Garbags
ACCESSORIES
(Map p72; www.garbags.eu; Rua do Salvador 56; ⊙11am-7pm) ✐ This ecofriendly outfit sells messenger bags, iPhone cases, wallets, handbags and zipper pouches cleverly made from former coffee sacks, potato chip bags, juice containers and other recycled materials. The gear seems durable (and waterproof) and the look is somewhat sleek, if you don't mind the corporate logos.

Cais do Sodré

Mercado da Ribeira
MARKET
(Map p68; ☑210 312 600; Av 24 de Julho; ⊙6am-2pm Mon-Sat) Lisbon's premier food market

buzzes with locals shopping for fruit and vegetables, crusty bread and silvery sardines fresh from the Atlantic.

Rato, Marquês de Pombal & Saldanha

Fashion Clinic
FASHION
(Map p80; www.fashionclinic.pt; Ave da Liberdade 192; ⊙10am-7.30pm Mon-Sat) Everything designer divas crave: ready-to-wear DKNY, Gucci and Prada, Jimmy Choo shoes, perfumes, accessories, fashion books and more.

Carbono
MUSIC
(Map p80; Rua do Telhal 6B; ⊙11am-7pm Mon-Sat) The staff may be grumpy, but it's hard not to like Carbono, with its impressive selection of new and secondhand vinyl and CDs. World music – West African boogaloo, Brazilian tropicalia – is especially well represented.

CE Livrarias
BOOKS
(Map p80; Rua Duque de Palmela 4; ⊙9am-8pm Mon-Fri, 10am-2pm Sat) Sizeable collection of literature in Portuguese, English, French and German, plus in-store readings and concerts.

Parque das Nações

Centro Vasco da Gama
MALL
(www.centrovascodagama.pt; Parque das Nações; ⊙8am-10pm Mon-Fri, 9am-9pm Sat & Sun) Glass-roofed mall sheltering high-street stores, cinema and a food court – upper-level restaurants have outdoor seating with a view.

ℹ Information

DANGERS & ANNOYANCES
Lisbon is generally a safe city with a low crime rate, though you'll want to mind your wallet on tram 28 – a major hot spot for pickpockets – and at other tourist hubs such as Rua Augusta. You're also certain to be offered hash and sunglasses from swarthy characters in Baixa and in Bairro Alto; a firm but polite 'no' keeps hawkers at bay. Main streets are relatively safe to walk along at night, but be wary around metro stations such as Anjos, Martim Moniz and Intendente, where there have been muggings. Take care in the dark alleys of Alfama and Graça.

EMERGENCY
Police, Fire & Ambulance (☑112)
Police Station (☑217 654 242; Rua Capelo 13)
Tourist Police (☑213 421 634; Palácio Foz, Praça dos Restauradores; ⊙24hr)

ⓘ LISBOA CARD

If you're planning on doing a lot of sightseeing, the **Lisboa discount card** represents excellent value. It offers unlimited use of public transport (including trains to Sintra and Cascais), entry to all key museums and attractions, and up to 50% discount on tours, cruises and other admission charges. It's available at **Ask Me Lisboa** (Map p64; Praça do Comércio; ◷9am-8pm) tourist offices, including the one at the airport. The 24-/48-/72-hour versions cost €19/32/39. You validate the card when you want to start it.

INTERNET ACCESS

Many cafes and some restaurants in Lisbon offer free wireless access. If you're travelling without a smartphone or laptop, a few internet cafes provide access (with prices around €2 to €4 per hour).

Skynet (Calçada Garcia 4; per hr €0.50; ◷9.30am-9pm) Only a few computers, but it's probably the cheapest internet cafe in town.

Cyber Bica (Rua dos Duques de Bragança; ◷11am-midnight Mon-Fri) Groovy cafe-bar.

Portugal Telecom (Praça Dom Pedro IV 68; ◷9am-10pm) Has rows of booths.

Web Café (Rua do Diário de Notícias 126; ◷7pm-2am) Internet access.

MEDIA

In addition to Portuguese dailies such as *Diario de Noticias* and the tabloid best-seller *Correio da Manhã*, the *Portugal News* (http://theportugalnews.com) is an English-language daily.

MEDICAL SERVICES

British Hospital (☎217 213 410; Rua Tomás da Fonseca; ◷8am-midnight) English-speaking staff and English-speaking doctors.

Clínica Médica Internacional (☎213 513 310; Avenida Sidónio Pais 14) A quick (though not cheap) private clinic with English-speaking doctors.

Farmácia Estácio (Praça Dom Pedro IV 62) A central pharmacy.

MONEY

Multibanco ATMs are widespread throughout the city.

Barclays Bank (☎217 911 100; Av da República 50)

Cota Câmbios (Praça Dom Pedro IV 41) The best bet for changing cash or travellers cheques is a private exchange bureau like this one.

POST

Main Post Office (Map p64; Praça do Comércio) Has poste restante.

Post Office (Map p64; Praça dos Restauradores) Central post office.

TELEPHONE

Equipped with a phone card, including the Portugal Telecom card, you can make international direct-dial (IDD) phone calls from most pay phones. At Portugal Telecom (p118) booths in post offices you can pay after you've made the call.

TOURIST INFORMATION

Ask Me Lisboa The largest and most helpful tourist office in the city faces Praça Restauradaures inside the Palácio Foz (Map p64; www.askmelisboa.com; Palácio Foz, Praça dos Restauradores; ◷9am-8pm) Staff here dole out maps and information, book accommodation and reserve rental cars. Nearby, the smaller Y Lisboa (Map p64; www.askmelisboa.com; Rua Jardim do Regedor 50; ◷10am-7pm) branch does much the same; there's also left luggage here and charged internet access. Lisboa Welcome Centre (Map p64; www.visitlisboa.com; Praça do Comércio; ◷9am-8pm) is another helpful branch.

Ask me Lisboa also runs several information kiosks, which are handy places for maps and quick information: Airport (Airport; ◷7am-midnight); Belém (Map p82; Largo dos Jernónimos, Belém; ◷10am-1pm & 2-6pm Mon-Sat); and Santa Apolónia (Map p72; Door 47, inside train station, Santa Apolónia; ◷8am-1pm Mon-Sat).

ⓘ Getting There & Away

AIR

Situated around 6km north of the centre, the ultramodern **Aeroporto de Lisboa** (Lisbon Airport; www.ana.pt) operates direct flights to major international hubs including London, New York, Paris and Frankfurt.

BOAT

The **Transtejo ferry line** (www.transtejo.pt) has several riverfront terminals.

Cais do Sodré (Map p64): service to Cacilhas (€1.20, 10 minutes, every 10 minutes all day), Montijo (€2.70, 30 minutes) and Seixal (€2.30, 30 minutes).

Terreiro do Paço (Map p64): service to Barreiro (€2.30, 30 minutes), for rail connections to the Alentejo, Algarve and Setúbal.

Belém (Map p82): service to Trafaria and Porto Brandão (€1.15, every 30 to 60 minutes), about 3.5km and 5km respectively from Costa da Caparica town.

BUS

Both information and tickets for international departures are scarce at weekends, so try to avoid that last-minute Sunday dash out of Portugal.

Sete Rios

Lisbon's long-distance bus terminal is **Sete Rios** (Rua das Laranjeiras), linked to both Jardim Zoológico metro station and Sete Rios train station. The big carriers, **Rede Expressos** (☑707 223 344; www.rede-expressos.pt) and **Eva** (☑707 223 344; www.eva-bus.com), run frequent services to almost every major town. You can buy your ticket up to seven days in advance. Services include the following:

Évora (€12, 1½ hours, 10 to 20 daily)
Coimbra (€14, 2½ hours, 15 to 25 daily)
Porto (€19, 3½ hours, 10 to 20 daily)
Faro (€20, 3½ hours, four to eight daily)

Buses to Sesimbra and Costa da Caparica also leave from here.

Gare do Oriente

The other major terminal is **Gare do Oriente** (near Parque das Nações), concentrating on services to the north and to Spain. On the 1st floor are bus company booths (mostly open from 9am to 5.30pm Monday to Saturday, and to 7pm Friday, closed for lunch; smaller operators only open just before arrival or departure).

The biggest companies operating from here are **Renex** (☑218 956 836; www.renex.pt) and the Spanish operator **Avanza** (☑218 940 250; www.avanzabus.com). Many Renex buses take passengers 20 minutes early at Campo das Cebolas in Alfama, before Gare do Oriente.

Eurolines (☑218 940 968; www.eurolines.com; Loja 203, Gare do Oriente) runs coaches to destinations all over Europe.

Terminal Campo Grande

Regional operators in the north – including **Mafrense** (☑217 582 212; www.mafrense.pt) for Ericeira and Mafra – operate from **Terminal Campo Grande** (☑217 582 212) outside Campo Grande metro station.

CAR & MOTORCYCLE

Motorbikes, ranging from 50cc to 700cc, are available for hire from **LX Rent a Scooter** (☑213 660 161; www.lxrentascooter.pt; Campo das Cebolas 20; ⊙10am-1pm & 2.30-7pm). Prices start at €30 for the day.

The big-name car-hire companies are all on hand, though you can often save by using local agencies; most offer pick-up and delivery service to the Palácio Foz tourist office on Praça dos Restauradores. The tourist offices have loads of car-rental fliers where you can compare prices. Staff will even call and book a vehicle for you.

Autojardim (☑800 200 613; www.auto-jardim.com)
Avis (☑800 201 002; www.avis.com.pt)
Europcar (☑219 407 790; www.europcar.pt)
Hertz (☑808 202 038; www.hertz.com)
Holidays Car (☑217 150 610; www.holidayscar.com)

TRAIN

Lisbon is linked by train to other major cities. Check www.cp.pt for schedules. Express services include the following:

Évora (€12, 1½ hours, three to four daily)
Coimbra (€20, two hours, 10 to 20 daily)
Faro (€21, three hours, three to six daily)
Porto C (€24, three hours, seven to 18 daily)

Lisbon has several major train stations. **Santa Apolónia** is the terminal for trains from northern and central Portugal. It has a helpful **information**

BIKING THE TEJO

With its steep, winding hills and narrow, traffic-filled lanes, Lisbon may not seem like the ideal place to hop on a bicycle. The city, however, is redefining itself with the addition of a biking/jogging path that opened in 2010. Coursing along the Tejo for nearly 7km, the path connects Cais do Sodré with Belém, and has artful touches – including the poetry of Pessoa printed along parts of it. It passes beside a rapidly changing landscape – taking in ageing warehouses that are being converted into open-air cafes, restaurants and nightspots.

A handy place to rent bikes is a short stroll from Cais do Sodré: **Bike Iberia** (Map p68; ☑213 470 347; www.bikeiberia.com; Largo Corpo Santo 5; bike hire per hr/day €4/14; ⊙9.30am-7.30pm). Those looking for a longer ride can bike out to Belém, catch the ferry to Trafaria, and then continue on another new bike path (separate from traffic) that runs for about 6km down to the pretty beach of Costa da Caparica.

You can also hire bikes for short spins along the Tejo out at Parque das Nações, where **Tejo Bike** (www.tejobike.pt; per hr from €5; ⊙10am-8pm) rents out bikes, kids' bikes and go-carts.

desk (☑ 808 208 208; ⏱ 7.30am-9pm Mon-Fri, 8pm-4.30pm Sat & Sun) at door 8.

Gare do Oriente is Lisbon's biggest station. Trains to the Alentejo and the Algarve originate from here. Note that all of Santa Apolónia's services also stop here. Ticket booths are on the 1st floor (platforms are on the 2nd) and car-rental offices, banks and shops are at street level. Left-luggage lockers are on the basement metro level.

If you're headed to the south, rather than going out to Gare do Oriente, you can also board at **Entrecampos** train station, connected to the metro station of the same name. Most, but not all, southbound trains also stop at **Sete Rios**, which is connected to the **Jardim Zoológico** metro station. Either of these stations provides services across the Ponte 25 de Abril to Setúbal, among other destinations.

Cais do Sodré is the terminal for train services to Cascais and Estoril.

Rossio, with its beautiful neo-Manueline facade, offers frequent services to Sintra via Queluz.

❶ Getting Around

TO/FROM THE AIRPORT

➥ The **Aeroporto metro station**, on the red line, opened in 2012, allowing convenient access to downtown. Change at Alameda (green line) to reach Rossio and Baixa.

---

❶ TICKETS & TRANSPORT CARDS

You'll pay more for transport if you buy your ticket on-board rather than purchasing a pre-paid card. On-board one-way prices are €1.80 for buses, €2.85 for trams and €3.60 (return) for funicular rides (one-way tickets not available). Santa Justa, however, costs €5 return.

To save money, purchase a **Viva Viagem card** (€0.50) from metro-station kiosks and add credit (in €5 denominations). Each ride will then deduct €1.40 per trip from the card for all transport, including the metro, except for Santa Justa. The other option is the **day pass**, which costs €6 and allows unlimited travel over a 24-hour period on the entire transport network.

There's also the Lisboa Card (p118), which is good for most tourist sights as well as bus, tram, funicular and metro travel.

➥ The **AeroBus** departs from outside Arrivals (adult/child €3.50/2, 25 to 35 minutes, roughly every 20 minutes from 7am to 11pm). It goes via Marquês de Pombal, Avenida Liberdade, Restauradores, Rossio and Praça do Comércio to Cais do Sodré. The ticket gives free passage on the entire city bus network for the rest of the day.

➥ Expect to pay about €10 for the 15-minute **taxi** ride into central Lisbon, plus €1.60 if your luggage needs to be placed in the boot. Avoid long queues by flagging down a taxi at Departures. Make sure the cabbie switches on the taximeter, and that you pay the listed fare.

CAR & MOTORCYCLE

Lisbon can be quite stressful to drive around, thanks to heavy traffic, maverick drivers and narrow one-way streets and tram lines. There are two ring roads useful for staying out of the centre: the inner Cintura Regional Interna de Lisboa (CRIL) and the outer Cintura Regional Externa de Lisboa (CREL).

Once in the centre, parking is the main issue. Spaces are scarce, parking regulations are complex, pay-and-display machines are often broken and car-park rates can be expensive (up to €25 per day). On Saturday afternoon and Sunday, parking is usually free.

A few good places for free parking: Campo de Santa Clara, near the Alfama, is good every day except Saturdays and Tuesdays, when the Feira da Ladra (p117) takes over the lot. You can also find free parking on Av 24 de Julho, west of Cais do Sodré. Always lock up and don't leave any valuables inside, as theft is a risk.

PUBLIC TRANSPORT
Bus, Tram & Funicular

Companhia Carris de Ferro de Lisboa (Carris; ☑ 213 613 054; www.carris.pt) operates all transport except the metro. Its buses and trams run from about 5am or 6am to about 10pm or 11pm; there are some night bus and tram services.

Pick up a transport map, *Planta dos Transportes Públicos da Carris* (including a map of night-time services) from tourist offices or Carris kiosks, which are dotted around the city. The Carris website has timetables and route details.

Don't leave the city without riding popular **tram 28** from Largo Martim Moniz or **tram 12** from Praça da Figueira through the narrow streets of the Alfama. Go early in the morning or at night to avoid the tourist mobs.

Two other useful lines are **tram 15**, which runs from Praça da Figueira and Praça do Comércio via Alcântara to Belém; and **tram 18** from Praça do Comércio via Alcântara to Ajuda. Tram 15 features space-age articulated trams with on-board machines for buying tickets and passes. Tram stops are marked by a small yellow *paragem*

DON'T MISS

A SURREAL MANSION & GARDENS

Exploring the **Quinta da Regaleira** (Map p124; www.regaleira.pt; Rua Barbosa du Bocage; adult/child €6/3; ◷10am-8pm) is like delving into another world. This neo-Manueline extravaganza was dreamed up by Italian opera-set designer Luigi Manini under the orders of Brazilian coffee tycoon, António Carvalho Monteiro, aka Monteiro dos Milhões (Moneybags Monteiro). Enter the villa to begin the surreal journey, with ferociously carved fireplaces, frescos and Venetian-glass mosaics. Keep an eye out for mythological and Knights Templar symbols.

The playful gardens are fun to explore – footpaths wriggle through the dense foliage to follies, fountains, grottoes, lakes and underground caverns. All routes seem to eventually end at the revolving stone door leading to the initiation well, **Poço Iniciáto**, plunging down some 30m. You walk down the nine-tiered spiral (three by three – three being the magic number) to mysterious hollowed-out underground galleries, lit by fairy lights.

(stop) sign hanging from a lamp post or from the overhead wires.

Metro

The **metro** (www.metrolisboa.pt; 1-/2-zone single €0.85/1.15; ◷6.30am-1am) is useful for short hops, and to reach the Gare do Oriente and nearby Parque das Nações.

Buy tickets from metro ticket machines, which have English-language menus. The Lisboa Card (p118) is also valid.

Entrances are marked by a big red 'M'. Useful signs include *correspondência* (transfer between lines) and *saída* (exit to the street). There is some impressive contemporary art on the metro, including Angelo de Sousa at Baixa-Chiado and Hundertwasser at Oriente.

Watch out for pickpockets in rush-hour crowds.

TAXI

Táxis in Lisbon are reasonably priced and plentiful. If you can't hail one, try the ranks at Rossio and Praça dos Restauradores, near stations and ferry terminals, and at top-end hotels, or call **Rádio Táxis** (☑218 119 000) or **Autocoope** (☑217 932 756).

The fare on the meter should read €2.50 (daytime flag-fall). You will be charged extra for luggage and an additional 20% for journeys between 9pm and 6am. Rip-offs occasionally occur (the airport route is the main culprit). If you think you may have been cheated, get a receipt from the driver, note the registration number and talk to the tourist police.

AROUND LISBON

When the city sizzles in summer, *lisboêtas* don't have to go far to keep their cool – it's all in their backyard. Enchanting beaches lie north and south of the capital. There are also rippling woods brushed with pine and eucalyptus, marshy reserves where bottlenose dolphins splash, hills studded with fanciful palaces, and limestone cliffs where dinosaurs left their footprints 150 million years ago. And you'll find it all within an hour of the capital.

Drenched in shades of green, Sintra is often touted as the must-do day trip and you can believe the hype – it's stunning. Moors, blue-blooded eccentrics and even Lord Byron let their vivid imaginations loose in above-the-clouds palaces, woods scattered with enormous boulders and subtropical gardens. To the southwest, Cascais is a cocktail of beach, culture and lively bars, and neighbouring Estoril might just tempt you to roll the dice at its once ritzy casino of James Bond 007 fame. Go northwest for royal decadence in Mafra's baroque palace of Versailles proportions.

Sintra

POP 26,000 / ELEV 280M

With its rippling mountains, dewy forests thick with ferns and lichen, exotic gardens and glittering palaces, Sintra is like a page torn from a fairy tale. Its Unesco World Heritage–listed centre, Sintra-Vila, is dotted with pastel-hued manors folded into luxuriant hills that roll down to the blue Atlantic.

Celts worshipped their moon god here, the Moors built a precipitous castle, and 18th-century Portuguese royals swanned around its dreamy gardens. Even Lord Byron waxed lyrical about Sintra's charms: 'Lo! Cintra's glorious Eden intervenes, in variegated maze of mount and glen', which inspired his epic poem *Childe Harold's Pilgrimage*.

Around Lisbon

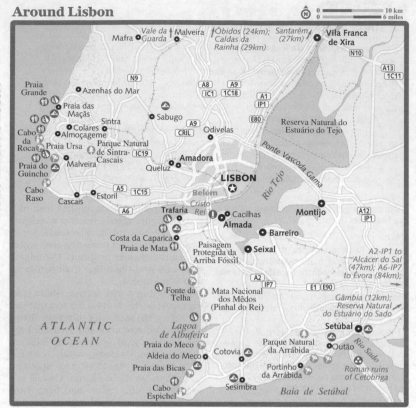

It's an unmissable day trip and, if time's not an issue, has enough allure to keep you there for several days.

Sintra has become quite popular in recent years, and it's hard to escape the tourist masses (especially in the summer). Go early in the day mid-week to escape the worst of the crowds.

If arriving by train, go to the last stop – Portela de Sintra – from which it's a pleasant 1km walk (or short bus ride) into the village.

◉ Sights

Palácio Nacional de Sintra   PALACE
(Map p126; Largo Rainha Dona Amélia; adult/child €9/7.50; ⊙9.30am-7pm) The star of Sintra-Vila is this historic palace, with its iconic twin conical chimneys and lavish interior. Of Moorish origins, the palace was first expanded by Dom Dinis (1261–1325), enlarged by João I in the 15th century (when the

kitchens were built), then given a Manueline twist by Manuel I in the following century.

The whimsical interior is a mix of Moorish and Manueline styles, with arabesque courtyards, barley-twist columns and 15th- and 16th-century geometric *azulejos* that figure among Portugal's oldest. Highlights include the octagonal Sala dos Cisnes (Swan Room), adorned with frescos of 27 gold-collared swans. Suspicious? You will be in the Sala das Pegas (Magpie Room), its ceiling emblazoned with magpies. Lore has it that the queen caught João I kissing one of her ladies-in-waiting. The cheeky king claimed the kisses were innocent and all '*por bem*' (for the good), then commissioned one magpie for every lady-in-waiting.

Other standouts are the wooden Sala dos Brasões, bearing the shields of 72 leading 16th-century families, the shipshape Galleon Room and the Palatine chapel featuring an Islamic mosaic floor. Finally, you reach the kitchen of twin-chimney fame, where the flutes work their magic. You can almost hear the crackle of a hog roasting on a spit for the king.

Castelo dos Mouros CASTLE
(Map p124; adult/child €7/6; ⊘9.30am-8pm) Soaring 412m above sea level, this mist-enshrouded ruined castle looms high above the surrounding forest. The 9th-century Moorish castle's dizzying ramparts stretch across the mountain ridges and past moss-clad boulders the size of small buses. When the clouds peel away, the vistas over Sintra's palace-dotted hill and dale to the glittering Atlantic are – like the climb – breathtaking.

The best walking route here from Sintra-Vila is not along the main road but the quicker, partly off-road route via Rua Marechal Saldanha. The steep trail is around 2km, but quiet and rewarding.

Parque da Pena GARDENS
(Map p124; ☑219 237 300; www.parquesdesintra. pt; adult/child €7/6, combined ticket with Palácio Nacional da Pena €13.50/11; ⊘9.30am-8pm) Parque da Pena is 200m up the road from Castelo dos Mouros, and is filled with tropical plants, huge redwoods and fern trees, camellias, rhododendrons and lakes (note the castle-shaped duck houses for web-footed royalty!). It's cheaper to buy a combined ticket if you want to visit Palácio Nacional da Pena too.

Buses (Map p126) to the **park entrance** leave from Sintra train station and near the *turismo* (tourist office). A taxi costs around €8 one way. The steep, zigzagging walk through pine and eucalyptus woods from Sintra-Vila is around 3km.

Palácio Nacional da Pena PALACE
(Map p124; adult/child €12.50/10; ⊘9.45am-7pm) Rising up from a thickly wooded peak and often enshrouded in swirling mist, Palácio Nacional da Pena is a wacky confection of onion domes, Moorish keyhole gates, writhing stone snakes and crenellated towers in pinks and lemons. Ferdinand of Saxe Coburg-Gotha, the artist-husband of Queen Maria II, commissioned Prussian architect Ludwig von Eschwege in 1840 to build the Bavarian-Manueline epic (and as a final flourish added an armoured statue of himself, overlooking the palace from a nearby peak).

The kitschy, extravagant interior is equally unusual, brimming with precious Meissen porcelain, Eiffel-designed furniture, trompe l'oeil murals and Dom Carlos' unfinished nudes of buxom nymphs.

Convento dos Capuchos MONASTERY
(Capuchin Monastery; ☑219 237 300; adult/child €6/5; ⊘9.30am-8pm) Hidden in the woods is the bewitchingly hobbit-hole-like Convento dos Capuchos, which was originally built in 1560 to house 12 monks who lived in incredibly cramped conditions, their tiny cells having low, narrow doors. Byron mocked the monastery in his poem *Childe Harold's Pilgrimage*, referring to recluse Honorius who spent a staggering 36 years here (before dying at age 95 in 1596).

It's often nicknamed the Cork Convent, because its miniscule cells are lined with cork. Visiting here is an Alice in Wonderland experience as you squeeze through to explore the warren of cells, chapels, kitchen and cavern. The monks lived a simple, touchingly well-ordered life in this idyllic yet spartan place, hiding up until 1834 when it was abandoned.

You can walk here – the monastery is 7.3km from Sintra-Vila (5.1km from the turn-off to Parque da Pena) along a remote, wooded road. There is no bus connection to the convent (taxis charge around €35 return; arrange for a pick-up ahead).

Palácio & Parque de Monserrate PALACE, GARDENS
(www.parquesdesintra.pt; adult/child €7/6; ⊘9.30am-8pm) At the centre of a lush, 30-hectare park, a manicured lawn sweeps up to the whimsical, Moorish-inspired *palácio*, the 19th-century romantic folly of English millionaire Sir Francis Cook. The wild and rambling gardens surrounding the building were created in the 18th century by wealthy English merchant Gerard de Visme, then enlarged by landscape painter William Stockdale (with help from London's Kew Gardens).

Its wooded hillsides bristle with exotic foliage, from Chinese weeping cypress to dragon trees and Himalayan rhododendrons. Seek out the Mexican garden nurturing palms, yuccas and agaves, and the bamboo-fringed Japanese garden abloom with camellias.

The park is 3.5km west of Sintra-Vila.

Museu do Brinquedo MUSEUM
(Toy Museum; Map p126; www.museu-do-brinque do.pt; Rua Visconde de Monserrate; adult/child €4.50/2.50; ⊘10am-6pm Tue-Sun) Sintra's toy story is Museu do Brinquedo. João Arbués

Sintra

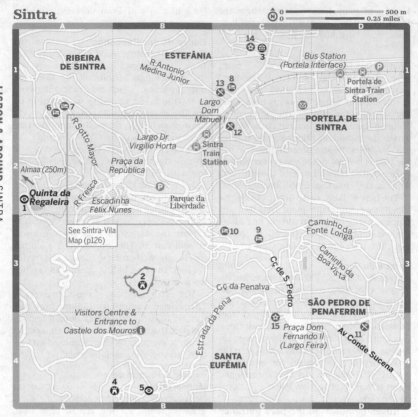

Moreira's fascinating 20,000-piece collection presents a chronological romp, from 3000-year-old Egyptian stone counters to a 1999 Barbie Burberry.

Museu de Arte Moderna MUSEUM
(Map p124; www.berardocollection.com; Avenida Heliodoro Salgado; ⊘10am-6pm Tue-Sun) FREE The Museu de Arte Moderna hosts rotating exhibitions covering the entire modern-art spectrum from kinetic and pop art to surrealism and expressionism. Sheltering Hockney, Lichtenstein and Warhol originals, the permanent collection is part of billionaire José Berardo's stash, which also graces the walls of Lisbon's Museu Colecção Berardo (p81).

Museu Anjos Teixeira MUSEUM
(Map p126; Alameda Volta do Duche; ⊘10am-6pm Tue-Fri, 2-6pm Sat & Sun) FREE Set in a former watermill, this small museum displays works by the father-and-son duo of Anjos Teixeira – two of Portugal's greatest sculptors. Most of the pieces here are the work of Pedro Augusto (1908–97), the son, who enjoyed greater success than his father, and was connected to the neorealism of the 1940s.

Some of his best works are on display here, from sensual Rodin-like works of feminine beauty to grand pastoral sculptures that capture the hardships of life in the countryside. Access is via steps, leading down from the main road opposite Parque da Liberdade.

🏃 Activities

Sintra is a terrific place to get out and stride, with waymarked **hiking trails** (look for red-and-yellow stripes) that corkscrew up into densely wooded hills strewn with giant boulders. Justifiably popular is the gentle 50-minute trek from Sintra-Vila to Castelo dos Mouros. You can continue to Palácio Nacional da Pena (another five minutes). From here you can ascend Serra de Sintra's highest point, the 529m Cruz Alta (High Cross), named after its 16th-century cross, with amazing views all over Sintra. It's possible to continue on foot to São Pedro de Penaferrim and loop back to Sintra-Vila. The *turismo* in Sintra-Vila can provide maps and info on various hiking trails.

Horseback riding is available in the Parque da Pena, from 30-minute teasers (€10) to six-hour excursions (€100).

Sintra Canopy   ZIPLINE
(☑ 219 237 300; www.parquesdesintra.pt; admission €29; ⊙ 11am-6.30pm) One of Sintra's newest activities is this zipline (flying fox), which takes visitors on a course through the treetops at heights of around 30m between 11 platforms. The whole course runs nearly 1km and takes one to two hours. Find it near the Moorish castle.

MuitAventura   ADVENTURE TOURS
(☑ 211 931 636; www.muitaventura.com; Rua Marquês Viana 31) This adventure outfitter has a regular schedule of organised activities, including mountain biking, rappelling, jeep tours, trekking and nighttime hikes. It's based in São Pedro.

Ozono Mais   ADVENTURE TOURS
(☑ 219 619 927; www.ozonomais.com) Offers a variety of outdoor excursions, including canoe-

ing, rafting, mountain biking and jeep tours. Call ahead for times and prices.

🎉 Festivals & Events

From late June to early July, the three-week-long **Festival de Sintra** (www.festivaldesintra. pt) features classical recitals, ballet and modern dance, world music and multimedia events, plus concerts for kids.

🛏 Sleeping

It's worth staying overnight, as Sintra has some magical guesthouses, from quaint villas to lavish manors. Book ahead in summer.

★ Nice Way Sintra Palace   HOSTEL €
(Map p126; ☑ 219 249 800; www.sintrapalace.com; Rua Sotto Mayor 22; dm €18-22, d with private/shared bathroom €60/50) In a rambling mansion north of the main square, you'll find stylishly outfitted rooms, great views of the countryside and a lovely garden. The flickering fireplace on cold nights sweetens the deal. There's a friendly vibe to the place, making it a good place to meet other travellers. There is also a fully equipped two-bedroom cottage available – excellent value for families at around €75 per night.

Almaa   HOSTEL €
(☑ 219 240 008; www.almaasintrahostel.com; Caminho dos Frades; dm/d/tr from €24/68/84) 🍃 Sustainably-minded Almaa is an idyllic spot to recharge for a few days, with a quirky design scheme (featuring recycled furniture) and an attractive setting. The surrounding 3.5 hectares of lush grounds is set with walking

---

SWEET DREAMS

Sintra is famous for its luscious sweeties. **Fábrica das Verdadeiras Queijadas da Sapa** (Map p126; Alameda Volta do Duche 12; ⊙ 9am-7pm Tue-Sun) has been fattening up royalty since 1756 with bite-sized *queijadas* – crisp pastry shells filled with a marzipan-like mix of fresh cheese, sugar, flour and cinnamon. Since 1952, **Casa Piriquita** (Map p126; Rua das Padarias 1-5; ⊙ 9am-8pm Thu-Tue) has been tempting locals with another sweet dream: the *travesseiro* (pillow), which is light puff pastry turned, rolled and folded seven times, then filled with delicious almond-and-egg-yolk cream and lightly dusted with sugar.

Sintra-Vila

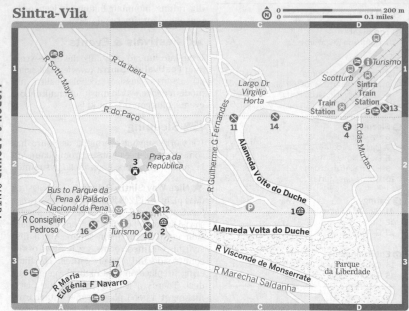

paths and an old spring-fed reservoir for swimming. It's a 10-minute walk from the village centre.

Casa de Hóspedes Dona
Maria da Parreirinha   GUESTHOUSE €
(Map p126; 219 232 490; Rua João de Deus 12-14; d €45-55) A short walk from the train station, this small, homely guesthouse has old-fashioned rooms with big windows, dark-wood furnishings and floral fabrics.

Monte da Lua   GUESTHOUSE €€
(Map p126; 219 241 029; www.montedalua.org; Av Dr Miguel Bombarda 51; d without breakfast €65-75;) Opposite the train station, this warm and welcoming marshmallow-pink villa offers clean and simple wood-floored rooms; the best overlook the wooded valley at the back.

Hotel Sintra Jardim   GUESTHOUSE €€
(Map p124; 219 230 738; hotelsintrajardim@gmail.com; Travessa dos Avelares 12; d €65-80;) This stately 1850s manor overlooks rambling gardens and an inviting pool, and offers captivating views to the castle. The bright, high-ceilinged rooms are decorated in crisp hues with shiny wood floors. Wake up to birdsong and a hearty breakfast.

Quinta das Murtas   GUESTHOUSE €€
(Map p124; 219 240 246; www.quintadasmurtas.com; Rua Eduardo Van Zeller 4; d/apt from €75/85;) A grand manor surrounded by lush greenery, this retreat charms with sweeping views, a trickling fountain and a grand lounge room with carved columns and an elaborate ceiling. The traditional, tiled-floor rooms are light and spacious; the roomier apartments also have kitchenettes.

Hotel Nova Sintra   GUESTHOUSE €€
(Map p124; 219 230 220; www.novasintra.com; Largo Afonso de Albuquerque 25; s/d €70/95;) This renovated late-19th-century mansion is set above the main road. The big drawcard is the sunny terrace overlooking Sintra, where you can take breakfast. Front-facing doubles offer picturesque views, back rooms more peaceful slumber. Some rooms are rather small.

Casa do Valle   B&B €€
(Map p124; 219 244 699; www.casadovalle.com; Rua da Paderna; d €90;) Just downhill from the historical centre, Casa do Valle has spacious rooms set around a garden with an inviting pool. Some rooms lack en-suite. There are fine views onto the lush hillsides rising above the valley and friendly multilingual service.

Sintra-Vila

Villa Mira Longa   B&B €€
(Map p126; ☑964 306 194; www.villamiralonga.
com; Estrada da Pena 4; d €80-120, 3-bedroom apt
€200; ☎) This restored villa, a short walk
from the centre, has comfortable rooms (the
best with panoramic views) and beautiful
common areas (including an antique-filled
dining room and an exquisitely manicured
garden). The kind hosts have a wealth of
knowledge about Sintra and offer a first-rate
breakfast.

Lawrence's Hotel   GUESTHOUSE €€
(Map p126; ☑219 105 500; www.lawrences
hotel.com; Rua Consiglieri Pedroso 38-40; s/d/
ste €110/120/145; ✳@☎) Lord Byron once
stayed at this 18th-century mansion turned
boutique hotel. It oozes charm with its
lanternlit, vaulted corridors and snug bar.
Wood floors creak in the individually designed rooms, decorated with *azulejos* and
antique trunks; some rooms have views over
the wooded valley. There's also an excellent
restaurant.

Casa Miradouro   GUESTHOUSE €€€
(Map p124; ☑219 107 100; www.casa-miradouro.
com; Rua Sotto Mayor 55; d €100-135, without
breakfast €80-115) This imposing Battenberg

cake of a house, built in 1890, has eight elegant, stuccoed rooms and panoramic views.
The best have small balconies.

✗ Eating

Saudade   CAFE €
(Map p126; Avenida Dr Miguel Bombardo 8; mains
€5-7; ⊙8.30am-8pm Sun-Wed, to midnight Thu-
Sat; ☎) This former bakery, where Sintra's
famous *queijadas* were made, has cherub-
covered ceilings and a rambling interior,
making it a fine spot for pastries or lighter
fare (with a different soup, salad, fish- and
meat-dish of the day). A gallery in the back
features changing art exhibitions.

Bica São Pedro   PORTUGUESE €
(Map p124; Rua 1 de Dezembro 16; mains €7-10;
⊙lunch & dinner) On a peaceful lane in São
Pedro, a friendly welcome and good-value
daily specials await – steak, salads, *bacalhau*
dishes, crepes and quiches are among the selections. There's garden dining in the back.

Tulhas   PORTUGUESE €€
(Map p126; Rua Gil Vicente 4; mains €10-17;
⊙lunch & dinner Thu-Tue) This converted grain
warehouse is dark, tiled and quaint, with
wrought-iron chandeliers and a relaxed,
cosy atmosphere. It's renowned for its *bacalhau com natas* (shredded cod with cream
and potato).

Tasca do Xico   TAPAS €€
(Map p126; Rua Arco do Teixeira 6; tapas €4-8;
⊙noon-10pm) On a narrow lane in the old
quarter, the petite Tasca do Xico prepares
tasty tapas plates (prawns with garlic, mussels in vinaigrette) as well as a few heartier
changing specials such as grilled fresh fish
of the day. Dine outside (or arrive early to
score the only table inside).

G-Spot   FUSION €€
(Map p124; ☑927 508 027; Alameda dos Combatentes da Grande Guerra 12; mains €16-18; ⊙7.30-
10.30pm Tue-Sat) The name may not whet
your appetite, but the cooking is top-notch
at this small, elegant restaurant just off the
beaten path, and features a changing selection of seasonally inspired dishes. Try the
multi-course tasting menu, a fair value at
€30. Reservations recommended.

Tacho Real   PORTUGUESE €€
(Map p126; ☑219 235 277; Rua da Ferraria 4;
mains €10-22; ⊙lunch & dinner Thu-Tue) At this
charming haunt, take a pew on the cobbled
patio or retreat to the 17th-century vaulted

interior, bedecked with century-old *azulejos*. Dapper waiters bring specialities, from juicy steaks to delicious stuffed king crab, to the table.

Dom Pipas PORTUGUESE €€
(Map p124; Rua João de Deus 62; mains €7-13; ⊘ lunch & dinner Tue-Sun) A local favourite, Dom Pipas serves up excellent Portuguese dishes, amid *azulejos* and rustic country decor. It's behind the train station (left out of the station, first left, then left again to the end).

Sabores da Vila PORTUGUESE €€
(Map p126; ☑ 219 242 855; Av Augusto Freire 2; mains €7-12; ⊘ lunch & dinner Mon-Sat; 🛜 ☑) Near the train station, this attractive space specialises in no-nonsense grilled meats and seafood (octopus, lamb chops, rump steak, salmon and the like).

🍷 Drinking & Nightlife

Sintra is a sleepy town, with little in the way of bar life. Most locals head to Lisbon for a big night out.

Fonte da Pipa BAR
(Map p126; ☑ 219 234 437; Rua Fonte da Pipa 11-13; ⊘ 9pm-2am) A tiled bar, this has craggy, cave-like rooms and comfy seats.

☆ Entertainment

Taverna dos Trovadores LIVE MUSIC
(Map p124; ☑ 219 233 548; Praça Dom Fernando II 18) This atmospheric restaurant and bar features live music (folk and acoustic) on Friday and Saturday nights – an institution that's been around for over two decades. Concerts run from 11.30pm to 2am. It's located in São Pedro de Penaferrim.

SPEEDY TRANSPORT

If you have limited time and you'd like to see some of the attractions beyond Sintra-Vila, **Sight Sintra** (Map p126; ☑ 219 242 856; Rua João de Deus; 2½hr tour €45; ⊘ 9.30am-8pm) rents out tiny two-person buggies that guide you by GPS along one of three different routes. The most popular takes you to Castelo dos Mouros and Palácio da Pena among other sites. It's located around the corner from the train station. You can also create your own itinerary, and hire it for €25 per hour.

Centro Cultural
Olga Cadaval CULTURAL CENTRE
(Map p124; ☑ 219 107 110; www.ccolgacadaval.pt; Praça Francisco Sá Carneiro) Sintra's major cultural venue stages concerts, theatre and dance.

ℹ Information

There's an ATM at the train station and in the tourism office.
Centro de Saúde (☑ 219 247 770; Rua Dr Alfredo Costa 34)
Police Station (☑ 219 247 850; Rua João de Deus 6)
Post Office Sintra-Vila (Map p126; Rua Gil Vicente, Sintra-Vila); Portela de Sintra (Map p124; Av Movimento das Forças Armadas, Portela de Sintra)
Turismo (Map p126; ☑ 219 231 157; Praça da Republica; ⊘ 9.30am-6pm Tue-Fri, 1.30-6pm Sat & Sun) Near the centre of Sintra-Vila, this helpful multilingual office has expert insights into Sintra and the surrounding areas. There's also a small train station (Map p126; ☑ 219 241 623; train station) branch, often overrun by those arriving by rail.

ℹ Getting There & Away

Buses run by **Scotturb** (Map p126; ☑ 214 699 100; www.scotturb.com; Av Dr Miguel Bombarda) or **Mafrense** (☑ 261 816 150; www.mafrense.pt) leave regularly for Cascais (€3.50, one hour), sometimes via Cabo da Roca (€3.35). Buses also head to Estoril (€3.50, 40 minutes), Mafra (45 minutes) and Ericeira (45 minutes). Most services leave from **Sintra train station** (Map p126) – which is *estação* on timetables – via **Portela de Sintra** (Map p124). Scotturb's useful information office, open from 9am to 1pm and 2pm to 8pm, is opposite the station.

Trains (€2.15, 40 minutes) run every 15 minutes between Sintra and Lisbon's Rossio station.

ℹ Getting Around

BUS
From the train station it's a 1km scenic walk into Sintra-Vila, or you can hop on bus 435, which goes from the station to Sintra-Vila (€0.85). This bus also continues on to Quinta da Regaleira and Palácio de Monserrate.

A handy bus for accessing the Castelo dos Mouros is the Scotturb bus 434 (€5), which runs frequently from the train station via Sintra-Vila to the castle (10 minutes), Palácio da Pena (15 minutes) and back. One ticket gives you hop-on, hop-off access (in one direction; no backtracking).

CAR & MOTORCYCLE

Driving can be a challenge on the narrow roads around Sintra. Parking is limited around town and there are very few spaces at Palácio Nacional de Pena, so it's better to avoid driving there in busy times. For parking near town, there's a free car park below Sintra-Vila; follow the signs by the *câmara municipal* (town hall) in Estefânia. Alternatively, park at Portela Interface and take the bus.

TAXI

Taxis are available at the train station or opposite Sintra-Vila post office. They are metered, so fares depend on traffic. Count on about €8 one way to Palácio Nacional da Pena. If you want them to wait, you'll have to negotiate a fare; expect to pay about €30 to €35 for a return visit to Convento dos Capuchos.

TRAM

On weekends, Sintra's restored electric tram, the **Elétrico de Sintra** (www.cm-sintra.pt; one-way €2; ☉ Fri-Sun) offers access to the coast, running from Rua Alves Roçadas near Portela de Sintra train station, arriving at Praia das Maçãs 45 minutes later. Trams depart hourly from 9am to 6pm from Friday to Sunday. The last tram back leaves the beach around 7pm.

West of Sintra

Precipitous cliffs and crescent-shaped bays pummelled by the Atlantic lie just 12km west of Sintra. Previous host of the European Surfing Championships, **Praia Grande** lures surfers and bodyboarders to its big sandy beach with ripping breakers. Clamber over the cliffs to spot dinosaur fossils. Family-friendly **Praia das Maçãs** has a sweep of gold sand, backed by a lively little resort. **Azenhas do Mar**, 2km further, is a cliff-hanger of a village, where a jumble of whitewashed, red-roofed houses tumble down the crags to a free saltwater pool (only accessible when the sea is calm).

En route to the beaches, ridgetop **Colares** makes a great pit stop with its panoramas, stuck-in-time village charm and wines dating back to the 13th century. The vines grown today are the only ones in Europe to have survived the 19th-century phylloxera plague, saved by their deep roots and sandy soil. To purchase some of the venerable wines, visit **Adega Regional de Colares** (☏ 219 291 210; Alameda Coronel, Linhares de Lima 32).

Wild and wonderful **Cabo da Roca** (Rock Cape) is a sheer 150m cliff, facing the roaring sea, 18km west of Sintra. It's Europe's westernmost point and a terrific sunset spot. Though a steady trickle of visitors come to see the lighthouse and buy an I've-been-there certificate at the *turismo,* it still has an air of rugged, windswept remoteness.

Just before reaching Cabo da Roca, there's a small sign indicating the turnoff to **Praia Ursa**. From here it's a 20-minute descent along a treacherous path (take care!) to a beautiful deserted beach (bring your own food and drinks). You might see a few nudists there in the summer. From here you can continue walking along the coast another 5km to Praia Grande.

🛏 Sleeping

Residencial Real   GUESTHOUSE €
(☏ 219 292 002; residencialreal.pmacas@gmail.com; Rua Fernão Magalhães, Praia das Maçãs; d with/without view €55/45; ☎) For spacious, immaculate rooms with expansive ocean views, you can't beat this homely guesthouse right on the beach at Praia das Maçãs. There's wi-fi in the lobby only and breakfast isn't included.

Estalagem de Colares   GUESTHOUSE €€
(☏ 210 445 167; Av Amilcar Augusto Gil 142, Colares; s/d from €60/80; P ❄) Peeking above lush greenery, this whitewashed villa is a calm retreat with large, clean rooms and a peaceful garden.

Hotel Arribas   HOTEL €€
(☏ 219 289 050; www.hotelarribas.pt; Av Alfredo Coelho 28, Praia Grande; d €72-100; P ❄ @ ☎ ≋) While this 39-room, scallop-shaped hotel isn't a pretty face, its sea views over Praia Grande and 100m-long ocean-water pool are magnificent. Light, breezy rooms feature fridges, TVs and balconies that are ideal for watching surfers ride the waves.

✗ Eating

Many cafes and seafood restaurants are scattered along Praia Grande; Praia das Maçãs also has a few options.

★ Adraga   SEAFOOD €€
(☏ 219 280 028; www.restaurantedaadraga.com; Praia da Adraga; seafood €25-45 per kg; ☉ 1-10pm) This legendary seafood restaurant sits on the edge of a small beach just below Almoçageme. The key to success: no fancy techniques or overdressed dining room – just incredibly fresh fish and seafood cooked to perfection, served up in a friendly, casual setting. Call ahead to reserve a table by the

window. Parking can be tough in the summer (go early if you're driving).

To get there, take the main road into Almoçageme, and just after the plaza, take the first left (Rua da Adraga), which leads down to the beach and restaurant.

Moinho Dom Quixote INTERNATIONAL €€
(☑219 292 523; Rua do Campo da Bola, Azoia; mains €7-12; ☉noon-2am) This colourfully decorated, kitsch-filled restaurant serves salads, quiches, burgers and bistro fare, but the real draw is the breezy terrace with magnificent views over the coast. Look for the large *moinho* (windmill) in Azoia, 2.5km south of the Cabo da Roca.

Colares Velho CONTEMPORARY €€
(☑219 292 727; Largo da Igreja, Colares; mains €15-20; ☉lunch & dinner Tue-Sat, lunch Sun) Clued-up foodies make sure there's rarely an empty table at this restaurant and tearoom, set in a converted grocery store and tavern. The country-style dining room, bedecked with 200-year-old pinewood dressers, is an elegant setting for flavours such as Roquefort steak and seafood *cataplana,* accompanied by full-bodied wines. Alternatively, sip Earl Grey and nibble on divine pastries in the tearoom.

Azenhas do Mar SEAFOOD €€€
(☑219 280 739; www.azenhasdomar.com; Azenhas do Mar; mains €18; ☉noon-10pm) Perched above the saltwater pool in Azenhas do Mar, you'll find delicious seafood dishes and grilled fish. The sea views are stunning, especially from the deck. A taxi from Sintra costs about €15.

❶ Getting There & Away

Bus 441 from Sintra's Portela Interface runs frequently via Colares to Praia das Maçãs (€3.25, 25 minutes) and on to Azenhas do Mar (€3.25, 30 minutes), stopping at Praia Grande (€3, 25 minutes) three times daily (more in summer). Bus 440 also runs from Sintra to Azenhas do Mar (€3.25, 35 minutes). On weekends, the Elétrico de Sintra (€2) goes from Sintra to Praia das Maçãs via Colares.

Bus 403 to Cascais runs regularly via Cabo da Roca (45 minutes) from Sintra station.

Cascais

POP 35,000

Cascais (kush-*kaish*) has rocketed from sleepy fishing village to much-loved summertime playground of wave-frolicking *lisboêtas* ever since King Luís I went for a dip in 1870. Its trio of golden bays attracts sun-worshipping holidaymakers, who come to splash in the ice-cold Atlantic. Don't expect to get much sand to yourself at the weekend, though.

There's plenty of post-beach life, with winding lanes leading to small museums, cool gardens, a shiny marina and a pedestrianised old town dotted with designer boutiques and alfresco fish restaurants. After dark, lively bars fuel the party. There's also great surfing at Praia do Guincho, 9km northwest, and running or cycling along the shoreline path.

The train station and nearby **bus station** are about 250m north of the main pedestrianised drag, Rua Frederico Arouca.

◉ Sights

Igreja de Nossa Senhora da Assunção CHURCH
(Largo da Assunção; ☉9am-1pm & 5-8pm) Weave through the back alleys west of the *câmara municipal* to the palm-fringed square that is home to the whitewashed Igreja de Nossa Senhora da Assunção, adorned with *azulejos* predating the 1755 earthquake.

Citadel FORTRESS
The citadel is where the royal family used to spend the summer. Today it houses a luxury hotel – the **Pousada de Cascais** (www.pousadas.pt) – which has surprisingly little of interest beyond hotel rooms and a courtyard restaurant. Beyond lies the modern **Marina de Cascais** with its postcard-perfect lighthouse, sleek yachts and lounge bars.

Casa das Histórias Paula Rego GALLERY
(www.casadashistoriaspaularego.com; Avenida da República 300; ☉10am-7pm) **FREE** The Casa das Histórias Paula Rego showcases the evocative paintings of one of Portugal's finest living artists. Exhibits span Rego's career, from early work with collage in the 1950s to the twisted fairy tale–like tableaux of the 1980s, and up to the disturbing realism of more recent years.

Parque Marechal Carmona PARK
(Avenida Rei Humberto II) The wild Parque Marechal Carmona provides a shady retreat from the seaside crowds, with a duck pond, birch and pine trees, palms and eucalyptus, rose gardens and flowering shrubs.

The grounds harbour the **Museu Condes de Castro Guimarães** (☉10am-5pm Tue-Sun) **FREE**, which sits in a whimsical early-19th-century mansion complete with castle turrets and Arabic cloister. The lavishly decorated interior houses 17th-century Indo-Portuguese cabinets, Oriental silk tapestries and 350-year-old *azulejos.*

Centro Cultural de Cascais   CULTURAL CENTRE
(Av Rei Humberto II de Itália; ☉10am-6pm Tue-Sun) FREE The colourful Centro Cultural de Cascais, in what was a barefooted Carmelite convent, hosts contemporary exhibitions and cultural events.

Museu do Mar   MUSEUM
(☑214 825 400; Rua Júlio Pereira de Mello; ☉10am-5pm Tue-Sun) FREE The small Museu do Mar spells out Cascais' maritime history with costumes, tools, nets and boats, accompanied by quotes (in English) from the fisherfolk.

Boca do Inferno   LOOKOUT
Atlantic waves pummel craggy Boca do Inferno (Mouth of Hell), 2km west of Cascais. It's about a 20-minute walk along the coast, or you can take a taxi (around €4 one-way). Expect a mouthful of small splashes unless a storm is raging.

🏄 Beaches

Cascais' three sandy bays – Praia da Conceição, Praia da Rainha and Praia da Ribeira – are fine for a sunbake or a tingly Atlantic dip, but don't expect much towel space in summer.

The best beach is wild, windswept Praia do Guincho, 9km northwest, a mecca to surfers and windsurfers with massive crashing rollers. The strong undertow can be dangerous for swimmers, but Guincho still lures nonsurfers with powder-soft sands, fresh seafood and magical sunsets.

🏃 Activities

If you're keen to ride the waves, grab your boardies and check out the surfing courses available at **Moana Surf School** (☑964 449 436; www.moanasurfschool.com; introductory 75min lesson €25, 4 lessons €85). It also rents boards and wetsuits. **Guincho Surf School** (☑917 535 719; 1/2/5 lessons €30/50/100) also offers classes.

Cascais Watersports Centre   WATER SPORTS
(☉10am-7.30pm) At Praia da Duquesa, midway between Cascais and Estoril, you can rent pedaloes, canoes and arrange waterskiing jaunts and windsurfing.

Cascais Dive Center   DIVING
(☑919 913 021; www.cascaisdivecenter.com) At Praia da Duquesa, this outfit can take you scuba-diving around the Cascais coastline and beyond with equipment rental and courses.

🎉 Festivals & Events

Festas do Mar   CULTURE
This festival in late August celebrates Cascais' maritime heritage with outdoor concerts, nautical parades and fireworks.

Festival de Música da Costa do Estoril   MUSIC
This festival brings classical and jazz concerts to both Cascais and Estoril in July.

🛏 Sleeping

It's worth booking in advance if you're visiting in summer, as the best places fill up in a flash.

Camping Orbitur do Guincho   CAMPGROUND €
(☑214 870 450; www.orbitur.pt; bungalows from €64, sites per adult/tent/car €6.50/7.40/6.50; 🛜) Set back behind the dunes of Praia do Guincho, 9km from Cascais, this pine-shaded site has a restaurant and tennis court. It gets busy in July and August. Buses run frequently to Guincho from Cascais.

Residencial Solar Dom Carlos   GUESTHOUSE €€
(☑214 828 115; www.solardomcarlos.pt; Rua Latino Coelho 104; s/d €50/70; P @🛜) Hidden down a sleepy alley, this 16th-century former royal residence turned guesthouse retains lots of original features from chandeliers to wood beams, *azulejos* and a frescoed breakfast room. The high-ceilinged rooms are spacious and traditional. Don't miss the 400-year-old chapel where Dom Carlos used to pray.

Residencial Parsi   GUESTHOUSE €€
(☑214 861 309; www.residencial-parsi.com; Rua Afonso Sanches 8; d without breakfast €50-75; 🛜) In a crumbling, characterful building near the waterfront, Parsi's seven rooms have wood floors set above a noisy Irish pub (light sleepers take note). The stuccoed front room (€100) has sea views. It's intimate and friendly.

Agarre o Momento   GUESTHOUSE €€
(☑214 064 532; www.agarreomomento.com; Rua Joaquim Ereira 458; d €60; @🛜) This welcoming guesthouse in a peaceful residential neighbourhood has bright, airy rooms plus

Cascais

a garden, shared kitchen and bike rental. Three rooms have en suite, while the other three share a bathroom. It's a 15-minute walk (1.5km) north of the station, or a €4.50 taxi ride.

Albatroz Bayside Villa
BOUTIQUE HOTEL €€€

(☑ 214 863 410; www.albatrozhotels.com; Rua Fernandes Tomás 1; d from €150; ✳ @ 🛜 ⛱) Facing the bay, this place has just 11 individually decorated rooms – some flowery, some with ornamental fireplace. The best rooms sport terraces, Jacuzzi tubs and ocean views.

Casa Vela
GUESTHOUSE €€€

(☑ 214 868 972; www.casavelahotel.com; Rua dos Bem Lembrados 17; d from €135; P ✳ 🛜 ⛱) The friendly Casa Vela has earned many admirers for its bright and attractive rooms set with modern furnishings. Some rooms have a balcony overlooking the lovely gardens and pool. It's in a peaceful neighbourhood about a 10-minute walk to the old town centre.

Casa da Pergola
B&B €€€

(☑ 214 840 040; www.pergolahouse.pt; Av Valbom 13; d €155) An oasis of calm with a lush garden and bougainvillea-draped facade, this century-old manor is a family heirloom. A marble staircase sweeps up to six classically elegant rooms with stucco, dark-wood trappings and sparkling bathrooms; several have garden-facing balconies. Relax in the antique-filled sitting room or with a glass of complimentary port in the evening.

🍽 Eating

You'll find a glut of restaurants with alfresco seating along pedestrianised Rua Frederico Arouca and cobbled Largo Cidade de Vitória. For seafood and sunsets, make for the ocean-facing restaurants in Guincho.

Santini
ICE CREAM €

(☑ 214 833 709; Av Valbom 28F; 2/3/4 scoops €2.60/4.50/5.80; ⏲ 11am-midnight) All hail

Cascais

Santini for its creamy, rich, 100% natural gelati, made to an age-old family recipe. Join the line, grab a cone and eat quickly before it melts.

House of Wonders CAFE €
(Largo da Misericordia; light meals €4-8; ⊙ 11am-8pm, until 11pm Jun-Aug; 🛜🐕) Tucked away in the old quarter, this charming Dutch-owned cafe is a traveller's delight. Aside from warm, welcoming ambience and an artwork-filled interior, you'll find beautifully presented salads, quiches, soups and desserts. Best of all is the rustic rooftop terrace, with picturesque views over Cascais – perfect for an afternoon or early evening drink.

Jardim dos Frangos CHICKEN €€
(📋 214 861 717; Av Marginal; mains €7-14; ⊙ noon-11pm) Whiffs of grilled chicken and piri-piri lure hungry locals to the pavement terrace of this no-frills joint.

Apeadeiro SEAFOOD €€
(Avenida Vasco da Gama 252; mains €7-12; ⊙ lunch & dinner Tue-Sun) With simple decor, this sunny restaurant is known for its superb char-grilled fish served up at reasonable prices.

Páteo do Petisco PORTUGUESE €€
(📋 214 820 036; Travessa das Amoreiras 5; tapas €5-9; ⊙ noon-11.30pm Tue-Sun) To escape the high prices and tourist masses in the old town, head out to this local favourite in the Torre neighbourhood. It's a buzzing place, with a friendly, tavern-like vibe and good-value Portuguese-style tapas – ideal for sharing with friends. It's about 3km northwest of the old town centre, best reached by taxi (around €5). Reserve ahead.

Casa da Guia INTERNATIONAL €€
(www.casadaguia.com; Av Nossa Senhora do Cabo 101) Among palm and pine trees, this lush waterfront complex contains a handful of shops, cafes and restaurants with outdoor terraces overlooking the deep blue Atlantic. Restaurants include a grillhouse, a sushi place and the quaint Bistro Garbo, serving pizzas, pastas and Swedish fare (mains €10 to €15). It's located on the main coastal road, about 3km west of the historic centre (and 1.3km west of Boca do Inferno).

Confraria Sushi JAPANESE €€
(Rua Luís Xavier Palmeirim 16; salads/sushi plates from €12/15; ⊙ noon-midnight Tue-Sun) It's hard to know where to look first at this bright, art-slung cafe, jazzed up with flower prints, zebra stripes and technicolour glass chandeliers. It's a fun spot for sushi and salads, and there's a handful of tables on the sunny patio.

Baía do Peixe SEAFOOD €€
(📋 214 865 157; Av Dom Carlos I 6; all-you-can-eat fish/shellfish €14/20; ⊙ lunch & dinner Tue-Sun) Seafood lovers take note: Baía do Peixe serves *rodizio* style, meaning waiters bring around either fish (four or five types, plus squid) or shellfish (including oysters, prawns, crab, cockles and clam dishes) and you select what you like from the plate. There's a two-person minimum for the shellfish option. Lunch specials (from €9) are also good value.

Mar do Inferno SEAFOOD €€€
(📋 214 832 218; Av Rei Humberto II de Italia; mains €16-25; ⊙ lunch & dinner Thu-Tue) Near the Boca

do Inferno, this humble-looking place serves superb seafood dishes to ocean views. Its mouth-watering mixed platters for two (€40 to €88) are legendary. The service, however, is so-so. Reserve ahead to score a table on the terrace.

Drinking & Nightlife

The pub-like bars huddling around Largo Luís de Camões fill with a good-time crowd after sundown.

Baluarte   LOUNGE
(☑214 865 157; Av Dom Carlos I 6; ⊙4pm-2am) Baluarte is an upscale, smoke-filled place with swirly gold wallpaper, tub chairs and bold purple splashes. It offers sea views, well-mixed cocktails and occasional DJ nights.

O Luain's   PUB
(☑214 861 627; Rua da Palmeira 4A) For the craic in Cascais, it has to be this cheery Irish watering hole. Pull up a stool for Guinness and live jam sessions on weekends.

O'Neill's   PUB
(☑214 868 230; Rua Afonso Sanches 8) An Irish number with banter and a passion for the pint, O'Neill's has live music at 11pm most nights.

Esplanada Rainha   OUTDOOR BAR
(Largo da Rainha; ⊙10am-10pm) For sundowners with a sea view, head to this outdoor place with a pleasant vista overlooking Praia da Rainha beach.

Jardim Cerveja   OUTDOOR BAR
(Parque Marechal Carmona; ⊙1pm-1am) On the edge of leafy Parque Marechal Carmona, this place has a large open-air terrace that makes a refreshing spot for a pint of Erdinger or

---

FREE WHEELS

For a spin out along the coast, take advantage of Cascais' **free bike hire**. The bikes are available from 8am to 7pm daily at various points around town, including Largo da Estação near the train station. Demand is naturally high, so arrive early and bring some form of ID. There's a bicycle path that runs the entire 9km stretch from Cascais to Guincho. A shorter route is along the attractive seafront promenade to Estoril, 2km east.

Guinness. There's live music on Friday and Saturday nights from 10pm.

Shopping

In the old quarter, Rua Frederico Arouca is sprinkled with boutiques and souvenir shops.

Cascais Villa
Shopping Centre   MALL
(Av Marginal; ⊙10am-11pm) Near the bus station, this mall shelters a cinema, supermarket and a string of other shops.

Mercado Municipal   MARKET
(Av Dom Pedro I & Rua Padre Moisés da Silva; ⊙6.30am-2pm Wed & Sat) Cascais' bustling municipal market tempts with fresh local produce such as juicy Algarve nectarines, glossy olives, wagon wheel–sized cheeses and bread.

Ceramicarte   ARTS & CRAFTS
(☑214 840 170; Largo da Assunção 3; ⊙10.30am-1.30pm & 3-6pm Mon-Fri, 10.30am-1pm Sat) This eye-catching gallery showcases Luís Soares' bright, abstract fused-glass creations, from jewellery to tableware.

Information

Banco Espírito Santo (☑214 864 302; Largo Luís de Camões 40) Has an ATM.

Cascais Hospital (☑214 827 700; Rua Padre JM Loureiro)

International Medical Centre (Instituto Médico de Cascais; ☑214 845 317; Av Pedro Álvares Cabral 242) English-speaking, pricey but fast, with 24-hour service available.

Main Police Station (☑214 861 127; Rua Afonso Sanches)

Post Office (Av Marginal; ⊙8.30am-6pm Mon-Fri) Also has NetPost.

Tourist Police Post (☑214 863 929; Rua Visconde da Luz) Next to the *turismo*.

Turismo (☑214 868 204; www.visiteestoril. com; Rua Visconde da Luz 14; ⊙9am-1pm & 2-7pm Mon-Sat) Surprisingly unhelpful. Sells a map of Cascais.

Getting There & Away

Bus 417 goes about hourly from Cascais to Sintra (€4.05, 30 minutes). For a more scenic view take bus 403 (€4.05, 40 minutes), which goes via Cabo da Roca (30 minutes).

Trains run from Lisbon's Cais do Sodré station to Cascais via Estoril (€2.15, 40 minutes, every 20 minutes).

It's only 2km to Estoril, so it doesn't take long to walk the seafront route.

Getting Around

Buses 405 and 415 go to Guincho (€2.60, 20 minutes, about hourly from 7am to 7pm).

For a taxi, call ☎ 214 660 101.

Estoril

POP 24,000

With its swish hotels, turreted villas and glitzy casino, Estoril (shtoe-*reel*) once fancied itself as the Portuguese Riviera. The rich and famous came here to frolic in the sea, stroll palm-fringed landscaped gardens and fritter away their fortunes. Though it still has a whiff of faded aristocracy, those heady days of grandeur have passed. Today, there isn't much to Estoril aside from its beach and casino, and overnight guests may end up wishing they'd stayed in livelier Cascais.

Estoril was where Ian Fleming hit on the idea for *Casino Royale,* as he stalked Yugoslav double agent Dusko Popov at its casino. During WWII, the town heaved with exiles and spies (including Graham Greene, another British intelligence man and author).

The bus and train stations are a stone's throw from the beach on Avenida Marginal, opposite the shady Jardim do Estoril. The casino is at the north end of the park.

Sights & Activities

Estoril's sandy Praia de Tamariz tends to be quieter than the bays in Cascais, and has showers, cafes, beachside bars and a free ocean swimming pool, east of the train station.

Estoril has a world-famous golf scene, including the nationally acclaimed **Golf do Estoril**.

Estoril Casino CASINO
(☎ 214 667 700; www.casino-estoril.pt; Praça José Teodoro dos Santos; gaming/slot machine rooms €4/free; ⏲ 3pm-3am) The temple-like casino has everything from roulette to poker, blackjack and the ubiquitous slot machines. Its cavernous main restaurant, **Preto e Prata** (☎ 214 684 521; show €21, dinner €35-44), stages a sparkly floor show nightly, and there's a first-rate Chinese restaurant on the ground floor.

Sleeping & Eating

Hotel Smart GUESTHOUSE €€
(☎ 214 682 164; www.hotel-smart.net; Rua Maestro Laçerda 6; d from €65; P 📶 ≋) The affable Bandarra family runs this 26-room guesthouse with pride – think manicured lawns, a clean swimming pool and gleaming marble floors. The light-filled rooms have lots of polished wood and tiny balconies.

Garrett do Estoril PORTUGUESE €
(☎ 214 680 365; Av de Nice 54; snacks €3-5; ⏲ 8am-7pm Wed-Mon) A block west of the park, this handsomely set *pastelaria* (pastry shop) and restaurant impresses with its teas, sandwiches, daily specials and pastries.

Praia de Tamariz PORTUGUESE €€
(☎ 214 681 010; Praia de Tamariz; mains €10-19; ⏲ 9am-midnight) Overlooking the beach of the same name, this traditional restaurant serves decent, if unsurprising, traditional fare. More memorable are the ocean views from the breezy terrace.

Information

Turismo (Av Aida near Av Marginal; ⏲ 10am-1pm & 2-6pm) Near the train station on the west side of the Jardim do Estoril.

Getting There & Away

Bus 412 goes frequently to Cascais (€1.80, five minutes), or it's a pleasant 2km walk or cycle along the seafront.

Queluz

Versailles' fanciful cousin-once-removed, the powder-puff **Palácio de Queluz** (☎ 214 343 860; adult/child €5/free; ⏲ 9.30am-5pm Wed-Mon) was once a hunting lodge, converted in the late 1700s to a royal summer residence. It's surrounded by queen-of-hearts formal gardens, with oak-lined avenues, fountains (including the *Fonte de Neptuno*, ascribed to Italian master Bernini) and an *azulejo*-lined canal where the royals went boating.

The palace was designed by Portuguese architect Mateus Vicente de Oliveira and French artist Jean-Baptiste Robillon for Prince Dom Pedro in the 1750s. Pedro's niece and wife, Queen Maria I, lived here for most of her reign, going increasingly mad. Her scheming Spanish daughter-in-law, Carlota Joaquina, was quite a match for eccentric British visitor William Beckford. On one occasion she insisted that Beckford run a race with her maid in the garden and then dance a bolero, which he did 'in a delirium of romantic delight'.

Inside is like a chocolate box, with a gilded, mirror-lined Throne Room and Pedro IV's bedroom where he slept under a circular ceiling, surrounded by *Don Quixote* murals. The palace's vast kitchens now house a palatial restaurant, **Cozinha Velha** (☑214 356 158; mains €22-28; ☺lunch & dinner).

Once you've seen the palace, live the life: the Royal Guard of the Court quarters have been converted into the dazzling **Pousada de Dona Maria I** (☑214 356 158; www.pousadas.pt; d incl breakfast from €123; ✷), with high-ceilinged rooms that will make you feel as if you're at home with the royals.

❶ Getting There & Away

Queluz (keh-*loozh*) is 12km northwest of Lisbon and makes an easy day trip. Frequent trains from Lisbon's Rossio station stop at Queluz-Belas (€1.55, 18 minutes).

Mafra

POP 11,000 / ELEV 250M

Mafra, 39km northwest of Lisbon, makes a superb day trip from Lisbon, Sintra or Ericeira. It is home to Palácio Nacional de Mafra, Portugal's extravagant monastery-palace hybrid with 1200 rooms. Nearby is the beautiful former royal park, Tapada Nacional de Mafra, once a hunting ground and still teeming with wild animals and plants.

The monumental palace facade dominates the town. Opposite is a pleasant square, Praça da República, which is lined with cafes and restaurants. Mafra's bus terminal is 1.5km northwest but buses also stop in front of the palace.

❍ Sights

Palácio Nacional de Mafra   PALACE
(☑261 817 550; adult/child €6/free, free 10am-2pm Sun; ☺10am-5.30pm Wed-Mon) Wild-spending Dom João V poured pots of Brazilian gold into this baroque palace, covering a mind-boggling 4 sq km and comprising a monastery and basilica. Begun in 1717, the exuberant mock-marble confection is the handiwork of German master Friedrich Ludwig, who trained in Italy and clearly had a kind of Portuguese Vatican in mind. No expense was spared: around 45,000 artisans worked on building its 1200 rooms and two bell towers, which shelter the world's largest collection of bells (92 in total).

When the French invaded Portugal in 1807, Dom João VI and the royals skedad-dled to Brazil, taking most of Mafra's furniture with them. Imagine the anticlimax when the French found nothing but 20 elderly Franciscan friars. General Junot billeted his troops in the monastery, followed by Wellington and his men. From then on the palace became a military haven. Even today, most of it is used as a military academy.

On a self-guided visit, you'll take in treasures such as the antler-strewn hunting room and a walled bed for mad monks (maybe sent over the edge by all those corridors!). The biggest stunner is the 83.6m-long barrel-vaulted library, housing some 40,000 15th- to 18th-century books, many hand-bound by the monks. It's an appropriate fairy-tale coda to all this extravagance that they're gradually being gnawed away by rats. The basilica of twin bell-tower fame is strikingly restrained by comparison, featuring multihued marble floors and Carrara marble statues.

Tapada Nacional de Mafra   FOREST
(☑261 817 050; www.tapadademafra.pt; walker €5, cyclist €10; ☺9.30am-5.30pm) The 819-hectare Tapada Nacional de Mafra is where Dom João V used to go a-hunting. Enclosed by an original 21km wall, the grounds are now an environmentally aware game park, home to free-roaming wild boar and red deer, plus smaller numbers of foxes, badgers and eagles.

To appreciate the different ecosystems, hike through its woodlands of Portuguese oak, cork oak and pine; don't miss the 350-year-old cork oak saved from fire in 2003. The 4km trail is a good introduction to the park, but you have a greater chance of spotting animals on one of the more remote 7.5km routes. Also on the grounds is a simple but pleasantly furnished guesthouse (singles/doubles €65/75). On weekends, many activities are on offer, including horse riding (by advance reservation), archery, wagon rides, and taking a tourist 'train' around the park.

The Tapada is about 7km north of Mafra, along the road to Gradil. It's best reached by private transport, as buses are erratic; from Mafra, taxis charge around €10 one way.

Sobreiro   MINIATURE VILLAGE
(☺9.30am-7pm) FREE At the village of Sobreiro, 4km northwest of Mafra (take any Ericeira-bound bus), sculptor José Franco has created an enchanting miniature, vaguely surreal craft village of windmills, watermills and traditional shops. Kids love it here; as do

A WOLF IN THE WOODS

There's no need to be afraid of the wolves at the **Centro de Recuperação do Lobo Ibérico** (Iberian Wolf Sanctuary; ☑ 261 785 037; http://lobo.fc.ul.pt; Vale da Guarda, Picão; adult/concession €5/3; ⊙ 4.30pm & 6pm Sat & Sun May-Sep, 3pm & 4.30pm Sat & Sun Oct-Apr), located near Malveira, 10km east of Mafra. The centre is home to a pack of around 20 wolves that can no longer live in the wild. Set in a forested valley, the centre aims to boost the rapidly dwindling numbers of Portugal's Iberian wolf population (now just 300 in the wild) by affording them safe shelter in a near-to-natural habitat. As the wolves are free to roam in their large enclosures, there's no guarantee that you'll spot them, but encounters are frequent. Visits are by 90-minute guided tours. The sanctuary is best reached by private transport.

some adults, especially when they discover the rustic *adega* (winery) serving red wine and snacks. Most folks bring a picnic.

🛏 Sleeping & Eating

Aldeia da Mata Pequena　　　RURAL INN €€
(☑ 219 270 908; www.aldeiadamatapequena.com; Rua São Francisco de Assis; house €70-130) Located 9km south of Mafra, this unique rural tourism option consists of attractive stone cottages, each with a kitchen, living room and sleeping area. It's set in a tiny village and is best reached by private car, which you'll need to explore the surrounding countryside.

Restaurante Sete Sóis　　　PORTUGUESE €€
(☑ 261 811 161; Largo Conde Ferreira 1; mains €7-12; ⊙ lunch & dinner) Conveniently located across from the plaza, this recommended local place serves good-value lunch specials (€7) and specialises in Portuguese classics like *bacalhau* (codfish) as well as wild game dishes like grilled wild boar.

❶ Getting There & Around

There are regular **Mafrense** (☑ 261 816 159; Av Dr Francisco Sá Carneiro) buses to/from Ericeira (€2.10, 20 minutes, at least hourly), Sintra (€3.55, 45 minutes) and Lisbon's Campo Grande terminal (€4.10, 75 minutes, at least hourly). Mafra's train station is 6km away from the town centre with infrequent buses; taxis charge around €9 from the station to the town centre. Go to Malveira station instead for easier connections (20 minutes) to Mafra.

Taxis are available in Praça da República.

SETÚBAL PENINSULA

As the mercury rises, the promise of sun, sea and mouth-watering grilled fish lures *lisboêtas* south to the Setúbal Peninsula

for weekends of ozone-enriched fun. Beach bums make for the Costa da Caparica's 8km sweep of golden sand to laze on a lounger, dip in the chilly Atlantic and unwind over sundowners in beachside cafes. The coast gets wilder the further south you venture and Cabo Espichel is wildest of all – a vertiginous cape thrashed by the Atlantic, where you can trace the footprints of dinosaurs.

Edging further south, the vibrant port of Setúbal provides a tonic for a UV overdose. It's a fine place to munch *choco frito* (fried cuttlefish) and spot bottlenose dolphins on a breezy cruise of the marshy Sado estuary. To the west lies Parque Natural da Arrábida, lined with scalloped bays flanked by sheer cliffs that are home to birds of prey. It leads to the fishing town and bay of Sesimbra, laced with cobbled backstreets and overshadowed by a Moorish castle. The coast is great for outdoorsy types, offering activities from scuba-diving and surfing to hiking and canyoning.

Costa da Caparica

Costa da Caparica's seemingly never-ending beach attracts sun-worshipping *lisboêtas* craving all-over tans, surfers keen to ride Atlantic waves, and day-tripping families seeking clean sea and soft sand. It hasn't escaped development, but head south and the high-rises soon give way to pine forests and mellow beach-shack cafes. The town has the same name as the coastline, and is a cheery place with shops and lots of inflatable seaside tack.

Costa da Caparica town focuses on Praça da Liberdade. West of the *praça*, pedestrianised Rua dos Pescadores, with hotels and restaurants, leads to the seaside and a helpful **tourist office** (p139). The main beach (called Praia do CDS, or Centro Desportivo de Surf), with cafes, bars and surfing clubs along its promenade, is a short walk north. The **bus terminal** (Av General Humberto Delgado) is 400m northwest of the Praça da Liberdade; additional stops are by the *praça*.

🏄 Beaches

During the summer a narrow-gauge railway runs most of the length of the beach and you can jump off at any one of 20 stops. The nearer beaches, including **Praia do Norte** and **Praia do São Sebastião**, are great for families, while the further ones are younger and trendier. **Praia do Castelo** (stop 11) and **Praia da Bela Vista** (stop 17) are more-secluded gay and nudist havens.

🏃 Activities

Among the hottest **surfing** spots are São João da Caparica, Praia da Mata and Praia da Sereia. Fonte da Telha (where the train terminates) is the best beach for **windsurfing** and has plenty of water-sports facilities. Check the handy *Tabela de Marés* booklet (available at the *turismo*), listing tide times, surf shops and clubs.

Da Wave (p138) rents out surf- and bodyboards, wetsuits and beach gear (footballs, frisbees and in-line skates).

Caparica Surfing School   SURFING
(☑ 212 919 078; www.caparicasurf.com; Praia do CDS; lessons €20; ⏰ 10am-6pm Sat & Sun) The main surfing school.

Hooked Surf School   SURFING
(☑ 913 615 978; www.hookedsurf.com; intro lesson €25, 4 lessons €80) Brian Trigg runs the excellent Hooked Surf School, offering lessons and a kids' surf club at Costa da Caparica, Praia do Guincho and Praia Grande. Call ahead for a pick-up from your accommodation. It also rents out boards and wetsuits.

Cabana Divers   DIVING
(☑ 919 390 278; www.cabanadivers.pt; Fonte da Telha) Cabana Divers, with a nicely set-up bar and wicker basket chairs by the beach, provides scuba-diving lessons and all the necessary equipment.

Bicla   CYCLING
(per hr/half-day €3/7.50; ⏰ 10am-7pm) You can rent bikes for cruising along the beach path from Bicla, which operates out of the beachside restaurant Dragão Vermelha.

🛌 Sleeping

**Centro de Lazer de
São João de Caparica**   HOSTEL €
(☑ 212 918 250; www.centrolazercaparica.com; Rua Bernardo Santareno 3; dm/s/d with shared bathroom €18/22/37; ☲) Popular with groups, this hostel offers clean and simple rooms and a sparkling swimming pool. There are bikes available for rent, which are useful as it's a bit out of the way (1km to the beach, 2km to Costa da Caparica town itself).

Costa da Caparica   CAMPGROUND €
(☑ 212 901 366; bungalows from €64, campsites per adult/tent/car €6.40/8.60/6.30; ☎) Orbitur's campground, 1km north of Costa da Caparica town, sits 200m from the beach and has a cafe, tennis court and playground.

Residencial Mar e Sol   GUESTHOUSE €€
(☑ 212 900 017; www.residencialmaresol.com; Rua dos Pescadores 42; s/d €50/65; ☒@☎) Mar e Sol offers simple yet comfy rooms in warm hues with parquet floors. There is free internet, bike hire (summer only) and a good Italian restaurant (p139) next door.

Real Caparica   GUESTHOUSE €€
(☑ 212 918 870; www.realcaparicahotel.com; Rua Mestre Manuel 18; s/d €45/65; ☒☎) A young crew runs this place, 30m from the beach. Rooms have simple wood furnishings, tile floors and patterned bedspreads; the upstairs rooms are brighter. You can snag a sea-view room for €75.

🍴 Eating & Drinking

In Costa da Caparica town, seafood restaurants line Rua dos Pescadores. Restaurants and open-sided bars on the beach crank up during the summer months.

A Merendeira   SANDWICHES €
(☑ 212 904 527; Rua dos Pescadores 20; sandwiches €2.20; ⏰ 10am-1am) This cafe on the main drag serves *merendeiras* (oven-baked sandwiches with chorizo, beef or cod), and filling daily soups and desserts.

Da Wave   CAFE €€
(Praia Nova; mains €9-11; ⏰ 10am-2am; ☎) One of many open-sided cafe-restaurants along the beach, Da Wave has a laid-back vibe with its beanbag chairs, loungers and reggae playing overhead. American-style breakfasts, sandwiches, pizzas and juices make up the menu. Find it by heading 500m from town in the direction of the narrow-gauge train.

Napoli   ITALIAN €€
(☑212 903 197; Rua dos Flores 1; mains €7-12; ☺dinner) Pizzas, pasta dishes and other Italian fare draw hungry locals to this unassuming (but smoky) Italian joint at Residencial Mar e Sol.

Bar Waikiki   BAR
(☑212 962 129; Praia da Sereia; sandwiches/salads/crepes from €3/10/6; ☺10am-4am Jun-Aug, 10am-7.30pm Mar-May & Sep-Oct) Nicely on its own, this beachfront bar is popular with surfers and has a cool lounge vibe. Great for sundowners, you'll find it at stop 15 on the train.

❶ Information

Turismo (☑212 900 071; ☺9.30am-1pm & 2-5.30pm Mon-Fri) Helpful staff in the modern brown building on the beach.

❶ Getting There & Away

Transportes Sul do Tejo (TST; ☑217 262 740; www.tsuldotejo.pt) runs regular buses (bus 153) to Costa da Caparica from Lisbon's Praça de Espanha (€2.90, 40 minutes, every 20 to 60 minutes).

The best way to get here is by ferry to Cacilhas (every 15 minutes) from Lisbon's Cais do Sodré, where bus 135 runs to Costa da Caparica town (€3.20, 30 to 45 minutes, every 30 to 60 minutes).

Those who prefer to cycle can do a bike-ferry-bike combo from Lisbon. Take the bike path along the Tejo out to Belém, board the ferry to Trafaria, and continue another 3km by bike from there along a bike path to Costa da Caparica.

❶ Getting Around

The train along the beach runs every half-hour from 9am to 7.30pm departing from Praia Nova and making over a dozen stops before reaching Fonte da Telha (adult/child €7.50/2 return), about 1km before the end of the county beach.

Setúbal

POP 114,000

Though hardly a classic beauty, the thriving port town of Setúbal (*shtoo-bahl*) makes a terrific base for exploring the region's natural assets. Top of the must-do list is a cruise to the marshy wetlands of the Sado estuary, the splashy playground of bottlenose dolphins, flocks of white storks (spring and summer), and wintering flamingos that make the water fizz like pink champagne.

You can hike or bike along the dramatic, pine-brushed coastline of Parque Natural da Arrábida, or simply soak up rays on nearby sandy beaches.

Back in town, it's worth taking a stroll through the squares in the pedestrianised old town and clambering up to the hilltop fortress for views over the estuary. The fish reeled the Romans to Setúbal in 412, so it's no surprise that seafood here is delicious. On Avenida Luísa Todi, locals happily while away hours polishing off enormous platters of *choco frito* and carafes of white wine.

Most sights are within easy walking distance of the pedestrianised centre. The bus station is about 150m north of the centre; the main train station is 700m north of the centre. Frequent ferries shuttle across the Rio Sado to the Tróia peninsula from terminals around Doca do Comércio.

◉ Sights

Casa da Cultura   CULTURAL CENTRE
(Rua Detrás da Guarda 26; ☺10am-midnight Tue-Sat, to 8pm Sun) FREE Opened in 2012, this sparkling new art space has a packed cultural calendar. Wander through changing exhibitions on the main floor, or stop in for an evening concert of jazz trios, classical quartets, world music and the like, which are held on the open-air Pátio do Dimas. The cinema upstairs has a mix of European arthouse fare, children's animated films and documentaries.

Prices are reasonable: exhibitions are free, films and concerts range from free to €5. Stop in the Cafe das Artes for a drink and to see what's on.

Praça do Bocage   PLAZA
All streets in the pedestrianised old town seem to lead to this mosaic-cobbled square, presided over by the arcaded pink-and-white town hall. It's a sunny spot for a wander amid the palms and fountains, or for coffee and people-watching on one of the pavement terraces.

Castelo São Filipe   CASTLE
(☺7am-10pm) Worth the 500m schlep uphill to the west, the castle was built by Filipe I in 1590 to fend off an English attack on the invincible Armada. Converted into a *pousada* (upmarket inn) in the 1960s, its hulking ramparts afford precipitous views and its chapel is festooned in blue-and-white 18th-century *azulejos*.

Setúbal

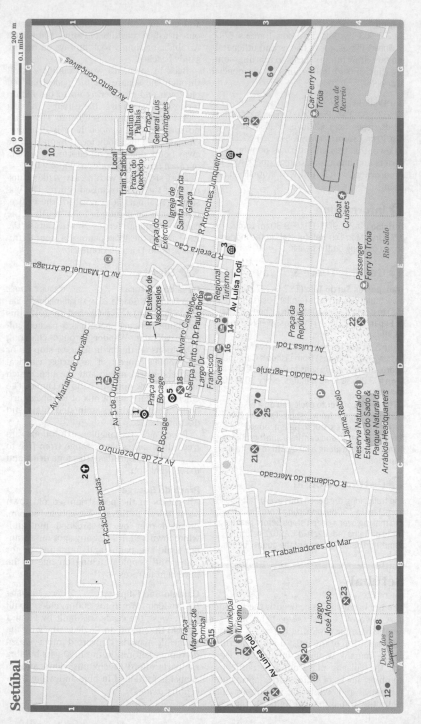

0   200 m
0   0.1 miles

Setúbal

Igreja de Jesus   CHURCH
(Praça Miguel Bombarda; ⊙9am-1pm & 2-5.30pm Tue-Sun) FREE Setúbal's architectural stunner is the sand-coloured Igreja de Jesus, one of the earliest examples of Manueline architecture, adorned with gargoyles and twirling turrets. Around the altar, 18th-century blue-and-white geometric *azulejos* contrast strikingly with the curling arches of the roof. Constructed in 1491, the church was designed by Diogo de Boitaca, better known for his later work on Belém's fantastical Mosteiro dos Jerónimos.

Museu do Trabalho
Michel Giacometti   MUSEUM
(Largo Defensores da República; adult/child €1.15/free; ⊙9am-12.30pm & 2-5.30pm Tue-Fri, 3-6pm Sat) How does the sardine get in the tin and 1001 other fishy mysteries are solved at this quirky, rarely visited museum, set in a former sardine-canning factory. There's also

an entire 1920s grocery, transported from Lisbon wholesale.

Museu de Arqueologia e
Etnografia   MUSEUM
(Museum of Archaeology & Ethnography; ☑265 239 365; Av Luísa Todi 162; ⊙9am-12.30pm & 2-5.30pm Tue-Sat) FREE This small, rambling museum showcases several intriguing pieces such as Roman mosaics and 19th-century devotional paintings on wood, showing invalids having holy visions.

Reserva Natural do
Estuário do Sado   NATURE RESERVE
This natural reserve protects the Sado estuary, a biologically rich area of wetlands extending east and south of Setúbal. With over 250 avian species, this is a prime spot for birdwatching. The little-visited **Moinho de Maré das Mouriscas** (☑914 162 354; ⊙10am-6pm Wed-Sun) FREE, located 8km east of Setúbal, has short walking trails and a bird observatory. It's set beside a former tide mill built in 1601, which also houses a gallery and cafe. You'll need a car to get here. Stop in the Municipal Turismo for exact directions.

🏖 Beaches

While Setúbal itself is a little underwhelming, the coastal scenery outside town is spectacular. Don't miss the chiselled cliffs, pine-brushed hills and picturesque beaches of Parque Natural da Arrábida (p144).

Alternatively, it's an easy 20-minute ferry ride – look out for dolphins on the way – to **Tróia**, where the soft sandy beaches are flanked by dunes.

⊂⊃ Tours

Bus Tours

Setúbal & Arrábida Bus Tour   BUS TOUR
(adult/child €10/5; ⊙10am-1pm Sat) The open-topped Setúbal & Arrábida Bus Tour provides hop-on hop-off service to attractions around Setúbal, taking in coastal scenery, village stops (in Azeitão) and clifftop lookouts. Catch the bus along Avenida Luísa Todi, near the Hotel Esperança.

Cycling Tours

To head off on your own, you can hire a bike from **Go Setúbal** (☑962 125 999; http://go setubal.pt; Av Luísa Todi 249; 1/3/8hr €3/7/10).

Blue Coast Bikes   CYCLING TOURS
(☑265 092 172; www.bluecoastbikes.travel; Rua das Fontaínhas 82; bike hire per day from €15, guid-

ed tours from €70) An American-Portuguese partnership, based in Setúbal, offers six- and eight-day guided tours through the Douro Valley, around the Alentejo and along the Costa Azul. Their mechanic is a former Portuguese downhill and cross-country champion.

Cruises & Dolphin-Watching

A highlight of any trip to Setúbal is the chance to spot resident bottlenose dolphins on a cruise of the **Sado estuary**. The frolicsome fellas show off their dorsal fins to a happy-snappy crowd; listen for their high-pitched clicking. Plenty of companies run half-day trips around the estuary (leaving from Doca do Comércio). Book ahead.

Nautur
CRUISE

(☑ 265 532 914; www.nautur.com; Rua Praia da Saúde 15E; cruises €28-55) Offers a variety of cruises, starting on the Sado estuary, then visiting Arrábida beach, before returning to the river for some dolphin-spotting.

Mil Andanças
DOLPHIN-WATCHING

(☑ 265 532 979; www.mil-andancas.pt; Av Luísa Todi 121) Runs dolphin-spotting river tours (€30 per person).

Troiacruze
CRUISE

(☑ 265 228 482; www.troiacruze.com; Rua das Barroças 34) Offers dolphin-spotting (€25) and other cruises, such as a sailing galleon along the Sado estuary.

Vertigem Azul
DOLPHIN-WATCHING

(☑ 265 238 000; www.vertigemazul.com; Rua Praia da Saúde 11D) 🕭 Offers sustainable three-hour dolphin-watching tours in the Sado estuary (€35). It's located 500m west of the centre.

4WD Tours

Mil Andanças offers 4WD tours in Arrábida (half-day €30).

Walking Tours

Sistemas de Ar Livre
WALKING TOUR

(SAL; ☑ 265 227 685; www.sal.pt; Av Manuel Maria Portela 40; per person from €8; ◷ 10am Sat & Sun Sep-Jun) 🕭 The ecotourism company Sistemas de Ar Livre arranges activities including three-hour guided walks in or around Setúbal.

Wine Tours

The tourist office has a free useful leaflet, *Rota de Vinhos da Costa Azul,* detailing all the wine producers you can visit in the area.

José Maria da Fonseca
WINE TOUR

(☑ 212 198 940; www.jmf.pt; Rua José Augusto Coelho 11, Vila Nogueira de Azeitão; visits €3; ◷ 10am-12.15pm & 2-5.30pm) Wine-lovers shouldn't miss the cellar tours of José Maria da Fonseca, the oldest Portuguese producer of table wine and Moscatel de Setúbal, in nearby Vila Nogueira de Azeitão. The winery is now run by the sixth generation of the family. Ring ahead to arrange a visit. From Setúbal, buses leave frequently to Vila Nogueira de Azeitão (20 minutes).

⊨ Sleeping

Parque de Campismo
CAMPGROUND €

(☑ 265 238 318; www.roteiro-campista.pt; Outão; campsites per adult/tent/car €4.50/6.50/3.20; 🕸) Situated 4km west of Setúbal, this shady site is right on the coast although it's mostly used by long-term caravanners. It's accessible by regular bus (25 minutes).

Blue Coast Hostel
HOSTEL €

(☑ 265 417 837; bluecoasthostel@gmail.com; Avenida 5 de Outubro 140; dm/d €19/40; 🕸@🕭) Opened in 2012, Blue Coast has colourful dorm rooms with wood floors, several of which are en suite (doubles, with worn carpeting, are less charming). There's a lounge, a concrete patio in the back and free bikes available. Daily lunches and dinners (€5 each) are a good place to meet other travellers.

Residencial Tody
GUESTHOUSE €

(☑ 265 220 592; http://residencialtodi.pt; Av Luísa Todi 244; s/d with shared bathroom €20/30; 🕭) If street noise doesn't affect your shut-eye, this is a decent cheapie on the main drag. The bare-bones rooms with TV and tiny bathrooms are tidy and clean.

Hotel Esperança
HOTEL €

(☑ 265 521 789; www.hotellunaesperanca.com; Av Luísa Todi 220; s/d €43/53; 🕸🕭) This shiny six-storey hotel, with its aquamarine paint job, is a bit of an eyesore, though it does have clean, carpeted rooms with big windows (which you can open to catch some fresh air) and efficient staff. Book higher floors to avoid street noise. Wi-fi is free in the lobby, but charged for in the rooms.

Aqualuz
HOTEL €€

(☑ 265 499 000; www.aqualuztroia.com; Tróia; d from €99; 🕸🕭🕮) A short stroll from lovely Tróia beach, this resort offers attractive modern rooms with balconies overlooking either the waterfront or the Arrábida mountains. The facilities are extensive, with a spa, restaurant, bar, pool and golf course. It's a good choice for families who want to be near the beach, but you'll need to take the ferry back to Setúbal if you tire of the handful of marina restaurants. Next door is the slightly pricier **Blue & Green Tróia Design Hotel** (265 498 000; www.troiadesignhotel.com; Tróia Marina, Tróia; d from €124; P ❋ 🤀 🕸).

Hotel Solaris
GUESTHOUSE €€
(265 541 770; www.solarishotel.com.pt; Praça Marquês de Pombal 12; s/d €50/60; ❋ @ 🤀) Overlooking a lively square, Solaris is a small and friendly option. Rooms have a neat, trim design with dark wood floors and red, quilted bedspreads; some have small balconies. Breakfast is above-par, with eggs and fresh fruit.

Pousada de São Filipe
LUXURY HOTEL €€€
(265 550 070; www.pousadas.pt; d from €145; ❋) Perched high and mighty above Setúbal is this green-shuttered retreat, hidden inside the town's hilltop fortress. Expect vaulted corridors filled with antiques, spacious quarters and dramatic ocean panoramas.

🍴 Eating & Drinking

Head to the western end of Avenida Luísa Todi, where alfresco restaurants serve lip-smacking, fresh-from-the-Atlantic seafood. Be sure to sample local specialities such as *caldeirada*, a hearty fish stew, and *choco frito* washed down with sweet Moscatel de Setúbal wine.

Mercado do Livramento
MARKET €
(Av Luísa Todi; 🕗 7am-2pm Wed-Sun) Amid life size statues of vendors (fruit sellers, fish-mongers etc), you can assemble a first-rate picnic at this enticing cast-iron market: cheese, olives, bread, seasonal fruits and more.

Taifa
CAFE €
(Av Luísa Todi 558; mains €6-8; 🕗 3pm-midnight Tue-Sun; 🤀🍴) A nice break from seafood restaurants, Taifa is a jazzy little cafe with outdoor tables and an eclectic menu that includes Thai dishes, Belgian beers, juices and appetisers. The soundtrack is equally diverse, encompassing blues, folk, swing, soul and salsa.

Duarte dos Frangos
CHICKEN €
(265 522 603; Av Luísa Todi 285; mains €5-10; 🕗 lunch & dinner Fri-Wed) This cosy spot just south of the old town whips up succulent

roast chicken. The yellow-and-blue decor is cheery, but service can border on matronly.

Botequim du Bocage
CAFE €
(265 534 077; Praça de Bocage 128; snacks €2-4) Pull up a chair at this cafe terrace on Setúbal's sunny main square. Light bites include quiche, pizza and sweets such as almond tart, and there are daily lunch specials (€5.50).

Portugália
PORTUGUESE €€
(Av Jaime Rebelo 31; mains €11-15; 🕗 noon-10.30pm Sun-Thu, to midnight Fri & Sat) The food is hit-or-miss, but its location on a leafy park overlooking the river makes it a fine destination for sunset drinks and snacks. Outdoor seating.

Xica Bia
SEAFOOD €€
(265 522 559; Av Luísa Todi 131; mains €11-13; 🕗 lunch & dinner Mon-Sat) Fado shawls, wrought-iron chandeliers and copper pots jazz up this brick-vaulted restaurant. Xica Bia serves market-fresh seafood.

Solar do Lago
PORTUGUESE €€
(265 238 847; Parque das Escolas 40; mains €8-12; 🕗 lunch & dinner) This high-ceilinged restaurant exudes rustic charm with its chunky wooden tables and terracotta tiles. Tasty seafood dishes include garlicky *caldeirada* (€25 for two) and grilled squid. A handful of outdoor tables overlook a quiet plaza.

Casa Santiago
SEAFOOD €€
(265 221 688; Av Luísa Todi 92; mains €7-13; 🕗 lunch & dinner Mon-Sat) Wafts of fish sizzling on the grill will reel you into this local favourite, where the hungry lunchtime crowds feast on huge portions of *choco frito*, served with a squirt of lemon and mounds of fries, rice and salad. It's the best along the strip with a covered terrace and plenty of buzz.

Baluarte da Avenida
SEAFOOD €€
(265 520 040; Av Luísa Todi 524; mains €10-13; 🕗 lunch & dinner) Baluarte serves excellent fish and seafood dishes, cooked to perfection without a lot of fuss. Start off with local Azeitão cheese, followed by grilled fish or *caldeirada* (seafood stew) for two, and finish with a glass of Setúbal moscatel. The downside: smoking is allowed inside the restaurant – quite aggravating for nonsmokers.

Pousada de São Filipe
SEAFOOD €€€
(265 550 070; mains €14-28; 🕗 lunch & dinner) This smart restaurant has a clifftop terrace with views. The food generally isn't worth

WORTH A TRIP

PARQUE NATURAL DA ARRÁBIDA

Thickly green, hilly and edged by gleaming, clean, golden beaches and chiselled cliffs, the Parque Natural da Arrábida stretches along the southeastern coast of the Setúbal Peninsula from Setúbal to Sesimbra. Covering the 35km-long Serra da Arrábida mountain ridge, this is a protected area rich in Mediterranean plants, from olive, pistachio and strawberry to lavender, thyme and chamomile, with attendant butterflies, beetles and birds (especially birds of prey such as eagles and kestrels), and 70 types of seaweed. Its pine-brushed hills are also home to deer and wild boar.

Highlights here are the long, golden beaches of windsurfer hot-spot **Figueirinha** and the sheltered bay of **Galapo**. Most stunning of all is **Portinho da Arrábida** with fine sand, azure waters and a small 17th-century fort built to protect the monks from Barbary pirates. There are some *quartos* (private rooms) right on the beach here.

Local honey is delicious, especially that produced in the gardens of the whitewashed, red-roofed **Convento da Arrábida** (📞212 197 620; arrabida@foriente.pt; admission €5; ⊙ Wed-Sun), a 16th-century former monastery overlooking the sea just north of Portinho (call ahead to schedule a visit). Another famous product is Azeitão ewe's cheese, with a characteristic flavour that owes much to lush Arrábida pastures and a variety of thistle used in the curdling process.

Public transport through the middle of the park is nonexistent; some buses serve the beach from July to September (around four daily to Figueirinha). Your best option is to rent a car or motorcycle, or take an organised trip by jeep and/or boat. Be warned: parking is tricky near the beaches, even in the low season.

the price tag, but it's a great setting for a sunset drink.

ℹ Information

Caixa Geral de Depósitos (Av Luísa Todi 190) Has an ATM.

Hospital São Berardo (📞265 549 000; Rua Camilo Castelo Branco) Near the Praça de Touros, off Avenida Dom João II.

Municipal Turismo (📞936 515 845; Av Luísa Todi 468; ⊙9am-8pm Mon-Fri, 10am-7pm Sat & Sun) Excellent information about Setúbal and attractions in the surrounding countryside.

Police Station (📞265 522 022; Av 22 de Dezembro)

Regional Turismo (📞265 539 130; www.costa-azul.rts.pt; Travessa Frei Gaspar 10; ⊙9.30am-12.30pm & 2-6pm Mon-Sat) Has a glass floor revealing the remains of a Roman *garum* (fish condiment) factory. Hands out leaflets on the area.

ℹ Getting There & Away

BOAT

Passenger-only catamarans to Tróia depart half-hourly to hourly every day (adult/child return €5.80/3.40). **Car ferries** (car and driver €13, additional passenger €3.20) run on a similar schedule. Note that car ferries, catamarans and cruises all have different departure points. See www.atlanticferries.pt for departure times.

BUS

Buses run between Setúbal and Lisbon's Praça de Espanha (€4.25 to €6.50, 45 to 60 minutes, at least hourly) – or from Cacilhas (€4.25, 50 minutes, every 15 minutes Monday to Friday, every two hours Saturday and Sunday).

TRAIN

From Lisbon's Sete Rios station at least six IC trains run daily to Setúbal (€9.65, one hour), with a change at Pinhal Novo. You can also catch a frequent ferry from Lisbon's Terreiro do Paço terminal to Barreiro station (€2.30, 30 minutes), from where there are cheaper, frequent *urbano* (urban) trains to Setúbal (€2.15, 30 minutes).

ℹ Getting Around

Cycling is a great way to discover the coast at your own pace. Hire a bike from Goper.

Car-rental agencies include **Avis** (📞265 538 710; Av Luísa Todi 96).

Sesimbra

POP 38,000

As well as fine sands, turquoise waters and a Moorish castle slung high above the centre, this former fishing village offers excellent seafood in its waterfront restaurants.

Though the beach gets packed in summer, the town has kept its low-key charm with narrow lanes lined with terracotta-roofed houses, outdoor cafes and a palm-fringed promenade for lazy ambles. Cruises, guided hikes and scuba-diving activities here include trips to Cabo Espichel, where dinosaurs once roamed. It's 30km southwest of Setúbal, sheltering under the Serra da Arrábida at the western edge of the beautiful Parque Natural da Arrábida.

◉ Sights

Castelo
CASTLE

(⊙8am-7pm) FREE For sweeping views over dale and coast, roam the snaking ramparts of the Moorish castle, rising 200m above Sesimbra. It was taken by Dom Afonso Henriques in the 12th century, retaken by the Moors, then snatched back by Christians under Dom Sancho I.

The ruins harbour the 18th-century, chalk-white Igreja Santa Maria do Castelo; step inside to admire its heavy gold altar and exquisite blue-and-white *azulejos*. The shady castle grounds are ideal for picnics.

Fortaleza de Santiago
CASTLE

FREE In the town centre, the grandest castle on the sand is 17th-century Fortaleza de Santiago, once part of Portugal's coastal defences and the summertime retreat of Portuguese kings. At research time it was closed for renovations.

✦ Activities

Sesimbra is a great place to get into the outdoors with a backyard full of cliffs for climbing, clear water for scuba diving, Atlantic waves for windsurfing, and miles and miles of unspoilt coastal trails for hiking and cycling. Adrenaline junkies get their thrills with vigorous pursuits from canyoning to rappelling.

Vertente Natural
ADVENTURE SPORTS

(☑210 848 919; www.vertentenatural.com; Santana; tours from €25) ✎ An eco-aware, one-stop shop for adventure sports, this Sesimbra-based outfitter offers trekking, canyoning, canoeing, diving and rappelling. It's headquartered a few kilometres northwest of town.

Aquarama
CRUISE

(☑965 263 157; www.aquarama.com.pt; Av dos Náufragos; adult/child from €18/10) Runs several trips per day to Cabo Espichel on a glass-bottomed partially submerged boat. Buy tickets at the office or on the boat.

Surf Clube de Sesimbra
SURFING

(☑210 875 139; www.scs.pt; Edificio Mar de Sesimbra, Rua Navegador Rodrigues Soromenho, Lote 1A, Loja 5; 90-minute private/group lesson €40/20) Offers lessons and board hire.

Best Dive
DIVING

(☑917 535 980; www.bestdive.pt; Av dos Náufragos; intro course €75-100, single dive incl equipment €46) PADI dive centre offering courses and dives in the Sesimbra area. It's on the beachfront road, 800m west of the Fortaleza de Santiago.

✺ Festivals & Events

Cabo Espichel Festival
RELIGIOUS

Spectacularly set, this festival celebrates an alleged apparition of the Virgin Mary during the 15th century; an image of the Virgin is carried through the parishes, ending at the Cape. It takes place on the last Sunday in September.

Senhor Jesus das Chagas
RELIGIOUS

On 4 May, a procession stops twice to bless the land and four times to bless the sea, carrying an image of Christ that is said to have appeared on the beach in the 16th century (usually kept in Misericórdia church).

⌴ Sleeping

Forte do Cavalo
CAMPGROUND €

(☑212 288 508; www.cm-sesimbra.pt; campsites per adult/tent/car €3.50/5.20/2.30; ⊙Mar-Oct) Camp under the pines at this hilltop municipal site, 1km west of town. It has sea views, a restaurant and a kids' playground.

Parque de Campismo de Valbom
CAMPGROUND €

(☑212 687 545; www.roteiro-campista.pt; campsite per adult/tent/car €4/4/3.50; ☀) Situated 5km north of Sesimbra off N378, this leafy site has excellent facilities for families including a swimming pool, a playground and minigolf. To get here from Sesimbra, take any Lisbon-bound bus.

Quinta do Rio
RURAL INN €€

(☑212 189 343; www.estalagemquintadorio.com; Alto das Vinhas; s/d €60/70; ☀) Nestled among orange groves and vineyards, this converted *quinta* (estate), 7km from Sesimbra, is a calm hideaway with light, spacious rooms and mountain views. Ideal for families, the country retreat offers horse riding, tennis and minigolf.

Residencial Náutico
GUESTHOUSE €€

(☑212 233 233; www.residencialnautico.com; Av dos Combatentes 19; d with/without breakfast €80/70; ❄) Set 500m uphill from the waterfront, this cheery guesthouse has airy tiled-floor double rooms in citrus shades. The best have terraces that overlook Sesimbra's sun-bleached red rooftops.

Sana Sesimbra
HOTEL €€

(☑212 289 000; www.sesimbra.sanahotels.com; Av 25 de Abril; d from €90-102; P ❄ 🛜 🏊) Overlooking the sea, Sana has attractive modern rooms with big windows that overlook the ocean or the town and hills beyond (it's worth paying an extra €12 for the sea views). The rooftop pool, bar and restaurant add to the appeal – and it's worth stopping for a drink even if you don't stay here. It's in a good central location, a short stroll east of the Fortaleza de Santiago.

✗ Eating

Sea-foodies are in heaven in Sesimbra, where what swims in the Atlantic in the morning lands on plates by midday. Check out the fish restaurants by the waterfront just east of the fort.

Isaías
SEAFOOD €

(☑914 574 373; Rua Coronel Barreto 2; mains €6-8; ☺lunch & dinner Mon-Sat) No menu, no frills, just *the* tastiest grilled fish and cheapest plonk in town at this *tasca* run with love and prowess by Senhor Isaías, his son Carlos and chip maven Maria. Sole, sardines, swordfish – it's all uniformly delicious.

DINO PAWS

Step back 150 million years while hunting for the footprints of dinosaurs on the craggy limestone cliffs just north of Cabo Espichel. The clearly visible imprints are near the small cove of Praia dos Lagosteiros. Rare and remarkably well preserved, the tracks date back to the Late Jurassic Age when this area was the stomping ground of four-legged, long-necked, herbivorous sauropods. Apparently, they were first discovered in the 13th century by fishermen who believed they were made by a giant mule that carried Our Lady of the Cape. Kids and dino fans should take a short ramble to see how many footprints they can find.

Tony Bar
SEAFOOD €€

(☑212 233 199; Largo de Bombaldes 19; mains €8-16; ☺lunch & dinner) This smart restaurant on the square serves up tasty grilled fish. Portions are generous and the service is attentive.

Ribamar
SEAFOOD €€

(☑212 234 853; Av dos Náufragos 29; mains €10-20; ☺lunch & dinner) One of Sesimbra's best, this sleek restaurant faces the beach. Feast away on large seafood platters for two. Choosing a bottle from the arm-long wine list is quite a challenge.

❶ Information

Near Fortaleza de Santiago, this helpful **turismo** (☑212 288 540; Largo da Marinha 26; ☺9.30am-1pm & 2-5.30pm) is set back slightly from the seafront.

❶ Getting There & Around

Buses operated by **Transportes Sul do Tejo** (www.tsuldotejo.pt) leave from Lisbon's Praça de Espanha (€4.25, 60 to 90 minutes, at least 10 daily); from Setúbal (€3.55, 45 minutes, at least nine daily Monday to Saturday, six Sunday); and from Cacilhas (€3.70, around one hour, at least hourly). There are runs to Cabo Espichel (€2.60, 25 minutes, two daily) and more frequent runs to the village of Azóia (€2.60, 10 daily Monday to Saturday, six Sunday), about 3km before the cape.

You can hire bikes or scooters from **Badger** (Av 25 de Abril; bike per half/full day €6/13), near the *turismo*.

Aldeia do Meco

This tiny village, 12km northwest of Sesimbra, is famous for its seafood restaurants.

Praia do Meco is an unspoilt sweep of golden sand, flanked by low-rise cliffs; try to catch one of its mesmerising sunsets.

The big summertime event is the **Super Bock Super Rock** (www.superbocksuperrock. pt) fest in mid-July, with three stages of top-name performers lighting up the crowds.

In a quiet wooded setting 1.4km north of the village, the big, fairly modern, whitewashed **Country House** (☑212 685 102; www.country house-meco.com; Rua Alto da Carona, Alfarim; d €50, 2-/4-person apt €65/80; ❄ 🛜) offers four spacious rooms (with coffeemakers and fridge) and three apartments, most with balconies. It's located 2km from the beach and is well signposted.

Right up on the clifftop, large **Campimeco** (☎212 683 374; www.campimeco.blogs.sapo.pt; campsites per adult/tent/car €4.05/3.55/3.55, bungalow from €51; 🛜🎿) is 3km from the village, above Praia das Bicas and close to several beaches. Simple bungalows with kitchens also available.

Beachfront **Bar do Peixe** (☎212 684 732; Praia do Meco; mains €7-12; ⊙11am-11pm Wed-Mon), north of Praia das Bicas, has a chilled vibe and a sea-facing terrace. It serves good grilled fish and refreshing carafes of white wine sangria. Other top restaurants are scattered throughout the village, particularly on the main street Rua do Comércio.

Buses run from Sesimbra to Aldeia do Meco (€2.60, 25 minutes, four to eight daily).

Cabo Espichel

At strange, bleak Cabo Espichel, frighteningly tall cliffs – some met by swaths of beach – plunge down into piercing blue sea. The only building on the cape is a huge church, the 18th-century **Nossa Senhôra do Cabo**, flanked by two arms of desolately empty pilgrims' lodges.

It's easy to see why Wim Wenders used this windswept spot as a location when he was filming *A Lisbon Story,* with its lonely, brooding atmosphere. It's worth your while trying to catch the **Cabo Espichel festival** if you are visiting in September.

Buses to Cabo Espichel run direct from Sesimbra (one-way/return €2.60/4.45, 25 minutes, two daily), while more frequent buses terminate at the village of Azóia (€2.60, 10 daily Monday to Saturday, six Sunday), about 3km before the cape.

The Algarve

Includes ➡

Best Places to Eat

Best Views

Why Go?

The Algarve is alluring. Coastal Algarve receives much exposure for its breathtaking cliffs, golden beaches, scalloped bays and sandy islands. But the letter 'S' (for sun, surf and sand) is only one letter in the Algarvian alphabet: activities, beach bars (and discos), castles (both sandy and real), diving, entertainment, fun...

Let's be frank: Portugal's premier holiday destination sold its soul to tourism in the '60s and never really looked back. Behind sections of the south coast's beachscape loom massive conglomerations of bland holiday villas and brash resorts. However the west coast is another story – it's more about nature and less about development.

And yet coastal Algarve is a 'drop in the ocean' for any visitor. The enchanting inner Algarve boasts pretty castle towns and historic villages, cork tree- and flower-covered hillsides, and birdlife. And the wonderful Via Algarviana walking track crosses its breadth.

When to Go

Lagos

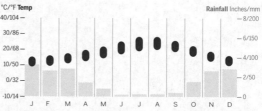

Anytime It's blessed with good weather; a mild winter and sun almost year-round.

Feb & Mar See and smell the abundance of almond and orange blossoms.

Apr & May Hike inland amid the wildflowers and leafy hillsides or get in preseason swims.

History

The Algarve has a long tradition of settlement. Phoenicians came first and established trading posts some 3000 years ago, followed by the Carthaginians. Next came the industrious Romans, who, during their 400-year stay, grew wheat, barley and grapes and built roads and palaces. Check out the remains of Milreu, near Faro.

Then came the Visigoths and, in 711, the North African Moors. They stayed 500 years, but later Christians obliterated what they could, leaving little trace of the era. Many place names come from this time, easily recognised by the article 'al' (eg Albufeira, Aljezur, Alcoutim). The Syrian Moors called the region in which they settled (east of Faro to Seville, Spain) 'al-Gharb al-Andalus' (western Andalucía), later known as 'Algarve'. Another Moorish legacy is the flat-roofed house, originally used to dry almonds, figs and corn, and to escape the night heat.

Trade, particularly in nuts and dried fruit, boomed, and Silves was the mighty Moorish capital, quite independent of the large Islamic emirate to the east.

The Reconquista (Christian reconquest) began in the early 12th century, with the wealthy Algarve as the ultimate goal. Though Dom Sancho I captured Silves and territories to the west in 1189, the Moors returned. Only in the first half of the 13th century did the Portuguese claw their way back for good.

Two centuries later the Algarve had its heyday. Prince Henry the Navigator chose the appropriately end-of-the-earth Sagres as the base for his school of navigation, and had ships built and staffed in Lagos for the 15th-century exploration of Africa and Asia – seafaring triumphs that turned Portugal into a major imperial power.

❶ Dangers & Annoyances

This is Portugal's most touristed area, and petty theft is prevalent. Never leave valuables unattended in the car or on the beach.

Swimmers beware of temperamental coast conditions, especially on the west coast, including dangerous ocean currents, strong winds and sometimes fog. Check the coloured flags: chequered means the beach is unsupervised, red means don't even dip your toe in as it's currently unsafe to do so, yellow means paddle but don't swim, and green means it's safe to swim. Blue is an international symbol that means the beach is smashing – safe, clean, good facilities.

Cliff instability is a problem, especially heading westwards from Lagos. Erosion is ongoing and serious rock falls and smaller landslides do occur. Heed the signs at the beaches and along the cliffs.

❶ Getting Around

BUS

A good bus network runs along the Algarve coast and to Loulé. From here, you can access inland Algarve, although services become more limited. Two big bus companies, **Eva Transportes** (✆ 289 899 700; www.eva-bus.com) and **Rede Expressos** (✆ 707 223 344; www.rede-expressos.pt) zip frequently between the Algarve and elsewhere in Portugal. Smaller lines include **Renex** (www.renex.pt) and **Frota Azul** (www.frotazul-algarve.pt).

Consider buying Eva's **Passe Turístico**, available from major bus stations and good for three days (€28.80) or seven days (€35.90) of unlimited bus travel on most main routes in one direction with Eva Transportes, and on Frota Azul between Lagos and Loulé. Bus service slows down considerably on weekends – particularly on Sunday.

CAR

Most main towns have reliable car-hire outlets.

TRAIN

Trains run along the coast between Faro and Vila Real de Santo António, and Faro and Lagos, and from the main towns to Lisbon.

Faro

POP 50,000

The Algarve's capital has a more distinctly Portuguese feel than most resort towns. Many visitors only pass through this underrated town – it makes an enjoyable stopover. It has an attractive marina, well-maintained parks and plazas, and a historic old town full of pedestrian lanes and outdoor cafes. Its student population of 8000 ensures a happening nightlife, and its theatre scene is strong. Marvellously preserved medieval quarters harbour curious museums, churches and a bone chapel. The lagoons of the Parque Natural da Ria Formosa and nearby beaches, including the islands of Ilha de Faro to the southwest and Ilha da Barreta (aka Ilha Deserta) to the south, add to Faro's allure.

History

After the Phoenicians and Carthaginians, Faro boomed as the Roman port Ossonoba. During the Moorish occupation it became the cultured capital of an 11th-century principality.

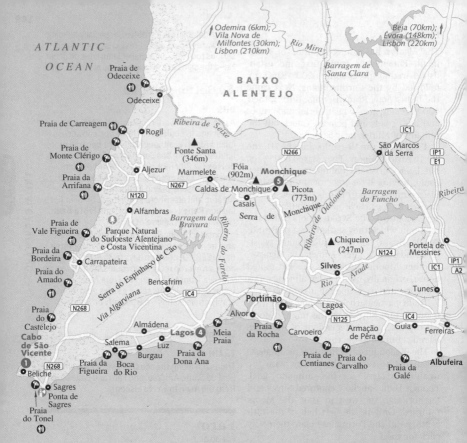

ATLANTIC OCEAN

Odemira (6km);
Vila Nova de
Milfontes (30km);
Lisbon (210km)

Beja (70km);
Évora (148km);
Lisbon (220km)

Rio Mira

Barragem de
Santa Clara

BAIXO
ALENTEJO

Praia de
Odeceixe

Odeceixe

Ribeira de Seixe

IC1

Praia de Carreagem

Rogil

São Marcos
da Serra

IP1

E1

Praia de
Monte Clérigo

Aljezur

Fonte Santa
(346m)

Marmelete

N266

N267

Fóia
(902m)

Monchique

5

Praia da
Arrifana

N120

Caldas de Monchique

Picota
(773m)

Barragem
do Funcho

Ribeira

Alfambras

Casais

Serra   de   Monchique

Ribeira de Odelouca

Praia de
Vale Figueira

Parque Natural
do Sudoeste Alentejano
e Costa Vicentina

Barragem da
Bravura

Ribeira do Farelo

Chiqueiro
(247m)

N124

Portela de
Messines

Praia da
Bordeira

Carrapateira

Silves

Rio   Arade

IC1

IP1

A2

Praia do
Amado

Serra do Espinhaço de Cão

Bensafrim

IC4

Portimão

Lagoa

Tunes

Praia
do
Castelejo

N268

Via Algarviana

Almádena

Alvor

Praia
da Rocha

Carvoeiro

N125

Armação
de Pêra

IC4

Guia

Ferreiras

Cabo
de São
Vicente

1

N268

Lagos

4

Meia
Praia

Praia de
Centianes

Praia do
Carvalho

Praia da
Galé

Albufeira

Beliche

Salema

Luz

Burgau

Praia da
Dona Ana

Sagres
Ponta de
Sagres

Praia
do Tonel

Praia da
Figueira

Boca
do Rio

ATLANTIC

OCEAN

The Algarve Highlights

1 Wind your way up the stunning – and secluded – west coast, after peering over the cliffs of **Cabo de São Vicente** (p195)

2 Lounge in waters off untouched sand islands in the **Parque Natural da Ria Formosa** (p161)

3 Explore the inner Algarve on foot, by bicycle or in a car, especially the villages of **Alte** and **Salir** in and around **Serra do Caldeirão** (p174)

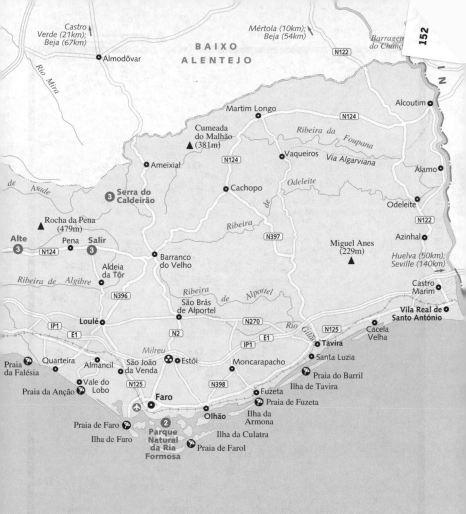

BAIXO ALENTEJO

Castro Verde (21km); Beja (67km)

Mértola (10km); Beja (54km)

Barragem do Chanç

Almodôvar

Martim Longo

Cumeada do Malhão (381m)

Ameixial

Ribeira da Foupana

Vaqueiros   Via Algarviana

Álamo

Cachopo

Odeleite

Odeleite

Serra do Caldeirão

Ribeira

Azinhal

Rocha da Pena (479m)

Alte   Pena   Salir

N124

Aldeia da Tôr

Barranco do Velho

Ribeira   de   Alportel

São Brás de Alportel

Miguel Anes (229m)

Huelva (50km); Seville (140km)

Castro Marim

Vila Real de Santo António

Ribeira de   Algibre

N396

Loulé

IP1   E1

N2

N270

IP1   E1

Rio   Gilão

N125

Cacela Velha

Milreu

Praia da Falésia

Quarteira

Almancil

São João da Venda   Estói

Moncarapacho

Tavira

Santa Luzia

Praia do Barril

Vale do Lobo

N125

Faro

Praia da Anção

Olhão

Ilha de Tavira

Fuzeta

Praia de Fuzeta

Ilha da Armona

Praia de Faro

Ilha de Faro

Parque Natural da Ria Formosa

Ilha da Culatra

Praia de Farol

N398

0   20 km

0   12 miles

④ Find your inner hedonist at the beaches and nightclubs of **Lagos** (p191)

⑤ Unwind in the spas of **Monchique** (p203) after hiking in the surrounding hills

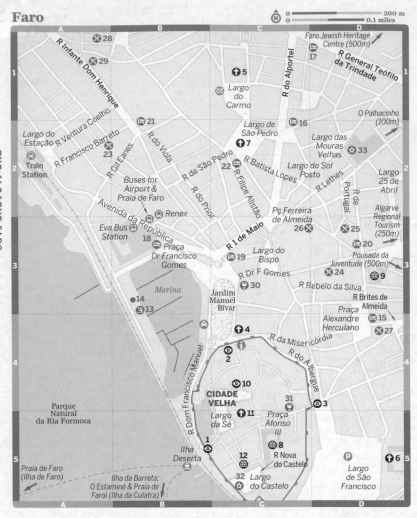

Afonso III took the town in 1249 – making it the last major Portuguese town to be recaptured from the Moors – and walled it.

Portugal's first printed works – books in Hebrew made by a Jewish printer – came from Faro in 1487.

A city from 1540, Faro had a brief golden age that slunk to a halt in 1596, during Spanish rule. Troops under the Earl of Essex, en route to England from Spain in 1597, plundered the city and carried off hundreds of priceless theological works from the bishop's palace, now part of the Bodleian Library in Oxford.

Battered Faro was rebuilt only to be shattered by an earthquake in 1722 and then almost flattened in 1755. Most of what you see today was built postquake, though the historic centre largely survived. In 1834 Faro became the Algarve's capital.

◎ Sights & Activities

◎ Cidade Velha

Within medieval walls, the picturesque Cidade Velha (Old Town) consists of winding, peaceful cobbled streets and squares,

Faro

reconstructed in a melange of styles following successive batterings – first by marauding British and then by two big earthquakes.

Arco da Vila　　　　　　　　LANDMARK
Enter the Cidade Velha through the neoclassical Arco da Vila, built by order of Bishop Francisco Gomes, Faro's answer to the Marquês de Pombal, who oversaw the city's reconstruction after the 1755 earthquake. The top of the street opens onto the orange tree-lined Largo da Sé, with the *câmara municipal* (town hall) on the left, the Paço Episcopal (Bishop's Palace) on the right and the ancient *sé* (cathedral) in front of you.

Sé　　　　　　　　　　CATHEDRAL
(admission €3; ⊙ 10am-5pm Mon-Fri, 10am-1pm Sat year-round, 10am-6pm Mon-Fri Jun-Aug) Housed within the walls of the Cidade Velha, the *sé* was completed in 1251, on what was probably the site of a Roman temple, then a Visigoth cathedral and then a Moorish mosque. Only the tower gate and several chapels remain of the original Romanesque-Gothic exterior – the rest was destroyed in 1755. It was rebuilt in a polygamy of Gothic, Renaissance and baroque styles, with intense gilded carving alongside elaborate tilework inside. The baroque organ is worth noting. Climb up to the rooftop *miradouro* (lookout) for views across the pretty walled town to the sea. If you're lucky, you might see storks nesting in the bell towers. The

cathedral buildings also house the **Museu Capitular**, with an assortment of sacred artwork (vestments, chalices, saint statues in glass boxes) and a small 18th-century shrine built of bones to remind you of your mortality.

Paço Episcopal　　　NOTABLE BUILDING
(Largo da Sé; admission €1.50) Facing the cathedral is the 18th-century Paço Episcopal (no longer open to visitors), with a pointy roof and an exterior finished in multicoloured *azulejos* (hand-painted tiles); it's the successor to the previous Episcopal dwelling trashed by British troops in 1596. At the southern end of the Largo da Sé is a small 15th-century town gate, the **Arco da Porta Nova**, leading to the ferry pier.

Museu Municipal　　　　　　MUSEUM
(☑ 289 897 400; adult/student €2/1; ⊙ 10am-7pm Tue-Fri, 11am-6pm Sat & Sun summer, 10am-6pm Tue-Fri, 10.30am-5pm Sat & Sun winter) Faro's domed and splendid 16th-century Renaissance **Convento de Nossa Senhora da Assunção**, in what was once the Jewish quarter, houses the Museu Municipal, formerly called the Museu Arqueológico. Highlights include the 3rd-century *Mosaic of the Ocean,* found in 1976 on a building site; 9th- to 13th-century domestic Islamic artefacts; and works by a notable Faro painter, Carlos Filipe Porfírio, depicting local legends. Ask for the informative pamphlets in English

about some of the exhibits, including the interesting *Paths of the Roman Algarve*, an atmospheric display of large rocks and plinths, and *Walks Around the Historic Centre (The Inward Village)*.

Trem Municipal Gallery of Art
GALLERY
(Rua do Trem; ⊙ 10am-6pm Tue-Fri, 10.30am-5pm Sat & Sun) FREE This attractively converted building houses temporary exhibitions by known local and international artists – painters, photographers, installation artists and sculptors. It's worth popping in to see what's on.

Arco de Repouso
LANDMARK
You can leave the Cidade Velha through the medieval Arco de Repouso (Gate of Rest) – apparently Afonso III, after taking Faro from the Moors, put his feet up and heard Mass nearby. Around the gateway are some of the town walls' oldest sections – Afonso III's improvements on the Moorish defences.

⊙ Elsewhere in Faro

Igreja de Nossa Senhora do Carmo & Capela dos Ossos
CHURCH
(Largo do Carmo; chapel admission €1; ⊙ 10am-1pm & 2-6pm Mon-Fri, 10am-1pm Sat) The twin-towered, baroque Igreja de Nossa Senhora do Carmo was completed in 1719 under João V and paid for (and gilded to death inside) with Brazilian gold. The facade was completed after the 1755 earthquake.

A more ghoulish attraction lies behind the church. The 19th-century Capela dos Ossos was built from the bones and skulls of more than 1000 monks as a blackly reverent reminder of earthly impermanence, and the ultimate in recycling. You can enter the church for free; entry to the chapel is €1.

Igreja de São Francisco
CHURCH
(Largo de São Francisco; ⊙ Mass 6.30pm) Features dazzling woodwork and a frenzied 18th-century baroque interior with tiles depicting the life of St Francis.

Igreja de Misericórdia
CHURCH
(⊙ Mass 9am) The 16th-century Igreja de Misericórdia, opposite the Arco da Vila, has a remarkable Manueline portico, the only remnant of an earlier chapel to withstand the 1755 earthquake.

Igreja de São Pedro
CHURCH
(⊙ 10am-1pm & 3-5pm Mon-Sat) At the southern end of Largo do Carmo is this 16th-century church. The plain exterior hides an interesting interior of 18th-century *azulejos* and fine-carved woodwork.

Faro Jewish Heritage Centre
CEMETERY
(☑ 289 829 525; ⊙ 9.30am-12.30pm & 2-5pm) The last vestiges of the first post-Inquisition Jewish presence in Portugal are found at the extraordinary Jewish cemetery, which has 76 beautiful marble gravestones. The small site also has a tiny museum and recreated synagogue (complete with a reconstructed wedding). Interested parties can ring in advance to arrange a guide. The centre is located north of town, near the Faro hospital; local buses (*circuito* bus 3) leave from in front of the Eva terminal. Alight at the Rotunda de Bombeiros bus stop and cross the road, the Estrada da Penha.

Museu Regional do Algarve
MUSEUM
(☑ 289 827 610; Praça da Liberdade; adult/concession €1.50/1; ⊙ 10am-1.30pm & 2.30-6pm Mon-Fri) Elements of old peasant life – such as a small fishing boat and a wooden water cart (used until the owner's death in 1974) – are on display, along with ceramics, fabrics and dioramas of typical interiors. Labelling is scarce – basic written information is available in English and other languages.

🏖 Beaches

The town's beach, **Praia de Faro**, with miles of sweeping sand, windsurfing operators and some cafes, is on the Ilha de Faro, 10km away. It's crammed in July and August. Take bus 14 or 16 from opposite the bus station (€1.95, half-hourly June to August, via the airport).

Ferries go out to **Praia de Farol** (on Ilha da Culatra) and **Ilha da Barreta** (aka Ilha Deserta), a stunning, remote, long and narrow strip of sand just off the mainland. Here, you will find **O Estaminé** (☑ 917 811 856; http://ilha-deserta.com) 🍴, an environmentally friendly restaurant built on boardwalks and run by solar power.

ᑕ Tours

Formosamar
BOAT TOUR
(☑ 967 073 846, 918 720 002; www.formosamar. com; Clube Naval, Faro Marina) 🍴 Ria Formosa and Lands are highly recommended outfits working under the name Formosamar to genuinely embrace and promote environmentally responsible tourism. Among the excellent tours it provides are two-hour bird-

watching trips around the Parque Natural da Ria Formosa (€25, minimum four people), two-hour guided cycling tours (€25), and numerous guided walking tours inland from Faro. Its 2½-hour boat trips take small boats (up to 12 people) in some of the narrower channels in the lagoon (€25), providing participants with a close-to-nature experience from Olhão. Two-hour kayaking trips depart from Olhão (€30).

Animaris
BOAT TOUR
(☎918 779 155, 917 811 856; www.ilha-deserta.com) Runs trips to Ilha da Barreta (Ilha Deserta). Boats leave from southeast of the marina, in front of the walls of Cidade Velha (Old Town).

✯ Festivals & Events

Seafood Festival
FOOD
Held annually at the end of July/beginning of August, this is the place for pescatarians and seafood-lovers. Fishers and others set up stalls and prepare their wares, from crustaceans to other ocean delights. Concerts add to the fun atmosphere.

FolkFaro
MUSIC
The city's big folk festival features lots of dance (with local and international folk groups), live music and street fests. It's held over a week in late August at various venues around town.

Feira de Santa Iria
RELIGIOUS
In late October Faro's biggest traditional event honours St Irene with fairground rides, stalls and entertainment. It takes place in a temporary fairground to the northeast, by the municipal fire station.

🛏 Sleeping
Outside high season, prices can halve.

Casa d'Alagoa
HOSTEL €
(☎289 813 252; booking@farohostel.com; Praça Alexandre Herculano 27; dm not incl breakfast €19-25, d €70; ☜) A welcome addition to Faro's budget scene, this place has all the elements of today's sophisticated hostel: it's funky, laid-back and cool. Housed in a renovated mansion, Casa d'Alagoa boasts a range of spacious dorms, a great communal area, and an upstairs terrace. There are electrical outlets at each bunk to charge your mobile and laptop, and a communal kitchen for all to use...but hey, why do you need it when dinner is on offer for €5?

Residencial Dandy
GUESTHOUSE €
(☎289 824 791; Rua Filipe Alistão 62; not incl breakfast s/d from €35/45, with shared bathroom €30/40; ✲☜) Truly one of the last of the older-style, rambling Portuguese guesthouses, this place has a charismatic owner, plus pot plants, plastic flowers, African masks and museum-style paraphernalia. The best of the 18 rooms have antique furniture, high ceilings and wrought-iron balconies. Smaller, tile-floored rooms are in the back.

Hotel Sol Algarve
HOTEL €€
(☎289 895 700; www.hotelsolalgarve.com; Rua Infante Dom Henrique 52; s/d/tr €60/70/95; P✲☜) This efficiently run hotel has wonderful staff and 38 bright, spick-and-span motel-style rooms, some with balconies. Parking costs €5 per night.

Hotel Adelaide
GUESTHOUSE €€
(☎289 802 383; www.adelaidehotel.eu; Rua Cruz dos Mestres 9; s/d €50/70; ✲☜) This modern, secure hotel has slightly worn but clean and light rooms, some with terraces and all with cable TV.

Hotel Dom Bernardo
HOTEL €€
(☎289 889 800; www.bestwesternhoteldombernardo.com; Rua General Teófilo da Trindade 20; s/d €90/97; P✲☜) Part of the Best Western chain, Dom Bernardo's rooms are spotless and modern, if a little 'a là the '80s' (although some rooms have been renovated). Prices are significantly less during low season; beware – it's a popular group option.

Hotel Faro
HOTEL €€€
(☎289 830 830; www.hotelfaro.pt; Praça Dr Francisco Gomes 2; s €138, d from €158; ✲) We're not

🅘 FINDING A BED
During July and August thousands of Portuguese and foreign visitors flock to the Algarve. Faro airport – the region's main transport hub – experiences tens of daily inbound and outbound flights a day. During this time, most visitors have prebooked package accommodation. For the independent traveller, it can be tricky to front up and expect to find a bed with no reservations; try and reserve a night or two in advance. Prices, too, are at their highest. In most places you can expect to pay considerably less in *mais tranquilo* (quieter) times. Check hotel websites for special deals.

sure how this modern cubist block made it past the town planners, but it has comfortable, sleek rooms with large beds, marble-filled bathrooms and flat-screen TVs. The small top-floor bar-restaurant with terrace is great for a sunset cocktail.

Hotel Eva HOTEL €€€
(☑ 289 001 000; www.tdhotels.pt; Av da República 1; s/d/ste €145/175/265; ✻ 🛜 🏊) The ever-so slightly worn 134-room hotel has spacious, pleasant rooms. Those facing east have balconies and views. There's a rooftop swimming pool for more marina-gazing. An extra €15 gets you a more upmarket 'superior' room – worth it for the plusher feel and space, but there's no balcony.

Hotel Santa Maria HOTEL €€€
(☑ 289 898 080; www.jcr-group.com; Rua de Portugal, 17; s €98-105, d €114-128; ✻ 🛜) Don't be fooled by the plain exterior – this modern motel-style option offers clean, though cramped, rooms with contemporary, stylish decor. Low-season prices are significantly cheaper.

🍴 Eating

Several midrange eateries are clustered around Praça Ferreira de Almeida. They serve similar fare in similar settings, mainly to travellers. Faro's big, daily *mercado municipal* (municipal market) is in Largo Mercado.

Algartalhos (Largo do Carmo) and small **Minipreço** (Praça Ferreira de Almeida 8) are centrally located supermarkets.

Gengibre e Canela VEGETARIAN €
(☑ 289 882 424; Travessa da Mota 10; buffet €7.50; ⊙ lunch Mon-Sat; 🥗) Give the taste buds a break from meat and fish dishes and veg out (literally) at this Zenlike vegetarian restaurant. The buffet changes daily; there may be

vegetable lasagne, *feijoada* (bean casserole) and tofu dishes.

Pastelaria Coelho PORTUGUESE €
(Brites de Almeida 2; mains €2-6; ⊙ 7.30am-midnight) This has to be the most deceptive spot in Faro. It looks like a *pastelaria* from the outside, yet inside, it morphs into a restaurant (the adjoining dining area gets packed to the gills) and serves up some hearty daily specials for a Portuguese song. Think everything from *xarém* (maize meal with meat or fish) to turkey stew for around €2 to €4 a plate. It's a favourite among the locals.

Restaurante Chefe Branco PORTUGUESE €
(Rua de Loulé 9/11A; €7.50-11.50; ⊙ lunch & dinner) A fabulous local spot with a cosy feel and lots of pot plants. The delightful staff serve honest, home-style fare including rabbit, goat and seafood dishes. The half portions are the biggest this side of the Rio Tejo. Serves excellent Algarvian desserts, too.

Restaurante O Murta SEAFOOD €
(Rua Infante D Henrique 136; mains €8.50-9; ⊙ lunch & dinner Mon-Sat) This simple place has been here for 32 years so it must be doing something right. Chefs grill up fish and prepare excellent seafood dishes such as *açorda de marisco* and the signature dish, *bacalhau* (cod prepared with piri-piri, chilli).

Gardy PATISSERIE €
(☑ 289 824 062; Rua de Santo António 16 & 33; mains €3-10; ⊙ Mon-Sat) The place to head for your patisserie fix and *the* place to be seen. Has a wide variety of homemade specialities.

Adega Nova PORTUGUESE €€
(www.restauranteadeganova.com; Rua Francisco Barreto 24; mains €7.50-18; ⊙ lunch & dinner) This popular place buzzes with tourists and country charm. It has a lofty beamed ceiling, rustic cooking implements on display and long, communal tables and bench seats. The meat and fish dishes can be a bit hit-and-miss, but service is efficient.

O Palhacinho PORTUGUESE €€
(Largo Dr Francisco Sá Carneiro; mains €8-13; ⊙ 7am-midnight Mon-Fri, lunch Sat) Located within the market complex, this unfancy treat-of-a-place is frequented by everyone and anyone, including – we are told – the town's lawyers. It serves traditional Portuguese cuisine – fish and meat dishes – in a pleasant, airy environment. Generous and tasty plates of the day are around €8.

Drinking

Faro's student-driven nightlife clusters around Rua do Prior and the surrounding alleys, with bars and clubs open most days till late, though things pick up considerably on weekends.

Jam Bar   BAR
(Rua do Rasquinho 26) Nestled in the history of the old town, this is a fun little bar that everybody's talking about.

Columbus Bar   BAR
(Rua Dr Francisco Gomes) A popular central place for a relaxing drink or three.

☆ Entertainment

O Castelo   BAR, PERFORMING ARTS
(Rua do Castelo 11; ⊙ 11am-4am winter, from 10am summer) Introducing Faro's smart O Castelo, which doesn't miss a beat. It's all things to all people: a bar-restaurant-nightclub-performance space. Start your day here with a coffee, grab a light meal or cheese platter with sangria for lunch, or take in the summer sunsets over a cocktail. In summer the outside morphs into a party and performance space and there are regular concerts. Its location, almost 'on' the historic walls of the old town, is superb.

Teatro Lethes   THEATRE
(☑ 289 820 300; www.teatrolethes.pt; Rua Lethes) This tiny and exquisite Italianate theatre hosts drama, music and dance performances. Adapted into a theatre in 1874 (from a building dating to 1603), it was once the Jesuit Colégio de Santiago Maior. Ask the tourist office for a list of what's on; outside performance times knock at the door. Other performances are often held in the modern Teatro Figuras.

ℹ Information

EMERGENCY & MEDICAL SERVICES
Hospital de Gambelas (☑ 289 892 000; www.hpalg.com; Urb Casal de Gambelas, Lote 2, Gambelas) A private hospital.
Police Station (☑ 289 822 022; Rua da Polícia de Segurança Pública 32) Around 100m southeast of Praça da Liberdade, before the Youth Hostel.

INTERNET ACCESS
Free wi-fi connection is available in Jardim Manuel Bívar and Alameda João de Deus.

POST
Main post office (Largo do Carmo)

TOURIST INFORMATION
Algarve Regional Tourism Administrative Office (☑ 289 800 400; www.visitalgarve.pt; Av 5 de Outubro 18; ⊙ 9am-12.30pm & 2-5.30pm Mon-Fri) Run by Turismo do Algarve (Algarve Tourism). Provides a map and leaflets of the region.
Faro Tourist Office (☑ 289 800 400; Rua da Misericórdia 8; ⊙ 9.30am-7pm Jun-Aug, 9.30am-1pm & 2-5.30pm Mon-Fri Dec-Feb) This efficient, busy place offers information on Faro. Helpful Fernanda has been here for over 30 years.
Turismo de Aeroporto Internacional (☑ 289 818 582; ⊙ 8am-11.30pm) Based at the airport and one of a series of offices run by Algarve Tourism around the region; good for basic information on arrival.

ℹ Getting There & Away

AIR
TAP (Air Portugal; ☑ 707 205 700; www.tap.pt) has multiple daily Lisbon–Faro flights (40 minutes). There's an office at the airport.
For flight inquiries call the **airport** (☑ flight information 289 800 801, general inquiries 289 800 800).

GETTING YOUR HEAD (& BODY) AROUND THE ALGARVE

The Algarve – both coastal and inland – comprises different areas. The coastline itself is 155km long and can be roughly categorised into distinct areas: the leeward coast (Sotavento), from Vila Real de Santo António to Faro, is largely fronted by a chain of sandy offshore *ilhas* (islands); the central coast, from Faro to Portimão, features the heaviest resort development; the increasingly rocky windward coast (or Barlavento), from Lagos to Sagres, culminates in the wind-scoured grandeur of the Cabo de São Vicente, Europe's southwesternmost corner; the Costa do Ouro (Golden Coast) borders the Costa de Sagres (Bay of Sagres), while the Costa Vicentina stretches for 110km north of Sagres and is part of the windy, wild national park, Parque Natural do Sudoeste Alentejano e Costa Vicentina. Elsewhere, in the hilly, thickly green interior, are two high mountain ranges, the Serra de Monchique and less-visited Serra do Caldeirão.

BUS

Buses arrive at and depart from **Eva bus station** (☑289 899 760; www.eva-bus.com; Av da República 5). Eva services run to Seville in Spain (€16, 4½ hours, four daily) via Huelva (€12, 3½ hours).

Renex (☑289 812 980; www.renex.pt; ⊙9-11.15am & 1.30-8pm Mon-Sat, 1.30-8pm Sun), located opposite the bus terminal, has express coaches to Lisbon (€19.20, five hours, at least hourly).

Services include:

Albufeira (€4.60, 1¼ hours, at least hourly) Some go on to Portimão (€5, 1½ hours,) and Lagos (€6, 1¾ hours).

Olhão (€3.25, 20 minutes, every 20 minutes weekdays, every 45 minutes weekends)

São Brás de Alportel (€4.05, 35 minutes, 11 daily) Via Estói (€3.25, 15 minutes).

Vila Real de Santo António (€5.45, 1¾ hours, seven to 11 daily) Via Tavira (€4.25, one hour).

CAR

The most direct route from Lisbon to Faro takes about five hours. An alternative to the motorway is the often traffic-clogged N125. Tolls apply.

Faro's easiest parking is in Largo de São Francisco (free).

Major car-rental agencies are at the airport.

Auto Jardim (☑289 800 881; www.auto-jardim.com)

Auto Rent (☑289 818 580, free call 800 212 011; www.autorent.pt) Efficient and helpful. The office is located in the car park 4.

Guerin (☑289 889 445; www.guerin.pt)

TRAIN

There are five trains from Lisbon daily (€21.20 to €22.20, three to 3¾ hours); 1st-class fares are slightly higher. You can also get to Porto (€51.50, six to eight hours, three daily), sometimes changing at Lisbon.

Regional services include the following:

Albufeira (€3.30, 30 minutes, nine daily)

Lagos (€7.20, 1¾ hours, nine daily)

Vila Real de Santo António (€5.15, 1¼ hours, 10 daily) Via Olhão (€1.40, 10 minutes).

ⓘ Getting Around

TO/FROM THE AIRPORT

Eva (☑289 899 740; www.eva-bus.com) buses 14 and 16 run from the airport to the bus station (€1.95, 20 minutes, half-hourly June to August, every two hours on weekends December to February). From here it's an easy stroll to the centre.

A taxi into town costs around €12 (20% more after 10pm and on weekends), plus around €2 for each luggage item.

BICYCLE & KAYAK

You can rent bikes (including kids' bikes) from Formosamar (p109;per hour/day €6/20) and kayaks from **Centro Nautico** (€3 per hour).

BOAT

Ilha Deserta (Animaris; ☑917 811 856; www.ilha-deserta.com) operates four ferries a day to/from Ilha da Barreta (€10 return). The same company also runs 1½-hour year-round boat trips (€25) through Parque Natural da Ria Formosa. Boats leave from the pier next to Arco da Porta Nova. Taxi boats also operate from here, or from the nautical centre.

TAXI

Ring for a **taxi** (☑289 895 790) or find one at the taxi rank outside the train station.

Milreu & Estói

Ten kilometres north of Faro, the Roman ruins at Milreu make a pleasant excursion. Several hundred metres up the road is the sleepy but attractive village of Estói, which boasts a derelict but charming 18th-century rococo palace and gardens, some of which has been recently renovated into a posh *pousada* (inn).

WALKING THE VIA ALGARVIANA

Covering some of the most beautiful scenery in the Algarve, the 300km Via Algarviana walking trail crosses the breadth of Portugal from Alcoutim to Cabo de São Vicente, taking in the wooded hillsides of the Serras de Caldeirão and Monchique. It takes about 14 days to walk the trail. You may hear the contrary, but walkers assure us that the Via Algarviana is definitely *not* yet fully marked and some signs have been vandalised. New military maps are accurate. The best times to walk the trail are between March and May; hunting season takes place on Thursday and Sunday from October to June – be careful on these days. For more information, visit www.viaalgarviana.org (run by environmental group Almargem) or www.algarveway.com (a private website run by enthusiasts). The official Via Algarviana route booklet (€7) is available from the Algarve Tourist Association's tourist offices.

◉ Sights

Milreu Ruins
ROMAN RUINS

(adult/under 25yr €2/1.80; ◷ 10.30am-1pm & 2-6.30pm May-Sep, 9.30am-1pm & 2-5pm Oct-Apr) Set in beautiful countryside, the ruins of this grand Roman villa provide a rare opportunity to gain insight into Roman life. The 1st-century-AD ruins reveal the characteristic form of a peristyle villa, with a gallery of columns around a courtyard. In the surrounding rooms geometric motifs and friezes of fish were found.

Tantalising glimpses of the villa's former glory include the **fish mosaics** in the bathing chambers, which are located to the west of the villa's courtyard. The remains of the bathing rooms also include the **apodyterium** (changing room; note the arched niches and benches for clothes and postbath massage) and the **frigidarium**, which had a marble basin to hold cold water for cooling off post-bath.

Other luxuries included underground heating and marble sculptures (now in Faro and Lagos museums).

To the right of the entrance is the site's **water sanctuary**, a temple devoted to the cult of water. The interior was once decorated with polychrome marble slabs and its exterior with fish mosaics. In the 6th century the late Romans converted it into a church, adding a baptismal font and a small mausoleum, and in the 8th century it was converted into a mosque. In the 10th century it collapsed, possibly due to an earthquake, and the site was abandoned. In the 15th century, a rural house was constructed within the abandoned site (the house you see today).

🛏 Sleeping & Eating

Simple local cafes front Estói's small main square but it's worth considering a snack at Pousada do Palácio de Estoi.

Pousada do Palácio de Estoi
LUXURY HOTEL €€€

(☏ 289 990 150; www.pousadas.pt; d €250) The rococo-style Pousada do Palácio de Estoi provides a luxurious stay. The incredible Versailles-style gardens are currently being restored. The public is permitted to visit the palace (free of charge) and wander through its delightful rooms. Whether you stay there or not, it's worth indulging in the smart restaurant (mains €10 to €21) or sampling snacks on the dreamy terrace.

ℹ Getting There & Away

Buses run from Faro to Estói, passing through Milreu (€3.40, 20 minutes, nine buses daily Monday to Friday, four on Saturday, one on Sunday), continuing to São Brás de Alportel. Estói is nearly 1km from Milreu.

São Brás de Alportel

POP 10,600

Seventeen kilometres north of Faro, this quiet country town provides a welcome break from the coast. São Brás de Alportel has few attractions in the town proper, but it's a pleasant place to stroll. There are some excellent activities in the surrounding area, including walks and a guided cork route. The town was a hot spot in the 19th-century heyday of cork and has stayed true to its agricultural roots. It lies in a valley in the olive-, carob-, fig- and almond-wooded Barrocal region, a lush limestone area sandwiched between the mountains and the sea.

◉ Sights & Activities

For a fine stroll, follow Rua Gago Coutinho south from the Largo to the 16th-century **igreja matriz** (parish church), which has breezy views of orange groves and surrounding valleys. Nearby, below what was once a bishop's palace, is **Jardim da Verbena**, a pretty garden with an interesting fountain. Also here is the **municipal swimming pool** (☏ 289 841 243; ◷ Jun-Sep) and a **playground**.

Museu Etnográfico do Trajo Algarvio
MUSEUM

(☏ 289 846 100; Rua Dr José Dias Sancho 61; admission €2; ◷ 10am-1pm & 2-5pm Mon-Fri, 2-5pm Sat, Sun & holidays) This constantly expanding and beautifully maintained museum, 200m east of the Largo (along the Tavira road, known as Rua Dr José Dias Sanco), is a labour of love for the curator and Friends of the Museum. It's housed in a former cork magnate's mansion (which is stunning in itself – note the original kitchen). The building displays a rambling collection of local costumes, while the garden has agricultural implements. In the stables, there is a fascinating exhibit, including a video, of the town's once-buoyant cork industry, which is part of the local cork route.

Calçadinha de São Brás de Alportel
WALKING

The Calçadinha de São Brás de Alportel is an ancient road constructed during Roman

(OVER)EXPOSING THE ALGARVE

Much of the tourism dollar into Portugal comes from the Algarve. Tourist numbers are not made up of international travellers alone; local visitors comprise a large part of the industry – numerous Portuguese have homes in this sun-kissed region – and many expats have moved here permanently. The massive influx of visitors has led to ongoing heavy development along much of the Algarve's southern coastline. While the Algarve's tourism industry provides work – albeit seasonal – to thousands of people, especially the young, some argue that the departure of Portuguese from their villages is causing an irreversible disintegration of traditions and village life. Concerns have also been raised about the impact on the environment caused by the construction of large (mainly concrete) hotels, apartments, shops and restaurants, and the building of major roads. Destruction of coastal areas including cliffs and beaches and pressure on water resources are among the issues cited. And while construction is said to be controlled, it is not always sensitive to its surrounds.

In recent years tourism authorities have focused their efforts on promoting special-interest activities beyond sun, surf and sand. Through this positive initiative the region's spectacular nature, walks and inland villages have increasingly been highlighted; however, this promotion has also seen thousands of tourists flock to visit some of the Algarve's 30-plus golf courses, which have a major environmental impact on an already stretched region, although some courses are adopting environmentally friendly maintenance practices.

When visiting the Algarve think carefully about the impact of your visit on this sensitive region: head inland (responsibly), be selective about the enterprises you select and consider the impact of the activities you undertake.

The Algarve Tourism Board has some excellent publications to help you get off the beaten track. These include *Rotas: Tours around the Algarve* (ideal for those with their own wheels) and *Trails in the Algarve,* which outlines some nature trails and cross-country day (or shorter) hikes. Both cost €7.

times, possibly linking Faro (Ossonoba) with Beja (Pax Julia). It was used by mules and shepherds until the 19th century. You can wander along two branches – one is around 100m, the other 500m. It starts near the **Centro da Calçadinha** (information centre; Rua do Matadouro 2; ⊙9.30am-1pm & 2-5.30pm Tue-Sat) FREE. The centre provides a text-heavy explanation of the route (in English and Portuguese).

Cork Route WALKING TOUR
(☑960 070 806; www.rotadacortica.pt; per person €26) An English-speaking guide from the municipality office leads a fascinating guided tour along a cork route, which includes anything and everything from visiting a traditional cork factory to cork stacks in the surrounding countryside, known as the *barrocal* (limestone) coastal region. Participants learn about the cork industry – from the extraction of cork from the trees to its production, processes and use. Minimum numbers may apply.

Sleeping

Hospedaria São Brás GUESTHOUSE €
(☑289 842 213; Rua Luís Bívar 27; s/d €30/50; ❄) Around the corner from the bus station (along the Loulé road), this guesthouse is jam-packed with attractive antiques (note the gramophone), pretty *azulejos* and plants. The delightful owner is happy to show you the full range of eclectic rooms.

Estalagem Sequeira HOTEL €
(☑289 843 444; Rua Dr Evaristo Gago 9; s/d €35/55; ❄🤶) Although its facade is uninspiring and its decor is a bit dated, this hotel's rooms are decent, with a trim if flowery design.

✕ Eating

Pastelaria O Ervilha PATISSERIE €
(Café Regional; Largo de São Sebastião 7; pastries from €1; ⊙breakfast, lunch & dinner Tue-Sun) In the centre of town and overlooking the square, this São Brás institution (it's been around since 1952) sells tasty pastries made

on the premises. (Don't miss the *Jesuítas*, comprising puff pastry and glaze).

Luís dos Frangos GRILL HOUSE €
(Churrasqueira Paraiso; ☏289 842 635; Estrada de Tavira 8150; mains €6-10; ☉ lunch & dinner Tue-Sun) Five hundred metres east of the Largo (beyond the museum), this is a local institution, famous for its grilled mains – particularly its chicken. It's a large, busy and friendly place.

❶ Information

Ponte de Informacão Turística (www.cm-sbras.pt; ☉9am-1pm & 2-5pm summer, 10am-1pm & 2-6pm winter) The municipality's tourist point, next to the municipal swimming pool and Jardim da Verbena, has some excellent resources including some maps of self-guided walking tours in the surrounding valleys and countryside.
Turismo (☏289 843 165; www.visitalgarve. pt; Largo de São Sebastião; ☉ 9.30am-1pm & 2-5.30pm Tue-Sat) Distributes maps and information on the region and town.

❶ Getting There & Away

Buses run to/from Faro (via Estói, €3.55, 30 minutes, nine daily) and to Loulé (€2.75, 25 minutes, three to five weekdays). There are fewer services on weekends.

Olhão & Around

POP 15,000

A short hop east of Faro, Olhão (pronounced *ol-yowng*) is the Algarve's biggest fishing port, with an active waterfront and pretty, bustling lanes in its old quarters. There aren't many sights, but the flat-roofed Moorish-influenced neighbourhoods and North African feel make it a pleasant place to wander. The town's fish restaurants draw the crowds, as does the morning fish and vegetable market on Av 5 de Outubro, best visited on Saturday.

Olhão is also a springboard for Parque Natural da Ria Formosa's sandy islands, Culatra and Armona, plus the park's environmental centre in Quinta Marim.

◉ Sights & Activities

Bairro dos Pescadores NEIGHBOURHOOD
Just back from the market and park is the Bairro dos Pescadores (Fishermen's Quarter), a knot of whitewashed, cubical houses, often with tiled fronts and flat roofs. Narrow lanes thread through the *bairro* (neighbour-

hood), and there's a definite Moorish influence, probably a legacy of long-standing trade links with North Africa. Similar houses are found in Fuzeta (10km east).

Quinta de Marim NATURE RESERVE
(☉8am-7pm Mon-Fri, 10am-7pm Sat & Sun, to 8pm daily summer) Three kilometres east of Olhão, is the beautiful 60-hectare Centro Educação Ambiental de Marim (Environmental Education Centre of Marim; commonly known as Quinta de Marim). A 3km nature trail takes you through various ecosystems – dunes, saltmarshes, pine woodlands. The Parque Natural da Ria Formosa (p116) headquarters and visitor interpretation centre is also here.

To get to Quinta Marim, take a municipal bus to the campground (200m before the visitor centre).

☂ Beaches

Fine beaches, sparsely sprinkled with holiday chalets, include those on the sandbank *ilhas* (islands) of Parque Natural da Ria Formosa: **Ilha de Farol**, **Ilha da Culatra** and **Ilha da Armona**. There are ferries to both islands from the pier just east of Jardim Patrão Joaquim Lopes.

☞ Tours

For around €12 per hour, you can grab a ride on a traditional boat through one of several private boat operators. Formosamar (p109), based in Faro, have tours departing from Olhão.

DON'T MISS

PARQUE NATURAL DA RIA FORMOSA

Ria Formosa Natural Park is mostly a lagoon system stretching for 60km along the Algarve coastline and encompassing 18,000 hectares, from west of Faro to Cacela Velha. It encloses a vast area of *sapal* (marsh), *salinas* (salt pans), creeks and dune islands. To the west there are several freshwater lakes, including those at Ludo and Quinta do Lago; the marshes are an important area for migrating and nesting birds. You can see a huge variety of wetland birds here, along with ducks, shorebirds, gulls and terns. This is the favoured nesting place of the little tern and rare purple gallinule.

Natura Algarve BOAT TOUR
(📞 918 056 674; www.natura-algarve.com; Av 5 do
Otubro) 🖋 This eco-responsible operator offers a range of mainly boat-related activities
from all-day boat tours exploring the Ria
Formosa (€52 excluding lunch, 5½ hours),
two-hour dolphin trips (€45), 2½ birdwatching trips (from the boat; €35) or the popular
'Natura' trip – a 2½ hour interpretative tour
with explanations about the history, traditions and local economy. You explore the
canals as well as Culatra Island.

✪ Festivals & Events

Festival do Marisco, a seafood festival featuring food and folk music, fills the Jardim
Patrão Joaquim Lopes some time in the middle of August.

🛏 Sleeping

Pensão Bicuar GUESTHOUSE €
(📞 289 714 816; www.pensionbicuar.com; Rua Vasco
da Gama 5; dm/s €20/38, d €49-68, f €68) This
guesthouse offers a range of pleasant rooms,
featuring old-fashioned details and quirky
idiosyncracies that visitors enjoy. Some
rooms have bathrooms, others don't. A guest
kitchen, a roof terrace and a book exchange
are handy services. Head to the left (east) of
the parish church.

**Parque de Campismo
de Fuzeta** CAMPGROUND €
(📞 289 793 459; camping@jf-fuseta.pt; Fuzeta;
camp sites per adult/tent/car €4.20/3.10/3.40;
☺year-round) This small, shady municipal
site is on the waterfront in peaceful Fuzeta,
about 10km east of Olhão.

Camping Olhão CAMPGROUND €
(📞 289 700 300; www.sbsi.pt; camp sites per adult/
tent/car €4.20/3.10/3.40, family bungalows €45;
🏊) This large, well-equipped, shady campground is 2km east of Olhão. The upside? It's
near Quinta Marim. The downside? It's by
a train line and trains run between 6.45am
and midnight. To get here, you can catch a
municipal bus from the bus station.

O Tartufo B&B €€
(📞 289 791 218; www.otartufo.com; Moncarapacho; s/d with shared bathroom €50/70, d €75-80,
apt €90; ☺Mar-Sep) Enthusiastic expatri-
ates Michelle and Theo have converted this
old *quinta* (farmhouse) into eight pleasant
rooms – a creative blend of traditional Moorish with a touch of contemporary hippy. The
B&B is set within a lovely garden, complete

with hammocks, mosaic paths and fountains.
A communal kitchen is a handy addition. It's
located in Moncarapacho, four kilometers inland from Fuzeta. Ring for directions.

🍴 Eating

Av 5 de Outubro has a **market** (☺7am-2pm
Mon-Sat) and is lined with seafood restaurants open for lunch and dinner (closed in
between). Follow your whim – nearly all
serve good *cataplanas* (seafood stews) and
xerém (similar to polenta) and charge between €8 and €16.

Sabores do Churrasco GRILL HOUSE €
(Av 5 de Outubro 162; mains €8-12) An authentic-
as-they-come Brazilian *churrasqueira* (grill
restaurant) and an incredible all-you-can-
eat carnivorous extravaganza – five different
kinds of grilled meats or, for an even greater
protein injection, 12 kinds in one sitting.

Pizza na Pedra ITALIAN €
(Av 5 de Outubro 50; mains €8-12) We know.
You're here to sate your yearnings for local
seafood, not necessarily foreign foods. It's
only that this little spot serves up authentic
Italian dishes that would make the harshest
of *mammas* proud.

ℹ Information

Centro de Saúde (📞289 700 260; Rua Associ-
ação Chasfa) For serious matters head to one
of the hospitals in Faro.
Police (📞289 710 770; Av 5 de Outubro 176)
Post office (Av da República) A block north
of the parish church, opposite a bank with an
ATM.
Turismo (📞289 713 936; Largo Sebastião
Martins Mestre; ☺9.30am-1pm & 3-6.30pm
Tue-Sat Jul & Aug, 9.30am-1pm & 2-5.30pm
Tue-Sat Sep-May) In the centre of the pedes-
trian zone; from the bus station bear right at
the fork beside the parish church.

ℹ Getting There & Away

BUS
Eva (www.eva-bus.com) express buses run to
Lisbon (€20, four hours, four to five daily), as do
Renex (Av da República 101).
  Buses run frequently to/from Faro (€3.25,
20 minutes), and to/from Tavira (€4.25, 40
minutes).

TRAIN
Regular trains connect to Faro (€1.60, 10 minutes, every one to two hours) or east to Fuzeta
(€1.60, 10 minutes) and Tavira (€2, 30 minutes).

ℹ Getting Around

Handy municipal buses run 'green and yellow routes' around town, including to the campground and supermarkets.

Ferries run out to the *ilhas* from the pier at the eastern end of Jardim Patrão Joaquim Lopes. Boats run to Ilha da Armona (€3.60 return, 15 minutes, at least nine daily June to mid-September, hourly July and August, around four daily mid-September to May); the last trip back from Armona in July and August leaves at 8.30pm.

Boats also go to Ilha da Culatra (€3.60 return, 30 minutes) and Praia de Farol (€4.20 return, one hour), with six daily from June to September and four daily from mid-September to May.

Tavira

POP 15,100

Set on either side of the meandering Rio Gilão, Tavira is a charming town. The ruins of a hilltop castle, an old Roman bridge and a smattering of Gothic and Renaissance churches are among Tavira's historic attractions. Its enticing assortment of restaurants and guesthouses makes it an excellent base for exploring the Algarve's eastern section.

Tavira is ideal for wandering; the warren of cobblestone streets hides pretty, historic gardens and shady plazas. There's a small, active fishing port and a modern market. Only 3km from the coast, Tavira is the launching point for the stunning, unspoilt beaches of Ilha de Tavira.

History

The Roman settlement of Balsa was just down the road from Tavira, near Santa Luzia (3km west). The seven-arched bridge the Romans built at Tavira (which was then called Tabira) was an important link in the route between Baesuris (Castro Marim) and Ossonoba (Faro).

In the 8th century, the Moors occupied Tavira. They built the castle, probably on the site of a Roman fortress, and two mosques. In 1242 Dom Paio Peres Correia reconquered the town. Those Moors who remained were segregated into the *mouraria* (segregated Moorish quarter) outside the town walls.

As the port closest to the Moroccan coast, Tavira became important during the Age of Discoveries, serving as a base for Portuguese expeditions to North Africa, supplying provisions (especially salt, wine and dried fish) and a hospital. Its maritime trade also expanded, with exports of salted fish, almonds, figs and wine to northern Europe. By 1520 it had become the Algarve's most populated settlement and was raised to the rank of city.

Decline began in the early 17th century when the North African campaign was abandoned and the Rio Gilão became so silted up that large boats couldn't enter the port. Things got worse when the plague struck in 1645, followed by the 1755 earthquake.

After briefly producing carpets in the late 18th century, Tavira found a more stable income in its tuna fishing and canning industry, although this too declined in the 1950s. Today, tourists have taken the place of fish as the biggest money-earners.

◎ Sights

◎ Old Town

Enter the old town through the **Porta de Dom Manuel**, built in 1520 when Dom Manuel I made Tavira a city. Around the back, along Calçada da Galeria, the elegant **Palácio da Galeria** (☎281 320 540; Calçada da Galeria; admission €2, joint ticket with Núcleo Islâmico adult/child €3/1.50; ☉10am-12.30pm & 3-6.30pm Tue-Sat winter, 10am-12.30pm & 3-6pm summer) holds exhibitions.

Largo da Porta do Postigo is by another old town gate and is in the town's Moorish quarter.

Castelo   CASTLE
(☉9am-7pm summer, 9am-5pm winter) FREE What's left of the castle is surrounded by a small and very appealing garden. The defence might date back to Neolithic times; it was rebuilt by Phoenicians in the 8th century and later taken over by the Moors. What stands today dates mostly from 17th-century reconstruction. The restored octagonal tower offers fine views over Tavira. Note: don't set the kids free here – ramparts and steps are without railing.

Igreja de Santiago   CHURCH
(☉Mass 9am Tue & Thu, 5pm Sun) Just south of Tavira's castle is the whitewashed 17th-century Igreja de Santiago, built where a small mosque probably once stood. The area beside it was formerly the Praça da Vila, the old town square.

Torre da Tavira   VIEWPOINT
(admission €4; ☉10am-5pm Mon-Sat) The Torre da Tavira, which was formerly the town's water tower (100m), now houses a camera obscura. A simple but ingenious object, the

Tavira

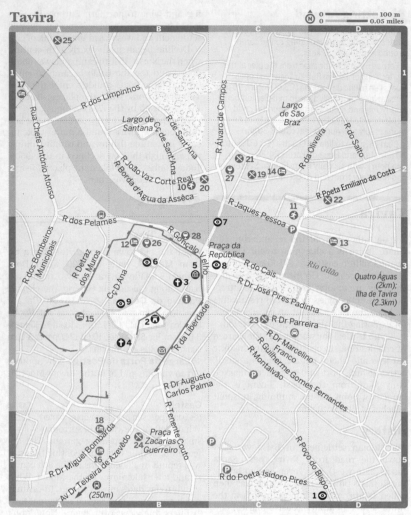

THE ALGARVE TAVIRA

camera obscura reveals a 360-degree panoramic view of Tavira, its monuments and local events, in real time – all while you are
stationary.

Igreja da Misericórdia   CHURCH
(Rua da Galeria) Built in the 1540s this church
is the Algarve's most important Renaissance
monument, with a magnificent carved,
arched doorway topped by statues of Nossa
Senhora da Misericórdia, São Pedro and
São Paulo. The church's stone mason, André Pilarte, also worked on Mosteiro dos
Jerónimos (p79).

Elsewhere in Tavira

Praça da República   PLAZA
For centuries this sociable town square on
the riverfront served as promenade and
marketplace, where slaves were traded
along with less ignominious commodities
such as fresh fish and fruit. The market
moved to Jardim do Coreto in 1887 in an effort to improve hygiene, only moving again
in 2000 to a new riverside location 500m
west of here (held mornings from Monday
to Saturday).

Tavira

THE ALGARVE TAVIRA

Ponte Romana   LANDMARK
This seven-arched bridge that loops away from Praça da República may predate the Romans but is so named because it linked the Roman road from Castro Marim to Tavira. The structure you see dates from a 17th-century reconstruction. The latest touch-up job was in 1989, after floods knocked down one of its pillars.

Núcleo Islâmico   MUSEUM
(Praça da República 5; adult/child €2/1, joint admission with Palácio Galeria €3/1.50; ⊙10am-12.30pm & 3-6pm summer, 10am-12.30pm & 2-5.30pm Tue-Sat winter) This small but modern museum exhibits impressive Islamic pieces – including a wall – discovered on the site in the 1990s during renovations of a former bank building. One of its important finds include a vase from the 11th century. While videos are in Portuguese, English handouts are invaluable.

**Biblioteca Municipal
Álvaro de Campos**   LIBRARY
(Rua da Comunidade Lusíada 21; ⊙10am-7pm Tue-Fri, 2-7.30pm Mon & Sat Apr-Oct) FREE Aspiring architects or anyone who appreciates modern design should pay a visit to Tavira's municipal library, which was originally the town prison. Architect João Luís Carrilho da Graça sympathetically and cleverly converted the former prison's facade and cells into a fabulous modern and harmonious cultural space. Opened in 2006, the building now houses books, exhibitions and computers.

Arraial Ferreira Neto Museum   MUSEUM
(⊙9am-6pm) FREE The original name of a former fishing community (between 1943 and around 1970) and now incorporated within the Hotel Vila Galé Albacora (p121) hotel resort, the site has maintained the original school and chapel. It also has the small but very quaint tuna fishing museum, which has little in the way of description but 45-minute guided tours are available (€5; ask at reception).

🏃 Activities & Tours

Kitesurf Eolis   KITESURFING
(☑962 337 285; www.kitsurfeolis.com; Ria Formosa 38, Centro Comercial, Shop 33, Cabanas de Tavira) Highly professional outfit based at Cabanas de Tavira, around 6km east of Tavira, offering kitesurfing classes and a range of other water sports.

**Salt Pans to
Quatro Águas**   WALKING, BIRDWATCHING
You can walk 2km east along the river, past the fascinating, snowlike salt pans to Quatro Águas. The salt pans produce tip-top table salt and attract feeding birds in summer, including flamingos. As well as being the jumping-off point for Ilha de Tavira, the seaside hub of Quatro Águas has a couple of seafood restaurants and Arraial Ferreira Neto Museum, a former tuna-canning village. A bus goes to Quatro Águas from the Tavira bus station from July to mid-September (eight daily). A taxi to Quatro Águas costs around €5.

THE ALGARVE TAVIRA

Tourist Train
TRAIN TOUR

(40min tour €3.50; ☺ hourly 10am-7pm Sep-May, to 8pm Jun, to midnight Jul & Aug) Starts from the northern side of Ponte Romana and visits the main sights.

✯ Festivals & Events

You can't go wrong with free sardines and that's what you'll get at **Festa de Cidade**, Tavira's biggest festival, held on June 23 and 24. Myrtle and paper flowers decorate the streets, and the dancing and festivities carry on till late.

🛏 Sleeping

Rates for some accommodation can halve in low season.

Tavira Youth Hostel
HOSTEL €

(☑ 281 326 731; www.hihostels.com; Rua Dr Miguel Bombarda 36; not incl breakfast dm €15, d €38-45) Up there with HI's newer hostels, this hip spot is perfect for the budget traveller. It features a lovely living room decked out in a Moorish theme, four-bed dorms, a fabulous kitchen and a laundry. Its ingenious design even allows for attractive hotel-style doubles. What's more, it's bang in the centre of town.

Pensão Residencial Lagôas
GUESTHOUSE €

(☑ 281 328 243; Rua Almirante Cândido dos Reis 24; s/d not incl breakfast from €25/30; 🖥) For those who are allergic to hostels, this is one of the few budget options around. It offers small (some cramped), spotless rooms. There's a plant-filled courtyard and a sunny terrace with views.

Ilha de Tavira
CAMPGROUND €

(☑ 281 321 709; www.campingtavira.com; camp sites per 1/2 people incl tent €12/17.50; ☺ May-Oct) Tavira's nearest camping site has a great location on the island. It gets crowded and noisy in the high season (mid-June to mid-September). There's no car access.

Calçada Guesthouse
GUESTHOUSE €€

(☑ 927 710 771, 926 563 713; www.calcadaguesthouse.com; Calçada de Dona Ana 12; r from €84; 🖥) Two British expats renovated and run this stylish, if ever-so-slightly cramped, spot. It has a modern, clean design and all the mod cons. It's centrally located and has a wonderful roof terrace. Breakfast costs extra (€8), and children are welcome (and often a feature). Minimum-night stays sometimes apply.

Tavira Inn
GUESTHOUSE €€

(Casa do Rio; ☑ 917 356 623; www.tavira-inn.com; Rua Chefe António Afonso 39; d not including breakfast €105; ✱🖥🏊) In a quirky spot nestled by the train bridge and in front of the river, the five rooms in this comfortable place have style...and effective double-glazed windows. There's a lot of terracotta, the owner's own artwork, a small saltwater swimming pool and a bar. Children are not permitted.

Hotel Residencial Princesa do Gilão
GUESTHOUSE €€

(☑ 281 325 171; www.residencial-gilao.com; Rua Borda d'Água de Aguiar 10; s/d/tr €52/58/68; ✱) This '80s-style place on the river has tight but neat rooms with identical decor. Get a room with a river view.

Hotel Vila Galé Albacora
HOTEL €€

(☑ 281 380 800; www.vilagale.pt; Quatro Águas; r from €100; ☺ Apr-Oct; ✱🖥🏊) Two kilometres east of town, overlooking Ilha de Tavira, this four-star 162-room hotel has been converted from, and cleverly incorporates, a former tuna village, complete with the original school and chapel. It has cheerful modern rooms (the former tuna workers' living premises), plus a spa, a pool and a restaurant.

Quinta da Lua
B&B €€€

(☑ 281 961 070; www.quintadalua.com.pt; Bernardinheiro, Santo Estevão; d/ste €185/225; ✱🖥🏊) Peace and serenity. Set among orange groves 4km northwest of Tavira, this delightful place has eight bright and very stylish rooms set around a large, saltwater swimming pool. The extensive gardens feature an outdoor lounge area. Superb breakfasts (anything from homemade muesli to eggs) included.

Quinta do Caracol
GUESTHOUSE €€€

(☑ 281 322 475; www.quintadocaracol.com; Rua do São Pedro; s/d €100/140; 🅿✱🏊🖥) This unpretentious, rambling 17th-century farmhouse is set in a lovely garden, despite the surrounding suburban development. Each of its nine apartments is uniquely kitted out in traditional Algarve furnishings and rustic artwork; all have kitchenettes. It's child- and pet-friendly.

From Tavira's train station, cross the railway and turn left at Rua de Sao Pedro. The entry is 200m further on to the left – look for the blue and white arch.

Tavira House Hotel BOUTIQUE HOTEL €€€
(☑281 370 307; www.tavirahousehotel.com; Rua Dr Miguel Bombarda 47-49; d/ste €150/190; ✳ 🌐) If this boutique number were an American movie icon, she'd be Zsa Zsa Gabor. It is tastefully 'campish' and the unique rooms beautifully incorporate the mansion's original features. Each room is named after a flower and the design reflects this in colour and quirky touches. It's clearly aimed at boutique-hotel–minded people, and does a good job of it.

Oh, and *Dahlinks*, there's even a tiny Roman-style dipping pool and a fabulous roof terrace!

Pousada Convento da Graça LUXURY HOTEL €€€
(☑281 329 040; www.pousadas.pt; Rua Dom Paio Peres Correia; d €250; ✳ 🖭) If you can get past the front door (there's a bit of attitude here), you'll find an elegant converted convent, with attractive and plush rooms – some with modern four-poster beds – a pool and a pricey restaurant.

✘ Eating

You can take your pick of eateries along the waterfront's well-trodden taste-bud path Rua Dr José Pires Padinha.

The modern **mercado municipal** (☉most stalls morning only), on the eastern edge of town, sells fish and vegetables. Large supermarkets are also at the eastern entrance to town.

A couple of reasonable, slightly more up market restaurants are in Quatro Aguas.

For tasty, alternative off-the-beaten-track eating experiences head to the fishing village of Santa Luzia, 3km southwest of Tavira. Here, *marisqueiras* (fish restaurants) serve up the speciality, *polvo* (octopus).

Churrasqueira O Manel GRILL HOUSE €
(☑281 323 343; Rua Dr António Cabreira 39; mains €6-9) *The* place to come for *frango no churrasco* (grilled chicken) with salad (it's spot on; the owner has been at the grill for decades). Takeaway also available.

Casa Simão PORTUGUESE €
(João Vaz Corte Real 10; mains €6-11; ☉lunch & dinner Mon-Sat) We'll be upfront: this old-style, barnlike eatery has harsh lighting and zero romance, but that's because the delightful family-owners concentrate on down-to-earth fare – they whip up great-value meals such as *javali estufado* (wild boar stew) and grills. Go for the daily specials.

Pastelaria Tavirense PATISSERIE €
(☑281 323 451; Rua Dr Marcelino Franco 17; snacks €2-7; ☉8am-midnight) Of all the *pastelarias*, this serves up the best pastries plus good soups and snacks for those on a budget.

Aquasul SEAFOOD €€
(☑281 325 166; Rua Dr Augusto Silva Carvalho 13; mains €12-16; set menus around €21; ☉dinner Tue-Sat winter, Mon-Sat summer; ☑) You won't hear too much Portuguese spoken here, given this place's popularity among foreigners and expats, but this Dutch-run place serves up some tasty international dishes in a cosy, mosaic-filled environment.

Restaurante O Ciclista SEAFOOD €€
(☑281 325 246; Rua João Vaz Corte Real; mains €8-12, fish per kg €25-50; ☉lunch & dinner Tue-Sun, lunch Mon) Just beyond the EN125 bridge, this isolated barnlike spot rightly stands out on its own. Seafood here is fresh, grilled and served by the kilo. It gets packed to the gills with locals.

Restaurante Avenida SEAFOOD €€
(☑281 321 113; Av Dr Mateus Teixeira de Azevêdo 6; mains €8-12; ☉lunch & dinner Wed-Mon) This very authentic, well-maintained Portuguese place with gold-and-blue tablecloths has an air of the 1960s, efficiency with a capital 'E' and a loyal clientele. Good home-style dishes include the seafood risotto and grilled tuna.

Jamie's Cozinha INTERNATIONAL €€
(www.jamiescozinha.com; Poeta Emiliano da Costa 6; ☉dinner Tue-Sun; ☑) This cheekily named spot (translate it into English) is a welcome

---

WORTH A TRIP

CACELA VELHA

Enchanting, small and cobbled, Cacela Velha is a huddle of whitewashed cottages edged with bright borders, and has a pocket-sized fort, orange and olive groves, and gardens blazing with colour. It's 12km east of Tavira, above a gorgeous stretch of sea, with a couple of excellent cafe-restaurants, splendid views and a meandering path down to the long white beach.

Unfortunately, there's no direct bus from Tavira, but Cacela Velha is located only 1km south of the N125 (2km before Vila Nova de Cacela; €1.75), which is on the Faro–Vila Real de Santo António bus route.

change to Tavira's standard cuisine scene. To start with, it's refreshing when the owner-chef proudly declares himself a vegetarian. But that's not to say there's not meaty fare; this place serves up sophisticated Mediterranean-focussed cuisine – including meats and sea-food – using local produce where possible and a seasonally changing menu.

 Drinking & Entertainment

Bars are interspersed throughout town; most are on the northern bank, with a couple along Rua Dr José Padinha.

For a higher-velocity night, head to the *mercado municipal,* which hosts a row of dancier, preclub bars that play music from hands-in-the-air house to African. The area buzzes in July and August.

Tavira Lounge   BAR, CAFE
(☑281 381 034; Rua Gonçalo Velho 16-18; ☺noon-2am Mon-Sat summer, noon-11.30pm Mon-Thu, to late Fri & Sat winter; ☎) By day it's a cafe-restaurant; by night a cafe-bar. Whatever it is, it's cosy and a lovely place to chill over delicious tapas snacks, or kick back with a cocktail or smoothie. Free internet and several cosy spaces ensure a long and comfortable visit. There are even distractions for the kids.

Refcafé   BAR
(Rua Gonçalo Velho 23; ☺Tue-Sun) A casual place where nothing is quite what it seems: it's more of a bar (despite its name, although it serves good smoked-salmon sandwiches), the space has a 1970s feel (but it plays contemporary music), and the ladies' bathroom is behind the blue (not yellow) curtain. Can be fun.

Távila   BAR
(Praça Dr António Padinha 50) Overlooking a small tree-filled plaza, this low-key spot is popular with locals. It has outdoor tables, ideal for an afternoon or evening drink.

 Information

Banks with ATMs lie around Praça da República and Rua da Liberdade.

Biblioteca Municipal Álvaro de Campos (Rua Comunidade Lusiada 21; ☺10am-7pm Tue-Fri, 2-7.30pm Mon & Sat Apr-Oct) Free access plus wi-fi.

Centro de Saude (☑281 329 000; Strada de Santa Luzia; ☺3-8pm) Public clinic; these hours are for tourists.

Espaço Internet (Câmara Municipal, Praça da República; ☺9am-noon, 12.30-5pm & 5.30-8pm Mon-Fri) Free access.

Police station (☑281 322 022; Rua da Atalaia 2)

Post office (Rua da Liberdade)

SOS Clinic (☑281 380 660; Rua Almirante Cândido dos Reis 226; ☺8am-midnight) Private clinic. Between midnight and 8am doors are closed but ring in an emergency as there's an on-duty practitioner.

Turismo (☑281 322 511; www.visitalgarve.pt; Rua da Galeria 9; ☺9.30am-7pm Mon-Fri Jul & Aug, 9.30am-1pm & 2-5.30pm Mon-Fri Sep-Jun) Provides local and some regional information and has accommodation listings. Changeable hours.

❶ Getting There & Around

BICYCLE

Casa Abilio (www.abiliobikes.com; Rua João Vaz Corte Real 23; per day €7)

Sport Nautica (Rua Jacques Pessoa 26; per day €6-8.50)

BUS

The **bus station** (☑281 322 546) has the following services:

Faro (€4.25, one hour, 11 daily weekdays, seven daily weekends) Via Olhão (€2.40).

Vila Real de Santo António (€4.25, 40 minutes, 11 weekdays, seven weekends) Express buses also go to Lisbon (€19.50 to €20, up to five hours, four to five daily) and Huelva (Spain; €15, two hours, twice daily), with connections to Seville (€17, three hours).

TRAIN

Trains run daily to Faro (€3.15, 40 minutes, 15 daily) and Vila Real (€2.65, 35 minutes, 12 daily).

TAXI

Taxis (☑281 321 544, 281 325 746) A reliable rank is located near the cinema on Rua Dr Marcelino Franco.

Ilha de Tavira

Sandy islands (all part of the Parque Natural da Ria Formosa) stretch along the coast from Cacela Velha to just west of Faro, and this is one of the finest. The huge beach at the island's eastern end, opposite Tavira, has water sports, a campground (p121) and cafe-restaurants. Outside high season, the island feels wonderfully remote and empty, but during July and August it's busy.

A kilometre west of the jetty is an unofficial nudist area. A few kilometres further west along the island is **Praia do Barril**, accessible by a **miniature train** that trundles over the mud flats from **Pedras d'el Rei**, a resort 4km southwest of Tavira. Praia do Barril has an extraordinary anchor cemetery; the anchors were left by the tuna boats that once fished these waters. There are some eateries where the shuttle train stops, then sand, sand, sand as far as the eye can see.

❶ Getting There & Away

Ferries make the five-minute hop to the *ilha* (€1.80 return) from Quatro Águas, 2km southeast of Tavira. Times are subject to change – ask the crew when the last one runs! In July and August they usually run till midnight and can be very busy. From June to mid-September a boat normally runs direct from Tavira from around 8am (return adult/child €2/1, 15 minutes) – ask at the *turismo* for details.

In addition to the local ferry, **Sequa Tours water taxi** (✆ 966 615 071; http://sequatours.com/watertaxiservice.html) operates 24 hours a day from July to mid-September, and until midnight from May to June. The fare from Quatro Águas-Tavira to the island is around €18 for five people.

A bus goes to Quatro Águas from the Tavira bus station from July to mid-September (eight daily). A taxi to Quatro Águas costs around €5.

For Praia do Barril, take a bus from Tavira to Pedras d'el Rei (10 minutes, around eight daily weekdays), from where the little train runs regularly to the beach (it runs all year, though the timetable varies out of high season).

Vila Real de Santo António

POP 11,900

Perched on the edge of wide Rio Guadiana, low-key but pleasant Vila Real de Santo António stares across at Spanish eyes. Its small pedestrian centre is architecturally impressive: within five months in 1774, the Marquês de Pombal stamped the town with his hallmark gleaming grid-pattern of streets (like Lisbon's Baixa district) after the town was destroyed by floods. From here you can head off to Castro Marim. The large, sandy Monte Gordo beach is 4km away.

🛏 Sleeping

Villa Marquês   HOTEL €
(✆ 281 530 420; Rua Dr José Barão 61; s/d €35/40; ❄) Two streets back from the waterfront, near the bus station, this modern, yellow place has bright and airy – if a little cramped – rooms and a rooftop terrace with views over town. The best value in town.

Casa de Hospedes Matos Pereira   GUESTHOUSE €
(✆ 281 543 325; Rua Dr Sousa Martins 57; s/d €35/50) This family-home guesthouse near the *turismo* has small, lace-filled rooms, some with a terrace and very steep steps.

Hospedaria Arenilha   GUESTHOUSE €
(✆ 964 722 018, 281 512 565; Rua Dom Pedro V, 53-55; s/d €50/60, tr €75-90; ❋) In the centre of town, this place was built to resemble a hotel but seems to have morphed into budget accommodation. Nevertheless, it has modern and clean rooms with all the mod cons. Rates fluctuate.

✕ Eating

Associação Naval do Guadiana   SEAFOOD €€
(Av da República; mains €8-14; ☺lunch & dinner) The recently remodelled waterfront building has a terrace with views over the river and good seafood, as attested by the locals.

Os Arcos   PORTUGUESE €€
(Av da República 45; mains €11-15; ☺lunch & dinner) Unpretentious and slightly barnlike, Os Arcos offers efficient service in a typically gruff Portuguese don't-mess-with-me-it's-service-time manner. Large selection of meat and fish.

❶ Information

Turismo (✆ 281 544 495; Av Marginal, Monte Gordo) The nearest tourist office is located in Monte Gordo, 4km away.

❶ Getting There & Away

BOAT
Ferries cross the river border every hour to whitewashed Ayamonte; buy tickets (person/car/bike €1.70/5/1.10) from the waterfront office, open 9am to 6.30pm Monday to Saturday, 9.15am to 5.40pm Sunday. Note: there is a one-hour time difference between Portugal and Spain.

BUS
Buses (✆ 281 511 807) service the following:
Faro (€5.45, 1¾ hours, six to nine daily)
Lisbon (€20, 4½ hours, around nine daily)
Mértola (€10.80, one hour, one to two daily)
Monte Gordo (€2.75, 10 minutes, seven to eight daily)

Tavira (€4.25, 30 to 45 minutes, six to nine daily)

To get to Spain, you must head to Huelva (€15, one hour, two daily), and connect there to Seville (total fare from Vila Real de Santo António €17, 3½ hours).

TRAIN

Trains to Lagos (€9.15, 3¾ hours, nine daily) require changes at Faro and/or Tunes. There are regular train services to Faro (€3.15, 45 minutes, hourly).

Castro Marim

POP 3100

Slumbering in the shadows of a 14th-century castle, Castro Marim is a picturesque village that sees few foreign visitors, but deserves to see more. It has a quaint, tree-shaded centre, several restaurants and impressive fortifications. These afford views across salt pans, the bridge to Spain, and the marshes of the Reserva Natural do Sapal de Castro Marim, which is famous for its flamingos. For walkers, there are some good trails around the area. It's 3km north of Vila Real de Santo António.

◉ Sights

Castelo & Around   HISTORIC SITE
(adult/child €1/.50; ⊙ 9am-7pm Apr-Oct, 9am-5pm Nov-Mar) In the 13th century, Dom Afonso III built Castro Marim's castle on the site of Roman and Moorish fortifications in a dramatic and strategic position for spying on the Spanish frontier. In 1319 it became the first headquarters of the religious military order known as the Order of Christ, the new version of the Knights Templar. Until they moved to Tomar in 1334, the soldiers of the Order of Christ used this castle to keep watch over the estuary of the Rio Guadiana

and the border with Spain, where the Moors were still in power.

The grand stretch of ruins today, however, dates from the 17th century, when Dom João IV ordered the addition of vast ramparts. At the same time **Forte de São Sebastião**, a smaller fort, was built on a nearby hilltop (closed to the public). Much of the area was destroyed in the 1755 earthquake, but the ruins of the main fort are still amazing.

Inside the wonderfully derelict castle walls is a 14th-century church, the **Igreja de Santiago**, where Henry the Navigator, also Grand Master of the Order of Christ, is said to have prayed. A small museum displays some pots and vases dating back to the Iron Age, discovered during excavations. A fun spectacle, the **Feira Mediéval**, takes place at the castle for four days encompassing the last weekend of August. There's a parade on the first (from the village to the castle) and last days (from the castle to the village), emulating medieval times). Food stalls with local products, music, fencing competitions and a medieval banquet create an authentic atmosphere.

Reserva Natural do Sapal de Castro Marim e Vila Real de Santo António   NATURE RESERVE
(☑ administrative office 281 510 680; Sapal de Venta Moínhos; ⊙ 9am-12.30pm & 2-5.30pm Mon-Fri) Established in 1975, this nature reserve is Portugal's oldest, covering 20 sq km of marshland and salt pans bordering the Rio Guadiana north of Vila Real. Important winter visitors are greater flamingos, spoonbills and Caspian terns. In spring it's busy with white storks.

Birdwatchers should also head to **Cerro do Bufo**, 2km southwest of Castro Marim, another rewarding area for spotting the park's birdlife.

> **WORTH A TRIP**
>
> ## ALMANCIL
>
> It's worth making a detour to Almancil, 13km northwest of Faro and about 6km south of Loulé, to visit the marvellous **Igreja de São Lourenço de Matos** (Church of St Lourenço). The church was built on the site of a ruined chapel after local people, while digging a well, had implored the saint for help and then struck water.
>
> The resulting baroque masterpiece, which was built by fraternal master-team Antão and Manuel Borges, is smothered in *azulejos* – even the ceiling is covered in them. The walls depict scenes from the life of the saint. In the earthquake of 1755, only five tiles fell from the roof.
>
> Buses between Albufeira (40 minutes) and Loulé (15 minutes) stop here.

The park's administrative office is 2km from Monte Francisco, a five-minute bus ride north of Castro Marim; get directions from the *turismo* at Castro Marim, as there are few signs.

ℹ Information

Turismo (☑ 281 531 232; Rua Dr José Alves Moreira; ⏱ 9.30am-1pm & 2-5.30pm Tue-Thu) Below the castle in the village centre.

ℹ Getting There & Away

Buses from Vila Real run to Castro Marim (€2.20, eight minutes) and go on to Monte Francisco, a short distance north. Weekend buses are extremely limited.

Alcoutim

POP 2900

Strategically positioned along the idyllic Rio Guadiana, Alcoutim (ahl-ko-*teeng*) is a small village just across the river from the Spanish town of Sanlúcar de Guadiana. What-are-you-looking-at fortresses above both villages remind one of testier times. Phoenicians, Greeks, Romans and Arabs have barricaded themselves in the hills here, and centuries of tension have bubbled across the river, which forms the Algarve's entire eastern boundary. In the 14th century, Dom Fernando I of Portugal and Don Henrique II of Castile signed a tentative peace treaty in Alcoutim. Tragically, today Alcoutim is struggling to stay on the map – it's population has been slowly diminishing. Nevertheless, it's worth a quick visit if you're passing between the Algarve and Alentejo, even if just for the quirky riverside beach and fascinating castle and churches.

◉ Sights & Activities

Castelo   CASTLE
(admission €2.50; ⏱ 9.30am-7pm Apr-Sep, to 5.30pm Oct-Mar) The flower-ringed, 14th-century *castelo* has sweeping views. Inside the grounds are the small, excellent **Núcleo Museológico de Arqueologia** (archaeological museum), displaying ruined medieval castle walls and other artefacts, and an exhibition on Islamic board games.

Entrance fee to the castle also includes entry to small museums (núcleos museológicos) in Alcoutim and around.

Riverside Beach   BEACH
The main attraction for most day-trippers is the small riverside beach, equipped with sand, palm-leaf umbrellas and even a lifeguard! The setting is breathtaking, but in summer it's hot, hot, hot. At the bridge, follow the signs to Praia Fluvial.

🛏 Sleeping

Pousada da Juventude   HOSTEL €
(☑ 281 546 004; www.pousadasjuventude.pt; dm €13, d €35-40, apt €75; ⏱ reception 8am-noon & 6pm-midnight; 🖭) On the river, 1km north of the square, past the new town, is this well-appointed hostel, with a pool and kitchen facilities, plus bikes and canoes for rent.

Ilda Afonso   GUESTHOUSE €
(☑ 281 546 411; Rua Dr João Dias 10A; r €30) Rooms are plain, but the owners are friendly and it's central. Private houses with beds. Breakfast not included.

Brisas do Guadiana   GUESTHOUSE €
(☑ 968 162 508; visitaralcoutim@gmail.com; Rua do Bairro das Casas Pré-Fabricadas; s €35, d €40-45) Contrary to the street name ('Prefabricated Houses St'), this smart yellow place on top of the hill behind the castle offers decent rooms. Breakfast not included.

✕ Eating

You can take a safe pick from one of the town's few eateries, all of which serve up traditional cuisine with Algarvian flavours.

Snack Bar
Restaurante O Soeiro   PORTUGUESE €
(☑ 281 546 241; Rua do Município; daily specials €6.50-9; ⏱ lunch Mon-Fri) Cheap and cheerful, but good for its grilled chicken and its setting near the river.

O Camané   PORTUGUESE €€
(Rua 1 de Maio; mains €8.50-12; ⏱ lunch & dinner Wed-Mon) Bursting with a range of Algarvian and Alentejan dishes, including *porco preto* (wild boar) and *açorda* (bread soup).

ℹ Information

Turismo (☑ 281 546 179; Rua 1 de Maio; ⏱ 9.30am-1pm & 2-5.30pm Mon-Fri Oct-Jun, Tue-Sat Jul-Sep) Behind the central square, this office distributes maps and other information.

ℹ Getting There & Around

Bus services run to/from Vila Real de Santo António (€4.25, 1¼ hours, one on Monday, Wednesday and Friday); on Monday and Friday these go to/from Beja (two hours, around €5) via Mértola (50 minutes).

Loulé

POP 26,700

One of the Algarve's largest inland towns, and only 16km northwest of Faro, Loulé (lo-lay) is a reasonable base from which to explore the inland Algarve. A busy commercial centre, it is one of the fastest-growing towns in Portugal, as people use this as a base to work (or seek work) in the Algarve. Loulé has an attractive old quarter and Moorish castle ruins and its history spans back to the Romans. A few of Loulé's artisan traditions still survive; crafty folk toil away on wicker baskets, copperworks and embroidery at hole-in-the-wall workshops about town. Loulé's small university lends it some verve, as does its wild Carnaval (just before Lent) and FestivalMed, an annual music festival.

If arriving by train, note that the train station is 5km southwest of town (take any Quarteira-bound bus).

◎ Sights & Activities

Museu Municipal   MUSEUM
(☑289 400 600; Largo Dom Pedro I; admission €1.50; ◎9.30am-5.30pm Mon-Fri, 9.30am-2pm & 3-5.30pm Sat) Housed within Loulé's restored castle, Museu Municipal contains beautifully presented fine fragments of Bronze Age and Roman ceramics (exhibitions change every few years). A glass floor exposes excavated Moorish ruins. The admission fee includes entry to a stretch of the castle walls and the **Cozinha Tradicional Algarvia**, a re-creation of a traditional Algarve kitchen, featuring a cosy hearth, archaic implements and burnished copper.

Nossa Senhora da Conceição   CHAPEL
(◎9am-12.30pm & 2-5.30pm Mon-Fri & 9.30am-2pm & 3-5.30pm Sat) Situated opposite Loulé's castle, and dating from the mid-17th century, the small chapel of Nossa Senhora da Conceição has a plain facade that nonchalantly hides a heavily decorated mid-18th-century interior with a magnificent gold altarpiece. During recent excavations an Islamic door, dating from the 3rd century, was uncovered under the floor, where it now stays, protected by glass.

Almargem   WALKING
(☑289 412 959; www.almargem.org) FREE The environmental group, Almargem, is responsible for the Via Algarviana and welcomes visitors on its Sunday walks.

✦ Festivals & Events

Carnaval   RELIGIOUS
Just before Lent, Loulé shimmies into something sexy and sequinned, with parades, tractor-drawn floats and lots of musical hijinks. Friday is the children's parade, and Sunday the big one. Held in late February or early March.

FestivalMed   WORLD MUSIC
(www.festivalmed.com.pt) Having been an attraction since 2006, FestivalMed is fast gaining a reputation as a quality world-music festival, attracting the likes of Jamaican performer Jimmy Cliff and other international performers. Held in late June.

Nossa Senhora da Piedade   RELIGIOUS
Linked to ancient maternity rites, this *romaria* (religious festival) is the Algarve's most important. On Easter Sunday a 16th-century image of Our Lady of Pity (or Piety) is carried down from its hilltop chapel, 2km north of town, to the parish church. Two weeks later, a procession of devotees lines the steep route to the chapel to witness its return.

⌷ Sleeping

Casa Beny   GUESTHOUSE €
(☑967 936 067, 289 417 702; casabeny.g@gmail.com; Rua São Domingos 13; d €50-55; ❋豢) In a pleasantly restored mansion dating from 1897, Casa Beny offers nine peachy rooms, each with Brazilian hardwood floors, a touch of '80s-style pine, tall ceilings and French doors. The rooftop terrace has castle views.

Hospedaria Dom Fernando   GUESTHOUSE €€
(☑289 415 553; Travessa do Mercado; s/d €45/65; ❋豢) This option offers two different choices: a newer section, above the owner's restaurant, with simple, modern rooms, or those in the neighbouring building, which are showing signs of age in the decor department, but are adequate and cheaper (these cost €10 less per person). In an excellent location, behind the market, although you'll be in the thick of it (think noise and action) during festival times.

Loulé Jardim Hotel   HOTEL €€
(☑289 413 094; www.loulejardimhotel.com; Praça Manuel D'Arriaga 25; s/d/tr €60/80/105, d with terrace €87; ❋豢❋) A late-19th-century building with tasteful, airy and spacious rooms, this well-run place overlooks a pretty square. Book ahead for a terrace.

Loulé

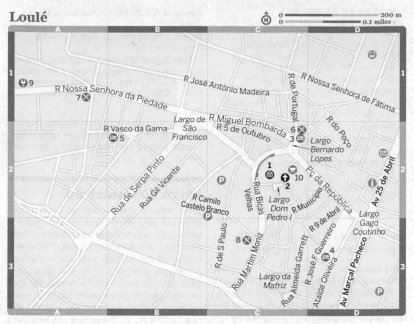

N 0 ─────── 200 m
0 ─────── 0.1 miles

Loulé

◎ Sights
1 Museu Municipal C2
2 Nossa Senhora da Conceição C2

🛏 Sleeping
3 Casa Reny C2
4 Hospedaria Dom Fernando D3
5 Loulé Jardim Hotel B2

✕ Eating
6 Cantina dos Sabores C2
7 Churrasqueira Angolana A1
8 Espaços Gastronómicos Perdição C3

🍷 Drinking & Nightlife
9 Bar Marroquia A1
10 Café Calcinha C2

✕ Eating & Drinking

Cantina dos Sabores VEGETARIAN €
(Rua de Portugal 22; ⊙ lunch & dinner Mon-Sat; 🖋)
You might have to queue to get a place at this
buzzing vegetarian eatery alongside everyone from professionals to butch-looking
meat-eating guys. (OK, so it has chicken on
the menu.) It's deservedly popular for its daily specials (around €6), juices and desserts.
Generous portions are filling and enjoyable.

Churrasqueira Angolana GRILL HOUSE €
(Rua Nossa Senhora da Piedade 63; ⊙ lunch &
dinner) It ain't pretty from the outside, but
you don't come here for the setting, nor for
the service – it's brusque, busy and food-
focussed. But you'll get a decent grill here,
from tuna steaks to chicken.

**Espaços Gastronómicos
Perdição** MEDITERRANEAN €€
(📞 919 669 953; Rua Camilo Castelo Branco; mains
€7-15; ⊙ lunch Mon-Sat, dinner Thu-Sat; 🖋) This
place lives up to its name: gastronomic delights in the form of daily vegetarian, fish,
meat and pasta dishes. Has a good selection
of juices, teas and desserts, too.

Monte da Eira PORTUGUESE €€
(📞 289 438 129; www.restaurantemontedaeira.
com; Clareanes; mains €12-18; ⊙ lunch & dinner;
🖋🚗) On Rte 396, 5km north of Loulé in the
village of Clareanes, is this smart restaurant,
the stables of a converted threshing mill,
now several rooms and two outdoor terraces.
People come from afar to feast on dishes of
javali (wild boar), lamb and bean casserole,
and stewed rabbit. To top it off, choose from

WALKS IN SERRA DO CALDEIRÃO

A walk well worth doing is **Rocha da Pena**, a limestone peak just east of Alte and off the N124. Walkers can do a signed 4.7km circuit walk up the mountain; follow the road signs to the mountain. A return walk takes about two to three hours. Carry water and snacks; there's a small shop-cafe at the base and another in Penina village but no other refreshment stops for miles. Note fire-danger times – bushfires occur in this area.

The *tourismo* at Salir may stock basic maps.

one of 96 wines – *hic* – and that's the red alone. Vegetarians are catered for, too.

Café Calcinha   CAFE
(☑ 289 415 763; Praça da República 67; snacks €1-7; ☺ 8am-11pm Mon-Fri, to 4pm Sat) This traditional 1920s-style cafe (Loulé's oldest) has marble-topped tables and sidewalk tables. The statue outside depicts António Aleixo, an early-20th-century poet and former regular of the cafe.

Bar Marroquia   BAR
(Rua Nossa Senhora da Piedade 122) Popular with Loulé's younger crowd, this bar has an Arabic theme and an international party philosophy.

🛍 Shopping

Loulé's excellent arts and crafts are made and sold in craft shops around and behind the castle (Rua Barbaca). The **mercado municipal** also has traditional craft stalls.

ℹ Information

Biblioteca Municipal de Loulé (Rua José Afonso; ☺ 2-7pm Mon, 9.30am-7pm Tue-Fri, 2.30-6pm Sat 15 Sep-15 Jun, Mon-Fri 16 Jun-14 Sep) Smart, new library with free internet.
Turismo (☑ 289 463 900; www.visitalgarve. pt; Av 25 de Abril 9; ☺ 9.30am-5.30pm Tue-Fri, 9.30am-1pm & 2-5.30pm Sat & Mon) Maps and brochures available here. Keeps longer hours in summer (and is open on Sundays).

ℹ Getting There & Around

BUS

Daily **bus** (☑ 289 416 655; Rua Nossa Senhora de Fátima) connections head to the following:

Albufeira (€4.25, 55 minutes, two to three daily)
Faro (€3.25, 40 minutes, hourly weekdays, fewer weekends)
If heading to Portimão on a weekday, change at Albufeira. On weekends there are three direct buses (€5.45, 1½ hours). Express buses head to Lisbon (€20, 3¾ hours, four to five daily).

CAR

If driving, parking can be tricky in Loulé – park on the edge of town. Note, however, never leave valuables in your car – travellers have reported theft.

Serra do Caldeirão

Lying around 30km north of Loulé is the stunning region of Serra do Caldeirão, a beautiful protected area of undulating hills, cork trees and harsh scrubland. The area is renowned for its bird varieties. It's an excellent place to hike – the Via Algarviana goes through here – and a wonderful spot to base oneself to meander through some ancient villages and enjoy the region's cuisine. A feature of the region are its *fontes* (traditional water sources, many of which comprise exquisite taps and fountains), highlighted by signs that have been erected in recent years.

Perched on a hillside on the edge of Serra do Caldeirão, **Alte**, located 45km northwest of Loulé, is a quaint and very pretty little village. In high season visitors are disgorged from buses for a quick-see experience. Boasting flower-filled streets, whitewashed buildings and several *fontes*, it's a pleasant place to wander for an hour or so. The *fontes* were traditionally used for the mills and former wells; a main *fonte*, Fonte Grande passes through dykes, weirs and watermills. Several *artesanatos* (handicrafts shops) are dotted around town, as are several restaurants and cafes.

Tourist information is available in **Pólo Museológico Cândido Guerreiro e Condes de Alte** (☑ 289 478 058; Rua Condes de Alte; ☺ 12.30-3pm Mon-Fri) **FREE**, a museum-cultural space that pays homage to Alte's famous poet, Guerreiro, and the Counts of Alte who lived there. It displays the books and paraphernalia of all.

If travelling by car, pass through the small, sleepy and attractive town of **Salir**. It's a pleasant, very genuine village set on two hills with castle walls dating from the 12th century and has an attractive church.

Salir has a small **tourismo** (☑289 489 137; Largo do Castelo; ⊙9am-12.30 & 2-5.30pm Mon-Fri) near the castle.

Buses depart Loulé for Alte (€3.55, 45 minutes, twice daily on weekdays) and Salir (€2.45, 30 minutes, six daily on weekdays, one Saturday).

🛏 Sleeping & Eating

Quinta do Coração GUESTHOUSE €
(☑289 489 959; www.algarveparadise.com; Carrasqueiro; s/d €35/55, self-catering studio €60, 2-person cottage €65; ☒) The setting of this converted farmhouse, in Carrasqueiro (7km east of Salir) is lovely – on a wooded hill, encircled by a eucalypt, olive-grove and cork-tree paradise. This ain't your gleaming white-tiled experience; the rooms, studios and cottage (with kitchenette) are rough-and-rustic, in a pleasant sort of way. The experience comes with a well-meaning 'touch of hippy'.

It's on the Via Algarviana.

Quinta do Freixo RURAL INN €€
(☑289 472 185; www.quintadofreixo.org; Benafim; s/d €48/65; ⊙Mar-Nov; ☒) This pleasant place – a converted barn – is located on Quinta do Freixo, a functioning farm well-known for producing traditional foodstuffs. Although a rural experience, accommodation errs on the 'moo', not the 'poo'; you can see animals from the comfortable communal areas, without leaving the complex's green lawns and swimming pool.

The 10 comfortable rooms feature Alentejan (painted wooden) furniture. Popular with small European groups. Travellers report unreliable opening months, however.

Casa da Mãe GUESTHOUSE €€
(☑289 489 179; www.casadamae.com; Almeijoafra; s €40-75, d/tr €70/85; @☒) This friendly

unpretentious complex offers a series of good-value, if slightly dated, rooms and apartments. It has a lovely garden – with pool – and superb views of greenery and Salir in the distance. Good breakfasts with homemade produce. The Via Algarviana passes close by.

Albufeira
POP 22,000

Once a scenic fishing village, Albufeira has tragically lost its vestiges to its past – fishing boats are now moored at the ultramodern marina southwest of town. These days, the town is a den of mass-market tourism; the old town – and its pretty cobblestone streets and Moorish influences – is concealed by neon signs, English menu boards and rowdy bars. It is the destination for cheap package deals, mainly catering to Brits and Germans and focused on cheap food, grog and fine nearby beaches.

Despite this, it has good transport links to lovely beaches, such as Praia da Galé to the west. To explore the pretty inland villages and the area's high-quality restaurants, you will need your own transport.

Arrival here can be slightly overwhelming. A snapshot orientation: the old town lies below the N526 (Av dos Descobrimentos), and 3km east of here is 'the Strip', a road with more shops and bars, leading up from crowded Praia da Oura.

◉ Sights

Museu Municipal de Arqueologia MUSEUM
(admission €1; ⊙9.30am-12.30pm & 1.30-5.30pm Tue-Sun) This museum showcases items excavated from the municipality and surrounds (such as the castle in the village of Paderne). Pieces date from the prehistoric era to the

---

WORTH A TRIP

VILA JOYA – JOY INDEED

★ **Vila Joya** (☑289 591 795; www.vilajoya.com; Apt 120 Praia da Galé; r incl breakfast from €385; P ☀ ☎ ☒ ♨) is a luxury resort and spa located several kilometres from Albufeira – yet a planet away in every respect – right on the beachfront near Praia da Galé. The decor and surrounds have a touch of Africa about them. Pool areas, lush green lawn, views of the sea and a health spa add to an ultraplush and relaxing experience. If your purse strings don't stretch to staying here, consider saving your pennies for a meal at the restaurant, one of only two eateries in the Algarve with Michelin stars (not one, but two!). You'll enjoy impeccable service, exquisite locally sourced produce and the best of the *best* cuisine from chef Dieter Koschina at **Vila Joya Restaurant** (mains €42-110; degustation menu €165; ⊙lunch & dinner).

16th century. A highlight is a beautifully complete Neolithic vase from 5000 BC.

Museum of Sacred Art MUSEUM
(☑289 585 526; admission €2; ⊙10.30am-4.30pm Sep-Jun & at night Jul-Aug) This tiny museum is housed in the beautifully restored 18th-century Chapel of San Sebastian. It has a stunning gold wooden altar and exhibits sacred art from surrounding churches that survived the 1775 earthquake.

☂ Beaches

Besides strolling cheek-to-jowl with others along the pedestrianised seafront, most come here for the beaches. **Praia do Peneco**, through the tunnel near the *turismo*, is usually head-to-toe with sunloungers. East and west of town are beautifully rugged coves and bays, though the nearest are heavily developed and often crowded. These include **Praia da Oura**, at the bottom of 'the Strip' 3km to the east and accessible by the blue (azul) line bus (catch it above the escalators by the old fishing quarter); **Praia da Falésia**, a long beach 10km to the east; **Balaia** and **Olhos de Água**. Buses run to Olhos de Água (10 minutes, half-hourly), mostly continuing to Praia da Falésia (20 minutes).

One of the best beaches to the west, **Praia da Galé**, about 6km away, is long and sandy, not so crowded and a centre for jet-skiing and water-skiing. Eva buses run to Praia da Galé (€3.40 one way) or the red line 1 and 2 head there every half hour in summer (€1.40).

🛏 Sleeping

Most places are associated with travel companies; bagging a room in July and August is impossible without reservations. Many places close in low season (November to March).

Dianamar GUESTHOUSE €
(☑289 587 801; www.dianamar.com; Rua Latino Coelho 36; s/tr €50/75, d €60-65; ⊙Apr-Oct) If you must stay in Albufeira, this is one good reason to do so. Friendly, Scandinavian-run Dianamar has lovely details, with fresh flowers and attractive rooms, many with balconies and two with sea views. Excellent and oh-so-generous breakfasts and afternoon teas. Best to reserve ahead.

THE ALGARVE FOR KIDS

The Algarve is a fun, kid-focused area with loads of attractions, family-friendly beaches and cultural activities. Try thrilling water parks such as Slide & Splash (p178) and Krazy World (p182); the great zoo (p187) in Lagos; and, at Silves, the imagination-firing castle (p179).

There are some excellent museums, too: in São Brás de Alportel there's a simple cork display in the Museu Etnográfico do Trajo Algarvio (p159), and in Portimão, the wonderful Museu de Portimão (p184) re-creates a former fish cannery.

Many towns along the coast run boat trips, and several have little trains.

Albufeira is particularly kid-friendly with a plethora of agencies in the area selling a variety of trips, from horse riding to cruising on pirate ships. Most boat trips leave from the marina. Other kid-friendly activities include the following:

Albufeira Riding Centre (☑289 542 870; Vale Navio Complex; 1hr ride €30) On the road to Vilamoura. Offers one- to three-hour horse rides for all ages and abilities.

Aqua Show (☑289 389 396; www.aquashowpark.com; adult/child €25/15; ⊙10am-6pm Jun-Sep, to 7pm Aug) In Quarteira, 10km east of Albufeira, with parrots, reptiles and a wave pool.

Aqualand (☑282 320 230; www.aqualand.pt; Alcantarilha; adult/child €20/15.50; ⊙10am-6pm Jun-Sep) Huge loop-the-loop slide and rapids.

Dolphins Driven (☑913 113 095; www.dolphins.pt; Marina de Albufeira) Offers three boat trips from Albufeira (from 2½ hours to full day) to caves, beaches, up the Rio Arade and to Ria Formosa.

Zoomarine (☑289 560 306; www.zoomarine.com; adult/child €24/15; ⊙10am-7.30pm Jul–mid-Sep, to 5pm rest of year, closed Dec) Will satisfy all desires for aqua-entertainment, with huge swimming pools and slides, as well as lakes, an aquarium and dolphin shows. Located at Guia, 8km northwest of Albufeira.

Vila São Vicente BOUTIQUE HOTEL €€€
(🖉289 583 700; www.hotelsaovicentealbufeira.
com; Largo Jacinto D'Ayet; r from €125, ste from
€175; ❉ @ ❉) This peaceful, classically decorated boutique-style hotel has handsome
rooms with polished-wood floors. It's a
welcome relief from the town's theme-park
atmosphere.

🍴 Eating & Drinking

British breakfasts? Thai curries? Tasty?
Bland? Albufeira has every conceivable
range of dining option. The small market has fruits, vegetables and fish. Browse
the menus near Largo Cais Herculano, the
main plaza or any streets leading off here,
for foodstuffs and flavours that will best appease your hunger pangs.

You can bar-hop your brain cells away in
Albufeira. Bars throng the area around Largo Engenheiro Duarte Pacheco and nearby
Rua Cândido dos Reis. Nearly all offer happy
hours (at various times of the day) and similar cocktails, and are open until at least 4am
in summer.

ℹ️ Information

HPP Albufeira (🖉797 275 275; www.hpp
algarve.pt; Largo da Correeira, Montechoro;
⊙24hr) Medical matters and emergencies.
Centro de Saúde (🖉289 598 400; ⊙24hr)
Two kilometres north of the old town.
GNR Police Station (🖉289 590 790; Av 25
de Abril) North of town, near the *mercado
municipal*.
Turismo (🖉289 585 279; www.visitalgarve.
pt; Rua 5 de Outubro 8; ⊙9.30am-1pm &
2-5.30pm Sep-Jun, 9.30am-7pm Jul & Aug)
Algarve Tourism office; by a tunnel that leads
to the beach.
Municipal Tourism Office (🖉289 515 973;
www.cm-albufeira.pt; Estrada de Santa Eulália;
⊙9am-6pm Mon-Fri, to 3pm Sat) Helpful local
tourist office with maps and info.

ℹ️ Getting There & Away

BUS
The **main bus station** (🖉289 580 611; Rua dos
Caliços) is 2km north of town. Passengers trav-
elling to Lisbon can purchase tickets at a more
conveniently located **bus shop** (🖉289 588 122;
Av da Liberdade), outside of which buses leave
for the main bus station (€1.40) every 30 min-
utes from 7am to 10pm.
Faro (€4.65, 40 minutes, half-hourly)
Lagos (€4.95, one to 1¼ hours, 12 daily)

Lisbon (€20, three hours, four to seven daily).
Loulé (€3.55, 40 minutes, four to seven daily).
Silves (€4.25, 40 minutes to one hour, three to
seven daily)
Buses also head to Huelva in Spain (€17, 4¼
hours, via Faro), and on to Seville (€19, 5½
hours).

TRAIN
Services from Albufeira:
Faro (€10.60 to €14.20, 35 minutes, 10 daily)
Lagos (€4.75, 1¼ hours, 10 daily)

ℹ️ Getting Around

To reach the train station, take the 'giro' city bus
(€1.40). The giro (red line numbers 1 or 2) also
leaves half-hourly for Praias de São Rafael, Galé
and Guia (€1.40). These depart from the top of
the escalators above the fishing quarter. Blue
line buses head to Praia Ouro, though you return
on the green line. (Check, however, as these may
change.)
For car hire, try the following:
Auto Jardim (🖉289 580 500; www.auto-
jardim.com; Edifício Brisa, Av da Liberdade)
Auto Prudente (🖉289 542 160; www.auto-
prudente.com; Estrada de Santa Eulália,
Edifício Ondas do Mar, Loja 1)

Carvoeiro

Carvoeiro is a cluster of whitewashed buildings rising up from tawny, gold and green
cliffs and backed by hills. Shops, bars and
restaurants rise steeply from the small arc
of beach that is the focus of the town, and
beyond lie hillsides full of sprawling holiday
villas. This diminutive seaside resort 5km
south of Lagoa is prettier and more laid-
back than many of the bigger resorts, but
its size means that it gets full to bursting in
summer.

🏖️ Beaches

The town's handkerchief-sized little sandy
beach, **Praia do Carvoeiro**, is surrounded
by the steeply mounting town. About 1km
east on the coastal road is the bay of **Algar
Seco**, a favourite stop on the tour-bus itinerary thanks to its dramatic rock formations.

If you're looking for a stunning swimming
spot, continue east along the main road, Estrada do Farol, to **Praia de Centianes**, where
the secluded cliff-wrapped beach is almost as
dramatic as Algar Seco. Buses heading for
Praia do Carvalho (nine daily and three on
weekends from Lagoa, via Carvoeiro) pass

THE ALGARVE CARVOEIRO

nearby – get off at Colina Sol Aparthotel, the Moorish-style clifftop hotel.

🏃 Activities

The nearest water park is **Slide & Splash** (☑282 341 685; www.slidesplash.com; Estrada Nacional 125; adult/child €18/14.50), situated 2km west of Lagoa.

Golf

Golfers can be choosy: there's the **Pestana Gramacho** (☑282 340 900; www.pestanagolf.com) and **Pestana Vale da Pinta** (☑282 340 900; www.pestanagolf.com), both at **Pestana Golf Resort** (Apartado 1011, Carvoeiro); and **Vale de Milho** (☑282 358 502; www.valedemilhogolf.com) near Praia de Centianes.

Diving

The (German) family-run **Divers Cove** (☑282 356 594; www.diverscove.de; Quinta do Paraíso; 3hr introduction €80, 1-day discovery €135, 2-day scuba diver €260, 4-day open water €440; ⊙9am-7pm) diving centre provides equipment, dives and PADI certification.

🛏 Sleeping

In July and August it may be impossible to find a room, so reserve well ahead. Some guesthouses may require a minimum three-night stay.

O Castelo GUESTHOUSE €
(☑282 357 416; www.ocastelo.net; Rua do Casino 59; d without view €55, d with view €65-85; ✹🛜) To the west of the bay, behind the *turismo*, this welcoming guesthouse with a justifiably proud owner was renovated in 2012. It gets the sunrise view and offers 12 smart, well-kept rooms (and one suite). Some rooms share a large terrace and sea views. Guests even have use of a kitchen.

Casa Luiz GUESTHOUSE €
(☑282 354 058; www.casaluiz.com; Rampa da Nossa Senhora da Encarnação; d/studios/apt €60/70/80) Four clean and modern rooms and studio (with kitchenette), all overlooking the beach.

🍴 Eating & Drinking

There are a handful of restaurants clustered near the beach and scattered along Estrada do Farol.

Marisqueira SEAFOOD, GRILL HOUSE €€
(Estrada do Farol; mains €13.50-25; ⊙lunch & dinner Tue-Sun) This simple, well-established

place has an outdoor terrace and is known for its seafood and grilled dishes.

Pimenta Preta MEDITERRANEAN €€€
(☑282 350 200; www.palmgardensalgarve.com; Pestana Palm Gardens Resort, Centeanes; ⊙lunch & dinner Tue-Sun) Yes, it's in a resort, so it's a little upmarket. But this smart eatery serves up great-quality Mediterranean cuisine – such as tiger prawns with saffron ginger sauce. But don't ask for this – the menu changes seasonally so there's always new gourmet surprises.

Restaurante Boneca Bar BAR
(☑282 358 391; ⊙10am-midnight summer) Hidden in the rock formations out at Algar Seco, this long-standing place is a novel spot for a cocktail.

ℹ Information

The post office and several banks are located on Rua dos Pescadores (the one-way road in from Lagoa).

Turismo (☑282 357 728; ⊙9.30am-1pm & 2-5.30pm Mon-Fri)

ℹ Getting There & Around

Buses run on weekdays from Portimão to Lagoa (€2.20, 20 minutes, hourly) and to Carvoeiro (€3.25, 10 minutes, one to seven daily).

You can rent scooters from **Motorent** (☑282 356 551; Rua do Barranco, Edificio Galeão, Loja 11) on the road back to Lagoa. Several car-rental agencies are also found along this stretch of road.

Note: parking is often very difficult in summer – you are best to head to Estrada do Farol and walk.

Silves

POP 11,000

Silves is an attractive town of jumbling orange rooftops scattered above the banks of the Rio Arade. It boasts one of the best-preserved castles in the Algarve, attractive red-stone walls and winding, sleepy backstreets on a hillside. Not much happens around town, but it's a good base if you're after a less hectic, noncoastal Algarvian pace. Around Silves, there are some lovely rural accommodation options. It's 15km northeast of Portimão.

The train station is located 2km south of town, but you'll need to catch a cab as it's along a major highway.

History

The Rio Arade was long an important route into the interior for the Phoenicians, Greeks and Carthaginians, who wanted the copper and iron action in the southwest of the country. With the Moorish invasion from the 8th century, the town gained prominence due to its strategic hilltop, riverside site. From the mid-11th to the mid-13th centuries, Shelb (or Xelb), as it was then known, rivalled Lisbon in prosperity and influence: according to the 12th-century Arab geographer Idrisi, it had a population of 30,000, a port and shipyards, and 'attractive buildings and well-furnished bazaars'.

The town's downfall began in June 1189, when Dom Sancho I laid siege to it, supported by a horde of (mostly English) crusaders, who had been persuaded (with the promise of loot) to pause in their journey to Jerusalem and give Sancho a hand. The Moors holed up inside their impregnable castle with their huge cisterns, but after three hot months of harassment they ran out of water and were forced to surrender. Sancho was all for mercy and honour, but the crusaders wanted the plunder they were promised, and stripped the Moors of their possessions (including the clothes on their backs) as they left, tortured those remaining and wrecked the town.

Two years later the Moors recaptured the town. It wasn't until 1249 that Christians gained control once and for all. But by then Silves was a shadow of its former self. The silting up of the river – which caused disease and stymied maritime trade – coupled with the growing importance of the Algarvian ports hastened the town's decline. Devastation in the 1755 earthquake seemed to seal its fate. But in the 19th century, local cork and dried-fruit industries revitalised Silves, hence the grand bourgeois architecture around town. Today tourism and agriculture are the town's lifeblood.

◉ Sights

Castelo
CASTLE

(☑ 282 445 624; adult/concession/under 10yr €2.50/1.25/free, joint ticket with Museu Municipal de Arqueologia €3.60; ☺ 9am-5pm Dec-Feb, to 6.30pm Jun-Aug) The russet-coloured, Lego-like castle has great views over the town and surrounding countryside. It was restored in the 1940s and you can walk around its chunky sandstone walls. In the north wall you can see a treason gate, an escape route through which turncoats would sometimes let the enemy in, typical of castles at the time. The Moorish occupation is recalled by a deep well and a rosy-coloured water cistern, 5m deep and constructed at the end of the 12th century. Inside, the cistern's four vaults are supported by 10 columns. Most probably built in the 11th century, the castle was abandoned by the 16th century. Recent restorations include the red-brick interior walkway.

Sé
CATHEDRAL

(admission €1; ☺ hours vary Mon-Fri) Just below the castle is the *sé* (cathedral), built in 1189 on the site of an earlier mosque, then rebuilt after the 1249 Reconquista and subsequently restored several times following earthquake damage. The stark, fortresslike building has a multiarched Portuguese-Gothic doorway, and some original Gothic touches left, including the nave and aisles and a dramatically tall, strikingly simple interior. There are several fine tombs, one of which is purported to be of João do Rego, who helped to settle Madeira.

Igreja da Misericórdia
CHURCH

(☺ 9am-1pm & 2-5pm Mon-Fri) The 16th-century Igreja da Misericórdia, plain apart from its distinctive, fanciful Manueline doorway (not the main entrance) is decorated with curious heads, pine cones, foliage and aquatic emblems.

Museu Municipal de Arqueologia
MUSEUM

(☑ 282 444 838; Rua das Portas de Loulé; adult/under 10yr €2/free, joint ticket with Castelo €3.60; ☺ 10am-6pm) Just below the cathedral is the impressive, well-laid-out Museu Municipal de Arqueologia. In the centre is a well-preserved 4m-wide, 18m-deep Moorish well surrounded by a spiral staircase, which was discovered during excavations. The find, together with other archaeological discoveries in the area, led to the establishment of the museum on this site; it shows prehistoric, Roman and Moorish antiquities. One wall is of glass, showing a section of the fort wall (also of Almohad origin) that is used to support the building.

⚗ Activities

Country Riding Centre
HORSE RIDING

(www.countryridingcentre.com; lessons from €30) Located about 4km east of Silves, left off the road to Messines (it is signposted); offers hour-long to half-day rides at all levels.

JOHN HARPER / GETTY IMAGES ©

1. Praia da Galé **2.** Praia da Dona Ana
3. Surfers, the Algarve **4.** Praia da Marinha

2

JUAMPITER / GETTY IMAGES ©

Beaches of the Algarve

The Algarve's extraordinary coastline – stretching for over 150km along the Atlantic ocean – is incredibly diverse, and offers an abundance of enticing choices.

Small, secluded coves to wide stretches of rugged, dune-backed shores. Simple rock-backed nooks with calm waters (great for kids) to rugged coasts with huge swells.

The coast's varied geography changes dramatically along its length and makes for some quirky beachscapes. From Vila Real de Santo António to the tiny village of Cacela Velha, the beaches are a dune system. The central coast sees kilometres of limestone cliffs. Think eroded rock towers, and plenty of nooks and caves.

The increasingly rocky coast, from Lagos to Sagres, culminates in the wind-scoured grandeur of the Cabo de São Vicente. Here, dramatic black cliffs, bordered by beautiful sandy stretches, head north along the Costa Vicentina Natural Park. This stretch is made for serious surfers.

Top 10 Beaches of the Algarve

Our (highly subjective) picks include:

➡ **Odeceixe** This beach has a river on one side and the ocean on the other.

➡ **Praia da Falésia** A posh 'resort' beach backed by high ochre-hued cliffs.

➡ **Praia da Marinha** Great snorkelling, with a novel entry via a long staircase.

➡ **Meia Praia** Vast, popular and scenic, with options for water sports.

➡ **Praia do Barril** Crown jewel of Ilha de Tavira, with an anchor cemetery.

➡ **Ilha da Barreta (Ilha Deserta)** Accessed by boat through nature-filled lagoons.

➡ **Praia de Vale Figueira** Long stretch of wild, little-frequented coast.

➡ **Praia da Bordeira** Wild untamed beauty (with surfing).

➡ **Praia da Dona Ana & Praia do Camilo** Enchanting, golden rock formations.

➡ **Praia de Vale do Lobo** Has all the tourist services within reach and on tap.

4

Krazy World
WATER PARK

(☎282 574 134; www.krazyworld.com; Algoz; adult/child €12/8; ☉10am-6pm) Near São Bartolomeu de Messines, about 17km northwest of Silves, this animal and crocodile park also has minigolf, ponies and two swimming pools.

🎉 Festivals & Events

Over one week each August (dates vary annually), Silves relives its past at the **Medieval Fair**. The town's important events and people are reconstructed, from Al Muthamid, the governor of Silves, to the town being awarded its charter. Think bawdy costumes, dances, jesters, feasts, traditional food and handicrafts...all evoking life in the 11th to 13th centuries.

🛏 Sleeping

Quinta da Figueirinha
RURAL INN €

(☎282 440 700; www.qdf.pt; 2-/4-/6-person apt from €56/96/138; 🐾) 🌿 This 36-hectare organic farm and botanic (drought-resistant) garden, run by the kindly agronomist Dr Gerhard Zabel, offers simple apartments in peaceful farmlike surroundings. The surrounding exotic orchards are yours (more than 50 species of plants) for picking and wandering. Leaving Silves and crossing the bridge, take the first left to Fragura and continue for 4km. The *quinta* (estate) is signposted. You can self-cater, or there is a basic restaurant serving delicious, wholesome buffet-style food.

Casa das Oliveiras
RURAL INN €

(☎282 342 115; www.casa-das-oliveiras.com; s €47-53, d €57-65; 🐾🖥) This peaceful place offers an old-style B&B with a British flavour, with five slightly dated rooms in a relaxed setting. There's a lovely garden and pool area. It's 4km from Silves train station. Ring for directions.

Vila Sodre
GUESTHOUSE €

(☎282 443 441; http://vilasodresilves.com.sapo.pt; Estrada de Messines; s €42.50, d €57; 🖥🐾) This modern blue-and-white villa is 1.4km east of the newer bridge. It's good value, with smart, if faded, rooms that overlook orange orchards. The highlight is the owner – ask to see his extraordinary wine collection.

Duas Quintas
RURAL INN €€

(☎919 729 799; www.algarveguesthouse.com; São Estevão; d/studios €95/115; 🐾🖥) This charm-

ing but unpretentious place in a converted farmhouse screams 'relax!' Set within greenery and rolling hills, it has six pleasant rooms, a living space, terraces and a pool. The friendly Irish owners serve up scrumptious gourmet breakfasts – great energy for the excellent walks in the surrounds. Prices are significantly less outside high season. To get here, head 5.5km northeast (en route to São Bartolomeu de Messines) to Sítio São Estevão.

🍴 Eating

There are plenty of cafe-restaurants in the pedestrianised streets leading up to the castle or down by the river, where you'll also find a reasonable *mercado municipal* (just west of the old pedestrian bridge).

Pastelaria Rosa
PATISSERIE €

(Largo do Município; pastries from €1.50; ☉7.30am-late Mon-Sat) On the ground floor of the townhall building, this quaint, tile-lined place is Silves' oldest cafe and the best place to try Algarvian sweets.

Tasca Béné
PORTUGUESE €€

(☎282 444 767; €8-12; ☉lunch & dinner Mon-Sat) This atmospheric traditional *tasca* (tavern) serves up all the Portuguese cliches – chequered cloths and old-world paraphernalia – and it's got a great reputation for doing so. The menu comprises daily meat and fish specials and by night, it's an *à la carte* menu. *Cataplanas* (seafood stews) are available for €25 (for two).

Café Ingles
INTERNATIONAL €€

(☎282 442 585; www.cafeingles.com.pt; mains €10-23; 🍴) Located below the castle entrance, the Café Ingles has a wonderful, shady terrace and is everyone's favourite spot. The food is excellent (don't miss the chocolate St Emilion dessert). One of the Algarve's liveliest restaurants north of the coast, it has an elegant interior and on weekends it occasionally has live jazz, fado and African music.

Recanto dos Mouros
PORTUGUESE €€

(☎282 443 240; Monte Branco; mains €9-14; ☉lunch & dinner Thu-Tue) Situated a kilometre or so behind the castle (follow the signs), this is one of Silves' most popular places. As the Portuguese attest, it's *bom preço-qualidade* (damn good value) for lots of hearty Algarvian delights.

ℹ PAYING TOLLS IN A HIRE CAR

In recent times the government has introduced charges to drive along the A22, the large motorway that runs along the Algarve. Frustratingly, there are no toll booths and, at the time of research, not all hire cars were fitted with electronic transformers. If you hire a car that is not fitted with an electronic transformer, you are responsible for paying the toll. To do this you must go to any Portuguese post office within five days of driving on the A22 (but after 48 hours), provide your hire car's license plate number and pay up (check first that you are covering your trips only). License plates are photographed on the A22 and if you fail to pay the tolls, the car-hire company is obliged to pass on your details to the appropriate authorities.

You will undoubtedly find yourself on this motorway; it's a far easier and safer alternative to the oft-crowded (albeit free-of-charge) N125, so if you are hiring a car, check with your car-hire company how toll fees will be paid on the A22.

★ Restaurante O
Barradas PORTUGUESE €€€
(☑ 282 443 308; www.obarradas.com; Palmeirinha; mains €9.50-25; ☉ dinner Thu-Tue) ⌀ The star choice for fine dining is this delightful spot (follow the road to Lagoa and then to Palmeirinha; it's 3km from Silves). The German chef creates her own Portuguese wonders, always using Mediterranean ingredients, sourced where possible from local suppliers. The country's finest organic meats and fresh, not farmed, fish are used. Desserts use seasonal fruits. An elegant atmosphere, gourmet dishes, and too many fine wines (did we mention her husband is a winemaker?) make for a taxi booking (seriously, think about it).

ℹ Information

Centro de Interpretaçao do Património
(Largo do Município; ☉ 9am-1pm & 2-5pm Mon-Fri) Although this interesting little spot promotes the network of Islamic routes through Portugal, Spain and Morocco, it acts as the pseudo municipal tourism office. Knowledgeable overseer, Miguel, knows a lot about the town, as well as its Islamic cultural heritage.
Post office (Rua Samora Barros)
Turismo (☑ 282 440 800; www.visitalgarve. pt; ☉ 9.30am-1pm & 2-5.30pm Mon-Fri) Next to the main car park. The unrelated but informative municipality website is www.cm-silves.pt.

ℹ Getting There & Around

Much of the hilly, compact centre of Silves is easily done on foot; many streets are pedestrianised areas only. Drivers are advised to park their car in the large car park on the city side (north) of the river and southwest of the city centre (no charge).

BUS
There are no direct buses between Lagos and Silves; change at Portimão (40 minutes).
Albufeira (€4.25, 40 minutes, four to seven daily)
Portimão (€3.25, 20 minutes, five to nine daily)
For Faro you must change at Lagoa (€4.40). All buses leave from the riverfront, with fewer running at weekends. The **bus ticket office** (☑ 282 442 338; ☉ 8.15am-1.30pm & 2.45-6pm Mon-Fri, to 1pm Sat, 10am-noon Sun) is on the western side of the market.

TRAIN
Local buses travel daily between Silves and its train station (three to five daily). Services from Silves:
Faro (€5.10, one hour, nine daily)
Lagos (€2.90, 35 minutes, nine daily)

Portimão

POP 50,000

Bustling Portimão is the western Algarve's main commercial centre and the second-most populous city in the Algarve. The messy outskirts of the city hide a small but friendly hub, whose focal points are the Praça Manuel Teixeira Gomes, a pleasant waterfront, an assortment of outdoor cafes, and sizzling fish restaurants in the old quarter and quayside. You can also arrange a boat cruise up the Rio Arade. Most tourists only pass through en route to Praia da Rocha.

Portimão was an important trading link for Phoenicians, Greeks and Carthaginians (Hannibal is said to have visited). It was called Portos Magnus by the Romans and was fought over by Moors and Christians. In 1189 Dom Sancho I and a band of crusaders sailed up the Rio Arade from here to besiege Silves. Almost destroyed in the 1755 earthquake, it regained its maritime importance in the 19th century. It became the region's fishing and canning centre before this, too, declined.

◉ Sights

Igreja Matriz CHURCH
The town's parish church stands on high ground to the north of the town centre and features a 14th-century Gothic portal – all that remains of the original structure after the 1755 earthquake.

Museu de Portimão MUSEUM
(☑ 282 405 230; admission €3; ⊘ 2.30-6pm Tue & 10am-6pm Wed-Sun 1 Sep-14 Jul, 7.30-11pm Tue & 3-11pm Wed-Sun 15 Jul-31 Aug) The modern Museu de Portimão, housed in a 19th-century fish cannery, is one excellent reason to visit Portimão. The museum focuses on three areas: archaeology, underwater finds and, the most fascinating, the re-creation of the fish cannery (mackerel and sardines). You can see former production lines, complete with sound effects – clanking and grinding and the like. An excellent video (in Portuguese) of the fishing industry reveals each step in the process, from netting the shoals to packaging.

🏃 Activities

Operators galore line the riverside promenade offering **boat trips**. These include cruises up the coast and/or the Rio Arade, visiting caves along the way. Prices start at around €30. There are also **dolphin-spotting** opportunities. Some trips are in fishing boats for 10 people, others are in sailing boats for 35. **Santa Bernarda** (☑ 967 023 840; www.santa-bernarda.com; adult/child from €30/15) runs trips visiting the caves and coast on a 23m wooden sailing ship with wheelchair access. The full-day trip includes a beach barbecue and time to swim.

🛏 Sleeping

Pousada de Juventude HOSTEL €
(☑ 282 491 804; www.hihostels.com; Rua da Nossa Senhora da Conceição; dm/d €17/45) This place is just out of the centre, but it's a good budget option.

Globo Hotel HOTEL €€
(☑ 282 405 030; www.hotelsalgarvesol.pt; Rua 5 de Outubro 26; s/d €69/85; ❄) Rooms here have a snazzy design, with contemporary fittings

and abundant natural light. Each floor has a colour scheme, from lilac to green.

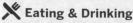 Eating & Drinking

The fountain-lined pedestrian street Rua Direita, about 300m west of the river, is a good destination for restaurant browsing. For open-air seafood grub, head to Largo da Barco – a strip of restaurants under the arches of the bridge – where for decades, charcoal-grilled sardines and barbecued fish were enjoyed by hungry fishermen and, in more recent years, hoards of visitors (OK, tourists).

A Casa da Isabel PATISSERIE €
(www.acasadaisabel.com; Rua Direita 61; ⊘ 9am-8pm, to midnight Jul-Aug) This pleasant little tea room is housed in a lovely tile-fronted mansion and churns out a mouthwatering array of conventual desserts, plus a range of teas.

Taska Porta Velha BAR
(☑ 918 053 169; Travessa Manuel Dias Barão; tapas €5-10; ⊘ 10pm-4am Mon-Sat) This atmospheric bar is the kind of place you can kick back and relax in. It's been lovingly restored and decorated; spread across several rooms are antique knick-knacks and modern artworks. The tables are made of wood and stone slabs and in one room the ceiling is made entirely of corks. *Petiscos* (snacks) and drinks only. It's near the modern square (an extension of Rua Direita).

ℹ Information

There are several banks with ATMs around the riverside Praça Manuel Teixeira Gomes.
Municipal turismo (☑ 282 430 165; www.cm-portimao.pt; Plaza 1 de Dezembro; ⊘ 10am-7pm Mon-Sat) Portimão's information office is housed in the wonderful Teatro Municipal de Portimão ('TEMPO'). Ask about performances.

ℹ Getting There & Around

BUS
Local buses (known as the *rede urbana*, or urban network) shuttle between Praia da Rocha and Portimão (€1.50) at least hourly.

To head further afield, Portimão has excellent bus connections. **Frota Azul** (www.frotazul-algarve.pt) has services to Monchique (€4.25, 45 minutes, six to eight daily), Silves (€3.25, 35 minutes, five to eight daily) and Lagos (€4.05, 40 minutes, hourly).

You can get information and tickets for Eva services at the **Eva office** (☑ 282 418 120;

www.eva-bus.com; Largo do Dique 3), located by the riverside. Eva buses leave from near the petrol station along the riverside on Av Guanaré. Services include the following:

Albufeira (€4.50, one hour, seven express services weekly)

Cabo São Vicente (€6.25, 1½ hours, one daily)

Faro (€5.45,1¾ hours, seven daily, four express services weekly)

Lagos (€4.25, 45 minutes, six daily, six express services weekly)

Lisbon (€20, 3¼ hours, five express services weekly)

Loulé (€5.45, 1¾ hours, four services, weekends only)

For Sagres and Salema you must change in Lagos.

Local buses cover some inner-city routes. Services are limited on weekends.

CAR
If you have your own wheels, the easiest parking is a free riverside area by the Repsol petrol station.

TRAIN
Eight daily trains connect Portimão with Tunes (€2.90, 45 minutes). Change at Tunes for Lisbon. Services also go to Silves (€1.50, 20 minutes, nine daily) and Lagos (€2, 20 minutes, seven daily).

Praia da Rocha

One of the Algarve's fine beaches, Praia da Rocha is a wide stretch of sand backed by ochre-red cliffs and the petite 16th-century **Fortaleza da Santa Catarina**, built in the 16th century to stop pirates and invaders from sailing up the Rio Arade to Portimão.

Behind the beach looms the town; this has long known the hand of development, with high-rise condos and luxury hotels sprouting along the cliffside, and a row of restaurants, bars and dance clubs packed along the main thoroughfare. If you look hard beyond the ugly concrete facade, Praia da Rocha has several vestiges from an elegant past, including some 19th-century mansions, which are now atmospheric guesthouses.

There's also a sleek marina, **Marina de Portimão**, painted autumnal colours (to match the cliffs) and a **casino** where you can double (or deplete) your savings.

🛏 Sleeping

Accommodation is almost impossible to find during the high season if you don't have a prior reservation.

Albergaria Vila Lido GUESTHOUSE €€€
(☑282 241 127; www.hotelvilalido.com; Av Tomás Cabreira; d €110-140; ❄ 🎧) Near the fort, this hotel is housed in a converted 19th-century mansion and has a slightly dated Brighton (UK) guesthouse feel, with great sea views and 10 bright rooms, most of which have terraces.

Bela Vista BOUTIQUE HOTEL €€€
(☑282 460 280; www.hotelbelavista.com; Tomás Cabreira; r €220-300, ste €400-500; ☺Mar-Nov; 🎧🏊) This beautiful spot – a renovated former mansion with two modern wings – adds a touch of class to Praia da Rocha. Portuguese interior-design team Graça Viterbo has gone to town here, using a quirky blend of contemporary and antique, all in a blue-and-yellow colour theme. It's uber-luxurious yet not-so-snobby-you-can't-sneeze, and professional yet fun.

The restaurant is open to the public and is worth checking out. Prices are significantly lower outside high season.

Hotel da Rocha LUXURY HOTEL €€€
(☑282 424 081; www.hoteldarocha.com; d from €150; 🅿❄@🏊) This modern spot is bang in the middle of a busy strip opposite the beach. The rooms are simple, yet sleek and with good light. All feature kitchenettes.

🍴 Eating

The marina has a row of romantic, upmarket dining and drinking spots, some of which stare across at the beautiful Praia Meia Grande. In summer, grab a sundowner at one of the beachside eateries.

Restaurante Marisqueira PORTUGUESE €€
(mains €14-20; ☺lunch & dinner Mon-Sat) An unusually traditional restaurant for Praia da Rocha, this popular and low-key place opposite Algarve Mor hotel offers decent Portuguese fare, with a hearty array of daily specials.

Dockside RESTAURANT €€
(www.restaurantedockside.com; mains €10-20; ☺10am-midnight) One of the best situated places on the marina. Serves up live shellfish and flambéed meat dishes.

🍷 Drinking & Entertainment

Praia da Rocha bristles with bars that are packed with sun-kissed faces, satellite TV, live music and karaoke. Many are owned or run by foreign residents. You might as well be in Dublin, for the plethora of Irish bars (just follow the craic). They're open all day (and nearly all night).

Voxx
DANCE

(Av Tomás Cabreira) This sleek discotheque makes good use of its waterside setting and plays anything from pop to African to hip-hop.

Discoteca Katedral
DANCE

(Rua António Feu) Monster Discoteca Katedral gets busy with pop house until 6am nightly during summer. The marina has some sleek, fun alternatives with karaoke and regular live music.

Casino
CASINO

(☑ 282 402 000; Av Tomás Cabreira; ⊙4pm-3am) FREE The glitzy casino, midway along the esplanade in Hotel Algarve, has the gaming lot.

❶ Information

The post office is near the *turismo*.

Tourist police (☑ 281 419 183; Av Tomas Cabrera; ⊙9am-12.30pm & 2-5pm Mon-Fri)

Turismo (☑ 282 419 132; Av Tomas Cabrera; ⊙9.30am-7pm Jul & Aug, 9.30am-5.30pm Mon-Fri, 9.30am-1pm & 3-5.30pm Sat Sep-Jun) In the centre of the esplanade.

Unicâmbio/Western Union (⊙9.30am-9pm) Next door to the *turismo*; has telephone booths and internet.

❶ Getting There & Around

BUS

A regular shuttle heads to Portimão (€1.50, every 15 to 30 minutes). Eva runs to/from Lisbon (€20, five daily). The bus terminus in Praia da Rocha is by Club Praia de Rocha.

CAR

Auto Rent (☑ 282 417 171; www.autorent.pt; Av Tomás Cabreira) offers good car-rental deals.

Lagos

POP 22,000

As far as touristy towns go, Lagos (*lah-goosh*) has got the lot. It lies along the bank of the Rio Bensafrim, with 16th-century walls enclosing the old town's pretty, cobbled streets and picturesque plazas and churches. Beyond these lies a modern, but not overly unattractive, modern sprawl. The town's good restaurants and range of fabulous beaches nearby add to the allure. With every activity under the sun (literally) on of-fer, plus a pumping nightlife, it's not surprising that people of all ages are drawn here. In season, with all the crowds and action, the town can feel hectic and claustrophobic.

Aside from its hedonistic appeal, Lagos has historical clout, having launched many naval excursions during Portugal's extraordinary Age of Discoveries.

History

Phoenicians and Greeks set up shop at this port (which later became Roman Lacobriga) at the mouth of the muddy Rio Bensafrim. Afonso III recaptured it from the Moors in 1241. In 1415 a giant fleet set sail from Lagos under the command of the 21-year-old Prince Henry the Navigator to seize Ceuta in Morocco, thereby setting the stage for the Age of Discoveries.

The shipyards of Lagos built and launched Prince Henry's caravels, and Henry split his time between his trading company here and his navigation school at Sagres. Local boy Gil Eanes left Lagos in 1434 as commander of the first ship to round West Africa's Cape Bojador. Others continued to bring back information about the African coast, along with ivory, gold and slaves. Lagos has the dubious distinction of having hosted (in 1444) the first sale of black Africans as slaves to Europeans, and the town grew into a slave-trading centre.

It was also from Lagos in 1578 that Dom Sebastião, along with the cream of Portuguese nobility and an army of Portuguese, Spanish, Dutch and German buccaneers, left on a disastrous crusade to Christianise North Africa, which ended in a debacle at Alcácer-Quibir in Morocco. Sir Francis Drake inflicted heavy damage on Lagos a few years later, in 1587.

Lagos was the Algarve's high-profile capital from 1576 until 1755, when the earthquake flattened it.

❍ Sights

Igreja de Santo António
CHURCH, MUSEUM

(Rua General Alberto da Silveira; ⊙10am-6pm Tue-Sun) The little Igreja de Santo António, bursting with 18th- and 19th-century gilded, carved wood, is a stupendous baroque extravaganza. Beaming cherubs and ripening grapes are much in evidence. The dome and *azulejo* panels were installed during repairs after the 1755 earthquake.

Enter from the adjacent **Museu Municipal** (Rua General Alberto da Silveira; admission/

concession €3/1.50; ⊙10am-6pm Tue-Sun), a glorious and fascinating historic mishmash. There's an entrancing haphazardness about it all, from Roman nails found locally and opium pipes from Macau to bits of the Berlin wall sharing a case with scary-looking surgical instruments.

Fortaleza da Ponta da Bandeira   FORT
(Av dos Descobrimentos; adult/concession €3/1.50; ⊙10am-6pm Tue-Sun) This little fortress, at the southern end of the avenue, was built in the 17th century to protect the port. Now restored, it houses an exhibition on the Portuguese discoveries and a quaint chapel, Santa Bárbara, Protector of Storms.

Ponta da Piedade   VIEW POINT
Protruding south from Lagos, Ponta da Piedade (Point of Piety) is a stunning, dramatic wedge of headland. Three windswept kilometres out of town, the point is well worth a visit for its contorted, polychrome sandstone cliffs and towers, complete with lighthouse and, in spring, hundreds of nesting egrets. The surrounding area is brilliant with wild orchids in spring. On a clear day you can see east to Carvoeiro and west to Sagres.

Parque Zoológico de Lagos   ZOO
(☑282 680 100; www.zoolagos.com; Quinta Figueiras; adult/child €16/12; ⊙10am-7pm Apr-Sep, 10am-5pm Oct-Mar, restaurant closed Mon; ⊛) This zoo is a shady 3-hectare kid-pleaser, with many small primates and a children's farm housing domestic animals. It's near the village of Barão de São João, 8km west of Lagos.

Town Walls   LANDMARK
Just south of Praça do Infante is a restored section of the stout town walls, built (atop earlier versions) during the reigns of Manuel I and Joao III in the 16th century, when the walls were enlarged to the existing outline. They extend intermittently, with at least six bastions, for about 1.5km around the central town.

Igreja de Santa Maria   CHURCH
(Praça do Infante) Igreja de Santa Maria was built during the 15th and 16th centuries and retains a 16th-century entrance; the rest of the remaining structure dates largely from the mid-19th century when it was restored after fire. Don't overlook the strange orange and purple battling angels mural behind the altar.

Rua da Barroca   HISTORI[C]
Rua da Barroca once formed the boun[d]... between the town and the sea and retains some Arabic features.

Castelo dos Governadores   HISTORIC BUILDING
(Governors Castle) Castelo dos Governadores was built by the Arabs. After the Reconquista in the 13th century, the Algarve's military government was established here in the 14th century. It's said that the ill-fated, evangelical Dom Sebastião attended an open-air Mass here and spoke to the assembled nobility from a small **Manueline window** in the castle, before leading them to a crushing defeat at Alcácer-Quibir (Morocco).

🦅 Beaches

Meia Praia, the vast expanse of sand to the east of town, has outlets offering sailboard rental and water-skiing lessons, plus several laid-back restaurants and beach bars. South of town the beaches – **Batata**, **Pinhão**, **Dona Ana**, **Camilo** among others – are smaller and more secluded, lapped by calm waters and punctuated with amazing grottoes, coves and towers of coloured sandstone. A ferry runs from the waterfront in Lagos to Meia Praia.

🏃 Activities

Water Sports

Lagos is a popular **surfing** centre and has good facilities; surfing companies head to the west coast for the waves.

Lagos Surf Center   SURFING
(☑282 764 734; www.lagossurfcenter.com; Rua da Silva Lopes 31; 1-/3-/5-day courses €55/150/225) Will help you catch a wave and head to where there are suitable swells. Children must be accompanied by a family member over 14 years of age. It also rents out wetsuits (€5 per day) and boards (€10 to €20) and offers beach kayaking trips (from €25 per person).

Blue Ocean   DIVING
(☑964 665 667; www.blue-ocean-divers.de) For those who want to go diving or snorkelling. Offers a half-day discovery experience (€30), a full-day dive (€90) and a divemaster PADI scuba course (€590). It also offers kayak safaris (half-/full day €30/45, child under 12 years half price).

Windsurf Point   WINDSURFING
(☑282 792 315; www.windsurfpoint.com; Bairro 1 de Maio, Meia Praia; ⊙9am-7pm) Windsurfing

Lagos

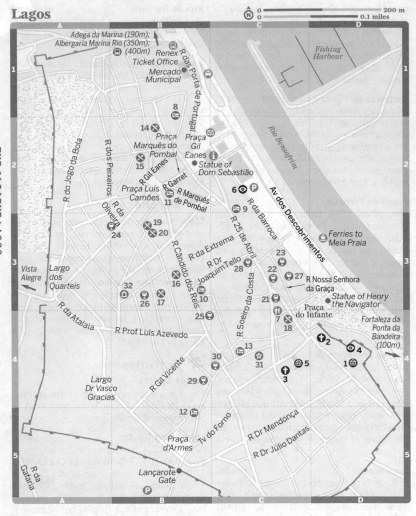

courses (beginners full-day €200) at Meia Praia, kitesurfing, board rental (per hour/half-day €35/70) and a shop.

Boat Trips & Dolphin Safaris

Numerous operators have ticket stands at the marina or along the promenade opposite. They operate a bit like sausage factories but offer some fun outings. Local fishermen offering jaunts to the grottoes by motorboat trawl for customers along the promenade and by the Fortaleza da Ponta da Bandeira.

Bom Dia　　　　　　　　　　BOAT TOUR

(☏ 282 087 587; www.bomdia-boattrips.com) The oldest operator and based at the marina, Bom Dia runs trips on traditional schooners, including a five-hour barbecue cruise (adult/child €49/25), with a chance to swim; a two-hour grotto trip (adult/child €22.50/12.50; four daily) or family fishing (adult/child €35/25).

Axessextreme　　　　　　　　KAYAKING

(☏ 919 114 649; www.axessextreme.com; 3hr tour per person €25) One of the first companies in the

Lagos

area to offer kayaking trips in the Algarve. Also offers mountain biking and wave surfing.

Algarve Dolphins   DOLPHIN WATCHING
(☑ 282 798 727; adult/child from €35/25) Offers dolphin-spotting trips and also supports the research and protection of dolphins.

Other Activities

Tiffany's   HORSE RIDING
(☑ 282 697 395; www.teamtiffanys.com; Vale Grifo, Almádena; ◷ 9am-dusk) About 10km west of Lagos this outfit charges €33 an hour for horse riding and has other options, including a three-/five-hour trip (€85/140); the latter includes a champagne picnic.

Mountain Bike Adventure   CYCLING
(☑ 918 502 663; www.themountainbikeadventure. com, Porta da Vila; rides from €25) Bike geeks will have some fun with this company, which offers a range of trips for all standards, from shorter scenic trips, to full-on technical rides with shoots, drops and jumps. Also offers accommodation packages.

🛏 Sleeping

Accommodation options are extensive in Lagos, with more places out on Meia Praia and on Praia da Dona Ana. Rooms are pricier and scarcer from July to mid-September. Locals often meet the buses to tout their private homes; head to the tourist office for a list of officially approved individuals.

★ **Hotel Mar Azul**   GUESTHOUSE €
(☑ 282 770 230; www.hotelmarazul.eu; Rua 25 de Abril 13; s €45-60, d €50-70; @ ☎) This little gem is one of Lagos's best-value spots. It's a central, well-run and delightfully welcoming place, with comfortable, neat rooms, some with sea views. Owner Rui (and helpful staff) are people-in-the-know. A simple breakfast is an added bonus.

Pousada da Juventude   HOSTEL €
(☑ 282 761 970; www.pousadasjuventude.pt; Rua Lançarote de Freitas 50; dm/d €17/45; @ ☎) This well-run hostel is a good place to meet other travellers. It is slightly worn, thanks to its popularity, but there's a kitchen and pleasant courtyard, and the reception is very helpful. It's open 24 hours.

Sol a Sol   HOTEL €€
(☑ 282 761 290; Rua Lançarote de Freitas 22; r €65-70) This central, small hotel has rooms with tiny balconies and views over the town; it's a bit dated but has had some recent renovations and the rooms are neat and clean. Prices are considerably less than stated outside high season.

Hotel Riomar   HOTEL €€
(☑ 282 763 091; www.hotelriomarlagos.com; Rua Cândido dos Reis 83; d €90; ❄) Rooms in this simple, unpretentious, but adequate spot, are small but comfortable, with parquetry wood floors and balconies (no view).

Inn Seventies
GUESTHOUSE €€

(Rua Marquês de Pombal; d €90-120; P ✻ ⊜ ⊠) There's a touch of Austin Powers here – a retro-mod spot that bills itself as 'boutique' in a converted 1970s bank building. The owner has flipped out on the decade's theme across its 10 'suites' – think psychadelic blues, limes, purples and reds. It's fun, if verging on 'nearly-but-not-quite-there'.

Having said that, views from the top terrace are superb, and it must be one of the few (if only) places in town with a rooftop pool. And it doesn't get more central than this – bang on the main plaza.

Hotel Lagosmar
HOTEL €€

(☑ 282 763 722; www.lagosmar.com; Rua Dr Faria da Silva 13; s/d €85/100; ✻ ⊜) Lagosmar boasts motel-style rooms that are simple, neat and comfortable. Some have tiny verandahs. Prices are considerably less than stated outside high season.

Vila Galé Lagos
LUXURY HOTEL €€€

(☑ 282 771 400; www.vilagalelagos.pt; Meia Praia; s/d from €275/320; P ✻ ⊠) This large place offers all the creature comforts for resort-loving visitors and business clients. Everything seems to come in multiples – pools, restaurants, activities and zeros (as in the price – but promotions are available).

Albergaria Marina Rio
HOTEL €€€

(☑ 282 780 830; www.marinario.com; Av dos Descobrimentos; s €111-122, d €114-125; P ✻ @ ⊜ ⊠) Overlooking the harbour, this hotel has comfortable rooms with contemporary decor and balconies. On the downside, it faces the road and backs onto the bus station. Most rooms are twins. There's a tiny pool and roof terrace.

✖ Eating

Lagos has some great dining spots, serving both Portuguese and international cuisine. Budget travellers should focus their attentions on lunchtime *pratos do dia* (daily specials), which often cost around €7. Many excellent cafes are dotted around town. A daily fish market sells its catch.

For self-caterers, there is a small but accessible **supermarket** (Av dos Descobrimentos 2; ⊙ 8am-9pm).

Panaderia Central
BAKERY €

(1 de Maio 29; snacks from €1.30; ⊙ 6.30am-8pm Mon-Fri, to 7pm Sat) Lagos' oldest bakery (it's been here since 1906!) still bakes the fresh-est goods in the Algarve. Great for early risers or party-goers who've seen the sun rise.

Mimar Café
CAFE €

(Rua António Barbosa Viana 27; snacks €3-8; ⊙ 7.30am-10pm Mon-Sat, to midnight Jun-Aug; ⊜) One of the town's best-value casual eateries, this is excellent for coffees and breakfasts, plus home-baked meals (accompanied by scrumptious salads). Daily luncheon specials are great deals for around €4. By night it's a tapas-cum-wine bar.

Bora Café
CAFE €

(www.boracafe.net; Rua Conselheiro Joaquim Machado 17; mains €3-7; ⊙ 8.30am-6pm; ⊜) Tiny Bora is the ideal place for your healthy fruit and vegie fix, delicious *batidos* (fruit milkshakes) and a cool outdoor setting.

Café Gombá
CAFE €

(☑ 282 762 188; Rua Cândido dos Reis 56; ⊙ 8am-7pm, closed Sun winter) This place has been around since 1964 and the friendly owner has a loyal local clientele who come for the coffee and cakes, all baked on the premises.

★ A Forja
PORTUGUESE €€

(Rua dos Ferreiros 17; mains €8-15; ⊙ lunch & dinner Sun-Fri) The secret is out. This buzzing place pulls in the crowds – locals, tourists, expats – for its hearty, top-quality traditional food served in a bustling environment at great prices. Plates of the day are always reliable, as are the fish dishes.

Cervejaria Dois Irmãos
TAPAS €€

(☑ 282 181 100; Travessa do Mar 2; €6.50-11; ⊙ lunch & dinner) Hordes of local businessfolk head to this relaxing and stylish place – which is housed in a quaint historical building on Praça do Infante. The sublime selection of *petiscos* (Portuguese tapas) includes everything from pipis to pork ear. Good mains are available, too.

O Camilo
SEAFOOD €€

(Praia do Camilo; €7.50-14; ⊙ lunch & dinner) Inland from Ponta da Piedade and above Praia do Camilo, 'Camilo' is synonymous with seafood dishes (the selection is overseen by the restaurant patriarch). Seafood specialties are on offer daily. The setting is light, bright and airy and has a large terrace. Definitely the place to linger.

Casinha do Petisco
SEAFOOD €€

(Rua da Oliveira 51; mains €7-13; ⊙ Mon-Sat) Blink – or be late – and you'll miss this tiny traditional gem. It's cosy and simply decorated and comes highly recommended by locals for its seafood grills and shellfish dishes.

Atlântico
PORTUGUESE €€

(www.restauranteatlantico.com; Estrada da Meia Praia; €7.50-21; ☺ lunch & dinner) Head to Meia Praia to experience this place where the owner is a character and the quality is high. There's a bar, a stunning terrace with beach views and a very old wine collection. Surf and sand nearby. The menu is extensive (erring on Portuguese). Now you just need time. So make some.

Adega da Marina
PORTUGUESE €€

(☏ 282 764 284; http://adegadamarina.grupoadm. pt; Av dos Descobrimentos 35; mains €6-13, fish per kg €35-52; ☺ lunch & dinner) This barnlike place is a bit like a Portuguese grandmother – she hasn't changed her hairstyle in a while. But she dishes out generous portions of reliable (and economical) tasty grilled chicken and seafood favourites to grateful guests (who queue to eat here in summer). Her accessories include iron chandeliers and farming implements.

🍷 Drinking & Nightlife

Dozens of bars – party palaces and local beer stops – litter the streets of Lagos, with some of the Algarve's most diverse and most clichéd drinking holes on hand. These gather plenty of surfers, backpackers and younger party animals. They are generally open until the wee hours of the morning, and a few are open during the day. Most offer a drinking gimmick – anything from 'happy hours' to sculling from funnels or guzzling progressive shots of hard liquor. Such bars include, but are by no means limited to: **Eddie's Bar** (Rua 25 de Abril 99), **Three Monkeys** (Rua Lançarote de Freitas 26), **Green Room** (Rua de Oliveira 44), **Irish Rover** (Rua do Ferrador 9) and **Inside Out** (Rua Cândido dos Reis 19).

Meia Praia has some beachfront gems just seconds from sun, swimming and sand, including **Linda's Bar** (São Roque, Meia Praia; ☺ 10am-11pm Thu-Tue summer, 11am-6pm Thu-Tue winter), with fab food, good salads, cocktails and tunes; and **Bahia Beach Bar** (www.bahiabeachbar.eu; ☺ 10am-late Apr-Oct, 10am-6pm winter), an essential hang-out with live music on Friday and Sunday. Further around the beach and side by side are **Bar Quim**, renowned for its prawn dishes, and **Pôr do Sol**, a great place to enjoy the Angolan dish, *muamba de galinha* (chicken in palm oil).

Taberna de Lagos
BAR

(Rua Dr Joaquim Tello 1) Boasting a stylish space and brooding electronic music, this airy and atmospheric bar attracts a somewhat savvier bar-goer (higher cocktail prices also keep some punters away).

Taverna Velha
BAR

(Rua Lançarote de Freitas 34) The snug Old Tavern is an old favourite and continues to haul in a lively, more mature crowd with its feel-good cocktail of pop classics.

Grand Café
BAR

(Rua Nossa Senhora da Graça; ☺ 6pm-2am) This classy place has three bars, lots of gold leaf, kitsch, red velvet and cherubs, over which are draped dressed-up local and foreign hipsters.

Amuras Bar
BAR

(Marina) One of half a dozen restaurant-bars overlooking the marina, this one attracts a slightly more staid crowd, that comes for fruity cocktails and live music most nights.

Duna Beach Club
BAR

(☏ 282 762 091; Meia Praia; ☺ 9pm-2am) Chill out with the smart set at this bar-restaurant, open day and night. It's located bang on Meia Praia beach, with a pool and attitude. At night it's the bar for the 'resort-chic' folk.

Bon Vivant
BAR

(Rua 25 de Abril 105; ☺ 4pm-4am) Thanks to its bright signage, it's hard to miss this long-standing bar. It's less seedy than some of the publike drinking holes and is spread across three levels with various terraces. Shakes up some great cocktails and it's pretty hot once it gets going (usually late).

Stevie Ray's Blues Jazz Bar
BAR

(www.stevie-rays.com; Rua da Senhora da Graça 9; ☺ 9am-4pm Wed-Sat) This intimate two-level candlelit joint is the best live-music bar in town. On weekends it has live blues, jazz and oldies. It attracts a smart-casual older crowd.

⭐ Entertainment

Centro Cultural
CULTURAL CENTRE

(☏ 282 770 450; Rua Lançarote de Freitas 7; ☺ 10am-8pm) This is Lagos' main venue for performances and contemporary art exhibitions.

🛍 Shopping

Owl Story
BOOKS

(☏ 282 792 289; Rua Marreiros Neto 67; ☺ 10am-7pm Mon-Fri, 10am-1pm Sat) Owl Story has an

LOCAL KNOWLEDGE

WALKING IN THE ALGARVE

Ana Carla Cabrita is a walking guide with **Walkin'Sagres** (p196).

Why do you like walking in the Algarve region? For many reasons! The region has a lot of untouched nature. You can walk long distances with the feeling of being on your own, without another soul. You also meet elderly, local people, see typical houses, get a sense of traditions. The feeling of being back in time is amazing!

What fauna and flora should travellers look out for when they are walking in the Algarve? From August to October, Sagres is the best place to look for raptors, vultures and the rare Black Stork just to name a few. In spring, flowers are everywhere, including wild orchids. Sagres' Biogenetic Reserve is protected because of its many endemic plants, such as *Biscutella Vicentina* and *Ulex erinaceus*.

Can you share your favourite 'secret' walking spot in the Algarve? This one is difficult! North of Aljezur, in Rogil, there's a small but really special walk – near local farms, clifftop sand dunes and an amazingly diverse flora. (Follow the "Esteveira" sign.) And at Serra do Caldeirão (p174), on the northeast Algarve, there are some marked walks around the small villages of Caixas Baixas and Mealha.

excellent supply of new and secondhand English books as well as sailing almanacs and boating books.

ℹ Information

Praça Gil Eanes has banks with ATMs.

Nova Câmbios (Praça Gil Eanes 11; ⊘9am-7pm Mon-Sat, 10am-5pm Sun) A private exchange bureau.

Cyber Café Gélibar (Rua Lançarote de Freitas 43A; per hr €2.50; ⊘9am-10pm) Cafe with internet.

Hospital (⊅282 770 100; Rua Castelo dos Governadores) Just off Praça do Infante. Free treatment in the public hospital if you're prepared to queue.

Police station (⊅282 780 240; EN125, eastern end of Lagos)

Post & telephone office (⊅282 770 240) Centrally located just off Praça Gil Eanes.

Hospital São Gonçalo (⊅282 790 700; www. hppsaude.pt; Av D Sebastião) Private hospital a few kilometres northwest of the town centre.

Turismo (⊅282 763 031; www.visitalgarve. pt; Praça Gil Eanes; ⊘9am-6pm daily, longer hours in summer) The very helpful staff offers excellent maps and leaflets.

ℹ Getting There & Away

BUS

From the **bus station** (⊅282 762 944; www. eva-bus.com; Rua Vasco da Gama) buses travel to the following:

Albufeira (€5.45, one hour, 10 daily weekdays, four on weekends)

Cabo de São Vicente (€4.10, one hour, one on weekdays only)

Lisbon (€20, 4¼ hours, 10 express daily)

Portimão (€4, 20 minutes, hourly)

Sagres (€3.80, one hour, nearly hourly on weekdays, one Saturday and Sunday) Via the crossroads to Salema (€2.60, 20 minutes; several run into Salema) from where you must walk for around 1km along a narrow road.

Vila do Bispo (€3.15, 1½ hours, nearly hourly on weekdays)

To get to/from Carrapateira or Monchique, change at Aljezur (€3.80, 50 minutes, one to two daily) or Portimão. Buses to Aljezur serve Odeceixe (€4.35, 1½ hours).

Renex also operates an express service from Lagos to Lisbon (€19.50); tickets are available from the **Renex ticket office** (⊅282 768 931, 282 768 932; Rua das Portas de Portugal 101).

Buses also go to Seville (via Huelva) in Spain (€21, 5½ hours, two to three times daily Monday to Friday, more frequently in summer).

TRAIN

Lagos is at the western end of the Algarve line, with direct regional services to the following:

Faro (€7.20, 1¾ to two hours, nine daily) Via Albufeira (€4.75).

Vila Real de Santo António (€5.15, 1¼ hours, 11 daily) Via Tavira (¾ hour).

Trains go daily to Lisbon (all requiring a change at Tunes; €26, four hours, five daily).

ℹ Getting Around

BOAT

In summer, ferries run to and fro across the estuary to the Meia Praia side from a **landing** just north of Praça do Infante.

BUS

Two local bus services provide useful connections around town, as well as to Meia Praia, Luz, Odiáxere and the zoo in Barão de João. The tourist office can provide information on the buses and their routes. Tickets cost between €1 and €2 (or buy a book of 10 tickets – this costs less; a one-day ticket with Onda costs €3). Buses run from Monday to Saturday between 7am and 8pm (7pm on Saturday). A few run on Sunday.

CAR & MOTORCYCLE

Drivers are advised to leave their cars in one of the free car parks on the outskirts of Lagos (look for the large parking signs). An alternative is the underground car park on Av dos Descobrimentos; but this road is usually congested. Street parking spaces close to the centre are metered – watch out or you'll be wheel-clamped.

Local agencies offering competitive car-rental rates:

Auto Jardim (☑282 769 486; www.auto-jardim.com; Rua Victor Costa e Silva 18A)

Luzcar (☑282 761 016; www.luzcar.com; Largo das Portas de Portugal 10)

Motorent (☑282 769 716; www.motorent.pt; Rua Victor Costa e Silva; bike/motorcycle per 3 days from €21/60) You can hire both bicycles (€10 per day, €21 three days) and scooters (50/125cc per three days from €55/65).

TAXI

You can call for **taxis** (☑282 763 587) or find them on Rua das Portas de Portugal.

Lagos to Sagres

To the west of Lagos, the coastline is sharp and ragged, and much less developed, though the area is certainly not undiscovered. Once-sleepy fishing villages set above long beaches have now woken up to the benefits of tourism and, in some cases, developers have moved in. Out of the high season, these places remain bewitchingly calm.

Luz

Six kilometres west of Lagos, the small resort of Luz is packed with Brits. It's fronted by a sandy beach that's ideal for families. Most accommodation is prebooked by those on a package deal. Luz is a convenient side trip from Lagos. Buses run frequently from Lagos (around €2, 15 minutes) and arrive by the village church on the waterfront.

If you do end up here for the night, you can try **Camping de Espiche** (☑282 789 265; www.turiscampo.com; sites per adult/tent/car €6.50/4/4; ☒), a Turiscampo-run, shady site 2km from Luz.

If there's only one reason to visit Luz (dare we stretch it to the Algarve), it's to dine at **Pastelaria Chicca** (☑282 761 334; www.pastelariachiccaluz.com; Rua da Várzea 3; meals €5-14; ⊙lunch & dinner Sun-Fri winter, dinner Sun-Fri summer; ☒) ∅. Both the owner, Chicca, and the cuisine have big personalities (think Nigella Lawson); her presentation of the dishes – all her creations – are as full-on as the treats themselves. All ingredients are organic, all are imaginatively combined, and all are superb. Think savoury bread-and-butter pudding, vegetable stacks (and other vegie options), amazing salads, fish and meats, and *the* best desserts (don't miss the white-chocolate-and-raspberry tart) and cakes. Come with time and an empty stomach. You can always work off the calories by walking back along the cliff track between Luz and Lagos.

Salema

This charmingly small coastal resort has an easygoing atmosphere; it's set on a wide bay 17km west of Lagos, surrounded by developments that manage not to overwhelm it. It's ideal for families, and there are several small, secluded beaches within a few kilometres – **Praia da Salema** by the village, **Praia da Figueira** to the west and **Boca do Rio** to the east. Dinosaur prints exist in the area.

🛏 Sleeping

Quinta dos Carriços   CAMPGROUND €
(☑282 695 201; www.quintadoscarricos.com; campsite per adult/tent/car €6/6/6, studio/apt €77/87; ☒) Just 1.5km north of Salema, this campground is in a peaceful, tree-filled setting with abundant birdlife (no radios allowed!). It has studios and apartments and a designated nudist camping area.

A Maré   GUESTHOUSE €€
(☑282 695 165; www.the-mare.com; s/d €64/80, self-catering apt €75-90) Just off the main road into town, this blue-and-white beach house has dated, but bright rooms, some with sea views, a pretty garden and a guests' kitchen. It's a short stroll downhill to the beach. There's a two-night minimum stay.

Hotel Residencial Salema   HOTEL €€
(☑282 695 328; www.hotelsalema.com; s/d €81/94; ⊙Apr-Oct; ❄) Fifty metres from the

ST VINCENT

Although not much is known about the life of the Spanish-born St Vincent, his death is of such legendary stuff that both Spain and Portugal claim him as their own. In Portugal he is considered the patron saint of wine and sea voyages.

St Vincent was a Spanish preacher who was killed by the Romans in 304. During his torturous death (he was burnt at the stake), he is said to have maintained such composure, praising God all the while, that he converted several of his torturers on the spot. Following his martyrdom, his remains were gathered, at which point two differing accounts emerge. Spain claims his final resting place is in Ávila. Portugal claims that his remains washed up on the shores of the Algarve, near Sagres, in a boat watched over by two protective ravens. A shrine in his honour, which Muslim chronicles refer to as the Crow Church, became an object of Christian pilgrimage, though it was destroyed by Muslim fanatics in the 12th century.

Afonso Henriques, Portugal's first king, had the remains moved by ship to Lisbon in 1173, again accompanied by ravens. St Vincent became Lisbon's patron saint (his remains now rest in the Igreja de São Vicente de Fora). A raven features in the city's coat of arms – some *lisboêtas* claim that ravens inhabited the church's bell tower for years afterwards.

beach, Salema offers bright rooms with terraces (most with sea views) in a modern whitewashed building.

✖ Eating

For a place of its size, Salema boasts excellent eateries.

Água na Boca   SEAFOOD €€
(☑ 282 695 651; Rua dos Pescadores; mains €14-18; ☻ lunch & dinner Mon-Sat) This is the upmarket choice in Salema and is said to be one of the best in town.

Restaurante Lourenço   SEAFOOD €€
(☑ 282 698 622; Rua 28 de Janeiro; mains €9.50-16; ☻ lunch & dinner Mon-Sat) Behind the car park, this unpretentious place is recommended for its fish (the owner happens to be a keen hobby fisherman).

❶ Getting There & Away

At least six buses daily connect Lagos and Salema (€2.60, 30 minutes). Some stop at the cross roads from where it's a 3km walk along the main road; others enter Salema.

Sagres

POP 1940

Overlooking some of the Algarve's most dramatic scenery, the small, elongated village of Sagres has an end-of-the-world feel with its sea-carved cliffs and empty, wind-whipped fortress high above the ocean. Despite its connection to Portugal's rich nautical past, there isn't much of historical interest in town. Its appeal lies mainly in its sense of isolation (refreshing after the hectic Algarve), plus access to fine beaches. It has a laid-back vibe, and simple, cheery cafes and bars. It's especially popular, particularly in the last decade, with a surfing crowd. Outside town, the striking cliffs of Cabo de São Vicente make for an enchanting visit.

One kilometre east of the square, past holiday villas and restaurants, is the port, still a centre for boatbuilding and lobster fishing, and the marina.

Sagres has milder temperatures than other parts of the Algarve, with Atlantic winds keeping the summers cool.

History

Sagres is where dashing Prince Henry the Navigator built a new, fortified town and a semimonastic school of navigation that specialised in cartography, astronomy and ship design, steering Portugal on towards the Age of Discoveries.

At least, that's according to history and myth. Henry was, among other things, governor of the Algarve and had a residence in its primary port town, Lagos, from where most expeditions set sail. He certainly did put together a kind of nautical think-tank, though how much thinking went on out at Sagres is uncertain. He definitely had a house somewhere near Sagres, where he died in November 1460.

In May 1587 the English privateer Sir Francis Drake, in the course of attacking supply lines to the Spanish Armada, captured and wrecked the fortifications around Sagres. The Ponta de Sagres was refortified following the earthquake of 1755, after which there was little of verifiable antiquity left standing.

◉ Sights

Fortaleza de Sagres   FORTRESS
(✐ 282 620 140; adult/child €3/1.50; ⊘ 9.30am-8pm May-Sep, 9.30am-5.30pm Oct-Apr) Blank, hulking and prisonlike, Sagres' fortress has a forbidding front wall balanced by two mighty bastions. Inside, a few buildings dot the vast, open expanse, but otherwise a visit here is mostly about the striking views over the sheer cliffs, and all along the coast to Cabo de São Vicente.

Splash out on the printed guide (€1, in English) that's sold at the entrance.

Inside the gate is a curious, huge stone pattern that measures 43m in diameter. Named the **rosa dos ventos** (literally, 'wind rose'), this strange paving pattern is believed to be a mariner's compass. Excavated in 1921, the paving may date from Prince Henry's time – probably the only thing that does apart from the foundations.

The village's oldest buildings, which include a cistern tower to the east; a house and the small, whitewashed, 16th-century **Igreja de Nossa Senhora da Graça**, with its golden altar (of wood), to the west; and the remnants of a wall, are possibly replacements added after the 1755 earthquake.

Many of the gaps you will see between buildings are the result of a 1960s spring-clean of 17th- and 18th-century ruins that was organised to make way for a reconstruction (later aborted) that was to coincide with the 500th anniversary of Henry's death.

Smack in the centre is a modern, rather unsightly exhibition hall (closed at the time of research). A small auditorium shows a short film (with English subtitles) on Sagres' role in maritime navigation history every

40 minutes. Near the southern end of the promontory is a **lighthouse**. Death-defying anglers balance on the cliffs below the walls, hoping to land bream or sea bass.

A wonderful boardwalk now follows the perimeter and bikes are permitted. Don't miss the 'temporary' art installation installed at the far end of the peninsula – a labyrinth by Portugal's famous sculpture-architect, Pancho Guedes.

Cabo de São Vicente   LANDMARK
A trip to Cabo de São Vicente (Cape St Vincent), Europe's southwesternmost point, is a must. At sunset you can almost hear the hissing as the sun hits the sea. This barren, thrusting headland is the bleak last piece of home that nervous Portuguese sailors would have seen as they launched into the unknown.

The cape – a revered place even in the time of the Phoenicians and known to the Romans as Promontorium Sacrum – takes its present name from a Spanish priest martyred by the Romans. The old fortifications, trashed by Sir Francis Drake in 1587, were later pulverised by the 1755 earthquake.

At the end of the cape there's a wind-whipped red **lighthouse** (hundreds of ocean-going ships round this point every day) and a former convent. On-site, and opened in 2010, is the small, but excellent, **Museu dos Faróis** (admission €1.50; ⊘ 10am-5pm Oct-Mar, to 6pm Tue-Sun Apr-Sep). It showcases the importance of Sagres in Portugal's maritime navigation history, along with replicas of 16th-century cartography and the history of the Cape's lighthouse.

At the 4.5km mark you'll pass the remains of **Fortaleza do Beliche**, built in 1632 on the site of an older fortress. It was once a hotel, but sadly it's crumbling, along with the cliff, and is now strictly off-limits.

🐦 Beaches

There are four good beaches a short drive or long walk from Sagres: **Praia da Mareta**, just below the town; lovely **Praia do Martinhal** to the east; **Praia do Tonel** on the other side of the Ponta de Sagres, and especially good for surfing; and the isolated **Praia de Beliche**, on the way to Cabo de São Vicente.

🏃 Activities

Surfing

Surfing is possible at all beaches except Praia do Martinhal and Praia da Baleeira.

Sagres

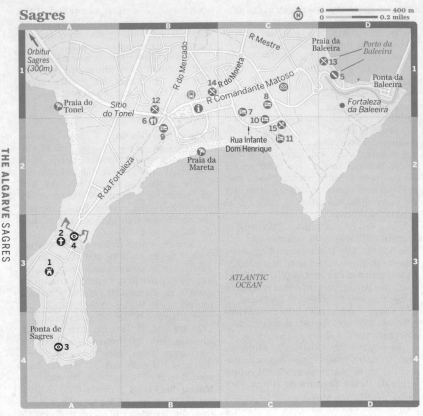

Several places offer surfing and bodyboarding lessons.

Sagres Natura
SURFING
(☎ 282 624 072; www.sagresnatura.com; Rua São Vicente) Recommended surf school. Also rents out bodyboards (€10 per day), surfboards (€15) and wetsuits (€5). The company also offers canoeing trips (€35). Bikes can also be hired (€15).

Free Ride Sagres Surfcamp
SURFING
(☎ 916 089 005; www.freeridesurfcamp.com; 1-/3-/5-day lessons €55/150/225) Offers lessons and free transport from Sagres and Lagos.

Walking

Walkin'Sagres
GUIDED WALKS
(☎ 925 545 515; www.walkinsagres.com) 🌿 If you are going to do anything in Sagres, you must do this – a guided walk around and/or near Sagres and Cabo de São Vicente. The delightful multilingual guide, Ana Carla (she

speaks English, French, Spanish and Portuguese) explains the history and other details of the surrounds. The walks head through pine forests to the Cape's cliffs and vary from shorter 6km options (€25; three hours) to a longer 8km walk (€40; 4½ hours). There's even a one-hour walk for parents with young children (€15, children free). In March and April you can walk among flowers, including orchids. Occasionally she takes themed walks, such as star gazing (see website).

Diving & Boating

DiversCape
DIVING
(☎ 965 559 073; www.diverscape.com; Porto da Baleeira) Diving centres are based at the port. Recommended is the PADI-certified DiversCape, which organises snorkelling expeditions (€25, two hours), plus dives of between 12m and 30m around shipwrecks. A dive and equipment costs €45/210/320 for one/six/10 dives, while the four-day

Sagres

PADI open-water course is €395. Beginners' courses (from €80) are available.

Mar Ilimitado　　　　　　　　　BOAT TOUR
(☑ 916 832 625; www.marilimitado.com; Porto da Baleeira) Mar Ilimitado, a team of marine biologists, offers a variety of 'educational' boat trips from dolphin-spotting trips (€32) to excursions up to Cabo de São Vicente (€20) and seabird watching (€40).

🛏 Sleeping

Sagres fills up in summer, though it's marginally easier to find accommodation here than in the rest of the Algarve during the high season, thanks partly to the number of private houses in Sagres that advertise private rooms or apartments and informal 'hostels'. Doubles generally cost around €40 and flats cost from €45 to €80.

Elsewhere prices can halve outside high season, including the top-end options.

Orbitur Sagres　　　　　　　CAMPGROUND €
(☑ 282 624 371; www.orbitur.pt) Situated some 2.5km from town, off the road to Cabo de São Vicente, this is a shady, well-maintained campground with lots of trees. You can hire bikes here.

Casa do Cabo de Santa Maria　GUESTHOUSE €€
(☑ 282 624 722; www.casadocabodesantamaria.com; Rua Patrão António Faústino; r/apt not incl breakfast from €50/80; 🛜🚬) You could eat off the floors of these squeaky-clean, welcoming rooms and apartments. They might not have sweeping views, but they are handsome and nicely furnished rooms – excellent value.

Aparthotel Navigator　　　　　HOTEL €€
(☑ 282 624 354; www.hotel-navigator.com; Rua Infante Dom Henrique; 1-/2-person apt not incl

breakfast €90/95; ℗🚿@🛜🚬) It certainly ain't five-star, yet it's large, with spacious, cheaply furnished apartments and million-dollar views over the cliffs. Each has a balcony and satellite TV. Prices halve outside high season.

Mareta View Boutique B&B　　BOUTIQUE HOTEL €€€
(☑ 282 620 000; www.maretaview.com; Praça da República; s/d from €118/128; 🚿@🛜) The Mareta View (and its neighbour Mareta Beach) brings sleek – and classy – attitude to Sagres. White- and aquamarine-hued decor gives it a futuristic feel (the rooms' funky mood lighting rivals the Cape Vincent lighthouse beacon). It has wonderful sea views (these rooms cost around €20 more), excellent breakfasts and a top location on the old plaza.

Pousada do Infante　　　LUXURY HOTEL €€€
(☑ 282 620 240, reservations 218 442 001; www.pousadas.pt; Rua Patrão Antonio Faustino; d from €180; ℗🚿@🛜🚬) This modern *pousada* has large rooms in a great setting near the clifftop. Count on green or orange interiors, handsome public areas and picture-perfect views from the terraces. A good price, quality pick.

Pontalaia　　　　　　　　APARTMENTS €€€
(☑ 282 620 280; www.pontalaia.com; Rua Infante Dom Henrique; apt from €125; 🚿🚬) This small, condolike complex offers attractive airy apartments set with blond woods and stylish furnishings, each with a balcony.

🍴 Eating & Drinking

Many places close or operate shorter hours during the low season (November to April). The *mercado municipal* provides great supplies for long beach days.

There are cafes on Praça de República and restaurants along the way to Cabo de São Vicente. Elsewhere, there are several inviting restaurants on the sands of Praia do Martinhal, including **Nortada** (☑918 613 410; mains €5-25; ⊘10am-10pm) and **Restaurante-Bar Martinhal** (☑282 624 032; Praia do Martinhal; dishes €10-15; ⊘10am-9pm Tue-Sun).

Rua Comandante Matoso

It's Groundhog Day (albeit a pleasant one) along Rua Comandante Matoso, with its row of four atmospheric, good-value cafe-bars located cheek-to-cheek.

Pau de Pita   CAFE €
(Rua Comandante Matoso; snacks €4-10; ⊘10am-late; ☋) The funkiest of its neighbours (at least in its design – think disco ball for tasteful mood lighting), this place has great salads and juices and plays pleasant house music.

Dromedário   CAFE €
(☑282 624 219; Rua Comandante Matoso; snacks €4-10; ⊘10am-late; ☋) The legitimate founder of such cafe-bars and still going strong (it's been going well over 25 years): good food, karaoke and 'mixology', aka creative cocktails.

Mitic   CAFE €
(Rua Comandante Matoso; snacks €4-10; ⊘10am-late; ☋) Hefty toasted sandwiches, good cocktails, friendly environment.

Agua Salgada   CAFE, BAR €
(☑282 624 297; Rua Comandante Matoso; snacks €4-10; ⊘10am-late; ☋) Said to have the best crêpes and has a DJ in the evenings.

Elsewhere in Town

A Casínha   PORTUGUESE €€
(Rua de São Vicente; mains €8-17; ⊘lunch & dinner Mon-Sat) This cosy terracotta-and-white spot – built on the site of the owner's grandparents' house – serves up some fabulous Portuguese cuisine, including a *cataplana* for two (€32) and *arroz de polvo* (octopus risotto, €23). A pleasant change from the seaside eateries.

A Tasca   SEAFOOD €€
(Porto da Baleeira; mains €12-17; ⊘lunch & dinner Thu-Tue) Overlooking the marina and out to sea, this converted fish warehouse specialises in, you guessed it, seafood. Travellers say its dishes can be a bit hit-and-miss, but the view from the sunny terrace is lovely and the atmospheric interior is filled with hanging strands of dried garlic and chillies.

A Sagres   PORTUGUESE €€
(mains €8-13; ⊘lunch & dinner Thu-Tue) This popular local restaurant offers great fish (such as *masinha de mar* for two, €26) and grilled meat fare that won't break the bank. It's on the roundabout as you turn off to the fort.

★A Eira do Mel   PORTUGUESE €€€
(☑282 639 016; www.eiradomel.com; Estrada do Castelejo, Vila do Bispo; mains €14.50-18; ⊘lunch & dinner Mon-Sat) It's worth driving 10km further north to Vila do Bispo to enjoy the fine foods of chef José Pinheiro at this charming, Michelin-listed restaurant. The meat leans towards the Algarvian; the seafood has a more contemporary touch. Think rabbit in red-wine sauce (€16), octopus *cataplana* with sweet potatoes (€35 for two people), curried Atlantic wild shrimps (€22) and *javali* (€17). Mouthwatering stuff.

Vila Velha   INTERNATIONAL €€€
(☑282 624 788; Rua Patrão António Faustino; mains €16-29; ⊘dinner Tue-Sun; ☑) In a house with a lovely garden in front, the upmarket Vila Velha offers consistently good seafood mains, rabbit, grilled salmon and good vegetarian dishes. It has a more international flavour; not for those who want 'real' Portuguese food.

ⓘ Information

There's a **bank and ATM** just beyond the **turismo** (☑282 624 873; www.cm-viladobispo. pt; Av Comandante Matoso; ⊘9.30am-1pm & 2-5.30pm Mon-Fri, hours subject to change), which is 100m east of Praça da República; the **post office** is just east of there.

Internet is available at many of the town's cafe-bars.

ⓘ Getting There & Around

The **bus stop** (☑282 762 944) is by the *turismo*. You can buy tickets on the bus.

Buses come from Lagos via Salema (€3.40, one hour, around 12 daily) and Portimão (€5.40, 1¾ hours, one on weekdays). On weekends there are fewer services. It's only 10 minutes to Cabo de São Vicente (twice daily on weekdays only; €1.95).

Bike rental is available at Sagres Natura (p149).

WILDLIFE OF THE ALGARVE

With five special protection areas (a birding initiative), eight special areas of conservation, two natural parks and one natural reserve (not to forget its sea life), the Algarve is one of the most flora- and fauna-rich regions of the country. The **purple gallinule** (aka the purple swamphen or sultan chicken) is one of Europe's rarest and most nattily turned-out birds – a large violet-blue water creature with red bill and legs. In Portugal it only nests in a patch of wetland spilling into the exclusive Quinta do Lago estate (www.quintadolago.com), at the western end of the Parque Natural da Ria Formosa (p116), 12km west of Faro. Look for it near the lake at the estate's São Lourenço Nature Trail.

Another bizarre Algarve resident is the **Mediterranean chameleon** (Chamaeleo chamaeleon), a 25cm-long reptile with independently moving eyes, a tongue longer than its body and skin that mimics its environment. It's the only chameleon found in Europe, its habitat limited to Crete and the Iberian Peninsula. Your best chance of seeing this shy creature is on spring mornings in the Quinta Marim area of the Parque Natural da Ria Formosa or in Monte Gordo's conifer woods, now a protected habitat for the species.

Bird-lovers should consider a trip to the Serra de Caldeirão foothills (p174). The dramatic Rocha da Pena, a 479m-high limestone outcrop, is a classified site because of its rich flora and fauna. **Orchids**, **narcissi** and **native cistus** cover the slopes, where **red foxes** and **Egyptian mongooses** are common. Among many bird species seen here are the huge **eagle owl**, **Bonelli's eagle** and the **buzzard**.

There's a *centro ambiental* (environmental centre) in Pena village, and you can walk up to the top of Rocha itself.

For a taxi, call one of three *taxistas* on ☏ 964 858 517, ☏ 282 624 501 or ☏ 282 624 450.

North of Sagres

Heading north along the Algarve's western coast you'll find some amazing beaches, backed by beautiful wild vegetation. Thanks to building restrictions imposed to protect the **Parque Natural do Sudoeste Alentejano e Costa Vicentina**, it's relatively well preserved. This protected area is rarely more than 6km wide, and runs for about 120km from Burgau to Cabo de São Vicente and up nearly the entire western Algarve and Alentejo shore. Here there are at least 48 plant species found only in Portugal, and around a dozen or so found only within the park.

It's home to otters, foxes and wild cats, and some 200 species of birds enjoy the coastal wetlands, salt marshes and cliffs, including Portugal's last remaining ospreys. Although the seas can be dangerous, the area has a growing reputation for some of Europe's finest surf and attracts people from all over the world.

Carrapateira

Surf-central Carrapateira is a tranquil, pretty, spread-out village, with two exhilarating beaches nearby whose lack of development, fizzing surf and strong swells attract both a hippy, surf-dude crowd and, more recently, *lisboetas*. The coast along here is wild, with copper-coloured and ash-grey cliffs covered in speckled yellow and green scrub, backing creamy, wide sands.

◉ Sights & Activities

For surfing courses (with accommodation package) contact **Algarve Surf School** (☏ 962 846 771; www.algarvesurfschool.com; 1-week incl breakfast & lunch, equipment hire, lessons from €485) or **Amado Surfcamp** (☏ 927 831 568; www.amadosurfcamp.com; 1-week incl breakfast, equipment hire & lessons €395-475, camping €325).

Carrapateira Land & Sea Museum MUSEUM (☏ 282 970 000; Rua de Pescador; adult/child €2.60/1.05; ⊙10am-5pm winter, 11am-6pm Tue-Sat summer) The Carrapateira Land & Sea Museum is a must for visitors – surfers or otherwise. Its contemporary design space has small exhibits covering everything from the fishing industry to daily life of the locals, and stunning photograph collages depicting Carrapateira of yesteryear (there's minimal English labelling). The vista from the museum's ingenious viewing window over the dunes is sublime.

🏖 Beaches

Praia da Bordeira (aka Praia Carrapateira) is a mammoth swath of sand merging into dunes, 2km off the road on the north side of the village, while the similarly stunning **Praia do Amado** (more famous for its surf) is at the southern end of the village.

🛏 Sleeping & Eating

Despite the number of campervans you see around the place, camping here is definitely illegal – please think twice before joining the camping fray; the dune system is particularly fragile.

Cafes and snack bars line the town's tiny plaza and keep long hours.

Pensão das Dunas GUESTHOUSE €
(☎282 973 118; www.pensao-das-dunas.pt; Rua da Padaria 9; d €40, 1-/2-room apt not incl breakfast €60/75; 🖲) This pretty guesthouse has basic but pleasant, colourful rooms overlooking a flower-filled courtyard. It's 100m from the road at the southern end of the village.

Bamboo GUESTHOUSE €€
(☎969 009 988, 282 973 323; Sítio do Rio; d/tr €60/85, 2-person apt €90; 🖲) 🍴 About 500m from Praia da Bordeira, on the main road, this friendly, ecologically minded guesthouse has four lovely, colourful rooms and friendly owners. It has a wonderful open-plan apartment.

Monte do Sapeiro GUESTHOUSE €€
(www.montedosapeiro.com; Vilarinha; r €90) You'll settle in here like pigs in a sty… which is exactly what these two rooms formerly were. Now they're contemporary and very sleek accommodation options, set on a grass lawn with views of fields beyond and lounging areas. The stunning kitchen is for communal use (and breakfasts with home-made goodies). It's located in Vilarinha, a small inland village just south of Carrapateira.

⭐ **Sítio do Rio** GRILL HOUSE, SEAFOOD €€
(☎282 973 119; mains €9-15; ⊙lunch & dinner Wed-Mon; 🍴) Right on the dunes near Praia da Bordeira, this restaurant cooks up excellent grilled fish and meat mains; there are also vegetarian choices. It has an appealing indoor area, with fishing nets on the walls, and outdoor seating under large umbrellas. It's hugely popular at weekends and is good value.

Sítio do Forno SEAFOOD €€
(☎282 973 914; mains €10-17; ⊙noon-9pm Tue-Sun Apr-Oct) On the cliff overlooking Praia do Amado, this large place grew from a tiny fisherman's cabana. The value is in the setting – the magnificent ocean views – not so much in the cuisine, though some fish dishes are delicious, depending on what's available.

Aljezur

POP 3300

Some 20km north of Carrapateira, Aljezur is an attractive village that straddles a river. The western part is Moorish, with a collection of cottages below a ruined 10th-century hilltop castle; the eastern side, called Igreja Nova (meaning 'new church'), is 600m up a steep hill. Aljezur is close to some fantastic beaches, edged by black rocks that reach into the white-tipped, bracing sea – surfing hot spots. The countryside around, which is part of the natural park, is a tangle of yellow, mauve and green wiry gorse and heather.

⊙ Sights & Activities

Hidden in the narrow backstreets of Aljezur, are a string of quaint museums (one entrance price of €2 permits you to visit all four museums!). All are well worth a visit.

Castelo CASTLE
FREE The polygonal-shaped castle, believed to have been occupied since the Iron Age, was used by the Moors in the 10th century. These days walls from the 13th century and two towers survive. A climb to the castle affords great views of the village and beyond.

Painter José Cercas House Museum MUSEUM
(entry to 4 museums €2; ⊙9am-6pm summer, 9am-1pm & 2-5pm winter) This quaint house belonged to Portuguese painter José Cercas (1914–1992) who left his home and belongings – an extraordinary collection of furniture, artworks and personal objects – to the town.

St Anthony Museum MUSEUM
(entry to 4 museums €2; ⊙9am-6pm summer, 9am-1pm & 2-5pm winter) Housed in a former chapel built in the 17th century (which was destroyed in the 1755 earthquake), this is now a museum devoted to St Anthony – think paintings, books, coins and icons all relating to the saint.

Municipal Museum
MUSEUM

(entry to 4 museums €2; ⊘ 9am-6pm summer, 9am-1pm & 2-5pm winter) This small museum displays everything from early archaeological remains from the area to Islamic ceramics from the Aljezur Castle, plus ethnographic items from a bygone era.

Museu de Arte Sacra
MUSEUM

(entry to 4 museums €2; ⊘ 9am-6pm summer, 9am-1pm & 2-5pm winter) Built in the 16th century and damaged in the 1755 earthquake, this small church was reconstructed in the 18th century. Its small religious art museum houses items donated by a locally-born Monsignor (Canon Manuel Franciso Paral).

Burros e Artes
DONKEY TOUR

(☑ 967 145 306, 282 998 331; http://donkey-trekking-algarve.com.blogspot.com) Get ready for something novel: for those who believe 'slow is beautiful' this might be your kind of travel – covering 10km to 15km per day on foot with nothing but you, your walking legs, stunning nature and your, err, *burro* (donkey) which carries your luggage. This company coordinates your trip – generally from two days to two weeks – including accommodation, food and optional guides (who speak German, English, French and Spanish). Prices depend on a number of factors, including the standard of accommodation you opt for, but allow around €90 per person per day for the donkey, €100 per person per day for the guide, and €20 to €65 per day for accommodation. Food is extra again. You can choose to 'go it alone' without a guide, in which case the added fun is to tend to the donkey (there are strict rules to follow regarding its care). Children can enjoy some shorter rides (a 1½-hour ride costs €30). Burro e Artes is located 4km northeast of Aljezur; ring for directions.

🏖 Beaches

Wonderful, unspoilt beaches near Aljezur include **Praia da Arrifana** (10km southwest, near a tourist development called Vale da Telha), a dramatic, curved black-cliff-backed bay with one restaurant, balmy pale sands and some big northwest swells (a surfer's delight); and **Praia de Monte Clérigo**, about 8km northwest. **Praia de Amoreira**, 6km away, is a wonderful beach where the river meets the sea. More difficult to reach but worth the effort getting there is the more remote **Praia de Vale Figueira**, about 15km southwest of Aljezur on rugged dirt roads.

Surfing lessons are offered by **Arrifana Surf School** (☑ 917 862 138; arrifanasurfschool.com; 1-/3-/4-/5-day course €55/150/200/225).

🛏 Sleeping

In Praia da Arrifana locals sometimes rent out private rooms (look for '*quartos*' signs). There are a few other options outside town.

Amazigh Hostel
HOSTEL €

(☑ 282 997 502; www.amazighostel.com; Rua da Ladeira 5; dm/d/f €25/79/139; @ 🖟) Meet the setting for *Gidget* with a Gen Y twist: this hip, hop and happening place is intelligently designed and clean (though admittedly, showing a few signs of wear). It has inbuilt lockers under the bunks, steel staircases, surfboard and gear storage, the coolest of living areas (including a sun terrace with superlative views), plus a communal kitchen.

Pousada da Juventude
HOSTEL €

(☑ 282 997 455; www.pousadasjuventude.pt; Praia da Arrifana; dm €17, d with bathroom €47) This grey-and-yellow hostel is decked out in plastic furniture that is of cutting-edge design. The hostel offers light and airy rooms, great communal areas including a sunny terrace, a storeroom for surf gear, and a washing and drying room. It's a few minutes' walk from Praia da Arrifana.

Restaurante-Bar A Lareira
GUESTHOUSE €

(☑ 282 998 440; Rua 3 de Janeiro; d/tr €60/75) Located in Igreja Nova, this place has 12 clean and tidy rooms with wood details, and each opens onto a shared terrace with lovely views. There's a good restaurant below.

Parque de Campismo Serrão
CAMPGROUND €

(☑ 282 990 220; www.parque-campismo-serrao.com; campsite per adult/tent/car €5.50/5/4; @ 🖟 🏊) This calm, shady site is 4km north of Aljezur, then 1km off the main road. It has wheelchair access, tennis courts, a playground and apartments, plus bike rental.

🍴 Eating & Drinking

Cafe-bars overlook the main square around Igreja Nova. In Praia da Arrifana there's a string of seafood restaurants (packed with Portuguese at weekends) on the road above the beach, where you can expect to pay around €10 for grilled fish.

Mercado Municipal
MARKET €

(⊘ 8am-2pm Mon-Sat) Located near the bridge, the municipal market is a good place to buy fresh fruit and vegies.

Restaurante-Bar A Lareira PORTUGUESE €€
(Rua 3 de Janeiro; mains €9-15; ☺lunch & dinner Sun-Fri) Warning: walk past here at lunch time and you'll be in like a shot, thanks to the wonderful aromas emanating from the doors. It's unpretentious and family-run, and (you guessed it) serves up some authentic, Portuguese fare.

Pontá Pé SEAFOOD, GRILL HOUSE €€
(✆282 998 104; Largo da Liberdade; mains €8-13; ☺lunch & dinner Mon-Sat) Friendly, with wooden floors and a beamed ceiling, this place does tasty fish dishes and good barbecue chicken.

❶ Information

Post office (Rua 25 de Abril)
Turismo do Algarve (✆282 998 229; Rua 25 de Abril 62; ☺9.30am-7pm Tue-Thu, 9.30am-1pm & 2-5pm Fri-Mon summer, 9.30am-5.30pm Tue-Fri, 9.30am-1pm & 2-5pm Sat winter)

❶ Getting Around

If you're driving, there's a free car park next to the *turismo*. Eva buses run between Lagos and Aljezur (€4, four on weekdays, one on Saturday). One bus runs on weekdays to/from Carrapateira (30 minutes). **Rede Expresso** (www.rede-expressos.pt) buses run north to Lisbon (€17.10, three daily) and south to Lagos (€7.60, two daily) and Portimão (€8.60, one daily). Unfortunately, at the time of research, no buses were running to/from Praia da Arrifana.

Odeceixe

Around here the countryside rucks up into rolling, large hills. As the Algarve turns into

the Alentejo, the last coastal settlement is Odeceixe, an endearing small town clinging to the southern side of the Ribeira de Seixe valley, and so snoozy it's in danger of falling off, except during high season, when Portuguese and European visitors pack the place.

The sheltered **Praia de Odeceixe**, 3.5km down the valley, is a wonderful bite of sand surrounded by gorse- and tree-covered cliffs. **Odeceixe Surf School** (✆963 170 493; www.odeceixesurfschool.com; 1-/3-/5-day courses €55/150/225) offers surfing classes (and board and wetsuit rental) – look for its signs on the beach.

🛏 Sleeping & Eating

There are a handful of unofficial, but well-advertised *quartos* (private rooms) in the village, especially along Rua Nova (en route to the beach). Expect to pay at least €35 to €40 for a double.

Several pleasant eateries are around Largo 1 Mai, a great spot to sit and watch the world amble by, and on Rua Estrada Nacional, the road into town. On the way to the beach there are a couple of restaurants, and at the beach there are snack-bars competing for hungry beachgoers.

Casa Hospedes Celeste GUESTHOUSE €
(✆282 947 150; www.casaceleste.web.pt; Rua Nova 9; d €60) This renovated, clean and bright spot is excellent value, in a great central location and run by delightful owners. Rooms are smallish, but have colourful bedspreads and TV.

Parque de Campismo São Miguel CAMPGROUND €
(✆282 947 145; www.campingsaomiguel.com; campsites per adult/tent/car €6.40/5.90/5.40, bungalows from €80; @⛺) Facility-loaded and pine-shaded, this campground-cum-miniresort is 1.5km north of Odeceixe; wooden bungalows are also available.

Pensão Luar GUESTHOUSE €€
(✆282 947 194; www.pensaoluar.blogspot.com; Rua da Várzea 28; d/tr €65/75) At the western edge of the village, this friendly place is good value (prices are almost half outside high season), with modern, white spick-and-span rooms.

Casa Vicentina RURAL INN €€€
(✆282 947 447; www.casavicentina.pt; Monte Novo; d/ste €125/165; 🖥⛺) For a touch of indulgence head to this stylish complex set in tranquil, rural surrounds. The owner has

---

MARKET MANIA

Look out for local specialities – warm woollens, brassware and Moorish-influenced ceramics – at the region's many markets. Check with tourist offices before you visit as days do change.

➡ **Every Saturday** São Brás de Alportel

➡ **First Saturday** Lagos

➡ **First Sunday** Olhão-Fuzeta

➡ **First Monday** Portimão

➡ **First and third Tuesday** Albufeira

➡ **Second Friday** Monchique

➡ **Third Monday** Aljezur, Silves

➡ **Third Thursday** Alte

gone to town in the rooms and suites; these are arranged around a lush green lawn, with pool and lily ponds. Some rooms have kitchenettes. It's 2km from Odeceixe, near Maria Vinagre and is signposted.

Taberna do Gabão PORTUGUESE €€
(☑ 282 947 549; Rua do Gabão 9; mains €6.50-13.50; ☉ lunch & dinner Wed-Mon) Odeceixe's best option, this welcoming restaurant features good-value traditional dishes served in a charming old-fashioned wooden dining room. There's outdoor seating.

❶ Getting There & Away

Express buses run between Lagos and Odeceixe (€4.35, 80 minutes, three to six on weekdays) via Aljezur (35 minutes). Buy tickets at the *papelaria* (newsagent; open from 9am to 1pm) next to the market.

Monchique

POP 2800

High above the coast, in cooler mountainous woodlands, the picturesque hamlet of Monchique makes a lovely base for exploring the surrounding area, with some excellent options for walking, biking and canoeing. Nearby Caldas de Monchique, an enticing spa town, is another alluring factor.

Set in the forested Serra de Monchique, the Algarve's mountain range, lying some 24km north of Portimão, Monchique is also known for having the best brews of the fiery *medronho,* a locally made liqueur.

Fires regularly affect this area during the summertime – the last major ones were in 2003 and 2004. These cause widespread damage and ongoing frustration at the lack of measures to prevent the devastation.

◉ Sights

A series of brown pedestrian signs starting near the bus station directs visitors up into the town's narrow old streets and major places of interest.

Igreja Matriz CHURCH
(Rua da Igreja) The local church has an extraordinary, star-shaped Manueline porch decorated with twisted columns that look like lengths of knotted rope. Inside you'll find a simple interior, with columns topped with more stony rope, and some fine chapels, including one whose vault contains beautiful 17th-century glazed tiles showing Sts Francis and Michael killing the devil.

Nossa Senhora do Desterro CONVENT
Overlooking the town from a wooded hilltop are the ruins of the 17th-century Franciscan monastery. It is on the path of the Via Algarviana and you can climb up here (though at the time of research, crude 'private' signs alluded to someone squatting here).

☞ Tours

All guided activities require advance reservations.

Outdoor Tours GUIDED TOURS
(☑ 282 969 520; www.outdoor-tours.com; Mexilhoeira Grande; trips from €20) This Dutch-run company offers biking (€29 to €48), kayaking (€25) and walking trips (from €5 per person) both in and around the Algarve and Serra de Monchique.

Alternativtour GUIDED TOURS
(☑ 965 004 337, 282 913 204; www.alternativtour.com) Alternativtour runs guided walks (€50 for two people), mountain-biking tours (€55 for two people), canoeing trips (€50 for two people) or combined mountain-biking and canoeing trips (€65 for two people). Prices decrease the more people there are. Bike hire costs €20 per day.

⛏ Sleeping

Miradouro GUESTHOUSE €
(☑ 282 912 163; Rua dos Combatentes do Ultramar; s/d from €30/40) Up steep Rua Engenheiro Duarte Pacheco (signposted to Portimão), near the *turismo*, this 1970s hilltop place, run with great seriousness, offers sweeping, breezy views and neat rooms, some with balcony.

Villa Vina RURAL INN €€
(☑ 966 765 644, 965 753 393; www.villvina.pt; r €78) Hidden up a tiny pathway (note: the only access is by steps) and signed as you cross the Ribeira do Banho, around 500m after the turn-off to Caldas de Monchique, this lovely rural villa with a pretty garden is perfect for those who crave seclusion, rather than village infrastructure. Reservations required.

Albergaria Bica-Boa GUESTHOUSE €€
(☑ 282 912 271; bica-bao@sapo.pt; d €72; ℗ ☂) One kilometre out of town on the Lisbon road, this modest, but pretty four-room place overlooks a wooded valley. Breakfast is included and there's a decent restaurant here, too (mains €8.50 to €12).

✖ Eating & Drinking

On the road to Fóia, many restaurants offer excellent piri-piri chicken.

A Charrette   PORTUGUESE €€

(Rua Dr Samora Gil 30-34; mains €10-17; ☺ lunch & dinner) Touted as the area's best eatery for its regional specialities (it recently won an award for its efforts to preserve culinary traditions), this place serves reliably good cuisine amid country rustic charm. A few favourites include cabbage with spicy sausages and an award-winning honey flan for dessert.

Restaurante O Parque   PORTUGUESE €€

(mains €7-13; ☺ lunch & dinner) Directly opposite the Monchique tourist office, this cosy local haunt serves good, honest, down-to-earth dishes. Many workers head here for lunch.

Barlefante   BAR

(Travessa das Guerreiras; mains €3-5; ☺ noon-2am Mon-Thu, 1pm-4am Fri-Sun) Monchique's coolest haunt, this fun place has a touch of the burlesque, with hot-pink walls, red-velvet alcoves, ornate mirrors and chandeliers.

🔒 Shopping

Distinctive, locally made 'scissor chairs' (wooden folding stools) are a good buy here (smaller children's versions start at around €25). Try shops along Rua Estrada Velha and Rua Calouste Gulbenkian.

ℹ Information

Turismo (✆ 282 911 189; Largo da São Sebastião; ☺ 9.30am-1pm & 2-5.30pm Mon-Fri) A useful spot for picking up maps, but frustratingly, limited (or no) information on walks. It's uphill from the bus stop, up Rua Engenheiro Duarte Pacheco.

ℹ Getting There & Away

Frota-Azul (www.frotazul-algarve.pt) buses run to/from Portimão (€4.25, 45 minutes, five to eight daily).

Around Monchique

Fóia

The 902m Fóia peak, 8km west of Monchique, is the Algarve's highest point. The road to the summit climbs through eucalyptus and pine trees and opens up vast views over the rolling hills. On the way are numerous piri-piri pit stops offering spicy chicken. Telecommunication towers spike the peak, but ignore them and look at the panoramic views. On clear days you can see out to the corners of the western Algarve – Cabo de São Vicente to the southwest and Odeceixe to the northwest.

We know that you shouldn't use the word 'gorgeous' too much. But that's all that comes to mind when describing **O Luar de Fóia** (Fóia; mains €6-12) – this 'g' word applies to the setting (slightly rustic), the view (cliff-edge expansive) and the cuisine (full-on traditional Portuguese using quality produce). Of course, chicken piri-piri is the go here, as is suckling pig, cow's cheek in a pot and some excellent-value, good wines. Well worth the extra grunt to get here.

Caldas de Monchique

Caldas de Monchique is a bit like the set of *The Truman Show*. It's a slightly sanitised, faintly fantastical hamlet, with a therapeutic calm, and pastel-painted buildings nestling above a delightful valley full of birdsong, eucalyptus, acacia and pine trees, 6km south of Monchique (and 500m below the main road).

It has been a popular spa for over two millennia – the Romans loved its 32°C, slightly sulphurous waters, which are said to be good for rheumatism, and respiratory and digestive ailments. Dom João II came here for years in an unsuccessful attempt to cure his dropsy.

Floods in 1997 led to the closure of the spa hospital, after which it was redeveloped into a spa resort, and its picturesque buildings repainted pale pink, green and yellow.

🏃 Activities

The most peaceful patch is a pretty, streamside garden above the hamlet's central square. Down the valley is the spa itself and below this is the huge unattractive bottling plant where the famous Caldas waters are bottled.

Termas de Monchique Spa   THERMAL SPRINGS

(✆ 282 910 910; www.monchiquetermas.com; admission €25, hotel guests €15; ☺ 10am-6pm Mon-Thu, to 7pm Fri & Sat, longer hours summer) In the wooded valley below town, admission allows access to the sauna, steam bath, gym and swimming pool with hydromassage jets. You can then indulge in special treatments, from a Cleopatra bath to a chocolate-mask wrapping.

Sleeping

Albergaria Lageado   HOTEL €
(282 912 616; www.albergariadolagado.com; s/d €45/55; ☉ May-Oct; ⌘) In the village, Albergaria Lageado is an attractive hotel with a red-sloped roof and cosy ambience. It provides spotless rooms, a small plant-surrounded pool and a restaurant. Packages with board are also available.

Termas de Monchique Hotels   HOTEL €€€
(Termas de Monchique; s/d €105/140) Termas de Monchique owns four hotels, all of which have the same room rates (and include breakfast). You can book weekend or week-long packages that include treatments. Prices are cheaper in low season.

Situated next to the Termas de Monchique spa, **Hotel Termal** is the oldest, biggest (and least modern) hotel of the spa's four hotels. Next to the spa's main reception, **Hotel Central** has 13 beautifully furnished rooms. **Estalagem Dom Lourenço** is the most luxurious option, but for style, **Hotel Dom Carlos** is the newest and most contemporary.

Eating

Café Império
(282 912 290; mains €6-12; ☉ Wed-Mon) From the outside particularly hot, although the of the valley is lovely. Locals flock place for what is reputedly the best piri-piri chicken in the region. Heading north, it's 700m on the left-hand side past the turn-off to Caldas – look for the tiled 'Schweppes' sign on the wall.

Restaurante 1692   RESTAURANT €€€
(mains €9-18; ☉ lunch & dinner) This upmarket place has tables in the tree-shaded central square, and a classy interior.

Information

At the Termas de Monchique reception (the first building on your left), you can book accommodation. Spa treatments and other luxuries are available at the spa.

Getting There & Away

The Monchique–Portimão bus service (Frota Azul) goes via Caldas de Monchique (€4.25); the bus stop is on the road above the hamlet near Restaurant Rouxinol. It's easy to miss – ask the driver to alert you.

The Alentejo

Why Go?

Go to be bewitched. Portugal's largest region, covering a third of the country, truly captivates. Think dry, golden plains, rolling hillsides and lime-green vines. A rugged coastline, traditional whitewashed villages, marble towns and majestic medieval cities. Plus a proud if melancholic people, who valiantly cling to their local crafts.

Centuries-old farming traditions – and cork production – continue here. Alentejo's rich past offers Palaeolithic carvings, fragments from Roman conquerors and solid Visigothic churches. There are Moorish-designed neighbourhoods and awe-inspiring fortresses built at stork-nest heights.

And the cuisine? Alentejo is 'it' for traditional food. Gastronomic delights are plentiful – pork, game, bread, cheese, wine, and seafood along the coastline. Bird life and rare plants are prolific, and walking opportunities abound.

The world is (finally) catching on to Alentejo. Get there before the crowds do.

Best Places to Eat

➡ Herdade do Esporão Restaurant (p220)

➡ Tasca do Celso (p255)

➡ Botequim da Mouraria (p217)

Best Places to Stay

➡ Albergaria do Calvario (p216)

➡ Quinta do Barrieiro (p240)

➡ Herdade do Touril (p256)

When to Go

Évora

°C/°F Temp / Rainfall Inches/mm

[Chart showing temperature and rainfall by month J F M A M J J A S O N D, temperature scale 40/104, 30/86, 20/68, 10/50, 0/32, -10/14; rainfall scale 8/200, 6/150, 4/100, 2/50, 0]

Apr & May Red and yellow flowers mingle with golden plains, and it's baby stork time!

Sep & Oct Enjoy festival frenzy while missing the crowds and the heat.

Jun & Jul Pre-August beaches await, plus Festas Populares, Évora's bounciest country fair.

History

Prehistoric Alentejo was a busy place, and even today it is still covered in megaliths. But it was the Romans who stamped and shaped the landscape, introducing vines, wheat and olives, building dams and irrigation schemes and founding huge estates called *latifúndios* to make the most of the region's limited rivers and poor soil for agriculture.

The Moors, arriving in the early 8th century, took Roman irrigation further and introduced new crops such as citrus and rice. By 1279 they were on the run to southern Spain or forced to live in *mouraria* (segregated Moorish quarters) outside town walls. Many of their hilltop citadels were later reinforced by Dom Dinis, who created a chain of spectacular fortresses along the Spanish border.

Despite Roman and Moorish development, the Alentejo remained agriculturally poor and backward – increasingly so when the Age of Discoveries led to an explosive growth in maritime trade, and seaports became sexy. Only Évora flourished, under the royal patronage of the House of Avis, but it too declined once the Spanish seized the throne in 1580.

During the 1974 revolution Alentejo suddenly stepped into the limelight: landless rural workers who had laboured on the *latifúndios* for generations rose in support of the communist rebellion and seized the land from its owners. Nearly 1000 estates were collectivised, although few succeeded and all were gradually re-privatised in the 1980s. Most are now back in the hands of their original owners.

Today Alentejo remains among Europe's poorest and emptiest regions. Portugal's entry into the EU (and its demanding regulations), increasing mechanisation, successive droughts and greater opportunities elsewhere have hit the region hard. Young people have headed for the cities, leaving villages – and their traditions – to die out. Although its cork, olives, marble and granite are still in demand, and the deep-water port and industrial zone of Sines is of national importance, this vast region contributes only a small fraction to the gross national product. Locals are still waiting for the benefits promised by the construction of the huge Barragem do Alqueva (Alqueva Dam) and its reservoir.

Getting Around

Buses are the best way to access the region's smaller towns and villages (the few operating train services were unreliable at the time of research). Two bus companies service the Alentejo: **Rede Expressos** (www.rede-expressos.pt) and the national company, **Rodalentejo** (www.rodalentejo.pt). Their websites publish up-to-date bus schedules. To get to remote places, including some mountaintop villages and the Alqueva Dam, a hire car is your best option.

ALTO ALENTEJO

The northern half of the Alentejo is a medieval gem, with a scattering of walled fortress towns (such as Elvas and Estremoz) and remote cliff-top castles (such as Marvão and Castelo de Vide). Only a handful of visitors to Alto Alentejo travel beyond Évora, so once outside the city you'll see traditional life at its most authentic.

Évora

POP 41,000

One of Portugal's most beautifully preserved medieval towns, Évora is an enchanting place to delve into the past. Inside the 14th-century walls, Évora's narrow, winding lanes lead to striking architectural works: an elaborate medieval cathedral and cloisters; the cinematic columns of the Templo Romano (near the intriguing Roman baths); and a picturesque town square, once the site of some rather gruesome episodes courtesy of the Inquisition. Aside from its historic and aesthetic virtues, Évora is also a lively university town, and its many attractive restaurants serve up hearty Alentejan cuisine. Outside town, Neolithic monuments and rustic wineries make fine day trips.

Évora climbs a gentle hill above the Alentejo plain. Around the walled centre runs a ring road from which you can enter the

INTERNET RESOURCES

A handy website about Alentejo is www.visitalentejo.pt, presented in several languages. Detailed maps show highlights, bike trails, restaurants, everything for the tourist. Choose your interest, from gastronomy, wine, nature, heritage or just the rhythm of the seasons.

The Alentejo Highlights

1 Sample the history, culture and cuisine of historically rich **Évora** (p207), a Unesco World Heritage–listed city

2 Walk the coastal or inland sections of the **Rota Vicentina** (p256) and stop overnight in **Vila Nova de Milfontes** (p254)

3 Watch the shadows play on the megaliths at **Cromeleque dos Almendres** (p221) and **Monsaraz** (p221)

4 Stroll with spirits of past civilisations and religions in **Mértola** (p241)

5 Gaze out over the countryside from the castle perches of enchanting **Marvão** (p239) and **Castelo de Vide** (p236)

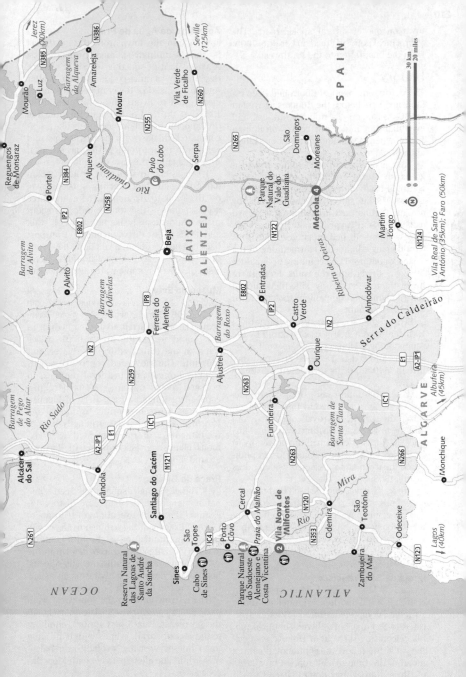

town on one of several 'spoke' roads. The town's focal point is Praça do Giraldo, 700m from the bus station to the southwest.

History

The Celtic settlement of Ebora had been established here before the Romans arrived in 59 BC and made it a military outpost, and eventually an important centre of Roman Iberia, when it was known as 'Ebora Liberalitas Julia'.

After a depressing spell under the Visigoths, the town got its groove back as a centre of trade under the Moors. In AD 1165 Évora's Muslim rulers were hoodwinked by a rogue Portuguese Christian knight known as Giraldo Sem Pavor (Gerald the Fearless). The well-embellished story goes like this: Giraldo single-handedly stormed one of the town's watchtowers by climbing up a ladder of spears driven into the walls. From there he distracted (some say killed) municipal sentries while his companions took the town with hardly a fight.

Évora's golden age was from the 14th to 16th centuries, when it was favoured by the Alentejo's own House of Avis, as well as by scholars and artists. Declared an archbishopric in 1540, it got its own Jesuit university in 1559.

When Cardinal-King Dom Henrique, last of the Avis line, died in 1580 and Spain seized the throne, the royal court left Évora and the town began wasting away. The Marquês de Pombal's closure of the university in 1759 was the last straw. French forces plundered the town and massacred its defenders in July 1808.

Ironically, it was decline itself that protected Évora's very fine old centre – economic success would have led to greater redevelopment. Today its population is smaller than it was in the Middle Ages.

◉ Sights

Igreja de São Francisco   CHURCH
(Praça 1 de Maio) FREE Évora's best-known church is a tall and huge Manueline-Gothic structure, completed around 1510 and dedicated to St Francis. Exuberant nautical motifs celebrating the Age of Discoveries deck the walls and reflect the confident, booming mood of the time. It's all topped by a cross of Christ's order and dome. Legend has it that the Portuguese navigator Gil Vicente is buried here.

Aqueduto da Água de Prata   AQUEDUCT
Jutting into the town from the northwest is the beguilingly named Aqueduto da Água de Prata (Aqueduct of Silver Water), designed by Francisco de Arruda (better known for Lisbon's Tower of Belém) to bring clean water to Évora, and completed in the 1530s. At the end of the aqueduct, on Rua do Cano, the neighbourhood feels like a self-contained village, with houses, shops and cafes built right into its perfect arches, as if nestling against the base of a hill.

It's possible to walk for around 8.5km along the aqueduct, starting outside town, on the road to Arraiolos. There are three access points – the tourist office provides maps. Unfortunately, it's not a circuit walk and heads in one direction only, so transport back can be a problem if you don't have your own wheels. Take plenty of liquids – ironically, there's no potable water along the way.

Museu do Évora   MUSEUM
(Largo do Conde de Vila Flor; adult/senior/youth €3/2/2; ⊙9.30am-5.30pm Tue-Sun winter, 10am-6pm summer) Adjacent to the cathedral, in what used to be the archbishop's palace (built in the 16th century), is this elegant museum. The cloistered courtyard reveals Islamic, Roman and medieval remains. In polished rooms upstairs are former Episcopal furnishings and a gallery of Flemish paintings. Most memorable is *Life of the Virgin*, a 13-panel series originally part of the cathedral's altarpiece, created by anonymous Flemish artists working in Portugal around 1500.

Praça do Giraldo   PLAZA
(🕿) The city's main square has seen some potent moments in Portuguese history, including the 1483 execution of Fernando, Duke of Bragança; the public burning of victims of the Inquisition in the 16th century; and fiery debates on agrarian reform in the 1970s. Nowadays it's still the city's focus, host to less dramatic activities such as sitting in the sun and coffee drinking.

The narrow lanes to the southwest were once Évora's *judiaria* (Jewish quarter). To the northeast, Rua 5 de Outubro, climbing to the *sé* (cathedral), is lined with handsome town houses wearing wrought-iron balconies, while side alleys pass beneath Moorish-style arches.

Palácio dos Duques de Cadaval   PALACE
(Palace of the Dukes of Cadaval) Just northwest of the Igreja de São João is the 17th-century

facade of a much older palace and castle, as revealed by the two powerful square towers that bracket it. The Palácio dos Duques de Cadaval was given to Martim Afonso de Melo, the governor of Évora, by Dom João I, and it also served from time to time as a royal residence. A section of the palace is still in use as the private quarters of the de Melo family; the other main occupant is the city's highway department.

Town Walls HISTORIC SITE
About one-fifth of Évora's residents live within the town's old walls, some of which are built on top of 1st-century Roman fortifications. Over 3km of 14th-century walls enclose the northern part of the old town, while the bulwarks along the southern side, such as those running through the *jardim público* (public gardens), date from the 17th century.

Largo da Porta de Moura PLAZA
The Moura Gate Sq stands just southeast of the cathedral. Near here was the original entrance to town. In the middle of the square is a strange-looking, globular 16th-century Renaissance **fountain**. Among the elegant mansions around the square is **Casa Cordovil** (Largo da Porta de Moura), built in Manueline-Moorish style; also have a look across the road to the west at the extraordinary knotted Manueline stone doorway of the **Igreja do Carmo** (Our Lady of Carmo Church).

Jardim Público GARDENS
For a lovely tranquil stroll, head to the light-dappled public gardens (with a small outdoor cafe) south of the Igreja de São Francisco. Inside the walls of the 15th-century **Palácio de Dom Manuel** is the **Galeria das Damas** (Ladies' Gallery), an indecisive hybrid of Gothic, Manueline, neo-Moorish and Renaissance styles. It's open when there are (frequent) temporary art exhibitions.

From the town walls you can see, a few blocks to the southeast, the crenellated, pointy-topped Arabian Gothic profile of the **Ermida de São Brás** (Chapel of St Blaise), dating from about 1490. It's possibly an early project of Diogo de Boitaca, considered the originator of the Manueline style.

Sé CHURCH
(Largo do Marquês de Marialva; admission €1.50-4.50; ⊙ 9am-12.20pm & 2-4.50pm) Évora's cathedral looks like a fortress, with two stout granite towers. It was begun around 1186, during the reign of Sancho I, Afonso Henriques' son – there was probably a mosque here before that – and was completed about 60 years later. The flags of Vasco da Gama's ships were blessed here in 1497.

You enter the cathedral through a portal flanked by 14th-century stone apostles, flanked in turn by asymmetrical towers and crowned by 16th-century roofs. Inside, the Gothic influence takes over. The chancel, remodelled when Évora became the seat of an archdiocese, represents the only significant stylistic change since the cathedral was completed. Golden light filters through the window across the space.

The cool **cloister** is an early-14th-century addition. Downstairs are the stone tombs of Évora's last four archbishops. At each corner of the cloister a dark, circular staircase (at least one will be open) climbs to the top of the walls, from where there are good views.

A **museum** is to the cathedral's right. Recently relocated here from the cathedral after its restoration, the building – the former 'College of the Choirboys' – houses an enormous collection of religious art, icons and ecclesiastical riches. A highlight is a jewelled reliquary (containing a fragment of the true cross), encrusted with emeralds, diamonds, sapphires and rubies. Enter the museum via a modern black electronic door (scan your ticket and make sure you keep it as you need it again to exit).

Templo Romano RUINS
(Temple of Diana; Largo do Conde de Vila Flor) Opposite the Évora Museum are the remains of a Roman temple dating from the 2nd or early 3rd century. It's among the best-preserved Roman monuments in Portugal, and probably on the Iberian Peninsula. Though it's commonly referred to as the Temple of Diana, there's no consensus about the deity to which it was dedicated, and some archaeologists believe it may have been dedicated to Julius Caesar.

How did these 14 Corinthian columns, capped with Estremoz marble, manage to survive in such good shape for some 18 centuries? The temple was apparently walled up in the Middle Ages to form a small fortress, and then used as the town slaughterhouse. It was uncovered late in the 19th century. Obviously these unwitting preservation techniques worked, as the imposing colonnade is stunningly complete.

Évora

Av de Lisboa

Porta
de Avis

Av D Manuel Trindade Salgueiro

R das Alcaçarias

◉1

P

P

Porta da
Lagoa

R do Muro

R do Cano

R de Santa Maria

Largo
de Aviz

Largo
do Chaõ das
Covas

R das Fontes

Av de Lisboa

R Cándido dos Reis

R do Armeiro

✕32

20

R do Cavalho

R do Apóstolo

Largo Dr
Evaristo
Cutileiro

R da Mouraria

Lg dos Duques
de Cadaval

36
✕

R José Elias Garcia

✕39

R 31 de Janeiro

R de Aviz

R do Menino Jesus

✕27

Jardim
de Diana

14 7

Pç Joaquim
António
de Aguiar

Rua dos Penedos

R dos Penedos

42

R de Olivença

17

R das Casas Pintadas

16

Largo do
Conde de
Vila Flor

R de Burgos

Lg do
Marques de
Marialva

11

R da Cal Branca

R João de Deus

Tv da Milheira

12

21

✕29

26

R 5 de Outubro

47

48

R de Diogo Cão

✕31

R Serpo Pinto

R da Moeda

25

Praça
do Giraldo

Bus to Camp Site

R de Valdevinos

44

R Miguel Bombarda

41 35 43 38

28

19

23

45

Porta de
Alconchel

P

R dos Mercadores

R do Raimundo

R do Lagar
dos Dízimos

R dos Touros

22

Tv da Cavaco

Tv de Landim

5

Cemitério
dos
Remédios

Av D Nuno Álvares Pereira

R Bernardo Matos

✕30

46

Praça 1
de Maio

R da República

6

✕37

R Romão Ramalho

33
✕

Capela
dos Ossos

R do Cicioso

Praça da
República

13

Jardim
Público

Porta do
Raimundo

Av Túlio Espanca

(250m)

Parque
Infantil

◉9

Av da

Porta de
Alconchel

R Gil Vicente

Av Marechal Carmona

◉2

Ramalho Ortigão

Rossio
de São
Brás

(530m)

✕40

Modelo

Termas Romanas ROMAN RUINS

(⊙9am-5.30pm Mon-Fri) **FREE** Inside the entrance hall of the *câmara municipal* on Praça de Sertório are more Roman vestiges, discovered only in 1987. These impressive Roman baths, which include a *laconicum* (heated room for steam baths) with a superbly preserved 9m-diameter circular pool, would have been the largest public building in Roman Évora. The complex also includes an open-air swimming pool, discovered in 1994.

Universidade de Évora UNIVERSITY

(☑ 266 740 800; ⊙ main building 9am-7pm Mon-Fri, 9am-1pm Sat) **FREE** Just outside the walls to the northeast is the university's main building (Colégio do Espírito Santo), a descendent (reopened in 1973) of the original Jesuit institution founded in 1559 (which closed when the Jesuits got shooed out by Marquês de Pombal in 1759). Inside are arched, Italian Renaissance–style **cloisters**, the Mannerist-style **Templo do Espírito Santo** and beautiful *azulejos* (hand-painted tiles).

Igreja de São João CHURCH

(Church of St John the Evangelist; admission €3, plus Salas de Exposição do Palácio €5; ⊙10am-12.30pm & 2-5pm Tue-Sun) The small, fabulous Igreja de São João, which faces the Templo Romano, was founded in 1485 by one Rodrigo Afonso de Melo, count of Olivença and the first governor of Portuguese Tangier, to serve as his family's pantheon. It is still privately owned, by the Duques de Cadaval, and notably well kept.

Behind its elaborate Gothic portal is a nave lined with fantastic floor-to ceiling *azulejos* produced in 1711 by one of Portugal's best-known tile-makers António de Oliveira Bernardes. The grates in the floor expose a surprising underworld: you can see a deep Moorish cistern that predates the church, and an ossuary full of monks' bones. In the sacristy beyond are fragments of even earlier *azulejos*.

Convento dos Lóios BUILDING

The former Convento dos Lóios, to the right of Igreja de São João, has elegant Gothic cloisters topped by a Renaissance gallery. A national monument, the convent was converted into a top-end *pousada* (upmarket inn) in 1965. If you want to wander around, wear your wealthy-guest expression – or have dinner at its upmarket restaurant.

Évora

Igreja da Nossa Senhora da Graça CHURCH
(Church of Our Lady of Grace; Largo da Graca) Down an alley off Rua da República is the curious baroque facade of this church, topped by four ungainly stone giants – as if they've strayed from a mythological tale and landed on a religious building. An early example of the Renaissance style in Portugal is found in the cloister of the 17th-century **monastery** next door.

Museu Relogio MUSEUM
(☏ 266 751 434; www.museudorelogio.com; Rua Serpa Pinto 6; admission €2; ☺ 2-5pm Tue-Sun, 10am-12.30pm Sat & Sun) This is one of two watch museums that houses one family's extraordinary private collection (the other is in Serpa). You name it – if it ticks, chimes, beeps and tells the time in some form or another, it's here. The highlight is watching a master watch repairer at work.

Aréna de Évora LANDMARK
Évora has a *praça de touros* (bullring) outside the southern walls, near the *jardim público*.

☞ Tours

Agia GUIDED TOUR
(☏ 963 702 392; www.alentejoguides.com; adult/under 12yr €12/free, minimum 2 people; ☺ 10am) Agia offers daily 90-minute guided tours of Évora from outside the *turismo* (tourist office) on Praça do Giraldo.

Cartuxa Winery TOUR
(☏ 266 748 383; www.cartuxa.pt; Estrada da Soeira; from €5; ☺ 11.30am, 3pm & 4pm Tue-Sun) For a taste of history, this is a fun visit – Cartuxa is one of the oldest wineries in Alentejo. Run by the well-known local philanthropic foundation Eugenio De Almeida, it produces some good wines at all prices, along with olive oils and other products. You must

reserve a tour (strictly at the times given); prices start at €5 and then vary according to how many wines you want to taste.

Ebora Megalithica
TOUR

(☑964 808 337; www.eboramegalithica.com; per person €25) If you're interested in the megaliths – Almendres, Zambujeiro and the Menir dos Almendres – this is a must. Young archaeologist enthusiast Mário makes the megalithic sites accessible in every sense, providing their 'where, what, why and how'. He succeeds in making the experience an educational yet relaxed one. Maximum seven people per tour.

Rota do Fresco
CULTURAL TOUR

(☑284 475 413; www.rotadofresco.com; per person €20) Offers fascinating cultural tours led by an art historian to local baroque sites filled with frescos and *azulejos* (tiles). Reservations required.

⭐ Festivals & Events

Rota de Sabores Tradicionais
FOOD

A gastronomic festival that lasts for months, celebrating game in January, pork in February, soups in March, lamb in April and desserts in May – traditional restaurants throughout the city serve specialities accordingly.

Festas Populares
RURAL

Évora's biggest, bounciest annual bash, and one of Alentejo's best country fairs, held in late June.

Évora Classical Music Festival
MUSIC

Despite its name, this five-day event encompasses a wide range of contemporary and world musical styles. Concerts are held at various indoor and outdoor venues in Évora. It's held in summer (dates change annually).

🛏 Sleeping

In high season it's advisable to book ahead.

Hostel Namaste
HOSTEL €

(☑266 743 014; www.hostelnamasteevora.pt; Largo Doutor Manuel Alves Branco 12; dm/s/d €17/30/40; 🛜📶) You kinda get the gist of a place when the scrawl on a reception wall says '...the best way to travel is to feel. Feel everything in every way. – Álvaro de Campos'. New in 2012, this welcoming guesthouse – a converted house in the historic Arabic quarter – is new age but not grungy, quirky but not gimmicky. It offers a good selection of rooms and dorms; the themed 'Fernando Pessoa' dorm appropriately has an antique desk as its showpiece (Pessoa was Portugal's famed poet).

Hostel Santantao
HOSTEL €

(☑266 708 182; www.hostelsantantao; 2nd fl, Praça do Giraldo 83; dm/d €18/38; 🛜) A good ol' fashioned hostel where small neat dorms with bunk beds are the norm (including a separate female dorm; there's one private room) and there's a communal kitchen. It's located right on the plaza and up a couple of flights of stairs. It sleeps 20 in total so it's not overwhelming, there's a small roof terrace, and the friendly owner, Nelson, will point you in the right direction. Price includes continental breakfast.

Casa dos Teles
GUESTHOUSE €

(☑266 702 453; http://casadosteles.planetaclix.pt; Rua Romão Ramalho 27; s/d €30/35, with shared bathroom €20/25; ✳🛜) These nine mostly light and airy rooms are reasonable *quartos* (rooms in private houses).

Parque de Campismo
CAMPGROUND €

(☑266 705 190; www.orbitur.pt; sites per adult/tent/car €5.80/8/5.50) Flat, grassy and tree-shaded, with disabled access, Orbitur's well-equipped campground is 2km southwest of town. Yellow line bus 41 from Praça do

THE ALENTEJO ÉVORA

THE WINE ROUTE

Wines here, particularly the reds, are fat, rich and fruity. But tasting them is much more fun than reading about them, so drop in on some wineries. The **Rota dos Vinhos do Alentejo** (Alentejan Wine Route) splits the region into three separate areas – the Serra de São Mamede (dark reds, full bodied, red fruit hints), Historic (around Évora, Estremoz, Borba and Monsaraz; smooth reds, fruity whites) and the Rio Guadiana (scented whites, spicy reds). Some wineries also have accommodation options.

You'll see brown signs all over the place announcing that you are on the wine trail, and you can pick up the booklet that lists wineries and their details at any local tourist office. Otherwise, visit the helpful Rota dos Vinhos do Alentejo headquarters (p219).

Giraldo, via Avenida de São Sebastião and the bus station, goes close by.

Hotel Riviera
HOTEL €€

(☑266 737 210; www.riviera-evora.com; Rua 5 de Outubro 49; s/d/ste €64/80/97; 🕸🛜) Only one block from the *praça* (town square), this charming and well-renovated place has bright, stylish rooms with *boveda* (brick-arched) ceilings and carved bedheads. Bathrooms are gleamingly tiled. Prices are significantly less outside high season.

Évora Inn
HOSTEL €€

(☑910 357 785; www.evorainn.com; Rua da República 11; s/d/f €48/58/65; 🛜) A welcome addition to Évora's midrange options, this funky, modern and spic-and-span spot, hidden behind a traditional facade, is smack bang on the main plaza. Each room – which has a different name and theme (think Che Guevara and the like) – is a designer's wet dream. It's a fun and bright spot; the only drawback for some might be that some rooms are on the squishy side. Breakfast costs €5.

Best Western Hotel Santa Clara
HOTEL €€

(☑266 704 141; www.bestwesternhotelsantaclara. com; Travessa da Milheira 19; r €74; P🕸🛜) A whitewashed building tucked away in a quiet back street, this efficiently run and reliable hotel has plain but comfortable rooms.

★Albergaria do Calvario
BOUTIQUE HOTEL €€€

(☑266 745 930; www.albergariadocalvario.com; Travessa dos Lagares 3; d from €108) Elegant (yet unpretentious), friendly (yet not in your face), comfortable (but not awkwardly can't-put-your-feet-up-uber-luxurious), this place has an ambience that travellers adore. The delightful staff leave no service stone unturned – anything, it seems, is possible. Breakfasts are among the region's best: locally sourced organic produce, from fresh fruit and healthy trimmings, to homemade cakes and egg dishes.

Gorgeous lounge areas are decked out with a tasteful melange of antique and modern furniture. Comfortable beds, flat-screen TVs, books, heating and air-conditioning ensure a homely, don't-want-to-leave kind of stay. It's located in a delightful part of town, near Porta Lagoa and the aqueduct, and has a pleasant garden patio area. The hotel also runs self-contained rural accommodation options several kilometres from town. These include a country apartment (with a pool; great for couples and you can still

have breakfast in the hotel) and a couple of houses (perfect for families).

Convento do Espinheiro
LUXURY HOTEL €€€

(☑266 788 200; www.conventodoespinheiro.com; r from €200) Housed in a restored 15th-century convent, several kilometres northeast of Évora, this elegant hotel and spa complex has facilities galore (heliport, anyone?). The rooms feature heavy fabrics and rugs, and there are several restaurants on the premises. Frequent deals available.

Pousada dos Lóios
LUXURY HOTEL €€€

(☑266 730 070; www.pousadas.pt; Largo do Conde de Vila Flor; d €250; 🕸🛜🛁) Occupying the former Convento dos Lóios, opposite the Templo Romano, this beautiful *pousada* has gorgeously furnished rooms in a contemporary style (mint green and white) set around the pretty cloister. Note the original walkie-talkie 'devices' in the room doors. There's a flash restaurant on the ground floor of the cloister (mains €22 to €20).

✖ Eating

Scattered around Praça do Giraldo are a handful of attractive cafes with outdoor seating. Most of the town's many snack bars serve basic cheap eats.

Salsa Verde
VEGETARIAN €

(☑266 743 210; www.salsa-verde.org; Rua do Raimundo 93A; from €4.85 or per kg €14.40; ☉lunch & dinner Mon-Fri; lunch Sat; 🍴) Vegetarians (and Portuguese pigs) will be thanking the owner for this veggie-popping paradise. Pedro, the owner, gives a wonderful twist to traditional Alentejan dishes (the famous bread dish, *migas*, is prepared with mushrooms). Don't be put off by the eatery's cafeteria-like appearance; come here for the food – all locally sourced fresh products and olive oil are used.

Pastelaria Conventual
Pão de Rala
PATISSERIE €

(Rua do Cicioso 47; pastries from €2; ☉7.30am-8pm) Out of the centre, but still within the walls, this delightful spot specialises in convent cakes, all made on the premises from recipes that originated in the local convents. Don't miss the *pão de rala* (we'll let you find out what it is) – it's sweet stuff (and wonderfully sinful).

Café Arcada
CAFE, RESTAURANT €

(Praça do Giraldo 10; meals €7-10; ☉8am-9.30pm) This busy, barn-sized cafe is an Évora institution, serving coffee, crêpes and cakes. You can sit at an outdoor table on the lovely plaza.

Mercado Municipal
MARKET €

(Municipal Market; Praça 1 de Maio; ⊗8am-5pm Tue-Sun) You can pick up fruit and vegetables at the municipal market. Or try Modelo Hypermarket, a supermarket beyond the town limits on the road to Alcáçovas.

★ Botequim da Mouraria
PORTUGUESE €€

(☑266 746 775; Rua da Mouraria 16a; mains €13-16.50; ⊗lunch & dinner Mon-Fri, lunch Sat) Local gastronomes believe this is Évora's culinary shrine. Poke around the old Moorish quarter to find this cosy spot serving some of Évora's finest food and wine (the owner currently stocks more than 150 wines from the Alentejo alone). There are no reservations, just 12 stools at a counter. The owner will cook customer by customer according to their (and often his!) whim.

Dom Joaquim
PORTUGUESE €€

(☑266 731 105; Rua dos Penedos 6; mains €12-15; ⊗lunch Tue-Sun, dinner Tue-Sat) Housed in a renovated building, award-winning Dom Joaquim offers fine dining in a smart, contemporary setting. Modern artworks line the stone walls, and cane chairs grace clothed tables. It's often full of local business people who gather here for excellent traditional cuisine. And Chef Joaquim adores his clients as much as they love his skills. He serves big tastes with great enthusiasm: meats, including game such as *perdiz* (partridge), and succulent, fall-off-the-bone lamb; and seafood dishes, such as *caçao* (dogfish). Desserts consist mainly of *doces conventuais* (traditional convent puddings). Oh so sweet.

Um Quarto Para as Nove
PORTUGUESE €€

(Rua Pedro Simões 9; mains €12-19; ⊗lunch & dinner Thu-Tue) We'll let you establish the reason for this eatery's name (the owner bought the object secondhand – it never worked). This cheerful place has clocked up 30 years experience and, with that, some of Évora's best seafood dishes. It's hard to go past the generous and tasty *arroz* (risotto) dishes; the daily specials are worth going for.

Vinho e Noz
PORTUGUESE €€

(Ramalho Orgigão 12; mains €11-12; ⊗lunch & dinner Mon-Sat) The delightful owner and family run this efficient and unpretentious place, which has professional service, a large wine list and good-quality cuisine. It's been going

for over 30 years and is one of the best value places in town.

Snack-Bar Restaurante A Choupana
PORTUGUESE €€

(☑266 704 427; Rua dos Mercadores 18; mains €6-15; ⊗lunch & dinner Mon-Sat) This is a tiled, busy place where many locals opt to sit on stools at a long bar. There's a TV, lots of knick-knacks and tasty, good-value daily mains (including generous half serves). Attached is an appealing restaurant served by efficient bow-tied waiters.

Cafe Restaurante Repas
PORTUGUESE €€

(☑266 708 540; Praça 1 de Maio 19; mains €6-12; ⊗breakfast, lunch & dinner Thu-Tue) Repas may be nothing special cuisine-wise, but its location near the Igreja São Francisco is pleasant. In summer, this is the spot for *caracois* (snails) and beer.

Café Alentejo
PORTUGUESE €€

(☑266 706 296; Rua do Raimundo 5; mains €10-15; ⊗lunch & dinner Mon-Sat) Housed in a 16th-century building, Café Alentejo is full of arches and smart decor (with beautiful floors). Not to mention the amazing aromas: a heady mix of red wine and herbs that hits you on entry.

Restaurante Cozinha de Santo Humberto
PORTUGUESE €€

(☑266 704 251; Rua da Moeda 39; mains €12.50-16; ⊗lunch & dinner Fri-Tue) This is a traditional, long-established place, in a grand arched, whitewashed cellar hung with brass and ceramics. It offers hearty servings of rich regional fare – with baked duck rice and boar stew as specialties.

Restaurante O Fialho
PORTUGUESE €€

(☑266 703 079; Travessa dos Mascarenhas 16; mains €14.50-18; ⊗lunch & dinner Tue-Sun) This is listed here because it would be obvious by its absence; it's Évora's long-standing culinary institution, with photos of visiting dignitaries lining the walls. It has wood panelling and white tablecloths and offers professional service and Alentejan cuisine.

Luar de Janeiro
PORTUGUESE €€€

(☑266 749 114; www.luardejaneiro.com; Travessa do Janeiro 13; mains €14-22; ⊗lunch & dinner Fri-Wed) We'll be upfront: you don't come here for the atmosphere (no soft lighting, no music). You do come here for attentive service and lashings of the freshest, top-quality produce. The shy but passionate owner, Paulo (he's the waiter, too), drives miles to source

> **PARKING IN ÉVORA**
>
> If you're driving it's best to park outside the walls at a signposted car park (eg at the southern end of Rua da República in Parking Rossio de São Brás). Spaces inside the walls are limited and usually metered, and driving here can be tricky due a web of narrow streets. Pricier hotels have some parking.

the best of everything, be it *presunto* (from Spain) to delicious meats (try the *cabrito no forno*, oven-roasted kid). Paulo lets the food do the talking; it will hit your hip pocket, but it's sustainable in every other sense.

Drinking & Nightlife

Most bars open late and don't close until at least 2am (4am at weekends). Some places may have cover charges.

Bar da Moeda Gastropub BAR
(☑266 785 047; Rua da Moeda 55; ☺ Tue-Sat; ☜) Nestle in under the attractive vaulted ceilings of this cool and popular spot, tucked away in the narrow Rua da Moeda. Offers great meals at reasonable prices (mains €7 to €9) and drinks, from beer on tap to spirits. Sometimes has live acoustic music.

Bar Oficina BAR
(Rua da Moeda 27; ☺7pm-3am Mon-Sat) Attracting all ages, this tiny, smoky but cosy spot with little wooden tables in a cave-like space attracts a loyal following who enjoy kicking back under the vaulted white ceilings for a beer or three.

Bar do Teatro BAR
(Praça Joaquim António de Aguiar; ☺8pm-2am) Next to the theatre, this small, inviting bar has high ceilings and old-world decor that welcomes a friendly mixed crowd. The music tends towards lounge and electronica.

Praxis CLUB
(☑266 707 505; Rua de Valdevinos; ☺midnight-6am) Praxis has one big dance floor, one small dance floor and DJs spinning house, R&B and hip hop. It's a lively, good-time crowd, but the place doesn't get busy until around 2am after the other places have closed.

☆ Entertainment

For theatre, film, concerts and art expositions, stop in at the imaginative cultural centre Sociedade Harmonia Eborense (☑266 746 874; Praça do Giraldo 72) to see what's on.

Shopping

Rua 5 de Outubro has rows of *artesanatos* (handicrafts shops) selling pottery, knick-knacks and cork products. A couple of shops in the modern *mercado municipal* sell pottery. On the second Tuesday of each month a vast open-air market sprawls across the big Rossio de São Brás, just outside the walls south of Rua da República.

Montsobro ARTS & CRAFTS
(www.montsobro.com; Rua 5 de Outubro 66) One of many shops along Rua 5 de Outubro, this was the first – and is still one of the best – that sells cork products.

Feiras no Largo MARKET
(Praça 1 de Maio; ☺8am-2pm Sat & Sun) Each weekend sees the Feiras no Largo, one of four different markets – antiquities, used books and collectables, art and *artesenato*.

Livraria Nazareth BOOKS
(☑266 741 702; Praça do Giraldo 46) Head up the stairs of Évora's oldest shop for maps, including *Alentejo & Évora* (€4.95), and some books in English.

Information

EMERGENCY & MEDICAL SERVICES
Évora District Hospital (☑266 740 100; Largo Senhor da Pobraza) East of the centre; Évora's public hospital.
Misericordia Hospital (Hospital da Misericordia; ☑266 760 630; www.hmevora.pt; Estrada de Viana) Évora's private hospital is a couple of kilometres south of town; it's good for emergencies.
PSP Police Station (☑266 160 450; Rua Francisco Soares Lusitano) Near the Templo Romano.

INTERNET ACCESS
Câmara Municipal (☺9am-12.30pm & 2-5pm Mon-Fri) Free internet access in the same building as the old Roman baths.
Cybercenter (Rua Serpa Pinto 36; per hr €2; ☺10.30am-11pm Mon-Fri, 2-10pm Sat & Sun)

MONEY
There are several banks with ATMs on and around Praça do Giraldo, including **Caixa de Crédito Agrícola** (Praça do Giraldo 13).
MundiTransfers (☑266 761 025; Rua Serpa Pinto 40A; ☺10am-2pm & 3-7pm Mon-Fri) The only place that changes travellers cheques.

POST

Branch Post Office (Largo da Porta de Moura)
Main Post Office (Rua de Olivença)

TOURIST INFORMATION

Rota dos Vinhos do Alentejo Headquarters
(Wine Route Office; ☑266 746 498; www.
vinhosdoalentejo.pt; Praça Joaquim António de
Aguiar 20-21; ☉2-7pm Mon, 11am-7pm Tue-Fri,
10am-1pm Sat) Head here for details of a *rota
dos vinhos* (wine route) to *adegas* (wineries)
in the Alentejo, plus wine tastings and cellar visits. Charges vary depending upon the
individual cellar; these generally range between
€5 and €30.

Turismo (☑266 777 071; www.cm-evora.
pt; Praça do Giraldo 73; ☉9am-7pm Apr-Oct,
9am-6pm Nov-Mar) Has a *Historical Itineraries* leaflet (€1.10), a great town map and the
listings guide *Viva por Cá*. Excellent tourist
guides can be downloaded from www.cm-evora.
pt/guiaturistico (in English, Spanish, French,
Russian and Portuguese).

ⓘ Getting There & Away

BUS

The **bus station** (☑266 738 120; Avenida São
Sebastião) is west of town. Services include:
Beja (express €8, 1½ hours, hourly)
Coimbra (€18.50, 4½ hours, four daily) Alter-
natively, change in Lisbon.
Elvas (express €12, 1¼ hours, two weekdays)
Estremoz (express €8, 30 minutes, six daily)
Faro (€17, four hours, three daily) Via Albufeira.
Lisbon (€12, 1½ to two hours, hourly)
Portalegre (normal/express €8, 30 minutes,
three to five daily)

Reguengos de Monsaraz (express €8, ¾ hour,
two weekdays, one weekends)
Vila Viçosa (normal/express €5.50/9, 1½/one
hour, one to six weekdays)

TRAIN

Évora station (☑266 742 336) The train
station is outside the walls, 600m south of the
jardim público. There are daily trains to/from
Lisbon (€12.50, 1½ hours, four daily). Trains
also go to/from Beja (change in Casa Branca;
€7.20, 2¼ hours, four daily), Lagos (€31.10, 4½
to five hours, three daily) and Faro (€29.30,
four to five hours, two daily).

ⓘ Getting Around

CAR & BICYCLE

Evora Adventure Bike (☑969 095 880, 266
702 326; Travessa do Barão 18; €8/40 half-
day/4 days; ☉9am-9pm) Half-day and multiday bike rental.

Europcar (☑266 742 627; Estrada de Viana,
Lot 10; ☉9am-1pm Mon-Fri, 3-6.30pm Mon-
Sat) For car hire. In front of Lidl supermarket
on the outskirts of town (direction of Viana).

TAXI

Taxis (☑266 734 734) Congregate in Praça do
Giraldo. On a weekday you can expect to pay
about €6 from the train station to Praça do
Giraldo.

Around Évora

Megaliths – the word is derived from the
ancient Greek for 'big stones' – are found
all over the ancient landscape that surrounds Évora. These prehistoric structures,

---

LOCAL KNOWLEDGE

SECRETS OF THE MEGALITHS

Mário Carvalho is a tour guide of the Alentejo megaliths with Ebora Megalithica (p215).

What's the big deal about the megaliths? They remain today the most tangible and
impressive remains of one of the most significant moments in human history – the Neolithic revolution.

What's your favourite megalith [in Alentejo] and why? The megalithic enclosure of
Almendres (near Évora)! Besides being the largest megalithic monument on the Iberian
Peninsula and one of the oldest monuments of humankind, its location (on a slope facing the eastern horizon) and surroundings (a cork oak forest) make this monument one
of a kind.

Can you share any 'secrets' about a megalith? One of the biggest misconceptions
about the standing stones is that they are phallic representations. It's a Freudian mis-
conception. Modern archaeology and the study of rock art have proven this wrong and
have gradually replaced it with an anthropomorphic perspective. In fact, they are possibly the first statues dedicated to the human figure.

built around 5000 to 7500 years ago, dot the European Atlantic coast, but here in Alentejo there is an astounding amount of Neolithic remains. Dolmens (Neolithic stone tombs – *antas* in Portuguese) were probably temples and/or collective tombs, covered with a large flat stone and usually built on hilltops or valleys, near water lines. Menhirs (individual standing stones) point to fertility rites – as phallic as skyscrapers, if on a smaller scale – and cromeleques, organised sets of standing stones, seem to incorporate basic astronomic orientations related to seasonal transitions (equinoxes and solstices).

Megalith devotees can buy the book *Paisagens Arqueologicas A Oeste de Évora* (€13), which has English summaries, available at the *turismo*.

You can see more megaliths around Reguengos de Monsaraz, Elvas and Castelo de Vide.

ℹ Getting There & Away

To get to this area, your only options are to rent a car or bike (note that about 5km of the route is rough and remote), hire a taxi for the day (around €60), or go on a guided tour (p215).

With your own wheels, head west from Évora on the old Lisbon road (N114) for 10km, then turn south for 2.8km to Guadalupe, then follow the signs to the Cromeleque dos Almendres (4.3km).

Return to Guadalupe and head south for 5km to Valverde, home of the Universidade de Évora's school of agriculture and the 16th-century Convento de Bom Jesus. Following the signs to Anta

---

WORTH A TRIP

REGUENGOS DE MONSARAZ

This small working-class town, once famous for its sheep and wool production, is a stopping point and transport hub for Monsaraz. It's also close to the pottery centre of São Pedro do Corval as well as to an impressive half-dozen dolmens and menhirs (out of around 150 scattered across the surrounding plains). It's worth a day trip for its excellent wineries alone.

The town's rocket-like local church was built in 1887 and designed by José António Dias da Silva, who was also responsible for Praça de Touros, the Lisbon bullring.

Also worth considering is **Fabrica Alentejana de Lanificios** (☑ 266 502 179; Rua Mendes; ☉ 9am-5pm Mon-Fri), the last remaining hand-loom producer of *mantas alentejanas* (handwoven woollen floor rugs) – only a few women are at the looms these days. The owner and/or weavers are happy to show you around. The factory is southeast of the *praça* (take the road to Monsaraz and turn right at Rua Mendes) and the factory's shop is in Monsaraz.

The small **turismo** (☑ 266 503 052; Rua 1 de Maio; ☉ 9am-12.30pm & 2-5.30pm Mon-Fri, 10am-1pm & 2.30-4.30pm Sat & Sun) can point you in the right direction for the wineries around Reguengos (part of the wine route), including the acclaimed **Herdade do Esporão** (☑ 266 509 280; www.esporao.com), 7km south of town. The property's border was defined in 1267 and it has vestiges of Roman times. It produces a wide variety of wines for the domestic and overseas markets, and its Australian-Portuguese winemaker, David Baverstock, was voted Portugal's Winemaker of the Year in 2013. Whatever you do, factor in a lunch stop either at the winery's very smart new eatery, the **Herdade do Esporão Restaurant** (mains €15.50 to €21, open for lunch) or its more casual cellar bar (the winery's main buildings were recently renovated to a smart, sleek look). Here you can admire artworks (many pieces produced for the reserve labels) while enjoying some top-class cuisine – traditional recipes with a modern twist and with vegetables sourced from the kitchen garden – and stupendous vineyard views. Wine matching is *de rigeur* with many older and special vintages (not only commercial wines) on offer.

The winery also offers various **tours** of the vineyards and extraordinary cellars (among the largest in Portugal; parts of the cellars were sourced from the same factory that supplied the metro in Lisbon). Birdwatching trips head to one of the two water courses, while history tours cover the archaeological excavations of the Herdad's neighbouring estate, Perdigões. Phone ahead to arrange a tour.

To get there, buses run daily to Évora (€7.40 express, normal/express 1¼ hours/45 minutes, two to nine daily) and direct to Lisbon (€13, 2½ hours, two daily).

Grande do Zambujeiro, turn into the school's farmyard and onto a badly potholed track. After 1km you'll see the Great Dolmen.

Cromeleque dos Almendres

Set within a beautiful landscape of olive and cork trees – unfortunately the dirt road almost impinges onto the site – is the Cromeleque dos Almendres (Almendres Cromlech). This huge, spectacular oval of standing stones, 15km west of Évora, is the Iberian Peninsula's most important megalithic group and an extraordinary place to visit.

The site consists of a huge oval of some 95 rounded granite monoliths – some of which are engraved with symbolic markings – spread down a rough slope. They were erected over different periods, it seems, with basic astronomic orientations and were probably used for social gatherings or sacred rituals back in the dawn of the Neolithic period.

Two and a half kilometres before Cromeleque dos Almendres stands **Menir dos Almendres**, a single stone about 4m high, with some very faint carvings near the top. Look for the sign; to reach the menhir you must walk a few hundred metres from the road.

Anta Grande do Zambujeiro

The Great Dolmen of Zambujeiro, 13km southwest of Évora, is Europe's largest dolmen. Under a huge sheet-metal protective shelter in a field of wildflowers and yellow broom, stand seven stones and a 'closing slab' that connects the chamber with the corridor. Each is 6m high and together they form a huge chamber around 5m in diameter.

Unfortunately, you can't get in; the entrance is blocked, but you can peer in from the high mound behind. Archaeologists removed the capstone in the 1960s. Most of the site's relics can be found in the Museu do Évora (p210).

Évoramonte

POP 700

Northeast of Évora, this tiny village, with its quaint 16th-century castle, makes an interesting detour on your way through the region. There are fine views all around across the low hills.

The interesting **castelo** (adult/senior €1.50/0.75; ⊙ 9am-12.30pm Wed-Sun, 2-5pm Tue-Sun, closed 2nd weekend of every month) dates from 1306, but was rebuilt after the 1531 earthquake. Exterior stone carving shows unwarlike small bows, the symbol of the Bragança family – the knot symbolises fidelity. The interior is neatly restored, with impressively meaty columns topped by a sinuous arched ceiling on each cavernous floor. The roof provides sweeping panoramas.

It also has an unexpectedly smart restaurant (mains €9 to €12) with indoor-outdoor seating and views. There are also several restaurants in the village below.

Unfortunately, at the time of research, no buses were heading to Évoramonte; you need to have your own wheels.

São Pedro do Corval

Known for its fine pottery traditions, this tiny village, 5km east of Reguengos de Monsaraz, has dozens of **pottery workshops** where you can see both the potters and artists in action and purchase a few pieces of cheap and cheerful plates, pots, jugs, candlesticks and floor tiles.

With more than 20 *olarias* (pottery workshops), the village is one of Portugal's largest pottery centres. It's difficult to recommend one *olaria* over another; wander along Rua da Primavera and the nearby streets (follow the '*olarias*' signs) and ask at the Reguengos and Monsaraz tourist offices for a map locating the *olarias*. Buses between Reguengos and Monsaraz stop here.

Monsaraz

POP 780 (CASTLE 20)

Perched high over the surrounding countryside, tiny Monsaraz is a charming village with a looming castle at its edge, great views over the Alqueva Dam and olive groves sprinkling the landscape. Its narrow streets are lined with uneven-walled, whitewashed cottages. Sadly, as with other villages in the region, Monsaraz struggles to retain its inhabitants; the permanent residents are mainly elderly people. But it has not lost its magic. In the streets, you'll see flat-capped men watching the day unfold and women chatting on stoops.

Today, the village prospers on tourism, with a handful of restaurants, guesthouses and artisan shops. It's worth coming to taste a slice of traditional Portugal, wander the slumbering streets and sample Alentejan cuisine. It's at its best as it wakes up in the morning, in the quiet of the evening, or during a wintry dusk.

Settled long before the Moors arrived in the 8th century, Monsaraz was recaptured by the Christians under Giraldo Sem Pavor (Gerald the Fearless) in 1167, and then given to the Knights Templar as a thankyou gift for their assistance. The castle was added in 1310.

As for your arrival? It will be just like historic times – on foot through one of the four arched entrances. Coaches and cars have to be parked outside the walled village.

◉ Sights & Activities

Igreja Matriz   CHURCH
(⊙10am-6pm) The parish church, near the *turismo,* was rebuilt after the 1755 earthquake and again a century later. Inside (if you can get in, hours can be vague) is an impressive nave and a 14th-century marble tomb carved with 14 saints. An 18th-century *pelourinho* (stone pillory) topped by a Manueline globe stands outside. The 16th-century **Igreja da Misericórdia** is opposite, but is rarely open.

Museu de Arte Sacra   MUSEUM
(Museum of Sacred Art; admission €1.80; ⊙10am-6pm) Housed inside a fine Gothic building beside the parish church, this museum has a small collection of 14th-century wooden religious figures and 18th-century vestments and silverware. Its most famous exhibit is a rare example of a 14th-century secular fresco, a charming piece depicting a good and a bad judge, the latter appropriately two-faced.

Castelo   CASTLE
(⊙24hr) The castle at the southwestern end of the village was one in the chain of Dom Dinis' defensive fortresses along the Spanish border. It's now converted into a small bullring, and its ramparts offer a fine panoramic view over the Alentejan plains.

Barragem do Alqueva   BOAT TOUR
(per person €50, discount for a group) A great way to explore the Barragem do Alqueva is by boat. **Capitão Tiago** (☑962 653 711; www.sem-fim.com; Telheiro; per person €50) runs excellent voyages in his 17m Dutch sail boat. Several trips are available – the standard

is two hours with the chance to swim and visit some of the islands. Other packages include a meal at Tiago's restaurant, **Sem Fim** (☑962 653 711; www.sem-fim.com; Rua das Flores 6A, Telheiro; ⊙lunch & dinner Fri-Sun Oct-May, Wed-Mon Jun-Sep). You can also rent bikes and canoes (per day €25). Telheiro is about 2km from Monsaraz.

✦ Festivals & Events

Accommodation must be booked far in advance at the times these events are on.

Museu Aberto   MUSIC
Monsaraz heaves with jollity during its week-long Museu Aberto (Open Museum) music festival, held in July in even-numbered years.

Festa de Nosso Senhor Jésus dos Passos   VILLAGE
Bullfights and processions feature in this festival, held around the second weekend of September.

🛏 Sleeping

Some villagers have converted their ancient cottages to guesthouses, most of which are along Rua Direita. Make sure you book ahead in high season.

Casa Pinto   B&B €€
(☑266 557 076; www.casapinto.net; Praça Dom Nuno Álvares Pereira 10; d €75-115; ❇🛜) A touch of class and the downright quirky hits Monsaraz. Each of the five rooms – decorated by the Spanish owner–interior designer – has a theme based around former Portuguese colonies, from Macau to Mombasa. We're talking themed touches, from a waterfall shower (Dili) to elephant tusks (Asilah, Morocco – no, the tusks are not real) and much more besides. Fabulous terrace views and pleasant living spaces.

Casa Saramago de Monsaraz   RURAL INN €€
(☑266 557 494; www.casasaramago-monsaraz.com.pt; Telheiro; r €65; P❇🐾) Based in Telheiro, at the foot of Monsaraz, this delightfully converted blue and white *quinta* is great value for money. Rooms are tastefully decorated in old-style – but not too twee – furniture. The Portuguese owners are friendly and accommodating. Rooms in the former *celeiros* (silos) have verandahs and face Monsaraz. Four-legged friends are welcome, too – a horse hotel and *cão* (dog) kennels are on the premises.

Casa Dona Antónia   B&B €€

(☑266 557 142; www.casadantonia-monsaraz.com; Rua Direita 15; d €60-75, ste €90; ✲) The eight rooms in this traditional house vary in size, but all are pleasant and comfortable; the suite is huge and includes a terrace.

St Condestável   B&B €€

(☑266 557 181; www.condestavel-monsaraz.com; Rua Direita 4; r/ste €55/80; ✲ 🛜) This old place has five cool rooms (great when the mercury hits 40°C). Decor errs on the masculine (it lacks a bit of colour), with wooden finishings. Subtract €5 per person if you don't want breakfast.

✕ Eating

Monsaraz has a handful of restaurants, all offering traditional Alentejan mains.

Cafe-Restaurante Lumumba   INTERNATIONAL €

(Rua Direita 12; mains €6-10; ☉lunch & dinner Tue-Sun) This small place has a more local, less touristy clientele as well as more atmosphere than other cafes. It also boasts a terrace with great views.

A Casa do Forno   PORTUGUESE €

(Travessa da Sanabrosa; ☑266 557 190; mains €8-10; ☉lunch & dinner Wed-Mon) The menu is fairly standard here (although the walls display lots of prizes for cuisine from previous decades), but the ambience is pleasant – there are checked tablecloths, attractive wooden chairs and an outdoor terrace with 'those' views.

Xarez   INTERNATIONAL €€

(www.xarez-monsaraz.com; Rua de Santiago 33; mains €7-12; ☉11am-8pm Sep-Oct & Dec-May, 11am-midnight summer) A tourist-magnet for its views and reasonable *petiscos* (snacks) and mains. Seems to be open when nothing else is.

🛍 Shopping

Loja da Mizette   HANDICRAFTS

(☑266 557 159; Rua do Celeiro; ☉9.30am-1pm & 2-7pm Mon-Fri, 10am-1pm & 2-8pm Sat & Sun) Sells Alentejano *mantas* made in its factory in nearby Reguengos by one of the few remaining female weavers. The last of its kind.

ℹ Information

Multibanco ATM (Travessa da Misericórdia 2) Off the main square.

Turismo (☑927 997 316; Rua Direita; ☉10am-12.30pm & 2-5.30pm) Stocked with some regional information, including bus timetables and basic maps of the area's megalithic monuments.

ℹ Getting There & Away

Buses run to/from Reguengos de Monsaraz (€3, 35 minutes, four daily on weekdays). The last bus back to Reguengos, where you can pick up connections to Évora, is around 6pm (check, however, as this changes).

Around Monsaraz

Neolithic megaliths are scattered throughout the landscape around Monsaraz – it is great to explore and discover them amid the

---

WORTH A TRIP

ARRAIOLOS: THE GREAT CARPETS OF PORTUGAL

About 20km north of Évora is the small town of Arraiolos, famed for its exquisite *tapetes* (carpets). These handwoven works show a marked influence from Persian rugs, and they have been in production here since the 12th century. It seems half the population is involved in this artistry, and on a casual stroll through town, you might encounter several women stitching in front of their homes. Rug patterns are based on abstract motifs, *azulejo* designs or flower, bird or animal depictions. Shops are abundant, and you can pay anything from €50 for a tiny runner to €2000 for the most beautiful pieces, which feature more elaborate designs.

The village itself dates from the 2nd or 3rd century BC, and is laid out along traditional lines, with whitewashed blue-trimmed houses topped with terracotta roofs and the ruins of a castle overlooking the town. The plain facade of the **Igreja da Misericórdia** hides a beautiful interior with a golden altar and 18th-century *azulejo*-lined walls.

Take a peek at the centuries-old dye chambers in the main square, which is also where you'll find the **turismo** (☑266 490 254; www.cm-arraiolos.pt; ☉9am-5pm Mon-Sat). There are cafes in Arraiolos for lingering, and a flashy **pousada** (☑266 419 340; www.pousadas.pt; d €220) just outside town.

tangles of olive groves and open fields of wildflowers (they're signposted, but finding each one is an adventure). Most spectacular is **Cromeleque do Xerez**, an ensemble with the triumphant 7-tonne menhir at its centre. The rocks once stood 5km south of Monsaraz but were moved before flooding by the massive Barragem do Alqueva. A remaining highlight is the **Menhir de Bulhoa**, another phallic stone with intriguing carved circles and lines; it's 4km north of Monsaraz off the Telheiro–Outeiro road. A map outlining the region's megalithic circuit is available at the tourist office.

Estremoz

POP 9000

Along with neighbouring Borba and Vila Viçosa, the very authentic, active town of Estremoz is one of the region's well-known marble hotspots and is worth visiting. The region's marble – rivalling that in Carrara, Italy – is used all over the place: even the cobbles are rough chunks of marble.

Ringed by an old protective wall, Estremoz has a centre set with orange tree–lined lanes, a 13th-century hilltop castle enclosed in an old quarter, and peaceful plazas (the main one being **Rossio Marquês de Pombal**, or 'the Rossio'). This simple provincial town is a busy trading centre, with lots of shops selling farm tools, though visitors can also load up on crafts, earthenware pottery and gourmet delights – all of which are available at the great market that fills the huge central square on Saturday. The town boasts some excellent eateries.

◉ Sights

◉ Lower Town

On the fringes of the Rossio are imposing old churches, former convents and, just north of the square, monastic buildings converted into **cavalry barracks**. Opposite these, by Largo General Graça, is a marble-edged water tank, called the **Lago do Gadanha** (Lake of the Scythe) after its scythe-wielding statue of Neptune. Some of the prettiest marble streets in town are south of the Rossio, off Largo da República.

Café Águias D'ouro   HISTORIC BUILDING
(268 339 100; Rossio do Marquês de Pombal) This stunning cafe – built in art-nouveau style between 1908 and 1909 – is worth see-ing for both the interior and exterior. At the start of the 20th century it was where the local *intelligencia* gathered to share ideas and local gossip.

◉ Upper Town

The upper town is surrounded by dramatic zigzagging ramparts and contains a gleaming white palace. The easiest way to reach it on foot is to follow narrow Rua da Frandina from Praça Luís de Camões and pass the inner castle walls through the Arco da Frandina.

Museu Municipal   MUSEUM
(268 339 219; Largo D Dinis; adult €1.55; ◉ 9am-12.30pm & 2-5.30pm Tue-Sun) This museum is housed in a beautiful 17th-century alms-house near the former palace. Pretty hand-painted furniture sits alongside endearing, locally carved wooden figures (charming rural scenes by Joaquim Velhinho) and a collection of typical 19th-century domestic Alentejan items. On the ground floor is an amazing display of the unique Estremoz pottery figurines – some 500 pieces covering 200 years, including lots of ladies with carnivalesque outfits, explosively floral headdresses (Primavera) and wind-rippled dresses. There's even an entire 19th-century Easter Parade.

Royal Palace &
Torre das Três Coroas   PALACE
At the top of the upper town is the stark, glowing-white, fortress-like former royal palace, now the Pousada de Santa Rainha Isabel. Dom Dinis built the palace in the 13th century for his new wife, Isabel of Aragon.

After her death in 1336 (Dinis had died 11 years earlier) it was used as an ammu-nition dump. An inevitable explosion, in 1698, destroyed most of the palace and the surrounding castle, though in the 18th century João V restored the palace for use as an armoury. The 27m-high keep, the Torre das Três Coroas (Tower of the Three Crowns), survived and is still the dominant feature. It's so called because it was apparently built by three kings: Sancho II, Afonso III and Dinis.

Visitors are welcome to view the public areas of the *pousada* and climb the keep, which offers a superb panorama of the old town and surrounding plains. The holes at the keep's edges were channels for boiling oil – a good way of getting rid of uninvited guests.

Estremoz

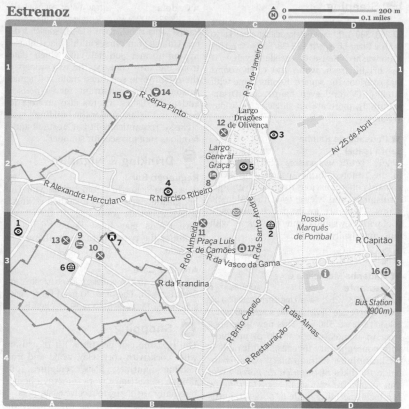

Estremoz

⊙ Sights
1	Afonso Ginja	A3
2	Café Águias D'ouro	C3
3	Cavalry Barracks	C2
4	Fátima Estróia	B2
5	Lago do Gadanha	C2
6	Museu Municipal	A3
7	Royal Palace & Torre das Três Coroas	B3

⊜ Sleeping
8	Hotel O Gadanha	C2
9	Pousada de Rainha Santa Isabel	A3

⊗ Eating
10	A Cadeia	A3
11	Adega do Isaías	B3
12	Gadanha Mercearia e Restaurante	C2
13	São Rosas	A3

⊜ Drinking & Nightlife
14	Até Jazz Café	B1
15	Reguengo Bar	B1

⊜ Shopping
16	Casa Galileu	D3
17	Irmãs Flores	C3

✿ Festivals & Events

The town's biggest event is the **Feira Internacional de Artesanato e Agro-Pecuária de Estremoz** (FIAPE), a baskets, ceramics, vegetables and livestock bonanza, held for several days at the end of April. **Cozinha dos Ganhões** (Festival de Gastronomia Alentejana), the town's fun culinary festival, is held from the end of November to the beginning of December.

Sleeping

Hotel O Gadanha
HOTEL €

(☑268 339 110; www.hotelogadanha.com; Largo General Graça 56; s/d/tr €23/38/50; ❄️🛜) This whitewashed house is excellent value. It has bright, fresh, white and clean rooms that overlook the square. Rooms come with satellite TV (and even hairdryers). Disappointingly, there are no single rates Friday to Sunday.

★Pousada de Rainha Santa Isabel
LUXURY HOTEL €€€

(☑268 332 075; www.pousadas.pt; d €220; ❄️📶) In the restored former palace, this lavish *pousada* offers spacious rooms with antique furnishings and views over the Alentejo plains. There are lovely palace gardens, a pool with views and common areas set with museum-quality tapestries.

Eating

★Gadanha Mercearia e Restaurante
RESTAURANT €€

(☑268 333 262; www.merceariagadanha.pt; Largo Dragões de Olivença 84A; snacks €6.50-13; ☺lunch & dinner Thu-Tue) This new little spot tries to merge traditional local products with contemporary touches. And it pulls it off beautifully. Extraordinary *petiscos* include the likes of *linguiça de porco preto* and *farinheira* with quail eggs (*farinheira* is a local speciality made of pork fat, herbs and flour). The daily luncheon menu for around €13 is highly recommended. Don't miss the desserts. (Our favourite? *Chocolate e avelã*.)

Adega do Isaías
PORTUGUESE €€

(Rua do Almeida 21; mains €11-13; ☺lunch & dinner Mon-Sat; 🍴) To enter this award-winning, rustic *tasca* (tavern), you pass by a sizzling grill cooking up tender fish, meat and Alentejan specialities. Inside, a wine cellar awaits, crammed with tables and huge wine jars.

São Rosas
INTERNATIONAL, PORTUGUESE €€

(☑268 333 345; Largo de Dom Dinis 11; mains €13-18; ☺lunch & dinner Tue-Sun) White tablecloths under whitewashed arches equal rustic-meets-smart, and the food is great, featuring some lovely starters (including smoked salmon and clams with oil, garlic and coriander), plus gazpacho in summer. It's near the former palace. The *borrego assado no forno* (roast lamb) is especially good (€15).

A Cadeia
INTERNATIONAL, PORTUGUESE €€

(☑268 323 400; www.cadeiaquinhentista.com; Rua Rainha Santa Isabel; mains €13-18; ☺lunch & dinner) Unlock your purses at this place, housed in the former judicial jail, which dates from the 16th century; the two storeys of the quadrangle separated male and female prisoners. The restaurant serves *petiscos* and main dishes. There's also an area for coffee and drinks under the building's arch, a classy, romantically lit bar upstairs and a fabulous roof terrace (for summer).

🍷 Drinking & Nightlife

Reguengo Bar
BAR

(Rua Serpa Pinto 126; ☺8am-2am Tue-Sun) This big barnlike space with a vaulted ceiling is where Estremoz youth kick up their heels. Live bands play most Friday nights. In summer the party continues in the garden outside.

Até Jazz Café
BAR

(☑268 083 459; www.atejazzcafe.com/home; Rua Serpa Pinto 65) The place to head for a varied schedule of jazz or fado most weekends.

🛍 Shopping

The *turismo* can provide a list of artisans who work with cork, clay, wood and iron, making figurines, bells, sculptures and unique pieces (most work from their homes, but many are happy to receive customers – it makes a great visit). Those who make *bonecas,* the clay dolls for which the town is famous, include **Irmãs Flores** (☑268 322 018; Largo da República 31-32; ☺9am-1pm Mon-Sat, 2-7pm Mon-Fri), **Afonso Ginja** (☑268 081 618; afonsoginja@gmail.com; Rua Direita 5) and **Fátima Estróia** (Rua Narciso Ribeiro).

The weekly Saturday market held on the Rossio provides a great display of Alentejan goodies and Estremoz specialities, from goat- and ewe-milk cheeses, to a unique style of unglazed, ochre-red pots.

Casa Galileu
HANDICRAFTS

(☑268 323 130; Rua Victor Cordon 16) If you miss the Saturday market, visit this shop southeast of the Rossio. It is crammed with locally made items, including essentials such as flat caps and cowbells.

ℹ Information

Caixa Geral de Depósitos Bank & ATM (Rossio Marquês de Pombal 43)
Centro de Saúde (☑268 332 042; Av 9 de Abril) At the northeastern end of town.

Police Station (📞268 338 470; Rua 31 de Janeiro)

Post Office (Rua 5 de Outubro; ⊙9am-6pm Mon-Fri)

Turismo (📞268 339 227; www.cm-estremoz. pt; Casa de Estremoz/câmara municipal, Rossio Marquês de Pombal; ⊙10am-1pm & 2-6pm)

❶ Getting There & Around

All buses stop at and depart from a smart, new, modern 'marble-mobic' **bus station** (📞938 876 333; Av Rainha Santa Isabel) off Av 25 de Abril (behind the *azulejo*-covered former train station).

Estremoz has services to Évora (six daily weekdays, one Saturday; €4.35), Évoramonte (four daily weekdays; €4.35), Portalegre (at least four daily; €8), Vila Viçosa (three daily weekdays; €2.50) and Elvas (five daily; €8.70). Regular buses also head further afield to Faro in the Algarve (€18.50; change in Albufeira or Évora), and Lisbon (at least six daily; €15).

Around Estremoz

Borba

POP 4500

Tiny Borba glows with a peculiar rosy light. Its marble wealth hasn't brought it many obvious riches, so its marble-lined houses and public buildings have a remarkable simplicity.

The town is encircled by marble quarries and is famous for its great red wines. The least visited of the marble towns, it is worth dropping into, if only to poke your head into the many antique shops.

◉ Sights

The Alentejo Wine Route lists several *adegas* in this region.

Adega Cooperativa de Borba   WINERY
(📞268 891 660; www.adegaborba.pt; Rua Gago Coutinho Sacadura Cabral; ⊙2-7pm Mon, 11am-7pm Tue-Fri, 10am-1pm Sat) This *adega* is one of the region's largest, producing the famous Borba full-bodied red and white *maduro* (mature) and rosé wines. Ring ahead to arrange a visit and tasting. You can buy wine at the Adega's large shop, 100m further up the road from the coop.

✖ Eating

Tasca Real   PORTUGUESE €
(Dr Ramos de Abreu 20; mains €6-8; ⊙lunch & dinner) Trade in the fancy settings for a cellarlike space, nouveau cuisine for plates of local *petiscos* and hearty mains, and snooty waiters for down-to-earth owners. One of the most authentic and delightful experiences you'll get in Alentejo. Pigs' trotters are a speciality. As for the price-to-quality ratio? The best value around.

❶ Getting There & Away

Buses stop just east of the *praça*.

Estremoz (€6, 15 minutes, around five buses daily) Obtain times and tickets from Café Brinquete, at Av do Povo 31.

Vila Viçosa (around €2) Buy tickets from the driver on the Rodovária do Alentejo bus.

Vila Viçosa

POP 8000

If you visit just one marble town in the region, Vila Viçosa is the one to target. It features Praça da República, a long attractive plaza set with orange trees, a marvellous marble palace (one of the country's largest) and a castle.

This was once home to the Bragança dynasty, whose kings ruled Portugal until it became a republic – Dom Carlos spent his last

---

USING YOUR MARBLES

The marble towns gleam with rosy-gold or white stone and the effect is enhanced by the houses, which have a Hollywood-smile brightness. As if locals hadn't found enough uses for the stone stuff, with their marble doorsteps, pavements and shoes (OK, we made that last one up), a process has been cooked up to create marble paint: marble is recrystallised limestone, so if you heat marble chips in a clay oven for three days they turn into calcium oxide, which is mixed with water to become whitewash. Cheaper than paint. People take pride in the whiteness of their houses and retouch them annually.

While we're on the subject of colour, apparently the yellow borders keep away fever, while blue is the bane of flies (you can add these colours to the oxide). The blue theory may have some truth, or at least international adherents – in Rajasthan (India) local people also apply pale blue to their houses to ward off mosquitoes.

night here before his assassination; it was also the birthplace of Catarina de Bragança (1638), who married Charles II to become Queen of England (and after whom Queens in New York was named). There are many sites and sights of marble (and non-marble) and a friendly laid-back citizenry who are proud of their sparkling town.

◉ Sights

Terreiro do Paço
PLAZA

The palace square covers 16,000 sq metres, and is ringed by the Paço Ducal, an enormous palace, the heavy-fronted Agostinhos Convent and graceful Chagas Nunnery. In the centre is a statue of Dom João IV.

Paço Ducal
PALACE

(⌨ 268 980 659; www.fcbraganca.pt; adult/under 10yr €6/free; ◷ 2.30-5.30pm Tue, 10am-1pm & 2.30-5.30pm Wed-Sun Apr-Sep; 2-5pm Tue, 10am-1pm & 2-5pm Wed-Sun Oct-Mar; 2.30-6pm Tue, 10am-1pm & 2.30-6.30pm Jul & Aug) The dukes of Bragança built their palace in the early 16th century when the fourth duke, Dom Jaime, decided he had had enough of his uncomfortable hilltop castle. The wealthy Bragança family, originally from Bragança in Trás-os-Montes, had settled in Vila Viçosa in the 15th century. After the eighth duke became king in 1640, it changed from a permanent residence to just another royal palace, but the family maintained a special fondness for it and Dom João IV and his successors continued to visit the palace.

The palace's best furniture went to Lisbon after Dom João IV ascended the throne, and some went on to Brazil after the royal family fled there in 1807, but there are still some stunning pieces on display, such as a huge 16th-century Persian rug in the Dukes Hall. Lots of royal portraits put into context the interesting background on the royal family.

The private apartments hold a ghostly fascination – toiletries, knick-knacks and clothes of Dom Carlos and his wife, Marie-Amélia, are laid out as if the royal couple were about to return (Dom Carlos left one morning in 1908 and was assassinated in Lisbon that afternoon).

A compulsory Portuguese-speaking guide leads the hour-long tours. English guidebooks cost €4.

Other parts of the Ducal Palace, including the 16th-century cloister, house more museums containing specific collections and with separate admission fees (armoury/ coach collection/Chinese Porcelain/treasury €3/2/2.50/2.50).

Castelo
CASTLE

The fascinating Dom Dinis walled hilltop castle was where the Bragança family lived before the palace was built. Part of it has been transformed into the **Museu de Arqueologia and Museu de Caça** (Archaeological Museum and Game & Hunting Museum; admission €3; ◷ 2.30-5.30pm Tue, 10am-1pm & 2.30-5.30pm Wed-Sun). A visit to these museums is a must – if only as an excuse to wander through the castle itself, with its 'secret' tunnels, giant fireplaces and wonderful vaulted ceilings.

The extraordinary (and under-promoted) archaeological collection is housed in the castle's many rooms and spans various eras from the Palaeolithic to the Roman. It even has Ancient Egyptian treasures. The less interesting hunting museum is stuffed with guns and the dukes' animal trophies.

Surrounding the castle is a cluster of village houses and peaceful overgrown gardens. There's a 16th-century Manueline *pelourinho* (pillory; the prison used to be nearby), with sculpted frogs.

Igreja de Nossa Senhora da Conceição
CHURCH

(◷ 8.30am-12.30pm & 2.30-6.30pm) Within the castle walls is this brilliantly tiled 15th-century church. It is also known as *Solar da Padroeira*, Home of the Patron Saint – the Virgin's image is found within. It was here that in 1646, King João IV offered the kingdom to Nossa Senhora Da Conceição who became then the patron saint of Portugal. From that time on, the kings of Portugal never wore the crown again, as it was now the Virgin's. Celebrations take place on 8 December.

🛏 Sleeping

Hospedaria Dom Carlos
GUESTHOUSE €

(⌨ fax 268 980 318; Praça da República 25; s/d/tr not incl breakfast €30/40/50; ✸) In an excellent location on the main square, the Dom Carlos offers tidy and comfortable rooms with wood finishing and a small, fancy lobby.

Casa do Colégio Velho
GUESTHOUSE €€

(⌨ 268 889 430; www.casadocolegiovelho.com; Rua Dr Couto Jardim 34; d €75-95, ste from €110; 🛜 ✸) You'll feel like Catarina Bragança herself in one of the seven plush rooms in this former family residence (home to the Jesuits in the 17th century). Decoration embraces a mélange of styles, including modern art deco and even rare rose marble in one of the bathrooms. The helpful English-speaking owner is handy with recommendations. The *casa* overlooks a lovely, neat garden, with lilies and a pool.

Herdade da Ribeira de Borba   RURAL INN €€
(☑268 980 709; www.hrb.com.pt; Ciladas; r €90-110; ✳ ❄) Five kilometres out of Vila Viçosa and on a working farm (think rural tranquillity, walks, birdwatching), this lovely option offers everything from contemporary apartments with kitchens in former workers' cottages, to plainer but pleasant rooms in the main building. Perfect for longer-term stays.

Pousada de Dom João IV   LUXURY HOTEL €€€
(☑268 980 742; www.pousadas.pt; d €220; ✳ ❄ ❄) Next to the Ducal Palace, this former royal convent was once the 'House of the Ladies of the Court'. Today, this regal spot offers spacious rooms – one with original frescos – terraces and classic furnishings. Rooms open onto a striking inner courtyard.

✗ Eating

Taverna dos Conjurados   PORTUGUESE €€
(Largo 25 de Abril 12; mains €10-15; ☺ weekends Nov-Mar, lunch & dinner Apr-Oct) This pleasant eatery is slightly more upmarket than the average taverna, yet it's by no means snobby. The attentive host is proud of his classic Portuguese cuisine, with some recipes going back to the Dukes' times (complete with time-consuming preparation). Regional meats, *baccalhau* (salted codfish) and *perdiz* (partridge) are favourites.

Os Cucos   PORTUGUESE €€
(☑268 980 806; mains €8-12; ☺ lunch & dinner Mon-Sat) Hidden in the pretty gardens near the *mercado municipal,* this is the pick for quality food and shady location. It has an airy, semicircular interior, and you can eat snacks at garden tables. The changing daily specials (Monday, *bacalhau;* Tuesday, *arroz de pato* etc) feature regional cuisine.

☆ Entertainment

Classical concerts (☑268 980 659; www.fcbraganca.pt; FREE) are held year-round in the chapel of the Ducal Palace on the last Friday of the month at 9pm.

ℹ Information

Espaço Internet (Rua Alferes Marcelino; ☺10am-1pm & 3.30-6.30pm Mon-Fri, 10am-12.30pm Sat) Free web access.

Turismo (☑268 889 317; www.cm-vilavicosa.pt; Praça da República 34; ☺9am-1pm & 2.30-5.30pm winter, 9.30am-1pm & 2.30-5.30pm summer) For town maps and information.

ℹ Getting There & Away

There are limited buses to/from Évora (1¾/one hour, two to three on weekdays), and Estremoz (35 minutes, two to three on weekdays).

Elvas

POP 25,000

Elvas' claim to fame is that it boasts the largest group of bulwarked dry-ditch land fortifications in the world. The impressive fortifications zigzagging around this pleasant little town – declared a UNESCO-heritage town in 2012 – reflect an extraordinarily sophisticated military technology. Its moats, fort and heavy walls would indicate a certain paranoia if it weren't for Elvas' position, only 15km west of Spain's Badajoz. Inside the stout town walls, you'll find a lovely town plaza, some quaint museums and very few foreign visitors – aside from the occasional flood of Spanish day trippers. Although there's not much to hold your attention beyond a day, Elvas is an interesting place to visit, with its evocative frontier-post atmosphere, its narrow medina-like streets and its extraordinary, forbidding walls and buttresses. It has a few excellent eateries.

History

In 1229 Elvas was recaptured from the Moors after 500 years of fairly peaceful occupation. The following centuries saw relentless attacks from Spain, interrupted by occasional peace treaties. Spain only succeeded in 1580, allowing Felipe II of Spain (the future Felipe I of Portugal) to set up court here for a few months. But the mighty fortifications were seldom breached: in 1644, during the Wars of Succession (1640-68), the garrison held out against a nine-day Spanish siege and, in 1659, just 1000 – an epidemic had wiped out the rest – withstood an attack by a 15,000-strong Spanish army.

The fortifications saw their last action in 1811, when the Duke of Wellington used the town as the base for an attack on Badajoz during the Peninsular War.

Elvas

200 m
0.1 miles

Forte de Santa Luzia (600m)

Portas de São Vicente

Portas de São Pedro

R Mouzinho de Albuquerque

Igreja de São Domingos

Igreja de São Pedro

R da Cadela

R de S Pedro

R Sa da Bandeira

R Espírito de Santo

Largo do Colégio

Biblioteca Municipal

Igreja de Salvador

R dos Chilões

Av S Domingos

R da Cadela

R Martim Mendes

R da Carreira

R de Olivença

R de Alcamim

Praça da República

R da Feira

R dos Arcos

R de Olivença

Largo de Santa Clara

Av Garcia de Orta

R do Tabalado

Av 14 de Janeiro

R de S Francisco

Praça 25 de Abril

R Pinto

R de Évora

Jardim Municipal

Hospital (500m)

Portas da Esquina

The Aqueduct

Av de Badajoz

Elvas

⊙ Sights

Museu de Arte Contemporânea de Elvas
GALLERY

(📞268 637 150; www.cm-elvas/mace; adult €2; ☉3-6.30pm Tue, 10am-1pm & 3-6.30pm Wed-Sun) The Museu de Arte Contemporânea de Elvas is a must-see (admittedly, it depends on what's on show). Opened in 2007, the museum is housed in a cleverly renovated baroque-style building from the 1700s, formerly the Misericórdia Hospital, and houses exhibitions of modern Portuguese artists from the collection of António Cachola. Each six months or so a different selection of the 300 contemporary pieces (installations, paintings and photographs) is on display. Artists include the likes of Francisco Vidal, Rui Patacho and Ana Pinto. One of the rooms contains the original chapel with exquisite tiles.

Aqueduto da Amoreira
AQUEDUCT

It took an unsurprising 100 years or so to complete this breathtakingly ambitious aqueduct. Finished in 1622, the huge cylindrical buttresses and several tiers of arches stalk from 7km west of town to bring water to the marble fountain in Largo da Misericórdia. It's best seen from the Lisbon road, west of the centre.

Castelo
CASTLE

(adult/concession €1.50/0.75; ☉9.30am-1pm & 2.30-5.30pm) You can walk around the battlements at the castle for dramatic views across the baking plains. The original castle was built by the Moors on a Roman site, and rebuilt by Dom Dinis in the 13th century, then again by Dom João II in the late 15th century.

Igreja de Nossa Senhora da Assunção
CHURCH

(Praça da República; ☉9.30am-12.30pm & 2-5pm winter, 10am-1pm & 3-6pm summer) **FREE** Francisco de Arruda designed this sturdy fortified church in the early 16th century, and it served as the town's cathedral until Elvas lost its episcopal status in 1882. Renovated during the 17th and 18th centuries, it retains a few Manueline touches, such as the south portal. Inside is a sumptuous 18th-century organ and some very pretty, but somewhat lost, 17th- and 18th-century tiling.

Igreja de Nossa Senhora da Consolação
CHURCH

(Largo de Santa Clara; ☉9.30am-12.30pm & 2-5pm winter, 10am-1pm & 3-6pm summer) **FREE** This plain church hides a thrilling interior. There are painted marble columns under a cupola, gilded chapels and fantastic 17th-century *azulejos* covering the surface. The unusual octagonal design was inspired by the Knights Templar chapel, which stood on a nearby site before this church was built in the mid-16th century. It was once the church of the Dominicans, and is all that is left of the original monastery.

Largo de Santa Clara
PLAZA

This delightful cobbled square facing the Igreja de Nossa Senhora da Consolação has a whimsical centrepiece – a polka-dotted **pelourinho**. This pillory was a symbol of municipal power: criminals would once have been chained to the metal hooks at the top. The fancy archway, with its own loggia at the top of the square, is pure Moorish artistry – a flourish in the town walls that once trailed past here.

THE ALENTEJO ELVAS

Museu Fotográfico João Carpinteiro
MUSEUM

(☑ 268 636 470; Largo Luis de Camões; adult/child €2/1; ⊙ 10am-1pm & 3-7pm Wed-Sun, 3-7pm Tue summer, 10am-1pm & 2-5pm Wed-Sun, 2-5pm Tue winter) Housed in the old town cinema is this photography museum, with an impressive collection of cameras; the oldest is a pocket-vest number dating from 1912. Changing photography exhibits are often the highlight of a visit here.

Fortifications
MUSEUM

(☑ 268 628 357) The wall encircling the town spans three periods – the first walls were constructed in the 8th century with the arrival of the Moors, and the second Muslim wall spans the 10th and 11th centuries (and onwards). The last (the majority of what you see) was constructed in the 17th century: Flemish Jesuit engineer Cosmander designed the formidable defences, adding moats, ramparts, seven bastions, four semibastions and fortified gates in the style of the famous French military architect the Marquis de Vauban.

To give an idea of the level of security: after crossing a drawbridge to get to the main gate, you come to a 150-sq-metre square, surrounded by bastions, turrets and battlements, a covered road and three lines of trenches, some of which are carved out of rock.

Fernandina Tower
TOWER

(☑ 268 636 470; Rua da Cadeia; ⊙ 10am-1pm Wed-Sun, 3-7pm Tue-Sun) **FREE** The Fernandina Tower was the result of alterations undertaken in the 14th century to the second Muslim wall. It served as a jail from the end of the 15th century. These days, you can climb the spiral staircase to the top for wonderful views. Note: the lighting is poor and it's a steep and winding climb up three levels. There's also an excellent video on Elvas and its fortifications.

Forte de Santa Luzia
FORT

This miniature, zigzag-walled fort, just 1.4km south of the *praça,* houses a **military museum** (☑ 268 628 357; admission €2; ⊙ 10am-1pm & 3-7pm Wed-Sun, 3-7pm Tue). The **Forte de Nossa Senhora da Graça,** 3km north of town, with a similar shape, was added in the following century; these days, it's in bad shape (abandoned and dilapidated so take care if visiting), although not completely out of bounds (it still has signs from its days as a former army base).

Tours

Agia
WALKING TOUR

(☑ 933 702 392; www.alentejoguides.com) This licensed guide association organises two-hour walking tours (€12) that explore Elvas' historic sites. Tours take place on Saturdays at 10am and depart from Praça 25 Abril. Sunset tours depart on Saturdays at 6.30pm (€10; May to September only).

★★ Festivals & Events

Elvas starts to tap its blue suede shoes in late September, celebrating the **Festas do Senhor da Piedade e de São Mateus,** with everything from agricultural markets and bullfights to folk dancing and religious processions (especially on the last day).

🛏 Sleeping

António Mocisso e Garcia Coelho Quartos
GUESTHOUSE €

(☑ 268 622 126; residencial.mocisso@hotmail.com; Rua Aires Varela 5; s/d/tr €25/35/48; ✳) The best of the budget places in the town centre has 14 small but clean rooms. Single rooms are less appealing and some rooms have small windows. Prices are a bit fluid.

Hotel São João de Deus
LUXURY HOTEL €€

(☑ 268 639 220; www.hotelsaojoaodeus.com; Largo João de Deus 1; s/d Sun-Thu €64/70, Fri & Sat €74/80; ✳@✳) Spanish-owned and -operated since 2004, this is Elvas' grandest hotel. It's a pleasant, although not always sympathetic, conversion of a 17th-century convent. Each room is different in size and decor – the larger ones are lovely, a couple of smaller ones less so. Most have handsome wood floors and heavy fabrics; one has a bedhead made of tiles.

Hotel Dom Luís
LUXURY HOTEL €€

(☑ 268 622 710; www.elpohoteis.com; Av de Badajoz; s/d €52/62; ✳🛜) This modern establishment is slightly tattered around the edges. There are two sections: older rooms with worn carpets and traditional Alentejano decor, and newer rooms with contemporary decor in browns and beiges. It's 700m west of the centre, just outside the town walls and near the aqueduct.

Eating

A Coluna
PORTUGUESE €€

(☑ 268 623 728; Rua do Cabrito 11; mains €7-11, tourist menu €10; ⊙ lunch & dinner Wed-Mon) Fancying itself as the town's 'gourmet' number, this tavern-cavern offers an elegant space with *azulejos* on the walls. Pork and *bacalhau* (cod fish) dishes are its forte.

O Lagar
PORTUGUESE €€

(☑ 966 038 995; Rua Nova da Vedoria 7; mains €8-15; ☺ lunch & dinner Fri-Wed) Smart and buzzing, O Lagar dishes up excellent regional cooking, with good-value, high-quality *açordas* (a kind of bread soup) and *bacalhau*. Service can be a bit slow, but it's a pleasant enough place to linger over a meal.

Adega Regional
PORTUGUESE €€

(☑ 268 623 009; www.adegaregional-elvas.com; Rua João Casqueiro 22B; mains €9.50-14; ☺ lunch & dinner Wed-Mon) Locals love this small place where it's all about the food – lashings of *plumas de porco preto* (pork) and *marisco* (shellfish) dishes of all kinds, or a good-value three-course daily meal for €10.

🛍 Shopping

The thing to buy here is Ameixas de Elvas, a type of sweet pickled plum, said to be author Agatha Christie's favourite dessert.

ℹ Information

Banco Espirito Santo & ATM (☑ 268 939 240; Praça da República) One of many banks with ATMs around town.

District Hospital (☑ 268 637 700; Av de Badajoz) Opposite the Pousada de Santa Luzia.

Espaço Internet (Praça da República; ☺ 10am-7pm Mon-Fri) Free internet access. Enter from Rua dos Sapateiros.

Police Station (☑ 268 639 470; Rua Isabel Maria Picão)

Post Office (Rua da Cadeia; ☺ 8.30am-6pm Mon-Fri, 9am-12.30pm Sat)

Turismo (☑ 268 622 236; www.cm-elvas.pt; Praça da República; ☺ 9am-7pm Apr-Oct, 9am-6pm Mon-Fri, 9am-12.30pm & 2-5.30pm Sat & Sun Nov-Mar) Usually has a town map and pamphlets.

ℹ Getting There & Around

Drivers be aware – it's possible to find central parking, but not always easy; if you don't like narrow one-way streets, park on the outskirts of town (or just inside Portas de Olivença).

The **bus station** is outside the city walls, on the road to Spain. It's an 800m walk mostly uphill (or a €6 taxi ride) to the main *praça*. Popular bus routes:

Estremoz (around €10, 45 minutes, one weekdays) Or change at Vila Viçosa.

Évora (around €13, 1¼ to 1¾ hours, four weekdays)

Portalegre (around €14, 1¼ hours, two weekdays)

Faro (€21, 6½ hours, one daily)

Lisbon (€17.10, 3¼ to 3½ hours, seven daily)

Portalegre

POP 15,200 / ELEV 520M

Alto Alentejo's capital, Portalegre, is bunched up on a hilltop at the foot of Serra de São Mamede. This pretty, whitewashed, ochre-edged city makes for a charming, low-key, off-the-beaten-track experience. It's worth stopping here at the very least, en route to mountaintop villages.

Inside the city walls are faded baroque mansions and relics of the town's textile-manufacturing heyday – wool was the mainstay in the 18th century, cork in the 19th century, and tapestries in the 20th. Even today, Portalegre stays true to its legacy of natty threads – the Portalegre Tapestry Factory still produces extraordinary tapestries of artworks by famous modern artists, and there's a fabulous museum showcasing the work.

The city is known for its jazzfest which takes place every February, and the International Theatre Festival where thespians strut their stuff each November.

◉ Sights

The town's former glory is recorded in stone: faded 17th-century baroque town houses and mansions dot Rua 19 de Junho to the southeast.

Sé
CHURCH

(☺ 2.30-6pm Tue, 9am-noon & 2.30-6pm Wed-Sun) In 1550 Portalegre became the seat of a new diocese and soon got its own cathedral. The pyramid-pointed, twin-towered 18th-century facade, with a broken clock, sombrely presides over the whitewashed Praça do Município. The sacristy contains an array of fine *azulejos*.

Castelo
CASTLE

(☺ 9.30am-1pm & 2.30-6pm Tue-Sun) FREE Portalegre's castle, off Rua do Carmo, dates from the time of Dom Dinis. Its three restored towers offer good views across the town. In the 1930s, part of the castle walls were destroyed to open the streets to traffic. In 2006, a controversial renovation was completed – a modern wooden structure now links the

Portalegre

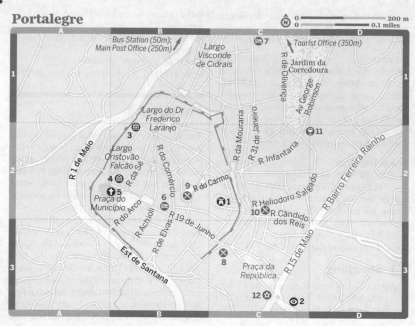

Portalegre

◎ Sights
1 Castelo	C2
2 Manufactura de Tapeçarias de Portalegre	C3
3 Museu da Tapeçaria de Portalegre Guy Fino	B2
4 Museu Municipal	B2
5 Sé	B2

🛏 Sleeping
6 Hotel Mansão Alto Alentejo	B2
7 Pensão Nova	C1

🍴 Eating
8 O Poeiras Restaurante	C3
9 Restaurante-Cervejaria Santos	B2
10 Solar do Forcado	C2

🍷 Drinking & Nightlife
11 Crisfal	D2

🎭 Entertainment
12 Centro de Artes do Espectáculo de Portalegre	C3

walls of the castle to the tower. Designed by Portuguese architect Cândido Chuva Gomes, the you-either-love-it-or-hate-it construction is intended to resemble rocks, marking the difference between the 13th and 21st centuries. There is a temporary exhibition gallery on the 1st floor.

Museu da Tapeçaria de Portalegre Guy Fino
MUSEUM
(Rua da Figueira 9; admission €2; ⊘ 9.30am-1pm & 2.30-6pm Tue-Sun) If there's one thing you must visit in Portalegre, it's this splendid museum. Opened in 2001, it contains brilliant contemporary creations from Portalegre's unique tapestry factory. It's named

after the factory founder, who created an innovative 'stitch' by hand weaving. The museum shows a selection of the 7000 colours of thread used.

French tapestry artist Jean Lurçat at first dismissed the technique, until the factory made a copy of one of his works – a cockerel – and asked him to identify the one made at Aubusson, in France. He chose the perfect Portalegre copy – you can see them juxtaposed in this museum. The huge tapestries are very expensive, and the museum includes works by some of the most famous names in Portuguese 20th-century art, including Almada Negreiros and Vieira de Silva. They are all hand-signed on the back by the artist, attesting their quality and authenticity.

Real aficionados can see the women at work at the **factory** (☑245 301 400; www.mtportalegre.pt; Rua de Iria Gonçalves 2) where they are made (its walls are also adorned with fabulous examples). Photography is prohibited and advance reservations are required.

Museu José Regio
MUSEUM

(Rua Poeta José Régio; ⊙9.30am-1pm & 2.30-6pm Tue-Sun) This small museum is in poet José Regio's former house, and shows his magpie-like collection of popular religious art, with around 400 Christ figures. There are lots of rustic ceramics from Coimbra, which 18th-century migrant workers used to swap for clothes.

Museu Municipal
MUSEUM

(Rua José Maria da Rosa; admission €2; ⊙9.30am-1pm & 2-6pm) The local museum exhibits religious art of the 17th and 18th centuries, including paintings and furniture from the Convento de Santa Clara (now a public library) and Monastero de São Bernardo (now the National Guard School), along with private collections.

⌂ Sleeping

Hotel Mansão Alto Alentejo
GUESTHOUSE €

(☑245 202 290; www.mansaoaltoalentejo.com.pt; Rua 19 de Junho 59; s/d €35/45; ✸) The stone staircase is steep, but it's the pick of the bunch for its small, bright rooms with traditional hand-painted Alentejan furniture and charming lounge area. Good, central location.

Pensão Nova
GUESTHOUSE €

(☑245 331 212; fax 245 330 493; Rua 31 de Janeiro 30; s/d €25/40; ✸) For real budget travellers, this is the town's only option. Pensão Nova is looking long in the tooth these days: small, slightly fuggy rooms crammed with large pieces of wooden furniture. If it's full, guests are housed in a similar abode, Pensão Residencial São Pedro.

★Convento da Provença
LUXURY HOTEL €€

(☑245 337 104; www.provenca.pt; Monte Paleiros; s/d/ste €85/95/105; ✸ ☎ ☲) Mother Superior may not have approved of this luxury sleeping option, but *we* do. This renovated former convent has an austere white exterior, but its interior is another story. Shiny sabres and suits of armour fill the grand lounge room and entrance hall. The spacious rooms and suites are decked out in masculine hues

and stylish wooden trimmings, and all have lovely green views. There's a massive games room (and kids' nursery). Light meals are available with advance warning. The Convento is located north of Portalegre at Monte Paleiros on the road to Marvão.

Quinta da Dourada
RURAL INN €€

(☑937 218 654; www.quintadadourada.com; d €75-85; P ✸ ☎ ☲) Seven kilometres northeast of Portalegre, in the Parque Natural da Serra de São Mamede, this picture-perfect, modern-looking place is surrounded by glorious vegetation – lime trees and flowers. The individual rooms are smartly furnished and have granite floors.

✕ Eating

Portalegre has some reasonable restaurants. Praça da República is the place for cheap eats.

★Solar do Forcado
PORTUGUESE €€

(☑245 330 866; Rua Cândido dos Reis 14; mains €7.50-13; ⊙lunch & dinner Mon-Fri, dinner Sat) The current owner and his father (sadly, recently deceased) were former *forcados* (performers of a specific style of Portuguese bullfighting), as attested by the many photos and paraphernalia that cover the walls of this cosy spot. It goes without saying that meat lovers should charge in here for hefty regional delights of *bovino* (bull meat) plus wild pig and deer, and great *doces conventuais* (convent desserts). Incredible value.

O Poeiras Restaurante
PORTUGUESE €€

(☑245 201 862; Praça da República 9-15; mains €8.50-13) This great value, popular restaurant on the plaza has a meaty smell and whips up good Alentejano cuisine, and chicken *piri-piri* (chilli).

Restaurante-Cervejaria Santos
PORTUGUESE €€

(☑245 203 066; Largo Serpa Pinto 4; mains €7.50-10; ⊙lunch & dinner Thu-Tue) Portalegre's only alfresco eating spot. Has good regional choices, including *migas* and the like.

♙ Drinking & Nightlife

For outdoor drinking, take your pick of the spots around Praça da República and to a lesser extent Largo do Dr Frederico Laranjo.

Crisfal
CLUB

(Av George Robinson) This renovated former cinema is the place to join the late-night disco crowd.

THE ALENTEJO PORTALEGRE

☆ Entertainment

**Centro de Artes do
Espectáculo de Portalegre**   THEATRE
(☑ 245 307 498; www.caeportalegre.blogspot.com; Praça da República 39) Overlooking Praça da República is Portalegre's major performance space, hosting fado singers, rock, jazz and acoustic groups, as well as dance and theatre. Ask at the tourist office for current shows.

ℹ Information

The Millennium, BPI and Montepio banks all have ATMs.

Hospital (☑ 245 301 000) About 400m north of town.

Main Post Office (Av da Liberdade, cnr Rua Alexandre Herculano; ☉ 8.30am-6pm Mon-Fri, 9am-12.30pm Sat) About 250m north of the Rossio.

Police Station (☑ 245 300 620; Praça da República) Just outside Porta de Alegrete.

Turismo (☑ 245 307 445; Rua Guilherme Gomes Fernandes 22; ☉ 9.30am-1pm & 2.30-6pm) Helpful staff dole out information and a town map. Also free internet access.

ℹ Getting There & Around

BUS

The **bus station** (☑ 245 330 723) has regular services to the following destinations:

Lisbon (around €19, 4½ hours, one daily)

Estremoz (€8, 50 minutes, one daily weekdays)

Évora (€8, 1½ hours, one daily weekdays)

Elvas (around €7, 1½ hours, two daily weekdays)

Marvão (around €3.50, 45 minutes, two to five weekdays)

Castelo de Vide (€2.60-3.35, two to four weekdays)

TAXI

There are sometimes **taxis** (☑ 245 202 375) outside the bus station and in the nearby Rossio.

Castelo de Vide

POP 4100 / ELEV 570M

High above lush, rolling countryside, Castelo de Vide is one of Portugal's most attractive and underrated villages. Its fine hilltop vantage point, dazzlingly white houses, flower-lined lanes and proud locals are reason alone to visit. There aren't many attractions in town, but there don't need to be. Absorb this pleasant place for a day and a night;

at dusk and early morning you can experience the town at its most disarming. You'll see elderly women crocheting on doorsteps, children playing in the narrow streets, and neighbours chatting out of upper-storey windows.

Castelo de Vide is famous for its crystal-clear mineral water, which spouts out of numerous pretty public fountains; several of these are surrounded by hedged gardens.

◎ Sights

Old Town & Judiaria   HISTORIC SITE
By the castle is a small *judiaria* – the former Jewish district. A sizeable community of Jews settled here in the 12th century, then larger waves came in the early 15th century after the expulsion of the Jews from Spain. At first they didn't have an exclusive district, but Dom Pedro I restricted them to specific quarters. The highlight of this area is the **synagogue and museum** (☉ 9.30am-1pm & 2-5.30pm Sep-May, to 6pm Jun-Aug).

Reopened in 2009 after being converted into a museum, the site comprises the original synagogue – two rooms (one for women and one for men), a wooden tabernacle and Holy Ark for Torah scrolls. The remaining rooms (part of the original village home from which the synagogue was originally converted) house a superb collection of items illustrating the history of the Jewish communities of Castelo de Vide. Following Manuel I's convert-or-leave edict in 1496, many Jews returned to Spain, though some headed to Évora.

Castelo   CASTLE
(☉ 9.30am-1pm & 2-5.30pm, to 6pm Jun-Aug) **FREE** Originally Castelo de Vide's inhabitants lived within the castle's sturdy outer walls; even now there remains a small inner village with a church, the 17th-century **Igreja da Nossa Senhora da Alegria**. You can take in some brilliant views from here over the town's red roofs, surrounded by green and olive hills.

The castle, built by Dom Dinis and his brother Dom Afonso between 1280 and 1365, is topped by a 12m-high brick tower, thought to be the oldest part. Feel like royalty and catch the great views from the roof of the tower's fine vaulted hall (the hall itself is unfortunately covered in graffiti).

Fonte da Vila   FOUNTAIN
In a pretty square just below and east of the *judiaria* is the worn-smooth 16th-century

Castelo de Vide

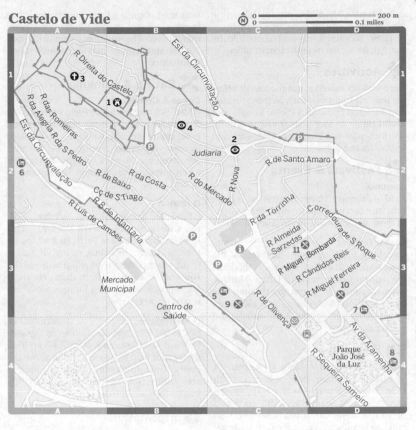

Castelo de Vide

◉ Sights
1 Castelo	B1
2 Fonte da Vila	C2
3 Igreja da Nossa Senhora da Alegria	A1
4 Old Town & Judiaria	B2
Synagogue & Museum	(see 4)

🛏 Sleeping
5 Casa Amarela	C3

6 Casa de Hóspedes Machado	A2
7 Casa de Hóspedes Melanie	D3
8 Casa do Parque	D4

🍴 Eating
9 Doces & Companhia	C3
10 O Alentejano	D3
11 O Miguel	C3

marble Fonte da Vila, with a washing area. This, along with several other fountains in the village, spouts the delicious mineral water for which Castelo de Vide is known.

Anta dos Coureleiros & Menhir da Meada   MEGALITHS
In the wild, boulder-strewn landscape around Castelo de Vide are dozens of an-cient megaliths. The two most impressive are the Anta da Melriça, northwest of town, and the 7m-high Menhir da Meada, around 13km north of town. This is supposedly the tallest menhir in the Iberian Peninsula – a large phallus for keeping the fields fertile and acting as a territory marker (one of the few believed to have done both jobs). The so

called Parque Megalítico dos Coureleiros is a collection of five different arrangements.

These megaliths are best accessible by car. Ask for a map from the tourist office.

🏃 Activities

Keen walkers should ask at the tourist office for walking trail maps such as those headed Torrinha and Serra de S Paulo. These wonderful three- to four-hour sojourns around the area pass old churches, fountains and megaliths and dolmens.

🎉 Festivals & Events

Carnaval   CARNIVAL
Held in February/March, this festival is great fun, with everyone out to watch processions of those in their home-made fancy dress.

Easter Festival   EASTER
Castelo de Vide's big bash – and one of the most traditional of its festivals – is the four-day fair on Good Friday to Easter Monday when a couple of lambs go through the highs and lows of blessings and slaughter. Processions, folk dances, band music and revelry take place.

🛏 Sleeping

Casa de Hóspedes Melanie   GUESTHOUSE €
(✆245 901 632; Largo do Paça Novo 3; s/d/tr €25/35/45; ❄) Situated near a leafy square, this clean spot is up there with Portugal's best-value accommodation. It has five neat and light rooms with cork-tile floors. Longer stayers are invited to enjoy the roof terrace.

Casa de Hóspedes Machado   GUESTHOUSE €
(✆245 901 515; Rua Luís de Camões 33; s/d/tr €25/30/35) On the western edge of town, this friendly and efficiently run place has airy, modern and spotless rooms. There's a small, shared kitchen and outdoor patio.

Casa do Parque   GUESTHOUSE €
(✆245 901 250; www.casadoparque.net; Av da Aramenha 37; s €35-45, d €40-65) Overlooking the park, and in a historic building (a former girls' school – even the receptionist has a school matron's manner), this spot has inviting, slightly worn rooms with tile floors and big windows. Prices are very changeable.

Casa Amarela   GUESTHOUSE €€
(✆245 905 878; www.casaamarelath.com; Praça Dom Pedro V 11; s €65-70, d €70-120, ste €140) This beautifully restored 18th-century building on the main square, with views over the *praça*, is a luxurious choice. It has stone staircases and antiques-filled common areas. The 10 rooms drip with rich fabrics and feature massive, marble-filled bathrooms.

🍴 Eating & Drinking

Doces & Companhia   PATISSERIE €
(✆245 901 408; Praça Dom Pedro V 6; mains €3-5; ☺breakfast, lunch & dinner Mon-Sat) Serving great cakes and ice creams, this is the place to ease your sugar cravings. Also on offer are set-menu lunches (around €8) and a lovely terrace (head through the restaurant to find it).

O Miguel   PORTUGUESE €€
(✆245 901 882; Rua Almeida Sarzedas 32-34; mains €9-11; ☺lunch & dinner Mon-Sat) This long-standing down-to-earth spot whips up regional dishes including *migas de batata* (potato dumplings), tripe and traditional flavours of the season (or festival) in a convivial atmosphere. Set lunches for around €9 are served on weekdays.

O Alentejano   PORTUGUESE €€
(✆245 901 355; Largos dos Mártires de República 14; mains €7-14; ☺lunch & dinner Tue-Sun) This pretty spot has the prime location above the pretty Fonte do Montorinho. It is a reasonable choice, serving traditional, if slightly tourist-focused, cuisine.

ℹ Information

Caixa Geral de Depósitos (✆245 339 100; Praça Valéncia de Alcántara)
Centro de Saúde (✆245 900 160; EN246-1) On the southern exit out of town.
Police Station (✆245 901 314; Av da Aramenha)
Post Office (Rua de Olivença)
Turismo (✆245 908 227; www.cm-castelo-vide.pt; Praça Dom Pedro V; ☺9am-12.30pm & 2-5.30pm winter, 9am-1pm & 3-6pm summer) Stocks some reasonable printed matter, including maps and leaflets.

ℹ Getting There & Away

BUS
Buses (✆245 901 510) run to/from Portalegre (€2.60 to €3.35, 20 minutes, one to three daily), and Lisbon (€17, 4¼ hours, two daily). For Marvão you must change in Portagem.

All buses stop beside the garden (Praça Valéncia de Alcántara). Ask at the *turismo* for bus times.

Taxis (☎ 245 901 271) are available from outside the *turismo*.

Marvão

POP 150 / ELEV 862M

On a jutting crag high above the surrounding countryside, the narrow lanes of Marvão feel like a retreat far removed from the settlements below. The whitewashed village of picturesque tiled roofs and bright flowers has marvellous views, a splendid castle and a handful of low-key guesthouses and restaurants. Since the 16th century, the town has struggled to keep inhabitants, and today the friendly locals survive mainly on tourism. It's worth spending a night here.

Arriving by car or bus you'll approach Portas de Ródão, one of the four village gates, opening onto Rua de Cima, which has several shops and restaurants. Drivers can park outside or enter this gate and park in Largo de Olivença, just below Rua de Cima.

History

Not surprisingly, this garrison town just 10km from the Spanish frontier has long been a prized possession. Romans settled here, and Christian Visigoths were on the scene when the Moors arrived in 715. It was probably the Moorish lord of Coimbra, Emir Maraun, who gave the place its present name.

In 1160 Christians took control. In 1226 the town received a municipal charter, the walls were extended to encompass the whole summit, and the castle was rebuilt by Dom Dinis.

Marvão's importance in the defence against the Castilians was highlighted during the 17th-century War of Restoration, when further defences were added. But by the 1800s it had lost its way, a garrison town without a garrison, and this lack of interest is why so many 15th- and 16th- century buildings have been preserved. Its last action was at the centre of the tug-of-war between the Liberals and Royalists; in 1833 the Liberals used a secret entrance to seize the town – the only time Marvão has ever been captured.

◉ Sights & Activities

You can make a brilliant 30km round-trip via Santo António das Areias and Beirã, visiting nearby *antas* (dolmens). Follow the *'antas'* signs through a fabulously quiet landscape of cork trees and rummaging pigs. Some megaliths are right by the roadside, while others require a 300m-to-500m walk. Be sure to bring refreshments: there's no village en route. You can continue north of Beirã to visit the megaliths in the Castelo de Vide area.

Castelo
CASTLE

(⊙ 24hr) FREE The formidable castle, built into the rock at the western end of the village, dates from the end of the 13th century, but most of what you see today was built in the 17th century. The views from the battlements are staggering. There's a huge vaulted cistern (still full of water) near the entrance and it's landscaped with hedges and flowerbeds. You can walk around the town on the castle walls. At the time of research there was talk of charging an entrance fee and providing maps with important highlights.

Museu Municipal
MUSEUM

(adult €1.30; ⊙ 9am-12.30pm & 2-5.30pm Tue-Sun) Just southeast of the castle, the Igreja de Santa Maria provides graceful surroundings for the small museum. At the time of research, the museum was reorganising its (previously) scattergun displays of muskets and bayonets, medieval grave markers, carved stonework dating from the 3rd millennium BC, costumes and Roman pottery shards.

Casa da Cultura
CULTURAL CENTRE

(Largo do Pelourinho; ⊙ 9.30am-1pm & 2-5.30pm) FREE In a restored building, this cultural centre hosts changing exhibitions, and you can check out the rustic upstairs courtroom, dating from 1809. There's also a small handicrafts shop on site (in what was a former prison).

Cidade de Ammaia
MUSEUM

(admission €2; ⊙ 9am-1pm & 2-5pm Mon-Fri, 10am-1pm & 2-5pm Sat & Sun) This excellent little Roman museum lies between Castelo de Vide and Marvão in São Salvador de Aramenha. From São Salvador head 700m south along the Portalegre road, then turn left, following the signs to Ammaia.

In the 1st century AD this area was a huge Roman city called Ammaia, flourishing from the area's rich agricultural produce (especially oil, wine and cereals). Although evidence was found (and some destroyed) in the 19th century, it wasn't until 1994 that thorough digs began.

Here you can see some of the finds, including engraved lintels and tablets, jewellery, coins and some incredibly well-preserved glassware. You can also follow paths across the fields to where the forum and spa once stood and see several impressive columns.

Walking Trail
WALKING TOUR

Ask at the tourist office for instructions on the interesting 7.5km circuit walk from Marvão to Portagem via Abegoa and Fonte Souto (or 2.5km direct to Portagem), following a medieval stone-paved route. Note: the return journey is steep.

🛏 Sleeping

Casa da João
GUESTHOUSE €

(☑ 245 993 437; Travessa de Santiago 1; r €30) One of two budget options in town, this offers two spotless double rooms with a shared bathroom.

Casa Rosado
GUESTHOUSE €

(☑ 963 838 532, 245 993 491; casa.rosado@sapo.pt; Rua das Portas da Vila 14; r €25) These budget digs – two rooms – are as basic (but clean) as they come, and have their own bathroom and good views.

★ Quinta do Barrieiro
GUESTHOUSE €€

(☑ 964 054 935, 245 964 308; www.quintado barrieiro.com; r from €85, 6-person apt €225; P ❄ 🗪 🎇) Special occasion anyone? Bah! You shouldn't need an excuse to come to this rural tourism abode. Home to two creative Portuguese – a sculptor and an architect – this superb place, made up of several *casinhas* (little houses) and rooms, provides comfort, creativity and the outdoors (there are some great walks around the property and to a dam).

The garden is full of the owner's sculptures, as are the light and airy communal living areas. The continental breakfasts are included (the fresh bread is delivered to your accommodation – all have kitchenettes). Ring for directions as it's 13km from Marvão, and 10km from Portalegre.

Hotel El Rei Dom Manuel
HOTEL €€

(☑ 245 909 150; www.turismarvao.pt; Largo da Olivença; s €40-65, d €50-95; 🗪) This is the pick for reliability. This charming, friendly and professional hotel has comfortable rooms with tiled floors, drapes and puffy pillows. The best rooms are the suites-with-a-view. Breakfast is served in the hotel restaurant.

Casa da Árvore
GUESTHOUSE €€

(☑ 245 993 854; I; Rua Dr Matos Magalhães 3; s/d €50/60) This elegant guesthouse has five country-home-style rooms and an attractive, comfortable lounge area with a stunning view. It's good value and great for kicking back in after pounding the streets.

Dom Dinis
GUESTHOUSE €€

(☑ 245 909 028; www.ter-domdinis.com; Rua Dr Matos Magalhães 7; s €40, d €60-70, with terrace €90; ❄ 🗪) Dom Dinis has eight smallish, but (refurbished) modern bedrooms decked out in masculine hues. The largest has a terrace with lovely views over the castle walls.

🍴 Eating

Surprisingly, for such a nice spot with a plethora of places to stay, Marvão is light on for great-quality restaurant options – the town's two main restaurants are the large **Bar-Restaurante Varanda do Alentejo** (☑ 245 993 272; Praça do Pelourinho 1; mains €8-12; ⏱ lunch & dinner Mon-Sat, lunch Sun), undergoing renovation at time of research, and **Restaurante Casa do Povo** (☑ 245 993 160; Rua de Cima; mains €8-13; ⏱ lunch & dinner Fri-Wed). From past experience, these serve up just passable dishes to the summer and weekend crowds. If cuisine rates over views, then you're better off heading to Portagem on the Rio Sever, several kilometres down the road.

Restaurante Sever
PORTUGUESE €€

(☑ 245 993 318; Portagem; mains €10-17.50; ⏱ lunch & dinner) The pick of local restaurants, this smart place is in a beautiful location, just over the bridge in Portagem, on the Rio Sever. It comes highly recommended by locals and serves first-class Alentejan cuisine. Specials include *perna de borrego do forno* (roast leg of lamb, €17.50). For both price and quality, it's at the higher end of the scale.

ℹ Information

There's a Caixa Geral do Depósitos bank (with ATM) on Rua do Espírito Santo. Access free internet at the Casa da Cultura (p239). After the gate entrance (not to be confused with a small information booth on the left as you enter the walls) is the helpful **turismo** (☑ 245 993 456; www.cm-marvao.pt; Rua de Baixo; ⏱ 9am-12.30pm & 2-5.30pm), which also has free internet.

ℹ Getting There & Away

BUS

Two buses run on weekdays between Portalegre and Marvão (45 minutes). There is a service to/from Castelo de Vide, but it may require a change of bus at Portagem, a major road junction 7.5km northeast.

TAXI
A **taxi** (☎ 245 993 272; Praça do Pelourinho) to Castelo de Vide costs around €15.

BAIXO ALENTEJO

Mértola
POP 2000

Spectacularly set on a rocky spur, high above the peaceful Rio Guadiana, the cobbled streets of medieval Mértola are a delightful place to roam. A small but imposing castle stands high, overlooking the jumble of dazzlingly white houses and a picturesque church that was once a mosque. A long bout of economic stagnation at this remote town has left many traces of Islamic occupation intact, so much so that Mértola is considered a *vila museu* (open-air museum). To let Mértola's magic do its thing, you need more than a quick visit here.

Mértola comes to life every two years in May (dates change but it's uneven numbered years) during the town's Islamic Festival, when it is decorated to resemble a souk.

Music, handicrafts and festivities continue for several days.

History

Mértola follows the usual pattern of settlement in this area: Phoenician traders, who sailed up the Guadiana, then Carthaginians, then Romans. Its strategic position, as the northernmost port on the Guadiana, and the final destination for many Mediterranean routes, led the Romans to develop Mértola (naming it Myrtilis) as a major agricultural and mineral-exporting centre. Cereals and olive oil arrived from Beja and copper and other metals from Aljustrel and São Domingos. It was a rich merchant town.

Later the Moors, who called it Martulah and made it a regional capital, further fortified Mértola and built a mosque. Dom Sancho II and the Knights of the Order of Santiago captured the site in 1238. But then, as commercial routes shifted to the Tejo, Mértola declined. When the last steamboat service to Vila Real de Santo António ended and the copper mines of São Domingos (the area's main employer) closed in 1965, its port days were over.

⊙ Sights

Stepping through the thick outer walls into the old town makes you feel as if you have stepped back in time. It's enchanting just

---

MÉRTOLA'S MUSEUMS

Mértola's wonderful group of **museums** (1 museum adult/concession €2/1, combined ticket €5/2.50; 9am-12.30pm & 2-5.30pm Tue-Sun) have the same opening hours and form an excellent tour of the town.

Casa Romana (Roman House; Largo Luís de Camões) In the cellar of the *câmara municipal* is the enchanting Casa Romana. This clever display allows the visitor to walk 'through' the foundations of the Roman house upon which the building rests, and brings it to life with its small collection of pots, sculpture and other artefacts.

Museu Islâmico (Largo de Misericordia) At the southern end of the old town, the Islamic Museum is a small but dramatic display of inscribed funerary stones, jewellery, pots and jugs from the 11th to 13th centuries.

Museu de Arte Sacra (Museum of Ecclesiastical Art; Largo da Misericórdia) Housed in the former Misericórdia church, the Museu de Arte Sacra exhibits religious statuettes from the 16th to 18th centuries and several impressive 16th-century retables from the village and castle churches; some portray the battle against the Moors.

Museu Paleocristão (Palaeo-Christian Museum; Rossio do Carmo) North of the old town is this museum, which features a partly reconstructed line of 6th-century Roman columns and poignant funerary stones, some of which are beautifully carved with birds, hearts and wreaths. It was the site of a huge Palaeo-Christian basilica, and the adjacent cemetery was used over the centuries by both Roman-era Christians and medieval Moors.

to wander around the snoozy, sun-baked streets (but take plenty of water).

Castelo & Torre de Menagem (Nucleo do Castelo) CASTLE

(⊘9am-12.30pm & 2-5.30pm Tue-Sun) Above the parish church looms Mértola's fortified castle, most of which dates from the 13th century. It was built upon Moorish foundations next to an Islamic residence, the *alcáçova* (citadel), which itself overlaid the Roman forum. For centuries the castle was considered western Iberia's most impregnable fortress.

From its prominent tower, the Torre de Menagem, and the walls, there are ultrafabulous views – the *alcáçova* is on one side, and the old town and the river on the other.

Largo Luís de Camões PLAZA

This is the administrative heart of the old town, a picturesque square lined with orange trees, with the *câmara municipal* at its western end. To reach the *largo* (small square), enter the old town and keep to the left at the fork in the road.

Torre do Relógio TOWER

This little clock tower, topped with a stork's nest and overlooking the Rio Guadiana, is northeast of Largo Luís de Camões. Alongside it is a municipal building with a rooftop worthy of Van Gogh.

Igreja Matriz CHURCH

(Rua da Igreja; ⊘Tue-Sun) **FREE** Mértola's striking parish church – square, flat-faced and topped with whimsical little conical decorations – is most known because in a former incarnation it was a mosque, one of the few in the country to have survived the Reconquista. It was reconsecrated as a church in the 13th century. Look out for an unwhitewashed cavity in the wall, behind the altar; in former times this served as the mosque's *mihrab* (prayer niche).

Note also the goats, lions and other figures carved around the peculiar Gothic portal and the typically Moorish horseshoe arch in the north door.

Torre do Rio TOWER

At the river's edge, near its confluence with the Ribeira de Oeiras, is the ruined, Roman-era Torre do Rio (River Tower), which once guarded the vital port.

Convento de São Francisco GARDENS

(☑286 612 119; www.conventomertola.com/en; admission €3; ⊘10am-6pm Sun) ✏ This 400-year-old former convent, across the Ribeira de Oeiras, 500m southwest of Largo Vasco da Gama, has been owned since 1980 by Dutch artist Geraldine Zwanikken and her family. In a true labour of love, they have gradually transformed the ruins into an extraordinary place, most simply described as an organic nature reserve full of herbs, rare plants and flowers, watered by a restored Islamic irrigation system. Locals have their vegetable gardens here.

It's also an art gallery – highlights include Geraldine's modern artworks and, gracing the former chapel (if they are not in temporary exhibitions elsewhere), the kinetic installations of renowned artist Christiaan Zwanikken. The nearby riverside is devoted to specially constructed nests for storks and lesser kestrels.

🏃 Activities

You can rent kayaks for trips down the lazy river at **Beira Rio Náutica** (☑286 611 190; www.beirario.pt; per hr/day from €5/15). It also offers boat tours (minimum four; €10 per person).

Parque Natural do Vale do Guadiana NATURE RESERVE

Created in 1995, this zone of hills, plains and deep valleys around Serpa and Mértola shelters the Rio Guadiana, one of Portugal's largest and most important rivers. Among its rich variety of flora and fauna are several rare or endangered species, including the black stork (sightings of the shy creatures are rare), lesser kestrel (most likely around Castro Verde and at Convento do São Francisco), Bonelli's eagle, royal owl, grey kite, horned viper and Iberian toad. The park also has many prehistoric remains. Ask at the **park headquarters** (☑286 610 090; Rua Don Sancho II; ⊘9am-12.30pm & 2-5.30pm Mon-Fri, 10am-1pm & 3-6pm Sat), in smart premises by the *câmara municipal,* for details of walking trails and where to spot wildlife – they can advise you and provide you with a basic map.

🛏 Sleeping

The *turismo* has a brochure listing more accommodation options in rural areas.

Casa da Tia Amalia HOSTEL €

(☑965 052 379, 918 794 579; www.mertola-hostel-low-cost-casa-da-tia-amalia.com; Além Rio 16; dm/d with shared bathroom €14/15, d €34) A welcome addition to Mértola's budget options, this hostel was just opening at the time of research and should be worth checking out. Homely, bright rooms await. Prices are higher during festivals and special occasions.

Residencial Beira Rio   GUESTHOUSE €
(☑286 611 190; www.beirario.pt; Rua Dr Afonso Costa 108; s/d/tr from €30/40/55; ✸ ⬙) Beira Rio offers simple, colourful rooms. Those with river views are slightly more expensive but they have breezy terraces.

Hotel Museu   HOTEL €€
(☑286 612 003; www.hotelmuseu.com; Rua Dr Afonso Costa 112; s €45, d €55-60; ✸ ⬙) This is the new sister of Beira Rio and is a more modern, neater option. Some rooms have lovely views; Roman ruins were found in the foundations and you and the public can visit (thus the hotel name).

Monte do Alhinho   RURAL INN €€
(☑286 655 115; www.omontedoalhinho.com/home. htm; Estrada Nacional 265; s/d €50/60; ✸ ✸) Try the appealing Monte do Alhinho, 8km from Mértola on the road to São Domingos. This tastefully converted farmhouse-cum-hacienda has massive rooms, fluffy white towels, and a superb kitchen, where breakfast – an onslaught of Alentejan delights – is served. Discounts apply for long-term stays.

Convento de São Francisco   GUESTHOUSE €€
(☑286 612 119; www.conventomertola.com; apt €70) ✐ For those who are happy with rustic and a more laissez-faire approach, this former convent overlooking Mértola and the Rio Guadiana is a lovely spot for hardier, artistic and/or tranquil souls. The fully equipped apartments are converted from former stables, arteliers and the like. There's a cottage (solar powered) on the grounds for those looking for complete seclusion. Single-night stays are not offered. An artist-in-residence program is also available.

✖ Eating

Mértola's speciality is game, including *javali* (wild boar) and the regional pork dish *migas* – great labouring fuel, but perhaps heavier than necessary for sightseeing.

Self-caterers should head to the **mercado municipal** (Municipal Market; Praça Vasco da Gama; ⊙8am-4pm Mon-Sat), which sells fresh fruit and vegetables and other produce. There's also a wonderful unsigned **bakery** (Rua Dr Afonso Costa 96), where you can buy fresh-baked bread (go early or in the evening for hot rolls).

DON'T MISS

ENTRADAS

The tiny village of Entradas is a photostop must. Entradas's main street features tiny, whitewashed homes and is a wonderful example of a working rural village. The name is said to have come from the fact that it was the gateway *(entrada)* to the Campos de Ourique, sought-after winter pastures for herds and herders. It has a stunning rural museum, **Museu da Ruralidade** (open 10am to 12.30pm and 2pm to 7pm Wednesday to Sunday, plus 2pm to 7pm Tuesday), which displays many elements of local cultural and agricultural practices.

Café-Restaurante Alentejo   PORTUGUESE €
(☑286 655 133; Moreanes; mains €7-11; ⊙lunch & dinner Tue-Sun) This attractive place in Moreanes, 10km from Mértola on the way to São Domingos, is almost a museum thanks to its antique exhibits (including the local clients themselves!) It serves great-value, hearty helpings of true Alentejan cuisine.

A Esquina   PORTUGUESE €€
(☑286 611 081; Rua Dr Afonso Costa 1; mains €10-15; ⊙10am-late) Several boars' heads mounted on the wall (not to mention the array of *presuntos* – hams hanging at the bar) attest to this eatery's hearty Alentejan cuisine, which is of high quality and served with gusto. It's situated on the roundabout into town.

Restaurante Alengarve   PORTUGUESE €€
(☑286 612 210; Av Aureliano Mira Fernandes; mains €9-14; ⊙lunch & dinner Thu-Tue) Run by the same family for over 40 years, this restaurant offers extremely consistent home-style Alentejan dishes.

O Brasileiro   PORTUGUESE €€
(Cerro de São Luís; mains €8-14; ⊙lunch & dinner) Set on a hill above Mertola, this pleasant spot serves great quality traditional cuisine. Known for its game dishes, including *javali* (wild pig) and *migas* (meat and bread stew) dishes.

🍷 Drinking & Nightlife

Lancelote Bar   BAR
(Rua Nossa Senhora da Conceição; ⊙9pm-4am) This vaguely medieval-feeling bar has friendly barkeeps and eclectic decor (colourful

paintings and a wall of skeleton keys), with a shady wooden terrace attached.

Alsafir
BAR

(☑286 618 049; Rua dos Combatentes da Grande Guerra 9; ⊘9pm-4am) A more tavern-like bar, Alsafir organises the occasional dance-party night.

🛍 Shopping

Oficina de Tecelagem
HANDICRAFTS

(Rua da Igreja; ⊘9am-5.30pm) A small wool-weaving workshop next to the *turismo,* this place hangs on by a thread through tourist sales of beautiful handmade products, including rugs and ponchos. Weaving is done onsite.

ℹ Information

Centro de Saúde (☑286 610 900; Cerca Carmo) Medical centre.

Millennium BCP Bank (Rua Dr Afonso Costa) Has an ATM. Three other banks are about town.

Police Station (☑286 612 127; Rua Dr Afonso Costa)

Post Office (Rua Alves Redol; ⊘9am-12.30pm & 2-5.30pm)

Turismo (☑286 610 109; Rua da Igreja 31; ⊘9am-12.30pm & 2-5.30pm mid-Sep–Jun, 9.30am-12.30pm & 2-6pm 1 Jul-15 Sep) Just inside the walled town, this place has a town map, list of *quartos* and free internet access. Also stocks brochures outlining nine different walks in the area, varying from one- to five-hour walks *(percurso pedestres).*

ℹ Getting There & Away

There are bus services by **Rede Expressos** (☑286 611 127; www.rede-expressos.pt) to Lisbon (€17, 4¼ hours, one daily), Beja (€10.80, one hour, one daily) and Vila Real de Santo António/Monte Gordo (€11, 1½ hours, one daily). **Rodoviária do Alentejo** (www.rodalentejo.pt)

offers a slower local Vila Real service (€6, two hours) via Alcoutim (50 minutes), which runs on Monday and Friday. It also has three weekday services to/from Beja (€5, 75 minutes).

São Domingos

The ghost town of São Domingos consists of desolate rows of small mining cottages. Once the mine closed in the 1960s, many miners emigrated or moved to Setúbal. But the nearby village is set amid beautiful countryside and next to a huge lake, where you can swim or rent a paddleboat or canoe.

The São Domingos mine itself is over 150 years old – though mining has been taking place here since Roman times – and is a deserted, eerie place to explore, with crumbling old offices and machinery. The rocks surrounding it are clouded with different colours, and the chief mine shaft is filled with deep, unnatural dark-blue water, shot through with it-doesn't-bear-thinking-about substances (read: contaminated). Locals have no fondness for the firm that established the mines, which kept its workers in line with a private police force.

A small museum, **Casa do Mineiro** (Rua Santa Isabel 31-33; ⊘9am-12.30pm & 2-5.30pm Mon-Fri, plus Sat & Sun Jun & Aug), recreates a typical miner's cottage.

Best visited with your own transport, São Domingos is 15km east of Mértola.

Castro Verde

The thriving village of Castro Verde has a big history. It was an ancient hill fort that soon grew into a settlement. The village is located near the site where the Battle of Ourique was fought (1139), when Afonso Henriques defeated the Moors and declared himself

---

BEJA'S LOVE LETTERS

A series of scandalous, passionate 17th-century love letters came from Beja, allegedly written by one of the convent's nuns, Mariana Alcoforado, to French cavalry officer Count Chamilly. The letters immortalised their love affair while the count was stationed here during the time of the Portuguese war with Spain.

The *Letters of a Portuguese Nun* first emerged in a French translation in 1669 and subsequently appeared in English and many other languages. Funnily enough, the originals were never found.

In 1972 three Portuguese writers, Maria Isabel Barreno, Maria Teresa Horta and Maria Velho da Costa, published *The Three Marias: New Portuguese Letters,* a collection of stories, poems and letters that formed a feminist update of the letters – for which they were prosecuted under the Salazar regime.

the first King of Portugal. In the 18th century Dom João V ordered the construction of the stunning Royal Basilica, whose tiles replicate the battle scenes. These days, its inhabitants are fiercely proud of the local traditions; their annual fair – Feira de Castro – is held on the third weekend of October.

It's worth the detour, especially if en route from Beja to Mértola or the Algarve.

◉ Sights & Activities

Basílica Real   CHURCH
(admission €1; ⊘9.30am-12.30pm & 2-5.30pm Wed-Sun) The 18th-century Royal Basilica features extraordinary gilded woodcarvings and a set of tiled panels depicting the Battle of Ourique. A small museum shows religious art. The highlight is the unique 13th-century silver head of Saint Fabian.

Largo da Feira Moinho de Vento   WINDMILL
This working museum proudly continues Castro Verde's old milling traditions in a surviving windmill that dates from the 1800s. The miller lives here so you can enter if it's in use.

Museu da Lucerna   MUSEUM
(⊘2-6pm Sat & Sun) FREE The building – a former factory – that houses this museum is as interesting as the beautiful collection of ancient Roman oil lamps from the 1st century that were found in the region. It also has exhibitions.

LPN Interpretative and Environmental Centre   BIRDWATCHING
(League for the Protection of Nature; www.lpn.pt; www.projectos.lpn.pt/birdscastroverde; ⊘9am-1pm & 2-6pm Tue-Sat) 𝄢 This environmental organisation is responsible for overseeing the protected area (85,000 hectares) known as the steppe – the flat, grassy land that distinguishes this area – and for implementing protection measures for the incredible steppe birds, including the great bustard and lesser kestrels. Staff at the information office are particularly welcoming; you can view displays and pick up information. This is *the* place for birdwatchers and it is also the departure point for walks in the steppe; ask at the office. It's located around 5km northeast of Castro Verde (on E802, the main road to Beja).

❶ Information

Turismo (📞286 328 149; www.cm-castro-verde.pt; ⊘9am-12.30pm & 2-5.30pm Tue-Fri,

10am-1pm & 3-6pm Sat & Sun) Has maps, information and a selection of local product for sale.

Beja
POP 21,600

Baixo Alentejo's principal town is easygoing, welcoming and untouristed, with a walled centre and some beguiling sights, all of which are within an easy walk of each other; these often follow old Roman routes. Often dismissed as Évora's 'plainer cousin', Beja has an inferiority complex, but it shouldn't. Its inexpensive guesthouses, quaint plazas and excellent eateries make it a relaxing place to stop and a very genuine Portuguese experience.

Beja is at the heart of the regional tourist area called Planície Dourada (Golden Plain) – meaning it's surrounded by a sea of wheat fields. On Saturday there's the bonus of a traditional market, spread around the castle.

History

Settlements have existed on the site of Beja since the Iron Age. Vestiges of this period have been discovered as recently as the 1990s, and some of these finds are proudly displayed in the town's archaeological museum. During Roman and Muslim times, Beja was considered an important administrative centre (locals will stress that this role was wrongly attributed to Évora alone). The Romans called the city Pax Julia (shortened to Pax, which then became Paca, Baca, Baju and finally Beja), after Julius Caesar restored peace between the Romans and rebellious Lusitanians. It became an important agricultural centre, booming on wheat and oil.

Little evidence remains of the 400 years of subsequent Moorish rule, except for some distinctive 16th-century *azulejos* in the Convento de Nossa Senhora da Conceição (now the Museu Regional). The town was recaptured from the Moors in 1162.

◉ Sights

Museu Jorge Vieira   MUSEUM
(Rua do Touro 33; ⊘9.30am-12.30pm & 2-6pm Tue-Sun) FREE A charming, small museum, devoted to the work of renowned Portuguese sculptor Jorge Vieira, who donated his works to Beja. His monumental bulbous figures and strange creatures capture the imagination, calling to mind Maurice Sendak's *Where the Wild Things Are*. Look

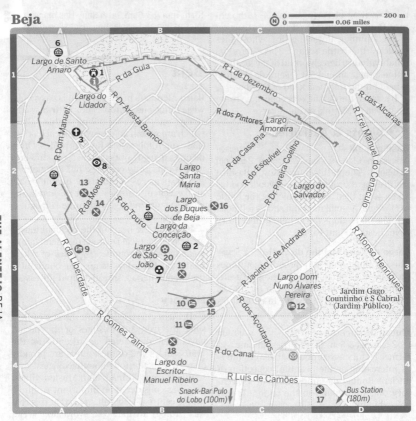

out for Viera's linked ellipses on Praça Diogo Fernandes de Beja.

Praça da República   PLAZA

This renovated attractive town square with a *pelourinho* (stone pillory) is the historic heart of the old city. Dominating the square is the 16th-century **Igreja de Misericórdia**, a hefty church with an immense porch – its crude stonework betrays its origins as a meat market. The **Planície Dourada** (☑284 310 150; www.rt-planiciedourada.pt; ⏰9am-12.30pm & 2-5.30pm) building features an elegant Manueline colonnade.

Convento de Nossa
Senhora da Conceição   MUSEUM

(Largo da Conceição; adult/child €2/free; ⏰9.30am-12.30pm & 2-5.15pm Tue-Sun) Founded in 1459, this Franciscan convent was the location for the romance between a nun and soldier that inspired *Letters of a Portuguese Nun*.

Indeed a romantic setting, it's a delicate balance between no-nonsense Gothic and Manueline flights of fancy. The interior is lavish – amazing highlights are the rococo chapel with 17th- and 18th-century gilded woodwork, and a chapel inlaid with intricate marble. The chapterhouse is incongruously Arabian, with a beautiful ceiling painted with unfurling ferns, 16th-century tiles and a carved doorway. The cloister has some splendid 16th- and 17th-century *azulejos*.

Tucked inside this convent is the **Museu Regional**, displaying Roman lamps, glass bottles and stelae, and 16th- and 17th-century paintings. The admission fee includes entry to the Museu Visigótico.

Núcleo Museológico da
Rua do Sembrano   ROMAN RUINS

(Rua do Sembrano; ⏰9.30am-12.30pm & 2-5.45pm) **FREE** Opened in 2008, this modern museum contains more than meets the eye – the exhibition is underfoot and

Beja

displayed through a glass floor. Iron Age finds were discovered here during building works in the 1980s, and the site was deemed important enough to excavate and protect. Peer through the glass floor at 2200-year-old remains, over which were laid subsequent Roman walls, indicating that this location was important for millennia. A curator will explain the site.

Museu Visigótico   MUSEUM
(Largo de Santo Amaro; adult/concession €2/1; ☉ 9.30am-12.30pm & 2-5pm Tue-Sun) Found just beyond the castle, the unusual Visigothic museum is housed in the former **Igreja de Santo Amaro**, parts of which date from the early 6th century when it was a Visigothic church – so it's one of Portugal's oldest standing buildings. Inside, the original columns display intriguing, beautiful carvings. The admission fee includes entry to the Museu Regional.

Castelo   CASTLE
FREE Dom Dinis built the castle on Roman foundations in the late 13th century. Eventually, the tower may (re)open to visitors. The *turismo* is located here.

Igreja de Nossa Senhora dos Prazeres e Museu Episcopal   MUSEUM
(adult/child €1.50/free; ☉ 10am-12.30pm Wed-Sun) Several museums of religious artworks opened in Beja in 2008. So great was the wealth of the Catholic Church that no single space can display all of the paintings and other items. The most attractive is housed in this restored church. While the church is

stunning, perhaps only those interested in religious art might appreciate the museum (enter from near the altar).

🛏 Sleeping

Hospedaria Rosa do Campo   GUESTHOUSE €
(☑ 284 323 578; Rua da Liberdade 12; s/d/tr €30/40/50; ✳ 🛜) This sparkling guesthouse has polished floors and mostly spacious rooms, each with a small refrigerator. Incredible value.

Hotel Bejense   GUESTHOUSE €
(☑ 284 311 570; www.hotelbejense.com; Rua Capitão João Francisco de Sousa 57; s/d/tr €35/45/60; ✳) This pleasant family-run option, with bright and airy rooms (slightly tizzy decor) is hard to beat for value. Front rooms have small balconies and the hallways are trimmed with tiles. Breakfast is a small but excellent buffet.

Hotel Santa Bárbara   GUESTHOUSE €
(☑ 284 312 280; www.hotelsantabarbara.pt; Rua de Mértola 56; s €30, d €45-48, tr €60; ✳ 🛜) This reliable and good-value choice has neat, motel-style rooms set in masculine tones – all dark woods and plaid curtains – and it's well located in the pedestrianised town centre.

Pousada de São Francisco   LUXURY HOTEL €€€
(☑ 284 313 580; www.pousadas.pt; Largo Dom Nuno Álvares Pereira; d €190; ✳ ▨) Located in the 13th-century São Francisco Convent, this *pousada* provides gorgeous rooms, formerly cells, and a restaurant (open all day) with a magnificent vaulted ceiling. A Gothic chapel, former chapter house and pleasant

WORTH A TRIP

ALVITO

Situated only 38km northwest of Beja and 37km southwest of Évora in Baixa Alentejo, beautiful Alvito (population 1260) is well worth visiting, for half a day at least. Be aware though, such is its appeal, it's the kind of place you get to and wished you'd packed your toothbrush (accommodation options abound). The town was the home of the Portuguese barons; the first baron, Dom João Fernandes da Silveira, decided to make Alvito an artistic landmark. (The Festa do Barão – Baron's Feast – is held every two years around June.)

You can visit parts of a 15th-century former **castle**, now a **luxury pousada** (☎ 284 480 700; www.pousadas.pt; r €270), and several important **churches**. The 16th-century **Ermida de Sao Sebastião** has some extraordinary revived frescos.

Throughout the village, you can see beautiful **Manueline features** – pick up a map from the **tourist office** (☎ 284 480 808; www.cm-alvito.pt; Rua dos Lobos 13; ☺ 9am-12.30pm & 2-5.30pm Mon-Fri, 10am-12.30pm & 2-5.30pm Sat) and play 'spot the Manueline doorway' (these are stunning).

The community-focused **Rota do Fresco** (Fresco Route; ☎ 284 475 413; www.rotado fresco.com; Rua 5 de Outubro 20, Vila Nova da Baronia) arranges fun and informative cultural and heritage tours, including – as the name suggests – trips to the region's extraordinary historic frescos.

If you decide to stay the night in Alvito, our pick is the delightful **Horta do Padre** (☎ 284 485 400, 961 865 052; Quinta da Esperança, Apartado 16; s/d €25/35; ✱) ✐, a renovated blue-and-white traditional Alentejan farmhouse 1km east of Alvito's centre (down Estrada de São Roman), with comfortable rooms and excellent breakfasts. The multilingual owners, Fernanda and Lino, are passionate about preserving Portuguese traditional practices and are fountains of knowledge about the region. Best to ring in advance. (If you love it you can consider renting the whole place – eight beds in total).

lounge areas add to the unique and luxurious atmosphere.

Eating

Salão de Chá Maltesinhas
PATISSERIE €

(☎ 284 321 500; Terreiro dos Valentes 7; snacks €1-5; ☺ 9am-7pm Mon-Fri, 9am-2pm Sat) It looks like a smart *pastelaria,* but there's an important difference. It's known for its delicious regional *doces conventuais* (desserts traditionally made by nuns). Try the *pasteis de toucinho,* a delicious thin pastry and almond creation with, believe it or not, a smidgen of pork lard. Worth the pig out.

Sabores do Campo
VEGETARIAN €

(Rua Bento de Jesus Caraça 4; ☺ lunch & dinner Mon-Thu, lunch Fri; ✐) This simple place serves 100% vegetarian food – perfect for those in need of some tasty pork-free tarts, vegetables and salads. Prices are by weight (€14 per kilogram).

Luiz da Rocha
CAFE €

(☎ 284 323 179; Rua Capitão João Francisco de Sousa 63; mains €6-11; ☺ lunch & dinner) Founded in 1893, this is one of Beja's oldest cafes and best-known institutions. It gathers a chatty neighbourhood crowd day and night and is justly famous for its cakes: *trouxas de ovos* (literally 'sweet egg yolks') and *porquinhos de doce* ('sweet little pigs'). It also serves up Alentejan staples.

Restaurante Alentejano
PORTUGUESE €

(☎ 284 323 849; Largo dos Duques de Beja 6; mains €7.50-10; ☺ lunch & dinner Sat-Thu) This lively local eatery is a good bet for filling Alentejan plates of roasted pork or cod dishes. Its plain exterior hides a dapper but relaxed interior. Popular among the lunching businessfolk.

Vovó Joaquina
INTERNATIONAL €€

(☎ 966 278 887; Rua do Sembrano 57; mains €7-12.50; ☺ lunch & dinner Tue-Sat) Modern meets traditional in this delightfully quirky place where old photos, chandeliers, marble-topped bales and a piano are the backdrops. It serves up a reasonable selection of pasta, French dishes and local favourites. Despite its cavernous size, the space is warm and inviting and, if there's a crowd, the buzz takes precedence over cuisine, which is good, but won't blow your socks off.

Adega Típica 25 Abril
PORTUGUESE €€

(☎ 284 325 960; Rua da Moeda 23; mains €7-15; ☺ lunch & dinner Tue-Sun) Packed to the basket-lined rafters with locals, this cavernous, rustic *adega* serves typical food, with good daily specials.

A Pipa PORTUGUESE €€
(✔284 327 043; Rua da Moeda 8; mains €8-12.50; ⊙lunch & dinner Mon-Sat) This rustic eatery has a wood-beamed ceiling, bright blue wooden chairs, checked tablecloths and serves excellent daily dishes. The meats – such as *febras de porco* (pork steaks) and *lombinhos de porco preto* – are delicious.

 Drinking & Nightlife

Snack-Bar Pulo do Lobo CAFE, RESTAURANT
(Av Vasco da Gama; ⊙8am-midnight Mon-Sun) A cafe and restaurant with outdoor seating, this is a favourite for an evening get-together over snails and *petiscos* and cold beer. Great quality plates of the day cost between €9 and €15.

 Entertainment

Pax Julia Teatro Municipal CINEMA, THEATRE
(✔284 315 090; www.paxjulia.org; Largo de São João 1) This cinema and theatre hosts regular concerts, dance performances and film screenings. A program guide is available at the theatre's box office.

 Shopping

Igreja de Misericórdia HANDICRAFTS
(Praça da República; ⊙10am-1pm Mon-Sat, 2-5.30pm Mon-Fri) An *artesenato* cooperative has a range of goods for sale within the Igreja de Misericórdia – a unique style of store.

ℹ **Information**

Biblioteca Municipal (Rua Luís de Camões; ⊙2.30-10.30pm Mon, 9.30am-12.30pm & 2.30-11pm Tue-Fri, 2.30-8pm Sat) Free internet and wi-fi.

Espaço Internet (Rua Luís de Camões; ⊙9am-12.30pm Mon-Fri, 2-5.30pm Mon-Sat) Free internet access. Enter through Casa da Cultura.

Hospital (✔284 310 200; Rua Dr António Covas Lima) Hospital José Joaquim Fernandes; centrally located.

Police Station (✔284 322 022; Largo Dom Nuno Álvares Pereira)

Post Office (Rua Luís de Camões; ⊙8.30am-6.30pm Mon-Fri)

Turismo (✔fax 284 311 913; Rua Capitão João Francisco de Sousa 25; ⊙10am-1pm & 2-6pm Apr-Oct, 9am-1pm & 2-5pm Nov-Mar) Within the castle premises; provides a city map but not much else.

ℹ **Getting There & Away**

BUS
From the **bus station** (✔284 313 620) buses run to regional towns and villages. Weekends see fewer services. The bus station is in the southern part of town, about 600m from the historic centre.

Buses run from Beja to local destinations and those further afield:
Albufeira (€13.30, three hours, three daily)
Évora (€8, 1¼ hours, hourly)
Faro (€14, three hours, three daily)
Lisbon (€13.30, 3¾ hours, hourly)
Mértola (€10.80, one hour, one daily)
Serpa (€6, 40 minutes, three daily) From Serpa, some continue to Moura (€5.10, 65 minutes, four daily).

CAR
Drivers are advised to park their cars in the clearly marked car parks outside the walled centre.

TRAIN
Trains head to Lisbon (€17, 2½ hours, four daily). You change to a connecting train at Casa Branca. At the time of research, the trains had a reputation as being a bit unreliable.

Serpa
POP 7000

Planted among the rolling hills of vineyards and dusty fields, Serpa is a sleepy, atmospheric town of bleached-white walls and narrow cobblestone streets. At its medieval heart is a small, pretty plaza carefully guarded by the elderly folk who have long called Serpa home. Locals are renowned for their love of food, and several factory outlets produce the town's culinary jewel, *queijo Serpa,* a cheese made from curdled sheep's milk.

It's worth a quick visit, or even an overnight stay if you want to experience life in the Portuguese slow lane.

◎ **Sights**

Castelo ⌐ CASTLE
FREE At the time of research, the castle was closed for works (due to reopen 2014). It has long views from the battlements: flat plains, the aqueduct, town walls, rooftops and orange trees, and the slow life of Serpa residents.

Town Walls & Aqueduto AQUEDUCT
Walls still stand around most of the inner town. Along the west side (follow Rua dos Arcos) run the impressive remains of an

Serpa

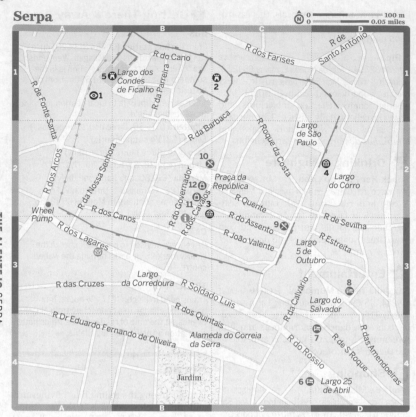

11th-century **aqueduct**. At the southern end is a huge 17th-century **wheel pump** (aka *noria*), once used for pumping water along the aqueduct to the nearby **Palácio dos Condes de Ficalho** (still used by the de Ficalho family as a holiday home).

Museu Etnográfico   MUSEUM
(Ethnographic Museum; Largo do Corro; ⊙9am-12.30pm & 2-5.30pm) FREE No traditional rural trade is left unturned in the exquisite exploration of Alentejan life found at Serpa's Museu Etnográfico. Occupying the former town market (in use from 1887 to 1986), the museum beautifully presents restored items donated by locals. Polished tools used by former wheelwrights, saddle makers, cheese makers, barrel makers and ironmongers – among others – are on display.

Museu do Relógio   MUSEUM
(☑284 543 194; www.museudorelogio.com; Rua do Assento 31; adult/under 10yr €2/free; ⊙2-5pm

Tue-Fri, 10am-noon & 2-5.30pm Sat & Sun) The Watch Museum houses an amazing collection of watches and clocks (shared with its sister museum in Évora), dating from a 1630 Edward East clock to the museum's own 2010 wristwatch model. Napoleonic gilded timepieces and Swiss cuckoo clocks are among the 2000 pieces ticking away in the cool surroundings of the former Convento do Mosteirinho.

✨ Festivals & Events

Festas de Senhora de Guadalupe   RELIGIOUS
Celebrations of Serpa's patron saint take place over Easter from Good Friday to the following Tuesday – there is .a pilgrimage to bring the saint's image down to the parish church, and on the last day a procession takes it back to the chapel. On Easter Tuesday, roast lamb is the traditional meal.

Serpa

Noites na Nora THEATRE
This festival features nightly local theatre and music shows on a terrace tucked behind the aqueduct. Check with the tourist office – dates change annually.

Sleeping

Residencial Beatriz GUESTHOUSE €
(☎284 544 423; www.residencialbeatriz.com; Largo do Salvador 10; s/d €35/45, apt €50-70; P❋⊛) Overlooking the pretty square, this small guesthouse provides simple but adequate rooms of varying sizes. If there's more than two of you, the apartments provide good-value stays.

Hotel Pulo do Lobo HOTEL €
(☎284 544 664; www.hotelpulodolobo.com; Estrada de São Brás 9A; s/d €30/45; ⊛) Handy to the bus station, this sparkling place and its house-proud owners provide plain but modern rooms. Excellent value if you don't mind being slightly out of the centre.

Casa de Hóspedes Vírginia GUESTHOUSE €
(☎284 549 145; Largo 25 de Abril; s/d €20/30) This small guesthouse has basic but spotless rooms and en-suite bathrooms, though the walls are somewhat thin. It faces a square dotted with orange trees.

Casa de Serpa GUESTHOUSE €€
(☎284 549 238; www.casadeserpa.com; Largo do Salvador 28; s €40, d €58-65) This friendly guesthouse has handsomely furnished rooms of varying sizes (some without external windows). Rooms at the back are small-

er but open onto a courtyard. Homemade breakfasts include local produce.

Eating

All the local restaurants serve *tapas de queijo de Serpa* (the salty and creamy local cheese) or *queijadas* (small cheesecakes). Cheap eats can be found in several decent snack bars at the roundabout near the bus station.

Molhó Bico PORTUGUESE €€
(☎284 549 264; www.molhobicoserpa.com; Rua Quente 1; mains €8.50-14; ⊗lunch & dinner Thu-Tue) This enticing place pulls a crowd; kitchen odours hit you on entry to its arched, rustic space. It has wagon-wheel lights, huge wine urns, and a friendly ambience. Eating here is a pure, traditional gastronomic experience. There are hearty half serves.

Pedra de Sal PORTUGUESE €€
(☎284 543 436; www.facebook.com/pages/Pedra-de-Sal-Restaurante-Serpa-Portugal/364403729621?fref=ts; Estrada da Circunvalaçao s/n; mains €10-16; ⊗lunch & dinner Tue-Sat, lunch Sun) This smart place is a win-win food-lover's scenario. The owner-chef conjures up Alentejano specialties using quality produce, including her own home-grown greens. Modern art, a candelabra and wood trim grace the interior, and in summer there's an attractive bamboo-covered outdoor patio.

Restaurante O Alentejano PORTUGUESE €€
(☎284 544 335; Praça da República; mains €10-13; ⊗lunch & dinner Tue-Sun) This handsome place, above a cafe of the same name in a former mansion, serves local cuisine. Go for the daily specials – anything from braised hare in red wine to pigs' trotters.

Shopping

Small artisan shops and delicatessens are dotted around town. You can buy good *queijadas* and a range of oils, honey, herbs and handicrafts at **Dom Luis** (Praça da República 15; ⊗8am-7pm) and **Casa de Artesenato** (☎968 100 150; Rua dos Cavalos 33; ⊗9.30am-7pm summer, 10am-6.30pm winter).

ⓘ Information

Caixa Geral de Depósitos Bank & ATM (Largo Conde de Boavista) Around the corner from the *turismo*.

Espaço Internet (Rua Pedro Anes 14; ⊙10am-6pm Mon-Fri, 10am-4pm Sat) Free internet access with helpful staff.

Post Office (Rua dos Lagares)

Turismo (☑284 544 727; www.cm-serpa.pt; Rua dos Cavalos 19; ⊙10am-7pm Apr-Sep, 9am-6pm Oct-Mar) Staff provide a map of the old town with good listings, and sell local handicrafts.

ⓘ Getting There & Away

Buses (☑284 544 740) run to/from Lisbon (€15.50, four hours, three to five daily) via Beja (€3.55). There are no direct buses to Évora. The bus station is a couple of kilometres south of town – head south on Avenida da Paz.

If arriving by car it's best to park outside the wall, or risk tight gateways into the old town and breathtakingly narrow streets.

Moura

POP 8500

This pleasant working-class city, a flattish fortified town, has an ageing castle, graceful buildings and a well-preserved Moorish neighbourhood. Well placed near water sources and rich in ore, Moura has been a farming and mining centre and a fashionable spa in previous incarnations. More recent developments? The world's largest

solar-power generation plant is located nearby and it's the nearest large town to the Barragem do Alqueva, 15km to the north.

The Moors' 500-year occupation came to an end in 1232 after a Christian invasion. Despite the reconquest, Moorish presence in the city remained strong – they only abandoned their quarter in 1496 (after Dom Manuel's convert-or-leave edict).

The town's name comes from a legend related to the 13th-century takeover. Moorish resident Moura Salúquiyya opened the town gates to Christians disguised as Muslims. They sacked the town, and poor Moura flung herself from a tower.

⊙ Sights & Activities

There are several cafes with outdoor seating around Praça Sacadura Cabral, where you'll also find the *mercado municipal* in a huge glass building.

Museu Municipal   MUSEUM
(☑285 253 978; Rua da Romeira; ⊙9.30am-12.30pm & 2.30-5.30pm Tue-Fri, 10am-noon & 2-4pm Sat & Sun) **FREE** In an appealing residential quarter off a lane about 200m east of the *praça* (head up Rua do Espírito Santo, behind the tourist office), this tiny museum contains local prehistoric and Roman remains, such as 1st- and 2nd-century needles,

---

DAM STATISTICS

The 250-sq-km Alqueva reservoir, Europe's largest and created by an enormous dam (Barragem do Alqueva) near Moura, is undeniably beautiful. But there is something strange and otherworldly about it: it's not so much a lake as drowned land, with islands poking out of the water and roads disappearing into nowhere.

It is hoped that this huge water mass will save the arid Alentejo. One of Portugal's major agricultural regions, and its poorest, it employs a host of irrigation schemes and reservoirs to bring water to the soil, as well as hydroelectricity that supplies the national grid. The most important source of water is the Rio Guadiana, which rises in Spain and flows through the Alentejo. Various agreements with Spain were meant to ensure that its waters were fairly shared. In 1998 the Portuguese finally started work on the giant dam. It flooded 2000 properties, including those of the village of Luz (rebuilt elsewhere but strangely antiseptic). The project cost €1.7 billion.

Critics say that the dam may not even fulfil its remit, that irrigation schemes are vastly expensive, and that it is an ecological disaster (many birds and animals had to be moved as part of the initial agreement). Ancient rock art was enveloped in the waters and menhirs were moved elsewhere.

Completed in 2002, the dam created an 83km-long reservoir, with a perimeter of 1100km. Only if you have time, and your own transport (no buses head here), it's worth driving to the dam wall for a look. **A Centro de Informação** (⊙10am-7pm Dec-Feb, 9.30am-6.30pm Jun-Aug, closed 1-2.30pm) provides technical (read: public relations) information.

A fun way to see the dam is out on a boat; head to the marina to see what day trips are on offer. Alternatively there are some decent organised trips from Monsaraz (p222).

as well as Moorish funerary tablets. The municipality's collection of ecclesiastical art is housed in the **Igreja de São Pedro** (☑285 251 421; ☺ 10am-1pm & 2.30-5.30pm Tue-Sun).

Lagar de Varas do Fojo (Museu do Azeite)   MUSEUM
(Rua João de Deus 20; ☺ 9.30am-12.30pm & 2.30-5.30pm Tue-Sun) FREE With a system of production that would have been similar to that of Roman times, an oil press here recreates the oil-pressing factory that functioned on this spot between 1841 and 1941, with giant wooden and stone-wheel presses, vats and utensils. Opposite is the recently opened **Jardim das Oliveiras**, with various varieties of olive trees and herbs, and reflective space. It's dedicated to Miguel Hernández, a Spanish poet and revolutionary who, upon fleeing Spain, entered the Moura district, only to be returned by Salazar to Franco's troops. He later died in prison.

Igreja de São Baptista   CHURCH
This 16th-century church has a remarkable Manueline portal. Set against the plain facade, it is a twisting, flamboyant bit of decoration, with carvings of knotted ropes, crowns and armillary spheres. Inside are some fine deep-blue and yellow 17th-century Sevillian *azulejos*. It's just outside Jardim Dr Santiago.

Jardim Dr Santiago & Spa   GARDENS
(☺ thermal spa 9am-noon) The lovely, shady Jardim Dr Santiago, at the eastern end of Praça Sacadura Cabral, is a delightful place. There are good views a bandstand and shady flowering trees, and it's a favourite spot for elderly men to sit and chat.

At the **thermal spa**, at the entrance to the garden, you can join the locals for a soak in a basic bath. Bicarbonated calcium waters, said to be good for rheumatism, burble from the richly marbled **Fonte das Três Bicas** (Fountain with Three Spouts) by the entrance to the *jardim*.

Mouraria   MOORISH QUARTER
(Poço Árabe) The old Moorish quarter lies at the western end of Praça Sacadura Cabral. It's a well-preserved tight cluster of narrow, cobbled lanes and white terraced cottages with chunky or turreted chimneys.

The **Núcleo Árabe** (Travessa da Mouraria 11; ☺ 9.30am-12.30pm & 2.30-5.30pm Tue-Fri) FREE, just off Largo da Mouraria, is a pocket collection of Moorish ceramics and other remains – carved stone inscriptions and a

14th-century Arabic well. Visits must be arranged through the Museu Municipal.

Castelo   CASTLE
(☺ 9am-2.30 & 2.30-5.30pm) FREE The castle offers fabulous views across the countryside. One of the towers is the last remnant of a Moorish fortress. Rebuilt by Dom Dinis in the 13th century and again by Dom Manuel I in 1510, the castle itself was largely destroyed by the Spanish in the 18th century. There's a ruined convent inside the walls.

🛏 Sleeping

There's a couple of good-value places around town if you do decide you enjoy small town life for a night or two.

Hotel Santa Comba   HOTEL €
(☑ 285 251 255; www.hotelsantacomba.com; Praça Sacadura Cabral 34; s/d from €24/38; ❄) This smart place opened in 2004 and has clean rooms overlooking the main square. There's disabled access and a pleasant dining room.

Hotel Passagem do Sol   HOTEL €
(☑ 285 250 080; www.hotelpassagemdosol.com; Largo José Maria dos Santos 40; s/d €26/38; ❄@🖧) The key holders – jugs embedded into walls – are the most novel things in this modern, but comfortable and spotless place. It's near the bus station – look for an ordered, green-shuttered house.

🍴 Eating & Drinking

Patos & Infantes   PORTUGUESE €
(☑ 285 254 402; Rua Primero Dezembro 34; mains €6.50-12; ☺ lunch & dinner Wed-Sun, lunch Mon) A bustling establishment offering *cozinha tradicional* (traditional cuisine), with a manageable (ie smaller) menu. Half servings are available for those who can't stomach consuming half an animal in one sitting.

O Trilho   PORTUGUESE €€
(☑ 285 254 261; www.otrilho.com; Rua 5 de Outubro 5; mains €8.50-13.50; ☺ lunch & dinner Tue-Sun) Three streets east of Rua Serpa Pinto, O Trilho is a local favourite, with excellent regional mains and mouth-watering daily specials in pleasant, starched tableclothed surroundings.

ℹ Information

There are banks on the *praça* and along Rua Serpa Pinto, directly north of the *turismo*.

Post Office (Rua da República) East of Rua Serpa Pinto.

THE ALENTEJO MOURA

Turismo (285 251 375; www.cm-moura.pt; ⊙9am-12.30pm & 2-5.30pm Mon-Fri, 9.30am-1pm & 2.30-6pm Sat & Sun) At the time of research, the office was relocating to the castle grounds.

ⓘ Getting There & Away

Buses run to/from Beja (around €5, one hour, six weekdays) via Serpa (€3.20, 40 minutes). Rede Expressos runs to Lisbon (€16.50, four hours, daily) via Évora (€7.60, 1½ hours); these leave from Praça Sacadura Cabral.

COASTAL ALENTEJO

Vila Nova de Milfontes

POP 3200

One of the loveliest towns along this stretch of the coast, Vila Nova de Milfontes has an attractive, whitewashed centre, sparkling beaches nearby and a laid-back population who couldn't imagine living anywhere else. Milfontes remains much more low-key than most resort towns, except in August when it's packed to the hilt with surfers and sunseekers (up to 50,000 people in town). It's located in the middle of the beautiful Parque Natural do Sudoeste Alentejano e Costa Vicentina and is still a port (Hannibal is said to have sheltered here) alongside a lovely, sand-edged limb of estuary.

Milfonte's narrow lanes and tiny plazas harbour varied eating and drinking options, with even more scenic restaurants out on the beach.

Beaches

Praia do Farol, the lighthouse beach just by the town, is sheltered but gets busy. Beaches on the other side of the estuary are less crowded. Be careful of the strong river currents running through the estuary. If you have your own transport, you could head out to the fantastic **Praia do Malhão**, backed by rocky dunes and covered in fragrant scrub, around 7km to the north (travel 2.5km to Bruinheras, turn left at the roundabout just before the primary school, then travel another 3km – at the time of research it was signed to the left). The more remote parts of the beach harbour nudist and gay areas. The sea can be quite wild here, but the rugged coast is strikingly empty of development.

🏃 Activities

Ecoalga　　　　　　　　　　　DIVING
(964 620 394; www.ecoalga.com; Rua 25 de Abril 5C) Based in nearby Porto Côvo, this is the place to go scuba diving; it also takes boat trips.

Sudaventura　　　　　　　　SURFING
(916 925 959; www.sudaventura.com; Rua Custódio Brás Pacheco 38A; ⊙10am-7pm, closed Sun

WORTH A TRIP

PORTO CÔVO

Worth popping in for a visit (though not to linger if you're short of time; it gets packed in summer) is the appealingly 'traditional cute' Porto Côvo. Perched on low cliffs with views over the sea, Porto Côvo (population around 1000) is a former fishing village with a pretty square and cobbled streets lined with sun-bleached houses.

Paths along the cliffs lead down to the harbour at the town's southern end and to interesting rock formations to the north, with access to various beaches such as the pretty **Praia do Somouqueira**. If you want to really let loose, head to the official 'nudie' beach, **Praia do Salto**.

The **turismo** (269 959 124; ⊙9am-noon & 1-5pm Mon-Fri winter, 10am-1pm & 3-7pm Mon-Sat summer) is on the edge of the old town, one block north of the main square by a car park. Diving trips can be arranged through **Ecoalga** (964 620 394; www.ecoalga.com). In summer, a boat shuttles between Porto Côvo and the diminutive island of Ilha do Pessegueiro (Fishermen's Island).

Overlooking the quaint square is **Cervejaria Marquês** (269 905 036; Largo Marquês de Pombal 10; mains €12-19; ⊙lunch & dinner Wed-Mon), overwhelmingly the favourite place to eat.

At least one Rede Expressos bus (more in summer) travels to/from Lisbon each day (€15.20, 2¾ hours). In summer there are regular connections to Vila Nova de Milfontes (€6, 25 minutes).

Dec-Feb) Offers a range of excursions, including canoe trips, and kayak, surfboard and bike rentals. Surf lessons cost €35 per class, body-board lessons €30 and paddle-board lessons €40.

🛏 Sleeping

The tourist office has a list of official sleeping options. High-season (August) prices are listed here; at other times of the year prices are significantly lower. In August, you'll need to book in advance.

Sol da Vila   GUESTHOUSE €
(www.soldavila.com; Rua Custódio Brás Pacheco 4; d/apt €55/90; 🛜) A centrally located, unpretentious spot with simple, spotless rooms... and much more. There's a lovely patio (with prolific lemon tree) and friendly owner on the premises to point you in the right direction. Three apartments are also available. Bike rental is €10 per day.

Campiférias   CAMPGROUND €
(✆283 996 140; www.roteiro-campista.pt; Rua da Praça; sites per adult/tent/car €3.95/3.20/4; 🛥) Shady, and 800m from the beach.

Casa do Adro   GUESTHOUSE €€
(✆283 997 102; www.casadoadro.com.pt; Rua Diário de Notícias 10; d €90; ❄🛜) Set in a house dating from the 17th century, this special option is chock-a-block with antiques and artwork. It has six elegantly furnished bedrooms, some with private balcony or shared terrace. Hospitality abounds and foodies will love the breakfasts – you can turn up to this scrumptious spread at any time in the morning (a nice touch).

Casa Amarela   HOSTEL €€
(✆283 996 632; www.casaamarelamilfontes. com; Rua Dom Luis Castro e Almeida; dm/d/tr/q €20/60/80/92.50; @🛜) This privately run, cheery yellow place is set with eclectic knick-knacks belonging to the genial English-speaking owner, Rui. You'll find bright rooms, a lounge space and shared (if slightly messy) kitchens. The annexe nearby was being renovated at the time of research – expect attractive dorm rooms, a courtyard and kitchen.

Hotel Casa dos Arcos   GUESTHOUSE €€
(✆fax 283 996 264; Rua do Cais; d/tr €70/85; ❄) Jauntily painted in blue and white, this airy and spotless (if dated) guesthouse has comfortable beds, tiled floors and small balconies.

OFF THE BEATEN TRACK

PADARIA IN VENDA FRIA

Bread lovers and those who appreciate traditional culinary practices shouldn't go past the very simple *padaria* (bakery; open 8am to 8pm) in the tiny village of Venda Fria on Strada R393, 4.5km from Vila Nova de Milfontes. Dona Ercilia Joaquina has baked bread here every day for over 20 years. You can't enter the kitchen for photographs, but you can pick up some steaming, straight-from-the oven loaves for around €1.50. Heading north, turn left after Cafe Venda Fria and continue for 200m. Look for a tiny black-and-white *'pão'* (bread) sign on the right.

🍴 Eating

Porto das Barcas   €
(✆283 997 160; Estrada do Canal; mains €6-14; ⏾lunch & dinner Thu-Sun winter, daily summer) With a wonderful outlook over the water and cliffs, this is a great place to kick back for a seafood lunch. Its light and airy ambience in a dreamy location are winners whatever your impression of the cuisine (which locals love). It's 2.5km north of town along the canal road.

★ Tasca do Celso   PORTUGUESE €€
(✆283 996 753; www.tascadocelso.com; Rua dos Aviadores; mains €13.50-26; ⏾lunch & dinner Tue-Sun) *The* choice. Locals and travellers from far and wide rave about the excellent cuisine produced within the kitchen of this charming, 'upmarket rustic' blue-and-white building. You're safe trying anything here. It's got great service, open fires and an appealing bar area, too.

Restaurante A Fateixa   SEAFOOD €€
(✆283 996 415; Largo do Cais; mains €8-15; ⏾lunch & dinner Thu-Tue) A Fateixa delivers good grills and seafood dishes – try the *tamboril* (monkfish) rice for two – and it has breezy outdoor tables. It's excellent value given its perfect setting down by the river.

Conversas com Sal   CONTEMPORARY €€
(✆283 998 078; Avenida Marginal Edifício Milfontes; mains €12-17; ⏾noon-2am Dec-Oct; 🛜) Milfontes goes cosmopolitan at this hip abode, which screams 'chill out' and where anything goes: candelabra, surfboards, retro sofas, guitars, board games. And we haven't

ROTA VICENTINA WALKING TRAIL

The recently opened Rota Vicentina comprises two walking trails – one coastal and one inland – and runs along the southwest coast between Santigao do Cacém and Cabo de São Vincente. The coastal walk is beautiful. It uses paths forged by beach goers and fishingfolk and passes through some of the harsher, yet stunning, coastal scenery and wilderness. The inland route (dubbed the 'historical way') is also fascinating. It runs through the Parque Natural do Sudoeste Alentejano e Costa Vicentina, plus rural towns and villages, cork tree forests and valleys.

Both trails are comprised of sections (together totalling about 350km). While promoted as being 'complete', at the time of research walkers stated that this was not the case, with some sections not functioning as well they might. Private companies have cottoned onto the route, but there's nothing to stop you from doing it alone if you're prepared to carry your things. Numerous accommodation options are along both routes. For further information see www.rotavicentina.com.

even got to the food, an esoteric range of *petiscos,* main meals, delicious desserts and tea infusions.

🍷 Drinking & Nightlife

Lua Cheia & Manjedoura   BAR
(☑ 964 923 571; Rua António Mantas; ⊙ 8.30pm-4am Mon-Sat) Try saying this place's name after a few drinks. Opened in 2013 and, at the time of research, Milfontes' trendiest drinking hole.

Café Azul   BAR
(Rossio 20) Always lively, whatever the time of year, even if the rest of the town is dead. This is a jovial bar with a pool table and lots of papier-mâché sharks, octopuses and squid hanging from the ceiling.

ℹ️ Information

Police Station (☑ 283 998 391; Rua António Mantas)
Turismo (☑ 283 996 599; Rua António Mantas; ⊙ 10am-1pm & 2-6pm) Off the main road, opposite the police station. Buses stop 100m along the same road.

ℹ️ Getting There & Away

Vila Nova has three bus connections daily on weekdays to/from Odemira (€6, 20 minutes). Rede Expressos buses run daily from Lisbon (€16, four hours, three daily, more in summer) via Setubal (€14.50) and at least once daily to/from Portimão (€13.50, two hours) and Lagos (€12.50, two hours). There are summer services to Sagres (€13, two hours). The ticket agent for **Rede Expressos** (☑ 919 136 225; www.rede-expressos.pt) is located in the sewing shop Travessa dos Amadores.

Zambujeira do Mar

POP 850

Enchantingly wild beaches backed by rugged cliffs form the setting of this sleepy seaside village. The main street terminates at the cliff; paths lead to the attractive sands below. Quieter than Vila Nova, Zambujeira attracts a backpacker, surfy crowd, though in August the town is a party place and hosts the massive music fest, **Festa do Sudoeste**. The high-season crowds obscure Zambujeira's out-of-season charms: fresh fish in family-run restaurants, blustering cliff-top walks and a dramatic, empty coast.

A 3km-long walking and biking path runs between Zambujeira do Mar and Porto de Pesca.

🛏️ Sleeping

★**Herdade do Touril**   RURAL INN €€
(☑ 937 811 627; www.herdadedotouril.pt; r from €90; @ 🐾) Four kilometres north of Zambujeira do Mar is this upmarket *quinta* building with rooms and apartments of the fluffy-pillow variety. Some are located within the original building (built in 1826), while others are converted farm cottages. The rustic and contemporary design of this tranquil place has an African safari-lodge feel – without the lions. Instead, storks nest in nearby cliffs (note, this area is not safe for children). There's a seawater pool, a buffet breakfast and free bikes. Good taste, good choice.

Residencial Mira Mar   GUESTHOUSE €€
(☑ 283 961 352; Rua Miramar; d €60-65) In Zambujeira's main street, next to a cafe of the same name. Rooms are basic, but tiled and

large and light. Some have access to balconies. No English is spoken.

Eating

Your best bet for great bites is to head to Porto de Pesca where there are a couple of wonderful fishers' tavernas.

A Barca
SEAFOOD €€

(☑ 283 961 186; Entrada da Barca, Porto de Pesca; meals €12-15.50; ☺ lunch & dinner Tue-Sun Feb-Nov, plus open Mon Jul & Aug) The owner's father once cooked lunch for the local fishermen after they came into port; these days, the former kiosk is an upmarket restaurant that serves great fish and *marisco* (shellfish) dishes to discerning diners. Lovely outdoor area and view of the sea, but (of course) expect the odd seagull.

Restaurante Sacas
SEAFOOD €€

(☑ 283 961 151; Entrada da Barca, Porto de Pesca; meals €8.50-16; ☺ lunch & dinner Thu-Tue, daily Jul & Aug) A family team adds colour to this fun, laid-back 'cabana'; Dona Ana Maria even creates her own seafood dishes. The fresh fish and shellfish more than make up for the car-park view (many years ago the cabana was at the base of the cliffs, but was destroyed by rough seas).

🛈 Information

There's a small **turismo** (☑ 283 961 144; ☺ 10am-6pm Tue-Sat) on the main street, which closes to traffic from July to mid-September.

🛈 Getting There & Away

In summer, Zambujeira has one daily connection with Vila Nova de Milfontes (€7.50, 45 minutes) and one with Lisbon (€15, 3¾ hours) through **Rede Expressos** (www.rede-expressos.pt) – buy tickets at **Pastelaria Doce Tentação** (ask for directions). Buses also run to Odemira (40 minutes) and Beja (three hours, one weekdays); for these you buy your ticket on the bus.

Estremadura & Ribatejo

Includes ➡

Best Places to Eat

➡ A Tasquinha (p274)

➡ Malagueta Afrodisíaca (p280)

➡ Mar à Vista (p262)

Best Places to Stay

➡ Casa do Outeiro (p278)

➡ Casa das Marés (p265)

➡ Casa d'Óbidos (p269)

Why Go?

Stretching from the Rio Tejo to the Atlantic Ocean, Estremadura and Ribatejo constitute Portugal's heartland, but their central importance goes beyond geography. These fertile lands have formed the backdrop for every major chapter in Portuguese history, from the building of key fortified settlements in the 12th century to the release of Salazar's political prisoners in 1974. Two of medieval Portugal's critical battles for autonomy – against the Moors at Santarém and the Spaniards at Aljubarrota – were fought and won here, and remain commemorated in the magnificent monasteries at Alcobaça and Batalha, both Unesco World Heritage sites. A third Unesco site, Tomar's Convento de Cristo, was long the stronghold of the Knights Templar.

These days the region draws visitors not only to these renowned monasteries, but also to its vineyards, beaches, castles and historic villages – and Fátima, modern Portugal's premier religious shrine.

When to Go

Leiria

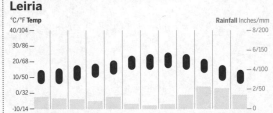

| **Apr & May** Beat summer heat with a springtime visit to the region's World Heritage sites. | **Jun & Sep** For warm beaches at cooler prices, visit the coast in early summer or autumn. | **Oct** World-class waves at Peniche, Ericeira and other prime surf spots. |

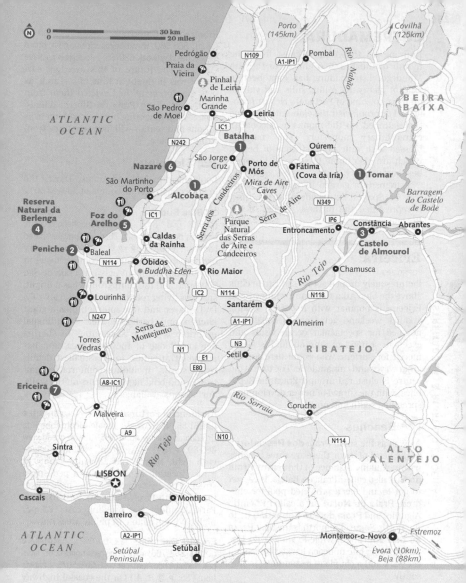

Estremadura & Ribatejo Highlights

1 Explore the region's three World Heritage sites: the monasteries at **Batalha** (p276), **Alcobaça** (p275), and **Tomar** (p290)

2 Watch the pros in action at Supertubos, the gnarliest spot in surfing **Peniche** (p264)

3 Survey the Rio Tejo from the crenellated heights of 12th-century **Castelo de Almourol** (p289)

4 Cross the narrow arched bridge to the island fort on **Berlenga Grande** (p266)

5 Sail across the lagoon at sunset in **Foz do Arelho** (p270)

6 Catch Carnaval or New Year's fireworks at **Nazaré** (p272), one of Estremadura's most picturesque beach-party settings

7 Feast on the region's best seafood at **Ericeira** (p260)

ESTREMADURA

Running up the Atlantic coast from the mouth of the Rio Tejo almost to the Rio Mondego, Estremadura has long been a land of plenty, its rolling hills and valleys offering up some of Portugal's richest farmland. For proof, visit the elaborate kitchens that fattened up the monks at Alcobaça's extraordinary monastery. The coast is blessed with miles-long strands of beach, which are also home to some of Europe's best surf waves.

Estremadura earned its name the same way as Spain's Extremadura: for a time, it represented the furthest reaches of the Reconquista.

Ericeira

POP 10,260

Picturesquely draped across sandstone cliffs above the blue Atlantic, sunny, whitewashed Ericeira is popular with *lisboêtas* seeking a quick weekend getaway. It's equally renowned for spectacular ocean vistas and excellent seafood restaurants and is also a mecca for surfers, who come here for the great waves and camaraderie. The town's old centre is clustered around Praça da República, with the sprawl of newer development spreading south and north.

Beaches

As well as the small **Praia dos Pescadores** in the heart of town, there are three beaches within walking distance of the centre. **Praia do Sul**, also called Praia da Baleia, is easiest to get to and has a protected pool for children. **Praia do Norte** (also called Praia do Algodio) and **Praia de São Sebastião** lie to the north. Some 5km north is unspoilt **Praia de São Lourenço**, while **Praia Foz do Lizandro**, a big bite of beach backed by a small car park and a couple of restaurants, is 3km south.

Activities

The big attraction in Ericeira is **surfing**. Serious aficionados congregate 3km north of town at **Praia da Ribeira d'Ilhas**, a World Qualifying Series (WQS) site and frequent host to Portuguese national surfing championships; most amateurs will find the waves at the nearer Praia de São Sebastião challenging enough.

Ribeira Surf Camp   SURFING

(261 869 590; www.ribeirasurfcamp.com; board rentals per day/week €20/95, 1-/5-lesson package €30/100) The future of this excellent surf school was in doubt at time of research, as new developments had evicted them from their location on Praia da Ribeira d'Ilhas. Still, it's worth getting in touch with them as lessons and rentals will likely continue from a different base.

Sleeping

Book ahead in July and August. During the low season, expect discounts of 30% to 50%.

★**Blue Buddha**   HOSTEL €

(910 658 849; www.bluebuddhahostel.com; Moinhos do Mar; dm €25-26, d with private/shared bathroom €69/55; P@奠) Like your very own beach house, this welcoming hostel in a condo development between Praia de São Sebastião and the campground has a bright, spacious living room with couches, cable TV, DVD player and free internet, plus a guest kitchen and barbecue area. Multilingual proprietress Luzia is generous in sharing her knowledge of the local area, and her abundant attention to the smallest details really shows, including comfortable mattresses and bold happy colours on the walls. Surf lessons available.

Residencial Fortunato   GUESTHOUSE €

(261 862 829; www.pensaofortunato.com; Rua Dr Eduardo Burnay 45; d €55-70, with ocean view €65-80; P奠) A well-run, well-kept place with light, bright and all-white rooms in a nice location at the end of a pedestrian street. The best digs upstairs have small terraces with lovely sea views for €10 extra. Parking under the building costs €3 per night. Wi-fi available in public areas only.

Ericeira Camping   CAMPGROUND €

(261 862 706; www.ericeiracamping.com; sites per adult/child/tent/car €6/3/6.50/3, cabins from €85; P@奠勤) On the coastal highway 800m north of Praia de São Sebastião, this high-quality site has two-bedroom cabins, lots of trees, a playground, disabled access and a municipal swimming pool next door.

Blue Buddha New   HOSTEL €

(910 658 849; www.bluebuddhahostel.com; Rua Florêncio Granate 19; dm €26-30, tw €70; 奠) This smart upmarket hostel is in a picturesque location in a lovely part of old Ericeira and has great sea views. Check in is at Blue Buddha hostel.

Ericeira

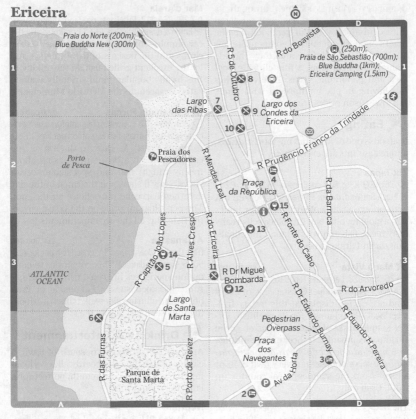

Ericeira

ESTREMADURA & RIBATEJO ERICEIRA

Residencial Vinnus   GUESTHOUSE **€€**
(📞 913 807 449; www.residencialvinnus.com; Rua Prudêncio Franco da Trindade 19; r not incl breakfast €65-70; 🛜) Friendly, bright, modern and centrally located, Residencial Vinnus offers great value, with simple and comfortable whitewashed rooms, some with pretty, blue-tiled bathrooms. It's worth the extra invest-ment for the spacious ones with kitchenette, but the pretty corner doubles have great light. Excellent overall with a good attitude.

Hotel Vila Galé   HOTEL **€€€**
(📞 261 869 900; www.vilagale.pt; Largo dos Nave-gantes; d €140, with view €168, with balcony & view €175; 🅿 ✳ @ 🛜 ⊗) Spiffy Vila Galé is an im-posing edifice whose green mansard roof

dominates Ericeira's skyline. Although its classic fin-de-siècle core has been rendered unrecognisable by recent remodelling, the hotel's modern amenities compensate for any lost historic charm, and they include comfortable bedrooms, a fine cliffside pool area and panoramic vistas. A few glitches like having to pay for in-room wi-fi grate, but low-season prices are terrific.

✖️ Eating

Seafood is one of Ericeira's big tourist draws, and restaurants are everywhere.

Tik Tapas
TAPAS €

(☑261 869 235; Rua do Ericeira 15; tapas €2-8; ⊙lunch Sat-Wed, dinner Fri-Wed; ☑) Decked out with orange walls, colourful wooden tables and a glowing blue bar, this place sells really tasty meat, fish and veggie tapas, full meals, sangria and draught beer.

★Mar à Vista
SEAFOOD €€

(☑261 862 928; Largo das Ribas 16; mains €12-20; ⊙lunch & dinner Thu-Tue) Crustaceans of every kind are on full display at this hearty frill-free local place known for its shellfish. Order simple *doses* of oysters, clams or garlic shrimp accompanied by beer on tap, indulge in a *massada, feijoada, açorda* or *cataplana* for two, or choose your very own crab or lobster from the stainless steel counter up front. Cash only.

Tik Tak
INTERNATIONAL €€

(http://restaurantetiktak.wordpress.com; Rua 5 de Outubro 7; mains €9-15; ⊙7-11pm daily, 12.30-3pm Sat & Sun; ☑) On a picturesque corner in the pedestrian zone, Tik Tak draws plenty of tourists and hip young locals to its open kitchen, jazzy music and atmospheric tables on the cobblestones. The varied menu offers a break for those unmoved by Ericeira's seafood fetish; there are more fresh vegetables than most, plus abundant nonfishy options: serious carnivores will love the *parrilhada real* – a cornucopia of grilled meat that'll feed two or three (€27).

Restaurante Prim
BRAZILIAN €€

(☑261 865 230; Rua 5 de Outubro 16; mains €8-15; ⊙lunch & dinner) This bright, contemporary place with outdoor seating dishes up high-quality, Brazilian-style grilled meats that smell of the wood stove, and potent caipirinhas. Side dishes such as rice and black beans make welcome alternatives to the ubiquitous Portuguese potato. The wine list is uninspired but this is a good spot.

Mar d'Areia
SEAFOOD €€

(☑261 862 222; Rua Fonte do Cabo; mains €9-13; ⊙lunch & dinner Tue-Sun; ☑) They keep the decor simple – blue-and-white checked table-cloths and tile designs of fish in nets – and let the excellent grilled fish do the talking at this locally popular, family-friendly seafood eatery adjacent to the Mercado Municipal.

★Esplanada Furnas
SEAFOOD €€€

(☑261 864 870; www.restaurantefurnasericeira. com; Rua das Furnas; fish & seafood per kg €15-60; ⊙lunch & dinner) As close to the sea as you can get without a boat, Furnas is all about freshly caught fish and spectacular ocean views. They'll show you the catch of the day and then barbecue your choice on the spot. The per-kilogram price on the board covers the fish, plus all the accompaniments.

A Canastra
SEAFOOD €€€

(Rua Capitão João Lopes 8A; grilled fish per kg €15-50; ⊙lunch & dinner) This romantic, reliable option specialises in grilled fish and *caldeiradas* (seafood stews). Eat inside or grab one of the alluring sidewalk tables overlooking the ocean just across the street.

🍸 Drinking & Entertainment

At Praia Foz do Lizandro, south of town, a cluster of bars line the boardwalk overlooking the beach and river mouth, perfect for a late afternoon drink.

Neptuno
PUB

(☑261 862 017; Rua Mendes Leal 12; ⊙7.30pm-2am) This cosy neighbourhood pub features live fado on Monday nights in summer.

Ouriço
NIGHTCLUB

(www.facebook.com/discotecaourico; Rua Capitão João Lopes 9; ⊙11pm-6am Fri & Sat, nightly Jul & Aug) One of Portugal's oldest discos caters to night owls of all ages, with a mix of pop, dance, oldies and dancefloor standards.

Jukebox
BAR

(www.facebook.com/jukeboxbarericeira; Rua Dr Miguel Bombarda 7; ⊙8pm-2am) This laid-back little spot specialises in jazz, blues and soul. They mix a decent cocktail and are also open for brunch at weekends from May to September.

Sunset Bamboo
BAR

(Travessa Jogo da Bola; ⊙noon-8pm Sun-Tue & Thu, noon-2am Fri & Sat; ☜) This casual place is almost summed up by its name. It offers a relaxed beach-town vibe and is a perfect spot for an afternoon drink, whether a fruit juice or a cocktail. There's a light menu of sandwiches and snacks and it is open until 2am all week in summer.

❶ Information

Espaço Multimédia (Biblioteca Municipal, Rua Mendes Leal; ☉10am-1pm & 2-6pm Tue-Sat) Free internet in the ornate blue-and-white public library, one block west of Praça da República.

Turismo (☑261 863 122; turismo.ericeira@cm-mafra.pt; Rua Dr Eduardo Burnay 46; ☉10am-6pm Sep–mid-Jul, 10am-10pm mid-Jul–Aug) Has internet access at €2.50 per hour.

❶ Getting There & Away

BUS

Mafrense (☑261 862 717; www.mafrense.pt) buses stop at the bus station 800m north of the *praça* (town square), off the N247 highway.

Connections to northern destinations such as Peniche and Coimbra are best made through Torres Vedras (€3.55, one hour, six on weekdays, three on Saturday and one on Sunday). Other destinations, with services roughly on the hour, are Lisbon–Campo Grande station (€6, 1¼ hours), Mafra (€2.10, 25 minutes) and Sintra (€3.35, 50 minutes).

❶ Getting Around

Regular local buses to Torres Vedras go past Praia da Ribeira d'Ilhas (€1.20). For Praia Foz do Lizandro (€0.90), take any Sintra-bound bus to a stop on the N247 above the beach.

You can rent bicycles from **Go Out** (☑925 307 317; www.goout.com.pt; Rua Prudêncio Franco da Trindade 1; per day/week €11/56; ☉9am-1pm & 3-6pm Apr-Sep). There's a **taxi stand** in Largo dos Condes da Ericeira.

Peniche

POP 14,700

Popular for its long, fabulous town beach, nearby surf strands and also as a jumping-off point for the beautiful Ilhas Berlengas nature reserve, Peniche, spectacularly set on a headland with the sea on all sides, remains a working port, giving it a slightly grittier, more 'lived-in' feel than its resort neighbours. The walled historic centre makes for pleasant strolling, and the seaside fort where Salazar's regime detained political prisoners is a must-see for anyone interested in Portuguese history. Outdoors enthusiasts will love the beaches east of town, where lessons and rentals for every sport under the sun are available.

From the bus station, it's a 10-minute walk west to the historic centre. Cross the Ponte Velha (Old Bridge) into the walled town. The fort, harbour and Av do Mar – where you'll find most of the seafood restaurants – are a short distance south.

◉ Sights

Fortaleza   FORT
(☉9am-12.30pm & 2-5.30pm Tue-Fri, from 10am Sat & Sun) **FREE** Dominating the south of the peninsula, Peniche's imposing 16th-century fortress was used in the 20th-century as one of dictator Salazar's infamous jails for political prisoners. By the entrance where prisoners once received visitors – the stark booths with glass partitions are preserved – is the **Núcleo-Resistência**, a grim but fascinating display about those times including Resistance leaflets and prisoners' poignant, beautifully illustrated letters to their children.

Housed inside the fortress complex, the **Museu Municipal's** (☑262 780 116; admission €1.55; ☉9am-12.30pm & 2-5.30pm Tue-Fri, from 10am Sat & Sun) most striking feature is the top floor, which has a row of cells for political prisoners from the dictatorship years, some used for solitary confinement. Floors below this contain a nonthrilling municipal mishmash, from Roman archaeological artefacts to shipwreck finds.

Headland   VIEWPOINT
While in Peniche, make sure you do the circuit of the whole headland, either in the car or by walking the six kilometres. At Cabo Carvoeiro, the very tip, there's a lighthouse and spectacular views of a rock stack and the Berlenga islands, as well as an excellent restaurant.

Baleal   BEACH
About 5km to the northeast of Peniche is this scenic island-village, connected to the mainland village of Casais do Baleal by a causeway. The fantastic sweep of sandy beach here offers some fine surfing. Surf schools dot the sands, as do several bar-restaurants.

Escola de Rendas de Bilros   ARTS & CRAFTS
(☉9am-12.30pm & 2-5.30pm Mon-Fri) At this school attached to Peniche's *turismo* (tourist office) building, you can watch the nimble (and chatty) ladies in action as the chaos of their bobbins produces exquisite lace.

🏃 Activities

Surfing

Long renowned as a prime surfing destination, Peniche burnished its celebrity status when **Supertubos** beach, south of town, was selected as a stop on the ASP World Tour, the most prestigious international circuit of competitive surfing.

Meanwhile, **Baleal** is a paradise of challenging but, above all, consistent waves that make it an ideal learners' beach.

Peniche is full of surfers' hostels and schools. Depending on the season, surf camps at Baleal charge from €240 to €500 for a week of classes, including equipment and shared self-catering lodging. You can also take individual two-hour classes (€35) and rent boards and wetsuits (€30/135 per day/week). Well-established operators include **Baleal Surfcamp** (📞262 769 277; www.balealsurfcamp.com; Rua Amigos do Baleal 2; 1/3/5 day course €60/95/145) and **Peniche Surfcamp** (📞962 336 295; www.penichesurfcamp.com; Av do Mar 162, Casais do Baleal).

Diving

There are good opportunities for diving, especially at Berlenga. Expect to pay about €65 to €75 (less around Peniche) for two dives with **Acuasuboeste** (📞918 393 444; www.acuasuboeste.com; Porto de Pesca) or **Haliotis** (📞262 781 160; www.haliotis.pt; Av Monsenhor Bastos, Hotel Praia Norte). Both companies also offer a range of PADI certification courses.

Kitesurfing

Kitesurfing is big. On the far side of high dunes about 500m east of the walled town, **Peniche Kite & Surf Center** (📞919 424 951; www.penichekitecenter.com; Av Monsenhor Bastos, Praia de Peniche de Cima) offers lessons with equipment for €40 if there are two of you.

Tours

From the harbourfront kiosks in Largo da Ribeira, an ever-increasing number of companies offer day tours to Berlenga, plus other activities such as fishing.

SURFING PORTUGAL

Portugal is a great surfing destination because, as continental Europe's westernmost spot, the coast is a swell magnet. Add to that mild weather, different breaks and conditions within a short distance, wild coastal stretches, great food, great night scene, and affordable prices. And did I mention the waves are great too?

Best is the Peniche area, for variety of conditions and for Supertubos (p264) alone, and Ericeira (p260) for the concentration of world-class breaks, including the best points and reefs in Europe. Sagres (p194) is another great option that offers good surf, the country's best weather, a wild coast and great nightlife in bars with live gigs of many sorts.

For beginners, Peniche offers a variety of options that let you gradually move up along the difficulty scale.

Surfing conditions? Windguru (www.windguru.cz) can be pretty accurate if you know how to read it. In Portugal (all in Portuguese), www.beachcam.pt has good cameras when they're working. The Instituto Hidrográfico has a forecast application on its website (www.hidrografico.pt/qual-e-a-tua-onda.php). There's also the fine work of a professional meteorologist and surfer on meteoceansurf.blogspot.pt.

Postsurf beers? I live in Ericeira, so I would have to go for local choices. Bandejas, Tubo, La Luna, Na Onda and Bamboo (p262) are all pretty cool. Done with talking and ready to hit the floor? Ouriço (p262) is an inevitable part of the Portuguese surfing experience.

Hungry surfers should try *bacalhau à braz* (an amazing mix of codfish with fried chips and eggs), *arroz de marisco* (seafood rice), *açorda de marisco* (mashed bread seasoned and mixed with prawns and shellfish) and classic *bitoque* (steak with fries, rice and a fried egg on top).

João Valente, Director, Surf Portugal website (www.surfportugal.pt)

Associação de Operadores
Marítimo-Turística
BOAT TRIPS

(☑262 789 997; associacaopescadesportiva@gmail.com; ✋) Runs cruises on demand throughout the year, ranging from €8.50 per person for a trip to Cabo Carvoeiro, to €50 per person to the Farilhões, the twin outer islands of the Berlenga chain. It also organises fishing trips: a full-day excursion for up to 11 people, including licences, bait and equipment costs €550; half-day excursions on a smaller boat cost €35 per person (maximum six passengers).

Nautipesca
FISHING

(☑917 588 358, 262 789 648; www.nautipesca.com.pt) Organises fishing trips from its kiosk at the harbour.

🛏 Sleeping

Expect discounts of up to 30% outside July and August. Surfers can also find cheap lodging at the many surf camps in Baleal and at numerous other hostels.

Katekero II
GUESTHOUSE €

(www.feriaskatekero.com; Av do Mar 68; d/apt €55/80; ✳🎤🐾✋) These appealing and spacious modern rooms sit above a popular seafood restaurant on the harbourfront. They are simple but attractive, with comfortable bed platforms, a fridge, and, in some cases, a small balcony. All have great views over the water, and are very reasonably priced for this location. There are also modern apartments with kitchen and options for sleeping up to four.

Nineteen Bed & Breakfast
HOSTEL €

(☑912 305 707; nineteen.peniche@gmail.com; Rua António da Conceição Bento 19; dm/d €23/55; 🎤) Alongside the municipal market, this new option is part-hostel, part-guesthouse, offering some very smart private rooms (with shared bathroom) as well as appealing dormitory accommodation. An excellent breakfast is included, and the couple that run it is extremely helpful.

Peniche Hostel
HOSTEL €

(☑969 008 689; www.penichehostel.com; Rua Arquitecto Paulino Montês 6; dm/d €20/50; @🎤) This cosy little hostel, only steps from the *turismo* and a five-minute walk from the bus station, has colourfully decorated and breezy rooms with tall windows overlooking the town wall. The friendly owners make you feel at home immediately, as do the comfortable common areas and small sun-

deck. Surfboards and bikes are available for hire, and there's an attached surf school.

Residencial Rimavier
GUESTHOUSE €

(☑262 789 459; www.rimavier.com; Rua Castilho 6; s/d €35/45) This immaculate *pensão* (guesthouse) – run by the helpful family in the souvenir shop downstairs – has small but spruce rooms, nautically-themed linens and hallways decorated with lovely tile paintings of Peniche.

Parque de Campismo
Peniche Praia
CAMPGROUND €

(☑262 783 460; www.penichepraia.pt; Estrada Marginal Norte; sites per adult/child/tent/car €3.80/1.90/3.80/3.40; P🎤✋✋) On the high, windy, north side of the peninsula, 1.7km from town and the beach, and 2km from Cabo Carvoeiro, this site has decent facilities but lacks shade. There's also a good selection of bungalows, apartments, and double rooms (from €49 to €79 in high season).

★Casa das Marés
B&B €€

(☑262 769 371, 262 769 200, 262 769 255; www.casadasmares2.com; Praia do Baleal; d €80-89; 🎤) At the picturesque, windswept tip of Baleal stands one of the area's most unique accommodation options. Three sisters inherited this imposing house from their parents and divided it into three parts – each of which now serves as its own little B&B. Breezy, inviting rooms all have great close-up sea views, and the sound of the breaking waves below is magical. Downstairs sitting areas are extremely cosy and the entire place is loaded with character. The breakfast in the middle one (II) is especially delicious. Worth reserving ahead.

Residencial Maciel
GUESTHOUSE €€

(☑262 784 685; www.residencial-maciel.com; Rua José Estêvão 38; d €45-65; 🎤) Spiffed up with new paint, blinds and soundproof windows to go with its polished wood floors and carpeted hallways, Maciel is a cut above the other downtown sleeping options. The annexe around the corner costs €10 less.

🍴 Eating

Restaurante A Sardinha
SEAFOOD €

(Rua Vasco da Gama 81; mains €6-14; ☉lunch & dinner) This simple place on a narrow street parallel to Largo da Ribeira does a roaring trade with locals and tourists alike. They can be a little pushy if you're walking by on the street but once inside things improve, and the fixed-price menu, featuring soup, bread, main course, dessert, wine and coffee, is a great deal at €7.50.

★ Restaurante Popular
SEAFOOD €€

(☑262 790 290; Largo da Ribeira 40; mains €8-12; ☉lunch & dinner Tue-Sun) This harbourside spot serves up really excellent seafood in a luminous, glassy light area. It's a great place offering top value. The tasty daily specials reflect what's been caught locally – the *espetos* (skewers) of mixed fish are very tasty.

Katekero II
SEAFOOD €€

(www.feriaskatekero.com; Av do Mar 68-70; mains €8-13; ☉lunch & dinner Wed-Mon) One of several restaurants forming a long strip near the harbour, this attractive and welcoming place serves good seafood without an excessive price tag, including an excellent seafood rice. Its land-based plates are also recommended, with particularly tasty pork dishes.

★ Nau dos Corvos
MODERN PORTUGUESE €€€

(☑262 783 168; www.naudoscorvos.com; Marginal Norte, Cabo Carvoeiro; mains €17-22; ☉lunch & dinner) It's just you and the sea out here at Cabo Carvoeiro, 2.5km from the centre of town at the tip of the peninsula. But as you gaze out at the Atlantic from the windy platform, it's nice to know that under your feet is an excellent seafood restaurant. With some of the best sunset views in Portugal, and great plates to share, it's a romantic, upmarket place to dine.

Drinking & Nightlife

The area around Igreja de São Pedro is the old town's drinking hub (think four walls, cold beer and a home stereo system). For nightlife, you're really better off in Baleal, where you'll find several laid-back surfer bars right on the beach.

Java House
CAFE, BAR

(Largo da Ribeira 14; ☉9am-3am Mon-Thu, 9am-4am Fri & Sat; ☜) The most popular joint in town, this deals in everything from early-morning coffees to sandwiches and crêpes. The lights dim later in the evening, and DJs strut their stuff. The cocktails and mixed drinks are let down by the service, but the terrace and the exposed rock interior are atmospheric.

❶ Information

Espaço Internet (☑969 195 895; Rua Dr João Matos Bilhau 28; ☉10am-1pm & 3-10pm Mon-

Sat, 10am-noon & 3-8pm Sun) Free internet access.

Turismo (☑262 789 571; turismo@cm-peniche.pt; ☉9am-1pm & 2-5pm) Main branch in the public garden alongside Rua Alexandre Herculano.

❶ Getting There & Away

BUS

Peniche's **bus station** (☑968 903 861; Rua Dr Ernesto Moreira) is served by **Rodotejo** (www.rodotejo.pt) and **Rede Expressos** (www.rede-expressos.pt). Destinations include Coimbra (€14.50, 2¾ hours, three daily), Leiria (€13, two hours, three daily), Lisbon (€9, 1½ hours, every one to two hours) and Óbidos (€3.15, 40 minutes, six to eight daily).

CAR & MOTORCYCLE

Driving into Peniche, the main highway (N114/IP6) reaches a roundabout shortly before town, where you can bear left towards the centre, right for Baleal and the eastern beaches, or straight for 3km along the northern cliffs to Cabo Carvoeiro and its lighthouse. Most days you can find ample free parking on the road that runs along the harbour.

❶ Getting Around

Local buses connect Peniche with Baleal (€1.50, 10 minutes) during the week, but service is spotty on weekends outside summer. Bikes are a good way to get around the beaches; hire them at **Stand Rádio Micro-Moto** (☑262 782 480; Rua António da Conceição Bento 19; day hire €7).

Reserva Natural da Berlenga

Sitting about 10km offshore from Peniche, **Berlenga Grande** is a spectacular, rocky and remote island, with twisting, shocked-rock formations and gaping caverns. It's the only island of the Berlenga archipelago you can visit – the group consists of three tiny islands surrounded by clear, calm, dark-blue waters full of shipwrecks that are great for snorkelling and diving.

In the 16th century Berlenga Grande was home to a monastery, but now the most famous inhabitants are thousands of nesting sea birds, especially guillemots. The birds take priority over human visitors: the only development that has been allowed includes housing for a small fishing community and a lighthouse. Paths are clearly marked to stop day trippers trespassing on the birds' domain.

Linked to the island by a narrow causeway is the 17th-century **Forte de São João Baptista**, now one of the country's most dramatic (but barren) hostels.

🛏 Sleeping & Eating

If you want to sleep on the island, you'll need to book well ahead. The two park facilities can only be reserved starting in May. Most places are already booked solid by the end of May.

There's a small grocery store on the island for self-catering.

Berlenga Campismo CAMPGROUND €
(☎262 789 571; turismo@cm-peniche.pt; 2-/3-/ 4-person tent sites €11/16/20; ☺May-Sep) This simple camping area is just above a pretty beach near the boat dock; book in advance at the Peniche *turismo*.

Forte de São João Baptista Hostel HOSTEL €
(☎912 631 426; www.facebook.com/aaberlenga; s/d/q €22/44/80; ☺Jun-Sep) This was once a fine historic inn but was abandoned for many years – and you can feel it. It's a dramatic but dead-basic hostel, with limited water supply and antiquated bathrooms; you need to bring your own sleeping bag and cooking equipment, although there is a small shop and a bar. Advance payment by wire transfer is required. Bring a torch, as the generator goes off at midnight.

Mar e Sol HOTEL €€
(☎262 750 331; www.restaurantemaresol.com; tw/f €100/140; ☺mid-Apr–Oct) The decent, if simple, rooms here would seem overpriced anywhere else, but when you consider the location just a few steps above Berlenga's boat dock and directly adjacent to its only restaurant, things appeal more. Prices halve at beginning and end of the season.

❶ Getting There & Away

Viamar (☎262 785 646; www.viamar-berlenga. com; day round-trip adult/child €18/10, one-way €11/6; ☺20 May-15 Sep) is the longest established of several harbourside outfits, all making the 40-minute trip to the island on roughly the same schedule and for the same round-trip fare. Viamar sails three times daily during July and August, at 9.30am, 11.30am and 5.30pm, returning at 10.30am, 4.30pm and 6.30pm. During the remainder of the season there's one sailing daily, departing at 10am, returning at 4.30pm.

Tickets tend to sell out q[...] only 300 visitors are all[...] ings are weather-depe[...] also offer add-ons suc[...] island or a sea cave [...]

If you're prone to [...] day carefully – the [...]

Óbidos

POP 3100 / ELEV 80M

Surrounded by a classic crenellated w[...] Óbidos' gorgeous historic centre is a labyrinth of cobblestoned streets and flower-bedecked, whitewashed houses livened up with dashes of vivid yellow and blue paint. It's a delightful place to pass an afternoon, but there are plenty of reasons to stay overnight, as there's excellent accommodation including a hilltop castle now converted into one of Portugal's most luxurious *pousadas* (upmarket hotels).

Hill-town aficionados looking to savour Óbidos' 'lost in time' qualities may find the main street ridiculously touristy, but wind your way away from it and you'll capture some of the town's atmosphere. There are pretty bits outside the walls too.

The main gate, Porta da Vila, leads directly into the main street, Rua Direita, lined with chocolate and cherry-liqueur shops.

History

When Dom Dinis first showed Óbidos to his wife Dona Isabel in 1228, it must have already been a pretty sight because she fell instantly in love with the place. The king decided to make the town a wedding gift to his queen, initiating a royal tradition that lasted until the 19th century.

Any grace it had in 1228 must be credited to the Moors, who had laid out the streets and had only recently abandoned the strategic heights. The Moors had chased out the Visigoths, who in turn had evicted the Romans, who also had a fortress here.

Until the 15th century Óbidos overlooked the sea; the bay gradually silted up, leaving the town landlocked.

◉ Sights

Castelo, Walls & Aqueduct HISTORIC SITE
FREE You can walk around the unprotected **muro** (wall) for uplifting views over town and surrounding countryside. The walls date from Moorish times (later restored), but the **castelo** (castle) itself is one of Dom

...t have the Taliban got to do with a rural winery 12km south of Óbidos? Well, when ...y blew up the Buddhas of Bamiyan in Afghanistan in 2001, the millionaire art collec-...or José Berardo was so incensed at the wanton destruction of culture that he decided to do something to balance it out and created a large sculpture park in the grounds of his winery. The result, **Buddha Eden** (www.buddhaeden.com; Carvalhal; admission €2.50; ☺9.30am-5.30pm Oct-Mar, 10.30am-6.30pm Apr-Sep), is an astonishing sight, with monu-mental Buddhist statues standing proud above the cork trees, a phalanx of terracotta warriors looking down on a duck-filled lake, modern contemporary sculpture among the vines, and a little **tourist train** (adult/child €3/free) doing the rounds for the sore-of-foot. It's a great place to relax, and there's a café here, as well as a wine shop. To make a day of it, there's an appealing restaurant in the nearby village – **Mãe d'Água** (www.restaurantemaedagua.com; Rua 13 Maio 26, Sobral do Parelhão; mains €10-18; ☺lunch Tue-Sun, dinner Tue-Sat) does confident modern Portuguese fare in a contemporary setting within a noble old building.

To get here, take the A8 motorway south from Óbidos and exit at junction 12, then follow signs for Carvalhal.

Dinis' 13th-century creations. It's a stern edifice, with lots of towers, battlements and big gates. Converted into a palace in the 16th century (some Manueline touches add levity), it's now a deluxe *pousada*.

The **aqueduct**, southeast of the main gate, dates from the 16th century and is 3km long.

Igreja de Santa Maria   CHURCH
(Praça de Santa Maria; ☺9.30am-12.30pm & 2.30-7pm) The town's elegant main church, near the northern end of Rua Direita, stands out for its interior, with a wonderful painted ceiling and walls done up in beautiful blue-and-white 17th-century *azulejos* (hand-painted tiles). Paintings by the renowned 17th-century painter Josefa de Óbidos are to the right of the altar. There's a fine 16th-century Renaissance tomb on the left, probably carved by French sculptor Nicolas Chanterène.

Museu Municipal   MUSEUM
(☎262 955 557; Solar da Praça de Santa Maria; ☺10am-1pm & 2-6pm) **FREE** Located in an 18th-century manor house just next to Igreja de Santa Maria, the town's museum houses a small collection of paintings spanning several centuries. The highlight is a haunting portrait by Josefa de Óbidos, *Faustino das Neves* (1670), remarkable for its dramatic use of light and shade.

Santuário do Senhor da Pedra   CHURCH
(Largo do Santuário; ☺9am-12.30pm & 2.30-7pm Tue-Sun, to 5pm Oct-Apr) Below town this im-posing, if a little ramshackle, hexagonal church is an 18th-century baroque gem in need of some tender loving care. It's worth the stroll down here for the unusual hexagonal interior; in the altar is the stone sculpture of Christ crucified that gives the place its name.

⭐ Festivals & Events

Festival Internacional do Chocolate   FOOD
(www.festivalchocolate.cm-obidos.pt; ⊡) This scrumptiously decadent 23-day celebration draws over 200,000 people each February to March with events for every age and taste, including a kids' playhouse made entirely from chocolate.

Mercado Medieval   MEDIEVAL FAIR
(www.mercadomedievalobidos.pt) This two-week medieval fair – held in July inside the castle grounds and below the town's western wall – includes live entertainment, jousting matches, plenty of grog and pigs roasting on spits, and the chance to try your hand at scaling the town walls with the help of a harness and rope. Dress in medieval attire and the €6 admission fee is halved; you can also rent an outfit for €6 and get in free.

🛌 Sleeping

Several places around town rent out private rooms; look for signs, or pick up a comprehensive list of accommodations at the *turismo*.

Hostel Argonauta
HOSTEL €

(☑262 958 088; www.hostelargonauta.com; Rua Adelaide Ribeirete 14; dm/d €25/50; 🛜) In a pretty spot just outside the walls, this excellent location feels more like staying at a friend's place than a hostel. Run with enthusiasm and good cheer, it has an arty, colourful dorm with stove and beds as well as bunks; there's also a cute double with a great view. The small capacity means it's a great personal, sociable experience. Breakfast is included.

★ Casa d'Óbidos
RURAL INN €€

(☑262 950 924; www.casadobidos.com; Quinta de São José; s/d €75/90, 2-/4-/6-person apt not incl breakfast €90/140/175; P🛜🏊) In a whitewashed, 19th-century villa below town, this delightful place features spacious, breezy rooms with good new bathrooms and period furnishings, plus tennis courts, a swimming pool and lovely grounds with sweeping views of Óbidos' bristling walls and towers. Home-produced honey and fruit are served at breakfast, and trails lead through orchards up to town. Head for the big baroque church below town and turn left after it.

Casa do Relógio
GUESTHOUSE €€

(☑262 958 554; www.casadorelogio.com; Rua da Graça 12; s/d/tr €45/60/80; 🛜🏊) Just east of the town walls this 18th-century house (named for a nearby sundial) has eight smallish, but spotless, traditionally furnished rooms with handsome tile floors, plus a pretty shared terrace.

Casas de São Thiago
D&B €€

(☑262 959 587; www.casas-sthiago.com; Largo de São Thiago 1; s/d €65/80; 🛜) This charming frilly labyrinth of snug, 18th-century rooms and tiled, flower-filled courtyards in the shadow of the castle has its own wine cellar and billiards room. Rooms vary, but all offer standard midrange comforts, plus some nice antique touches. There are six more, slightly cheaper rooms in another building near the principal entrance to town.

Pousada do Castelo
HISTORIC HOTEL €€€

(☑262 955 080; www.pousadas.pt; d/ste from €210/297; P🛜@🛜) One of Portugal's best *pousadas* occupies a charming convent hidden within the town's forbidding 13th-century castle. The whitewashed rooms are mostly done up with sleek contemporary furnishings. Book well in advance for the split-level rooms in the two castle towers –

especially room 203, which is popular with honeymooners.

Casa das Senhoras Rainhas
BOUTIQUE HOTEL €€€

(☑262 955 360; www.senhorasrainhas.com; Rua Padre Nunes Tavares 6; d with/without balcony €150/140, ste €170; ✳🛜) Tucked away inside the walls in the lower part of town – bear right as you enter the main gate – is this most enticing option with an excellent restaurant. Rooms are just lovely, with a classy, restrained elegance that evokes a bygone age without laying it on. Most have cute balconies looking at the walls: these can be your venue for breakfast if you choose. Little touches like an honesty bar plus fruit and homemade liqueur chocolates in the rooms add charm.

Hotel Real d'Óbidos
HOTEL €€€

(☑262 955 090; www.hotelrealdobidos.com; Rua Dom João de Ornelas; s €112-150, d €137-188; P✳🛜🏊) It's all medieval here, with suits of armour, shields riveted to the walls and staff in tunics, but modern comforts aren't lacking. Just outside the town walls, this is an atmospheric and well-equipped aristocratic dwelling converted to a small upmarket hotel. Rooms are spacious and commodious, and the summertime pool is great, as is the four-poster suite.

✖ Eating & Drinking

In touristy Óbidos, restaurants are generally long on atmosphere but short on value. The larger hotels, including the Pousada do Castelo, have good, but pricey, dining rooms.

Senhor da Pedra
PORTUGUESE €

(Largo do Santuário; mains €6-9; ⊙lunch & dinner) Behind the striking church of Senhor da Pedra below town, this simple white-tiled eatery (the one on the right as you look at the row of restaurants) is a recommended place to try low-priced authentic Portuguese cuisine. It's a classic affair with Mum in the kitchen, and Dad and the boy on tables. The name isn't signed – it just says 'Snack Bar', but if these are snacks, we'd hate to see what they consider a full meal.

Alcaide
PORTUGUESE €€

(☑262 959 220; Rua Direita 60; mains €12-17; ⊙lunch & dinner Thu-Tue) This upstairs restaurant with windows overlooking the town features creative dishes such as *requinte de bacalhau* (cod with cheese, chestnuts and apples). It's better than most of the main street options.

Cozinha das Rainhas
CONTEMPORARY, PORTUGUESE €€€

(✒ 262 955 360; www.senhorasrainhas.com; Rua Padre Nunes Tavares 6; mains €19-23; ☺ lunch Thu-Mon, dinner Wed-Mon) Attached to the Casa das Senhoras Rainhas hotel, this elegant restaurant offers some of the finest dining in Óbidos, with main courses like *bacalhau das rainhas* (codfish in a *fines herbes* crust with extra-virgin olive oil) and desserts like *dueto de chocolate* (white and dark chocolate mousse scented with orange and lime peel).

ⓘ Information

Espaço Internet (Rua Direita 107; ☺10am-7pm Mon-Fri Sep-Jul, 10am-8pm Mon-Fri, 11.30am-6.30pm Sat & Sun Jul & Aug) Free internet access opposite the church.

Turismo (✒ 262 959 231; posto.turismo@cm-obidos.pt; ☺ 9.30am-7.30pm Apr-Oct, 9.30am-6pm Mon-Fri, 9.30am-12.30pm & 1.30-5.30pm Sat & Sun rest of year) Just outside Porta da Vila near the bus stop, helpful multilingual staff offer town brochures and maps in four languages. Bike rentals (per day/half day €10.10/5.05) are also available; it also rents strange little buggies that aren't a great match to the medieval town.

ⓘ Getting There & Away

BUS
Buses stop on the main road just outside Porta da Vila. There are frequent departures for Peniche (€3.15, 40 minutes) and hourly weekday runs to Lisbon (€8.15, 65 minutes), plus five on Saturday and Sunday.

CAR & MOTORCYCLE
There is a fee-charging car park just outside the gate, while the one just across the road is free.

TRAIN
There are at least six daily trains to Lisbon (€8.45 to €9.30, 2½ hours) mostly via connections at Mira Sintra-Meleças station on the suburban Lisbon line. The station is located at the foot of the castle end of town. It's a pretty but uphill walk to town.

Foz do Arelho

POP 1300

With a vast, lovely beach backed by a rivermouth estuary ideal for windsurfing, Foz do Arelho remains remarkably undeveloped. It makes a fine place to laze in the sun, and

outside July and August it'll often be just you and the local fishermen. The beach has a row of relaxed bars and restaurants; the town is a 15-minute walk inland.

🏃 Activities

Escola de Vela da Lagoa
WATERSPORTS

(✒ 962 568 005; www.escoladeveladalagoa.com; ☺daily Apr-Sep, weekends Oct-Mar) Hires out sailboards (from €15 for one hour), sailboats (€16), kayaks (€8) and catamarans (from €20). The school also provides windsurfing and sailing lessons (two hours, €60 for one, €90 for two) and group kayak lessons (€14 per person for a three-hour session), and houses a bar serving snacks and drinks with lagoon views. From the Foz do Arelho village, it's 2.8km: turn left on the road that follows the lagoon's inland edge past the curious rock called Penedo Furado and continue.

🛏 Sleeping

Parque de Campismo Foz do Arelho
CAMPGROUND €

(✒ 262 978 683; www.orbitur.pt; sites per adult/child/tent/car €5.80/2.90/8/5.50, 5-person cabins €107; [P][🛜][🏊][♿]) This good, shady campsite, 2km from the beach, is run by Orbitur. It has a restaurant, a bar, laundry facilities and a market.

Hotel Penedo Furado
HOTEL €€

(✒ 262 979 610; www.hotelpenedofurado.com; Rua dos Camarções 3; s/d €65/80; [P][🛜]) Situated in the Foz do Arelho village, this modern hotel offers bright rooms that are a little bland but spacious and decent, with comfortable beds. Some have verandahs and distant lagoon views. There's a breezy, summery feel about this friendly, tiled place.

O Facho
HOTEL €€

(✒ 262 979 110; ofachoguesthouse@hotmail.com; Rua Francisco Almeida Grandela 3; d rear-view/ocean-view €65/85; [P]) This funky 100-year-old pink waterfront hotel has seen better days, but still retains lots of historic character, including high ceilings, creaky wooden floors, and checkerboard tiles and tubs in some bathrooms. The best rooms are the front-facing ones on the 2nd floor, with terrific ocean views.

🍴 Eating & Drinking

Tavola de Pedra
PORTUGUESE €€

(www.tavoladepedra.pai.pt; Rua Francisco Almeida Grandela 135A; mains €9-18; ☺lunch & dinner, closed Tue Oct-Mar) In the village, at the entrance from the east, this place features excellent local cooking, with tasty seafood stews and soups as well as good-quality meat dishes and some African dishes. Don't confuse it with the bar out the front; this is down the driveway to the side of it.

Cais da Praia
CAFE €€

(www.caisdapraia.com; Av do Mar; mains €9-19; ☺9am-3am Jun-Aug, to 2am Sep-May; 🤖📶) The trendiest of Foz do Arelho's waterfront joints, this is right on the beach and serves everything from sandwiches to full meals with great lagoon views and a good-value drinks list. It's very family-friendly.

Cabana do Pescador
SEAFOOD €€€

(☑262 979 451; Av do Mar; mains €12-25; ☺noon-4pm & 7-10.30pm) This renowned restaurant with its ocean-view terrace serves excellent meals featuring every imaginable form of sea life. It's not a frilly place, but the fish on a slab and central fountain with crustaceans scuttling about show what it's all about. Though it's not the cheapest, it's really good.

Trombone
JAZZ BAR

(Largo do Arraial 3; ☺8pm-2am) In the village, this characterful, spacious jazz bar has tasty mixed drinks and a pleasant terrace. It may not be the liveliest bar in town, but it's the best.

ℹ Getting There & Away

Buses connect Foz do Arelho with Caldas da Rainha (€2.05, 20 minutes, nine daily, fewer on weekends), from where you can connect to larger towns.

São Martinho do Porto

POP 2700

In contrast to nearby Nazaré, São Martinho do Porto is no party town, but a happy place where families and older paddlers enjoy the gentle lap of the waves on the omega-shaped bay ringed by sheltered, safe, sandy beaches.

🛏 Sleeping & Eating

Colina do Sol
CAMPGROUND €

(☑262 989 764; www.colinadosol.pt; sites per adult/child/tent/car €5/2.50/5-7/4; 🅿🤖🏊📶) This well-equipped, friendly campsite is 2km north of town, and about the same distance from the beach, with disabled access, a children's playground, a pool and some sections shaded by pine trees.

THE BIGGEST WAVE

A tiny black dot on a massive wall of water: footage of surfers riding monster waves at Nazaré has captivated the world in recent years. Given the right conditions, the big ones here can be over 30m high – think an eight-storey office building. The official world record of 23.77 metres for the biggest wave surfed was set here in 2011 by Garrett McNamara, who nearly bettered the feat with another giant in 2013. The waves are so fast and tall that surfers get towed in by jet-ski.

Why so big? Storms and winds in the Atlantic can generate mighty waves by themselves, but Nazaré has a peculiarity that multiplies this potential: an offshore underwater canyon some 5km deep pointing right at Praia do Norte beach. The energy of the ocean swells is concentrated by this feature, producing the massive waves.

Palace do Capitão
B&B €€

(☑262 985 150; www.palacecapitao.com; Rua Capitão Jaime Pinto 6; d €100-140, ste €180; 🅿✳🤖) This perfectly preserved 19th-century sea captain's home directly across from the beach is a place of distinction, with much of its original Victoriana still intact. Rooms are all different and beautiful, with lots of character. Room 4 is particularly lovely and light, while the upstairs suite (room 6) has its own sun terrace, accessed by a whimsical spiral staircase. Service is helpful here.

Hotel Atlântica
HOTEL €€

(☑262 980 151; www.residencial-atlantica.com; Rua Miguel Bombarda 6; d €75; @🤖) In a modern building, this welcoming place has spotless white-and-blue rooms with tiled floors to match. Rooms have low beds, little balconies and a summery feel. The mattresses could be firmer, but the friendliness of the owners makes up for it. Downstairs, the restaurant has a great terrace and serves simple but good fish and meat dishes. Room rates drop dramatically outside July and August.

ℹ Information

Turismo (☑262 989 110; www.cm-alcobaca.pt; Rua Vasco da Gama; ☺10am-1pm & 3-7pm May-Sep, 10am-1pm & 2-6pm Oct-Apr) In the heart of the village; in the same building is an elevator that takes you up to the top of the town.

❶ Getting There & Away

The train station is about 700m southeast of the centre. Buses stop on Rua Conde de Avelar, a block inland from the waterfront.

BUS

Rede Expressos runs at least five buses daily to/from Lisbon (€11, 1½ hours).

TRAIN

There are five daily trains northbound to Leiria (€4.15 to €4.55, 40 to 45 minutes) and southbound to Caldas da Rainha (€1.55, 15 minutes), with onward connections in both directions.

Nazaré

POP 10,500

With a warren of narrow, cobbled lanes running down to a wide, cliff-backed beach, Nazaré is Estremadura's most picturesque coastal resort. The sands are packed wall-to-wall with multicoloured umbrellas in July and August, but the party atmosphere isn't limited to the summer beach scene – Nazaré is one of Portugal's top draws for New Year's Eve and Carnaval celebrations as well.

The town centre is jammed with seafood restaurants, bars and local women in traditional dress hawking rooms for rent, especially near seafront Av da República. To get a different perspective, take the funicular up to Promontório do Sítio, where picture-postcard coastal views unfold from the cliffs.

Nazaré has hit the headlines in recent years for the monster waves that roll in just north of town and the record-breaking feats of the gutsy surfers that ride them (see box, p271).

◉ Sights

Promontório do Sítio   HISTORIC AREA

Until the 18th century the sea covered the present-day site of Nazaré; locals lived at this clifftop area 110m above the beach. Today this tourist-filled promontory is popular for its tremendous views and its religious associations. From Rua do Elevador, north of the *turismo*, an **ascensor** (funicular; adult/child €1.20/0.90; ⊙every 15min 7.15am-9.30pm, every 30min 9.30pm-midnight) climbs up the hill to Promontório do Sítio; it's nice to walk back down, escaping the crowds of trinket-sellers. There are plenty of places to stay and eat up on the clifftop too.

On a foggy day in 1182, local nobleman Dom Fuas Roupinho was in pursuit of a deer when the animal disappeared off the edge of the Sítio precipice. Dom Fuas cried out to the Virgin, whose sculpture was venerated in a nearby cave, for help, and his horse miraculously stopped right at cliff's edge; the mark of one of its horseshoes is still visible. In what is a much-repeated story in the Iberian peninsula, Dom Fuas built the small Hermida da Memória chapel on the edge of the drop-off to commemorate the event and house the sculpture. It was later visited by a number of VIP pilgrims, including Vasco da Gama. The statue is now housed in the grander church across the square.

Igreja de Nossa Senhora da Nazaré   CHURCH

(⊙9am-7pm Apr-Sep, 9am-6pm Oct-Nov) The 17th-century, baroque Igreja de Nossa Senhora da Nazaré, decorated with attractive Dutch *azulejos*, is on the Promontório do Sítio and holds the much-venerated sculpture of the Virgin, said to have been made by Joseph himself in Nazareth when Jesus was a baby: hence the name of the town. For €0.50, you can get up close and personal with the statue itself – it's not too often that you get the chance to appear in the middle of an altarpiece.

Look out for paintings of a deer in midair that refer to the legend of the Virgin's appearance here. Though the fall was tragic for the animal itself, its look of surprise is difficult not to snigger at.

✨ Festivals & Events

Carnaval   MARDI GRAS

One of Portugal's brashest Mardi Gras celebrations, with lots of costumed parades and general irreverence. Lots of people dress up and the nights go loud and long.

Festa do Mar   RELIGIOUS

Held every year on the first weekend in May, this festival features fireworks at midnight, a parade with floats dedicated to local patron saints and a procession of decorated boats around Nazaré's harbour.

Nossa Senhora da Nazaré   RELIGIOUS

This annual pilgrimage, held in Sítio on 8 September and the following weekend, is Nazaré's big religious festival, featuring sombre processions, folk dances and bullfights.

ESTREMADURA & RIBATEJO NAZARÉ

Nazaré

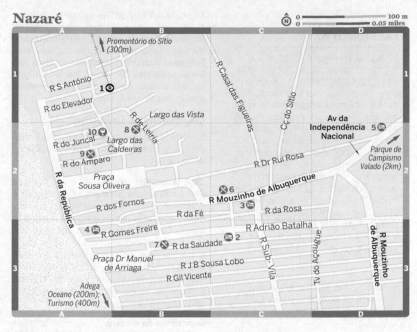

Nazaré

◎ Sights
1 Ascensor A1

🛏 Sleeping
2 Hospedaria Ideal C3
3 Magic Art Hotel C2
4 Ribamar A3
5 Vila Conde Fidalgo D2

✖ Eating
6 A Lanterna C2
7 A Tasquinha B3
8 Conchinha da Nazaré B2
9 Maria do Mar A2

🍷 Drinking & Nightlife
10 Casa O Santo A2

🛏 Sleeping

You'll likely be hit up by local women offering rooms for rent. It never hurts to bargain and see what the going rate is. Expect to pay 30% to 50% less outside July and August.

★ Vila Conde
Fidalgo GUESTHOUSE, APARTMENTS €
(☎ 262 552 361; http://condefidalgo.planetaclix.pt; Av da Independência Nacional 21A; d/apt from €50/60; ❋ ⊗ 🐾) Built around a series of courtyards and patios decorated with broken-china mosaics and adorned with flowers and plants, this pretty family-run complex a few blocks up from the beach was a former fishermen's colony. Friendly manager Ana offers 10 clean, colourful and comfortable rooms with minifridges, plus a dozen apartments of varying sizes. Breakfast (freshly squeezed orange juice, bread and seasonal fruit) is €5 extra, served in your room or on the terrace outside.

Hospedaria Ideal GUESTHOUSE €
(☎ 262 551 379; www.hospedariaideal.com.sapo.pt; Rua Adrião Batalha 98; d with shared bathroom €40, with full board €75) The charming landlady has a little restaurant downstairs and six humbly old-fashioned rooms upstairs that are little bigger than the beds. Doubles cost as little as €20 most of the year. It's booked solid in August, when full board is mandatory. She also has a good-value little seafront house for €300 a week in summer.

Parque de Campismo Valado CAMPGROUND €
(☎ 262 561 111; www.orbitur.pt; Rua dos Combatentes do Ultramar 2; sites per adult/child/tent/car €5.80/2.90/8/5.50; 🅿 ⊗ 🐾 🛶) This shady, well-equipped year-round Orbitur site has

FISHING, THE OLD-FASHIONED WAY

Long gone are Nazaré's days as a traditional fishing village, but tourists can still get a taste of the old ways on Saturdays throughout May and June during the **Arte Xávega** festival. In the morning, locals set off in pointy-prowed *xávega* boats to lay out the gigantic nets typical of this stretch of coast, a process that takes many hours. Then at 4pm, townspeople gather on the beach, men in berets and women in shawls and kerchiefs, and begin to draw the nets in – sometimes with the help of teams of oxen. Watching is colourful enough, but tourists are also welcome to help haul. Fish is sold on the spot as soon as it comes out of the net.

a restaurant, bar and excellent swimming pool as well as bungalows and fixed tents available. It's 2km east of town, off the Alcobaça road.

Magic Art Hotel   HOTEL €€
(☑ 262 569 040; www.hotelmagic.pt; Rua Mouzinho de Albuquerque 58; s/d Aug €85/90, Jul €70/75; P ❋ ❀ ☎) Close to the action, this breezy newish hotel has gone for the chic modern look. Clean-lined, well-equipped white rooms with artily presented photos of oldtime Nazaré contrast with appealing black slate bathrooms. Despite the guest lounge looking like a design showroom, this is an unpretentious, attractive and friendly place. As everywhere in this party town, expect some street noise. Great value in winter, when a double is only €45.

Adega Oceano   GUESTHOUSE €€
(☑ 262 561 161; www.adegaoceano.com; Av da República 51; d Aug €85; ❋ ☎) This cordial little oceanfront place offers much nicer amenities than you'd expect from the exterior appearance. The rooms should all have been remodelled by the time you read this; they are compact, with flatscreen TV and excellent modern bathrooms. Those at the front have nice views across the beach to the cliffs and waterfront. As with any place this close to the action, street noise can be a problem.

Ribamar   HOTEL €€
(☑ 262 551 158; www.ribamar.pai.pt; Rua Gomes Freire 9; d €70-90; ❋ ☎) Rooms at this seafront hotel are brighter, frillier and airier than the musty and lugubrious halls might suggest. Bathrooms are clean and nicely tiled, and the two corner rooms (11 and 21) have little balconies with great ocean views. Price varies according to the vistas; low-season you can bag a room for half the rate. Streetside revelry can be noisy here.

🍴 Eating & Drinking

Seafood is the star in Nazaré. To drink with the locals, check out the bars around Travessa do Elevador.

★ A Tasquinha   SEAFOOD €
(Rua Adrião Batalha 54; mains €6-10; ☉ lunch & dinner Tue-Sun) This exceptionally friendly family operation serves excellent seafood in a pair of snug but pretty tiled dining rooms. High quality and reasonable prices make it hugely popular. Expect queues on summer nights but however many people there are, the delightful owners always try and squeeze you in, even if it's at someone else's table! Top value.

Conchinha da Nazaré   SEAFOOD €
(☑ 262 186 156; Rua de Leiria 17D; mains €7-12; ☉ lunch & dinner) This authentic, simple place on a backstreet square serves good-value seafood, including wood-grilled fish and delicious *açorda de marisco* (thick bread soup with seafood; €11). Many nights there are more locals than tourists.

Maria do Mar   SEAFOOD €€
(Rua do Guilhim 13; mains €8-12; ☉ lunch & dinner daily) Tucked away in a dark backstreet, this place does an excellent fish stew served in its rustic nautical dining room. There's a welcoming host and good atmosphere.

A Lanterna   SEAFOOD €€
(☑ 262 562 215; Rua Mouzinho de Albuquerque 59; mains for 2 €20-32; ☉ lunch & dinner) This cosy, if touristy, place specialises in paella-like *cataplana* (seafood simmered with herbs, tomatoes, onions and wine), served in its low-ceilinged dining room. We're not so sure about the Lonely Planet sign outside though...

Casa O Santo   BAR
(☑ 262 085 128; Travessa do Elevador 11; seafood appetisers from €5; ☉ noon-late) An immensely enjoyable *cervejaria* (beer house) serving beer, wine and tasty seafood snacks – especially recommended are the garlicky steamed *ameijoas* (clams). Grab

a table on the pavement, or eat under the stone arches of the cosy interior rooms beside the bustling bar.

ℹ Information

Espaço Internet (Biblioteca Municipal, Av do Municipio; ⏰9.30am-6pm Mon-Fri, 3-6pm Sat & Sun; 📶) Free internet and wi-fi in Nazaré's spiffy new public library.

Turismo (📞262 561 194; www.cm-nazare.pt; Av Manuel Remígio, Centro Cultural da Nazaré; ⏰9.30am-1pm & 2.30-6pm Oct-Mar, 9.30am-12.30pm & 2.30-6.30pm Apr-Jun & Sep, 9am-9pm Jul-Aug) It's found on the beachfront strip, located in the cultural centre in the old fish market.

ℹ Getting There & Away

BUS

Rodotejo (www.rodotejo.pt) and **Rede Expressos** (www.rede-expressos.pt) serve the following destinations several times daily from Nazaré's bus station, a couple of blocks in from the ocean: Alcobaça (€2.20, 20 minutes), Leiria (express/local €6.80/3.80, 40/60 minutes), Lisbon (€11, 1¾ hours) and Peniche (€9.80, 70 minutes).

Alcobaça

POP 17,800

Only 100km north of Lisbon, the little town of Alcobaça has a charming if touristed centre with a little river and bijou bridges. All however yields centre stage to the magnificent 12th-century Mosteiro de Santa Maria de Alcobaça, one of Portugal's memorable Unesco World Heritage sites.

⊙ Sights

Mosteiro de Santa Maria de Alcobaça   MONASTERY

(📞262 505 126; www.mosteiroalcobaca.pt; church free, monastery adult/child €6/free, with Tomar and Batalha €15; ⏰9am-7pm Apr-Sep, 9am-5pm Oct-Mar) One of Iberia's great monasteries utterly dominates the town of Alcobaça. Hiding behind the imposing baroque facade lies a high, austere, monkish church with a forest of unadorned 12th-century arches. But make sure you visit the rest too: the atmospheric refectory, vast dormitory and other spaces bring back the Cistercian life, which, according to sources, wasn't quite as austere here as it should have been.

➡ History

The monastery was founded in 1153 by Afonso Henriques, first king of Portugal, honouring a vow he'd made after the reconquest of Santarém in 1147. The monastery estate became one of the richest and most powerful in the country, apparently housing 999 monks, who held Mass nonstop in shifts.

In the 18th century however, it was the monks' growing decadence that became famous, thanks to the writings of 18th-century travellers such as William Beckford, who, despite his own tendency to exaggerate, was shocked at the 'perpetual gormandising... the fat waddling monks and sleek friars with wanton eyes...' The party ended in 1834 with the dissolution of the religious orders.

➡ Church

Much of the original facade was altered in the 17th and 18th centuries. However, once you step inside, the combination of Gothic ambition and Cistercian austerity hits you

---

LOVE, POLITICS & REVENGE

As moving as *Romeo and Juliet* – and far more gruesome – is the tragic story of Dom Pedro. Son of the king, Dom Afonso IV, Pedro fell madly in love with his wife's Galician lady-in-waiting, Dona Inês de Castro, with whom he had several children. Even after the death of Pedro's wife, his father forbade Pedro from marrying Inês, wary of her Spanish family's potential influence. Suspicious nobles continued to pressure Dom Afonso IV until finally he sanctioned Inês' murder in 1355, unaware that the two lovers had already secretly married.

Two years later, when Pedro succeeded to the throne, he exacted his revenge by ripping out and eating the hearts of Inês' murderers. He then exhumed and crowned her body, and ordered the court to pay homage to his dead queen by kissing her decomposing hand.

The couple are buried in elaborate tombs in the Mosteiro de Santa Maria de Alcobaça. Inês' tomb rests, not on lions but on the animal-like figures of the men that assassinated her.

immediately: the nave is a breathtaking 106m long but only 23m wide, with huge pillars and truncated columns. It is modelled on the French abbey of Clairvaux.

Occupying the south and north transepts are two intricately carved 14th-century tombs, the church's greatest possessions, which commemorate the tragic love story of Dom Pedro and Dona Inês de Castro. Although the tombs themselves were badly damaged by rampaging French troops in search of treasure in 1811, they still show extraordinary narrative detail. The tombs are inscribed Até ao Fím do Mundo (until the end of the world) and, on Pedro's orders, placed foot to foot so that, when the time comes, they can rise up and see each other straight away.

Nearby, look at the remarkable clay figures in the chapel of St Bernard and the unusual arching in the ambulatory.

➡ Kitchen & Refectory

The grand kitchen, described by Beckford as 'the most distinguished temple of gluttony in all Europe', owes its immense size to alterations carried out in the 18th century, including a water channel built through the middle to divert wild fish right into the kitchen.

The adjacent refectory, huge and vaulted, is where the monks ate in silence while the Bible was read to them from the pulpit, reached by a photogenic arched staircase. The monks entered through a narrow door on their way to the refectory; those too fat to pass through were forced to fast.

➡ Claustro do Silencio & Sala dos Reis

The beautiful Cloister of Silence dates from two eras: Dom Dinis built the intricate lower storey, with its arches and traceried stone circles, in the 14th century; the upper storey, typically Manueline in style, was added in the 16th century. Off the northwestern corner of the cloister is the 18th-century Sala dos Reis (Kings' Room), so called because statues of practically all the kings of Portugal line the walls. Below them are *azulejo* friezes depicting stories relevant to the abbey's construction. Upstairs, make sure you see the vast vaulted dormitory.

🛏 Sleeping & Eating

Hotel Santa Maria   HOTEL €

(☑262 590 160; www.hotelsantamaria.com. pt; Rua Dr Francisco Zagalo 20-22; s/d/tr/ste €39/49/64/70; P🌸🛜) Popular with tour groups, this modern place sits just across

from the Mosteiro de Santa Maria de Alcobaça. It's unexciting but has a great location and offers decent value. Book ahead for the front rooms with impressive views of the monastery's facade and square.

★ Challet Fonte Nova   B&B €€€

(☑262 598 300; www.challetfontenova.pt; Rua da Fonte Nova 8; s/d/ste €85/120/145; P🌸🛜) Set amid pretty gardens, this elegant, charming, 19th-century chalet has grand common areas with gleaming wood floors, carpets and period furnishings. The main house is especially attractive: sumptuously decorated rooms with big plush beds and not a hair out of place, tall French windows, and a downstairs self-serve bar with billiard table. There's also a whitewashed modern annexe with suites and a small spa complex.

A Casa   PORTUGUESE €€

(Praça 25 de Abril 51-54; mains €8-14; ⊙9am-7pm) Enjoy the local speciality, *frango na púcara* (stewed chicken) in the attractive beamed dining room just off the main square or escape the crowds on the pretty back patio. This is a reliable, welcoming place to eat. There's a second location just around the corner on Travessa da Cadeia.

ℹ Information

Biblioteca Municipal de Alcobaça (www.cm-alcobaca.pt; Rua Araujo Guimarães; ⊙2-6pm Mon, 10am-6pm Tue-Fri, 2-7pm Sat Sep–mid-Jul, 10am-6pm Mon-Fri mid-Jul & Aug) Free internet at the local library.

Turismo (☑262 582 377; www.rt-leiriafatima. pt; Rua 16 de Outubro 7; ⊙10am-1pm & 2-6pm Oct-Apr, 10am-1pm & 3-7pm May-Sep) Across the square from the monastery, this provides assistance in multiple languages.

ℹ Getting There & Away

Coming from Leiria it's possible to see both Batalha and Alcobaça in a single, carefully timed day. All buses run less frequently on weekends. Destinations include Batalha (€3.15, 30 minutes, every hour or two), Lisbon (€11.20, two hours, six per weekday), Leiria (€3.55, 50 minutes, six per weekday) and Nazaré (€2.20, 20 minutes, every hour or two).

Batalha

POP 8500 / ELEV 120M

Among the supreme achievements of Manueline architecture, Batalha's monastery transports visitors to another world, where solid rock has been carved into forms as delicate as snowflakes and as pliable as twisted rope.

⊙ Sights

Mosteiro de Santa
Maria da Vitória
MONASTERY

(☑ 244 765 497; www.mosteirobatalha.pt; church free, rest adult/child €6/free, with Alcobaça and Tomar €15; ⊙ 9am-6.30pm Apr-Sep, 9am-5.30pm Oct-Mar) This extraordinary abbey was built to commemorate the 1385 Battle of Aljubarrota (fought just south of here). Most of the monument was completed by 1434 in Flamboyant Gothic, but Manueline exuberance steals the show, thanks to additions made in the 15th and 16th centuries.

➡ History

At the Battle of Aljubarrota, 6500 Portuguese, commanded by Dom Nuno Álvares Pereira and supported by a few hundred English soldiers, repulsed a 30,000-strong force of Juan I of Castile, who had come claiming the throne of João d'Avis.

João called on the Virgin Mary for help and vowed to build a superb abbey in return for victory. Three years later he made good on his promise, as work began on the Dominican abbey.

➡ Exterior

The glorious ochre-limestone building bristles with pinnacles and parapets, flying buttresses and balustrades, and late-Gothic carved windows, as well as octagonal chapels and massive columns. The spectacular western doorway's layered arches pack in apostles, angels, saints and prophets, all topped by Christ and the Evangelists.

➡ Interior

The vast, vaulted Gothic interior is plain, long and high, warmed by light from the deep-hued stained-glass windows. To the right as you enter is the intricate Capela do Fundador (Founder's Chapel), an achingly beautiful, lofty, star-vaulted square room lit by an octagonal lantern. In the centre is the joint tomb of João I and his English wife, Philippa of Lancaster, whose marriage in 1387 cemented the alliance that still exists between Portugal and England. The tombs of their four youngest sons line the south wall of the chapel, including that of Henry the Navigator (second from the right).

➡ Claustro Real

Afonso Domingues, master of works during the late 1380s, built the fabulous Claustro

ℹ MULTI-MONASTERY TICKET

If you're planning to visit the monasteries at Alcobaça and Batalha, as well as the Convento de Cristo in Tomar, you can get (from any one of them) a combined ticket for €15 (a saving of €3) that will let you in to all three and is valid for a week.

Real (Royal Cloisters) in a restrained Gothic style, but it's the later Manueline embellishments by the great Diogo de Boitac that really take your breath away. Every arch is a tangle of detailed stone carvings of Manueline symbols, such as armillary spheres and crosses of the Order of Christ, entwined with writhing vegetation, exotic flowers and marine motifs – ropes, pearls and shells. Three graceful cypresses echo the shape of the Gothic spires atop the adjacent chapter house.

➡ Claustro de Dom Afonso V

Anything would seem austere after the Claustro Real, but the simple Gothic Claustro de Dom Afonso V is like being plunged into cold water – sobering you up after all that frenzied decadence. Between the two cloisters is a modern exhibition and audiovisual presentation.

➡ Sala do Capítulo

To the east of the Claustro Real is the early-15th-century chapterhouse, containing a beautiful 16th-century stained-glass window. The huge vault was considered so outrageously dangerous to build that only prisoners on death row were employed in its construction. A guard of honour overwatches the tomb of unknown soldiers.

➡ Capelas Imperfeitas

The roofless Capelas Imperfeitas (Unfinished Chapels) are perhaps the most astonishing aspect of Batalha. Only accessible from outside the abbey, the octagonal mausoleum with its seven chapels was commissioned in 1437. However, the later Manueline additions by the architect Mateus Fernandes overshadow everything else.

Although Fernandes' plan was never finished, the staggering ornamentation is all the more dramatic for being open to the sky. Most striking is the 15m-high doorway, a mass of stone-carved thistles, ivy, flowers, snails and all manner of 'scollops and twistifications', as William Beckford noted. Dom Duarte can enjoy it for all eternity: his tomb, and that of his wife, lie opposite the door.

Batalha de Aljubarrota
Centro de Interpretação
BATTLEFIELD

(www.fundacao-aljubarrota.pt; admission €7; ⊙10am-5.30pm Tue-Sun Oct-Apr, 10am-7pm May-Sep) For Portuguese people Aljubarrota conjures up a fierce sense of national pride, a 1385 battle where they defeated an odds-on favourite Castilian force and established the foundations for the Portuguese golden age. We thought the entry fee to the modern interpretation centre here, 2km south of Batalha, was steep until we saw the audiovisual, a no-expenses-spared blood-and-thunder half-hour medieval epic (available in English) that brings the whole thing to vivid life.

The display on bones is also fascinating – one skull still has the tip of an arrowhead in it. The battlefield itself is freely accessible and has some English explanations, but to really understand what went on here, you'll want the audioguide (€3) from the interpretation centre.

MCCB
MUSEUM

(Museu da Comunidade Concelhia da Batalha; www.museubatalha.com; Largo Goa, Rua Damão e Diu 4; admission €2.50; ⊙10am-1pm & 2-6pm Wed-Sun) This modern municipal museum in the centre of town is well worth the visit, taking you through the prehistory and history of the region, including some well-presented Roman remains and sections on the battle of Aljubarrota and Mosteiro de Santa Maria da Vitória's construction.

🍴 Sleeping & Eating

Pensão Gladius
GUESTHOUSE €

(☑919 103 044, 244 765 760; Praça Mouzinho de Albuquerque; s/d/tr not incl breakfast €25/30/40) In the square right next to the abbey, friendly older proprietor Dona Eglantina runs this snug but attractive place. It's got a vaguely alpine feel, with flower-filled window boxes and spotless, modern rooms tucked under the eaves. Some upstairs rooms overlook the equestrian statue in the abbey square. You'll probably pick up the wi-fi signal from the free council zone outside.

★Casa do Outeiro
BOUTIQUE HOTEL €€

(☑244 765 806; www.casadoouteiro.com; Largo Carvalho do Outeiro 4; s/d/tr €58/63/75; 🅿✳@ 🛜🏊) One of our favourite hotels in central Portugal, this excellent place would be worth a detour even if there wasn't a monastery looming in plain view of some of the rooms. This place feels in parts like a casual contemporary gallery – stylish and colourful, with the owners' original artworks decorating the rooms and passageways. Rooms are modern, commodious and attractive, and all a little different.

Balconies, coffee-tray and minifridge are standard, as is the excellent breakfast with homemade jams and a welcome drink on arrival. And did we mention the sizeable swimming pool, minigym and pool table? A standout.

Churrasqueira Vitória
GRILL HOUSE €

(☑244 765 678; Largo da Misericórdia; mains €6.50-9; ⊙lunch & dinner) In the square beside the smaller church near the monastery, this simple, friendly place serves excellent grilled meat and other Portuguese standards. Grab half a chicken for €6.50 and go home happy.

★Vinho em Qualquer
Circunstância
MODERN PORTUGUESE €€

(☑244 768 777; www.circunstancia.com.pt; Estrada de Fátima 15; mains €10-16; ⊙5pm-1am Mon-Sat) Sleek and stylish, this wine bar serves delicious tapas and full meals along with an amazing array of Portuguese wines displayed all around the modern dining area. Food is contemporary and innovative, and reliably excellent. Service, particularly from the sommelier, is very helpful.

ℹ Information

There's a free wi-fi zone around the centre of town.

Turismo (☑244 765 180; www.rt-leiriafatima. pt; Praça Mouzinho de Albuquerque; ⊙10am-1pm & 3-7pm May-Sep, 10am-1pm & 2-6pm Oct-Apr) Very helpful, facing the back side of the monastery.

ℹ Getting There & Away

BUS

Rodotejo (www.rodotejo.pt) and **Rede Expressos** (www.rede-expressos.pt) leave from the stop in Largo 14 de Agosto, behind the police station, very near the abbey and *turismo*. Express services go to major cities, including Lisbon (€11.50, two hours) four to five times daily – buy tickets online or at cafe Frazão behind the church nearby. For closer destinations such as Alcobaça, Fátima, Leiria, Nazaré and Tomar, you can pay on the bus.

Leiria

POP 55,000

Leiria is an agreeable mixture of medieval and modern, a lively university town built at the foot of a promontory fortified since Moorish times. The town's dramatically sited castle is a commanding presence above the narrow streets and red-tiled roofs of the historic centre, built along the lazy curves of the Rio Lis.

Dom Afonso III convened a *cortes* (Portugal's early parliament) here in 1254; Dom Dinis established his main residence in the castle in the 14th century; and in 1411 the town's sizeable Jewish community built Portugal's first paper mill. Modern-day Leiria has a pleasant, low-key urban buzz and makes a convenient base for visiting nearby

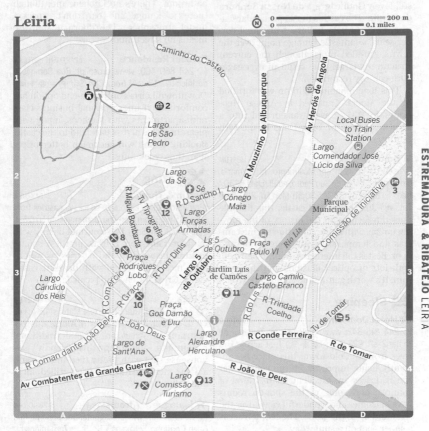

Leiria

◎ Sights
1 Castelo	A1
2 M|i|mo	B1

🛏 Sleeping
3 Eurosol Residence	D2
4 Hostel Leiria	B4
5 Hotel Dom Dinis	D3
6 Hotel Leiriense	B3

🍴 Eating
7 A Toca	B4
8 Cardamomo	B3
9 Malagueta Afrodisíaca	B3
10 Martin & Thomas	B3

🍷 Drinking & Nightlife
11 Club Glam	C3
12 Pharmácia	B2
13 Suite	B4

ESTREMADURA & RIBATEJO LEIRIA

sights, including Alcobaça, Batalha, Fátima and the Pinhal de Leiria – all easily accessible by bus.

◉ Sights

Castelo
CASTLE

(☑ 244 813 982; www.cm-leiria.pt; adult/child €2/1; ☉ 10am-6pm Tue-Sun Apr-Sep, to 5.30pm Oct-Mar) Inside the walls of Leiria's castle is a peaceful overgrown garden and the ruined but still lovely Gothic **Igreja de Nossa Senhora da Penha**. The castle's most spectacular feature, however, is a **gallery** with small corner seats: a fantastic vantage point over the town's red-tiled roofs, though the current structure is largely the result of over-eager 20th-century restoration.

This long-inhabited clifftop was fortified by the Moors. Captured by Afonso Henriques in 1135, it was transformed into a royal residence for Dom Dinis in the 14th century.

M|i|mo
MUSEUM

(Museu da Imagem em Movimento; http://mimo. cm-leiria.pt; Largo de São Pedro; adult/child €2.10/ free; ☉ 10am-1pm & 2-5.30pm Mon-Fri, 2-5.30pm Sat; ⊞) Just below the castle, this likeable museum focuses on the history of the moving image, with a fine collection of cine cameras and temporary exhibitions on the top floor. Best is the interactive floor in between, with lots of optical illusions and things to spin. It's worth getting the audioguide (free).

⌁ Sleeping

★ Hotel Dom Dinis
HOTEL €

(☑ 244 815 342; www.hotelddinis.pt; Travessa de Tomar 2; s/d €28/45; P ⊞ @ �) Just across the river from the old town, this place is constantly being improved by the couple that run it. Prices are excellent for this level of comfort, and some of the spot-on rooms have balconies and wonderful views over the river and up to the castle. The roof terrace is a super spot on a sunny day.

Hotel Leiriense
HOTEL €

(☑ 244 823 054; www.hotelleiriense.com; Rua Afonso de Albuquerque 6; s/d €40/55; ⊞ ଵ) On a cobbled street in the historic centre, this dignified place has a great location and small but decent rooms with double-glazing to keep out street noise. There's a retro appeal to its marble steps, tiled hallways and parquet wood floors. It's heated but can still be cold in winter, when rates are much cheaper, but don't include breakfast.

Hostel Leiria
GUESTHOUSE, HOSTEL €

(☑ 244 812 802; www.hostelleiria.com; Rua Dr Correia Mateus 30; dm €18-20, s/d €35/45; P ⊞ ଵ) In a characterful 1920s blue building on a very central corner, this is part-guesthouse, part-hostel and a curious mixture of old and new. The elegance of public areas extends to the spacious private rooms, some of which have balconies. Dorms are essentially the same, except with bunks; all have en-suite bathroom. There's no kitchen, and, though there's a lounge and bar, don't expect a hostel atmosphere. The 'doormat' staircase means no street mud.

Eurosol Residence
APARTMENT HOTEL €€

(☑ 244 860 460; www.eurosol.pt; Rua Commisão de Iniciativa 13; s/d from €84/96; P ⊞ @ ଵ ≋) Downtown Leiria's only high-end option has comfortable if unexceptional business-class mini-apartments with kitchens, many with pleasant views across parkland to the castle. Booking online will get much better prices than these rack rates.

✗ Eating

Martin & Thomas
BAKERY €

(Praça Rodrigues Lobo 8-9; snacks & pastries from €1; ☉ 8am-7.30pm Mon-Thu, 8am-midnight Fri & Sat, 9.30am-7.30pm Sun) This gourmet bakery with outdoor tables on Leiria's prettiest square features tasty bread and pastries, as well as light meals, all served with dazzling castle views. Great for day-trip picnic fare too.

A Toca
PORTUGUESE €

(☑ 244 832 221; Rua Dr Correia Mateus 42; mains €6-11; ☉ lunch & dinner Sun-Fri) Along this pedestrianised street are several traditional restaurants, including this friendly, no-nonsense spot with pretty tiled interior and a long menu featuring wood-grilled meat and fish.

★ Malagueta Afrodisíaca
FUSION €€

(☑ 244 831 607; www.malaguetaafrodisiaca.pt; Rua Gago Coutinho 17; mains €12-15; ☉ 7pm-midnight; ⌁) For a rare deviation from standard Portuguese fare, head to this trendy, slinkily decorated place, tucked down a narrow street in the historic centre. The eclectic 15-page menu features aphrodisiac teas, flaming desserts, mixed drinks, and a dizzying collection of Brazilian, Mexican and other overseas-influenced dishes.

Cardamomo
INDIAN, PORTUGUESE €€

(☑ 244 832 033; Rua Barão de Viamonte 43; mains €10-12; ☉ lunch & dinner Tue-Sun; ⌁) The owner's Goan roots are clearly on display at this air-conditioned upstairs restaurant serving a fusion of Indian and Portuguese cuisine. Start with bacon-wrapped asparagus or salad greens with apples and honey, then feast on stuffed eggplant, sea bass with mango, Goan *xacuti* curry or arugula-beet risotto.

Drinking

Bars are scattered throughout the historic centre, and the student population keeps things hopping.

Pharmácia PUB
(Largo da Sé 9; ⊙9.30pm-2am Mon-Sat) Set inside a marvellously tiled 19th-century pharmacy, this Irish-style bar features a mellow vibe, darts and a extensive collection of drinks.

Suite NIGHTCLUB
(www.clubesuite.com; Rua Machado dos Santos; ⊙10pm-5am Tue-Sat) Party into the wee hours at this club in the heart of town. Tuesday and Thursday are student nights, while the big club night is Saturday.

Club Glam NIGHTCLUB
(www.facebook.com/glamclubleiria; Jardim Luís de Camões; ⊙10pm-5am Fri & Sat) A popular Latino dance club in the riverfront park.

❶ Information

Biblioteca Municipal (Largo Cândido dos Reis 6; ⊙2-8pm Mon & Sat, 10am-8pm Tue-Fri) Free internet access at the public library.
Hospital de Santo André (☏244 817 016; www.chlp.pt; Rua das Olhalvas) About 1.5km east of town.
Turismo (☏244 848 770; www.rt-leiriafatima. pt; Jardim Luís de Camões; ⊙10am-1pm & 2-6pm Mon-Fri Oct-Apr, 10am-1pm & 3-/pm May-Sep) Provides a free town map. Might be moving location; check the website for the current address.

❶ Getting There & Away

BUS

Rodotejo (www.rodotejo.pt) and **Rede Expressos** (www.rede-expressos.pt) both serve the **bus station** (Largo 5 de Outubro) in the heart of town. Buses run every hour or two to Alcobaça (€3.55, 50 minutes), Batalha (€1.95, 20 minutes), Coimbra (€9, 50 minutes), Fátima (€3.35 to €6, 25 to 45 minutes), Lisbon (€12.50, two hours) and Nazaré (express/local €6.80/3.80, 40/60 minutes).

TRAIN

Leiria is on the train line that runs about three times daily from Figueira da Foz (€5, one hour) to the Mira Sintra-Meleças station near Lisbon (€10.35 to €11.40, 2½ to 3½ hours). The station is 4km northwest; **bus 4** runs here frequently from Largo Comendador José Lúcio da Silva (€1.25, 10 minutes). A **taxi** costs about €5.

Pinhal de Leiria

First planted by a forward-looking monarch some 700 years ago, the Pinhal de Leiria is a vast forest of towering pines whose fragrance and stippled shade make this one of the loveliest stretches of Portugal's Atlantic coast. Dom Dinis expanded it significantly as a barrier against encroaching dunes and also as a source of timber for the maritime industry – a great boon during the Age of Discoveries.

Today, the protected forest covers more than 100 sq km along the coast west of Leiria. Narrow roads and well-maintained bike paths cut through it, leading to a number of really excellent beaches and three resort towns: **São Pedro de Moel**, 20km west of Leiria; **Praia da Vieira**, 16km north of São Pedro along the coastal highway; and **Pedrógão**, 2km further north.

🛏 Sleeping & Eating

São Pedro de Moel is the most appealing of the three towns.

Orbitur CAMPGROUND €
(☏244 599 168; www.orbitur.pt; São Pedro de Moel; sites per adult/child/tent/car €6.40/ 3.20/8.40/5.90; ⓟ 🤖 ﹫ ﹢) In among the pine trees but in the centre of town, this well-equipped, pretty site includes a swimming pool, disabled facilities and a playground. Two-/four-/five-person bungalows cost €92/ 102/107 in August or €67/77/82 the rest of the summer.

Hotel Mar e Sol HOTEL €€
(☏244 590 000; www.hotelmaresol.com; Av da Liberdade 1, São Pedro de Moel; r €85-130; ﹡ 🤖) This well-refurbished seafront hotel is comfortable and sparkling clean, with minimalist modern decor. It's in a great position; the best rooms, with balconies and grand views over the tussling sea, cost €35 to €45 extra. There's a rooftop sundeck and a gym and spa complex (which costs extra) and good low-season discounts. Wi-fi is free in the lobby, but costs extra in the rooms.

Bambi Café CAFE €

(☑244 599 020; Av de Liberdade, São Pedro de Moel; ⊙11am-3am Jul-Sep, 1pm-2am Thu-Sun Oct-Jun; 🛜) Guinness on tap, wi-fi, and comfy couches on an outdoor deck are the big draws at this cool glass-walled cafe behind the *turismo*.

O Pai dos Frangos PORTUGUESE €€

(☑244 599 158; Praia Velha, São Pedro de Moel; mains €9-15; ⊙lunch & dinner Tue-Sun) 'The Father of Chickens' sits in splendid isolation right on the fabulous sands of Praia Velha, a kilometre north of São Pedro de Moel. Specialities include *arroz de marisco* (paella-like rice and seafood stew) and, naturally, grilled chicken.

★**Estrela do Mar** SEAFOOD €€€

(☑244 599 245; Av Marginal, São Pedro de Moel; mains €14-22; ⊙lunch & dinner) In an utterly memorable position on the water, this place scores top marks for location: the dining room is right over the waves above São Pedro's town beach. Seafood prices here partly reflect the unbeatable view, but the quality and atmosphere are great.

ℹ Information

Turismo de São Pedro de Moel (Av da Liberdade, São Pedro de Moel; ⊙10am-1pm & 3-7pm Tue-Sun Jul & Aug) Summer only. There's a year-round tourist office in the museum in nearby Marinha Grande.

ℹ Getting There & Away

From Leiria there are at least six daily buses to São Pedro de Moel (€3, 40 minutes) and Praia da Vieira (€3.35, 45 minutes). If driving from Leiria, follow signs for Marinha Grande first.

Fátima

POP 11,600 / ELEV 320M

Whatever your beliefs, you can't help but be impressed by the vast reserves of faith that every year lead as many as six million people to the glade where, on 13 May 1917, the Virgin Mary is said to have first appeared to three awestruck peasant children (p481). Where sheep once grazed there are now two huge churches on opposite ends of a vast 1km-long esplanade.

Aesthetically, it's hard to get past the town's bland and monolithic architecture, and outside the main pilgrimage dates (the 12th and 13th of each month from May to October) the vast parking lots ringing the

basilicas have the feel of a forlorn desert. Yet for Catholic pilgrims Fátima has a magnetic appeal like few places on earth, and a trip here will provide any visitor with new insights into Portugal's religious culture.

The focus of the pilgrimages, known as Cova da Iria, is just east of the A1 motorway. Several major roads ring the area, including Av Dom José Alves Correia da Silva to the south, where the bus station and *turismo* are located.

The town itself is packed with boarding houses and restaurants for the pilgrim masses, and shop windows crowded with glow-in-the-dark Virgins and busts of the Pope.

◉ Sights

Santuário de Fátima CHRISTIAN

(www.santuario-fatima.pt) It's difficult to believe that a century ago, this was pastureland outside an insignificant village. This vast complex is now one of Catholicism's major shrines; the focus of enormous devotion and pilgrimage. At the eastern end is the 1953 basilica, a triumphantly sheer-white building with colonnade reminiscent of St Peter's. Nearby, the Capela das Aparições (Chapel of the Apparitions) marks the site where the Virgin appeared. At the precinct's western end is the 2007 Basílica da Santíssima Trindade.

The **chapel** is the focus of the most intense devotion. Supplicants who have promised penance (for example, in return for helping a loved one who is sick, or to signify a particularly deep conversion) shuffle on their knees across the vast esplanade, following a long marble runway polished smooth by previous penitents. Near the chapel is a blazing pyre where people can throw offerings on the fire, leave gifts – donated to charities – or light candles in prayer. The sound of hundreds of candles is like a rushing waterfall.

Inside the older church, the **Basílica de Nossa Senhora do Rosário de Fátima**, attention is focused on the tombs of the three children, Os Três Pastorinhos (the three little shepherds): Francisco (died 1919, aged 11) and Jacinta (died 1920, aged 10), both victims of the flu epidemic, were beatified in 2000. Lúcia, the third witness of the apparition, entered a convent in Coimbra in 1928, where she died in 2005. Her beatification is underway.

The **new basilica** was inaugurated in 2007, and, while impressive, has something of a conference-centre feel. A central passageway hung with golden angels leads to a long etched-glass window spelling out scriptural verses in dozens of languages. Twelve 9m bronze doors run around the edges of the monumental round marble structure, each with a Biblical quote dedicated to one of Jesus' disciples. Inside, the impersonal feel is redeemed by Irish artist Catherine Green's striking altarpiece depicting a wild-haired and gaunt Crucifixion, backed by Slovenian artist Marko Ivan Rupnik's beautiful mosaic work.

At the sanctuary entrance is a segment of the Berlin Wall, a tribute to 'God's part in the fall of communism'. Twin wax museums on either side of the old basilica give a blow-by-blow account of the story of Fátima; and represent 33 scenes from the life of Christ.

Masses are held roughly hourly in the basilicas or at the Capela das Apariçoes. At least two daily are held in English; check at the information booth by the chapel.

Museu de Arte Sacra e Etnologia MUSEUM
(☑249 539 470; http://masefatima.blogspot.com; Rua Francisco Marto 52; adult/child €2.50/1.50; ☺10am-7pm Tue-Sun Apr-Oct, 10am-5pm Tue-Sun Nov-Mar) The most interesting of Fátima's several religious exhibitions and museums, this has a wide display of religious art and artefacts from around the world.

🛏 Sleeping & Eating

There are dozens of restaurants, *pensões* (guesthouses) and pilgrim lodges amid the shops east of the basilica, very few with any character.

★ Avenida de Fátima HOTEL €
(☑249 534 171; www.hotelavenidadefatima.com; Av José Alves Correia da Silva; s/d €30/45; [P] [❄] [🌐]) Modern and comfortable, with spick-and-span rooms with every contemporary comfort, this is an excellent deal not far from the basilica. Prices are a steal for this standard, and there are convenient family rooms available.

Residencial Aleluia GUESTHOUSE €
(☑249 531 540; www.residencialaleluia.com; Av Dr José Silva 120; s/d €35/44, breakfast €3) As bland as everything else in Fátima but squeaky clean and directly across from the basilica, this offers cosy en-suite rooms. Other pluses

include the friendly English-speaking owner and in-house laundry service (€10 per load).

O Crispim PORTUGUESE €€
(☑249 532 781; www.ocrispim.com; Rua S João Eudes 23; mains €10-20; ☺lunch & dinner Tue-Sun) It's worth seeking this place out for an atmosphere full of good cheer without any ostentatious piety. It's a comfortably, rustic sort of place serving house wine in wooden tankards and whose speciality is grilled meats – Iberian pork, and succulent beef from the north of Portugal, flame-grilled on the back patio. Prices are by weight, but are reasonable; the starters and accompaniments can add up though.

ⓘ Information

Turismo (☑244 848 770; www.rt-leiriafatima. pt; Av Dom José Alves Correia da Silva; ☺10am-1pm & 3-7pm daily Apr-Oct, 10am-1pm & 2-6pm Mon-Fri Nov-Mar) Near the sanctuary.

ⓘ Getting There & Away

BUS

Fátima (sometimes called Cova da Iria on timetables) is a stop on most major north–south bus runs. The following destinations are served at least hourly: Coimbra (€11, one to 1¼ hours), Leiria (€3.35 to €6, 25 to 45 minutes), Lisbon (€11.50, 1½ hours) and Porto (€17, two hours).

TRAIN

Fátima's train station is 21km east: buses are a much better option.

Porto de Mós

POP 6000 / ELEV 260M

Dominated by a 13th-century hilltop castle, Porto de Mós is an untouristy town on the little Rio Lena that makes a good launchpad for exploring the mountains and caves of the adjacent Parque Natural das Serras de Aire e Candeeiros.

Porto de Mós became a major Roman settlement whose residents used the Lena to ferry millstones from a nearby quarry. The region remains an important centre for quarrying the black-and-white stones used in *calçada portuguesa,* the mosaic-style pavements seen throughout Portugal.

⊙ Sights

Castelo CASTLE
(over/under 26 €1.50/0.75; ☺10am-12.30pm & 2-6pm Tue-Sun May-Sep, to 5.30pm Oct-Apr) The

green-towered castle was originally a Moorish stronghold. Conquered definitively in 1148 by Dom Afonso Henriques, it was largely rebuilt in 1450 and again after the 1755 earthquake. These days it's too pristine to be convincingly medieval, but is fun to climb around and has pleasant views across the valley to the Serras de Aire e Candeeiros. Stick around till closing and watch 'em lock up with a key the size of your forearm.

Estrada Romana
ROMAN RUINS

Fifteen minutes northeast of Porto de Mós by car, a section of ancient Roman road has been converted into a walking trail. Marked with red and yellow blazes, the old road bed meanders through the hills for 9km; the most impressive section is at the signposted trailhead just above the town of Alqueidão da Serra.

🛏 Sleeping & Eating

There's currently nowhere to stay in Porto de Mós itself, but Rio Alcaide is only a 10-minute walk away.

Quinta de Rio Alcaide
RURAL APARTMENTS €€

(✆966 164 342; www.rioalcaide.com; Rio Alcaide; d €60; P ⊠) One kilometre southeast of Porto de Mós, this rustic inn is set in a converted 18th-century paper mill. The rooms and apartments are charming, including one in a hilltop windmill, and another that, in 1973, served as a meeting place for Portuguese captains plotting the Revolution of the Carnations. The grounds feature a pool, citrus trees, hiking trails and a cascading stream. Management is welcoming but pretty much let you get on with things, so don't expect hotel-standard maintenance or service.

Esplanada Jardim
CAFE €

(✆244 403 004; Jardim Público; lunch €5-7; ◷10am-2am) This pleasant cafe in the leafy municipal gardens near the *turismo* serves excellent, reasonably priced lunches on weekdays.

Adega do Luis
PORTUGUESE €€

(✆964 103 287; www.adegadoluis.pt; Rua Principal, Livramento; mains €12-20; ◷lunch & dinner Wed-Mon) Three kilometres southeast of town, this delightful place with high ceilings, stone walls and a roaring fire in the brick oven serves grilled bacon, lamb chops, Iberian pork and *picanha* (rump steak), with pear tart for dessert. Call ahead outside summer as hours fluctuate according to demand.

ⓘ Information

Turismo (✆244 491 323; Jardim Público; ◷10am-1pm & 3-7pm Mon-Sat Apr-Sep, 10am-1pm & 2-6pm Mon-Sat Oct-Mar) Near the town's main roundabout; also has free internet terminals.

ⓘ Getting There & Away

There are at least three buses each weekday to/from Leiria (€3, 45 minutes) via Batalha (€2.10, 15 minutes). There are also three to four daily buses to Alcobaça (€3, 35 minutes).

Parque Natural das Serras de Aire e Candeeiros

With its barren limestone heights crisscrossed by hiking trails, this natural park east of Porto de Mós is a popular place for outdoor pursuits.

Once the haunt of dinosaurs, the park is famous for its cathedral-like caves, but above ground it's also scenic, particularly the high Planalto de Santo António (starting 2km south of the Grutas de Santo António). Gorse- and olive grove–covered hills are divided by dry-stone walls and threaded by cattle trails, all making for tempting rambles. Numerous *percursos pedestres* (walking trails), ranging from 1km to 17km, are described in the English-language *Guide to Walking Tours in the Aire and Candeeiros Mountain Ranges,* available for €5 from the park offices.

◉ Sights

Monumento Natural das Pegadas dos Dinossáurios
DINOSAUR FOOTPRINTS

(✆249 530 160; www.pegadasdedinossaurios.org; Bairro; adult/child €3/1.50; ◷10am-12.30pm & 2-6pm Tue-Sun, until 8pm Sat & Sun Apr-Sep; ⓖ) On the N357 10km south of Fátima in the village of Bairro, this quarry has more than a thousand individual prints, and is one of the most important locations for sauropod prints in the world. The visit starts with a 20-minute video in Portuguese, then you take a 1.5km walk around the quarry, first seeing the prints from above then walking among them.

These, the oldest and longest sauropod tracks in the world, record walks in the mud a trifling 175 million years ago. The dinos would have been stepping through carbonated mud, later transformed into limestone. As you walk across the slope you can clearly see the large elliptical prints made by the hind feet and the smaller, half-moon prints made by the forefeet.

Mira de Aire
CAVES

(☑244 440 322; www.grutasmiradaire.com; Mira de Aire; adult/child €6.20/3.60; ☉9.30am-8pm Jul-Aug, 9.30am-7pm Jun & Sep, 9.30am-6pm Apr-May, 9.30am-5.30pm Oct-Mar; ⛟) Portugal's largest cave system, 14km southeast of Porto de Mós is very touristy and old-fashioned, although the caves themselves are impressive. The 45-minute tour's spiralling 110m descent leads through psychedelically-lit chambers to a final cavern containing a lake with a rather hokey fountain display. There's also a children's zoo here and an aquapark. There are three buses weekdays from Porto de Mós (€2.45, 35 minutes). From July to mid-September there's also weekend service.

Grutas de Alvados & Grutas de Santo António
CAVES

(☑249 841 876, 244 440 787; www.grutasalvados.com; adult/child per cave €5.80/3.80, both caves €9/6; ☉10am-7pm Jun-Aug, 10am-5pm Mon-Fri, 10am-5.30pm Sat & Sun Sep-May) These caves are about 15km southeast of Porto de Mós, and 2km and 3.5km, respectively, south of the N243 from Porto de Mós to Mira de Aire. Discovered in 1964, they are the spiky smaller cousins of Mira de Aire, with similarly disco-flavoured lighting.

Buses between Porto de Mós and Mira de Aire can drop you at the caves turn-off on the N243, but it's a steep uphill walk from there.

🛏 Sleeping

Pousada de Juventude Alvados
HOSTEL €

(☑244 441 202; www.pousadasjuventude.pt; Barreira de Água, Alvados; dm €13, d with private/shared bathroom €36/32; ☉Dec-Oct; Ⓟ🐶) This friendly, sparkling modern place 8km southeast of Porto de Mós has four-bed dorms, doubles with and without private bathrooms, kitchen and wheelchair-accessible facilities. Weekday buses from Leiria (€4.25, 55 minutes) stop in front twice daily.

Parque de Campismo
CAMPGROUND €

(☑campground 244 450 555, reservations 243 999 481; sites per adult/child/tent €2.50/1.25/0.75; ☉Jun–mid-Oct) Remote, basic and beautifully set by a little lake in the village of Arrimal, 17km south of Porto de Mós, this campground has only 30 pitches, so book ahead.

It's accessible by a weekday bus to Porto de Mós (€2.75, 35 minutes).

ℹ Information

Ecoteca (☑244 491 904; ecoteca@gmail.com; Alameda Dom Afonso Henriques, Porto de Mós; ☉9.30am-12.30pm & 2-6pm Tue-Sat) Park office near the Porto de Mós *turismo*, where you can pick up information and hiking maps.

Park Headquarters (☑243 999 480; www.icnf.pt; Rua Dr Augusto César Silva Ferreira, Rio Maior; ☉9am-12.30pm & 2-5.30pm) In Rio Maior, south of the park.

RIBATEJO

Literally meaning 'Above the Tejo', Ribatejo is the only Portuguese province that doesn't border either Spain or the open ocean. A string of Templar castles are proof of its strategic importance, though these days its clout is economic, thanks to industry along the Tejo and the rich agricultural plains that spread out from the river's banks. This is also bull country – most of Portugal's fighters are bred in and around the capital, Santarém.

Santarém

POP 29,200 / ELEV 110M

Contemplating the staggering views from Santarém's Portas do Sol atop the old town walls, it's easy to understand why Roman, Visigoth, Moorish and Portuguese armies all wanted to claim this strategic stronghold above the Rio Tejo. Dom Afonso Henriques' storming of these heights in 1147 marked a turning point in the Reconquista and quickly became the stuff of Portuguese national legend.

A group of beautiful Gothic buildings recalls Santarém's glory days, though it was quickly eclipsed by Lisbon. These days, the traditional centre with its venerable stores and workshops still functioning amid a general air of genteel decay makes it worth a visit, as do the heart-lifting vistas. It's rather short on accommodation though.

History

One of the most important cities of Lusitania under Julius Caesar, and prized by the Moors under the name Xantarim for almost 400 years, Santarém already had centuries of history under its belt before passing to Portuguese rule in 1147. So great was Dom

Santarém

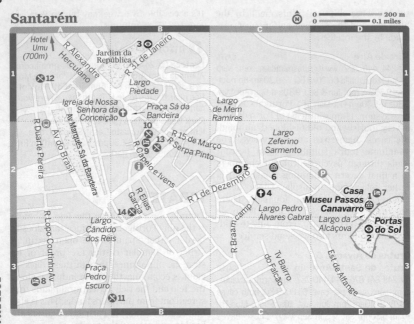

Santarém

⊙ Top Sights
1 Casa Museu Passos
  Canavarro D2
2 Portas do Sol D3

⊙ Sights
3 Convento de São Francisco B1
4 Igreja da Santa Maria Graça C2
5 Igreja de Marvila C2
6 Museu Arqueológico C2

⊙ Sleeping
7 Casa da Alcáçova D2
8 Hotel Vitória A3
9 Pensão José Rodrigues B2

⊗ Eating
10 O Saloio B2
11 Taberna do Quinzena B3
12 Taberna do Quinzena II A1
13 Taberna e Mercearia Sebastião B2
14 Tascá B2

Afonso Henriques' joy at conquering this legendarily impenetrable citadel that he built the magnificent Mosteiro de Santa Maria de Alcobaça in gratitude.

⊙ Sights

★Portas do Sol   GARDEN
(Gates of the Sun; ⊙ 9am-11pm May-Sep, 9am-8pm Oct-Apr) Occupying the site of the Moorish citadel, the Portas do Sol garden proffers utterly majestic views over the Rio Tejo and the great spread of plains that surround it. The garden's shady walks make a fine place for a picnic or afternoon linger. It's particularly spectacular at sundown.

★Casa Museu Passos Canavarro   MUSEUM
(www.fundacaopassoscanavarro.pt; Largo da Alcáçova 1; admission €5; ⊙10am-1pm & 3-6pm Tue-Sun) Right by the Portas do Sol and sharing some of the same privileged views, this is a unique place to visit for lovers of art and beauty. The historic house, once home to 19th-century liberal politician Passos Manuel, is stocked with artistic treasures and curios, from Japanese furniture and *netsuke* to 16th-century maps and collections of 20th-century art.

But the best part about it is that you are shown around by the multilingual, urbane and delightful owner, a direct descendant of Passos, and it's his personal explanations and love for the items in his home that make this such an enchanting place to visit.

Museu Arqueológico
MUSEUM

(Largo Zeferino Sarmento; ⊙9am-12.30pm & 2-5.30pm) FREE This archaeological museum is housed in the enchanting 12th-century Igreja de São João de Alporão. Among the stone carvings, *azulejos* and rotating exhibits is the elaborate tomb of Dom Duarte de Menezes, who died in 1464 in a battle against the Moors in North Africa. It's quite grand – especially considering that once the Moors had finished with him, all that was left for burial was a tooth!

Convento de São Francisco
MONASTERY

(Rua 31 de Janeiro; admission €2; ⊙9am-12.30pm & 2-5.30pm Sun-Thu, to 10pm Fri & Sat) This restored 13th-century Franciscan monastery is a fine example of Portuguese Gothic. Especially lovely is the cloister, with graceful twinned columns and arches. It's also a venue for temporary exhibitions.

Igreja de Marvila
CHURCH

(Largo de Marvila; ⊙9am-12.30pm & 2-5.30pm) Dating from the 12th century but with 16th-century additions, this endearing little church has a fine, twisted Manueline doorway, while the interior is completely awash in brilliant, dramatically patterned *azulejos* dating from the 17th century.

Igreja da Santa Maria Graça
CHURCH

(Largo Pedro Álvares Cabral; ⊙9am-12:30pm & 2-5.30pm) This early-15th-century church, with its delicately carved facade of multilayered arches, is a jewel. Inside, a rose window spills light across the beautifully spare interior of stone columns and white walls. Note the tombs of Pedro Álvares Cabral (the 'discoverer' of Brazil, who lived in Santarém) and Dom Pedro de Menezes. The de Menezes family founded the church, which explains Dom Pedro's more elaborate tomb.

✪ Festivals & Events

Feira Nacional da Agricultura
LIVESTOCK

(www.cnema.pt; ⚑) Famous nationwide for its merriment, horse races, bullfights and night-time bull-running. It lasts 10 days in the first half of June and mostly takes place 2km west of the town centre. There are lots of associated children's events.

Festival Nacional de Gastronomia
FOOD

(www.festivalnacionaldegastronomia.com) Held over a fortnight in October/November at the Casa do Campino, the Festival Nacional de Gastronomia encourages you to eat as much traditional Portuguese fare as you can.

🛏 Sleeping

Hotel Vitória
GUESTHOUSE €

(☑243 309 130; hotelvitoriasantarem@gmail.com; Rua Segundo Visconde de Santarém 21; s/d €35/50; ❄🖥) This night-at-your-great-aunt's-type place is run by Dona Vitória, assisted by various elderly hangers-on. It has clean and well-kept rooms with old-fashioned amenities.

Hotel Umu
HOTEL €

(☑243 377 240; www.umu.pt; Av Bernardo Santareno 38; s/d/ste €42/52/90; ℗❄@🖥) This place is undergoing modernization, so the smallish rooms with decent services will offer value once they are renovated. The location in a high-rise district 2km north of the centre leaves a lot to be desired.

Pensão José Rodrigues
GUESTHOUSE €

(☑962 837 909; Travessa do Froes 14; r per person not incl breakfast €15-20) On a quiet cobbled alley between Santarém's two pedestrianised thoroughfares, Dona Arminda rents out a few simple rooms, most with shared bathroom. Look for the '*quartos/dormidas*' sign out front.

★ Casa da Alcáçova
HISTORIC HOTEL €€€

(☑243 304 030; www.alcacova.com; Largo da Alcáçova 3; s from €85, d €125-160; ℗❄🖥🏊) With the atmosphere of a stylish country retreat, but right in the city, this historic secluded manor house is set by its own section of the city walls, offering utterly spectacular views from the ramparts and many of the rooms. The interior is just as special, with antique furniture, an atmosphere of classy but relaxed elegance, and sumptuous rooms with good bathrooms.

Extras include a lovely pool area and a summer lounge with the foundations of a Roman temple in the middle of it. Service is faultless and welcoming. Rooms by the pool are cheaper and good for families. Did we mention the views? Yes, but they're worth mentioning again.

✗ Eating & Drinking

As you'd expect of a student-packed agricultural town, Santarém is well off for good-value restaurants.

Taberna do Quinzena PORTUGUESE €
(www.quinzena.com; Rua Pedro de Santarém 93; mains €6-9; ⊙ lunch & dinner Mon-Sat) If you don't mind drawing a few locals' stares, this atmospheric neighbourhood hang-out is well worth a visit. Walls plastered with brightly coloured bullfighting posters are a reminder that this was once a macho refuge, though women can now join the boys for a simple but delicious plate of grilled pork or fish, washed down with cheap local Ribatejo wine straight from the barrel. A second branch, **Taberna do Quinzena II** (Cerca da Mecheira 20; mains €6-9; ⊙ lunch & dinner Mon-Sat) is near the bus station.

O Saloio PORTUGUESE €
(☏ 243 327 656; Travessa do Montalvo 11; mains €6-12; ⊙ lunch & dinner Mon-Fri, lunch Sat) This cosy, tiled, family-friendly *tasca* (tavern) is a neighbourhood favourite thanks to its authentic Portuguese dishes. Drop your inhibitions and discover local specialities like *caldeirada de enguias* (eel stew).

★ **Tascá** PETISCOS €€
(www.tascana.net; Rua Arco de Manços 8; petiscos €4-6) Bright, fun and contemporary, this loosely Spanish-themed bar does innovative *petisco* (snack) portions high on presentation and taste from its open kitchen. Most of the socialising goes on around the barrels or on the great terrace outside. Friday lunch has delicious *cozido*, Saturday sees roast kid, Sunday *bacalhau* and Sunday evening changes the theme with sushi.

Taberna e Mercearia Sebastião PORTUGUESE, BAR €€
(www.tabernaemerceariasebastiao.blogspot.com; Travessa do Froes 13; mains €8-16; ⊙ noon-1am) This 19th-century grocer's shop has had a sympathetic modern refit and now presents

---

THE KNIGHTS TEMPLAR

Founded in about 1119 by French crusading knights to protect pilgrims visiting the Holy Land, the Templars got their name when King Baldwin of Jerusalem housed them in his palace, which had once been a Jewish temple. The Knights soon became a strictly organised, semireligious gang. Members took vows of poverty and chastity, and wore white coats emblazoned with a red cross – a symbol that eventually came to be associated with Portugal itself. By 1139 the Templars were the leading defenders of the Christian crusader states in the Holy Land.

In Portugal, Templar knights played a key role in expelling the Moors. Despite vows of poverty, they accepted land, castles and titles in return for military victories. Soon the order had properties all over Europe and the Middle East. This geographically dispersed network enabled them to take on another influential role: bankers to kings and pilgrims.

By the early 14th century, the Templars had grown so strong that French King Philip IV – eager for their wealth or afraid of their power – initiated an era of persecution (supported by the French pope Clement V). He arrested all of the knights, accusing many of heresy and seizing their property. In 1314 the last French Grand Maître (Master) was burned at the stake.

In Portugal, Dom Dinis followed the trend by dissolving the order, but a few years later he cannily re-established it as the Order of Christ, though now under the royal thumb. It was largely thanks to the order's wealth that Prince Henry the Navigator (Grand Master from 1417 to 1460) was able to fund the Age of Discoveries. In the 16th century, Dom João III took the order into a humbler phase, shifting it towards monastic duties. In 1834, with the dissolution of the monasteries, the order's lands were confiscated, but it still lives on to some extent: these days the Grand Master is the Portuguese president.

a cool, characterful, intimate space. You can eat well here – best are the specials – and for just a snack, the miniplate with a quarter of wine goes down a treat for €3.50.

ℹ Information

Esp@çonet (Sala de Leitura Bernardo Santareno, Rua Pedro Canavarro; ◷10am-6pm Mon-Fri) Free internet.

Hospital (☏243 300 200; Av Bernardo Santareno) On the northern edge of town.

Turismo (☏243 304 437; www.cm-santarem.pt; Rua Capelo e Ivens 63; ◷10am-2pm & 3-7pm Mon-Fri, 9am-1pm & 2-6pm Sat & Sun)

ℹ Getting There & Around

The train station is 2.4km northeast and steeply downhill from the centrally located **bus station** (Av do Brasil). Local buses run regularly between the two stations on weekdays and Saturday mornings (€1.25, 10 minutes). Taxis charge about €4.

BUS

Rede Expressos (www.rede-expressos.pt) and **Rodotejo** (www.rodotejo.pt) operate at least three times daily (more frequently to Lisbon) to: Coimbra (€14.30, 2¼ hours), Fátima (€9.50, 45 minutes), Leiria (€12.50, 1¼ hours), Lisbon (€8, one hour).

TRAIN

Very frequent IC (€11.70) and local (€6.55) trains go to Lisbon (45 minutes to one hour).

Constância & Castelo de Almourol

POP 1000

Constância's compact cluster of whitewashed houses, cobbled lanes and narrow staircases spills picturesquely down a steep hillside to the confluence of the Rios Tejo and Zêzere. It's a sleepy, pretty village whose leafy riverfront promenade, main square and gardens make a lovely place for lunch or a stroll before moving on to the biggest draw in these parts, nearby Castelo de Almourol.

◉ Sights

Castelo de Almourol   CASTLE
(◷10am-1pm & 2.30-7.30pm Mar-Oct, 10am-1pm & 2.30-5.30pm Nov-Feb) Like the stuff of legend, 10-towered Castelo de Almourol stands tantalisingly close to shore but just out of reach in the Rio Tejo. The castle is 5km from Constância. Boats (€2, five minutes) leave regularly from a riverside landing directly opposite the castle. Once on the island, a short walk leads up to the ramparts, where you're free to linger as long as you like.

The island, almost jumping distance from land, was once the site of a Roman fort; the castle was built by Gualdim Pais, Grand Master of the Order of the Knights Templar, in 1171. It's no surprise that Almourol has long caught the imagination of excitable poets longing for the Age of Chivalry.

You can also go to the castle by boat from the town of **Tancos** (☏249 712 093; jftancos@gmail.com; €2.50), with the same hours, which must be prebooked. Buses run between Constância and Tancos, passing near the castle.

🛏 Sleeping & Eating

A local speciality, *queijinhos do Céu* (sweets from heaven), is still made by local nuns from almond meal and egg yolks (delicious!).

Casa João Chagas   GUESTHOUSE €
(☏249 739 403; www.casajoaochagas.com; Rua João Chagas, Constância; s/d €39/50; P❄☞) Set in the former town hall and another building opposite, this excellent place offers large, simple, modernized rooms with comfortable beds and a good attitude. It's right in the centre of things just off the main square near the river.

Remédio d'Alma   PORTUGUESE €€
(☏249 739 405; Largo 5 de Outubro, Constância; mains €11-15; ◷lunch Tue, lunch & dinner Wed-Sun) For fine regional cooking, try this elegant little place, set in a pretty stucco house with a lovely garden shaded by orange trees. It's 200m upriver from Constância's main square.

ℹ Information

Turismo (☏249 730 052; www.cm-constancia.pt; Av das Forças Armadas; ◷9am-6pm Mon-Fri, 11am-1pm & 2-6pm Sat & Sun) Beside the river in the centre of town.

ℹ Getting There & Away

BUS

Constância is easily reached by bus from Tomar (€2.45, 40 minutes). **Rodotejo** (www.rodotejo.pt) run four buses weekdays to Tancos (20 minutes), which will drop you at the turnoff to the castle, from where its a 10-minute walk. You can also book a boat to the castle from Tancos itself, a better option for onward transport.

CAR & MOTORCYCLE

If driving your own vehicle, exit the A23/IP6 at Constância and follow signs to the castle.

TRAIN

To visit the castle only, take a local train (changing at Entroncamento) from Tomar (€3.25, 55 minutes) or Santarém (€4, 45 minutes, some direct services) to tiny Almourol station, then walk 1km downhill to the ferry landing. The train station nearest Constância – known as Praia do Ribatejo – is 2km outside town, so the bus is a better option if you're only visiting Constância.

Tomar

POP 16,000

Tomar is one of central Portugal's most appealing small towns. With its pedestrian-friendly historic centre, its pretty riverside park frequented by swans, herons and families of ducks, and its charming natural setting adjacent to the lush Mata Nacional dos Sete Montes (Seven Hills National Forest), it wins lots of points for aesthetics.

But to understand what makes Tomar truly extraordinary, cast your gaze skyward to the crenellated walls of the Convento de Cristo, which forms a beautiful backdrop. Eight-and-a-half centuries after its founding, this venerable headquarters of the legendary Knights Templar is a rambling concoction of Gothic, Manueline and Renaissance architecture that bears extravagant witness to its integral role in centuries of Portuguese history, from the founding of Portugal as a nation-state to the Age of Discoveries.

◎ Sights

★ **Convento de Cristo**   MONASTERY
(www.conventocristo.pt; Rua Castelo dos Templários; adult/child €6/free, with Alcobaça and Batalha monasteries €15; ☺9am-6.30pm Jun-Sep, to 5.30pm Oct-May) Wrapped in equal parts splendour and mystery, the Knights Templar held enormous power in Portugal from the 12th to 16th centuries, largely bankrolling the Age of Discoveries. Their headquarters are set on wooded slopes above the town and enclosed within 12th-century walls. The Convento de Cristo is a stony expression of magnificence, founded in 1160 by Gualdim Pais, Grand Master of the Templars. It has chapels, cloisters and choirs in widely diverging styles, added over the centuries by successive kings and Grand Masters.

➡ **Charola**
This extraordinary 16-sided Templar church, thought to be in imitation of the Church of the Holy Sepulchre in Jerusalem, dominates the complex. Its eastern influences give it a very different feel to most Portuguese churches; the interior is otherworldly in its vast heights – an awesome combination of simple forms and rich embellishment. It's said that the circular design enabled knights to attend Mass on horseback. In the centre stands an eerily Gothic high altar while wall paintings date from the early 16th century. A huge funnel to the left is an ancient organ pipe (the organ itself is long gone).

➡ **Church**
Dom Manuel was responsible for tacking the nave on to the west side of the Charola and for commissioning a two-level choir. The *coro alto* (upper choir) is a fabulous Manueline work, with intricate decor on the vaulting and windows. The main western doorway into the nave is a splendid example of Spanish *plateresque* style.

Seeming to have grown from the wall, the window on the church's western side is the most famous and fantastical feature of the monastery. It's the ultimate in Manueline extravagance, a celebration of the Age of Discoveries: a Medusa tangle of snaking ropes, seaweed and cork boats, atop of which floats the Cross of the Order of Christ and the royal arms and armillary spheres of Dom Manuel. It's best seen from the roof of the adjacent Claustro de Santa Bárbara. Follow signs to the *janela* (window). Unfortunately obscured by the Claustro Principal is an almost-equivalent window on the southern side of the church.

➡ **Claustro do Cemitério & Claustro da Lavagem**
Two serene, *azulejo*-decorated cloisters to the east of the Charola were built during the time when Prince Henry the Navigator was Grand Master of the order in the 15th century. The Claustro do Cemitério (Burial-Ground Cloisters) contains two 16th-century tombs and pretty citrus trees, while the two-storey Claustro da Lavagem (Ablutions Cloisters) affords nice views of the crenellated ruins of the Templars' original castle.

➡ **Claustro Principal**
The elegant Renaissance Claustro Principal (Great Cloisters) stands in striking contrast to the flamboyance of the monastery's Manueline architecture. Commissioned during the reign of João III, the cloisters were probably designed by the Spaniard Diogo de Torralva but completed in 1587 by an Italian, Filippo Terzi. These foreign architects were

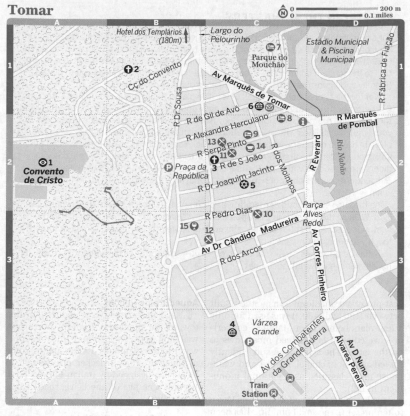

Tomar

Tomar

◎ Top Sights
1 Convento de Cristo	A2

◎ Sights
2 Ermida de Nossa Senhora da Conceição	B1
3 Igreja de São João Baptista	C2
4 Museu dos Fósforos	C4
5 Museu Luso-Hebraico Abraham Zacuto	C2
6 Núcleo De Arte Contemporânea	C1

🛏 Sleeping
7 Estalagem de Santa Iria	C1
8 Hotel Cavaleiros de Cristo	C2
9 Residencial União	C2

✖ Eating
10 Calça Perra	C3
11 La Bella	C2
12 O Infante	C3
13 Restaurante Tabuleiro	C2

🍷 Drinking & Nightlife
14 Café Paraíso	C2
15 Theatro	B3

among several responsible for introducing a delayed Renaissance style into Portugal. The Claustro Principal is arguably the country's finest expression of that style: a sober ensemble of Greek columns and pillars, gentle arches and sinuous, spiralling staircases.

Museu Luso-Hebraico Abraham Zacuto
MUSEUM

(Rua Dr Joaquim Jacinto 73; ◎10am-7pm Tue-Sun Apr-Sep, 10am-1pm & 2-5pm Tue-Sun Oct-Mar) FREE On a charming cobbled lane in the old town, you'll find the country's

THEATRE IN THE MONASTERY

For a completely different take on Tomar's Convento de Cristo (p290), catch a performance of Umberto Eco's *The Name of the Rose* by hometown theatre troupe Fatias de Cá (p294). From the first strains of Gregorian chants wafting through the monastery's entry hall, to the torch-lit finale in the Great Cloisters, this performance takes you to places (literally and figuratively) that you won't get to during a daytime tour.

Not for the faint of heart or weak of leg, the play is a multihour experience. Although it is performed in Portuguese, the plot is easy enough to follow for anyone who has read the novel, and roaming the monastery by night is a wonderful experience regardless of your linguistic abilities. The presentation is punctuated by five meal breaks, each taking place in the old refectory, where chanting black-robed monks preside at the head of long stone tables. The first course involves a little tongue-in-cheek medieval humour: diners are presented with a rock and a pile of walnuts and left to their own devices. Subsequent courses are much more substantial and accompanied by free-flowing wine.

As the sun sets, a mood of meditative contemplation creeps in with the crepuscular light. Walking the hallways in this altered state, it's easier to summon up images from centuries past. The last few scenes, staged in obscure atticlike spaces, are guaranteed to jolt you out of this reverie.

Fatias de Cá stages performances in other atmospheric sites throughout Portugal; for full details, see www.fatiasdeca.net.

best-preserved medieval synagogue. Built between 1430 and 1460, it was used for only a few years before Dom Manuel's convert-or-leave edict of 1497 forced most Jews to do the latter. The synagogue subsequently served as prison, chapel, hayloft and warehouse until classified as a national monument in 1921.

Mostly thanks to the efforts of Luís Vasco (often present), the small building has been remodelled to look something like it would have in the 15th century. It's named after the Jewish mathematician and royal astrologer who helped Vasco da Gama plan his voyages. Inside, among various stones engraved with 13th- and 14th-century Hebraic inscriptions, is a rose-coloured limestone block from the Great Synagogue of Lisbon, dating from 1307. An excellent personal explanation from the person on duty brings this place and its history to life.

Museu dos Fósforos   MUSEUM
(www.museudosfosforos.vidasmundanas.net; Av General Bernardo Faria; ⊙ 10am-5pm) FREE This museum, reached via the lovely courtyard of the Convento de São Francisco, contains Europe's largest collection of matchboxes. Amassed by local 'phillumenist' Aquiles da Mota Lima, the 40,000-plus matchboxes from countries around the world depict everything from bullfighters to bathing beauties, dinosaurs and French cuisine.

Aqueduto de Pegões   AQUEDUCT
FREE This impressive aqueduct, striding towards the monastery from the northwest, was built between 1593 and 1613 to supply water to thirsty monks. Its 180 arches, some of which are double-decker, are thought to have been designed by Italian Filippo Terzi. It's best seen just off the Leiria road, 2.3km from town.

Igreja de São João Baptista   CHURCH
(Praça da República; ⊙ 10am-7pm Tue-Sun) FREE
The old town's most striking church faces Praça da República, itself an eye-catching ensemble of 17th-century buildings alive with the echo of cooing pigeons. The church dates mostly from the late 15th century. It has an octagonal spire and richly ornamented Manueline doorways on its northern and western sides. Inside are 16th- and 17th-century *azulejos;* Gregório Lopes, one of 16th-century Portugal's finest artists, painted the six panels.

Ermida de Nossa Senhora da Conceição   CHURCH
(⊙ 11am-6pm Apr-Sep, 11am-5pm Tue-Sun Oct-Mar) FREE Downhill from the monastery is this strikingly simple Renaissance chapel in a lovely position. It's attributed to Diogo de Torralva, architect of the Convento de Cristo cloisters.

Núcleo De Arte Contemporânea GALLERY
(Rua de Gil de Avô; ⊙11am-6pm Apr-Sep, to 5pm Tue-Sun Oct-Mar) FREE This modern museum showcases the work of 20th-century modernists and surrealists as well as contemporary artists from all over Portugal.

 Activities

Via Aventura KAYAKING
(🗐916 444 026; www.via-aventura.com; Rua Principal 45D) Organises kayak trips on the Rio Nabão as well as to Constância and Castelo de Almourol (€18 per person).

Festivals & Events

Festa dos Tabuleiros TOWN FESTIVAL
(Festa do Espírito Santo; www.tabuleiros.org) Tomar's most famous event is the quadrennial Festa dos Tabuleiros, next scheduled for June/July 2015 and 2019.

Nossa Senhora da Piedade RELIGIOUS
This important religious festival features a candlelit procession and a parade of floats decorated with paper flowers. It's held on the first Sunday in September.

Sleeping

Camping Redondo CAMPGROUND €
(🗐249 376 421; www.campingredondo.com; sites per adult/child/tent/car €3.50/2/3/2.50, 4-person chalet €95, 2-person caravan €40; P🗐🏊🐾) This lovely Dutch-run campground with four chalets plus two additional units in a stone cottage is 10km northeast at Poço Redondo. Amenities include a bar, pool and sun terrace.

For transport details and driving directions in English, consult the website.

Residencial União GUESTHOUSE €
(🗐249 323 161; www.residencialuniao.pt; Rua Serpa Pinto 94; s/d €30/50; 🗐) Tomar's most atmospheric budget choice, this once-grand town house with a good location on the main pedestrian thoroughfare has been a hotel since the 19th century and features large and sprucely maintained rooms with antique furniture and fixtures. Especially pleasant are the elegant breakfast room, serve-yourself bar and kindly owners. It's better value in summer than winter, when it can feel a little chilly.

Hotel Cavaleiros de Cristo HOTEL €
(🗐249 321 203; www.cavaleirosdecristo.pt; Rua Alexandre Herculano 7; s/d €35/55; ❄🗐) Down a side street near the river, this place offers comfortable, modern rooms with writing desks and minibars.

Quinta do Valle RURAL HOTEL €€
(🗐249 381 165; www.quintadovalle.com; 2-/4-person apt not incl breakfast €75/92; P🗐🏊) With parts dating back to the 15th century, this manor house 8km south of Tomar, together with its outbuildings, has been turned into upmarket rural accommodation, with large grounds, chapel, swimming pool and quaint two- to four-bedroom apartments featuring fireplaces and kitchenettes. It's got a lovely out-of-the-way feel and is a venue for utter relaxation. Breakfast is available for €6 extra per person.

To get here from Tomar, take the N110 south, exit at Guerreira, pass through the village and turn right, following the *turismo de habitação* signs.

Estalagem de Santa Iria INN €€
(🗐249 313 326; www.estalagemsantairia.com; Parque do Mouchão; s/d/ste €65/85/125; P🗐) Centrally located on an island in Tomar's lovely riverside park, this curious, slightly kitsch, old-fashioned inn has large careworn but comfortable rooms, most with balconies overlooking the leafy grounds or the river.

ESTREMADURA & RIBATEJO TOMAR

FESTA DOS TABULEIROS

Tomar's Festival of the Trays is a weeklong celebration with music, drinking, dancing and fireworks. But the highlight is definitely the procession of about 400 young, white-clad women (traditionally virgins) bearing headdresses of trays stacked as tall as they are with loaves of bread and ears of wheat, decorated with colourful paper flowers and, finally, topped with a crown, cross or white paper dove. Young male attendants, dressed in black and white, help the girls balance the load, which can weigh up to 15kg. The following day, bread and wine are blessed by the priest and handed out to local families. The festival is believed to have roots in pagan fertility rites, though officially it's related to the saintly practices of 14th-century Dona Isabel (Dom Dinis' queen).

The festival is held every four years in June or July. Upcoming years for the festival are 2015, 2019 and 2023.

Downstairs are a restaurant and bar, both with roaring winter fireplaces. It's a friendly place, albeit with a few glitches, and the location is great.

★**Hotel dos Templários** HOTEL €€€
(☑249 310 100; www.hoteldostemplarios.pt; Largo Cândido dos Reis 1; s/d €112/132; P☀⊛≋) At the river's edge, just outside the historic centre, this spacious, efficient hotel offers excellent facilities including gym, sauna, and indoor and outdoor pools, the latter adjacent to a small but stylish hotel bar. The rooms are large and very comfortable; most have balconies, some of which overlook the river. Try for a room in the modern wing. Room rates are normally lower than the rack rates listed here; check the hotel website.

✖ Eating

O Infante PORTUGUESE €
(Av Dr Cândido Madureira 106; mains €6-13; ☉lunch & dinner) This very attractive local restaurant features a neo-medieval dining room. It has great daily specials for €6 to €7, and good-value à la carte dishes, with tasty cuts of meat. The house red is a bit syrupy so go for a better local drop. Friendly and attentive service.

Calça Perra PORTUGUESE €€
(www.calcaperra.pt; Rua Pedro Dias 59; mains €12-15; ☉10.30am-3pm & 6.30pm-midnight Mon-Sat, 10.30am-3pm Sun) At this charming backstreet eatery you can dine in the pretty pink-walled dining room or the breezy courtyard below. Seasonal specials such as lamprey rice back up the list of reliable meat and fish dishes and a selection of tasty pastas.

Restaurante Tabuleiro PORTUGUESE €€
(☑249 312 771; Rua Serpa Pinto 140; mains €8-12; ☉lunch & dinner Mon-Sat; ⚑) Located just off Tomar's main square, this family-friendly local hang-out features warm, attentive service, good traditional food and ample portions.

La Bella ITALIAN €€
(☑249 322 996; Rua Serpa Pinto 149; mains €7-14; ☉lunch & dinner Tue-Sun) People flock to this brightly lit, mirror-walled pizzeria just behind Igreja de São João Baptista for excellent pasta, pizza and meat dishes.

♬ Drinking & Entertainment

Theatro BAR
(Rua do Teatro; ☉10pm-4am Wed, Fri & Sat, 10pm-2am Sun) Next door to the cinema, this eclectic bar features jazz, classical music and weekend DJ sets running the gamut from electronic to lounge to alternative sounds.

Café Paraíso CAFE
(cafeparaisotomar.com; Rua Serpa Pinto 127; snacks from €3; ☉9am-2am Mon, 8am-2am Tue-Sat, 8pm Sun) This old-fashioned, high-ceilinged deco cafe serves as a refuge for anyone in need of a midafternoon snack and a shot of caffeine or whisky.

Fatias de Cá THEATRE COMPANY
(☑960 303 991; www.fatiasdeca.net) This Tomar-based theatre company presents highly innovative and entertaining weekend performances of works such as *The Name of the Rose* and *The Tempest*, often in amazing locations.

ℹ Information

Espaço Internet (☑249 312 291; Rua Amorim Rosa; ☉10.30am-12.30pm & 2.30-7pm Mon-Sat) Free internet.

Hospital Nossa Senhora da Graça (☑249 320 100; Av Maria de Lourdes Mello e Castro) A kilometre east of town.

Turismo (☑249 329 823; www.cm-tomar.pt; Rua Serpa Pinto; ☉10am-1pm & 3-7pm Apr-Sep, 9.30am-1pm & 2.30-6pm Oct-Mar) Offers a good town map and an accommodation list.

ℹ Getting There & Away

The **bus** (☑249 312 738) and **train** stations are next door to each other, about 500m south of the *turismo*. You will also find several large car parks here.

BUS

Two to four daily buses serve, among other places, Lisbon (€9.80, 1¾ hours), Fátima (€4, one hour), Batalha (€5.50, two hours), Alcobaça (€7, two to 2½ hours) and Leiria (€4, one hour).

TRAIN

Trains run to Lisbon (€9.85 to €10.85, 1¾ to two hours) via Santarém (€5.05 to €5.55, 40 to 55 minutes) every hour or two between 6am and 10pm.

The Beiras

Best Places to Stay

➡ Casa das Penhas Douradas (p336)

➡ Casa da Sé (p342)

➡ Aveiro Rossio Hostel (p319)

Best Places to Eat

➡ Fangas Mercearia Bar (p306)

➡ Pedra de Sal (p312)

➡ Tres Pipos (p340)

Why Go?

Three worlds rolled into one, the Beiras offer as much diversity as any region in Portugal.

Along the Atlantic, the Beira Litoral lures surfers and sun-seekers with scores of sandy beaches. Here, the sophisticated university city of Coimbra and the brash casino-party town of Figueira da Foz arm-wrestle for visitors' attention.

Move inland to the Beira Alta highlands and the mood shifts entirely. Stoic stone villages cling to the slopes of Portugal's highest mountains – the Serra da Estrela – casting their gaze down at the fertile wine country of the Dão valley.

East of the mountains, in the hypnotically beautiful Beira Baixa, vast expanses of olive and cork oak forest spread across a hotter, lonelier landscape. Here, surveying the borderlands from the ramparts of nearly abandoned medieval fortress-towns, you feel centuries away from the coast you just left behind.

When to Go
Coimbra

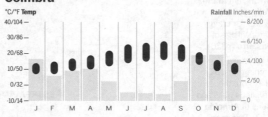

Early May Queima das Fitas fills Coimbra's streets with students in dashing capes.

Jun Before summer crowds descend, and beaches are warm enough for a swim.

Jul Clear mountain air and low-season prices in the Serra da Estrela.

The Beiras Highlights

1 Explore the hilltop labyrinth that is **Coimbra** (p298), a home of fado, lip-smacking food, fabulous views and a marvellous historic university.

2 Hike alongside the glistening Rio Zêzere outside **Manteigas** (p334), past shepherds' huts and soaring peaks.

3 Admire the art nouveau facades lining the canals of **Aveiro** (p318), then hit the streets for some of the Beiras' most animated nightlife.

4 Zig-zag your way up terraced slopes to **Piódão** (p323), the most picturesque of the Beiras' stone villages.

5 Conjure up a vanished civilisation at the Roman ruins of **Conímbriga** (p309).

6 Sip fine Dão wine in the flowery civic gardens of **Viseu** (p340).

7 Savour the golden light in the cork oak forest as you climb from ancient **Idanha-a-Velha** (p327) to the spectacular craggy cliff-top village of **Monsanto** (p326).

8 Whistle a marching tune as you explore the marvellous walls and castles of **Almeida** (p350), **Trancoso** (p347) and other Planalto fortress towns.

BEIRA LITORAL

Coimbra

POP 101,455

The medieval capital of Portugal for over a hundred years, and site of the country's greatest university for the past five centuries, Coimbra wears its weighty importance in Portuguese history with dignity. Its atmospheric, beautiful historic core cascades down a hillside in a lovely setting on the east bank of the Rio Mondego: it's a multicoloured collage of buildings spanning nearly a millennium.

If you visit during the academic year, you'll be sure to feel the university's influence. Students throng bars and cafes; posters advertise talks on everything from genetics to genocide; and graffiti scrawled outside *repúblicas* (communal student dwellings) address the political issues of the day. If you can, come during the Queima das Fitas in early May, a raucous weeklong celebration featuring live music every night. Or stroll the streets on a summer evening, when the city's old stone walls reverberate with the haunting metallic notes of the *guitarra* (Portuguese guitar) and the full, deep voices of fado singers.

Take a few steps outside the historic centre and you'll also see the city's modern side – a modern riverfront park with terrace bars and restaurants, a spiffy pedestrian bridge across the Mondego, and vast shopping complexes offering everything you'd expect in a major European city.

The city also makes a fine base for day visits to the remarkable Roman ruins at Conímbriga, the medieval hilltop fortress of Montemor-o-Velho or the outlandishly ornate Palace Hotel do Buçaco.

History

The Romans founded a city at Conímbriga, though it was abruptly abandoned in favour of Coimbra's more easily defended heights. The city grew and prospered under the Moors, who were evicted definitively by Christians in 1064. The city served as Portugal's capital from 1139 to 1255, when Afonso III decided he preferred Lisbon.

The Universidade de Coimbra, Portugal's first university (and among the first in Europe), was actually founded in Lisbon by Dom Dinis in 1290 but settled here in 1537. It attracted a steady stream of teachers, artists and intellectuals from across Europe. The 16th century was a particularly heady time thanks to Nicolas Chanterène, Jean de Rouen (João de Ruão) and other French artists who helped create a school of sculpture here that influenced styles all over Portugal.

Today Coimbra's university remains Portugal's most prestigious – and one of its most traditional. Students still attend class in black robes and capes – often adorned with patches signifying course of study, home town or other affiliation – while a rigorously maintained set of rites and practices called the *codigo de praxe* governs all aspects of student life.

◉ Sights

Crowning Coimbra's steep hilltop is the university, around and below which lies a tangle of old town lanes. The new town, locally called 'Baixa', spreads at the foot of the hill and along the Rio Mondego.

◎ Upper Town

Long a Moorish stronghold and for a century the seat of Portugal's kings, Coimbra's upper town rises abruptly from the banks of the Rio Mondego. The most picturesque way to enter Coimbra's labyrinth of lanes is via Arco de Almedina – the city's heavy-duty Moorish gateway – and up the staggered stairs known as Rua Quebra Costas (Backbreaker).

People have been gasping up this hill (and falling down it) for centuries; local legend says that it was the 19th-century writer Almeida Garrett who persuaded the mayor to install the stairs.

Up Rua Sub Ripas is the grand Manueline doorway of the early-16th-century Palácio de Sub Ripas (Rua Sub Ripas), signposted Torre da Contenda; its Renaissance windows and stone ornaments are the work of Jean de Rouen, whose workshop was nearby. Further on is the Torre de Anto (Rua Sub Ripas), a tower that once formed part of the town walls. This is soon to become the Museu da Guitarra do Fado de Coimbra (Coimbra Fado Guitar Museum), which should be open by the time you read this.

For a glimpse of student life, stroll along any of the alleys around the Sé Velha (old cathedral) or below the Sé Nova (new cathedral). Flags, offbeat art and graffiti mark the cramped houses known as *repúblicas*, each housing a dozen or so students from the same region or faculty.

THE BEIRAS COIMBRA

★ **Velha Universidade** UNIVERSITY
(Old University; www.uc.pt; admission €7, incl tower €10; ⊙ 9.30am-1pm & 2-5.30pm Mon-Fri, 10.30am-4.30pm Sat & Sun Nov–mid-Mar, 9am-7.30pm daily mid-Mar–Oct) In every way the city's high point, the Old University consists of a series of remarkable 16th to 18th-century buildings, all set around the vast **Patio des Escolas**, entered by way of the elegant 17th-century **Porta Férrea**, which occupies the same site as the main gate to Coimbra's Moorish stronghold. The highlight is the magnificent library.

In the square itself is a **statue of João III**, who turns his back on a sweeping view of the city and the river. It was he who re-established the university in Coimbra in 1537 and invited big-shot scholars to teach here in what had previously been a royal palace.

The square's most prominent feature is the much-photographed 18th-century **clock tower**. This tower is nicknamed *a cabra* (the goat) because, when it chimed to mark the end of studies, the first-year undergrads were pounced upon by swaggering older students and humiliated without mercy – that is, unless they leapt their way home like mountain goats in order to avoid them.

From the courtyard gate take the stairway on the right up to the rather grand **Sala dos Capelos** (Graduates' Hall), a former examination room hung with dark portraits of Portugal's kings, and heavy quiltlike decoration. The adjacent passageway affords visitors excellent city views.

Back outside, to the left below the clock tower, you'll find the entrance to fanciful **Capela de São Miguel**, an ornate baroque chapel with brightly painted ceiling, ornate tilework, Manueline features and a gilded organ. Concerts still take place here on occasion – ask at the *turismo* (tourist office).

However, all else pales before **Biblioteca Joanina** (João V Library; ✆booking 239 859 818; reservas@ci.uc.pt; Velha Universidade; adult/senior/student €3.50/1.75/2.45 or with Sala dos Capelos €5/2.50/3.50 9am-7pm May-Sep, to 5pm Oct-Apr) next door. A gift from João V in the early 18th century, it seems too extravagant and distracting for study with its rosewood, ebony and jacaranda tables, elaborately frescoed ceilings and gilt chinoiserie bookshelves. Its 300,000 ancient books deal with law, philosophy and theology. A lower floor has more tomes and the **Prisão Acadêmica**, a lock-up for misbehaving students.

Visitors are admitted in small numbers and on a timetable, and you may find that some rooms are closed during degree ceremonies. Buy your ticket in the shop in the square just outside the Porta Férrea. Individuals and small groups can generally get in with minimal waiting time.

★ **Sé Velha** CATHEDRAL
(Old Cathedral; ✆239 825 273; Largo da Sé Velha; admission €2; ⊙10am-5.30pm Mon-Sat, to 6pm Apr-Oct) Coimbra's stunning old cathedral is one of the finest examples of Romanesque architecture in Portugal. Its crenellated exterior and narrow, slitlike lower windows serve as reminders of the nation's embattled early days, when the Moors were still a threat. These buildings were designed to be useful as fortresses in times of trouble. The exceptional main portal and facade are striking.

The church was financed by the first king of Portugal, Afonso Henriques, in the 12th century. The high, barrel-vaulted nave preserves its main Romanesque features; side altars and well-preserved Gothic tombs of bishops are backed by bright Andalusian tiles. The high gilt retable is in ornate late-Gothic style and depicts the Assumption of Mary. Contrast this with the Renaissance Capela do Santíssimo Sacramento alongside. If you want to visit on a Sunday, duck in just before or after 11am Mass.

★ **Museu Nacional de Machado de Castro** MUSEUM
(✆239 853 070; www.mnmachadodecastro.imc-ip.pt; Largo Dr José Rodrigues; adult/child €6/free, cryptoportico only €3; ⊙10am-12.30pm & 2-6pm Tue-Sun Oct-Mar, 10am-6pm Tue-Sun Apr-Sep) Recently reopened, this great museum is a highlight of central Portugal. It's fitting that it has become a real centre of the local community, with people gathering to admire the views from its patio and cafe, for it's built over the Roman forum, the remains of which you can see. The artistic collection is wide-ranging and superb.

Part of the visit takes you down to the vaulted galleries of the cryptoportico that allowed the forum to be level on such a hilly site. It's spooky and immensely atmospheric. The route through the museum section starts with sculpture, from the architectural (column capitals) through Gothic religious sculpture and on. Highlights include a section of the delicate cloister of São João de Almedina and some exquisite alabaster

Central Coimbra

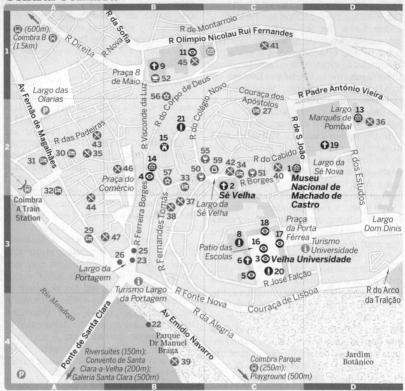

pieces from England. Renaissance masters arriving in Coimbra from other parts of Europe brought their own styles and contributed to the establishment of a distinctive Coimbra tradition. A whole chapel has even been reassembled here. The section downstairs includes impressive 16th-century terracotta figures from Hodart's Last Supper, while paintings on the higher floors include stunning Flemish panels by Metsys. A collection of gold monstrances, furniture, and Moorish-influenced pieces are almost too much by the time you reach them.

Sé Nova
CATHEDRAL
(New Cathedral; ☎ 239 823 138; Largo da Sé Nova; admission €1; ☺ 9.30am-12.30pm & 2-6.30pm Tue-Sat) The large, severe 'new' cathedral, started by the Jesuits in 1598 but only completed a century later, dominates the square of the same name high in the old town. Its sober Renaissance lines contrast with the gilt side panels and ornate baroque altarpiece. Down

the side is a gallery of reliquaries featuring bones and worse from minor saints and bishops, including St Francis Xavier and, harder to believe, St Luke. Climb to the platform for uplifting city views.

Museu da Ciência
MUSEUM
(☎ 239 854 350; www.museudaciencia.org; Largo Marquês de Pombal; adult/student €4/2; ☺ 10am-6pm Tue-Sun) This wonderful science museum occupies a centuries-old former monastery converted by Pombal into the university's chemical engineering building. It features intriguing state-of-the-art interactive science displays coexisting with 18th-century lab sinks; don't miss the giant glowing globe in a room paved with medieval stones, or the psychedelic insect's-eye view of flowers. Displays are in English/Portuguese. There's also a great cafe with terrace and views down to the new town. A combined ticket including the Velha Universidade costs €9, a €2 saving.

2-6pm Tue-Sat) Housed in the medieval tower directly above the Arco de Almedina, this historical museum displays a plaster reproduction of Coimbra's old-town layout, complete with castle. A multilingual audiovisual presentation takes you step by step around the 2km of walls. There's an exhibition and city views upstairs, but the real fun is looking down through the *matacães* (embrasures), through which hot oil was traditionally poured on enemies below.

◉ Praça da República & Around

Leafy Praça da República is a social centre. The surrounding neighbourhood, laid out in the 19th century and still dominated by prim bourgeois homes of the period, is a relaxing break from the high density of both the university and the Baixa area.

Jardim Botânico   GARDEN
(☑239 855 233; www.uc.pt; ⊙9am-5.30pm Mon-Fri, 11am-5.30pm Sat & Sun Oct-Mar, 9am-5.30pm Mon-Fri, 2-8pm Sat & Sun Apr-Sep) 🅿 FREE A serene place to catch your breath, the lovely university-run botanic garden sits in the shadow of the 16th-century **Aqueduto de São Sebastião**. Founded by the Marquês de Pombal, the gardens combine formal flowerbeds, meandering paths and elegant fountains. The green-fingered can also visit the lush **greenhouses** and the adjacent **Museu Botânico** (Botanical Museum; ☑239 855 210; www.uc.pt; Calçada Martim de Freitas; adult/student €2/1.50; ⊙9am-noon & 2-5pm Mon-Fri), while **Skygarden** (www.skygardenadventure.com; Calçada Martim de Freitas; adult/child €17/13; ⊙10am-8pm Tue-Sun Apr-Sep, 10am-5.30pm Tue-Sun Mar & Oct, weekends only Nov & Feb; ⊛) has a series of ziplines here.

Casa Museu Bissaya Barreto   MUSEUM
(☑239 853 800; www.fbb.pt; Rua Infantaria 23; adult/child or senior €2.50/1.25; ⊙11am-1pm Tue-Fri, 3-6pm Tue-Sun) Bissaya Barreto was a local surgeon, scholar and obsessive hoarder of fine arts, and his handsome, late-19th-century mansion has been turned into an art museum. A guide (not necessarily English-speaking) accompanies guests through rooms jam-packed with Portuguese sculpture and painting, Chinese porcelain, old *azulejos* and period furniture.

◉ Along & Across the River

In an ecclesiastical counterweight to the university, a cluster of convents, together with

◉ Baixa & Around

Igreja de Santa Cruz   CHURCH
(Praça 8 de Maio; adult/student €2.50/1.50; ⊙9am-noon & 2-5pm Mon-Sat, 4-5.30pm Sun) From the trendy shops outside, this church plunges you back to Portugal's past. Step through the Renaissance porch and flamboyant 18th-century arch to discover some of the Coimbra School's finest work, including an ornate pulpit and the elaborate tombs of Portugal's first kings, Afonso Henriques and Sancho I. The most striking Manueline work is in the restrained 16th-century cloister.

Behind the church is the **Jardim da Manga** and its curious fountain: a lemon-yellow, four-buttressed affair.

Núcleo da Cidade Muralhada & Torre de Almedina   MUSEUM
(☑239 833 771; www.cm-coimbra.pt; Pátio do Castilho; adult/student €1.80/1.20; ⊙10am-1pm &

Central Coimbra

several other sights, sits on the far side of the Rio Mondego. Lovely green spaces stretch south from the Ponte de Santa Clara along the eastern bank of the river. **Parque Dr Manuel Braga** provides a haven of serene shade under stately rows of old sycamores, while the **Parque Verde do Mondego** (www.parqueverdedomondego.pt; ⟐) features riverfront bars and eateries, a pedestrian bridge across the Rio Mondego and a small playground for kids.

Convento de Santa Clara-a-Velha CONVENT (⟐239 801 160; http://santaclaraavelha.drcc.pt; Rua das Parreiras; adult/student €5/3; ⟐10am-7pm Tue-Sun May-Sep, to 5pm Oct-Apr) This Gothic convent was founded in 1330 by the saintly Dona Isabel, Dom Dinis' wife; it served as her final resting place until flooding forced her to be moved uphill. The ad-

jacent **museum** displays archaeological finds and shows two films, one about the nuns who lived here, the other documenting the 20-year renovation that cleared the river ooze that had drowned it since the 17th century.

Convento de Santa Clara-a-Nova CONVENT (⟐239 441 674; Calçada de Santa Isabel; admission cloister €1.50; ⟐8.30am-6pm) Begun on higher ground in the 17th century to replace its flooded twin, this convent is devoted almost entirely to the saintly Queen Isabel's memory. Aisle panels tell her life story, while her solid-silver casket is enshrined above the altar, and even her clothes hang in the sacristy. Her statue is the focus of the Festa da Rainha Santa. At the time of research it was closed for emergency stabilisation works.

Portugal dos Pequenitos   THEME PARK
(☑239 801 170; www.portugaldospequenitos.
pt; Rossio de Santa Clara; adult/3-13yr/family
€8.95/5.50/23.95; ☉10am-7pm Mar-May & mid-
Sep–mid-Oct, 9am-8pm Jun–mid-Sep, 10am-5pm
mid-Oct–Feb; ☉) The brainchild of local col-
lector Bissaya Barreto, this is an impossibly
cute theme park where kids clamber over,
into and through doll's-house versions of
Portugal's most famous monuments, while
parents clutch cameras at the ready. There's
an extra charge to visit marginally interesting minimuseums of marine life, clothing
and furniture.

Quinta das Lágrimas   GARDEN
(Rua Vilarinho Raposo; admission €2; ☉10am-5pm
Tue-Sun mid-Oct–mid-Mar, 10am-7pm mid-Mar–
mid-Oct) Legend says Dona Inês de Castro
met her grisly end (p275) in the gardens
of this private estate. It's now a deluxe hotel, although anyone can take a turn about
the grounds and track down the Fonte dos
Amores (Lovers' Fountain), which marks the
spot where the prince's unwitting mistress
was struck down. Also note the sequoia tree
planted by the Duke of Wellington.

🏃 Activities

Several organisations offer opportunities for
canoeing, rafting and other outdoor sports
in the Coimbra region.

O Pioneiro do Mondego   KAYAKING
(☑239 478 385; www.opioneirodomondego.com;
per person €22.50) 🛶 Rents out kayaks for
paddling the Mondego between Penacova
and Torres de Mondego, an 18km trip.

Transserrano   ADVENTURE, CULTURAL
(☑235 778 938; www.transserrano.com) 🛶 Excursions in the nearby Serra da Lousã and
Serra do Açor, including hiking, climbing,

and tours focused on traditional cheese-
making and olive-oil production.

Tours

Go Walks   WALKING TOURS
(☑910 163 118; www.gowalksportugal.com; €10)
🛶 Various walking tours including a nightlife one run by enthusiastic, knowledgeable
Coimbra students who speak good English
(French and Spanish also bookable). Some
require prebooking, but a guaranteed one
leaves Largo de Portagem Monday to Friday
at 9am, 11am, 2.30pm and 4.30pm.

Basófias   BOAT TOURS
(☑969 830 664; www.odabarca.com; €6.50;
☉Tue-Sun) Boat trips (50 minutes) on the Rio
Mondego. They depart from beside Parque
Dr Manuel Braga hourly from 3pm to 7pm
May to September, and at 3pm and 4pm
only October to April.

Tuk-Tuk City Tour   CITY TOURS
(☑969 830 664; www.odabarca.com; adult/child
€7.50/4.50; ☉10.30am, 11.30am, then hourly 2.30-
5.30pm mid-Apr–mid-Oct; ☉) This hour-long
circuit takes you whizzing deftly through
the old town's narrow streets aboard an
six-seater Thai *tuk-tuk,* then explores the
city's outskirts before depositing you back at
the embarkation point, Largo da Portagem.
Tickets are purchased from the driver.

Yellow Bus Tours   BUS TOURS
(☑239 801 100; www.yellowbustours.com; adult/
child €10/5; ☉Sat & Sun mid-Mar–mid May, Tue-Sun
mid-May–Oct) Hour-long hop-on, hop-off tours
of Coimbra with multilingual commentary.
The double-decker buses originate near the
turismo at Largo da Portagem. You can pay
on board or buy tickets at the *turismo* and
hotels. An extra €2 buys a riverboat tour.

FIRED UP

In the first week of May, Coimbra marks the end of the academic year with Queima das
Fitas (p304), a weeklong party that serves as the country's biggest and best excuse to
get roaring drunk. Literally, the name means 'Burning of the Ribbons', because graduates ritually torch the colour-coded ribbons worn to signify particular courses of study.

In the wee hours of Friday morning, the Queima kicks off with the **Serenata Monumental**, a hauntingly beautiful midnight fado performance on the steps of the Sé Velha.
The agenda continues with sports events, private black-tie balls, nightly concerts at the
so-called **Queimodromo** across the Ponte de Santa Clara, and a beer-soaked Sunday-
afternoon parade called the **Cortejo dos Grelados** that runs from the university down
to Largo da Portagem.

In their rush to sponsor the various festivities, Portuguese breweries provide ultra-
cheap beer, which is distributed and drunk in liberal quantities.

RAINHA-SANTA ISABEL

One of Portugal's most popular saints, Queen-Saint Isabel is most often depicted with a scattering of roses falling across her garments. Legend has it that one day while she was bringing food to the poor, her less-than-saintly husband (Dinis I) accused her of stealing food from the royal kitchens. When the king angrily demanded to see the contents of her apron, out fell nothing but flowers. Rainha Isabel – not surprisingly, given the apocryphal tale – is credited with founding homes for abused wives and abandoned children. When eldest son Afonso challenged Dom Dinis for the throne, Isabel rode on horseback between the two lines of opposing forces, daring both father and son to attack her first.

✖✥ Festivals & Events

Queima das Fitas   STUDENT
(www.queimadasfitas.org) Coimbra's biggest bash celebrates the end of the academic year in great style. The festivities take place every year during the first week in May.

Festa da Rainha Santa   RELIGIOUS, FIESTA
(www.rainhasantaisabel.org) Held around 4 July in even-numbered years, this festival commemorates Santa Isabel. A Thursday-night candlelit procession carries her statue from the Convento de Santa Clara-a-Nova across the Ponte de Santa Clara to Largo da Portagem and through the streets to Igreja do Carmo; a second procession the following Sunday returns her to the convent. The festival also coincides with the yearly **Festa da Cidade** (Town Festival), celebrated with music, folk dancing and fireworks.

Festival das Artes   ARTS
(www.festivaldasartes.com) This two-week festival in late July brings classical music to the Quinta das Lágrimas, jazz to the riverboats, guest chefs to local restaurants and other forms of merriment to Coimbra's streets.

🛏 Sleeping

There are numerous cheap *residenciais* on Avenida Fernão de Magalhães near the Coimbra A train station.

★**Riversuites**   HOTEL €
(☑239 440 582; www.riversuiteshotel.com; Av João das Regras 82; r €39; ✻ 🙲) Just across the bridge from the centre, with easy parking alongside, this excellent new hotel has slick rooms (not suites), modern stylings and comforts. A decent breakfast is included, and the showers are just great. Don't worry about the busy road outside; the windows are so well soundproofed it's almost unnerving. The price may rise, but at time of research it offered unbeatable value.

★**Serenata Hostel**   HOSTEL €
(☑239 853 130; www.serenatahostel.com; Largo da Sé Velha 21; dm/d not incl bathroom €24/55, d €60; @🙲) In the pretty heart of the old town, this noble building with an intriguingly varied history is now a fabulous hostel, chock-full of modern comforts and facilities while maintaining a period feel in keeping with this historic zone. Great lounge areas, a cute secluded sun terrace, several computers, spacious dorms, friendly staff and a modern kitchen complete a very happy picture. Prices are often lower than listed here.

Hotel Vitória   HOTEL €
(☑234 824 049; www.hotelvitoria.pt; Rua da Sota 9; s/d €35/48; ✻🙲🖩) This friendly family-run *residencial* in the heart of the eating district has had a major upgrade, with a modern wing tacked on. The old rooms are perhaps a touch larger and still look very good, while the newer ones have a clean-line Nordic feel; all have lots of light. The views over rooftops and up to the old town, or down to the river, are a highlight, so try to get a room on the 3rd floor if possible. There's a great family room available too, and a downstairs restaurant.

Residencial Botânico   GUESTHOUSE €
(☑239 714 824; residbotanico@gmail.com; Bairro de São José 15; s/d/tr €36/46/65; ✻ @🙲🖩) This irreproachably kept guest house is a 15-minute stroll from the centre through the botanic gardens and boasts friendly staff and elegantly sparse rooms, including some family suites. Rooms vary in size – some are very spacious, with newly fitted bathrooms. The overall package is excellent, there's easy street parking around the corner, and double-paned glass to keep out street noise.

Quebra-Luz   GUESTHOUSE €
(☑912 278 779; www.quebra-luz.com; Rua Quebra Costas 18; s/d €40/45, not incl bathroom €35/40; 🙲) Right on the old town's 'back-breaking'

stairs, this isn't easy to find but makes a good central haven, though you won't be able to park too close. It's an apartment with four rooms decorated with attractive fabrics that give the place an optimistic feel. Two share a bathroom (another has exterior private bathroom) and there's a kitchen and book exchange. It's reasonably well soundproofed so those noisy students won't disturb your rest. Don't be put off by the dingy staircase.

Hotel Domus
GUESTHOUSE €

(☑239 828 584; www.residencialdomus.com; Rua Adelino Veiga 62; s/tw/q €30/38/60; ※ ᯧ) Clean, well-maintained Domus is a family-run place in a quiet pedestrian shopping zone near Coimbra A train station. There are some nice old features and furnishings and friendly management. The best rooms are the front-facing ones upstairs, which get plenty of natural light.

Grande Hostel de Coimbra
HOSTEL €

(☑239 108 212; www.grandehostelcoimbra.com; Rua Antero de Quental 196; dm/d €18/40; ᯧ) You won't find a hostel more laid-back than this – in fact, service may be too lax for some – but it's hard to beat the location in a grand, century-old town house with views near the nightlife of Coimbra's university campus. Rooms can get hot in summer, but there's a garden area to wind down in.

★ Casa Pombal
GUESTHOUSE €€

(☑239 835 175; www.casapombal.com; Rua das Flores 18; s/d €58/68, not incl bathroom €44/54; @ ᯧ) In a lovely old-town location, hidden down a narrow lane but very close to the museum and the top of the lift, this winning guest house squeezes tons of charm into a small space. Nine cosy wood-floored rooms – some with shared bathroom – are individually decorated in historic style; a couple boast magnificent views.

There are numerous nice touches like a flask of port in the rooms and a small roof terrace. The friendly owners provide multilingual advice about local cultural events, plus a delicious breakfast with vegetarian options in the gorgeous blue-tiled breakfast room. Book ahead from Easter to October.

Hotel Oslo
HOTEL €€

(☑239 829 071; www.hotel-oslo.web.pt; Av Fernão de Magalhães 25; s/d €55/65; P ※ @ ᯧ) This comfortable, reliable hotel near the Coimbra A station has well-maintained rooms, a free garage with complimentary valet parking, satellite TV, double-paned windows and a

popular 5th-floor bar with views up to the university. Recently remodelled 'superior' rooms have larger bathrooms, flatscreen TVs and balconies for not much of an extra investment. The standards are compact but fine too.

Hotel Astória
HOTEL €€

(☑239 853 020; www.almeidahotels.com; Av Emídio Navarro 21; s/d €72/92, superior s/d €97/117, ste €130; ※ ᯧ) The Astória's unmistakable art nouveau facade contemplates the river and Largo da Portagem. It has personality and professional staff; it's all delightfully old-fashioned but that goes for the dog-eared rooms too. It won't be to everyone's taste. The round tower rooms have wraparound views and a little balcony in a prime location. Wi-fi is only in the lobby.

Residencial Alentejana
GUESTHOUSE €€

(☑239 825 903; www.residencialalentejana.com; Rua Dr António Henriques Seco 1; s €39-55, d €45-68; ※ ᯧ) Worth the uphill walk, this prominent old town house offers wood-panelled, high-ceilinged older rooms, plus some less charming but still comfortable newer ones. It's a characterful place with kindly owners and a good-value local restaurant downstairs.

★ Quinta das Lágrimas
HOTEL €€€

(☑239 802 380; www.quintadaslagrimas.pt; Rua António Augusto Gonçalves; s/d annexe €194/215, palace €223/247; P ※ ᯧ ⊠) This splendid historical palace is now one of Portugal's most enchanting upper-crust hotels. Choose between richly furnished rooms in the old palace, or Scandinavian-style minimalist in the modern annexe – complete with jacuzzi. A few rooms look out onto the garden where

DON'T MISS

TOP FIVE VIEWS IN COIMBRA

Coimbra's picturesque hillside position means there are some great spots to enjoy magnificent views. Our pick of the vistas:

➡ Cafe of Museu Nacional de Machado de Castro (p306)

➡ On the roof of the Sé Nova (p300)

➡ Cafe at the Museu da Ciência (p300)

➡ Top of the tower at Patio des Escolas (p299)

➡ Belvedere of Santa Clara-a-Nova (p302)

THE BEIRAS COIMBRA

Dona Inês de Castro reputedly met her tragic end. Significant discounts are sometimes available online, even in high season, and it's cheaper midweek. Other facilities include a pitch 'n' putt course and driving range.

✖ Eating

The atmospheric narrow streets between Praça do Comércio and Coimbra A train station are full of characterful Portuguese eateries; just wander down here and smell what's cooking.

Porta Larga   SANDWICHES €
(📞239 823 619; Rua das Padeiras 35; sandwiches €4.50; ⊙9am-8pm Mon-Sat) For a quick snack with a hefty dose of local flavour, António's *sandes de leitão* (roast pork sandwiches) can't be beat, although it's best avoided if you're squeamish about little piggies turning on spits.

Adega Paço dos Condes   PORTUGUESE €
(📞239 825 605; Rua do Paço do Conde 1; mains €5-10; ⊙lunch & dinner Mon-Sat) Usually crowded with students and Coimbra locals, this straightforward family-run grill is one of the city's best budget eateries. It's like something from a bygone era; prices are great and there's a long list of daily specials which are usually your best way forward.

Cafetaria do Museu   CAFE, BAR €
(Rua dos Estudos; light meals €4-9; ⊙10.30am-7pm Sun-Thu, 10.30am-4am Fri & Sat; ✏) Tucked away in a remote part of the top of town, the science museum's cafe offers a large interior warmed by log fire and an excellent terrace with views over the town below. It does light meals, juices and salads during the day and has regular DJ sets and events at weekends, when it's a popular bar.

Restaurante Jardim da Manga   PORTUGUESE €
(📞239 829 156; Rua Olímpio Nicolau Rui Fernandes; mains €6-9; ⊙lunch & dinner Sun-Fri) Student-friendly and tailored to tight budgets, this cafeteria-style restaurant serves up tasty meat and fish dishes, with pleasant outdoor seating beside the Jardim da Manga fountain.

Mercado Municipal Dom Pedro V   MARKET €
(Rua Olímpio Nicolau Rui Fernandes; ⊙Mon-Sat) 🍃 A colourful stop for self-caterers, this market is full of lively fruit and vegetable stalls and butcher shops displaying Portuguese cuts of meat, hooves, claws and all.

★Zé Manel dos Ossos   TASCA €€
(Beco do Forno 12; mains €7-15; ⊙lunch & dinner Mon-Fri, lunch Sat) Tucked down a nondescript alleyway, this little gem, which is papered with scholarly doodles and scribbled poems, is easy to miss. Despite its location, it's highly popular, so come early or be ready to wait. Try the good *feijoada á leitão* (a stew of beans and suckling pig). The charismatic service makes dining here a delight.

★Fangas Mercearia Bar   PETISCOS €€
(📞934 093 636; Rua Fernandes Tomás 45; petiscos €4-7; ⊙noon-4pm & 7pm-1am Tue-Sun; ✏) Top-quality deli produce is used to produce delightful *petiscos* (like Portuguese tapas) in this bright and beautiful dining room, the best place to eat in the old town. Service is slow but friendly and will help you choose from a delicious array of tasty platters – sausages, stuffed vegetables, conserves – and interesting wines. Book ahead as this small space always fills quickly.

Loggia   PORTUGUESE, BAR €€
(📞239 853 076; www.loggia.pt; Largo Dr José Rodrigues, Museu Nacional de Machado de Castro; mains €12; ⊙10am-6pm Tue-Sun, 7.30-10.30pm Wed-Sat) This museum restaurant has one of the town's most enviable locations, on a flat deck with stunning views over the cascading roofs of the old city. It's a romantic, candlelit dining scene by night, and great value for its confident modern Portuguese mains with a Roman twist (the lunchtime €7 special is also a steal). At other times, it's a venue for coffees or beers in the sunshine with the best vistas in town.

Restaurante Giro   PORTUGUESE €€
(📞239 833 020; www.restaurantegiro.com; Rua das Azeiteiras 39; mains €9-15; ⊙lunch & dinner Mon-Sat) This back-alley place serves toothsome traditional Portuguese fare in a pleasant tiled dining room. The grilled meats are excellent, and though portions aren't as large as in some places, that's probably a good thing.

O Trovador   PORTUGUESE €€
(📞239 825 475; Largo da Sé Velha 15; mains €9-13; ⊙lunch & dinner Mon-Sat) In a wonderful position right opposite the majestic old cathedral, this restaurant sees many tourists but nevertheless offers up good-value regional cuisine supplemented by daily specials in a likeable setting. The walls are decorated with tiles, quotations and photos of old

Coimbra, and the atmosphere is traditional. Regular fado performances.

Restaurante Zé Neto
PORTUGUESE €€

(Rua das Azeiteiras 8; mains €9-11; ⊘lunch & dinner Mon-Sat) This marvellous family-run place specialises in homemade Portuguese standards, including *cabrito* (kid). Come in the late morning and you'll catch the elderly owner – a fixture here since 1952 – tapping out the menu on a typewriter of similar vintage.

Itália
ITALIAN €€

(www.grupovalentinorestaurantes.com; Parque Dr Manuel de Braga; mains €8-15; ⊘noon-midnight; 🖟) Cheery Itália serves reasonably good Italian food – including tasty pizza – but what really draws the crowds is its incomparable location. The sunny glass-walled dining room is cantilevered over the Rio Mondego, while breezy outdoor tables bask in the shade of giant sycamores in the adjacent riverside park.

Dona Especiaria
PORTUGUESE €€€

(Restaurante do Gil; ☑922 040 194; www.dona especiaria.pt.vu; Rua Joaquim António d'Aguiar 49; set lunch/dinner €7.50/30; ⊘lunch Tue-Sun, dinner Mon-Sat) We really can't decide whether to recommend this weird place or not. A small dining room is the stage for a charismatic chef's caprices. Start with fruit and follow with Portuguese cuisine with numerous twists; it's almost a surreal experience. It's not gourmet, more an enthusiastic friend's dinner party. It's very personal and intimate, some dishes hit heights, and it's always interesting, though service can be painfully slow. Lunch is simpler. No sign. Book dinner ahead.

 Drinking & Nightlife

Coimbra has some great bars. In the old town, around Praça da Sé Velha, students spill onto the cobblestones outside classic pubs like **Bigorna** (Rua Borges Carneiro 11) and **O Moelas** (Rua dos Coutinhos 14). The area around Praça da República is chock-full of bars and clubs.

★ Galeria Santa Clara
BAR, CAFE

(☑239 441 657; www.galeriasantaclara.com; Rua António Augusto Gonçalves 67; ⊘2pm-2am Mon-Fri, 2pm-3am Sat & Sun) Arty tearoom by day and chilled-out bar at night, this terrific place across the Mondego has good art on the walls, a series of sunny rooms and a fine riverfront terrace. It's got a great indoor-outdoor vibe and can feel like a party in a private house when things get going.

★ Café Santa Cruz
CAFE

(www.cafesantacruz.com; Praça 8 de Maio; ⊘7.30am-2am Mon-Sat) Few cafes in Portugal offer such an atmospheric backdrop. The interior, set in a dramatically beautiful high-vaulted former chapel, features stained-glass windows, graceful stone arches, and a Ché mosaic where the altar would have been,

LOCAL KNOWLEDGE

COIMBRA FADO

If Lisbon represents the heart of Portuguese fado music, Coimbra is its head. The 19th-century university was male-only so the town's womenfolk, immortalised in song as *tricanas*, were of great interest to the student body. Coimbra fado developed partly as a way of communicating with these heavily chaperoned females, usually in the form of serenades sung under the bedroom window. For this reason, fado is traditionally sung only by men, who must be students or ex-students.

The Coimbra style is considered more lyrical and pure than the Lisbon variety, though it was influenced over the decades by musical traditions from all over Portugal and the Portuguese-speaking world thanks to the varied origins of the student body. It ranges from hauntingly beautiful serenades and lullabies to more boisterous students-out-on-the-piss type of songs. The singer is normally accompanied by a 12-string *guitarra* (Portugese guitar) and perhaps a Spanish (classical) guitar too. Due to the clandestine nature of these bedroom-window concerts, audience appreciation is traditionally indicated by softly coughing rather than clapping.

There are several excellent venues in Coimbra to hear fado. A couple of tracks to get you in the mood are: 'Balada da Despedida', the most famous of the farewell songs traditionally composed and sung by graduating classes; and 'Canção de Embalar', by the legendary singer and antidictatorship activist José (Zeca) Afonso.

THE BEIRAS COIMBRA

while the outdoor patio area affords one of the city's best vantage points over Praça 8 de Maio. Popular with tourists and locals alike, the cafe has regular free fado. You'll pay a bit extra for the atmosphere, but it's worth it.

Feitoconceito
BAR

(www.feitoconceito.pt; Rua Alexandre Herculano 16A; ⊘2pm-2am Mon-Wed, 2pm-4am Thu-Sat) Entered through the Tabacaria Pavão, this hip little hideaway near Praça da República woos a crowd with regular DJ sets, plus ridiculously low prices on caipirinhas, mojitos, gins-and-tonic, vodka and beer. Hang out at the bar, or decamp to one of the high-ceilinged back rooms, all decorated with eye-catching, one-of-a-kind wallpaper. Don't confuse it with the other bar in this green-tiled building.

Aqui Base Tango
BAR

(Rua Venâncio Rodrigues 8; ⊘9pm-4am Tue-Sat) This offbeat house holds one of Coimbra's most enticing bars, a quirky space with extremely original decor and a relaxed, inclusive vibe. Music ranges from jazz to alternative rock and there's always something interesting going on or in the pipeline.

Bar Quebra Costas
BAR

(☑239 821 661; www.quebra.eu; Rua Quebra Costas 45; ⊘noon-4am Mon-Fri, 2pm-4am Sat) In the perfect position to sip a cold beer as you watch people puff and pant up the Quebra Costas, this Coimbra classic has a sunny cobblestoned terrace, an artsy interior, friendly service and chilled-out tunes playing on the sound system.

AAC Bar
BAR

(Bar Associação Académica de Coimbra; Av Sá da Bandeira; ⊘9am-4am) Join the black-cape-clad students at their student-union bar, where beers are cheap and everyone is welcome. The esplanade out back, with wood decking and a grassy lawn, makes an agreeable refuge.

Noites Longas
CLUB

(Rua Almeida Garrett 7; ⊘11pm-6am Mon-Sat) This club plays mainly rock and goes loud and very late. It's not subtle but it's a reliable local favourite.

☆ Entertainment

Free fado performances take place periodically at Café Santa Cruz – consult the weekly schedule of events posted at the cafe. From late June to mid-September, you'll also find evening folk music and dancing in Praça 8 de Maio.

★ Á Capella
FADO

(☑918 113 307; www.acapella.com.pt; Rua Corpo de Deus; admission incl 1 drink €10; ⊘9pm-2am) A 14th-century chapel transformed into candlelit cocktail lounge, this regularly hosts the city's most renowned fado musicians. The setting is as intimate as the music itself, with heart-rendingly good acoustics. These shows cater directly to a tourist crowd, but atmosphere and music are both superb. There's a show every night at 10pm.

★ Fado ao Centro
FADO

(☑913 236 725; www.fadoaocentro.com; Rua Quebra Costas 7; show incl drink €10) At the bottom of the old town, this friendly fado centre makes a good place to introduce yourself to the genre. There's a performance every evening at 6pm (and other shorter ones during the afternoon). Shows include plenty of explanation in Portuguese and English about the history of Coimbra fado and the meaning of each song. It's tourist-oriented, but the performers enjoy it and do it well. You can chat with them afterwards over a glass of port (included).

Teatro Académico de Gil Vicente
THEATRE, CONCERT VENUE

(TAGV; ☑239 855 630; www.tagv.info; Praça da República) This university-run auditorium is an important theatre, cinema and concert venue.

🛍 Shopping

Coimbra is famous for its distinctive hand-painted pottery depicting whimsical, stylised hunting scenes with twirling tendrils and graceful animals. The best place to watch a painter at work and pick up some ceramics is the shop and studio of **Carlos Tomás** (☑239 812 945; carlostomas_ceramica artesanal@hotmail.com; Largo da Sé Velha 4). It can also custom-paint items and arrange well-padded delivery worldwide.

ℹ Information

INTERNET ACCESS

Ciberespaço (Loja 4, Av Sá da Bandeira; per hr €2.20; ⊘10am-10pm Mon-Sat, 1-9pm Sun) Plenty of computers, on the ground floor of an old-fashioned shopping centre.

Espaço Internet (www.integrar.org; Praça 8 de Maio 37; ⊘10am-8pm Mon-Fri, 10am-10pm Sat & Sun) Free access.

MEDICAL SERVICES

Hospital da Universidade de Coimbra (☑239 400 400; Praceta Mota Pinto) Located 1.5km northeast of the centre.

POST

Main post office (Rua Olímpio Nicolau Rui Fernandes; ◷9am-6pm Mon-Fri, 10am-6pm Sat) There's also a branch on Praça da República (◷9am-6pm Mon-Fri, 10am-6pm Sat).

TOURIST INFORMATION

These offices offer good town maps as well as the *Agenda de Atividades* cultural diary.

Turismo Largo da Portagem (☑239 488 120; www.turismodecoimbra.pt; Largo da Portagem; ◷9am-6pm Mon-Fri, 9.30am-12.30pm & 1.30-5.30pm Sat & Sun mid-Sep–mid-Jun, 9am-8pm Mon-Fri, 9am-6pm Sat & Sun mid-Jun–mid-Sep) By the bridge in the centre of things.

Turismo Praça República (www.turismo decoimbra.pt; Praça da República; ◷10am-1pm & 2-6pm Apr-Oct, 9.30am-1pm & 2-5.30pm Mon-Fri Nov-Mar) On the eastern side of town.

Turismo Universidade (☑239 834 158; www.turismodecoimbra.pt; Praça da Porta Férrea; ◷9am-5pm Mon-Fri, 10am-4pm Sat & Sun Nov-Mar, 10am-1pm & 2-6pm daily Apr-Oct) Adjacent to the Velha Universidade ticket desk, just outside the Porta Férrea.

❶ Getting There & Away

BUS

From the rather grim **bus station** (Av Fernão de Magalhães) a 15-minute walk northwest of the centre, **Rede Expressos** (☑239 855 270; www.rede-expressos.pt) runs at least a dozen buses daily to Lisbon (€14.50, 2½ hours) and to Porto (€12.50, 1½ hours), with almost as many to Braga (€14, 2¾ hours) and to Faro (€27, six to nine hours). There's also a regular service (more frequent in summer) that runs to Seia (€10.50, 1¾ hours), Guarda (€13.50, two to three hours) and other points around the Parque Natural da Serra da Estrela.

CAR

Several car-rental agencies are concentrated just south of the bus terminal.

Auto Jardim (☑239 827 347; www.auto-jardim.com; Rua Abel Dias Urbano 6)

Hertz (☑219 426 300; www.hertz.pt; Edifício Tricana, Rua Padre Estevão Cabral)

TRAIN

Long-distance trains stop only at **Coimbra B** station, north of the city. Cross the platform for quick, free connections to more-central **Coimbra A** (called just 'Coimbra' on timetables).

Coimbra is linked by regular Alfa Pendular (AP) and *intercidade* (IC) trains to Lisbon (AP/IC €22.80/19.20, 1¾/two hours) and Porto (€16.70/13.20, one/1¼ hours); IC trains also stop at intermediate destinations north and south. Trains run roughly hourly to Figueira da Foz (€2.65, one hour).

❶ Getting Around

BICYCLE

The Parque Verde do Mondego has free bikes that you can grab for the day from April to October.

BUS

Between them, buses 27, 28 and 29 run about every half-hour from the main bus station and the Coimbra B train station to Praça da República.

You can purchase multiuse tickets (three/five/10 trips €2.20/3.15/5.80; day ticket €3.50), which are also usable on the *elevador*, at the **SMTUC office** (www.smtuc.pt; Largo do Mercado; ◷7am-7pm Mon-Fri, 8am-1pm Sat) at the foot of the *elevador*, at official kiosks and also at some *tabacarias* (tobacconists-cum-newsagents). Tickets bought on board cost €1.60 per trip.

You'll also see *patufinhas* (electric minibuses) crawling around pedestrian areas in the centre of Coimbra, between Baixa and Alta Coimbra and through the medieval heart of the city. These accept the same tickets as other SMTUC buses.

CAR

If you come by car, prepare for snarled traffic and scarce parking. The best free parking near the Baixa is on the west bank of the river, in a dirt lot just across Ponte de Santa Clara from Largo da Portagem. Nearer the university, free street parking is available on side streets around Praça da República.

ELEVADOR DO MERCADO

The **elevador** (€1.60; ◷7.30am-9pm Mon-Sat, 10am-9pm Sun) – a double elevator connected by walkway, between the market and the university – can save you an uphill climb. Use city bus tickets or buy a ticket from the lift operator.

Around Coimbra

Conímbriga

Hidden amid humble olive orchards in the rolling country southwest of Coimbra, Conímbriga boasts Portugal's most extensive and best-preserved Roman ruins, and ranks with the best-preserved sites on the entire Iberian Peninsula. It tells the poignant tale of a town that, after centuries of security, was first split in two by quickly erected walls and then entirely abandoned as the Roman Empire disintegrated.

History

Conímbriga actually dates back to Celtic times (*briga* is a Celtic term for a defended area). But when the Romans settled here in the 1st century AD, it blossomed into a major city on the route from Lisbon (Olisipo) to Braga (Bracara Augusta). Its prosperity is revealed by well-to-do mansions carpeted with elaborate mosaics and scattered with fountains.

In the 3rd century the townsfolk, threatened by invading tribes, desperately threw up a huge defensive wall right through the town centre, abandoning the residential area. But this wasn't enough to stop the Suevi (Sueves) seizing the town in 468. Inhabitants fled to nearby Aeminius (Coimbra) – thereby saving Conímbriga from destruction.

◉ Sights

★ Roman Ruins
RUINS
(⊙10am-7pm) The sprawling Roman ruins (included in the admission fee for the town's museum) tell a vivid story. On the one hand, their domesticity is obvious, with elaborate mosaics, heated baths and trickling fountains that evoke delightful, toga-clad dalliances. But smack through the middle of this scene runs a massive defensive wall, splitting and cannibalising nearby buildings in its hasty erection to fend off raids.

It's the disproportionately large wall that will first draw your attention, followed by the patchwork of exceptional mosaic floors below it. Here you'll find the fabulous **Casa dos Repuxos** (House of Fountains); though partly destroyed by the wall, it contains cool pond-gardens, fountains and truly extraordinary mosaics showing the four seasons and various hunting scenes. With a 50-cent coin you can turn on the fountains.

The site's most important villa, on the other side of the wall, is said to have belonged to one Cantaber, whose wife and children were seized by the Suevi in an attack in 465. It's a palace of a place, with baths, pools and a sophisticated underground heating system.

Excavations continue in the outer areas. Eye-catching features include the remains of a 3km-long aqueduct, which led up to a hilltop bathing complex, and the forum, once surrounded by covered porticoes.

Museu de Conímbriga
MUSEUM
(www.conimbriga.pt; admission €4, free Sun before 2pm; ⊙10am-7pm) To get your head around Conímbriga's history, begin at the small, somewhat old-fashioned museum. Displays present every aspect of Roman life from mosaics to medallions. There's a sunny cafe-restaurant at the back, open summer only.

❶ Getting There & Away

Buses run from Coimbra directly to the ruins (€2.30, 45 minutes) at 9am or 9.30am (only 9.30am on weekends). The return trip is at 12.45pm and 5.45pm (only 5.45pm on weekends). There are also half-hourly buses to Condeixa-a-Nova, which is a half-hour stroll from the ruins.

Luso & Buçaco

A retreat from the world for almost 2000 years, the slopes of the Serra do Buçaco are now home to the 105-hectare Mata Nacional do Buçaco (or Bussaco). Harbouring an astounding 700 plant species, from huge Mexican cedars to tree-sized ferns, this national forest is equally fecund in terms of the poetry it has inspired. Generations of Coimbra's literary types have enshrined the forest in the national imagination with breathless hymns to its mystical marriage of natural and spiritual beauty.

The high stone walls that for centuries have encircled the forest have no doubt helped reinforce its sense of mystery. And in the midst of the forest stands a royal palace completed in 1907; despite the extravagance of its fairy-tale neo-Manueline facade, the dynasty fell just three years later.

Outside the forest walls lies the old-fashioned little spa town of Luso, whose waters are considered a balm for everything from gout to asthma. The forest and spa make an easy day trip from Coimbra. If you want to linger, Luso has a handful of *residenciais* (guest houses), or a more sizeable investment can see you sleeping right in the astonishing royal palace itself, in the heart of the forest.

History

The Luso and Buçaco area probably served as a Christian refuge as early as the 2nd century AD, although the earliest known hermitage was founded in the 6th century by Benedictine monks. In 1628 Carmelite monks embarked on an extensive program of forestation. They planted exotic species, laid cobbled paths and enclosed the forest within high stone walls. The forest grew so renowned that in 1643 Pope Urban VIII decreed that anyone damaging the trees would be excommunicated.

The peace was briefly shattered in 1810, when Napoleon's forces under Masséna were soundly beaten here by the Anglo-Portuguese army of the future Duke of Wellington (the battle is re-enacted here every 27 September). In 1834, when religious orders throughout Portugal were abolished, the forest became state property.

◎ Sights & Activities

★ **Mata Nacional do Buçaco** FOREST
(www.fmb.pt; car/cyclist/pedestrian €5/free/free; ⊙ 8am-8pm Apr-Sep, 8am-6pm Oct-Mar) ⚐ The aromatic forest is crisscrossed with trails, dotted with crumbling chapels and graced with ponds, fountains and exotic trees from palms to sequoias. Popular paths lead to the pretty **Vale dos Fetos** and the **Fonte Fria**, where swans swim beneath a grand staircase. Among several fine viewpoints is **Cruz Alta** (545m).

What most visitors come to see is the fairy-tale **Palace Hotel do Buçaco.** Now a luxury hotel, it was built in 1907 as a royal summer retreat on the site of a 17th-century Carmelite monastery. This wedding cake of a building is over-the-top in every way: outside, its conglomeration of turrets and spires is surrounded by rose gardens and swirling box hedges in geometrical patterns; inside (nonguests are more or less prohibited entry) are neo-Manueline carving, suits of armour on the grand staircases and *azulejos* (tiles) illustrating scenes from Os Lusiados (The Lusiads), in which Portuguese armies win glorious battles at sea amid the dismayed looks of their stupefied opponents.

Tucked away behind the hotel, **Santa Cruz do Bussaco** (www.fmb.pt; adult/child €2/1; ⊙ 10am-1pm & 2-5pm Oct-Mar, to 6pm Apr-Sep) is what remains of a convent where the Duke of Wellington-to-be rested after the Battle of Bussaco in 1810. The atmospheric interior has decaying religious paintings, an unusual passageway right around the chapel, some guns from the battle, and the much-venerated image of Nossa Senhora do Leite (Our Lady of Milk), with ex-voto offerings.

By road the Portas das Ameias, the nearest gate into the forest, is 900m from the centre. The hotel is 2.1km from the Portas das Ameias.

Maloclinic Spa SPA
(www.maloclinicspa.com; Rua Álvaro Castelões; ⊙ 10am-6pm Mon-Fri, 9am-6pm Sat & Sun, extended hours summer) Just the ticket after a long walk in the forest, the Termas de Luso welcomes drop-in visitors for therapies ranging from full-body massages (€45) and steam baths (€15) to body wraps. People come from far and wide to fill their bottles for free at the adjacent natural spring.

🛏 Sleeping

Rua Emídio Navarro, Luso's main street, is lined with several *pensões* and *residenciais*.

Astória GUESTHOUSE €
(☑ 231 939 182; pensaoastorialuso@sapo.pt; Rua Emídio Navarro 144, Luso; s/d €30/40; ☎) Beside the *turismo*, this rambling, homely place features clean, comfortable rooms with wood floors, slightly tired-looking beds and frilly decor. The restaurant downstairs serves traditional Portuguese standards.

Alegre Hotel BOUTIQUE HOTEL €€
(☑ 231 930 256; www.alegrehotels.com; Rua Emídio Navarro 2, Luso; s €45-55, d €60-86; 🅿🛜🏊) This grand, atmospheric, pinkish-coloured 19th-century town house wears its age much better than Luso's other in-town lodgings. Replete with period touches, its large doubles boast plush drapes, decorative plaster ceilings and polished period furniture. Its appeal is enhanced by an elegant entryway, formal parlour and pretty vine-draped garden with pool.

Palace Hotel do Buçaco HOTEL €€€
(☑ 231 937 970; www.almeidahotels.com; Mata Nacional do Buçaco; s €120-150, d €150-200; 🅿❄) This sumptuous royal palace sits in the middle of the forest and offers a delightfully ostentatious place to stay. Common areas are stunning – particularly the tilework above the grand staircase – though some rooms feel a little musty and threadbare. Don't expect flatscreen TVs or period furniture, but do expect stunning marble bathrooms.

Some of the furniture around the place is a little disappointing, there's lots of stuff from the mid-20th century that's neither comfortable nor historic, just outdated. Nevertheless, the opulent beauty of the building and its fairytale location make this worth

THE BEIRAS AROUND COIMBRA

the stay, and meals here are truly memorable. Significant discounts are sometimes available for bookings via the hotel's website.

✕ Eating

Restaurante Imperial PORTUGUESE €
(☏ 231 937 570; Rua Emídio Navarro 25, Luso; mains €7-11; ☉ lunch & dinner) The grilled meats and other simple Portuguese fare are good value, but steer clear of the vinegary house red.

★ Pedra de Sal PORTUGUESE €€
(☏ 231 939 405; www.restaurantepedradesal.com; Rua Francisco A Dinis 33, Luso; mains €10-16) Winningly done out in dark wood, this is the best restaurant in Luso by quite a distance. It specialises in succulent cuts of pork from the Iberian pig, has some excellent wines to wash them down with and top service to boot. Book ahead at weekends.

Palace Hotel do Buçaco PORTUGUESE €€€
(☏ 231 937 970; www.almeidahotels.com; Mata Nacional do Buçaco; 7-/8-course meal €35/40; ☉ lunch & dinner; ☜) For a truly memorable dinner, it's hard to beat the elegant spread at the Palace Hotel's dining room. Better come hungry – the meal spans seven to eight courses: appetisers, soup, pasta, fish and/or meat, salads, local cheeses, dessert trolley and finally a *cafezinho* (espresso). The dining room itself is a work of art, with natural light pouring over the parquet wood floors through a graceful faux-Manueline window studded with rosettes and overlapping arches.

ⓘ Information

Turismo (☏ 231 939 133; info.luso-bucaco@turismodocentro.pt; Rua Emídio Navarro 136, Luso; ☉ 9am-12.30pm & 2-5.30pm Oct-May, 9.30am-1pm & 2.30-6pm Jun-Sep) Has accommodation information, town and forest maps, internet access, and is helpful.

ⓘ Getting There & Away

BUS
Buses (handier than the train) run four to five times each weekday and twice daily on Saturdays from Coimbra's main bus station to Luso (€3.55, 40 minutes) and the Palace Hotel do Buçaco (€3.75, 50 minutes).

CAR
If driving from Coimbra, ignore your GPS and make sure to take the lovely foresty N235, which comes off the IP3: you'll save a toll, too.

TRAIN
Trains run three times daily from Coimbra B station to Luso/Buçaco station (€3.60, 25 minutes), but the inconvenient schedule makes a same-day round-trip nearly impossible. From Luso/Buçaco station it's a 15-minute walk to central Luso, plus another half-hour uphill through the forest to the Palace Hotel.

Montemor-o-Velho

Perched high atop a rugged hill 25km west of Coimbra, glowering **Castelo do Montemor-o-Velho** (☉ 10am-6.30pm, to 5.30pm Oct-Mar) **FREE** dominates the surrounding marshland. Whether seen from a distance or from atop the castle walls themselves, it's easy to imagine this site as an early Reconquista bastion. Fernando I of Castilla y León recaptured Montemor-o-Velho from the Moors in 1064, and in less than a century his greatgrandson Afonso Henrique claimed it as part of his new Kingdom of Portugal. Over the intervening centuries the castle was rebuilt and expanded several times, with most of the current structure dating from the 14th century.

Today you can walk the crenellated battlements and survey lush rice fields lying alongside the Rio Mondego far below. Inside little remains but part of the ruined **Paço das Infantas** (Princesses' Palace), built by Afonso Henrique's aunt Urraca, and the beautifully tiled **Igreja de Santa Maria de Alcáçova**, a small Romanesque church with 16th-century Manueline touches. It conserves some 18th-century wall paintings. The site's strategic importance as a fortification dates back at least two millennia; today, it makes a fine spot for a picnic.

The village below is also picturesque. Recently renovated **Hotel Abade João** (☏ 239 687 010; www.hotelabadejoao.com; Rua dos Combatentes da Grande Guerra 15; s/d €35/50; P ☜) is a cool, attractive option sitting above the sleepy, pretty town square. Comfortable rooms are a steal at this price and breakfast is included.

Trains between Coimbra B (€1.90, 40 minutes) and Figueira da Foz (€2.05, 25 minutes) stop every hour or two at Montemor station, 4km southeast of the castle. **Moisés Correia de Oliveira** (www.moises-transportes.pt) buses between Coimbra (€3.15, 50 minutes) and Figueira (€2.30, 30 minutes) stop closer to the castle, five to eight times daily (fewer on Sunday).

Figueira da Foz

POP 27,742

Popular with Portuguese holidaymakers for over a century, the beach resort of Figueira da Foz (fi-*guy*-ra da *fosh;* Figueira) continues to attract big summer crowds – including Spaniards lured by easy motorway access, and surfers drawn to championship-calibre waves at Cabedelo. For most visitors, the star attractions are Figueira's outlandishly wide beach and a casino featuring big-name acts on summer evenings. The local sands are so vast that it takes a five-minute walk across creaky boardwalks simply to reach the sea. Out of season, the place has a lonelier charm, but come here in summer and things are upbeat, with sizzling bodies and candy-striped beach huts filling every square inch of beach.

◉ Sights & Activities

At the time of research, the fortress area was the object of major redevelopment, with a pedestrian promenade, water features and an open-air theatre planned.

Museu Municipal Santos Rocha   MUSEUM
(☑ 233 402 840; Rua Calouste Gulbenkian; adult/child €2/free; ⊙ 9.30am-5pm Tue-Fri, 2-7pm Sat) This modern museum, beside Parque das Abadias, houses a wonderfully wide-ranging collection featuring local archaeological finds, Roman coins, medieval statues, outlandish Indo-Portuguese furniture, objects documenting Portugal's early African explorations, and rotating art exhibits. It opens until 6pm weekdays in July and August.

Serra da Boa Viagem   HEADLAND
(◧) For those with wheels, this headland, found 4km north of Figueira and carpeted in pines, eucalyptus and acacias, is a fine place for panoramas, picnics, mountain-biking and cool walks. Take the coastal road to Buarcos, turn right at the lighthouse and follow the signs to Boa Viagem. Up here, **Luso Aventura** (☑ 915 536 555; www.lusoaventura.com; €10-16; ⊙ Apr-Oct; ◧) has a series of zipline-style routes between trees offering great entertainment for all levels.

🏄 Beaches

Despite its size, Figueira's main city beach gets packed in August. For more character and some terrific surf, head north to **Buarcos**. From Figueira's *turismo* it's a 2km stroll along the pleasant beachfront prom-

enade to the south end of Buarcos. Alternatively, **AVIC** (☑ 233 422 828) runs buses (€1.35) every 45 minutes or so.

For more seclusion, continue around Cabo Mondego headland to **Praia de Quiaios**, about 10km north of Figueira da Foz. **Joalto** (☑ 233 422 648) buses run here from the bus station (€2.40, 30 minutes) seven times daily (less at weekends).

South across the mouth of the Rio Mondego is **Praia de Cabedelo**, Figueira's prime surfing venue; classes and rentals are available from **Escola de Surf da Figueira da Foz** (☑ 918 703 363; www.surfingfigueira.com; Rua do Cabedelo 36, São Pedro; group/individual class €30/40, short-/longboard rental per day €20/30).

A little further is **Praia de Gala**. AVIC buses run from the train station via the centre to Cabedelo and Gala (both €1.35) every hour or so on weekdays (less often on weekends).

🎊 Festivals & Events

Festas da Cidade   FIESTA
The town festival carries on for two weeks at the end of June, with folk music, parades and concerts.

🛏 Sleeping

Prices listed are for high season (July and August). Expect discounts of up to 40% in winter. You may be approached in summer by locals offering private rooms: often a decent deal.

★ Paintshop Hostel   HOSTEL €
(☑ 233 436 633, www.paintshophostel.com; Rua da Clemência 9; dm/d €20/50; @ 🤏) Set in a characterful blue house in the old part of town, this top-of-the-line hostel offers great facilities for backpackers and surfers, including bike, board and wetsuit rental, DVD library, free wi-fi and breakfast, kitchen, pool table, and a great bar area out the back. There are weekly BBQs and other events so you've got an instant social scene. The high-ceilinged dorms are comfy and there are quiet private rooms at the top of the building. The English owners and their friendly dog Star have an excellent attitude and offer great advice on anything from biking routes to nightlife.

Orbitur Gala   CAMPGROUND €
(☑ 233 431 492; www.orbitur.pt; Praia de Gala; sites per adult/child/tent/car €6.40/3.20/8.40/5.90; P 🤏 ◧) The best of the local campgrounds, this flat, shady spot is next to a great beach. It's south of Foz do Mondego and 1km from

Figueira da Foz

THE BEIRAS FIGUEIRA DA FOZ

200 m
0.1 miles

Rua do Hospital
Rua Mercês
R da Clemência
Rua Restauração
R Gonçalo Velho
R dos Combatentes da Grande Guerra
R M Pinto
R dos Bombeiros Voluntários
Pç General Freire de Andrade
Pç 8 de Maio
Rua República
Doca de Recreio
R Fernandes Coelho
Rua Paço
R Calouste Gulbenkian
Passeio Infante Dom Henrique
Passeio Infante Dom Henrique
Jardim Municipal
Mercado Municipal
Av Foz do Mondego
Parque das Abadias
Av do Dr Manuel Gaspar de Lemos
R Dr F A Diniz
R Poeta Acácio Antunes
Parque de Campismo Figueira da Foz (1.8km); Discoteca Pessidónio (2.2km)
R Dr L Carriço
R da Fonte
R Bernado Lopes
R Académico Zagalo
R Joaquim Sotto Mayor
R da Liberdade
R M Bombarda
R Maestro David de Sousa
R Dr Calado
R Cândido dos Ries
R Dr A L Guimarães
Buarcos (2km)
Praia da Figueira da Foz
Av 25 de Abril
Temporary Municipal Market
Forte de Santa Catarina

Figueira da Foz

the nearest bus stop. Bungalows cost €92 for two in high season, half that outside summer.

★ **Residencial Aviz**   GUESTHOUSE €€
(☑ 233 422 635; www.residencialaviz.pt.to; Rua Dr A Lopes Guimarães 16; s/d €50/65; ✳🐾) Run by a charming, well-travelled couple, this squeaky-clean guest house two blocks from the beach has lovely wood floors, high ceilings and some nice period details. Reserve ahead in summer. It halves in price in the low-season.

Lazza Hotel   HOTEL €€
(☑ 233 425 105; www.lazzahotel.com; Travessa Nova 2; s/d €70/85; P✳🐾) A short block from the beach, this modernised hotel has a great position that's also right by the main nightlife zone. Rooms are typical of this type of refit, with minimalist decor and modish whites, greys, browns and blacks. Breakfast is a little extra.

Hotel Wellington   HOTEL €€
(☑ 233 426 767; www.lupahoteis.com; Rua Dr Calado 25; s/d/ste €75/85/120; P✳🐾) Near the beach and casino action, this comfortable hotel is right in the heart of things and offers immaculate rooms with huge beds, minibars and writing desks, along with off-street parking nearby (€7 per night).

Sweet Atlantic Hotel   HOTEL €€€
(☑ 233 408 900; www.sweethotels.pt; Av 25 de Abril 21; r not incl breakfast €124; P✳@🐾) Rising over the beachfront promenade, this excellent modern hotel contrasts chocolatey and dark cherry colours with the bright magnificence of the strand-and-sea views from its comfortable rooms. All have some sea view, those that are front-on are stunning. Small kitchenettes, smart bathrooms, and a spa

complex (€15 for a 90-minute circuit) are other good extras.

✖ Eating

Núcleo Sportinguista   PORTUGUESE €
(☑ 233 434 882; Rua Praia da Fonte 14; mains €7.50-8; ⊘ lunch & dinner) Sitting under the awning, surrounded by enthusiastic locals and a sea of tables draped in checked tablecloths, feels a bit like crashing a Portuguese family's private barbecue. Don your best green and white clothes – it's a supporters' club for the Lisbon football team Sporting Clube – and enjoy the delicious grilled meats and cheap pitchers of wine. A great deal.

Pizzeria Claudio   PIZZERIA €
(Largo do Carvão 11E; pizzas from €7; ⊘ noon-2.30pm, 7-10.30pm Tue-Sun) Figueira's best pizzeria generates lines out the door in summer.

A Grega   PORTUGUESE €
(Rua da Restauração 30; mains €7-8; ⊘ lunch & dinner Tue-Sun) This simple neighbourhood restaurant does tasty grilled meats, including an Argentine-style *parrillada* (mixed grill, €18.50) that two will struggle to finish. There's also toothsome calamari and mixed fish dishes.

Restaurante Caçarola I   SEAFOOD €€
(☑ 233 424 861; Rua Cándido dos Reis 65; specials €7-8, mains €10-15; ⊘ lunch & dinner) Figueira isn't the Atlantic coast's finest place to eat, but this spot by the casino does things well. Locals belly up to the island bar all day long for good-value *combinados do dia balcão* (daily lunch-counter specials) at this popular seafood restaurant. In addition to the counter seating, there are tables on the pedestrian boulevard outside. There's another **branch** (Rua Bernardo Lopes 85; mains €10-15;

THE BEIRAS FIGUEIRA DA FOZ

lunch & dinner) around the corner. Little extras mount up if you're going à la carte.

Restaurante Forte de Santa Catarina
SEAFOOD €€€

(233 428 530; Tennis Club, Av 25 de Abril; all-you-can-eat per person €21, min 2 people; 12.30-3pm, 7.30-10.30pm) At this seafront eatery, crowds pack in nightly for the *rodízio de mariscos* (all-you-can-eat seafood) and to chat with the turbaned owner, who is something of a local celebrity. Dinner reservations are recommended in summer and on weekends.

Drinking & Nightlife

Zeitgeist Caffé
BAR

(Rua Francisco António Dinis 82; 4pm-4am;) Glamorous Zeitgeist features comfy couches and chairs, wi-fi and windows overlooking the popular strip of bars that line adjacent Rua Académico Zagalo. There's regular live music and DJs in a wide range of styles.

Ricky's on the Beach
BAR

(Rua São Lourenço; daily Jun-Aug, weekends only Sep-Apr) Not actually on the beach, but not far from it, this cheerful Australian/Portuguese-run spot gets things moving on summer nights with its tiki theme and excellent cocktails including delicious caipirinhas.

Complexo Piscina de Mar
BAR, POOL

(Av 25 de Abril; 10am-8pm Jul & Aug) Relax by the pool at this waterfront bar with great beach views, resident DJ and a big-screen TV for those must-see football matches.

Discoteca Pessidónio
CLUB

(233 435 637; Rua Estrada da Serra, Condados, Tavarede; Fri & Sat Jul & Aug) Still going strong after four decades, Pessidónio is in the suburbs east of the municipal campground. Its four distinct dance venues include the Capela Club, whose poolside Sala da Piscina is popular for tropical drinks on hot summer nights.

Bergantim Discoteca
CLUB

(967 647 910; Rua Dr A Lopes Guimarães 28; Fri & Sat) This lively disco/nightclub spinning mostly pop, rock and electronica has a party atmosphere and a perfect downtown location one block from the beach. Entry is normally around €6 to €8, including a drink.

Entertainment

Casino Figueira
CASINO

(233 408 400; www.casinofigueira.pt; Rua Dr Calado 1; 3pm-3am Sun-Thu, 4pm-4am Fri & Sat) Shimmering in neon and acrylic, Figueira's casino is the epicentre of the city's nightlife. Crawling with cash-laden holidaymakers in search of a quick buck, it has roulette and slot machines, occasional free cabaret shows and a sophisticated piano bar with live music after 11pm most evenings. Dress up at night – beach attire, thongs (flip-flops) or sports shoes may keep you out.

Centro de Artes e Espectáculos
ARTS CENTRE

(233 407 200; www.cae.pt) Behind the museum, CAE hosts big-name bands, theatre and art-house cinema. Check the website or pick up a schedule at the *turismo*.

Information

Biblioteca Municipal (Rua Calouste Gulbenkian; 2-7.30pm Mon, 9.30am-7.30pm Tue-Fri, 2-7pm Sat) Free internet at the town library.

Turismo (233 422 610; www.figueiraturismo.com; Av 25 de Abril; 9.30am-1pm & 2.30-6pm)

Getting There & Away

The train and bus stations are right next to each other, 1.5km east of the beach.

BUS

Figueira is served by two long-distance companies. **Moisés Correia de Oliveira** (233 426 703; www.moises-transportes.pt) has at least hourly service (fewer on weekends) via Montemor-o-Velho to Coimbra (€3.90, 1½ hours).

Rede Expressos (www.rede-expressos.pt) has buses to Lisbon (€15.50, 2¾ hours, at least three daily) via Leiria; and to Aveiro (€8.50, one hour, two to four daily).

TRAIN

Train connections to/from Coimbra (€2.65, one hour, hourly) are superior to buses. There are also direct trains to Leiria (€5, one hour, three daily), with connecting service to Mira Sintra-Meleças station on the suburban Lisbon line. For Porto, change in Coimbra.

Praia de Mira

For a few days of sunny, windblown torpor, head for Praia de Mira, the best-equipped town along the 50km coastal strip between Figueira da Foz and Aveiro. Sandwiched between a long, clean beach and a canal-fed lagoon, this small resort has little to distract you from the main business at hand: sun, sea and seafood.

Praia de Mira is 7km west of Mira on the N109, itself 35km north of Figueira da Foz.

Activities

Secret Surf School
SURFING
(☎968 422 146; www.secretsurfschool.com; Duna Bar; 2hr class per person €20; ⊙daily Jul & Aug, weekends Sep-Jun) Located on the beach in the centre of town; these people can teach you how to get out there riding waves.

🛏 Sleeping

Rates given here are for the high season (mid-July to August). At other times they drop by up to 40%. In summer, private *quartos* (rooms) are typically €30 to €40 per double. Watch for signs, or contact the *turismo*.

Orbitur
CAMPGROUND €
(☎231 471 234; www.orbitur.pt; Estrada Florestal 1-km 2, Dunas de Mira; sites per adult/child/tent/car €5.80/2.90/8/5.50; ⊙mid-Mar–Sep; P ☏ 🚻) This well-equipped, shady site is at the southern end of the lagoon. Bungalows are available from €84 in August, or €59 the rest of the summer.

Hotel Maçarico
HOTEL €€
(☎231 471 114; www.macaricobeachhotel.com; Rua Raúl Brandão; P 🛁) This stylish new beachfront hotel, a refurbishment of an old favourite, has very recently opened its doors. It was looking very sleek, with a sudoku-like facade containing modern rooms with excellent sea-view balconies. The pool deck has more great vistas.

✗ Eating & Drinking

Restaurante Caçanito
SEAFOOD €€
(☎231 472 678; Av do Mar; mains €10-15; ⊙lunch & dinner Apr-Sep, closed Mon Oct-Mar) Neighbourhood cats wait expectantly outside the door of this great little restaurant, an unadorned wood and glass cube right on the beach. Caçanito wins universal acclaim from locals for its superb charcoal-grilled seafood.

Jôbaló
GRILL HOUSE €€
(Av Manuel Milheirão 115; all-you-can eat rodízio €14.50; ⊙12.30-3.30pm &, 7.30pm-1am) Fans of grilled meat should make the 1.5km trek inland to this Brazilian-style *churrasqueria* (barbecue house) with indoor-outdoor seating on the town's main entrance road. House specialities such as *picanha* (rump steak, served with or without garlic) are excellent. Better yet, try the all-you-can-eat *rodizio*, where itinerant waiters ply you with every grilled meat imaginable till you beg for mercy. It also does takeaway portions.

Marisqueira Tezinho
SEAFOOD €€
(☎231 471 162; Av da Barrinha 9; mains €8-13; ⊙lunch & dinner, closed Tue Sep-Jun) Bustling and friendly, with only two small rooms, this place opposite the lagoon is recommended for its ultrafresh seafood.

Sixties Irish Pub
PUB
(☎231 472 475; Travessa Arrais Manuel Patrão 14; ⊙8pm-2am Mon-Thu, 7.30pm-4am Fri & Sat, 3pm-2am Sun) Tucked into a classic pub-crawler's alley a block from the beachfront, this cosy spot has multiple beers on tap and a lively old-school Irish atmosphere.

ℹ Information

The **turismo** (☎231 480 550; turismo@cmmira.pt; Av da Barrinha; ⊙9am-1pm & 2-5pm Tue-Sat, 2-5.30pm Sun, daily & extended hours in high summer), 450m south of the main drag, beside the lagoon, shares a wooden house with a little ethnographic exhibition.

DON'T MISS

ALIANÇA UNDERGROUND MUSEUM

Between Aveiro and Coimbra, in the village of Sangalhos in the Bairrada wine-producing region, is this extraordinary **location** (☎234 732 045, 916 482 226; www.alianca.pt; Rua do Comercio 444, Sangalhos; admission €3; ⊙daily 90min visits 10am, 11.30am, 2.30pm, 4pm): part *adega* (winery), part repository of an eclectic, enormous, and top-quality art and artefact collection. Vast vaulted chambers hold sparkling wine, barrels of maturing *aguardente* (distilled spirits), and a series of galleries displaying a huge range of objects. The highlight is at the beginning: a superb collection of African sculpture, ancient ceramics and masks, but you'll also be taken by the spectacular mineral and fossil collection and the beauty of some of the spaces. Other pieces include *azulejos*, a rather hideous collection of ceramic and faience animals, and an upstairs gallery devoted to India. The only complaints are that there's no information on individual pieces, and you don't have time to linger at leisure. Phone to book your visit, which can be in English and includes a glass of sparkling wine.

ℹ Getting There & Away

Most transport only stops inland at Mira (7km east). **Joalto** (☏ 233 422 648; www.transdev. pt) runs from Coimbra to Praia de Mira via Mira three to five times daily, with extra services in summer. There are two buses on weekdays from Aveiro to Praia de Mira (€3.70, one hour); otherwise you'll have to change (or get a taxi) in Mira. Buses also run regularly from Figueira da Foz to Mira (€3.80, one hour).

Aveiro

POP 54,400

Hugging the edge of the Ria, a shallow coastal lagoon rich in bird life, Aveiro (uh-*vey*-roo), whose name might come from the Latin *aviarium* (place of birds), is a prosperous town with a youthful, energetic buzz. It's occasionally dubbed the Venice of Portugal thanks to its high-prowed boats, humpbacked bridges and small network of picturesque canals. It's a lovely little place best explored on foot or aboard a *moliceiro* – the traditional seaweed-harvesting boat now converted to tourist use.

A prosperous seaport in the early 16th century, Aveiro suffered a ferocious storm in the 1570s that blocked the mouth of the Rio Vouga, closing it to ocean-going ships and creating fever-breeding marshes. Over the next two centuries, Aveiro's population shrank by three-quarters. But in 1808 the Barra Canal forged a passage back to the sea, and within a century Aveiro was rich once more, as evidenced by the spate of art nouveau houses that still define the town's old centre. Salt harvested here was taken to Newfoundland to preserve cod that came back as *bacalhau* (dried salt-cod).

⊙ Sights & Activities

Museu de Aveiro   MUSEUM
(Museu de Santa Joana; ☏ 234 423 297; www. ipmuseus.pt; Av Santa Joana; admission €4, 10am-2pm Sun free; ⊙ 10am-5.30pm Tue-Sun) This fine, if somewhat single-minded, museum in the former Mosteiro de Jesus opposite the Catedral de São Domingos owes its finest treasures to Princesa (later canonised) Joana, daughter of Afonso V. In 1472, 11 years after the convent was founded, Joana 'retired' here and, though forbidden to take full vows, she stayed until her death in 1490.

Her tomb, a 17th-century masterpiece of marble mosaic, takes centre stage in an equally lavish room (actually the remodelled choir stalls). The adjacent chapel is decorated with *azulejos* depicting Princesa Joana's life. The museum's paintings include a late-15th-century portrait of her, attributed to Nuno Gonçalves.

Museu Arte Nova   MUSEUM
(www.cm-aveiro.pt; Rua Dr Barbosa Magalhães 9; adult/child €1/0.50; ⊙ 9.30am-12.30pm Tue-Fri, 2-6pm Tue-Sun) Set in Aveiro's most eye-catching art nouveau building, this small museum above a cafe has a modest one-room exhibition in Portuguese on art nouveau design and architecture. Larger temporary displays upstairs rotate every three months. Ask for the multilingual brochures mapping and detailing all the town's art nouveau highlights.

Reserva Natural das
Dunas de São Jacinto   NATURE RESERVE
🌿 Stretching north from São Jacinto, between the sea and the lagoon west of Aveiro, is this supremely peaceful 6.7-sq-km wooded nature reserve, equipped with trails and birdwatching hides. A meandering 7km loop trail with information boards runs through the pines and dunes and can be walked at any time. At the trailhead, 1.5km north of the ferry on the N327, is a map, as well as a small helpful **interpretative centre** (www. icnf.pt; Estrada Nacional 327; ⊙ 9am-noon & 2-5pm Mon-Wed & Fri-Sat) FREE. The best birdwatching is from November to February.

To get here, take a bus from Aveiro to Forte da Barra (single/return €2.50/4), where there is a ferry to São Jacinto (passenger/car return €3/5). Schedules for boats are at www.moveaveiro.pt; bus schedules are at www.transdev.pt. Drivers can also circumnavigate the lagoon and arrive from the north via Ovar, but it's a much longer journey.

Oficina do Doce   CULINARY CENTRE
(www.oficinadodoce.com; Rua João Mendonça 23; tour €2; ⊙ 10am-7pm Jun-Sep, 10am-5pm Oct-May, weekends only Dec-Feb) Part living museum, part cooking school, Oficina do Doce aims to introduce visitors to Aveiro's proudest culinary tradition – *ovos moles*: eggy, sugary sweets originally developed by local nuns. You can watch as modern-day confectioners work their magic or, better yet, learn about the process first-hand by making your own. It's best to reserve your visit ahead in the Aveiro Welcome Center.

🏄 Beaches

The surfing venues of **Praia da Barra** and **Costa Nova**, 13km west of Aveiro, are good for a day's outing. Prettier Costa Nova has a beachside street lined with cafes, kitsch gift shops and picturesque candy-striped cottages. Buses go (€2.50/4 single/return, hourly) from Aveiro's Rua Clube dos Galitos.

Wilder and more remote is **Praia de São Jacinto**, on the northern side of the lagoon. The vast beach of dunes is a 1.5km walk from São Jacinto port, through a residential area at the back of town. Take a bus from Aveiro to Forte da Barra (single/return €2.50/4), where there is a ferry to São Jacinto (passenger/car return €3/5). Schedules for boats are at www.moveaveiro.pt; bus schedules are at www.transdev.pt. Drivers can also circumnavigate the lagoon and arrive from the north via Ovar, a much longer trip.

☞ Tours

O Cicerone
WALKING TOUR
(☎ 234 094 074; www.o-cicerone-tour.com; per person/additional person €7.50/5) ✐ This dynamic young company leads two-hour walking tours (English spoken) of downtown Aveiro; there are various themed tours as well as a general one, depending on your interests. It also runs cultural tours elsewhere in the region. Book by phone or at the Aveiro Welcome Centre.

Ecoria
BOAT TOUR
(www.ecoria.pt; adult/child €6/4; ☉ daily; ♿) Near the *turismo,* this is one of several canalside operators offering 45-minute trips on traditional seaweed-collecting boats *(moliceiros)* around the Ria, with departures subject to passenger numbers. Longer trips to São Jacinto also run in July and August.

Viva a Ria
BOAT TOUR
(☎ 969 008 687; www.vivaaria.com; adult/child €6/4; ♿) Offers trips in traditional seaweed-gathering boats on the Ria. Trips leave throughout the day.

🎉 Festivals & Events

Feira de Março
FIESTA
Held from 25 March to 25 April, this festival dates back five and a half centuries. Nowadays it features everything from folk music to rock concerts.

Festas do Município
FIESTA
Aveiro sees two weeks of merrymaking around 12 May in honour of Santa Joana.

Festa da Ria
FIESTA
Aveiro celebrates its canals and *moliceiros* in late August. Highlights include folk dancing and a *moliceiros* race.

🛏 Sleeping

Look for private rooms (*quartos*) around town in summer by asking at the *turismo* or searching for signs in windows.

★ Aveiro Rossio Hostel
HOSTEL €
(☎ 234 041 538; www.aveirorossiohostel.com; Rua João Afonso de Aveiro 1; dm €16-25, r €45-68; ✳ @ 🛜) ✐ This superb ecologically minded hostel breaks frontiers in the quality of its accommodation, furnishings, welcome and services. Every traveller-friendly facility you could dream of is here, and the relaxed, stylish decor has to be seen to be believed. Creatively decorated with family heirlooms, recycled furniture and found objects, it also overflows with homey touches (from the waffle iron to the honour-system minibar) and splashes of colour.

There's a back patio for lounging, and breakfast often includes fresh croissants or organic fruit from the family farm. Solar energy is used wherever possible, earning the hostel recognition as Portugal's first 'green hostel'. Dorm rooms come with plush mattresses and individual reading lamps, and there are a couple of air-conditioned rooms under the eaves with beds rather than bunks.

Hospedaria dos Arcos
GUESTHOUSE €
(☎ 234 383 130; hospedariadosarcos@gmail.com; Rua José Estevão 47, Rua dos Mercadores 24; s/d €25/35; 🛜) One of several budget options along José Estevão, Hospedaria dos Arcos has a just-like-grandma's-house atmosphere, with several floors of spotless little chambers with bathroom. Get an exterior room for more light. Handily, there's another entrance on the pedestrian drag.

Pensão Avenida
GUESTHOUSE €
(Tricana de Aveiro; ☎ 234 423 366; Av Dr Lourenço Peixinho 256; d €35, s/d with shared bathroom €20/25) This handsome art nouveau building is directly across from the train station, about a 15-minute walk from the centre. The owners, who also run the adjacent *pastelaria* (pastry and cake shop), have fixed up the bright, high-ceilinged rooms simply but tastefully.

Aveiro

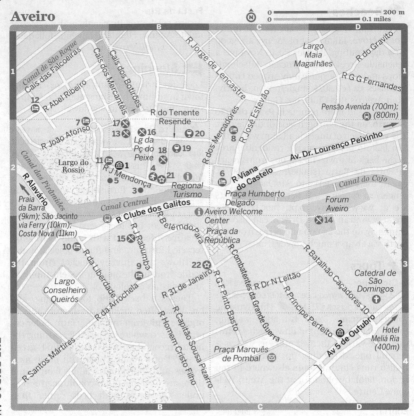

Wake in Aveiro
GUESTHOUSE €

(☑964 398 194; www.booking.com; Rua das Tricanas 5; d not incl breakfast €40-80; ❋ 🎧) A great option for couples, this beautifully renovated house has compact but stylish rooms, created with an eye for colour and design. The themed superior rooms on the top floor are worth the upgrade. Check in at Aveiro Rossio Hostel around the corner.

Praia da Barra Camping
CAMPGROUND €

(☑234 369 425; www.campingbarra.com; Rua Diogo Cão 125, Praia da Barra; sites per adult/child/tent/car €3.90/2.10/4.05-4.80/4.15, apt €66-86; P @ 🎧 ⛲) A well-equipped, sandy and flat site next to the beach about 10km from Aveiro. There's a dedicated tent area as well as facilities such as minigolf, a restaurant and cybercafe.

Hotel Aveiro Center
HOTEL €€

(☑234 380 390; www.hotelaveirocenter.com; Rua da Arrochela 6; s/d/superior d incl breakfast €48/70/80; P 🎧) This small hotel is a short stroll from the heart of town but it has a quiet backstreet location. Little extras such as tea trays in the rooms and a welcome drink back up the cordial service. The massive superior rooms are worth the small extra investment.

Aveiro Palace Hotel
HOTEL €€

(☑234 423 001; www.hotelaveiropalace.com; Rua Viana do Castelo 4; s/d €69/79; P ❋ @ 🎧) A smart remodelling job has converted Aveiro's most central hotel, overlooking the heart of town, into a more upmarket option with comfortable modern rooms. Four stars might be pushing it a bit, but the price is right and location unrivalled. It's worth paying an extra €10 for a superior and getting views over the street and canal outside. There's a pretty 1st-floor lounge, and you can leave the car for only €5 a day in the nearby underground parking.

Aveiro

Hotel das Salinas
HOTEL €€

(☑ 234 404 190; www.hoteldassalinas.com; Rua da Liberdade 10; s/d €48/70, apt for 1/2/4 people €58/85/125; ☎) This comfortable little hotel feels downright homey. Angle for one of the 'studio' units, complete with kitchenettes, couches and plasma TVs for little more than a regular double; great for families. Some rooms offer nice canal views. Breakfast is served in a pleasant patio in summer.

★ Hotel Moliceiro
HOTEL €€€

(☑ 234 377 400; www.hotelmoliceiro.com; Rua Barbosa de Magalhães 15; s/d €110/125; ⓟ✳@☎) This central hotel is so well cared for it feels like it just opened. Solicitous staff run a stylish set-up in a primo position, with well-equipped, spacious chambers offering original art on the walls, sturdy but stylish furnishings and decent-sized bathrooms. Higher grade rooms add views over the park and canal, more space and zippier decor.

Hotel Meliã Ria
HOTEL €€€

(☑ 234 401 000; www.meliaria.com; Cais da Fonte Nova; s/d €116/126; ⓟ✳@☎✖) This spiffy four-star sits alone at the eastern end of the main canal. Its cubelike exterior is shrouded in intriguing brises-soleil, while inside it's all contemporary lines and business-friendly comforts. Check online for specials, as you can generally beat the rack rates we list here by a considerable margin. There's a spa too; guests pay extra to use the facilities.

✖ Eating

Every cafe and *confitaria* in town advertises *ovos moles*, a sticky-sweet egg-yolk-and-sugar blend encased in a crisp white wafer case. The **Forum Aveiro** (www.forumaveiro.com; Rua Batalhão de Caçadores 10) shopping centre has a food court and large supermarket.

Adega Típica O Telheiro
PORTUGUESE €

(☑ 234 429 473; Largo da Praça do Peixe 20-21; mains €7-9; ⊙ lunch & dinner Tue-Sun) A charismatic old-style place with hanging curios and rather nifty stools with proper footrests at the bar for comfier eating. The food is reliably tasty, with cheap daily specials and abundant doses of fish and grilled meat.

O Bairro
MODERN PORTUGUESE €€

(☑ 234 338 567; www.obairro.pt; Largo da Praça do Peixe 24; mains €10-18; ⊙ lunch & dinner Tue-Sun) Artfully blending the traditional and the modern, the formal and the whimsical, this great new restaurant specialises in produce from the deeps – fittingly, given its location opposite the fish market. The talented young chef produces fresh modern cuisine, giving confident new outfits to longtime local staples. Book for the popular Sunday brunch.

Maré Cheia
SEAFOOD €€

(Rua José Rabumba 8-12; fish per kg €36; ⊙ lunch & dinner Thu-Tue) *Maré cheia* means 'high tide' in Portuguese, but the adjective *cheia* (full) applies equally to the counter and dining room at this fabulously popular seafood eatery, complete with 'meet-your-meal' fishtanks. You'll often have to elbow your way through a crowd of locals just to get your name on the waiting list. It's a great place to try the local *enguias* (eels), served fried, grilled or *caldeirada* (stewed).

THE BEIRAS AVEIRO

A Peixaria
SEAFOOD €€

(📞234 331 165; www.restauranteapeixaria.pt; Rua Mestre Jorge Pestana, São Jacinto; mains €14-18, fish per kg €25-40; ⊙lunch & dinner Tue-Sun) 🍴 A block back from the waterfront in São Jacinto, this no-frills family restaurant has the best fish in town and, many say, the region. There's always a big variety of Atlantic species, simply and deliciously done – try the eel stew too.

O Batel
PORTUGUESE €€

(Travessa Tenente Resende 21; fish per kg €30-45; ⊙lunch & dinner Mon-Sat, lunch Sun) This narrow, nautically themed restaurant in a skinny alley is worth tracking down. Its good-value daily specials (€7) are backed up by a seafood-heavy menu with great quality and some innovative touches. Service is professional and friendly.

Mercado do Peixe
PORTUGUESE €€

(📞234 383 511; www.mercadodopeixe.web.pt; Largo da Praça do Peixe; mains €10-18; ⊙lunch daily, dinner Mon-Sat) Perched above the city's homely fish market, this industrial-chic restaurant has large windows overlooking the canal and the adjacent square. The seafood is excellent, and low-priced lunch specials Monday to Friday include homemade bread, soup and a main course.

🍷 Drinking & Nightlife

A big student population and summer holiday crowds make for some raucous nightlife. Action radiates from Largo da Praça do Peixe, with several places clustered on Rua do Tenente Resende.

Casa de Chá
CAFE, BAR

(www.casadechaartenova.com; Rua Dr Barbosa Magalhães 9; ⊙9am-2am Tue-Thu, 9am-3am Fri & Sat, 11am-9pm Sun; 🛜) In the town's most striking art nouveau building, this casual cafe-bar invites relaxation with brightly coloured beanbags to flop into. It's got a fine range of tea and infusions and livens up at night with excellent caipirinhas, Friday night DJs and a perky summer scene.

Decante Wine Bar
WINE BAR

(Rua do Tenente Resende 28; ⊙from 5pm) People congregate on the streetside tables to sip wine during the early evening, then move inside for live music most nights, including everything from Latin rhythms, rock and blues to jazz and world music.

Clandestino
PUB

(www.facebook.com/clandestinoaveiro; Rua do Tenente Resende 35; ⊙9pm-2am or later Mon-Sat) A cosy little pub attracting a youthful crowd with chilled-out music and imported DJs.

☆ Entertainment

Forum Aveiro (p321) has a popular cinema.

Teatro Aveirense
THEATRE

(📞234 400 920; www.teatroaveirense.pt; Rua Belem do Para) Celebrating 125 years at the heart of Aveiro's cultural scene, this recently renovated historic theatre regularly hosts dance, music and theatre performances.

Mercado Negro
PERFORMING ARTS

(www.mercadonegro-aveiro.blogspot.com; Rua João Mendonça; ⊙3pm-12.30am Tue-Sun) 🍴 With a high-ceilinged upstairs cafe overlooking the canal, and a performance venue on the floor below, this quirky alternative artspace attracts a largely bohemian crowd.

ℹ Information

Aveiro Digital (Praça da República; ⊙9am-7pm Mon-Fri, 10am-6pm Sat) Free internet. Check the timetable as it's sometimes occupied by classes.

Aveiro Welcome Center (📞234 377 761; www.aveiro.eu; Rua Clube dos Galitos 2; ⊙9.30am-7pm Mon-Fri, 9.30am-12.30pm & 2-6pm Sat & Sun Oct-Dec, 9.30am-7pm Jul-Sep) Helpful tourist office that can book excursions and give good info on things to do around town.

Hospital Infante Dom Pedro (📞234 378 300; www.hip.min-saude.pt; Av Artur Ravara)

Regional Turismo (📞234 420 760; www.turismodocentro.pt; Rua João Mendonça 8; ⊙9am-8pm Mon-Fri, 9am-6pm Sat & Sun Jun-Sep, 9am-6pm Mon-Fri, 9.30am-12.30pm & 1.30-5.30pm Sat & Sun Oct-May) In an art nouveau gem beside the Canal Central.

ℹ Getting There & Away

BUS

Few long-distance buses terminate here – there isn't even a bus station. Catch buses at the stop on Rua Clube dos Galitos; many also stop at the train station.

Rede Expressos has five to six daily services to/from Lisbon (€16.50, three to four hours) via Coimbra (€6, 45 minutes) or Figueira da Foz (€8.50, 1¼ hours). Transdev runs a slower but cheaper coastal service to Figueira da Foz via some intermediate beaches. Other buses run to Viseu (€8.50, one hour) and on to Guarda and Castelo Branco.

TRAIN

Trains run from the modern station, which has superseded the beautiful old tiled one alongside. Aveiro is within Porto's *urbano* network, which means there are commuter trains there at least every half-hour (€3.35, 50 to 60 minutes); much pricier IC/AP links (€11.70/14.20, 30 to 40 minutes) are only slightly faster. There are also at least hourly links to Coimbra (regional/intercity/ AP €5.20/11.70/14.20, 30 to 60 minutes) and several daily IC (€20.20, 2½ hours) and AP (€26.30, two hours) trains to Lisbon.

ⓘ Getting Around

BICYCLE

Loja BUGA (Bicicleta de Utilização Gratuita de Aveiro; www.moveaveiro.pt; ☺ 9am-6pm Mon-Fri, 10am-1pm & 2-6pm Sat & Sun) provides free bikes. Leave a document as deposit at the kiosk beside the Canal do Cojo, take a bike and ride it within the town limits, then return it to the kiosk before it shuts, all for free. Open until 7pm in summer.

BUS

Catch buses to the coast at the stop on Rua Clube dos Galitos. It's an easy 15-minute walk southwest from the train station into town.

Piódão

POP 178 / ELEV 690M

Remote Piódão (pee-*oh*-downg) offers a chance to see rural Portugal at its most pristine. This tiny traditional village clings to a terraced valley in a beautiful, surprisingly remote range of vertiginous ridges, deeply cut valleys, rushing rivers and virgin woodland called the Serra de Açor (Goshawk Mountains).

Until the 1970s you could only reach Piódão on horseback or by foot, and it still feels as though you've slipped into a time warp. The village is a screne, picturesque composition in schist stone and grey slate; note the many doorways with crosses over them, said to offer protection against curses and thunderstorms.

Houses descend in terraces to the square, where you'll find the fairy-tale parish church, the **Igreja Nossa Senhora Conceição**, and a low-key touristy scene selling local liqueurs and souvenirs.

◉ Sights & Activities

Núcleo Museológico de Piódão   MUSEUM
(Largo Cónego Manuel Fernandes Nogueira ; admission €1; ☺ 10am-1pm & 2-6pm Jun-Sep, 9am-1pm,

2-5pm Oct-May) This tiny museum above the *turismo* displays reconstructions of typical rooms in local homes, complete with tools, pottery and furniture. There are also historic photos of Piódão and its residents.

Walks   WALKING
A signposted network of hiking trails connects Piódão to the nearby villages of Foz d'Égua (two-hour loop hike) and Chãs d'Égua (one hour each way). Foz d'Égua has some lovely old stone bridges, schist houses and a precarious-looking footbridge over the river gorge. Chãs d'Égua is home to more than a hundred examples of rock art from the Neolithic to the Iron Age.

✖ Festivals & Events

The area's patron saint, São Pedro do Açor, is honoured with a Mass, religious procession, ball, and a handicrafts fair during the **Santos Populares no Piódão** in late June or early July.

⌇ Sleeping & Eating

There are *quartos* everywhere, but quality is uneven. A full list is available from Piódão's *turismo*. Cafes around the square do light meals.

Casa da Padaria   B&B €
(☑ 235 732 773; http://casa-da-padaria.planetaclix. pt; d €45) On the far side of the village from where you arrive, this handsome house has an exceptionally friendly host and offers good value for simple rustic rooms.

Casa de Xisto Piódão   COTTAGE €
(☑ 933 403 055; www.casadexistopiodao.com; Rua Francisco Pacheco; s/d/q not incl breakfast €50/55/75) This tall, narrow house in the heart of the village sleeps up to six in comfort. There's not a lot of space, but it's colourful and cosy. Minimum two-night stay.

Casas da Aldeia   COTTAGE €
(☑ 919 189 195; www.casasaldeiapiodao.com; r not incl breakfast €40-50; ℗) ✿ Piódão's improvement committee has kitted out these schist houses across a little valley from the centre, with great views of the village. Each has two rooms with TV, private bathroom, kitchenette and fireplace. You can rent just a room, or an entire house.

Estalagem do Piódão   HOTEL €€
(☑ 235 730 100; www.inatel.pt; r €70-90; ℗ ☜ 🞅) Looming unaesthetically on a ridge above the village, this government-run caricature

of a local schist house has rather luxurious, modern rooms and a decent restaurant with vistas. It's a helpful, friendly place with an indoor pool. Rates vary according to demand and you'll usually get a cheaper deal online.

O Fontinha PORTUGUESE €
(mains €8; ⊘ lunch & dinner Tue-Sun) A schist house in the heart of the village, this is a good venue for simple, tasty local food like pork chops, trout or *bacalhau*.

❶ Information

There's no ATM in town.

Turismo (☑235 732 787; www.cm-arganil. pt; Largo Cónego Manuel Fernando Nogueira; ⊘10am-1pm & 2-6pm Jun-Sep, 9am-1pm & 2-5pm Oct-May) On the square. Provides info on Piódão and walks in the surrounding area.

❶ Getting There & Away

The only public transport is a bus from Arganil (41km west) to Piódão (€4.30, 1¼ hours) on Thursday and Sunday. Check current times with Piódão's *turismo*.

The area's breathtaking views, narrow roads and sheer drops are a lethal combination for drivers.

BEIRA BAIXA

Beira Baixa closely resembles the neighbouring Alentejo, with hospitable locals, fierce summer heat and rolling plains stretching to the horizon. It's also home to sprawling agricultural estates, humble farming hamlets and several stunning fortress towns that for centuries guarded the vulnerable plains from Spanish aggression.

Castelo Branco

POP 35,242

Sweltering Castelo Branco isn't Portugal's most charming provincial capital but makes a good jumping-off point for outlying attractions such as Monsanto and Idanha-a-Velha. The best reasons to visit nowadays are the town's excellent museum and gardens. Still, there are some charming medieval streets clustered in the centre, and the town's modern development includes an attractive series of tree-lined squares and boulevards.

From the bus station, turn right down Rua do Saibreiro to central Alameda da Liber-

dade. From the train station the Alameda is 500m north on Avenida Nuno Álvares.

Sights

Paço Episcopal MUSEUM
(www.ipmuseus.pt; Largo Dr José Lopes Dias; adult/under 14yr/student €2/free/1; ⊘10am-5.30pm Tue-Sun Oct-Apr, 10am-7pm Tue-Sun May-Sep) The bishop's palace, in the north of town, is a sober 18th-century affair housing the **Museu de Francisco Tavares Proença Júnior**. Downstairs, the centrepiece is an excellent display of local archaeological finds. If you're a fan of embroidery you'll also love the upstairs exhibition of Castelo Branco's famous *colchas*: silk-embroidered linen bedspreads and coverlets inspired by fabrics brought back by Portuguese explorers. There's a stunning collection of Asian originals, plus an area where you can watch artists at work (weekdays only).

Jardim do Paço Episcopal GARDEN
(Rua Bartolomeu da Costa; admission €2; ⊘9am-5pm Oct-Apr, 9am-7pm May-Sep) This delightful, unusual retreat next to the museum is the garden of the bishop's palace, a baroque whimsy of clipped box hedges and little granite statues representing virtues, seasons, kings, saints, months and continents among other things. Notice that the statues of Portugal's Spanish-born kings Felipe I and II are smaller than those of the Portuguese monarchs.

At the bottom of the kings' stairway, there's a hidden, clap-activated fountain, sadly out of order at the time of research. It was built by a loutish 18th-century bishop who liked to surprise maidens by soaking their petticoats. Ask the attendant if it's back in operation.

Castelo CASTLE
FREE There's little left of the castle, which was built by the Knights Templar in the 13th century and extended by Dom Dinis. A phone mast now stands where the chapel once was. However, the garden, which has supplanted the walls, offers grand views over town and countryside. The old lanes that lead back to the town centre are also picturesque.

🛏 Sleeping

Residencial Arraiana HOTEL €
(☑272 341 637; residencialarraiana@gmail. com; Av 1 de Maio 18; s/d/tr €25/40/50; ❄ 🛜) A few blocks southwest of the centre, Ar-

raiana provides good value, with 30 well-kept rooms with little minibar. It's an old-fashioned, dignified little place, and you can always bank on finding a room.

Tryp Colina do Castelo   HOTEL €€
(272 349 280; www.trypcolinacastelo.com; Rua da Piscina; s/d €56/66; P ✴ @ 🛜 🏊) Soulless but nicely positioned on the hillside northwest of the *castelo,* the city's top choice is a huge, modern, business hotel affording fine views from most of its comfy, bright rooms. Amenities include a nice indoor pool, squash and tennis courts and a gymnasium. There are good family rooms, and some higher-grade rooms come with gym equipment.

Eating & Drinking

Frei Papinhas   GRILL HOUSE €
(272 323 090; Rua dos Prazeres 31; mains €8-12; ⊙lunch & dinner Tue-Sun) Appealingly rustic decor characterises this superfriendly meat restaurant on a quiet street in the centre of town. The genial host runs the grill, and will bring your order bit by bit to keep it warm. He'll also press various delicious little free morsels on you throughout your meal so don't expect to have room for dessert. This is basically behind the post office on the central Largo da Sé.

Praça Velha   PORTUGUESE €€
(272 328 640; www.pracavelha.com; Praça Luís de Camões 17; dishes €13-16; ⊙lunch & dinner Tue-Sat, lunch Sun) This atmospheric former Knights Templar abode in the old town includes a medieval wooden ceiling, stone floors and pillars, and a long buffet table heaped with platters. Try the all-inclusive lunch specials (€13) or the fantastic Sunday buffet (€19). It's got a great location on the old town's prettiest square. If you book online you can even choose your table.

❶ Information

Biblioteca Municipal (Praça do Município; ⊙10am-4.30pm Mon-Fri) Free internet in the public library.

Cyber Centro Municipal (Praça do Município; internet per hr €1; ⊙9am-11pm Mon-Fri) Across the courtyard from the library.

Parque Natural do Tejo Internacional Office (272 348 140; pnti@icnb.pt; 2nd fl, Centro de Interpretação Ambiental Bldg, Rua da Bela Vista s/n) In a spiffy new white building in the centre. There's also a nature exhibition here.

Turismo (272 330 339; www.cm-castelo branco.pt; cnr Av Nuno Alvares & Rua Cadetes de Toledo; ⊙9.30am-7.30pm Mon-Fri, 9.30am-1pm & 2-6pm Sat & Sun) Just off the town's main square.

❶ Getting There & Away

BUS

Rede Expressos (272 340 126; www.rede-expressos.pt) services from Castelo Branco:

Coimbra (€14, two to three hours, one to four daily)

Covilhã (€6, 50 minutes, at least six daily)

Guarda (€10.80, 1½ hours, at least six daily)

Lisbon (€14.50, 2¾ hours, one to four daily)

TRAIN

Castelo Branco is on the Lisbon–Covilhã line. Three daily IC trains to Lisbon (€14.70, 2¾ hours) are supplemented by slower regional services (€14.20, 3¾ hours). IC/regional trains also serve Covilhã (€6.60/6.30, 50 minutes/one hour).

Parque Natural do Tejo Internacional

Still one of Portugal's wildest landscapes, this 230-sq-km natural park shadows the Rio Tejo and the watersheds of three of its tributaries. While not aesthetically remarkable, it shelters some of the country's rarest bird species, including black storks, Bonelli's eagles, royal eagles, Egyptian vultures, black vultures and griffon vultures. The park was established in 2000, after a major push by private environmental organisation Quercus.

The park office in Castelo Branco can provide background information. The best-marked hiking trail, the Rota dos Abutres (Route of the Vultures), descends from Salvaterra do Extremo (60km east of Castelo Branco) into the dramatic canyon of the Rio Erges.

Drivers can get a taste of the park's natural beauty by following the unnumbered road between Monforte da Beira and Cegonhas (southeast of Castelo Branco), which passes through a beautiful cork oak forest on either side of the Ribeira do Aravil. It doesn't appear on all maps: pass through Monforte da Beira if coming from Castelo Branco, and turn right after 2km. Alternatively, a signposted turnoff to the park just short of Monforte takes you down a rough circular route through part of the park, but the way's not well indicated.

WORTH A TRIP

PENHA GARCIA

A good side trip from Monsanto takes you 14km north then east along the N239 towards the Spanish border to Penha Garcia. It's a picturesque spot with a dam and lake behind it. From the church, a charming 3km circular walking route, the Rota dos Fósseis, takes you past old mills and various fossil finds. You can also walk to Penha Garcia along the GR-12 path from Monsanto.

Monsanto

POP 200 / ELEV 600M

Like an island in the sky, the stunning village of Monsanto towers high above the surrounding plains. A stroll through its steeply cobbled streets, lined with stone houses that seem to merge with the boulder-strewn landscape, is reason enough to come. But to fully appreciate Monsanto's rugged isolation, climb the shepherds' paths above town to the abandoned hilltop castle, whose crumbling walls command vertiginous views in all directions. Walkers will also appreciate the network of hiking trails threading through the vast cork-oak-dominated expanses below.

◉ Sights

Village   VILLAGE

Since winning a competition in 1938 as the country's most 'Portuguese' village, Monsanto has been largely shielded from modernisation. Several houses are surprisingly grand, some sporting Manueline doorways and stone crests. Halfway to the castle you'll come across the **gruta**, a snug cavern apparently once used as a drinking den; other caves around town double as barns for the local sheep and goats. Startlingly enormous boulders are perched precariously throughout, looking like detritus from a clash of the titans.

Castelo   CASTLE

This formidable stone fortress seems almost to have grown out of the boulder-littered hillside that supports it. It's a beautiful site, windswept and populated by lizards and wildflowers. Immense vistas include Spain to the east and the Barragem da Idanha dam to the southwest.

There was probably a fortress here even before the Romans arrived, but after Dom Sancho I booted out the Moors in the 12th century it was beefed up. Dom Dinis refortified it, but after centuries of attacks from across the border it finally fell into ruin.

Just below the castle stands what's left of the Romanesque **Capela de São Miguel**, with its cluster of tombs carved into solid rock eerily lying just outside the chapel portal.

✻ Activities

Monsanto is crisscrossed by long-distance hiking trails, including the GR-12 from Lisbon to Bulgaria, and the GR-22, a 540km circuit of Portugal's historic villages. For a beautiful, relatively easy walk (one hour return), descend the GR-12 along the stone road to the **Capela de São Pedro de Vira-Corça**, a medieval chapel surrounded by giant boulders. You can follow this same trail all the way to Idanha-a-Velha, a beautiful but exposed 7km walk best in cooler weather.

✸ Festivals & Events

On 3 May each year Monsanto comes alive in the **Festa das Cruzes**, commemorating a medieval siege. The story goes that the starving villagers threw their last lonely calf over the walls, taunting their besiegers as if they had plenty to spare. The hoodwinked attackers promptly abandoned the siege. These days, young girls throw baskets of flowers instead, after which there's dancing and singing beside the castle walls.

⌷ Sleeping & Eating

Accommodation in Monsanto is limited. Advance reservations are advisable in high season.

There are souvenir shops selling homemade honey cakes, some laced with a wicked *aguardente* (alcoholic 'firewater').

★ **Casa da Tia Piedade**   GUESTHOUSE €
(🖉 966 910 599; www.casadatiapiedade.com; Rua da Azinheira 21; s/d not incl breakfast €45/50; ❄ ⛶) You've just about got your own house attached to this warmly welcoming spot in the heart of the village, with discreet entrance, terrace and kitchen/lounge. There are two lovely bedrooms – one's a little bigger, one has a view – but only one is let at a time unless you're a family or group, so the exterior bathroom is private. The owners are helpful and kind but also respect

privacy. Breakfast's available for an extra €5 per couple.

Casa do Chafariz
GUESTHOUSE €

(☑914 253 793; casadochafariz1@sapo.pt; Rua Marquês da Graciosa; s/d/tr €35/45/50) A stone's throw from the *turismo*, these four rooms in a renovated old house cluster around an unadorned cobblestone courtyard. All have nice wood floors and massive slabs of exposed stone, plus TV and electric heat. The two upstairs units are nicest, with high ceilings and atmospheric – if nonfunctioning – fireplaces. Penny-pinchers can save €5 by staying in the rather claustrophobic smaller room at the foot of the stairs.

Adega Típica O Cruzeiro
PORTUGUESE €€

(☑277 314 528; Rua Fernando Namora 4; mains €10-12; ⊘12.30-3pm Thu-Tue, 7-9pm Thu-Mon) Just below the old town, this likeable place is a rather surprising find as you descend into the bowels of a modern municipal building. The attractive dining area boasts spectacular views over the plains below, and the superfriendly staff serve very tasty meals from a seasonal menu – if you spot a dish with wild mushrooms *(cogumelos silvestres)*, go for it.

Petiscos e Granitos
PORTUGUESE €€

(☑277 314 029; Rua Pracinha; mains €10-16; ⊘lunch & dinner) Wedged between gigantic boulders, Petiscos e Granitos' back terrace provides a fantastic backdrop for sipping a *copo de vinho* (glass of wine) at sunset, with incomparable views over the plains below. Waiters sometimes move at a geological pace, but specialities like game dishes and grilled lamb chops with roasted potatoes are delicious. Closed Mondays in winter.

ℹ Information

Turismo (☑277 314 642; www.turismode natureza.com; Rua Marquês da Graciosa; ⊘9.30am-1pm & 2-5.30pm Tue-Sun Oct-Mar, 10am-1pm & 2-6pm Apr-Sep) The website has details of accommodation in the area.

ℹ Getting There & Away

Without a car, Monsanto can be difficult to reach. **Rodoviária da Beira Interior** (RBI; ☑272 340 126; www.transdev.pt) has one direct bus daily between Castelo Branco and Monsanto (€5.60, one hour), leaving Castelo Branco at 5.15pm weekdays and 11.35am on weekends, returning from Monsanto at 7.15am daily. Ask at the *turismo* in either Monsanto or Castelo Branco for the latest schedules.

Idanha-a-Velha

Extraordinary Idanha-a-Velha is a very traditional small village with a huge history. Nestled in a remote valley of patchwork farms and olive orchards, it was founded as the Roman city of Igaeditânia (Egitania). Roman ramparts still define the town, though it reached its apogee under Visigothic rule: they built a cathedral and made Idanha their regional capital. It's also believed that their legendary King Wamba was born here.

Moors were next on the scene, and the cathedral was turned into a mosque during their tenure. They, in turn, were driven out by the Knights Templar in the 12th century. It's believed that a 15th-century plague virtually wiped out the town's population, with survivors going on to found Idanha-a-Nova about 20km to the southwest. However, the townspeople's misfortune is our luck, since they left the town virtually intact. Today a small population of shepherds and farmers live amid the Roman, Visigothic and medieval ruins.

⊙ Sights

Catedral
CATHEDRAL

(⊘24hr) Tucked into a corner of the walled town sits the 6th-century Visigothic cathedral, surrounded by a jigsaw puzzle of scattered archaeological remains. The church has undergone heavy restoration, but its early roots are evident everywhere: foundation stones bearing Latin inscriptions, Moorish brick arches, salvaged Roman columns and Visigothic elements such as the baptistry visible through glass near the entrance. Of the frescos within, the best preserved features São Bartolomeu with a demon at his feet.

Lagar de Varas & Museu Epigráfico Egitaniense
MUSEUM

(⊘9.30am-1pm & 2-5.30pm Tue-Sun Oct-Mar, 10am-1pm & 2-6pm Tue-Sun Apr-Sep) FREE The Lagar de Varas, near the cathedral, hosts an impressive olive-oil press made in the traditional way with ruddy great tree trunks providing the crushing power. In the same complex you'll find a narrow epigraphic museum densely packed with more than 200 stones from the area bearing Latin inscriptions. Touch-screen displays explain the context of the collection, with in-depth studies of three noteworthy stones.

Ruins

RUINS

FREE The only evidence of the Knights Templar is the Torre des Templários, made of massive chunks of stone and now surrounded by clucking hens. It sits on top of what was likely the pedestal of a Roman temple. Other Roman remains include the gracefully arched bridge on the east side of town and the old wall and gate on the north side.

Sleeping & Eating

Idanha-a-Velha has no tourist accommodation and only a couple of small cafes serving snacks and drinks. Monsanto (16km northeast) and the pretty hill town of Idanha-a-Nova (20km southwest) are your best bets for a hot meal and a place to bed down. The latter has a comfortable **hostel** (☑ 277 208 051; www.pousadasjuventude.pt; Praça da República 32, Idanha-a-Nova; dm €12, d without/ with bathroom €26/30, f €52; ☺ Dec-Oct; ☜) in a prime position.

ⓘ Information

Turismo (☑ 277 914 280; Rua da Sé; ☺ 9.30am-1pm & 2-5.30pm Tue-Sun Nov-Mar, 10am-1pm & 2-6pm Tue-Sun Apr-Oct) Staff lead free guided town visits daily if there are enough people. It's opposite the cathedral in the museum complex.

ⓘ Getting There & Away

There's a daily bus service to/from Idanha-a-Nova (40 minutes), from where you can catch onward buses to Castelo Branco (€3.85, 45 minutes, two to three daily). Alternatively, you can hike the beautiful but exposed 7km trail from Monsanto or get a pricey taxi from Idanha-a-Nova (around €30).

Sortelha

POP 444 / ELEV 760M

Perched on a rocky promontory, Sortelha is the oldest of a string of fortresses guarding the frontier east of Guarda and Covilhã. Its fortified 12th-century castle teeters on the brink of a steep cliff, while immense walls encircle a village of great charms. Laid out in Moorish times, it remains a winning combination of stout stone cottages, sloping cobblestone streets and diminutive orchards.

'New' Sortelha lines the Santo Amaro–Sabugal road. The medieval hilltop fortress is a short drive, or a 10-minute walk, up one of two lanes signposted '*castelo*'.

◉ Sights

Old Town

HISTORIC AREA

FREE The entrance to the fortified old village is a grand, stone Gothic gate. From here, a cobbled lane leads up to the heart of the village, with a *pelourinho* (stone pillory) in front of the remains of a small castle to the left and the parish church to the right. Higher still is the bell tower – climb it for a view of the entire village. For a more adventurous and scenic climb, tackle the ramparts around the village (beware precarious stairways and big steps).

Sleeping

Sortelha boasts several atmospheric rustic cottages complete with kitchens, thick stone walls and heating. The *turismo* has a full list.

Casa da Lagariça & Casa da Calçada

COTTAGE €€

(☑ 271 388 116; www.casalagarica.com; Calçada de Santo Antão 11; d €55 Sep-Jun, €80 Jul & Aug; Ⓟ) These cute stone cottages just below the old town make fine bases. The larger, Lagariça, has two doubles and a twin as well as sofabed; the smaller has two doubles. You can rent out just a room or the whole house; the houses come with kitchen but breakfast is included.

Casas do Campanário

COTTAGE €€

(☑ 271 388 198; luispaulo55@sapo.pt; Rua da Mesquita; d €50, house for 4/6 people €100/150; ☜) Nicely sited at the top of the village, adjacent to the bar of the same name, is Sortelha's 'inside-the-walls' lodging option. Ask at Bar Campanário, just above the bell tower.

✗ Eating & Drinking

★ Bar As Boas Vindas

BAR €

(meals €5-9; ☺ noon-late Fri-Sun) Uphill and to the right of the *turismo*, this little stone house with couches, rustic farm decor, a cat curled up by the fire and a well-stocked bar makes a great place to get cosy in winter or kick back on the cute terrace on a hot summer afternoon.

Dom Sancho I

PORTUGUESE €€

(☑ 271 388 267; Largo do Corro; mains €10-16; ☺ lunch & dinner Tue-Sat, lunch Sun) Sortelha's favourite eatery sits just inside the main Gothic gates. Prices for the regional cuisine – with several game options – are high, but the food is renowned and the dining room rustically elegant. For lighter snacks and drinks, head to the beamed, stone-walled bar (with cosy fireplace in winter) downstairs.

ℹ Information

Turismo (📞 271 750 080; turismo@sabu galmais.com; Largo do Corro; ⊙ 9am-1pm & 2-5.30pm Tue-Fri, 10am-1pm & 2.30-5.30pm Sat & Sun) Just inside the old town gate. Opens until 6pm in the summer months.

ℹ Getting There & Away

The only bus service is on a school bus that takes kids to and from Sabugal, from where you can connect to Guarda.

Regional trains on the Covilhã–Guarda line (three to four daily) stop at Belmonte-Manteigas station, 12km to the northwest, where you can catch a **taxi** (📞 936 259 107) to Sortelha (around €20).

PARQUE NATURAL DA SERRA DA ESTRELA

Fascinating both for its natural and cultural history, Parque Natural da Serra da Estrela was one of Portugal's first designated parks, and at 1011 sq km remains the country's largest protected area. The rugged boulder-strewn meadows and icy lakes of its high country form one of Portugal's most distinct and unexpected landscapes. It's a glorious, seasonal beauty: the *altiplano* (upland) area is stunning in the morning or evening light. On the slopes below, rushing rivers historically provided hydro power to spin and weave the Serra's abundant wool into cloth. Nowadays, shepherds still roam a landscape of terraced fields and traditional one-room, stone *casais* (huts) thatched with rye straw, but traditional sheep-herding is fast giving way to a service economy catering to week ending tourists.

The presence of the 1993m Torre – Portugal's highest peak – at the centre of the park is both a blessing and a curse. It forms an undeniably dramatic backdrop, but as the only place in Portugal where snow dependably falls, it also tends to lure vast winter hordes with little consciousness of their impact on the high country's ecosystems.

The Serra abounds in hiking and climbing opportunities; these mountains are one of Portugal's most alluring destinations for outdoors enthusiasts. Hikers – and everyone else – will also appreciate the Serra's excellent mountain cheese and hearty rye bread.

◉ Sights & Activities

Wildlife

The park harbours many endangered or vulnerable species including the black stork, Montagu's harrier, chough, turtle dove and 10 species of bats. If you're lucky you may also catch a glimpse of miniature high-altitude frogs, mountain geckos or rare birds such as the peregrine falcon, eagle owl and black-shouldered kite.

The flora, too, is interesting. Several of the park's plants have been put in the list of endangered or vulnerable species due to their popularity as medicinal remedies, including mountain thrift *(Armeria transmontana)*, great yellow gentian *(Gentiana lutea)* and juniper *(Juniperus communis)*.

Walking

Crisp air and immense vistas make this a trekking paradise. In part because of limited infrastructure, surprisingly few people get off the main roads. Even in summer, walkers will generally feel they have the park to themselves.

While still very chilly and possibly damp, late April has the hillsides bright with wildflowers. The weather is finest from May to October. Winter is harsh, with snow at the higher elevations from November or December to April or May.

Whenever you come, be prepared for extremes: scorching summer days give way to freezing nights, and chilling rainstorms blow through with little warning. Mist is a big hazard not only because it obscures walking routes and landmarks, but because it can also stealthily chill you to the point of hypothermia.

There are three main 'official' routes through the park, as well as branches and alternative trails. The TSE1 runs the length of the park (about 90km) and is the easiest to follow, taking in every kind of terrain, including the summit of Torre. TSE2 and TSE3 (both around 80km) run respectively along the western and eastern slopes. All of the trails pass through towns and villages, each of which offers some accommodation. Many of the finest walks start around Manteigas. Other good routes head off the N339 south of Sabugueiro – the day walks along Lagoa Comprida or to Covão do Lagoacho are worthwhile at any time of year.

Parque Natural da Serra da Estrela

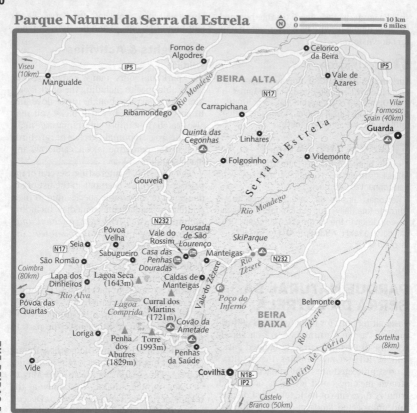

By far the best resource is Centro de Interpretaçaõ da Serra da Estrela in Seia. Multilingual staff here are experts on hiking in the Serra and are goldmines of route information. They'll give you personalised advice and can also organise guided hikes.

Within a zone of special protection, camping and fires are strictly prohibited except at designated sites, all of which are on the main trails.

Skiing

The ski season typically runs from January to March, with best conditions in February.

Biking & Other Activities

Several companies specialise in outdoor activities in the park, including **Adriventura** (www.adriventura.com), which organises groups for biking, rock climbing, hiking and more. The Vodafone Bike Park around Torre (half/full day €15/20) has three runs, available once the snow has melted. SkiParque, east of

Manteigas, offers many activities, including summertime 'dry skiing', paragliding, rock climbing, mountain biking and hiking.

Sleeping

While Seia, Gouveia, Manteigas, Covilhã and Guarda all provide useful bases with comfortable accommodation options, those wanting a true mountain experience should opt for Manteigas, because the others – situated as they are on the Serra's outer slopes – feel as if they are more a part of the surrounding plains.

Whereas camping grounds drop their rates or close in winter, many hotels, *pensões* and *residenciais* actually increase their rates, typically from late December to March.

There are hostels at Penhas da Saúde and Guarda, and at least eight camping grounds near the centre of the park. Turismo Habitação properties can be booked through local *turismo*s.

❶ Information

There are park offices at Manteigas (headquarters), Seia, Gouveia and Guarda; local *turismos* can also provide park information.

By far the most reliable place for maps and walking info is Seia's Centro de Interpretaçaõ da Serra da Estrela. The best available map for the central *planalto* (plateau) is the 1:30,000 one that comes within a Portuguese booklet called *Rotas e Percursos da Serra da Estrela* (€10). It describes some walking routes but is worth it for the map alone. Other maps available are the military 1:50,000 ones, on sale at €7.50.

❶ Getting There & Around

Express buses run daily from Coimbra to Seia, Guarda and Covilhã, and from Aveiro, Porto and Lisbon to Guarda and Covilhã. There are daily IC trains from Lisbon and Coimbra to Guarda (plus IR services calling at Gouveia) and from Lisbon to Covilhã (with IR services on to Guarda).

There are regular, though infrequent, bus services around the edges of the park but none directly across it.

Driving can be hairy, thanks to mist and wet or icy roads at high elevations, and stiff winds. The Gouveia–Manteigas N232 road is one of the most tortuous in all of Portugal. Be prepared for traffic jams around Torre on weekends.

Seia

POP 5700 / ELEV 532M

Despite its sweeping views over the surrounding lowlands, modern Seia feels largely like a charmless strip of contemporary buildings slapped onto a hillside. The best reasons to visit are the local museums, especially the Serra da Estrela interpretative centre, and the attractive rural lodgings in the surrounding hills. The town itself is also a handy place to buy cheese, cured meats and woolly slippers.

◉ Sights & Activities

Centro de Interpretaçaõ da
Serra da Estrela   MUSEUM
(CISE; ☑ 238 320 300; www.cise-seia.org.pt; Rua Visconde Molelos; adult/child €4/2.50; ☺ 10am-6pm Tue-Sun) ✦ This regional museum provides an excellent introduction to the Serra da Estrela region. A nine-minute 3D film in English or Portuguese takes you flying around the mountains' main points of interest. Multimedia displays include an interactive scale model of the Serra. CISE also has very helpful information on hiking and is the best place in the region to buy maps.

Museu do Pão   MUSEUM
(☑ 238 310 760; www.museudopao.pt; adult/child €5/3; ☺ 10am-6pm Tue-Fri & Sun, 10am-10pm Sat; ▣) This museum, set in a huge complex with mill wheels, restaurant and rustic buildings, has all the information you'll ever need on local bread production. The highlight is the traditional-style shop. It's 1km northeast of the centre on the road to Sabugueiro.

Museu do Brinquedo   MUSEUM
(☑ 238 082 015; museu.brinquedo@cm-seia.pt; Largo de Santa Rita; adult/child €3/2; ☺ 10am-6pm Tue-Sun; ▣) Near the *turismo*, this museum traces the history of Portuguese toys, from

THE BEIRAS SEIA

A SHEPHERD'S BEST FRIEND

Any animal lover travelling through the Serra da Estrela will be hard-pressed to resist the 'take me-home-now' feeling prompted by the regioñs indigenous Cão da Serra da Estrela, or **Estrela mountain dog** (EMD). It's not just the adorable fuzzy golden and black puppies; the massive adults are as handsome as they are strong, smart, loving and loyal.

Widely recognised as one of the most ancient breeds on the Iberian Peninsula, the EMD is thought to have descended from dogs brought by the Romans or Visigoths. Over the centuries, shepherds chose the best dogs to guard their goats and sheep and perform in harsh mountain conditions. Fiercely resisting any predator daring enough to attack its flock, the EMD can also be gentle as a lamb, especially in its nurturing attitude towards the young of both the human and goat/sheep variety. Traditionally the dogs were outfitted with spiked collars to protect their throats against an attacking wolf or bear.

While today the EMD is a popular Portuguese pet, its traditional use has declined drastically. Ironically, the wolf-recovery organisation **Grupo Lobo** (http://lobo.fc.ul.pt) has become a leading advocate for reviving the EMD's role as herd guardian. Conservationists worldwide now see herd-guarding dogs as one of the best strategies for protecting flocks while promoting wolf recovery.

the Victorian to the contemporary. There's a playroom, a collection of toys from other countries and a workshop where kids can watch toys being made or repaired.

🛏 Sleeping

Casas da Ribeira   COTTAGE €
(☑238 311 221, 919 660 354; www.casasdaribeira.com; Póvoa Velha; 2-person cottages €50-70, 4-person €100; 🕾) *✐* Close to Seia's services but feeling a million miles away, this charming collection of vine-draped stone cottages sits in the hills above town. The six houses are similar, rustic and beautifully restored with kitchens and fireplaces (firewood included). A delicious breakfast with home-baked bread is provided. There's normally a two-night minimum stay; prices drop with extra nights. From Seia, climb the Sabugueiro road for about 5km, then turn left 1km to Póvoa Velha. Call ahead. Wi-fi at reception only.

★Casas da Lapa   BOUTIQUE HOTEL €€
(☑935 550 500; www.casasdalapa.pt; Rua da Eira de Costa 10, Lapa dos Dinheiros; s/d midweek €75/90, weekend €85/100; 🅿❄@🕾❄) This lovely boutique inn 9km south of Seia is a study in contrasts, blending ancient stone architecture with colourful modern decor. There are eight rooms in the renovated main house, with two larger self-catering units off-site in the same village. Guests have access to a sauna, Turkish bath, massage room and weight room, although plenty of folks are happy just chilling by the infinity pool, on a sunny terrace where the rush of a nearby waterfall provides the background music.

To get here, follow signs from Seia to São Romão and keep going. It's then a left turn up to Lapa dos Dinheiros, which has narrow, very steep streets. This is at the very top of the village.

Casa das Tilias   RURAL HOTEL €€
(☑238 080 765; www.solarcasadastilias.com; Rua das Tilias, São Romão; s/d midweek €45/60, weekends €55/70, apt €70-120; 🅿🕾❄) This gorgeous 1850s-era mansion with polished wooden floors and high ceilings (some with lovingly restored friezework) has six rooms and a grand parlour in the main building, plus three self-catering apartments in the modern adjacent annexe. Service is efficient and businesslike, and there's a spacious garden area. It's 4km from Seia – follow signs to São Romão.

Hotel Eurosol   HOTEL €€
(☑238 310 100; www.eurosol.pt; Av 1 de Maio 16; s/d €43/57, winter weekends €57/80; 🅿❄@🕾❄🛗) This well-equipped, friendly hotel in the centre of town has large rooms, pink-marble bathrooms with abundant hot water, a large sandy children's play area, a summer pool with lounge chairs and free off-street parking. We list rack rates here, but you can normally get a better deal via the website. Two-night minimum on winter weekends. Wi-fi is extra.

✗ Eating

Restaurante Regional da
Serra   PORTUGUESE €
(☑238 312 717; Av dos Combatentes da Grande Guerra 14; mains €6-11; ⊙noon-3pm & 7-9.30pm) This trim place is well known for hearty regional specialities, including local cheeses and sausages as well as *chanfana à serrana* (highland goat).

Restaurante Borges   PORTUGUESE €€
(☑238 313 010; Travessa do Funchal 7; mains €9-14; ⊙lunch & dinner Fri-Tue, lunch Wed) Tucked away in a tight corner off the main street, this country-style place offers large portions of delicious traditional Portuguese fare and is popular with locals celebrating special events. The TV conspicuously blaring in other Portuguese restaurants is blessedly absent here.

❶ Information

Biblioteca (Rua da Caínha; ⊙9am-noon & 2-6pm Mon-Fri) Free internet in the heart of town at the local library.

Parque Natural da Serra da Estrela Office (☑238 310 440; pnse@icnb.pt; Praça da República 30; ⊙9am-12.30pm & 2-5.30pm Mon-Fri) Tough to spot, this park office is in the centre of town. There's better information at the park interpretation centre though.

Turismo (☑238 317 762; turismo@cm-seia.pt; Rua Pintor Lucas Marrão; ⊙9am-12.30pm & 2-5.30pm Mon-Sat, 9am-1pm Sun) Helpful and central.

❶ Getting There & Away

Rede Expressos (☑238 313 102; www.rede-expressos.pt) buses go to Lisbon (€19, four hours), Coimbra (€10.50, 1½ hours) and Guarda (€10.50, 70 minutes). It also runs two direct buses weekly to Covilhã (€13.20, 1¾ hours).

Marques (☑232 421 954; www.marques.pt) has buses to Viseu and local villages several times each weekday.

Sabugueiro

POP 700 / ELEV 1050M

Attracting tourists from far and wide thanks to its title as Portugal's highest village, Sabugueiro is more noteworthy as a place to shop for *queijo da serra* (mountain cheese) and Serra da Estrela dogs than as a destination in itself. You can buy some excellent cheese here, although it's mostly made with milk from outside the Serra da Estrela due to diminishing local supply and skyrocketing demand. If you like the centre runny, ask for a cheese that's *amanteigado* – delicious!

Dog lovers will find it hard to resist stopping to look at the impossibly cute Serra da Estrela puppies peering wistfully from their roadside cages. Local families also sell delicious smoked ham, rye bread, juniper-berry firewater and cosy fleece slippers for the chilly mountain nights.

Sabugueiro is a 15-minute drive uphill from Seia. A taxi from Seia costs around €12.

Gouveia

POP 3800 / ELEV 650M

Gouveia, draped across a hillside 5km from the N17, is a charming blend of the contemporary and historic in a small-town setting. Pleasantly laid out, with parks and public gardens, it offers sufficient accommodation, food and transport to be a good base for exploring the northwestern side of the *parque natural*. Sights are few, but the pretty *azulejo*-clad church and the splendid views keep the eyes interested.

🛏 Sleeping & Eating

Parque de Campismo
Curral do Negro   CAMPGROUND €
(📞961 350 810; EN 232, Km 79; sites per adult/child/tent/car €3.20/1.80/2.80/4; 🅿🚻🛗) Generously shaded with oaks, pines and chestnuts, this scenically located place offers camp sites plus three modern bungalows sleeping six to eight. It's reached via a steeply winding climb 3km southeast of town.

Casas do Toural   COTTAGE €€
(📞927 971 221; www.casasdotoural.pt; Rua Direita 74; 2-person cottage €55-70, 4-person cottage €100-108; 🚻🛗) 🍴 This gorgeous ensemble of restored houses surrounds an immaculately kept hillside farm-garden in the centre of town. Most rooms feature exposed stone walls, kitchens, fireplaces and living rooms.

Book in advance on weekends. For longer-term guests, owner Maria José offers guided hikes into the Serra da Estrela. Apartments are self-catering, but if you want breakfast, it's available for a little extra.

Quinta das Cegonhas   B&B, CAMPGROUND €€
(📞238 745 886; www.cegonhas.com; Nabainhos; sites per 2 adults, tent & car €17.50, d €61, apt €69-91; @🛜🏊🛗) This restored 17th-century *quinta* (country estate) 6km northeast of Gouveia has nice views, terraced tent sites, private rooms and self-catering apartments. The Dutch owners offer a wealth of information about local hikes and can arrange multiday excursions. If you'd rather just kick up your feet and relax, head to the pool and lounge area. Sociable evening meals are available.

Hotel Monteneve   HOTEL €€
(📞238 490 370; www.montenevehotel.com; Av Bombeiros Voluntários 12; s/d €65/90, not incl breakfast €55/80; 🅿🌀🛜) This old granite building in the heart of town has been converted into a rigorously clean hotel with comfortable rooms and a pleasant breakfast area. Prices are more usually around €55 for a double: a good deal.

Restaurante O Júlio   PORTUGUESE €€
(📞238 498 016; Travessa do Loureiro 6; dishes €9-11; ⏰lunch & dinner Wed-Mon) Tucked away in a narrow downtown street, this place is popular for its regional cuisine. House specialities include *cabrito à serrana* (mountain-style kid) and *batatinhas do céu* (heavenly potatoes). The *prato do dia* (daily special)for €6 is a steal.

ℹ Information

Centro do Cidadão Espaço Net (Rua da República; ⏰9.30am-12.30pm & 2-6pm Mon-Fri) Free internet across the square from the *turismo*.

Parque Natural da Serra da Estrela Office (📞238 492 411; pnse@icnb.pt; Av Bombeiros Voluntários 8; ⏰9am-12.30pm & 2-5.30pm Mon-Fri) Right in the centre of town by the *pelourinho* (whipping post).

Turismo (📞238 083 930; turismo@dlcg.pt; Jardim da Ribeira; ⏰10am-12.30pm & 2-6pm Mon-Sat, 10am-12.30pm & 2-5pm Sun) On a pleasant square five minutes' walk downhill from Praça de São Pedro.

ℹ Getting There & Away

BUS

Rede Expressos (📞238 493 675; www.rede-expressos.pt) and **Marques** (www.marques.pt)

HILL TOWNS OF THE NORTHERN SERRA

Two of the Serra da Estrela's prettiest towns are tucked high in the hills between Gouveia and Guarda. Neither has much tourist infrastructure – part of their appeal.

Linhares, designated an *aldeia histórica* (historic village) by the Portuguese government, is best known for its imposing grey castle, which commands remarkable bird's-eye views over the surrounding countryside. Poke around in the warren of stone houses, terraced hillsides and twisting lanes below the castle and you'll find signs advertising rooms for rent; **Casa Pissarra** (☑ 271 776 180; mariarpvpires@sapo.pt; Rua Direita; r €35-45, house €120) is a good option offering two typical village houses. There's also an Inatel hotel. Below the church on Largo da Igreja is **Cova da Loba** (☑ 271 776 119; www.covadaloba.com; Largo da Igreja, Linhares da Beira; mains €11-17; ☺ lunch Fri-Tue, dinner daily), serving tasty contemporary Portuguese cuisine. Friendly **Cafe Mimoso** (Largo da Igreja, Linhares da Beira; light meals €2-5; ☺ 8am-11pm Wed-Mon) on the same square is good for toasted sandwiches and coffee.

The biggest draw of **Folgosinho**, aside from its miniature castle, is its pretty main square, where you'll find **O Albertino** (☑ 238 745 266; www.oalbertino-folgosinho.com; set menus €11-16; ☺ lunch & dinner Tue-Sat, lunch Sun), a cosy stone-walled restaurant specialising in down-to-earth mountain cuisine. Dinner is an all-you-can-eat affair, featuring gamey favourites such as *feijoada de javali* (beans stewed with wild boar). Albertino also rents rooms around town from €40.

stop at Gouveia's **bus station** (Rua Cidade da Guarda), a 10-minute walk north of the centre. Marques runs to Seia (€2.55, 25 minutes, four per weekday) and Guarda (€4.35, 1½ hours, one daily). Rede Expressos goes two or three times daily to Coimbra (€13.20, two hours) and Lisbon (€19, 4¾ hours).

TRAIN

The Gouveia railway station, 14km north near Ribamondego, is on the Beira Alta line between Coimbra (€8.90, 1¾ hours) and Guarda (€5.60, 50 minutes) – regional trains stop here two to four times daily. A taxi between Gouveia and the station will cost around €10.

Manteigas

POP 3430 / ELEV 720M

Cradled at the foot of the beautiful Vale do Zêzere, with high peaks and forest-draped slopes dominating the horizon in all directions, Manteigas feels more like a true mountain town than any of the other major Serra da Estrela gateways. There has been a settlement here since at least Moorish times, probably because of the nearby Caldas de Manteigas hot springs.

Manteigas makes an excellent base for hikers looking to explore the region. Walk through the glacial valley above town and you'll still encounter terraced meadows, stone shepherds' huts and tinkling goat-bells, while in Manteigas itself cobblestone

streets and older homes still hold their own against the high-rise development that has taken root on the Serra's fringes.

From Seia or Gouveia you approach Manteigas down a near-vertical switchback road, the N232. South of town, the N338 snakes up the Zêzere valley into the high country between Torre and Penhas da Saúde.

◉ Sights & Activities

Poço do Inferno   WATERFALL
In springtime, this waterfall in a craggy gorge makes a beautiful sight. From Manteigas, drive approximately 4km along the signposted main road towards Torre. Just beyond Caldas de Manteigas, turn left for Poço do Inferno (Hell's Well) and climb a further 6km to the falls through lush evergreen forest.

There's also a hiking trail from Manteigas to the falls, starting with a long descent along the cobbled road between the *turismo* and petrol station.

In summer the waterfall slows to a trickle.

★ Trilhos Verdes   WALKING
(www.manteigastrilhosverdes.com) ✐ This excellent network of marked trails in the Manteigas area makes the town a great base for hiking. There are 16 routes, all with their own leaflet at the park office in town. You can browse the trails online.

➡ **Vale do Zêzere**

The relatively easy ramble through this magnificent, glacier-scoured valley, one of the park's most beautiful and noteworthy natural features, is a highlight of any trip to Manteigas. Its only drawback: the trail is shadeless and baking in clear summer weather.

From Manteigas, follow the N338 for 2.8km towards Caldas de Manteigas, leaving the road at the 'Roteiro Rural Palhotas' sign just beyond the spa hotel. From here, a part-cobbled, part-dirt road leads upstream through irrigated fields dotted with typical stone *casais* (huts). About 4km along, the unpaved road crosses the Rio Zêzere just above a popular local swimming hole.

From here, the 4km trail follows the Rio Zêzere upstream along its eastern bank, climbing gradually through a wide-open landscape dotted with stone shepherds' huts and backed by spectacular views of the looming mountains on either side. Eventually the path narrows and steepens as you scramble up to meet the N338 (11km from Manteigas).

Once at the N338, backpackers wanting to stay overnight amid this dazzling scenery can continue uphill on the paved road 1.1km to the Covão d'Ametade campground. Thirsty day trippers should descend 900m along the road to Fonte Paulo Luís Martins, a crystalline spring whose delightfully cold water (constantly 6°C) is bottled in Manteigas and sold nationally. If you've left a car at the swimming hole, you can walk an additional 3.2km back downhill along the N338, although it's usually easy to hitch a ride from someone filling bottles at the springs.

➡ **Penhas Douradas**

A medium-difficulty walk from Manteigas goes to Penhas Douradas, on a ridge high above. The track climbs northwest out of town via Rua Dr Afonso Costa to join a sealed, switchback forestry road and, briefly, a wide loop of the Seia-bound N232. Branch left off the N232 almost immediately, on another forestry road to the Meteorological Observatory. From there it's a short, gentle ascent to Penhas Douradas.

You're about 700m above Manteigas here, and mustn't miss the stunning view from a stub of rock called Fragão de Covão; just follow the signs. You can also drive up the N232 just for the view.

Walking back the same way makes for a return trip of about 5½ hours.

SkiParque   DRY SKIING

(☑ 275 980 090; www.skiparque.pt; N232; ☉ 10am-6pm) A dry-ski run 8km east of Manteigas, friendly SkiParque has a lift, gear rental, snowboarding, a cafe and a treeless, functional campground. The price for lifts and equipment rental is €14/23 per one/four hours in high season. Lessons (one/two people €25/35) are also available.

SkiParque organises other outdoor activities such as **rock climbing**, **hiking**, **mountain biking** and **paragliding** lessons for first-timers.

🛏 Sleeping

⭐**Parque Campismo**
Covão d'Ametade   CAMPGROUND €

(www.covaodametade.wix.com/home;   Covão d'Ametade; sites €1.50-2.50 plus per adult/child €1.50/1; Ⓟ) ☞ The wilder of two idyllic, bare-bones campgrounds tucked away in the mountains surrounding Manteigas, this tents-only site sits in a grove of birch trees near the head of the Vale do Zêzere, with awe-inspiring views up to the looming Cántaro Magro. It's signposted at a hairpin bend 12km west of Manteigas along the N338. There are basic toilets, picnic tables and cement barbecues, but don't expect electricity or hot water.

Pensão Estrela   GUESTHOUSE €

(☑ 275 981 288; www.residencialestrela.web.pt; Rua Doutor Sobral 5; s/d €20/30; ☞) This recommended mother-and-son team in the heart of the village offers very clean, comfortable heated rooms with good bathrooms at a great price. Breakfast is simple but decent, with tasty mountain *chouriço* (spicy sausage), and there's a sociable bar downstairs.

Covão da Ponte   CAMPGROUND €

(www.covaodaponte.com; sites per adult/child/tent/car €1.50/1/1.50/1; Ⓟ) At this lovely, shaded spot along the Mondego, you can wade, picnic or simply relax by the river's tranquil headwaters. Hikers can also explore the surrounding fields and mountains on three loop trails of varying lengths. To get here, take the N232 5.4km uphill from Manteigas, then continue an additional 5km from the signposted turn-off. The poorly marked park entrance is on the right. There's an intermittently open snack bar as well as showers.

Pensão Serradalto   GUESTHOUSE €

(☑ fax 275 981 151; paragem_serradalto@hotmail.com; Rua 1 de Maio 15; s/d/ste winter €35/45/60,

THE BEIRAS MANTEIGAS

summer €25/35/50 ; ⊘Wed-Mon; 🐾) In the heart of town, the Serradalto offers rooms with wood floors and simple antique furnishings, plus fine valley views from a sunny, grapevine-shaded upstairs terrace. Multinight stays earn a €5 discount.

★Casa das Obras — RURAL INN €€

(🖉275 981 155; www.casadasobras.pt; Rua Teles de Vasconcelos; r summer/winter €68/80; 🐾🌊) Elegant and friendly, Manteigas's nicest in-town lodging is a lovely 18th-century town house that has been carefully renovated to preserve its original grandeur and stone-walled charm. It's all historic feel and noble elegance but it's no shrine, rather a relaxed spot with a top welcome from the family who has owned this place for centuries.

The antique-filled rooms are classy and stylish, but the real joy are the public areas, including a wonderful breakfast room where you all eat around a lord-of-the-manor-style long table, and an atmospheric 16th-century cellar bar. There's also a pool in a grassy courtyard across the street.

Hotel Berne — HOTEL €€

(🖉275 981 351; www.hotelberne.com; Quinta de Santo António; s/d €55/70; 🅿@🐾🌊🏠) Going for a Swiss feel, this lovely hotel at the bottom of town has cheerful, spotless, wood-accented rooms. Many units have balconies and double-hinged windows opening onto views of Manteigas and the mountains above. The restaurant is locally known, the spacious lounge is a great spot, complete with pool table, and there are good family options.

★Casa das Penhas Douradas — HOTEL €€€

(🖉275 981 045; www.casadaspenhasdouradas.pt; Penhas Douradas; s €120-140, d €135-155; 🅿❄@🐾🌊) Near the top of the mountain between Manteigas and Seia, this superb hotel gets everything right. Though its high, lonely location and spectacular views are appealing enough, this would be an excellent place to stay in any location. The rooms all have great natural light, views, and some come with cosy sloping ceiling or have a most appealing little terrace. Bathrooms are modern and stylish, and the downstairs heated pool area is great in both summer and winter.

An enlightened attitude to guest comfort means there are all sorts of welcome details, such as a free snack buffet all afternoon, bikes and kayaks to use, books, DVDs and spa and massage treatments available. There's a top network of marked trails up here too, so you can hike from the hotel doorstep.

Pousada de São Lourenço — INN €€€

(🖉275 980 050; www.pousadas.pt; Penhas Douradas; s/d €145/155, with mountain view €176/186; 🅿🐾) In a splendid position high on the mountainside, this inn has a great location but at last visit the rooms looked a little tired and the atmosphere, like in so many *pousadas* (upmarket inns), was a bit staid. It's 13km above and north of Manteigas, topping the wiggly switchbacks on the N232. Though comfortable, the hotel isn't value-packed – and wi-fi in the rooms is extra – but the setting and, especially, the views are memorable.

🍴 Eating & Drinking

O Trenó — PORTUGUESE €

(🖉275 982 020; Estrada da Lapa; mains €8-11; ⊘lunch & dinner Tue-Sat, lunch Sun) South of the centre of Manteigas, in the San António district near a couple of hotels, this unpretentious place offers a genuine welcome. It's a good spot to try typical mountain dishes such as *chanfana* (stewed goat) or *feijoca* (bean and pork stew) and chat about local issues with the friendly staff.

Pastelaria Padaria Floresta — BAKERY, CAFE €

(Rua 1 de Maio; ⊘6am-midnight Mon-Sat, 8am-1pm Sun) Open bright and early, this little bakery is a hiker's best friend, with simple sandwiches on homemade bread plus delicious trail snacks for sale for around €1. Taste the *empadas de frango* (pastry dough filled with chicken), *queijadas de requeijão* (half-sweet, half-savoury cheese tarts) and the house speciality *pastéis de feijoca* (bean cakes).

Luso Pizza — PIZZERIA €

(🖉275 982 930; Rua Dr Manuel Duarte Leitão; small pizzas €7-9; ⊘11am-11pm) This tiny place makes great pizza; pasta appears on the menu but isn't always available.

Santa Luzia — PORTUGUESE €€

(🖉963 968 013; Rua Dr Esteves Carvalho 4; mains €8-15; ⊘lunch & dinner) The crisp reds-and-whites of the dining area blend seductively with the dark-wood tables at this main-street eatery whose bar always buzzes with locals enjoying a beer or two. The menu is aimed more at visitors, but features tasty-enough mountain specialities such as trout and roast goat. There's polite service and a great outdoor terrace with mountainside perspectives.

Grannitus
BAR

(Rua Sobral 3) All you could want in a mountain-village bar is here: log fire, pool table, cheap drinks, good atmosphere. Just don't take on the locals at darts unless you're pretty good at it.

ℹ️ Information

Parque Natural da Serra da Estrela Office
(☑275 980 060; pnse@icnb.pt; Rua 1 de Maio 2; ⊙9am-12.30pm & 2-5.30pm Mon-Fri) On the main road in the centre of town. Has useful leaflets on walking routes in the Manteigas area and little else.

Turismo (☑275 981 129; Rua Dr Esteves de Carvalho 2; ⊙9am-12.30pm & 2-5.30pm Tue-Sat) Friendly; on the main road near the petrol station.

ℹ️ Getting There & Away

Two weekday buses connect Manteigas with Guarda. Check with Manteigas' *turismo* for up-to-the-minute details.

Manteigas is a fairly easy 20-minute drive from the IP2, or a more winding 40-minute drive from Covilhã.

Torre

In winter, Torre's road signs are so blasted by freezing winds that horizontal icicles barb their edges. Portugal's highest peak at 1993m, Torre (Tower) produces a winter freeze so reliable that it's got a small **ski resort** (☑275 314 727; www.skiserradaestrela.com; Torre; half-/full day Sat & Sun Nov-Apr €15/25, other times €10/15; ⊙9am-5pm ski season), with mainly beginners' slopes (there's one 'black' run). Ski-gear (€25 per day) and snowboard (€15 per day) rental is available, and there's a supervised kids' play park.

Outside the snow season (mid-December to mid-April), Portugal's pinnacle is rather depressing – tired and tacky, occupied by several ageing golf-ball radar domes, and a sweaty, smelly shopping arcade. The 7m-high, neoclassical obelisk was erected by João VI in the early 19th century so that Portugal could cheekily claim its highest point was exactly 2000m.

Redeeming the summit is the **Centro de Interpretação do Parque Natural da Serra da Estrela** (admission €2.50), a park visitor centre filled with maps, photos and displays about the region's natural and cultural history.

Even if you give Torre itself a miss, it's worth making the trip in this direction just to survey the astoundingly dramatic surroundings. The drive from Manteigas or Covilhã is especially breathtaking, passing through the Nave de Santo António – a traditional high-country sheep-grazing meadow – before climbing through a surreal moonscape of crags and gorges. Visible near the turn-off for Torre is Cántaro Magro, a notable rock formation. Rising 500m straight from the valley below, it's a spectacular spot, popular with rock-climbers.

In August, **Autotransportes do Fundão** (☑275 336 448) runs a 2pm bus service from Covilhã's bus station to Torre (€2.85, 1½ hours), arriving around 3.30pm and returning down the mountain an hour later.

Penhas da Saúde

Penhas, the closest spot in which to hunker down near Torre (about 10km from Covilhã), isn't a town but a weather-beaten collection of chalets sited striplike along the N339 at an elevation of about 1500m. Supplies are limited; if you plan to go walking, do your shopping in Covilhã.

🛏️ Sleeping

Pousada da Juventude
HOSTEL €

(☑275 335 375; www.pousadasjuventude.pt; dm/d summer €13/45; ⊙Oct-Aug; P@🖥️) 🌿 Penhas' first-rate mountaintop hostel has a communal kitchen and cafeteria, giant stone fireplaces and a games room featuring billiards and table tennis. The deluxe doubles in the annexe are especially nice, but those in the main building are cosy too. Dorms have eight berths and plenty of space; meals are available. Book well ahead in winter.

ℹ️ Getting There & Away

Daily throughout August, and on weekends in late July and early September, buses run from Covilhã's bus station to Penhas (€2.20) at 8.50am and 2pm, returning down the mountain at 5.35pm.

A taxi from Covilhã to Penhas costs around €20.

Covilhã

POP 36,700 / ELEV 700M

Modern Covilhã is awash in suburban sprawl, its 18th-century textile factories having given way to high-rise apartment blocks. Despite dreary outskirts, Covilhã's pleasant historic core remains intact, and the

THE BEIRAS TORRE

Covilhã

Companhia Club (300m)
Ponte Pedonal Penedos Altos (200m)
Av Frei Heitor Pinto
Jardim Público
Largo Infantaria XXI
R C Campos Melo
R Rui Faleiro
R das Flores
Praça do Município
(1.5km); (1.7km)
R António Augusto d'Aguiar
Museu de Lanifícios (500m)

vanishing history of wool production and cloth dyeing in the Serra da Estrela.

A map shows the 100-plus wool producers that once thrived in this region, while other displays demonstrate how cochineal and indigo from the New World were used to dye Portuguese soldiers' uniforms. Even if yarn makes you yawn, you may be impressed by the gigantic old looms and dyeing vats. Admission includes entry to two adjacent exhibitions, which can also be visited separately.

Igreja de Santa Maria   CHURCH
(Rua 1 Dezembro) The narrow, winding streets west of Praça do Município have a quiet charm, and in the midst of them is the Igreja de Santa Maria, with a startling facade covered in *azulejos*.

Ponte Pedonal Penedos Altos   BRIDGE
This striking pedestrian bridge spans the valley east of the old town. It's immediately noticeable for its loftiness (52m at its top point) and unusual zigzag trajectory. Built by João Luís Carrilho da Graça, it's won rave reviews in architecture circles since its opening in 2009.

🛏 Sleeping

★**Hotel Covilhã Jardim**   HOTEL €
(☎275 322 140; www.hotelcovilhajardim.com; Jardim Público 40; s/d Apr-Dec €30/45, Jan-Mar €35/55; ❋@☎) This amiable, bright, modern family-run place sits on the municipal gardens. All rooms have lots of natural light and leafy views of the park or sweeping panoramas of the surrounding mountains (room 110 has both), and one is wheelchair-accessible. The cafe downstairs is another

---

presence of the Universidade da Beira Interior lends it an air of modern urban vitality. The city's geographic setting on steeply canted terraces provides phenomenal views eastward towards Spain.

◉ Sights

Commanding fabulous views, the leafy **Jardim Público**, just north of Praça do Município, is a popular local gathering place and a pleasant spot for a drink at sunset.

Museu de Lanifícios   MUSEUM
(Museum of Wool-Making; ☎275 319 700; www.museu.ubi.pt; Rua Marquês d'Ávila e Bolama; adult/16-25yr €5/2.50; ◷9.30am-noon & 2.30-6pm Tue-Sun) Covilhã used to be the centre of one of Europe's biggest wool-producing regions but stray outside the centre and you'll see the town's ghostly mills standing empty and forlorn. Sited in the former royal textile factory, this museum traces the proud but

plus. Note: though we employ the wi-fi icon here, access is by cable.

Hotel Solneve
HOTEL €

(☎275 323 001; www.solneve.pt; Rua Visconde da Coriscada 126; s/d €25/51; 🅿 ❋ ❋ 🛋) With views of Covilhã's main square, this grand pink hotel in the heart of town has spotless, high-ceilinged rooms that have been recently modernised and offer great value. Facilities are good, with minibars, a decent restaurant and a swimming pool downstairs, plus off-street parking (€2.50). Pricier rooms include jet baths.

Residêncial Panorama
GUESTHOUSE €

(☎275 323 952; www.residencialpanorama.pt; Rua Bombeiros Voluntários 9; r €40-60; ❋ ❋) In a quiet location on a backstreet behind the church, this friendly place has rather sweet rooms and a popular bar-restaurant.

Hotel Covilhã Parque
HOTEL €€

(☎275 329 320; www.covilhaparquehotel.com.pt; Av Frei Heitor Pinto; s/d/tr €35/60/72; 🅿 ❋ ❋) Ten floors of uninspired but comfortable rooms enjoy nice city views in this modern apartment block next to the *turismo*. The rack rates are high at s/d €80/100, but the rates are more usually what we list here, which represents decent value.

🍴 Eating

Pastelaria Restaurante Montiel
CAFE, PORTUGUESE €

(☎275 322 086; Praça do Município 33-37; mains €7-12, snacks €1-3; ❋ cafe all day, restaurant lunch & dinner) The upstairs dining room serves decent regional cooking, with an emphasis on meat dishes. The downstairs cafe is a Covilhã social hub and serves tasty snacks: chicken empanadas, sausage rolls and the like.

ComFusão
PORTUGUESE €€

(☎275 098 902; Rua de São Tiago 13; dishes €6-14; ❋4pm-2am Mon-Sat) This comfortable and convivial spot is winningly decorated in wood and stone and offers a short selection of typical northern Portuguese dishes and *petiscos* (tapas) presented with modern flair and design.

Restaurante Zé do Sporting
PORTUGUESE €€

(Rua Comendador Mendes Veiga 19; mains €8-14; ❋lunch & dinner Tue-Sat, lunch Sun) Grilled meats – including local favourites such as *coelho* (rabbit) and *cabrito* (kid) – share the menu with other Portuguese classics.

Try the *feijoada á transmontana,* a hearty stew of beans, cabbage, pork and smoky sausage.

🍷 Drinking & Nightlife

Covilhã Jardim Café-Bar
CAFE

(☎275 322 140; Jardim Público 40; snacks €2-4; ❋8am-10pm) With comfy couches inside and tree-shaded tables on its parkside terrace, this trendy little cafe makes an enjoyable place to watch the world go by.

Companhia Club
CLUB

(www.companhiaclub.com; Rua da Indústria 33) This surprisingly sleek and modern DJ bar and club is one of a cluster of late-night venues popular with students, set in the abandoned-looking mill zone in the north of town. To get there, head along Avenida Frei Heitor Pinto past the *turismo* and veer right down Rua da Indústria.

ℹ️ Information

Ponto Já (Rua da Olivença, cnr Rua António Augusto d'Aguiar; ❋10am-7pm Mon-Fri) Free internet on the ground floor of the market building.

Turismo (☎275 319 560; www.turismo serradaestrela.pt; Av Frei Heitor Pinto; ❋9am-5.30pm Mon-Fri, 9am-12.30pm & 2-5.30pm Sat)

ℹ️ Getting There & Away

BUS

From the long-distance **bus station** (☎275 313 506; Avenida da Anil), **Rede Expressos** (www.rede-expressos.pt) runs regularly to Guarda (€6, 45 minutes, several times daily), and via Castelo Branco (€6, one hour) to Lisbon (€15.50, 3¾ hours) at least three times daily. There are also multiple daily services to Porto (€16.80, 3¾ hours).

TRAIN

Three daily IC trains run to/from Lisbon (€17.20, 3¾ hours) via Castelo Branco (€6.60, 50 minutes). Regional trains serving Castelo Branco are slightly slower and slightly cheaper.

ℹ️ Getting Around

From the train and long-distance bus stations, it's a punishing 2km climb to Praça do Município, the town centre. A taxi up the hill from either station will cost about €5, or you can catch a **local bus** (Covibus; ☎275 098 097; www.covi bus.com) for €1.20: take bus 10 or 11 for Praça do Município.

WINES OF THE DÃO REGION

The velvety reds of the Dão region, south and east of Viseu, have been cultivated for over 2000 years, and are today among Portugal's best drops. Vineyards are mostly sheltered in valleys at altitudes of 200m to 900m just west of the Serra da Estrela, thus avoiding the rain of the coast but also the harsh summer heat that comes further inland. This, together with granitic soil, helps the wines retain their natural acidity. Dão wines are often called the burgundies of Portugal because they don't overpower but, rather, are subtle and full of finesse.

Some three dozen Dão vineyards and producers offer multilingual cellar tours and tastings; most require advance booking. You can pick up a list in Viseu's *turismo*. Two popular wineries near Viseu are **Casa da Ínsua** (☑232 642 222; www.casadainsua.pt; Penalva do Castelo), 30km east on the IP5 and N329-1, and **Casa de Santar** (☑232 942 937; http://casadesantar.com; Santar; ⊘ guided visits 11am & 3pm Tue-Sat), 15km southeast on the N231. Both have fine grounds and lovely architecture, and the former operates a plush five-star country hotel.

For a hearty meal on the wine trail, head straight to **Tres Pipos** (☑232 816 851; www.3pipos.pt; Rua de Santo Amaro 966, Tonda; mains €9-16; ⊘lunch Tue-Sun, dinner Tue-Sat), which is found in the small village of Tonda, 20km south of Viseu near Tondela. Excellent regional cuisine is served in atmospheric dining rooms with old wooden ceilings and thick stone walls. There's a good selection of Dão wines on the list and also a shop selling wine.

The **Comissão Vitivinícola Regional do Dão** (CVRD; ☑232 410 060; www.cvrdao. pt; Rua Aristides Sousa Mendes, Viseu) regulatory body eventually plans to open its headquarters – Viseu's 16th-century Antigo Paço Episcopal – as a posh Solar do Dão where the public can sample Dão wines.

White Dão wines are also available, though the full-bodied reds are generally better. But do try the sparkling white wines of the separate, small Lafões region, northwest of Viseu.

BEIRA ALTA

Heading north and west from the Serra da Estrela, mountains give way quickly to rolling plains that stretch up to the Douro valley and east to Spain. Threat of invasion from its not-always-friendly neighbour marks both the region's history and its landscape. A series of fearsome fortress-towns are the biggest draw for travellers, though the cities of Viseu and Guarda also have charms, from excellent local wines to troves of Renaissance art.

Viseu

POP 47,250

One of the Beiras' most appealing cities, Viseu rivals more-visited Coimbra for sheer charm and vitality. Its well-preserved historical centre offers numerous enticements to pedestrians: cobbled streets, meandering alleys, leafy public gardens and a central square – Praça da República, aka the 'Rossio' – graced with bright flowers and fountains. Sweeping vistas over the surrounding plains unfold from the town's highest point, the square fronting the cathedral, built on the site of a former mosque, while some of Portugal's standout Renaissance art is on show alongside. Viseu is also a great place to eat and drink: the reds from the surrounding Dão region are considered to be some of Portugal's finest.

History

According to legend, Viriato, chief of the Lusitani tribe, took refuge in a cave here before the Romans hunted him down in 139 BC. The Romans built a fortified camp just across the Rio Pavia from Viseu. The town, conquered and reconquered in the struggles between Christians and Moors, was definitively taken by Fernando I, king of Castilla y León, in 1057.

Afonso V completed Viseu's sturdy walls in about 1472. The town soon spread beyond them, and grew fat from agriculture and trade. An annual 'free fair' declared by João III in 1510 carries on today as one of the region's biggest agricultural and handicrafts expositions.

⊙ Sights

Sé   CATHEDRAL

(⊙9am-noon & 2-7pm) Resplendent on a high rock is the 13th-century granite cathedral, whose gloomy Renaissance facade conceals a splendid 16th-century interior, including an impressive Manueline ceiling.

Panoramas of Viseu's historic centre are available from the upper gallery of the adjacent cloister. The lower level, handsome with tiles, Ionic columns, tombstone fragments and round arches, is one of Portugal's earliest Italian Renaissance structures. Note the amazing Romanesque-Gothic portal on one corner, rediscovered during restoration work in 1918.

Stairs in the northern transept of the cathedral climb to the **Museu de Arte Sacra**. The museum itself is a lacklustre assemblage of vestments and religious paraphernalia, but its lofty setting offers a nice perspective on the church's architecture.

Facing the cathedral is the 1775 **Igreja da Misericórdia**, whose bright rococo exterior contrasts markedly with its neoclassical, severe and rather dull interior, which contains another museum and a treasury.

⭐**Museu Grão Vasco**   MUSEUM

(www.imc-ip.pt; Adro da Sé; admission €4, Sun morning free; ⊙2-5.30pm Tue, 10am-5.30pm Wed-Sun) Adjoining the cathedral, the severe granite box of the Paço de Três Escalões (Palace of Three Steps), was originally built as the bishop's palace. It's now a splendid museum featuring Viseu's own Vasco Fernandes, known as Grão Vasco (the Great Vasco; 1480–1543) – one of Portugal's seminal Renaissance painters.

There are two principal floors, one with religious art and 19th-century Portuguese works (check out the moustached lady by José de Almeida Furtado). The top floor has Vasco's majestic canvases and works of other bright lights of the so-called Viseu School. Vasco's colleague, collaborator and rival Gaspar Vaz merits special attention. Together they spurred each other on to produce some of Portugal's finest artwork. After five centuries their rich colours and luminous style are still as striking as ever.

Around the Sé   NEIGHBOURHOOD

North of the cathedral along Rua Silva Gaio is the longest remaining stretch of the old **town wall**. To the east, across Avenida Emídio Navarro, is another old town gate, the **Porta dos Cavaleiros**.

South of the cathedral beneath the **Passeio dos Cônegos** (Curates Walk, on part of the old wall) is **Praça de Dom Duarte**, named after the Portuguese monarch born in Viseu. Several noble mansions adorn the square.

Southward is **Casa de Dom Duarte** (Rua Dom Duarte; ⊙closed to public), a house with a beautiful Manueline window and traditionally regarded as the king's birthplace.

Rua Augusto Hilário runs southeast through the former **judiaria** (14th-to-16th-century Jewish quarter). **Rua Direita**, Viseu's most appealing street and once the most direct route to the hilltop, is a lively melee of shops, souvenir stands, restaurants and old town houses.

Around the Rossio   NEIGHBOURHOOD

At the southern end of Praça da República is the late-18th-century **Igreja dos Terceiros**, all heavy, gilded baroque but for the luminous *azulejos* portraying the life of St Francis.

Fine modern **azulejos** at the northern end of the Rossio depict scenes from regional life, and beyond these is the *azulejo*-adorned **Museu Almeida Moreira** (apoio.municipe@cm-viseu.pt; Rua Soar de Cima; ⊙10am-noon & 2-5pm Tue-Sun) 𝗙𝗥𝗘𝗘, genteel home to the first director of the Museu Grão Vasco, with fine furnishings and art.

From here the grandest route into the old town is through the **Porta do Soar de Cima**, a gate set into a section of Afonso V's town walls.

Parque do Fontelo   PARK

A haven of woodland and open space sprawls beyond the Portal do Fontelo. Here are the 16th-century **Antigo Paço Episcopal** (former Bishop's Palace), now home to the Dão Regional Vintners' Commission (CVRD), together with once-lovely Renaissance gardens, a stadium and a recreation complex.

✿ Festivals & Events

Feira de São Mateus   TOWN FESTIVAL

(www.feirasaomateus.pt) Viseu's biggest annual get-together is a jamboree of agriculture and handicrafts from mid-August to mid-September, augmented by folk music, traditional food, amusement-park rides and fireworks. This direct descendant of the town's old 'free fair' still takes place in the riverside Campo da Feira de São Mateus, set aside for the event by João III in 1510.

Viseu

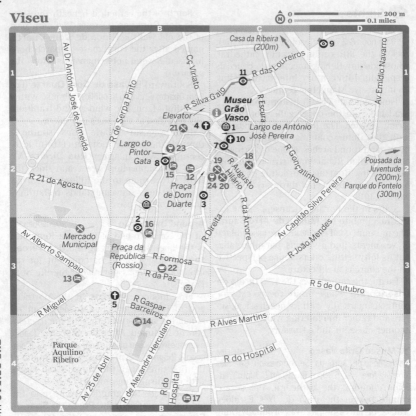

N 0 — 200 m
0 — 0.1 miles

🛏 Sleeping

Campismo
Moinhos do Dão CAMPGROUND, COTTAGE €
(☑ 232 610 586; www.moinhosdodao.nl; Tibaldinho, Mangualde; sites per adult/child/car €3.50/1.75/1, tent €3-4; P) ⊘ This amazingly located, utterly tranquil spot sits at the end of a very rutted – walk if you value your vehicle – 1.6km dirt road 20km southeast of Viseu and offers camping right on the banks of the Rio Dão, plus rustic indoor lodgings. Built amid a cluster of restored water-mills, it's a place where you truly get away from it all – swimming and boating by day, dining by candlelight at outdoor tables by night. Closed for the 2014 season for renovations.

Pensão Rossio Parque GUESTHOUSE €
(☑ 232 422 085; www.pensaorossioparque.com; Rua Soar de Cima 55; s €30, d €30-35, tw €40-50; ✳🖤) A no-brainer for budget-minded travellers, this small, old-fashioned hotel directly

above the Rossio features a bright, bustling restaurant downstairs and nice views from the front rooms. All rooms have bathroom and are discounted for longer stays.

Pousada da Juventude HOSTEL €
(☑ 232 413 001; www.pousadasjuventude.pt; Rua Aristides Sousa Mendes; dm €12, d with shared/private bathroom €25/27; 🖤) A 10-minute walk east of the centre, Viseu's boxy and rather basic hostel has friendly, helpful staff but no cooking facilities. You'll find free internet and a decent restaurant across the street.

★Casa da Sé BOUTIQUE HOTEL €€
(☑ 232 468 032; www.casadase.net; Rua Augusta Cruz 12; s/ste €79/155, d €89-113; ✳🖤) Right in the heart of old Viseu, this handsome boutique hotel is owned by an antique dealer, so the historic building is full of period furniture and *objets d'art*, all of which are for sale, so you can take the bed with you when

Viseu

you check out. All rooms are different and exceedingly well-decorated. Staff are helpful, and there's a warm, hospitable feel to the place. It also has an elegant little cafe and shop. Some street noise at weekends.

★ **Quinta dos Três Rios**　　　RURAL INN €€
(☑ 232 959 189; www.minola.co.uk; Rua Francisco de Oliveira 239, Parada de Gonta; 2-/4-person apt from €100/150; P 🛜) At this remarkable getaway 10km southwest of Viseu, every room is a suite with 5m-high ceilings and 4m French doors opening onto a symphony of frogs and nightingales by night, and vistas of the surrounding olive trees, vineyards and river by day. The hosts make fabulous dinners with homemade olive oil and wine.

They also lead impromptu tours of the surrounding area that encompass everything from wineries to traditional fishing and barrel-making to grape stomping during the harvest season. When you get to Parada de Gonta, go through the village and down the hill towards the river – you'll see the *quinta* on your right.

Palácio dos Melos　　　BOUTIQUE HOTEL €€
(☑ 232 439 290; www.hotelpalaciodosmelos.pt; Rua Chão Mestre 4; s/d €80/90, ste €125-145; P ✳ @ 🛜) This very central hotel enjoys a remarkable location, in a renovated mansion built right into the town walls. Rooms incorporate all the modern comforts you'd expect from a five-star place, but the most atmospheric rooms in the original older building also have grand high ceilings, carpets and chandeliers that speak of a different time.

Guests have access to a small grassy yard where drinks are served, reached by a catwalk across the top of the old town gate. Look for money-saving packages online, including meals in the hotel's gourmet restaurant.

Hotel Avenida　　　HOTEL €€
(☑ 232 423 432; www.hotelavenida.com.pt; Av Alberto Sampaio 1; s/d €50/70; @ 🛜) Proudly proclaiming its presence with a vintage neon sign visible from the Rossio, this friendly, modestly elegant hotel has a grand spiral staircase, stately common areas and darkish, plush old rooms decorated in regal colours.

Hotel Grão Vasco　　　HOTEL €€
(☑ 232 423 511; www.hotelgraovasco.pt; Rua Gaspar Barreiros; s/d €65/75; P ✳ @ 🛜 🏊) It's a little retro, but there's something nice about this huge old-school place, with black noticeboards with white clip-on letters and weird items for sale in a dusty display case. The service is good and the low-bedded rooms are pretty comfortable. Go for one on the top floor if available – if not, grab one on the garden side of the building.

★ **Pousada de Viseu**　　　HOTEL €€€
(☑ 232 457 320; www.pousadas.pt; Rua do Hospital; s €110, d €120-144; P ✳ @ 🛜 🏊) This superbly refashioned *pousada* is set in a monumental 19th-century hospital and is a top luxury option. The original three floors, all with ridiculously high ceilings and spacious rooms, have been enhanced with a 4th floor dedicated to special suites with panoramic terraces. The enormous central courtyard,

complete with bar, is a neoclassical delight, while the elegant former pharmacy has been converted into a cosy lounge. Indoor and outdoor pools, plus spa complex complete the picture. Excellent value.

Eating

O Hilário
PORTUGUESE €

(Rua Augusto Hilário 35; mains €5-9; ⊙ lunch & dinner Mon-Sat) Fantastically friendly and welcoming, this slice of old Portugal is named for the 19th-century fado star who once lived down the street. Great value *doses* (portions) will feed one hungry person, but halves are available for lighter appetites. If your favourite grandparents owned a restaurant this would be it.

Casa dos Queijos
PORTUGUESE €

(Travessa das Escadinhas da Sé 7; mains €6-9; ⊙ lunch & dinner Mon-Sat) Despite the owner's rather gruff attitude, this stone-walled old place, hidden up narrow stairs, gets top marks for atmosphere and for its carefully prepared grills and *cozidos* (stews). The shop downstairs, stacked high with tempting wines and cheeses, is a neighbourhood hang-out where locals chat all afternoon over glasses of wine.

O Cortiço
PORTUGUESE €€

(☑232 423 853; Rua Augusto Hilário 45; mains €11-17; ⊙ lunch & dinner) This heartily recommended stone-walled eatery specialises in traditional recipes collected from surrounding villages. Generous portions are served in heavy tureens, and the good house wine comes in medieval-style wooden pitchers. Finish your meal with a glass of the local firewater made from olives.

Restaurante Muralha da Sé
PORTUGUESE €€€

(☑232 437 777; www.muralhadase.pt; Adro da Sé 24; mains €18-21; ⊙ lunch & dinner Tue-Sat, lunch Sun) This unabashedly upper-crust spot under the looming Igreja da Misericórdia boasts fine regional cuisine made with ingredients from the nearby Serra da Estrela, plus cathedral-square views from its terrace.

Drinking & Entertainment

Bars in the streets around the cathedral overflow making for a merry atmosphere.

Palato
WINE BAR

(☑232 435 081; www.noitebiba.pt/palato; Praça de Dom Duarte 1; ⊙8pm-4am Mon-Sat) A trendy locale, this comfortably posh spot has a long list of Dão and Douro wines by the bottle,

with 30-odd available by the glass at fair prices given the quantity they pour. The interior blends plush fabrics with exposed stone, and there's a cosy downstairs as well. Service is solicitous, and snacks and rolls are served until 3.30am.

Irish Bar
PUB

(Largo do Pintor Gata 8; ⊙9am-2am Mon-Sat, 1pm-2am Sun) Smoky and atmospheric, this offers Guinness on tap, occasional live Irish music and terrace seating on a charming square near the old town gate.

Brothers
CAFE, BAR

(Rua da Paz 26) This stylish cafe-bar in an attractive area of the new town has a bohemian-style Paris atmosphere, good beers and coffee, and regular live music.

Shopping

Casa da Ribeira
HANDICRAFTS

(☑232 429 761; Largo Nossa Senhora da Conceição; ⊙9am-12.30pm & 2-5.30pm Tue-Sat) In this municipal space, local artisans work and sell their products, including lace, ceramics and the region's distinctively black earthenware.

Information

Espaço Internet (Solar dos Condes de Prime, Rua dos Andrades; ⊙10am-8pm Mon-Fri, 10am-1pm & 2-7pm Sat, 2-7pm Sun) Free internet in a centrally located historic mansion.

Welcome Center Viseu (☑232 420 950; www.turismodocentro.pt; Adro da Sé; ⊙9am-6pm Mon-Fri, 9.30am-12.30pm & 1.30-5.30pm Sat & Sun) Viseu's tourist office is by the cathedral square. It opens half an hour later at weekends in summer.

Getting There & Away

Rede Expressos (☑232 422 822; www.rede-expressos.pt) serve the following destinations regularly from the **bus station** at the western edge of town.

Coimbra (€8.50, 1¼ hours)
Guarda (€8.90, one hour)
Lisbon (€17.50, 3½ hours)
Porto (€11.50, 1¾ hours)
Vila Real (€10.30, 1¼ hours)

Guarda

POP 26,000 / ELEV 1056M

Fria, farta, forte e feia (cold, rich, strong and ugly): such is the popular description of Portugal's highest full-fledged city. Hunkered down on a hilltop, it was founded in

1197 to guard young Portugal against both Moors and Spaniards (hence the name).

Nowadays this district capital is a delightful place to spend an afternoon. Old Guarda is perched on a steep hill, a rambling climb from the IP5 or the train station, both roughly 5km northeast of the old centre. From the bus station on Rua Dom Nuno Álvares Pereira, it's 800m northwest to the cathedral square and the heart of the old town.

◉ Sights

Sé CATHEDRAL
(Praça Luís de Camões; ◷9am-noon & 2-5pm) Powerful in its sobriety, this grey Gothic fortress squats heavily over the central square. The earliest parts date from 1390 but it's also dotted with Manueline and Renaissance ornamentation. The most striking feature in the immense, granite interior is a four-storey Renaissance altarpiece attributed to Jean de Rouen (João de Ruão).

Museu da Guarda MUSEUM
(http://museudaguarda.imc-ip.pt; Rua Alves Roçadas 30; adult/child €2/free, Sun morning free; ◷10am-5.30pm Tue-Sun) The museum occupies the severe, 17th-century Episcopal Seminary, adjacent to the old bishop's palace. The collection runs from Bronze Age swords to Roman coins, from Renaissance sculpture to 19th- and 20th-century Portuguese painting.

In the adjacent, 18th-century courtyard, the handsome **Paço da Cultura** (◷irregular hours) features temporary art exhibitions. Check out its beautiful patio.

Old Town HISTORIC AREA
With its 16th-to-18th-century mansions and its overpowering cathedral, **Praça Luís de Camões** is the town's centrepiece. Plenty of medieval atmosphere survives in the cobblestone lanes and huddled houses north of the cathedral, centred around Rua de São Vicente.

Of the old walls and gates, the stalwart **Torre dos Ferreiros** (Blacksmiths' Tower; Rua Tenente Valadim) is still in good condition. Two other surviving gates are **Porta d'El Rei**, which you can climb for views over town, and **Porta da Erva**. A walk between these two gates takes you through the heart of Guarda's historic **judiaria** (Jewish quarter). Sharp-eyed visitors will notice crosses and other symbols scratched into doorframes: these identified the homes of *marranos* (New Christians) during the Inquisition.

Torre de Menagem TOWER
(◷10am-1pm & 2-6pm Apr-Oct, 9am-1pm & 2-5pm Nov-Mar) FREE Guarda's castle keep, on a hilltop above the cathedral, is open for daily tours; visit for the views up top, all the way to Spain and the Serra da Estrela. Check in for the visit at **Guarda Patrimonium** FREE just down the hill, which houses a very small collection of archaeological finds from the surrounding area. The tour includes a rather overproduced kid-focused 3D movie that sends you soaring through virtual renditions of Guarda's main monuments. There are three full visits a day (they take an hour) but you can go up top for the views at any time.

◪ Sleeping

★Hotel Santos HOTEL €
(☎271 205 400; www.hotelsantos.pt; Rua Tenente Valadim 14; s €30-40, d €40-60; ☏) Santos is warmly recommended for its spotless, newly furnished rooms, good prices, generous breakfast and welcoming staff. Its ultramodern interior resembles an Escher drawing, with interconnecting walkways, stairs and glass walls that incorporate both a handsome 19th-century granite building and the town's medieval walls. For nice views of the cathedral, book ahead for room 307 on the top floor.

Residência Filipe GUESTHOUSE €
(☎271 223 658; www.residencia-filipe.com; Rua Vasco da Gama 9; s/d/tr €20/35/45; P) This funny mix of old and new offers mostly bright, attractive rooms, brisk service and garage parking across the street (€2.50).

Parque Municipal de Campismo CAMPGROUND €
(☎271 221 200; Rua do Estádio Municipal; sites per adult/child/car €2.50/2/3, tent €2.50-3.50; P) Very close to the town centre and next to a leafy park, this municipal site has free hot showers and plenty of shade. It's open all year but you'll freeze in winter.

Solar de Alarcão RURAL INN €€
(☎271 214 392; solaralarcao@gmail.com; Rua Dom Miguel de Alarcão 25-27; d €80; P) Easily Guarda's most refined choice, this beautiful 17th-century granite mansion has its own courtyard and loggia, sits within spitting distance of the cathedral, and offers a handful of gorgeous rooms stuffed with antique furniture.

✖ Eating

Rua Francisco de Passos is the historic centre's best street for restaurant-browsing.

Guarda

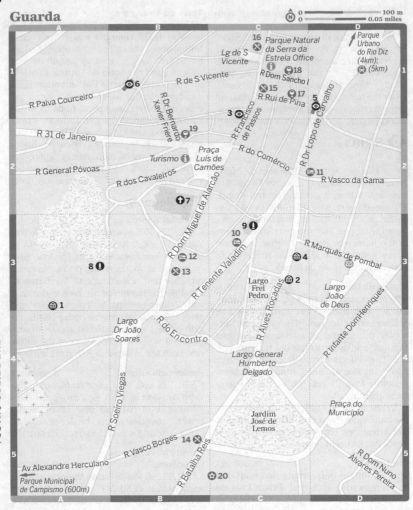

Parque Urbano
do Rio Diz
(4km);
(5km)

Parque Natural
da Serra da
Estrela Office

Lg de S
Vicente

R de S Vicente

R Dom Sancho I

18

R Paiva Courceiro

6

15

R Rui de Pina

17

5

R Dr. Bernardo Xavier Freire

R Francisco de Passos

3

R Dr Lopo de Carvalho

R 31 de Janeiro

19

Turismo

Praça
Luís de
Camões

R do Comércio

R General Póvoas

R dos Cavaleiros

11

R Vasco da Gama

R Dom Miguel de Alarção

7

9

10

R Marquês de Pombal

8

12

4

R Tenente Valadim

13

Largo
Frei
Pedro

R Alves Roçadas

2

Largo
João
de Deus

1

Largo
Dr João
Soares

R do Encontro

R Infante Dom Henriques

R Soeiro Viegas

Largo General
Humberto
Delgado

Praça do
Município

Jardim
José de
Lemos

R Vasco Borges

14

Av Alexandre Herculano

R Batalha Reis

20

Parque Municipal
de Campismo (600m)

R Dom Nuno
Álvares Pereira

O Bule
CAFE €

(271 211 275; Rua Dom Miguel de Alarcão; 8am-8pm Mon-Fri, 9am-8pm Sat, 10am-8pm Sun) This lovely, traditional cafe near the cathedral specialises in local pastries, including delicious *queijadas de canela,* cinnamon-tinged sheep's milk tarts.

Restaurante Belo Horizonte
PORTUGUESE €€

(271 211 454; Largo de São Vicente 1; mains €8-15; lunch & dinner Mon-Sat, lunch Sun) Granite-fronted Belo Horizonte does a great line in regional specialities such as *cabrito grelhado* (grilled kid). The solicitous husband-and-wife team here do everything right. There are *bacalhau* specials every day.

O Caçador
SEAFOOD €€

(271 211 702; Rua Batalha Reis 121; mains €8-13; lunch & dinner Tue-Sun) Drawing in dinner guests with a happy red neon sign and a glass-walled front room vaguely reminiscent of Parisian brasseries, O Caçador, despite its name ('the hunter'), specialises in seafood brought straight from the coast.

Restaurante A Floresta
PORTUGUESE €€

(271 212 314; Rua Francisco de Passos 40; mains €8-14; lunch & dinner) Just north of the cathedral, this snug and friendly place serves hearty regional cuisine, including the marvellous *chouriçada,* a heaping portion

Guarda

of grilled sausages from the nearby Serra da Estrela. *Meia-doses* (half-portions) of most items are available for €6 to €9.

🍷 Drinking & Nightlife

Aqui Jazz   BAR
(Rua Rui de Pina 29; ⏱11pm-3am Wed-Sat) Attracts arty types with live jazz in its attractive stone-walled interior.

Bar Noctis   BAR
(Rua Dom Sancho I 9; ⏱10.30pm-3am) In the dark streets of the old town is this popular late-night hang-out.

Praça Velha   BAR
(Rua Augusto Gil 17; ⏱10am-2am Mon-Sat; 🛜) This cute little place is a fine spot for free wifi or an evening drink while you wait for the late-openers to get their act together. There's pleasant outdoor seating in a great location.

☆ Entertainment

Teatro Municipal da Guarda   THEATRE
(📞271 205 240; www.tmg.com.pt; Rua Batalha Reis 12) Guarda's shiny new theatre complex, a boxy modern building of greyish-green glass just south of the historic centre, regularly hosts high-quality theatre, dance and music, including frequent international acts.

ⓘ Information

Parque Natural da Serra da Estrela Office
(📞271 225 454; pnse@icnb.pt; Rua Dom Sancho I 3; ⏱9am-12.30pm & 2-5.30pm Mon-Fri) Modestly helpful.

Ponto Já (Av Alexandre Herculano; ⏱9am-6pm Mon-Fri) Free internet.

Turismo (📞271 205 530; postodeturismo@ mun-guarda.pt; Praça Luís de Camões;

⏱10am-1pm & 2-6pm Jun-Sep, to 5pm Oct-May) Helpful; free internet access.

ⓘ Getting There & Away

BUS
Rede Expressos (📞271 212 720; www.rede-expressos.pt) runs services at least three times daily to the following destinations:
Castelo Branco (€10.80, 1¾ hours)
Coimbra (€13.50, 2¾ hours)
Covilhã (€6, 45 minutes)
Lisbon (€17.50, 4½ hours)
Porto (€14, three hours)
Viseu (€8.90, one hour)

Marques (📞238 312 858; www.marques.pt) goes daily via Gouveia (€4.35, 1½ hours) and Seia (€4.75, two hours). Rede Expressos also goes to Seia (€10.50, 70 minutes) once daily Sunday to Friday.

TRAIN
Guarda's modern train station is served by at least two fast IC trains daily from Lisbon (€20.70, 4¼ hours) and Coimbra (€12.70, 2¼ hours). For Porto change at Pampilhosa.

ⓘ Getting Around
Buses (€0.90) between the train station and the centre are infrequent; if one isn't waiting, you're probably better off taking a **taxi** (€4 to €5).

Trancoso
POP 3100 / ELEV 870M

A warren of cobbled lanes squeezed within Dom Dinis' mighty 13th-century walls makes peaceful, hilltop Trancoso a delightful retreat from the modern world.

THE JEWS OF BELMONTE

When the Moors ruled Portugal, it's estimated that 10% of the country's population was Jewish. Jews remained vital to the young Christian state, serving as government ministers and filling key roles in Henry the Navigator's school devoted to overseas exploration. The current Duke of Bragança, hereditary king of Portugal, proudly acknowledges his own Jewish parentage.

When Portugal embraced Spain's Inquisitorial zeal beginning in the 1490s, thousands of Jews from both Portugal and Spain fled to northeast Portugal, including the Beiras and Trás-os-Montes, where the arm of the Inquisitors had not yet reached. However it wasn't too long before the Inquisitors made their presence felt even here, and Jews once again faced conversion, expulsion or death.

However, in the 1980s it was revealed that in the town of Belmonte, 30km south of Guarda, a group of families had been practising Jewish rites in secret since the Inquisition – over 500 years. While many such communities continued in secrecy well into the Inquisition, most slowly died out. But Belmonte's community managed to survive five centuries by meticulously ensuring marriages were arranged only among other Jewish families. The transmission of Jewish tradition was oral and passed from mother to daughter. Each Friday night families descended into basements to pray and celebrate the Sabbath. Now that the community is out in the open, they have embraced male-dominated Orthodox Judaism, though the women elders have not forgotten the secret prayers that have been doggedly transmitted these past 500 years.

The **Museu Judaico de Belmonte** (☑ 275 913 505; Rua Portela 4; adult/child €2.50/1.50; ☉ 9am-12.30pm & 2-5.30pm Tue-Sun mid-Sep–mid-Apr, 9.30am-1pm & 2.30-6pm Tue-Sun mid-Apr–mid-Sep) is a well-presented display of Jewish artefacts, mostly modern, with some history about the 20th-century re-establishment of Judaism in Portugal. Ask here about visiting the town's synagogue.

There are several other little museums in Belmonte, one on olive oil, and one on Portugal's New World discoveries – the explorer Pedro Álvares Cabral, known as the discoverer of Brazil, was born here. See www.cm-belmonte.pt for more details.

There are frequent daily bus connections between Belmonte and Guarda.

Although it's predominantly a medieval creation, the town's castle also features a rare, intact Moorish tower, while just outside the walls are what are believed to be Visigothic tombs.

Dinis underscored the importance of this border fortress by marrying the saintly Dona Isabel of Aragon here in 1282. But the town's favourite son is Bandarra, a lowly 16th-century shoemaker and fortune-teller who put official noses out of joint by foretelling the end of the Portuguese monarchy.

Sure enough, shortly after Bandarra's death, the young Dom Sebastião died, heirless, in the disastrous Battle of Alcácer-Quibir in 1558. Soon afterwards, Portugal fell under Spanish rule.

◉ Sights

Old Town　　　　　　　　　　HISTORIC AREA

The **Portas d'El Rei** (King's Gate), surmounted by the ancient coat of arms, was always the principal entrance, whose guillotine-like door sealed out unwelcome visitors. The walls run intact for over 1km around the medieval core, which is centred on the main square, **Largo Padre Francisco Ferreira**. The square, in turn, is anchored by an octagonal *pelourinho* (pillory) dating from 1510. Another important gate, **Portas do Prado**, serves as the western entrance to the walled town.

Like many northern towns, Trancoso acquired a sizeable Jewish community following the expulsion of Jews from Spain at the end of the 15th century. As elsewhere along the border, you can generally spot Jewish houses by looking for a pair of doors: a smaller one for the private household and a larger one for a shop or warehouse. The old **judiaria** (Jewish quarter) covered roughly the southeast third of the walled town. Among dignified reminders of that time is a former rabbinical residence called the **Casa do Gato Preto**, decorated with the gates of Jerusalem and other Jewish images.

About 150m northward is Trancoso's prettiest church, the 13th-century **Capela de San-**

ta Luzia, with heavy Romanesque door arches and unadorned dry-stone construction. Trancoso abounds with other churches heavy with baroque make-up, most prominently the Igreja de São Pedro, behind the *pelourinho* on Largo Padre Francisco Ferreira.

Castelo
CASTLE

(⊙9.30am-12.30pm & 2-6pm Apr-Sep, 9.30am-12.30pm, 2-5.30pm Tue-Fri, to 5pm Sat, to 4.30pm Sun Oct-Mar) FREE On a hill in the northeast corner of town is the tranquil castle, with its crenellated towers and the distinctively slanted walls of the squat, Moorish Torre de Menagem, which you can climb for views. The friendly office here is a good source of local information in English.

Visigothic Tombs
TOMBS

FREE Across the road from the Portas do Prado, beside the courthouse, is an untended rock outcrop carved with eerie, body-shaped cavities, thought to be Visigothic tombs dating to the 7th or 8th century.

★ Festivals & Events

Feira Medieval de Trancoso
MEDIEVAL

In late June Trancoso heads back to its past with lots of dressing up, a medieval market in the castle area, jousting and more. It's lots of fun.

🛏 Sleeping

Ask at the *turismo* about *quartos* for rent.

Residencial Dom Dinis
GUESTHOUSE €

(🖉 271 811 525; www.domdinis.net; Av da República 10; s/d/tr €24/32/41; P 🖥) In a drab apartment block behind the post office, the Dom Dinis has spotless, if spiritless, remodelled rooms with wooden floors, plus a downstairs bar and restaurant. Breakfast is an extra €4.50 per person.

AROUND THE PLANALTO

While Trancoso and Almeida are the quintessential Planalto fortress-villages, three other towns are well worth a gander, though only if you have your own wheels – bus connections would be maddening in this sparsely populated region. With a car, you could see all three in a single, long day.

Located 30km northwest of Trancoso, **Sernancelhe** has a wonderfully preserved centre fashioned out of warm, beige-coloured stone. Sights include a 13th-century church that boasts Portugal's only free-standing Romanesque sculpture; an old Jewish quarter with crosses to mark the homes of the converted; several grand 17th- and 18th-century town houses, one of which is believed to be the birthplace of the Marquês de Pombal; and hills that bloom with what are considered to be Portugal's best chestnuts.

Heading northeast another 16km, you arrive at little **Penedono**, with its small but splendid **castle** (⊙9.30am-6pm Oct-Mar, 10am-7pm Apr-Sep) FREE. This irregular hexagon, with its picturesque crenellation, has fine views over the Planalto. It probably dates back to the 13th century and is a remarkable sight. The **turismo** (⊙9am-1pm & 2-5pm Mon-Fri, 9am-12.30pm & 2.30-5pm Sat, 2.30-5pm Sun) is below the castle.

Perhaps most impressive of all is **Marialva**, 25km southeast of Penedono. The beautiful upper part of the old town is dominated by a forbidding, 12th-century **castelo** (castle; adult/15-25yr €1.50/0.75, Sun morning free; ⊙10am-1pm & 3-7pm May-Sep, 9.30am-12.30pm & 2-6pm Oct-Apr) that guards over the rugged valley of the Rio Côa. Below its walls lies a haunting little village populated almost exclusively by black-clad widows knitting in the timeless shade. The castle ticket office functions as the *turismo*.

If you want to make an overnight trip of it, consider staying at Sernancelhe's 17th-century **Casa da Comenda de Malta** (🖉 254 559 189; www.casadacomendademalta.com; d from €65; 🏊), near the church in the old town, with well-equipped rooms, walled gardens and a pool. In Penedono, **Residencial Flora** (🖉 254 504 411; flora.residencial@gmail.com; Bairro do Prazo, Penedono; s/d €20/35), a short walk downhill from the *castelo*, offers plain but modern rooms with bathroom. The downstairs restaurant serves hearty Portuguese fare (mains €8 to €10). The hotel opposite the castle has a great location but mixed reviews from readers. Marialva has several appealing options, including the cushiest digs of all, at the luxurious **Casas do Côro** (www.casasdocoro.com.pt; s/d from €130/145; 🖥🏊), with a great location on the cobbled square by the castle.

Hotel Turismo de Trancoso
HOTEL €€

(☑ 271 829 200; www.hotel-trancoso.com; Rua Professora Irene Avillez; s/d €89/99; P⚙@🌐🏊) This welcoming modern hotel a short stroll from the old town has comfortable, Nordic-style rooms with blond wood, good space and balconies. It's attractively set around an interior atrium. Facilities are good, including an indoor pool and small gym. Good deals are usually available online, with prices midweek or in winter especially attractive.

✕ Eating & Drinking

Dom Gabriel
PORTUGUESE €

(Av Engenheiro Frederico Ulrich; mains €8-9; ☺ lunch & dinner Tue-Sun) Just outside the city walls, this is the town's best-value restaurant for solid local fare, with well-prepared meat dishes and a friendly attitude.

Casa da Prisca
DELI €

(☑ 271 811 196; www.casadaprisca.com; Rua da Corredoura 1; ☺ 9am-7pm) This centenarian shop specialising in regional cheeses and smoked meats just inside the Portas d'El Rei is a fun place to browse. Try the *sardinhas doces* (sweet sardines), a local fish-shaped confection made with eggs, almonds, cinnamon and chocolate.

Área Benta
PORTUGUESE €€

(☑ 271 817 180; www.areabenta.pt; Rua dos Cavaleiros 30A; mains €9-15; ☺ lunch & dinner) For regional cuisine presented with contemporary flair, try this swish, minimalist restaurant in an ancient stone town house. Specialities include *feijoada à transmontana* (a stew of red beans, pork and cabbage) and *cabrito assado com castanhas* (roast kid with chestnuts). Its lofty reputation isn't always matched by quality and service but it's still the town's best option. Downstairs is a lounge bar, an appealing place for a pre- or postdinner drink.

Bar Água Benta
BAR

(Rua dos Cavaleiros 36A; ☺ 10pm-3am Mon-Thu, to 4am Fri & Sat) Tucked away in the backstreets is this little cafe-bar, with a cheerful and youthful atmosphere, international beers, and occasional live music and karaoke.

ℹ Information

Espaço Internet (☑ 271 829 300; ☺ 9am-12.30pm & 1.30-6pm Mon-Fri) Free internet in Trancoso's Centro Cultural, two blocks south of the *turismo*.

Turismo (☑ 271 811 147; www.cm-trancoso.pt/turismo; ☺ 9am-12.30pm & 2-5.30pm Mon-Fri, to 5pm Sat, to 4.30pm Sun Oct-May, 9.30am-12.30pm & 2-6pm daily Jun-Sep)

ℹ Getting There & Away

BUS
From Trancoso's **bus station** (Av Calouste Gulbenkian), just northwest of the walled town, **Rede Expressos** (www.rede-expressos.pt) has services to Viseu (€6.80, 70 minutes, two to three daily), with connections via Celorico da Beira to Guarda (€8.90, 1¼ to 1¾ hours, daily).

TRAIN
The closest train station is at Celorico da Beira, 15km to the south.

Almeida

POP 1500 / ELEV 760M

After Portugal regained independence from Spain in the 1640s, the country's border regions were on constant high alert. Almeida, along with Elvas and Valença do Minho, became a principal defence against Spanish incursions. Almeida's vast, star-shaped fortress – completed in 1641 on the site of its medieval predecessor, 15km from Spain – is the least famous but the most handsome of the three.

When its military functions were largely suspended in 1927, Almeida settled into weedy obscurity. Nowadays, the fortified old village – designated as a national monument and recently scrubbed up for tourism – is a place of great charm: the town may have the disquieting calm of a museum, but it also has enough history and muscular grandeur to set the imagination humming.

◎ Sights

The **fortress** is on the northern side of 'new' Almeida. Most visitors arrive via the handsome **Portas de São Francisco**, two long tunnel-gates separated by an enormous dry moat.

The long arcaded building just inside the Portas de São Francisco is the 18th-century **Quartel das Esquadras**, the former infantry barracks. Make sure you also see the attractive **Picadero d'el Rey**, once the artillery headquarters, now a stable and riding school. Near this, the fort's **castle** was blown to smithereens during a French siege in 1810, when Britain's and Portugal's own ammunition supplies exploded. You can still see the foundations from an ugly catwalk.

Museu Histórico
Militar de Almeida   MUSEUM

(adult/child €3/free, with Sala de Armas & CEAMA €3.50/free; ⊙ 9am-5.30pm Tue-Sun Oct-Jun, 10am-6.30pm Tue-Sun Jul-Sep) This interesting museum is built into the *casamatas* (casemates or bunkers), a labyrinth of 20 underground rooms used for storage, barracks and shelter for troops in times of siege. In the 18th century these *casamatas* also served as a prison. Piles of cannonballs fill a central courtyard of the museum, with British and Portuguese cannons strewn about nearby.

Sala de Armas   MUSEUM

(adult/child €1/free; ⊙ 9.15am-5.15pm Tue-Sun Oct-Jun, 10am-6.30pm Tue-Sun Jul-Sep) This small display of swords and muskets in the exterior entrance to the Porta de São Francisco is an annexe of the town's historical museum.

CEAMA   MUSEUM

(Centro de Estudos de Arquitectura Militar de Almeida; adult/child €1/free; ⊙ 9am-5.30pm Tue-Sun Oct-Jun, 10am-6.30pm Tue-Sun Jul-Sep) This annexe of the historical museum has details on the construction of the fortress.

🛏 Sleeping & Eating

Pensão-Restaurante
A Muralha   GUESTHOUSE, RESTAURANT €

(✆ 271 574 357; www.amuralha.pt; Bairro de São Pedro; s/d €25/40; 🅿 ❄ 🛜) This functional, modern place sits 250m outside the Portas de São Francisco on the Vilar Formoso road. It has quiet, personality-free rooms that offer decent value and a large restaurant serving excellent local food (mains €7 to €11). The specials (€10 to €14) cost a little more but are definitely worth it.

★ Hotel Fortaleza de Almeida   HOTEL €€

(✆ 271 574 250; www.hotelfortalezadealmeida.com; s €75-100, d €85-110; 🅿 ❄ @ 🛜) This excellent hotel sits on the site of former cavalry quarters near the north bastion. A genuine personal welcome is offered and rooms are large and comfortable, all with giant windows and/or balconies; some have great views over the walls. Natural light and plenty of space is key to the relaxing feel, and there's a lovely restaurant area and terrace. Room 215 is a particular favourite.

Casa de Pedra   APARTMENT €€

(✆ 919 625 138; www.casadepedra.com.pt; Praça da Liberdade 9; apt €85-95; ❄ 🛜) On the same pretty square as Almeida's town hall, courthouse and post office, this comfortable apartment occupies a restored 17th-century stone house smack in the historic centre. Full of natural light and smartly done up with modern furnishings, it's a great spot. You can rent each floor separately or take the whole house. Breakfast is an extra €5.

ⓘ Information

The **turismo** (✆ 271 570 020; turismo.almeida@ cm-almeida.pt; ⊙ 9am-12.30pm & 2-5.30pm, from 10am Sat & Sun) is impressively located in an old guard-chamber within the Portas de São Francisco. Here you can get a map of the fortress and town.

ⓘ Getting There & Around

Nondrivers will almost certainly have to stay the night due to limited bus connections. There's weekday bus service to Celorico da Beira, from where you can change for destinations such as Coimbra and Viseu. There's also a daily bus to and from Guarda (€5.20, one hour).

Porto, the Douro & Trás-os-Montes

Why Go?

It's the dynamic Rio Douro that brings diversity to the province it has defined, with its granite bluffs, wine caves, medieval stone houses and steep, terraced vineyards. Porto, Portugal's second-largest city, is at its mouth; the world's oldest demarcated vineyards are close to the source; and scores of friendly villages in between have always relied on it for water, food and commerce. Come for the intricately carved cathedrals, baroque churches, palatial *quintas* (country villas), beaux-arts boulevards and 18th-century wine cellars.

Sandwiched between the Rio Douro and the Spanish border in Portugal's extreme northeast corner, ruggedly beautiful Trás-os-Montes is named for its centuries-long isolation 'behind the mountains'. Here, rural life is still the region's heart and soul, from the southwest's steep vineyard-clad hillsides, to the olive groves, almond orchards and rugged canyonlands of the sun-baked east, and the chestnut-shaded, heathery highlands of the north.

Best Places to Eat

➡ A Grade (p370)
➡ Casa de Pasto da Palmeira (p372)
➡ DOC (p394)

Best Places to Stay

➡ Guest House Douro (p366)
➡ 6 Only (p368)
➡ Quinta do Vallado (p391)

When to Go
Porto

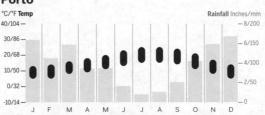

Jun 24 Festa de São João, Porto's biggest party: music, fireworks and plastic mallets.

Aug–Sep Lamego's Festa de Nossa Senhora dos Remédios runs for weeks.

Sep Hillsides of Trás-os-Montes hang heavy with grapes; hiking opportunities abound in parks.

Porto

POP 237,580

From across the Rio Douro at sunset, romantic Porto looks like a pop-up town. A colourful tumbledown dream with medieval relics, soaring bell towers, extravagant baroque churches and stately beaux-arts buildings piled on top of one another, illuminated by streaming shafts of sun. If you squint you might be able to make out the open windows, the narrow lanes and staircases zigzagging to nowhere.

Porto's historic centre is the Ribeira district, a Unesco World Heritage site where *tripeiros* (Porto residents) mingle before old storefronts, on village-style plazas and in the old houses of commerce where Roman ruins lurk beneath the foundations. On the downside, here and in other parts of the city centre stand many dilapidated early-20th-century town houses, left to crumble as the young and moneyed flee to the sprawling suburbs by the sea.

Yet despite signs of decay, in the last two decades Porto has undergone a remarkable renaissance – expressed in the hum of its efficient metro system and the gleam of Álvaro Siza Vieira's Museu de Arte Contemporânea and Rem Koolhaas' Casa da Música. More recently, the arrival of low-cost airlines has turned Porto into a popular weekend getaway; hence the boom in tourism.

Culturally, Porto holds its own against much larger global cities. The birthplace of port, it's a long-standing mecca for wine aficionados. Riverside wine caves jockey for attention in nearby Vila Nova de Gaia, with scores of cellars open for tastings. With appealing new kitchens springing up regularly, its palate is slowly growing more cosmopolitan. And thanks to a number of superb venues, Porto residents dance to many of the world's top rock, jazz and electronic artists. On warm summer nights many a plaza can feel like one enormous block party.

Of course, you'll be forgiven if what you remember most are the quiet moments: the slosh of the Douro against the docks; the snap of laundry lines drying in river winds; the shuffle of a widow's feet against cobblestone; the sound of wine glasses clinking under a full moon; the sight of young lovers discreetly tangled under a landmark bridge, on the rim of a park fountain, in the crumbling notch of a graffiti-bombed wall...

History

Porto put the 'Portu' in 'Portugal'. The name dates from Roman times, when Lusitanian settlements straddled both sides of the Rio Douro. The area was briefly in Moorish hands but was reconquered by AD 1000 and reorganised as the county of Portucale, with Porto as its capital. British-born Henri of Burgundy was granted the land in 1095, and it was from here that Henri's son and Portuguese hero Afonso Henriques launched the Reconquista (Christian reconquest), ultimately winning Portugal its status as an independent kingdom.

In 1387 Dom João I married Philippa of Lancaster in Porto, and their most famous son, Henry the Navigator, was born here. While Henry's explorers groped around Africa for a sea route to India, British wine merchants – forbidden to trade with the French – set up shop, and their presence continues to this day, evidenced in port-wine labels such as Taylor's and Graham's.

Over the following centuries Porto acquired a well-earned reputation for rebelliousness. In 1628 a mob of angry women attacked the minister responsible for a tax on linen. A 'tipplers riot' against the Marquês de Pombal's regulation of the port-wine trade was savagely put down in 1757. And in 1808, as Napoleon's troops occupied the city, Porto citizens arrested the French governor and set up their own short-lived junta. After the British helped drive out the French, Porto radicals were at it again, leading calls for a new liberal constitution, which they got in 1822. Demonstrations in support of liberals continued to erupt in Porto throughout the 19th century.

Meanwhile, wine profits helped fund the city's industrialisation, which began in earnest in the late 19th century, at a time when the elite in the rest of Portugal tended to see trade and manufacturing as vulgar. Today the city remains the economic capital of northern Portugal and is surpassed only by much-larger Lisbon in terms of economic and social clout.

Sights & Activities

Ribeira

The Ribeira district – Porto's riverfront nucleus – is a remarkable window into Porto's history. Along the riverside promenade, *barcos rabelos* (the traditional boats used to

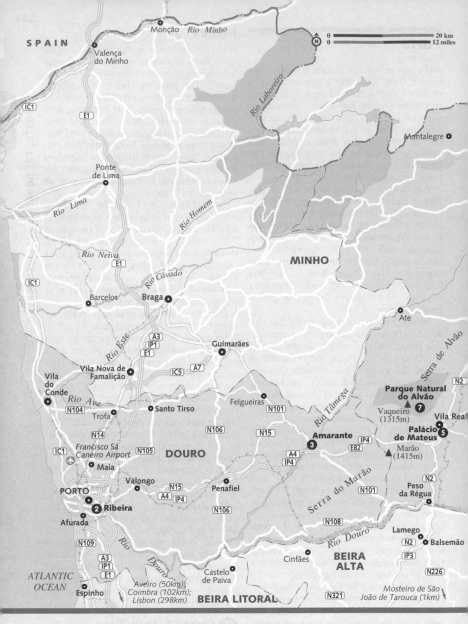

Porto, the Douro & Trás-os-Montes Highlights

1 Wine-taste your way around the picturesque vineyards of the **Alto Douro** (p392)

2 Lose yourself amid the medieval alleys of Porto's

cinematic district, **Ribeira** (p373)

3 Relax beside the Rio Tâmega and its medieval bridge in the charming town of **Amarante** (p385)

4 Come face to face with Palaeolithic artwork at **Parque Arqueológico do Vale do Côa** (p395)

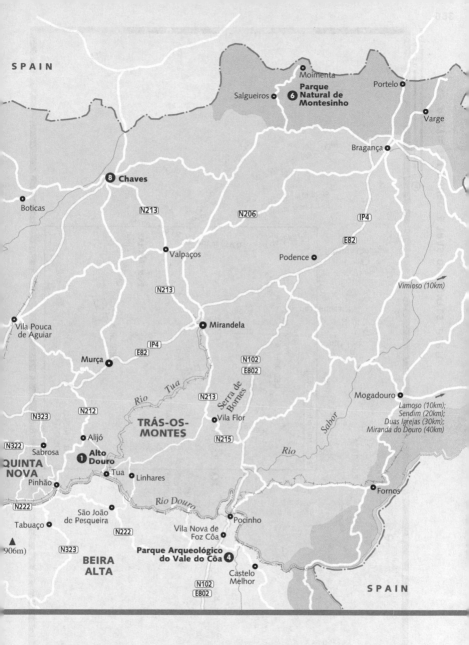

Moimenta

Parque Natural de Montesinho 6

Salgueiros

Portelo

Varge

Bragança

8 **Chaves**

Boticas

N213

N206

IP4

E82

Valpaços

Podence

Vimioso (10km)

N213

Mirandela

Vila Pouca de Aguiar

IP4

E82

Murça

N102

E802

Rio Tua

Serra de Bornes

N213

N323

N212

TRÁS-OS-MONTES

Vila Flor

Mogadouro

Lamoso (10km);
Sendim (20km);
Duas Igrejas (30km);
Miranda do Douro (40km)

N322

Sabrosa

Alijó

N215

Rio Sabor

QUINTA NOVA

1 **Alto Douro**

Pinhão

Tua

Linhares

Fornos

N222

São João de Pesqueira

Rio Douro

Tabuaço

N222

Pocinho

906m)

N323

BEIRA ALTA

Vila Nova de Foz Côa

Parque Arqueológico do Vale do Côa 4

Castelo Melhor

N102

E802

5 Stroll the formal gardens and taste fine wines at the stately 18th-century **Palácio de Mateus** (p397)

6 Hike across a medieval bridge or climb heather-draped hills to 21st-century windmills in **Parque Natural de Montesinho** (p411)

7 Swim in natural pools above the dramatic **Fisgas de Ermelo** (p400) waterfall in **Parque Natural do Alvão** (p400)

8 Take in the medieval tower and the 17th-century fortifications from the Roman bridge in **Chaves** (p403)

Porto

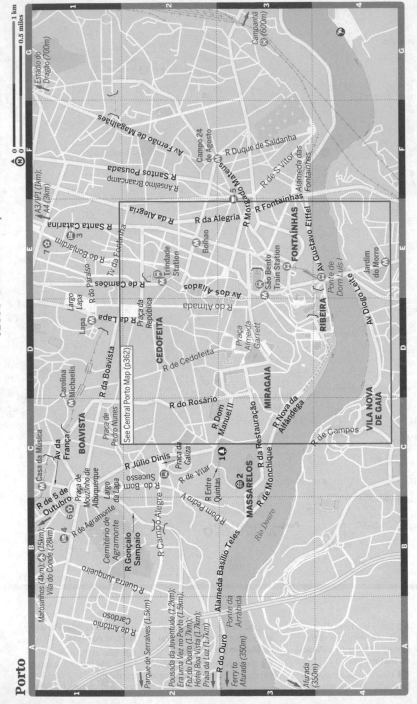

Porto

ferry port wine down the Douro) bob beneath the shadow of the photogenic Ponte de Dom Luís I. From here you have a fine perspective of the port-wine lodges across the river in Vila Nova de Gaia. It's also packed with flocks of tourists.

Sé
CATHEDRAL
(Map p362; Terreiro da Sé; cloisters adult/student €3/2; ⊙9am-12.15pm & 2.30-6.30pm daily Apr-Oct, to 5.30pm Nov-Mar) FREE From Praça da Ribeira rises a tangle of medieval alleys and stairways that eventually reach the hulking, hilltop fortress of the cathedral. Founded in the 12th century, it was largely rebuilt a century later and then extensively altered during the 18th century. However, you can still make out the church's Romanesque contours. Inside, a rose window and a 14th-century Gothic cloister remain from its early days.

Igreja de São Francisco
CHURCH
(Map p362; ☎222 062 100; Praça Infante Dom Henrique; adult/student €3.50/2.50; ⊙9am-8pm Jul-Aug, to 7pm Mar-Jun & Sep-Oct, to 6pm Nov-Feb) Sitting on Praça Infante Dom Henrique, Igreja de São Francisco looks from the outside to be an austerely Gothic church, but inside it hides one of Portugal's most dazzling displays of baroque finery. Hardly an inch escapes unsmothered, as otherworldly cherubs and sober monks are drowned by nearly 100kg of gold leaf.

Palácio da Bolsa
MONUMENT
(Stock Exchange; Map p362; Rua Ferreira Borges; tours adult/concession €7/4; ⊙9am-6.30pm Apr-Oct, 9am-12.30pm & 2-5.30pm Nov-Mar) This splendid neoclassical monument (built from 1842 to 1910) honours Porto's past and present money merchants. Just past the entrance hall is the glass-domed **Pátio das Nações** (Hall of Nations), where the exchange once operated. But this pales in comparison with rooms deeper inside, and to visit these you must join one of the half-hour guided tours, which set off every 30 minutes and are given in Portuguese, English, French, German and Spanish.

The highlight is a stupendous ballroom called the Salão Árabe (Arabian Hall), with stucco walls that have been teased into complex Moorish designs, then gilded with some 18kg of gold. There's also a restaurant and wine bar (the appropriately named 'O Comercial') for lingering amid the elegance.

Casa do Infante
HISTORICAL BUILDING
(Map p362; Rua Alfândega 10; adult/student €2.20/1.10, Sat & Sun free; ⊙10am-5pm Tue-Sun) Just back from the river is the handsomely renovated medieval town house where, according to legend, Henry the Navigator was born in 1394. The building later served as Porto's first customs house. Today it houses three floors of exhibits on the complex activities of the customs house throughout the centuries. In 2002 the complex was excavated, revealing Roman foundations as well as some remarkable mosaics – all of which are now on display.

Instituto dos Vinhos do Douro e do Porto
NOTABLE BUILDING
(Map p362; www.ivdp.pt; Rua Ferreira Borges 27; with wine tasting €5; ⊙11am-7pm Mon-Fri) When area vintners apply for the certification that ultimately christens their casks with the term 'Port' they bring vials to the labs set in this attractive relic just uphill from the river. The labs are off-limits to visitors, but you're welcome to explore the lobby exhibits, and the attached wine shop offers free tastings.

Igreja da Misericórdia
CHURCH
(Map p362; ☎222 074 710; Rua das Flores 5; adult/student €2/free; ⊙9am-noon & 2-5pm Tue-Fri, 9am-noon Sat & Sun) North of Largo de S Domingos on the distinctly Parisian Rua das Flores, you'll find the rococo facade of this 16th-century church, designed by the Italian baroque architect Nicolau Nasoni. The church's original nucleus is now a museum boasting a superb Renaissance painting known as *Fons Vitae* (*Fountain of Life*). The painting depicts Dom Manuel I and his

family around a fountain of blood from the crucified Christ.

Praça da Ribeira   SQUARE
(Map p362) Down by the river, narrow streets open out onto a plaza framed by austerely grand, tiled town houses overlooking a picturesque stretch of the Rio Douro. From here you have fine views of the port-wine lodges across the river as well as the monumental, double-decker Ponte de Dom Luís I.

Ponte de Dom Luís I   BRIDGE
(Map p362) Completed in 1886 by a student of Gustave Eiffel, the bridge's top deck is now reserved for pedestrians as well as one of the city's metro lines; the lower deck bears regular traffic, with narrow pedestrian walkways lining the road.

Its construction was significant, as the area's foot traffic once travelled across a bridge made from old port boats lashed together. To make matters worse, the river was wild back then, with no upstream dams. When Napoleon invaded in 1809, scores were crushed and drowned in the rushing river as a panicked stampede proved too much for the makeshift bridge.

Palacio das Artes   PALACE
(Map p362; Largo de S Domingos 16-22; ⊙9.30am-7pm Mon-Fri) Rotating exhibitions of mixed media, sculpture, photography and video art are curated by the cultural ministry and are usually worth a peek.

Igreja de Santa Clara   CHURCH
(Map p362; ☑222 054 837; Largo 1 de Dezembro; ⊙9.30-noon & 3.30-6pm Mon-Fri, 3-6pm Sat, 10am-11am Sun) East of the Sé, this humbler (but not too humble) church was part of another Franciscan convent. Gothic in shape, with a fine Renaissance portal, its interior is dense with elaborately gilded woodwork.

◉ City Centre

Rua Santa Catarina   STREET
(Map p362) Rua Santa Catarina is absurdly stylish and romantic with trim boutiques, striped stone pavements and animated crowds. At its southern end it opens out onto the lovely, eclectic Praça da Batalha, framed by Nasoni's gracefully baroque Igreja de Santo Ildefonso (Map p362; ☑222 004 366; Praça da Batalha; ⊙3pm-6pm Mon, 9am-noon & 3-6.30pm Tue-Fri, 9am-noon & 3-8pm Sat, 9am-12.45pm & 6-7.45pm Sun) with its twin bell towers, and the lavishly romantic Teatro Nacional São João, built in the style of Paris' Opéra-Garnier.

Avenida dos Aliados   STREET
(Map p362) Lined with bulging, beaux-arts facades and capped by the stately câmara

---

THE AZULEJO HUNTER'S GUIDE TO PORTO

Porto has some stunning tilework, with a wide range of stories unfolding on the city's old walls. One of the largest and most exquisite displays of *azulejos* (hand-painted tiles) covers the Igreja do Carmo. Silvestre Silvestri's magnificent 1912 panel illustrates the legend of the founding of the Carmelite order.

Along pedestrianised Rua Santa Catarina, the Capela das Almas (Map p362; Rua Santa Catarina 428; ⊙7.30am-1pm & 3.30-7pm Mon, Tue & Sat, 7.30am-7pm Wed-Fri, 7.30am-1pm & 6-7pm Sun) is a close second to Igreja do Carmo. Magnificent panels here depict scenes from the lives of various saints, including the death of St Francis and the martyrdom of St Catherine. Interestingly, Eduardo Leite painted the tiles in a classic 18th-century style, though they actually date back to 1929.

Hidden inside the Sé (p357), on the upper storey of the cloister (reached via a Nasoni-designed stairway), is Vital Rifarto's 18th-century masterpiece of *azulejos* that lavishly illustrate scenes from the *Song of Songs*.

Just off Av dos Aliados lies São Bento train station (Map p362). Completed in 1903, it seems to have been imported straight from 19th-century Paris, thanks to its mansard roof and imposing stone facade. But the dramatic *azulejos* in the front hall are the real attraction. Designed by Jorge Colaço in 1930, some 20,000 tiles depict historic battle scenes (including Henry the Navigator's conquest of Ceuta), as well as a history of transport.

Bringing the art of the *azulejo* up to date, the modernist, polychromatic *Ribeira Negra* by Júlio Resende celebrates life in the Ribeira district in a huge, tiled mural. Created in 1987, it's located at the mouth of the tunnel to the lower deck of the Ponte de Dom Luís I.

municipal (municipal council), this *avenida* recalls grand Parisian imitators like Buenos Aires and Budapest. Its central plaza was restored a few years back and often hosts pop-up-book, comic and art festivals and exhibitions.

Torre dos Clérigos
TOWER

(Map p362; Rua de S Filipe de Nery; admission €2; ⊙9am-6.30pm) Just uphill from Aliados you can get your bearings and bird's-eye photographs from the vertigo-inducing Torre dos Clérigos. Italian-born baroque master Nicolau Nasoni designed the 76m-high tower in the mid-1700s. To reach the top you must scale its 225-step spiral staircase.

Jardim da Cordoaria
PARK

(Map p362) Uphill from Aliados and past the Torre dos Clérigos lies the pleasantly leafy park known simply as 'Cordoaria'. Check out the four haunting sculptures by Spanish sculptor Juan Muñoz. The romantic, narrow lanes that run north from the Cordoaria and the Torre are the domain of Porto's hippest bars.

Centro Português de Fotografia
MUSEUM

(Portuguese Photography Centre; Map p362; www.cpf.pt; Campo dos Mártires da Pátria; ⊙exhibition hall 10am-12.30pm & 2-6pm Tue-Fri, 3-7pm Sat & Sun) FREE On the south side of Cordoaria is a stately yet muscular building (1796) that once served as a prison and now houses a photography museum. You actually walk through the thick iron gates and into the cells to see the work, which lends the intriguing exhibits even more gravitas. Immediately south of the museum are the narrow, atmospheric lanes that were once part of Porto's *judiaria* (Jewish quarter).

Igreja do São João Novo
CHURCH

(Map p362; ⊙8am-11am & 3-5pm Mon-Fri, 4.30-6.30pm Sat, 8am-10am Sun) FREE Set up a narrow maze of stone stairs, this medieval church with magnificent views was built in 1539 on land that was originally part of Porto's old Jewish quarter. It's a nice place to stop, take a breath and listen to sad fado tunes riding the wind.

Igreja do Carmo
CHURCH

(Map p362; Rua do Carmo; ⊙8am-noon & 1-6pm Mon & Wed, 9am-6pm Tue & Thu, 9am-5.30pm Fri, 9am-4pm Sat, 9am-1.30pm Sun) FREE Almost adjacent to the Cordoaria stands this striking *azulejo*-covered church, and one of Porto's best examples of rococo architecture.

Museu Nacional Soares dos Reis
MUSEUM

(Map p362; Rua Dom Manuel II 44; adult/student €5/2, 10am-2pm Sun free; ⊙10am-6pm Wed-Sun, 2-6pm Tue) A short walk west of Cordoaria lands you at the town's most comprehensive art collection, which ranges from Neolithic carvings to Portugal's take on modernism, all housed in the formidable Palácio das Carrancas.

Requisitioned by Napoleonic invaders, the neoclassical palace was abandoned so rapidly that the future Duke of Wellington found an unfinished banquet in the dining hall. Transformed into a museum of fine and decorative arts in 1940, its best works date from the 19th century, including sculptures by António Soares dos Reis (see especially his famous *O Desterrado, The Exile*) and António Teixeira Lopes, and the naturalistic paintings of Henrique Pousão and António Silva Porto.

◉ Boavista & West Porto

The sprawling roundabout at Praça de Mouzinho de Albuquerque roughly marks the boundary between 'old' and 'new' Porto. Here you'll find Casa da Música (p377), Porto's extraordinary concert hall.

Museu de Arte Contemporânea
MUSEUM

(www.serralves.pt; Rua Dom João de Castro 210; museums & park €7, park €3; ⊙10am-5pm Tue-Fri year-round, to 8pm Sat & Sun Apr-Sep, to 7pm Sat & Sun Oct-Mar) Set in a leafy, upmarket neighbourhood, off the grand Av da Boavista, is this arrestingly minimalist construction of vast, whitewashed spaces bathed in natural light, designed by the eminent Porto-based architect Álvaro Siza Vieira. Most of the museum is devoted to cutting-edge exhibitions, on show in nearby **Casa de Serralves**, a delightful pink art-deco mansion, though there's also a fine permanent collection featuring works from the late 1960s to the present.

Both museums are accessible on a single admission fee and are located within the marvellous 18-hectare **Parque de Serralves**. Lily ponds, rose gardens, formal fountains and whimsical touches – such as a bright-red sculpture of oversized pruning shears – make for a bucolic outing in the city. The estate and museum are 6km west of the city centre; take bus 201 from in front of Praça Dom João I, one block east of Av dos Aliados.

LOCAL KNOWLEDGE

CONTEMPORARY ARCHITECTURE HIGHLIGHTS

Álvaro Siza Vieira (Matosinhos, b 1933) and Eduardo Souto de Moura (Porto, b 1952) are two of Portugal's most acclaimed contemporary architects, both honoured with the prestigious Pritzker Prize.

Here, architect Bernardo Amaral, owner of Casa do Pinheiro (www.casadopinheiro porto.com), guides you through some of their most emblematic buildings, many of which are in Porto.

Álvaro Siza Vieira's Matosinhos

Start with Álvaro Siza Vieira's **Boa Nova Tea House** (1958–63; Av da Liberdade) in Leça da Palmeira, dramatically nestled in the rocks above the Atlantic, now sadly abandoned. Nearby is the **Tides Swimming Pool** (1961–66; Av da Liberdade), another Siza creation virtually invisible from the seafront boulevard, except for its horizontal copper cladding. A ramp leads the way through parallel walls of rough concrete, defining a sensorial promenade to the seashore. A must-stop for those with curiosity about Siza and his *oeuvre* is the family house he renovated in the 1960s, which now hosts the **Casa da Arquitectura** (Rua Roberto Ivens 582), an association that promotes architecture and organises exhibitions and tours.

Álvaro Siza Vieira's Porto

In **Serralves Contemporary Art Museum** (1991–99; Rua D João Castro 210), check out the fascinating dialogue that Siza created between the exhibition spaces and the modernist garden originally designed in the 1930s. Next pop by the Faculty of Architecture of Porto (1986–93), a fragmented building that faces the Douro, with a library that showcases a symmetrical skylight. Another hotspot on the Siza circuit is **Bouça Housing Cooperative** (1973–76, 2003–2006; Rua das Águas Férreas), originally conceived after the Carnation Revolution as a response to people's request for a place to live in.

Souto de Moura's Porto

Souto de Moura's **Burgo office tower** (1991–2007; Av da Boavista 1837) is a free interpretation of Mies van der Rohe's Seagram Building in Porto's urban landscape. Souto de Moura was also in charge of the most recent design of Porto's subway network (1997–2005); pay attention to the light and proportions of **Trindade** (Rua das Águas Férreas) and **Casa da Música stations** (Avenida de França), which also feature contemporary interpretations of Porto's traditional materials, such as granite stone and ceramic tiles. Souto de Moura is also behind the marvellous design of **4Rooms** (www.4rooms.org), an intimate guesthouse in the historic heart of Foz.

Souto de Moura's Braga

For more buildings designed by Souto de Moura, take a drive up north to Braga, which features some of his best works, including the **Municipal Stadium** and the **Carandá Cultural Market**. Nearby, in the village of Sta Maria do Bouro, you can experience a stay in **Pousada do Gerês – Amares**, ruins from a 12th-century Cistercian monastery that were rehabilitated by Souto de Moura into a lodge.

Bernardo Amaral runs guided tours, as do **Cultour** (www.cultour.com.pt) *and* **Porto Architourism** (www.portoarchitourism.com). *For a self-guided tour, pick up an architecture map of Siza and Souto de Moura's works, available at turismo offices in Porto.*

👁 Palácio de Cristal to Foz do Douro

Palácio de Cristal and, beyond it, the suburb of Foz do Douro, are both to the west of the city centre along the Douro. While it can get jumping on weekends, Foz do Douro is often peaceful on weekdays, especially if wisps of fog blow in off the Atlantic, bathing the cobbled upper reaches in cool mist.

Museu dos Transportes MUSEUM
(Map p362; www.amtc.pt; Rua Nova da Alfândega; adult/student €3/1.50; ⊘10am-1pm & 2-6pm

Tue-Fri, 3-7pm Sat & Sun) Set in the gorgeous 19th-century riverside customs house, this museum traces the motor car from its inception to the future. It does the same for radio and telecommunication.

Museu do Vinho do Porto
MUSEUM

(Port Wine Museum; Map p362; Rua de Monchique 45; admission €2.20, weekends free; ⊙10am-5.30pm Tue-Sat, 10am-12.30pm & 2-5.30pm Sun) Down by the river in a remodelled warehouse, this modest museum explores the impact of the famous tipple on the region's history in a series of largely interactive displays, though it doesn't offer much insight into the wine itself.

Jardim do Palácio de Cristal
PARK

(Map p356; Rua Dom Manuel II; ⊙8am-9pm Apr-Oct, 8am-7pm Nov-Mar) Sitting atop bluffs just west of Porto's old centre, this leafy park is home to a domed sports pavilion, the hi-tech Biblioteca Municipal Almeida Garrett and pleasant tree-lined footpaths with fantastic river views.

Museu Romântico
MUSEUM

(Quinta da Macieirinha; Map p356; Rua Entre Quintas 220; admission €2.20, Sat & Sun free; ⊙10am-5.30pm Mon-Sat, 10am-12.30pm & 2-5.30pm Sun) Nestled on the southern slopes of Jardim do Palácio de Cristal, beneath cathedral oaks and sycamores, is the small but stately home where the exiled king of Sardinia spent his final days holed up in 1843. The upstairs has been turned into a modest museum featuring the king's belongings and dainty period furnishings. Downstairs is the wonderful Solar do Vinho do Porto (Map p356; Rua Entre Quintas 220; ⊙4pm-midnight Mon-Sat).

◉ Vila Nova de Gaia

While technically its own municipality, Vila Nova de Gaia ('Gaia') sits just across the Rio Douro from Porto and is woven into the city's fabric both by a series of stunning bridges and by its shared history of port-wine making. Since the mid-18th century, port-wine bottlers and exporters have been obliged to maintain their 'lodges' – basically dressed-up warehouses – here. Today some 30 of these lodges clamber up the steep riverbank.

From Porto's Ribeira district, a short walk across Ponte de Dom Luís I lands you on Gaia's inviting riverside promenade. Lined with beautiful *barcos rabelos* – flat-bottomed boats specially designed to carry wine down

the Douro's once-dangerous rapids – the promenade offers grandstand views of Porto's historic centre. Here you'll find Gaia's turismo (Map p362; ☑223 703 735; www.cmgaia.pt; Av Diogo Leite 242; ⊙10am-6pm Mon-Fri, 10am-1pm & 2-6pm Sat), which dispenses a good town map and a brochure listing all the lodges open for tours.

Most people come here to taste the tipple, of course, and about 17 lodges oblige them. If you come in high season (June to September), you may feel yourself rushed in the largest lodges. Then again, you won't have to wait long for a tour in your native tongue. Note that most large houses charge for their tours (€2 to €3), though these invariably include free tastings.

Don't miss a ride on Teleférico de Gaia (Map p362; www.gaiacablecar.com; one-way/return €5/8; ⊙10am-8pm summer, 10am-6pm winter), an aerial gondola that provides fine views over the Douro and Porto on its short, five-minute jaunt. It runs between the southern end of the Ponte Dom Luís I and the riverside.

Espaço Porto Cruz
NOTABLE BUILDING

(Map p362; ☑220 925 340; www.myportocruz. com; Largo Miguel Bombarda 23) This swanky port wine emporium inside a restored 18th-century riverside building celebrates all things port. In addition to a shop where tastings are held (€5 for three ports), there are exhibition halls, a rooftop terrace with panoramic views and the DeCastro Gaia restaurant on the third floor, with renowned chef Miguel Castro Silva.

Mosteiro da Serra de Pilar
MONASTERY

(Map p362) Watching over all is this severe 17th-century hilltop church, with its striking circular cloister. Requisitioned by the future Duke of Wellington during the Peninsular War (1807–14), it still belongs to the Portuguese military and is closed to the public. The church is open for Mass every Sunday morning from 10am to noon.

Graham's
WINE TASTING

(Map p362; ☑223 776 484; www.grahamsportlodge.com; Rua do Agro 141; tours €5; ⊙9.30am-6.30pm daily) One of the original British-founded Gaia wine caves, recently renovated and now boasting a small museum, Graham's is a popular choice for tours, which include a tasting of three reserve wines. The brand-new Vinum restaurant (Map

Central Porto

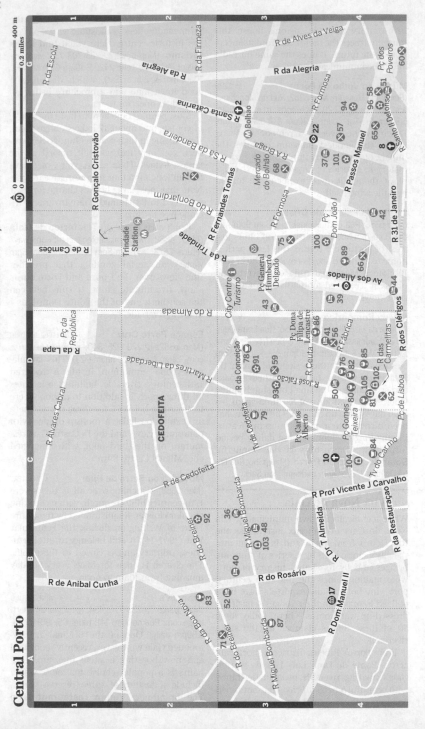

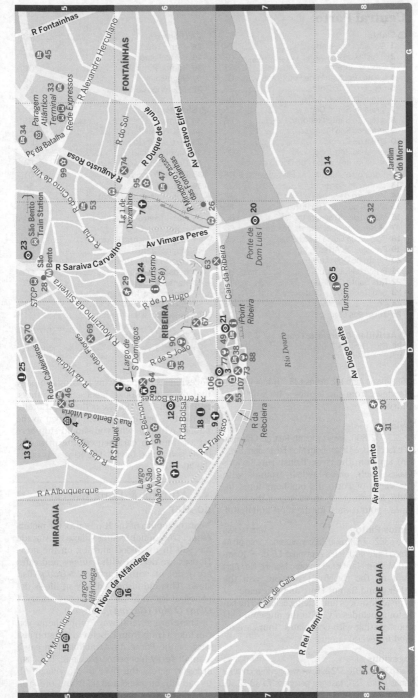

Central Porto

◉ Sights
1 Avenida dos Aliados E4
2 Capela das Almas G3
3 Casa do Infante D7
4 Centro Português de Fotografia C5
5 Espaço Porto Cruz................................E8
6 Igreja da Misericórdia..........................D6
7 Igreja de Santa Clara E6
8 Igreja de Santo Ildefonso F4
9 Igreja de São Francisco........................C6
10 Igreja do Carmo C4
11 Igreja do São João Novo C6
12 Instituto dos Vinhos do Douro e
 do Porto C6
13 Jardim da Cordoaria.............................C5
14 Mosteiro da Serra de Pilar F8
15 Museu do Vinho do Porto A5
16 Museu dos Transportes B6
17 Museu Nacional Soares dos Reis B4
18 Palácio da Bolsa...................................C6
19 Palacio das Artes D6
20 Ponte de Dom Luís I E7
21 Praça da Ribeira D7
22 Rua Santa Catarina...............................F4
23 São Bento Train Station........................E5
24 Sé E6
25 Torre dos Clérigos D5

◉ Activities, Courses & Tours
26 Blue Dragon Tours................................E6

27 Graham's...A8
28 Living Tours...E5
29 Porto Tours E6
30 Ramos Pinto..C8
31 Sogevinus..C8
32 Teleférico de Gaia.................................E8

⬤ Sleeping
33 6 Only...G5
34 B&B Hotel Porto F5
35 Dixo's Oporto Hostel.............................D6
36 Gallery Hostel..B3
37 Grande Hotel do Porto...........................F4
38 Guest House Douro................................D7
39 Hotel Aliados...E4
40 Hotel Eurostars das Artes.....................B3
41 Hotel Infante de Sagres........................D4
42 Hotel Teatro E4
43 Hotel Vera Cruz.....................................E3
44 InterContinental Porto...........................E4
45 Magnólia Hostel.....................................G5
46 Oporto Poets Hostel..............................D5
47 Pensão Astória.......................................F6
48 Pensão Favorita.....................................B3
49 Pestana Porto Hotel...............................D7
50 Porto Downtown Hostel.........................D4
51 Residencial Santo André.......................G4
52 ROSA ET AL Townhouse........................B3
53 Tattva Design Hostel..............................E5
54 Vinum A8

p362; Rua do Agro 141; mains €16-29) has incredible views from the terrace – it's worth the splurge.

Taylor's WINE TASTING
(☑223 742 800; www.taylor.pt; Rua do Choupelo 250; tours €3; ◷10am-6pm Mon-Fri, to 5pm Sat & Sun) Up from the river, British-run Taylor's boasts lovely, oh-so-English grounds with fine views of Porto. Its one-hour tours include a tasting of three top-of-the-range wines – your reward for the short huff uphill.

Ramos Pinto WINE TASTING
(Map p362; ☑936 809 283; www.ramospinto.pt; Av Ramos Pinto 400; tours & tastings €5-15; ◷10am-6pm Mon-Fri May-Oct, 9am-5pm Mon-Fri Nov-Apr) Right on the riverfront you can visit the rather grand Ramos Pinto and take a look at its historic offices and ageing cellars. The basic tour includes a visit to the museum plus a port tasting with chocolates. Tours are offered in several languages.

Sogevinus WINE TASTING
(Map p362; ☑916 372 896; www.sogevinus.com; Av Ramos Pinto 280; tastings per glass €1.30-22.50; ◷10am-7pm May-Oct, 10am-6pm Mon-Fri Nov-Apr)

Sogevinus is the port-wine holding company that owns the Kopke label, among others. Founded in 1638, Kopke is the oldest brand on the hill, but its lodge is not open to the public. Which is why you should stop here for the smooth caramelised bite of a seriously good aged tawny. The 10-year is tasty; the 20-year is spectacular.

◉ Afurada & Praia Estrela do Mar

Near the mouth of the Rio Douro, the picturesque, traditional fishing village of Afurada has salt in the blood and fog on the nose. Houses are decked with *azulejos* and cafes are redolent with hearty *caldeirada* (fish stew). This old-fashioned way of life is depicted in Pedro Neves' 2007 documentary *A Olhar O Mar* (*Gazing out to Sea*).

There are several ways to get here. You can take a tram from Ribeira to the stop just west of the Ponte da Arrábida, then catch a small **ferry** (per person/bicycle €1/1; ◷6am-midnight) across the river to the village. Alternatively, buses 93 and 96 from Cordoaria stop just across the bridge in Vila Nova de

Gaia. From here, it's a short walk along the boardwalk to Afurada.

Or you could rent a bicycle, propel yourself to the ferry, and continue west. You'll come upon the last swath of intact estuary, which runs into the back of a wide blonde beach that arcs perfectly to receive rolling surf.

Soft, golden, sheltered **Praia Estrela do Mar** is the best swimming beach in Porto. It's a 15-minute bike ride or 40-minute walk from Afurada, or you can take bus 902 from Boa Vista bound for Lavadores (via Ponte Arrábida), get off at the pedestrian path and walk 800m south.

🚶 Tours

Eco Tours WALKING TOUR
(☎220 108 096; www.ecotours.com.pt; Rua do Passeio Alegre 20; 4hr tour per person €70; ⊙9am-6pm Mon-Fri) This outfit offers English-walking excursions that take in the highlights of historic Porto before heading to Vila Nova de Gaia for port tasting. They also offer cruises (from €10).

Porto Tours TOUR
(Map p362; ☎222 000 045; www.portotours.com; Calçada Pedro Pitões 15, Torre Medieval; ⊙10am-7pm Mon-Fri, 9am-6pm Sat & Sun) Situated next to the cathedral, this excellent municipal service provides details of all the recommended tour operators, from city walking tours, Douro cruises and jaunts by Segway, bike and scooter to private taxi tours or helicopter rides over the city. As well as providing impartial advice, Porto Tours will make bookings for you

Living Tours TOUR
(Map p362; ☎228 320 992; www.livingtours.pt; Rua Mouzinho da Silveira 352-4; ⊙9am-7pm daily) A great range of sightseeing options are on offer at this friendly agency, from city tours (starting at €12) to fado dinners (€16.50) and day trips (€90) to the Douro and Minho.

Blue Dragon Tours TOUR
(Map p362; ☎222 022 375; www.bluedragon.pt; Avenida Gustavo Eiffel 280; tours from €10) A good range of bike tours of Porto and surrounds, as well as tours on foot and by Segway.

The Worst Tours
WALKING TOUR

(www.theworsttours.weebly.com) FREE A trio of out-of-work architects got together to offer free offbeat tours of Porto on foot, each with a different theme – from romantic to Sunday blues. Pay as much as you wish. Tours meet at Praça do Marquês.

River Cruises

Several outfits offer cruises in ersatz *barcos rabelos*, the colourful boats that were once used to transport port wine from the vineyards. Cruises last 45 to 55 minutes and depart at least hourly on summer days. You can board at Porto's Cais da Ribeira or Cais da Estiva, or at Vila Nova de Gaia's Cais de Gaia or Cais Amarelo. By far the largest carrier is **Douro Azul** (☑ 223 402 500; www.douroazul.com); **Barca Douro** (www.barcadouro.pt) and **Douro Acima** (www.douroacima.pt) are also solid choices.

🎆 Festivals & Events

There's a stream of cultural events throughout the year; check the main tourism website, www.portoturismo.pt, for details.

Fantasporto
FILM

(Porto International Film Festival; www.fantasporto.com) Two weeks of fantasy, horror and just plain weird films in February/March.

Festival Internacional de Teatro de Expressão Ibérica
THEATRE

(International Theatre Festival of Iberian Expressions; www.fitei.com) Two weeks of contemporary theatre in Spanish and Portuguese; held in late May/early June.

Serralves Em Festa
CULTURE

(www.serralvesemfesta.com) This huge event runs for 40 hours nonstop over one weekend in early June. Parque de Serralves hosts

---

PORTO FOR CHILDREN

The best spots for kids to let off some steam are Porto's numerous parks – the fenced, expansive Parque de Serralves (p359) is particularly kid-friendly. For beach fun, head to **Praia Estrela do Mar**. Kids might also enjoy a rattling journey in one of Porto's old **trams** (p380). The *turismo* offers a brochure called *Famílias Nos Museus* (*Families in Museums*), which lists a wide variety of activities designed just for kids throughout the city's museums.

---

the main events, with concerts, avant-garde theatre and kiddie activities; other open-air events happen all over town.

Festa de São João
RELIGIOUS

(St John's Festival) Porto's biggest party. For one night in June the city erupts into music, competitions and riotous parties; this is also when merrymakers pound each other on the head with squeaky plastic mallets (you've been warned).

Festival Internacional de Folclore
MUSIC

(International Folk Festival) A week-long festival in late July/early August attracting international groups.

Noites Ritual Rock
MUSIC

A weekend-long rock extravaganza in late August.

🛏 Sleeping

Porto's sleeping scene has experienced an incredible renaissance in the last couple of years, due to the influx of weekend visitors arriving with low-cost flights. Time-worn *residenciales* are slowly being replaced by contemporary hostels and guesthouses; and cool tourist apartments (look for the 'AL' sign) are now plentiful.

🛏 Ribeira

Dixo's Oporto Hostel
HOSTEL €

(Map p362; ☑ 222 444 278; www.dixosoportohostel.com; Rua Mouzinho da Silveira 72; dm €20, d €50; @ 🛜) Cool and colourful hostel on the 1st floor of a townhouse just up from the Ribeira. The staff are super-friendly, there's a shared kitchen with a top-floor terrace and a common lounge with games. Dorms, which have lockers, are clean and cosy, plus there's free breakfast and all-day tea and coffee.

★ Guest House Douro
GUESTHOUSE €€€

(Map p362; ☑ 222 015 135; www.guesthousedouro.com; Rua de Fonte Taurina 99-101; s €130-170, d €150-185; 🌸 @ 🛜) In a restored relic overlooking the Douro, these eight rooms have been blessed with gorgeous wood floors, plush queen beds and marble baths; the best have river views. There's a 1am curfew.

Pestana Porto Hotel
BOUTIQUE HOTEL €€€

(Map p362; ☑ 223 402 300; www.pestana.com; Praça da Ribeira 1; s/d €135/160; 🌸 🛜) Right on the Douro, this is one of Porto's most sophisticated sleeps. Rooms maintain a fine

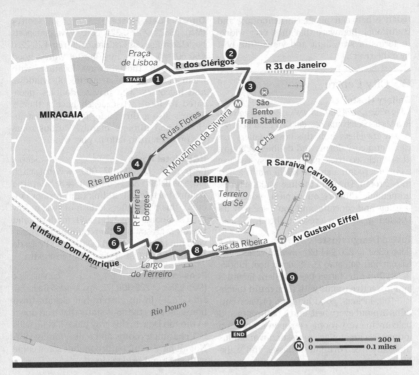

🏃 Walking Tour
Porto by Foot

START TORRE DE CLÉRIGOS
FINISH VILA NOVA DE GAIA RIVERFRONT
LENGTH 2KM, TWO TO THREE HOURS

Begin at the baroque **❶ Torre de Clérigos** (p359), which offers unrivalled views over Porto. Next, head down Rua dos Clérigos, passing the foot of **❷ Avenida dos Aliados** (p358) and pausing to admire the avenue's beaux-arts splendour. Just ahead, you'll see the French-inspired **❸ São Bento train station** (p358). Check out the astounding *azulejos* in its main hall. Now cross over to Rua das Flores, a lovely street dotted with second-hand booksellers, old-fashioned stationers and some enticing cafes.

Near the end of the street is Nicolau Nasoni's baroque masterpiece, the **❹ Igreja da Misericórdia** (p357). Cross Largo São Domingos to Rua Ferreira Borges, where you will pass the neoclassical **❺ Palácio da Bolsa** (p357). You can check out its main courtyard – once Porto's stock exchange – for free or stay on for a tour of its elaborate

interior. Just next door is the **❻ Igreja de São Francisco** (p357), with a severe Gothic facade hiding a jaw-dropping golden interior.

Head back up Rua Infante Dom Henrique and turn right on Rua da Alfândega, where you'll find the medieval **❼ Casa do Infante** (p357), the birthplace of Henry the Navigator and the site of some remarkable Roman ruins. Continue into the shadowy Ribeira district, following narrow, medieval Rua de Fonte Taurina as it opens onto the lovely **❽ Praça da Ribeira** (p358). From here, take a stroll along the Rio Douro, admiring Vila Nova de Gaia's port-wine lodges across the river. Next, walk across the Eiffel-inspired **❾ Ponte de Dom Luís I** (p358) to Gaia's **❿ waterfront esplanade**. Grab an outdoor table at one of the waterfront cafes and enjoy the splendid city views across the Ribeira over a much-deserved drink.

balance between plush contemporary and traditional. Be aware that they vary widely in terms of size, light and views (the best face the river).

City Centre

Gallery Hostel
HOSTEL €

(Map p362; ☑224 964 313; www.gallery-hostel.com; Rua Miguel Bombarda 222; dm €20-22, d €60; ⊚) A true travellers' hub, this hostel-gallery has clean and cosy dorms and doubles; a sunny, glass-enclosed back patio; a grassy terrace; a cinema room; a shared kitchen and a bar-music room. Throw in the free walking tours, homemade dinners on request, port wine tastings and concerts, and you'll see why it's booked up so often – reserve ahead.

Tattva Design Hostel
HOSTEL €

(Map p362; ☑220 944 622; www.tattvadesignhostel.com; Rua do Cativo 26-28; dm/d from €15/45; ⊚⊚) Top-rate Tattva has excellent facilities and attractive rooms with thoughtful touches – big lockers, good lighting, privacy curtains around every bed, and a bathroom and balcony in every room. The open-air rooftop lounge is a great place for a sundowner. Plus there are free Portuguese classes and walking tours.

Porto Downtown Hostel
HOSTEL €

(Map p362; ☑222 018 094; www.portodowntown hostel.com; Praça Guilherme Gomes Fernandes 66; dm €14-16, d €42; ℗⊚⊚) This popular hostel has large sunlit dorms with new beds, and common areas with shag rugs and beanbag chairs strewn about.

Magnólia Hostel
HOSTEL €

(Map p362; ☑222 014 150; www.magnoliahostel. com; Av Rodrigues de Freitas 387; dm €17-19, d €44-48; ⊚⊚) You'll find an excellent ambience at this attractive, well-maintained hostel with a range of rooms spread over three floors of a converted town house. There's a lounge with a spooky, out-of-tune piano, and a leafy outdoor space that sometimes hosts concerts. Breakfast is included, as are free walking tours.

Residencial Santo André
GUESTHOUSE €

(Map p362; ☑222 000 115; Rua Santo Ildefonso 112; s/d €20/35; ⊚) A charming four-floor walk-up with spiralled staircase and 10 oddly curvaceous rooms, some with bathrooms. They're all spic and span, but it's the smaller rooms that catch the most light. Set on a quiet street, it's a splendid cheapie.

Oporto Poets Hostel
HOSTEL €

(Map p362; ☑223 324 209; www.oportopoets hostel.com; Rua dos Caldeireiros 261; dm €20-22, d €50-60; ⊚) Lovely little hostel with a good central (but tucked-away) location, with clean and cosy dorms featuring big windows and balconies. The private doubles, decorated by local artists, each have a theme. There's also a tiny patio, free breakfast included and dinners nightly. Various tours are on offer, from fado to port wine.

B&B Hotel Porto
HOTEL €

(Map p362; ☑220 407 000; www.hotelbb.pt; Praça da Batalha 32-34; d €49; ℗❋⊚) Set in a restored art-deco building (and former cinema), this place offers a dash of style at low prices. Rooms are trim and modern, and there's a grassy if rather minimalist courtyard out the back. Good location on Praça da Batalha. Breakfast and parking cost extra.

Pensão Astória
GUESTHOUSE €

(Map p362; ☑222 008 175; Rua Arnaldo Gama 56; s/d €25/35) In an austere but elegant town house atop vertiginous stairs that lead down to the Rio Douro, this cosy place has no frills but charming rooms and a nice family vibe. Not all have a full bathroom but some come with river and bridge views.

★6 Only
GUESTHOUSE €€

(Map p362; ☑222 013 971; www.6only.pt; Rua Duque de Loulé 97; s/d €50/75; @⊚) This beautifully restored guesthouse has just six rooms, all with simple but stylish details that effortlessly blend old (such as wrought-iron decorative balconies) with contemporary. There's a lounge, a Zen-like courtyard and friendly staff.

★Pensão Favorita
GUESTHOUSE €€

(Map p362; ☑220 134 157; www.pensaofavorita. pt; Rua Miguel Bombarda 267; s/d €60/80; ⊚) An artful addition to Porto, Pensão Favorita has inviting rooms of ample size with big windows, mid-century furnishings and wide plank floors. The rooms in the redbrick addition out the back overlook the garden; there's also a lounge and restaurant (open Tuesday to Sunday) with outdoor seating, which does great lunch specials.

Castelo Santa Catarina
BOUTIQUE HOTEL €€

(Map p356; ☑225 095 599; www.castelosantacatarina.com.pt; Rua Santa Catarina 1347; s/d €65/75; ℗@⊚) This whimsical, late-19th-century, pseudo-Gothic castle is a fabulously over-the-top hideaway with palm-shaded, *azulejo*-smothered gardens and its own chapel. Choose between more elegant, period-furnished doubles in the castle and smaller rooms in a modern annexe. Reserve well in advance.

Hotel Eurostars das Artes
HOTEL €€

(Map p362; ☑ 222 071 250; www.eurostars hotels.com; Rua do Rosário 160-164; s/d €80/90; P ✳ @ ☎) This stylish hotel has a boutique feel with handsomely outfitted rooms featuring spare contemporary furnishings, sparkling marble bathrooms and wi-fi. There's also a lounge and a peaceful outdoor deck ideal for an afternoon drink. The rooms in the back are quieter.

Hotel Aliados
HOTEL €€

(Map p362; ☑ 222 004 853; www.hotelaliados.com; 2nd Fl, Rua Elísio de Melo 27 ; s/d €55/65; ✳ @ ☎) Set in one of Porto's beaux-arts buildings, this affordable hotel offers out-of-date and pokey but still decent rooms with wooden floors and dark-stained wood furnishings. Plaza-facing rooms are bright but can be noisy.

Hotel Vera Cruz
HOTEL €€

(Map p362; ☑ 223 323 396; www.veracruzporto hotel.com; Rua Ramalho Ortigâo 14; s/d from €50/60; ✳ @ ☎) Homey rooms with high ceilings off the *avenida*. The carpeting can be a bit aged, but suites have wood-tiled floors. The top-floor breakfast room is special.

InterContinental Porto
LUXURY HOTEL €€€

(Map p362; ☑ 220 035 600; www.ihg.com; Praça da Liberdade 25; r €245; P ✳ @ ☎) In a painstakingly restored former palace on the central Praça da Liberdade, this is a top choice for business and leisure visitors, with classic decor that nods to the building's history, a full spectrum of amenities and outstanding service.

ROSA ET AL Townhouse
GUESTHOUSE €€€

(Map p362; ☑ 916 000 081; www.rosaetal.pt; Rua do Rosário 233; s/d €129/169; ☎) This gorgeously done up town house in the thick of Porto's art district has six suites with hardwood floors and free-standing claw-foot tubs, and a lovely garden out the back. The restaurant serves delicious brunch from Wednesday to Sunday. There are rotating exhibits, cooking workshops and other fun events. It's pricey but worth the splurge. Rates exclude breakfast.

Grande Hotel do Porto
HOTEL €€€

(Map p362; ☑ 222 076 690; www.grandehotelporto. com; Rua Santa Catarina 197; s €74-145, d €74-155;

P ✳ ☎) Open since 1880, this proud old institution preserves a good deal of its grandeur, especially in its cavernous dining room and gilded parlour. Its renovated rooms are less distinguished but still plush.

Hotel Infante de Sagres
BOUTIQUE HOTEL €€€

(Map p362; ☑ 223 398 500; www.hotelinfante sagres.pt; Praça Dona Filipa de Lencastre 62; s/d from €162/180; P ✳ @ ☎) A time warp with well-coiffed doormen, crystal chandeliers and ornately decorated common areas, this place is a plush getaway in the heart of the city. Digs are modern with all the trimmings, though standard rooms are a little careworn and dark.

Hotel Teatro
BOUTIQUE HOTEL €€€

(Map p362; ☑ 220 409 620; www.hotelteatro.pt; Rua Sá Bandeira 84; s/d from €113/125; ✳ @ ☎) This design hotel stands in the spot of the 1859 Teatro Baquet, a swanky hideaway done up by interior designer Nini Andrade e Silva. The theatre theme prevails – the reception resembles a box office, while the rooms and suites come with weighty curtains, large mirrors, and bronzes and golds.

🛏 Boavista & Foz do Douro

Pousada da Juventude
HOSTEL €

(☑ 226 177 257; www.pousadasjuventude.pt; Rua Paulo da Gama 551; dm €15, d €36, d with private bathroom €42; P @ ☎) In a bright, modern building above the Rio Douro, the crown jewel of Portugal's hostels offers handsome doubles with balconies and sweeping river views, plus well-maintained four-person dorms. There's a restaurant and a supermarket nearby, but no kitchen. The hitch: it's 4km from central Porto. Take bus 207 from Campanhã station or bus 500 from Aliados.

Hospedarla Boavista
GUESTHOUSE €

(Map p356; ☑ 226 098 376; Av da Boavista 880; d €20-35; ☎) Eight spacious budget rooms await in your Porto grandma's house. The carpet may be industrial but the furniture is antique, the ceilings are high, the bathrooms gleaming, and the beds are firm in this solid cheapie. Rooms overlook *senhora*'s blooming veggie garden.

Hotel Boa Vista
HOTEL €€

(☑ 225 320 020; www.hotelboavista.com; Esplanada do Castelo 58; s/d €75/83; P ☎ ✳) A classic, 19th-century seaside inn outside and a modern, if somewhat characterless, hotel inside, the Boa Vista sits at the mouth of the

PORTO, THE DOURO & TRÁS-OS-MONTES PORTO

Douro, one block from the beach in the tiny neighbourhood of Foz do Douro. It's worth the extra €13 for a view of the fort and the sea. There are bikes for hire.

⭐ Vila Nova de Gaia

⭐Yeatman   RESORT €€€
(☑220 134 200; www.the-yeatman-hotel.com; Rua do Choupelo; s/d €248/263; ❄✿❄♨) Named for one of Taylor's original founders, the Yeatman is Porto's only true five-star resort, terraced and tucked into the Gaia hillside with massive Douro and Porto views. There's a Michelin-starred chef, huge guest rooms and suites with private terrace, a decanter-shaped pool, sunken Roman baths in the fantastic Caudalie spa, and all the amenities you desire. Discounts available for online bookings.

✖ Eating

Porto's restaurant scene has grown in leaps and bounds in recent years. Diners can enjoy traditional recipes from the north, contemporary Portuguese fusion fare or a medley of Italian, Indian and vegetarian dishes, and even sublime sushi. For dessert or breakfast, the cafes and patisseries around town keep locals in *pastéis de nata* (custard tarts).

Those wanting to self-cater should check out Porto's fantastic municipal market, the Mercado do Bolhão (p371), which is most alive in the morning and is a bastion of fresh fruit, flowers and fish.

✖ Ribeira & Around

Mercearia Das Flores   PORTUGUESE €
(Map p362; Rua das Flores 110; snacks €2.50-5.50; ⊙10am-7.30pm Mon-Thu, to 9pm Fri & Sat) This rustic-chic delicatessen food store serves all-day snacks made with organic regional products on the three tables and two

counters of its bright and airy interior. You can also order wines by the glass, tea from the Azores and locally brewed Sovina beer. Try the spicy sardines and salad on dark, sweet *broa* cornbread.

⭐Miss'Opo   PORTUGUESE €€
(Map p362; ☑222 082 179; www.missopo.com; Rua dos Caldereiros 100; small plates €2-9, Sun brunch €8-12; ⊙dinner Tue-Sun, brunch Sun) Don't miss dinner at this cool guesthouse in the maze of alleyways up from the Ribeira, with a stylishly rough-around-the-edges look and delicious small plates churned out of the tiny kitchen, which also serves Sunday brunch. Reserve ahead, especially on weekends. There are six lovely apartments upstairs, featuring blond wood and kitchenettes.

⭐A Grade   PORTUGUESE €€
(Map p362; ☑223 321 130; Rua da São Nicolau 9; mains €10-17.50; ⊙lunch & dinner Mon-Sat; ✍) Both a humble mum-and-dad operation and a masterwork of traditional fare, with generously portioned standouts such as baked octopus in butter and wine, and grilled seafood casseroles. Reservations recommended.

Don Tonho   SEAFOOD €€€
(Map p362; ☑222 004 307; Cais da Ribeira 13-15; mains €13-29; ⊙lunch & dinner) Built into ancient riverside ramparts, this elegant restaurant serves traditional Portuguese fare prepared with a contemporary twist. It serves up solid seafood, including fine *bacalhau* (dried salt-cod), and also boasts one of Porto's most extensive wine lists.

Ode Porto Wine House   PORTUGUESE €€€
(Map p362; ☑913 200 010; Largo do Terreiro 7; mains €19-21; ⊙dinner Tue-Sun) A slow-food hideaway just up from the Ribeira, with chestnut wood beams, exposed stone walls and slate tables on wine barrels. The

---

PORTO'S GRAFFITI ART

It glows everywhere. Alien words contorted into a visual language that all see and few understand. This three-dimensional scrawl appears on garage doors, crumbling ancient walls, empty storefront glass and neglected stucco. Maybe it's some postmodern, evolutionary art cycle, where the city chooses its worthy, salvageable relics and lets the bandit artists fix the rest. Usually they do it with loud blocky neon melting into a signature. Other times it's all straight lines and clear images: a stencilled pilgrim here, a cloaked bodhisattva there. These 'statements' (and what else can you call them?) are left untouched for days, weeks and sometimes years. There's no getting around it – when graffiti tolerance is this high, it becomes a sort of passive celebration. And in Porto the graffiti art deserves to be celebrated. It's massive, ubiquitous and spectacular – especially at the Lapa metro station.

GAY & LESBIAN PORTO

Porto's gays and lesbians keep it discreet in the streets, but let their hair down in Porto's numerous gay-friendly night spots. Most venues are clustered around Jardim da Cordoaria. Gay Pride festivities take place in the first or second weekend in July. Consult www.portugalgay.pt for listings, events and other information. Note that while there are no exclusive women's bars or clubs, all the places listed here are at least somewhat mixed.

Zoom (Map p362; Beco Passos Manuel; ⊙ 11pm-4am Fri & Sat) Located in an old warehouse, this is the gay dance hall of the moment, with some of the best electronic dance music in town and an often-mixed crowd.

Pride Bar (Map p356; ☑ 964 936 791; www.pride-bar.blogspot.com; Rua do Bonjardim 1121; ⊙ midnight-late Fri-Sun) Another favourite has live music, drag shows and go-go boys. Open very late.

Café Lusitano (Map p362; www.cafelusitano.com; Rua José Falcão 137; ⊙ noon-1.30am Mon-Thu, to 3.30am Fri & Sat) In a handsomely designed throwback to 1950s Paris, this intimate space hosts a mixed gay-straight crowd. Live music on Wednesday nights.

ingredients are all Portuguese – bread from Bragança, oregano from Algarve, smoked pork from Minho and sheep's cheese from Alentejo – and the dishes have a story. Reservations required.

Kyodai
SUSHI €€€

(Map p362; ☑ 936 335 483; Rua dos Mercadores 36; per person €17-25; ⊙ lunch & dinner Tue-Sun) Top-notch sushi is served in this back-alley Porto hole-in-the-wall and prepared by Brazilian chefs who collectively have 54 years of fish-carving and rolling experience. They hand-select their fish every day, and create an ever-changing set menu. Reserve ahead.

DOP
PORTUGUESE €€€

(Map p362; ☑ 222 014 313; www.ruipaula.com; Largo de S Domingos 18; mains €29-30; ⊙ lunch & dinner Tue-Sat, dinner Mon) Sit at the 'long table' and watch the chef prepare tapas tableside, or find a romantic corner and linger over duck risotto and a bottle of Douro red. Porto's upper crust digs it.

✗ Central Porto

★ Casa Guedes
TASCA €

(Map p362; Praça dos Poveiros 130; mains €3.75-5.50; ⊙ lunch & dinner Mon-Sat) Come for tasty, filling and cheap meals, or for the famous pork sandwiches, served all day. Space is tight and this no-frills *tasca* is among Porto's favourites, so be prepared to wait for a table, inside or on the nice little terrace on the square.

Mercado do Bolhão
MARKET €

(Map p362; Rua Formosa; ⊙ 7am-5pm Mon-Fri, to 1pm Sat) Just east of Aliados lies the 19th-century, wrought-iron Mercado do Bolhão, where earthy vendors sell fresh produce, including cheeses, olives, smoked meats, fresh flowers and more.

O Buraco
PORTUGUESE €

(Map p362; Rua do Bolhão 95; mains €5-7; ⊙ lunch & dinner Mon-Sat) As old school as old school gets, this longstanding restaurant on the ground floor of an unassuming office building seems frozen in time, with its polished wood interiors and chequered tablecloths. It draws in a mix of neighbourhood locals and architects for its big cheap portions of simple fish and meat dishes.

Casa Santo António
TAPAS €

(Map p362; Rua S Bento da Vitória 80; snacks €1-5; ⊙ lunch & dinner Tue-Sat) Behind the blue door of this traditional hole-in-the-wall, you can fill up on simple but deliciously prepared *petiscos*. If you find a spot, that is (it gets very busy in the evenings). Their new location on Rua da Fábrica is a more contemporary clean-lined version of the original, serving small bites from 4pm till 2am.

Cafe Santiago
CAFETERIA €

(Map p362; Rua Passos Manuel 226; mains €8.75-12; ⊙ lunch & dinner Mon-Sat) One of the best places to try Porto's classic belly-filling treat, the *francesinha* – a thick open-faced sandwich, piled with cheese, sausage, egg and/or assorted other meats, plus a tasty rich sauce.

Padeirinha Doce
CAFE €

(Map p362; Rua Augusto Rosa 46; pastries €1-3; ⊙ breakfast & lunch daily, dinner Mon-Sat) The croissants are stuffed with ham and cheese, and the muffins are packed with walnuts. The chocolate éclairs are sinful, *pastéis de nata* flaky and sweet, the orange juice fresh squeezed and the espresso rocket-fuelled. Naturally this hole-in-the-wall is crammed with locals every morning.

Pedro dos Frangos
GRILL HOUSE €
(Map p362; Rua do Bonjardim 223; mains €4.50-9.50; ⊘ lunch & dinner) *Frango no espeto* (spit-roasted chicken) is the name of the game at this extremely popular and inexpensive grill. Grab a spot at the stand-up counter and join the good ol' boys for a filling meal (abundant chips included).

Nakité
VEGETARIAN €
(Map p362; Rua do Breiner 396; mains €5-9.50; ⊘ lunch & dinner; 🖫) 🍃 This pleasant vegetarian restaurant has satisfying daily specials featuring tofu, seitan and tempeh paired with goat cheese, shiitake mushrooms and other fresh ingredients. Dine inside (amid piped-in New Age tunes) or on the back patio next to a gurgling fountain.

Clérigos Vinhos e Petiscos
PORTUGUESE €€
(Map p362; Passeio dos Clérigos, Rua das Carmelitas 151; small bites €2-10; ⊘ lunch & dinner Tue-Sun) The tapas bar is the best thing about this swanky new spot in the spruced-up Clérigos centre. The restaurant is decent but it's the *petiscos* that steal the show, from Kobe *picanha* to shellfish *açorda*. Sit on the black-and-white stools sampling the small bites and pair them with your pick of wine by the glass from a vending machine.

Flor dos Congregados
PORTUGUESE €€
(Map p362; Travessa dos Congregados 11; mains €8-15; ⊘ lunch Tue-Sat, dinner Mon-Sat) Tucked away in an alley, and through a narrow iron-and-glass entry is this two-floor dining room with exposed stone walls, wooden beams and a frequently changing blackboard menu. Great €6 lunch specials and all-day layered sandwiches.

Café Vitória
INTERNATIONAL €€
(Map p362; Rua José Falcão 156; mains €7.50-15; ⊘ noon-midnight Mon, Wed & Thu, 2pm-2am Fri & Sat) Head to this little-known gem for lighter fare in the cafe downstairs (good-value weekday lunch specials) and heartier Portuguese dishes in the elegant upstairs dining room (open Wednesday to Saturday evenings). There's a pleasant garden out the back, and a festive cocktail-sipping scene on weekends.

Casa d'Oro
ITALIAN €€
(Alameda Bastio Teles 797; pizzas €8-12; ⊘ lunch & dinner) This concrete-and-glass clay-oven pizzeria leaning over the Rio Dour, just up-river from the mouth, does terrific pizzas including *diavola* (spicy salami and oregano), *Vesuvio* (sausage and broccoli) and *fichi e prosciutto* (prosciutto and fig).

Book
PORTUGUESE €€€
(Map p362; 🖉 917 953 387; Rua do Aviz 10; mains €10.50-23) One of Porto's hottest tables, this place has a library theme and buzzes with a mix of well-heeled locals and tourists. The decor is a mix of industrial and classic, and dishes are modern takes on Portuguese mainstays, like baked kid goat with turnip greens, and partridge pie with a ginger and orange sauce. Service can be slow. Book ahead.

Escondidinho
PORTUGUESE €€€
(Map p362; www.escondidinho.com.pt; Rua Passos Manuel 144; mains €15-28; ⊘ lunch & dinner) Amid *azulejos*, dark wood furnishings and starched white place settings, Escondidinho serves solid traditional cuisine to a mainly tourist clientele, hence the slightly inflated prices. Chefs here combine fresh ingredients and a wood-burning oven to create classic dishes.

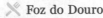

Afurada

Taberna São Pedro
SEAFOOD €€
(Rua Agostinho Albaño 84, Afurada; mains €6-10; ⊘ lunch daily, dinner Mon-Sat) Fado scales the *azulejo* walls, toddlers tear through the dining room, plump and oily sardines (and other fresh fish) are roasted on pavement grills, and you can almost smell the tart snap of *vinho verde* in the air. There's much to love in this forever-packed, salt-of-the-earth local seafood house. It's located one block inland from the ferry pier.

Foz do Douro

★ Casa de Pasto da Palmeira
PORTUGUESE €€
(Rua do Passeio Alegre 450; mains €6.30-13.70; ⊘ lunch & dinner Tue-Sun) An adorable eatery right on the waterfront with two small colourful rooms featuring contemporary artwork and a few tables on the front patio. The creative small-size dishes change daily – think hake and shrimp *moqueca* with banana and coriander, and *alheira* rolls with turnip sprouts. A cool local find.

Bar Tolo PORTUGUESE €€

(☎224 938 987; Rua Senhora da Luz 185; mains €10-17) A fun little spot in a tall, narrow, sky-blue corner building, with a tiny rooftop terrace sporting an ocean view, a rustic-chic vibe and a menu of creative *petiscos* and mains.

Shis FUSION €€€

(☎226 189 593; www.shisrestaurante.com; Praia do Ourigo; mains €20-25; ☺lunch & dinner) Perched above the thrashing sea is this fashionable white dining room with funky Chinese lanterns, Eames chairs and lighthouse views. The sushi bar is very good, and so are the creative mains, such as duck ravioli and tuna with balsamic-infused teriyaki sauce. There's also a cafe, if you don't want to splurge.

🍸 Drinking & Nightlife

They may have a strong work ethic, but that doesn't stop *tripeiros* from partying – the city has a club scene that is at once sophisticated and largely devoid of elitism. Porto also boasts a rich theatre and music scene. To keep pace pick up *Agenda do Porto*, a monthly cultural events brochure, or scan the daily *Jornal de Notícias*.

🍷 Ribeira

Vinologia WINE BAR

(Map p362; Rua de São João 46; ☺4pm-midnight) This cosy wine bar is an excellent place to sample the fine quaffs of Porto, with over 200 different ports on offer. If you fall in love with a certain wine, you can usually buy a whole bottle (or even send a case home).

Café Bar O Cais BAR

(Map p362; Rua Fonte Taurina 2a; ☺9pm-3am daily) A loyal clientele crowds this funky, classic-rock-drenched basement bar with old stone walls and vinyl booths.

Sahara LOUNGE

(Map p362; Caís da Estiva 4; ☺6pm-2am Mon-Thu, 11am-2am Fri-Sun) Decked out like an Arabian hideaway, this loungey place has hookahs in its nooks and crannies, a young garrulous crowd, the occasional belly dancer and pavement seating for taking in the passing people parade.

🍷 City Centre

Nightlife rules in central Porto with some eclectic bar-gallery spaces leading the way. It's worth exploring the narrow cobblestone streets just north of Rua das Carmelitas, which become an all-out street party (especially Rua Galeria de Paris, Cândido dos Reis and Conde de Vizela) on warm summer nights and on weekends throughout the year. Nearby, there is also a lively (downmarket) scene at open-air cafe-restaurants on Praça de Parada Lentão, around the corner from the Jardim da Cordoaria.

Café Candelabro CAFE

(Map p362; Rua da Conceição 3; ☺10am-2am Mon-Sat) Cool cafe-bar in a former bookstore, with a boho crowd and a retro vibe featuring black-and-white mosaic tile floors, bookcases with old books and magazines, and big windows opening out to the street. It gets busy, with blasting techno on weekend nights.

Duas de Letra CAFE

(Map p356; Passeio de Sao Lázaro 48; ☺10am-8pm Tue-Thu & Sun, to 2am Fri & Sat) Artsy cafe overlooking a leafy square, with a low-key vibe, wooden ceilings, an old bike mounted on the ceiling, an exhibition space upstairs with rotating exhibits and two patios. The snacks are delicious, and there's a great tea selection.

Casa do Livro LOUNGE

(Map p362; Rua Galeria de Paris 85; ☺6pm-3am Mon-Thu, 6pm-4am Fri & Sat) Vintage wallpaper, gilded mirrors and walls of books give a discreet charm to this nicely lit beer and wine bar. On weekends, DJs spin funk, soul, jazz and retro sounds in the back room. There's a €5 door charge.

Rota do Chá TEAHOUSE

(Map p362; www.rotadocha.pt; Rua Miguel Bombarda 457; tea €2.50; ☺11am-8pm Mon-Thu, noon-midnight Fri & Sat, 1-8pm Sun) This proudly bohemian cafe has a verdant but rustic back garden where students and the gallery crowd sit around low tables sampling from an enormous 300+ tea menu divided by region. Tasty snacks include quiches, muffins, scones and toast. They serve weekend brunches and weekday lunch specials.

Piolho Douro CAFE

(Map p362; Praça Parada Leitão 41; ☺8am-midnight Mon-Thu, to 2am Fri & Sat) Old school, still cool, and crazy popular on weekends when college kids pack the communal tables, lean against thick columns, and sip cold, cheap draughts or strong coffee. Take your poison inside or out in the glass box dining room on the plaza.

PORT WINE 101

With its intense flavours, silky textures and appealing sweetness, port wine is easy to love, especially when it is taken with its proper accompaniments: cheese, nuts and dried fruit. Ports are also wonderfully varied, and even non-connoisseurs can quickly learn to tell an aged tawny from a late-bottled vintage (LBV). For a friendly primer on all things port, head to the convivial Vinologia (p373), where the learned owner gives an enlightening lesson with each glass he pours (English and French spoken). From here, you can also head across the Douro to Vila Nova de Gaia to taste the output of particular houses. Finally, impress friends and loved ones by leading your own tour through the offerings at the remarkable Solar do Vinho do Porto (p361).

History

It was probably Roman soldiers who first planted grapes in the Douro valley some 2000 years ago, but tradition credits the discovery of port itself to 17th-century British merchants. With their own country at war with France, they turned to their old ally Portugal to meet their wine-drinking needs. The Douro valley was a particularly productive area, though its wines were dark and astringent. According to legend, the British threw in some brandy with grape juice, both to take off the wine's bite and to preserve it for shipment back to England – and port wine was the result. In fact, the method may already have been in use in the region, though what's certain is that the Brits took to the stuff. Their influence has been long and enduring, a fact that is still evidenced by some of port's most illustrious names including Taylor's, Graham's and Cockburn's.

The Grapes

Port-wine grapes are born out of adversity. They manage to grow on rocky terraces with hardly any water or even soil, and their roots must reach down as far as 30m, weaving past

Praça BAR
(Map p362; Praça D Filipa de Lencastre 193; ⊙ 6pm-2am Mon-Sat) The busiest of a string of usually happening bars across from Hotel Infante do Sangres. It is a bit too bright inside, but the white walls, marble bar, reggae tunes and tropical cocktails (think mojitos, margaritas and *caipirinhas*) keep the young and hip lubricated and happy.

Plano B BAR
(Map p362; Rua Cândido dos Reis 30; ⊙ closed Aug; 🛜) This creative space has an art gallery in front, a tall-ceilinged cafe (with free wireless access) in the back, and a cosy downstairs where DJs and live bands hold court. Much like the crowd, the programming is truly eclectic, with performance art, theatre and art openings held regularly.

Galeria de Paris BAR
(Map p362; Rua Galeria de Paris 56) The original on the strip that's now synonymous with the Porto party scene, this whimsically decorated spot has toys, thermoses, old phones and other assorted memorabilia lining the walls. In addition to cocktails and draught beer, you'll find tapas at night.

Café Au Lait BAR
(Map p362; Rua Galeria de Paris 44; ⊙ 11.30am-2am Mon-Sat) A narrow, intimate bar attracting a lively but unpretentious artsy crowd. In addition to cocktails, there are snacks and salads, including vegetarian fare. DJs spin from Wednesday to Saturday night, adding to the good cheer.

Casa de Lo CAFE
(Map p362; Tv de Cedofeita 20 A; ⊙ 2pm-2am Mon-Sat, to 8pm Sun) Hidden off a narrow alley is this boho coffee house beloved by area hipsters. Think thick stone walls, old timber-beamed ceilings, a nice little patio out the back, funky downbeat tunes and a pretty and pouty artsy crowd. DJs spin on Friday and Saturday.

Café Guarany CAFE
(Map p362; www.cafeguarany.com; Av dos Aliados 89; ⊙ 9am-midnight) With a sunny, tiled interior, marble-top tables and an Afro-Brazilian mural, this classy affair has attracted the business and literary elite since the 1930s. It regularly has live music, and serves full meals.

Café Majestic CAFE
(Map p362; Rua Santa Catarina 112; snacks €2-4; ⊙ 9.30am-midnight Mon-Sat) Porto's best-known

layers of acidic schist (shale-like stone) to find nourishment. Vines endure both extreme heat in summer and freezing temperatures in winter. These conditions produce intense flavours that stand up to the infusions of brandy. The most common varietals are hardy, dark reds such as *touriga, tinto cão* and *tinto barroca*.

The Wine

Grapes are harvested in autumn and immediately crushed (often still by foot) and allowed to ferment until alcohol levels reach 7%. At this point, one part brandy is added to every five parts wine. Fermentation stops immediately, leaving the unfermented sugars that make port sweet. The quality of the grapes, together with the ways the wine is aged and stored, determines the kind of port you get. The most common include the following:

Ruby – made from average-quality grapes, and aged at least two years in vats; rich, red colours and sweet, fruity flavours.

Tawny – made from average-quality grapes, and aged for two to seven years in wooden casks; mahogany colours, drier than ruby, with nuttier flavours.

Aged tawny – selected from higher-quality grapes, then aged for many years in wooden casks; subtler and silkier than regular tawny; drinks more like brandy or cognac than wine.

Vintage – made from the finest grapes from a single year (and only select years qualify), aged in barrels for two years, then aged in bottles for at least 10 years (and up to 100 or more); dark ruby colours, fruity yet extremely subtle and complex.

Late-bottled vintage (LBV) – made from very select grapes of a single year, aged for around five years in wooden casks, then bottled; similar to vintage, but ready for immediate drinking once bottled, and usually smoother and lighter bodied.

tea shop is packed with prancing cherubs, opulently gilded woodwork, leather seats and gold-braided waiters who'll serve you an elegant set breakfast, afternoon tea or any number of snacks and beverages.

Villa CLUB
(Map p362; Travessa dos Congregados 64; ⊙ vary) This block-long club was opened by Ibiza promoters. It can feel empty on any given night, but it is known to get wild when they pack the place for special events.

Era Uma Vez no Porto BAR
(Map p362; Rua das Carmelitas 162) Artwork lines the walls of this cosy, low-lit Baixa bar popular with a younger grungy crowd. There's a mellow buzz to the place, making it a fine retreat from the mayhem of nearby Rua Galeria de Paris. Step onto the tiny balcony for views of the Torre dos Clérigos across the way.

Palácio de Cristal to Foz do Douro

All of the places listed here can be reached via the night bus 1M from Aliados.

Praia da Luz BAR
(Av Brasil; ⊙ 9am-2am) Praia da Luz is a worthwhile stop when out exploring Porto's coastline. It rambles over tiered wooden decks to its own private rocky cove, and while you should probably skip the food, you should definitely enjoy a cocktail. Bring a sweater. It's about 500m north of the Castelo de São João.

Gato Vadio BAR
(Map p362; Rua do Rosário 281; ⊙ 5pm-midnight Thu-Sun summer & spring, 7pm-midnight Wed-Sun autumn & winter) This cultural association runs an artsy cafe-bar that does film screenings, readings and occasional dinner parties. There's a nice little patio out the back, and you can order cakes, cookies and nice teas, and a full bar is also on offer.

Indústria CLUB
(www.industria-club.com; Av do Brasil 843; ⊙ 11.30pm-4am Thu-Sat) This basement club – owned by Antonio Pereira (aka DJ Vibe), his girlfriend and Portugal celebrity, Merche Romero – was recently re-modelled and still serves up deep house to a crowd that generally skews young. Take bus 1M and get off at the Molhe stop.

Twins
CLUB

(Passeio Alegre 1000; ⊙ 11pm-6am Thu-Sat) Set in a quaint 19th-century seaside home, this club rumbles into the wee hours as great house tunes keep the party rolling for the moneyed pretty people. It's a bit out of the way, but that breeze does feel good at dawn. There's also a downtown Twins lounge on Cândido dos Reis.

Elsewhere in Porto

Vogue
CLUB

(www.vogueporto.com; Av Fontes de Pereira de Melo 481; ⊙ 11.30pm-4am Wed-Sat) This was the only place to dance on Wednesday nights at research time. The crowd is often trendy, and the music bounces from electronica to house.

☆ Entertainment

Fado

Porto has no fado tradition of its own, but you can enjoy the Lisbon or Coimbra versions of 'Portuguese blues' into the wee hours at several places in town. **Restaurante O Fado** (Map p362; ☎ 222 026 937; www. ofado.com; Largo de São João Novo 16; ⊙ 8.30pm-2am Mon-Sat) is a great option, but an even greater spot is **Casa da Mariquinhas** (Rua S Sebastião 25; ⊙ 5pm-1am Wed-Thu, 5pm-2am Fri-Sat), which has fado nightly from Wednesday to Saturday. Another good stop on the fado circuit is **O Mal Cozinhado** (Rua do Outeirinho 13; ⊙ 8.30pm-midnight Mon-Sat).

Music & Theatre

The Casa da Música has quickly become the city's premier music venue.

Maus Hábitos
PERFORMING ARTS

(Map p362; www.maushabitos.com; 4th Fl, Rua Passos Manuel 178) This creatively decorated multiroom space hosts a culturally ambitious agenda. Changing art exhibits and imaginative installations adorn the walls, while live bands and DJs work the small stage. Hidden within, there's also an inexpensive vegetarian pizzeria (open for lunch Monday to Friday).

Breyner 85
LIVE MUSIC

(Map p362; www.breyner85.com; Rua do Breiner 85; ⊙ 3-9pm Mon, to 2am Tue-Sun) This creative space in a two-floor town house features an eclectic line-up of bands covering rock, jazz and blues. The large grassy terrace is a treat. Concerts start at around 11pm. Sunday night's jam sessions are particularly popular.

Armazém do Chá
LIVE MUSIC

(Map p362; www.armazemdocha.com; Rua José Falcão 180; ⊙ Mon-Sat) This space downtown once housed a roasting company – it's called 'Tea Warehouse' – and now lives on as an alternative cafe-bar with an industrial-chic vibe and a weekly program of live concerts and DJ-spun tunes.

Hot Five Jazz & Blues Club
JAZZ

(Map p362; www.hotfive.eu; Largo Actor Dias 51; ⊙ 10pm-3am Wed-Sun) True to its name, this spot hosts live jazz and blues as well as the occasional acoustic, folk or all-out jam session. It's a modern but intimate space, with seating at small round tables, both fronting the stage and on an upper balcony.

Teatro Nacional São João
PERFORMING ARTS

(Map p362; ☎ 223 401 900; www.tnsj.pt; Praça da Batalha) One of Porto's premier performing-arts organisations hosts international dance, theatre and music groups. Set in an old synagogue turned church, shows are scheduled sporadically and take place in a spectacular interior courtyard framed by 50ft stone walls.

Coliseu do Porto
CONCERT VENUE

(Map p362; www.coliseudoporto.pt; Rua Passos Manuel 137) This frayed, yet still stylish, art-deco theatre hosts major names – like Air and Slash – as well as grand theatre productions. If something big is going on down here, you'll see posters all over town.

Teatro Rivoli
THEATRE

(Map p362; Praça Dom Joáo I; ♿) In the mood for a musical? This stage serves up mainstream, translated classics, such as *Annie*, from Broadway's yesteryear.

Teatro de Belmonte
THEATRE

(Map p362; www.marionetasdoporto.pt; Rua Belmonte 57) Specialises in puppet shows that range from fairy tales like Cinderella to non-violent political theatre.

Football

The flashy, fairly new, 52,000-seat Estádio do Dragão is home to heroes-of-the-moment **FC Porto** (www.fcporto.pt). It's northeast of the centre, just off the VCI ring road (metro stop Estádio de Dragão).

Boavista FC (www.boavistafc.pt) is FC Porto's worthy cross-town rival. Its home turf is the Estádio do Bessa, which lies west of the centre just off Av da Boavista (take bus 3 from Praça da Liberdade). Check the local

PORTO'S MUSIC MECCA

Grand and minimalist, sophisticated yet populist, dreamt up by a local cultural elite and beloved by young bohemians, skate punks and ravers, Porto's **Casa da Música** (House of Music; Map p356; ☑ 220 120 220; www.casadamusica.com; Av da Boavista 604; tours per person €3; ☉ tours 4pm daily) opened its doors in 2005. Like a gigantic piece of raw crystal, the cloud-white concrete exterior is at once rigorously geometric and defiantly asymmetrical. But that monolithic sheathing doesn't prepare you for the surprisingly varied delights inside.

At the building's heart is a classic shoebox-style concert hall, meticulously engineered to accommodate everything from jazz duets to Beethoven's Ninth. It's also home to most of the building's right angles. The rest of the rooms – from classrooms to group rehearsal spaces to professional soundproof practice studios to a light-filled VIP lounge – wind around the central hall in a progression of trapezoids and acute angles. It's as if architect Rem Koolhaas has deliberately crushed and twisted the sombre geometry of high modernism, then added narrative touches such as *azulejos* and gilded furnishings – though always refracted through his own peculiar vision.

The hall holds concerts most nights of the year, from classical to jazz, and fado to electronica (look out for one of the Casa's all-night raves popular among local beat freaks), with occasional summer concerts staged outdoors in the adjoining plaza. It also offers one-hour guided **tours** in English led by students from Porto's highly regarded school of architecture.

Other ways to interact with the space include having a coffee or a light meal in the ground-floor cafe **Bar dos Artistas** (Map p356; ☉ 9.30am-7pm Mon-Sat, 10am-6pm Sun; 🛜), heading to the 7th floor for fine dining at the stylish **Restaurant Casa Da Musica** (Map p356; ☑ 220 107 160; ☉ lunch & dinner Mon-Sat), or jacking into the lobby's dozenseat digitopia where you can tickle keyboards linked to Macs souped up with pro-grade mixing and beat-making software, and leave with a demo CD, all for free.

editions of *Jornal de Notícias* for upcoming matches.

🛍 Shopping

Porto shopping ranges from dusty food shops to chic fashion boutiques. In some areas, entire streets specialise in particular items (try Rua da Fábrica for bookshops). Rua Santa Catarina near Praça da Batalha is a bustling, all-purpose shopping street, and style hounds will love Rua da Bombarda, home to nearly a dozen art galleries and a growing collection of clothing and interior boutiques.

It's great fun buying direct from the warehouses in Vila Nova de Gaia, but for vintage port and high-quality wines at reasonable prices you can also try **Garrafeira do Carmo** (Map p362; Rua do Carmo 17).

A Vida Portuguesa　　SOUVENIRS
(Map p362; www.avidaportuguesa.com; Rua Galeria de Paris 20; ☉ 10am-8pm Mon-Sat) This lovely store in an old fabric shop showcases a medley of stylishly repackaged vintage Portuguese products – classic toys, old-fashioned

soaps and retro journals, plus those emblematic ceramic *andorinhas* (swallows).

Porto Signs　　SOUVENIRS
(Map p362; Rua Alfândega 17; ☉ 10am-8pm Mon-Sat) A nice twist on the traditional tourist shop, Porto Signs has unique, locally designed graphic T-shirts, as well as Portuguese wine, tea, photography books, cork products and that ever-present Barcelos rooster.

CC Bombarda　　MALL
(Map p362; Rua Miguel Bombarda; ☉ noon-8pm Mon-Sat) Amid the galleries along Rua Miguel Bombarda, this small, unique shopping mall is a highlight. Inside you'll find stores selling locally designed urban wear, bonsai trees, stylish home knick-knacks, Portuguese indie rock and other hipster-pleasing delights. There's a shop (Frida) where you can order a doll made to your own likeness, and a cafe (Pimenta Rosa) serving light fare on an inner courtyard.

Livraria Lello　　BOOKS
(Map p362; Rua das Carmelitas 144; ☉ 10am-7.30pm Mon-Fri, 10am-7pm Sat) Even if you're not after books, don't miss this 1906 neo-

Gothic confection that's stacked to the rafters with new, secondhand and antique books, including foreign-language guidebooks and some literature. Up the curving staircase is a pleasant cafe.

Prometeu Artesano HANDICRAFTS
(Map p362; Muro dos Bacalhoeiros 125; ☺ 9.30am-8pm) Promoting a collective of artisans from across Portugal, this antiquated stonehouse riverside shop has a fun collection of *azulejos*. While not everyone will be a fan of the Jesus sticks (passion of the twigs, if you will), you shouldn't miss the lovely ceramic dishes downstairs.

Lobo Taste HANDICRAFTS
(Map p362; Largo de S Domingos 20; ☺ 10am-8pm) A small but groovy shop set in the Palacio das Artes. It specialises in contemporary handicrafts, including ceramic sculpture, wooden radios and a terrific selection of baskets and sun hats.

Information

EMERGENCY
Police Station (☎ 222 092 000; Largo 1 de Dezembro)
Tourist Police (☎ 222 081 833; Rua Clube dos Fenianos 11; ☺ 8am-2am) Multilingual station beside the main city *turismo*.

INTERNET ACCESS
Biblioteca Municipal Almeida Garrett (Jardim do Palácio de Cristal; ☺ 2-6pm Mon, 10am-6pm Tue-Sat) A public library with free internet access.

INTERNET RESOURCES
O Porto Cool (www.oportocool.wordpress. com) Excellent blog with up-to-date info and listings in and around Porto. Worth a browse.

 PORTO CARD

If you intend to do a lot of sightseeing, the **Porto Card** (1-/2-/3-day card €10.50/17.50/21.50) may save you money. It allows holders free or discounted admission to city museums, free travel on public transport, and discounts on cruises, tours and cultural events, as well as discounts at some restaurants and shops. The card is sold at *turismos* (tourist offices) throughout Porto and some other authorised places. There's also a walker's version, without public transport, which costs €5 for one day.

MEDICAL SERVICES
Santo António Hospital (☎ 222 077 500; Largo Prof Abel Salazar) Has English-speaking staff.

MONEY
There is a currency exchange, open from 7am to 8pm, as well as several 24-hour ATMs, in the airport Arrivals Hall.
Intercontinental (☎ 222 005 557; Rua de Ramalho Ortigão 8; ☺ 9am-noon & 2-6.30pm Mon-Fri, 9am-noon Sat)
Unicâmbio (☎ 222 010 807; www.unicambio. pt; Rua Sá da Bandeira 7; ☺ 8.30am-6pm Mon-Fri, 9am-1pm & 2-5pm Sat & Sun) Currency exchange, Western Union services, plus internet access (€2.50 per hour) and phone booths for international calls.

POST
Post Office (Map p362; Praça General Humberto Delgado) Across from the main tourist office.
Post Office (Map p362; Praça da Batalha; ☺ 8.30am-6pm Mon-Fri)

TELEPHONE
Post offices, kiosks and newsagents sell Portugal Telecom phone cards, which can be used from most public phones.
Portugal Telecom Office (PT; ☎ 225 001 117; www.telecom.pt; Rua Tenente Valadim 431; ☺ 8am-8pm Mon-Sat, 10am-8pm Sun) The handiest place for long-distance calls using card phones or pay-afterward *cabines* (phone boxes).

TOURIST INFORMATION
City Centre Turismo (Map p362; ☎ 223 393 472; www.visitporto.travel; Rua Clube dos Fenianos 25 ; ☺ 9am-8pm daily Jun-Oct, to 7pm daily Nov-May) The main city *turismo* has a detailed city map, a transport map and the *Agenda do Porto* cultural calendar, among other printed materials.
Turismo (Sé) (Map p362; ☎ 223 393 472; www.visitporto.travel; Terreiro da Sé; ☺ 9am-8pm daily)
iPoint Ribeira (Map p362; www.visitporto. travel; Praça da Ribeira; ☺ noon-7pm daily mid-July–mid-Sep) Useful *turismo*-run information point on Praça da Ribeira, open seasonally.
iPoint Campanhã (www.visitporto.travel; Estação de Comboio de Campanhã; ☺ 10am-6pm daily Jun-Oct) Seasonal information point run by the *turismo* at the Campanhã train station.

TRAVEL AGENCIES
When booking a tour, see government-run organisation Porto Tours (p365), which acts as an impartial intermediary between tour operators and travellers.

ANDANTE CARD

For maximum convenience, Porto's transport system offers the rechargeable **Andante Card** (www.linhandante.com), allowing smooth movement between tram, metro, funicular and many bus lines.

The card itself costs only €0.50 and can be recharged for one year. Once you've purchased the card, you must charge it with travel credit according to which zones you will be travelling in. A Z2 trip covers the whole city centre east to Campanhã train station, south to Vila Nova de Gaia and west to Foz do Douro. And each 'trip' allows you a whole hour to move between different participating methods of transport without additional cost. Your time begins from when you first enter the vehicle or platform: just wave the card in front of a validation machine marked 'Andante'.

Places to purchase credit are widely available, including metro ticket machines and staffed TIP booths at central hubs such as Casa da Música and Trindade, as well as the STCP office, the funicular, the electric tram museum and a scattering of other authorised sales points.

One/11 'trips' in Z2 (including central Porto, Boavista and Foz do Douro) cost €1.15/12. Alternatively, you can choose to roam freely for 24 hours for €6. If you want to go further out than two zones, pick up a map and an explanation of zones at any metro station.

Tagus (☑ 226 094 146; www.taguseasy.pt; Rua Rainha D Estefânia 244, Loja 8; ☺ 9am-6pm Mon-Fri, 10am-1pm Sat) Youth-oriented agency selling discounted tickets, rail passes and international youth and student cards.

ⓘ Getting There & Away

AIR

The gleaming Francisco Sá Carneiro airport (p506), ominously named after a beloved politician who was killed in a plane crash, is 19km northwest of the city centre. **Portugália** (www.portugalia-airlines.pt) and **TAP** (www.flytap.com) have multiple daily flights to/from Lisbon. There are also low-cost carriers, such as **easyJet** (www.easyjet.com) and **Ryanair** (www.ryanair.com), with nonstop services to London, Madrid, Paris, Frankfurt, Amsterdam and Brussels. Note that there is a left-luggage facility on the 3rd floor (€2 per day for a 10kg bag).

BUS

As in many Portuguese cities, bus services in Porto are regrettably dispersed, with no central bus terminal. The good news is that there are frequent services to just about everywhere in northern Portugal, as well as express service to Coimbra, Lisbon and points south.

Domestic

Renex (www.renex.pt; Campo Mártires de Pátria 37) is the choice for Lisbon (€20, 3½ hours), with the most direct routes and eight to 12 departures daily, including one continuing on to the Algarve. Renex also has frequent services to Braga (€6, 1¼ hours). Buses depart from Campo Mártires da Patria 37.

Rede Expressos (Map p362; ☑ 222 006 954; www.rede-expressos.pt; Rua Alexandre Herculano 366) has services to the entire country from the smoggy **Paragem Atlântico terminal** (Map p362).

For fast Minho connections, mainly on weekdays, three companies run from around Praceta Régulo Magauanha, off Rua Dr Alfredo Magalhães. **Transdev-Norte** (www.transdev.pt) runs chiefly to Braga (€6, 1¼ hours) and Guimarães (€6, one hour). **AV Minho** (www.avminho.pt) goes mainly via Vila do Conde (€2.45, one hour) to Viana do Castelo (€5.60, 2¼ hours). **Rodonorte** (☑ 222 005 637; www.rodonorte.pt; Travessa Passos Manuel) has multiple daily departures (fewer on Saturday) for Amarante (€6.30, one hour), Vila Real (€9, 1½ hours) and Bragança (€14, 3½ hours).

International

There are Eurolines departures from Interface Casa da Música (Rua Capitão Henrique Calvão). Northern Portugal's own international carrier, **Internorte** (Map p356; www.internorte.pt), departs from the same terminal. Most travel agencies can book outbound buses with either operator.

CAR & MOTORCYCLE

All major Portuguese and international car-hire companies have offices at the airport (some have offices in town, as well) including the always helpful and reliable **Cael** (☑ 229 964 269; www.cael.pt; Av Arquitecto Fernando Tavora 2021; per day from €62) and **Europcar** (☑ 222 057 737; www.europcar.com; Rua Antonio Bessa Leite 1478; per day from €40).

TRAIN

Porto is the principal rail hub for northern Portugal. Long-distance services start at **Campanhã station** (☉ 9am-7pm), which is 3km east of the centre. Most *urbano*, regional and *interregional* (IR) trains depart from the stunning indoor-outdoor **São Bento station** (Praça Almeida Garrett), though all these lines also pass through Campanhã.

For destinations on the Braga, Guimarães and Aveiro lines, or up the Douro valley as far as Marco de Canaveses, take one of the frequent *urbano* trains. Don't spend extra money on *interregional*, *intercidade* (IC) or Alfa Pendular (AP) trains to these destinations as the *urbano* trains take around the same amount of time; Porto to Braga costs €2.20 by *urbano*, but €13 by AP train.

Direct IC destinations from Porto include Lisbon (2nd class €20, three hours, hourly).

There are information points at both São Bento and Campanhã stations. Alternatively, call toll-free ☑ 808 208 208 or consult www.cp.pt.

ⓘ Getting Around

TO/FROM THE AIRPORT

The metro's 'violet' line provides a handy service to the airport. A one-way ride from the city centre costs €1.80 and takes about 45 minutes.

A daytime taxi costs €20 to €25 to/from the centre. Taxis authorised to run *from* the airport are labeled 'Maia' and/or 'Vila Nova de Telha'; the rank is just outside the Arrivals Hall. In peak-traffic time, allow an hour or more between the city centre and the airport.

BICYCLE

Despite the narrow alleyways, steep hills and cobbled streets, cyclists are ubiquitous in Porto, and there are some particularly great rides along the Douro on dedicated bike paths from the Ribeira to Foz or from Vila Nova de Gaia to Afurada and beyond.

Vieguini (☑ 914 306 838; www.vieguini.pt; Rua Nova da Alfandega 7; bikes per hr/day €5/12; ☉ 10am-7pm) Vieguini has a great selection of high-quality mountain bikes and rents out motor scooters (per day €22.50), too.

CAR & MOTORCYCLE

Avoid driving in central Porto if possible. Narrow, one-way streets, construction and heavy traffic can turn 500m into half a morning. Street parking is tight, with a two-hour maximum stay on weekdays. There is no limit on weekends and parking spaces are more readily available. Most squares have underground, fee-charging lots – follow the blue Ps. Beware that men may guide you into places and then expect tips. They can be very disagreeable if you don't comply. They also may direct you into an illegal spot – be sure to double-check signs.

PUBLIC TRANSPORT

Bus

Porto's transport agency **STCP** (Sociedade de Transportes Colectivos do Porto; Map p362; ☑ 808 200 166; www.stcp.pt) runs an extensive bus system, with central hubs at Praça da Liberdade (the southern end of Av dos Aliados), Praça Almeida Garrett (in front of São Bento train station) and Cordoaria. Special all-night lines also run approximately hourly, leaving Aliados on the hour and returning on the half-hour from 1am to 5.30am. City *turismos* have maps and timetables for day and night routes.

A ticket bought on the bus (one way to anywhere in the STCP system) costs €1.50. All the lines accept the Andante Card (p379).

Also available is the *bilhete diário* (day pass), valid for unlimited trips within the city on buses and trams. For 24/72 hours, it costs €5/11.

Funicular

The restored **Funicular dos Guindais** (one way/with Metro transfer €0.95/1.45; ☉ 8am-10pm Sun-Wed Jun-Sep, 8am-8pm Sun-Wed Oct-May, 8am-midnight Thu-Sat year-round) shuttles up and down a steep incline with tremendous river and bluff views from Av Gustavo Eiffel opposite Ponte de Dom Luís I, to Rua Augusto Rosa, near Batalha and the cathedral. The funicular is part of the Andante Card (p379) scheme.

Metro

Porto's fairly new metro system provides speedy service around town. The central hub is Trindade station, a few blocks north of the Aliados corridor. Three lines – Linha A (blue, to Matosinhos), Linha B (red, to Vila do Conde and Póvoa de Varzim) and Linha C (green, to Maia) – run from Estádio do Dragão via Campanhã train station through the city centre, and then on to far-flung northern and western suburbs. Linha D (yellow) runs north–south from Hospital São João to João de Deus in Vila Nova de Gaia, crossing the upper deck of Ponte de Dom Luís I. Key stops include Aliados and São Bento station. Linha E (violet) connects Linha B with the airport.

Metro trains run from approximately 6am to 1am daily.

Tram

Porto's trams used to be one of its delights. Only three lines remain but they're very scenic. The Massarelos stop, on the riverfront near the foot of the Palácio de Cristal, is the tram system's hub. From here, line 1 trundles along the river to nearby Praça Infante Dom Henrique (Ribeira). Line 1E (appears as a crossed-out '1') heads down the river in the opposite direction, towards Foz do Douro. And line 18 heads uphill to the Igreja do Carmo and Jardim do Cordoaria. Trams run approximately every 30 minutes from 9am to 7pm.

TAXI

There are taxi ranks throughout the centre, or you can call a **radio taxi** (☏ 225 076 400). Count on paying around €5 to €7 for trips within the centre during the day, with a 20% surcharge at night. There's an extra charge if you leave the city limits, which includes Vila Nova de Gaia.

Vila do Conde

POP 30,000

With its quaint historic heart, poetic folk hero, glassy river mouth, luscious beaches and salty past, you can understand why Vila do Conde is a popular weekend getaway for Porto residents. An important salt exporter during Roman times and a prime shipbuilding port during the Age of Discoveries, the town still drips history. Looming over it is the immense hilltop Mosteiro de Santa Clara, which, along with surviving segments of a long-legged medieval aqueduct, lends the town an air of monumentality. In addition to this, Vila do Conde's beaches are some of the best north of Porto, and a metro link makes getting here an easy afternoon jaunt from downtown Porto.

Vila do Conde sits on the northern side of the Rio Ave, where it empties into the sea. From the metro station, look for the aqueduct (about 100m away) and follow it towards the large convent (another 400m). From here it's a few steep blocks downhill to the town's historic centre. From the centre it's another kilometre via Av Dr Artur Cunha Araújo or Av Dr João Canavarro to Av do Brasil and the 3km-long beach.

◉ Sights & Activities

Mosteiro de Santa Clara   MONASTERY

Peering down over the town centre and the Rio Ave, the imposing Mosteiro de Santa Clara, founded in 1318, still has a severe-looking Gothic chapel, though the main building is an 18th-century affair. Currently the entire complex is closed to visitors.

Casa do Barco   MUSEUM

(Cais das Lavandeiras; ⏱ 10am-6pm Tue-Sun) **FREE** This glass-box museum is on the southwest corner of Praça Republica. The basement level offers up models, photo displays, old fishing gear and one full-sized boat that provide a glimpse into the city's shipbuilding past.

Casa de José Régio   MUSEUM

(Centro de Memória, Largo S Sebastião 14; ⏱ 10am-6pm Tue-Sun) **FREE** Religious art, antique furnishings, ceramics and early 20th-century contemporary art – including some stunning Julio canvases – can be glimpsed at the Casa de José Régio. Named after the distinguished local-born poet, playwright and healer José Régio (1901–69), who lived and worked here, admission includes a guided tour (in Portuguese) through each floor of the town house. Highlights include the stunning upstairs office and library, and the rooftop garden.

Alfandega Resia
Museu da Construção Naval   MUSEUM

(Museum of Shipbuilding; Largo da Alfândega; adult/child €1/0.50; ⏱ 10am-6pm Tue-Sun) Shipbuilding has been in Vila do Conde's bones since at least the 13th century. This museum on the banks of the Rio Ave, just west of Praça da República, has exhibits on trade and models of hand-built *nau* (a sort of potbellied caravel once used for cargo and naval operations). The real attraction, however, is the replica of a 16th-century *nau* moored opposite the museum.

Visitors can wander across the various decks of the ship, peeking in rooms that provide a glimpse of ship life during the 1500s.

Museu das Rendas de Bilros   MUSEUM

(Museum of Bobbin Lace; Rua São Bento 70; admission €1; ⏱ 10am-noon & 2-6pm Mon-Fri) It's no accident that seafaring fingers, so deft at making nets, should also be good at lace making. Vila do Conde is one of the few places in Portugal with an active school of the art, founded in 1918. Housed in a typical 18th-century town house in the town centre, the school includes the Museu das Rendas de Bilros, which displays eye-popping examples of work from Portugal and around the world.

🏖 Beaches

Vila do Conde's two best beaches, **Praia da Forno** and **Praia de Nossa Senhora da Guia**, are wide, blonde and picturesque even when the winds howl. Most of the year seas are calm and suitable for young children. Buses marked 'Vila do Conde' from Póvoa de Varzim stop at the station and continue to the beach, about half-hourly all day from Monday to Friday (fewer on weekends).

Surfers can sometimes ride swells near the 17th-century Castelo de São João Baptista,

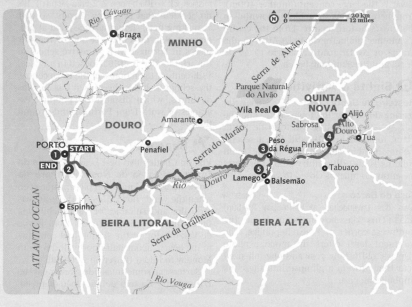

MATTES RENÉ, HEMIS.FR/ GETTY IMAGES ©

1 WEEK Wines of the Douro

Wine lovers have their work cut out for them on a leisurely journey through the Douro Valley, Portugal's premier 'wine country'.

Not only is it the world's oldest demarcated wine region, bearing the title since 1756, it's also dazzling – steep terraced vineyards rise sharply from the banks of the Douro River, whitewashed *quintas* perch high up in the hills. Visitors are just as wowed by these dramatic vistas as they are by the area's viticulture, which has been turning out some of Portugal's premier wines for centuries.

Any self-respecting wine tour will begin in **Porto** (p353), gateway to the world's most famous port-wine region. Across the river is the historic **Vila Nova de Gaia** (p361), where you can sample countless varieties at its many port-wine lodges. Spend at least an afternoon tasting the sweet tipple in Gaia's lodges – the recently spruced up **Graham's** (p361) has a small museum and does excellent tours and tastings. Continue the journey east following the Douro, all the way to **Peso da Régua** (p390), a riverside town set in the heart of vineyard country. Make sure you stop by for a tasting at the nearby **Quinta do Vallado** (p391), a winery since 1716 and now a swank little rural hotel where you can have a fine wine-paired meal, and stay the night. Continue on to the quaint riverside village of **Pinhão** (p392), a great base for a few nights.

From the village head out to explore the **Alto Douro** (Upper Douro; p392), a spectacular area that Unesco designated a World Heritage site. A drive along the winding mountain roads reveals some of the most scenic views out to the vineyards, guesthouses and restaurants that sprinkle the area. Stop in for a tour and tasting at some of the wine estates; **Quinta Nova** (p392) and **Quinta do Crasto** (p393) are the most breathtaking, both offering a taste of their wines paired with magnificent views.

On the way back to Porto, visit the attractive food- and wine-loving town of **Lamego** (p388), producer of a fine sparkling wine.

OGPHOTO / GETTY IMAGES ©

Top: Vineyards, Rio Douro
Bottom: Terraced vineyard, Rio Douro

at the river mouth. Once a castle, it's now a small deluxe hotel (p384) with a glamorous, hard-partying reputation.

Festivals & Events

Festival Ollin Kan Portugal
MUSIC
(www.ollinkanportugal.com) Held in June on the shores of the Rio Ave. Musicians from the Americas, Africa and throughout Europe rock Vila do Conde with three nights of free music.

Festa de São João
RELIGIOUS
The town's biggest event takes place on the days leading up to 23 June, with fireworks, concerts, a traditional boat parade and a religious procession through the streets.

Curtas
FILM
(www.curtas.pt) For 18 years running, this seaside hamlet has been hosting an edgy and popular short film fest each July.

Feira Nacional de Artesanato
HANDICRAFTS FAIR
(http://fna.vconde.org) A major fair showcasing Portuguese handicrafts is on during the last week of July and the first week of August.

Sleeping

Parque de Campismo da Árvore
CAMPGROUND €
(252 633 225; www.cnm.org.pt; Rua do Cabreiro, Árvore; sites per adult/tent €6/5; 🐾🏊) Tightly packed and well shaded, this campsite is 3km from town, right next to Praia da Árvore.

Pensão Patarata
GUESTHOUSE €
(252 631 894; Cais das Lavandeiras 18; s/d €30/40; 🏊) Looking over the river, off the southwest corner of the square, this place has simple but sweet rooms with high ceilings and wooden furnishings, and all have river views. Breakfast is served at extra cost.

Forte São João Baptista
HOTEL €
(252 240 600; www.fortesaojoao.pt; Av Brasil; s/d €50/60; 🅿🏊) Hidden within the forbidding, metres-thick stone walls of a 17th-century fort is this oasis of luxury. The hotel's eight rooms are cosy but plush, and popular on party nights (p385), even if you do have to forfeit your keys until 6am.

Estalagem do Brazão
GUESTHOUSE €€
(252 642 016; www.estalagemdobrazao.com; Av Dr João Canavarro; s/d €58/82; 🅿🏊@🏊) Set in a restored 16th-century nobleman's house,

this guesthouse has been added onto at various times over the years, making it a patchwork of old and new. Rooms are spacious and comfortable, with sea-green carpeting and crown mouldings. Situated 200m west of the Rua 25 de Abril *turismo*, it's excellent low-season value.

Villa C Hotel & Spa
BOUTIQUE HOTEL €€
(252 240 420; www.villachotel.com; Av Mouzinho de Albuquerque, Azurara; s/d €95/120; 🅿✳🏊🏊) A boutique property set on the hill above town, rooms here are minimalist and stylish with wooden floors and marble baths. Those on the seaside have spectacular views, but you can glimpse lovely village views from the street side. Stay off the 1st floor to avoid the roaring highway.

Eating & Drinking

Around the corner from the *turismo* is Praça José Régio, a rather ugly modern plaza in the middle of the quaint old town. Here, there's an assortment of outdoor cafes, bars and restaurants, and on weekends pop-up bars sprout to serve sugary *caparinhas* to the masses.

Adega Gavina
SEAFOOD €
(Rua Cais das Lavandeiras 56; meals €5-7; ⏱ lunch & dinner Mon-Sat) The top choice in town offers tremendous roast-chicken lunches for a song, and cooks some damn good steaks, but first and foremost it's a seafood grill. Step one: stroll into the kitschy interior and peruse the chalkboard menu. Step two: choose your catch and watch the chef grill it perfectly on his streetside barbecue. Excellent value lunch specials (€5 to €7) come with potatoes, rice and steamed greens.

O Canghalho
SEAFOOD €€
(Rua Cais das Lavandeiras 48; meals €10-15; ⏱ lunch & dinner Mon-Sat) The funky, tricked-out vintage Land Rover parked out front may catch your eye, and as you come close you'll notice the stylish bistro interior and fresh fish on ice. Great style, great vibe, tasty seafood.

Restaurante Le Villageois
FRENCH-PORTUGUESE €€
(Praça da República 94; meals €9-18; ⏱ lunch & dinner Tue-Sun) The popular Villageois has been preparing terrific steaks and fresh seafood in French-Portuguese style since 1977. The airy dining room is appointed with *azulejos*, the appealing sun-drenched patio is classy and the bar is full. It hosts live fado on Friday and Saturday nights.

Caximar
SEAFOOD €€
(www.restaurantecaximar.pai.pt; Av Brasil; mains €9-16; ☺ lunch & dinner Tue-Sun) For tasty seafood in a modern, unfussy place with tables overlooking the crashing waves, head to the beach, 1km west of Forte São João Baptista.

Cacau
BAR
(Praca de Republica 42; ☺ 9am-2am) Running deep into the hollowed-out ground floor of an old stone relic, Cacau is a cafe by day and a bar by night, with electro-funky tunes and a young crowd.

Forte São João Baptista
CLUB
(www.fortesaojoao.pt; Av Brasil; ☺ Jul-Sep) The best party spot in Vila do Conde. Think mighty, seasonal blinged-out electronica throwdowns with international DJs, Bedouin tents, spinning disco balls and up to 2000 people spilling onto the windswept sands and dancing on the ancient fortress walls. Parties last until 6am. Make arrangements in advance to get on the door list.

❶ Information

The friendly Vila do Conde **turismo** (☎ 252 248 473; www.cm-viladoconde.pt; Rua 25 de Abril 103; ☺ 9am-7pm Mon-Fri, 9.30am-1pm & 2.30-6pm Sat & Sun) has maps and some nice examples of local lace, but the staff do not speak much English.

❶ Getting There & Away

Vila do Conde is 33km from Porto, and is a straight shot on the IC1 Hwy. It's served by Porto's Linha D (red) metro line to Póvoa de Varzim, stopping about 400m from the town centre. A one-way trip from central Porto costs €2.30 and takes about an hour – the trip is a little faster if you catch the express service.

Buses stop on Rua 5 de Outubro, near the *turismo*. AV Minho express buses stop hourly (fewer on weekends) en route to Porto (€3, 50 minutes) and Viana do Castelo (€4, one hour).

Amarante

POP 11,260
Handsomely set on a bend in the Rio Tâmega, the sleepy village of Amarante is dominated by a striking church and monastery, which sit theatrically beside a rebuilt medieval bridge that still bears city traffic. The willow-lined riverbanks lend a pastoral charm, as do the balconied houses and switchback lanes that rise quickly from the narrow valley floor.

The town enjoys some small degree of fame for being the hometown of São Gonçalo. Portugal's St Valentine, he is the target for lonely hearts who make pilgrimages here in the hope of finding true love. Surrounded by prized vineyards, Amarante is also something of a foodie mecca. As well as wine, the region produces excellent cheeses, smoked meats (*fumeiros*) and rich eggy pastries.

Self-drivers can use Amarante as an alternate base to explore the *quintas* (estates) of the Alto Douro.

There is free parking just east of the *turismo* where the *mercado municipal* (municipal market) is held; avoid parking there overnight before crowded market days (Wednesday and Saturday).

History

The town may date back as far as the 4th century BC, though Gonçalo, a 13th-century hermit, is credited with everything from the founding of the town to the construction of its first bridge.

Amarante's strategically placed bridge (Ponte de São Gonçalo) almost proved to be its undoing in 1809, when the French lost their brief grip on Portugal. Marshal Soult's troops retreated to the northeast after abandoning Porto, plundering as they went. A French detachment arrived here in search of a river crossing, but plucky citizens and troops held them off, allowing residents to escape to the far bank. The French retaliated by burning down much of the town.

Amarante has also suffered frequent natural invasions by the Rio Tâmega. Little *cheia* (high water level) plaques in Rua 31 de Janeiro and Largo Conselheiro António Cândido tell the harrowing story.

◉ Sights & Activities

Ponte de São Gonçalo
BRIDGE
A symbol of the town's heroic defence against the French (marked by a plaque at the southeastern end), the granite Ponte de São Gonçalo is Amarante's visual centrepiece. The original bridge, allegedly built at Gonçalo's urging in the 13th century, collapsed in a flood in 1763; this one was completed in 1790.

Mosteiro de São Gonçalo
MONASTERY
(☺ 9am-7pm summer, 9am-5.30pm winter) Founded in 1543 by João III, the Mosteiro de São Gonçalo and Igreja de São Gonçalo weren't completed until 1620. Above the

church's photogenic, Italian Renaissance side portal is an arcaded gallery, 30m high, with 17th-century statues of Dom João and the other kings who ruled while the monastery was under construction: Sebastião, Henrique and Felipe I.

The bell tower was added in the 18th century. The best view of the royal statues is from the steep lane just west of the church entrance. Within the lofty interior is an impressive gilded baroque altar, pulpits, an organ casing held up by fishtailed giants, and Gonçalo's tomb in a tiny chapel (left of the altar). Tradition has it that those in search of a mate will have their wish granted within a year if they touch the statue above his tomb. Sure enough, its limestone toes, fingers and face have been all but rubbed away by hopefuls.

Museu Amadeo de Souza-Cardoso   MUSEUM
(Alameda Teixeira de Pascoaes; adult/student/child €1/0.50/free; ☉10am-12.30pm & 2-6pm Tue-Sun summer, 9.30am-12.30pm & 2-5.30pm winter) Hidden in one of the Mosteiro de São Gonçalo's cloisters is this delightfully eclectic collection of modernist and contemporary art, a pleasant surprise in a town of this size. The museum is named after Amarante's favourite son, artist Amadeo Souza-Cardoso (1889–1918) – one of the best-known Portuguese artists of the 20th century – who abandoned naturalism for home-grown versions of impressionism and cubism. The museum is full of his sketches, cartoons, portraits and abstracts.

Solar dos Magalhães   RUINS
This burned-out skeleton of an old manor house situated above Rua Cândido dos Reis, near the train station, has been left in ruins – a stark and uncaptioned memento from Napoleon's troops.

Igreja de São Domingos   CHURCH
(Praça da República; cloister €1; ☉3pm-7pm summer, 3pm-5.30pm winter) Rising beside São Gonçalo are several impressively steep switchbacks topped by this round, 18th-century church. The views from here are stunning.

Igreja de São Pedro   CHURCH
(Largo de São Pedro; ☉2.30-6pm summer, to 5.30pm winter) The nave of this baroque church is decorated with beautiful 17th-century blue-and-yellow *azulejos*.

Rio Tâmega   WALKING, BOATING
(boat hire per 30min/1hr €5/10; ☉boat hire 9am-8pm) For an idyllic river stroll, take the cobbled path along the north bank. A good picnic or daydreaming spot is the rocky outcropping overlooking the rapids 400m east of the bridge. You can also potter about the peaceful Rio Tâmega in a paddle or row boat; boat hire is available along the riverbank.

✵ Festivals & Events
Held during the first weekend in June, **Festas de Junho** highlights include an all-night drumming competition, a livestock fair, a handicrafts market and fireworks, all rounded off with Sunday's procession in honour of the main man – São Gonçalo.

🛏 Sleeping

Parque de Campismo de
Penedo da Rainha   CAMPGROUND €
(☏255 437 630; ccporto@sapo.pt; Rua Pedro Avelos; sites per adult/tent/car €3.50/2.75/2.25; ☉Feb-Nov; ☀) A big, shady site that cascades down to the river, this campground has a *minimercado* (grocery shop) and bar. It's about 1km upstream (and uphill) from the town centre.

Residencial Estoril   GUESTHOUSE €
(☏255 431 291; mnestoril@hotmail.com; Rua 31 de Janeiro 150-152; s €30, d €35-50) Jutting out over the riverbank, Estoril has basic wood-floor rooms with small bathrooms, a couple of them with sweet views of São Gonçalo's bridge. It is one of the only spots to offer rooms year round. There's an extra charge for breakfast.

★Casa da Calçada   LUXURY HOTEL €€€
(☏255 410 830; www.casadacalcada.com; Largo do Paço 6; s/d €175/186; ⓟ❄🛜☀) Oozing class and boasting every creature comfort, this 16th-century palace (rebuilt following Napoleon's destructive campaign) rises royally above the Ponte de São Gonçalo. Past the antique-filled parlours lie spacious, elegantly furnished rooms with marble bathrooms. The Jacuzzi and pool overlook the hotel's vineyards. This Relais & Châteaux property is easily Amarante's top choice.

✗ Eating
You can get picnic supplies at shops along Rua 31 de Janeiro or at the **mercado municipal** (Rua Capitão Augusto Casimiro; ☉8.30am-1pm).

Bar dos Pauzinhos CAFE €
(Rua dos Pauzinhos; snacks €1.50-8.50; ☺noon-2am Mon-Thu, noon-4am Fri & Sat) This new three-floor hotspot has daytime drinks and snacks, such as sandwiches and burgers, plus an alfresco terrace at the top. The crowd is young, the decor contemporary and the TV screen huge.

Cafe Principe CAFE €
(Largo Conselheiro Atónio Candido 73; sandwiches €3-5; ☺lunch & dinner) If you're hankering to try the smoked meats Amarante is famous for, you might consider this modernised bar and cafe, where the barman makes his sandwiches with great respect and keeps his Sintra beer icy.

Confeitaria da Ponte BAKERY €
(Rua 31 de Janeiro 186; pastries €1.10-1.50; ☺8.30am-8.30pm daily) Boasting a peaceful, shaded terrace overlooking the bridge, this traditional bakery has the best ambience for enjoying Amarante's famous pastries and eggy custards.

Adega Quelha PORTUGUESE €€
(Rua de Olivença; mains €5-14.50; ☺lunch daily, dinner Tue-Sun) One of several low-key *adegas* (wine taverns) proffering Amarante's fine smoked meats and cheese, Adega Quelha is a good place to sample the local delicacies among locals. Grab a bite and a jug of red wine at the bar, or sit down to a simple but filling meal.

Zé da Calçada PORTUGUESE €€
(Rua 31 de Janeiro; mains €8-12; ☺lunch & dinner) Excellent northern cuisine served in an elegant country-style dining room or on a verandah with idyllic views of the Moistero and the bridge. Top picks here include duck rice and grilled goat. Weekday lunch specials are great value.

Lusitano PORTUGUESE €€
(Rua 31 de Janeiro; mains €7.50-14; ☺lunch & dinner Wed-Mon) Roasted kid goat and stewed tripe are house specialities at this traditional Portuguese restaurant with a pretty riverside terrace.

 Drinking & Nightlife

Open-air cafes and bars pop up every summer along the riverside on Av General Silveira, opposite the Mosteiro de São Gonçalo.

Travo & Canela WINE BAR
(Rua Cândido dos Reis; ☺11.30am-2am) This inviting wine bar combines trim decor with festive red-and-yellow walls. DJs spin and live bands perform on occasion. The inviting sunken stone terrace is Amarante's hipster hangout of choice.

 Information

Banks with ATMs are along Rua 5 de Outubro and Rua António Carneiro.

Biblioteca Municipal Albano Sardoeira (☑255 420 236; Largo de Santa Clara; ☺10am-12.30pm & 2-6.30pm Mon-Sat) Free internet access.

Hospital (☑255 410 500; Quinta da Lama, Telões) North of the centre.

Police Station (☑255 437 790; Rua Capitão Augusto Casimiro)

Post Office (Rua João Pinto Ribeiro; ☺8.30am-6pm Mon-Fri)

Turismo (☑255 420 246; www.amarante. pt/turismo; Alameda Teixeira de Pascoaes; ☺9am-5.30pm Mon-Fri) Next to the museum, in the former cloisters of São Gonçalo. It offers city maps, but very little English is spoken.

Getting There & Away

BUS

At the small but busy **Estacão Quemado** (www. rodonorte.pt; Rua Antonio Carneiro), buses stop at least five times daily from Porto (€6.40, one hour) en route to Vila Real (€6.30, 40 minutes) and Bragança (€12, 2¾ hours). There are also daily buses to Braga (€7.80, 1½ hours) and Lisbon (€18, 4¼ hours).

Lamego

POP 26,690 / ELEV 550M

Most people come to Lamego – a prim, prosperous town 10km south of the Rio Douro – to see (and possibly to climb) the astonishing baroque stairway that zigzags its way up to the Igreja de Nossa Senhora dos Remédios. The old town centre itself has a mix of winding narrow lanes and tree-lined boulevards, with uplit medieval landmarks looming from almost every angle. Connoisseurs also swear by Lamego's *raposeira*, the town's famously fragrant sparkling wine, which provides a fine break between bouts of port.

Though often quiet midweek, Lamego is a university town, and there's usually some fun to be had in area bars on weekends. It's also a natural base for exploring the half-ruined monasteries and chapels in the surrounding environs, one of which dates back to the time of the Visigoths.

Self-drivers take note: parking can be tight in Lamego.

History

Lamego was an important centre even in the time of the Visigoths and has had a cathedral since at least the 6th century. The city fell to the Moors in the 8th century and remained in their hands until the 11th. In 1143 Portugal's first *cortes* (parliament) was convened here to confirm Afonso Henriques as Portugal's first king. The little town grew fat thanks to its position on trading routes between the Douro and the Beiras and, thanks to its wine, was already famous in the 16th century.

⊙ Sights & Activities

Igreja de Nossa Senhora dos Remédios   CHURCH

(⊙7.30am-8pm May-Sep, 7.30am-6pm Oct-Apr) One of the country's most important pilgrimage sites, this twin-towered 18th-century church has a trim blue-and-white stucco interior with a sky-blue rococo ceiling and a gilded altar. The church, however, is quite overshadowed by the zigzagging monumental **stairway** that leads up to it. The 600-plus steps are resplendent with *azulejos,* urns, fountains and statues, adding up to one of the great works in Portuguese rococo style.

It's a dramatic sight at any time, but the action peaks in late summer when thousands of devotees arrive and ascend the steps in search of miracles during the Festa de Nossa Senhora dos Remédios. Most offerings are made at the rear altar where Mother Mary reigns supreme. If you can't face the climb by foot, a road (turn off 1km out on the Viseu road) winds up the hill for about 3km before reaching the top.

Sé   CATHEDRAL

(Largo da Sé; ⊙9am-1pm & 3-6.30pm) Older than Portugal itself, Lamego's striking *sé* has been declared a national monument. There is little left of its 12th-century original except the base of its square belfry. The rest of the structure, including the brilliantly carved Gothic triple portal, dates mostly from the 16th and 18th centuries. Arresting biblical frescoes and the high choir stalls are the work of 18th-century Italian baroque architect Nicolau Nasoni, who left his mark all over Porto. With luck you will find the door open to the peaceful 16th-century cloisters, located just around the corner.

Igreja Santa Maria de Almacave   CHURCH

(Rua das Cortes 2; ⊙8am-noon & 4-7pm) This unassuming little church is Lamego's oldest surviving building, much of it dating back to the 12th century. It's thought that after winning independence from Spain, Portugal's first king assembled his initial *cortes* (an early version of Portugal's proto-democratic assembly of nobles and clergy) here from 1142 to 1144. It occupies the site of a Moorish cemetery; some of its grave markers are now in the Museu de Lamego.

Museu de Lamego   MUSEUM

(Largo de Camões; admission €2; ⊙10am-6pm Tue-Sun) Occupying a grand, 18th-century Episcopal palace, the Museu de Lamego is one of Portugal's finest regional museums. The collection features five entrancing works by renowned 16th-century Portuguese painter Vasco Fernandes (Grão Vasco), richly worked Brussels tapestries from the same period, and an extraordinarily diverse collection of heavily gilded 17th-century chapels rescued in their entirety from the long-gone Convento das Chagas.

Castelo   CASTLE

(Rua do Castelo; admission by donation; ⊙10am-12.30pm & 2-5.30pm) Climb the narrow, winding Rua da Olaria to the modest medieval castle, encircled by a clutch of ancient stone houses. What little remains – some walls and a tower – has belonged to the Boy Scouts ever since their mammoth 1970s effort to clear the site after years of use as a glorified rubbish tip. Unfortunately, it isn't always open. Still, walk through narrow stone lanes and you'll be treated to glorious views from the castle's perch.

✺ Festivals & Events

Lamego's biggest party, the **Festa de Nossa Senhora dos Remédios**, runs for several weeks from late August to mid-September. In an afternoon procession on 8 September, ox-drawn carts rattle through the streets carrying *tableaux vivants* (religious scenes represented by costumed people), and devotees slowly ascend the stairway on their knees. Less-pious events in the run-up include rock concerts, folk dancing, car racing, parades and at least one all-night party.

⊨ Sleeping

Residencial Solar da Sé   GUESTHOUSE €

(☎254 612 060; Av Visconde Guedes Teixeira 7; s/d €24/39; ✳ ⊛ ♠) There are great deals to be had on rooms with French windows opening onto the *sé*. The carpet is a bit aged, but there's a funky modernist groove you might like. Or love.

Hotel Solar do Espírito Santo HOTEL €

(☑254 655 233; Rua Alexandre Herculano 8; s/d €22/39; P ❋ @ ☎) The common areas feature old-world touches like wooden floors and *azulejo*-lined walls. Rooms are cramped but clean, with parquet floors.

Hotel São Paulo HOTEL €

(☑254 613 114; www.hotelsaopaulo.pt; Av 5 de Outubro 22; s/d €30/40; P ❋ ☎) Although it's a bit out of the way, this recently upgraded guesthouse – now a hotel – is one of the best lodging options. The rooms are clean and bright, with parquet floors. Corner units have extra windows and verandahs, and some rooms even have views.

Hotel Solar dos Pachecos HOTEL €€

(☑254 600 300; Av Visconde Guedes Teixeira 27; s/d €40/65; P ❋ @ ☎) Occupying an impressive 18th-century nobleman's city home, this central place offers clean, carpeted rooms with exposed stone walls, ample light, high ceilings and wide terraces out the back.

✕ Eating & Drinking

Like most regions that produce good wines, Lamego delivers food to match. Its *fumeiros* (smoked meats) are justly famous and can be found in one of several wonderful gourmet food shops on Rua de Olaria. Hit the **mercado municipal** (Av 5 de Outubre; ⊙7.30am-6pm Mon-Fri, 7.30am-5pm Sat) early for fresh fruit and veggies if you're packing a picnic.

Restaurante Trás da Sé PORTUGUESE €

(☑254 614 075; Rua Virgílio Correia 12; mains €5-6; ⊙lunch & dinner) Congratulations to the chef line the walls at this *adega*-style place, where the atmosphere is friendly, the menu short and simple, the food good and the *vinho maduro* (matured wine) list long.

Scala Cafe CAFE €

(Av Visconde Guedes Teixeira; pastries €1-2; ⊙breakfast, lunch & dinner) The charming wooden booths and tables are almost always crammed with locals who descend for great coffee and better pastries.

Sé Christia PORTUGUESE €€

(Rua do Mazeda 11-12; mains €8-13; ⊙lunch & dinner) Lamego's best restaurant occupies an elegant dining room, with outdoor tables above a small plaza. The menu is traditional Portuguese, and the service is excellent.

Pau de Café BAR

(Rua Alexandre Herculano; ⊙8am-2am; ☎) Students tend to gather for billiards, beer and thumping Euro tunes at this expansive patio cafe turned bar. The music isn't for all, but there is a scene here most nights.

Casa do Castelo BAR

(Rua do Castelinho 25; ⊙noon-2am Tue-Sun) A hidden drinking spot lies inside the walls of the *castelo*. This atmospheric landmark bar is subdued during the week, but packs in a festive student crowd on weekends.

☆ Entertainment

Teatro Ribeiro Conceição THEATRE

(☑962 116 119; www.teatroribeiroconceicao.com; Largo de Camões; tickets €5-20) This handsomely restored theatre and cultural space hosts a wide range of programs throughout the year, from children's puppet shows to classical concerts, orchestral concerts and ballets. There's also a cafe with outdoor seating.

❶ Information

Biblioteca Municipal (Municipal Library; Rua de Almacave 7; ⊙9am-12.30pm & 2-5.30pm Mon-Fri) Provides free internet access in 30-minute chunks.

Hospital (☑254 609 980; Lugar do Frazio)

Police Station (☑254 656 739; Rua António Osório da Mota)

Post Office (Av Dr Alfredo de Sousa; ⊙8.30am-6pm Mon-Fri)

Turismo (☑254 615 770; www.cm-lamego. pt; Av Visconde Guedes Teixeira; ⊙9.30am-12.30pm & 2-6pm daily) This fantastic tourist office is full of solid suggestions from warm, knowledgeable, English-speaking staff.

❶ Getting There & Away

The most appealing route to Lamego from anywhere in the Douro valley is by train to Peso da Régua and by bus or taxi from there. A taxi from Régua costs about €15 to €20.

From Lamego's bus station, Joalto/EAVT and Rede Expressos are the only operators. Buses travel about hourly to Peso da Régua (€2.30, 30 minutes) and daily to Viseu (€8.90, 1¼ hours) and Lisbon (€18.50, 5¾ hours). The Lisbon bus also passes through Chaves (€11.40, 2¼ hours) and Vila Real (€6, one hour). **Copy Print** (☑254 619 447; Av Visconde Guedes Teixeira; ⊙8am-8pm), a newsagent beside the *turismo*, sells tickets for these services.

Around Lamego

Capela de São Pedro de Balsemão

Older than Portugal itself, this mysterious little **chapel** (⊙ 10am-12.30pm & 2-5.30pm Wed-Sun, 2-5.30pm Mon-Tue) was probably built by Visigoths as early as the 6th century. With Corinthian columns, round arches and intriguing symbols etched into the walls, it certainly predates the introduction of even Romanesque architecture to Portugal. More ornate 14th-century additions were commissioned by the Bishop of Porto, Afonso Pires, who is buried under a slab in the floor. Check out the ancient casket dominating the entrance chamber: supported by lions and intricately engraved, it depicts the Last Supper on one side and the Crucifixion on the other.

The chapel is tucked away in the hamlet of Balsemão, 3km southeast of Lamego above the Rio Balsemão. It's a pleasant downhill walk from Lamego through an old world village, then a riparian corridor full of flowers, grapevines and wild shrubs, though it is a rather steep return trip. From the 17th-century Capela do Desterro at the end of Rua da Santa Cruz, head southeast over the river and follow the road to the left.

Mosteiro de São João de Tarouca

The stunning, massive yet skeletal remains of Portugal's first Cistercian monastery, the **Mosteiro de São João de Tarouca** (☑254 678 766; ⊙ 9.30am-12.30pm & 2-5.30pm Oct-Apr, 10am-12.30pm & 2-6pm May-Sep), founded in 1124, stand eerily in the wooded Barosa valley below the Serra de Leomil, 15km southeast of Lamego. There is beauty in the decay, as a stream bisects the walls backed by a bowl of terraced hills. The monastery fell into ruin after religious orders were abolished in 1834.

Only the church, considerably altered in the 17th century, stands intact among the ghostly ruins of the monks' quarters. Its treasures include the gilded choir stalls, 18th-century *azulejos,* and the church's pride and joy – a luminous *São Pedro* painted by Gaspar Vaz, contemporary and colleague of Grão Vasco.

From Lamego, Joalto/EAVT has several services each weekday (fewer on weekends) to Tarouca (€2.30).

Mosteiro de Salzedas

With pink stone arches picturesquely mouldering in the sun, the Cistercian **Mosteiro de Salzedas** (admission €3; ⊙9.30am-1pm & 2.30-6pm Wed-Sun, 2.30-6pm Mon-Tue) is located 3km up the Barosa valley from Ucanha in Vila Salzedas.This was one of the grandest monasteries in the land when it was built in 1168 with funds from Teresa Afonso, governess to Afonso Henriques' five children. The enormous church, which was extensively remodelled in the 18th century, is today a bit scruffy with decay, particularly its roofless cloisters next door; the faux crystal chandeliers are an odd sight, too. Across from the church lies the old *judiaria,* with dark narrow lanes skirting around the gloomy centuries-old dwellings.

From Lamego, Joalto/EAVT runs three buses each weekday to Vila Salzedas (€2.75).

Peso da Régua
POP 17,131

Lamego's businesslike alter ego, the sun-bleached town of Régua, abuts the Rio Douro at the western edge of the demarcated port-wine region. As the region's largest riverside town, it grew into a major port-wine *entrepôt* in the 18th century, and remains an important transport junction – thanks in part to the hulking IP3 bridge that soars above the river valley. The town itself, set along a busy highway above the river, doesn't have a lot of charm, and most visitors stop in just long enough to get recommendations, maps and directions to nearby wineries. However, it makes a convenient base to visit the port-wine country, cruise the Rio Douro and ride the Corgo railway line to Vila Real. Most tourists stick to the scenic riverfront, but the quaint old town one block uphill is an almost exclusively local scene, and well worth a wander.

There is a public car park at the eastern end of the riverfront promenade, a few blocks from the *turismo.*

◉ Sights & Activities

Museu do Douro   MUSEUM
(www.museudodouro.pt; Rua Marqués de Pombal; adult/student €6/3; ⊙10am-6pm daily May-Oct, 10am-6pm Tue-Sun Nov-Apr) It's not all about the wine. Sometimes it's about contemporary canvases, impressionist landscapes, old leather-bound texts, vintage port-wine posters and the remains of an old flat-bottomed port hauler. You'll find it all in a gorgeous

converted riverside warehouse, with a restaurant and bar on site. The gift shop, stocked with wine, handmade soaps and some terrific silver, is brilliant.

Boat Trips   CRUISE
(☑222 081 935; www.viadouro-cruzeiros.com; cruises from €10) Peso da Régua is a major stop on the Douro cruise line. Your best bet is to reserve through Porto Tours (p365) in Porto. You could also try hopping aboard one of the frequent daily 50-minute cruises to Pinhão offered by Tomaz do Douro. You'll find them at the pier. Locals also operate smaller boats from the pier, which can be less comfortable, yet more intimate and often a better choice for an hour's cruise.

Steam Train to Tua   TRAIN TRIP
(Comboio Vapor; www.cp.pt; one-way €3.95; ☉4 daily) While the gorgeous Linha da Tua line remains out of service, you can still ride in this lovingly restored steam train, which travels along the Douro from Régua to Tua, making a 20-minute stop in Pinhão.

🛏 Sleeping

Hotel Dom Quixote   HOTEL €
(☑254 321 151; residencialdquixote@sapo.pt; 1st fl, Av Sacadura Cabral 1; s/d €30/45; P❋☎) Located 1.5km west of the *turismo*, the modern Dom Quixote is arguably Régua's best budget option. It offers simple but comfortable – if forgettable – rooms.

Hotel Régua Douro   HOTEL €€
(☑254 320 700; www.hotelreguadouro.pt; Largo da Estação; s/d €70/88; P❋@☎☀) This industrial-sized hotel sits by the river and is steps from the train station. It has plush, carpeted rooms in ruby (or is that tawny?) colour schemes and windows overlooking the Douro. The pool is much appreciated on hot days.

★Quinta do Vallado   RURAL INN €€€
(☑254 323 147; www.quintadovallado.com; Vilalinho dos Freiras; s/d from €120/130; P❋☀) About 3km from Régua, this 70-hectare winery offers five rooms in an old stone manor and eight swanky new rooms decked out with chestnut and teak wood, each complete with a balcony. They all share a common living room and a gorgeous pool. Guests get a free tour of the winery, with a tasting.

Aquapura   RESORT €€€
(☑254 660 600; www.aquapurahotels.com; Quinta Vale de Abraão; r €250; P❋☎) This stunning 50-room property is the grand dame of the Douro, nestled on an idyllic bend in the river 5km from Régua, wrapped by terraced vineyards and dotted with swaying palms. Chic modernist rooms are set in an antiquated villa that's also outfitted with a top-shelf spa and stunning black-bottom infinity pool.

🍴 Eating

Dom Quixote   PORTUGUESE €
(Av João Franco; mains €5-6; ☉lunch & dinner) Run in conjunction with the guesthouse (but in a different location (next to EuropCar), this humble diner serves all the fish and roasted-meat dishes you crave, along with a nice selection of table wines.

Taberna do Jéréré   PORTUGUESE €€
(Rua Marquês de Pombal 38; mains €9-16; ☉lunch daily, dinner Mon-Sat) Excellent Portuguese dishes, including *bacalhau á Jéréré* (dried salt-cod with shrimp, mushroom and spinach), served in a tastefully rustic dining room with a beamed ceiling and granite floors. Great-value lunch specials.

Douro In   PORTUGUESE €€
(☑254 323 951; Av Joáo Franco; mains €15-19.50; ☉lunch & dinner) A step up in price and quality from most Régua options is the stylish Douro In. Elegant place settings and sizeable windows overlooking the river set the scene for feasting on monkfish skewers with citrus rice and other flavourful dishes. It has a superb wine list, and an upstairs wine bar with an outdoor terrace. Book ahead.

Castas e Pratos   PORTUGUESE €€€
(Rua José Vasques Osorio; mains €13.50-25.90; ☉lunch & dinner) The coolest dining room in town is set in a restored wood-and-stone railyard warehouse with exposed original timbers. You can order grilled *alheira* sausage or octopus salad from the tapas bar downstairs or have the seabass on seafood fumet with saffron filaments, or kid goat in port with fava beans in the mezzanine.

ℹ Information

Pick up a town map and local information at the **turismo** (www.douroturismo.pt; Rua da Ferreirinha 505; ☉9.30am-12.30pm & 2-6pm daily Jul–mid-Sep, Mon-Fri mid-Sep–Jun), 1km west of the station.

ℹ Getting There & Around

Joalto buses run regularly to/from Lamego (€2.30, 20 minutes) and Tâmega/Rodonorte has four daily departures to Vila Real (€6, 30 minutes).

There are around 12 trains daily from Porto (€10, two hours); some continue up the valley to Pinhão (€2.75, 25 minutes, five daily). Around six trains depart daily for Tua (€3.95, 40 minutes). If you've taken a train this far and suddenly realise you need a car to visit the vineyards, your best bet is **Europcar** (☎254 321 146; www.europcar. com; Av João Franco; per day from €82).

To get to the *cais fluvial* (river terminal) from the *turismo*, bear left at the Residencial Império.

Alto Douro

Heading upriver from Peso da Régua, terraced vineyards blanket every hillside, with whitewashed *quintas* perched high above the Douro. This dramatic landscape is the jaw-dropping by-product of over 2000 years of winemaking. While villages are small and architectural monuments few and far between, it's worth the trip simply for the ride itself (scenic by car, train or boat), with panoramic vistas lurking around nearly every bend. Its allure has clearly not gone unnoticed. In 2001 Unesco designated the entire Alto Douro wine-growing region a World Heritage site.

Further east towards Spain, the soil is drier, and the sculpted landscape gives way to more rugged terrain. But despite the aridity – and the blisteringly hot summers – the land around Vila Nova de Foz Côa produces fine grapes and excellent olives and nuts.

Many port and table wine *quintas* offer rural accommodation, though rooms grow scarce in late September and early October during the *vindima* (grape harvest).

Daily trains run from Porto, with a change at Régua, up to Pinhão, Tua and Pocinho. Travellers with their own wheels can take the river-hugging N222 from Régua to Pinhão, beyond which the roads climb in and out of the valley.

Pinhão & Around

POP 1000

Encircled by terraced hillsides that produce some of the world's best port – and some damn good table wines too, little Pinhão sits on a particularly lovely bend of the Rio Douro, about 25km upriver from Peso da Régua. Wineries and their competing signs dominate the scene. Even the delightful train station has *azulejos* depicting the grape harvest. The town itself, cute though

it is, holds little of interest, but does makes a fine base for exploring the many surrounding vineyards.

In addition to drinking your fill, this is a good setting for country walks, and there are some fine day-trip possibilities. Except on high-season weekends, street parking is straightforward. Look around the train station or down by the river (first left after passing the train station).

🏃 Activities

Driving the Alto Douro   DRIVING TOUR
(Hwy N222 & N322) One of the region's biggest thrills is simply driving the Douro's winding roads, navigating hairpin turns, climbing terraced ridges and cruising village back roads patrolled by mobs of latter-day Romeos. This road teases the adventurous driver, taking you away from the river and into the shadows of another impossibly huddled village, then back into direct sunlight that streams through trees and bathes the steep drop to the river in surreal golden light. In between, of course, you will need to stop at a *quinta* or three.

Quinta Nova   HIKING
(☎254 730 430; www.quintanova.com; winery visit €12, geocaching per person €10; ☺winery tours 11am, 3pm & 5pm) Set on a stunning ridge, surrounded by luscious, ancient vineyards, overlooking the deep green Douro river with mountains layered in the distance, the Quinta Nova estate is well worth an in-depth exploration. The three hiking trails (the longest is 2.5 hours) are the best in the region, and fans of *The Amazing Race* will want in on the Geocaching Challenge. Guests use a GPS to locate five wine caches, replacing the corks in each. If you complete the task, you'll win a prize! To get here, head 9km west of Pinhão, along the northern bank of the Douro (EN322-2). Hotel guests roam free.

Train to Pocinho   TRAIN TRIP
(one-way €4.65; ☺ departs 5 times daily) With the Linha do Tua still out of service, the most beautiful train trip in the area is this one-hour chug upriver along the most stunning section of the Tua line. Trains depart from the Pinhão train station twice per day.

Douro-a-Vela Boat Trips   CRUISE
(☎918 793 792; www.douro-a-vela.pt; per person €25) One of the cheapest, easiest and sweetest thrills in the area demands that you cruise upriver into the heart of the Alto Douro aboard a traditional flat-bottomed port boat. Catch the

boat from the Folgosa do Douro pier, just outside DOC. Cruises last an hour and cost €25.

Quinta Nova Wine Museum & Shop
WINE TASTING

(Aris Douro; ☎254 730 030; www.quintanova.com; Largo da Estacão 14; tours & tastings €5; ⊙tours 11am, 3pm & 5pm Mon-Sat, 11am & 3pm Sun Apr-Oct) This collection of vintage winemaking gear offers a glimpse into the early days of viniculture and cooperage (bottling and labelling), but is only available by 25-minute tours offered three times a day. It's owned and operated by Quinta Nova, and you can taste the table and port wines here, too.

🛌 Sleeping

★ **Casa Cimeira**
RURAL INN €

(☎254 732 320; www.casacimeira-douro.com; s/d €45/60; P❋❂⛱) Set in a 200-year-old home

at the top of the hilltop town of Valença – its cobbled streets wrapped with vineyards and olive trees and alive with old country warmth – this is the domain of the charming Nogueira family. Rooms are spotless, there's a small pool, a sun deck and family-style dinners featuring the casa's own house wine.

Hotel Douro
HOTEL €

(☎254 732 404; www.hotel-douro.pt; Rua Antonio Manuel Saraiva 39; s/d €45/60; ❋@❂) This cheery, well-kept hotel – the nicest of its kind in Pinhão – has several river-facing rooms, other large rooms facing a quiet rear courtyard, and a miniterrace covered with vines.

Quinta de Santo António
RURAL INN €€

(☎254 789 177; www.quintasantoantonio.pt; s/d €80/90; P❋@❂⛱) This stunning 25-hectare property is owned by the former winemaker for Sandeman. The drive up the

---

DRINKING IN THE DOURO

Pinhão offers some enticing exploring for wine-lovers, with picturesque 18th-century manor houses overlooking steeply terraced vineyards leading down to the Rio Douro. To explore the *quintas* on your own, you'll need a vehicle. Ask the tourist office in Peso da Régua about lodges open for tours and tastings. A few good places to start the viticultural journey:

Quinta do Panascal (☎254 732 321; www.fonseca.pt; tours €3; ⊙10am-6pm daily May-Oct, 10am-6pm Mon-Fri Nov-Apr) Producer of Fonseca ports, this lovely estate offers self-guided audio tours (in many languages) through some beautifully situated vineyards, with a tasting of three wines. It's located about 10 minutes' drive west of Pinhão, well signed from the N222.

Quinta do Portal (☎259 937 000; www.quintadoportal.com; tours €5; ⊙10am-7pm daily mid-May–mid-Oct) This award-winning vineyard produces ports, red and white table wines, and a little-known muscatel wine. The surrounding region is one of the only places in the country producing muscatel (the other is Setúbal). Tours include a visit to the cellar with a tasting of three wines. There's a restaurant and guest house (doubles from €125). The winery lies about 12km north of Pinhão, along EN323, in the direction of Vila Real. Call ahead.

Quinta do Crasto (☎934 920 024; www.quintadocrasto.pt; tours €18; ⊙9am-6pm Mon-Fri) They've been making wine since 1615 on this gorgeous property set high in the Alto Douro with delicately laced vineyards overlooking the river and layers of mountains. Their dusty hounds are sweet, the wine is special and they do receive guests, but only during the week and with advance reservation. The tour includes a tasting of five wines.

Quinta Seara D'ordens (☎254 906 415; www.searadordens.com; tours & tasting €5; ⊙9am-noon & 2-6pm daily) A 60-hectare property run by three charming brothers who make some of the most quaffable and affordable table wines in the valley. Make an appointment and they'll guide you through their product line, pouring glass after glass, and if you buy a bottle the tasting is free.

Quinta do Tedo (☎934 609 671; www.quintadotedo.com; ⊙10am-7pm daily) Blessed with sublime real estate carved by two rivers – the Douro and Tedo – this American-French-Portuguese-owned estate is equipped with a restaurant and winery, which you can see on a short 20-minute tour with eight excellent table wines and a port to sample in the tasting room. Be warned, they do get some package tourists, but service is excellent even for indie types.

steep, rutted dirt road is exciting, the perch high, the river and mountain views jaw-dropping, and the price fair. Don't leave until you've sipped their 25-year-old tawny. Get here via the road to Tabuaço.

Casa de Casal de Loivos
RURAL INN €€

(☑254 732 149; www.casadecasaldeloivos.com; s/d €85/110; @☀) The house has been in this winemaking family for nearly 350 years. The halls are enlivened by museum-level displays of folkloric dresses, and the perch-high above the Alto Douro and 7km from Pinhão, with vineyard-terraced hills spread out in all directions – is spectacular. It closes from December to February.

Casa do Visconde de Chanceleiros
RURAL INN €€€

(☑254 730 190; www.chanceleiros.com; s €125-140, d €135-150; P ☎ ☀) This gorgeous 250-year-old manor house up in the hills of Alto Douro has spacious standard and superior rooms featuring classic decor and patios. The expansive views of the valley and lush terraced gardens steal the show but so does the outdoor pool, tennis court, Jacuzzi and sauna in a wine barrel. Delicious dinners are served on request.

Quinta Nova
RURAL INN €€€

(☑254 732 430; www.quintanova.com; s €134-152, d €152-173; ☎ ☀) This 120-hectare vineyard offers first-rate lodging on a historic estate on the northern side of the Douro, 9km from Pinhão. Rooms are sizeable and plush. Views are massive and the atmosphere – in the rooms, by the pool, throughout the grounds – is extremely romantic. The restaurant (open for lunch Tuesday to Sunday, and dinner Tuesday to Saturday) is fair at best, but the wine is special. There are also walking trails.

DON'T MISS

SAN SALVADOR DEL MUNDO

San Salvador del Mundo makes for a stunning diversion between Pinhão and Foz Côa. Follow the signs to a short series of stone turnouts with special hill, vineyard and river views. Some have stone slab tables and benches that demand a picnic, surrounded by wildflowers and serenaded by birdsong. After lunch continue to the top of the road and stroll to the chapel on the pinnacle. Spectacular.

Vintage House
BOUTIQUE HOTEL €€€

(☑254 730 230; www.hotelvintagehouse-douro.com; Lugar da Ponte; s €158-178, d €165-230; P ✴ @ ☎ ☀) Occupying a string of 19th-century buildings right on the river, this luxurious sleep is actually very modern once you get past the distinctly English facade (a reminder of the key role Brits played in the port trade). This is where BB King stayed when he rocked the Douro. All rooms have terraces or balconies with river views.

✖ Eating

Veladouro
PORTUGUESE €

(Rua Praia; mains €6-8; ☺lunch & dinner Mon-Sat) Simple Portuguese food, such as wood-grilled meats, is served inside this quaint schist building or outside under a canopy of vines. From the train station, turn left and go along the main road for 150m, then left again under a railway bridge, and right at the river.

Ponte Romana
PORTUGUESE €€

(Rua Santo António 2; mains €8-12; ☺lunch & dinner Mon-Sat) For nicely prepared traditional Portuguese food, Ponte Romana is the place to go, with tasty fresh grilled sea bass, tender and buttery grilled octopus, and *cabrito assado* (roasted kid goat). From the train station, turn left and follow the main road for 600m; cross the stone bridge and you'll see it on the right.

★DOC
PORTUGUESE €€€

(☑254 858 123; www.ruipaula.com; Folgosa; mains €27.50-29; ☺lunch & dinner daily summer, closed Mon & dinner Sun winter) DOC serves haute cuisine to the well-to-do (check out the Ferraris and Astons in the parking lot) on an outdoor deck over the Douro. The changing menu features creative dishes such as monkfish with scallops, and Portuguese sausage samosa. It's located 13km west of Pinhão, on the southern side of the river. For a real splurge, order the €70 tasting menu.

❶ Getting There & Away

Regional trains go to and from Peso da Régua (€2.75, 25 minutes, five daily), where you can catch one to Porto.

Vila Nova de Foz Côa
POP 3200

In the heart of the Douro's *terra quente* (hot land), this once-remote, whitewashed town has been on the map since the 1990s.

That's when researchers – during an environmental impact study for a proposed dam – stumbled across an astounding collection of Palaeolithic art. These mysterious rock engravings, which number in the thousands, blanket the nearby Rio Côa valley. Archaeologists brought the petroglyphs to the world's attention, and the dam builders backed down when the whole valley was declared a Unesco World Heritage site.

You may find the climate startlingly Mediterranean if you've just come from the mountains. Summers here are infernally hot, with temperatures regularly exceeding 45°C. But if you come in late March, you'll be treated to cooler climes, wildflowers and blooming almond trees.

Long-distance coaches stop at the bus station about 150m north of the *turismo* at Av Gago Coutinho. From here the town stretches eastward along Av Gago Coutinho, pedestrianised Rua Dr Juiz Moutinho de Andrade, Rua São Miguel and Rua Dr Júlio de Moura to the old town's centre, Praça do Município.

There is usually plenty of free parking along Av Gago Coutinho between the *turismo* and the Parque Arqueológico do Vale do Côa headquarters.

◎ Sights & Activities

Parque Arqueológico do
Vale do Côa
ARCHAEOLOGICAL SITE

(www.arte-coa.pt; Av Gago Coutinho 19 A, Foz Côa; park €10, museum €5 [on Sun afternoons €1]; park & museum €12; ☉ museum 10am-1.30pm & 2-5.30pm Tue-Sun, park 9am-12.30pm & 2-5.30pm Tue-Sun) Most visitors to Vila Nova de Foz Côa come for one reason: to see its world-famous gallery of rock art. Although the park is currently an active research zone, three sites are open to the public: **Canada do Inferno**, with departures at around 9.30am from the park museum in Vila Nova de Foz Côa; **Ribeira de Piscos**, with departures at around 9.30am from the Muxagata visitor centre on the western side of the valley; and **Penascosa**, with departures from the Castelo Melhor visitor centre on the eastern side, which also offers night tours (€17).

While Castelo Melhor has some of the most significant etchings, Canada do Inferno – which sits by the half-constructed dam – is the ideal place to understand just how close these aeons-old drawings came to disappearing.

Because the entire valley is a working archaeological site, all visitors must enter with a guided tour. Visitors gather at the various visitor centres, where they're taken, eight at a time, in the park's own 4WDs, for a guided tour of one of the sites (two hours at Canada do Inferno, which includes 1km of walking; one hour at Penascosa; 2½ hours at Ribeira de Piscos, with 2km of walking). You can take in two sites in one day – one in the morning and one in the afternoon. Visitors with mountain bikes may go on guided bike tours (bring your own bike) in similar-sized groups.

Visitor numbers are strictly regulated, so from July to September book a tour well in advance or you may miss out; reservations are accepted from Tuesday to Friday. You must book at least a few weeks ahead for bicycle trips at any time. You can make bookings through the park office.

Make sure you bring comfortable shoes and a hat, sunblock and water in summer months, as it gets boiling hot in the valley.

Old Town
NEIGHBOURHOOD

The sleepy old quarter makes for a pleasant stroll in the early evening. Highlights are the Praça do Município, with its impressive granite *pelourinho,* and the elaborately carved portal of the Manueline-style parish church. Just east off the square is the tiny Capela de Santa Quitéria, once the town's synagogue.

Museu da Casa Grande
MUSEUM

(adult/student €2/1; ☉ 9am-noon & 2-6pm Tue-Sun) Archaeological finds from the Stone Age to the 18th century have been uncovered in the region around Freixo de Numão, 12km west of Vila Nova de Foz Côa. A good little display can be viewed in this baroque town house with Roman foundations. Some English and French are spoken. Guided tours are available by arrangement with the museum.

🛏 Sleeping & Eating

Pousada da Juventude
HOSTEL €

(☑ 279 764 041; www.pousadasjuventude.pt; Caminho Vicinal Currauteles 5; dm/d €13/32; ⓟ @ 🛜) This hostel, in a modern pink-brick building, is well worth the 800m-walk north from the town centre (1.4km by road). Its basic but handsome doubles have views over a rugged valley; four-bed dorms are clean and well maintained. Amenities include bar, open kitchen, laundry, cafeteria, games room and large patio with sweeping views.

MATEUS REVISITED

If 'Mateus' conjures up images of sickly sweet pink 'starter wine' and ubiquitous 1970s wine-bottles-as-candleholders, think again and try a sip of Alvarelhão. This distinctive Portuguese grape is the original base for Mateus rosé, which in the 1950s was retooled for mass marketing in North America, where palates were considerably less sophisticated. Now the growers and vintners of Lavradores de Feitoria, whose numbers include the current Count of Vila Real and heir to the famous Palácio de Mateus itself, are producing an Alvarelhão rosé that more fully honours the legacy of this uniquely Iberian varietal.

Some growers describe Alvarelhão as a grape that is impractical and near-impossible to grow. It matures late, well into October, and is easy prey to mildews and other pathogens – so much so that growers traditionally grew it closest to their homes and estates so they could be more easily alerted to possible outbreaks of disease. As one Lavradores producer puts it, 'Here in Portugal, we love tradition. But we are not efficient. We are not practical. We grow something because our fathers and our grandfathers and their grandfathers did. It's said that because of this we still have hundreds of varietals which have died out in other places. So we are still growing this Alvarelhão because we love it.'

Because of its temperamental nature, Alvarelhão – like many of Portugal's best wines – is bottled in small quantities, mostly for use in Portugal. Until these delicious and deserving wines get wider international distribution, do yourself a favour while touring the Palácio de Mateus (p397) and sip it while you can!

Hotel Vale do Côa
HOTEL €

(☎279 760 010; www.hotelvaledocoa.net; Av Cidade Nova 1A; s/d €42/55; P❄) This modern hotel opposite the tourist office offers comfortable, air-conditioned rooms with clean-swept wooden floors. Most rooms have verandahs with views of the hilly countryside.

Cafenteria Ritz
PORTUGUESE €

(Rua de São Miguel 14; mains €5-7; ☺breakfast, lunch & dinner Mon-Sat) Popular among the locals for locally styled roast-meat (and only roast meat) dishes. Ritz stays open until midnight.

António & Julia
SELF-CATERING €

(Rua de São Miguel 50; ☺breakfast & lunch Mon-Sat) Top-quality local hams, sausages, cheese and honey are available for picnics at this charming shop on the São Miguel strip.

Restaurante A Marisqueira
PORTUGUESE €€

(Rua de São Miguel 35; mains €7-25; ☺lunch & dinner Mon-Sat) Located on a pleasant pedestrian street in the old town, this cheery place serves good Portuguese meat dishes and just enough *mariscos* (shellfish) to justify the name in a small but bright contemporary dining room.

☆ Entertainment

Although there isn't a lot going on in Foz Côa, the **Centro Cultural** (☎279 760 324; www.fozcoactiva.pt; Av Cidade Nova 2) hosts concerts, temporary art exhibitions and film screenings throughout the year. It's in the same building as the *turismo*.

ℹ Information

Biblioteca Municipal de Vila Nova de Foz Côa (☎279 760 300; Av Cidade Nova 2; ☺9amnoon & 2-5.30pm Mon-Fri) Free internet access in the same building as the *turismo*.
Municipal Turismo (☎279 760 329; www.cm-fozcoa.pt; Av Cidade Nova 2; ☺9am-12.30pm & 2-5.30pm) Opposite Albergaria Foz Côa.

ℹ Getting There & Away

One daily bus connects Vila Nova de Foz Côa with Bragança (€8.30, 1¾ hours) and another with Miranda do Douro (€6, 2½ hours). Three buses per day travel via Trancoso (€4.40) from Viseu (€9.20, two hours).

Five daily trains run to Pocinho, at the end of the Douro valley line, from Porto (€10.65, 3½ hours) and Peso da Régua (€6) through Pinhão (€3.20). A taxi between Pocinho and Vila Nova de Foz Côa costs about €6 to €8, and there are two daily buses (€2 to €4.40, 20 minutes).

ℹ Getting Around

A twice-daily bus passes the outskirts of Castelo Melhor (€1.90, 15 minutes); from there it's an easy walk to the Parque Arqueológico do Vale do Côa visitor centre. Alternatively, there is a taxi stand on the square in front of the parks office in

Vila Nova de Foz Coa, and park guides often help organise carpools, too.

Vila Real

POP 19,200 / ELEV 445M

Clinging to steep hillsides above the confluence of the Rios Corgo and Cabril, the university town of Vila Real in Trás-os-Montes is short on charm, although its historic centre, dotted with picturesque old churches, is pleasant enough. Its key attractions lie just beyond the city limits: the dramatically rugged highlands of the Parque Natural do Alvão; and the resplendent Palácio de Mateus, one of Europe's most elegant country houses, surrounded by lovely vineyard country east of town.

◎ Sights

Palácio de Mateus   PALACE
(☑ 259 323 121; www.casademateus.com; gardens €6.50, palace & gardens €10; ☉ 9am-1pm & 2-7pm) Famously depicted on bottles of Mateus rosé, the 18th-century Palácio de Mateus is one of Portugal's great baroque masterpieces – probably the work of Italian-born architect Nicolau Nasoni. Guided tours of the mansion (in English, French, Spanish and German) take you through the main quarters, which combine rusticity with restrained grandeur.

Its granite wings ('advancing lobster-like towards you', wrote English critic Sir Sacheverell Sitwell) shelter a lichen-encrusted forecourt dominated by an ornate stairway and guarded by rooftop statues. Surrounding the palace is a fantasy of a garden, with tiny boxwood hedges, prim statues and a fragrant cypress tunnel that's blissfully cool on even the hottest days. (Don't miss the fanciful 5m-tall curved ladders used to prune the tunnel's exterior branches!)

Inside, the library contains one of the first illustrated editions of Luís Vaz de Camões' *Os Lusíadas*, Portugal's most important epic poem, while another room houses an unintentionally droll collection of religious bric-a-brac, including three dozen macabre relics bought from the Vatican in the 18th century: a bit of holy fingernail, a saintly set of eyeballs, and the inevitable piece of the true cross – each with the Vatican's proof of authenticity.

Near the guided tour starting point, a wine shop offers tastings of three locally produced wines for €4. Especially interesting is the Alvarelhão, which is essentially the same fine rosé originally bottled by Mateus in the 1940s.

The palace is 3.5km east of the town centre. Take local Corgobus bus 1 (€1, 20 minutes) towards the university (UTAD). It leaves from Largo de Camões, just north of the *turismo*, roughly half-hourly between 7.30am and 8pm, with fewer buses on weekends. Ask for 'Mateus' and the driver will set you down about 250m from the palace (if you don't ask, he may not stop).

Churches   CHURCH
Once part of a Dominican monastery, the Gothic **sé** (Cathedral; Travessa de São Domingos) has been given a lengthy facelift that has restored the 15th-century grandeur of its rather spare interior.

Northeast of the cathedral is the magnificent baroque facade of the 17th-century **Capela Nova** (cnr Ruas Central & Direita). Inside are fine 18th-century *azulejos* and large-headed cherubs with teddy-boy coifs.

More baroque, and more *azulejos*, are on view at the **Igreja de São Pedro** (Largo de São Pedro), one block north of Capela Nova.

Museu Etnográfico de Vila Real   MUSEUM
(Avenida 1º de Maio; ☉ 9.30am-12.30pm & 2-6pm) **FREE** This small but colourful museum documents the traditional culture of the surrounding highlands, with exhibits on linen-making, ceramics, farming techniques, games, musical instruments and local festivals.

Miradouro de Trás-do-Cemitério   VIEWPOINT
For a fine view across the gorge of the Rio Corgo and Rio Cabril, walk south to this panoramic viewpoint, just beyond a small cemetery and chapel.

⌷ Sleeping

Appealing budget and midrange options in downtown Vila Real are in short supply. The best accommodation, including some charming semirural guesthouses, is on the city's outer fringes.

Residencial Real   GUESTHOUSE €
(☑ 259 325 879; www.residencialreal.com; Rua Central 5; s/d €30/40) The most appealing of the limited budget options downtown, this family-run place is nicely positioned in the middle of a pedestrian zone, above a popular *pastelaria* (pastry shop). Some of the bright, neatly kept rooms have high ceilings and French windows.

Vila Real

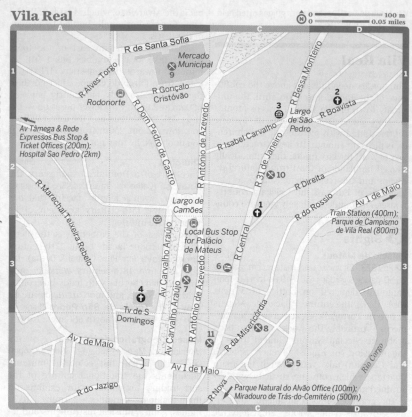

Vila Real

◉ Sights
1 Capela Nova C2
2 Igreja de São Pedro D1
3 Museu Etnográfico de Vila Real C1
4 Sé B3

🛏 Sleeping
5 Hotel Miracorgo C4
6 Residencial Real C3

✖ Eating
7 Café Pastelaria Nova Pompeia B3
8 Casa Lapão C4
9 Mercado Municipal B1
10 Terra de Montanha C2
11 Transmontano C4

Parque de Campismo de
Vila Real   CAMPGROUND €
(☎ 259 324 724; camping.vilareal@gmail.com; Rua Dr Manuel Cardona; sites per adult/child/tent/car €3.75/1.88/2.30/2.65; ☺ Mar-Nov) This simple, shady hillside campsite above the Rio Corgo, 1.2km northeast of the centre, has a municipal pool nearby, which guests are allowed to use for €0.50.

Casa Agrícola da Levada   RURAL INN €€
(☎ 259 322 190; www.casadalevada.com; Rua da Capela, Timpeira; s/d €60/75; P 🛜 🏊) Just north of the centre, at the end of a long, shady drive lies this little gem of an inn. A collection of tastefully renovated old houses surrounds grounds that include rose gardens, a large grassy lawn and a swimming pool. The friendly, multilingual owners have deep roots in the region and are generous in sharing their knowledge of the area's highlights.

Quinta de São Martinho   RURAL INN €€
(☎ 259 323 986; www.quintasaomartinho.com; Lugar de São Martinho, Mateus; s/d €55/65; P 🛜 🏊) Only 400m from the Palácio de

Mateus, this rambling granite farmhouse-turned-inn is surrounded by pretty gardens. Rooms aren't fancy but have wood-beamed ceilings and are traditionally furnished. Three-course dinners can be arranged with advance notice.

Hotel Miracorgo   HOTEL €€
(☑ 259 325 001; www.hotelmiracorgo.com; Av 1 de Maio 78; s/d/ste €49/71/98; ⓟ❉@⛱☒) Boasting fine views of the Rio Corgo canyon, this central, modern, midrise business hotel has well-appointed if unexciting rooms in two buildings, all with large verandahs. Get a room with the bridge or the river view.

✖ Eating

Numerous eateries are clustered in the historic centre, along the narrow streets just east of Av Carvalho Araújo.

Transmontano   PORTUGUESE €
(Rua Teixeira de Sousa 35-37; mains €6.50-9.50; ⊙ lunch & dinner Mon-Sat) Popular with locals, this plain-faced, family-run place in the central pedestrian zone serves delicious, belly-filling regional dishes. At lunchtime, *pratos do dia* (daily specials) go for €5.

Casa Lapão   TEAHOUSE €
(Rua de Misericórdia 51-54; pastries from €1; ⊙ 8.30am-7pm daily) This spruce tearoom specialises in traditional local sweets, including *cristas de galo* (almond and egg paste in a buttery pastry dough), *pitos de Santa Luzia* (made with pumpkin and cinnamon) and *pastéis de Santa Clara* (made with eggs, almond and cinnamon).

Café Pastelaria Nova Pompeia   BAKERY €
(Av Carvalho Araújo 82; mains €4.10-9.90; ⊙ 8am-8pm Mon-Sat, 8am-1pm Sun; ☏) A few doors down from the tourist office, this large, bright cafe and bakery serves omelettes and light meals at reasonable prices. Free wi-fi is icing on the cake.

Mercado Municipal   MARKET €
(Rua de Santa Sofia; ⊙ Mon-Sat) Self-caterers can stock up on rural produce at the market.

Terra de Montanha   PORTUGUESE €€
(Rua 31 de Janeiro 16; mains €10.50-13.50; ⊙ lunch & dinner Mon-Sat, lunch Sun; ☏) From the black crockery to the halved wine casks that serve as booths, everything here is rigorously *transmontana*. The hearty local cuisine

includes specialities such as *posta barrosã* (grilled veal steak). Weekday lunch specials are a great deal, plus they have vegetarian options – a rarity in these parts.

☆ Entertainment

Teatro de Vila Real   ARTS CENTRE
(☑ 259 320 000; www.teatrodevilareal.com; Alameda de Grasse) This slick, modern building, in a parklike area across the Corgo from the city centre, stages high-quality dance and theatre performances, as well as classical, jazz and world music. It also screens biweekly films and serves as a venue for the **Douro Jazz Festival** (www.douro jazz.com) during wine harvest season. At the back, the theatre's bright cafe overlooking the Corgo is popular with Vila Real's beau monde.

ⓘ Information

Hospital de São Pedro (☑ 259 300 503; Av da Noruega, Lordelo)
Parque Natural do Alvão Office (☑ 259 302 830; pnal@icnb.pt; Rua dos Freitas; ⊙ 9am-12.30pm & 2-5.30pm Mon-Fri)
Police Station (☑ 259 330 240; Largo Conde de Amarante)
Post Office (Av Carvalho Araújo; ⊙ 8.30am-6pm Mon-Fri)
Regional Turismo (☑ 259 322 819; www.douro-turismo.pt; Av Carvalho Araújo 94; ⊙ 9am-12.30pm & 2-5.30pm) Located in a Manueline house in the town centre.

ⓘ Getting There & Around

BUS
Several companies serve Vila Real. **Rodonorte** (☑ 259 340 710; www.rodonorte.pt) buses leave from a station on Rua Dom Pedro de Castro, 300m northwest of the *turismo*. **AV Tâmega** (☑ 259 322 928; www.avtamega.pt) and **Rede Expressos** (☑ 962 060 655; www.rede-expressos.pt) both operate from a lot slightly west of the Rodonorte station, at the corner of Rua Dr António Valente Fonseca and Av Cidade de Ourense. Destinations served by these companies include Bragança (€10.80, two hours), Chaves (€8, 70 minutes), Lamego (€6, 45 minutes), Lisbon (€20.50, five to 5½ hours), Miranda do Douro (€12.70, three to 3½ hours) and Porto (€9, 1½ hours).

CAR & MOTORCYCLE
There is pay parking downtown along Av Carvalho Araújo and in the parking garage below the *câmara municipal* (town hall).

GHOST TOWNS: THE TRANSMONTANA EXODUS

Portugal is one of the few European countries to experience mass emigration well into the 20th century. In the 1970s alone, it's estimated that 775,000 people left the country – nearly 10% of the total population.

With difficult agricultural conditions and very little industry, it is of little surprise that Trás-os-Montes (along with the neighbouring Minho) contributed more than its share of residents to the exodus. The region's population shrank by nearly 33% between 1960 and 2001. To get an idea of the kinds of conditions they were fleeing, consider this: 60% of the region's workforce was engaged in agriculture into the 1990s – a figure that is much higher than found in many developing nations.

At the turn of the 20th century, the lion's share of emigrants headed to Brazil, which was undergoing a coffee boom. Later, many left for Portugal's African possessions, which received increased investment and interest during Salazar's regime. Then, as Europe's postwar economy heated up in the 1960s and '70s, *transmontanas* began to stick closer to home, finding work as labourers in Germany, Belgium, Switzerland and especially France.

The effect of this mass exodus is still visible, especially in many rural areas. There are many villages that have been abandoned wholesale, left to a handful of widows and a clutch of chickens. Around others you'll find a ring of modern construction, almost always paid for by money earned abroad rather than the fruit of the land. And don't be surprised to meet a villager, scythe in hand and oxen in tow, who speaks to you in perfect Parisian argot.

Parque Natural do Alvão

With its rock-strewn highlands, schist villages, waterfalls and verdant pockets where cows graze in stone-walled pastures, the pristine Parque Natural do Alvão comes as a delightful revelation to travellers climbing from the hotter, drier country below. A drive of less than half an hour brings you from Vila Real to this extraordinary park straddling the central ridgeline of the Serra de Alvão, whose highest peaks reach more than 1300m. The small (72 sq km) protected area remains one of northern Portugal's best-kept secrets and shelters a remarkable variety of flora and fauna, thanks to its position in a transition zone between the humid coast and the dry interior.

The Rio Ôlo, a tributary of the Rio Tâmega, rises in the park's broad granite basin. A 300m drop above Ermelo gives rise to the spectacular Fisgas de Ermelo falls, the park's major tourist attraction.

Exploring the park on your own is not simple, as maps, accommodation and public transport are limited. Whether you plan to walk or drive in the park, it's worth visiting one of the park offices, located in Vila Real and Mondim de Basto, beforehand.

◉ Sights

Fisgas de Ermelo
WATERFALL

Just north of the town of Ermelo, on the N304 between Vila Real and Mondim de Basto, is a turn-off to the dramatic Fisgas de Ermelo waterfalls. From this junction, the road climbs 4km to an overlook with picture-perfect views of the falls and the rugged terrain surrounding them.

To see the falls from above, return to the main road and climb to a T-junction with a right-hand turn marked Varzigueto. Follow the Varzigueto road a short distance until you see signs on the right-hand side for Piocas de Cima. There are actually two footpaths: the first is marked '1.5km', the second is marked '600m'. Either path leads down into the river gorge, where you'll find not only hair-raising views of the river plunging off a cliff face, but also (further up) a natural waterslide and a series of pools perfect for cooling off on a hot day.

Ermelo
VILLAGE

The 800-year-old village of Ermelo is famous for its schist cottages capped with fairy-tale slate roofs that seem to have been constructed from broken blackboards. Once the main village of the region, it boasts traditional *espigueiros* (stone granaries), an ancient chapel, a sturdy granite *pelourinho* (pillory), a workshop that still practises the ancient local art of linen-making, and Ponte de Várzea – a Roman bridge rebuilt in medieval times.

The Ermelo turn-off is about 16km south of Mondim de Basto on the N304. The heart of town is about 1km uphill.

Lamas de Ôlo
VILLAGE

Set in a wide, verdant valley some 1000m above sea level, somnolent Lamas de Ôlo is the park's highest village, best known for its photogenic thatched roofs, as well as a nearby mill that was long driven by water from a crude aqueduct.

✖ Activities

There are a number of fine hikes in the park. A 7km, three-hour jaunt around the southern village of **Arnal** is described in the Portuguese-language leaflet *Guia do Percurso Pedestre,* available at park offices. The signposted hike delivers views east beyond Vila Real to the Serra do Marão. While you're in Arnal, track down the slate-roofed centre for traditional handicraft techniques.

Another popular route is the 13km, five-hour loop through the high country starting just north of the Cimeira dam along the Vila

Real–Lamas de Ôlo road. The trail, marked with red and yellow blazes, traverses the rock-strewn *planalto* (high plateau) for 8km to the village of Barreiro. From here, you can return 5km by road to your starting point, passing through Lamas de Ôlo en route.

With your own vehicle it's much easier to explore the network of small hillside villages within the park's borders. A particularly attractive drive connects Lamas de Ôlo to Ermelo via the traditional agricultural communities of **Pioledo**, **Varzigueto** and **Fervença**.

🛏 Sleeping & Eating

Camping is prohibited in the natural park, and other food and lodging options are scarce. It's worth inquiring at the Mondim de Basto *turismo* (p403) for possible bookings of private houses within the park. Otherwise, your best bet is to use Vila Real or Mondim de Basto as your base.

Dona Benedita
GUESTHOUSE €

(☑ 255 381 221; s/d €25/50) In Ermelo, Dona Benedita rents out three rooms, one of which is an en-suite.

Tasquinha d'Alice
PORTUGUESE €

(☑ 255 381 381; snacks €2.50-6; ⊙ Oct-Aug) In Bobal, halfway between Lamas de Ôlo and

---

THE HILLS ARE ALIVE: STRANGE WAYS IN TRÁS-OS-MONTES

For centuries, the remoteness of Trás-os-Montes has insulated it from central authority, helping its people preserve nonconformist ways that sometimes raise eyebrows in other parts of Portugal.

A number of licentious – and blatantly pagan – traditions still survive in the countryside. Witness the antics of the **Caretos of Podence** (near Macedo de Cavaleiros) – where gangs of young men in *caretos* (leering masks) and vividly striped costumes invade the town centre, bent on cheerfully humiliating everyone in sight. Prime targets are young women, at whom they thrust their hips and wave the cowbells hanging from their belts. Similar figures are to be seen in Varge, in the Parque Natural de Montesinho.

Colourful festivals derived from ancient Celtic solstice rituals take place in many villages in the two weeks between Christmas Eve and Dia dos Reis (Epiphany). During the so-called **Festa dos Rapazes** (Festival of the Lads), unmarried men over 16 light all-night bonfires and rampage around in robes of rags and masks of brass or wood. Un-Christian indeed!

Then there are the *pauliteiros* (stick dancers) of the Miranda do Douro region, who look and dance very much like England's Morris dancers. Local men deck themselves out in kilts and smocks, black waistcoats, bright flapping shawls, and black hats covered in flowers and ribbons, and do a rhythmic dance to the complex clacking of *paulitos* (short wooden sticks) – a practice that likely survives from Celtic times. The best time to see *pauliteiros* in Miranda is during the **Festas de Santa Bárbara** (also called Festas da Cidade, or City Festival), which is held on the third weekend in August.

Finally, there are the region's so-called crypto-Jews. During the Inquisition, Jews from Spain and Portugal found that they could evade ecclesiastical authorities here. Many families continued to observe Jewish practices in secrecy well into the 20th century.

Mondim de Basto, Tasquinha d'Alice is recommended for its all-day snacks, such as great *alheira* as well as *salpicão* omelette. Staff can also arrange full meals for groups of six or more with advance notice. The back room has lovely vistas.

Sabores do Alvão   PORTUGUESE €
(mains €7-11) A good option for food in Ermelo is Sabores do Alvão, a family-run restaurant by the church with nice valley views and hearty staples like spare ribs cooked in wine and garlic, served with rice.

ℹ Information

There are park offices in Vila Real (p399) and Mondim de Basto.

ℹ Getting There & Away

Public transport within the park is extremely limited.

FROM VILA REAL

Rodonorte (☑ 259 340 710) operates weekday buses at noon and 6.30pm to Lamas de Ôlo (€2.45, 30 minutes), returning to Vila Real at 12.30pm.

FROM MONDIM DE BASTO

Auto Mondinense (☑ 255 381 296) runs from Mondim de Basto to Ermelo (€2.35, one hour) three times each weekday, and to Lamas de Ôlo (€3.20, 50 minutes) twice on Tuesdays and Fridays.

Mondim de Basto

POP 7493 / ELEV 200M

Sitting in the Tâmega valley at the intersection of the Douro, Minho and Trás-os-Montes regions, low-lying Mondim de Basto has no compelling sights beyond a few flowery squares, but it makes an attractive base from which to explore the heights of the Parque Natural do Alvão. The vineyards surrounding town cultivate grapes used in the fine local *vinho verde* (young wine).

🏃 Activities

Hiking

Hikers wanting to feel a little burn in their thighs should consider the long haul up to the 18th-century Capela da Senhora da Graça on the summit of pine-clad Monte Farinha (996m). It takes about two hours to reach the top. The path starts east of town on the N312 (the *turismo* has a rough map). By car, turn off the N312 3.5km from

Mondim towards Cerva; from there it's a twisting 9.5km to the top.

Swimming

At **Senhora da Ponte**, 2km south of town on the N304, there's a rocky swimming spot by a disused watermill on the Rio Cabril. Follow the signs to the Parque de Campismo de Mondim de Basto and then take the track to the right.

Wine Tasting

Eight kilometres north of town in Atei, the 17th-century Casa Santa Eulalia (www.casa santaeulalia.com) is set amid 32 hectares of vineyards, and offers tastings of their refreshing local *vinho verde* with advance notice.

🛏 Sleeping

Residencial Carvalho   GUESTHOUSE €
(☑ 259 470 547; j3.carvalho@gmail.com; Av Dr Augusto Brito; s/d/ste €20/30/45; ❈ @ 🛜) For low-cost indoor accommodation, your best bet is this graceless, modern *residencial* (guesthouse) west of the *turismo*, next to the GALP petrol station.

Casa das Mourôas   GUESTHOUSE €€
(☑ 938 711 272, 255 381 394; Rua José Carvalho Camões; s/d €50/55) Occupying an old stone house on the same flower-filled square as the *turismo*, this little place has three humble but neat rooms arranged around a delightful, vine-covered terrace. English is spoken. Reservations are recommended on weekends and in summer.

Quinta do Fundo   RURAL INN €
(☑ 255 381 291; www.quintadofundo.com; Vilar de Viando; s/d/ste €40/50/75; 🅿 🛜 🏊) This pleasant spot, set amid a sea of vineyards 2km south of town on the N304, has decent rooms (if you can overlook the shiny, vinyl-like flowered bedspreads), fine mountain vistas, a tennis court, bikes for rent and a swimming pool. The *quinta* (estate) also produces its own *vinho verde*. Ask about discounts for multinight stays.

Casa do Barreiro de Cima   RURAL INN €€
(☑ 255 386 491; www.casadobarreirodecima.com; Rua do Barreiro de Cima 15; s/d €50/60; 🅿 🛜 🏊) Chirping birds and fragrant boxwood hedges greet you at this agreeable hideaway, tucked down a side road in the wine country 6km north of Mondim de Basto. The 17th-century granite manor house is full of period charm, although the rooms are a little on the small side.

More appealing are the secluded and grassy grounds across the street from the inn – punctuated with an *espigueiros* (granary) and a cool blue pool that offers lovely views over the surrounding hills and nearby vineyards.

Casa do Campo RURAL INN €€
(☑ 255 361 231; www.casadocampo.pt; Celorico de Basto, Molares; s/d/ste €75/90/110; [P][≋]) If you have wheels, consider this antique-packed, whitewashed 17th-century manor house with its own crenellated stone tower, chapel and extravagant topiary gardens. Rooms are modest but pleasant, with wood floors and plain country furnishings. Suites include a small living room with TV and *frigobar*. It's 7km west of Mondim. There's an outdoor pool and tennis court.

Eating

Adega Sete Condes PORTUGUESE €€
(Rua Velha; mains €7.50-12; ☺ lunch & dinner Tue-Sun, lunch Mon) Tucked into a tiny corner near the *turismo*, this rustic, granite-walled spot has a small menu of well-prepared traditional dishes, including *bacalhau* (dried salt-cod) and a very tasty *feijoada* (pork and bean stew).

Adega São Tiago PORTUGUESE €€
(Zona Velha; mains €7.50-11; ☺ lunch & dinner Mon-Sat) Adega São Tiago features a traditional Portuguese menu; the all-inclusive lunch special is a good deal at €6.

❶ Information

Parque Natural do Alvão Office (☑ 255 381 209; pnal@icnb.pt; Lugar do Barrio; ☺ 9am-12.30pm & 2-5.30pm Mon-Fri) About 700m west of the *turismo*.

Turismo (☑ 255 389 370; www.cm-mondim debasto.pt; Praça do Municipio; ☺ 9am-1pm & 2-5pm Mon-Fri, 10am-1pm & 2-5pm Sat, 9am-1pm Sun) Has loads of local information and rents out bikes (per hour/day €1/5).

❶ Getting There & Around

BUS
Buses stop behind the *mercado municipal*, 150m east of the *turismo* and what remains of the old town. **Auto Mondinense** (☑ 255 381 296) has seven weekday and two to three weekend buses to Porto (€6.05, 2¾ hours) via Guimarães (€4, 1½ hours). For Vila Real, take a Mondinense bus to Campeã (€3.40, 50 minutes, three daily) and change there for the short-hop Rodonorte bus to Vila Real.

CAR & MOTORCYCLE
There is street parking just west of the centre along Av Augusto Brito.

Chaves

POP 18,000 / ELEV 340M
A spa town with a long and fascinating history, Chaves (*shahv*-sh) is a pretty and engaging place, straddling the mountain-fringed banks of the Rio Tâmega only a few kilometres south of the Spanish border. Its well-preserved historic centre is anchored at the edges by a 16-arched Roman bridge dating back to Trajan's reign, a beautiful medieval tower and the rock-solid Forte de São Francisco.

All of these remnants testify to Chaves' earlier strategic importance in controlling the small but fertile plain that surrounds it. Romans built a key garrison here, that was subsequently contested by the Visigoths, Moors, French and Spanish. The city saw particularly fierce fighting during the Napoleonic invasion, when it was at the forefront of the resistance against French domination.

Nowadays Chaves is a placid backwater, where the Portuguese come not to defend the national honour but to pamper themselves in the natural hot springs that bubble up in the city's heart.

The backbone of Chaves' old town is Rua de Santo António, which runs southeast from the *turismo* to the Roman bridge. The spa is near the river, just south of the centre.

◉ Sights & Activities

Forte de São Francisco FORT
Reached by a drawbridge and bordered by a park with floral designs, hedges and grand old oaks, the 17th-century Forte de São Francisco is the centrepiece of Chaves' old town. The fort, with its thick walls, was completed in 1658 around a 16th-century Franciscan convent. These days it's a top-end hotel (p405), though nobody minds if you snoop around inside the walls.

Torre de Menagem TOWER
The lovely Torre de Menagem (castle keep) stands alone on a grassy embankment behind the town's main square, the only major remnant of a 14th-century castle built by Dom Dinis. Around the tower are attractive manicured flowerbeds and a stretch of old defensive walls, with views over the town and countryside.

Chaves

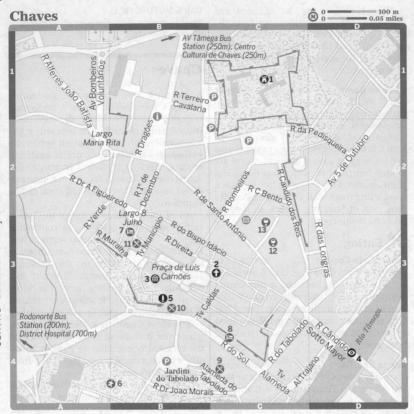

The *torre* now houses a motley collection of military gear in the **Museu Militar** (admission incl Museu da Região Flaviense €1; ⊘ 9am-12.30pm & 2-5.30pm, closed holidays), accessed via a series of creaky stairs.

Ponte Romana
BRIDGE

Chaves' handsome, 140m-long, Roman-era bridge makes a lovely place for a car-free stroll. The span was completed in AD 104 by order of Emperor Trajan (hence its other name, Ponte Trajano). It likely served as a key link on the important road between Braga and Astorga (Spain), as two engraved Roman milestones on the centre of the bridge indicate.

Museu da Região Flaviense
MUSEUM

(Praça de Luís Camões; admission incl Museu Militar €1; ⊘ 9am-12.30pm & 2-5.30pm) Small but interesting, this regional archaeological-ethnographic museum has lots of Roman artefacts, plus a collection of pre-Roman jewellery, bronze tools, grinding stones and menhirs, some dating back over 2500 years. There are also temporary art displays upstairs.

Termas de Chaves
SPA

(☑ 276 332 445; www.termasdechaves.com; Largo das Caldas) The warm waters of the Termas de Chaves, which emerge from the ground at 73°C, are said to relieve everything from rheumatism to obesity. After shelling out the initial €35 medical consultation fee, you have access to a plethora of reasonably priced treatments (€5 to €23), ranging from steam baths to massage. In the rotunda just outside the baths, spa employees distribute free glasses of the warm, bicarbonate-heavy waters, though they taste pretty awful.

🛏 Sleeping

Budget accommodation is clustered along Rua do Sol in the historic centre. For a bit

Chaves

more character and charm, consider the slew of attractive rural inns in the hills surrounding town. Book ahead in summer, when the spa is in full swing. Most places offer big discounts from September to May.

Hospedaria Florinda   GUESTHOUSE €
(☑276 333 392; www.hospedariaflorinda.com; Rua dos Açougues; s/d €30/40; ⊙lunch & dinner; ✳🛜) On a narrow street near the Torre de Menagem, Florinda has pleasant rooms with hardwood floors and tiny tubs. Some overlook a light-flooded inner courtyard. The lady of the house prepares meals on request.

Hotel Kátia   HOTEL €
(☑276 324 446; Rua do Sol 28; s/d €35/45; ✳🛜) Recently upgraded from guesthouse to hotel, this family-run place offers small stylish rooms – some with verandahs – plus a decent restaurant downstairs. Get one of the rooms facing the street.

Quinta do Rebentão   CAMPGROUND €
(☑276 322 733; www.cccchaves.com; Vila Nova de Veiga; sites per adult/child/tent/car €3.20/2.70/2.60/3, 2-/4-person bungalows €40/52; ⊙Jan-Nov; @🛜≋) Six kilometres southwest of Chaves, just off the N2, is this grassy, partly shaded, suburban camping facility with free hot showers, pool access and basic supplies.

Quinta da Mata   RURAL INN €€
(☑276 340 030; www.quintadamata.net; Estrada Nacional 213; s/d €70/80; P@🛜≋🍴) This isolated, family-friendly country haven, just 4.5km southeast of Chaves off the N213, centres on a lovingly restored and elegantly appointed 17th-century manor house with terracotta tile floors and stone walls. The grounds include tennis courts, a sauna and beautiful, flower-filled gardens on the lush hills overlooking the city. The excellent breakfast includes local ham and other regional specialities. Bikes are free for guests.

Hotel Rural Casa de Samaiões   RURAL INN €€
(☑276 340 450; www.hotel-casasamaioes.com; Samaiões; s/d/ste €83/93/134; P✳🛜≋) Set amidst spacious grounds at the foot of lovely mountains, this manor house turned luxury hotel in the village of Samaiões (5km south of Chaves) is replete with historic decor, including a full suit of armour in the front parlour, and a 19th-century chapel. The rooms, while comfortable, are blandly modern by contrast.

Quinta de Santa Isabel   RURAL INN €€
(☑936 452 043; www.quintadesantaisabel.com.pt; Santo Estevão; self-catering 2-/4-person apt €60/90; P🛜) This cluster of lovely stone houses – some dating back to the 16th century and converted from haylofts or stables – sits at the foot of a vineyard-covered hillside in the tiny town of Santo Estevão, 7km northeast of Chaves. The five apartments – each with a fireplace or wood-stove, plus kitchenette or kitchen – are filled with historic charm, including ancient wood floors, stone walls and antique furniture.

The common rooms, including billiards and foosball tables, are built around the massive, old wine press downstairs. Pets are welcome, there are hiking trails out the back and the proprietor speaks flawless English.

Forte de São Francisco   LUXURY HOTEL €€
(☑276 333 700; www.fortesaofrancisco.com; s/d/ste from €75/85/145; P✳@≋) For stylish digs in downtown Chaves, look no further than this remarkable historic inn. Housed in a 16th-century convent within the walls of the city's 17th-century fort, this extraordinary blend of four-star hotel and national monument has flawless rooms, tennis courts and a sauna, plus a rare-bird aviary, a centuries-old private chapel and an upscale restaurant and bar.

★ Pedras Salgadas
CABIN €€€

(☎259 437 140; www.pedrassalgadaspark.com; Bornes de Aguiar; 2 people €180, 3-4 people €190; P❄❀➔☎) 🖉 Seven fully equipped eco-bungalows are scattered around the woodlands of a spa park on the edge of Bornes de Aguiar, 30km south of Chaves. Shaded by tall trees, each spare and stylish cabin comes with grey slate tiled walls, private decks and lots of glass surfaces. Take to the waters at the spa or grab a free bike to explore the forest trails. Breakfast (extra charge) comes delivered in a basket.

Vidago Palace
LUXURY HOTEL €€€

(☎276 990 920; www.vidagopalace.com; Parque de Vidago, Apartado 16; s/d €220/240; P❄@➔☎) This recently opened salmon-pink grand palace in the spa town of Vidago, 12km south of Chaves, quickly shot up to the top rungs of Portugal's luxury hotels. The Belle Epoque grand dame showcases opulent rooms and suites, a gourmet restaurant in a ballroom, an 18-hole golf course and a white-marble spa for taking in the natural spring waters.

✗ Eating

For self-caterers, there's a supermarket upstairs from the AV Tâmega bus station.

O Cândido
PORTUGUESE €

(Rua da Tulha 14; mains €5-9; ☺lunch & dinner) Come to this no-frills restaurant to mingle with locals over typical dishes like *rancho*, *alheira* and *pataniscas*. The full menu with soup, salad, main and dessert is a steal at €9.

Maria
BAKERY €

(Largo do Municipio 4; snacks €0.55; ☺6.30am-6.30pm Mon-Sat, 1-6.30pm Sun) Look for the bright blue door of this tiny bakery, which whips up the best *pasteis de Chaves* (flaky turnovers filled with ground meat).

João Padeiro
BAKERY €

(Rua do Postigo; ☺9am-8pm) Snack on tasty regional treats at this corner bakery, including the trademark *folar de Chaves* (big pillowy loaves filled with bacon, *linguiça* and local *salpicão* sausage).

Carvalho
PORTUGUESE €€

(☎276 321 727; Largo das Caldas 4; mains €8-17; ☺lunch & dinner Tue-Sat, lunch Sun) Carvalho's top-notch regional dishes have earned recognition as some of Portugal's best. It's hidden away amid the cluster of parkside cafes opposite the Jardim do Tabolado.

🍷 Drinking & Entertainment

There's a cluster of lively bars across from the park and the spa at the bottom of town, and another on Travessa Cándido dos Reis near the fort.

Adega Faustino
WINE BAR

(Travessa Cândido dos Reis; snacks €4-9; ☺noon-11pm Mon-Sat) Resembling a fire station from the outside, this cavernous ex-winery oozes atmosphere inside, with cobblestoned floors and gigantic wine casks lined up behind the bar. The menu features a long list of carefully prepared regional snacks, from *salpicão* (small rounds of smoked ham) to pig's ear in vinaigrette sauce, plus an excellent selection of quaffable local wines.

Biblioteca
BAR

(Travessa Cândido dos Reis) This bar-disco with a name meaning 'library' attracts a raucous and decidedly nonliterary younger crowd.

Centro Cultural de Chaves
PERFORMING ARTS

(☎276 333 713; Largo da Estação) Chaves' brand-new cultural centre stages regular concerts, plays and other events, most of them free of charge. For details on current shows, see the monthly *Agenda Cultural,* available at the tourist office.

ℹ Information

Biblioteca Municipal (Largo General Silveira; ☺9am-7pm Mon-Fri) Free internet at the town library.

Hospital (☎276 300 900; Av Francisco Sá Carneiro) Northwest of the centre.

Police Station (☎276 323 125; Avenida Xavier Teixeira)

Post Office (Largo General Silveira; ☺8.30am-1pm & 2-5.30pm Mon-Fri)

Regional Turismo (☎276 348 180; turismo@portoenorte.pt; Terreiro de Cavalaria; ☺9am-12.30pm & 2-5.30pm Mon-Sat; ➔) Helpful multilingual tourist office.

ℹ Getting There & Around

BUS

AV Tâmega (☎276 332 384; www.avtamega.pt) and **Rodonorte** (☎276 328 123; www.rodonorte.pt; Av de Santo Amaro) have terminals just north and west of the centre respectively. Only Tâmega serves all of the following destinations: Bragança (€11.60, three hours, one daily at 4pm), Coimbra (€13.40, 3¾ hours, three daily), Lisbon (€21.60, six to seven hours, three daily), Porto (€13.40, 2¼ hours, several daily) and Vila Real (€8, 1¼ hours, several daily).

PIG MYSTERIES

Hundreds of crudely carved granite pigs or boars, known as *berrões*, are still scattered around the more remote parts of Trás-os-Montes and over into Spain. While they're widely acknowledged to be Celtic in origin, nobody knows for sure what purpose they served. Theories abound: they may have been symbols of fertility or prosperity, grave guardians, offerings to Iron Age gods, manifestations of the gods themselves or simply property markers.

You can see these mysterious pigs in museums in Bragança, Chaves and Miranda do Douro, or in situ in Bragança's citadel, where a weather-beaten porker supports a medieval pillory. The best-preserved example sits heavily atop a pedestal in the central square of tiny Murça, 30km northeast of Vila Real.

CAR & MOTORCYCLE
There's plenty of free public parking below the Torre da Menagem and around Jardim do Tabolado.

Bragança

POP 20,000 / ELEV 650M

The historical capital of Trás-os-Montes, Bragança is at once a modern city of broad sterile avenues and suburban high-rises, and an overgrown medieval village from whose crenellated heights one can still survey the surrounding countryside and see small farms, fields and oak-chestnut forest. While many streets – especially some in the older *centro* – give the appearance of a town down on its luck, new construction and civic projects express Bragança's enduring pride and dynamism. Recent additions to the city's cultural life include a municipal theatre, museums dedicated to contemporary art and regional folk traditions, and eye-catching public sculptures such as the bronze postman outside the *correio* (post office) and the massive fighting bulls in the Rotunda do Lavrador Transmontano.

For the visitor, the main attraction remains the ancient walled Cidadela (citadel), high atop the hill at Bragança's eastern edge. Walk through the arched gates into this extraordinarily well-preserved medieval quarter, with its tangle of narrow streets, multistorey keep and towering pig pillory, and it's easy to imagine life in the Middle Ages unfolding around you. The view from the topmost tower – for those brave enough to climb a steep, ancient wooden ladder – is truly astounding.

The city's main axis road – alternately called Av João da Cruz, Rua Almirante Reis, Rua Combatentes da Grande Guerra and Rua Trindade Coelho – winds southeast from the bus station up to the citadel. The town centre is Praça da Sé, the square in front of the old cathedral.

History

Known as Brigantia to the Celts and Juliobriga to the Romans, Bragança is an ancient city. Its location, mere kilometres from the Spanish border, made it an important post in the centuries-long battles between Spain and Portugal. The walled citadel was built in 1130 by Portugal's first king, Afonso Henriques I. His son and successor, Sancho I, improved the fortifications by building Bragança's castle, with its watchtowers, dungeons and keep, in 1187, after reclaiming the city from the king of León.

In 1442 Afonso V created the Duchy of Bragança for his uncle, an illegitimate son of the first Avis king João I, thus launching one of Portugal's wealthiest and most powerful noble families. The Braganças assumed the Portuguese throne in 1640, ending Spain's 60-year domination of Portugal. The family went on to reign in Portugal until the dissolution of the monarchy in 1910.

During the Napoleonic Wars, Bragança again served as an important strategic point against foreign invaders: it was from here that Sepúlveda launched his call to resistance against French forces.

◉ Sights

Museu do Abade de Baçal　MUSEUM
(www.ipmuseus.pt; Rua Abílio Beça 27; admission €2, 10am-2pm Sun free; ◉ 10am-5pm Tue-Fri, to 6pm Sat & Sun) Set in a restored 18th-century bishop's palace, the Museu do Abade de Baçal is one of Portugal's best regional museums. Its diverse collections include local artefacts from the Celtic and Roman eras, along with objects, paintings and photographs depicting daily life in Trás-os-Montes to the present.

Bragança

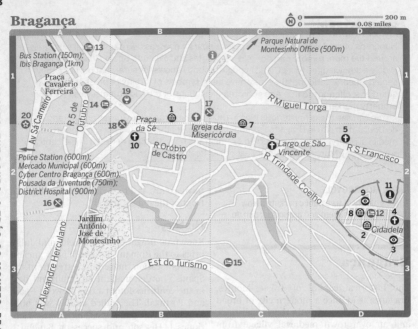

Bragança

◎ Sights

1 Centro de Arte Contemporânea
  Graça Morais B1
2 Cidadela D3
3 Domus Municipalis D3
4 Igreja de Santa Maria D3
5 Igreja de São Bento D2
6 Igreja de São Vicente C2
7 Museu do Abade de Baçal C2
8 Museu Ibérico da Máscara e do
  Traje D2
  Museu Militar .... (see 11)
9 Pelourinho D2
10 Sé B2
11 Torre de Menagem D2

🛏 Sleeping

12 Arco da Velha D2
13 Hotel Tulipa A1
14 Pensão Rucha A1
15 Pousada de São Bartolomeu C3

🍴 Eating

16 O Pote A2
17 Restaurante Lá Em Casa B1
18 Solar Bragançano B2

🍷 Drinking & Nightlife

19 Moderno B1

🎭 Entertainment

20 Teatro Municipal A2

Of particular interest are the handful of Iron Age stone pigs called *berrões*. The museum also features works by Portuguese naturalist painter Aurelia de Sousa and her contemporaries, as well as Christian pieces from India, which depict Jesus in a style highly influenced by Hindu and Buddhist art.

Cidadela   HISTORIC BUILDING
Climb uphill from Largo de São Vicente and you'll soon set foot inside the astonishingly well-preserved 12th-century citadel. People still live in its narrow, atmospheric lanes, unspoilt by the few, low-key handicrafts shops and cafes that have crept in.

Within the ruggedly ramparted walls is the original castle – built by Sancho I in 1187 and beefed up in the 15th century by João I, then heavily restored in the 1930s. The stout **Torre de Menagem** was garrisoned up until the early 20th century. It now houses a **Museu Militar** (Military Museum; admission €2,

Fri morning free; ⊙9am-noon & 2-5pm Tue-Sun), whose four floors are filled with swords, guns and suits of armour spanning several centuries, from medieval times to WWI and the Salazar dictatorship's colonial exploits. The price of admission is well worth the chance to climb to the top of the crenellated tower, with great views all around. In front of the *torre* is an extraordinary, primitive **pelourinho** (stone pillory) atop a granite boar similar to the *berrões* found around the province.

Squatting at the rear of the citadel is an odd pentagonal building known as the **Domus Municipalis** (Town House; Terreiro do Castelo; ⊙9am-5pm Tue-Sun) FREE, the oldest town hall in Portugal – although its precise age is a matter of scholarly disagreement – and one of the few examples of civil Romanesque architecture on the Iberian Peninsula. Bragança's medieval town council once met upstairs in an arcaded room studded with weathered faces of man and beast and scratched with symbols of the stonemasons.

Beside the Domus Municipalis is the early-16th-century **Igreja de Santa Maria**. Of particular interest are its brick Mudéjar columns, vividly painted ceiling, and a 17th-century Santa Maria Madalena at the high altar, with her traditional long hair and ragged garb.

Museu Ibérico da Máscara e do Traje   MUSEUM

(Iberian Mask & Costume Museum; Rua Dom Fernão o Bravo 24/26; adult/child €1/free; ⊙9am-1pm & 3-6pm Tue-Sun summer, 9am-12.30pm & 2-5.30pm Tue-Sun winter) This visually appealing little museum displays a colourful and fascinating collection of masks and costumes from the ancient pagan-based solstice and Carnaval festivities celebrated in Trás-os-Montes and neighbouring Zamora (Spain). Costumes are displayed across three floors, with the upper exhibits dedicated to the work of local artisans.

Centro de Arte Contemporânea Graça Morais   MUSEUM

(Rua Abílio Beça 105; adult/student €2/1, mornings & Sundays free; ⊙10am-12.30pm & 2-6.30pm Tue-Sun) This cross-border collaboration between Portugal and Spain has a permanent collection that features local painter Graça Morais' haunting portraits of Trás-os-Montes residents, alongside more abstract work. The modern annexe showcases rotating special exhibitions, and there's a cafe with a lovely patio.

Igreja de São Bento   CHURCH

(Rua São Francisco) Bragança's most attractive church has a Renaissance stone portal, a wonderful *trompe l'œil* ceiling over the nave and an Arabic-style inlaid ceiling above the chancel.

Igreja de São Vicente   CHURCH

(Largo de São Vicente) Romanesque in origin but rebuilt in the 17th century, this church may have played host to a chapter in Portugal's favourite – and grisliest – love story. Tradition has it that the future Dom Pedro secretly married Inês de Castro here around 1354.

Sé   CATHEDRAL

(Praça da Sé) Bragança's modest old cathedral started out in 1545 as the Igreja de São João Baptista, but moved up the ranks to become a cathedral in 1770 when the bishopric moved here from Miranda do Douro. It was then downgraded again when Bragança's contemporary cathedral, the **Igreja de Nossa Senhora Rainha**, opened just west of the centre.

Festivals & Events

Bragança's biggest annual market, **Feira das Cantarinhas**, runs for three days in early May. It's a huge street fair of traditional handicrafts (a *cantarinha* is a small terracotta pitcher) held in and around the Cidadela.

Sleeping

Bragança's central hotels are largely dreary low-budget affairs whose glory days seem to have been sometime in the early 1970s. There are also two campgrounds in the nearby Parque Natural de Montesinho.

Hotel Tulipa   HOTEL €

(☑273 331 675; www.tulipaturismo.com; Rua Dr Francisco Felgueiras 8-10; s/d/tr €40/50/60; ✳🖧) Nicely remodelled in 2010, the Tulipa offers clean and comfortable contemporary rooms, most with flat-screen TVs, and some adapted for visitors with disabilities. Another plus is the central location between the bus station and downtown. The downstairs restaurant serves great-value weekday lunch specials.

Pousada da Juventude   HOSTEL €

(☑273 304 600; braganca@movijovem.pt; Av 22 de Maio; dm €13, d with private/shared bathroom €32/28; ℗@🖧) This modern – if sometimes inattentively run – hostel offers self-service laundry, free wi-fi, comfy common areas, and an on-site bar and restaurant. The two-bedroom apartment (€64), with its own kitchen and washer-dryer, is a great option for families. It's located in the nondescript suburbs west of the centre, about a 30-minute walk from the Cidadela.

Pensão Rucha   GUESTHOUSE €
(☑273 331 672; Rua Almirante Reis 42; s/d with shared bathroom €17.50/27.50) The kind proprietor at this simple *pensão* (guesthouse) offers nine lacklustre rooms with shared bathroom, some overlooking a leafy garden, at a good price. No breakfast.

Ibis Bragança   HOTEL €
(☑273 302 520; www.ibishotel.com; Rotunda do Lavrador Transmontano; r without breakfast €59; P❄️🛜) Just off the IP4 north of town, the Ibis is nicer than most hotels in the centre, despite its bland chain-hotel predictability. The rooms are small but bright and cheery. Wi-fi is available in the lobby (free) or in the rooms (€5 per hour), and breakfast costs €5 extra. Rates drop dramatically outside the summer season.

Arco da Velha   APARTMENT €€
(☑966 787 784; www.turismobraganca.com; Rua Dom Fernão o Bravo; 2-bedroom apt €90; P) The only place to stay within Bragança's atmospheric medieval citadel, this comfy split-level apartment sleeps up to four, allows pets and has its own parking spot just outside. The original stone-walled building has been thoroughly remodelled, with modern furniture and a wood-pellet stove for chilly winter evenings. Minimum stay is two nights.

Pousada de São
Bartolomeu   LUXURY HOTEL €€€
(☑273 331 493; www.pousadas.pt; Estrada do Turismo; s/d €130/140; P❄️@🛜🏊) This whitewashed modern affair may not be the most arresting *pousada* (upmarket inn) in Portugal, but its views over the Cidadela and countryside are way up there. It sits proudly alone, on a hilltop 1.5km southeast of the centre, and boasts lots of creature comforts, including a great restaurant and bright contemporary rooms with balconies overlooking the pool and the castle.

✗ Eating

Mercado Municipal   MARKET €
(⊙8am-6pm Mon-Sat) It's a longish walk to this recent, rather antiseptic market behind the *câmara municipal*.

Restaurante Lá Em Casa   PORTUGUESE €
(Rua Marquês de Pombal 7; mains €6-12.50; ⊙lunch & dinner) This place serves platters heaped with excellent, wood-grilled local meats in a stone-walled, pine-panelled dining room with fireplace. The veal and lamb are especially savoury. Daily lunch specials are well-priced.

★Don Roberto   PORTUGUESE €€
(☑273 302 510; Rua Coronel Álvaro Cepeda, Gimonde; mains €9-15; ⊙lunch & dinner daily) It's worth catching a cab out to this traditional roadside tavern, 7km from town, in the village of Gimonde en route to Montesinho. The ambience is down-home rural – think wooden beams and smoked ham hanging off the walls – and the food is the real deal. Try the steak, starters such as *alheira* and *salpicão*, and the delicious *milho doce* dessert.

Solar Bragançano   PORTUGUESE €€
(Praça da Sé 34; mains €9.50-14.50; ⊙lunch & dinner daily summer, Tue-Sun rest of year) Upstairs in a manor house opposite the cathedral square, this elegant eatery boasts oak-panelled rooms, chandeliers, wide plank floors, a leafy and sun-dappled outdoor terrace and a seasonal menu weighted towards local game, with specialities including wild boar, partridge with grapes and pheasant with chestnuts.

O Pote   PORTUGUESE €€
(Rua Alexandre Herculano 186; mains €7.50-14; ⊙lunch & dinner Mon-Sat) This friendly eatery is divided into a formal upstairs dining room and a more relaxed downstairs cafe, both serving excellent regional specialities. The olive oil, some of the wine and much of the produce is sourced from the owners' farm outside town. The weekday lunch menu for €7.50 is a great deal.

♟ Drinking & Nightlife

There are atmospheric bars in the Cidadela where you can down shots of *ginja* (cherry liqueur) with Bragança's version of good ole boys.

Moderno   BAR
(☑273 327 766; Rua Almirante Reis; ⊙midnight-4am) This is the city's principal bar and disco, with DJs spinning an eclectic mix of tunes.

☆ Entertainment

Teatro Municipal   PERFORMING ARTS
(☑273 302 744; http://teatromunicipal.cm-bragan ca.pt; Praça Cavaleiro Ferreira) The boxy Teatro

Municipal has given the city's cultural life a great boost by hosting high-quality music, theatre and dance shows, plus afternoon performances for children. There's a multi-screen cinema next door.

❶ Information

Biblioteca Municipal (☎273 300 854; Praça Camões; ⊗9am-12.30pm & 2-7pm Mon-Fri) Free internet (one hour maximum) at the public library.

Cyber Centro Bragança (1st fl, Mercado Municipal; per hr €1; ⊗10am-11pm Mon-Fri, 10am-7pm Sat, 2-7pm Sun) Evening and weekend internet access.

Hospital (☎273 310 800; Av Abade Baçal) West of the centre.

Parque Natural de Montesinho Office (☎273 300 400; pnm@icnb.pt; Rua Cónego Albano Falcão 5; ⊗9am-12.30pm & 2-5.30pm Mon-Fri) Northeast of the *turismo*.

Police Station (☎273 303 400; Rua Dr Manuel Bento 4) Just north of the *câmara municipal*.

Post Office (Largo dos Correios; ⊗8.30am-5.30pm Mon-Fri, 9am-12.30pm Sat) Doubles as a telephone office.

Turismo (☎273 381 273; www.cm-braganca. pt; Av Cidade de Zamora; ⊗9am-12.30pm & 2-5pm Mon-Fri, 10am-12.30pm Sat) An extremely helpful office.

❶ Getting There & Away

BUS

Bragança's spiffy modern bus station, housed in the former train depot at the top of Av João da Cruz, is served by **Rede Expressos** (☎966 482 215; www.rede-expressos.pt), **Rodonorte** (☎273 326 552; www.rodonorte.pt) and **Euro-lines** (☎273 326 211, 273 327 122; www.euro lines.com). Station offices tend to be open only at departure times. Services to the following destinations are daily, except as noted:

Braga (€13.50, four hours, Rodonorte)
Guimarães (€13.50, 3½ hours, Rodonorte)
Lisbon (€18.50, seven hours, Rede Expressos)
Nice, France (€112, 23 hours, Eurolines, three times a week)
Paris, France (€86, 19 hours, Eurolines, daily except Sunday)
Porto (€12, three hours, Rodonorte and Rede Expressos)
Vila Nova de Foz Côa (€7.50, 1¾ hours, Rede Expressos)
Vila Real (€9.10, two hours, Rodonorte)
Viseu (€13, 3¼ hours, Rede Expressos)
Trancoso (€9.80, 2¼ hours, Rede Expressos)

CAR & MOTORCYCLE

Parking is generally not difficult. There are lots of paid spots in the square just south of the *sé*, with free overnight parking for motor homes in the lot just east of the Cidadela.

Parque Natural de Montesinho

The peaceful highlands along Portugal's northeastern border with Spain constitute one of Trás-os-Montes' most appealing natural and cultural landscapes – it's a patchwork of rolling grasslands, giant chestnut trees, oak forests and deep canyons, sprinkled with ancient stone villages where an ageing population still ekes out a hard-scrabble existence.

The 750-sq-km Parque Natural de Montesinho was established to protect the area's 88 lean villages as much as their natural setting. This harsh, remote *terra fria* inspired early Portuguese rulers to establish a system of collective land tenure and then leave the villagers to their own devices, allowing for a remarkably democratic, communal culture, which persists today.

Unfortunately, remote villages continue to be deserted by their young, and many have not a single resident under the age of 60. However, these settlements – mostly just small clusters of granite houses roofed in slate and sheltering in deep valleys – retain an irresistible charm, especially in late April, when cherry and chestnut trees are in flower. In some towns, the government has helped preserve traditional slate-roofed stone houses as well as churches, forges, mills and the characteristic, charming *pombals* (dovecotes).

Villages that retain lashings of character include Pinheiro Novo, Sernande, Moimenta and Dine in the west, and Montesinho, Varge, Rio de Onor and Guadramil in the east.

The natural base from which to explore the park is Bragança. Smaller villages within the park also offer accommodation, but public transport is patchy. A great resource for info about the park is www.amontesinho.pt.

❍ Sights & Activities

The most famous inhabitant of the eastern Serra de Montesinho is the rust-coloured Iberian wolf. Indeed, this natural park and the adjoining Spanish park together form the last major refuge for this seriously endangered

Parque Natural de Montesinho

animal. Other threatened species include the royal eagle and the black stork.

In vast forests of Iberian oak and chestnut, and among riverside alders, willows, poplars and hazel, there are also roe deer, otters and wild boar; in the grasslands are partridges, kites and kestrels. Above 900m the otherwise barren ground is carpeted in heather and broom in spring.

There are plenty of biking and hiking opportunities. Park offices in Bragança (p411) and Vinhais (p414) offer free brochures detailing 11 marked **hiking trails** around the park (although some of these seem to be chronically out of print!).

If you come here in the summer, you can cool off in the park's plentiful (if chilly) rivers and streams. Look for signs pointing to *praias fluviais* (river beaches) throughout the park; one of the nicest such swimming spots is near the centre of the park, just northwest of the town of Fresulfe.

Rio de Onor   VILLAGE

This lovely little town of 70 souls, situated in the eastern half of the park, is entirely unfazed by the Spanish–Portuguese border splicing it down the middle. It's interesting not just for its rustic stone buildings, whose ground floors still house straw-filled stables for goats, sheep and donkeys, but also for its staunch maintenance of the communal lifestyle once typical of the region. Spend an afternoon here and you'll see elderly locals trundling wheelbarrows from the well-tended community gardens surrounding town, pitchforking hay onto horse-drawn carts, stopping in at the local cafe whose communally shared proceeds are used to

fund town festivals, or trading jobs with each other – one cousin staying to mind the store while the other goes to bring in the sheep. The twinned village also has one other claim to fame – a hybrid Portuguese–Spanish dialect known as Rionorês.

The border runs east–west through the middle of the village, while the Rio de Onor trickles along perpendicular to it. The road from Bragança continues north through town into Spain, branching right just before the border to cross an old stone bridge to the prettiest part of the village, where you'll find the community cafe.

From Bragança, STUB bus 5 (€1.20, 45 minutes) heads to Rio de Onor three times daily.

Montesinho   VILLAGE

Hidden at the end of the road in a narrow valley wedged between forbidding granite heights, this tiny village is one of the park's best-preserved, thanks to a program to restore old dwellings and stop construction of new ones. The village is also the jumping-off point for the 8km **Porto Furado hiking trail** through the rugged hills to a nearby dam. STUB bus 7 (€1.20, one hour) runs from Bragança to Montesinho at least once daily.

Dine & Moimenta   VILLAGES

Dine and Moimenta, two of the prettiest villages in the western half of the park, are connected by a high-altitude road with panoramic views of the windmill-speckled hills along the Spanish border. In well-preserved Dine, you can visit a tiny **archaeological museum**, which documents the 1984 find by a Danish diplomat of Iron Age remains in a nearby cave. The museum is usually locked, but just ask around and someone will rustle up the French-speaking caretaker, Judite, who may also lead you around to the cave itself – pointing out traditional lime kilns and wild-growing medicinal herbs along the way.

Moimenta has a lovely core of granite houses roofed in terracotta, plus a small baroque church – a rare dose of luxury in this austere corner of Portugal. The pretty 7km **Calçada loop trail** descends from town into the nearby river gorge, following sections of an old stone roadway across a remarkably well-preserved **medieval bridge** with a single impressive arch.

🛏 Sleeping & Eating

Park headquarters rents out several houses throughout the park. Known as *casas-retiro* and *casas-abrigo,* these generally sleep six or more people. Check with the park offices for price details, or search 'casas retiro abrigo Montesinho' online and click on the 'Onde Ficar – ICNB' link for photos.

For a more complete list of local sleeping options, check out the *Alojamento* (lodging) section of the free *Nordeste Transmontano* booklet available from Bragança's tourist office (p411).

🛏 Eastern Park

There are a number of self-catering stone cottages in the village of Montesinho. Note that rooms book up in July and August.

Casa Alta ROOMS €
(✐273 927 128; Rio de Onor; r without breakfast €35) Senhor António Preto rents out three simple rooms in this old stone house on the western side of the river in downtown Rio de Onor.

Casa de Onor ROOMS €
(✐937 592 762, 273 927 163; www.casadeonor.com; Rio de Onor; s/d €30/60) In a pretty stone house overlooking the river in the centre of Rio de Onor, Senhora Rita Rego rents out five rooms sleeping one to six people, each with private bathroom. Breakfast is included, and additional meals are available upon request for €15 per person.

Casa das Pedras COTTAGE €
(✐919 860 500; www.casadaspedras.com; Montesinho; cottage €55-60) Senhor Antero Pires rents out four rustic stone and wood cottages ranging from a basic studio to multi-room units with kitchenettes.

Inatel Parque de Campismo de Bragança CAMPGROUND €
(✐273 001 090; pc.braganca@inatel.pt; N103-7, km 6; sites per adult/child/tent/car €5/4/3.50/5; ☺Jun–mid-Sep) The nicest of the local campgrounds, tucked into a cottonwood grove on the banks of the Rio Sabor, has featureless but shady and quiet sites, plus hot showers and a restaurant. From Bragança take STUB bus 7 (€1.20, 20 minutes, four daily).

★ **A Lagosta Perdida** B&B €€€
(✐273 919 031; www.lagostaperdida.com; Rua do Cimo 4, Montesinho; d €125; P ☎ ⊠ ⋈) The region's most luxurious accommodation is this refurbished stone-walled house, run by a friendly Anglo-Dutch couple. It retains numerous period features, including high, beamed ceilings and an old stone water trough downstairs. The comfortable rooms come equipped with cable internet connections, tea-making facilities, flat-screen TVs and beautifully tiled modern bathrooms with tubs.

Other amenities include mountain bikes, a nice piano, a library full of books about local trails, flora and fauna, a swimming pool heated by solar power and incinerated olive pits, and six hiking trails right out the back. Two meals a day from the vegetarian-friendly kitchen are included in the price. Kids will love the ping-pong table, not to mention the sheepdogs, cats, bunny, Scottish Highland ponies, horse and donkey. Prices with breakfast and dinner are €125.

Café Montesinho CAFE €
(✐273 919 219; Montesinho) A cosy spot in the hub of the village, stone-walled Café Montesinho serves snacks and drinks, and also rents an upstairs two-bedroom apartment (€50) that sleeps up to four people, complete with kitchen and a pleasant verandah.

🛏 Western Park

Casa dos Marrões RURAL INN €
(✐273 999 550; www.casadosmarroes.com; Vilarinho; s/d €47.50/50, self-catering house €100; P ⊠) In Vilarinho, 17km northwest of Bragança, this 18th-century home built of oak, chestnut and schist has lovely beamed ceilings and exposed-stone walls. Across the street is a self-catering house sleeping up to six. A spring-fed outdoor pool, plus nearby

hiking trails and riverside beaches, enhance its appeal.

Casa da Bica
RURAL INN €

(☑273 323 577; www.montesinho.com/casadabica; Rua do Lameiro 9, Gondesende; d €35; P) In Gondesende, 12km northwest of Bragança, this schist cottage offers five rather spartan rooms upstairs, plus a downstairs sitting area with fireplace, where breakfast is served.

Estúdio da Moimenta
APARTMENT €

(☑273 300 400; pnm@icnb.pt; Moimenta; d €41) The smallest and least expensive of the park-administered lodgings, this two-person studio, complete with kitchenette, is right in the heart of Moimenta village. There are also larger houses available.

Parque de Campismo Cepo Verde
CAMPGROUND €

(☑273 999 371; www.montesinho.com; Gondesende; sites per adult/child/tent/car €2.80/1.50/2.80/1.80; ⊠) This medium-sized rural facility is 12km west of Bragança near the tiny village of Gondesende on the park's southern border. Sixty campsites, some shaded and some in full sun, are set on a hillside above a central cafe and swimming pool (€1.50). STUB bus 4 from Bragança passes within 1km of the campground (€1.20, 40 minutes).

Moinho do Caniço
RENTAL HOUSE €€

(☑273 323 577; www.montesinho.com/moinho; N103, km 251, Castrelos; house with/without breakfast €70/60; P) This tastefully refurbished watermill – complete with centuries-old kitchen and open fireplace – is 12km west of Bragança on the N103. The rustically furnished stone-floored cottage sleeps up to four people, with trout fishing in the Rio Baceiro just outside the door. STUB bus 2 (€1.20, 55 minutes) stops nearby.

❶ Information

Park offices at Bragança (p411) and **Vinhais** (☑273 771 416; cipnm@cm-vinhais.pt; Casa da Vila, Centro Histórico; ⊙9am-12.30pm & 2-5.30pm daily) distribute a free park map. Brochures on flora, archaeology, handicrafts and park walks are in Portuguese, although English-speaking staff at Bragança are happy to answer questions.

❶ Getting Around

Exploring the park is difficult without a car, a bike or sturdy feet. The free park map clearly indicates which roads are paved – unpaved roads can be dicey both during and after rains.

Only parts of the park are served by bus. For up-to-date schedules, check with Bragança's municipal bus company, **STUB** (www.stub.com.pt). Trips to towns within the park cost €1.20 and generally take an hour or less.

Miranda do Douro

POP 7482 / ELEV 560M

A fortified frontier town hunkering on the precipice of the gorgeous Rio Douro canyon, Miranda do Douro was long a bulwark of Portugal's 'wild east'. With its crumbling castle still lending an air of medieval charm, modern-day Miranda has now taken on a decidedly different role – receiving weekending Spanish tourists, as opposed to repelling Castilian attacks.

The town's beautifully hulking, 16th-century church may seem all out of proportion to the rest of the town, but it once served as cathedral for the entire region. Visitors shouldn't miss Miranda's ethnographic museum, which sheds light on the region's border culture, including ancient rites such as the 'stick dancing' of the *pauliteiros*.

Street signs around town are written in Mirandês, an ancient language that developed during Miranda's long centuries of isolation from the rest of Portugal. Romance-language buffs will enjoy names like 'Rue de la Santa Cruç', which read like a fantastical blend of French, Spanish and Portuguese.

Largo do Menino Jesus da Cartolina, a roundabout perched at the edge of the river gorge, roughly divides the old and new town. The *turismo* sits on the northern edge of the roundabout. The bus station lies just downhill, on the road descending towards the bridge to Spain.

Uphill (southwest) from the roundabout, past the old walls and castle ruins, are the old town and what was once the citadel. The main axis is Rua da Alfândega (also called Rua Mouzinho da Albuquerque), which runs into central Praça de Dom João III and, a little further on, Largo da Sé and the cathedral.

The new town's commercial hub is Rua do Mercado, running northeast from the roundabout and parallel to the Rio Douro gorge.

History

Miranda was a vital stronghold during Portugal's first centuries of independence, and the Castilians had to be chucked out at least twice: in the early days by Dom João I, and again in 1710, during the War of the Spanish Succession. In 1545, perhaps as a snub to the increasingly powerful House of Bragança, a diocese was created here – hence the oversized cathedral.

During a siege by French and Spanish troops in 1762, the castle's powder magazine exploded, pulverising most of the castle and killing some 400 people. Twenty years later, shattered Miranda lost its diocese to Bragança. No one paid much attention to Miranda again until the nearby dam was built on the Douro in the 1950s.

◉ Sights & Activities

It's possible to see the sights of Miranda do Douro in a couple of hours, but the vagaries of public transport make it almost essential for nondrivers to stay longer.

Museu da Terra de Miranda   MUSEUM
(Praça de Dom João III; admission €2, Sun morning free; ⊘ 9.30am-12.30pm & 2-6pm Wed-Sun, 2.30-5.30pm Tue summer, 9am-12.30pm & 2-5.30pm Wed-Sun, 2-5.30pm Tue winter) This modest but attractive museum sheds light on a unique culture that has preserved millennial traditions into the 21st century. The handsome 17th-century building (formerly Miranda's city hall) houses a fascinating collection of local artefacts: ceramics, textiles, clothing, furniture, musical instruments and tribal-looking masks, along with re-creations of a traditional kitchen, a blacksmith's forge and a room dedicated to traditional wool and linen weaving, complete with massive looms.

Old Town   NEIGHBOURHOOD
The backstreets in the old town hide some dignified **15th-century facades** on Rua da Costanilha (which runs west off Praça de Dom João III) and a **Gothic gate** at the end of it.

Inside the right transept of the handsomely severe 16th-century **sé** (cathedral), look for the doll-like Menino Jesus da Cartolinha, a Christ child in a becoming top hat whose wardrobe rivals Imelda Marcos', thanks to deft local devotees. It's open Tuesday afternoons and daily from Wednesday to Sunday.

Barragem de Miranda & River Cruises   BOAT TOUR
A road crawls across this 80m-high dam about 1km east of town, and on to Zamora, 55km away in Spain. Even dammed, the gorge is dramatic.

You can take a one-hour boat trip through the gorge with **Europarques** (☑ 273 432 396; www.europarques.com; adult/child under 10yr €16/8; ⊘ trips 4pm daily, plus 11am Sat & Sun). Boats leave from beside the dam on the Portuguese side. Occasional two-hour trips

SPEAKING MIRANDÊS

France has Provençal, Britain has Welsh and Gaelic, and Italy has dozens of distinct regional dialects. Portugal, by contrast, is one of Europe's most monolingual countries, thanks both to its long-stable borders (unchanged since the 13th century) and to the fact that it was conquered and consolidated within a very short period of time (less than 200 years).

The region around Miranda do Douro is a significant exception. Because of its proximity to Spain and long isolation from the rest of Portugal, residents of the towns and villages around Miranda still speak what linguists now recognise as an entirely distinct language. Closely related to Astur-Leonese – the regional language of the adjacent Spanish province – Mirandês is in fact closer to Iberian Latin, the language spoken during the Roman period, than it is to either Portuguese or Spanish.

While Mirandês has largely died out in the city of Miranda do Douro itself, it's still the first language of some 10,000 people in the surrounding villages. The Portuguese government officially recognised it as a second language in 1998, and increasingly the region's road signs are bilingual.

In 1882 Portuguese linguist José Leite de Vasconcelos described Mirandês as 'the language of the farms, of work, of home and love'. The same is true today.

Resurgent local pride in the language is evident in the window display of Miranda do Douro's Papelaria Andrade, whose collection of Mirandês-language titles includes translations of *Asterix* comic books.

(€20) are also offered but for larger groups only; check with Europarques for details.

🛏 Sleeping

Hotel A Morgadinha
HOTEL €

(☎273 438 050; www.hotelmorgadinha.pai.pt; Rua do Mercado 57/59; s/d €25/45; ❄🔊) This simple hotel – one of several budget options along the same street – features spacious rooms with parquet wood floors and bathtubs. There are nice river views from the upstairs breakfast area and from many of the rooms; avoid those facing the street, which are noisier and more claustrophobic.

Hotel Turismo
HOTEL €

(☎273 438 030; www.hotelturismomiranda.pt; Rua 1 de Maio 5; s/d €30/50; ❄🔊) Offering terrific comfort for a modest price, this place opposite the *turismo* features large, spotless rooms – most including a separate sitting room – with cable TV, minibars and marble bathrooms. Front rooms have large windows with views across to the castle ruins, while the back rooms are more quiet.

Hotel Parador Santa Catarina
HOTEL €€

(☎273 431 005; www.hotelparadorsantacatarina.pt; Largo da Pousada; s/d midweek €82.50/92.50, weekend €92/102; P❄@🔊) Every guest gets a private verandah with spectacular views of the gorge at this luxurious hotel perched on the canyon's edge. Rooms are a handsome mix of traditional and contemporary, with hardwood floors, flat-screen TVs and large marble bathrooms. The attached restaurant is the most upmarket in town.

🍴 Eating

O Moinho
PORTUGUESE €

(Rua do Mercado 47D; pizzas €4.50-7, mains €6.50-10.50; ☺lunch & dinner) Despite lacklustre service, this new-town spot serves up glorious Douro views along with a wide-ranging menu featuring pizza, pasta, salads and Portuguese standards.

São Pedro
PORTUGUESE €€

(Rua Mouzinho de Albuquerque; mains €7.50-12.50; ☺lunch daily, dinner Tue-Sun) This spacious restaurant, just in from the main old-town gate, serves up a fine *posta á São Pedro* (grilled veal steak dressed with garlic and olive oil). The €11 tourist menu comes with soup, main, dessert, wine and coffee.

O Mirandês
PORTUGUESE €€

(Rua Dom Dinis 7; mains €7-14) Below the castle, just to the right of the main road leading into the old town, this unassuming light-filled spot is popular with locals for its great-value lunch specials and tasty dinners.

Capa d'Honras
PORTUGUESE €€

(Travessa do Castelo 1; mains €10-15; ☺lunch & dinner) Named after the sinister-looking cape that is traditional to the region, this upmarket place just inside the old town gates serves local specialities such as *posta* (veal steak) as well as very good *bacalhau*.

🍷 Drinking & Nightlife

Face Loungebar
BAR

(☎965 447 802; Largo do Castelo; ☺8pm-4am) Miranda's neon-lit, old-school disco serves up pop and dance standards.

ℹ Information

Centro de Saúde (☎273 430 040; Rua Dom Dinis) Health centre with 24-hour emergency service.

Espaço Internet (Rua Mousinho de Albuquerque; ☺10am-12.30pm & 2-6pm Mon-Sat) Free internet in the Casa da Cultura Mirandesa.

Parque Natural do Douro Internacional Office (☎273 431 457; Largo do Castelo; ☺9.30am-12.30pm & 2-5.30pm Mon-Fri) Around the block from the cathedral and across from a baroque church that has been converted into a public library.

Police (☎273 430 010; Largo de São José)

Post Office (Rua do Paço; ☺9am-12.30pm & 2-5.30pm Mon-Fri)

Turismo (☎273 430 025; www.rt-nordeste.pt; Largo do Menino Jesus da Cartolinha; ☺9am-12.30pm & 2-5.30pm Mon-Sat)

ℹ Getting There & Around

BUS

Rodonorte (☎273 432 667; www.rodonorte.pt) offers service daily except Saturday to Mogadouro (€6.20, 45 minutes), with onward connections to Vila Nova de Foz Côa (€7.40, 2½ hours), Vila Real (€12.70, three to four hours) and Porto (€14.90, 4½ to six hours).

CAR & MOTORCYCLE

The quickest road from Bragança to Miranda do Douro is the N218 and N218-2, a winding 80km trip. The slower but lovelier 80km route (N216/N221) from Macedo de Cavaleiros via Mogadouro crosses a *planalto* (high plateau) dotted with olive, almond and chestnut groves and includes a dramatic switchbacking descent into the Rio Sabor valley. Miranda has plenty of free parking around Largo do Menino Jesus da Cartolina.

Parque Natural do Douro Internacional

Tucked into Portugal's far northeast corner, this 852-sq-km, Chile-shaped park runs for 120km along the Rio Douro and the monumental canyon it has carved along the border with Spain. The canyon's towering, granite cliffs are the habitat for several threatened bird species, including black storks, Egyptian vultures, griffon vultures, peregrine falcons, golden eagles and Bonelli's eagles.

The human habitat is equally fragile. In the plains that run up to the canyon lip, there are some 35 villages, many inhabited by descendants of banished medieval convicts, as well as Jews who fled the Inquisition. The region's isolation has enabled its people to preserve even more ancient roots, such as the Celtic *dança dos paulitos*. Many villagers still speak Mirandês, a language distinct from both Spanish and Portuguese that linguists believe descends directly from Iberian Latin; you'll see town names written in Portuguese and Mirandês throughout the park's northern reaches.

As you move south along the river, the terrain gains a distinctly Mediterranean air, with rolling orchards of olives and chestnuts and, in the southernmost reaches, land demarcated for port-wine grapes.

Park maps, as elsewhere in Portugal, are in short supply. At the time of research, a free park overview map was available, as were a couple of detailed trail maps (€0.50 each); all other print resources had run out, with only reference copies or photocopies available. English-speaking staff at the Mogadouro headquarters can answer general questions, but printed materials are in Portuguese only.

Miranda do Douro and Mogadouro are the best places from which to explore the park.

✖️ Activities

There are four marked trails in the park. The most convenient for nondrivers – and one of the most beautiful – is the 19km **Miranda do Douro to São João das Arribas loop**, starting and ending at Miranda do Douro's cathedral. The trail – open to hikers, cyclists and horses – passes through mixed oak woodlands and small villages, and includes striking vistas of the river at São João.

Another stunning option near the southern end of the park is the **Vale da Ribeira do Mosteiro loop**, which passes through vineyards and rugged canyon country along a small tributary of the Douro.

For fabulous, near-aerial views of the gorge and its birdlife, you can also visit six **panoramic overlooks** throughout the park. North to south, with the nearest village in parentheses, these are **Penha das Torres** (Paradela), **São João das Arribas** (Aldeia Nova), **Fraga do Puio** (Picote), **Carrascalinho** (Fornos), **Penedo Durão** (Poiares) and **Santo André** (Almofala).

Without your own transport, the easiest way to see the Douro gorge is on Europarques' hour-long cruise (p415) from Miranda do Douro.

In Torre de Moncorvo, near the park's southern end, **Sabor Douro e Aventura** (☑ 964 801 280; www.sabordouro.com; Rua Abade Tavares, Torre de Moncorvo) offers guided tours by jeep, motorbike, bike and on foot, as well as water sports such as jet-skiing and canoeing. Prices range from €10 for a canoeing lesson to €35 for a half-day jet-boat tour with lunch. Also availabe is a six-room rural house, Casa da Avó.

🛏️ Sleeping & Eating

With its impressive views of the river gorge, Miranda do Douro (p414) is the most attractive base for exploring the park. Mogadouro also offers tourist services, but at nearly 15km from the Douro, it's a far less scenic option.

Casa de l Bárrio   RURAL INN €€

(☑ 273 738 088; www.casadelbarrio.com; Rue de l Bárrio 7, Picote; house €120, d €60; 🅿❄🛜) 🚲 This great rural option in the village of Picote, 17km southwest from Miranda do Douro, is run by a linguist and a biologist, who offer free guided nature walks for their guests. This cosy solar-energy-powered house sleeps up to five and features lots of pine wood, a fireplace and a small patio out front. Breakfast (included) is delivered every morning, and there are free bikes for guests.

A Lareira   PORTUGUESE €€

(Av Nossa Senhora do Caminho 58-62, Mogadouro; mains €8-13; 🕑lunch & dinner Tue-Sun) This recommended restaurant offers outstanding local beef, veal and mushrooms grilled on an open fireplace by the French-trained proprietor. The small, well-equipped rooms upstairs (single/double €25/30) are also excellent value.

ℹ Information

The most informative park office is in Miranda do Douro (p416), with another in **Mogadouro** (☑ 279 341 596; Av do Sabor 49, Mogadouro; ◷ 9am-1pm & 2-5pm Mon-Fri).

ℹ Getting There & Around

Rodonorte (www.rodonorte.pt) offers regular bus services to Miranda do Douro and Mogadouro. However, public transport to smaller villages within the park is extremely limited, and mostly designed to serve schoolchildren; check with the park offices for current schedule information.

The Minho

Best Places to Stay

➡ Margarida da Praça (p438)

➡ Portuguez Inn (p425)

➡ Carmo's Boutique Hotel (p447)

➡ Pousada do Gerês-
Caniçada/São Bento (p456)

Best Places to Eat

➡ Taberna do Félix (p426)

➡ Cor de Tangerina (p433)

➡ Taberna do Valentim (p439)

➡ O Abocanhado (p458)

Why Go?

The Minho delivers world-class natural beauty with a knowing smile. Here are lush river valleys, sparkling beaches and granite peaks patrolled by locals – who seem particularly in tune with their homeland, whether they are charging 2m waves along the Costa Verde or shepherding their flock into high mountain meadows. This is, after all, the birthplace of the Portuguese kingdom, and it would be hard to find better-preserved landmarks than those uplit and on display in the Minho's gorgeous old cities.

Then there's the bold, sharp and fruity *vinho verde* to consider. This young wine is fashioned from the fruit of miles of vineyards that wind along rivers, over foothills and into Minho mountain villages. The crops are eventually crushed and bottled in community *adegas* (wineries), giving each destination its own flavour. Of course, if you sip enough along the way, they may all blend into one delicious memory.

When to Go
Braga

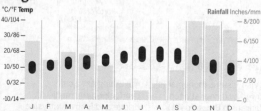

May In the first week of the month, Festa das Cruzes turns Barcelos into a fairground.

23 & 24 Jun Braga's Festas de São João bursts with pagan energy and fireworks.

Sep Festas de Senhora, Peneda, features candlelit processions and a gushing waterfall.

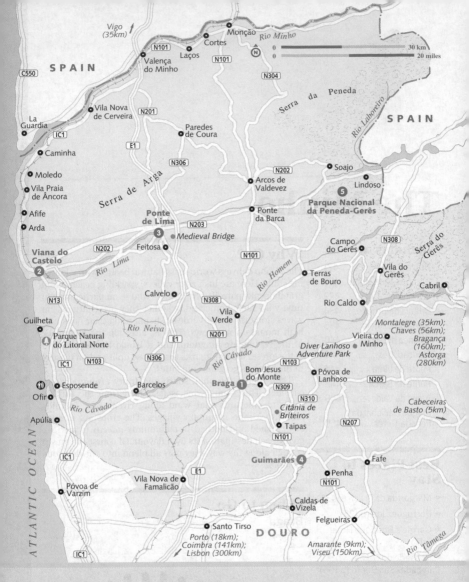

The Minho Highlights

1 Visit historic monuments, followed by dinner at a top restaurant in **Braga** (p421)

2 Stroll the atmospheric streets of **Viana do Castelo** (p435), then catch sunset on the beach

3 Lounge at a cafe overlooking the medieval bridge and lush countryside beyond in **Ponte de Lima** (p444)

4 Explore the contemporary art and culture in buzzing **Guimarães** (p429)

5 Hike the boulder-strewn peaks and gorse-clad moorlands of the **Parque Nacional da Peneda-Gerês** (p450)

Braga

POP 71,750 / ELEV 200M

Portugal's third-largest city is an elegant town laced with ancient narrow lanes closed to vehicles, and strewn with plazas and a splendid array of baroque churches. The constant chiming of bells is a reminder of Braga's age-old devotion to the spiritual world. Its religious festivals – particularly the elaborately staged Semana Santa (Holy Week) – are famous throughout Portugal. But don't come expecting piety alone: Braga's upscale old centre is packed with lively cafes and trim boutiques, some excellent restaurants and low-key bars catering to students from the Universidade do Minho. In fact, it's such a young city that in 2012 it was pronounced the European Youth Capital.

Just outside the city stands the magnificent, much-visited hillside church and sanctuary of Bom Jesus do Monte.

History

Founded by Romans, Braga was settled in the 1st century BC, named Bracara Augusta and made capital of the Roman province of Gallaecia. Braga's position at the intersection of five Roman roads helped it grow fat on trade, but it fell to the Suevi around AD 410, and was sacked by the Visigoths 60 years later. The Visigoths' conversion to Christianity in the 6th century and the founding of an archbishopric in the next century put the town atop the Iberian Peninsula's ecclesiastical pecking order.

The Moors moved in around 715, sparking a long-running tug of war that ended when Fernando I, king of Castilla y León, definitively reconquered the city in 1040. The archbishopric was restored in 1070, though prelates bickered with their Spanish counterparts for the next 500 years over who was Primate of All Spain. The pope finally ruled in Braga's favour, though the city's resulting good fortune began to wane in the 18th century, when a newly anointed Lisbon archdiocese stole much of its thunder.

Not surprisingly, it was from conservative Braga that António de Oliveira Salazar, with his unique blend of Catholicism and fascism, gave the speech that launched his 1926 coup, introducing Portugal to half a century of dictatorship.

◎ Sights & Activities

Sé
CHURCH

(Rua Dom Paio Mendes; ⊙9am-6pm winter, 8am-7pm summer) FREE Braga's extraordinary cathedral, the oldest in Portugal, was begun when the archdiocese was restored in 1070 and completed in the following century. It's a rambling complex made up of differing styles, and architecture buffs could spend half a day happily distinguishing the Romanesque bones from Manueline musculature and baroque frippery.

The original Romanesque style is the most interesting and survives in the cathedral's overall shape, the southern entrance and the marvellous west portal, which is carved with scenes from the medieval legend of Reynard the Fox (now sheltered inside a Gothic porch). The most appealing external features are the filigree Manueline towers and roof – an early work by João de Castilho, who went on to build Lisbon's Mosteiro dos Jerónimos.

You can enter the cathedral through the west portal or via a courtyard and cloister that's lined with Gothic chapels on the north side. The church itself features a fine Manueline carved altarpiece, a tall chapel with *azulejos* (hand-painted tiles) telling

---

EASTER IN BRAGA

Braga hosts the most elaborate Easter celebrations in Portugal. It kicks off with Semana Santa, when Gregorian chants are piped throughout the city centre and makeshift candlelit altars light the streets at night. The action heats up during Holy Thursday's Procissão do Senhor Ecce Homo, when barefoot, hooded penitents – members of private Catholic brotherhoods (think Opus Dei) – march through the streets spinning their eerie rattles. The Good Friday Mass in the cathedral is a remarkable, elaborately staged drama with silk canopies, dirgelike hymns, dozens of priests and a weeping congregation. On Saturday evening, the Easter Vigil Mass begins dourly, the entire cathedral in shadow, only to explode in lights and jubilation. Finally, on Sunday, the people of Braga blanket their thresholds with flowers, inviting passing priests to enter and give their home a blessing.

Braga

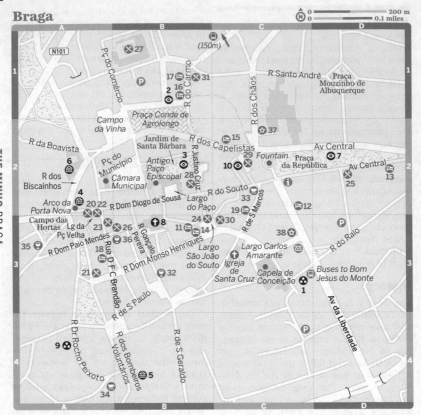

the story of Braga's first bishop, and fantastic twin baroque organs held up by formidable satyrs and mermen, which are played at mass every Sunday at 11.30am.

Connected to the church is the **treasury** (adult/child €3/2; ⏱ 9am-12.30pm & 2-6.30pm summer, 9am-12.30pm & 2-5.30pm), housing a goldmine of ecclesiastical booty, including the lovely Nossa Senhora do Leite of the Virgin suckling Christ, attributed to 16th-century French sculptor Nicolas Chanterène. Other highlights are the iron cross that was used in 1500 to celebrate the very first Mass in Brazil.

To visit the **choir** (adult/child €2/1), visitors must purchase a separate ticket and join a guided tour (some guides speak English), which gives an up-close look at the mesmerising organs and gilded choir stalls. Visitors will then be led downstairs and into the cathedral's showpiece Capela dos Reis (Kings' Chapel), home to the tombs of Henri of

Burgundy and Dona Teresa, parents of the first king of Portugal, Afonso Henriques. You'll also visit the *azulejo*-covered Capela de São Geraldo (dating from the 12th century but reworked over the years) and the 14th-century Capela da Glória, whose interior was painted in unrepentantly Moorish geometric motifs in the 16th century.

Museu Dom Diogo de Sousa   MUSEUM

(Rua dos Bombeiros Voluntários; admission €3, 10am-2pm Sun free; ⏱ 10am-5.30pm Tue-Sun) The archaeological museum houses a nicely displayed collection of fragments from Braga's earliest days. The four rooms feature pieces from Palaeolithic times (arrowheads, funerary objects and ceramics) through the days of Roman rule and on up to the period dominated by the Suevi-Visigoth kingdom (5th to 7th centuries). The most fascinating pieces are the huge *miliários* (milestones), carved with Latin inscriptions, that marked the Roman roads.

Braga

Termas Romanas do Alto Cividade   ROMAN RUINS

(Rua Dr Rocha Peixoto; adult/student €1.70/free; ☺9am-12.30pm & 2-5.30pm Tue-Fri, 11am-5pm Sat & Sun) These ruins of an extensive bathing complex – with an attached theatre – date from the 2nd century AD, and were probably abandoned in the 5th century. See the quick seven-minute introductory video in English or Portuguese.

Fonte do Ídolo   ROMAN RUINS

(Idol Spring; Rua do Raio; adult/student €1.85/0.90; ☺9am-12.30pm & 2-5.30pm Tue-Fri, 11am-5pm Sat & Sun) Another Roman ruin recently opened to the public, this spring is set underneath a mod lobby. An essential community water source, it was carved into a fountain during pre-Roman times by Celicus Fronto, an immigrant from the city-state of Arcobriga. One carving is of a toga-clad pilgrim thought to be holding the horn of plenty. There's an introductory video, too.

GNRation   CULTURAL CENTRE

(www.gnration.pt; Praça Conde de Agrolongo; ☺10am-6.30pm) Braga's new cultural centre lives inside an 18th-century building that once housed police headquarters. Enter through the modern entrance with a glass sliding door and you're inside an incubator

of the city's creative industry, with concerts, film screenings, workshops and theatre performances.

Museu dos Biscainhos   MUSEUM

(Rua dos Biscainhos; admission €2, Sun morning free; ☺10am-12.15pm & 2-5.30pm Tue-Sun) An 18th-century aristocrat's palace is now home to the enthusiastic municipal museum, with a nice collection of Roman relics and 17th-to-19th-century pottery and furnishings. The palace itself is the reason to come, with its polychrome, chestnut-panelled ceilings and 18th-century *azulejos* depicting hunting scenes. The ground floor is paved with deeply ribbed flagstones on which carriages would have once rattled through to the stables.

Praça da República   SQUARE

The cafes and restaurants on this broad plaza are a pleasant place to start or finish your day. An especially mellow atmosphere descends in the evening, when coloured lights appear and people of all ages congregate to enjoy the night air.

The square-shaped, crenulated tower behind the cafes is the walled-up **Torre de Menagem** (Largo Terreiro do Castelo), which is all that survives of a fortified medieval palace.

Museu da Imagem
MUSEUM

(Campo das Hortas 35-37; ☉11am-7pm Tue-Fri, 2.30-6pm Sat & Sun) **FREE** A minimalist, ancient and beautiful stone relic, outfitted tastefully with steel and wood stairs, shows off impeccably lit, international photography exhibits on three floors.

Jardim de Santa Bárbara
GARDEN

(Rua Justino Cruz) This 17th-century square has narrow paths picking their way through a sea of flowers and topiary. On sunny days, the adjacent pedestrianised streets Rua Justino Cruz and Rua Francisco Sanches fill with buskers and cafe tables.

Tourists' Affairs
GUIDED TOURS

(☑253 253 169; www.thetouristsaffairs.com) A brand-new tour agency started by a pair of young enthusiastic locals, an architect and an archaeologist, it specialises in all things Minho. The free walking tours (at 9.30am and 3pm daily) are a delight – call a day ahead to reserve a spot. Other options include a cultural half-day tour and a variety of à la carte tours of the region.

🎊 Festivals & Events

Semana Santa
RELIGIOUS

Elaborate Easter celebrations.

Festas de São João
CULTURAL

A pre-Christian solstice bash dressed up to look like holy days, this festival still bursts with pagan energy. Held on 23 and 24 June, it features medieval folk plays, processions, dancing, bonfires, spectacular fireworks – and thousands of little pots of basil. Basil is the symbol of São João (John the Baptist), and traditionally people write poems to loved ones and then conceal them in their pots. Oddly, locals also bust out squeaky plastic hammers and whack each other mercilessly.

🛏 Sleeping

Reservations are essential during Semana Santa.

Pop Hostel
HOSTEL **$**

(☑253 058 806; www.bragapophostel.com; Rua do Carmo 61; dm/d from €17/40; @🛜) This small cosy hostel in a top-floor apartment is a great recent addition to Braga, with a colourfully decked lounge, a hammock on the balcony and a friendly owner who knows all the great eating and drinking spots in town. Bike hire and tours available.

Truthostel
HOSTEL **$**

(☑253 609 020; www.truthostel.com; 2nd floor, Av da Liberdade 738; s/d €23/45; @🛜) Cobbled together from a few big apartments in an art-deco building, this friendly place was recently converted from guesthouse to hostel. Rooms are fresh and clean, decent and simply furnished. They vary greatly in size and light; some have balconies and private bathrooms.

Casa de Santa Zita
GUESTHOUSE **$**

(☑253 618 331; braga@osz.pt; Rua São João 20; s/d €25/36; 🛜) This impeccably kept pilgrim's lodge (look for the small tile reading 'Sta Zita') is open to all and has an air of palpable serenity. The sweet sisters offer bright spotless rooms with ironed cotton sheets and hardwood floors, and breakfast served in a stone arched dining room. The only drawback is a midnight curfew.

Hotel Dos Terceiros
HOTEL **$**

(☑253 270 466; www.terceiros.com; Rua dos Capelistas 85; s/d €35/45; ✳🛜) On a quiet pedestrian street near Praça da República, this simple hotel has great deals on recently updated rooms overlooking a small square, some with tiny balconies. Most rooms have one full and single bed each, and can sleep up to three people.

Truthotel
HOTEL **$**

(☑253 277 177; www.truthotel.com; Rua de São Marcos 80; s/d €45/55; P✳@🛜) This recently renovated place in a fine old town house has individually decked out rooms with high ceilings and parquet floors. Five of the rooms are decorated by artists; a few have terraces. There are rotating art exhibits in the lobby, and the staff is welcoming and friendly.

Hotel Dona Sofia
HOTEL **$$**

(☑253 263 160; www.hoteldonasofia.com; Largo São João do Souto 131; s/d €50/65; P✳@🛜) On a pretty central square, Dona Sofia has functional, if a bit dated, carpeted rooms of varying sizes. Aim for one of the airy rooms with nice French windows overlooking the square.

Hotel Ibis
HOTEL **$$**

(☑253 204 800; www.ibishotel.com; Rua do Carmo 38; s/d €61/67; P✳@🛜) The rooms in this smart, modern midranger all have wood floors, floating desks, bathtubs and queen beds. They aren't huge, but have all the mod cons, and those on the upper reaches have panoramic views of surrounding monuments. Walk-in prices dip as low as €45, at which it's a steal.

Hotel Bracara Augusta BOUTIQUE HOTEL $$
(☑253 206 260; www.bracaraaugusta.com; Av Central 134; s/d €79/99; P❄@🛜) This stylish, grand town house offers bright, modern rooms with parquet floors, classic decor and marble bathrooms. The suites have French doors opening onto decorative balconies. Its otherwise pricey restaurant has an excellent breakfast buffet, with open-air dining by a gurgling fountain in the back.

★Portuguez Inn GUESTHOUSE $$$
(☑962 130 549; www.portuguezinn.pt; Rua Dom Frei Caetano Brandão 154; per 2/4 people €160/260; P❄🛜) This hideaway in the historic centre bills itself as 'the world's smallest guesthouse'. Small it is but its six levels offer a stylish micro-world that features a 1st-century Roman sewer in the basement, a cosy top-floor living room and Portuguese products throughout, such as woollen blankets, ceramic swallows, handmade soaps and cotton dolls. The house sleeps up to four people, who get breakfast delivered in a basket every morning and can rent bikes, book tours, have their laundry done and lots more.

✖ Eating

The boisterous **mercado municipal** (Praça do Comércio; ☺8am-3pm Mon-Fri, 6am-1pm Sat) buzzes on weekdays and Saturday mornings, and is ideal for self-caterers. You can also hit one of several fruit-and-vegetable shops along Rua de São Marcos.

Spirito ICE CREAM $
(Largo São João do Souto 19; cup €2-3.50, cone €2-4; ☺1.30-7pm & 9pm-midnight Tue-Sat) Don't miss the artisanal gelato at this always buzzing shop, where lines form out the door for a cup or cone of oatmeal-, cookie- or bubblegum-flavoured ice creams, and great cupcakes and coffees, too.

Mercado da Saudade CAFE $
(Rua Dom Paio Mendes 59; snacks €2-3.50; ☺10am-8pm Wed-Thu, 10am-1am Fri & Sat, 2-7pm Sun) Colourful little grocery store-cafe with a few storefront and sidewalk tables, where you can buy a variety of Portuguese products – from cork items, shoes and soaps to edibles such as chocolates and sardines. The snacks are delicious; try the Portuguese pork sandwich and wash it down with a glass of wine or Sovina, the local handcrafted beer.

Livraria Centésima Página CAFE $
(Av Central 118-120; snacks €2.60-4.90; ☺9am-7.30pm Mon-Sat) Tucked inside Centésima Página, an absolutely splendid bookshop with foreign-language titles, this charming cafe serves a rotating selection of tasty quiches along with salads and desserts, and has outdoor tables in the pleasantly rustic garden. The lunch specials are a steal.

Silvas PORTUGUESE $
(Largo do Terreiro do Castelo; mains €6-8; ☺lunch & dinner Mon-Sat, lunch Sun) Cosy little spot in the shadow of Torre de Menagem, this has a narrow glass-enclosed interior with a counter and a few tables outside. The well-prepared dishes change daily and include duck rice, rolled veal and always a fresh fish dish.

Taberna Velhos Tempos PORTUGUESE $
(Rua do Carmo 7; mains €7.50-11; ☺lunch & dinner Mon-Sat) Rustic tavern with wooden beams, lots of bric-a-brac and a menu of tasty mainstays. Try the *bacalhau con natas* or duck rice. The portions are huge so order only half.

Frigideiras do Cantinho CAFE $
(Largo São João do Souto 1; mains €4-7; ☺breakfast, lunch & dinner) Set on a sweet, quiet plaza, with pleasant indoor and outdoor seating, this humble cafe is favoured by loyal locals for its *frigideiras* (€1.50 per pop): meat pies with pork and veal, a tradition from 1796.

Salão de Chá Lusitana TEAROOM $
(Rua Justino Cruz 127; mains €7-10; ☺8am-8pm) Next to sweet-smelling Jardim de Santa Bárbara, this sunny, well-preserved art-deco tearoom is a local favourite with all, but especially ladies who lunch.

Anjo Verde VEGETARIAN $
(Largo da Praça Velha 21; mains €7.50-8.60; ☺lunch & dinner Mon-Sat; 🍴) Braga's vegetarian offering serves generous, elegantly presented plates in a lovely, airy dining room. Vegetarian lasagne, risotto and vegetable tarts are among the choices. Mains can be bland, but the spiced chocolate tart is a superstar.

Cozinha da Sé PORTUGUESE $$
(Rua Dom Frei Caetano Brandão 95; mains €10-14; ☺lunch & dinner Wed-Sun, dinner Tue) Contemporary artwork hangs from the exposed stone walls at this intimate cheery Braga dining room. Sé serves traditional, high-quality

dishes (including one vegetarian selection), with flavourful standouts such as baked *bacalhau* (dried salt-cod) and *açorda de marisco* (seafood stew in a bread bowl).

Copo e Meio
PORTUGUESE $$

(☑253 265 475; Rua Dom Frei Cateano Brandão 118; tapas €2-9, mains €11-19; ☺lunch & dinner Mon-Sat) This swanky, gourmet tapas bar-restaurant, with two cute upstairs stone dining rooms and a streetside deck, gets packed with local moneyed types. Come for the tapas and wine.

Taberna do Félix
PORTUGUESE $$

(☑253 617 701; Largo da Praça Velha 18-19; mains €10.75-16.75; ☺dinner Mon-Sat) Savour terrific Portuguese dishes in this attractive country-style tavern with two cosy dining rooms showcasing lots of bric-a-brac. The menu is small but dishes are delicious, including breaded sardines, duck rice and codfish *a minha moda*.

BRAC
PORTUGUESE $$

(Campo das Carvalheiras; snacks €3-9, mains €13-17; ☺dinner Mon-Sat) Braga's gourmet hotspot offers tasty *petiscos* at the backlit bar and more elaborate dishes like prawn curry and roasted black pork in the swanky dining room with stone columns and exposed stone walls. There's happy hour every night from 5.30pm to 7pm.

🍷 Drinking & Nightlife

Estúdio 22
BAR

(Rua Dom Paio Mendes 22; ☺10.30am-1am) Loungey cafe-bar on a bustling strip by the cathedral, great for coffee drinking during the day and sampling the speciality gin and tonics at night to the sound of live bands or DJs spinning funk and bossa.

Domus Vinum
WINE BAR

(www.domus-vinum.com; Largo da Nossa Senhora da Boa Luz 12; tapas €4-6.50; ☺6pm-2am Tue-Sun) With Brazilian beats, a lantern-lit front patio and excellent wines by the glass, Domus Vinum draws a stylish crowd. The Portuguese and Spanish tapas are excellent. It's just west of the old town entrance portal, Arco da Porta Nova.

Café A Brasileira
CAFE

(Largo do Barão de São Marinho 17; ☺7am-8pm Mon-Sat) A Braga classic, this 19th-century cafe is a converging point for the old and new generations. Try the *café de saco* (small shot of filtered coffee).

Taberna Svbvra
BAR

(Rua Dom Frei Caetano Brandão 101; ☺9pm-2am) Buzzy bar hidden behind a saloon-like wooden door, with a local low-key vibe and occasional live music. If the door is locked, knock and you'll be let into the smoky interior with guitars gracing the walls.

Colinatrum
CAFE

(☑253 215 630; www.colinatrum.com; Rua Damião de Góis 11; ☺8am-2am; 🤖) On a hill overlooking the countryside, this sleek glass-and-wood cafe is a fine meeting spot for a coffee or two, sunset cocktails or late-night bites. From the muslin-shaded outdoor terrace, you'll have a splendid view of Bom Jesus do Monte.

Barhaus
BAR

(Rua Dom Gonçalo Pereira 58; ☺noon-2am Tue-Sat) Popular bar with two indoor bars and a huge open-air patio, which draws a crowd with posh pretensions. DJs spin '80s music on weekends, when there's a €3 cover.

Sardinha Biba
CLUB

(www.sardinhabiba.com; Praça Dr Cândido da Costa Pires; ☺Wed, Fri & Sat 11pm-6am) One of Braga's oldest disco clubs, southeast of the historical centre, in the Mercado do Carandá. It churns out house and techno tunes to a party-happy crowd.

☆ Entertainment

Espaço Quatorze
PERFORMING ARTS

(Rua dos Chãos 14; ☺10pm-2am Tue-Sun) This youthful arts space hosts exhibitions, concerts, film screenings and other cultural fare. There's also a shop selling fair-trade items and a cafe where you can linger over a bite or a drink.

Teatro Circo de Braga
THEATRE

(☑253 203 800; www.teatrocirco.com; Av da Liberdade 697) One of the most dazzling theatres in the country, inside a grand fin de siècle building, where you can catch concerts, theatre and dance, with offerings ranging from the staid to the truly avant-garde.

ℹ Information

Biblioteca Lúcio Craveiro da Silva (www.blcs. pt; Rua de São Paulo 1; ☺9.30am-6pm Mon-Fri summer, 9.30am-12.30pm & 2-6pm Mon & Sat, 9am-8pm Tue-Fri winter) Free wi-fi and internet access on public computers.

Hospital Escala Braga (☑253 027 000; Sete Fontes – São Victor) A block west of Av da Liberdade.

BUSTLING BARCELOS

Thursday Market

The Minho is famous for its sprawling outdoor markets, and the largest, oldest and most celebrated is the **Feira de Barcelos** (Campo da República; ⊘7am-7pm Thu), held every Thursday in the ancient town of Barcelos, on the banks of the Rio Cávado. Tour buses arrive by the dozen, spilling their contents into the already brimming marketplace. You'll need at least a couple of hours to see all the goods.

Despite attracting travellers, the market retains its rural soul. Villagers hawk everything from scrawny chickens to hand-embroidered linen, and Roma women bellow for business in the clothes section. Snack on sausages and homemade bread as you wander among the brass cowbells, hand-woven baskets and carved ox yokes.

Pottery is what most outsiders come to see, especially the yellow-dotted *louça de Barcelos* ware and the gaudy figurines à la Rosa Ramalho, a local potter known as the Grandma Moses of Portuguese pottery – her work put Barcelos on the map in the 1950s. Once you've taken in the market, you'll find that Barcelos has a pleasant medieval core, with old stone towers perched over the river.

Rooster Rescue

His colourful crest adorns a thousand souvenir stalls – and you will notice the great and brilliant cocks sprinkled along the Barcelos streets like bigger-than-life chess pieces – but just how and why did the proud Portuguese cockerel become a national icon? It seems that a humble pilgrim, plodding his way to Santiago de Compostela in the 16th (some say 14th) century, stopped to rest in Barcelos, only to find himself wrongfully accused of theft and then swiftly condemned to be hanged. The outraged pilgrim told the judge that the roast on the judge's dinner table would affirm the pilgrim's innocence. And, just as the judge was about to tuck in, the cooked cock began to crow. The pilgrim was set free.

Sleeping & Eating

Accommodation is always tight on Wednesday and Thursday because of the market. Try the remarkable **Quinta do Convento da Franqueira** (☑253 831 606; www.quintada franqueira.com; s/d €75/100; ⊘Apr-Oct; P🕸📶🏊) in a 16th-century convent turned vineyard and inn, 6km north of town. Or in the town centre, stay in one of the stylish rooms at **Hotel do Terço** (☑253 808 380; www.hoteldoterco.com; Rua de São Bento 7; s/d €50/65; P🕸📶), a sleek modern option sitting atop its namesake shopping centre. There are plenty of equally inviting cafes and bakeries on the Old Town walking-only streets and plazas. The best food is to be had at **Galliano** (www.restaurantegalliano.com; Campo 5 de Outubro 20; mains €9-17; ⊘lunch & dinner Mon-Sat, lunch Sun), which features regional delicacies like *barrosã grelhado* (grilled steak), plus great-value lunch specials (€7).

Getting There & Away

Transdev Norte/Arriva (☑253 209 401; Av Dr Sidónio País 445) has the only reliable bus service to/from Barcelos, with at least eight buses to Braga (€2.60, one hour) on weekdays and about four on weekends. It also has services to Ponte de Lima (€3.10, one hour). Barcelos' station is on the Porto–Valença do Minho line. There are three to five direct trains a day to/from Porto (€4.70, one hour), and commuter trains every hour or two that change at Nine (€4, 1¼ hours). There is a similar service via Nine to Braga (€2.90, 45 to 60 minutes).

Police Station (☑253 200 420; Largo São Tiago 6)

Post Office (Rua Gonçalo Sampaio; ⊘8.30am-6pm Mon-Fri, 9am-12.30pm Sat) Just off Av da Liberdade.

Turismo (☑253 262 550; www.cm-braga.pt; Avenida da Liberdade 1; ⊘9am-1pm & 2-6.30pm Mon-Fri, 10am-1pm & 2-6pm Sat & Sun) Braga's helpful tourist office is in an art-deco-style building facing the fountain.

❶ Getting There & Around

BUS

Braga has a centralised bus station that serves as a major regional hub.

Airport Bus (☑253 262 371; www.getbus.eu) About nine buses daily do the 50-minute run between the Porto airport and Braga, in each direction. One-way fare is €8 (€4 for children), return is €14 (€6 for children).

Empresa Hoteleira do Gerês (☑253 262 033) Serves Vila do Gerês (€4.25, 1½ hours) about hourly during the week and six times on Saturday and Sunday.

Rede Expressos (www.rede-expressos.pt) Has up to 12 daily buses to Lisbon (€18.50, 4½ hours).

Transdev Norte/Arriva (☑253 209 401) Has at least eight buses per day to Viana do Castelo (€4.35, 1½ hours), Barcelos (€2.60, one hour), Guimarães (€3.15, 50 minutes) and Porto (€4.80, one hour), plus four per day to Campo do Gerês (€4.10, 1½ hours). Service drops by half at weekends.

CAR & MOTORCYCLE

The A3-IP1 motorway makes Braga an easy day trip from Porto. The N101 from Braga to Guimarães is a good road for a slow ride.

Because of one-way and pedestrian-only streets, driving in central Braga is tricky, and most parking incurs a fee. There is a large, fee-charging car park under Praça da República. You might also try side streets east of Av da Liberdade.

Avic (☑253 203 910; Rua Gabriel Pereira de Castro 28; ☉9am-7pm Mon-Fri, 9am-12.30pm Sat) is an efficient agency for several car-rental companies, with prices starting at €35 per day.

TRAIN

Braga is at the end of a branch line from Nine and also within Porto's *suburbano* network, which means commuter trains travel every hour or so from Porto (€3.10, about one hour); don't waste €32.80 on an Alfa Pendular (AP) train.

Useful AP links include Coimbra (€19, 2¼ hours, five to seven daily) and Lisbon (€31, four hours, two to four daily).

Bom Jesus do Monte

The goal of legions of penitent pilgrims every year, Bom Jesus do Monte is one of Portugal's most recognisable icons. A rather windswept and glamorous pilgrimage site, lying 5km east of central Braga, the sober neoclassical church stands atop a forested hill that offers grand sunset views across the city. But most people don't come simply for the church or even the view. They come to see the extraordinary baroque staircase, **Escadaria do Bom Jesus.**

The photogenic climb is made up of tiered staircases, dating from different decades of the 18th century. The lowest is lined with chapels representing the Stations of the Cross. **Escadaria dos Cinco Sentidos** (Stairway of the Five Senses) features allegorical fountains with water gurgling from the ears, eyes, nose and mouth of different statues. Highest is **Escadaria das Três Virtudes** (Stairway of the Three Virtues), with chapels and fountains representing faith, hope and charity.

The area around the church has become something of a resort, with fancy hotels, tennis courts, flower gardens and a lake. It's choked with tourists on summer weekends, who come to explore the church, cobblestone roads and trails on foot or bicycle.

🛏 Sleeping

Reservations are recommended in summer.

Hotel Grande   HOTEL **$**
(☑253 281 222; www.grandehotelbomjesus.com; Largo Mãe da Água, Bom Jesus, Tenões; s/d €39/55; 🅿❄🤖) This sleek hotel, with its minimalist exterior and nouveau Renaissance interior, is 1km from the church (at the fork before reaching Bom Jesus, veer left). Its spacious doubles (most complete with balconies) are by far the best choice in the area.

Hotel do Elevador   HOTEL **$$**
(☑253 603 400; www.hoteisbomjesus.pt; Bom Jesus do Monte; s/d €85/102; 🅿❄@🤖) Set in an antiquated villa, this is one of four Bom Jesus hotels owned by the same company. Its rooms have romantic old-world touches and magical views. The restaurant (mains €10 to €16) has a stunning perch.

✖ Eating

Aside from the hotel restaurants, eating options are scarce. For good homemade food, try **Adega Regional de Tenões**, on the road to Bom Jesus.

❶ Getting There & Away

City bus 2 runs from Braga's Av da Liberdade to the bottom of the Bom Jesus steps (€1.65, 20 minutes) – the end of the line – every half-hour all day (hourly on Sunday). From here you can hoof it up the steps or hop aboard the newly restored **ascensor** (funicular; Largo Mãe da Água; one way €1.20; ☉8am-8pm), which whisks visitors to the top every half hour. Alternatively, a taxi from central Braga to the top of the steps costs €7 to €10.

Guimarães

POP 8200 / ELEV 400M

Beautifully preserved Guimarães has an illustrious past. It's the proud birthplace of Afonso Henriques, the first independent king of Portugal and, thus, the Portuguese Kingdome. He was born here in 1110 and later used the city to launch the main thrust of the Reconquista against the Moors.

Its medieval centre is a warren of labyrinthine lanes and picturesque plazas framed by 14th-century edifices, while on an adjacent hill stands a 1000-year-old castle and, next to it, the massive palace built by the first duke of Bragança in the 15th century. Guimarães' glory was officially recognised in 2001, when Unesco declared its old centre a World Heritage site. More recently, in 2012, the city was the European Capital of Culture, which has led to several new openings on the cultural front and given the city a more creative edge.

On top of the city's historical treasures, museums and cutting-edge cultural institutions, there are cafe-filled plazas, atmospheric guesthouses and delightful restaurants. Plus, Guimarães is a university town, and its students lend much vitality to the place – particularly during the celebratory Festas de Cidade e Gualterianas in August.

⊙ Sights

Paço dos Duques de Bragança PALACE
(Ducal Palace; Rua Conde D Henrique; adult/child €5/free; ⊙10am-6pm) Looming over the medieval city on Guimarães' hilltop, with its crenulated towers and cylindrical brick chimneys, Paço dos Duques was first built in 1401 and later pompously restored as a

---

ON THE ART TRACK IN GUIMARÃES

Rui Torrinha is a cultural programmer for A Oficina, an entity that runs Centro Cultural Vila Flor (p430). He is also a cultural instigator, mainly in the urban music field, where he helps break new artists.

What are your favourite Guimarães art collectives and hotspots that visitors should keep on their radar?

The list of associations in Guimarães is endless but I particularly love Convívio (p433), a pivotal cultural hub founded in 1961 that has since launched some of the most important events in the city – and it's still reinventing itself within the city's new context. Laboratório das Artes (on the upper floors of the Café Milenário building on Largo do Toural) is a great example of resilience through art. This visual-arts collective has been really supportive of established artists but also newcomers, allowing the city to connect with new kinds of expression. Another important association is **Cineclube** (2nd floor, Largo da Misericórdia 19; www.cineclubeguimaraes.org), who have a space in a gorgeous building near Convívio, with a rooftop where they sometimes project films. Finally, there's Center for Art & Architecture Affairs (p430), an old factory reconverted in a multidisciplinary venue that offers a particular look at contemporary art, not only as a presentation space but also as an artistic residency for creators who need a place to work in Guimarães.

To which cafe-bars/clubs in Guimarães would you send people who are interested in the art scene?

My regular summer cafe for meeting the art crowd is Medieval at Praça da Oliveira. If you're looking for underground vibes, Projecto is the place to hit, where the crowd's modern punk attitude celebrates contemporary culture in a club context. Make sure to pay a visit to São Mamede CAE (p434), an old cinema and now a cultural centre that offers all kinds of shows and has a bar that attracts an artsy crowd.

Which festivals and events in Guimarães do you love most?

I love Guimarães Jazz (p432) and GUIdance, the international contemporary dance fest in early February. Manta, the annual open-air event in CCVF's garden, has shows by local and international bands.

Guimarães

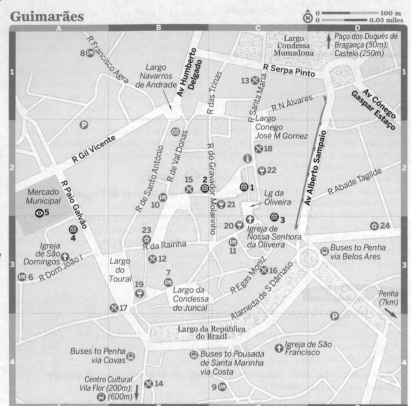

presidential residence for Salazar. Today it's open to visitors who can wander through the rooms, which house a collection of Flemish tapestries, medieval weapons, a chapel with glittering stained-glass windows and enormous tapestries which relate various episodes in the Portuguese attempt to conquer North Africa.

Castelo
CASTLE

(⏱10am-6pm) **FREE** Built in the 11th century and still in fine form, the seven-towered castle is thought to be the birthplace of the great man himself, Afonso Henriques. Walk around the windswept ramparts of the castle and scale the narrow steps to the bird's-nest heights of Countess Mumadona's keep.

Centro Cultural Vila Flor
CULTURAL BUILDING

(📞253 424 700; www.ccvf.pt; Avenida D Afonso Henriques 701) CCVF kick-started the city's cultural revival when it opened in 2005 in a striking modern building added onto a con-

verted 18th-century palace. Events at this culture powerhouse include movie screenings, cafe concerts, theatre and art exhibits.

Platform for Arts and Creativity
CULTURAL BUILDING

(adult/student €4/3; free Sun mornings; ⏱10am-7pm) For the 2012 European Capital of Culture, the old market square was revamped into a multipurpose cultural centre inside a shimmering three-floor metallic building that looks like a bunch of stacked-up boxes. Inside is a permanent exhibit by Portuguese painter José de Guimarães, with items from his private collection of pre-Colombian, African and Chinese art. Check out the room called Spells, with an impressive display of African masks.

Center for Art & Architecture Affairs
CULTURAL BUILDING

(www.centroaaa.org; Rua Padre Augusto Borges de Sá; ⏱2.30-7pm) Inside a former textile factory,

Guimarães

this non-profit collective promotes interaction between various fields of creative expression, including visual arts, design, film, literature, media, performing arts and architecture. Events include film screenings, theatre performances, concerts and workshops.

Igreja de São Gualter   CHURCH
(Church of St Walter; Largo São Gualter; ⊙8am-noon & 3-5pm Mon-Sat, 8am-noon Sun) This slender 18th-century construction, with its 19th-century twin spires and blooming run-up from central Guimarães, has the most striking appeal of all the city's churches.

Museu Alberto Sampaio   MUSEUM
(Rua Alfredo Guimaraes; adult/child €3/free, Sun morning free; ⊙10am-6pm Tue-Sun) Built around the serene Romanesque cloister of Igreja de Nossa Senhora da Oliveira, this museum has an excellent collection of ecclesiastical art and religious finery. Highlights include the tunic reputedly worn by João I at the Battle of Aljubarrota (1385).

Antigos Paços do Concelho   HISTORIC BUILDING
Guimarães' 14th-century former town hall sits above an arcaded portico providing a most graceful communication between cosy Largo da Oliveira and the more rambling Praça de Santiago.

**Museu Arqueológico
Martins Sarmento**   MUSEUM
(🕾253 415 969; www.csarmento.uminho.pt; Rua Paio Galvão; admission €3; ⊙9.30am-noon & 2-5pm Tue-Sat, 10am-noon & 2-5pm Sun) This fantastic collection of mostly Celtiberian

artefacts is housed in a former convent and named after the archaeologist who excavated Citânia de Briteiros in 1875. Hefty stone artefacts, including thick Roman columns and milestones, and a mossy Celtic sarcophagus, are spread around the cloister. Look for the impressive *pedras formosas* (beautiful stones) thought to have adorned Celtiberian bathhouses in the surrounding region, and the impressive case of Palaeolithic and Neolithic tools.

Penha   PARK
Some 7km southeast up a twisting, cobbled road – or a short ride on an ageing cable car – is the wooded summit of Penha (617m) overlooking Guimarães, the highest point for miles. Its cool woods make it a wonderful escape from the city and summer heat. Kids love losing themselves amid the massive boulders, many cut with steps, crowned with flowers and crosses, or hiding in secret grottoes.

On the lower slopes of the hill lies the Mosteiro de Santa Marinha da Costa, 1.5km east of Penha's centre. It dates from 1154, when Dona Mafalda, wife of Afonso Henriques, commissioned it to honour a vow she made to the patron saint of pregnant women. Rebuilt in the 18th century, it's now a flagship Pousada de Portugal.

The easiest and finest route to the top of Penha is aboard the **Teleférico da Penha** (Cable Car; one way/return €2.70/4.40; ⊙10am-7pm Mon-Fri, to 8pm Sat & Sun Jun-Sep), which starts from Parque das Hortas, 600m east of Guimarães' old centre. You can also get there by Mondinense bus (€2.45, eight daily Monday to Saturday), which departs from the bus station. A taxi costs €10.

Galeria de Arte Jose Gomes Alves GALLERY
(Rua do Gravador Molarinho; ⊙ 10.30am-1pm & 3.30-7pm Tue-Sat) FREE A bright airy gallery in a medieval stone compound, with intriguing rotating exhibitions of modern work.

✦ Festivals & Events

Festas de Cidade e Gualterianas CULTURAL
(www.aoficina.pt) Marked by a free fair (held in Guimarães since 1452 to honour its patron saint), this festival also features folk dancing, rock concerts, fireworks and parades. It takes place on the first weekend in August.

Guimarães Jazz MUSIC
One of the country's top festivals, this jazz extravaganza runs for about three weeks in November.

🛏 Sleeping

TM Hostel 2 HOSTEL $
(☎ 253 433 504; www.tmhostels.com; Rua da Rainha D Maria II 144; dm €14-15, d €39-42; @🛜) The newer branch of this hip hostel chain by fashion designer Tony Miranda houses the reception for both branches. Rooms vary in size and configuration. All are bright and colourful and feature fabrics from the designer's old creations; some have French balconies. There's a kitchen and a living room, plus a rooftop terrace. Book ahead for weekends.

My Hostel HOSTEL $
(☎ 253 414 023; www.myhostel-guimaraes.web node.pt; Rua Francisco Agra 135; dm €15-17, €38-42; 🛜) Stylish new hostel with eight colourful bright rooms that include dorms and doubles with swanky shared and private bathrooms. There's a nice shared kitchen-living room and a terrace. Towels cost €1 but breakfast is included. You can order food and massages.

TM Hostel 1 HOSTEL $
(☎ 253 433 504; www.tmhostels.com; Rua Val de Donas 11; dm €19-20, €38-44; 🛜) Fashion-inspired hostel with curtains and sheets made of old dresses, and squeaky-clean rooms – from four-bed dorms with shared or private bathroom to twins and doubles. Some rooms come with balconies and there's a shared terrace with astroturf. Reserve ahead; check-in is between 9am and 11am only.

Pousadas da Juventude HOSTEL $
(☎ 253 421 380; www.pousadasjuventude.pt; Largo da Cidade 8; dm/d/apt €14/38/70; @🛜) Set in the palatial 18th-century home of a prosperous factory owner, this terrific hostel in the historic Couros district has hardwood floors, bright six-bed dorms and spacious doubles that are downright stylish. It also has kitchen and laundry facilities and a huge living room with pool tables.

Hotel Toural HOTEL $$
(☎ 253 517 184; www.hoteltoural.com; Largo A L de Carvalho; s/d €65/86; P🅿@🛜) In a complex of two connected historic buildings, this four-star hotel accessed through a leafy alleyway entrance has well-appointed rooms overlooking the square, the patio or the mountains in the distance.

Hotel de Guimarães HOTEL $$
(☎ 253 424 800; www.hotel-guimaraes.com; Rua Eduardo Manuelde Almeida; s/d €80/90; P🅿@ 🛜🖥) A business hotel near the train station, with large rooms with lush linens, chic paint jobs and flat-screen TVs, along with a health club and spa. It's a bit removed from the old town, but still excellent value and an easy two-minute walk to the train.

Hotel Mestre d'Avis HOTEL $$
(☎ 253 422 770; www.hotelmestredeavis.pt; Rua Dom João I 40; s/d €45/70; P🅿🛜) Fronted by curlicue ironwork, this renovated hotel has bright rooms on a quiet cobbled street in the centre. The contemporary rooms come in three categories – standard, superior and deluxe. Some have balconies and alcoves; all feature a dash of style.

Pousada de Santa Marinha RURAL INN $$$
(☎ 253 511 249; www.pousadas.pt; s/d €180/190; P🅿🖥) This former monastery overlooking the city from the slopes of Penha is a magnificent, sprawling structure. The gardens are stunning and you'll want to wander around the cloister, past dribbling fountains and masterful *azulejos*. The rooms inside the former monks' cells feel cramped, so book a room in the modern wing.

🍴 Eating

Adega dos Caquinhos PORTUGUESE $
(Rua da Arrochela; mains €6-9; ⊙ lunch & dinner Mon-Sat) Family-run tavern with a small menu of two to three dishes daily, prepared the home-style way. Whatever's fresh at the market you get served on your plate in this down-home cash-only spot with bits of

broken ceramics gracing the walls. Try the homemade cookies ice cream.

Danúbio Bar
CAFE $

(Avenida Dom Afonso Henriques 15; snacks €1-3.50; ⊙ 7.30am-midnight) This corner kiosk draws in a local crowd (of mostly old men) for its simple but tasty snacks at low prices. Try the delicious hamburgers with arugula and herb fries and *patanisca* sandwiches. Wash it down with beer either inside or on the tiny cobblestone square in front.

Manifestis Probatum
TAPAS $

(Rua Egas Moniz 57-63; snacks €3-7.50; ⊙ 12.30pm-midnight Tue-Thu & Sun, 12.30pm-2am Fri & Sat) Stylish new wine and tapas bar that serves all-day Spanish tapas and Portuguese *petiscos* that focus on canned fish – from trout in white wine to smoked mackerel. Pick between many Portuguese wines by the glass or sip a Sovina craft beer on the wooden bar or the clean-lined airy back room with leafy views.

Pastelaria Clarinha
BAKERY $

(Largo do Toural 86-88; pastries €0.70-3.20; ⊙ breakfast, lunch & dinner Tue-Sun) Guimarães' best pastry shop has filled its window with fresh-baked tarts and cakes to tempt passers-by since 1953. There are a few pavement tables and a heavenly *toucinho do ceu* (almond cake).

★ Cor de Tangerina
VEGETARIAN $$

(Largo Martins Sarmento 89; mains €6-12; ⊙ noon-11pm Tue-Sat, noon-7pm Sun;) This charming restaurant whips up a good selection of cuisine you won't find elsewhere in Guimarães. Changing art exhibitions decorate the walls, while the wild, jazz-washed garden (with tangerine tree) produces most of the herbs used in the ancient stone kitchen. The chef is something of a herbal alchemist, capable of brewing all manner of teas and tonics, too.

Solar do Arco
PORTUGUESE $$

(253 513 072; Rua de Santa Maria 48-50; mains €9.50-13; ⊙ lunch & dinner Mon-Sat, lunch Sun;) With a handsomely panelled dining room under a graceful arcade, this is a top central choice. Portuguese classics made with straight-from-the-market ingredients add to the allure. Touristy it is though, and hence pricier.

Histórico by Papaboa
PORTUGUESE $$

(www.papaboa.pt; Rua de Val Donas 4; mains €9.50-14; ⊙ lunch & dinner) The setting – in a medieval fort with breezy courtyard seating and glassed-in stone dining room – is tremendous. Service is top-notch and the fare is dressed up yet traditional, such as black pork with prawns and mustard sauce. The weekday lunch menu is a steal. On Saturday afternoons (5pm to 9pm) it serves regional *petiscos*.

🍷 Drinking & Entertainment

Coconuts
BAR

(www.coconuts.com.pt; Largo da Oliveira 1-3; ⊙ 8am-2am Wed-Sat, 8am-midnight Sun-Tue) Popular bar on the Oliveira square, with *azulejo*-filled interiors and tables on the cobblestone square. It serves coffee, snacks and a low-key vibe during the day and turns into a happening hotspot at night, with DJs on Fridays and Saturdays.

Tásquilhado
BAR

(Rua de Santa Maria 42; ⊙ 9pm-2am Wed-Sat, to midnight Sun) One of a swathe of bar-hopping venues in the historic centre, this cosy, ever-popular bar plays alternative sounds and offers enticing drink specials during the week.

El Rock
BAR

(Praça de Santiago 31; ⊙ 2pm-2am) Dug into a narrow stone room and spreading onto the plaza is this funky beer bar. It hosts occasional live bands, and is the destination for many a pretty, wild-haired hipster when night falls.

Tunel 29
BAR

(www.tunel29.com; Praça de Santiago 29; ⊙ 6pm-close) A reggae- and electronica-infused, mosaic-tiled cave that sees its share of Guimarães party people.

Cervejaria Martins
BEER HALL

(Largo do Toural 32-35; ⊙ 10am-2am Mon-Sat) Always bustling cafe-bar where sports blast on TV and lots of men sit around the circular counter. A long-standing favourite, going strong since the 1950s. It serves snacks till late.

Convívio Associação
PERFORMING ARTS

(Largo da Misericórdia 7-8; ⊙ 3-7pm Mon-Fri, 9pm-midnight Mon-Thu, 9pm-2am Fri & Sat) Started 52 years ago, this creative cultural association – also a jazz school – is still going strong. Its program includes classic music concerts, jazz sessions, exhibits, theatre and workshops. Fridays and Saturdays are the busiest nights, when an older boho crowd descends to the bar and small open-air patio.

São Mamede CAE PERFORMING ARTS
(www.sao-mamede.com; Rua Dr José Sampaio 17-25; ☺10am-midnight Mon-Tue & Thu, 10am-2am Wed, Fri & Sat) This converted old cinema-cultural centre draws a student crowd for its range of events, from performances to film screenings, cheap weekday lunches served at the funky 1st-floor cafe and a loungey wine bar on the top floor.

ℹ Information

Espaço Internet (Praça de Santiago; ☺10am-8pm Mon-Sat Sep-Jul, 10am-2pm Mon-Sat Aug) Free internet access. It's up a flight of stairs near Largo da Oliveira. There's also free wi-fi on the main squares in town.
Hospital (☎253 540 330; Rua dos Cutileiros, Creixomil) Opposite the bus station.
Livraria Ideal (Rua da Rainha 34; ☺10am-1pm & 3-7pm Mon-Fri, 10am-1pm Sat) The city's best bookshop has a terrific selection of area maps.
Police Station (☎253 513 334; Av Dr Alfredo Pimenta) Next to the fire department.
Post Office (Rua de Santo António 138; ☺8.30am-6pm Mon-Fri)
Turismo (☎253 518 394; www.guimaraes turismo.com; Praça de Santiago; ☺9.30am-6.30pm Mon-Fri, 10am-1pm & 1.30-6.30pm Sat, 10am-1pm Sun) The excellent, informative staff speaks English, French and Spanish.

ℹ Getting There & Around

There is street parking in front of the Convento do Carmo at the foot of the Paço dos Duques. If you wish to explore Guimarães and surrounds on two wheels or four, go to **Quality Tours** (☎253 527 144; www.qualitytours.pt; Largo Martins Sarmento 89; ☺9am-7pm), which rents out bikes (€15 per day) as well as scooters and four-wheelers; it also organises guided walking tours (€25 per person).

BUS

Transdev (☎253 516 229) has buses leaving at least every hour for Braga (€3.15, 50 minutes) Monday to Saturday, and runs eight buses on Sunday. Transdev also has services to Porto (€5.10, 50 minutes) running approximately every hour on weekdays but less often on weekends, and to Lisbon (€20.50, five hours) daily.
Rodonorte (☎253 423 500; www.rodonorte. pt) heads for Amarante (€7.60, one hour), Vila Real (€8.50, two hours) and Bragança (€14.50, four hours).
   Get Bus (www.getbus.eu) has six buses daily that do the 50-minute run between the Porto airport and Guimarães, in each direction. The

ne-way fare is €8 (€4 for children); return is €14 (€8 for children).

TRAIN

Guimarães is the terminus of a branch of Porto's wide *suburbano* network. Commuter trains potter out to Guimarães from Porto (€3.10, 75 minutes) 11 to 16 times daily. Try to avoid the once-daily *intercidade* (express) train, which costs €11.70 and departs at 7.43am.

Citânia de Briteiros

◉ Sights & Activities

One of the most evocative archaeological sites in Portugal, **Citânia de Briteiros** (admission incl museum adult/student €3/1.50; ☺9.30am-6pm May-Sep, to 5pm Oct-Apr), 15km north of Guimarães, is the largest of a liberal scattering of northern Celtic hill settlements called *citânias* (fortified villages), which date back at least 2500 years. It's likely that this sprawling 3.8-hectare site, inhabited from about 300 BC to AD 300, was the Celt-iberians' last stronghold against the invading Romans.

When the archaeologist Dr Martins Sarmento excavated the site back in 1875, he discovered the foundations and ruins of more than 150 rectangular, circular and elliptical stone huts, all linked by paved paths and a water distribution system, and cocooned by multiple protective walls. Highlights of the site include two reconstructed huts that evoke what it was like to live in the settlement and, further down the hill, a bathhouse with a strikingly patterned stone doorway.

Some artefacts are on display in the Sede e Museu Arqueológico in Guimarães, but the **Museu da Cultura Castreja** (Museum on Pre-Roman Culture; Solar da Ponte; adult/student €3/1.50; ☺9.30am-12.30pm & 2-6pm) also has important artefacts from various sites housed in Sarmento's 18th- and 19th-century manor house. It's about 2km back down the hill towards Guimarães in the village of Briteiros Salvador.

ℹ Getting There & Away

From Guimarães, **Transdev/Arriva** (☎253 423 500) has about eight weekday buses that pass within 1km of the site; get off between the towns of Briteiros Salvador and Santa Leocádia. Check at the bus station for current schedule information.

Viana do Castelo

POP 15,600

The jewel of the Costa Verde, Viana do Castelo is blessed with both an appealing medieval centre and lovely beaches just outside the city. The old quarters showcase leafy, 19th-century boulevards and narrow lanes crowded with Manueline manors and rococo palaces. The town's setting just by the Rio Lima estuary means that Viana do Castelo is only a short hop from some excellent beaches, and also makes it a handy base for exploring the lower Lima valley and the nearby Serra d'Arga mountain.

History

The remains of Celtic hill settlements on Monte de Santa Luzia, overlooking the contemporary town centre, and the name Viana – a nod to its Roman past when this once-humble settlement was called Diana – convey Viana do Castelo's deep historical roots, while its Manueline mansions and monasteries recall its 16th-century prosperity as a major cod-fishing port. In fact, by the mid-17th century it had bloomed into Portugal's biggest overall port, with merchants trading as far afield as Russia.

More riches arrived in the 18th century, with the advent of the Brazilian sugar and gold trade. But with Brazil's independence and the rising importance of Porto, Viana's golden age stuttered and faded. These days Viana earns much of its current living and reputation as the Minho's favourite resort town.

◉ Sights & Activities

Praça da República   SQUARE

This fine hub of seven narrow laneways is at the heart of the old town's zone of mansions and monuments. An especially elegant example is the **Chafariz**, a Renaissance fountain that was built in 1554. The fountain is topped with Manueline motifs of an armillary sphere and the cross of the Order of Christ. The fortresslike **Antigos Paços do Concelho** is the old town hall – a 16th-century creation that sometimes hosts contemporary art exhibitions.

Igreja Matriz   CHURCH

(Rua Santos Cabral; ◉9am-6pm) This elegant parish church – also known as the *sé* – dates from the 15th century, although it has been through several reincarnations since then. Check out its unusually sculpted Romanesque towers and Gothic doorway, carved with figures of Christ and the Evangelists.

Museu de Arte e Arqueologia   MUSEUM

(www.cm-viana-castelo.pt; Rua Manuel Espregueira; admission €2; ◉10am-1pm & 3-7pm Jun-Sep, to 6pm Oct-May) The 18th-century Palacete Barbosa Maciel bears witness to Viana's affluent past. It houses an impressive collection of 17th- and 18th-century ceramics (especially blue Portuguese china) and furniture. Most impressive are three 2nd-floor rooms lined with *azulejos,* depicting scenes of hunting and palace life.

Museu do Traje   MUSEUM

(Costume Museum; Rua da Picota; admission €2; ◉10am-1pm & 2-6pm) This attractive museum houses the traditional wear used for farming, fishing and seaweed harvesting in centuries past. You'll see costumes worn during the Romaria de Nossa Senhora d'Agonia and cool antique looms. The then-and-now mural-sized photos on the 2nd floor are pretty special, too.

SURFING & KITESURFING IN MINHO

Praia do Cabedelo (p437) is an excellent kitesurfing destination, with consistent on-shore wind year-round. It's a great teaching site, but also fun for intermediate surfers thanks to the lagoonlike conditions created by the southern headland and harbour breakwater, which is a full kilometre north. South of Cabedelo 17km, there's good kiting and some traditional surfing at **Esposende**, but conditions are iffy.

Among the fine beaches strung north along the 25km of coast between Viana do Castelo and Caminha, **Afife** has the best surf breaks, with waves topping out at 2m during peak swells. Four daily regional trains (€1.40, 13 minutes) make their way up the coast to Afife from Viana. Advanced kitesurfers will want to drive a bit further north to **Moledo** where the wind and waves are at their fiercest and finest. For tips and gear rental, stop by **Viana Locals** (p437) at Praia do Cabedelo.

Viana do Castelo

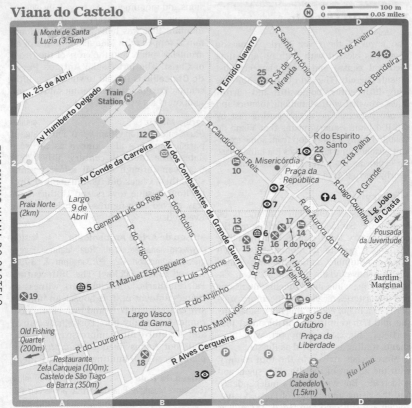

Castelo de São Tiago da Barra CASTLE
(Campo de Castelo; ⊙9am-6pm) You can still
scoot around the ramparts of this squat castle, a short walk west of the centre, which
began in the 15th century as a smallish fort.
It was integrated into a larger fort, commissioned by Felipe II of Spain (Felipe I of Portugal) in 1592, to guard the prosperous port
against pirates.

Monte de Santa Luzia HILL
There are two good reasons to visit Viana's
228m, eucalyptus-clad hill. One is the wondrous view down the coast and up the Lima
valley. The other is the fabulously over-the-
top, 20th-century, neo-Byzantine **Templo
do Sagrado Coração de Jesus** (Temple of
the Sacred Heart of Jesus; ⊙11am-1pm & 3-8pm)
FREE. You can get a little closer to heaven on
its graffiti-covered roof, via a lift, followed by
an elbow-scraping stairway (€0.80) – take
the museum entrance on the ground floor.

Behind the Pousada do Monte de Santa
Luzia is another attraction, the **Ruinas da
Cidade Velha** (admission €3; ⊙9am-noon &
2-6pm), ruins of a Celtiberian *citânia* from
around the 4th century BC. You'll see the
stones peeking above the wind-blown savannah. Most of the site is accessible via a
boardwalk.

You can get up the mountain by the restored **funicular** (one way/return €2/3; ⊙9am-
8pm Jun-Sep, 8am-6pm Oct-May), which departs
from near the train station every 15 minutes.
You can also drive or take a taxi (3.5km) to
the top, or hike 2km of steps (only for the
fit and/or penitent). The road starts by the
hospital, and the steps begin about 200m up
the road.

Gil Eannes LANDMARK
(☎258 809 710; www.fundacaogileannes.pt; Doca
Comercial; admission €2; ⊙9am-7pm) Demanding attention on the waterfront near Largo
5 de Outubro is a pioneering naval hospital

Viana do Castelo

ship, the *Gil Eannes (zheel yan-ish)*. Now restored, the ship once provided on-the-job care for those fishing off the coast of Newfoundland. Visitors can clamber around the steep decks and cabins, though a scattering of old clinical equipment may make your hair stand on end.

River Trips   BOAT TRIPS
(www.passeiofluvial.com; ⊙ May-Sep) If there are enough passengers, boats run up and down the Rio Lima daily in summer, from the pier south of Largo 5 de Outubro (the same dock where ferries depart to Praia do Cabedelo). The most common trip takes 40 minutes (adult/child €7.50/4). Longer excursions (adult/child €12/6.50) take in the old shipyards; these must be booked at least a day ahead.

Serra d'Arga   GUIDED TOUR
(☑ 969 220 704; www.serradearga.com) Don't miss a trip to this nearby mountain, just a 25-minute drive away, with its eight scenic villages and protected nature that includes diverse fauna such as the Iberian frog and the Garrano horse. The local guides can take you on day hikes and even on full-moon night treks. Reserve ahead.

Praia do Cabedelo   BEACH
This is one of the Minho's best beaches: a 1km-long arch of blond powdery sand, which folds into grassy dunes backed by a grove of wind-blown pines. It's across the river from town. Get there by passenger ferry (one-way adult/child €1.40/0.70) from

the pier south of Largo 5 de Outubro; the five-minute trip goes hourly between 9am and 6pm. Alternatively, TransCunha has multiple daily buses to Cabedelo (€1) from the bus station.

Viana Locals   SURFING
(☑ 258 325 168; www.vianalocals.com; Praia do Cabedelo) A friendly, full-service board-sports outfitter and school right on Praia do Cabedelo. It has surfboards, kite gear and paddle boards for rent and sale, and does overnight repairs too.

Festivals & Events

Viana has a knack for celebrations. The Romaria de Nossa Senhora d'Agonia, held in August, is the region's biggest annual bash and **Carnaval** festivities here are considered northern Portugal's best. The town also goes a little nuts in mid-May during **Semana Acadêmica** (or Queima das Fitas), a week of end-of-term student madness. The *turismo* has details of other annual events.

Encontros de Viana   FILM
A week-long festival of documentaries and short films; held in the first half of May.

Festival Maio   CULTURE
A national folk-dance extravaganza that takes place at the end of May.

Sleeping

Ó Meu Amor   GUESTHOUSE $
(☑ 258 406 513; www.omeuamor.com; Rua do Poço 19; s/d €25/45; @ 🛜) Top choice in town

CELEBRATION OF SORROWS

Streets decorated with coloured sawdust. Women decked out in traditional finery of scarlet and gold. Men drinking till they keel over. Viana do Castelo's **Romaria de Nossa Senhora d'Agonia** (Festival of Our Lady of Sorrows; www.festas-agonia.com) is one of the Minho's most spectacular festivals. Expect everything from emotive religious processions to upbeat parades with deafening drums and lumbering carnival *gigantones* (giants) and *cabeçudos* (big heads). The festival takes place for three or four days around 20 August. Accommodation is very tight at this time, so book well ahead.

right in the historic centre, this new hideaway in a rambling town house full of nooks and crannies has nine adorable rooms with shared bathrooms. Each has a theme – such as India and Africa rooms in the attic – and some have tiny balconies with rooftop and mountain views. Guests can use the kitchen and cosy living room.

O Laranjeira GUESTHOUSE $
(☑ 258 822 258; www.olaranjeira.com; Rua Manuel Espregueira 24; s/d €40/50; ✳ 🛜) This bright town house is a fantastic choice in the old centre, a cosy family-run spot with seven small but soulful rooms, each with a theme and some with patios. There's an attractive restaurant on the ground floor, where guests enjoy discounted meals.

Hotel Jardim HOTEL $
(☑ 258 828 915; www.residencialjardim.com.sapo.pt; Largo 5 de Outubro 68; s/d €40/55; P ✳ @ 🛜) In a stately 19th-century town house, this quirky place has spacious rooms with wooden floors, stone-framed French windows overlooking the historic centre or the river, and sizeable bathrooms. Nab one of the lighter rooms on the top floors, for better views.

Pousada da Juventude HOSTEL $
(☑ 258 800 260; www.pousadasjuventude.pt; Rua da Lima; dm €13, d with private bathroom/shared €34/28; P @ 🛜) This Carrilho Graça–designed hostel overlooks the marina 1km from the centre. The exterior may need a paint job, but the interiors are swanky, with

black concrete floors and chic marble baths. Four-bed dorms have lockers.

Orbitur CAMPGROUND $
(☑ 258 322 167; www.orbitur.com; Praia do Cabedelo; per site/person €21.60/6.40; ⏱ Apr-Sep; 🛜 ⛵) Nestled on the inland side of lovely sand dunes, this shady site is within walking distance of the ferry pier, and has two- to six-person bungalows (€92 to €127). It heaves with holidaymakers in summer, and is a two-minute walk to the sea.

★**Margarida da Praça** GUESTHOUSE $$
(☑ 258 809 630; www.margaridadapraca.com; Largo 5 de Outubro 58; s/d €55/65; @ 🛜) Fantastically whimsical, this boutique inn offers thematic rooms in striking pinks, sea greens and whites, accented by stylish floral wallpaper, candelabra lanterns and lush duvets. The equally stylish lobby glows with candlelight in the evening. Staff are warm and helpful, and there's a TV room and a small top-floor terrace. The 3rd-floor suite (€10 more) is a charmer. Book ahead.

Hotel Laranjeira HOTEL $$
(☑ 258 822 261; www.residencialaranjeira.com; Rua Candido dos Reis 45; s/d €60/70; P 🛜) This well-managed place was recently upgraded to hotel status and now has 26 contemporary if poky rooms with pine floors and glass-partitioned bathrooms. Some have balconies, and others great views of Santa Luzia.

Melo Alvim HOTEL $$$
(☑ 258 808 200; www.meloalvimhouse.com; Av Conde da Carreira 28; s/d €117/130; P ✳ @ 🛜) Deluxe rooms in a stately 16th-century mansion, individually decked out with hardwood floors, four-poster beds, original stone accents and marble bathrooms. No two rooms are alike, but it is worth paying the extra €9 for the deluxe rooms, which have more space, huge ceilings and ornately carved beds.

Flôr de Sal BOUTIQUE HOTEL $$$
(☑ 258 800 100; www.hotelflordesal.com; Av de Cabo Verde 100, Praia Norte; s/d from €135/165; P ✳ 🛜 ⛵) Perched on a windswept stretch of rocky coastline, this sleek designer offering has whitewashed rooms, all the modern touches and huge balconies with ocean views. There's a spa, gym, indoor pool and pleasant restaurant on-site. It's 2km west of the centre.

Pousada do Monte de
Santa Luzia
HISTORIC HOTEL **$$$**

(Pousada de Viana do Castelo; ☑ 258 800 370; www.pousadas.pt; s/d €170/180; P ❀ @ 🛜 🛋) This regal 1918 hotel sits squarely atop Monte de Santa Luzia, peering down at the basilica's backside and beyond it to some of the best coastal views in Portugal. Common areas are splendid, while the rooms themselves are comfortable, if less inspired than the views.

🍴 Eating

Viana do Castelo whips up some excellent seafood – among the region's best. Although you can find fresh fish at restaurants throughout the old town, the best joints are around the old fishing quarter on the west side of town.

Freguez
CAFE **$**

(Rua do Poço 42; snacks €1.50-7; ⊙ 10am-2am daily Jun-Oct, noon-midnight Mon-Tue, noon-2am Wed-Sat Nov-May) A cool cafe-bar with a fado soundtrack, hip vibe and outdoor tables on the pedestrian lane. Also sells a few Portuguese edibles (wine, sardines, jam) and handicrafts, and serves delicious *petiscos*. There are occasional fado concerts and poetry readings.

Dolce Vianna
PIZZA **$**

(☑ 258 824 860; Rua do Poço 44; pizzas €6-7.25; ⊙ lunch & dinner) This popular pizzeria buzzes at lunch time, when there's a special weekday menu for €5.50 and a range of cheesy thick-crust pizzas churned out of the woodburning oven in the corner. It also has a set of pleasant clean rooms upstairs.

O Marques
PORTUGUESE **$**

(Rua do Marques 72; meals from €5.50; ⊙ lunch & dinner Mon-Fri, lunch Sat) Another tremendous backstreet find, this place is absolutely jammed with locals for the *platos do dia* (plates of the day; €5.50). Think baked cod with white beans or roasted turkey leg with potatoes and salad. It's a friendly, satisfying, family-run affair.

Confeitaria Natário
BAKERY **$**

(Rua Manuel Espregueira 37; pastries €2-3) This popular bakery is the place to try the delicious *bolas de Berlim* (cream-filled donuts), which are so good that you may have to wait in line to get some.

⭐ Taberna do Valentim
SEAFOOD **$$**

(Campo do Castelo; mains €9.75-12.50; ⊙ lunch & dinner Mon-Sat) This bright and buzzing seafood restaurant is right outside the old fishing quarter. Fresh grilled fish is available by the kilo, and equally well loved are the rich seafood stews – *arroz de tamboril* (monkfish rice) and *caldeirada* (fish stew). In a good eating town, Valentim is a top choice.

O Pescador
SEAFOOD **$$**

(☑ 258 826 039; Largo de São Domingos 35; mains €9.50-15.50; ⊙ lunch & dinner Mon-Sat, lunch Sun) A simple, friendly, family-run restaurant admired by locals for its good seafood and tasty lunch specials (from €6.50).

Zefa Carqueja
GRILL HOUSE **$$**

(Campo do Castelo; mains €8-25; ⊙ lunch & dinner) Barbecue aficionados should head for this grill house for some of the best barbecue chicken and ribs in northern Portugal. You can also get barbecued seafood – including lobster. Dine in or line up at the grill and take it away.

🍷 Drinking & Nightlife

There is a handful of upmarket bars, trendy beer bars and more casual open-air spots on the waterfront.

Mau Maria
BAR

(Rua do Hospital Velho 16; ⊙ 6pm-2am daily Jul-Aug, 10pm-2am Mon-Sat Sep-Jun) The historic centre's coolest bar by far, with a funky all-white interior and a vintage vibe. It sometimes hosts DJs and concerts. Don't miss the ace champagne sangrias.

Republica
BAR

(Praça da Erva 17-19; ⊙ 9pm-2am daily summer, closed Sun & Mon rest of year) This is where the action happens on weekend nights, at this cosy bar on the old town's main square. Tables spill out and crowds hang out till closing time.

Foz
CAFE

(Praça da Liberdade; ⊙ noon-2am) This glass-box cafe, with a massive menu and even better views, is a gathering point for locals late in the evening. It's a good place for a sundowner, a crêpe or even an ice cream. The wine list is substantial.

Nazoni
CLUB

(Rua Espirito Santo; ⊙ 10pm-4am Thu-Sat) Underground indie rock fills the historic 18th-century rococo environs of the Capula Malheiras, where you can shake your arse free of all sin and self-doubt.

Fiori Klub CLUB

(Rua de Monserrate 384; cover €5-10; ☺midnight-6am Thu-Sat) This dance spot hosts resident and occasional international DJs spinning pop and house tunes.

Prosak CLUB

(Av Cabo Verde 36, Praia Norte; ☺11pm-8am Thu-Sat) A good choice if you're looking to groove into the wee hours. This boxy space has a spacious dance floor ringed by an upstairs gallery for checking out the scene below. It's next door to the Flôr de Sal hotel.

☆ Entertainment

Glamour LIVE MUSIC

(Rua da Bandeira 179-185; ☺10.30pm-4am Tue-Sat) This nightlife mainstay is Viana's longest-running nightclub, featuring live acts that usually cover the rock and blues classics. Bands take the stage at midnight.

Teatro Municipal Sá de Miranda THEATRE

(☑258 809 382; www.cm-viana-castelo.pt; Rua Sá de Miranda) Viana Do Castelo's cultural epicentre, this pink-washed neoclassical theatre hosts a regular line-up of music, theatre, dance and the occasional opera.

ℹ Information

Hospital (☑258 802 100; Estrada de Santa Luzia) North of the train station.

Police Station (☑258 809 880; Rua de Aveiro)

Post Office (Av dos Combatentes da Grande Guerra 323; ☺8.30am-6pm Mon-Fri)

Viana Welcome Centre (☑258 098 415; www.vivexperiencia.pt; Rotunda da Liberdade; ☺10am-7pm mid-Jun–mid-Sep, 10am-11pm Aug, 10am-5pm Tue-Sun mid-Sep–mid-Feb, 10am-6pm Tue-Sun mid-Feb–mid-Jun) This private outfit offers creative city tours (€15 on foot, €20 by bike) in multiple languages, as well as regional food, wine and culture itineraries in the Douro and Minho. Canyoneering, surfing and hiking are also available, as is bike rental (per hour/day €2.50/11) and rickshaw carts for €9 per hour.

ℹ Getting There & Around

BUS

Long-distance *expresso* buses operate from the shiny, centralised bus station, which is just across the tracks from the train station.

AV Cura/Transcolvia (☑258 800 340) Runs up the Lima valley to Ponte de Lima (€3, one hour), Ponte da Barca (€3.75, 1½ hours) and Arcos de Valdevez (€4, 1½ hours) at least hourly on weekdays (less at weekends).

AV Minho (☑258 800 341) Runs a line from Porto (€6, 2¼ hours) at least four times daily, passing through Esposende (€3, 40 minutes); one to three daily buses run to Valença do Minho (€4, 1¼ hours) and Monção (€5, 1½ hours).

Transdev Norte (☑258 825 047) Has at least eight weekday and four weekend runs to Braga (€4, 1½ hours).

CAR & MOTORCYCLE

Parking can be a challenge – most locals opt for paid underground lots sprinkled about the centre (including lots on either end of Av dos Combatentes da Grande Guerra). There's ample free parking next to the Castelo de São Tiago da Barra. If you need wheels to hit the beaches north of Viana, **Orbita** (☑258 813 513; www.orbitaviagens.com; Rua Alves Cerqueria 216; ☺9am-6pm) rents out cars from €29 per day, but they must be reserved at least one day in advance.

TRAIN

Daily direct services from Porto include five IR/international trains (€6.65, 1½ hours) and five regional services (€4.95, two hours). For Braga (€4.35, 1½ to two hours, 12 daily), change at Nine. There are also seven to 10 daily trains to Valença do Minho (€3.45, 45 minutes to one hour).

Valença do Minho

POP 3400

Now you're really in the Minho, where all is green, fertile and rustling in shared Spanish–Portuguese winds and waters. And no place has a better view of it all than this atmospheric fort village occupying strategic heights above the picturesque Rio Minho. Valença do Minho (Valença) sits just a cannonball shot from Spain, and its impressive pair of citadels long served as the Minho's first line of defence against Spanish aggression. But history insists on repeating itself, and these days the town is regularly overrun by Spanish hordes. They come armed with wallets and make away with volumes of towels and linens from the high stacks that line the cobbled streets.

The good news is that on even the busiest days (which tend to be Wednesdays and weekends), you can sidestep the towel touts and discover that these two interconnected forts also contain a fully functioning village where locals shop, eat, drink and gossip among pretty squares and narrow, medieval lanes. And when, in the evening, the weary troops retreat to Spain with their loot, the empty watchtowers return to their silent contemplation of their ancient enemy – the glowering Spanish fortress of Tui just across the river.

Visitors can easily see the sights of Valença as a day trip, but there are two atmospheric places to sleep within the fortress walls that allow you to see and feel peaceful Valença when it empties at sunset. That's when you can hear the footsteps of kittens in the laneways while birdsong echoes off ancient stone walls.

An uninspiring new town sprawls at the foot of the fortress. From the bus station it's 800m north via Av Miguel Dantas (the N13) and the Largo da Trapicheira roundabout (aka Largo da Esplanada) to the *turismo*. The train station is just east of Av Miguel Dantas.

◉ Sights & Activities

There are in fact two **fortresses**, bristling with bastions, watchtowers, massive gateways and defensive bulwarks, connected by a single bridge. The old churches and Manueline mansions inside testify to the success of the fortifications against several sieges, some as late as the 19th century. The earliest fortifications date from the 13th-century reign of Dom Afonso III, though largely what you see today was built in the 17th century, its design inspired by the French military architect Vauban.

Zip past the tacky gift shops and towel merchants, and follow the cobbled lanes to the far end of the larger northern fortress, which incorporates Dom Afonso's original stronghold and contains almost everything else that's of interest. From Praça da República bear right, then left, into Rua Guilherme José da Silva (which turns into Rua Dr Pedro Augusto Dias). On the left, opposite the post office, is the **Casa da Eira**, with a handsome Manueline window somewhat marred by a horrendous corrugated tin room that peeks above the crenulated walls. The 14th-century **Igreja de Santo Estevão**, with its neoclassical facade, is at the end of the street. From the church, take a left and you'll see the 1st-century Roman milestone from the old Braga–Astorga road.

From the milestone continue north to the end of Rua José Rodrigues and the now-decrepit Romanesque parish church, **Igreja de Santa Maria dos Anjos** (Church of St Mary of the Angels), dating from 1276. At the back is a tiny **chapel** with Romano-Gothic inscriptions on the outside. To the left of the parish church is the **Capela da Misericórdia** and beyond it the Pousada de São Teotónio.

But the best fun can be had rambling on and around the series of exterior walls. In fact, if you turn right by the *pousada* you'll descend the atmospheric lane through one of the **original gates**, with a trickling stream running below, and an impressive echo. Keep going and you'll pass through several thick, mossy layers to the outside world.

🛏 Sleeping

Residencial Portas do Sol   GUESTHOUSE $
(☏ 251 837 134; www.residencialportasdosol.com; Rua Conselheiro Lopes da Silva 51; s/d €30/45; ✳@🛜) One of two options in the fortress is set in an antiquated stone building that's been refurbished and outfitted with all things IKEA-esque, but that's not necessarily a bad thing. The ceilings are high, and the old stone window frames lend enough old-world panache. It's in the north fort, a half block from the bridge.

Hotel Lara   HOTEL $
(☏ 251 824 348; www.hotellara.com; Av dos Bombeiros Voluntarios; s/d €35/45; P✳🛜) The ageing bones of this business hotel in the new town cloak some great-value and spacious rooms, with Japanese wallpaper and tremendous views from the upper reaches. It's directly opposite the fort.

Pousada de São Teotónio   LUXURY HOTEL $$$
(☏ 251 800 260; www.pousadas.pt; Rua de Baluarte do Socorro; s/d €135/145; P✳🛜) Perched on the outermost post of the fortress and surrounded by green ramparts, this bright, modern *pousada* has large, luxurious rooms, most with prime views overlooking the walls and river to Spain; a few have balconies.

🍴 Eating

Churrasqueira Valenciana   GRILL HOUSE $
(Rua Maestro Sousa Morais 6-8; mains €5-14; ⊙lunch Tue-Sun) Come to this cavernous and always bustling dining room if you're looking for tasty and cheap grilled chicken. There's no patio dining, which means there's no view, but the local scene inside is worthy of your contemplation.

O Limoeiro
PORTUGUESE $$

(Rua da Oliveira 23; mains €6.50-14) Lunch-only spot on the outer ramparts, popular with locals for its good codfish on the grill and seafood rice. Downstairs is a tiny bar area with a few tables, upstairs a rustic dining room accessed along a vine-covered staircase. Tables spill onto the esplanade on warm days.

Fortaleza
PORTUGUESE $$

(Rua Apolinário da Fonseca 5; meals €9-15; ☺ lunch & dinner Fri-Wed) Set in the south fortress, with tables inside and on a wide patio with views overlooking the edge of the fort, this place does decent grilled meats and fish, and rice with river eel in springtime. They have another more modern restaurant down the street, Fortaleza 2.

Baluarte
PORTUGUESE $$

(Rua Apolinário da Fonseca; mains €7-18; ☺ lunch & dinner) Baluarte enjoys a peaceful fortress setting with outdoor tables fronting a plaza, contempo glass-enclosed interiors and good service. A decent assortment of Minho dishes are on hand, including lots of codfish, their speciality.

❶ Information

Turismo (☎ 251 823 374; www.cm-valenca. pt; ☺ 9.30am-12.30pm & 2-5.30pm Mon-Sat) Helpful tourism office to the left of the main entrance into the old town, right by the main parking lot.

❶ Getting There & Around

BUS
AV Minho (☎ 258 800 340) has three daily weekday runs and two daily weekend runs beginning in Monção (€2, 20 minutes) and going all the way to Porto (€9, 3½ hours) via Viana do Castelo (€6, 1¼ hours).

CAR & MOTORCYCLE
There is free parking in lots just west of the fortresses, though they can fill to capacity at weekends. If you're spending the night inside, you should be able to find free street parking within the fort.

TRAIN
Five to 10 trains run daily to Valença from Porto (€9.30, 3½ hours), two of which continue as far as Vigo in Spain.

Monção
POP 2500

Like Valença do Minho to the west, Monção (mohng-*sowng*) was once an important fortification along the border with Spain. It's a modest but attractive historic centre, which includes the remains of its 14th-century fortifications still watching over the river, that sees far fewer visitors than Valença's. The

---

GOING GREEN IN VINHO VERDE COUNTRY

Outside Portugal, *vinho verde* (literally 'green wine') gets a bum rap, but often for good reason – exports tend to sit on shelves far too long. The stuff is made to be drunk 'green' – that is, while it is still very young, preferably less than one year old.

While the wine is made from fully ripe rather than still-green grapes, as is sometimes believed, the straw-coloured whites can indeed achieve greenish tints – a visual reminder of the green landscape from which they come. Served well chilled on a hot summer day, its fruity nose, fine bubbles and acidic bite make *vinho verde* one of the great delights of travelling in northern Portugal.

Vinho verde is grown in a strictly demarcated region of the Minho that occupies the coastal lowlands between the Rio Douro and the Spanish border. There are actually more vines here than in the Douro, but the *quintas* (estates) are subdivided to such a degree that most growers simply sell their fruit, or their wine, to community *adegas* (wineries).

Traditionally the vines are trained high, both to conserve land and to save the grapes from rot, and you can still see great walls of green in the summer months. Like German wines, *vinho verde* tends to be aromatic, light-bodied and low in alcohol. There are red *vinho verdes*, though you may find them chalky and more of an acquired taste. White is both the most common and the easiest to appreciate. Alvarinho grapes, grown around Monção, are also used to make a delightful *vinho verde*.

For more information about the wine, its history and visiting particular regions and vineyards, check out www.vinhoverde.pt.

town's big claim to fame is its fine *vinho verde*, with signs touting Monção as the cradle of the refreshing Alvarinho wine (Spain's Galicia makes similar claims).

It is said that during a siege by Castilian soldiers in 1368, a local townswoman named Deu-la-Deu Martins managed to scrabble together enough flour from starving citizens to make a few loaves of bread, and in a brazen show of plenty tossed them to the enemy with the message, 'if you need any more, just let us know'. The disheartened Spaniards immediately withdrew to Spain.

From the bus station it's 600m east to the defunct train station, then another two blocks north up Rua General Pimenta de Castro to the first of the town's two main squares, Praça da República. Praça Deu-la-Deu and the heart of the old town lie just one block further.

◎ Sights & Activities

Old Monção   NEIGHBOURHOOD
The best part of Monção's old town is the utter lack of tourism. It's almost exclusively a local scene in chestnut-shaded **Praça Deu-la-Deu**, where a hand-on-breast statue of its namesake tops a **fountain** and looks hungrily down over the surrounding cafes.

The **Senhora da Vista** bastion at the northern end offers a gentle view across the sinuous Rio Minho into Spain. The **Capela da Misericórdia** at the square's southern end has a coffered ceiling painted with cherubs.

East of the square is the snug, cobbled old quarter. Two blocks along Rua da Glória is the pretty little Romanesque **igreja matriz** (parish church), where Deu-la-Deu is buried (look for the stone-carved alcove to the left of the entrance).

Palácio da Brejoeira   PALACE
(☑ 251 666 129; www.palaciodabrejoeira.pt; Quinta da Brejoeira, Pinheiros; tours €3-7.50, wine tasting €2.50; ⊙ 9.30am-noon & 2-5.30pm Tue-Sun) On the N101 toward Arcos de Valdevez, this grand neoclassical palace built in the early 19th century has been open to the public since 2010, even though the current owner, a nonagenarian heir, still lives inside. Visits are by guided tour only, which run every 30 minutes.

You can choose the half-hour tour that takes in the opulent interiors (€5), such as the Empire furniture–filled king's room and the dining room where Franco and Salazar had a meeting in 1950, as well as the family's chapel and the gardens with 20 species of camellia. Or you can opt for the half-hour tour of the surroundings (€3), that include a forest, a plane-tree avenue, a romantic lake and the vineyards – the estate has 18 hectares of vineyards planted with Alvarinho. The hour-long tour (€7.50) takes in all of the highlights. Carriage rides are also available, for €15.

Adega Cooperativa de Monção   WINERY
(☑ 251 652 167; www.adegademoncao.pt; ⊙ 9am-12.30pm & 2-6pm Mon-Fri, 8.30am-1pm Sat) Alvarinho is the delicious, tart and full-bodied variety of white *vinho verde* produced around Monção and neighbouring Melgaço. If you'd like a tasting, stop by this *adega* 1.8km south of Monção on the N101 to Arcos de Valdevez. Otherwise, the clutch of bars around Monção's principal squares will be happy to oblige.

Termas de Monção   THERMAL SPRINGS
(www.tesal.com; Av das Caldas; admission €12-15; ⊙ 9.30am-8.30pm Mon-Sat, to 8pm Sun) Monção's *termas* (thermal springs) have a large aquatic area with jacuzzis, tiny waterfalls and a children's swimming area. In addition to dips in the warm springs, a wide variety of spa treatments are available, with day packages starting at €49. Those wanting the aquatic experience without the fuss can head across the road to the *piscina municipal*, a handsomely designed 25m indoor pool, with a smaller pool for younger swimmers.

★☆ Festivals & Events

Feira do Alvarinho   CULTURE
(www.feiraalvarinho.pt.vu) The self-described cradle of Alvarinho, Monção hosts a three-day fair in late May in honour of its wine. Music, folk dancing and much eating and drinking rule the day.

Festa do Corpo de Deus   RELIGIOUS
The town's biggest party is held on Corpus Christi, which generally falls in May or June, depending on the year. Events include a religious procession and medieval fair, with a re-enactment of St George battling the dragon.

Festa da Nossa Senhora das Dores   RELIGIOUS
A big five-day celebration in the third week of August, headed by a pious procession.

THE MINHO MONÇÃO

🛏 Sleeping

Hospedaria Beco da Matriz GUESTHOUSE $
(📞251 651 909; Beco da Matriz; r €35) Just left of the facade of the *igreja matriz*, this place offers simple but impeccable rooms, with comfortable beds and spotless tile floors. Some rooms have excellent views over the adjacent ramparts to Spain. Check in at the bar downstairs if there's no answer at the door.

Solar de Serrade RURAL INN $$
(📞251 648 363; www.solardeserrade.pt; Mazedo; d from €65; P🕏) One of two manor houses on area estates producing Alvarinho grapes and delicious wines, this rather magnificent 17th-century mansion on the road towards Arcos de Valdevez has whimsical gardens and eight elaborately furnished rooms and suites. Good for romantic getaways.

Fonte da Vila BOUTIQUE HOTEL $$
(📞251 656 269; www.fontedavila.com; Estrada de Melgaço; s/d €65/80; P❋🕏) The Spanish-owned Fonte da Vila has cheerfully painted rooms with wooden floors and a clean-lined contemporary look in a renovated and re-modelled manor house with a garden patio. There's an upscale seafood restaurant on the ground floor. It's in the new town, right across from the gas station.

Convento dos Capuchos BOUTIQUE HOTEL $$$
(📞251 640 090; www.conventodoscapuchos.com; Quinta do Convento de São Antonio, Estrada de Melgaço; s/d from €90/147; P🕏🏊) Monção's most captivating property is set in a restored 18th-century hilltop monastery with a glimmering infinity pool overlooking the river below. The deluxe rooms have wooden floors and French doors opening onto a splendid river-front terrace. Less expensive rooms are set in a newly constructed annexe; they are large with chic furnishings, but lack the former's majesty and views. The premises include a small spa and gym, as well as a restaurant.

🍴 Eating

For the pick of local specialities, try fresh shad, salmon and trout from the Rio Minho, and lamprey eels in spring.

Bard Rock Cafe CAFE $
(Rua da Boavista; snacks €3-5; ⊙10am-2am) Right on the ramparts is this two-floor music-themed cafe-bar with a few plastic chairs outside featuring views out to Spain across

the river. Snacks like sandwiches, burgers and *francesinhas* (overstuffed sandwich) are served all day; at nighttime come for beers and cocktails. From the main square, go all the way to the river and then turn left.

Escondinho CAFE $
(Praça Deu-la-Deu 18; pastries €0.60-1.20; ⊙break-fast, lunch & dinner) Monção's best pastry shop has tempting fresh-baked goods with out-door tables overlooking the plaza.

Cabral PORTUGUESE $$
(Rua de Zenbro 1; mains €6-18; ⊙lunch & dinner) Cabral grills fresh fish and offers a tasty *arroz do marisco* (rice and seafood stew). It's all served in an attractive stone-walled dining room, almost always packed at lunch, down a narrow lane from Praça Deu-la-Deu.

Sete á Sete PORTUGUESE $$
(📞251 652 577; Rua Conselheiro João da Cunha; mains €8.50-15; ⊙lunch & dinner Tue-Sun) At the entrance to the old centre, this stone-walled dining room serves top-notch Minho speci-alities made with the finest, freshest ingre-dients, such as the seasonal river eel and *cabrito* (kid).

ℹ Information

Turismo (📞251 652 757; www.portoenorte. pt; Praça Deu-la-Deu; ⊙9.30am-12.30pm & 2-6pm Mon-Sat) Housed in the Casa do Curro, the *turismo* also sells a small but high-quality selection of pottery and lacework from artisans of northern Portugal.

ℹ Getting There & Around

You'll find street parking around Praça da Repú-blica and Praça Deu-La-Deu.

AV Minho (📞258 800 341) operates one weekend and two weekday buses that stop here en route from Melgaço (€3.70, 35 minutes) to Porto (€9, four hours) via Viana do Castelo (€5.50, 1½ hours).

Ponte de Lima

POP 2800 / ELEV 175M

This photogenic town by the sweet and mel-low Rio Lima springs to life on weekends, when Portuguese tourists descend in droves, and every other Monday, when a vast mar-ket spreads along the riverbank. All the ac-tion happens within sight of Portugal's fin-est medieval bridge. Even if you can't make the market, Ponte de Lima's small, historic centre, dotted with cafes and vast riverside gardens and greenways, is well worth visiting. Even the outskirts are romantic: vineyards tumble to bustling avenues, and at sunset swallows take flight, singing and diving until night finally falls.

When a Roman regiment first passed through here, soldiers were convinced that the Rio Lima was Lethe itself – the mythical 'river of oblivion'. Alas, no such luck. Decimus Junius Brutus forced his men to plunge ahead, but they still remembered all their sins upon reaching the far side. The impressive Ponte Romana (Roman Bridge) – part of the Roman road from Braga to Astorga in Spain, and the town's namesake – supposedly marks their crossing. Though largely rebuilt in medieval times, it still contains traces of its Roman antecedent.

◉ Sights

Ponte Romana   LANDMARK
The city's pièce de résistance, this elegant 31-arched bridge across the Rio Lima is now limited to foot traffic. Most of it dates from the 14th century, though the segment on the north bank by the village of **Arcozelo** is bona fide Roman. **Largo de Camões**, with a fountain resembling a giant bonbon dish, makes a fine spot to watch the sun set over the bridge.

Town Walls & Towers   LANDMARK
Two crenulated towers (part of the fortifications made in the 14th century) face the river at the end of Rua Cardeal Saraiva. The **Torre da Cadeia Velha** (Old Prison Tower; ⊙ 9.30am-12.30pm & 2-6pm) FREE now houses temporary art exhibitions and the *turismo*.

Fragments of the walls survive behind and between this and the other tower, the **Torre de São Paulo**. Note the somewhat bizarre *azulejo* image on its front wall, entitled Cabras são Senhor! (They're goats m'lord!) – a reference to a local story in which Dom Afonso Henriques almost attacked a herd of goats, apparently mistaking them for Moors.

Behind the tower is the rather staid, mostly 15th-century **igreja matriz** (Rua Cardeal Saraiva; ⊙ 7.30am-7pm), sporting a pretty Romanesque doorway.

Museu dos Terceiros   MUSEUM
(www.museudosterceiros.com; Av 5 de Outubro; admission €2.50; ⊙ 10am-12.30pm & 2-6pm Tue-Sun) Downriver, the 18th-century Igreja de São Francisco dos Terceiros is now a rambling museum full of ecclesiastical and folk treasures, although the highlight is the church

itself, with its gilded baroque interior. The Renaissance-style **Igreja de Santo António dos Frades**, once a convent church, is now a wing of the museum.

Museu do Brinquedo Português   MUSEUM
(Casa do Arnado, Largo da Alegria, Arcozelo; adult/student & over 3yr €4.50/2.50; ⊙ 10am-12.30pm & 2-6pm Tue-Sun) Dedicated to the Portuguese toy, this museum is in a gorgeous red mansion right after the Roman bridge in Arcozelo. The focus is on toys made between the late 19th century and 1986. Displays in different rooms include raw materials and manufacturing techniques, and toys arranged by decade, from brightly painted wooden beach buckets to papier-mâché dolls and tinplate cannons. There's also a play room, and a toy workshop accessed through the garden.

**Lagoas de Bertiandos e
São Pedro de Arcos**   NATURE RESERVE
(www.lagoas.cm-pontedelima.pt; ⊙ 10am-12.30pm Mon-Fri, 2-5.30pm daily) FREE This 350-hectare nature reserve is set in a wildlife-rich humid zone just north of the Rio Lima. There's a wildlife interpretation centre and eight hiking trails, ranging from an easy lakeside loop (1.6km) to a longer 12.5km hike. Get there on the A27, 4km west from Ponte de Lima, taking exit 3.

Jardins Temáticos   GARDEN
(Thematic Gardens; adult/under 12yr €2/1; ⊙ 1.30-7pm Mon, 10am-12.30pm & 1.30-7pm Tue-Fri, 10am-7pm Sat & Sun May-Jun & Sep, 1.30-8pm Mon, 10am-8pm Tue-Sun Jul-Aug, 1.30-6pm Mon, 10am-6pm Tue-Sun Oct) Green space is abundant in Ponte de Lima, but this small, intriguing garden with rose bushes and lemon-filled trellises is notable because each May it hosts a competition where 12 artists create temporary gardens built around a theme. The winning garden is chosen in October and remains rooted for the year. Jardins Temáticos is next to a public swimming pool on the western side of the river.

🏃 Activities

Ecovia   WALKING
On both sides of the Rio Lima you'll find riverside paths. Given the distances it's best to explore them by bike or horse. Rent wheels (per hour €2) at Clube Náutico or at Passeig 25 de April (per hour €2, per day €8).

On the right bank the paths follow the river west for 9km to Fontão and east for 8km to the settlement of Refóios do Lima. West of Ponte de Lima, the *ecovia* (greenway) begins again off Av dos Plátanos and runs 13.3km to Vitorino das Donas. The big government dream is to eventually follow the Lima all the way to Viana do Castelo, but for a day's whirl, this will do just fine.

Village Walks WALKING

There are several charming walks through the countryside, past ancient monuments and along cobbled lanes trellised with vines. The *turismo* has literature on routes ranging from 5km to 14km. Pack water and a picnic – cafes and restaurants are rare.

A steep 5km climb north of Arcozelo yields panoramic views up and down the Lima valley from a tiny and bizarre **chapel** (open irregular hours) dedicated to Santo Ovídio, patron saint of ears. Yes, you read that right. The interior is covered with ear-shaped votive candles offered in hope of, or as thanks for, the cure of an ear affliction. You can also drive up; the turn-off from the N202 is about 2.5km upstream of the N201 bridge.

Clube Náutico WATER SPORTS

(☎258 944 899; www.cnplima.com; kayak & canoe per 1.5 hr €3; ⏲9.30am-12.30pm & 2-8pm) Across the river and 400m downstream from town, this aquatic outfitter rents out canoes and plastic kayaks for exploring the mellow river as it spreads over willowed sand bars, glistens blue in the sun and fades to deep green at dusk. It also rents out bicycles (per 1½ hours €5).

Festivals & Events

Vaca das Cordas & Corpus Christi CULTURE

The ninth Friday after Easter is the date for a tradition that probably dates back at least to Roman times and possibly has Phoenician origins. It features a kind of bull-running in which young men goad a hapless bull (restrained by a long rope) as it runs through the town. It's followed the next day by the more pious Festa do Corpo de Deus, with religious processions and flowers carpeting the streets.

Feiras do Cavalo CULTURE

(www.feiradocavalo.com) Held annually in the third week of June, this horse fair is one of the town's most raucous festivals, when the Expo Lima (the riverside fairgrounds), becomes a race track and stage for horses, carriages and musicians.

Feiras Novas CULTURE

(New Fairs) Held here since 1125, this is one of Portugal's most ancient ongoing events. Stretching over three days during the third week of September it centres on the riverfront, with a massive market and fair, and features folk dances, fireworks, brass bands and all manner of merrymaking. Book accommodation well ahead.

Sleeping

Pousada da Juventude HOSTEL $

(☎258 943 797; www.pousadasjuventude.pt; Rua Papa João Paulo II; dm €12, d €26-30; P @ ᯤ) Built of concrete, wood and glass, this striking, contemporary youth hostel is a pleasant 10-minute walk from the centre of town along the river. Facilities are limited, but the dorms and doubles (with private and shared bathroom) are clean and attractive.

Quinta de Pentieiros CAMPGROUND $

(☎258 240 202; www.lagoas.cm-pontedelima.pt; site adult/child €3.50/2, casas €55; P ≋) Inside the Lagoas nature reserve, this estate has campsites and more comfortable bungalows and *casas* with kitchen units that work well for families. There's also an inviting swimming pool (€2 on weekdays, €3 on weekends), horse riding and bike rental. Prices are lower (and crowds fewer) on weekdays.

Residencial São João GUESTHOUSE $

(☎258 941 288; alojamento_s.joao@sapo.pt; Largo de São João; s/d €35/40; ᯤ) This welcoming, family-run guesthouse offers a decent collection of clean, serviceable and mostly bright rooms with wooden floors. Most have private bathrooms. Quarters are tight and there's no TV but the location can't be beat.

Mercearia da Vila GUESTHOUSE $$

(www.merceariadavila.pt; Rua Cardeal Saraiva 34-36; d/ste €65/80; ᯤ) Six rooms hide above this charming old grocery-store-turned-cafe. Each comes with a theme (from green tea to chocolate), as well as hardwood floors and original furniture. Some have balconies, and the top-floor suite has a window overlooking the river. There's also a shared living room and kitchen. Don't miss the delicious *petiscos* and homemade cakes downstairs.

Casa do Pinheiro GUESTHOUSE $$

(☎258 943 971; www.manorhouses.com/manors/portugal/casadopinheiro.html; Rua General Norton de Matos 629; s/d €55/65; ❄ ᯤ ≋) A stunning place set in a painstakingly restored private house from the 1700s, whose seven elegant rooms boast high ceilings, antique beds, hardwood floors and touches of religious art. Some rooms have balconies, while others open onto the splendid back garden with a small pool and fruit trees. Breakfast is fabulous.

InLima Hotel & Spa BOUTIQUE HOTEL **$$**
(☑258 900 050; www.inlimahotel.com; Rua Agostinho José Taveira 6; s/d €65/85; ✸@⊛) Floating above the *ecovia* like some white-washed frosted glass pod from the future is the swankiest, most contemporary hotel in town. The 30 chic rooms all have woven floors, blond-wood desks, lush linens, rain showers and wide terraces. At these prices, it's a steal.

Casa do Arrabalde RURAL INN **$$**
(☑258 742 442; www.casadoarrabalde.com; Arcozelo; s/d €60/80, cottage €140; P⊛⊛) This terrific option sits conveniently just across the Ponte Romana in Arcozelo. The main quarters are still inhabited by the family who built the place in the 18th century. Rooms are grand and furnished with period antiques; the cottages are more contemporary. There are huge verdant grounds and an inviting pool.

Casa do Barreiro RURAL INN **$$**
(☑258 948 137; www.casadobarreiro.com; Gemeira; s/d €45/75, apt €70-120; P⊛⊛) Particularly elegant, this 17th-century yellow manor house about halfway between Ponte de Lima and Ponte de Barca features original details, including stone mantles and *azulejos*. The six rooms and two apartments are spare but lovely, and the grounds gush with fountains, are surrounded by vineyards and include a pool and tennis courts. It's open from May to September.

★ **Carmo's Boutique Hotel** BOUTIQUE HOTEL **$$$**
(☑258 938 743; www.carmosboutiquehotel.com; Estrada Nacional 203, Gemeira; d/ste €220/320; P✸⊛⊛) The area's best hotel, this boutique hideaway is in the village of Gemeira en route to Ponte da Barca and has 15 stunning rooms, two pools and a small basement spa inside a contemporary two-wing structure. Inside, it is all about casual and cosy chic, breakfast is served till noon and rates include dinner at the restaurant, which whips up great regional dishes. Definitely worth a splurge.

✗ Eating

A Tulha PORTUGUESE **$**
(☑258 942 879; Rua Formosa; mains €6-10; ⊙lunch & dinner Tue-Sat, lunch Sun; ✸) All dark wood, stone and terracotta tiles inside, this restaurant serves excellent meat and fish dishes with plenty of vegetables. Try the *medalhão á Tulha* – a thick steak wrapped in bacon.

Muralha PORTUGUESE **$$**
(Largo da Picota; mains €8.50-12; ⊙lunch & dinner Wed-Mon, lunch Tue) Tucked into an alcove behind one of the town's old towers, this somewhat divey dining room serves tasty octopus and meat dishes. It brags about its *cabrito* too.

Manuel Padeiro PORTUGUESE **$$**
(Rua do Bonfim 20; mains €7.50-14; ⊙lunch & dinner Mon-Tue & Thu-Sun) The speciality at this simple local tavern with a 60-year tradition is *sarrabulho*, a hearty rice dish with pork blood, meat and entrails. Other dishes are well-prepared too, including the daily weekday lunch specials, which are a steal.

Vaca Das Cordas PORTUGUESE **$$**
(Rua Padre Francisco Pacheco 39-41; mains €10-13; ⊙11am-2am Mon-Sat) On a narrow lane near Largo de Camões, you'll find a long dark restaurant and bar that serves juicy grilled steak and lots of meaty appetisers. Bullfighting murals and cowboy accoutrements adorn the walls.

Sabores do Lima PORTUGUESE **$$**
(☑258 931 121; Largo de António Magalhães 64; mains €8-13; ⊙lunch & dinner Tue-Sun) A few steps from the river, the inviting Sabores do Lima has exposed stone walls that give a dash of style to its open dining room. The first-rate cooking features grilled meats, cod dishes and a few assorted seafood plates.

A Carvalheira PORTUGUESE **$$**
(☑258 742 316; mains €12-18; ⊙lunch & dinner Tue-Sun; P✸) On the N202 at the northern end of Arcozelo, country-style A Carvalheira has a reputation for serving the area's best food. Order ahead if you want the regional favourite – *arroz de sarrabulho* (stewed rice with pork and pork blood).

🍷 Drinking & Nightlife

Arte e Baco WINE BAR
(Rua Formosa 19; ⊙5pm-2am Mon-Fri & Sun, 5pm-4am Sat) The hippest bar in town is a black-floored, chalkboard-walled lounge featuring rotating art exhibitions, the finest wine from

the Minho (mostly *vinho verde*) and Douro, fine cigars, better port and occasional live music.

Bar Che
BAR

(Rua Formosa 37; ⏰2pm-2am Mon-Thu & Sun, 2pm-4am Fri & Sat) Images of the bar's namesake revolutionary decorate this cosy place, which has long attracted alternative types.

☆ Entertainment

Teatro Diogo Bernardes
THEATRE

(✆258 900 414; www.cm-pontedelima.pt; Rua Agostinho José Taveira) Behind the Museu dos Terceiros, the galleried Teatro Diogo Bernardes, built in 1893, is the pride of the town, with interesting music and theatre performances throughout the year.

ⓘ Information

Espaço Internet (✆258 900 400; Av António Feijó 16; ⏰1-8pm Mon-Fri) Free internet access. If phoning, use extension 415.

Hospital (✆258 909 500; Rua Conde de Bertiandos)

Police Station (✆258 900 380; Rua Dr Luís da Cunha Nogueira)

Post Office (Praça da República; ⏰8.30am-5.30pm Mon-Fri)

Turismo (✆258 942 335; www.cm-pontede lima.pt; Torre da Cadeia Velha; ⏰9.30am-12.30pm & 2-6pm summer, 9am-12.30pm & 2-5.30pm winter) This exceptionally friendly and well-organised tourist office shares space with a small handicrafts gallery. The lower floor has glass walkways over the excavated layers of an ancient tower.

ⓘ Getting There & Away

There is street parking uphill from Praça da República; higher up still, it's free.

Board long-distance buses on Av António Feijó (buy tickets on board) or at the bus station. All services thin out on Sunday.

AV Cura/Transcolvia (✆258 800 340) has a service to Viana do Castelo (€3.50, 50 minutes).

Rede Expressos (✆258 942 870) has one daily run to Braga (€4, 30 minutes), Valença do Minho (€7, 25 minutes) and Lisbon (€19, 6½ hours) via Porto (€8, 2¼ hours).

Ponte da Barca

POP 2870 / ELEV 178M

Peaceful and friendly Ponte da Barca, named after the *barca* (barge) that once ferried pilgrims and others across the Rio Lima, has an idyllic, willow-shaded riverfront (perfect for cycling into the wooded valley), a handsome 16th-century bridge, a tiny old centre and the best source of information on the Parque Nacional da Peneda-Gerês.

The old town, just east of the bridge, is packed into narrow lanes on both sides of the main road, Rua Conselheiro Rocha Peixoto. Wednesday is market day.

⊙ Sights & Activities

The riverfront is the focal point of the town (and a good place for a picnic), with picturesque weeping willows lining the banks of the Rio Lima, and a green lawn that beckons sunbathers. The lovely, 10-arched **ponte** (bridge) originally dates from the 1540s. Beside it is the old arcaded marketplace and a little garden, **Jardim dos Poetas**, dedicated to two 16th-century poet brothers, Diogo Bernardes and Agostinho da Cruz, who were born in Ponte da Barca. It's now a strip of occasionally happening bars with ample, shady park-bench riverside seating.

The *turismo* has a booklet called *Historia, Patrimonia & Cultura*, with regional information, including details of **hikes** in the surrounding valley, some of them punctuated with ancient sites. A simple stroll west for 4km leads to **Bravães**, a village famous for its lovely, small Romanesque **Igreja de São Salvador**. Its west portal is adorned with intricate carved animals, birds and human figures; its interior shelters simple frescos of the Virgin and the Crucifixion.

✷ Festivals & Events

Festa de São Bartolomeu
CULTURE

Held from 19 to 24 August, this festival sees folk music and dancing aplenty, not to mention parades and fireworks.

⌂ Sleeping

Pensão Restaurante Gomes
GUESTHOUSE $

(✆258 452 288; Rua Conselheiro Rocha Peixoto 13; s/d with shared bathroom €20/25) Welcome to your sweet Barca granny's house. Incredibly cheap, old-world rooms have worn wooden floors, sloping ceilings and tons of charm, and there are fabulous river and bridge views from the rooftop terrace.

Residencial San Fernando
GUESTHOUSE $

(✆258 452 580; www.residencialsfernando.com; Rua de Sto Antonio; d from €38; Ⓟ) At the very top of the new town, about 800m beyond Pensão Restaurante Gomes, this more-modern *residencial* has smart, bright rooms with up-to-date comforts, up a marble staircase. If you can't find anyone at the desk, pop into the furniture shop next door.

Residencial Os Poetas GUESTHOUSE $
(☑258 453 578; Largo dos Poetas 49; s/d from €32/36; ☺Jul-Sep) A short stroll east of the bridge, this summer-only place has 10 pleasant rooms and an excellent riverside location.

Casa Nobre do Correio Mor INN $$
(☑258 452 129; www.laceme.pt; Rua Trás do Forno 1; s/d from €48/75; ☏▨) Lovingly restored, this 17th-century manor house on the street above the town hall offers 10 gorgeous rooms, most with stone-framed windows, wide timber floors, antique furnishings and French windows with city and river views.

✗ Eating & Drinking

Belião Bar CAFE $
(Jardim dos Poetas; mains €6-8; ☺10am-2am Sun-Thu, to 4am Fri & Sat; ☞) From a pretty plaza overlooking the bridge, diners can enjoy vegetable lasagne, Mexican burritos, vegetable quiche, hamburgers and big salads made with market-fresh ingredients. At night the bar frequently hosts live bands and DJs.

Veranda do Lima PORTUGUESE $$
(Campo do Cúrro; mains €9-18; ☺lunch & dinner) The recently remodelled main dining room is one of Barca's grandest options, with fresh fish and all the traditional meat dishes served on pressed tablecloths. If you want something lighter, pop into the restaurant's popular cafe next door.

❶ Information

ADERE Peneda-Gerês (☑258 452 250; www. adere-pg.pt; ☺9am-12.30pm & 2.30-6pm Mon-Sat Jul-Aug, 9am-12.30pm & 2.30-6pm Mon-Fri Sep-Jun)

Espaço Internet (Rua Doutor José Lacerda Emegre 17; ☺9am-12.30pm & 2-5.30pm Mon-Sat) Free internet access.

Post Office (Rua das Fontaínhas; ☺9am-12.30pm & 2-5.30pm Mon-Fri)

Turismo (☑258 452 899; www.pontedabarca. com.pt; Rua Dom Manuel I; ☺9.30am-12.30pm & 2-6pm Mon-Sat summer) The tourist office is about 750m east of the bridge down a small street, and has a town map and accommodation information.

❶ Getting There & Away

You'll find free parking in the shady square at the western end of the bridge.

AV Cura buses run to Arcos de Valdevez (€1.15, 15 minutes), Ponte de Lima (€3.15, 40 minutes) and Viana do Castelo (€4.25, 1½ to two hours) four to seven times daily from Monday to Friday, and once or twice a day on weekends.

Salvador buses travel through Ponte da Barca twice a day Monday to Friday on their way from Arco de Valdevez to Soajo (€2.75, 45 minutes) in Parque Nacional da Peneda-Gerês. Buses stop in front of Churasqueira Barquense restaurant on Rua Dr Francisco Sá Carneiro. Enquire at the *turismo* for the current schedule. Salvador buses also travel to Braga daily (€3.80, one hour).

Arcos de Valdevez

POP 2300 / ELEV 200M

Drowsy little Arcos de Valdevez is home to a couple of interesting old churches and several stately homes in a small, almost tourist-free old centre. It also has a vibrant, willow-shaded riverfront. While it doesn't merit a special trip, it's a handy gateway to the northern end of Parque Nacional da Peneda-Gerês.

🛏 Sleeping

Residencial Tavares GUESTHOUSE $
(☑258 516 253; Rua Padre MJ Cunha Brito; s/d from €20/35; ✳☏) In the historic centre, Tavares is excellent value for its clean, bright rooms, though the building itself is modern and unappealing. Some rooms have balconies. Take a right from the *turismo*, go up to the square with the Lapa church and Tavares is to your right.

Hotel Ribeira HOTEL $
(☑258 531 358; www.hotelribeira.pt; Largo dos Milagres; s/d €50/60; ℙ✳@☏) Except for its picturesque fairy-pink facade, this early-1900s town house has, unfortunately, been largely gutted of its original character, but it does have spotless, comfortable rooms with big windows, high ceilings and an excellent position by the river.

★Paço da Glória RURAL INN $$
(☑258 947 177; www.pacodagloria.com; Jolda-Madalena; s/d from €70/80; ℙ▨) A restored 18th-century manor house, built on 13th-century foundations in what was then the cradle of Portuguese nobility, can be your nest in the vineyard-draped hills outside Arcos. Rooms inside the house are massive, with stone fireplaces and huge marble bathrooms, while those in the 17th-century staff annexe are older and cosier. There's a fantastic 1730s chapel with a gilded altar,

PROTECTED AREAS OF PENEDA-GERÊS

The government is working hard to ensure that Peneda-Gerês' largely undisturbed ecosystems remain that way. To help protect the area the park has a high-elevation inner zone, partly set aside for research and closed to the public, and an outer buffer zone, where development is controlled. Most villages, roads, tracks and trails are in the latter area.

The most assiduously protected area is the Mata de Albergaria, north of Vila do Gerês. Ironically, it's crossed by the N308 highway, which, because it serves an EU-appointed border crossing, cannot simply be closed. Motorised traffic is tolerated on a 6km stretch of road above Gerês but travellers are forbidden to linger. At checkpoints at either end, drivers must pay €1.50 to enter the road from June to September. Daily patrols ensure that motorists don't park on the road. Two side roads are also no-go areas for non-residents: southwest down the Rio Homem valley and east from Portela do Homem into the high Serra do Gerês.

Campers must use designated sites or risk the wrath of park rangers. There are also restrictions on the type of boats allowed in the park's *albufeiras* (reservoirs), and no boats at all are allowed on the Vilarinho das Furnas and Paradela. Even swimming is prohibited in Vilarinho das Furnas.

and the pool is glorious. Reserve via www.manorhousesofportugal.com.

Casa da Breia RURAL INN $$
(☑ 258 751 751; www.casadabreia.com; São Paio de Jolda; cottage €60-110; P ☁ ☳) This sweeping 17th-century *quinta*, nestled in a village just 10km from Arcos, is owned by a sweet family who offer the charming, historic stone cottages (former staff quarters) to guests. The hosts offer terrific tips for visiting the nearby national park.

✖ Eating

Doçaria Central BAKERY $
(☑ 258 515 215; Rua General Norton de Matos 47; pastries €1; ☺breakfast & lunch) Founded in 1830, this wonderful confectioner stocks the town's favourite sweet, *rebuçados dos arcos* (enormous, jaw-breaking, hard-boiled sweets), and pastry, *charutos dos arcos* (preserved egg wrapped in a sugary dough). To get here take the street to the right of the tourist office, past the post office.

Minho Verde PORTUGUESE $$
(Rua Mário Júlio Almeida Costa 37; mains €6-16; ☺lunch & dinner Mon-Sat) One of Arcos' finest restaurants is in an unlikely location in an ugly block down the waterfront from the *turismo*. However, it serves excellent Minho specialities ranging from *posta de vitela* (veal steak) to *arroz de sarrabulho*. On Saturdays in spring and summer, it serves *feijão terrestre*, a local bean along with Barrosã beef.

Casa Real Matadouro STEAKHOUSE $$
(Pedrosas – Guilhadeses; mains €9-18; ☺lunch & dinner) Set in a stately house on the riverside, Matadouro serves some of the best steaks in the Minho. It's located about 500m south of the *turismo* on the river.

ℹ Information

Turismo (☑ 258 520 530; www.portonorte.pt; Rua Professor Doutor Mário Júlio Almeida Costa; ☺9.30am-12.30pm & 2-6pm Mon-Sat summer, 9am-12.30pm & 2-5.30pm Mon-Sat winter) This helpful, English-speaking tourist office is across from the town fountains (legless horses).

ℹ Getting There & Away

The bus station is almost 1km north of the town centre, but regional buses will stop on request in front of the *turismo*.

AV Cura buses run to Ponte da Barca (€1.35, 15 minutes), Ponte de Lima (€3.35, 50 minutes) and Viana do Castelo (€4, 1½ hours) eight times daily Monday to Friday, and once or twice on weekends.

Salvador buses roll at least twice on weekdays to Soajo (€2.75, 40 minutes) in Parque Nacional da Peneda-Gerês. There is no weekend service into the park.

Parque Nacional da Peneda-Gerês

Spread across four impressive granite massifs in Portugal's northernmost reach, this 703-sq-km park encompasses boulder-strewn peaks, precipitous valleys and lush forests of oak and fragrant pine. It also shelters more than 100 granite villages that, in many ways, have changed little since Portugal's founding in the 12th century. Established in 1971, Parque Nacional da Peneda-Gerês – Portugal's first and only national park – has helped preserve not just a unique set of ecosystems but also an endangered way of life for its human inhabitants.

Many of the park's oldest villages are found in the Serra da Peneda and remain in a time warp, with oxen being trundled down cobbled streets by black-clad widows, and horses shod in smoky blacksmith shops. You can get the good kind of lost amid the hard-handed, open-hearted shepherds of old Portugal, who still maintain the practice of moving livestock, and even entire villages, to high pastures for up to five months each year. Yet, despite joint governmental and private initiatives, this rustic scene is in danger of fading away, as young people head for the cities, and village populations continue to shrink. The steeper, more pristine Serra do Gerês sees the most tourism, in the form of hiking and water sports such as kayaking and rafting.

◉ Sights & Activities

The ancient, remote granite villages, still inhabited by farmers and shepherds (and now small doses of tourists), are the park's real treasure. So are their distinctive *espigueiros* (stone granaries).

There is a scattering of **Stone Age dolmens** and **antas** (megaliths) on the high plateaux of the Serra da Peneda and Serra do Gerês, near Castro Laboreiro, Mezio, Paradela, Pitões das Júnias and Tourém. Not all are easily accessible, but there is a good road from the park gateway in Mezio to **Gião**. Once home to the Mezio people, it's considered to be one of the most important rock compounds in the northwest Iberian peninsula.

Parque Nacional da Peneda-Gerês

Wildlife

In the more remote areas a few wolves still roam, as do wild boar, badgers and otters. With luck, you may catch a quick glimpse of roe deer and a few wild ponies. Closer to the ground are grass snakes and the rare venomous black viper. Birders should look out for red kites, buzzards, goshawks, golden eagles and several species of owl.

The park's domestic animals are also of interest – and don't tend to run away so quickly. In particular, primitive local breeds of long-horned cattle (the mahogany-coloured *barrosã* and darker *cachena*), goats, sheep, and the huge, sturdy Castro Laboreiro sheepdog are all unique to the area.

Sheltered valleys hold stands of white oak, arbutus, laurel and cork oak. Forests of black oak, English oak and holly give way at higher elevations to birch, yew and Scots pine, and in alpine areas to juniper and sandwort. The endemic Gerês iris grows in a small patch of the Serra do Gerês.

Outdoor Activities

The park is alive with adventure options. Hiking trails ranging in length from 1km to 30km abound in all sections of the park. Signage is solid, mountain-bike rental is easy to source, and swimming holes beckon. Rio Caldo is the centre for water sports, and the thermal springs of Vila do Gerês are worth a dip.

ⓘ Information

An EU-assisted consultancy, Adere Peneda-Gerês (p449), which was formed to spur ecotourism in the region, is the best resource on the park. Materials available include pamphlets on the park's natural, architectural and human landscapes, and about village-to-village walks on marked trails. There's also a booklet on accommodation.

Adere Peneda-Gerês is also the booking agent for many campgrounds, shelters and rural houses located in the park. You can peruse pictures, read about and book accommodation online at www.adere-pg.pt.

The park has five information gateways, each created to welcome visitors in the five municipalites of the park, with a thematic display about an aspect of the park and maps to take away. The **Lindoso** (☑258 578 141; portalindoso@cmpb.pt; ⊙10am-12.30pm & 2-5pm Tue-Sun Oct-Mar, 10am-6pm Tue-Sun Apr-Jun & Sep, 10am-7pm daily Jul-Aug) gate is the gateway for the Ponte da Barca municipality. The **Campo do Gerês** (☑253 351 888; museu@cm-terrasdebouro.pt; Campo do Gerês; ⊙10am-7pm Tue-Fri, 10am-5.30pm Sat-Sun mid-Jun–mid-Sep, 10am-12.30pm & 2-5pm Tue-Sun mid-Sep–mid-Jun) gate represents the Terras de Bouro municipality. The **Lamas de Mouro** (☑251 465 010; portadelamas@cm-melgaco.pt; ⊙10am-12.30pm & 2-7pm Jul-Aug, 10am-12.30pm & 2-6pm Apr-Jun & Sep, 10am-12.30pm & 2-5pm Oct-Mar) gateway, on the way to Castro Laboreiro, is the info point for Melgaço municipality. Another info point is at **Mezio** (☑258 522 157; portadomezio@ardal.pt; ⊙9.30am-1pm & 2-6pm Mon-Fri, 10am-1pm & 2-7pm Sat-Sun Apr-Sep, 9.30am-1pm & 2-5pm Oct-Mar), 13km from Arcos de Valdevez. Lastly, the gateway for the eastern part of the park is at **Montalegre** (☑276 518 320; Terreiro do Açougue, Montalegre; ⊙9am-12.30pm & 2-5.30pm Mon-Fri).

ⓘ Getting There & Around

Empresa Hoteleira do Gerês (☑253 262 033) buses go from Braga to Vila do Gerês (€4.25, 1½ hours) hourly during the week, five times on Saturday and four times Sunday.

On weekdays there are eight Salvador buses from Braga to Arcos de Valdevez (€4, one hour); on weekends, three. Two Salvador buses also go on weekdays from Arcos de Valdevez to Soajo (€2.75, 50 minutes) and Lindoso (€3.55, one hour) in Parque Nacional da Peneda-Gerês; there are no buses on weekends.

Paved roads are well maintained throughout the park, but back roads can be be tricky to navigate.

Serra da Peneda

The lesser-visited, northernmost end of the park is ripe for exploration. Lower-lying forested hills fade into massive glacially formed peaks, some topped with powerful 21st-century windmills; others sit idly watching over vast boulder fields. Old stone houses huddle in the shadows, wild horses and cattle gather and wander free, and stone fences sprout haphazardly and wind through wildflower prairies.

◉ Sights & Activities

Hiking is the principal activity in this end of the park, but there's a certain amount of old-world history to explore on these trails, too. The easiest walk can be found opposite the Lamas de Mouro gate. This **interpretative trail** winds past watermills, stone churches and community ovens, and along a stream for 4km.

Driving from here, bear right at the intersection and you'll head into the somewhat sprawling village of **Castro Laboreiro**, named for its endemic sheepdogs but more notable for the picturesque ruins of its 16th-century **castle**, built in 1505 on the foundations of a 12th-century Moorish castle. You can access it from a short and faint 800m trail. Views from the castle are stunning.

Castro Laboreiro has three other trails to explore. The shortest is a moderate 3km **interpretative trail**, but more strenuous and spectacular is the **Trilho Castrejo**, a 17km ramble over some of the oldest trails in these mountains. The there's the equally beautiful but less demanding **Pertinho do Céu** from the village of Gavieira. Maps and brochures with trail descriptions are available in Lamas de Mouro, but you can also download the brochures for free from the website www.cm-melgaco.pt.

Further south, almost halfway between Lamas De Mouro and Soajo, is one of the park's most stunning mountain villages, and the *serra's* namesake. Set on both sides of a deep ravine, and backed by a domed mountain and gushing waterfall, **Peneda** is a stunner. The village's only hotel, a former pilgrims' lodge, is set next to the **Igreja Senhora de Peneda**. This historic church is the centre of the **Festas de Nossa Senhora da Peneda**, which takes place during the first week of September when villagers converge on the plaza for candlelit processions and long nights of music, dance and prayer.

It's possible to **climb** the face of Peneda's gorgeous domed peak, but you'll need to bring your own climbing gear. Otherwise, a short but steep **1km trail** begins from behind the church and winds past, up and over the dome to an artificial but still scenic **lake** high in the hills where wild horses graze the savannah. If you stay on the trail past the lake you can make an 8km loop that leads back to the main highway just uphill from Peneda.

🛏 Sleeping & Eating

Parque Campismo
Lamas de Mouro   CAMPGROUND **$**
(🖉251 466 041; www.camping-lamas.com; Lamas de Mouro; per adult/tent/car €4.20/3.70/3, bungalow for 2 people €65; ☺Jul-Sep) This tremendous private campground near boulder fields and flowering meadows has shady creekside pitch sites plus four cosy pine-clad

bungalows with kitchenettes. It rents out mountain bikes and offers treetop adventures, canyoning and hikes with shepherds. There are a couple of restaurants not too far away, in the Lamas do Mouro village northwest of the park gate.

Miracastro   GUESTHOUSE **$**
(🖉251 460 020; www.albergariamiracastro.com; s/d €25/40; P ✽ 🛜) Friendly family-run guesthouse in the village of Castro Laboreiro, with simple rooms blessed with lots of light and gorgeous vistas from the balconies. The restaurant serves huge portions of tasty traditional dishes (€5 to €10), such as oven-baked *cabrito* and codfish with *broa* cornbread.

Miradouro do Castelo   GUESTHOUSE **$**
(🖉251 466 041; www.miradourodocastelo.com; d from €50; P 🛜) What steals the show at this simple guesthouse in Castro Laboreiro are the beautiful, sweeping views from the simple rooms with hardwood floors. Of the seven rooms, three have the wow view, and cost €10 more. The downstairs restaurant serves good local staples (€7 to €12).

Hotel Castrum Villae   HOTEL **$$**
(🖉251 460 010; www.castrumvillae.com; s/d €53/63; P 🛜) A fairly modern, comfy hotel in Castro Laboreiro, a short hoof to the *castro* (castle). The tiled rooms are bright and have accent wallpaper but are just a cut above basic. However, the hotel also has a restaurant and rents out bikes.

Hotel de Peneda   HOTEL **$$**
(🖉251 460 040; www.hotel.peneda.net; Lugar da Peneda; s/d €70/75; P 🛜) Once a nest for Igreja Senhora de Peneda's pilgrims, this mountain lodge features a waterfall backdrop, a gushing creek beneath and ultra-cosy rooms with blond-wood floors, French windows and views of quaint Peneda village across the ravine. If you'd rather save a few bucks, stay in the more atmospheric but less improved stone quarters in the Anjo de Guarda wing (singles/doubles €50/55), open only in summer. The hotel also has a decent restaurant.

ⓘ Getting There & Away

This is self-driving country. The five park offices provide general park information and can supply a map, but you'll get more specific hiking advice at the brilliant Lamas de Mouro gate.

ESPIGUEIROS

They look hauntingly like mausoleums, but *espigueiros* are in fact the stuff of life. New World corn was a great innovation in these low-yielding lands when it was introduced in the 18th century. But there was a catch – it ripened late, when autumn rains threatened harvests with rot. *Espigueiros* – granite caskets on stilts with slotted sides – were created to dry and store the valuable kernels. Usually built in clusters, covered with moss and topped with little crosses, they look like the village graveyard. Neither the washing lines lashed to them nor the squat, long-horned cattle grazing at their feet can entirely dispel their eerie charm.

Serra do Soajo

POP 980 / ELEV 300M

Sturdy Soajo (soo-*ahzh*-oo), high above the upper Rio Lima, is best known for its photogenic *espigueiros*. It has splendid views over the surrounding countryside, with scenic walks providing a fine opportunity to take in the beauty of this protected region. Although it lacks the majesty of the Serra da Peneda high country, it's accessible by public transport and, thanks to village enterprise and the Turismo de Aldeia, you can stay in one of Soajo's restored stone houses and glimpse a vanishing way of life.

Soajo is 21km northeast of Ponte da Barca on the N203 and N530, or the same distance from Arcos de Valdevez via the scenic N202 and N304. Buses stop by Restaurante Videira at the intersection of these two roads. A few hundred metres down the N530 towards Lindoso are Soajo's trademark *espigueiros*.

Soajo's small main square, Largo do Eiró – with a *pelourinho* topped by what can only be described as an ancient smiley face – is down a lane in the opposite direction from the bus stop.

🏃 Activities

Soajo is filled with the sound of rushing water, a resource that has been painstakingly managed over the centuries. A steep walk on the eastern slopes shows just how important these streams once were.

On the N304, 250m north of the bus stop, is the signed trailhead for the Trilho do Ramil. Initially paved with immense stones and grooved by centuries of ox-cart traffic, it ascends through a landscape shaped by agriculture, taking in granite cottages, *espigueiros* and superb views. Further up are three derelict watermills for grinding corn, stone channels that once funnelled the stream from one mill to the next, and the reservoir that fed them. Once you reach the old guardhouse at 500m, the trail parallels Laceiras Creek and runs through oak and pine groves to Branda Ramil (a *branda* was a settlement of summer houses for villagers, who drove their livestock to high pastures and lived with them all summer).

Another walk, along the Caminho do Pão and Caminho da Fé, takes you downhill from Soajo village to the Ponte da Ladeira, a simple medieval bridge. Hike another 500m upstream and you'll find perfect swimming holes at Poço do Luzio, an ideal antidote for Soajo's soaring summer mercury. Ask for a map at the info gate.

🛏 Sleeping & Eating

Village Houses   RURAL INN $

(cottage €45-200) About a dozen houses (sleeping two to eight) are available for tourist accommodation under the Turismo de Aldeia scheme. Each has a fireplace or stove (with firewood in winter) and a kitchen stocked with breakfast food, including fresh bread on the doorstep each morning. Casas de Soajo are a particularly great option, plus they accept bookings for one night only; not all village houses do (especially on weekends). Book through Adere Peneda-Gerês (p449) in Ponte da Barca or directly through www.casasdesoajo.com.

Casa do Adro   RURAL INN $

(☑ 258 576 327; www.casadoadroturismorural.com; s/d €50; P ✳ @) This manor house (rather than a cottage), located off Largo do Eiró by the parish church, dates to the 18th century. Rooms are huge, furnished with antiques, and blessed with sweet vineyard and village vistas. There is a minimum two-night stay in August.

Videira   PORTUGUESE $

(☑ 258 576 205; mains €8.50-10; ☺ lunch Thu-Mon Jul-Sep, Fri-Mon Oct-Jun) Locals rave about Videira's authentic regional smoked meats and sausage and the homemade mainstays. The shady, arched patio of this family-run tavern is outfitted with sturdy, polished wooden tables. It's situated by the bus stop. Most of the portions easily feed two so order less. Try the delicious *cachena* beef and the *feijão terrestre* bean stew.

Saber ao Borralho
PORTUGUESE $$

(☑ 258 577 296; www.saberaoborralho.com; plates for 2 €18-20; ☺ lunch & dinner Wed-Sun) A further 200m beyond Espigueiro, this handsomely set place features excellent local dishes like the Minho *barrosã* steak as well as three codfish dishes and a tempting dessert counter. Village house rentals are available here (€50 per night).

Espigueiro de Soajo
PORTUGUESE $$

(☑ 258 576 136; espiguerodosoajo@hotmail.com; Av 25 de Abril; mains €8-13; ☺ lunch & dinner Tue-Sat, lunch Sun) This modern place serves terrific Minho meat, and has outdoor seating on a vine-covered terrace. Management is English speaking (local by way of Boston) and very friendly. It's about 200m north of the centre on the N304.

❶ Information
There's an ATM below the parish council office, off the far side of the square – it's the only one in the entire park.

❶ Getting There & Away
On weekdays there are one to two Salvador buses from Arcos de Valdevez (€2.75, 50 minutes) via Ponte da Barca (€2.20, 35 minutes). A taxi from Arcos or Ponte da Barca costs €20 to €25.

Serra do Gerês
POP 800 / ELEV 350M

Big nature rises in steep wooded pinnacles, gushes with cold streams, and pools into crystalline swimming holes in the Gerês end of the park. This is the busiest section, which in summer months sees droves of tourists, and car traffic can jam up the roads. Its beating heart is the tourist resort town of Vila do Gerês, commonly referred to simply as Gerês. It's the park's busiest, most developed and unseemly settlement.

VILA DO GERÊS
Sandwiched tightly into the Rio Gerês valley, this spa town has a rather charming fin de siècle core surrounded by a ring of less appealing, modern *pensões* (guesthouses). Most accommodation remains shuttered from November to April, as does the spa itself. It's packed in July and August.

The town is built on an elongated, one-way loop, with the *balneário* (spa centre) in the pink buildings on the lower road. The original hot spring and some baths are in the staid colonnade at the northern end (where the road takes a sharp U-turn). Buses stop at a traffic circle just south of the loop.

🏃 Activities
There are several hiking trails within a short drive.

Cascata do Arado
HIKING

This scenic and somewhat challenging 12km trail penetrates a gorgeous highland boulder field and thick fern gullies to a waterfall. It begins in Pedra Bela, 200m north of the park office.

Roman Road Trails
HIKING

There are several trails that link to an old Roman road that once stretched 320km between Braga and Astorga (in Spain), and now has World Heritage status. Most are marked only as Trilho da Geira.

The trail at Portela de Homem is an out-and-back 6km round-trip in the steep, wooded Mata de Albergaria range. Milestones – inscribed with the name of the emperor during whose rule they were erected – remain at miles XXIX, XXX and XXXI. Another Trilho de Geira, in the Terras de Bouro region, leaves from São Sebastiao, roughly 6km from Campo do Gerês.

Trilho da Preguiça
HIKING

This park-maintained loop trail starts on the N308 about 3km above Gerês. For 5km it rolls through the valley's oak forests. A leaflet about the walk is available from the park office (€0.60). You can also carry on – or hitch – to the **Portela de Leonte**, 6km north of Gerês.

Águas do Gerês
THERMAL SPRINGS

(www.aguasdogeres.pt; admission €3; ☺ 8am-noon & 2.30-6pm May-Oct) After a long hike, finish the day by soaking away aches and pains in the town's thermal springs. In addition to the sauna, steam bath and pool (available with basic admission), you can indulge with a full range of treatments, including massages and facials.

🛏 Sleeping
Gerês has plenty of *pensões*, though in summer you may find some are block-booked for spa patients and other visitors. Outside July and August, prices plummet.

Parque de Campismo de Vidoeiro
CAMPGROUND $

(☑ 253 391 289; www.adere-pg.pt; per adult/tent/car €4/3.60/3.75; ☺ mid-May–mid-Oct) This cool and shady, hillside, park-run facility is next to the river, about 1km north of Vila do Gerês. Reception is open from 8am till noon and 3pm to 7pm. Avoid it in August, when screaming school children descend in droves.

Adelaide Hotel
HOTEL $

(☑ 253 390 020; www.adelaidehotel.pt; Rua de Arnaço 45; s/d €45/59; P ❋ ☎ ☲) This big, modern, lemon-yellow hotel wins for value. The rooms are spacious, with parquet floors and new beds. Make sure you get a room with a balcony and views. It is uphill from the southern end of the town loop, and has a swimming pool on the other side of town and a shuttle to take you there.

Hotel Baltazar
HOTEL $

(☑ 253 391 131; www.baltazarhotel.com; Rua Emy José Lagrifa Mendes 6; s/d €40/50; ☎) In a fine old granite building, this friendly, family-run hotel just up from the hot springs has spacious rooms, many of which look onto a pleasant wooded park. The downstairs restaurant is excellent.

Hotel Universal
HOTEL $$

(☑ 253 390 220; www.ehgeres.com; Av Manuel F Costa 115; s/d €45/60; P ❋ ☎ ☲) Yes, it's kitschy, but it's still got class. The mosaic stone atrium is leafy and filled with light; rooms are large and sport headboard radios of a bygone era.

Hotel Águas do Gerês
HOTEL $$

(☑ 253 390 190; www.aguasdogeres.pt; Av Manuel F Costa 136; s/d €66/86; P ❋ ☎) In a grand fin de siècle building, this slightly upmarket place has decent, spacious, carpeted rooms with high ceilings and modern decor that doesn't live up to the exterior. It also runs the hot springs and offers special packages.

✗ Eating & Drinking

Lurdes Capela
PORTUGUESE $

(Rua Dr Manuel Gomes de Almeida 77; mains €6-13; ☺ lunch & dinner) Family owned and operated, and almost always packed. Expect top-end service and even better food. We're talking massive fresh-fish platters with buttered potatoes and vegetables, fluffy, savoury omelettes and all the beef and cod dishes, too.

Adega Regional
PORTUGUESE $$

(Av Manuel F Costa 115; mains €10-18; ☺ lunch & dinner Tue-Sun) Set behind Hotel Universal, and just above a roaring stream, this historic stone *adega* serves tapas and wine. Saturday-night karaoke kicks off at 10pm.

❶ Information

Espaço Internet (Av Manuel F Costa; ☺ 9.30am-12.30pm & 2-5.30pm Mon-Fri) Free internet access up the stairs across from Hotel Universal.

Park Office (☑ 253 390 110; www.adere-pg.pt; Centro de Educação Ambiental do Vidoeiro; ☺ 9am-noon & 2-5.30pm Mon-Fri) About 1km north of the village on the track leading to the campground. There are several tour operators nearby that offer water sports, bike rental, horseback riding, canoeing and canyoning.

Turismo (☑ 253 391 133; www.portoenorte.pt; Av 20 de Junho 45A; ☺ 9.30am-12.30pm & 2-6pm summer, 9am-12.30pm & 2-5.30pm winter) On the road into town, right where the road forks.

❶ Getting There & Away

Empresa Hoteleira do Gerês (☑ 253 390 220; www.ehgeres.com) runs between six and 10 buses daily from Braga to Gerês (€4.25, 1½ hours), passing through Rio Caldo (€1.25, 1¼ hours). Buy tickets at Hotel Universal.

RIO CALDO
POP 900 / ELEV 160M

Just below Vila do Gerês, this tiny town sits on the back of the stunning Albufeira de Caniçada, making it the park's centre for water sports.

The English-run **Água Montanha Lazer** (AML; ☑ 253 391 779; www.aguamontanha.com; Lugar de Paredes) rents out single/double kayaks for €6/9 per hour, plus pedal boats and small motorboats. It will also take you wakeboarding (€50 per 20 minutes), or organise kayaking trips along the Albufeira de Salamonde. AML also rents out three attractively furnished cottages, all with verandahs, kitchen units and water views.

There are now dozens of guesthouses set on the ridge encircling the Albufeira de Caniçada, but none have a more spectacular setting than the lovely **Pousada do Gerês-Caniçada/São Bento** (☑ 253 649 150; www.pousadas.pt; Caniçada; s/d €160/170; P ❋ ☲). High above the Albufeira, it offers a splendid retreat at eagle's-nest heights. The rooms have wood-beamed ceilings and comfy furnishings, and some have verandahs with

BEAUTY BEYOND: BARROSO

This small northeast region of upper Trás-os-Montes, shared by the Montalegre and Boticas municipalities, packs a punch with its pretty villages where time seems to have stood still for centuries and endangered Iberian wolves roam the thick oak forests. It's known to have some of the best *fumeiro* (smoked meats) in the entire region, mainly due to the cold and dry climate and the food the villagers give the pigs, such as chestnuts, pumpkin and cabbage. Particularly good are the *alheira*, *chouriço de abóbora* and *sangueira* sausages. Also look out for *feijoada à transmontana* or *leitão à transmontana*, both traditional dishes involving pork.

Of the villages in the region, **Pitões das Júnias** is the most scenic, set on a plateau surrounded by endless mountain vistas. It has an ancient monastery nearby, Santa Maria das Júnias, and a pretty waterfall, both an easy hike away. Several village houses have rooms to rent, including the best-known restaurant, **Casa do Preto** (☑276 566 158; www.casadopreto.com; Pitões das Júnias; s/d €40/50; ℗ ☎), which makes mean *cabrito* and Barroso beef steaks (mains €7.50 to €10); the eight rooms above the restaurant are clean and spacious with big bathrooms. Don't miss **Taberna Terra Celta** (Largo do Eiro; ☺9am-midnight Tue-Sun) on the main village square, in an old wooden and stone home with an upstairs fireplace. On weekends it serves *fumeiro*, soups and salads; otherwise it's a great stop for a drink. Make sure you grab some rye bread at the village bakery and some jars of heather honey, available for sale in restaurants.

Another great lodging option in Barroso is **Casa dos Braganças** (☑276 579 138; www.casadosbragancas.com; Rua dos Braganças 8-10, Tourém; s/d €45/60; ℗ ☎) in the village of **Tourém**, a delightful rural inn run by a friendly live-in family. Inside this 18th-century house, rooms feature original details such as handpainted ceilings, stone walls, custom-made wood furniture and countryside views. There are free bikes, great birdwatching in the area (featuring some rare birds) and dinners on request.

For excellent nature tours of Barroso and beyond, but with focus on Trás-os-Montes, turn to **Portugal Ecotourism** (☑259 433 146; www.portugalecotourism.pt), a nature tourism specialist that offers short and multiday hikes, biking jaunts and wildlifewatching trips. The wolf tour is particularly interesting.

magnificent views. There's a pool, gardens, a tennis court and an excellent restaurant serving local delicacies (eg trout, roasted goat). To get there, head south 3km from Rio Caldo, along the N304, following signs to Caniçada.

CAMPO DO GERÊS
POP 160 / ELEV 690M

Campo do Gerês (called São João do Campo on some maps, and just Campo by most) is a humble huddle of stone houses high in the mountains in the middle of a wide, grassy basin. It sees more hikers than shepherds once the weather turns warm, thanks to easy access to some spectacular trails.

Coming from Vila do Gerês, you first arrive at a little traffic circle. The tiny village centre is another 1.5km straight on, while the youth hostel is 1km up the road to the left.

◉ Sights

The neighbouring village of **Vilarinho das Furnas** was for centuries a remarkably democratic and fiercely independent village, with a well-organised system of shared property and decision-making. But the entire town was submerged by the building of a dam in 1972. In anticipation of the end of their old way of life, villagers collected stories and objects for a moving memorial that is on display at the **Museu Etnográfico** (www.visitgeres.com; adult/student €2/1; ☺10am-7pm Tue-Fri, 10am-5.30pm Sat Sun mid-Jun–mid-Sep, 10am-12.30pm & 2-5pm Tue-Sun mid-Sep–mid-Jun), located at the park gate. The museum also offers exhibits on local flora and fauna. All exhibit explanations are in Portuguese.

In late summer and autumn, when the reservoir level falls, the empty village walls rise like spectres from the water. You can visit the spooky remains about 2.5km beyond the dam, which is a comfortable three-hour return hike.

☆ Activities

There are several well-marked hiking trails around Campo do Gerês; hikes last from three to six hours. You can pick up maps and trail information (€0.90 to €1.50) at the information desk of the Museu Etnográfico.

Trilho da Cidade da Calcedónia HIKING

A narrow, sealed road snakes over the ridge from Vila do Gerês to Campo do Gerês, offering short but spectacular high-elevation walks from just about anywhere along its upper reaches. One of these is the Cidade da Calcedónia trail, a moderate, signposted, 7km (four-hour) loop that climbs a 912m viewpoint called the Cabeço Calcedónia, with views to knock your socks off.

Trilho dos Currais HIKING

The 'Corrals Trail' is a moderate 10km loop that takes about four hours to complete. Along the way you'll wind beneath oak and pine and glimpse boulder fields, sublime valley views and – if you leave early enough and get lucky – resident deer, wolf or wild boar. The trailhead is located and signposted in Vidoeiro.

Equi Campo HIKING

(☎253 161 405; www.equicampo.com; ◷9am-7pm daily Jun-Aug, 9am-7pm weekends Sep-May) One of two Campo-based outfitters located on the right just before you arrive in town. Guides lead horse-riding trips (one/two hours €17/30), hikes (half-day €7 per person) and treetop adventures (€12). You can also rent mountain bikes here if you'd like to head off on your own (€5/17 per hour/day). The wooden shack also has a few tables outside, where snacks are served.

🛏 Sleeping & Eating

Parque Campismo de Cerdeira CAMPGROUND $

(☎253 351 005; www.parquecerdeira.com; per person/tent/car €5.50/4.80/4.90, bungalow €68, dm per person €17.50; ◷year-round; P🐾🛜🏊) This private facility has oak-shaded sites, a laundry, a pool, a *minimercado* (grocery shop), tennis courts, a swimming pool (closed Mondays), a good restaurant (open to the public) and bikes to hire (€15 for half a day). Best of all are the lovely ecofriendly bungalows, with French doors opening onto unrivalled mountain views. Book ahead in August. Look for the turn-off to the right after passing the village, which is about 500m away.

Pousada da Juventude Vilarinho das Furnas HOSTEL $

(☎253 351 339; www.pousadasjuventude.pt; Rua da Pousada 1; dm/d/bungalow €14/38/80;

P@🛜) Campo's woodland hostel, 1km from the main roundabout, began life as a temporary dam-workers' camp and now offers a spotless selection of spartan four-bed dormitories in wooden buildings at the bottom of the hill, stylish doubles (with huge bathrooms) in the main building and roomier bungalows (that sleep four) with kitchen units. Meals are also available, upon request.

Albergaria Stop GUESTHOUSE $

(☎253 350 040; www.albergariastop.com; Rua de São João 915; s €45, d €48-70; P🛜🏊) More mountain motel than lodge, this guesthouse has spotless rooms, wooden floors and mountain views. Most rooms have balconies, plus there is a pool and tennis courts. The modest restaurant and bar is what passes for Campo nightlife. It's located just before the village.

O Abocanhado PORTUGUESE $$

(☎253 352 944; www.abocanhado.com; Brufe; mains €15-18; ◷lunch & dinner daily mid-Jul-Aug, Sat & Sun Sep–mid-Jul) This beautifully situated restaurant is a temple to the finest ingredients that the surrounding countryside has to offer, including *javali* (wild boar), *veado* (venison) and *coelho* (rabbit), as well as beef and goat raised in the adjacent fields. Finish with *requeijão* – a soft goat's cheese so fresh it's actually sweet.

The only drawback: off-season, the restaurant keeps irregular hours, so call ahead before making the trip. It's located 9km east of Campo do Gerês (across the dam), in the village of Brufe, on a panoramic spot above the Rio Homem.

ℹ Getting There & Away

From Braga, Transdev has four daily buses (€4.10, 1½ hours; fewer at weekends) that stop at the museum crossroad and the village centre.

Eastern Peneda-Gerês

Cabril, on the eastern limb of the national park, and Montalegre, just outside the park, are actually in Trás-os-Montes, but you're unlikely to visit either unless you're coming in or out of the park.

CABRIL
POP 550 / ELEV 400M

Although it hardly looks the part, peaceful Cabril – set with its outlying hamlets in a wide, fertile bowl backed by soaring peaks – is the administrative centre of Portugal's biggest *freguesia* (parish), stretching up to the

Spanish border. Your best reference point is **Largo do Cruzeiro**, with its old *pelourinho*. To one side is the squat but stately **Igreja de São Lourenço**, said to have been moved five centuries ago, brick by brick, by villagers of nearby São Lourenço. Some 400m southwest is a bridge over an arm of the Albufeira de Salamonde where you'll find **Restaurante Ponte Nova** (mains €7-13; ☺ breakfast, lunch & dinner). It services good river trout (in season) and, if you order ahead, *cabrito* or *javali assada*. There's an outdoor deck right over the water. While Cabril is a lovely place to stop for lunch, there's no reason to stay the night.

There are no buses to Cabril, but you could take any Braga–Montalegre or Braga–Chaves bus service and get off at the Ruivães bus stop, then hike the last 4km. Drivers can cross into the park from the N103 via the Salamonde dam; alternatively, a longer but far more scenic route is via the Venda Nova dam, 14km east of Salamonde at Cambedo.

Further west in nearby **Fafião**, you'll find the adventure outfitter, **Javsport** (☎ 252 850 621; www.javsport.pt). It operates popular canyoning expeditions down the Rio Arado and Rio Conho for €50 per person.

MONTALEGRE

POP 1800 / ELEV 1000M

Montalegre is the park's eastern gateway, and if ever there was a picturesque hamlet with a castle on the hill, this is it. The small but particularly striking **castle**, part of Dom Dinis' 14th-century ring of frontier outposts, looms over the town and the surrounding fertile plains fed by so many rivers. The future Duke of Wellington made use of it in his drive to rid Portugal of Napoleon's troops in 1809. Today visitors can only wander around its perimeter, taking in the lovely views. Just below the castle lies the old town centre.

The town comes alive each Friday the 13th, for the **Noite das Bruxas**, a night-long celebration that attracts thousands for the raucous feast that involves street performances and much drinking of *queimada*, a slow-brewed drink with strong *bagaço* (Portuguese firewater) and honey, said to wash away the evil spirits.

From the bus station it's 500m uphill on Rua General Humberto Delgado to a five-way roundabout, beside which you'll find the town hall and *turismo*. Keep heading uphill to reach the crown.

◉ Sights

Barroso Eco Museu MUSEUM
(☎ 276 518 645; www.ecomuseu.org; Praça do Município; ☺ 10am-12.30pm & 2-6pm) **FREE** Next to the castle, this museum hosts exhibits that showcase regional history, rural traditions and folklore. There are also exhibits highlighting local flora and fauna, and a gallery rotating contemporary canvases from local artists.

⌁ Sleeping & Eating

Casa Zé Maria GUESTHOUSE $
(☎ 276 512 457; www.zemaria.centrobarrosao.com; Rua Dr Victor Branco 21; d from €40; P🅿🛜) This converted 19th-century granite manor features old-fashioned charm in its wooden-floored rooms with lacy bedspreads and dark-wood furnishings. It's located just one block east and one block south of the *turismo*.

O Castelo GUESTHOUSE $
(☎ 276 511 237; Terreiro do Açougue 1; s/d €35/45) This simple family-run guesthouse, right by the castle, has rooms featuring hardwood floors and stone walls; some have terraces with views of the castle. Rates include breakfast.

Montalegre Hotel HOTEL $$
(☎ 276 510 220; www.montalegrehotel.com; Rua de Avelar 100; s/d €60/78; P🅿❄🛜🏊) Situated just southwest of the roundabout at the top of town, this somewhat out-of-place business hotel with functional but soulless rooms has seen better days. However, it does have an indoor swimming pool, sauna and gym. Oh, and did we mention that it used to be a political prison during Salazar's reign?

Tasca do Açougue PORTUGUESE $
(Terreiro do Açougue; mains €7-10, snacks €3-7; ☺ lunch & dinner) In a charming stone cottage just below the castle, Tasca do Açougue serves tasty Iberian tapas dishes, including grilled octopus and smoked meats, as well as heartier plates. It's a lively place for a drink in the evening.

Pastelaria São Paulo BAKERY $
(Rua Direita 27; pastries €0.75-2; ☺ breakfast, lunch & dinner) If you're just in town long enough for a cup of something strong and a nibble of something sweet, then search out this bakery.

THE MINHO PARQUE NACIONAL DA PENEDA-GERÊS

ⓘ Information

Biblioteca Municipal (Rua General Humberto Delgado 385; ⊙1-7pm Mon & Wed, 9am-12.30pm & 2-5.30pm Tue-Fri) Free internet access.

Post Office (⊙9am-12.30pm & 2-5.30pm Mon-Fri) Located 400m northeast of the roundabout, down Av Dom Nuno Álvares Pereira.

Park Information Office (☑276 518 320; www.adere-pg.pt; Praça do Municipal; ⊙9am-12.30pm & 2-5.30pm Mon-Fri) Next door to the Barroso Eco Museu.

Turismo (☑276 510 205; www.cm-montalegre.pt; ⊙10am-12.30pm & 2-6pm) In the Eco Museu complex.

ⓘ Getting There & Away

Transdev (☑253 209 400; www.transdev.pt) runs three daily buses from Braga to Montalegre (€6.40, 2½ hours) from Monday to Thursday, and four on Friday; they run less frequently on weekends.

Understand Portugal

Portugal Today

Since the global financial crisis of 2008 Portugal's economy has been in freefall, with a shrinking GDP and surging unemployment, which reached 18% in 2013. The government's response – cutting public spending and other austerity measures – has not gone down well, with mass protests erupting across the nation. It's not all bad news though: Portugal is reaping the benefits of its investments in green energy and tourism is on the rise.

Best in Film

A Lisbon Story (1994) Wim Wenders' love letter to Lisbon.

Letters from Fontainhas (1997–2006) Pedro Costa's art-house trilogy set in Lisbon.

Capitães de Abril (*Captains of April*; 2000) Overview of the 1974 Carnation Revolution.

Best in Print

The Inquisitor's Manual (António Lobo Antunes; 1996) Story about life under Salazar.

Baltasar & Blimunda (José Saramago; 1982) Darkly comic 18th-century love story.

The Book of Disquietude (Fernando Pessoa; 1982) Literary masterpiece by Portugal's greatest poet.

Best Albums

Fado em Mim (2002) Mesmerising fado album by the legendary Mariza.

Art of Amália (1998) Compilation by one of fado's greats.

Best of Rui Veloso (2000) Portugal's legendary rock-balladeer.

Economic Crisis

Portugal's economy wasn't particularly strong in the years before the economic crisis, making the downturn all the more destructive: GDP growth has averaged just 1% annually over the past decade. Placed into the economically failing eurozone nations known as PIIGS (representing Portugal, Italy, Ireland, Greece and Spain), in 2011 Portugal – in dire financial straits – accepted an EU bailout worth €78 billion.

The younger generation has born the heaviest toll from the crisis, with unemployment above 40% for workers under the age of 25. In addition to this, there are the underemployed and those scraping by on meagre wages; in Portugal, the minimum wage is €566 per month, less than half that of the UK or France.

Mass Demonstrations & Protests

The EU bailout came with the stipulation that Portugal improve its budget deficit by reducing spending and increasing tax revenues. Austerity measures followed and the public took to the streets to protest against higher taxes, slashed pensions and benefits, coupled with record-high unemployment. Mass demonstrations and general strikes have grown, with the largest attracting an estimated 1.5 million people nationwide in 2013 – an astounding figure given Portugal's small size. Those in industries most affected by government policy – including education, healthcare and transport – have joined ranks with the unemployed and pensioners to protest in the largest gatherings since the Carnation Revolution in 1974.

Yet, unlike in Greece or Spain, protests have remained fairly peaceful thus far – some chalk this up to the more melancholy, less fiery Portuguese temperament. Where other southern Europeans throw Molotov cocktails, the Portuguese, well, sing: in one much-publicised protest, opera singer Ana Maria Pinto led the crowd in song ('*Acordai*' meaning 'Wake up'), drowning out a speech by President Aníbal Cavaco Silva on Portugal's Republic Day).

Daily Struggles & Political Upheavals

Despite the bailout package, Portugal remains in its most severe recession since the 1970s. Every day, Portuguese are confronted with depressing headlines announcing freezes on public spending, cuts in healthcare, removal of free school lunches, curtailing of police patrols and rising suicides, among many other issues. Pensioners living on 200-odd euros a month struggle to feed themselves without family financial support, and poverty and hunger affect untold millions; according to TNS Global roughly three out of four people in Portugal struggle to make their money last through the month. What began as a financial crisis has now turned into a political crisis, as successive government ministers have failed to ameliorate the growing problems. With anger growing on the streets, key government ministers have resigned and a wary public has clamoured for the resignation of Prime Minister Pedro Passos Coelho.

A Green Economy

While most of the economy has been floundering, Portugal has been transforming itself into one of the greenest economies in Europe. In 2013 renewable energy supplied some 70% of Portugal's total consumption. Owing in part to the recession, energy consumption has fallen every year since 2010. Long-term investments that began back in 2005 in hydroelectricity and wind energy, among other sources, have yielded dividends in recent years. Unfortunately, the economic crisis has created uncertainty over continued investment in renewable energy.

Growth in Tourism

One more bright note amid all the dour talk is the continued growth of Portugal's tourism sector. The country received 8% more visitors from 2012 to 2013. Tourism contributes nearly 10% of the nation's GDP, and international businesses continue to invest in Portugal. In 2013 Aman Resorts announced plans to construct a €92 million complex in the Alentejo, the largest tourism investment in a decade.

POPULATION: **10.7 MILLION**

AREA: **88,323 SQ KM**

UNEMPLOYMENT: **18%**

HIGHEST POINT: **TORRE (1993M)**

PORTUGUESE SPEAKERS WORLDWIDE: **260 MILLION**

if Portugal were 100 people

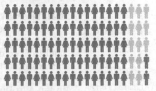

85 would be Roman Catholic
9 would be other
4 would be no religion
2 would be other Christian

occupation of workforce
(% of population)

Services 60

Industry 28

Agriculture 12

population per sq km

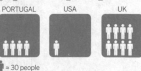

PORTUGAL   USA   UK

≈ 30 people

History

This small nation at the edge of Europe has seen a long line of conquerors and foreign princes over the last 3000 years. Celts, Romans, Visigoths, Moors and Christian crusaders all made contributions to Portugal's early identity. In the 15th century, sea captains and intrepid explorers helped transform Portugal into the seat of a vast global empire. The centuries that followed saw devastation (the Lisbon earthquake of 1755) and great changes (industrialisation, dictatorship, decolonisation) before Portugal became a stable democracy in the 1980s.

Early Peoples

Prehistoric Sights

Vila Nova de Foz Côa, Douro

Citânia de Briteiros, Minho

Cromeleque dos Almendres, Alentejo

Anta Grande do Zambujeiro, Alentejo

Cromeleque do Xerez, Alentejo

One of Europe's earliest settlements, the Iberian Peninsula was first inhabited many millennia ago, when hominids wandered across the landscape some time before 200,000 BC. During the Palaeolithic period, early Portuguese ancestors left traces of their time on earth in the fascinating stone carvings in the open air near Vila Nova de Foz Côa in the Alto Douro. These date back some 30,000 years and were only discovered by accident, during a proposed dam building project in 1992. Other signs of early human artistry lie hidden in the Alentejo, in the Gruta do Escoural, where cave drawings of animals and humans date back to around 15,000 BC.

Homo sapiens weren't the only bipeds on the scene. Neanderthals co-existed alongside modern humans in a few rare places like Portugal for as long as 10,000 years. In fact, some of the last traces of their existence were found in Iberia.

Neanderthals were only the first of a long line of inhabitants to appear (and later disappear) from the Iberian stage. In the 1st millennium BC Celtic people started trickling into the Iberian Peninsula, settling northern and western Portugal around 700 BC. Dozens of *citânias* (fortified villages) popped up, such as the formidable Citânia de Briteiros. Further south, Phoenician traders, followed by Greeks and Carthaginians, founded coastal stations and mined metals further inland.

TIMELINE	5000 BC	700 BC	197 BC
	Little-understood Neolithic peoples build protected hilltop settlements in the lower Tejo valley. They leave behind stone monuments, including megaliths scattered around Évora in present-day Alentejo.	Celtic peoples, migrating across the Pyrenees with their families and flocks, sweep through the Iberian Peninsula. They settle in fortified villages, known as *citânias*, and intermarry with local tribes.	After defeating Carthage in the Second Punic Wars, the Romans invade Iberia, expanding their empire west. They face fierce resistance from local tribes, including the Lusitani, but eventually conquer them.

Roman Settlement

When the Romans swept into southern Portugal in 210 BC, they expected an easy victory. But they hadn't reckoned on the Lusitani, a Celtic warrior tribe, who settled between the Rio Tejo and Rio Douro and resisted the Romans ferociously for half a century. Unable to subjugate the Lusitani, the Romans offered peace instead and began negotiations with Viriato, the Lusitanian leader. Unfortunately for Viriato and his underlings, the peace offer was a ruse, and Roman agents, posing as intermediaries, poisoned him. Resistance collapsed following Viriato's death in 139 BC.

For a vivid glimpse into Roman Portugal, you won't see a better site than Conímbriga, near Coimbra, or the monumental remains of the so-called Temple of Diana in Évora.

By the 5th century, when the Roman Empire had all but collapsed, Portugal's inhabitants had been under Roman rule for 600 years. So what did the Romans ever do for them? Most usefully, they built roads and bridges. But they also brought wheat, barley, olives and vines; large farming estates called *latifúndios* (still found in the Alentejo); a legal system; and, above all, a Latin-derived language. In fact, no other invader proved so useful.

Roman Sights

Conímbriga, Beiras

Milreu, Algarve

Termas Romanas, Évora

Núcleo Arqueológico, Lisbon

Cidade de Ammaia, Alentejo

Moors & Christians

The gap left by the Romans was filled by barbarian invaders from beyond the Pyrenees: Vandals, Alans, Visigoths and Suevi, with Arian Christian Visigoths gaining the upper hand in 469.

THE MYSTERY OF THE NEANDERTHALS

Scientists have never come to an agreement about the fate of the Neanderthals – stout and robust beings who used stone tools and fire, buried their dead and had brains larger than those of modern humans. The most common theory was that homo sapiens drove Neanderthals into extinction (perhaps in some sort of genocidal warfare). A less-accepted theory is that Neanderthals and humans bred together and produced a hybrid species. This idea gained credence when Portuguese archaeologists found a strange skeleton – the first complete Palaeolithic skeleton ever unearthed in Iberia – just north of Lisbon in 1999. In what was clearly a ritual burial, the team led by João Zilhão, director of the Portuguese Institute of Archaeology, discovered the 25,000-year-old remains of a young boy with traits of both early humans (pronounced chin and teeth) and of Neanderthals (broad limbs). Some believe this kind of relationship (love-making rather than war-making) happened over the span of thousands of years, and that some elements of Neanderthals entered the modern human gene pool.

AD 100	400	711	800
Romans collect taxes to build roads, bridges and other public works. They cultivate vineyards, teach the natives to preserve fish by salting and drying, and grant local communities much autonomy.	Rome crumbles as German tribes run riot in southern Europe. The Suevi, peasant farmers from the Elbe, settle in present-day Porto. Christian Visigoths follow suit, conquering the land in 469.	Visigoth King Witiza is assassinated. When oldest son Agila is blocked from the throne he sends for help from North African Berbers. The Muslim force arrives, establishes peace and puts down roots.	The Umayyad dynasty rules the Iberian Peninsula. The region flourishes under the tolerant caliphate. The Arabs introduce irrigation, bring new crops (including oranges and rice) and establish schools.

Portugal: A Traveller's History (2004), by Harold Livermore, explores some of the richer episodes from the past – taking in cave paintings, vineyards and music, among other topics.

Internal Visigothic disputes paved the way for Portugal's next great wave of invaders, the Moors – North African Muslims invited in 711 to help a Visigoth faction. They quickly occupied large chunks of Portugal's southern coast.

Southerners enjoyed peace and productivity under the Moors, who established a capital at Shelb (Silves). The new rulers were tolerant of Jews and Christians. Christian small-holding farmers, called Mozarabs, could keep their land and were encouraged to try new methods and crops, especially citrus and rice. Arabic words filtered into the Portuguese language, such as *alface* (lettuce), *arroz* (rice) and dozens of place names (including Fatima, Silves and Algarve), and locals became addicted to Moorish sweets.

Meanwhile in the north, Christian forces were gaining strength and reached as far as Porto in 868. But it was in the 11th century that the Reconquista (the Christian reconquest) heated up. In 1064 Coimbra was taken and, in 1085, Alfonso VI thrashed the Moors in their Spanish heartland of Toledo; he is said to have secured Seville by winning a game of chess with its emir. But in the following year, Alfonso's men were driven out by ruthless Moroccan Almoravids who answered the emir's distress call.

Alfonso cried for help and European crusaders came running – rallying against the 'infidels'. With the help of Henri of Burgundy, among others, Alfonso made decisive moves towards victory. The struggle continued in successive generations, and by 1139 Afonso Henriques (grandson of Alfonso VI) won such a dramatic victory against the Moors at Ourique (Alentejo) that he named himself Dom – King of Portugal – a title confirmed in 1179 by the pope (after extra tribute was paid, naturally). He also retook Santarém and Lisbon from the Moors.

The Portuguese were the first Westerners to reach Japan in 1543. They founded Nagasaki, introduced the mosquito net and brought new words to the Japanese language, including *pan* (bread) and, possibly, *arrigato* (thank you).

By the time he died in 1185, the Portuguese frontier was secure to the Rio Tejo, though it would take another century before the south was torn from the Moors.

The Burgundian Era

During the Reconquista, people faced more than just war and turmoil: in the wake of Christian victories came new rulers and settlers.

The Church and its wealthy clergy were the greediest landowners, followed by aristocratic fat cats. Though theoretically free, most common people remained subjects of the landowning class, with few rights. The first hint of democratic rule came with the establishment of the *cortes* (parliament). This assembly of nobles and clergy first met in 1211 at Coimbra, the then capital. Six years later the capital moved to Lisbon.

Afonso III (r 1248–79) deserves credit for standing up to the Church, but it was his son, the 'Poet King' Dinis (r 1279–1325), who really shook

1147	1242	1297
The Reconquista is underway as Christians attain decisive victories over the Moors. Portugal's first king Afonso Henriques (crowned in 1139) leads the attack, laying siege to Lisbon.	The last remaining Moors are driven out in the battle of Tavira. Portugal later establishes its border with Castile (Spain), aided by Dom Dinis: 50 fortresses line the eastern frontier.	The boundaries of the Portuguese kingdom – much the same then as they are today – were formalised with neighbouring Castile. The kingdom of Portugal had arrived.

→ Afonso Henriques statue

KRZYSZTOF DYDYNSKI / GETTY IMAGES ©

Portugal into shape. A far-sighted, cultured man, he took control of the judicial system, started progressive afforestation programs and encouraged internal trade. He suppressed the dangerously powerful military order of the Knights Templar, refounding them as the Order of Christ. He cultivated music, the arts and education, and founded a university in Lisbon in 1290, which was later transferred to Coimbra.

Dom Dinis' foresight was spot-on when it came to defence: he built or rebuilt some 50 fortresses along the eastern frontier with Castile, and signed a pact of friendship with England in 1308, the basis for a future long-lasting alliance.

It was none too soon. Within 60 years of Dinis' death, Portugal was at war with Castile. Fernando I helped provoke the clash by playing a game of alliances with both Castile and the English. He dangled promises of marriage to his daughter Beatriz in front of both nations, eventually marrying her off to Juan I of Castile, and thus throwing Portugal's future into Castilian hands.

On Fernando's death in 1383, his wife, Leonor Teles, ruled as regent. But she too was entangled with the Spanish, having long had a Galician lover. The merchant classes preferred unsullied Portuguese candidate João, son (albeit illegitimate) of Fernando's father. João assassinated Leonor's lover, Leonor fled to Castile and the Castilians duly invaded.

The showdown came in 1385 when João faced a mighty force of Castilians at Aljubarrota. Even with Nuno Álvares Pereira (the Holy Constable) as his military right-hand man and English archers at the ready, the odds were stacked against him. João vowed to build a monastery if he won – and he did. Nuno Álvares, the brilliant commander-in-chief of the Portuguese troops, deserves much of the credit for the victory. He lured the Spanish cavalry into a trap and, with an uphill advantage, his troops decimated the invaders. Within a few hours the Spanish were retreating in disarray and the battle was won.

> King João II financed voyages by Vasco da Gama and others, but he is also known for rejecting Christopher Columbus. The Italian navigator approached Portugal first (in 1485) before turning to Spain.

UNFORGETTABLE RIVER

When Roman soldiers reached the Rio Lima in 137 BC, they were convinced they had reached the River Lethe, the mythical river of forgetfulness that flowed through Hades and from which no man could return. Unable to persuade his troops to cross the waters leading to certain oblivion, the Roman general Decimus Junius Brutus Callaicus forged the river alone. Once on the other side he called out to his men, shouting each of their names. Stunned that the general could remember them, they followed after him and continued their campaign. Incidentally, Brutus, who led legions to conquer Iberia after Viriato's death, was later named proconsul of Lusitania.

1348	1385	1411	1415
The Plague arrives in Portugal (most likely carried on ships that dock in Porto and Lisbon). As in other parts of Europe, the disease devastates, killing one in three.	Intermarriage between Castilian and Portuguese royal families leads to complications. Juan I of Castile, claiming the throne, invades. The Portuguese, with English help, rout the invaders at Aljubarrota.	Newly crowned Dom João builds an elaborate monastery to commemorate his victory at Aljubarrota. João marries John of Gaunt's daughter, ushering in an English alliance lasting centuries.	Dom João's third son, Prince Henry the Navigator, joins his father in the conquest of Ceuta in North Africa. Thus begins the colonial expansion of Portugal.

The victory clinched independence and João made good his vow by commissioning Batalha's stunning Mosteiro de Santa Maria da Vitória (aka the Mosteiro da Batalha or Battle Abbey). It also sealed Portugal's alliance with England, and João wed John of Gaunt's daughter. Peace was finally concluded in 1411.

CR Boxer's classic text, *The Portuguese Seaborne Empire* (1969), is still one of the best studies of the explorations by Portuguese mariners and the complex empire that unfolded as a result.

The Age of Discoveries

João's success had whetted his appetite and, spurred on by his sons, he soon turned his military energies abroad. Morocco was the obvious target, and in 1415 Ceuta fell easily to his forces. It was a turning point in Portuguese history, a first step into its golden age.

It was João's third son, Henry, who focused the spirit of the age – a combination of crusading zeal, love of martial glory and lust for gold – into extraordinary explorations across the seas. These explorations were to transform the small kingdom into a great imperial power.

The biggest breakthrough came in 1497 during the reign of Manuel I, when Vasco da Gama reached southern India. With gold and slaves from Africa and spices from the East, Portugal was soon rolling in riches. Manuel I was so thrilled by the discoveries (and resultant cash injection) that he ordered a frenzied building spree in celebration. Top of his list was the extravagant Mosteiro dos Jerónimos in Belém, later to become his pantheon. Another brief boost to the Portuguese economy at this time came courtesy of an influx of around 150,000 Jews expelled from Spain in 1492.

Spain, however, had also jumped on the exploration bandwagon and was soon disputing Portuguese claims. Christopher Columbus' 1492 'discovery' of America for Spain led to a fresh outburst of jealous conflict. It was resolved by the pope in the bizarre 1494 Treaty of Tordesillas, by which the world was divided between the two great powers along a line 370 leagues west of the Cape Verde islands. Portugal won the lands to the east of the line, including Brazil, officially claimed in 1500.

The rivalry spurred the first circumnavigation of the world. In 1519 the Portuguese navigator Fernão de Magalhães (Ferdinand Magellan), his allegiance transferred to Spain after a tiff with Manuel I, set off in an effort to prove that the Spice Islands (today's Moluccas) lay in Spanish 'territory'. He reached the Philippines in 1521 but was killed in a skirmish there. One of his five ships, under the Basque navigator Juan Sebastián Elcano, reached the Spice Islands and then sailed home via the Cape of Good Hope, proving the earth was round.

As its explorers reached Timor, China and eventually Japan, Portugal cemented its power with garrison ports and trading posts. The monarchy, taking its 'royal fifth' of profits, became stinking rich – indeed the

1418	1419	1443	1494
Shipbuilding advances lead to the development of the *caravel*, a fast, agile ship that changed the face of sailing. Portuguese mariners put it to brilliant use on long voyages of exploration.	Portuguese sailors discover Madeira. More discoveries follow suit, including the Azores in 1427 and Cape Verde Islands in 1460. Explorers also chart the west coast of Africa.	Explorers bring the first African slaves to Portugal; it marks the beginning of a long, dark era of slavery in Europe and later the new world.	The race for colonial expansion is on: Spain and Portugal carve up the world, with the Treaty of Tordesillas drawing the line 370 leagues west of Cape Verde.

Exploration by the Portuguese

NORTH AMERICA

ATLANTIC OCEAN

PACIFIC OCEAN

SOUTH AMERICA

Brazil

Cape Horn

Demarcation Line Dividing the World (Treaty of Tordesillas in 1494)

Azores

Madeira

Portugal

Ceuta

EUROPE

AFRICA

Cape Verde Islands

São Jorge da Minta

São Tomé & Príncipe

ATLANTIC OCEAN

Congo

Angola

Mombasa

Malindi

Mozambique

Cape of Good Hope

SOUTHERN OCEAN

ASIA

Hormoz

India

Goa

Cochin

INDIAN OCEAN

China

Macau

Japan

PACIFIC OCEAN

AUSTRALIA

1. Gomes & de Noli (1460)
2. Cão (1482–85)
3. Dias (1487–88)
4. Vasco da Gama (1497–99)
5. Cabral (1500)
6. Albuquerque (1503–15)
7. Magellan & Elcano (1519–22) – for Spain
8. Melgueiro (1660)

INDIA AHOY!

Fed up with the Venetian monopoly on overland trade with Asia, Portuguese explorer Vasco da Gama set sail from Lisbon in 1497 for distant shores, with a motley crew aboard his handsome caravel. He skirted the coast of Mozambique and Mombasa before finally washing up on the shore of Calicut, India, in May 1498. The bedraggled crew received a frosty welcome from the Zamorin (Hindu ruler) and when tensions flared, they returned from whence they came. The voyage was hardly plain sailing – monsoon tides were fraught with danger, scurvy was rife and more than half of Vasco da Gama's party perished. For his pains and success at discovering a sea route to India, Manuel I made him a lord when he returned in 1499 and he was hailed 'Admiral of the Indian Ocean'.

But in 1502, mounting hostilities (with Muslim merchants who considered da Gama a rival) meant the Portuguese sea captain was forced to return to establish control. No more mister nice guy, he seized an Arab ship and set it alight with hundreds of merchants onboard, then banished Muslims from the port. He returned to Europe with coffers full of silk and spices. Luís Vaz de Camões recounts the fascinating adventures of Portugal's *facundo Capitão* (eloquent captain) in the epic poem *The Lusiads*.

wealthiest monarchy in Europe, and the lavish Manueline architectural style symbolised the exuberance of the age.

It couldn't last, of course. By the 1570s the huge cost of expeditions and maintaining an empire was taking its toll. Young, idealistic Sebastião took the throne, and the final straw came in 1578 when, determined to take Christianity to Morocco, he rallied a force of 18,000 and set sail from Lagos, to be disastrously defeated at the Battle of Alcácer-Quibir (also known as the Battle of Three Kings). Sebastião and 8000 others were killed, including much of the Portuguese nobility. His aged successor, Cardinal Henrique, drained the royal coffers ransoming those captured.

On Henrique's death in 1580, Sebastião's uncle, Felipe II of Spain (Felipe I of Portugal), fought for and won the throne. This marked the end of centuries of independence, Portugal's golden age and its glorious moment on the world stage.

Spain's Rule & Portugal's Revival

Spanish rule began promisingly, with Felipe vowing to preserve Portugal's autonomy and attend the long-ignored parliament. But commoners resented Spanish rule and held on to the dream that Sebastião was still alive (as he was killed abroad in battle, some citizens were in denial); pretenders continued to pop up until 1600. Though Felipe was honourable, his successors proved to be considerably less so, using Portugal to raise money and soldiers for Spain's wars overseas, and appointing Spaniards to govern Portugal.

An uprising in Catalonia gave fuel to Portugal's drive for independence (particularly when the Spanish King Felipe III ordered Portuguese troops to quell the uprising), and finally in 1640 a group of conspirators launched a coup. Nationalists drove the female governor of Portugal and her Spanish garrison from Lisbon. It was then that the duke of Bragança reluctantly stepped forward and was crowned João IV.

With a hostile Spain breathing down its neck, Portugal searched for allies. Two swift treaties with England led to Charles II's marriage to João's daughter, Catherine of Bragança, and the ceding of Tangier and Bombay to England.

In return the English promised arms and soldiers: however, a preoccupied Spain made only half-hearted attempts to recapture Portugal, and recognised Portuguese independence in 1668.

João IV's successors pursued largely absolutist policies (particularly under João V, an admirer of French King Louis XIV). The crown hardly bothered with parliament, and another era of profligate expenditure followed, giving birth to projects such as the wildly extravagant monastery-palace in Mafra.

Cementing power for the crown was one of Portugal's most revered (and feared) statesmen – the Marquês de Pombal, chief minister to the epicurean Dom José I (the latter more interested in opera than political affairs). Described as an enlightened despot, Pombal dragged Portugal into the modern era, crushing opposition with brutal efficiency.

Pombal set up state monopolies, curbed the power of British merchants and boosted agriculture and industry. He abolished slavery and distinctions between traditional and New Christians (Iberian Muslims and Jews who converted to Christianity), and overhauled education.

When Lisbon suffered a devastating earthquake in 1755, Pombal swiftly rebuilt the city. He was by then at the height of his power, and succeeded in dispensing with his main enemies by implicating them in an attempt on the king's life.

He might have continued had it not been for the accession of the devout Dona Maria I in 1777. The anticlerical Pombal was promptly sacked, tried and charged with various offences, though never imprisoned. While his religious legislation was repealed, his economic, agricultural and educational policies were largely maintained, helping the country back towards prosperity.

But turmoil was once again on the horizon, as Napoleon swept through Europe.

TREATY OF WINDSOR

The Treaty of Windsor (1386), which established a pact of mutual assistance between Portugal and England, is widely considered to be the oldest-surviving alliance in the world.

1578	1580	1622	1640
King Sebastião raises an army and invades Morocco. The expedition ends at the Battle of Alcácer-Quibir. Sebastião and many nobles are killed; the king leaves no heir, destabilising the country.	Sebastião's weak successor, the former cardinal Henrique, dies. King Felipe II of Spain invades Portugal and becomes king. Spain will rule for 80 years, draining Portugal's coffers and ending its golden age.	Portugal's empire is slipping out of Spain's grasp. The English seize Hormoz. Later, in the 1650s, the Dutch take Malacca, Ceylon (Sri Lanka) and part of Brazil.	When Catalonia rebels against the oppressive monarchy, Felipe III sends Portuguese troops to quell the uprising. Portuguese noblemen stage a coup and overthrow Spain. Dom João IV is crowned.

A DEVASTATING EARTHQUAKE

Lisbon in the 1700s was a thriving city, with gold flowing in from Brazil, a thriving merchant class and grand Manueline architecture. Then on the morning of 1 November 1755, a devastating earthquake levelled much of the city, which fell like a pack of dominoes, never to regain its former status; palaces, libraries, art galleries, churches and hospitals were razed to the ground. Tens of thousands died, crushed beneath falling masonry, drowned in the tsunami that swept in from the Tejo or burned in the fires that followed.

Enter the formidable, unflappable, geometrically minded Marquês de Pombal. As Dom José I's chief minister, the Marquês de Pombal swiftly set about reconstructing the city, good to his word to 'bury the dead and heal the living'. In the wake of the disaster, the autocratic statesman not only kept the country's head above water as it was plunged into economic chaos, but he also managed to propel Lisbon into the modern era.

Together with military engineers and architects Eugenio dos Santos and Manuel da Maia, the Marquês de Pombal played a pivotal role in reconstructing the city in a simple, cheap, earthquake-proof way that created today's formal grid, and Pombaline style was born. The antithesis of rococo, Pombaline architecture was functional and restrained: azulejos (tiles) and decorative elements were used sparingly, building materials were prefabricated, and wide streets and broad plazas were preferred.

Dom José I, for his part, escaped the earthquake unscathed. Instead of being at residence in the royal palace, he had ridden out of town to Belém, with his extensive retinue. After seeing the devastation, the eccentric José I refused to live in a masonry building ever again, and he set up a royal residence made of wood outside of town, on the hills of Ajuda, north of Belém. What was known as the Real Barraca (Royal Tent), became the site of the Ajuda Palace (Palácio Nacional de Ajuda; p80) after the king's death.

The Dawn of a Republic

In 1793 Portugal found itself at war again when it joined Britain in sending naval forces against revolutionary France. Before long, Napoleon threw Portugal an ultimatum: close your ports to British shipping or be invaded.

There was no way Portugal could turn its back on Britain, upon which it depended for half of its trade and the protection of its sea routes. In 1807 Portugal's royal family fled to Brazil (where it stayed for 14 years), and Napoleon's forces marched into Lisbon, sweeping Portugal into the Peninsular War (France's invasion of Spain and Portugal, which lasted until 1814).

To the rescue came Sir Arthur Wellesley (later Duke of Wellington), Viscount Beresford and their seasoned British troops, who eventually drove the French back across the Spanish border in 1811.

1690	1703	1717	1755
With the economy in tatters and the empire fading, the Portuguese pray for a miracle. The prayer is answered when gold is discovered in Brazil; incredible riches soon flow into the royal coffers.	France and Britain are at war. Facing (disastrous!) wine shortages, the English sign a new treaty with Portugal, and become a major player in the Portuguese economy, with port production growing exponentially.	Brazilian gold production nears its peak, with over 600,000oz imported annually. Dom João V becomes Europe's richest monarch, lavishing wealth on ostentatious projects like Mafra Palace.	Lisbon suffers Europe's biggest natural disaster in recorded history. On All Saint's Day, three massive earthquakes destroy the city, followed by a tsunami and ravaging fires that kill tens of thousands.

Free but weakened, Portugal was administered by Beresford while the royals dallied in Brazil. In 1810 Portugal lost a profitable intermediary role by giving Britain the right to trade directly with Brazil. The next humiliation was João's 1815 proclamation of Brazil as a kingdom united with Portugal – he did this to bring more wealth and prestige to Brazil (which he was growing to love) and, in turn, to him and the rest of the royal family residing there. With soaring debts and dismal trade, Portugal was at one of the lowest points in its history, reduced to a de facto colony of Brazil and a protectorate of Britain.

Meanwhile, resentment simmered in the army. Rebel officers quietly convened parliament and drew up a new liberal constitution. Based on Enlightenment ideals, it abolished many rights of the nobility and clergy, and instituted a single-chamber parliament.

Faced with this fait accompli, João returned and accepted its terms – though his wife and son, Miguel, were bitterly opposed to it. João's elder son, Pedro, had other ideas: left behind to govern Brazil, he snubbed the constitutionalists by declaring Brazil independent in 1822 and himself its emperor. When João died in 1826, the stage was set for civil war.

Offered the crown, Pedro dashed out a new, less liberal charter and then abdicated in favour of his seven-year-old daughter, Maria, provided she marry uncle Miguel and provided uncle Miguel accept the new constitution. Miguel took the oath but promptly abolished Pedro's charter and proclaimed himself king. A livid Pedro rallied the equally furious liberals and forced Miguel to surrender at Évoramonte in 1834.

After Pedro's death, his daughter Maria, now queen of Portugal at just 15, kept his flame alive with fanatical support of his 1826 charter. The radical supporters of the liberal 1822 constitution grew vociferous over the next two decades, bringing the country to the brink of civil war. The Duke of Saldanha, however, saved the day, negotiating a peace that toned down Pedro's charter, while still radically modernising Portugal's infrastructure.

The latter half of the 19th century was a remarkable period for Portugal, and it became known as one of the most advanced societies in southern Europe. Casual visitors to Lisbon, such as Hans Christian Andersen, were surprised to find tree-lined boulevards with gas street lamps, efficient trams and well-dressed residents. Social advances were less anecdotal. The educational reformer João Arroio dramatically increased the number of schools, doubling the number of boys' schools and quadrupling the number of girls' schools. Women gained the right to own property; slavery was abolished throughout the Portuguese empire, as was the death penalty; and even the prison system received an overhaul – prisoners were taught useful trades while in jail so they could integrate into society upon their release.

CUP OF TEA?

It was the Portuguese who started England's obsession with tea: their explorers introduced it to Europe in the mid-17th century and tea enthusiast Catherine of Bragança did the rest.

1770	1803	1807	1815
The king's powerful prime minister, the Marquês de Pombal, rebuilds Lisbon following a modern grid. He abolishes slavery, builds schools and develops the economy, crushing those in his way.	Britain and France are again at war. Portugal sides with Britain and refuses Napoleon's call to close its ports to the British. French troops are on the march across Iberia.	Napoleon invades Portugal. The Portuguese royal family and several thousand in their retinue pack up their belongings and set sail for Brazil. British warships guard their passage.	Having fallen hard for Brazil, Dom João VI declares Rio the capital of the United Kingdom of Portugal and Brazil and the Algarves, relegating Lisbon to second-class status.

Professional organisations, such as the Literary Guild, emerged and became a major impetus to the advancement of ideas in public discourse, inspiring debate in politics, religious life and the art world.

As elsewhere in Europe, this was also a time of great industrial growth, with a dramatic increase in textile production, much of it to be exported. Other major works included the building of bridges and a nationwide network of roads, as well as a flourish of major architectural works such as the Pena Palace above Sintra.

However, by 1900 the tides of discontent among workers began to grow. With increased mechanisation, workers began losing jobs (some factory owners began hiring children to operate the machines), and their demand for fair working conditions went unanswered. Those who went on strike were simply fired and replaced. At the same time, Portugal experienced a dramatic demographic shift: rural areas were increasingly depopulated in favour of cities, and emigration (especially to Brazil) snowballed.

Much was changing, and more and more people began to look towards socialism as a cure for the country's inequalities. Nationalist republicanism swept through the lower-middle classes, spurring an attempted coup in 1908. It failed, but the following month King Carlos and Crown Prince Luis Filipe were brutally assassinated in Lisbon.

Carlos' younger son, Manuel II, tried feebly to appease republicans, but it was too little, too late. On 5 October 1910, after an uprising by military officers, a republic was declared. Manuel, dubbed 'the Unfortunate', sailed into exile in Britain where he died in 1932.

The Rise & Fall of Salazar

After a landslide victory in the 1911 elections, hopes were high among republicans for dramatic changes ahead, but the tides were against them. The economy was in tatters, an issue only exacerbated by an economically disastrous decision to join the Allies in WWI. In postwar years the chaos deepened: republican factions squabbled, unions led strikes and were repressed, and the military grew more powerful.

The new republic soon had a reputation as Europe's most unstable regime. Between 1910 and 1926 there were an astonishing 45 changes of government, often resulting from military intervention. Another coup in 1926 brought forth new names and faces, most significantly António de Oliveira Salazar, a finance minister who would rise up through the ranks to become prime minister in 1932 – a post he would hold for the next 36 years.

Salazar hastily enforced his 'New State' – a corporatist republic that was nationalistic, Catholic, authoritarian and essentially repressive. All political parties were banned except for the loyalist National

Some historians believe Portuguese explorers reached Australia in the 1500s, 250 years before its 'official' discoverer, Captain James Cook. For the inside scoop, read Kenneth McIntyre's *The Secret Discovery of Australia* (1977).

PORTUGUESE AUSTRALIA?

1822		1832 ⟩	1865 ⟩
In Brazil – after his father, Dom João VI, returns to Portugal, to reclaim his crown – Prince Regent Pedro leads a coup d'état and declares Brazilian independence with himself the new 'emperor'.		Dom Pedro I returns to Portugal where he must contest his throne with his brother Miguel. Two years of civil war end with Miguel's banishment. Dom Pedro's daughter becomes queen.	Portugal enjoys a period of peace and prosperity. Railways connect villages with Lisbon and Porto, now cities enriched by maritime trade. Advancements are made in industry, agriculture, health and education.

➡ Dom Pedro I statue

Union, which ran the show, and the National Assembly. Strikes were banned and propaganda, censorship and brute force kept society in order. The sinister new secret police, Polícia Internacional e de Defesa do Estado (PIDE), inspired terror and suppressed opposition by imprisonment and torture. Various attempted coups during Salazar's rule came to nothing. For a chilling taste of life as a political prisoner under Salazar, you could visit the 16th-century Fortaleza at Peniche – used as a jail by the dictator.

The only good news was a dramatic economic turnaround. Through the 1950s and 1960s Portugal experienced an annual industrial growth rate of 7% to 9%.

Internationally, the wily Salazar played two hands, unofficially supporting Franco's nationalists in the Spanish Civil War, and allowing British

BEWARE THE ECONOMICS PROFESSOR

When General António Carmona was named Portugal's president in 1926, he inherited a country in serious debt. Fearing economic catastrophe, Carmona called in an expert, a man by the name of António de Oliveira Salazar. At the time, Salazar was a 37-year-old bachelor, sharing spartan quarters with a priest (who would later become cardinal of Lisbon). Salazar himself was no stranger to religious life. He spent eight years studying to become a priest, and some residents from his small native village even called him 'father' on his visits. Only a last-minute decision led him to veer into law instead.

One of the country's first economists, Salazar garnered wide respect for his articles on public finance. When General Carmona approached him with the job of finance minister, Salazar accepted on one condition: that the spending of all government ministries fall under his discretion. The general agreed.

Salazar achieved enormous success at firing up the national economy. He severely curtailed government spending, raising taxes and balancing the budget during his first year. Unemployment decreased significantly. Salazar quickly became one of Carmona's star ministers. He also took on adjoining posts as other ministers resigned. In this way he consolidated power until Carmona eventually named him prime minister.

Salazar set the tone for civilian life that would last for many decades to come. Under his authoritarian rule, he did bring stability and prosperity to the country, though at enormous cost: censorship, imprisonment and, in some cases, torture of political opponents. Among his most damning attributes was his attitude towards the working class. He believed in giving them a diet of 'fado, Fátima and football' to keep them happily compliant, but had no intention of bettering their lot; at the end of his rule, Portugal had the highest rate of illiteracy and tuberculosis in Western Europe, and women were still not allowed to vote. Given the socially backward condition of the nation when Salazar relinquished power, the advancements of the last 40 years seem all the more startling.

1890	1900	1908	1910
Portugal takes a renewed interest in its African colonies. Britain wants control of sub-Saharan Africa, and threatens Portugal with war. Cowed, Portugal withdraws, causing a crisis at home.	The republican movement gains force. The humiliating Africa issue is one among many grievances against the crown. Others include rising unemployment and growing social inequalities.	The Braganças fail to silence antimonarchist sentiment by shutting down newspapers, exiling dissidents and brutally suppressing demonstrations. King Carlos and his eldest son, Luís Filipe, are assassinated.	King Carlos' younger son, 18-year-old Manuel, takes the throne but is soon ousted. Portugal is declared a republic. Chaos rules, and the country will see 45 different governments in 16 years.

use of Azores airfields during WWII despite official neutrality (and illegal sales of tungsten to Germany). It was later discovered that Salazar had also authorised the transfer of Nazi-looted gold to Portugal – 44 tonnes according to Allied records.

Officially neutral in WWII, Portugal was a major intersection of both Allied and Nazi spying operations. British secret-service agents based there included Graham Greene, Ian Fleming and double agent Kim Philby.

But it was something else that finally brought the Salazarist era to a close – decolonisation. Refusing to relinquish the colonies, he was faced with ever more costly and unpopular military expeditions. In 1961 Goa was occupied by India, and nationalists rose up in Angola. Guerrilla movements also appeared in Portuguese Guinea and Mozambique.

Salazar, however, didn't have to face the consequences. In 1968 he had a stroke, and died two years later.

His successor, Marcelo Caetano, failed to ease unrest. Military officers sympathetic to African freedom fighters grew reluctant to fight colonial wars – the officers had seen the horrible living conditions in which the colony lived beneath the Portuguese authorities. Several hundred officers formed the Movimento das Forças Armadas (MFA), which on 25 April 1974 carried out a nearly bloodless coup, later nicknamed the Revolution of the Carnations (after victorious soldiers stuck carnations in their rifle barrels). Carnations are still a national symbol of freedom.

From Revolution to Democracy

Despite the coup's popularity, the following year saw unprecedented chaos. It began where the revolution had begun – in the African colonies. Independence was granted immediately to Guinea-Bissau, followed by the speedy decolonisation of the Cape Verde islands, São Tomé e Príncipe, Mozambique and Angola.

The word Portugal comes from Portus Cale, a name the Romans gave to a town near present-day Porto. The word morphed into Portucale under Visigoth rule and expanded significantly in meaning.

The transition wasn't smooth: civil war racked Angola, and East Timor, freshly liberated in 1975, was promptly invaded by Indonesia. Within Portugal, too, times were turbulent, with almost a million refugees from African colonies flooding into Portugal.

The country was an economic mess, with widespread strikes and a tangle of political ideas and parties. The communists and a radical wing of the MFA launched a revolutionary movement, nationalising firms and services. Peasant farmers seized land to establish communal farms that failed because of in-fighting and poor management. While revolutionaries held sway in the south, the conservative north was led by Mário Soares and his Partido Socialista (PS; Socialist Party).

It took a more moderate government, formed in 1975, to unite the country after a coup by radical leftists was crushed. At last, the revolution had ended.

1916	1932	1935	1943
Despite initial neutrality, Portugal gets drawn into the WWI, and sends 55,000 troops; nearly 10,000 perish. The war effort is devastating for the economy, creating a long postwar recession.	António de Oliveira Salazar seizes power. The Portuguese economy grows but at enormous human cost. Salazar uses censorship, imprisonment and torture to silence his opponents.	The largely unpublished 47-year-old poet Fernando Pessoa dies, leaving a trunk containing a staggering collection of writing. Critics later describe him as one of the greatest poets of the 20th century.	Portugal, neutral during WWII, becomes a crossroads for intelligence activities of Allied and Axis operatives. Salazar works both sides, selling tungsten to the Nazis while allowing Britain use of airfields.

The Rocky Road to Stability

Portugal was soon committed to a blend of socialism and democracy, with a powerful president, an elected assembly and a Council of the Revolution to control the armed forces.

Mário Soares' minority government soon faltered, prompting a series of attempts at government by coalitions and nonparty candidates, including Portugal's first female prime minister, Maria de Lourdes Pintasilgo. In the 1980 parliamentary elections a new political force took the reins – the conservative Aliança Democrática (AD; Democratic Alliance), led by Francisco de Sá Carneiro.

After Carneiro's almost immediate (and suspicious) death in a plane crash, Francisco Pinto Balsemão stepped into his shoes. He implemented plans to join the European Community (EC).

It was partly to keep the EC and the International Monetary Fund (IMF) happy that a new coalition government under Soares and Balsemão implemented a strict programme of economic modernisation. Not surprisingly, the belt-tightening wasn't popular. The loudest critics were Soares' right-wing partners in the Partido Social Democrata (PSD; Social Democrat Party), led by the dynamic Aníbal Cavaco Silva. Communist trade unions organised strikes, and the appearance of urban terrorism by the radical left-wing Forças Populares de 25 Abril (FP-25) deepened unrest.

In 1986, after nine years of negotiations, Portugal joined the EC. Flush with new funds, it raced ahead of its neighbours with unprecedented economic growth. The new cash flow also gave Prime Minister Cavaco Silva the power to push ahead with radical economic reforms. These included labour law reforms that left many workers disenchanted; the 1980s were crippled by strikes – including one involving 1.5 million workers – though all to no avail. The controversial legislation was eventually passed.

Unfortunately, however, the economic growth wouldn't last. In 1992 EC trade barriers fell and Portugal suddenly faced new competition. Fortunes dwindled as recession set in, and disillusionment grew as Europe's single market revealed the backwardness of Portugal's agricultural sector.

Strikes, crippling corruption charges and student demonstrations over rising fees only undermined the PSD further, leading to Cavaco Silva's resignation in 1995. The general elections in 1995 brought new faces to power, with the socialist António Guterres taking over power. Despite hopes for a different and less conservative administration, it was business as usual, with Guterres maintaining the budgetary rigour that qualified Portugal for the European Economic & Monetary Union (EMU) in 1998. Indeed, for a while Portugal was a star EMU performer

---

HISTORY THE ROCKY ROAD TO STABILITY

The law allowing all Portuguese women to vote was only established in 1975.

Former Colonies & Year of independence

Brazil, 1822

Goa, 1961

Guinea-Bissau, 1974

Angola, 1975

Cape Verde, 1975

Mozambique, 1975

São Tomé e Príncipe, 1975

East Timor, 1975

Macau, 1999

1961	1974	1986	1998
The last vestiges of Portugal's empire begin to crumble as India seizes Goa. Independence movements are underway in the former African colonies of Angola, Mozambique and Guinea-Bissau.	Army officers overthrow Salazar's successor in the Revolution of the Carnations. Portugal veers to the left, and communists and moderates struggle for power in the unstable country.	In a narrow second-round victory, Mário Soares is elected president of Portugal, becoming its first civilian head of state in 60 years. The same year, Portugal joins the EC along with Spain.	José Saramago receives the Nobel Prize in Literature for his darkly humorous tales about ordinary characters facing fantastical obstacles. A lifelong communist, his work was condemned by the church.

Portugal only narrowly missed claiming Europe's first female prime minister: in 1979 Margaret Thatcher snatched the honour just three months before Maria de Lourdes Pintasilgo (1930–2004).

producing steady economic growth that helped Guterres win a second term. But it didn't last. Corruption scandals, rising inflation and a faltering economy soon spelt disaster. Portugal slipped into economic stagnation by the dawn of the 21st century. The next 10 years were ones of hardship for the Portuguese economy, which saw little or negative GDP growth, and rising unemployment from 2001 to 2010. As elsewhere in Europe, Portugal took a massive hit during the global financial crisis. Ultimatums from the EU governing body to rein in its debt (to avoid a Greece-style meltdown) have meant that the Portuguese government has had to institute unpopular austerity measures – pension reform, raising taxes, public sector hiring freezes – which have led to protests and strikes.

For more on the latest in Portugal, see Portugal Today (p462).

JAVIER LARREA / GETTY IMAGES ©

Oceanário (p83), Lisbon

1998
Lisbon hosts Expo 98, showcasing new developments, including Santiago Calatrava's cutting-edge train station, Europe's largest oceanarium and its longest bridge (Ponte de Vasco da Gama).

2004
Hosting the European Football Championship, Portugal makes it to the final only to be defeated in an agonising loss to Greece. Over €600 million is spent remodelling and constructing stadiums.

2013
Fed up with rising unemployment, soaring taxes and a proposed €4 billion in government spending cuts, 1.5 million protestors take to the streets of Portugal.

Religion

Christianity has been a pivotal force in shaping Portugal's history, and religion still plays an important role in the lives of its people. Churches and cathedrals are sprinkled about every town and city across the country, and Portugal's biggest celebrations revolve around religious events, with a packed calendar of colourful parades and concerts held on important feast days. Portugal is also home to a number of pilgrimage sites, the most important of which, Fátima, attracts several million pilgrims each year.

Church & State

Portugal has a long and deep connection to the church. Even during the long rule of the Moors, Christianity flourished in the north – which provided a strategic base for Christian crusaders to retake the kingdom. Cleric and king walked hand in hand, from the earliest papal alliances of the 11th century through to the 17th century, when the church played a role both at home and in Portugal's expanding empire.

Things ran smoothly until the 18th century, when the Marquês de Pombal, a man of the Enlightenment, wanted to curtail the power of the church – specifically the Jesuits, whom he expelled in 1759. He also sought to modernise the Portuguese state (overseeing one of the world's first urban 'grid' systems) and brought education under the state's control. State–church relations see-sawed over the next 150 years, with power struggles including the outright ban of religious orders in 1821, and the seizing by the state of many church properties.

The separation of church and state was formally recognised during the First Republic (1910–26). But in practice the church remained intimately linked to many aspects of life. Health and education were largely under the domain of the church, with Catholic schools and hospitals the

Portugal's favourite holy man, Santo António, is the go-to for lonely hearts. Unmarried women and men light candles to him to find love, and on his feast day in June, Lisbon hosts free mass marriages for those too poor to spring for a private celebration.

LIFE UNDER MUSLIM RULE

The Moors ruled southern Portugal for almost 400 years, and some scholars describe that time as a golden age. The Arabs introduced irrigation, previously unknown in Europe. Two Egyptian agronomists came to Iberia in the 10th century and wrote manuals on land management, animal husbandry, plant and crop cultivation and irrigation designs. They introduced bananas, rice, coconuts, maize and sugar cane. They also encouraged small-scale cooperatives – in olive-oil and wine production, and food markets – which are still embraced in many parts of Portugal.

The Moors opened schools and set about campaigns to achieve mass literacy (in Arabic, of course), as well as the teaching of mathematics, geography and history. Medicine reached new levels of sophistication. There was also a degree of religious tolerance that evaporated when the Christian crusaders came to power. Much to the chagrin of Christian slave owners, slavery was not permitted in the Islamic kingdom – making it a refuge for runaway slaves. Muslims, Christians and Jews all peacefully coexisted – at times even collaborated together, creating one of the most scientifically and artistically advanced societies the world had ever known up until that time.

norm. Social outlets for those in rural areas were mostly church-related. And the completion of any public-works project always included a blessing by the local bishop.

In 1932 António de Oliveira Salazar swept into power, establishing a Mussolini-like *Estado Novo* (New State) that lasted until the Carnation Revolution of 1974. Salazar had strong ties to the Catholic church – he spent eight years studying for the priesthood before switching to law. His college roommate was a priest who later became the Cardinal Patriarch of Lisbon. Salazar was a ferocious anticommunist, and used Roman Catholic references to appeal to people's sense of authority, order and discipline. He described the family, parish and larger institution of Christianity as the foundations of the state. Church officials who spoke out against him were silenced or forced into exile.

Following the 1974 revolution, the church found itself out of favour with many Portuguese; its support of the Salazar regime spelled its undoing in the topsy-turvy days following the government's collapse. The new constitution, ratified in 1976, again emphasised the formal separation of church and state, although this time the law had teeth, and Portugal quickly transitioned into a more secular society. Today, only about half of all weddings happen inside a church. Divorce is legal, as is abortion (up to 10 weeks; a law that went into effect following a 2007 referendum). In 2010 same-sex marriage was legalised, making Portugal the sixth European nation to permit it (with several other nations joining the ranks in recent years).

The Inquisition

'After the earthquake, which had destroyed three-fourths of the city of Lisbon, the sages of that country could think of no means more effectual to preserving the kingdom from utter ruin than to entertain the people with an auto-da-fé, it having been decided by the University of Coimbra that burning a few people alive by a slow fire, and with great ceremony, is an infallible secret for preventing earthquakes.'

Candide *(Voltaire, 1759)*

One of the darkest episodes in Portugal's history, the Inquisition was a campaign of church-sanctioned terror and execution that began in 1536 and lasted for 200 years, though it was not officially banned until 1821. It was initially aimed at Jews who were either expelled from Portugal or forced to renounce their faith. Those who didn't embrace Catholicism risked facing the auto-da-fé (act of faith), a church ceremony consisting of a Mass, a procession of the guilty, the reading of their sentences and later, their burning at the stake.

'Trials' took place in public squares in Lisbon, Porto, Évora and Coimbra in front of crowds sometimes numbering in the thousands. At the centre atop a large canopied platform sat the Grand Inquisitor, surrounded by his staff of aristocrats, priests, bailiffs, torturers and scribes, who meticulously recorded the proceedings.

The victims usually spent years in prison, often undergoing crippling torture, before seeing the light of day. They stood accused of a wide variety of crimes – such as skipping meals on Jewish fast days (signs of 'unreformed' Jews), leaving pork uneaten on the plate, failing to attend mass or observe the Sabbath, as well as straight-up blasphemy, witchcraft and homosexuality. No matter how flimsy the 'evidence' – often delivered to the tribunal by a grudge-bearing neighbour – very few were found innocent and released. After a decade or so in prison, the condemned were finally brought to their auto-da-fé. Before meeting their judgement, they were

AUTO-DA-FÉ

The last auto-da-fé was held in 1765, which ironically enough was levied against 10 Jesuit priests who dared oppose the autocratic and anticlerical Marquês de Pombal.

dressed in a *san benito* (yellow penitential gown painted with flames) and *coroza* (a high conical cap) and brought before the tribunal.

After the sentence was pronounced, judgement was carried out in a different venue. By dawn the next morning, for instance, executioners would lead the condemned to a killing field outside town. Those who repented were strangled first before being burned at the stake. The unrepentant were simply burned alive.

During the years of the Inquisition, the church executed over 2000 victims and tortured or exiled tens of thousands more. The Portuguese even exported the auto-da-fé to the colonies – burning Hindus at the stake in Goa, for instance.

As Voltaire sardonically suggested, superstition played no small part in the auto-da-fé. Some believers thought that the earthquake of 1755 was the wrath of God upon them – and that they were being punished not for their bloody auto-da-fés, but because the Holy Office hadn't done quite enough to punish the heretics.

The Apparitions at Fátima

For many Portuguese Catholics, Fátima represents one of the most momentous religious events of the 20th century, and it transformed a tiny village into a major pilgrimage site for Catholics across the globe. On 13 May 1917, 10-year-old Lúcia Santos and her two younger cousins, Jacinta and Francisco Marto, were out tending their parents' flocks in the fields outside the village of Fátima. Suddenly a bolt of lighting struck the earth, and a woman 'brighter than the sun' appeared before them. According to Santos, she came to them with a message exhorting people to pray and do penance to save sinners. She asked the children to pray the rosary every day, which she said was key to bringing peace to one's own life and to the world. At the time, peace was certainly on the minds of many Portuguese, with the country already deeply enmeshed in WWI. She then told the children to come again on the 13th of each month, at the same time and place, and that in October she would reveal herself to them.

Word of the alleged apparition spread, although most who heard the tale of the shepherd children reacted with scepticism. Only a handful of observers came to the field for the 13 June appearance, but on the month following several thousand showed up. That's when the apparition apparently entrusted the children with three secrets. In the weeks that followed, a media storm raged, with the government accusing the

Portugal still has a few good old-fashioned pagan celebrations. The most famous is the *Festa dos Rapazes* (Festival of the Lads), which features young men in rags and wooden masks rampaging around Miranda do Douro.

FESTIVAL OF THE LADS

CRYPTO JEWS

When Manuel I banned the practice of Judaism, most Jews fled or converted. Some however, simply hid their faith from public view and wore the facade of being a New Christian (the name given to Jewish converts). Religious ceremonies were held behind closed doors, with the Sabbath lamp placed at the bottom of a clay jar so that it could not be seen from outside. Within their Catholic prayer books they composed Jewish prayers, and even overlaid Jewish prayers over Catholic rituals (like the making of the sign of the cross). Clever food preparations also helped hide their faith, such as the eating of pork-free *alheiras,* which were seasoned garlicky sausages made of a mixture of chicken, rabbit, partridge or veal mixed with bread dough for consistency.

One Crypto Jewish community in Belmonte managed to maintain its faith in hiding for over 400 years, and was only revealed in 1917. Through centuries of endogamy (intermarriages), many of the 200 Jews in this community suffer from hereditary diseases. No longer underground (Belmonte now has its own synagogue and Jewish cemetery), they still remain quite secretive about the practices they maintained in hiding.

FAITH ON THE DECLINE

The percentage of Portuguese who consider themselves Catholics (around 85%) ranks among the highest in Western Europe. The number of the faithful, however, has been on a steady decline since the 1970s, when over 95% of the nation was Catholic. Today nearly half a million residents describe themselves as agnostic, and less than 20% of the population are practising Catholics.

Regional differences reveal a more complicated portrait: around half of northern Portugal's population still attend Sunday Mass, as do more than a quarter in Lisbon – with noticeably fewer churchgoers on the southern coast.

Religious Events

Semana Santa, Braga

Festa de São João, Porto & Braga

Festa de Santo António, Lisbon

Fátima Romaris, Fátima

Romaria de Nossa Senhora d'Agonia, Viana do Castelo

Festa de Nossa Senhora dos Remédios, Lamego

church of fabricating an elaborate hoax to revive its flagging popularity. The church for its part didn't know how to react. The children were even arrested and interrogated at one point, but the three refused to change their story.

On 13 October 1917, some 70,000 gathered for what was to be the final appearance of the apparition. Many witnesses there experienced the so-called Miracle of the Sun, where the sun seemed to grow in size and dance in the sky, becoming a whirling disc of fire, shooting out multi-coloured rays. Some spoke of being miraculously healed; others were frightened by the experience; still others claimed they saw nothing at all. The three children claimed they saw Mary, Jesus and Joseph in the sky. Newspapers across the country reported on the event, and soon a growing hysteria surrounded it.

Only Lúcia made it into adulthood. Jacinta and Francisco, both beatified by the church in 2000, were two of the more than 20 million killed during the 1918 influenza epidemic. Lúcia later became a Carmelite nun and died at the age of 97 on 13 February 2007.

The Three Secrets

Much mystery surrounds the three secrets told to the children at Fátima on 13 July 1917. Lúcia revealed the first two in 1941 at the request of the Bishop of Leira, who was publishing a book on Jacinta. The first secret depicted a vision of demons and human souls suffering in the fires of hell. The second secret predicted that an even more disastrous war would follow WWI should the world – and in particular Russia – not convert. Given months before the Bolshevik takeover in St Petersburg, this secret was considered particularly inflammatory, as it went on to say that if her call for repentance goes unheeded Russia will spread its terrors through the world, causing wars and persecution of the church. Lúcia was reluctant to reveal the third secret, claiming that she was told by the Virgin Mary never to reveal it. Stricken with illness and convinced she was going to die – and under pressure from the Bishop of Leira – Lúcia finally agreed to write the secret down in 1944.

The bishop who received the secret then passed it on to the Vatican, who kept it hidden away for decades. Lúcia requested that the last secret be revealed in 1960 or upon her death, whichever came first. She picked 1960 as she figured that by then the secret would be more clearly understood. The Vatican, however, had other plans and announced in 1960 that the secret would probably remain sealed forever. Fátima followers meanwhile offered wild speculations on what the third secret might reveal – from nuclear holocaust to WWIII, catastrophic global financial crisis, famine or the apocalypse. The church kept them in suspense until 2000, when it was finally revealed.

The last secret was the most mystical and controversial of the three. Lúcia described seeing an angel holding a flaming sword who pointed at the earth and cried out 'penance'. Then she saw a ruined city full of corpses and beyond that a steep mountain, up which climbed a bishop dressed in white – whom she took to be the pope. At the top he knelt before a cross made of rough-hewn tree trunks, and was killed by soldiers who gunned him down.

Some claim that this predicted the assassination attempt on Pope John Paul II in 1981. The attempt happened on 13 May – the anniversary of the apparitions – and the pope himself claimed the Virgin of Fátima saved him from death. (According to some reconstructions of the shooting, the assassin's bullet followed a bizarre elliptical path rather than a straight line, thereby avoiding the pope's vital organs.) Conspiracy theorists, meanwhile, claim that the church was hiding the 'real' third secret, which related to the apocalypse and a great apostasy within the church – a breakdown that begins at the top. Recent scandals, including the Catholic sex-abuse cases in various parts of the world, have only fuelled the speculation among some 'Fátimists' that the third secret has yet to be revealed.

Fátima Books & Films

The Fourth Secret of Fátima (2006), written by Antonio Socci

The 13th Day (2009), directed by Ian and Dominic Higgins

Miracle of Our Lady of Fátima (1952), directed by John Brahm

RELIGION THE APPARITIONS AT FÁTIMA

Architecture & the Arts

Portugal has a long and storied art history. Neolithic tribes, Celtic peoples, Romans, Visigoths, Moors and early Christian crusaders have all left their mark on the Iberian nation. Around 1500, the Age of Discoveries ushered in a rich era of grand cathedrals and lavish palaces. In the 500 years that followed, Portugal became a canvas for a dizzying array of architectural styles – Manueline, mannerist, baroque, art nouveau, modernist and postmodernist. Meanwhile, painters, sculptors, poets and novelists have all made contributions to Portugal's artistic heritage.

The Palaeolithic Palette

Prehistoric Relics

Vila Nova de Foz Côa, the Douro

Citânia de Briteiros, the Minho

Cromeleque dos Almendres, the Alentejo

A most mysterious group of 95 huge monoliths forms a strange circle in an isolated clearing among Alentejan olive groves near Évora. It's one of Europe's most impressive prehistoric sites: the Cromeleque dos Almendres.

All over Portugal, but especially in the Alentejo, you can visit such ancient funerary and religious structures, built during the Neolithic and Mesolithic eras. Most impressive are the dolmens: rectangular, polygonal or round funerary chambers, reached by a corridor of stone slabs and covered with earth to create an artificial mound. King of these is Europe's largest dolmen, the Anta Grande do Zambujeiro, near Évora, with six 6m-high stones forming a huge chamber. Single monoliths, or menhirs, often carved with phallic or religious symbols, also dot the countryside like an army of stone sentinels. Their relationship to promoting fertility seems obvious.

With the arrival of the Celts (800–200 BC) came the first established hilltop settlements, called *castros*. The best-preserved example is the Citânia de Briteiros in the Minho, where you can literally step into Portugal's past. Stone dwellings were built on a circular or elliptical plan, and the complex was surrounded with a dry-stone defensive wall. In the *citânias* (fortified villages) further south, dwellings tended to be rectangular.

The Romans

Roman Ruins

Conímbriga, the Beiras

Temple of Diana, Évora

Teatro Romano, Lisbon

Milreu, the Algarve

The Romans left Portugal their typical architectural and engineering feats – roads, bridges, towns complete with forums (marketplaces), villas, public baths and aqueducts. These have now largely disappeared from the surface, though the majority of Portugal's cities are built on Roman foundations. Today you can descend into dank foundations under new buildings in Lisbon and Évora, and see Roman fragments around Braga. At Conímbriga, the country's largest Roman site, an entire Roman town is under excavation. Revealed so far are some spectacular mosaics, along with structural or decorative columns, carved entablatures and classical ornamentation, giving a sense of the Roman high life.

Portugal's most famous and complete Roman ruin is the Templo Romano, the so-called Temple of Diana in Évora, with its flouncy-topped

Corinthian columns, nowadays echoed by the complementary towers of Évora cathedral. This is the finest temple of its kind on the Iberian Peninsula, its preservation the result of having been walled up in the Middle Ages and later used as a slaughterhouse.

Architectural Movements

Great Gothic

Cistercians introduced the Gothic trend, which reached its pinnacle in Alcobaça, in one of Portugal's most ethereally beautiful buildings. The austere abbey church and cloister of the Mosteiro de Santa Maria de Alcobaça, begun in 1178, has a lightness and simplicity strongly influenced by Clairvaux Abbey in France. Its hauntingly simple Cloisters of Silence were a model for later cathedral cloisters at Coimbra, Lisbon, Évora and many other places. This was the birth of Portuguese Gothic, which flowered and transmuted over the coming years as the country gained more and more experience of the outside world. For centuries Portugal had been culturally dominated and restricted by Spain and the Moors.

By the 14th century, when the Mosteiro de Santa Maria da Vitória (commonly known as Mosteiro da Batalha or Battle Abbey) was constructed, simplicity was a distant, vague memory. Portuguese, Irish and French architects worked on this breathtaking monument for more than two centuries. The combination of their skills and the changing architectural fashions of the times, from Flamboyant (late) Gothic to Renaissance and then Manueline, turned the abbey into a seething mass of carving, organic decorations, lofty spaces and slanting stained-glass light. It's a showcase of High Gothic art. It exults in the decorative (especially in its Gothic Royal Cloisters and Chapter House), while the flying buttresses tip their hat to English Perpendicular Gothic.

Secular architecture also enjoyed a Gothic boom, thanks to the need for fortifications against the Moors and to the castle-building fervour of the 13th-century ruler, Dom Dinis. Some of Portugal's most spectacular,

Gothic Sites

Mosteiro de Santa Maria de Alcobaça, Estremadura

Convento do Carmo, Lisbon

Mosteiro de Santa Maria da Vitória, Estremadura

A SERENDIPITOUS DISCOVERY

In 1989 researchers were studying the rugged valley of the Rio Côa, 15km from the Spanish frontier, to understand the environmental impact of a planned hydroelectric dam that was to flood the valley. In the course of their work, they made an extraordinary discovery: a number of petroglyphs (rock engravings) dating back tens of thousands of years.

Yet it wasn't until 1992, after dam construction was underway, that the importance of the find began to take root. Archaeologists came across whole clusters of petroglyphs, mostly dating from the Upper Palaeolithic period (10,000 to 40,000 years ago). Local people joined the search and the inventory of engravings soon grew into the thousands. In 1998 the future of the collection was safeguarded when Unesco designated the valley a World Heritage site.

Today Rio Côa (p395) holds one of the largest-known collections of open-air Palaeolithic art in the world. Archaeologists are still puzzling over the meaning of the engravings – and why this site was chosen. Most of the petroglyphs depict animals: stylised horses, aurochs (extinct ancestors of domesticated cattle) and long-horned ibex (extinct species of wild goat). Some animals are depicted with multiple heads – as if to indicate the animal in motion – while others are drawn so finely that they require artificial light to be seen. Later petroglyphs begin to depict human figures as well. The most intriguing engravings consist of overlapping layers, with successive artists adding their touches thousands of years after the first strokes were applied. A kind of Palaeolithic palimpsest in which generations of hunters worked and reworked the engravings of their forebears.

huddled, thick-walled castles – for example, Estremoz, Óbidos and Bragança – date from this time, many featuring massive double-perimeter walls and an inner square tower.

Manueline

Manueline is a uniquely Portuguese style: a specific, crazed flavour of late Gothic architecture. Ferociously decorative, it coincided roughly with the reign of Dom Manuel I (r 1495–1521) and is interesting not just because of its extraordinarily imaginative designs, burbling with life, but also because this dizzyingly creative architecture skipped hand in hand with the era's booming confidence.

During Dom Manuel's reign, Vasco da Gama and fellow explorers claimed new overseas lands and new wealth for Portugal. The Age of Discovery was expressed in sculptural creations of eccentric inventiveness, drawing heavily on nautical themes: twisted ropes, coral and anchors in stone, topped by the ubiquitous armillary sphere (a navigational device that became Dom Manuel's personal symbol) and the cross of the Order of Christ (symbol of the religious military order that largely financed and inspired Portugal's explorations).

Manueline first emerged in Setúbal's Igreja de Jesus, designed in the 1490s by French expatriate Diogo de Boitaca, who gave it columns like trees growing into the ceiling, and ribbed vaulting like twisted ropes. The style quickly caught on, and soon decorative carving was creeping, twisting and crawling over everything (aptly described by 19th-century English novelist William Beckford as 'scollops and twistifications').

Outstanding Manueline masterpieces are Belém's Mosteiro dos Jerónimos, masterminded largely by Diogo de Boitaca and João de Castilho; and Batalha's Mosteiro de Santa Maria da Vitória's otherworldly Capelas Imperfeitas (Unfinished Chapels).

Other famous creations include Belém's Torre de Belém, a Manueline-Moorish cake crossed with a chess piece by Francisco de Arruda, and his brother Diogo de Arruda's fantastical organic, seemingly barnacle-encrusted window in the Chapter House of Tomar's Convento de Cristo, as well as its fanciful 16-sided Charola – the Templar church, resembling an eerie *Star Wars* set. Many other churches sport a Manueline flourish against a plain facade.

The style was enormously resonant in Portugal, and reappeared in the early 20th century in exercises in mystical romanticism, such as Sintra's Quinta da Regaleira and Palácio Nacional da Pena, and Luso's over-the-top and extraordinary neo-Manueline Palace Hotel do Buçaco.

Baroque

With independence from Spain re-established and the influence of the Inquisition on the wane, Portugal burst out in baroque fever – an architectural style that was exuberant, theatrical and fired straight at the senses. Nothing could rival the Manueline flourish, but the baroque style – named after the Portuguese word for a rough pearl, *barroco* – cornered the market in flamboyance. At its height during the 18th century (almost a century later than in Italy), it was characterised by curvaceous forms, huge monuments, spatially complex schemes and lots and lots and lots of gold.

Financed by the 17th-century gold and diamond discoveries in Brazil, and encouraged by the extravagant Dom João V, local and foreign (particularly Italian) artists created mind-bogglingly opulent masterpieces. Prodigious *talha dourada* (gilded woodwork) adorn church interiors all over the place, but it reached its most extreme in Aveiro's Mosteiro de Jesus, Lisbon's Igreja de São Roque and Porto's Igreja de São Francisco.

Portugal has few Renaissance buildings, but some examples of the style are the Great Cloisters in Tomar's Convento de Cristo, designed by Spanish Diogo de Torralva in the late 16th century; the nearby Igreja de Nossa Senhora da Conceição; and the Convento de Bom Jesus at Valverde, outside Évora.

Manueline Sites

Mosteiro dos Jerónimos, Belém

Torre de Belém, Belém

Chapter House, Tomar

Igreja de Jesus, Setúbal

Baroque Sites

Palácio Nacional de Mafra, Mafra

Igreja de São Roque, Lisbon

Igreja de São Francisco, Porto

Palácio de Mateus, Vila Real

The baroque of central and southern Portugal was more restrained. Examples include the chancel of Évora's cathedral and the massive Palácio Nacional de Mafra. Designed by the German architect João Frederico Ludovice to rival the palace-monastery of San Lorenzo de El Escorial (near Madrid), the Mafra version is relatively sober, apart from its size – which is such that at one point it had a workforce of 45,000, looked after by a police force of 7000.

Meanwhile, the Tuscan painter and architect Nicolau Nasoni (who settled in Porto around 1725) introduced a more ornamental baroque style to the north. Nasoni is responsible for Porto's Torre dos Clérigos and Igreja da Misericórdia, and the whimsical Palácio de Mateus near Vila Real (internationally famous as the image on Mateus rosé wine bottles).

In the mid-18th century a school of architecture evolved in Braga. Local artists such as André Soares built churches and palaces in a very decorative style, heavily influenced by Augsburg engravings from southern Germany. Soares' Casa do Raio, in Braga, and much of the monumental staircase of the nearby Bom Jesus do Monte, are typical examples of this period's ornamentation.

Only when the gold ran out did the baroque fad fade. At the end of the 18th century, architects flirted briefly with rococo (best exemplified by Mateus Vicente's Palácio de Queluz, begun in 1747, or the palace at Estói) before embracing neoclassicism.

Alvaro Siza: Complete Works 1952–2013, by Philip Jodidio is an excellent monograph on the great contemporary architect, and includes a full catalogue of his work produced both in Portugal and abroad.

The Modern Era

The Salazar years favoured decidedly severe, Soviet-style, state commissions (eg Coimbra University's dull faculty buildings, which replaced elegant 18th-century neoclassical ones). Ugly buildings and apartment blocks rose on city outskirts. Notable exceptions dating from the 1960s are Lisbon's Palácio da Justiça in the Campolide district, and the glori-

TWO LEGENDARY ARCHITECTS

Porto is home to not one but two celebrated contemporary architects: Álvaro Siza Vieira (born 1933) and Eduardo Souto de Moura (born 1952). Both remain fairly unknown outside their home country, which is surprising given their loyal following among fellow architects and their long and distinguished careers. Both have earned the acclaimed Pritzker Prize, the Nobel of the architecture world (Siza Vieira in 1992; Souto de Moura in 2011). The two men are quite close, and they even have offices in the same building. They have collaborated on a handful of projects (prior to going out on his own, Souto de Moura also worked for Siza).

On the surface, Siza's work may seem less than dazzling. Stucco, stone, tile and glass are his building materials of choice. Place means everything in Siza Vieira's work, with geography and climate carefully considered before any plans are laid, regardless of the size or scale of the project. Many of his works reside outside the country, although the Serralves Museum of Contemporary Art in Porto and the cliffside Boa Nova Casa Chá near Matosinhos are two of his most famous works in Portugal.

Like Siza, Souto de Moura spurns flashy designs. His works feature minimalist but artful structures that utilize local building materials. The Braga stadium (the Estádio Municipal de Braga), built for the 2004 European football championship, is set in a former granite quarry (with granite from the site being used to make concrete for the structure). The rock walls of the quarry lie behind one goal; the other side opens to views of the city. Better known is Souto de Moura's design for the Paula Rego museum in Cascais. This work in red concrete is distinguished by its two pyramid-shaped towers, giving a modern reinterpretation to classic Portuguese shapes (which appear in chimneys, lighthouses, towers and in old palaces such as the Palacio Nacional de Sintra).

Modern Architecture

Casa da Música, Porto

Casa das Histórias Paula Rego, Cascais

Gare do Oriente, Lisbon

Torre Vasco da Gama, Lisbon

ously sleek Museu Calouste Gulbenkian. The beautiful wood-panelled Galeto cafe-restaurant is a time capsule from this era.

The tendency towards urban mediocrity continued after the 1974 revolution, although architects such as Fernando Távora and Eduardo Souto de Moura have produced impressive schemes. Lisbon's postmodern Amoreiras shopping complex, by Tomás Taveira, is another striking contribution.

Portugal's most prolific contemporary architect is Álvaro Siza Vieira. A believer in clarity and simplicity, his expressionist approach is reflected in projects such as the Pavilhão de Portugal for Expo 98, Porto's splendid Museu de Arte Contemporânea and the Igreja de Santa Maria at Marco de Canavezes, south of Amarante. He has also restored central Lisbon's historic Chiado shopping district with notable sensitivity, following a major fire in 1988.

Spanish architect Santiago Calatrava designed the lean organic monster Gare do Oriente for Expo 98, architecture that is complemented by the work of many renowned contemporary artists. The interior is more state-of-the-art spaceship than station. In the same area lies Lisbon's architectural trailblazer the Parque das Nações, with a bevy of unique designs, including a riverfront park and Europe's largest aquarium. The longest bridge in Europe, the Ponte de Vasco da Gama, built in 1998, stalks out across the Tagus river.

Since the turn of the millennium, Portugal has seen a handful of architecturally ambitious projects come to fruition. One of the grander projects is Rem Koolhaas' Casa da Música in Porto (2005). From a distance, the extremely forward-looking design appears like a solid white block of carefully cut crystal. Both geometric and defiantly asymmetrical, the building mixes elements of tradition (like *azulejos* hidden in one room) with high modernism (enormous curtains of corrugated glass flanking the concert stage).

PESSOA'S MANY PERSONALITIES

'There's no such man known as Fernando Pessoa', swore Alberto Caeiro, who, truth be told, didn't really exist himself. He was one of more than a dozen heteronyms (identities) adopted by Fernando Pessoa (1888–1935), Portugal's greatest 20th-century poet.

Heralded by literary critics as one of the icons of modernism, Pessoa was also among the stranger characters to wander the streets of Lisbon. He worked as a translator by day (having learned English while living in South Africa as a young boy), and wrote poetry by night – but not just Pessoa's poetry. He took on numerous personas, writing in entirely different styles, representing different philosophies, backgrounds and levels of mastery. Of Pessoa's four primary heteronyms, Alberto Caeiro was regarded as the great master by other heteronyms Alvaro de Campos and Ricardo Reis. (Fernando Pessoa was the fourth heteronym, but his existence, as alluded to earlier, was denied by the other three.) Any one style would have earned Pessoa renown as a major poet of his time, but considered together, the variety places him among the greats of modern literature.

Pessoa for many is inextricably linked to Lisbon. He spent his nights in cafes, writing, drinking and talking until late into the evening, and many of his works are set precisely in Lisbon's old neighbourhoods. Among Pessoa's phobias: lightning and having his photograph taken. You can see a few of the existing photos of him at the Café Martinho da Arcada, one of his regular haunts.

Despite his quirks and brilliance, Pessoa published very little in his lifetime, with his great work *Livro do Desassossego* (*Book of Disquietude*) only appearing in 1982, 50 years after it was written. In fact, the great bulk of Pessoa's work was discovered after his death: thousands of manuscript pages hidden away inside a wooden trunk. Scholars are still poring over his elusive works.

Literary Giants

In 2010, Portugal lost one of its greatest writers when José Saramago died at the age of 87. Known for his discursive, cynical and darkly humorous novels, Saramago gained worldwide attention after winning the Nobel Prize in 1998. His best works mine the depths of the human experience and are often set in a uniquely Portuguese landscape. Sometimes his quasi-magical tales revolve around historic events – like the Christian Siege of Lisbon or the building of the Mafra Palace – while at other times he takes on grander topics (writing, for instance, of Jesus' life as a fallible human being) or even creates modern-day fables (in *Blindness*, everyone on earth suddenly goes blind). As a self-described libertarian communist, Saramago's political views sometimes landed him in trouble. After his name was removed from a list of nominees for a European literary prize, he went into self-imposed exile, spending the last years of his life in the Canary Islands.

In the shadow of Saramago, António Lobo Antunes is Portugal's other literary great – and many of his admirers say the Nobel committee gave the prize to the wrong Portuguese writer. Antunes produces magical, fast-paced prose, often with dark undertones and vast historical sweeps; some critics compare his work to that of William Faulkner. Antunes' writing reflects his harrowing experience as a field doctor in Angola during Portugal's bloody colonial wars, and he often turns a critical gaze on Portuguese history – setting his novels around colonial wars, the dark days of dictatorship and the 1974 revolution. Slowly gaining an international following, Antunes is still active today, and many of his earlier novels have finally been translated into English.

The Sin of Father Amaro is a powerful 19th-century novel by Eça de Queirós. The book is set in Portugal, though it was relocated for a popular Mexican film, El Crimen del Padre Amaro (2002).

ARCHITECTURE & THE ARTS LITERARY GIANTS

Fine Arts

As Gothic art gave way to more humanistic Renaissance works, Portugal's 15th-century painters developed their own style. Led by the master Nuno Gonçalves, the *escola nacional* (national school) took religious subjects and grounded them against contemporary backgrounds. In Gonçalves' most famous painting, the panels of Santo Antonio, he includes a full milieu of Portuguese society – noblemen, Jews, fishermen, sailors, knights, priests, monks and beggars.

Some of Portugal's finest early paintings emerged from the 16th-century Manueline school. These artists, influenced by Flemish painters, developed a painting style known for its incredible delicacy, realism and luminous colours. The most celebrated painter of his time was Vasco Fernandes, known as Grão Vasco (1480–1543). His richly hued paintings (still striking five centuries later) hang in a museum in Viseu dedicated to his work – as well as that of his Manueline school colleague Gaspar Vaz. Meanwhile sculptors including Diogo de Boitaca went wild with Portuguese seafaring fantasies and exuberant decoration on some of Portugal's icons.

The 17th century saw a number of talented Portuguese artists emerge. One of the best was Josefa de Óbidos, who enjoyed success as a female artist – an extreme rarity in those days. Josefa's paintings were unique in their personal, sympathetic interpretations of religious subjects and for their sense of innocence. Although she studied at an Augustine convent as a young girl, she left without taking the vows and settled in Óbidos (where she got her nickname). Still she maintained close ties to the church, which provided many of her commissions, and remained famously chaste until her death in 1684. Josefa left one of the finest legacies of work of any Portuguese painter. She excelled in richly coloured still lifes and detailed religious works, ignoring established iconography.

METRO ART

The Lisbon metro is not just about transport – it's an art gallery, showcasing the best of Portuguese contemporary art and architecture, with especially wonderful azulejos. Check out Metro Lisboa's website at www.metrolisboa.pt.

THE EVOCATIVE WORLD OF PAULA REGO

The conservative Salazar years of the mid-20th century didn't create the ideal environment to nurture contemporary creativity, and many artists left the country. These include Portugal's best-known living artist, Paula Rego, who was born in Lisbon in 1935 but has been a resident of the UK since 1951. Rego's signature style developed around fairy-tale paintings given a nightmarish twist. Her works deal in ambiguity and psychological and sexual tension, such as *The Family* (1988), where a seated businessman is either being tortured or smothered with affection by his wife and daughter. Domination, fear, sexuality and grief are all recurring themes in Rego's paintings, and the mysterious and sinister atmosphere, heavy use of chiaroscuro (stark contrasting of light and shade) and strange distortion of scale are reminiscent of surrealists Max Ernst and Giorgio de Chirico.

Rego is considered one of the great early champions for painting from a female perspective and she continues to add to a substantial volume of work. Her acclaim continues to grow, particularly with the opening of a new museum in Cascais that showcases her work.

Museums for Art

Museu Nacional do Azulejo, Lisbon

Casa das Histórias Paula Rego, Cascais

Museu Nacional de Arte Antiga, Lisbon

Museu Amadeo de Souza-Cardoso, Amarante

Museu Grão Vasco, Viseu

In the 19th century, naturalism was the dominant trend, with a handful of innovators pushing Portuguese art in new directions. Columbano Bordalo Pinheiro, who hailed from a family of artists, was a seminal figure among the Portuguese artists of his time. He played a prominent role in the Leã d'Ouro, a group of distinguished artists, writers and intellectuals who gathered in the capital and were deeply involved in the aesthetic trends of the day. A prolific artist, Pinheiro painted some of the luminaries of his day, including the novelist Eça de Queirós and Teófilo Braga (a celebrated writer who later became president of the early republic). One of his best-known works is a haunting portrait of the poet Antero de Quental, who later committed suicide.

Building on the works of the naturalists, Amadeo de Souza-Cardoso lived a short but productive life, experimenting with new techniques emerging in Europe. Raised in a sleepy village outside of Amarante, he studied architecture at the Academia de Belas Artes in Lisbon, but soon dropped out and moved to Paris. There, he found his calling as a painter, and mingled with the leading artists and writers of the time, including Amedeo Modigliani, Gertrude Stein, Max Jacob and many others. He experimented with impressionism, and later cubism and futurism, and created a captivating body of work, though he is little known outside of Portugal.

José Sobral de Almada Negreiros delved even deeper into futurism, inspired by the Italian futurist Filippo Tommaso Marinetti. His work encompassed richly hued portraits with abstract geometrical details (such as his famous portrait of Fernando Pessoa from 1954), and he was also a sculptor, writer and critic. He managed to walk a fine line during the Salazar regime, creating large-scale murals by public commission as well as socially engaged works critical of Portuguese society.

The Art of the Tile

Portugal's favourite decorative art is easy to spot. Polished painted tiles called *azulejos* (after the Arabic *al zulaycha,* meaning polished stone) cover everything from churches to train stations. The Moors introduced the art, having picked it up from the Persians, but the Portuguese wholeheartedly adopted it.

Portugal's earliest tiles are Moorish, from Seville. These were decorated with interlocking geometric or floral patterns (figurative representations aren't an option for Muslim artists for religious reasons). After the Portuguese captured Ceuta in Morocco in 1415, they began exploring the art themselves. The 16th-century Italian invention of majolica, in which colours are painted directly onto wet clay over a layer of white enamel, gave works a frescolike brightness and kicked off the Portuguese *azulejo* love affair.

The earliest home-grown examples, polychrome and geometric, date from the 1580s, and may be seen in churches such as Lisbon's Igreja de São Roque, providing an ideal counterbalance to fussy, gold-heavy baroque.

The late 17th century saw a fashion for huge panels, depicting everything from saints to seascapes. As demand grew, mass production became necessary and the Netherlands' blue-and-white Delft tiles started appearing.

Portuguese tile-makers rose to the challenge of this influx, and the splendid work of virtuoso Portuguese masters António de Oliveira Bernardes and his son Policarpo in the 18th century springs from this competitive creativity. You can see their work in Évora, in the impressive Igreja de São João.

By the end of the 18th century, industrial-scale manufacture began to affect quality, coupled with the massive demand for tiles after the 1755 Lisbon earthquake. (Tiling answered the need for decoration, and was cheap and practical – a solution for a population that had felt the ground move beneath its feet.)

From the late 19th century, the art-nouveau and art-deco movements took *azulejos* by storm, providing fantastic facades and interiors for shops, restaurants and residential buildings. Today, *azulejos* still coat contemporary life, and you can explore the latest in *azulejos* in the Lisbon metro. Maria Keil (1914–2012) designed 19 of the stations, from the 1950s onwards – look out for her wild modernist designs at the stations of Rossio, Restauradores, Intendente, Marquês de Pombal, Anjos and Martim Moniz. Oriente also showcases extraordinary contemporary work by artists from five continents.

Azulejos – Obras do Museu Nacional do Azulejo (2009) is a colourful showcase of Portugal's dazzling tiles, with works spanning five centuries. Find it for sale inside Lisbon's Museu Nacional do Azulejo.

ARCHITECTURE & THE ARTS FINE ARTS

AZULEJOS

Saudade: the Portuguese Blues

The Portuguese psyche is a complicated thing, particularly when it comes to not easily translatable concepts like *saudade*. In its purest form, *saudade* is the nostalgic, often deeply melancholic longing for something: a person, a place or just about anything that's no longer obtainable. *Saudade* is deeply connected to this seafaring nation's history and remains deeply intertwined with Portuguese identity. The elusive emotion has played a starring role in some of Portugal's great works of art – in film, literature and, most importantly, music.

Roots of Saudade

In Brazil, 30 January is set aside as the *Dia de Saudade* (Saudade Day). It's a fine day to engage in a bit of nostalgic longing for past lovers, distant homelands and better days.

Scholars are unable to pinpoint exactly when the term '*saudade*' first arose. Some trace it back to the grand voyages during the Age of Discoveries, when sailors, captains and explorers spent many months out at sea, and gave voice to the longing for the lives they left behind. Yet even before the epic sea voyages across the ocean, Portugal was a nation of seafarers, and *saudade* probably arose from those on terra firma – the women who longed for the men who spent endless days out at sea, some of whom never returned.

Naturally, emigration is also deeply linked to *saudade*. Long one of Europe's poorest peoples, the Portuguese were often driven by hardship to seek better lives abroad. Until recently, this usually meant the men leaving behind their families to travel to northern Europe or America to find work. Families sometimes waited years before being reunited, with emigrants experiencing years of painful longing for their homeland – for the familiar faces, the food and village life. Many did eventually return, but of course things had changed and so *saudade* reappeared, this time in the form of longing for the way things were in the past.

A Nation of Emigrants

Goa, India, still has vestiges of its Portuguese colonial past. In Margão, on the street named 'Rua das Saudades', there are Christian and Muslim cemeteries and a Hindu cremation ground.

The great discoveries of Portuguese seafarers had profound effects on the country's demographics. With the birth and expansion of an empire, Portuguese settled in trading posts in Africa and Asia, but the colony of Brazil drew the biggest numbers of early Portuguese emigrants. They cleared the land (harvesting the Brazil wood that gave the colony its name), established farms, and set about the slow, steady task of nation-building – with help, of course, from the millions of slaves stolen from Africa. Numbers vary widely, but an estimated half a million Portuguese settled in Brazil during the colonial period, prior to independence in 1822, and over 400,000 flooded in during the second half of the 19th century.

By the 1900s, Portuguese began emigrating in large numbers to other parts of the world. The US and Canada received over half a million immigrants, with huge numbers heading to France, Germany, Venezuela and Argentina. The 1960s saw another upsurge of emigrants, as young men fled the country in order to avoid the draft that would send them to fight bloody colonial wars in Africa. The 1974 revolution also preceded a big exodus as those associated with the Salazar regime went abroad rather than face reprisals.

What all these emigrants had in common was the deep sadness of leaving their homeland to struggle in foreign lands. Those left behind were also in a world of heartache – wives left alone to raise children, villages deserted of young men, families torn apart. The numbers are staggering: over three million emigrants between 1890 and 1990; aside from Ireland, no other European country lost as many people to emigration.

Saudade in Literature

One of the first great Portuguese works of literature that explores the theme of *saudade* is *Os Lusiadas* (*The Lusiads*, aka *The Portuguese*). Luiz Vaz de Camões mixes mythology with historical events in his great verse epic about the Age of Discoveries of the 15th and 16th centuries. The heroic adventurer Vasco da Gama and other explorers strive for glory but many never return, facing hardship (sea monsters, treacherous kings) along the way. First-hand experience informed Camões' work. He served in the overseas militia, lost an eye in Ceuta in a battle with the Moors, served prison time in Portugal and survived a shipwreck in the Mekong (swimming ashore with his unfinished manuscript held aloft, according to legend).

The great 19th-century Portuguese writer Almeida Garrett wrote an even more compelling take on the Age of Discoveries. In his book *Camões*, a biography of the poet, he describes the longings Camões felt toward Portugal while in exile. He also captured the greater sense of *saudade* that so many felt as Portugal's empire crumbled in the century following the great explorations.

More recent writers also explore the notion of *saudade*, though take radically different approaches from their predecessors. Contemporary writer António Lobo Antunes deconstructs *saudade* in cynical tales that expose the nostalgic longing for something as being a form of neurotic self-delusion. In *The Return of the Caravels* (1988), he turns the discovery myth on its head when, four centuries after da Gama's voyage, the great explorers, through some strange time warp, become entangled with the *retornados* (who returned to Portugal in the 1970s, after the loss of the country's African empire) as the Renaissance-era achievements collapse in the poor, grubby, lower-class neighbourhoods of Lisbon.

The most famous Portuguese emigrant to Brazil was the future king himself. When Napoleon invaded in 1807, the royal family and their extensive retinue fled to Brazil, where they installed themselves in Rio de Janeiro. Many royal retainers never returned home; Dom João VI returned only in 1822.

SAUDADE OF THE JEWS

Until the end of the 15th century, Jews enjoyed a prominent place in Portuguese society. The treasurer of King Afonso V (1432–81) was Jewish, as were others who occupied diplomatic posts and worked as trade merchants, physicians and cartographers. Jews from other countries were welcomed in Portugal, such as those expelled from Spain in 1492. Eventually, pressure from the church and from neighbouring Spain forced the king's hand, and in 1497 Manuel I decreed that all Jews convert to Christianity or leave the country. A catalogue of horrors followed, including the massacre of thousands of Jews in 1506 by mobs running riot and two centuries of bloody Inquisition that kicked off in 1536.

Aside from a secretive Crypto-Jewish group in Belmonte that managed to successfully preserve their faith, the Judaic community slowly withered and perished. Those who converted felt the heart-rending *saudade* of deep loss: essentially the loss of one's identity. Once flourishing Jewish neighbourhoods died as neighbours went into exile or perhaps suffered arrest, torture and even execution. The personal losses paralleled the end of a flourishing and tolerant period in Portugal's history, and effectively ended Jewish presence in Portugal.

Saudade in Film

Portugal's oldest and most prolific film-maker, Manoel de Oliveira, is known for his carefully crafted, if slow-moving, films that delve deep into the world of *saudade* – of growing old, unrequited loves and longing for things that no longer exist. In *Voyage to the Beginning of the World* (1997), several companions make a nostalgic tour through the rugged landscapes and traditional villages of the north – one in search of a past that he knows only in his dreams (having heard only of his ancestral land from his Portuguese-born father), and another haunted by a world that no longer exists (the places of his childhood uprooted). Past and present, nostalgia and reality collide in this quiet, meditative film. It stars a frail, 72-year-old Marcello Mastroianni as Oliveira's alter ego, in the actor's final film before he died.

One of the finest love letters to the capital is the sweet, meandering *Lisbon Story* (1994) directed by German filmmaker Wim Wenders. The story follows a sound engineer who goes in search of a missing director, discovering the city through the footage his friend left behind. Carefully crafted scenes conjure up the mystery and forlorn beauty of Lisbon (and other parts of Portugal, including a wistful sequence on the dramatic cliffs of Cabo Espichel). *Saudade* here explores many different realms, inspired in large part by the ethereal soundtrack by Madredeus – band members also play supporting roles in the film.

The film *Fados* (2007) is Spanish director Carlos Saura's love letter to the great Portuguese music. The film features the singing of fado legends like Camané and Mariza as well as genre-defying singers not often associated with the art – Brazilian signers Caetano Veloso and Chico Buarque, among others.

Fado

> 'I don't sing fado. It sings me.'
>
> *Amália Rodrigues*

Portugal's most famous style of music, fado (Portuguese for 'fate'), couldn't really exist without *saudade*. These melancholic songs are dripping with emotion – and revel in stories of the painful twists and turns of fate, of unreachable distant lovers, fathomless yearning for the homeland, and wondrous days that have come and gone. The emotional quality of the singing plays just as an important role as technical skills, helping fado to reach across linguistic boundaries. Listening to fado is perhaps the easiest way of understanding *saudade*, in all its evocative variety.

Although fado is something of a national treasure – in 2011 it was added to Unesco's list of the World's Intangible Cultural Heritage – it's really the music of Lisbon. (In the university town of Coimbra, fado exists in a different, slightly more cerebral form: it's exclusively men, often students or alumni, who sing of love, bohemian life and the city itself.) No one quite knows its origins, though African and Brazilian rhythms, Moorish chants and the songs of Provençal troubadors may have influenced the sound. What is clear is that by the 19th century, fado could be heard all

The national music of Cape Verde, a former Portuguese colony, is *morna*, a distant cousin of fado, with plaintive songs revolving around lost loves and homesickness. Renowned 'barefoot diva' Cesária Évora (1941–2011) produced many hits including 'Sodade' (Creole for 'saudade').

BRAZILIAN SAUDADE & BOSSA NOVA

Brazilian identity is also deeply connected to *saudade*, which is not surprising given the influence Portugal has had on the country – nearly every inhabitant in Brazil can trace Portuguese roots somewhere in the family tree. In Brazil, *saudade* means much the same thing, and it has played a role in shaping the country's music – in particular, bossa nova. The 1958 hit 'Chega de Saudade' (often poorly translated as 'No More Blues') by legendary song-writing team Tom Jobim and Vinícius de Moraes is considered one of the first bossa nova songs ever recorded. In it, the singer pines for his lover who has left him, and commands his sadness to go out and bring her back. Melancholic chords and a slow, wistful singing style are hallmarks here, as they are of nearly all bossa nova tunes. And even if you can't understand Portuguese, you'll still feel the sadness and deep sense of loss.

over the traditional working-class neighbourhoods of Mouraria and the Alfama, usually in brothels and seedy taverns. It was the anthem of the poor, and maintained an unsavoury reputation until the late 19th century when the upper classes took an interest in the music and brought it into the mainstream.

Fado remained an obscure, mostly local experience until the 20th century, when it received national and, later, international attention. One singer who played a major role in its popularisation was Amália Rodrigues, the 'queen of fado', who became a household name in the 1940s. Born to a poor family in 1920, Amália took the music from the tavern to the concert hall and then into households via radio, and onto film screens (starring in the 1947 film *Capas Negras*). She had some of Portugal's best poets and writers of the day writing songs for her. Yet, along the way, she had her share of ups and downs – depression, illness, failed love affairs – and her heart-rending fado was more than an abstraction.

Amália enjoyed wide acclaim, although her reputation was sullied following the 1974 revolution – when she was criticised for tacitly supporting the Salazar regime (although there is little evidence of that). Fado's popularity slid off the map in the post-revolution days when the Portuguese were eager to make a clean break from the past. (Salazar spoke of throwing the masses the three F's – fado, football and Fátima – to keep them happily occupied.) The 1990s, however, saw a resurgence of fado's popularity, with the opening of new fado houses and the emergence of new fado voices. Amália's reputation was also rehabilitated. Upon her death at age 79 in 1999, Portugal declared three days of national mourning and suspended the general election campaign in her honour. Today she is buried in the National Pantheon.

While fado may bring to mind dark bars of the Salazar years, this is not a musical form stuck in time. Contemporary performers and exponents of a new fado style include the dynamic *fadista* Mísia, who broke new ground by experimenting with full band instrumentation. The Mozambique-born singer Mariza has earned accolades for her extraordinary voice and fresh eclectic approach. She continues to break new ground in albums like *Terra* (2008) that bring in world music – African rhythms, flamenco, Latin sounds and jazz. Another one to watch is Carminho, a young singer with a powerful and mournful voice. Fado runs deep in her veins – her mother was the owner of one of Lisbon's most traditional fado houses (now closed), where as a young girl she heard the best *fadistas* of the time. The men aren't outdone: one of the great male voices in traditional fado these days is Camané.

Fados are traditionally sung by one performer accompanied by a 12-string Portuguese *guitarra* (a pear-shaped guitar). When two *fadistas* perform, they sometimes engage in *desgarrada,* a bit of improvisational one-upmanship where the singers challenge and play off one another. At fado houses, there are usually a number of singers, each one traditionally singing three songs.

For more on Amália Rodrigues, check out the fine documentary *The Art of Amália* (2000), directed by Bruno de Almeida. The biopic *Amália* (2008) by Carlos Coelho da Silva provides an in-depth portrait of Rodrigues that few ever saw.

SAUDADE: THE PORTUGUESE BLUES FADO

AMÁLIA RODRIGUES

Survival Guide

Directory A–Z

Accommodation

There's an excellent range of good-value accommodation in Portugal. Budget places provide some of Western Europe's cheapest rooms, while you'll find atmospheric accommodation in farms, palaces, castles, mansions and rustic town houses – usually giving good mileage for your euro.

Turismos (tourist offices) hold lists of accommodation and *quartos* (private rooms), but they overlook places not registered with them, some of which are excellent options. Good websites for browsing include www.manorhouses.com and www.innsofportugal.com.

Seasons

In popular tourist destinations prices rise and fall with the seasons. Mid-June to mid-September are firmly high season (book ahead); May to mid-June and mid-September to October are midseason; and other times are low season, when you can get some really good deals. Outside the resorts, prices don't vary much between seasons.

In the Algarve, you'll pay the highest premium for rooms from mid-July to the end of August, with slightly lower prices from June to mid-July and all of September, and substantially less (as much as 50%) if you travel between November and April. Note that a handful of places in the Algarve close in winter.

We list July (high-season) prices in reviews.

Camping & Caravan Parks

Camping is popular in Portugal; there are many campgrounds, often in good locations and near beaches. Prices for sites are typically calculated per person, per tent and per vehicle – usually €4 to €6 for each. Keep in mind that many sites get crowded and noisy at busy times (especially July and August).

➡ Nearly all campgrounds have hot showers, electrical hookups and a cafe. The best campgrounds also have a pool, restaurant, laundry service, children's playgrounds and perhaps a tennis court.

➡ Generally, campgrounds run by **Orbitur** (www.orbitur.pt) offer the best services. Some towns have municipal campgrounds, which vary in quality.

➡ For detailed listings of campgrounds nationwide, pick up the **Roteiro Campista** (www.roteiro-campista.pt; €7), updated annually and sold at *turismos* and bookshops. It contains details of most Portuguese campgrounds, with maps and directions.

Guesthouses

Guesthouses are small-scale budget or midrange accommodations, with a personal feel that can be lacking in larger hotels. Most are family-run places.

There are various types of guesthouses; prices typically range from €50 to €90 for a double room with private bathroom (and as little as €35 for the simplest lodgings with shared bathrooms).

➡ The *residencial* is generally the most expensive type of guesthouse, with breakfast usually included.

➡ The *pensão* (pension) is a slight step down in comfort and quality. These typically offer some rooms with shared bathrooms or rooms with only a shower or sink.

➡ The *hospedaria* or *casa de hóspedes* is at the bottom of the heap, with low prices and very basic rooms, usually with shared bathrooms; breakfast is not typically served here.

Hostels

Portugal has scores of hostels, particularly in Lisbon and Porto. If you're thinking bare-bones smelly backpacker lodging, think again. Lisbon's hostels are among the best in Europe, with stylish design in heritage buildings and excellent amenities.

➡ High-season dorm beds typically cost around €20. Many hostels also offer simple doubles with shared bathrooms, and some have small apartments.

➡ Bed linen and breakfast are usually included in the price. Standard features are kitchens, lounges with wi-fi access, and computers for guest use.

➡ In summer, reserve ahead, especially for doubles.

➡ Many of the hostels outside Lisbon are part of the **Pousadas de Juventude** (youth hostels; http://microsites.juventude.gov.pt) network affiliated with Hostelling International (HI).

➡ If you don't have a HI card, you can get a guest card, which requires six stamps (€2 per time) – one from each hostel you stay at – after which you have paid for your membership.

Pousadas

In 1942 the government started the **pousadas network** (www.pousadas.pt), turning castles, monasteries and palaces into luxurious hotels, roughly divided into rural and historic options. July prices range from €120 to €250; prices in August are €10 to €20 more. Most *pousadas* are cheaper during the week; they have lots of discounts and deals, plus

reduced prices for those aged over 55.

Private Rooms

In coastal resorts, mostly in summer, you can often rent a *quarto* (private room) in a private house. These usually have a shared bathroom, are cheap and clean, and might remind you of a stay with an elderly aunt. If you're not approached by an owner or don't spot a sign (*se aluga quarto*), try the local *turismo* for a list. Prices are generally from €35 to €45 per double.

Rental Accommodation

Plenty of villas and cottages are available for rent. **Air BnB** (www.airbnb.com) and **Choose Portugal** (www.chooseportugal.com) list hundreds of private houses and apartments for rent.

Turihab Properties

These charming properties are part of a government scheme, through which you can stay in a farmhouse, manor house, country estate or rustic cottage as the owner's guest.

High-season rates for two people, either in a double room or a cottage range from €70 to €140. Some properties have swimming pools, and most include breakfast (often with fresh local produce).

There are three types of Turihab lodgings:

Solares de Portugal (www.solaresdeportugal.pt) Grand manor houses, some of which date from the 17th- or 18th century.

Aldeias de Portugal (www.aldeiasdeportugal.pt) Lodgings in rural villages in the north, often in beautifully converted stone cottages.

Casas no Campo (www.casasnocampo.net) Country houses, cottages and luxury villas.

Business Hours

Opening hours vary throughout the year. We provide high-season opening hours; hours will generally decrease in the shoulder and low seasons.

Restaurants noon–3pm & 7–10pm

Cafes 9am–7pm

Shops 9.30am–noon & 2–7pm Mon–Fri, 10am–1pm Sat

Bars 7pm–2am

Nightclubs 11pm–4am Thu–Sat

Malls 10am–10pm

Banks 8.30am–3pm Mon–Fri

Children

The great thing about Portugal for children is its manageable size and the range of sights and activities on offer. There's so much to explore and to catch the imagination, even for those with very short attention spans.

The Algarve has to be the best kid-pleasing destination in Portugal, with endless beaches, zoos, water parks, horse riding and boat trips.

Kids will also be happy in Lisbon and its outlying provinces. There are trams, puppet shows, a huge aquarium, a toy museum, horse-drawn carriages, castles, parks and playgrounds.

As for fairy-tale places, Portugal has these in spades. Some children enjoy visiting churches if they can light a candle. They'll enjoy the make-believe of the castles and palaces sprinkled about the country.

Kids are welcome just about everywhere. They can even get literary: Nobel Prize–winner José Saramago, the great Portuguese novelist, has written a charming children's fable, *The Tale of the Unknown Island*, available in English.

➜ In towns, hop-on, hop-off tours can be good for saving small legs, and miniature resort trains often cause more excitement than you would have thought possible.

➜ The Portuguese are generally quite laid-back about breast-feeding in public as long as some attempt at discretion is made.

➜ Formula (including organic brands) and disposable nappies (diapers) are widely available at most pharmacies and grocery stores.

➜ *Turismos*, as well as most hotels and guesthouses, can recommend babysitters.

➜ For an entertaining guide packed with information and tips, turn to Lonely Planet's *Travel with Children*.

Customs Regulations

You can bring as much currency as you like into Portugal, though €10,000 or more must be declared.

The duty-free allowance for travellers more than 17 years old from non-EU countries is as follows:

➜ 200 cigarettes or the equivalent in tobacco

➜ 1L of alcohol that's more than 22% alcohol, or 2L of wine or beer

The allowance for nationals of EU countries is the following:

➜ 800 cigarettes or the equivalent

➜ 10L of spirits, 20L of fortified wine, 60L of sparkling wine or a mind-boggling 90L of still wine or 110L of beer

Discount Cards

➜ Portugal's network of *pousadas da juventude* is part of the HI network. An HI card from your hostelling association at home entitles you to the standard cheap rates.

➜ A student card will get you reduced admission to almost all sights. Likewise, those aged over 65 with proof of age will save cash.

➜ If you plan to do a lot of sightseeing in Portugal's main cities, the Lisboa Card and Porto Card are sensible investments. Sold at tourist offices, these cards allows discounts or free admission to many attractions and free travel on public transport.

Electricity

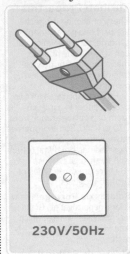

230V/50Hz

Embassies & Consulates

Your embassy or consulate is the best first stop in any emergency. Most can provide lists of reliable local doctors, lawyers and interpreters.

There's no New Zealand consulate in Portugal. The nearest New Zealand embassy is in **Madrid** (☑91 523 02 26; www.nzembassy.com/spain; 3rd fl, Calle de Pinar 7, Madrid).

Australian Embassy (☑213 101 500; www.portugal. embassy.gov.au; 2nd fl, Av da Liberdade 200, Lisbon)

Canada Lisbon (☑213 164 600; www.canadainternational. gc.ca; Avenida da Liberdade 196, Edifício Victoria); Faro (☑289 803 757; Rua Frei Lourenço de Santa Maria 1)

France Lisbon (☑213 939 294; www.ambafrance-pt.org; Rua Santos-o-Velho 5, Lisbon); Porto (☑226 078 220; Av da Boavista 1681, Porto)

German Embassy (☑218 810 210; www.lissabon.diplo.de; Campo dos Mártires da Pátria 38, Lisbon)

Irish Embassy (☑213 308 200; www.embassyofireland. pt; 4th fl, Av Liberdade 200, Lisbon)

Netherlands Embassy
(☎213 914 900; http://portu
gal.nlembaixada.org; Av Infante
Santo 43, Lisbon)

Spain Lisbon (☎213 472 381;
www.exteriores.gob.es; Rua do
Salitre 1, Lisbon); Porto (☎225
363 915; Rua de Dom João IV
341, Porto)

UK Embassy (☎213 924
000; www.gov.uk/government/
world/portugal; Rua de Saõ
Bernardo 33, Lisbon) Also in
Portimaõ (☎808 203 537; Ave
Guanaré).

US Embassy (☎217 273 300;
http://portugal.usembassy.gov;
Av das Forças Armadas, Lisbon)

Gay & Lesbian Travellers

In 2010 Portugal legalised
gay marriage, becoming the
sixth European country to
do so. Most Portuguese pro-
fess a laissez-faire attitude
about same-sex couples,
although how out you can be
depends on where you are
in Portugal. In Lisbon, Porto
and the Algarve, acceptance
has increased, whereas in
most other areas, same-sex
couples would be met with
incomprehension. In this
conservative Catholic country, homosexuality is still
outside the norm. And while
homophobic violence is extremely rare, discrimination
has been reported in schools
and workplaces.

Lisbon has the country's
best gay and lesbian network
and nightlife. Lisbon and
Porto hold Gay Pride march-
es, but outside these events
the gay community keeps a
discreet profile.

Health

Prevention is the key to staying healthy while abroad.
A little planning before
departure, particularly for
pre-existing illnesses, will
save trouble later. See your
dentist before a long trip,
carry a spare pair of contact
lenses and glasses, and take
your optical prescription with
you. Bring medications in
their original, clearly labelled,
containers. A signed and
dated letter from your physician describing your medical
conditions and medications,
including generic names, is
also a good idea. If carrying
syringes or needles, be sure
to have a physician's letter
documenting their medical
necessity.

Availability of Health Care

Good health care is read-
ily available and for minor
illnesses pharmacists can
give valuable advice and sell
over-the-counter medica-
tion. Most pharmacists
speak some English. They
can also advise when more
specialised help is required
and point you in the right
direction.

Health Insurance

Citizens of the EU are eligible
for free emergency medi-
cal treatment if they have a
European Health Insurance
Card (EHIC), which replaces
the no-longer-valid E111
certificate. In the UK, you
can apply for this card online
(www.nhs.uk/NHSEngland/
Healthcareabroad) or pick
up an application at a post

office. It will not cover you for
nonemergencies or emer-
gency repatriation.

Citizens from other coun-
tries should find out if there
is a reciprocal arrangement
for free medical care be-
tween their country and Portugal. If you do need health
insurance, consider a policy
that covers you for the worst
possible scenario, such as an
accident requiring an emergency flight home. Find out
in advance if your insurance
plan will make payments
directly to providers or reim-
burse you later for overseas
health expenditures.

Heat Exhaustion & Heat Stroke

Heat exhaustion occurs following excessive fluid loss
with inadequate replacement
of fluids and salt. Symptoms
include headache, dizzi-
ness and tiredness. To treat
heat exhaustion, replace
lost fluids by drinking water
and/or fruit juice or an oral
rehydration solution, such as
Dioralyte, and cool the body
with cold water and fans.

Heat stroke is much more
serious, resulting in irrational
and hyperactive behaviour
and eventually loss of consciousness and death. Rapid
cooling by spraying the body
with water and fanning is
ideal. Emergency fluid and
electrolyte replacement by
intravenous drip is recommended.

Jellyfish & Sea Urchins

Stings from jellyfish are painful but not dangerous. Douse
the wound in vinegar to
deactivate any stingers that
haven't 'fired'. Applying cala-
mine lotion, antihistamines
or analgesics may reduce the
reaction and relieve the pain.

Watch for sea urchins
around rocky beaches. If you
get their needles embedded
in your skin, immerse the
limb in hot water to relieve
the pain. To avoid infection
visit a doctor and have the
needles removed.

TRAVEL HEALTH WEBSITES

It's a good idea to consult your government's travel
health website before departure, if one is available:

Australia (www.smartraveller.gov.au)

Canada (www.hc-sc.gc.ca)

UK (www.fitfortravel.nhs.uk)

USA (wwwnc.cdc.gov/travel)

Rabies

Rabies, though rare in Portugal, is a risk, and is transmissible via the bite of an infected animal. It can also be transmitted if the animal's saliva comes in contact with an open wound. If you've been bitten by a wild animal, a treatment of shots must begin at once.

Tap Water

Tap water is generally safe to drink in Portugal.

Traveller's Diarrhoea

If you develop diarrhoea, be sure to drink plenty of fluids, preferably an oral rehydration solution (eg Dioralyte). A few loose stools don't require treatment, but if you start having more than four or five stools a day, you should start taking an antibiotic such as Norfloxacin, Ciprofloxacin or Azithromycin. Antidiarrhoeal agents such as loperamide are just 'stoppers' and don't get to the root of the problem. If diarrhoea is bloody, persists for more than 72 hours or is accompanied by fever, shaking, chills or severe abdominal pain you should seek medical attention.

Insurance

Don't leave home without a travel-insurance policy to cover theft, loss and medical problems. You should get insurance for the worst-case scenario; for example, an accident or illness requiring hospitalisation and a flight home.

Check the small print as some policies specifically exclude 'dangerous activities' such as scuba diving, motorcycling or even trekking. If you have these activities planned, either find another policy or ask about an amendment (usually available for an extra premium) that includes them.

Make sure you keep all documentation for any claims later on. Some policies ask you to call back (reverse charges) to a centre in your home country, where an immediate assessment of your problem is made.

Worldwide travel insurance is available at www.lonelyplanet.com/travel-insurance. You can buy, extend and claim online anytime – even if you're already on the road. For information about health insurance, see p501.

Internet Access

We use the icon @ to indicate places that have a physical computer where guests can access the internet. The icon ⊙ indicates where wireless access (wi-fi) is available.

Free internet access is growing in Portugal. If you have your own laptop, most hotels, hostels and midrange guesthouses offer wireless access. It is usually – but not always – free, so inquire before booking. Many cafes also offer free wi-fi.

Other places to access the internet include the following:

➡ *Bibliotecas municipais* (municipal libraries)

➡ Municipal Espaços Internet (www.espacosinternet.pt)

➡ Cybercafes, which are growing rarer in the age of smart phones, charge from around €2 per hour

Legal Matters

➡ Fines for illegal parking are common. If you're parked illegally you'll be towed and will have to pay around €100 to get your car back. Be aware of local road rules, as fines for other transgressions will also be enforced.

➡ Narcotic drugs were decriminalised in 2001 in an attempt to clear up the public-health problems among drug users, and to address the issue as a social rather than a criminal one. You may be brought before a commission and subject to fines or treatment if you are caught with up to 10 doses of a drug.

➡ Drug dealing is still a serious offence and suspects may be held for up to 18 months before coming to trial. Bail is at the court's discretion.

➡ It's illegal in Portugal to drive while talking on a mobile phone.

Maps

National and natural park offices usually have simple park maps, though these are of little use for trekking or cycling. The following offer a good range of maps:

Omni Resources (www.omnimap.com) US company that sells excellent maps, including 1:25,000 topographic maps.

Stanfords (www.stanfords.co.uk) Good selection of Portugal maps and travel products in the UK.

GOVERNMENT TRAVEL ADVICE

The following government websites offer travel advisories and information on current hot spots:

Australian Department of Foreign Affairs (www.smarttraveller.gov.au)

British Foreign Office (www.fco.gov.uk/countryadvice)

Canadian Department of Foreign Affairs (www.dfait-maeci.gc.ca)

US State Department (http://travel.state.gov)

PRACTICALITIES

➡ Portugal uses the metric system for weights and measures. Decimals are indicated by commas, thousands by points.

➡ Portugal uses the PAL video system, incompatible with both the French SECAM system and the North American NTSC system.

➡ Main newspapers include *Diário de Notícias*, *Público*, *Jornal de Notícias* and the tabloid best-seller *Correio da Manhã*.

➡ English-language media includes the long-running daily, the **Portugal News** (www. theportugalnews.com), and the weekly **Algarve Resident** (www.algarveresident.com).

➡ TV channels in Portugal include Rádio Televisão Portuguesa (RTP-1 and RTP-2), Sociedade Independente (SIC) and TV Independente (TV1), with RTP-2 providing the best selection of foreign films and world news coverage. Other stations fill the airwaves with a mix of Portuguese and Brazilian soaps, game shows and dubbed or subtitled foreign movies.

➡ Portugal's national radio stations include state-owned Rádiodifusão Portuguesa (RDP), which runs the stations Antena 1, 2 and 3 and plays Portuguese broadcasts and evening music (Lisbon frequencies are 95.7, 94.4 and 100.3). For English-language radio there is the BBC World Service (Lisbon 90.2) and Voice of America (VOA), or a few Algarve-based stations, such as Kiss (95.8 and 101.2).

➡ Smoking is allowed in some restaurants and most bars. Restaurants that allow smoking are supposed to have separate smoking sections, but inadequate ventilation means nonsmokers will be breathing in the fumes. Meanwhile, many hotels still offer smoking rooms.

Money

➡ Portugal uses the euro, along with most other European nations.

➡ Banks and *bureaux de change* are free to set their own rates and commissions, so a low commission might mean a skewed exchange rate.

➡ For information on tipping, see p23.

ATMs & Credit Cards

The most convenient way to get your money is from an ATM. Most banks have a Multibanco ATM, with menus in English (and other languages), that accept Visa, Access, MasterCard, Cirrus and so on. You just need your card and PIN. Your home bank will usually charge around 1% to 2% per transaction. But it's wise to have a back-up source of money; sometimes ATMs temporarily stop accepting a certain type of card, usually a hiatus lasting a day or so.

Credit cards are accepted at smarter hotels and restaurants and in larger towns, but won't be any use to pay for things in the budget arena or in rural outposts.

Travellers Cheques

Travellers cheques are a safe way to carry money, as they will be replaced if lost or stolen, but are less convenient than the card-in-machine method. Amex, Thomas Cook and Visa are most widely recognised. It's best to get cheques in euros, and keep a record of the ones you've cashed in case you do mislay them. However, although travellers cheques are easily exchanged, with better rates than for cash, they are poor value because commission is so high.

Post

Post offices are called **CTT** (www.ctt.pt). *Correio normal* (ordinary mail) goes in the red letterboxes, *correio azul* (airmail) goes in the blue boxes. Automated red postal stands dispense stamps, saving you the hassle of waiting in line at the post office. Post to Europe takes up to five working days, and the rest of the world up to seven. Economy mail (or surface airlift) is about a third cheaper, but takes a week or so longer.

Public Holidays

Banks, offices, department stores and some shops close on the public holidays listed here. On New Year's Day, Easter Sunday, Labour Day and Christmas Day, even *turismos* close.

New Year's Day 1 January

Carnaval Tuesday February/March – the day before Ash Wednesday

Good Friday March/April

Liberty Day 25 April – celebrating the 1974 revolution

Labour Day 1 May

Corpus Christi May/June – ninth Thursday after Easter

Portugal Day 10 June – also known as Camões and Communities Day

Feast of the Assumption 15 August

Republic Day 5 October – commemorating the 1910 declaration of the Portuguese Republic

All Saints' Day 1 November

Independence Day 1 December – commemorating the 1640 restoration of independence from Spain

Feast of the Immaculate Conception 8 December

Christmas Day 25 December

Safe Travel

Once behind the wheel of a car, the otherwise mild-mannered Portuguese change personality. Macho driving, such as tailgating at high speeds and overtaking on blind corners, is all too common. Portugal has one of the highest road accident rates in Europe. Police have responded by aggressively patrolling certain dangerous routes, such as on the cheerfully named 'highway of death' from Salamanca in Spain.

Compared with other European countries, Portugal's crime rate remains low, but some types of crime – including car theft – are on the rise. Crime against foreigners is of the usual rush-hour-pickpocketing, bag-snatching and theft-from-rental-cars variety. Take the usual precautions: don't flash your cash; keep valuables in a safe place; and, if you are challenged, hand it over – it's not worth taking the risk.

Take care in the water; the surf can be strong, with dangerous ocean currents.

Telephone

To call Portugal from abroad, dial the international access code (☑00), then Portugal's country code (☑351), then the number. All domestic

numbers have nine digits, and there are no area codes. Most public phones accept phone cards only – available at most news stands – though a few coin-operated phones are still around. You can also make calls from booths in Portugal Telecom offices and some post offices – pay when your call is finished.

Long-distance and international calls are cheaper from 9pm to 9am weekdays, all weekend and on holidays.

Directory Inquiries & Reverse-Charge Calls

Portugal's directory inquiries number is ☑118; operators will search by address as well as by name. The international directory inquiries number is ☑177.

To make a *pagar no destino* (reverse-charge call) with the help of a multilingual operator, dial ☑120.

International Calls & Cards

From Portugal Telecom, you can get a PT Hello Card in denominations of €5 or €10, which offer good long-distance rates. You call an access number then key in the code on the back of the card. There are lots of competing cards offering much the same service. Note that peak and off-peak periods vary from company to company.

Local, Regional & National Calls

The cheapest way to call within Portugal is with a Portugal Telecom *cartão telefónico* (phone card). These are available for €3, €5 and €10 from post and telephone offices and many newsagents. A youth or student card should get you a 10% discount.

Local calls cost around €0.10 per minute to land lines and €0.30 per minute to mobile phones. Numbers starting with 800 (*linha verde;* green line) are toll free. Those starting with 808

(*linha azul;* blue line) are charged at local rates from anywhere in the country.

Mobile Phones

Portugal uses the GSM 900/1800 frequency, the same as found in Australia, the UK and the rest of the EU. Mobile-phone usage is widespread in Portugal, with extensive coverage provided in all but the most rural areas. The main domestic operators are Vodafone, Optimus and TMN. All of them sell prepaid SIM cards that you can insert inside a GSM mobile phone and use as long as the phone is not locked by the company providing you service. If you need a phone, you can buy one at the airport and shops throughout the country with a package of minutes for under €20. This is generally cheaper than renting a phone. Note that mobile-phone numbers usually begin with a 9.

It's illegal in Portugal to drive while talking on a mobile phone.

Time

Portugal, like Britain, is on GMT/UTC in winter and GMT/UTC plus one hour in summer. This puts it an hour earlier than Spain year-round (which is a strange thought when you are crossing the border). Clocks are set forward by an hour on the last Sunday in March and back on the last Sunday in October.

Tourist Information

➡ Turismo de Portugal, the country's national tourist board, operates a handy website: www.visitportugal.com.

➡ Locally managed *postos de turismo* (tourist offices, usually signposted 'turismo') are everywhere, offering brochures and varying degrees of help with sights and accommodation.

Travellers with Disabilities

➜ The term *deficientes* (Portuguese for 'disabled') gives some indication of the limited awareness of disabled needs. Although public offices and agencies are required to provide access and facilities for people with disabilities, private businesses are not.

➜ Lisbon airport is wheelchair accessible, while Porto and Faro airports have accessible toilets.

➜ Parking spaces are allotted in many places but are frequently occupied. The EU parking card entitles visitors to the same street-parking concessions given to disabled residents. If you're in the UK, contact the **Department for Transport** (☎020-7944 8300; www.gov.uk/government/policies/making-transport-more-accessible-to-all).

➜ Newer and larger hotels tend to have some adapted rooms, though the facilities may not be up to scratch; ask at the local *turismo*. Most campgrounds have accessible toilets and some hostels have facilities for people with disabilities.

➜ Lisbon, with its cobbled streets and hills, may be difficult for some travellers with disabilities, but not impossible. The Baixa's flat grid and Belém are fine, and all the sights at Parque das Nações are accessible. For more information, contact the following organisations:

Accessible Portugal (☎926 910 989; www.accessibleportugal.com; Rua Jorge Barradas 50, 4th fl) This Lisbon-based tour agency offers a wide range of itineraries and can arrange accommodation, transfers, overnight trips and outdoor activities such as tandem skydiving and hot-air balloon trips.

Cooperativa Nacional de Apoio Deficientes (☎218 595 332; www.cnad.org.pt; Praça Dr Fernando Amado, Lote 566-E, Lisbon) This is a private organisation that can help with travel needs.

Dial-a-ride Disabled Bus Service Lisbon (☎217 585 676); Porto (☎226 006 353)

Secretaria do Nacional de Reabilitação (☎217 929 500; www.inr.pt; Av Conde de Valbom 63, Lisbon) The national governmental organisation representing people with disabilities supplies information, provides links to useful operations and publishes guides (in Portuguese) that advice on barrier-free accommodation, transport, shops, restaurants and sights.

Taxi Services for Disabled Persons Braga (☎253 684 081); Coimbra (☎239 484 522)

Visas

Nationals of EU countries don't need a visa for any length of stay in Portugal. Those from Canada, New Zealand, the USA and (by temporary agreement) Australia can stay for up to 90 days in any half-year without a visa. Others, including nationals of South Africa, need a visa unless they're the spouse or child of an EU citizen.

The general requirements for entry into Portugal also apply to citizens of other signatories of the 1990 Schengen Convention (Austria, Belgium, Denmark, Finland, France, Germany, Greece, Iceland, Italy, Luxembourg, the Netherlands, Norway, Spain and Sweden). A visa issued by one Schengen country is generally valid for travel in all the others, but unless you're a citizen of the UK, Ireland or a Schengen country, you should check visa regulations with the consulate of each Schengen country you plan to visit. You must apply for any Schengen visa while you are still in your country of residence.

To extend a visa or 90-day period of stay after arriving in Portugal, contact the **Foreigners' Registration Service** (Serviço de Estrangeiros e Fronteiras; ☎213 585 500; Av António Augusto de Aguiar 20 , Lisbon); major tourist towns also have branches. As entry regulations are already liberal, you'll need convincing proof of employment or financial independence, or a pretty good story if you want to stay longer.

Women Travellers

Women travelling alone in Portugal report few serious problems. As when travelling anywhere, women should take care – be cautious where you walk after dark and don't hitch.

If you're travelling with a male partner, people will expect him to do all the talking and ordering, and pay the bill. In some conservative pockets of the north, unmarried couples will save hassle by saying they're married.

If you're a victim of rape or violence while you're in Portugal, you can contact the **Associação Portuguesa de Apoio à Vítima** (APAV; Portuguese Association for Victim Support; ☎213 587 900; www.apav.pt; Rua José Estêvão 135, Lisbon), which offers assistance for rape victims. Visit the website for office locations nationwide.

Work

The most likely kind of work you will be able to find is teaching English, if you have Teaching English as a Foreign Language (TEFL) certification. If you're in the UK, contact the British Council, or get in touch with language schools in the area where you want to teach as possible avenues of work.

Bar work is a possibility in the Algarve, particularly in Lagos; ask around. You can also try looking in the local English press for job ads.

Transport

GETTING THERE & AWAY

Entering the Country

From within Europe, you'll have no problems entering Portugal by land or air. If arriving from further afield, check if you need a visa before arrival.

Flights, tours and rail tickets can be booked online at lonelyplanet.com.

Air

Most international flights arrive in Lisbon, though Porto and Faro also have some. For more information, including live arrival and departure schedules, see www.ana.pt.

TAP (www.flytap.com) is Portugal's international flag carrier and main domestic airline.

Lisbon (LIS; ☏218 413 500; www.ana.pt)

Porto Airport (OPO; ☏229 432 400; www.ana.pt)

Faro Airport (FAO; ☏289 800 800)

Land

Bus

The major long-distance carriers that serve European destinations are **Busabout** (www.busabout.com) and **Eurolines** (www.eurolines.com). Though these companies serve Portugal, it is not currently included in either company's multicity travel passes.

For some European routes, Eurolines is affiliated with the big Portuguese operators **Internorte** (www.internorte.pt) and **Eva Transportes** (www.eva-bus.com).

CONTINENTAL EUROPE

Eurolines has services to Portugal from destinations all across Europe, typically running about twice a week. From Paris, hefty surcharges apply to one-way or return tickets for most departures from July to mid-August and also on Saturday year-round.

UK–Portugal and France–Portugal Eurolines services cross to Portugal via northwest Spain. Spanish lines with services to Portugal include the following:

Alsa (www.alsa.es)

Avanza (www.avanzabus.com)

Damas (www.damas-sa.es)

UK

Eurolines runs several services to Portugal from Victoria coach station in London, with a stopover and change of bus in France and sometimes Spain. These include two buses a week to Viana do Castelo (34 hours), five to Porto (33 hours), five via Coimbra to Lisbon (35 hours) and two via Faro to Lagos (38

CLIMATE CHANGE & TRAVEL

Every form of transport that relies on carbon-based fuel generates CO_2, the main cause of human-induced climate change. Modern travel is dependent on aeroplanes, which might use less fuel per kilometre per person than most cars but travel much greater distances. The altitude at which aircraft emit gases (including CO_2) and particles also contributes to their climate change impact. Many websites offer 'carbon calculators' that allow people to estimate the carbon emissions generated by their journey and, for those who wish to do so, to offset the impact of the greenhouse gases emitted with contributions to portfolios of climate-friendly initiatives throughout the world. Lonely Planet offsets the carbon footprint of all staff and author travel.

CONTINENTAL EUROPE BUSES TO PORTUGAL

FROM	TO	FREQUENCY	DURATION (HR)	COST (€)
Amsterdam	Porto	3 times weekly	32	155
Amsterdam	Faro	3 times weekly	36	180
Barcelona	Lisbon	3 times weekly	19	86
Brussels	Porto	3 times weekly	28	137
Brussels	Faro	3 times weekly	32	169
Hamburg	Porto	3 times weekly	38	156
Hamburg	Lisbon	3 times weekly	40	159
Hamburg	Faro	3 times weekly	42	185
Madrid	Porto	daily	8½	54
Madrid	Lisbon	daily	8	47
Paris	Faro	3 times weekly	27	118-125
Paris	Lisbon	daily	26	96-118
Paris	Porto	daily	22	91-108
Seville	Lisbon	daily	7	44
Seville	Faro	daily	2	25

hours). These services cost around £89 one way.

Car & Motorcycle

Of more than 30 roads that cross the Portugal–Spain border, the best and biggest do so near Valença do Minho (E01/A3), Chaves (N532), Bragança (E82/IP4), Vilar Formoso (E80/IP5), Caia (E90/A6/IP7), Serpa (N260) and Vila Real de Santo António (E1/IP1). There are no longer any border controls. Petrol is cheaper in Spain.

LICENCES & INSURANCE

Nationals of EU countries, the USA and Brazil need only their home driving licence to operate a car or motorcycle in Portugal. Others should get an International Driving Permit (IDP) through an automobile licensing department or automobile club in their home country.

If you're driving your own car or motorcycle into Portugal, you need the following:

➡ vehicle registration (proof of ownership)

➡ insurance documents

➡ motor vehicle insurance with at least third-party cover.

Your home insurance policy may or may not be extendable to Portugal, and the coverage of some comprehensive policies automatically drops to third party outside your home country unless the insurer is notified.

If you hire a car, the rental firm will provide you with registration and insurance papers, plus a rental contract.

UK

The quickest driving route from the UK to Portugal is by car ferry to northern Spain. **Brittany Ferries** (www.brittany-ferries.com) runs three routes, each of which depart twice weekly from mid-March through October.

➡ Portsmouth to Santander (24 hours; from £1088 return)

➡ Portsmouth to Bilbao (24 to 32 hours; from £1128 return)

➡ Plymouth to Santander (20 hours; from £1008 return)

From Bilbao or Santander it's roughly 1000km to Lisbon, 800km to Porto and 1300km to Faro.

An alternative is to catch a ferry across the Channel – or

the **Eurotunnel** (www.eurotunnel.com) – vehicle train beneath it) to France and motor down the coast. The fastest sea crossings are between Dover and Calais, and are operated by **P&O Ferries** (www.poferries.com).

Train

Trains are a popular way to get around Europe – comfortable, frequent and generally on time. But unless you have a rail pass the cost can be higher than flying.

There are two standard long-distance rail journeys into Portugal. Both take the *TGV Atlantique* from Paris to Irún (in Spain), where you change trains. From there the *Sud-Expresso* crosses into Portugal at Vilar Formoso (Fuentes de Oñoro in Spain), continuing to Coimbra and Lisbon; change at Pampilhosa for Porto. The other option runs from Irún to Madrid, with a change to the *Talgo Lusitânia*, crossing into Portugal at Marvão-Beirã and on to Lisbon. For trips to the south of Portugal, change at Lisbon.

Two other Spain–Portugal crossings are at Valença do Minho and at Caia (Caya in Spain), near Elvas.

CONTINENTAL EUROPE TRAINS TO PORTUGAL

FROM	TO	FREQUENCY	DURATION (HR)	COST (€)
Vigo	Porto	twice daily	3¼	15
Madrid	Lisbon	daily	10½	61-84
Paris	Lisbon	daily	21	130

You will have few problems buying long-distance tickets as little as a day or two ahead, even in the summer. For those intending to do a lot of European rail travel, the exhaustive *Thomas Cook European Timetable* is updated monthly and is available from **Thomas Cook Publishing** (www.thomascooktimetables.com).

TRAIN PASSES

Many of the passes listed here are available through **Rail Europe** (www.raileurope.co.uk); most travel agencies also sell them, though you will save a little by buying directly from the issuing authority. Note that even with a pass you must still pay for seat and couchette reservations and express-train supplements.

InterRail Pass (www.interrail.eu) allows a certain number of travel days within a set time frame. The network includes 30 countries. A pass for five days of travel over 10 days costs €276 for 2nd class, €434 for 1st class. A month of unlimited travel runs €658/1034. The InterRail Pass is available to anyone residing in Europe for six months before starting their travels. You cannot use it in your home country.

Eurail (www.eurail.com) sells passes to non-European residents. The Global pass is valid for unlimited travel in 21 European countries, including Portugal, and ranges from 10 days (adult/under 26 US$908/591) to three months (US$2127/1384). The Select pass allows you to travel between three, four or five of your chosen Eurail countries (though France is no longer part of the deal). You can choose from five to 10 travelling days (or up to 15 days for five countries), which can be taken at any point within a two-month period.

The **Portugal-Spain rail pass** (www.raileurope.com) available only to non-European residents, is also valid for a specified period of 1st-class travel in Spain and Portugal during a two-month period, from three days (US$340) to 10 days (US$661).

CONTINENTAL EUROPE

The train journey from Paris (Gare d'Austerlitz) to Lisbon takes 21 hours and stops in a number of Spanish cities along the way. You can buy tickets direct from **SNCF** (www.voyages-sncf.com).

UK

The fastest and most convenient route to Portugal is with **Eurostar** (www.eurostar.com) from London Waterloo to Paris, and then onward by TGV.

River

Transporte Fluvial del Guadiana (www.rioguadiana.net) operates car ferries across the Rio Guadiana between Ayamonte in Spain and Vila Real de Santo António in the Algarve every hour (half-hourly in the summer) from 8.30am to 7pm Monday to Saturday, and from 9.30am to 5.30pm on Sunday. Buy tickets from the waterfront office (€1.70/5/1.10 per person/car/bike).

Sea

There are no scheduled sea-going ferries to Portugal, but many to Spain. The closest North African ferry connections are from Morocco to Spain; contact **Trasmediterranea** (www.trasmediterranea.es) for details. Car ferries also run from Tangier to Gibraltar.

GETTING AROUND

Air

Flights within mainland Portugal are expensive and, for the short distances involved, not really worth considering. Nonetheless, **TAP Air Portugal** (www.flytap.com) has multiple daily Lisbon–Porto and Lisbon–Faro flights (taking less than one hour) year-round. For Porto to Faro, change in Lisbon.

Bicycle

Mountain biking is popular in Portugal, even though there are few dedicated bicycle paths. Possible itineraries are numerous in the mountainous national/natural parks of the north (especially Parque Nacional da Peneda-Gerês), along the coast or across the Alentejo plains. Coastal trips are easiest from north to south, with the prevailing winds. More demanding is the Serra da Estrela (which serves as the Tour de Portugal's 'mountain run'). You could also try the Serra do Marão between Amarante and Vila Real.

Local bike clubs organise regular Passeio BTT trips; check their flyers at rental agencies, bike shops and *turismos* (tourist offices). Guided trips are often available in popular tourist destinations.

Cobbled roads in some old-town centres may jar your teeth loose if your tyres aren't fat enough; they should be at least 38mm in diameter.

Documents

If you're cycling around Portugal on your own bike, proof of ownership and a written description and photograph of it will help police in case it's stolen.

Hire

There are numerous places to rent bikes, especially in the Algarve and other touristy areas. Prices range from €8 to €25 per day.

Information

For listings of events and bike shops, buy the bimonthly Portuguese-language *Bike Magazine*, available from larger newsagents.

For its members, the UK-based **Cyclists' Touring Club** (CTC; www.ctc.org.uk) publishes useful and free information on cycling in Portugal, plus notes for half a dozen routes around the country. It also offers tips, maps, topography guides and other publications by mail order.

Transporting Your Bicycle

Boxed or bagged-up bicycles can be taken free on all *regional* and *interregional* trains as accompanied baggage. They can also go unboxed on a few suburban services on weekends or for a small charge outside the rush hour. Most domestic bus lines won't accept bikes on board.

Boat

Other than river cruises along the Rio Douro from Porto and the Rio Tejo from Lisbon, Portugal's only remaining waterborne transport are cross-river ferries. Commuter ferries include those across the Rio Tejo to/from Lisbon, and across the mouth of the Rio Sado between Setúbal and Tróia.

Bus

A host of small private bus operators, most amalgamated into regional companies, run a dense network of services across the country. Among the largest are **Rede Expressos** (www.rede-expressos.pt), **Rodonorte** (www.rodonorte.pt) and the Algarve line **Eva Transportes** (www.eva-bus.com).

Bus services are of four general types:

Alta Qualidade A fast deluxe category offered by some companies.

Carreiras Marked 'CR'; slow, stopping at every crossroad.

Expressos Comfortable, fast buses between major cities.

Rápidas Quick regional buses.

Even in summer you'll have little problem booking an *expresso* ticket for the same or next day. A Lisbon–Faro express bus takes four hours and costs €20; Lisbon–Porto takes about four hours for around €19. By contrast, local services can thin out to almost nothing on weekends, especially in summer when school is out.

Don't rely on *turismos* for accurate timetable information. Most bus-station ticket desks will give you a little computer printout of fares and all services.

Car & Motorcycle

Portugal's modest network of *estradas* (highways) is gradually spreading across the country. Main roads are sealed and generally in good condition. The downside is your fellow drivers: the country's per-capita death rate from road accidents has long been one of Europe's highest, and drinking, driving and dying are hot political potatoes. The good news is that recent years have seen a steady decline in the

road toll, thanks to a zero-tolerance police crackdown on accident-prone routes and alcohol limits.

Driving can be tricky in Portugal's small walled towns, where roads may taper to donkey-cart size before you know it, and fiendish one-way systems can force you out of your way.

A common occurrence in larger towns is down-and-outers, who lurk around squares and car parks, waving you into the parking space you've just found for yourself, and asking for payment for this service. It's wise to do as Portuguese do, and hand over some coins (€0.50) to keep your car out of 'trouble' (scratches, broken windows, etc).

Accidents

If you are involved in a minor 'fender bender' with no injuries, the easiest way for drivers to sort things out with their insurance companies is to fill out a *Constat Aimable* (the English version is called a European Accident Statement). There's no risk in signing this: it's just a way to exchange the relevant information and there's usually one included in rental-car documents. Make sure it includes any details that may help you prove that the accident was not your fault. To alert the police, dial ☏112.

Assistance

Automóvel Club de Portugal (ACP; ☏213 180 100; www.acp.pt), Portugal's national

PARKING

Parking is often metered within city centres, but is free on Saturday evening and Sunday. Lisbon has car parks, but these can get expensive (upwards of €20 per day). See individual town listings for parking tips.

ROAD DISTANCES (KM)

	Aveiro	Beja	Braga	Bragança	Castelo Branco	Coimbra	Évora	Faro	Guarda	Leiria	Lisbon	Portalegre	Porto	Santarém	Setúbal	Viana do Castelo	Vila Real	Viseu
Aveiro	---																	
Beja	383	---																
Braga	129	504	---															
Bragança	287	566	185	---														
Castelo Branco	239	271	366	299	---													
Coimbra	60	329	178	314	191	---												
Évora	305	78	426	488	191	251	---											
Faro	522	166	643	732	437	468	244	---										
Guarda	163	369	260	197	102	161	291	535	---									
Leiria	126	273	244	402	179	72	195	412	233	---								
Lisbon	256	183	372	530	264	202	138	296	402	146	---							
Portalegre	276	178	403	390	93	222	100	344	193	172	219	---						
Porto	71	446	58	216	308	123	368	585	202	189	317	339	---					
Santarém	188	195	309	464	181	134	117	346	295	78	80	147	251	---				
Setúbal	299	143	420	575	316	246	105	256	406	189	47	186	362	123	---			
Viana do Castelo	144	519	56	241	382	191	441	658	275	262	387	412	73	324	435	---		
Vila Real	169	528	94	120	261	199	450	683	159	282	412	352	98	349	460	150	---	
Viseu	86	415	185	228	177	86	366	554	75	158	288	268	127	220	331	241	113	---

auto club, provides medical, legal and breakdown assistance for its members. Road information and maps are available at ACP offices, including the head office in Lisbon and branches in Aveiro, Braga, Bragança, Coimbra, Évora, Faro, Porto and elsewhere.

If your national auto club belongs to the Fédération Internationale de l'Automobile or the Alliance Internationale de Tourisme, you can also use ACP's emergency services and get discounts on maps and other products. Among clubs that qualify are the AA and RAC in the UK, and the Australian, New Zealand, Canadian and US automobile associations.

The 24-hour ACP emergency help number is ☎707 509 510.

Fuel

Fuel is expensive – about €1.65 (and rising) for a litre of *sem chumbo* (unleaded petrol) at the time of writing. There are plenty of self-service stations, and credit cards are accepted at most. If you're near the border, you can save money by filling up in Spain, where it's around 20% cheaper.

Highways & Toll Roads

Top of the range are *auto-estradas* (motorways), all of them *portagens* (toll roads); the longest of these are Lisbon–Porto and Lisbon–Algarve. Toll roads charge cars and motorcycles a little over €0.06 per kilometre (around €20 from Lisbon to Porto and €19 from Lisbon to Faro).

Nomenclature can be baffling. Motorway prefixes indicate the following:

A prefixes Indicate Portugal's toll roads.

E prefixes Europe-wide designations.

N prefixes Indicate main two-lane *estradas nacionais* (national roads); prefix letter used on some road maps only.

IC (itinerário complementar) Indicates subsidiary highways.

IP (itinerário principal) Indicates main highways.

Numbers for the main two-lane *estradas nacionais* have no prefix letter on some road maps, whereas on other maps they're prefixed by N.

Hire

To rent a car in Portugal you should be at least 25 years old and have held your driving licence for more than a year (some companies allow younger drivers at higher rates). The widest choice of car-hire companies is at Lisbon, Porto and Faro airports. Competition has driven Algarve rates lower than elsewhere.

Some of the best advance-booking rates are offered by internet-based brokers such as **Holiday Autos** (www.holidayautos.com). Other bargains come as part of 'fly/drive' packages. The worst deals tend to be those done with international firms on arrival, though their prepaid promotional rates are competitive. Book at least a few days ahead in high season. For on-the-spot rental, domestic firms such as **Auto Jardim** (www.auto-jardim.com) have some of the best rates.

The average price for renting the smallest and cheapest available car for a week in high season is around €300 (with tax, insurance and unlimited mileage) if booked from abroad, and a similar amount through a Portuguese firm.

For an additional fee you can get personal insurance through the rental company, unless you're covered by your home policy. A minimum of third-party coverage is compulsory in the EU.

Rental cars are especially at risk of break-ins or petty theft in larger towns, so don't leave anything of value visible in the car.

Motorcycles and scooters can be rented in larger cities,

and all over coastal Algarve. Expect to pay from €30/60 per day for a scooter/motorcycle.

Road Rules

Despite the sometimes chaotic relations between drivers, there are rules. To begin with, driving is on the right, overtaking is on the left and most signs use international symbols. An important rule to remember is that traffic from the right usually has priority. Portugal has lots of ambiguously marked intersections, so this is more important than you might think.

Except when marked otherwise, speed limits for cars (without a trailer) and motorcycles (without a sidecar) are 50km/h in towns and villages, 90km/h outside built-up areas and 120km/h on motorways. By law, car safety belts must be worn in the front and back seats, and children under 12 years may not ride in the front. Motorcyclists and their passengers must wear helmets, and motorcycles must have their headlights on day and night.

The police can impose steep on-the-spot fines for speeding and parking offences, so save yourself a big hassle and remember to toe the line.

The legal blood-alcohol limit is 0.5g/L, and there are fines of up to €2500 for drink-driving. It's also illegal in Portugal to drive while talking on a mobile phone.

Hitching

Hitching is never entirely safe anywhere, and we don't recommend it. In any case it isn't an easy option in Portugal. Almost nobody stops on major highways, and on smaller roads drivers tend to be going short distances so you might only advance from one field to the next.

Local Transport

Bus

Except in Lisbon or Porto, there's little reason to take municipal buses, as most attractions are within walking distance. Most areas have regional bus services, for better or worse.

Metro

Both Lisbon and Porto have ambitious underground systems that are still growing.

Taxi

Taxis offer fair value over short distances, and are plentiful in large towns and cities. Ordinary taxis are usually marked with an 'A' (which stands for *aluguer*, for hire) on the door, number plate or elsewhere. They use meters and are available on the street and at taxi ranks, or by telephone for a surcharge of €0.75.

The fare on weekdays during daylight hours is about €2.50 *bandeirada* (flag fall) plus around €0.80 per kilometre, and a bit more for periods spent idling in traffic. A fare of €6 will usually get you across bigger towns. It's best to insist on the meter, although it's possible to negotiate a flat fare. If you have a sizeable load of luggage you'll pay a further €1.50.

AUTOMATED TOLLS

Portugal's main toll roads now have automated toll booths, meaning you won't be able to simply drive through and pay an attendant. You'll need to hire an electronic tag to pay for the tolls. Many car-rental agencies hire out the small electronic devices (for around €6 per week, less on subsequent weeks), and it's worth inquiring if one is available before renting a car. If you don't use the device, and go through a toll, you may receive a fine (via your car-hire agency) after your trip. The other option is simply to avoid the *auto-estradas*, which isn't always easy to do, especially when travelling across the Algarve. For more information, including locations where you can hire electronic tag devices throughout the country (useful if your car hire doesn't have them or you're driving your own vehicle), visit the government-run site **Via Verde** (☎707 503 503; www.viaverde.pt).

Train Routes

Rates are about 20% higher at night (9pm to 6am), and on weekends and holidays. Once a taxi leaves the city limits you also pay a surcharge or higher rate.

In larger cities, including Lisbon and Porto, meterless taxis marked with a T (for *turismo*) can be hired from private companies for excursions. Rates for these are higher but standardised; drivers are honest and polite, and speak foreign languages.

Tram

Tram lovers shouldn't miss the charming relics rattling through the narrow streets of Lisbon and Porto.

Tours

Bus

Cityrama (Map p80; ☑213 191 090; www.cityrama.pt; hop-on hop-off tour €12-25), and the following companies offer bus tours:

AVIC (www.avic.pt) Runs tours in Porto, the Douro and the Minho.

Diana Tours (www.dianatours.pt) Specialises in Lisbon and Sintra.

Megatur (www.megatur.pt) Offers a variety of Algarve tours.

Train

Caminhos de Ferro Portugueses (CP; www.cp.pt), the state railway company, organises Saturday day trips up the Douro valley on an old steam engine during the summer months.

Specialist Tours

Locally run adventure tours are noted in individual town listings; activity-based tours are listed in Portugal Outdoors (p40). Try the following for special-interest tours:

Destination Portugal (www.destination-portugal. co.uk) Will tell you all you need to know and can help with flights, car hire and accommodation, separately or together.

Martin Randall Travel (www.martinrandall.com) UK cultural specialist that arranges first-rate escorted tours, including a historical and architectural tour of central Portugal.

Naturetrek (www.naturetrek. co.uk) Specialist in birdwatching and botanical tours; runs an eight-day excursion around southern Portugal.

Train

Portugal has an extensive railroad network, making for a scenic way of travelling between destinations; see www.cp.pt.

Three of the most appealing old railway lines on narrow-gauge tracks climb out of the Douro valley:

Linha da Corgo From Peso da Régua to Vila Real.

Linha da Tâmega From Livração to Amarante.

Linha da Tua From Tua to Mirandela.

Discounts

Children aged under five travel free; those aged five to 12 travel for half price. A youth card issued by Euro26 member countries gets you a 20% discount on *regional* and *interregional* services on any day. For distances above 100km, you can also get a 20% discount on *intercidade* (express) services and a 10% discount on Alfa Pendular (AP) trains – though the latter applies only from Tuesday to Thursday. Travellers aged 65 and over can get 50% off any service by showing some ID.

Information & Reservations

You can get hold of timetable and fare information at all stations and from www.cp.pt. You can book *intercidade* and Alfa Pendular tickets up to 30 days ahead, though you'll have little trouble booking for the next or even the same day. Other services can only be booked 24 hours

in advance. A seat reservation is mandatory on most *intercidade* and Alfa trains; the booking fee is included in the price.

Types & Classes of Service

There are four main types of long-distance service. Note that international services are marked IN on timetables.

Regional (R) Slow, stop everywhere.

Interregional (IR) Reasonably fast.

Intercidade (IC) *Rápido* or express trains.

Alfa Pendular Deluxe This service is marginally faster than express and much pricier.

Lisbon and Porto have their own *urbano* (suburban) train networks. Lisbon's network extends to Sintra, Cascais and Setúbal, and up the lower Tejo valley. Porto's network takes the definition of 'suburban' to new lengths, running all the way to Braga, Guimarães and Aveiro. *Urbano* services also travel between Coimbra and Figueira da Foz. The distinction matters where long-distance services parallel the more convenient, plentiful and considerably cheaper *urbanos*.

Only the Faro–Porto *Comboio Azul* and international trains like *Sud-Expresso* and *Talgo Lusitânia* have restaurant cars, though all IC and Alfa trains have aisle service and most have bars.

Train Passes

The One Country Portugal Pass from **InterRail** (www. interrailnet.com) gives you unlimited travel on any three, four, six or eight days over a month (2nd class is €71/89/119/139; 1st-class costs about 35% more). It's available to all travellers who hail from outside of Portugal, and can be purchased from many travel agents in Portugal or in advance from the website.

Language

Portuguese pronunciation is not difficult because most sounds are also found in English. The exceptions are the nasal vowels (represented in our pronunciation guides by ng after the vowel), which are pronounced as if you're trying to make the sound through your nose; and the strongly rolled r (represented by rr in our pronunciation guides). Also note that the symbol zh sounds like the 's' in 'pleasure'. The stress generally falls on the second-last syllable of a word. In our pronunciation guides stressed syllables are indicated with italics. If you keep these few points in mind and read our coloured pronunciation guides as if they were English, you won't have problems being understood.

Portuguese has masculine and feminine forms of nouns and adjectives. Both forms are given in this chapter where necessary, and indicated with 'm' and 'f' respectively.

BASICS

Hello.	*Olá.*	o·*laa*
Goodbye.	*Adeus.*	a·de·*oosh*
How are you?	*Como está?*	ko·moo shtaa
Fine, and you?	*Bem, e você?*	beng e vo·*se*
Excuse me.	*Faz favor.*	faash fa·*vor*
Sorry.	*Desculpe.*	desh·*kool*·pe
Yes.	*Sim.*	seeng
No.	*Não.*	nowng
Please.	*Por favor.*	poor fa·*vor*

WANT MORE?

For in-depth language information and handy phrases, check out Lonely Planet's *Portuguese Phrasebook*. You'll find it at **shop.lonelyplanet.com**, or you can buy Lonely Planet's iPhone phrasebooks at the Apple App Store.

Thank you.	*Obrigado.*	o·bree·*gaa*·doo (m)
	Obrigada.	o·bree·*gaa*·da (f)
You're welcome.	*De nada.*	de *naa*·da

What's your name?
Qual é o seu nome? kwaal e oo se·oo *no*·me

My name is ...
O meu nome é ... oo *me*·oo *no*·me e ...

Do you speak English?
Fala inglês? *faa*·la eeng·*glesh*

I don't understand.
Não entendo. nowng eng·*teng*·doo

ACCOMMODATION

Do you have a single/double room?
Tem um quarto de teng oong *kwaar*·too de
solteiro/casal? sol·*tay*·roo/ka·*zal*

How much is it per night/person?
Quanto custa *kwang*·too *koosh*·ta
por noite/pessoa? poor *noy*·te/pe·*so*·a

Is breakfast included?
Inclui o pequeno eeng·*kloo*·ee oo pe·*ke*·noo
almoço? aal·*mo*·soo

air-con	*ar condicionado*	aar kong·dee·syoo·*naa*·doo
bathroom	*casa de banho*	*kaa*·za de ba·*nyoo*
bed	*cama*	*ka*·ma
campsite	*parque de campismo*	*paar*·ke de kang·*peezh*·moo
cot	*cama de grades*	*ka*·ma de *graa*·desh
guesthouse	*casa de hóspedes*	*kaa*·za de *osh*·pe·desh
hotel	*hotel*	o·*tel*
youth hostel	*pousada de juventude*	poh·*zaa*·da de zhoo·*veng*·too·de
window	*janela*	zha·*ne*·la

DIRECTIONS

Where's (the station)?
Onde é (a estação)? ong·de e (a shta·*sowng*)

What's the address?
Qual é o endereço? kwaal é oo eng·de·re·soo

Could you please write it down?
Podia escrever poo·*dee*·a shkre·*ver*
isso, por favor? ee·soo poor fa·*vor*

Can you show me (on the map)?
Pode-me mostrar po·de·me moosh·*traar*
(no mapa)? (noo *maa*·pa)

at the corner	na esquina	na shkee·na
at the traffic lights	nos semáforos	noosh se·*maa*·foo·roosh
behind ...	atrás de ...	a·*traash* de ...
in front of ...	em frente de ...	eng *freng*·te de ...
far	longe	*long*·zhe
left	esquerda	*shker*·da
near	perto	*per*·too
next to ...	ao lado de ...	ow *laa*·doo de ...
opposite ...	do lado oposto ...	doo *laa*·doo oo·*posh*·too ...
right	direita	dee·*ray*·ta
straight ahead	em frente	eng *freng*·te

EATING & DRINKING

What would you recommend?
O que é que oo ke e ke
recomenda? rre·koo·*meng*·da

What's in that dish?
Quais são os kwaish sowng oosh
ingredientes eeng·gre·dee·*eng*·tesh
daquele prato? da·ke·le *praa*·too

I don't eat ...
Eu não como ... e·oo nowng *ko*·moo ...

Cheers!
Saúde! sa·*oo*·de

That was delicious.
Isto estava eesh·too shtaa·va
delicioso. de·lee·see·o·zoo

Bring the bill/check, please.
Pode-me trazer po·de·me tra·*zer*
a conta. a *kong*·ta

I'd like to reserve a table for ...	Eu queria reservar uma mesa para ...	e·oo ke·*ree*·a rre·zer·*vaar* oo·ma me·za *pa*·ra ...
(eight) o'clock	as (oito da noite)	ash (oy·too da noy·te)
(two) people	(duas) pessoas	(doo·ash) pe·so·ash

KEY PATTERNS

To get by in Portuguese, mix and match these simple patterns with words of your choice:

When's (the next bus)?
Quando é que sai kwang·doo e ke sai
(o próximo (oo pro·see·moo
autocarro)? ow·to·kaa·rroo)

Where do I (buy a ticket)?
Onde é que eu ong·de e ke e·oo
(compro o bilhete)? (kong·proo oo bee·*lye*·te)

I'm looking for (a hotel).
Estou à procura de shtoh aa proo·*koo*·ra de
(um hotel). (oong o·*tel*)

Do you have (a map)?
Tem (um mapa)? teng (oong *maa*·pa)

Please bring (the bill).
Pode-me trazer po·de·me tra·zer
(a conta). (a *kong*·ta)

I'd like (the menu).
Queria (um menu). ke·*ree*·a (oong me·noo)

I'd like (to hire a car).
Queria (alugar ke·*ree*·a (a·loo·gaar
um carro). oong *kaa*·rroo)

I have (a reservation).
Eu tenho e·oo ta·nyoo
(uma reserva). (oo·ma rre·zer·va)

Could you please (help)?
Pode (ajudar), po·de (a·zhoo·daar)
por favor? poor fa·*vor*

Do I need (a visa)?
Preciso de pre·see·zoo de
(um visto)? (oong veesh·too)

Key Words

appetisers	aperitivos	a·pe·ree·*tee*·voosh
bar	bar	baar
bottle	garrafa	ga·*rraa*·fa
bowl	ligela	tee·*zhe*·la
breakfast	pequeno almoço	pe·*ke*·noo aal·*mo*·soo
children's menu	menu das crianças	me·noo dash kree·*ang*·sash
cold	frio	free·oo
delicatessen	charcutaria	shar·koo·ta·ree·a
dinner	jantar	zhang·taar
food	comida	koo·*mee*·da
fork	garfo	gar·foo
glass	copo	ko·poo
hot (warm)	quente	keng·te
knife	faca	faa·ka

Signs

Aberto	Open
Encerrado	Closed
Entrada	Entrance
Fechado	Closed
Informação	Information
Lavabos/WC	Toilets
Proibido	Prohibited
Saída	Exit

lunch	almoço	aal·mo·soo
main course	prato principal	praa·too preeng·see·paal
market	mercado	mer·kaa·doo
menu (in English)	menu (em inglês)	me·noo (eng eeng·glesh)
plate	prato	praa·too
restaurant	restaurante	rresh·tow·rang·te
spicy	picante	pee·kang·te
spoon	colher	koo·lyer
vegetarian food	comida vegetariana	koo·mee·da ve·zhe·ta·ree·aa·na
wine list	lista dos vinhos	leesh·ta doosh vee·nyoosh
with/without	com/sem	kong/seng

Meat & Fish

beef	carne de vaca	kaar·ne de vaa·ka
chicken	frango	frang·goo
duck	pato	paa·too
fish	peixe	pay·she
lamb	cordeiro	kor·day·roo
pork	porco	por·koo
turkey	peru	pe·roo
veal	novilho	noo·vee·lyoo

Fruit & Vegetables

apple	maçã	ma·sang
apricot	alperce	aal·per·se
artichoke	alcachofra	aal·ka·sho·fra
asparagus	espargos	shpar·goosh
beetroot	beterraba	be·te·rraa·ba
cabbage	couve	koh·ve
capsicum	pimento	pee·meng·too
carrot	cenoura	se·noh·ra
celery	aipo	ai·poo
cherry	cereja	se·re·zha
corn	milho	mee·lyoo
cucumber	pepino	pe·pee·noo
fruit	fruta	froo·ta
grapes	uvas	oo·vash
lemon	limão	lee·mowng
lettuce	alface	aal·faa·se
mushrooms	cogumelos	koo·goo·me·loosh
nut	oleaginosa	o·lee·a·zhee·no·za
onion	cebola	se·bo·la
orange	laranja	la·rang·zha
peach	pêssego	pe·se·goo
peas	ervilhas	er·vee·lyash
pineapple	ananás	a·na·naash
plum	ameixa	a·may·sha
potato	batata	ba·taa·ta
prune	ameixa seca	a·may·sha se·ka
pumpkin	abóbora	a·bo·boo·ra
spinach	espinafres	shpee·naa·fresh
strawberry	morango	moo·rang·goo
tomato	tomate	too·maa·te
turnip	nabo	naa·boo
vegetable	hortaliça	or·ta·lee·sa
watermelon	melancia	me·lang·see·a

Other

bread	pão	powng
butter	manteiga	mang·tay·ga
cheese	queijo	kay·zhoo
egg	ovo	o·voo
honey	mel	mel
lentils	lentilha	leng·tee·lya
noodles	massas	maa·sash
oil	óleo	o·lyoo
pepper	pimenta	pee·meng·ta
rice	arroz	a·rrosh
salt	sal	saal
sugar	açúcar	a·soo·kar
vinegar	vinagre	vee·naa·gre

Drinks

beer	cerveja	ser·ve·zha
coffee	café	ka·fe
juice	sumo	soo·moo
milk	leite	lay·te
red wine	vinho tinto	vee·nyoo teeng·too

tea	*chá*	shaa
(mineral) water	*água (mineral)*	aa·gwa (mee·ne·*raal*)
white wine	*vinho branco*	vee·nyoo brang·koo

EMERGENCIES

Help!	*Socorro!*	soo·ko·rroo
Go away!	*Vá-se embora!*	vaa·se eng·bo·ra
Call ...!	*Chame ...!*	shaa·me ...
a doctor	*um médico*	oong me·dee·koo
the police	*a polícia*	a poo·lee·sya

I'm lost.
Estou perdido. shtoh per·dee·doo (m)
Estou perdida. shtoh per·dee·da (f)

I'm ill.
Estou doente. shtoh doo·eng·te

It hurts here.
Dói-me aqui. doy·me a·kee

I'm allergic to ...
Eu sou alérgico/ e·oo soh a·ler·zhee·koo/
alérgica a ... a·ler·zhee·ka a ... (m/f)

Where are the toilets?
Onde é a casa ong·de e a kaa·za
de banho? de ba·nyoo

SHOPPING & SERVICES

I'd like to buy ...
Queria comprar ... ke·ree·a kong·praar ...

I'm just looking.
Estou só a ver. shtoh so a ver

Can I look at it?
Posso ver? po·soo ver

I don't like it.
Não gosto. nowng gosh·too

How much is it?
Quanto custa? kwang too koosh·ta

It's too expensive.
Está muito caro. shtaa mweeng·too kaa·roo

Can you lower the price?
Pode baixar o preço? po·de bai·shaar oo pre·soo

Question Words		
How?	*Como?*	ko·moo
What?	*Quê?*	ke
When?	*Quando?*	kwang·doo
Where?	*Onde?*	ong·de
Who?	*Quem?*	keng
Why?	*Porquê?*	poor·ke

There's a mistake in the bill.
Há um erro na conta. aa oong e·rroo na kong·ta

ATM	*caixa automático*	kai·sha ow·too· maa·tee·koo
credit card	*cartão de crédito*	kar·towng de kre·dee·too
internet cafe	*café da internet*	ka·fe da eeng·ter·ne·te
post office	*correio*	koo·rray·oo
tourist office	*escritório de turismo*	shkree·to·ryoo de too·reezh·moo

TIME & DATES

What time is it?
Que horas são? kee o·rash sowng

It's (10) o'clock.
São (dez) horas. sowng (desh) o·rash

Half past (10).
(Dez) e meia. (desh) e may·a

morning	*manhã*	ma·nyang
afternoon	*tarde*	taar·de
evening	*noite*	noy·te
yesterday	*ontem*	ong·teng
today	*hoje*	o·zhe
tomorrow	*amanhã*	aa·ma·nyang
Monday	*segunda-feira*	se·goong·da·fay·ra
Tuesday	*terça-feira*	ter·sa·fay·ra
Wednesday	*quarta-feira*	kwaar·ta·fay·ra
Thursday	*quinta-feira*	keeng·ta·fay·ra
Friday	*sexta-feira*	saysh·ta·fay·ra
Saturday	*sábado*	saa·ba·doo
Sunday	*domingo*	doo·meeng·goo
January	*Janeiro*	zha·nay·roo
February	*Fevereiro*	fe·vray·roo
March	*Março*	maar·soo
April	*Abril*	a·breel
May	*Maio*	maa·yoo
June	*Junho*	zhoo·nyoo
July	*Julho*	zhoo·lyoo
August	*Agosto*	a·gosh·too
September	*Setembro*	se·teng·broo
October	*Outubro*	oh·too·broo
November	*Novembro*	no·veng·broo
December	*Dezembro*	de·zeng·broo

TRANSPORT

Public Transport

boat	barco	baar·koo
bus	autocarro	ow·to·kaa·roo
plane	avião	a·vee·owng
train	comboio	kong·boy·oo
tram	eléctrico	ee·le·tree·koo

I want to go to (Braga).
Queria ir a (Braga).   ke·ree·a eer a (braa·ga)

Does it stop at (Amarante)?
Pára em (Amarante)?   paa·ra eng (a·ma·rang·te)

What time does it leave/arrive?
A que horas sai/chega?   a ke o·rash sai/she·ga

Please tell me when we get to (Évora).
Por favor avise-me   poor fa·vor a·vee·ze·me
quando chegarmos   kwang·doo she·gaar·moosh
a (Évora).   a (e·voo·ra)

Please stop here.
Por favor pare aqui.   poor fa·vor paa·re a·kee

aisle seat	lugar na coxia	loo·gaar na koo·shee·a
cancelled	cancelado	kang·se·laa·doo
delayed	atrasado	a·tra·zaa·doo
platform	plataforma	pla·ta·for·ma

Numbers		
1	um	oong
2	dois	doysh
3	três	tresh
4	quatro	kwaa·troo
5	cinco	seeng·koo
6	seis	saysh
7	sete	se·te
8	oito	oy·too
9	nove	no·ve
10	dez	desh
20	vinte	veeng·te
30	trinta	treeng·ta
40	quarenta	kwa·reng·ta
50	cinquenta	seeng·kweng·ta
60	sessenta	se·seng·ta
70	setenta	se·teng·ta
80	oitenta	oy·teng·ta
90	noventa	no·veng·ta
100	cem	seng
1000	mil	meel

ticket office	bilheteira	bee·lye·tay·ra
timetable	horário	o·raa·ryoo
train station	estação de caminhos de ferro	shta·sowng de ka·mee·nyoosh de fe·rroo
window seat	lugar à janela	loo·gaar aa zha·ne·la

a ... ticket	um bilhete de ...	oong bee·lye·te de ...
1st-class	primeira classe	pree·may·ra klaa·se
2nd-class	segunda classe	se·goong·da klaa·se
one-way	ida	ee·da
return	ida e volta	ee·da ee vol·ta

Driving & Cycling

I'd like to hire a ...	Queria alugar ...	ke·ree·a a·loo·gaar ...
bicycle	uma bicicleta	oo·ma bee·see·kle·ta
car	um carro	oong kaa·rroo
motorcycle	uma mota	oo·ma mo·ta

bicycle pump	bomba de bicicleta	bong·ba de bee·see·kle·ta
child seat	cadeira de criança	ka·day·ra de kree·ang·sa
helmet	capacete	ka·pa·se·te
mechanic	mecânico	me·kaa·nee·koo
petrol/gas	gasolina	ga·zoo·lee·na
service station	posto de gasolina	posh·too de ga·zoo·lee·na

Is this the road to ...?
Esta é a estrada   esh·ta e a shtraa·da
para ...?   pa·ra ...

(How long) Can I park here?
(Quanto tempo)   (kwang·too teng·poo)
Posso estacionar   po·soo shta·see·oo·naar
aqui?   a·kee

The car/motorbike has broken down (at ...).
O carro/A mota   oo kaa·rroo/a mo·ta
avariou-se (em ...).   a·va·ree·oh·se (eng ...)

I have a flat tyre.
Tenho um furo no   ta·nyoo oong foo·roo noo
pneu.   pe·ne·oo

I've run out of petrol.
Estou sem gasolina.   shtoh seng ga·zoo·lee·na

I'd like my bicycle repaired.
Queria consertar a   ke·ree·aa kong·ser·taar a
minha bicicleta.   mee·nya bee·see·kle·ta

GLOSSARY

For terms for food, drinks and other culinary vocabulary, see p521. For additional terms and information about the Portuguese language, see the Language chapter on p514.

adegas – wineries

Age of Discoveries – the period during the 15th and 16th centuries when Portuguese sailors explored the coast of Africa and finally charted a sea route to India

albergaria – upmarket inn

albufeira – reservoir, lagoon

aldeia – village

alta – upper

anta – see dolmen

arco – arch

armillary sphere – celestial sphere used by early astronomers and navigators to chart the stars; a decorative motif in Manueline architecture and atop *pelourinhos*

arrayal, arraiais (pl) – street party

artesanato – handicrafts shop

avenida – avenue

azulejo – hand-painted tile, typically blue and white, used to decorate buildings

bairro – town district

baixa – lower

balneário – health resort, spa

barcos rabelos – colourful boats once used to transport port wine from vineyards

barragem – dam

beco – cul de sac

biblioteca – library

bilhete diário/turístico – day pass/tourist ticket

câmara municipal – city or town hall

caldas – hot springs

Carnaval – Carnival; festival that takes place just before Lent

casa de hóspedes – boarding house, usually with shared showers and toilets

casais – huts

castelo – castle

castro – fortified hill town

cavaleiro – horseman

CCI – Camping Card International

Celtiberians – descendants of Celts who arrived in the Iberian Peninsula around 600 BC

centro de saúde – state-administered medical centre

cidade – town or city

citânia – Celtic fortified village

claustro – cloisters

concelho – municipality, council

cortes – Portugal's early parliament

CP – Caminhos de Ferro Portugueses (the Portuguese state railway company)

cromeleque – circle of prehistoric standing stones

cruz – cross

direita – right; abbreviated as D, dir or Dta

dolmen – Neolithic stone tomb (*anta* in Portuguese)

Dom, Dona – honorific titles (like Sir, Madam) given to royalty, nobility and landowners; now used more generally as a very polite form of address

elevador – lift (elevator), funicular

espigueiros – stone granaries

esplanada – terrace, seafront promenade

estação – station (usually train station)

estalagem – inn; more expensive than an *albergaria*

expressos – comfortable, fast buses between major cities

estradas – highways

fadista – singer of *fado*

fado – traditional, melancholic Portuguese style of singing

feira – fair

festa – festival

fortaleza – fortress

GNR – Guarda Nacional Republicana, the national guard (the acting police force in rural towns without PSP police)

guitarra – guitar

gruta – cave

hospedaria – see *casa de hóspedes*

IC (intercidade) – express intercity train

ICEP – Investimentos, Comércio e Turismo de Portugal, the government's umbrella organisation for tourism

igreja – church

igreja matriz – parish church

ilha – island

IR (interregional) – fairly fast train that doesn't make too many stops

jardim – garden

judiaria – quarter in a town where Jews were once segregated

largo – small square

latifúndios – Roman system of large farming estates

litoral – coastal

livraria – bookshop

Lisboêtas – Lisbon dwellers

loggia – covered area or porch on the side of a building

lugar – neighbourhood, place

Manueline – elaborate late Gothic/Renaissance style of art and architecture that emerged during the reign of Dom Manuel I in the 16th century

mantas alentejanas – handwoven woollen blankets

marranos – 'New Christians', ie Jews who converted during the Inquisition

menhir – standing stone monument typical of the late Neolithic Age

mercado municipal – municipal market

mesa – table

minimercado – grocery shop or small supermarket

miradouro – viewpoint

Misericórdia – derived from Santa Casa da Misericórdia (Holy House of Mercy), a charitable institution founded in the 15th century to care for the poor and the sick; it usually designates an old building that was founded by this organisation

moliceiro – high-prowed, shallow-draft boats traditionally used for harvesting seaweed in the estuaries of Beira Litoral

mosteiro – monastery

mouraria – the quarter where Moors were segregated during and after the Christian *Reconquista*

museu – museum

paço – palace

parque de campismo – camping ground

parque nacional – national park

parque natural – natural park

pelourinho – stone pillory, often ornately carved; erected in the 13th to 18th centuries as symbols of justice and sometimes as places where criminals were punished

pensão, pensões (pl) – guesthouse, the Portuguese equivalent of a B&B, though breakfast is not always served

planalto – high plain

pombal – dovecote, a structure for housing pigeons

ponte – bridge

portagem – toll road

pousada – government-run upmarket inn, often a converted castle, convent or palace

pousada da juventude – youth hostel; usually with kitchen, common rooms and sometimes rooms with private bathroom

praça – square

praia – beach

PSP – Polícia de Segurança Pública, the local police force

quinta – country estate or villa; in the Douro wine-growing region it often refers to a wine lodge's property

R (regional) – slow train

Reconquista – Christian reconquest of Portugal (718–1249)

reservas naturais – nature reserves

residencial, residenciais (pl) – guesthouse; slightly more expensive than a *pensão* and usually serving breakfast

ribeiro – stream

rio – river

romaria – religious pilgrimage

rua – street

saudade – melancholic longing for better times

sé – cathedral

sem chumbo – unleaded (petrol)

senhor – man

senhora – woman

serra – mountain, mountain range

solar – manor house

tasca – tavern

termas – spas, hot springs

terra quente – hot country

torre de menagem – castle tower, keep

Turihab – short for Turismo Habitação, a scheme for marketing private accommodation (particularly in northern Portugal) in cottages, historic buildings and manor houses

turismo – tourist office

vila – town

FOOD GLOSSARY

a conta – the bill

açorda – bread-based stew, usually served with mixed *mariscos* (shellfish) or *camarão* (prawn)

agua – water, usually offered *sem gas* (still) or *com gas* (bubbly)

amêijoas – clams

arroz – rice

arroz de marisco – rich shellfish and rice mixture

arroz de tamboril – monkfish rice

atum – tuna

azeite – olive oil

azeitonas – olives

bacalhau – salted codfish

bacalhau à brás – shredded fried cod with potato and scrambled egg

bacalhau com – shredded cod with cream and potatoes

bica – espresso

bife – steak

borrego – lamb

caldeirada – fish and shellfish stew, not unlike bouillabaisse

camarão/camarões – prawn/ prawns

carapau – a type of (small) mackerel

carne – meat

carne de porco – pork

carne de vaca – beef

cataplana – seafood stew cooked in a copper pot

cerveja – beer

choco – cuttlefish

choriço – smoked pork sausage

couvert – bread, cheese, olives brought to you table before your meal

cozido à portuguesa – stew of sausages, meats and vegetables

dose – a portion, usually big enough for two

ementa – menu

entradas – appetizers

espadarte – swordfish

especialidade da casa – house speciality

espetada – kebab

feijoada – bean and sausage stew, usually made with white beans

frango – chicken

frutos do mar – seafood

galão – tall weak coffee with milk

lula – squid

mariscos – shellfish

meia de leite – coffee with milk

meia dose – half-portion, usually serves one

migas – fried breadcrumbs flavoured with sausage

pão – bread

pastel de nata – custard tart

pastelaria – pastry shop and bakery

peixe – fish

pernil no forno – roast leg of pork

petiscos – small (tapas-sized) plates

piri piri – spicy chilli sauce

polvo – octopus

prato do dia – plate of the day

prato principal – main course

queijada – cheesecake

queijo – cheese

salmão – salmon

sandes – sandwiches

sardinhas – sardines

sobremesa – dessert

vinho – wine

vinho blanco – white wine

vinho tinto – red wine

vinho verde – semi-sparkling young wine

vitela – veal

Behind the Scenes

SEND US YOUR FEEDBACK

We love to hear from travellers – your comments keep us on our toes and help make our books better. Our well-travelled team reads every word on what you loved or loathed about this book. Although we cannot reply individually to postal submissions, we always guarantee that your feedback goes straight to the appropriate authors, in time for the next edition. Each person who sends us information is thanked in the next edition – the most useful submissions are rewarded with a selection of digital PDF chapters.

Visit **lonelyplanet.com/contact** to submit your updates and suggestions or to ask for help. Our award-winning website also features inspirational travel stories, news and discussions.

Note: We may edit, reproduce and incorporate your comments in Lonely Planet products such as guidebooks, websites and digital products, so let us know if you don't want your comments reproduced or your name acknowledged. For a copy of our privacy policy visit lonelyplanet.com/privacy.

OUR READERS

Many thanks to the travellers who used the last edition and wrote to us with helpful hints, useful advice and interesting anecdotes:

Ana Alvarez, Sara Amado, Irene Ax, Marisa Batista, Julie Bergeron, Roberta Bernardi, Simone Bizzozzero, Guido Braschi, Bianca-Maria Braunshofer, Elisabete Brigadeiro, Louis Bronne, Amy Camus, Cheryl Coimbra, Bernard Cotter, Janet Danziger, Tom Day, Bjorn de Koeijer, Jean Paul Derveaux, Jaime Diniz, Tine Dusauchoit, Jan Dziubecki, Jeroen Klein Egelink, Robin Eyre, Steve Fleming, Holly Fletcher, Marie Flynn, Louisa Maria Fry, Alessandra Furlan, Emma Gallo, Sylvia Geerlings, Norman Gray, Mary Hanna, Sarah Hatherell, Marg Heidebrecht, Pirko Hosoda, Geoff Hughes, Sandie Jackson, Anders Jeppsson, Andrew Lee, Dror Leviner, Gillian Main, Jiva Masheder, Annamaria Mauramati, Eric McCoy, Kevin McCue, Wally McDonald, Colin McGill, Michael Monson, Kevin Nead, Uwe Kjær Nissen, Peter O'Brien, John Osman, Guido Paola, Lidia Paulo & Joaquim Camacho, Georghios Paraskeva, Andy Parrett, Cláudia Isabel Penedo, John Penston, Blanca Pérez, Paulo Pires, Jan Polatschek, Nathalie Potvin, Esther Priest, Philip Prowse, Stacey Rawlinson, Ricardo Reis da Silva, Sarah Richardson & Zachary Jackson, Sara Riedl, Paul Rouse, Nadezhda Saleh, Sandra Santos, Ariane Senecal, Vitor Silva, Harald Smit, Meryl Steinberg, Carmen Swanwick-Roa, Filipe Tavares, Mindi & Mark Theberge, Ashveena Tirvassen, Karin Torsdotter, Alessandro Tosi, Gemma Ufton, Michiel van Dam, Jeroen van der Weijden, Joris van Empel, Leontine van Ooij, Vitor Vasconcelos, Kris Walewijns, Amy Williamson, Christopher Woods, Els Wyns

AUTHOR THANKS

Regis St Louis

In Lisbon, I'd like to thank Guida Moura for her friendship and hospitality, chef Michael Guerrieri for insight into the dining scene, and João Teixeira for his local knowledge and the generous use of the VW. Thanks also to Ljubomir Stanišić and staff for dining tips and to the helpful tourism officials around the Lisbon region, especially in Setúbal. As always, *beijos* to my family Cassandra, Magdalena and Genevieve for their support.

Kate Armstrong

As always, a huge *obrigada* to my Portuguese family – Dom Antonio Pedro and Dona Mina for their friendship, Ana Palma for her expertise; in Lagos, Rui, plus staff at Lagos Tourism; in Faro, Maria Manuel Delgado e Silva; and in Evora, Peter and Nina Brinkman and Michelle

Azinheira. Thanks to Regis, Angela Tinson, and Dora Whitaker for the opportunity. And finally, thanks to the beautiful, generous-hearted Portuguese – as modest as they are – and whose country deserves so much.

Anja Mutić

Obrigada, Hoji, for coming along for the ride and making life on and off the road a lot more fun. A huge thank you to Miguel Carvalho of the Portuguese National Tourist Office in New York, who's always such a stellar source of up-to-the-minute info about Portugal. Thanks to all the great people I have crossed paths with in Portugal over the years. Finally, to my always-laughing mom and the inspiring memory of my father.

Andy Symington

I owe a long-time debt of gratitude for wonderful hospitality to my uncle and aunt James and Penny Symington. Thanks go to

staff at numerous tourist offices, especially Figueira and Coimbra, and especially to João Valente, Patrick, Lisl and Francis Thompson, Pedro Canavarro, Debbie and Steve, Anja Ligtenbarg, Else Denninghoff Stelling, João Tomás, José Guerra, and a friendly couple from Asheville, NC. Also to Regis and my fellow authors and lastly, love and *muito obrigado* to Elena, for listening to my shocking fado voice and much more.

ACKNOWLEDGMENTS

Climate map data adapted from Peel MC, Finlayson BL & McMahon TA (2007) 'Updated World Map of the Köppen-Geiger Climate Classification', *Hydrology and Earth System Sciences*, 11, 163344.

Cover photograph: Rooster weather vane, Ferragudo, Algarve, Portugal, Richard Cummins/Getty Images

THIS BOOK

This 9th edition of Lonely Planet's *Portugal* guidebook was researched and written by Regis St Louis, Kate Armstrong, Anja Mutić and Andy Symington. Regis and Kate also worked on the previous two editions alongside Gregor Clark, Adam Skolnick and Kerry Christiani, while the following authors made significant contributions to previous editions: Robert Landon, Dr Caroline Evans, Abigail Hole, Charlotte Amelines, Richard Sterling, John King and Julia Wilkinson.

This guidebook was commissioned in Lonely Planet's London office, and produced by the following:

Commissioning Editor Dora Whitaker

Coordinating Editors Lauren Hunt, Ross Taylor

Senior Cartographers Valentina Kremenchutskaya, Anthony Phelan

Coordinating Layout Designer Adrian Blackburn

Managing Editors Martine Power, Angela Tinson

Senior Editor Karyn Noble

Managing Layout Designer Jane Hart

Assisting Editors Susie Ashworth, Kate Evans, Kirsten Rawlings

Assisting Cartographers Drishya C, Jeff Cameron, Michael Garrett, Rachel Imeson, Nithya Kalyani, Anoop Shetty

Assisting Layout Designer Carlos Solarte

Cover Research Naomi Parker

Internal Image Research Rebecca Skinner

Language Content Branislava Vladisavljevic

Thanks to Anita Banh, Sasha Baskett, Laura Crawford, Ryan Evans, Larissa Frost, Chris Girdler, Genesys India, Jouve India, Korina Miller, Wayne Murphy, Catherine Naghten, Trent Paton, Saralinda Turner, Dianne Schallmeiner, Clifton Wilkinson

Index

Map Pages **000**
Photo Pages **000**

Map Legend

Sights
- Beach
- Buddhist
- Castle
- Christian
- Hindu
- Islamic
- Jewish
- Monument
- Museum/Gallery
- Ruin
- Winery/Vineyard
- Zoo
- Other Sight

Activities, Courses & Tours
- Diving/Snorkelling
- Canoeing/Kayaking
- Skiing
- Surfing
- Swimming/Pool
- Walking
- Windsurfing
- Other Activity/ Course/Tour

Sleeping
- Sleeping
- Camping

Eating
- Eating

Drinking
- Drinking
- Cafe

Entertainment
- Entertainment

Shopping
- Shopping

Information
- Post Office
- Tourist Information

Transport
- Airport
- Border Crossing
- Bus
- Cable Car/ Funicular
- Cycling
- Ferry
- Monorail
- Parking
- S-Bahn
- Taxi
- Train/Railway
- Tram
- Tube Station
- U-Bahn
- Underground Train Station
- Other Transport

Routes
- Tollway
- Freeway
- Primary
- Secondary
- Tertiary
- Lane
- Unsealed Road
- Plaza/Mall
- Steps
- Tunnel
- Pedestrian Overpass
- Walking Tour
- Walking Tour Detour
- Path

Boundaries
- International
- State/Province
- Disputed
- Regional/Suburb
- Marine Park
- Cliff
- Wall

Population
- Capital (National)
- Capital (State/Province)
- City/Large Town
- Town/Village

Geographic
- Hut/Shelter
- Lighthouse
- Lookout
- Mountain/Volcano
- Oasis
- Park
- Pass
- Picnic Area
- Waterfall

Hydrography
- River/Creek
- Intermittent River
- Swamp/Mangrove
- Reef
- Canal
- Water
- Dry/Salt/ Intermittent Lake
- Glacier

Areas
- Beach/Desert
- Cemetery (Christian)
- Cemetery (Other)
- Park/Forest
- Sportsground
- Sight (Building)
- Top Sight (Building)

OUR STORY

A beat-up old car, a few dollars in the pocket and a sense of adventure. In 1972 that's all Tony and Maureen Wheeler needed for the trip of a lifetime – across Europe and Asia overland to Australia. It took several months, and at the end – broke but inspired – they sat at their kitchen table writing and stapling together their first travel guide, *Across Asia on the Cheap*. Within a week they'd sold 1500 copies. Lonely Planet was born.

Today, Lonely Planet has offices in Melbourne, London and Oakland, with more than 600 staff and writers. We share Tony's belief that 'a great guidebook should do three things: inform, educate and amuse'.

OUR WRITERS

Regis St Louis

Coordinating Author; Lisbon & Around Regis' long-time admiration for wine, rugged coastlines and soulful music made him easy prey for Portugal – a country he has travelled extensively over the past decade. Favourite memories from recent trips include borrowing a friend's VW van to explore the wild beaches and back roads outside of Lisbon; chatting with shepherds in the mountains near Manteigas; hearing avant-garde fado in Lisbon; and feasting on ole *percebes* in the Algarve. Regis has written more than 40 guidebooks for Lonely including the last three editions of Lonely Planet *Portugal* – and his travel articles and have appeared in the *Los Angeles Times* and the *Chicago Tribune* among numerous other tions. He lives in Brooklyn, New York. Regis also wrote the Plan Your Trip, Understand l and Survival Guide sections.

Read more about Regis at:
lonelyplanet.com/members/RegisStLouis

Kate Armstrong

The Algarve; The Alentejo A regular visitor to Portugal, Kate first backpacked around the country more than 20 years ago and fell for the Alentejan countryside, Algarvian seafood and Portuguese hospitality. Lured by the language of fado, she later returned to study Portuguese. For this edition Kate bodysurfed her way along the Algarve, 'mixed' with the megaliths, hiked sections of the Costa Vicentina, and consumed quantities (ahem, kilos) of convent cakes. She is published regularly in Australian and international publications – see www.katearmstrong.com.au.

Anja Mutić

Porto, the Douro & Trás-os-Montes; The Minho Croatia-born New York–based writer Anja Mutić has had a full-blown love affair with Portugal for nearly a decade. On her first visit in 2005, she fell head over heels; on the second visit in 2006, she met her partner in life and travel and has been returning ever since for stints and longer stays. Anja has covered many a city and corner of Portugal for various publications but has a particularly soft spot for the north and deems Porto among the most poignant cities on earth. Anja is online at www.everthenomad.com.

Read more about Anja at:
lonelyplanet.com/members/AnjaMutic

Andy Symington

Estremadura & Ribatejo; The Beiras Though he hails from Australia, Andy's great-grandfather emigrated to Porto in the 19th century and that side of his family still call Portugal home. This connection means that he's been a frequent visitor to the country since birth, and now nips across the border even more regularly from his base in Spain. He has authored and co-authored many Lonely Planet and other guidebooks.

Published by Lonely Planet Publications Pty Ltd

ABN 36 005 607 983

9th edition – March 2014

ISBN 978 1 74220 052 1

© Lonely Planet 2014   Photographs © as indicated 2014

10 9 8 7 6 5 4 3 2 1

Printed in China